Prentice Hall

Psychology

Second Edition

Prentice Hall
Psychology
Second Edition

William J. Elmhorst
Marshfield High School, Wisconsin

Katherine P. Minter
Westwood High School, Texas

Mary Spilis
Sylvania City Schools, Ohio *(retired)*

PEARSON

Boston   Columbus   Indianapolis   New York   San Francisco   Amsterdam
Cape Town   Dubai   London   Madrid   Milan   Munich   Paris   Montréal   Toronto
Delhi   Mexico City   São Paulo   Sydney   Hong Kong   Seoul   Singapore   Taipei   Tokyo

Executive Editor: Erin Mitchell
Editorial Assistant: Sarah Henrich
Program Manager: Reena Dalal
Program Team Lead: Amber Mackey
Project Manager: Crystal McCarthy, Sherry Lewis
Project Manager Team Lead: Linda Behrens
Operations Manager: Mary Fischer
Senior Operations Specialist: Diane Peirano
Director of Marketing: Brandy Dawson
Associate Director of Design: Blair Brown
Cover Designer: Kathryn Foot
Cover Photo: Mikael Damkier/Alamy
Digital Media Director: Sacha Laustsen
Digital Media Product Manager: Caroline Fenton
Digital Media Project Manager: Pamela Weldin
Full-Service Project Management: Lumina Datamatics
Composition: Lumina Datamatics
Text and Cover Printer/Binder: LSC Communications
Text Font: Sabon LT Std 10/12.5

Library of Congress Cataloging-in-Publication Data
Minter, Katherine P.
  Psychology / Katherine P. Minter, William J. Elmhorst. — 2nd edition.
    pages cm
  Includes bibliographical references and index.
  ISBN 978-0-13-398057-8—ISBN 0-13-398057-X
  1. Psychology.   I. Elmhorst, William J.   II. Title.
  BF121.M5776 2014
  150—dc23
                                    2014043397

www.PearsonSchool.com

High School Binding
ISBN-13: 978-0-133-98057-8
ISBN-10: 0-133-98057-X

Brief Contents

Scientific Inquiry Domain

Biopsychology Domain

Developmental and Learning Domain

Social Context Domain

Contents

Scientific Inquiry Domain

Biopsychology Domain

Developmental and Learning Domain

Social Context Domain

Cognition Domain

Individual Variations Domain

Applications of Psychological Science Domain

Learner-Centered, Achievement-Driven Approach

Prentice Hall Psychology 2nd Edition celebrates the fascinating field of psychology—its science, its history, its mysteries, its applications—by focusing on today's students. This learner-centered approach encourages dialogue and recognizes the importance of active engagement inside *and* outside the classroom. The second edition of *Prentice Hall Psychology* is uniquely integrated textbook with a media program that awakens students' curiosity and energizes their desire to learn and succeed.

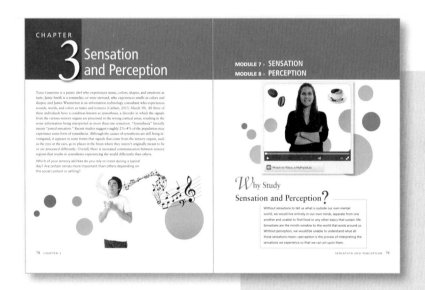

Chapter Opening Prologues are designed to capture student interest immediately. Taken from a case study or recent events in the news, these openers engage students in the material from the very start. The design truly captures students' imagination and adds to the appeal of the chapter content.

Chapter Opening Student Voice Videos Chapters now open with videos in which psychology students share personal stories about how the chapter theme directly applies to their lives.

Each module is structured around detailed **Module Goals and Learning Objectives** based on APA recommendations. These goals and objectives, which correspond to the APA's newest National Standards for High School Psychology Curricula, provide students and teachers with an overview of the major concepts and questions they will encounter. The phrasing of the learning objectives encourages students to think critically about key concepts. Teachers can refer to the module goals and learning objectives to determine which sections of the text to emphasize in their courses.

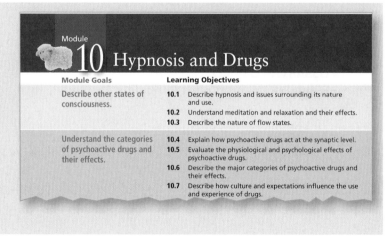

Student Voice Questions encourage students to stop, to clarify, and to think critically. Written by students for students, these questions create a dialogue between the text and the reader and encourage students to ask similar questions.

How long has psychology been around? ▶

ogy's beginnings, th
next section, we'll ta
Psychology is a
about 130 years old
before then; on the
ologists† thought ab
and Descartes wrote
(Durrant, 1993; Ev
doctors and physio
the body and the br
Helmholtz, 1852, 1
auditory (hearing) p

Being brought up in an individualist or collectivist culture can also influence how people think of others. In the United States, we tend to attribute other people's behavior to their personalities and other internal characteristics rather than to their social positions and other external situations. (Remember the fundamental attribution error Westerners tend to make.) (L)(I)(N)(K) *to Chapter Seven: Social Psychology, p.242.* But people raised in more collectivist cultures are more likely to attribute others' behavior to situational factors (Miller, 1984). For example, imagine that a man is walking quickly down the sidewalk, pushing aside people who stand in his way and not pausing to excuse himself or apologize. How would you explain this behavior? People from individualist cultures might say that the man is a rude, thoughtless person, whereas people from collectivist cultures would be more likely to consider external reasons for the man's behavior: They may think that he is late for an important meeting, or he is about to miss his train, or his wife is giving birth and he is trying to get t

LINK feature It is often difficult for students to make connections from one chapter to topics in other chapters. To help students identify interrelated concepts, through each chapter, whenever one topic has a relationship to another within the text, a (L)(I)(N)(K) symbol is shown, followed by specific chapter and page number cross references. These links refer to content covered within the same chapter, in earlier chapters, or in subsequent chapters—giving students a real sense of the connections throughout the text material.

Thinking Critically discussion prompts are new to the second edition. These prompts encourage students to take what they've learned from the text and think about it in more depth, creating a deeper understanding of the topic covered.

ght frontal lobe.) More specifically, this
ly and fluently. It is called *Broca's area*
ul Broca, who first provided widely ac-
fluent and articulate speech result from
mage to Broca's area causes a person to
, connected fashion. You can remember
rea causes "broken" speech. People with

Thinking Critically
Phineas Gage went from a mild-mannered railroad worker to a short-tempered and highly aggressive individual after a steel rod was driven through his frontal lobe. Discuss the extent to which his injuries and subsequent behavior change were a

👁 Watch the Video, *In the Real World: Are Stereotypes and Prejudices Inevitable?: Defining Prejudice,* at **MyPsychLab**

stereotype a set of characteristics that people believe is shared by all members of a particular social category; a concept held about a person or group of people that is based on superficial, irrelevant characteristics.

an unsupported and often negati
ticular social group, it is called p
types and Prejudices Inevitable?:
stereotypes and prejudice.
When prejudicial attitudes
treated differently than others i
discrimination. Prejudice is the a
result from that attitude.
While laws exist to prevent
some people from holding disc
eliminate, discrimination have
dressed are the prejudicial attit

Types of Prejudice and Dis

Vocabulary Terms and Running Glossary To help students recognize and understand the important terms introduced in each chapter, **Vocabulary Terms** are set in bold at first use and explained in the text. Additionally, the terms appear in a **Running Glossary** in the margin of the same page on which they are introduced; the term appears in bold along with its definition. In addition, **Support Vocabulary** definitions for tricky terms are provided as footnotes throughout the text.

Glossary/Glosario

A

absolute threshold: the lowest level of stimulation that a person can consciously detect 50 percent of the time the stimulation is present. 81
umbral absoluto: nivel más bajo de estimulación que puede percibir la persona de manera consciente el 50 por ciento de las veces que la estimulación está presente.

acculturation: the process of adapting to a new or different culture. 267
aculturación: proceso de adaptación a una cultura nueva o diferente.

acculturative stress: stress resulting from the need to change and adapt a person's ways to the majority culture. 478
estrés cultural: estrés que resulta de la necesidad de cambiar y adaptar la manera de ser de una persona a la cultura mayoritaria.

acquired (secondary) drives: those drives that are learned

trastorno de estrés agudo: trastorno que se produce tras someterse a un factor estresante mayor, y que produce síntomas de ansiedad, disociación, pesadillas recurrentes, perturbaciones del sueño, problemas de concentración y momentos en los que la persona parece "revivir" el suceso en sueños y revivisencias durante periodos de hasta un mes después de ocurrido el evento.

adaptive theory: theory of sleep proposing that animals and humans evolved sleep patterns to avoid predators by sleeping when predators are most active. 125
teoría de adaptación: teoría del sueño que propone que los animales y los seres humanos desarrollaron patrones de sueño para evitar a los depredadores, al dormir cuando los depredadores están más activos.

adolescence: the period of life from about age 13 to the early 20s, during which a young person is no longer physically a child but is not yet an independent, self-supporting adult. 176

All vocabulary terms set in bold in the text also appear in a **Glossary** at the end of the book. To provide further support for students, including those whose first language is Spanish, the **Glossary/Glosario** at the end of the book lists key terms and definitions in English along with those same key terms and definitions in Spanish.

MyPsychLab icons indicate that students can find related video, podcasts, simulations, practice quizzes, and more within MyPsychLab to expand their learning. There are many more resources available within MyPsychLab than those highlighted in the book, but the icons draw attention to some of the most high interest materials available at **www.mypsychlab.com**.

For a complete overview of MyPsychLab, see pages xxiv-xxv.

☑ **Study** and **Review** at **mypsychlab**

((**Listen** to the **Audio File** at **mypsychlab**

👁 **Watch** the **Video** at **mypsychlab**

⊚ Map the **Concepts** at **mypsychlab**

✳ **Complete** the **Survey** at **mypsychlab**

⊛ **Participate** in the **Experiment** at **mypsychlab**

Practice Quizzes are included at the end of each module. Each quiz features 10 multiple-choice questions designed to assess students' comprehension of module material. Practice quizzes encourage students to stop, review, and reinforce their learning before moving on to a new module. Answers are provided in the Teacher Edition of this text.

Practice Quiz

Study Help Note: These practice quizzes are spaced throughout each chapter to give you an opportunity to check your understanding of the material in each section and provide practice for exams.

Pick the best answer.

1. In the definition of psychology, *mental processes* means
   a. internal, covert processes
   b. unconscious processes
   c. outward or overt actions and reactions
   d. only human behavior

2. Dr. Baker designs an experiment for studying lab rats' reactions to energy drinks in relation to problem solving. Dr. Baker is most interested in the goal of
   a. description
   b. explanation

6. Which perspective offers the best explanation for schizophrenia?
   a. psychodynamic
   b. behavioral
   c. biopsychological
   d. humanistic

7. Wesley has learned that if he cries with his mother in public, she will often get him a new toy or a piece of candy to quiet him. Which of the following perspectives is associated with John Watson's ideas to explain Wesley's behavior?

CHAPTER 2 **Summary**

((**Listen** to an **Audio File** of your chapter at **MyPsychLab**

Module 4: The Nervous System
Understand the structure and function of the nervous system.

4.1 Describe the parts of the neuron and understand the basic process of neural transmission.
- Neurons have four primary components: dendrites that receive input, a soma or cell body, axons that carry the neural message to other cells, and axon terminals that are the site of neurotransmitter release.

4.2 Describe the major divisions of the human nervous system.
- The central nervous system consists of the brain and the spinal cord.
- There are two systems within the peripheral nervous system, the somatic nervous system, and the autonomic nervous system.

4.3 Identify the mechanisms of, and the importance of, plas...

Each chapter contains a content **Summary** and a comprehensive list of **Vocabulary Terms** used in that chapter, allowing students to review key terms quickly and locate each term within the text.

Assessments are also found at the end of each chapter. These end-of-chapter tests assess students' comprehension of key points and provide students a variety of opportunities to strengthen their analytical skills. Each test features a **vocabulary review** section; a **project assignment** that allows students to participate in a hands-on project or experiment related to the chapter material; a **tech alternative** that integrates technology into assessing and applying the content; a short essay question that encourage students to think critically about psychology topics; and an extensive **multiple-choice assessment** aligned to the chapter learning objectives.

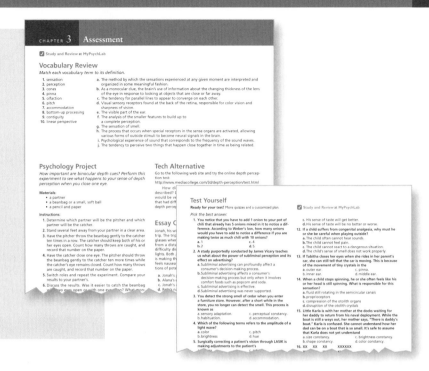

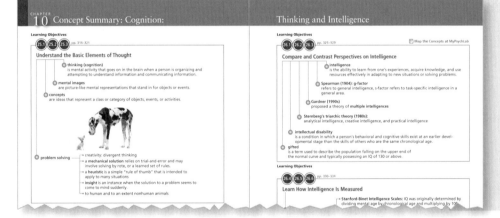

Concept Summaries, at the end of each chapter, provide students with a graphic summary of the chapter's content. By pulling the content together in this highly visual manner, students will better understand the connections and grasp how the chapter material fits together.

Other features of each chapter include special sections covering interesting topics related to the material, especially topics of diversity and cultural interest: *Classic Studies in Psychology, Psychology in the News,* and *Issues in Psychology*. These are not set off from the text in boxes, making it more likely that students will read the enriching material. Questions for Further Study allow students to think critically about the content they have just read.

Issues in Psychology: Workplace Violence

Acts of violence in the workplace have increased dramatically in the past few decades—nearly tripling in the 1980s alone (Baron, 1993). Psychologists are devoting time and energy to studying the reasons for this violence and are looking for ways to recognize and prevent future incidents. Some highlights from research in workplace violence show that people in some types of jobs face a higher probability of becoming a victim of a crime because of the characteristics of the job. For example, three of the most likely occupations are police officers, corrections officers, and taxi drivers (Centers for Disease Control and Prevention, 2009). For taxi drivers (along with convenience-store clerks), it is the availability of cash and the solitary nature of the job that entices many criminals to attempt robbery. In the case of police and correctional officers, violence is part of the very nature of their job. Consider the following statistics:

- Between 1992 and 2006, there were 11,613 workplace homicide victims reported.
- Of those homicides, 11.6 police officers out of every 100,000 were killed on the job compared to the national average for all occupations of 4.0 out of every 100,000.
- From 2004 to 2008 there was an average of 564 work-related homicides each year—10 percent of all fatal work injuries.
- Four out of every 5 homicide victims in 2008 were male.
- Men were more likely to be killed by a stranger, whereas women were more likely to be killed by a relative or personal acquaintance.

Teaching and Learning Package

The **Teacher's Edition** of **Prentice Hall Psychology** 2nd Edition contains teaching tips, classroom activities, and other valuable materials designed to support teachers as they use this program in the classroom. Each page of the Student Edition is reproduced in this wraparound edition and annotated with additional information developed by high school teachers for high school teachers—including lesson-plan ideas, discussion questions, background information that expands on the material presented in the Student Edition, and strategies for adapting instruction to meet the needs of diverse learners. The supplementary information and creative teaching ideas in the Teacher's Edition help teachers save valuable time before, during, and after class.

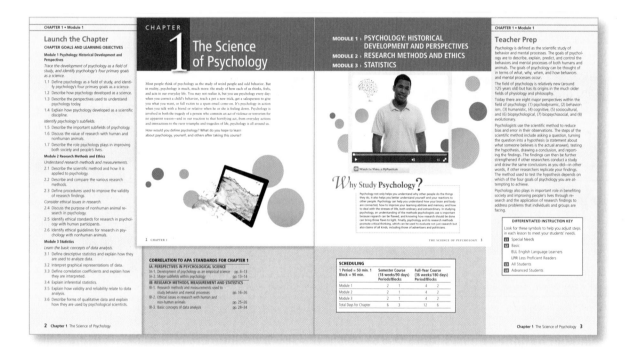

Teacher's Resource DVD with Interactive PowerPoint Slides The Teacher's Resource Manual, Test Bank, *TestGen®*, and PowerPoint Slides, are available on the Teacher Resource DVD, which provides a convenient way for teachers to access key supplementary materials at home or at school. The DVD includes **Interactive PowerPoint Slides**. The slides are designed to bring the text's powerful design right into the classroom, drawing students into the lesson and providing wonderful interactive activities, visuals, and videos.

The **Teacher's Resource Manual** offers an in-depth collection of resources. For each module, you'll find activities, exercises, assignments, and handouts for in-class use, as well as guidelines on integrating the many Pearson media resources into your classroom and syllabus. The electronic format features click-and-view hot links that allow teachers to quickly review or print any resource from a particular chapter. This resource saves prep work and helps maximize classroom time.

The **Test Bank** contains a primary test bank with more than 3,000 questions. Each chapter includes a Total Assessment Guide that lists all of the test items in an easy-to-reference grid. The Total Assessment Guide organizes all test items by learning objective and question type (remember the facts, understand the concepts, and apply what you know).

An additional feature of this test bank is the inclusion of rationales for the correct answer and the key distracter in the multiple-choice questions. The rationales help teachers further evaluate the questions they are choosing for their tests, giving them the option to use the rationales as an answer key for their students.

The *Prentice Hall Psychology* test bank comes with **TestGen®**, a powerful assessment-generation program that allows teachers to create and print quizzes and exams. This easy-to-use, customizable program enables teachers to view, edit, and add questions; transfer questions to test; print multiple tests for each chapter; and print multiple versions of tests.

TOTAL ASSESSMENT GUIDE

Chapter 1
The Science of Psychology

Learning Objectives	Remember the Facts	Understand the Concepts	Apply What You Know	Analyze It
1.1 Define psychology as a field of study, and identify psychology's four primary goals as a science.	1, 2, 6, 183, 221	3, 8, 11, 12, 13, 14, 184	4, 5, 7, 9, 10, 15, 222	
1.2 Describe psychology's emergence as a scientific discipline.	16, 17, 19, 21, 25, 26, 27, 30, 31, 32, 37, 39, 42, 44, 47, 185, 186, 187, 223, 224	18, 22, 23, 24, 28, 29, 34, 35, 36, 40, 45, 46, 188	20, 33, 38, 41, 43, 48, 245	243, 244
1.3 Describe the perspectives used to understand psychology today.	49, 51, 53, 56, 57, 58, 189, 226	54, 55, 225	50, 52, 59, 60, 61	
1.4 Explain how psychology developed as a scientific discipline.	62, 63	64, 190, 191	65, 227, 228	
1.5 Describe the important subfields of psychology.	66, 67, 68, 69, 70, 192, 193, 194, 229		71, 72, 73, 74, 75, 76, 195	
1.6 Discuss the value of research with human and nonhuman animals.	77	79, 196, 197, 230	78	
1.7 Describe the role psychology	80, 200	81, 198, 199		

Answer Key

1. d Explanation: These goals adequately help uncover the mysteries of behavior. (Topic: Trace the development of psychology as a science., Remember the Facts, LO 1.1 - Define psychology as a field of study, and identify psychology's four primary goals as a science.)

2. b Explanation: William James was a functionalist. (Topic: Trace the development of psychology as a science., Remember the Facts, LO 1.2 - Describe psychology's emergence as a scientific discipline.)

3. b Explanation: Freud studied repressed conflict and Watson studied observable behavior. (Topic: Trace the development of psychology as a science., Understand the Concepts, LO 1.2 - Describe psychology's emergence as a scientific discipline.)

Interactive PowerPoint Slides bring the text's powerful design right into the classroom, drawing students into the lesson and providing wonderful interactive activities, visuals, and videos. The slides are built around the program learning objectives and offer multiple pathways or links between content areas.

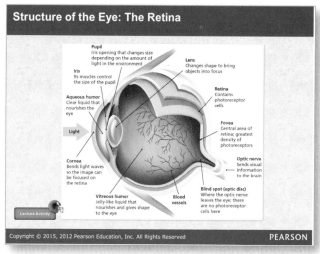

How to Access Resources

Most of the teacher supplements and resources for this text are available electronically for download to qualified adopters from the Pearson Instructor Resource Center (IRC). Upon adoption or to preview, please go to **www.pearsonschool.com/access_request**, select "We need IRC Access", then complete the form under Option 1. Teachers will be required to complete a brief one-time registration subject to verification of educator status. Upon verification, access information and instructions will be sent via email. Once logged into the IRC, enter 9780133980578 in the "Search our Catalog" box to locate these resources.

MyPsychLab
Engage, Assess, Succeed

What is **MyPsychLab**? **MyPsychLab** is a dynamic, easy-to-use learning and assessment tool that provides a wealth of resources for *Prentice Hall Psychology* 2nd Edition geared to meet the diverse needs of today's students and teachers. **MyPsychLab** offers many accessible tools that encourage students to read their text and help them improve results. It combines original online materials with powerful online assessments to engage students, assess their learning, and help them succeed. **MyPsychLab** helps ensure students are always learning and always improving.

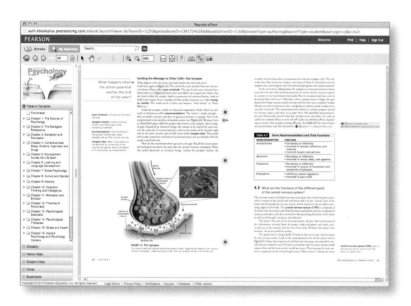

Pearson eText and Audio Textbook

- **Pearson eText** offers a complete interactive student text online. Students can navigate page-by-page, move directly to a chapter or section, or use the search feature to locate all references throughout the entire book. Pearson's interactive eText allows students to highlight, add study notes, bookmark pages, and access multimedia—videos, simulations, glossary—all at the point of use.

- **Audio Textbook** provides the complete *Prentice Hall Psychology* text in audio format.

- The audio text can be used stand-alone or in conjunction with the print textbook to help students read and understand each concept.

Interactive Study Tools and Assignments

MyPsychLab provides a wealth of interactive study tools to support a variety of student learning styles. Students will find video clips, simulations, animations, podcasts, flash cards, and more.

- **Downloadable Flash Cards** are another quick and easy way for students to quiz themselves on key content.

- **Psychology Library** offers numerous student tools and resources, including study skills and plagiarism tutorials, an APA documentation guide, and more.

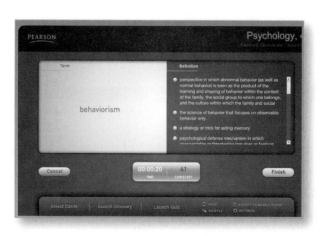

NEW! Dynamic Study Modules, which assess student performance and activity in real time, and using data and analytics, personalize content to reinforce concepts that target each student's strengths and weaknesses.

NEW! Writing Space, a single place to create, track, and grade writing assignments, provide writing resources, and exchange meaningful, personalized feedback with students, quickly and easily, including autoscoring for practice writing prompts. Plus, Writing Space has integrated access to Turnitin, the global leader in plagiarism prevention.

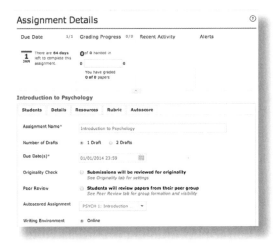

Assessments and Pearson GradeBook

For each chapter of the book, MyPsychLab offers a pre-test, post-test, and chapter exam. Based on the results of the pre-test, MyPsychLab creates a customized study plan for each student, identifying areas of strength and weakness and providing extra support where needed. With the Pearson GradeBook, students can follow their own progress and teachers can monitor the work of the entire class. Automated grading of these tests and assignments helps both students and teachers save time and improve results.

How to Access MyPsychLab

MyPsychLab with Pearson eText is an online homework, tutorial, and assessment system that improves results by helping students better master concepts and by providing educators a dynamic set of tools for gauging individual and class performance. Its immersive experiences truly engage students in learning, helping them to understand course material and improve their performance. And MyPsychLab comes from Pearson—your partner in providing the best digital learning experiences.

Upon textbook purchase, students and teachers are granted access to MyPsychLab with Pearson eText. High school teachers can obtain preview or adoption access for MyPsychLab in one of the following ways:

Preview Access

- Teachers can request preview access by visiting **PearsonSchool.com/access_request**. Select Initial Access then using Option **2**, select your discipline and title from the drop-down menu and complete the online form. *Preview Access* information will be sent to the teacher via e-mail.

Adoption Access

- With the purchase of a textbook program that offers a media resource, a *Pearson Adoption Access Card*, with student and teachers codes and a complete Instructor's Manual, will be delivered with your textbook purchase. ISBN 9780133540871

- Ask your sales representative for an *Adoption Access Code Card/Instructor Manual package* ISBN: 9780133540871

Or

- Visit **PearsonSchool.com/access_request**. Select Initial Access then using Option **3**, select your discipline and title from the drop-down menu and complete the online form. Access information will be sent to the teacher via e-mail.

Students, ask your teacher for access.

About the Authors

WILLIAM ELMHORST is a psychology teacher at Marshfield High School in Marshfield, Wisconsin. He received his Master of Arts in Education from Viterbo University in La Crosse, Wisconsin, and his Master of Science in Education Administration from the University of Wisconsin-Superior in Superior, Wisconsin. Will has been teaching Psychology for 24 years and is also a reader for the College Board's AP Psychology exam. He served as the National Chair of the APA affiliate board TOPSS in 2009, has published several articles on best practices in teaching psychology, and has authored Pearson Education's *AP* Test Prep Series: AP Psychology* workbook. Will also teaches an online Introduction to Psychology class for the University of Wisconsin Colleges. His research interests are diverse, and he is currently researching late 19th century science fiction, with a focus on psychology in the works of H. G. Wells. During time off from teaching, he enjoys travel with his sons and spending time outdoors.

KATHERINE MINTER, BS, MA, served as National Chair of the American Psychological Association's Teachers of Psychology in Secondary Schools (APA-TOPSS) in 2010 and has shared her knowledge and ideas with fellow teachers since 1992. Experienced in classroom teaching at high schools and community colleges, she currently teaches at Westwood High School, Round Rock Independent School District, near Austin, Texas. Katherine has taught Psychology, Advanced Placement (AP) Psychology, and International Baccalaureate (IB) Psychology at both the Standard Level and Higher Level. She has been a College Board Consultant since 1994, an AP Reader for many years, and an IB Trainer and IB Examiner. Katherine has been recipient of the College Board "Teaching Excellence Award" (1996), named "Westwood Teacher of the Year" (2001), and selected for the 2008 APATOPSS National Award for "Excellence in Teaching." She is also author of a teacher's manual for AP Psychology. In addition to teaching and writing, Katherine enjoys spending time with her family, as well as reading, traveling, and gardening.

MARY SPILIS is a retired high school teacher of 31 years in Sylvania, Ohio. During her tenure as an educator, she taught Psychology I & II and AP Psychology. She served as Chair of TOPSS, a member committee of the American Psychological Association. Mary has received numerous accolades during her career, and is a recipient of the National High School Psychology Teacher of the Year (awarded by the American Psychological Association), Teacher of the Year (Sylvania City Schools), Outstanding Teacher award (Miami University). She is a designated Master Teacher of the National Science Foundation, and authored the Treatment Unit, a lesson plan designed specifically for high school psychology teachers. Mary has been a consultant for the College Board for more than 20 years, has served as a reader for the AP Psychology exam for many years, and continues to teach AP Psychology teachers at workshops throughout the country. She also served as the AP Psychology content editor for the 4th edition of *AP Psychology* (Prentice Hall).

Preface

From beginning to end, *Prentice Hall Psychology* 2nd Edition was developed with high school students' and teachers' unique goals and concerns in mind. An engaging, clearly written textbook can motivate students to learn, so we wrote in a style that draws students to an ongoing dialogue and introduces them to psychology—its history, its breadth, its mysteries, and its applications. Examples and explanations are tailored to high school students' interests and needs to help them understand the fundamental concepts of psychology and show them that psychology is a current, relevant, and endlessly fascinating field. In *Prentice Hall Psychology* 2nd Edition, students will find the academic support they need to succeed in class—and the current references, accessible language, and humor that will motivate them to explore how psychological principles play a role in their everyday lives.

Organization and Curriculum Standards

We understand, too, that high school teachers value a flexible curriculum that addresses key learning objectives and standards. *Prentice Hall Psychology* is organized around and collated to the latest National Standards for High School Psychology Curricula, put forth by the American Psychological Association (APA). To ensure that *Prentice Hall Psychology* 2nd Edition reflects the current concerns of high school educators and the larger psychology community, each Learning Objective in this text is linked to a specific national standard. In fact, the organization of our text mirrors the organization of the standards. Like the standards, this book is divided into seven domains, and each chapter of this book addresses one or two standards from the 20 Standards Areas, providing complete and comprehensive coverage. Teachers can feel comfortable knowing that when they use *Prentice Hall Psychology* 2nd Edition in their classrooms, they are addressing key standards in a way that is both academically rigorous and student friendly.

The modular design of *Prentice Hall Psychology* 2nd Edition provides teachers the flexibility they need to structure their courses around their unique classroom goals. Every effort has been made to ensure that each module stands alone and may be taught in any order. Students do not need to read earlier modules to fully understand later modules. Because these modules are much shorter than traditional textbook chapters, they help students focus on a few pages of text at a time without feeling overwhelmed with information. Learning Objectives at the beginning of each module give students and teachers at-a-glance information about the topics covered within, and practice quizzes at the end of each module encourage students to review frequently and retain the material they've learned.

These carefully crafted features, along with the others described, make *Prentice Hall Psychology* 2nd Edition an innovative and invaluable resource for students and teachers alike. We are deeply indebted to the reviewers who have taken the time to give insightful feedback and suggestions for this program, especially the numerous high school psychology teachers who have helped us shape this book.

Acknowledgements

This program reflects the input and feedback of many educators and students who shared their thoughts with us. We are especially grateful to the many high school teachers who contributed to decisions about text organization, content coverage, and pedagogical innovation, helping us keep focused on what is most important to teachers and students in the classroom. We are indebted to the teachers who gave us their time, their energy, and their invaluable feedback as we developed this text and its supplementary materials. We are gratified with the results and hope that you find this text as inviting as we do!

Reviewers

Ruth Anderson, Clovis West High School

Alan Feldman, Glen Rock High School

Michael Hamilton, Hopkinton High School

Rachel Rosenbaum, Mercy College; Kingsborough Community College

In addition to the many reviewers who guided this book, we would like to extend our grateful acknowledgment to our extraordinary content advisors, Saundra Ciccarelli and Noland White, the authors of *Psychology*, a college-level introductory psychology course. Sandy and Noland's love of psychology, their dedication to students, and their humor inspired us and this book in countless ways.

Without the dedicated team at Pearson, this book would not have been possible. We would like to extend our thanks to Erin Mitchell, Executive Editor; Amber Mackey, Program Team Lead; and Linda Behrens, Project Manager Team Lead for their support of this project. Reena Dalal, Program Manager and Crystal McCarthy, Project Manager, managed the project with the help of editorial assistant Sarah Henrich. Elaine Shema, Product Management/Marketing for Humanities School, guided the project with expertise. Brandy Dawson, Sacha Laustsen, Caroline Fenton, and Pamela Weldin all contributed greatly to making the book the best that it could be. Sherry Lewis, Senior Production Project Manager, expertly directed the project through the production process, along with Diane Peirano, Operations Specialist. Blair Brown, Kathryn Foot, and Lumina Datamatics provided art direction for the book's wonderful design.

Will Elmhorst: I would like to thank the team at Pearson and Lumina Datamatics for their guidance and support, especially Abigail Perrine, for her wonderful leadership and kindness during the project, and Sherry Todd for her wisdom and excellent "coaching" that kept the tasks at hand moving forward successfully. I would also like to extend my thanks to my fellow psychology teachers for sharing their insights. Heartfelt thanks go to Kay Minter and Mary Spilis for giving so very generously from their experience and expertise toward the goal of making our final product such a student and teacher friendly textbook. Special thanks to my sons Noah, Taylor and Collin for all the love and support they gave their sometimes frazzled dad this past year. Finally, and most importantly, my love and thanks to my co-adventurer in life, Carla, for being there, at my side every step of the way on this journey. (URW!:))

Katherine Minter: My heartfelt gratitude goes to my students, who have been my greatest teachers over many years. Special thanks to my colleagues Will El-mhorst and Mary Spilis for being easy to work with, incredibly knowledgeable, and lovers of psychology just like me. For giving a public school teacher an opportunity to contribute to the broader teaching of the science of psychology, my thanks go to the whole team at Pearson and Lumina Datamatics, especially Abigail Perrine and Sherry Todd, who helped us navigate through the intricacies of a second edition. My deep appreciation particularly goes to Amber Mackey, who encouraged me to take on this project and who, with expertise, flexibility, and good humor, skillfully guided this project to its conclusion. Finally, my love goes to my husband, Larry, my children, Sarah and Andrew, and my grandson, Jedidiah, for always supporting my adventures.

Mary Spilis: Psychology has always been my passion; I deeply appreciate the opportunity to be a member of this team. The leadership at Pearson and Lumina Datamatics are amazing. Abigail Perrine continues to be the best project director on the planet; her knowledge and dedication in the production of an outstanding high school textbook as always is appreciated! Sherry Todd, also a member of Lumina Datamatics, kept us moving ever so forward and her advice was always just an email away! Heartfelt thanks to both of them! Thank you goes to Will Elmhorst for his gifted writing and insight into the needs of high school psychology teachers. Kay Minter continues to be a tremendous asset to the team. Her wisdom and understanding of high school psychology teachers, is exemplary. A special thank you to my most ardent supporter in the adventures of my life, Michael, my in-house editor and love of my life!

William Elmhorst
Marshfield High School
Marshfield, Wisconsin

Katherine Minter
Westwood High School
Austin, Texas

Mary Spilis
Sylvania City Schools *(retired)*
Sylvania, Ohio

Important Dates in Psychology

Use this timeline to get a better understanding of key dates in the history of psychology.

360 Plato writes the *Theaetetus* examining theories of perception, knowledge, and truth.

350 Aristotle writes *De Anima* about the relationship of the soul to the body.

1848 Phineas Gage suffers brain damage and provides a famous case study of the effects of brain damage.

1859 Charles Darwin publishes the theory of natural selection, which influences the field of evolutionary psychology.

B.C.E. 400　　　**C.E. 1650**　　　**1860**

430 Hippocrates proposes that mental illnesses are caused by an imbalance of four major fluids in the human body.

1649 Descartes publishes *The Passion of the Soul,* outlining the pineal gland as the seat of the soul.

1860 Gustav Fechner is often credited with performing the first scientific experiments that would form the basis for experimentation in psychology.

1861 Broca's Area and its role in speech production is discovered.

1874 Wernicke's Area and its role in language comprehension is discovered.

1879 Wilhelm Wundt establishes the first laboratory of psychology in Leipzig, Germany.

1884 James-Lange theory of emotion proposed.

1900 Freud publishes *The Interpretation of Dreams.*

1906 Ivan Pavlov publishes his findings on classical conditioning.

1906 Ramon y Cajal discovers that the nervous system is composed of individual cells.

1908 Yerkes-Dodson law proposed to explain relationship between performance and arousal.

1920 Francis Sumner becomes the first African American to receive a PhD in psychology at Clark University.

1920 Watson and Rayner publish the "Little Albert" experiment.

1921 The first neurotransmitter, acetylcholine, is discovered.

1921 The Rorschach Inkblot Test is developed.

1921 Allport proposes a trait theory of personality.

1900

1890 William James publishes his book, *Principles of Psychology.*

1892 American Psychological Association (APA) founded and G. Stanley Hall elected first president.

1894 Margaret Floy Washburn is the first woman to receive a PhD in psychology at Cornell University.

1904 Spearman proposes a general factor of intelligence.

1905 Mary Whiton Calkins becomes the first female president of the APA.

1905 The first widely used IQ test, the Binet-Simon, was created.

1905 Freud proposes his psychosexualtheory of personality development.

1920

1911 Thorndike proposes the Law of Effect.

1912 Gestalt psychology first developed by Max Wertheimer.

1912 The intelligence quotient is developed by William Stern.

1913 Carl Jung develops his theory of the collective conscious.

1915 Freud first proposes the concept of defense mechanisms.

1929 Hans Berger introduces EEG method for studying the human brain.

1938 B.F. Skinner introduces the concept of operant conditioning.

1938 Electroconvulsive shock first used on a human patient.

1939 Clark and Clark classic study on prejudice conducted.

1950 Erik Erikson proposes his psychosocial stages of personality development.

1951 Soloman Asch's classic study on conformity conducted.

1952 The first edition of the *Diagnostic and Statistical Manual of Mental Disorders (DSM)* is published.

1952 Chlorpromazine first drug treatment introduced for the treatment of schizophrenia.

1942 Carl Rogers develops client-centered therapy.

1942 The Minnesota Multiphasic Personality Inventory is created.

1961 Carl Rogers creates the concepts of ideal self, real self, conditional positive regard, and unconditional positive regard.

1961 Muzafer Sherif conducts the "Robber's Cave" study.

1967 Seligman demonstrates learned helplessness in dogs.

1967 Holmes and Rahe create the Social Readjustment Rating Scale.

1967 Beck proposes a cognitive theory for explaining depression.

1968 Roger Sperry demonstrates hemispheric specialization with split-brain patients.

1940

1960

1970

1930 Tolman and Honzik demonstrate latent learning in rats.

1930 Jean Piaget proposes four stages of cognitive development.

1933 Sigmund Freud proposes the concepts of id, ego, and superego.

1934 Lev Vygotsky proposes concept of zone of proximal development.

1935 Henry Murray creates the Thematic Apperception Test.

1935 Prefrontal lobotomy developed by Dr. Antonio Egas Moniz.

1948 Alfred Kinsey begins survey research on sexual behavior.

1953 The American Psychological Association publishes the first edition of *Ethical Standards in Psychology*.

1954 Abraham Maslow proposes a hierarchy of needs to describe human motivation.

1955 Albert Ellis proposes rational emotive behavioral therapy.

1956 Hans Selye proposes the General Adaptation Syndrome to describe responses to stress.

1959 Festinger and Carlsmith publish their study on cognitive dissonance.

1959 Harlow and Zimmerman demonstrate the importance of contact comfort with their study on infant monkeys.

1962 Cognitive arousal theory of emotion proposed by Schachter and Singer.

1963 Albert Bandura's "Bobo doll" study is conducted.

1963 Stanley Milgram conducts his classic study on obedience.

1963 Lawrence Kohlberg creates his theory of moral development.

1966 Masters and Johnson introduce four stages of sexual response cycle.

1977 The stress-vulnerability model of schizophrenia proposed by Zubin and Spring.

1977 Thomas and Chess conduct studies of different types of infant temperament.

1978 Elizabeth Loftus puts into question the validity of eyewitness testimony with discovery of misinformation effect.

1979 Mary Ainsworth uses the Strange Situation experiment to study infant attachment styles.

1979 Thomas Bouchard begins the Minnesota study of twins reared apart to identify the influence of genetics and the environment on personality traits.

1994 Herrnstein and Murray publish *The Bell Curve*.

1995 Goleman proposes idea of emotional intelligence.

2000 Genetic researchers finish mapping human genome.

2002 Steven Pinker publishes *The Blank Slate* arguing the concept of *tabula rasa*.

2002 New Mexico is the first state to allow licensed psychologists to prescribe drug treatments for psychological disorders.

1990

2010

1981 David Wechsler begins to devise IQ tests for specific age groups.

1983 Gardner first proposes his theory of multiple intelligences.

1985 Robert Sternberg proposes the triarchic theory of intelligence.

1989 Albert Bandura proposes the concept of reciprocal determinism.

1996 McCrae and Costa propose the Big Five Personality dimensions.

1997 Elisabeth Kubler-Ross publishes *On Grief and Grieving*, exploring the process of grieving through expansion of her theory of the five stages of death from *On Death and Dying* (1969)

2004 Alexander Storch presents possibility of obtaining stem cells from adults to repair damaged neural tissue.

2005 FDA mandates black box warnings of increased suicide risk on antidepressants.

2008 Law passed requiring insurance companies to provide equal coverage for mental health services.

2009 US President Barack Obama lifts federal funding limits on scientific research involving human stem cells.

2013 *DSM-5* published.

1974 Friedman and Rosenman discover link between heart disease and Type-A personality.

1974 The PET scan is first introduced as a brain imaging technique.

Correlation to APA's *National Standards for High School Psychology Curricula*

Prentice Hall Psychology 2nd Edition provides complete and comprehensive coverage of the APA's *National Standards for High School Psychology Curricula*.* The chart below lists the standards and shows which pages in *Prentice Hall Psychology* 2nd Edition focus on each standard.

APA NATIONAL STANDARDS FOR HIGH SCHOOL CURRICULA	SE PAGE(S)
I. SCIENTIFIC INQUIRY DOMAIN	
IA: PERSPECTIVES IN PSYCHOLOGICAL SCIENCE	
IA-1: Development of psychology as an empirical science	
I-A-1.1 Define psychology as a discipline and identify its goals as a science.	4-6
I-A-1.2 Describe the emergence of psychology as a scientific discipline.	6-10
I-A-1.3 Describe perspectives employed to understand behavior and mental processes.	10-12
I-A-1.4 Explain how psychology evolved as a scientific discipline.	12-13
IA-2: Major subfields within psychology	
I-A-2.1 Discuss the value of both basic and applied psychological research with human and non-human animals.	14
I-A-2.2 Describe the major subfields of psychology.	13-14
I-A-2.3 Identify the important role psychology plays in benefiting society and improving people's lives.	14
IB: RESEARCH METHODS, MEASUREMENT AND STATISTICS	
IB-1: Research methods and measurements used to study behavior and mental processes	
IB-1.1 Describe the scientific method and its role in psychology.	16-18
IB-1.2 Describe and compare a variety of quantitative (e.g., surveys, correlations, experiments) and qualitative (e.g., interviews, narratives, focus groups) research methods.	18-23
IB-1.3 Define systematic procedures used to improve the validity of research findings, such as external validity.	23-25
IB-1.4 Discuss how and why psychologists use non-human animals in research.	26
IB-2: Ethical issues in research with human and non-human animals	
IB-2.1 Identify ethical standards psychologists must address regarding research with human participants.	25-26
IB-2.2 Identify ethical guidelines psychologists must address regarding research with non-human animals.	26
IB-3: Basic concepts of data analysis	
IB-3.1 Define descriptive statistics and explain how they are used by psychological scientists.	28-29
IB-3.2 Define forms of qualitative data and explain how they are used by psychological scientists.	34
IB-3.3 Define correlation coefficients and explain their appropriate interpretation.	33
IB-3.4 Interpret graphical representations of data as used in both quantitative and qualitative methods.	30-32
IB-3.5 Explain other statistical concepts, such as statistical significance and effect size.	33
IB-3.6 Explain how validity and reliability of observations and measurements relate to data analysis.	33-34
II. BIOPSYCHOLOGICAL DOMAIN	
IIA: BIOLOGICAL BASES OF BEHAVIOR	
IIA-1. Structure and function of the nervous system in human and non-human animals	
IIA-1.1 Identify the major divisions and subdivisions of the human nervous system.	46-48
IIA-1.2 Identify the parts of the neuron and describe the basic process of neural transmission.	42-46
IIA-1.3 Differentiate between the structures and functions of the various parts of the central nervous system.	58-64
IIA-1.4 Describe lateralization of brain functions.	64-65
IIA-1.5 Discuss the mechanisms of, and the importance of, plasticity of the nervous system.	48-50

---

*American Psychological Association (APA) 750 First St. NE, Washington, DC 20002-4242 National Standards for High School Curricula dated August 2011

(continued)

(continued)

(continued)

The Science of Psychology

Most people think of psychology as the study of weird people and odd behavior. But in reality, psychology is much, much more: the study of how each of us thinks, feels, and acts in our everyday life. You may not realize it, but you use psychology every day: when you correct a child's behavior, teach a pet a new trick, get a salesperson to give you what you want, or fall victim to a spam email come-on. It's psychology in action when you talk with a friend or relative when he or she is feeling down. Psychology is involved in both the tragedy of a person who commits an act of violence or terrorism for no apparent reason—and in our reaction to that horrifying act, from everyday actions and interactions to the rarer triumphs and tragedies of life, psychology is all around us.

How would you define psychology? What do you hope to learn about psychology, yourself, and others after taking this course?

Watch the Video, at **MyPsychLab**

*W*hy Study **Psychology**?

Psychology not only helps you understand why other people do the things they do, it also helps you better understand yourself and your reactions to other people. Psychology can help you understand how your brain and body are connected, how to improve your learning abilities and memory, and how to deal with the stresses of life, both ordinary and extraordinary. In studying psychology, an understanding of the methods psychologists use is important because research can be flawed, and knowing how research should be done can bring those flaws to light. Finally, psychology and its research methods promote critical thinking, which can be used to evaluate not just research but also claims of all kinds, including those of advertisers and politicians.

1 Psychology: Historical Development and Perspectives

Module Goals	Learning Objectives
Trace the development of psychology as a science.	**1.1** Define psychology as a field of study, and identify psychology's four primary goals as a science.
	1.2 Describe how psychology developed as a science.
	1.3 Describe the perspectives used to understand psychology today.
	1.4 Explain how psychology developed as a scientific discipline.
Identify psychology's subfields.	**1.5** Describe the important subfields of psychology.
	1.6 Discuss the value of research with human and nonhuman animals.
	1.7 Describe the role psychology plays in improving both society and people's lives.

Trace the Development of Psychology as a Science

1.1 Define psychology as a field of study, and identify psychology's four primary goals as a science.

Some people believe psychology is just the study of people and what motivates their behavior. Psychologists do study people, but they study animals as well. To better understand what motivates behavior, psychologists study not only what people and animals do but also what happens in their bodies and in their brains as they do it. Before examining the field of psychology, take the survey *What Do You Know About Psychology?* to understand more about your own preconceived notions of people and human behavior.

Psychology is the scientific study of behavior and mental processes. *Behavior* includes all of our outward or overt actions and reactions, such as talking, facial expressions, and movement. The term *mental processes* refers to all the internal, covert (hidden) activity of our minds, such as thinking, feeling, and remembering. Why "scientific"? To study behavior and mental processes in both animals and humans, researchers have to observe them. Whenever a human being is observing anyone or anything, there's always a possibility the observer will see only what he or she expects to see. Psychologists don't want to let these possible biases* cause them to make faulty observations. They want to be as precise as possible and measure as carefully as they can, so they use the scientific method to study psychology.

❀ **Complete** the Survey, *What Do You Know About Psychology?*, at MyPsychLab

psychology scientific study of behavior and mental processes.

---

*biases: personal judgments based on beliefs rather than facts.

Psychology's Goals Every science has the common goal of learning how things work. The goals specifically aimed at uncovering the mysteries of human and animal behavior are description, explanation, prediction, and control.

Description: What Is Happening? The first step in understanding anything is to describe it. *Description* involves observing a behavior and noting everything about it: what is happening, where it happens, to whom it happens, and under what circumstances it seems to happen. For example, a psychologist might wonder why so many computer programmers seem to be male. She makes further observations and notes that many "non-techies" stereotypically perceive the life and environment of a computer programmer as one in which someone lives and breathes at the computer, surrounds himself with computer games, junk food, and science-fiction gadgets—characteristics that add up to a very masculine* ambience†. That's what *seems* to be happening. The psychologist's observations are a starting place for the next goal: Why do females seem to avoid going into this environment?

▲ *Is this an environment that you would want to study in? Some researchers have wondered if your answer might be influenced by your gender.*

Why Is It Happening? Based on her observations, the psychologist might try to come up with a tentative explanation, such as "women feel they do not belong in such stereotypically masculine surroundings." In other words, she is trying to understand or find an *explanation* for the lower proportion of women in this field. Finding explanations for behavior is a very important step in the process of forming theories of behavior. A **theory** is a general explanation of a set of observations or facts. The goal of description provides the observations, and the goal of explanation helps to build the theory.

The preceding example comes from a real experiment conducted by psychologist Sapna Cheryan and colleagues (Cheryan et al., 2009). Professor Cheryan (who teaches psychology at the University of Washington in Seattle) set up four experiments with more than 250 female and male student participants who were not studying computer science. In the first experiment, students came into a small classroom that had one of two sets of objects: either Star Trek® posters, video-game boxes, and Coke™ cans; or nature posters, art, a dictionary, and coffee mugs (among other things). Told to ignore the objects because they were sharing the room with another class, the students spent several minutes in the classroom. While still sitting in the classroom, they were asked to fill out a questionnaire asking about their attitude toward computer programming. Although the attitudes of male students were not different between the two environments, women exposed to the stereotypically masculine setup were less interested in computer programming than those who were exposed to the nonstereotypical environment. The three other similar experiments yielded the same results.

When Will It Happen Again? Determining what will happen in the future is making a *prediction*. In the Cheryan et al. study, the prediction is clear: If we want more women to go into computer programming, we must do something to change either the environment or the perception of the environment typically associated with this field. This is the purpose of the last of the four goals of psychology: changing or modifying behavior.

theory a general explanation of a set of observations or facts.

---

*masculine: characteristic of a male.
†ambience: climate, mood, feeling, atmosphere.

Control: How Can It Be Changed? The focus of *control*, or the modification of some behavior, is to change a behavior from an undesirable one (such as women avoiding a certain academic major) to a desirable one (such as more equality in career choices).

Professor Cheryan suggests that changing the image of computer programming may help increase the number of women choosing to go into this field. Not all psychological investigations will try to meet all four of these goals. In some cases, the main focus might be on description and prediction, as it would be for a personality theorist who wants to know what people are like (description) and what they might do in certain situations (prediction). Some psychologists are interested in both description and explanation, as is the case with experimental psychologists who design research to find explanations for observed (described) behavior. Therapists may be more interested in controlling or influencing behavior and mental processes, although the other three goals would be important in achieving this objective.

Although these goals have not really changed over the years since psychology's beginnings, the methods of achieving them certainly have changed. In the next section, we'll take a look at the early pioneers in psychology.

Psychology is a relatively new field in the realm of the sciences; it is only about 130 years old. It's not that no one thought about what makes people tick before then; on the contrary, many philosophers,* medical doctors, and physiologists† thought about little else. Famous philosophers such as Plato, Aristotle, and Descartes wrote about the relationship of the soul (or mind) and the body (Durrant, 1993; Everson, 1995; Jackson, 2001; Kenny, 1968, 1994). Medical doctors and physiologists wondered about the physical connection between the body and the brain. For example, physician Hermann von Helmholtz (von Helmholtz, 1852, 1863) performed groundbreaking experiments in visual and auditory (hearing) perception.

How long has ▶ psychology been around?

1.2 Describe how psychology developed as a science.

In the Beginning: Wundt, Titchener, and James The efforts to understand human behavior actually began in several different places around the world, and the people who were psychology's pioneers came from very different backgrounds. Eventually these varied ideas were recognized as the beginnings of a new field of inquiry, psychology.

It really all started to come together in a laboratory in Leipzig, Germany, in 1879. It was here that Wilhelm Wundt (VILL-helm Voont, 1832–1920), a physiologist, attempted to apply scientific principles to the study of the human mind. In his laboratory, students from around the world were taught to study the structure of the human mind. Wundt believed that consciousness, the state of being aware of external events, could be broken down into thoughts, experiences, emotions, and other basic elements. To inspect these nonphysical elements, students had to learn to think objectively about their own thoughts—after all, they could hardly read someone else's mind. Wundt called this process *objective introspection* (the prefix *intro* means inside and the root word *spect* means to look), the process of objectively examining and measuring one's own thoughts and mental activities (Rieber & Robinson, 2001). For example, Wundt might place an object, such as a rock, into a student's hand and have the student tell him everything that he

---

*philosophers: people who seek wisdom and knowledge through thinking and discussion.
†physiologists: scientists who study the physical workings of the body and its systems.

was feeling as a result of having the rock in his hand—all the sensations stimulated by the rock. (Objectivity* was—and is—important because scientists need to remain unbiased. Observations need to be clear and precise, but unaffected by the individual observer's beliefs and values.)

This was really the first attempt by anyone to bring objectivity and measurement to the concept of psychology. This attention to objectivity, together with the establishment of the first true experimental laboratory in psychology, is why Wundt is known as the "father of psychology."

Titchener and Structuralism in America
One of Wundt's students was Edward Titchener (1867–1927), an Englishman who eventually took Wundt's ideas to Cornell University in Ithaca, New York. Titchener expanded on Wundt's original ideas, calling his new viewpoint *structuralism* (the root word *struct* means to build) because the focus of study was the structure of the mind. He believed that every experience could be broken down into its individual emotions and sensations (Brennan, 2002). Although Titchener agreed with Wundt that consciousness could be broken down into its basic elements, Titchener also believed that objective introspection could be used on thoughts as well as on physical sensations. For example, Titchener might have asked his students to introspect about things that are blue rather than actually giving them a blue object and asking for reactions to it. Such an exercise might have led to something like the following: "What is blue? There are blue things, like the sky or a bird's feathers. Blue is cool and restful, blue is calm," and so on.

In 1894, one of Titchener's students at Cornell University became famous for becoming the first woman to receive a Ph.D. in psychology (Goodman, 1980; Guthrie, 2004). Her name was Margaret F. Washburn, and she was Titchener's only graduate student for that year. In 1908, she published a book on animal behavior that was considered an important work in that era of psychology, *The Animal Mind* (Washburn, 1908).

Structuralism was a dominant force in the early days of psychology, but it eventually died out in the early 1900s. A competing view arose not long after Wundt's laboratory was established, shortly before structuralism came to America.

William James and Functionalism
Harvard University was the first school in America to offer classes in psychology in the late 1870s. These classes were taught by one of Harvard's most illustrious instructors, William James (1842–1910). James began teaching anatomy and physiology, but as his interest in psychology developed, he began teaching psychology almost exclusively (Brennan, 2002). His comprehensive† textbook on the subject, *Principles of Psychology*, is so brilliantly written that copies are still in print (James, 1890, 2002).

Unlike Wundt and Titchener, James was more interested in the importance of consciousness to everyday life rather than just the analysis of it. He believed that the scientific study of consciousness itself was not yet possible. Conscious ideas are constantly flowing in an ever-changing stream, and once you start thinking about what you were just thinking about, what you were thinking about is no longer what you *were* thinking about, it's what you *are* thinking about, and . . . excuse me, I'm a little dizzy. I think you get the picture, anyway.

Instead, James focused on how the mind allows people to *function* in the real world—how people work, play, and adapt to their surroundings. He called this

▲ German physiologist Wilhelm Wundt. Wundt's father was a Lutheran minister; Wundt studied medicine, served as an army doctor, and was chair of the philosophy department at Leipzig University.

▲ Structuralists would be interested in all of the memories and sensations this woman is experiencing as she smells the rose.

---

*objectivity: expressing or dealing with facts or conditions as they really are without allowing the influence of personal feelings, prejudices, or interpretations.
†comprehensive: including all parts of a topic.

▲ Mary Whiton Calkins, despite being denied a Ph.D. degree by Harvard because she was a woman, became the first female president of the American Psychological Association and had a successful career as a professor and researcher.

Is functionalism ▶ still an important point of view in psychology?

functionalism early perspective in psychology associated with William James, in which the focus of study is how the mind allows people to adapt, live, work, and play.

viewpoint **functionalism** (the root word *funct* means to do, work, or perform). James was heavily influenced by Charles Darwin's ideas about *natural selection*, in which physical traits that help an animal adapt to its environment and survive are passed on to its offspring, becoming part of the animal's traits. If physical traits could aid in survival, why couldn't behavioral traits do the same? Animals and people whose behavior helped them to survive would pass those traits on to their offspring, perhaps by teaching or even by some mechanism of heredity.* For example, a behavior such as avoiding the eyes of others in an elevator can be seen as a way of protecting one's personal space—a kind of territorial protection that may have its roots in the primitive need to protect one's home and source of food and water from intruders[†] (Manusov & Patterson, 2006) or as a way of avoiding what might seem like a challenge to another person (Brown et al., 2005; Jehn et al., 1999).

One of James's early students was Mary Whiton Calkins, who completed every course and requirement for earning a Ph.D. but was denied that degree by Harvard University because she was a woman. Calkins eventually established a psychological laboratory at Wellesley College. Her work was some of the earliest research in the area of human memory and the psychology of the self. In 1905, she became the first female president of the American Psychological Association (Furumoto, 1979, 1991; Zedler, 1995).

Women were not the only minority to make contributions in the early days of psychology. In 1920, Francis Cecil Sumner became the first African American to earn a Ph.D. in psychology at Clark University. He eventually became the chair of the psychology department at Howard University and is assumed by many to be the father of African American psychology (Guthrie, 2004). Kenneth and Mamie Clark worked to show the negative effects of school segregation on African American children (Lal, 2002). Hispanic psychologist Jorge Sanchez conducted research in the area of intelligence testing, focusing on the cultural biases in such tests (Tevis, 1994). Although psychology recently has seen an increase in the contributions of all minorities, the percentages are still small when compared to the population at large.

In the new field of psychology, functionalism offered an alternative viewpoint to the structuralists. But like so many of psychology's early ideas, it is no longer a major perspective[‡]. Instead, one can find elements of functionalism in the modern fields of *educational psychology* (studying the application of psychological concepts to education) and *industrial/organizational psychology* (studying the application of psychological concepts to businesses, organizations, and industry), as well as other areas in psychology. Functionalism also played a part in the development of one of the more modern perspectives, evolutionary psychology, discussed later in this chapter.

Two Influential Approaches While the structuralists and functionalists argued with each other and among themselves, other psychologists were looking at psychology in other ways.

Sigmund Freud's Theory of Psychoanalysis It should be clear by now that psychology didn't start in one place and at one particular time. People of several different viewpoints were trying to promote their own perspective on the study of the human mind and behavior in different places all over the world.

---

*heredity: the transmission of traits and characteristics from parent to offspring through the actions of genes.
[†]intruders: person going into a place they are not invited.
[‡]perspective: philosophical interpretation of a topic.

Up to now, this chapter has focused on the physiologists and philosophers who became interested in psychology, with a focus on understanding consciousness but little else. The medical profession took a whole different approach to psychology.

Sigmund Freud had become a noted physician in Austria while the structuralists were arguing, and the functionalists were specializing. He was a medical doctor—a neurologist, someone who specializes in disorders of the nervous system—and he and his colleagues had long sought a way to understand the patients who were coming to them for help.

Freud's patients suffered from nervous disorders for which he and other doctors could find no physical cause. Therefore, it was thought, the cause must be in the mind, and that is where Freud began to explore. He proposed that there is an *unconscious* (unaware) mind into which we push, or *repress*, all of our threatening urges and desires. He believed that these repressed urges, in trying to surface, created the nervous disorders in his patients (Freud et al., 1990).

Freud stressed the importance of early childhood experiences, believing that personality was formed in the first six years of life; if there were significant problems, those problems must have begun in the early years.

Freud's ideas are still influential today, although in a somewhat modified form. He had a number of followers and many of them became famous by altering his theory to fit their own viewpoint, but his basic ideas are still discussed and debated today.

Pavlov, Watson, and the Dawn of Behaviorism Ivan Pavlov, like Freud, was not a psychologist. He was a Russian physiologist who, working with dogs, had shown that a reflex (an involuntary reaction) such as salivation, which is normally produced by actually having food in one's mouth, could be caused to occur in response to a totally new and formerly unrelated stimulus* such as the sound of a ticking metronome (a device used by musicians to keep a consistent tempo). He would turn on the metronome, give the dogs food, and they would salivate. After several repetitions, the dogs would salivate to the sound of the metronome *before* the food was presented—a learned (or "conditioned") reflexive response (Klein & Mowrer, 1989). This process was called *conditioning*.

In the early 1900s, psychologist John B. Watson had tired of the arguing among the structuralists; he challenged the functionalist viewpoint, as well as psychoanalysis, with his own "science of behavior," or **behaviorism** (Watson, 1924). Watson wanted to bring psychology back to a focus on scientific inquiry, and he felt that the only way to do that was to ignore the whole "consciousness" issue and focus only on *observable behavior*—something that could be directly seen and measured. He had read of Pavlov's work and thought that conditioning could form the basis of his new perspective of behaviorism.

Watson was certainly aware of Freud's work and his views on unconscious repression. Freud believed that all behavior stems from unconscious motivation, whereas Watson believed that all behavior is learned.

Watson believed that phobias are learned through the process of conditioning, and he set out to prove it. Along with his colleague Rosalie Rayner, he took a baby, known as "Little Albert," and taught him to fear a white rat by making a loud, scary noise every time the infant saw the rat, until finally just seeing the rat caused the infant to cry and become fearful (Watson & Rayner, 1920). Even though "Little Albert" was not afraid of the rat at the start, the experiment worked very well—in fact, "Little Albert" became afraid of other fuzzy things, including a rabbit, a dog, and a sealskin coat.

behaviorism the science of behavior that focuses on observable behavior only.

◄ Are Freud's ideas still in use?

This sounds really bizarre—what does scaring a baby have to do with the science ◄ of psychology?

---

*stimulus: anything that causes an organism to have a reaction or response.

▲ Mary Cover Jones, one of the early pioneers of behavior therapy, earned her master's degree under the supervision of John Watson. Her long and distinguished career also included the publication in 1952 of the first educational television course in child development (Rutherford, 2000).

👁 **Watch** the **Video**, *The Basics: Diverse Perspectives*, at **MyPsychLab**

psychodynamic perspective modern version of psychoanalysis that is more focused on the development of a sense of self and the discovery of motivations behind a person's behavior other than sexual motivations.

behaviorist perspective the science of behavior that focuses on observable behavior only.

humanistic perspective the "third force" in psychology that focuses on those aspects of personality that make people uniquely human, such as subjective feelings and freedom of choice.

Watson wanted to prove that all behavior was a result of a stimulus–response relationship such as that described by Pavlov. Because Freud and his ideas about unconscious motivation were becoming a dominant force, Watson felt the need to show the world that a much simpler explanation could be found. Although scaring a baby sounds a little cruel and such an experiment would not be conducted today, he felt that the advancement of the science of behavior was worth the baby's relatively brief discomfort.

One of Watson's students was Mary Cover Jones, who completed her master's degree in 1920 under Watson's supervision (Rutherford, 2000). She duplicated the "Little Albert" study with another child, "Little Peter," successfully conditioning Peter to be afraid of a white rabbit (Jones, 1924). She then began a process of *counterconditioning*, in which Peter was exposed to the white rabbit from a distance while eating a food that he really liked. The pleasure of the food outweighed the fear of the faraway rabbit. Day by day, the situation was repeated with the rabbit being brought closer each time, until Peter was no longer afraid of the rabbit. Jones went on to become one of the early pioneers of behavior therapy. Behaviorism is a major perspective in psychology today. It has also influenced the development of other perspectives, such as *cognitive psychology*.

1.3 Describe the perspectives used to understand psychology today.

Even in the twenty-first century, there isn't one single perspective that is used to explain all human behavior and mental processes. There are actually eight modern perspectives.

Modern Perspectives Two of psychology's modern perspectives are updated versions of psychoanalysis and behaviorism, while the others focus on people's goals, thought processes, social and cultural factors, biology, and genetics.

Psychodynamic Perspective Psychoanalysis has become the more modern **psychodynamic perspective.** Although the focus still includes the unconscious mind and its influence over conscious behavior and on early childhood experiences, there is less emphasis on sex and sexual motivations and more emphasis on the development of a sense of self, social, and interpersonal relationships, and the discovery of other motivations behind a person's behavior.

Behavioral Perspective The **behaviorist perspective** also remains very influential. When its primary supporter, John B. Watson, moved on to greener pastures in the world of advertising, B. F. Skinner became the new leader of the field.

Skinner not only continued research in classical conditioning, but he also developed a theory of how voluntary behavior is learned called *operant conditioning* (Skinner, 1938). In this theory, behavioral responses that are followed by pleasurable consequences are strengthened, or *reinforced*. For example, a child who cries and is rewarded by getting his mother's attention will cry again in the future. Skinner's work is discussed in much greater depth in Chapter Six. In addition to the psychodynamic and behavioral perspectives, six newer perspectives have developed within the last 50 years.

Humanistic Perspective Often called the "third force" in psychology, the **humanistic perspective** was really a reaction to both psychoanalytic theory and behaviorism. If you were a psychologist in the early to mid-1900s, you were either a psychoanalyst or a behaviorist—there weren't any other major viewpoints to rival those two.

In contrast to the psychoanalytic focus on sexual development and behaviorism's emphasis on external forces in guiding personality development, some professionals began to develop a perspective that would allow them to focus on people's ability to direct their own lives. Humanistic psychologists held the view that people have *free will*, the freedom to choose their own destiny, and that they strive for *self-actualization*, the achievement of one's full potential.

Two of the earliest and most famous founders of this view were Abraham Maslow (1908–1970) and Carl Rogers (1902–1987). Today, humanistic psychology exists as a form of psychotherapy aimed at self-understanding and self-improvement. Ⓛⓘ ⓃⓀ *to Chapter Fourteen: Psychological Therapies and Treatments, pp. 443–445.*

Cognitive Perspective Cognitive psychology, which focuses on how people think, remember, store, and use information, became a major force in the field in the 1960s. The development of computers (which just happened to make ideal models of human thinking), the work of other psychologist with children and language, and discoveries in biological psychology all stimulated an interest in studying the processes of thought. The **cognitive perspective** with its focus on memory, intelligence, perception, thought processes, problem solving, language, and learning has become a major force in psychology. Ⓛⓘ ⓃⓀ *to Chapter Ten: Cognition: Thinking and Intelligence, pp. 325–329.*

Within the cognitive perspective, the relatively new field of *cognitive neuroscience* includes the study of the physical workings of the brain and nervous system when engaged in memory, thinking, and other cognitive processes. Cognitive neuroscientists use tools for imaging the structure and activity of the living brain, such as magnetic resonance imaging (MRI), functional magnetic resonance imaging (fMRI), and positron emission tomography (PET). The continually developing field of brain imaging is important in the study of cognitive processes.

Sociocultural Perspective Another modern perspective in psychology is the *sociocultural perspective*, which actually combines two areas of study: *social psychology*, which is the study of groups, social roles, and rules of social actions and relationships; and *cultural psychology*, which is the study of cultural norms,* values, and expectations. These two areas are related in that both are about the effect that people have on one another, either individually or in a larger group such as a culture (Peplau & Taylor, 1997). Ⓛⓘ ⓃⓀ *to Chapter Seven: Social Psychology, pp. 228–261.*

The sociocultural perspective is important because it reminds people that the way they and others behave (or even think) is influenced not only by whether they are alone, with friends, in a crowd, or part of a group but also by the social norms, fads, class differences, and ethnic identity concerns of the particular culture in which they live. *Cross-cultural research* also fits within this perspective. In cross-cultural research, the contrasts and comparisons of a behavior or issue are studied in at least two or more cultures. This type of research can help illustrate the different influences of environment (culture and training) when compared to the influence of heredity (genetics, or the influence of genes on behavior).

Biopsychological Perspective *Biopsychology*, or the study of the biological bases of behavior and mental processes, isn't really as new a perspective as one might think. Also known as physiological psychology, biological psychology, psychobiology, and behavioral neuroscience, the **biopsychological perspective** is

▲ *Behaviorist B. F. Skinner puts a rat through its paces. What challenges might arise from applying information gained from studies with animals to human behavior?*

cognitive perspective modern perspective in psychology that focuses on memory, intelligence, perception, problem solving, and learning.

biopsychological perspective perspective that attributes human and animal behavior to biological events occurring in the body, such as genetic influences, hormones, and the activity of the nervous system.

---

*norms: standards or expected behavior.

part of the larger field of neuroscience: the study of the physical structure, function, and development of the nervous system. Also, the previously discussed field of cognitive neuroscience often overlaps with biopsychology and the sociocultural perspective.

Biopsychosocial Perspective The **biopsychosocial perspective** was theorized by psychiatrist George L. Engel at the University of Rochester. A fairly new approach to understanding and explaining human behavior, the biopsychosocial approach combines three major facets of an individual—biology, psychology, and social interactions—in trying to help explain a person either medically or psychologically. Dr. Engel expressed how genetics, behaviors, and environmental aspects interact to explain an individual. The third factor, a person's social interactions, can affect both body and mind. The mind and body also influence social interaction. In other words, all three factors are intertwined and need to be examined to treat the whole person (thereby making this approach a holistic* one). Consider the following example of how the three factors can interact:

Joe, a high school senior, has been having severe headaches for the past three weeks. His parents have also noted that he seems withdrawn and sad. The family doctor believes that Joe's headaches are run-of-the-mill migraines. Unsatisfied with this diagnosis, Joe's parents take him to a psychiatrist, who interviews Joe about the past month of his life. As it turns out, Joe had been kicked off the basketball team, which alienated him from his group of friends. Since Joe was unable to socialize as usual, he started to spend more time alone, which led to him feeling sad and withdraw. The stress of being alone eventually started to impact his body in the form of headaches.

Evolutionary Perspective The **evolutionary perspective** focuses on the biological bases for universal mental characteristics that all humans share. It seeks to explain general mental strategies and traits, such as why we lie, how attractiveness influences mate selection, why fear of snakes is so common, or why people universally like music and dancing. This approach may also overlap with biopsychology.

▲ *Psychologists with an evolutionary perspective would be interested in how this couple selected each other as partners.*

1.4 Explain how psychology developed as a scientific discipline.

As you can probably tell, psychology has changed over time, and it will continue to change in the future as new technologies are developed, new theories are adopted, and new discoveries are made. Lately, psychologists have performed significant research in several new or developing areas of psychology, including positive psychology.

Psychologist Martin Seligman, a psychology professor at the University of Pennsylvania, is widely recognized as one of the founders of *positive psychology*, a perspective that recommends shifting the focus of psychology away from the negative (abuse, anxiety, depression, all the things that can go wrong) to a more **positive perspective** or focus on strengths, well-being, and the pursuit of happiness (Myers, 1993). Positive psychologists' research findings may help more people learn how to live happy and satisfying lives.

You may have realized as you read through the various perspectives that no one perspective has all the answers. Some perspectives are more scientific (e.g., behavioral and cognitive), whereas others are based more in thinking about human behavior (e.g., psychodynamic and humanistic). Some, like sociocultural,

biopsychosocial perspective perspective in which behavior is seen as the result of the combined and interacting forces of biological, psychological, social, and cultural influences.

evolutionary perspective perspective that focuses on the biological bases of universal mental characteristics that all humans share.

positive perspective perspective in psychology that shifts focus away from the negative and instead focuses on well-being.

---

*holistic: broad and inclusive.

biopsychological, biopsychosocial, and evolutionary perspectives, are related to each other. Psychologists will often take an *eclectic* perspective—one that uses the "bits and pieces" of several perspectives that seem to best fit a particular situation.

Identify Psychology's Subfields

1.5 Describe the important subfields of psychology.

Why do psychologists perform research? Psychology is a large field, and the many professionals working within it have different training, different focuses, and perhaps different goals from the typical psychologist.

A *psychologist* has no medical training but has a doctorate degree. Psychologists undergo intense academic training, learning about many different areas of psychology before choosing a specialization. Because the focus of their careers can vary so widely, psychologists work in many different vocational* settings as described in the video *What Do Psychologists Do? **Figure 1.1a** shows the types of settings in which psychologists work. Remember, not all psychologists are trained to do counseling! Psychologists in the counseling specialization must also be licensed to practice in their states.

⊙ **Watch** the **Video**, *What Do Psychologists Do?*, at **MyPsychLab**

In contrast, a *psychiatrist* has a medical degree (M.D. or D.O.) and is a medical doctor who has specialized in the diagnosis and treatment (including the prescription of medications) of psychological disorders. A *psychiatric social worker* is trained in the area of social work and usually possesses a master's degree in that discipline. These professionals focus more on the environmental conditions that can have an impact on mental disorders, such as poverty, overcrowding, stress, and drug abuse.

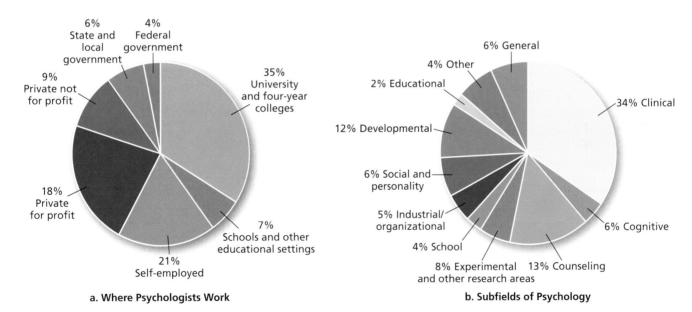

a. Where Psychologists Work

b. Subfields of Psychology

FIGURE 1.1 Work Settings and Subfields of Psychology
(a) There are many different work settings for psychologists. Although not obvious from the chart, many psychologists work in more than one setting. For example, a clinical psychologist may work in a hospital setting as well as teach at a university or college (Tsapogas et al., 2006). (b) This pie chart shows the specialty areas of psychologists who recently received their doctorates (Hoffer et al., 2007).

---

*vocational: having to do with a job or career.

1.6 Discuss the value of research with human and nonhuman animals.

You said not all psychologists do counseling. But I thought that was all that psychologists do—what else is there?

Thinking Critically

Do you believe that violence is a part of human nature? Is violent behavior something that can someday be removed from human behavior or, at the very least, controlled? Think about this question from each of the perspectives discussed in this chapter.

Although many psychologists do participate in delivering therapy to people who need help, there is a nearly equal number of psychologists who do other tasks: researching, teaching, designing equipment and workplaces, and developing educational methods, for example. Also, not every psychologist is interested in the same area of human—or animal—behavior, and most psychologists work in several different areas of interest, as shown in **Figure 1.1b**, Subfields of Psychology. (L)(I)(N)(K) *to Chapter Sixteen: Applied Psychology and Psychology Careers, pp. 500–519.*

Those psychologists who do research have two types of research to consider: basic research versus applied research. *Basic research* is research for the sake of gaining scientific knowledge. For example, a researcher might want to know how many "things" a person can hold in memory at any one time. The other form of research is *applied research*, which is research aimed at answering real-world, practical problems. An applied researcher might take the information from the basic researcher's memory study and use it to develop a new study method for students. Some of the subfields in Figure 1.1b tend to do more basic research, such as experimental and cognitive psychologists, whereas others may focus more on applied research, such as educational, school, and industrial/organizational psychologists.

1.7 Describe the role psychology plays in improving both society and people's lives.

There are many other areas of specialization: Psychology can also be used in fields such as health, sports performance, legal issues, business concerns, and even in the design of equipment, tools, and furniture. However, all psychologists have one important mission in common: to help others. Through research, counseling, treatment, and teaching, psychologists aim to understand how the human mind works and use that understanding to improve people's lives. Research into tough social issues such as racial prejudice and violence can lead to strategies for minimizing these issues in real communities. Research in the field of human factors psychology, which focuses on interactions between humans and machines, can lead to engineering improvements such as designing airline cockpits that help pilots perform their jobs more accurately and efficiently. Psychologists' increasing understanding of developmental issues during childhood can strengthen school curriculums and guide parents' approaches to raising their children. And well-trained counselors and therapists can help people work through difficult personal issues and overcome the challenges of psychological disorders. These are only a few of the many ways in which psychology can improve the daily lives of people around the world.

Study Help Note: These practice quizzes are spaced throughout each chapter to give you an opportunity to check your understanding of the material in each section and provide practice for exams.

Pick the best answer.

1. In the definition of psychology, *mental processes* means

   a. internal, covert processes
   b. unconscious processes
   c. outward or overt actions and reactions
   d. only human behavior

2. Dr. Baker designs an experiment for studying lab rats' reactions to energy drinks in relation to problem solving. Dr. Baker is most interested in the goal of

   a. description
   b. explanation
   c. prediction
   d. control

3. Who was the first woman to complete the coursework for a doctorate at Harvard University?

   a. Mary Whiton Calkins
   b. Mary Cover Jones
   c. Margaret Washburn
   d. Eleanor Gibson

4. Which of the following early psychologists would have been most likely to agree with the statement, "The study of the mind should focus on how it functions in everyday life"?

   a. Wilhelm Wundt
   b. William James
   c. John Watson
   d. Sigmund Freud

5. Which of the following perspectives focuses on the biological bases of universal mental characteristics?

   a. humanistic
   b. behavioral
   c. psychodynamic
   d. evolutionary

6. Which perspective offers the best explanation for schizophrenia?

   a. psychodynamic
   b. behavioral
   c. biopsychological
   d. humanistic

7. Wesley has learned that if he cries with his mother in public, she will often get him a new toy or a piece of candy to quiet him. Which of the following perspectives is associated with John Watson's ideas to explain Wesley's behavior?

   a. psychodynamic
   b. cognitive
   c. behavioral
   d. biopsychological

8. Which perspective would a researcher be taking if she were studying a client's early childhood experiences and his resulting development of self?

   a. psychodynamic
   b. cognitive
   c. behavioral
   d. evolutionary

9. Which of the following professionals in psychology has no medical training but has a doctoral degree?

   a. psychiatrist
   b. psychiatric nurse
   c. psychiatric social worker
   d. psychologist

10. If Dr. Swasey is like most psychologists, where does she probably work?

   a. university/college
   b. self-employed
   c. federal government
   d. state or local government

Module Goals	Learning Objectives
Understand research methods and measurements.	**2.1** Describe the scientific method and how it is applied to psychology. **2.2** Describe and compare the various research methods. **2.3** Define procedures used to improve the validity of research findings.
Consider ethical issues in research.	**2.4** Identify ethical standards for research in psychology with human participants. **2.5** Discuss the purpose of nonhuman animal research in psychology. **2.6** Identify ethical guidelines for research in psychology with nonhuman animals.

scientific method system of gathering data so that bias and error in measurement are reduced.

Understand Research Methods and Measurements

Have you ever tried to guess what people do for a living based only on their appearance? People's guesses sometimes reveal the biases that they may have about certain physical appearances: Men with long hair are musicians, people wearing suits are executives, and so on. Psychology is about trying to determine facts and reduce uncertainty and bias.

2.1 Describe the scientific method and how it is applied to psychology.

▲ *The scientific method can be used to determine if children who watch violence on television are more likely to be aggressive than those who do not.*

In psychology, researchers want to see only what is really there, not what their biases might want them to see. The way to do that is by using the **scientific method**, a system for reducing bias and error in the measurement of data. The scientific method is a way to accomplish the goals of psychology as discussed earlier: description, explanation, prediction, and control.

The first step in any investigation is to have a question to investigate, right? So the first step in the scientific method is this:

1. **Formulating the Question:** You notice something interesting happening in your surroundings for which you would like to have an explanation. An example might be that you've noticed that children seem to get a little more aggressive with each other after watching a particularly violent children's cartoon program. You wonder, is the violence in the cartoon creating the aggressive behavior in the children?

Once you have a question, you will want to look for an answer. The next logical step is to form a tentative* answer or explanation for the behavior you have seen based on your theory. This tentative explanation is known as a **hypothesis**.

hypothesis tentative explanation of a phenomenon based on observations.

2. **Forming a Hypothesis:** Based on your initial observations about what's going on in your surroundings, you form an educated guess about the explanation for your observations, putting it into the form of a statement that can be tested in some way. Going back to the previous example, you might say, "Children who watch violent cartoons will become more aggressive." (Forming a hypothesis based on observations is related to the goals of *description* and *explanation*.)

The next step is testing the hypothesis. People have a tendency to notice only things that agree with their view of the world, a kind of selective perception called *confirmation bias*. The scientific method is designed to overcome the tendency to look at only the information that confirms people's biases by forcing them to actively seek out information that might *contradict* their biases (or hypotheses). So when you test your hypothesis, you are trying to determine if the factor you suspect has an effect and that the results are not due to luck or chance. That's why psychologists keep doing research over and over—to get more evidence that hypotheses are "supported."

3. **Testing the Hypothesis:** The method you use to test your hypothesis will depend on exactly what kind of answer you think you might get. In the example, the best method would probably be an experiment in which you select a group of children, show half of them a cartoon with violence and half of them a cartoon with no violence, and then find some way of measuring aggressive behavior in the two groups.

4. **Drawing Conclusions:** Once you know the results of your hypothesis testing, you will find that either your hypothesis was supported—which means that your little experiment worked, and your measurements supported your initial observations—or it wasn't supported, which means that you need to go back to square one and think of another possible explanation for what you have observed. (Could it be that having to sit still in front of a TV makes children a little more aggressive? Or seeing bright colors flashing on a screen stimulates children to be aggressive?)

The results of any method of hypothesis testing won't be just the raw numbers or measurements. Any data that come from your testing procedure will be analyzed with some kind of statistical method that helps to organize and refine the data. Drawing conclusions can be related to the goal of *prediction*: If your hypothesis is supported, you can make educated guesses about future similar scenarios.

5. **Reporting Your Results:** You have come to some conclusion about your investigation's success or failure, and you want to let other researchers know what you have found.

Just because one experiment or other study did not find support for ◄ the hypothesis does not necessarily mean that the hypothesis is incorrect. Your study might have been poorly designed, or there might have been factors not under your control that interfered with the study. But other researchers are asking the same kinds of questions that you might have asked. So the final step in any scientific investigation is reporting the results.

Why tell anyone ◄ what happened if it failed?

---

*tentative: something that is not fully worked out or completed as yet.

At this point, you would want to write up exactly what you did, why you did it, how you did it, and what you found. If others can *replicate* your research (meaning, do exactly the same study over again and get the same results), it gives much more support to your findings. This allows others to predict behavior based on your findings and to use the results of those findings to modify or *control* behavior, the last goal in psychology.

In psychology, researchers try to find the answers to empirical questions. They can use a variety of research methods depending on the scientific question to be answered as seen in the video *Research Methods*.

Watch the Video, *Research Methods*, at MyPsychLab

2.2 Describe and compare the various research methods.

There are a number of different ways to investigate the answers to research questions, and which one researchers use depends on the kind of question they want to answer. If they want to simply gather information about what has happened or what is happening, they would want a method that gives them a detailed description.

Naturalistic Observation Sometimes all researchers need to know is what is happening to a group of animals or people. The best way to look at the behavior of animals or people is to watch them behave in their normal environment. With people, researchers might want to observe them in their workplaces, homes, or on playgrounds. For example, if someone wanted to know how adolescents behave with members of the opposite sex in a social setting, that researcher might go to the mall on a weekend night.

What is the advantage of naturalistic observation? It allows researchers to get a realistic picture of how behavior occurs because they are actually watching that behavior. In a more artificial setting, like a laboratory, they might get behavior that is contrived* or artificial rather than genuine. Of course, precautions must be taken. An observer should have a checklist of well-defined and specific behavior to record, perhaps using a laptop or tablet to log each piece of data. In many cases, animals or people who know they are being watched will not behave normally anyway, in a process called *observer effect*, so often the observer needs to remain hidden from view. When researching humans, this is often a difficult thing to do. In the mall setting with the teenagers, a researcher might find that pretending to read a book is a good disguise. In other cases, researchers might use one-way mirrors, or they might actually become participants in a group, a technique called *participant observation*.

Are there disadvantages? Unfortunately, yes. One of the disadvantages of naturalistic observation is the possibility of *observer bias*. That happens when the person doing the observing has a particular opinion about what he or she is going to see or expects to see. If that is the case, sometimes that person sees only those actions that support that expectation and ignores actions that don't fit. For example, if you think girls initiate flirting, you might not see the boys who initiate flirting. One way to avoid observer bias is to use the procedure called *blind observers*: people who do not know what the research question is and, therefore, have no preconceived notions about what they "should" see. It's also a good idea to have more than one observer so that the various observations can be compared.

Laboratory Observation Sometimes observing behavior in animals or people is simply not practical in a natural setting. For example, a researcher might want to observe the

▼ *This researcher is studying the behavior of a group of meerkats. Is this naturalistic observation? Why or why not?*

---

*contrived: deliberately created.

reactions of infants to a mirror image of themselves and record the reactions with a camera mounted behind the one-way mirror. That kind of equipment might be difficult to set up in a natural setting. In a laboratory observation, the researcher would bring the infant to the equipment, controlling the number of infants and their ages as well as everything else that goes on in the laboratory. As mentioned previously, laboratory settings have the disadvantage of being an artificial situation that might result in artificial behavior—both animals and people often react differently in the laboratory than they would in the real world. The main advantage of this method is the degree of control that it gives to the observer.

Both naturalistic and laboratory observations can lead to the formation of hypotheses that can later be tested.

Case Studies Another descriptive technique is called the **case study**, in which one individual is studied in great detail. In a case study, researchers try to learn everything they can about that individual. For example, Sigmund Freud based his entire theory of psychoanalysis on numerous case studies of his patients.

The advantage of the case study is the tremendous amount of detail it provides. It may also be the only way to get certain kinds of information. One famous case study is that of Phineas Gage, who in the mid-1800s accidentally had a large metal rod driven through his head because of an explosion that occurred while working on a railroad construction site and suffered a major personality change as a result (Damasio et al., 1994). Case studies are also good ways to study rare conditions such as multiple personality (now called dissociative identity disorder). ⓛⓘⓝⓚ *to Chapter Thirteen: Psychological Disorders, pp. 422–423.*

The disadvantage of the case study is that researchers can't really apply the results to other similar people. In other words, they can't assume that a person having the same kind of experiences as the person in their case study would turn out just like the subject of the case study. People are unique and have too many complicating factors in their lives to be that predictable. So what researchers find in one case won't necessarily apply or generalize to other cases.

Surveys Sometimes psychologists want to know very personal things—such as what people do in private lives, which may be embarrassing or even socially unacceptable. The only way to find out about very private (covert) behavior is to ask questions.

In the survey method, researchers will ask a series of questions about the topic they are studying. Surveys can be conducted in person in the form of interviews or on the telephone, the Internet, or with a questionnaire. In this way, researchers can ask lots of questions and survey literally hundreds of people. To gain a better understanding of what it is like to complete a survey, try your hand at *Participating in a Research Survey.*

That is the big advantage of surveys, aside from their ability to elicit private information. Researchers can obtain a tremendous amount of data on a very large group of people. Of course, there are disadvantages. For one thing, researchers have to be very careful about the group of people they survey. If they want to find out what high school freshmen think about how useful an app for a smart phone is, for example, they can't really ask every single high school freshman in the entire United States. But they can select a **representative sample** from that group. A representative sample has the same general characteristics of the larger group that the research is interested in learning more about. They can randomly* select a certain number of freshmen from several different high schools

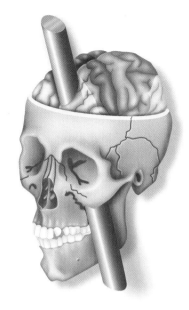

▲ *Phineas Gage survived a steel tamping rod going through his head after some explosive powder went off unexpectedly. Visible above the left side of his mouth is the entry point of the steel rod, and the exit point is at the top of the skull.*

✳ **Complete** the **Survey**, *Participating in a Research Survey*, at **MyPsychLab**

case study study of one individual in great detail.

representative sample randomly selected sample of subjects from a larger population of subjects.

---

*randomly: in this sense, selected so that each member of the group has an equal chance of being chosen.

"Next question: I believe that life is a constant striving for balance, requiring frequent tradeoffs between morality and necessity, within a cyclic pattern of joy and sadness, forging a trail of bittersweet memories until one slips, inevitably, into the jaws of death. Agree or disagree?"

▶ What good is all this focus on science and research going to do for me? I live in the real world, not a laboratory.

correlation a measure of the relationship between two variables.

across the United States by drawing names from a hat or flipping a coin while going down an attendance list.

That brings up the other major disadvantage of the survey technique: People don't always give researchers accurate answers. People tend to misremember things, distort the truth, and may lie outright—even if the survey is an anonymous* questionnaire. Other people deliberately give what they think is the more socially correct answer rather than their true opinion in order not to offend anyone; this process is called courtesy bias. Researchers must therefore take their survey results with a big grain of salt.†

Both the wording of survey questions and the order in which they appear on the survey can affect the outcome. It is difficult to word questions so that everyone who reads them will understand them in exactly the same way. For example, questions can be phrased in such a way that the desired answer becomes obvious (often resulting in courtesy bias–type answers). For example, "Do you agree that the new procedures for registering for classes online are too complicated?" is obviously looking for a confirmation, whereas "What is your opinion of the new procedures for registering for classes online?" is much more open to differing responses.

Thinking Critically about Psychology The real world is full of opportunities for scientific thinking. Think about all the commercials on television for miracle weight loss, hair restoration, or herbal remedies for arthritis, depression, and a whole host of physical and mental problems. Wouldn't it be nice to know how many of these claims people should believe? Wouldn't you like to know how to evaluate statements like these and possibly save yourself some time, effort, and money? That's exactly the kind of "real-world" problem critical "scientific" thinking can help sort out.

Correlations: Finding Relationships The methods discussed so far only provide descriptions of behavior. Actually, only two methods give researchers more than just a description of what has happened: correlations and experiments. Correlation is a statistical technique, a particular way of organizing numerical information so that it is easier to look for patterns in the information. This method will be discussed here because correlation, like the experiment, is about finding relationships. In fact, the data from the descriptive methods just discussed are often analyzed using the correlational technique.

A **correlation** is a measure of the relationship between two or more variables. A *variable* is anything that can change or vary—scores on a test, temperature in a room, gender, and so on. For example, researchers might be curious to know whether or not cigarette smoking is connected to life expectancy—the number of years a person can be expected to live. Obviously, the scientists can't hang around people who smoke and wait to see when those people die. The only way (short of performing a really unethical and lengthy experiment) to find out if smoking behavior and life expectancy are related to each other is to use the medical records of people who have already died. (For privacy's sake, personal information such as names and social security numbers would be removed, with only facts such as age, gender, and weight available to researchers.) Researchers

---

*anonymous: not named or identified.
†grain of salt: a phrase meaning to be skeptical; to doubt the truth or accuracy of something.

would look for two facts from each record: the number of cigarettes the person smoked per day and the age of the person at death.

Now the researcher has two sets of numbers for each person in the study that go into a mathematical formula, to produce a number called the *correlation coefficient**. The correlation coefficient represents two things: the direction of the relationship and its strength.

In terms of the correlation coefficient (represented by the small letter *r*), the number researchers get from the formula will either be a positive number or a negative number. If positive, the two variables increase in the same direction— as one goes up, the other goes up; as one decreases, the other also decreases. If negative, the two variables have an inverse† relationship. As one increases, the other decreases. If researchers find that the more cigarettes a person smoked, the younger that person was when he or she died, that would mean that the correlation between the two variables is negative. (As smoking goes up, life expectancy goes down—an inverse relationship.)

The strength of the relationship between the variables will be determined by the actual number itself. That number will always range between +1.00 and −1.00. The reason that it cannot be greater than +1.00 or less than −1.00 has to do with the formula and an imaginary line on a graph around which the data points gather, a graph called a scatterplot (see **Figure 2.1**). If the relationship is a strong one, the number will be closer to +1.00 or to −1.00. A correlation of +.89, for example, would be a very strong, positive correlation. That might represent the relationship between scores on the SAT and an IQ test, for example. A correlation of −.89 would be equally strong but negative. That would be more like the correlation researchers would probably find between smoking cigarettes and the age at which a person dies.

◀ Direction? How can a mathematical relationship have a direction?

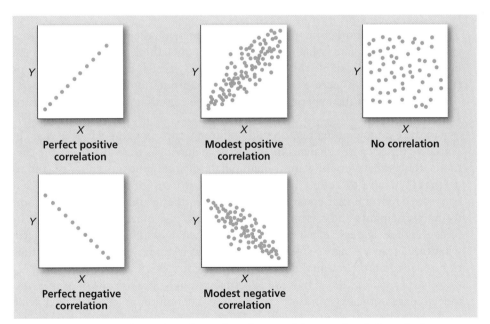

FIGURE 2.1 Scatterplots Showing Direction and Strength of Correlation
It should be noted that perfect correlations, whether positive or negative, rarely occur in the real world.

---

*coefficient: a number used to show a measurement.
†inverse: opposite in order.

Go back to the cigarette example—if we found that the correlation between cigarette smoking and life expectancy was high, does that mean that smoking causes your life expectancy to be shortened?

Notice that the closer the number is to zero, the weaker the relationship becomes. Researchers would probably find that the correlation coefficient for the relationship between people's weight and the number of freckles they have is pretty close to zero, for example.

Not exactly. The biggest error that people make concerning correlation is to assume that it means one variable is the cause of the other. Remember that *correlation does not prove causation*. Although adverse* health effects from cigarette smoking account for approximately 438,000 deaths each year in the United States alone, correlation by itself cannot be used to prove causation (Centers for Disease Control and Prevention, 2009b).

To sum up, a correlation will tell researchers whether there is a relationship between the variables, how strong the relationship is, and in what direction the relationship goes.

The Experiment The only research method that will allow researchers to determine the cause of a behavior is the **experiment**. In an experiment, researchers deliberately manipulate (change in some purposeful way) the variable they think is causing some behavior while holding all the other variables that might interfere with the experiment's results constant and unchanging. That way, if they get changes in behavior (an effect, in other words), they know that those changes must be due to the manipulated variable.

Selection First, researchers might start by selecting the children they want to use in the experiment. The best method to do that would be to make a random selection of a sample of children from a certain population as determined by the researchers—just as a sample would be selected for a survey. Ideally, researchers would decide on the age of child they wanted to study—say, children who are 3 to 4 years old. Then researchers would go to various day care centers and randomly select a certain number of children of that age. Of course, that wouldn't include the children who don't go to a day care center.

The Variables Another important step is to decide on the variable the researchers want to manipulate (which would be the one they think will cause changes in behavior) and the variable they want to measure to see if there are any changes (this would be the effect on behavior of the manipulation). Often the decision on the variables in the experiment comes before selection of the participants or subjects.

In the example of aggression and children's cartoons, the variable that researchers think causes changes in aggressive behavior is the violence in the cartoons. Researchers would want to manipulate that variable in some way, and to do that they have to define the term *violent cartoon*. They would have to find or create a cartoon that contains violence. Then they would show that cartoon to the participants and try to measure their aggressive behavior afterward. In measuring the aggressive behavior, the researchers would have to define exactly what they mean by "aggressive behavior" so that it can be measured. This definition is called an **operational definition** because it specifically names the operations (steps or procedures) that the experimenter must use to control or measure the variables in the experiment. An operational definition of aggressive behavior might be a checklist of very specific actions such as hitting and pushing that an observer can mark off as the children do the items on the list. If the observers were just told to look for "aggressive behavior," the researchers would probably get half a dozen or more different interpretations of what aggressive behavior is.

experiment a deliberate manipulation of a variable to see if corresponding changes in behavior result, allowing the determination of cause-and-effect relationships.

operational definition definition of a variable of interest that allows it to be measured.

---

*adverse: preventing or harmful.

The name for the variable that is manipulated in any experiment is the **independent variable** because it is independent of anything the participants do. The participants in the study do not get to choose or vary the independent variable, and their behavior does not affect this variable at all. In the preceding example, the independent variable would be the presence or absence of violence in the cartoons.

The participants' response to the manipulation of the independent variable is a dependent relationship, so the response of the participants that is measured is known as the dependent variable. Their behavior, if the hypothesis is correct, should depend on whether or not they were exposed to the independent variable, and in the example, the **dependent variable** would be the measure of aggressive behavior in the children. The dependent variable is always the thing (response of subjects or result of some action) that is measured to see just how the independent variable may have affected it.

▲ The act of hitting each other with toy swords could be part of an operational definition of aggressive behavior.

The Groups No, what has been described so far is not enough. The researchers may find that the children who watch the violent cartoon are aggressive, but how would they know if their aggressive behavior was caused by the cartoon or was just the natural aggressive level of those particular children or the result of the particular time of day they were observed? Those sorts of *confounding variables* (variables that interfere with each other and their possible effects on some other variable of interest) are the kind researchers have to control for in some way. For example, if most children in this experiment just happened to be from a fairly aggressive family background, any effects the violent cartoon in the experiment might have had on the children's behavior could be confused (confounded) with the possible effects of the family background.

The best way to control for confounding variables is to have two groups of participants: those who watch the violent cartoon, and those who watch a nonviolent cartoon for the same length of time. Then the researchers would measure the aggressive behavior in both groups. If the aggressive behavior is significantly greater in the group that watched the violent cartoon (statistically speaking), then researchers can say that in this experiment, violent cartoon watching caused greater aggressive behavior.

The group that is exposed to the independent variable (the violent cartoon in the example) is called the experimental group, because it is the group that receives the experimental manipulation. The other group that gets either no treatment or some kind of treatment that should have no effect (like the group that watches the nonviolent cartoon in the example) is called the control group because it is used to control for the possibility that other factors might be causing the effect that is being examined.

◄ If researchers do all of this and find that the children's behavior is aggressive, can they say that the aggressive behavior was caused by the violence in the cartoon?

2.3 Define procedures used to improve the validity of research findings.

The Importance of Randomization As mentioned previously, random selection is the best way to choose the participants for any study. Participants must then be assigned to either the experimental group or the control group. Not surprisingly, *random assignment* of participants to one or the other conditions* is the best way to ensure control over other interfering, or *extraneous*, variables,

independent variable variable in an experiment that is manipulated by the experimenter.

dependent variable variable in an experiment that represents the measurable response or behavior of the subjects in the experiment.

---

*condition: the state or environment that participants are placed in for the experiment.

Watch the Video, *A Sample Experiment*, at MyPsychLab

possible variables that could influence the results that are not being studied. Random assignment means that each participant has an equal chance of being assigned to each condition. So researchers want to take the entire participant group and assign each person randomly to one or the other of the groups in the study. Sometimes this process is as simple as picking names out of a hat. See how these pieces all fit together to form an experiment in the video, *A Sample Experiment*.

Experimental Hazards and Controlling for Effects A few other problems might arise in any experiment, even with the use of control groups and random assignment. These problems are especially likely when studying people instead of animals, because people are often influenced by their own thoughts or biases about what's going on in an experiment.

The Placebo Effect and the Experimenter Effect Let's say there is a new drug that is supposed to improve memory in people who are in the very early stages of *Alzheimer's* disease (a form of mental deterioration that occurs in some people as they grow old). Researchers wanting to test the drug to see if it really is effective in helping to improve memory would get a sample of people who are in the early stages of the disease, divide them into two groups, give one group the drug, and then test for improvement. They would probably have to do a test of memory both before and after the drug was given to be able to measure improvement.

The group that gets ▶ the drug would be the experimental group, and the one that doesn't is the control group, right?

Correct, and getting or not getting the drug is the independent variable, whereas the measure of memory improvement is the dependent variable. But there's still a problem with doing it this way. What if the researchers do find that the drug group had greater memory improvement than the group that received nothing? Can they really say that the drug itself caused the improvement? Or is it possible that the participants who received the drug knew that they were supposed to improve in memory and, therefore, made a major effort to do so? The improvement may have had more to do with participants' belief in the drug than the drug itself, a phenomenon* known as the placebo effect: The expectations and biases of the participants in a study can influence their behavior.

Another way that expectations about the outcome of the experiment can influence the results, even when the participants are animals rather than people, is called the experimenter effect. It has to do with the expectations of the experimenter, not the participants. As discussed earlier in the sometimes observers are biased—they see what they expect to see. Observer bias can also happen in an experiment. When the researcher is measuring the dependent variable, it's possible that he or she could give the participants clues about how they are supposed to respond—with body language, tone of voice, or even eye contact. Although not deliberate, it does happen. It could go something like this in the example: You, the Alzheimer's patient, are in the experimenter's office to take your second memory test after trying the drug. The experimenter seems to pay a lot of attention to you and to every answer that you give in the test, so you get the feeling that you are supposed to have improved a lot. So you try harder, and any improvement you show may be caused only by your own increased effort, not by the drug. That's the experimenter effect: The behavior of the experimenter caused the participant to change his or her response pattern.

Controlling for Effects: Single-Blind and Double-Blind Studies
Fortunately, there are ways to control for these effects. The classic way to control for the placebo effect is to give the control group an actual placebo—some

---

*phenomenon: an observable fact or event.

kind of treatment that doesn't affect behavior at all. In the drug experiment, the placebo would have to be some kind of pill or solution that looks like and is administered just like the actual drug. The participants in both the experimental and the control groups would not know whether they got the real drug or the placebo. That way, if their expectations have any effect at all on the outcome of the experiment, the experimenter will be able to tell by looking at the results for the control group and comparing them to the results of the experimental group. Even if the control group improves a little, the drug group should improve significantly more if the drug is working. This is called a *single-blind study* because the participants are "blind" to the treatment they receive.

For a long time, that was the only type of experiment researchers did in psychology. But researchers Robert Rosenthal and Lenore Jacobson reported in their 1968 book, *Pygmalion in the Classroom*, that when teachers were told that some students had a high potential for success and others a low potential, the students showed significant gains or decreases in their performance on standardized tests depending on which "potential" they were supposed to have (Rosenthal & Jacobson, 1968). Actually, the students had been selected randomly and randomly assigned to one of the two groups, "high" or "low." Their performances on the tests were affected by the attitudes of the teachers concerning their potential. This study and similar studies after it highlighted the need to have the experimenter as well as the participants in research be "blind." So in a double-blind study neither the participants nor the person or persons measuring the dependent variable know who got what. That's why everything in a double-blind experiment gets coded in some way, so that only after all the measurements have been taken can anyone determine who was in the experimental group and who was in the control group.

▲ This elderly woman has Alzheimer's disease, which causes a severe loss of recent memory. If she were given a new drug in the very early stages of her disease in the attempt to improve her memory, the researcher could not be certain that any improvement shown was caused by the drug rather than by the elderly woman's belief that the drug would work. The expectations of any person in an experimental study can affect the outcome of the study, a phenomenon known as the placebo effect.

Consider Ethical Issues in Research

2.4 Identify ethical standards for research in psychology with human participants.

Actually, as psychology began to grow and more research with people was being done, psychologists began to realize that some protections had to be put in place. No one wanted to be thought of as a "mad scientist," and if studies were permitted that could actually harm people, the field of psychology might die out pretty quickly. Scientists in other areas of research were also realizing that ethical treatment of the participants in studies had to be ensured in some way. Ethical treatment, of course, means that people who volunteer for a study will be able to expect that no physical or psychological harm should come to them. The video *Ethical Guidelines for Research* explains how researchers in the field of psychology draw the line between what is ethical and what is not and explains some of the safeguards in place today.

Universities and colleges (where most psychological research is carried out) have *institutional review boards (IRB)*, groups of psychologists or other professionals who look over each proposed research study and judge it according to its safety and consideration for the participants in the study. These review boards look at all aspects of the proposed research, from the written materials that explain the research to the potential subjects to the equipment that may be used in the study itself.

The study that Dr. Watson did with "Little Albert" and the white rat seems pretty cruel when you think about it. Do researchers today do that kind of study?

👁 **Watch** the **Video**, *Ethical Guidelines for Research*, at **MyPsychLab**

The Guidelines for Doing Research with People Quite a few ethical concerns arise when dealing with human subjects in an experiment or other type of study. Here is a list of the APA's Ethical Guidelines:

1. Rights and well-being of participants must be weighed against the study's value to science.
2. Participants must be allowed to make an informed decision about participation.
3. Deception must be justified.
4. Participants may withdraw from the study at any time.
5. Participants must be protected from risks or told explicitly of risks.
6. Investigators must debrief participants, telling the true nature of the study and expectations of results.
7. Data must remain confidential.
8. If for any reason a study results in undesirable consequences for the participant, the researcher is responsible for detecting and removing, or correcting, these consequences.

2.5 Discuss the purpose of nonhuman animal research in psychology.

Psychologists also study animals to find out about behavior, often drawing comparisons between what the animals do and what people might do under similar conditions.

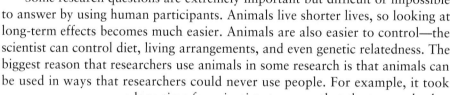

But why not just study ▶ people in the first place?

Some research questions are extremely important but difficult or impossible to answer by using human participants. Animals live shorter lives, so looking at long-term effects becomes much easier. Animals are also easier to control—the scientist can control diet, living arrangements, and even genetic relatedness. The biggest reason that researchers use animals in some research is that animals can be used in ways that researchers could never use people. For example, it took a long time for scientists to prove that the tars and other harmful substances in tobacco cause cancer because they had to do correlational studies with people and experiments only with animals.

2.6 Identify ethical guidelines for research in psychology with nonhuman animals.

There are also ethical considerations when dealing with animals in research, just as there are with humans. With animals, though, the focus is on avoiding exposing them to any *unnecessary* pain or suffering. So if surgery is part of the study, it is done under anesthesia. If the research animal must die for the effects of some drug or other treatment to be examined in necropsy (autopsy performed on an animal), the death must be accomplished humanely. Animals are used in only about 7 percent of all psychological studies (Committee on Animal Research and Ethics, 2004).

"He says he wants a lawyer."

Pick the best answer.

1. **In the scientific method, the final step is**
   a. reporting your results.
   b. perceiving a question.
   c. drawing conclusions.
   d. testing the hypothesis.

2. **Which of the following is an example of observer bias?**
   a. You ask your fellow students to be participants in a study of adult memory.
   b. You ask people from your church to participate in a study of family values.
   c. You develop an opinion of what you expect to see in an experiment.
   d. You allow a student to quit an experiment simply because he or she is bored.

3. **The greatest advantage to using a case study is that**
   a. researchers can gather data from large groups of people.
   b. there is a tremendous amount of detail that can be gathered.
   c. it can help in forming a hypothesis which can later be tested.
   d. it uses animals instead of humans and therefore does not endanger the subjects.

4. **The main advantage of a survey is that**
   a. only a small number of subjects need to be accessed.
   b. a large amount of data can be gathered.
   c. the chance of experimenter error is removed.
   d. subjects will not know if they are part of a control or experimental group.

5. **By using _____, researchers can maximize the likelihood of a representative sample.**
   a. very few individuals from a larger group
   b. random selection from a larger group
   c. case studies
   d. participant observation

6. **Which of the following would indicate the weakest relationship and thus be close to complete randomness?**
   a. +1.04
   b. −0.89
   c. +0.01
   d. −0.98

7. **In an experiment to examine the effects of sleep deprivation on completion of a puzzle, one group is allowed to sleep eight hours while another group is made to stay awake. In this experiment, the control group is**
   a. the group that gets to sleep.
   b. the group that remains awake.
   c. the puzzle.
   d. the difference in time for each group to complete the puzzle.

8. **In a _____ study, the participants do not know if they are part of the control group or the experimental group. Only the experimenter knows who is in each group.**
   a. placebo
   b. single-blind
   c. double-blind
   d. triple-blind

9. **What is the first guideline for doing research with people?**
   a. Participants have to give informed consent.
   b. Deception cannot be used in any studies with human beings.
   c. The rights and well-being of the participants must come first.
   d. Data must remain confidential.

10. **What is the biggest reason why we use animals in research?**
    a. Animals have simple behavior that makes it easy to see changes.
    b. Animals don't live as long as humans.
    c. We can do things to animals that we can't do to people.
    d. Animals are easier to control.

3 Statistics

Module Goal

Learn the basic concepts of data analysis.

Learning Objectives

3.1 Define descriptive statistics and explain how they are used to analyze data.

3.2 Interpret graphical representations of data.

3.3 Define correlation coefficients and explain how they are interpreted.

3.4 Explain inferential statistics.

3.5 Explain how validity and reliability relate to data analysis.

3.6 Describe forms of qualitative data and explain how they are used by research psychologists.

Learn the Basic Concepts of Data Analysis

Many students wonder why the science of psychology requires knowledge of mathematical concepts like statistics. The answer is simple: Psychologists base their conclusions on research findings. Data are collected (using the various research methods discussed in the previous module), and they have to be analyzed. Statistics is the field that gives us the tools to do that. An understanding of basic statistics can help you think critically about psychological research. It can also help you understand the statistical claims you read or hear about every day from sources like advertisements, political polls, and salespeople. Psychologists have to be able to do two things with the data they collect. The first is to summarize the information from a study or experiment. This is the role of **descriptive statistics**. The second is to make judgments and decisions about the data. We are interested in whether groups differ from each other. We are also interested in how one group of variables is related to another. This second emphasis is known as **inferential statistics**. Statistical analysis is a way of trying to account for the error that exists in almost any body of data, and **statistics** is the branch of mathematics that is concerned with the collection and interpretation of data from samples (Agresti & Finlay, 1997; Aron et al., 2005). Psychology is only one of many fields that use descriptive and inferential statistics.

3.1 Define descriptive statistics and explain how they are used to analyze data.

Descriptive statistics are a way of organizing numbers and summarizing them so that they can be understood. There are two main types of descriptive statistics:

- Measures of central tendency are used to summarize the data and give you one score that seems typical of your sample.
- Measures of variability are used to indicate the range of data. Are most data close to the average, or are they spread out more widely?

descriptive statistics a way of organizing numbers and summarizing them so that patterns can be determined.

inferential statistics statistical analysis of two or more sets of numerical data to reduce the possibility of error in measurement and to determine if the differences between the data sets are greater than chance variation would predict.

statistics branch of mathematics concerned with the collection and interpretation of numerical data.

Measures of Central Tendency One way to sum up numerical data is to find out what a "typical" score might be, or some central number around which all the others seem to fall. This kind of summation is called a *measure of central tendency*. There are three different measures of central tendency: the mean, the median, and the mode. The most commonly used measure of central tendency is the **mean**. To find the mean, you add up all the numbers in a particular set and then divide them by how many numbers there are. This is usually the way teachers get the grade point average for a particular student, for example. If Rochelle's grades on the tests she has taken so far are 86, 92, 87, and 90, then the teacher would add $86 + 92 + 87 + 90 = 355$, and then divide 355 by 4 (the number of scores) to get the mean, or grade point average, of 88.75.

Yes, the mean does not work as well when there are extreme scores, as you would have if only two students out of an entire class had a perfect score of 100 and everyone else scored in the 70s or lower. If you want a truer measure of central tendency in such a case, you need one that isn't affected by extreme scores. The **median** is just such a measure. A median is the score that falls in the middle of an *ordered* distribution of scores. Half of the scores will fall above the median, and half of the scores will fall below it. If the distribution contains an odd number of scores, it's just the middle number, but if the number of scores is even, it's the average of the two middle scores. Look at **Table 3.1** for an example of the median.

The mean IQ of this group would be 114.6, but the median would be 101 (the average between Evan with 102 and Fethia with 100, the average of the two middle numbers).

The **mode** is another measure of central tendency in which the most frequent score is taken as the central measure. In the numbers given in Table 3.1, the mode would be 100 because that number appears more times than any other. Three people have that score. This is the simplest measure of central tendency.

Measures of Variability Descriptive statistics can also determine how much the scores in a distribution differ, or vary, from the central tendency of the data. These *measures of variability* are used to discover how "spread out" the scores are from each other. The more the scores cluster around the central scores, the smaller the measure of variability will be, and the more widely the scores differ from the central scores, the larger this measurement will be. There are two ways that variability is measured. The simpler method is by calculating the *range* of the set of scores, or the difference between the highest score and the lowest score in the set of scores. The range is somewhat limited as a measure of variability when there are extreme scores in the distribution. For example, if you look at Table 3.1, the range of those IQ scores would be 240 to 95, or 145. But if you just look at the numbers, you can see that there really isn't that much variation except for that one high score of 240.

The other measure of variability that is commonly used is called the **standard deviation**. The standard deviation is a number that represents how far away the scores in a data set are from the mean.

◀ I remember that sometimes my teacher would "curve" the grades for a test, and it was always bad when just one person did really well and everyone else did lousy.

mean the arithmetic average of a distribution of numbers.

median the middle score in an ordered distribution of scores, or the mean of the two middle numbers; the 50th percentile.

mode the most frequent score in a distribution of scores.

standard deviation the square root of the average squared deviations from the mean of scores in a distribution; a measure of variability.

Table 3.1	Intelligence Test Scores for 10 People		
NAME	IQ	NAME	IQ
Allison	240	Fethia	100
Ben	105	George	100
Carol	103	Hal	100
Denise	103	Inga	98
Evan	102	Jay	95

3.2 Interpret graphical representations of data.

How do psychologists analyze the data they collect during research? Just looking at a long list of numbers isn't usually very helpful, so researchers make a graph or chart and search for patterns. Whereas statistical calculations represent research findings in the form of numbers, graphs and charts represent these same findings in a visual form. What type of graph or chart is best? It depends on the data: Researchers try to choose the graph or chart that most accurately represents the data they have found.

Frequency Distributions   A *frequency distribution* is a table or graph that shows how often different numbers, or scores, appear in a particular set of scores. For example, let's say that you have a sample of 30 people, the size of a psychology class. You ask them how many glasses of water they drink each day. You could represent the answers as shown in **Table 3.2**. Just by looking at this table, it is clear that typical people drink between four and eight glasses of water a day.

Tables can be useful, especially when dealing with small sets of data. Sometimes a more visual presentation gives a better "picture" of the patterns in a data set, and that is when researchers use graphs to plot the data from a frequency distribution. One common graph is a *histogram*. **Figure 3.1** shows how the same data from Table 3.2 would look in a histogram.

Another type of graph used in frequency distributions is the *polygon*, a line graph. **Figure 3.2** shows the same data in a polygon graph.

The Normal Curve   Frequency polygons allow researchers to see the shape of a set of data easily. For example, the number of people drinking glasses of water in Figure 3.2 is easily seen to be centered about six glasses (central tendency) but drops off below four glasses and above eight glasses a day (variability). Our frequency polygon has a high point, and the frequency decreases on both sides. A common frequency distribution of this type is called the *normal curve*. It has a very specific shape and is sometimes called the *bell curve*. Look at **Figure 3.3**. This curve is almost a perfect normal curve, and many things in life are not that perfect. The normal curve is used as a model for many things that are measured,

Table 3.2	A Frequency Distribution
NUMBER OF GLASSES PER DAY	NUMBER OF PEOPLE OUT OF 59 (FREQUENCY)
1	0
2	1
3	2
4	4
5	5
6	6
7	5
8	4
9	2
10	1

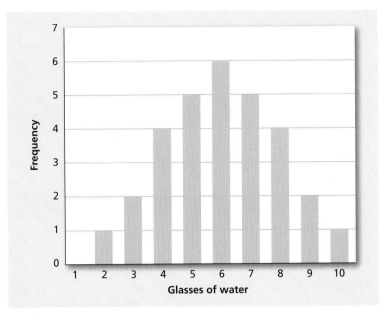

FIGURE 3.1 A Histogram
Histograms, or bar graphs, provide a visual way to look at data from frequency distributions. In this graph, for example, the height of the bars indicates that most people drink between 4 and 8 glasses of water (represented by the five highest bars in the middle of the graph).

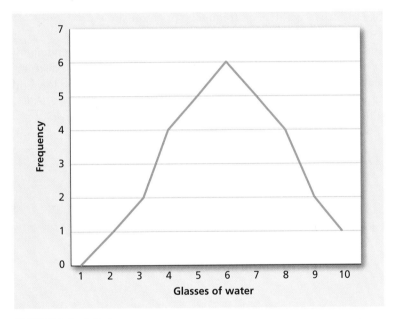

FIGURE 3.2 A Polygon
A polygon is a line graph that can represent the data in a frequency distribution in much the same way as a bar graph but allows the shape of the data set to be easily viewed.

such as intelligence, height, or weight, but even those measures only come close to a perfect distribution (provided large numbers of people are measured). One of the reasons that the normal curve is so useful is that it has very specific relationships to measures of central tendency and to the standard deviation.

Distributions aren't always normal in shape. Some distributions are described as *skewed*. This occurs when the distribution is not equal on both sides of a central score with the highest frequency (like in our example). Instead, the scores have a *skew* and are concentrated toward one side of the distribution. For

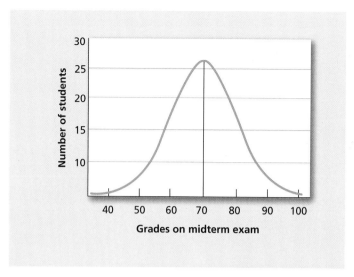

FIGURE 3.3 A Normal Curve
The normal curve, also known as the bell curve because of its unique shape, is often the way in which certain characteristics such as intelligence or weight are represented in the population. The highest point on the curve typically represents the average score in any distribution.

example, what if a study of people's water-drinking habits in a different class revealed that most people drank around seven to eight glasses of water daily, with no one drinking more than eight? The frequency polygon shown in **Figure 3.4** reflects this very different distribution.

Skewed distributions are called positively or negatively skewed, depending on where the scores are concentrated. A concentration in the high end of the distribution would be called *negatively skewed*, whereas a concentration in the low end would be called *positively skewed*. In Figure 3.4, most of the scores are concentrated in the high end of the distribution, so this distribution is negatively skewed.

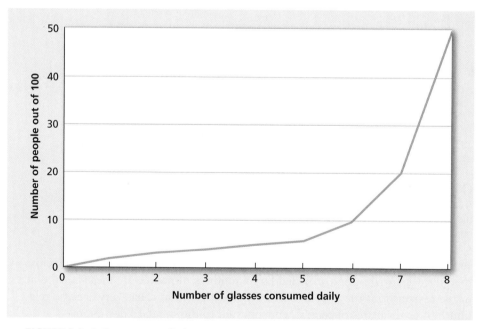

FIGURE 3.4 A Frequency Polygon
Skewed distributions are those in which the most frequent scores occur at one end or the other of the distribution, as represented by this frequency polygon in which most people are seen to drink at least 7 to 8 glasses of water each day.

3.3 Define correlation coefficients and explain how they are interpreted.

A *correlation* is a measure of the relationship between two or more variables. For example, if you wanted to know if scores on the SAT are related to grade point average, you could get SAT scores and GPAs from a group of people and enter those numbers into a mathematical formula, which will produce a number called the correlation coefficient. The correlation coefficient represents the strength and direction of the relationship between variables. The correlation coefficient that researchers get from the formula will either be a positive number or a negative number. If positive, the two variables increase in the same direction—as one goes up, the other goes up; as one decreases, the other also decreases. If negative, the two variables have an inverse (or opposite) relationship. As one increases, the other decreases. If researchers find that the more cigarettes a person smoked, the younger that person was when he or she died, that would mean that the correlation between the two variables is negative. (As smoking goes up, life expectancy goes down—an inverse relationship.)

3.4 Explain inferential statistics.

In any analysis that compares two or more sets of data, there is always the possibility of error in the data, and it is always possible that luck, or chance, has played a role in the experiment. When researchers want to know if the differences they find in data are large enough to be caused by the experimental manipulation and *not* just by chance, they have to use a kind of statistical technique that can take those chance variations into account. These kinds of statistical analysis use inferential statistics. All inferential statistics have one thing in common: They look for differences in group measurements that are **statistically significant**. Statistical significance is a way to test differences to see how likely those differences are to be real and not just caused by the random variations in behavior that exist in everything animals and people do.

Tests of significance give researchers the probability that the results of their experiment were caused by chance and not by their experimental manipulation. There are many different types of tests that researchers use to calculate statistical significance. In general, researchers are satisfied when these tests indicate that there is a 95 percent likelihood that their experimental results did not occur by chance. In reading scientific journals, you may see an equation that represents this significance as $p < .05$. In words, this states that the probability that these results have occurred by chance is less than 5 out of 100, thus the results are statistically significant.

3.5 Explain how validity and reliability relate to data analysis.

In psychology, as in other scientific fields, it's important that research results be both reliable and valid. The term **reliability** describes how consistent a result is. For example, if you perform an experiment five times and get similar results each time, you can say that your experiment is reliable. **Validity**, on the other hand, describes whether an experiment measures the thing that it is supposed to measure. Imagine that you decide to test young children's knowledge of U.S. geography by having them solve arithmetic problems. This test would not be valid because scores on a math test do not measure geographical knowledge.

You may not need to perform statistical calculations yourself during your time in high school, but if you are interested in exploring psychology further in college or as a career, you will likely use all of these statistical concepts to analyze

statistically significant referring to differences in data sets that are larger than chance variation would predict.

reliability the tendency of a test to produce the same scores again and again each time it is given to the same people.

validity the degree to which a test actually measures what it's supposed to measure.

your own research and the research of others. For now, just remember that statistical analysis is one of a psychologist's most important and helpful tools.

3.6 Describe forms of qualitative data and explain how they are used by research psychologists.

Qualitative data can offer a more holistic view of the topic being studied by a researcher. Forms of qualitative data include interviews, self reports by participants, responses to open ended questions on a survey, source material like journals or diaries, and anecdotes. The value of qualitative data is that it can be very in-depth and may be used to determine common themes (factors) and insights that experiments cannot be used to obtain. Qualitative data may used to prompt ideas for experiments or other ideas for further investigation of the topic.

Practice Quiz

Pick the best answer.

1. One type of bar graph is a

a. polygon.
b. histogram.
c. normal curve.
d. line graph.

2. A table that shows how often different scores appear in a set of scores is called a

a. frequency distribution.
b. bell curve.
c. bar graph.
d. central tendency.

3. In the set of numbers 2, 2, 2, 3, 5, 5, 6, 8, 15, what is the median?

a. 2
b. 3
c. 5
d. 15

4. In the set of numbers 2, 2, 2, 3, 5, 5, 6, 8, 15, what is the mode?

a. 2
b. 3
c. 5
d. 15

5. In a skewed distribution, the scores

a. have two high points instead of one.
b. fall to one side of the distribution.
c. are evenly distributed around the mean.
d. are all identical to each other.

6. The normal curve is a special kind of

a. inferential statistic.
b. frequency distribution.
c. measure of central tendency.
d. correlational coefficient.

7. Which of the following lets researchers know how spread out their data are?

a. measures of central tendency
b. measures of variability
c. inferential statistics
d. significant statistics

8. When a researcher wants to know if her results are likely to be caused by something other than chance, she wants to determine the results'

a. correlation coefficient.
b. statistical significance.
c. measure of variability.
d. median score.

9. When you add up all the numbers in a set of scores and divide the total by how many numbers there are, you are finding the

a. mean.　　　　　c. mode.
b. median.　　　　d. range.

10. Which of the following correlation co-efficients represents a strong negative correlation?

a. +0.85　　　　　c. −0.10
b. 0.00　　　　　　d. −0.79

(((Listen to an **Audio File** of your chapter at **MyPsychLab**

Module 1: Psychology: Historical Development and Perspectives
Trace the development of psychology as a science.

1.1 Define psychology as a field of study, and identify psychology's four primary goals.
- Psychology is the scientific study of behavior and mental processes.

1.2 Describe how psychology developed as a science.
- In 1879 psychology began as a science of its own in Germany with the establishment of Wundt's psychology laboratory.
- James proposed a countering point of view, functionalism.
- Freud proposed that the unconscious mind controls much of our conscious behavior.
- Watson proposed a science of behavior called behaviorism.

1.3 Describe the perspectives used to understand psychology today.
- Psychology includes eight perspectives.

1.4 Explain how psychology developed as a scientific discipline.
- Psychology has evolved; recent trends in positive psychology focus on strengths and happiness.

Identify psychology's subfields.

1.5 Describe the important subfields of psychology.
- There are many different areas of specialization in psychology, including clinical, counseling, developmental, social, and personality as areas of work or study.

1.6 Discuss the value of research with human and nonhuman animals.
- The goal of basic research is to gain scientific knowledge; the goal of applied research is to solve real-world problems.

1.7 Describe the role psychology plays in improving both society and people's lives.
- All psychologists share a mission to help others.

Module 2: Research Methods and Ethics
Understand research methods and measurements.

2.1 Describe the scientific method and how it is applied to psychology.
- The scientific method is a way to determine facts and control the possibilities of error.

2.2 Describe and compare the various research methods.
- Researchers use descriptive methods, naturalistic observation, case studies, correlational methods, and experiments to study behavior.

2.3 Define procedures used to improve the validity of research findings.
- Random assignment helps to control for individual differences.
- In a single-blind study, the subject doesn't know which group they are in. In a double-blind study, neither the subject nor the experimenter knows.

2.4 Identify ethical standards for research in psychology with human participants.
- Guidelines include the protection of rights and well-being of participants and informed consent.

2.5 Discuss the purpose of nonhuman animal research in psychology.
- Animals in psychological research make useful models because they are easier to control than humans.

2.6 Identify ethical guidelines for research in psychology with nonhuman animals.
- Animals must be protected and treated humanely.

Module 3: Statistics
Learn the basic concepts of data analysis.

3.1 Define descriptive statistics and explain how they are used to analyze data.
- Descriptive statistics include measures of central tendency and measures of variability.

3.2 Interpret graphical representations of data.
- Frequency distribution tables, histograms (bar graphs), and polygons (line graphs) can all be used to represent data.

3.3 Define correlation coefficients and explain how they are interpreted.
- The correlation coefficient measures the direction and strength of a relationship between two variables.

3.4 Explain inferential statistics.
- Inferential statistics help determine whether effects are caused by experimental manipulation or by chance.

3.5 Explain how validity and reliability relate to data analysis.
- Reliability describes how consistent a result is; validity describes whether an experiment measures what it is supposed to measure.

3.6 Describe forms of qualitative data and explain how they are used by research psychologists.
- Qualitative data is subjective and comes in many forms.

Vocabulary Terms

psychology p. 4
theory p. 5
functionalism p. 8
behaviorism p. 9
psychodynamic perspective p. 10
behaviorist perspective p. 10
humanistic perspective p. 10
cognitive perspective p. 11

biopsychological perspective p. 11
biopsychosocial perspective p. 12
evolutionary perspective p. 12
positive perspectives p. 12
scientific method p. 16
hypothesis p. 17
case study p. 19

representative sample p. 19
correlation p. 20
experiment p. 22
operational definition p. 22
independent variable p. 23
dependent variable p. 23
descriptive statistics p. 28
inferential statistics p. 28
statistics p. 28

mean p. 29
median p. 29
mode p. 29
standard deviation p. 29
statistically significant p. 33
reliability p. 33
validity p. 33

Study and Review at **MyPsychLab**

Vocabulary Review

Match each vocabulary term to its definition

1. functionalism
2. statistics
3. behaviorism
4. evolutionary psychology
5. psychoanalysis
6. hypothesis
7. case study
8. experiment
9. reliability
10. validity

a. The tendency of a test to produce the same scores again and again each time it is given to the same people.

b. The branch of mathematics concerned with the collection and interpretation of numerical data.

c. The theory and therapy based on the work of Sigmund Freud.

d. The early perspective in psychology associated with William James, in which the focus of study is how the mind allows people to adapt, live, work, and play.

e. A study of one individual in great detail.

f. The degree to which a test actually measures what it is supposed to measure.

g. A tentative explanation of a phenomenon based on observations.

h. A perspective that focuses on the biological bases of universal mental characteristics that all humans share.

i. A deliberate manipulation of a variable to see if corresponding changes in behavior result, allowing the determination of cause-and-effect relationships.

j. The science of behavior that focuses on observable behavior only.

Psychology Project

Although women and members of minority groups were not always fully represented in the early days of psychology, they have always made important contributions to the field. This project will give you a chance to study one psychologist's contributions in depth.

Materials:
- access to print or electronic reference resources
- a pencil and paper, or other note-taking materials
- poster board, markers, and craft supplies (optional)

Instructions:

1. Choose an influential psychologist to research. The psychologist may be historical or current, but he or she must be a woman or a member of a minority group. You may want to choose one of the psychologists discussed in this textbook, or you may ask your teacher or librarian for help finding a list of possible psychologists to research.

2. Once you have chosen your psychologist, use print or electronic resources to learn as much as you can about the person you have chosen. Ask yourself, "How did this person begin a psychology career? What are his or her areas of interest? Why is his or her research important? What is one challenge to his or her most important research? What is one strength of his or her most important research? Did this person have to overcome any special challenges?" Take notes as you gather information.

3. Share what you have learned with your classmates by delivering a short oral presentation about your psychologist or creating a poster filled with the information you've collected.

Tech Alternative

Select an early figure in psychology (example: John Watson).

Research the person you selected using the Internet and learn about the person's early life, education, career, contributions to psychology, and so on. Based on your findings, describe what this person's social networking page would look like. Be creative and think about selfies, postings, background, and other "friends," and explain your choices using information from your research. For example: Watson's selfie is of him and his favorite white stuffed animal, because he used furry white things in his research with "little Albert." Address five components of a social networking page and write up your response.

Essay Question

Qing is a 12-year-old girl who has just moved to the United States from China. She is struggling academically and socially, and she has trouble learning the traditions and expectations of her new home. She has become withdrawn and moody. However, she has always enjoyed painting, and art class is the one thing that still brings a smile to her face. In an essay, discuss how two of the following psychological perspectives would explain Qing's behavior:

a. Psychodynamic
b. Behavioral
c. Cognitive
d. Biopsychological

Test Yourself

Ready for your test? More quizzes and a customized plan.

☑ Study and Review at MyPsychLab

Pick the best answer.

1. **In the definition of psychology, the term *behavior* means**
   a. internal, covert processes.
   b. measurable behavior.
   c. overt actions and reactions.
   d. only animal behavior.

2. **A psychologist is interested in finding out why married couples seemingly begin to look like each other after several years of marriage. This psychologist is most interested in the goal of**
   a. description.
   b. explanation.
   c. prediction.
   d. control.

3. **Who is considered to be the father of African American psychology?**
   a. Charles Henry Thompson
   b. Robert V. Guthrie
   c. Francis Cecil Sumner
   d. Howard Hale Long

4. **Sigmund Freud's psychoanalysis focused on**
   a. observable behavior.
   b. Gestalt perceptions.
   c. introspection.
   d. early childhood experiences.

5. **Which psychologist focused on observable behavior?**
   a. Ivan Pavlov
   b. John Watson
   c. Sigmund Freud
   d. Abram Rogers

6. **Which perspective is often referred to as the "third force" in psychology and focuses on freedom of choice?**
   a. biopsychological perspective
   b. behaviorism
   c. cognitive psychology
   d. humanistic

7. **Which perspective best explains the bystander effect whereby individuals will be less likely to help someone in need because of the presence of others close by?**
   a. psychoanalysis
   b. behaviorism
   c. cognitive psychology
   d. sociocultural

8. **If Dr. Byers uses an eclectic approach in her clinical treatment of children, what is it that she is doing?**
   a. She is relying primarily on one psychological perspective to treat all her patients.
   b. She is using medications with all her patients.
   c. She relies heavily on the Freudian psychodynamic perspective to help children who show abnormal behavior.
   d. She is using a combination of perspectives to treat different clients.

9. **Dr. Colton identifies himself with the largest subfield of psychology. What kind of psychologist is he?**
   a. developmental
   b. clinical
   c. school
   d. experimental

10. **Micah has recently been diagnosed with a psychological disorder that is best addressed initially with medication. He would likely benefit the most by first seeing a**
    a. psychiatrist.
    b. psychoanalyst.
    c. psychiatric social worker.
    d. psychologist.

11. **Which step in the scientific method is derived from the goal of description?**
    a. reporting your results
    b. perceiving a question
    c. drawing conclusions
    d. forming a hypothesis

12. **Brianne wants to find an explanation for the behavior of her lab rats in her study. Which step in the scientific method is she currently focusing on?**
    a. testing a hypothesis
    b. perceiving the question
    c. drawing conclusions
    d. reporting her results

13. **The famous study of Phineas Gage, who survived when a metal rod pierced his skull, is an example of a**
    a. laboratory experiment
    b. correlation
    c. case study
    d. survey

14. **A researcher finds that as her subjects increased the number of hours they spent exercising, the overall weight of her subjects decreased. This would be an example of a _____ correlation.**
    a. positive
    b. negative
    c. zero
    d. causal

15. **A researcher wants to study the effects of texting on driving. Students in Group A drive a car in a computer game and see how many virtual accidents they have. Students in Group B are asked to drive the same virtual car but they must respond to and send at least three texts. The number of virtual accidents is measured for each group. What is the independent variable?**
    a. the virtual car
    b. texting
    c. the number of virtual accidents
    d. the group assignment

16. **A researcher asks an assistant to conduct a study on her behalf. She specifically tells her assistant to not let the participants know what group they are in (experimental or control). Such an experiment would be considered a**
    a. double-blind experiment.
    b. single-blind experiment.
    c. correlational study.
    d. laboratory observation.

17. **Double-blind studies control for**
    a. the placebo effect.
    b. the experimenter effect.
    c. the placebo effect and the experimenter effect.
    d. extrinsic motivation.

18. **If a chart shows that more than 80 percent of the students received either an A or B in the class, one would describe the chart as**
    a. normal distribution.
    b. positively skewed.
    c. negatively skewed.
    d. bell-shaped.

19. **The mean, median, and mode are all measures of**
    a. correlations.
    b. inferential statistics.
    c. variability.
    d. central tendency.

20. **_____ is a way of organizing numbers and summarizing them so that they can be understood whereas _____ allows researchers to draw conclusions about the results of research.**
    a. Descriptive statistics; inferential statistics
    b. Inferential statistics; descriptive statistics
    c. Correlational research; mean statistics
    d. Inferential statistics; mean, medium, and mode

Learning Objectives

(1.1) (1.2) (1.3) (1.4) pp. 4–13

Trace the Development of Psychology as a Science

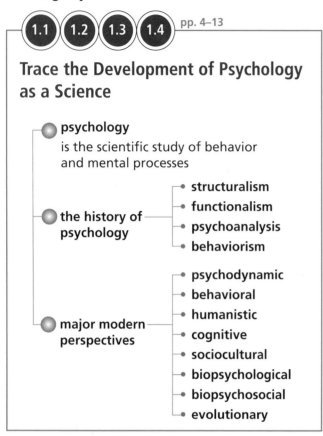

- **psychology**
  is the scientific study of behavior and mental processes

- **the history of psychology**
  - structuralism
  - functionalism
  - psychoanalysis
  - behaviorism

- **major modern perspectives**
  - psychodynamic
  - behavioral
  - humanistic
  - cognitive
  - sociocultural
  - biopsychological
  - biopsychosocial
  - evolutionary

Learning Objectives

(1.5) (1.6) (1.7) pp. 13–14

Identify Psychology's Subfields

- **major subfields of psychology**
  - clinical psychology
  - counseling psychology
  - developmental psychology
  - experimental psychology
  - social psychology
  - personality psychology
  - physiological psychology
  - comparative psychology
  - industrial/organizational (I/O) psychology

Learning Objectives

(2.1) (2.2) (2.3) pp. 16–25

Understand Research Methods and Measurements

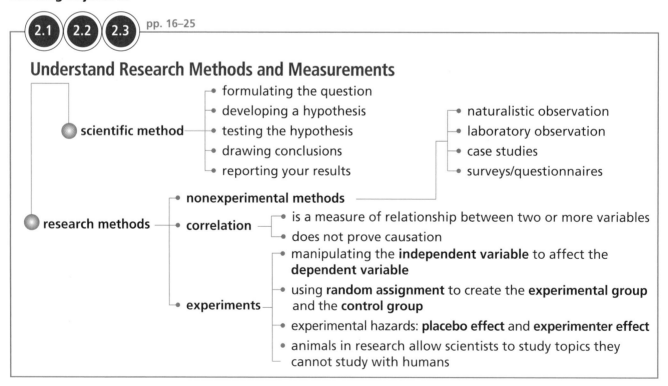

- **scientific method**
  - formulating the question
  - developing a hypothesis
  - testing the hypothesis
  - drawing conclusions
  - reporting your results

- **research methods**
  - **nonexperimental methods**
    - naturalistic observation
    - laboratory observation
    - case studies
    - surveys/questionnaires
  - **correlation**
    - is a measure of relationship between two or more variables
    - does not prove causation
  - **experiments**
    - manipulating the **independent variable** to affect the **dependent variable**
    - using **random assignment** to create the **experimental group** and the **control group**
    - experimental hazards: **placebo effect** and **experimenter effect**
    - animals in research allow scientists to study topics they cannot study with humans

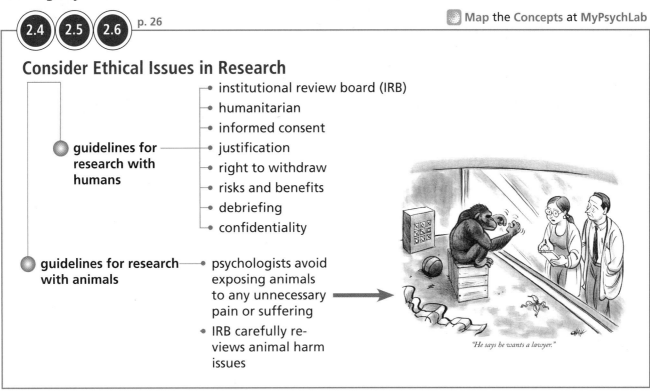

2.4 2.5 2.6   p. 26

Consider Ethical Issues in Research

guidelines for research with humans
- institutional review board (IRB)
- humanitarian
- informed consent
- justification
- right to withdraw
- risks and benefits
- debriefing
- confidentiality

guidelines for research with animals
- psychologists avoid exposing animals to any unnecessary pain or suffering
- IRB carefully reviews animal harm issues

"He says he wants a lawyer."

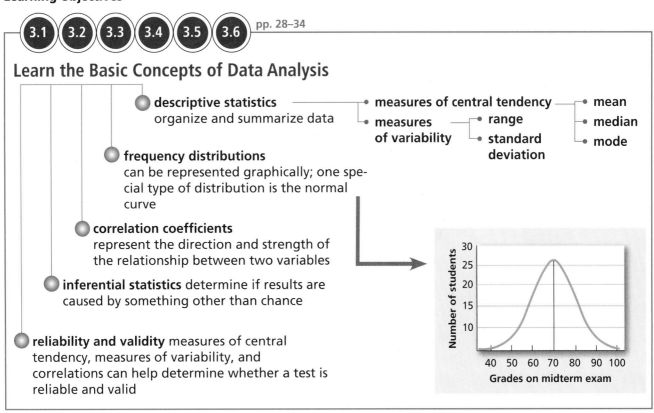

3.1 3.2 3.3 3.4 3.5 3.6   pp. 28–34

Learn the Basic Concepts of Data Analysis

descriptive statistics organize and summarize data
- measures of central tendency
  - mean
  - median
  - mode
- measures of variability
  - range
  - standard deviation

frequency distributions can be represented graphically; one special type of distribution is the normal curve

correlation coefficients represent the direction and strength of the relationship between two variables

inferential statistics determine if results are caused by something other than chance

reliability and validity measures of central tendency, measures of variability, and correlations can help determine whether a test is reliable and valid

Number of students: 10, 15, 20, 25, 30
Grades on midterm exam: 40 50 60 70 80 90 100

THE SCIENCE OF PSYCHOLOGY   **39**

2 The Biological Perspective

The Ironman® competition consists of a 2.4-mile swim, a 112-mile bike ride, and a 26.2-mile run. Dick Hoyt pulls his son Rick in a boat that is attached to a bungee cord, then he peddles Rick on a special two-seater bicycle, and finally he pushes Rick across the finish line in a customized running chair.

Why the unusual approach? Rick was born with spastic quadriplegia and cerebral palsy as the result of anoxia during birth. Unable to walk or talk, Rick learned to communicate by tapping his head against a head piece on his wheelchair when specific letters of the alphabet were highlighted on a specially designed computer screen. He eventually graduated from Boston University with a degree in special education.

Current research to help individuals with brain injuries or neurological conditions has moved far beyond the computer that assisted Rick. Some of the most promising areas are in brain–computer interfaces (BCI) that use the brain's electrical activity to communicate with others. It is possible that in the future, brain activity will enable individuals to control such assistive devices as prosthetic limbs or wheelchairs.

What do you see as the brain's role in our behavior? How much do you think your behavior is influenced by hormones and chemicals in the nervous system?

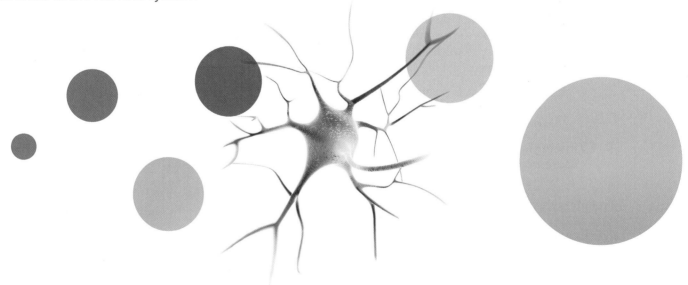

Watch the Video, at MyPsychLab

*W*hy Study the Nervous System and the Glands?

How could we possibly understand any of our behavior, thoughts, or actions without knowing something about the incredible organs that allow us to act, think, and react? If we can understand how the brain, the nerves, and the glands interact to control feelings, thoughts, and behavior, we can begin to truly understand the complex organism called a human being.

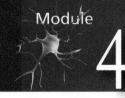

4 The Nervous System

Module Goals	Learning Objectives
Understand the structure and function of the nervous system.	**4.1** Describe the parts of the neuron and understand the basic process of neural transmission. **4.2** Describe the major divisions of the human nervous system. **4.3** Identify the mechanisms of, and the importance of, plasticity of the nervous system, and describe advances made in neuroscience.
Understand the structure and function of the endocrine system.	**4.4** Explain how the endocrine glands interact with the nervous system. **4.5** Outline how hormones influence behavior and mental processes. **4.6** Explain how hormones interact with the immune system.

neuron the basic cell that makes up the nervous system and that receives and sends messages within that system.

dendrites branchlike structures of a neuron that receive messages from other neurons.

soma the cell body of the neuron responsible for maintaining the life of the cell.

👁 Watch the Video, *The Basics: How the Brain Works, Part 1: The Neuron,* at **MyPsychLab**

Understand the Structure and Function of the Nervous System

This chapter will explore a complex system of cells, organs, and chemicals that work together to produce behavior, thoughts, and actions. The first part of this complex arrangement is the *nervous system*, a network of cells that carries information to and from all parts of the body. The field of *neuroscience* is a branch of the life sciences that deals with the structure and functioning of the brain and the neurons, nerves, and nervous tissue that form the nervous system.

4.1 Describe the parts of the neuron and understand the basic process of neural transmission.

In 1887, Santiago Ramón y Cajal, a doctor studying slides of brain tissue, first theorized that the nervous system was made up of individual cells (Ramón y Cajal, translation, 1995). Although the entire body is composed of cells, each type of cell has a special purpose and function and, therefore, a special structure. For example, skin cells are flat, but muscle cells are long and stretchy. Most cells have three things in common: a nucleus, a cell body, and a cell membrane holding it all together. The **neuron** is the specialized cell in the nervous system that receives and sends messages within that system. Neurons are one type of messenger in the body, and that means that they have a very special structure, which we will explore in the video *The Basics: How the Brain Works, Part I: The Neuron.*

The parts of the neuron that receive messages from other cells are called the **dendrites**. The name *dendrite* means "tree-like," or "branch," and this structure does indeed look like the branches of a tree. The dendrites are attached to the cell body, or **soma**, which is the part of the cell that contains the nucleus and is responsible for maintaining the life of the neuron. The **axon** (from the Greek for "axis") is a tube-like fiber attached to the soma and carries electrical messages from the cell body (soma) to the terminal knobs. The end of the axon branches out into several shorter fibers (terminals) that have swellings or little knobs on the ends called *axon terminal bulbs*, which are responsible for communicating with other nerve cells by releasing neurotransmitters.

Two special types of glial cells generate a layer of fatty substances called **myelin**. Myelin wraps around the shaft of the axons in sections, with tiny spaces between sections, forming an insulating and protective sheath.

The myelin sheath is a very important part of the neuron. It not only insulates the neuron, but it also offers a little protection from damage and speeds up the neural message traveling down the axon. In the disease called *multiple sclerosis* (MS), the myelin sheath is destroyed (possibly by the individual's own immune system), which leads to diminished or complete loss of neural functioning in those damaged cells, particularly associated with muscle control and movement. Early symptoms of MS may include fatigue, changes in vision, balance problems, and numbness, tingling, or muscle weakness in the arms or legs.

Generating the Message Within the Neuron—The Neural Impulse

A neuron that's at rest—not currently firing a neural impulse or message—is actually electrically charged. The inside of the cell is really a semiliquid (jelly-like) solution in which there are charged particles, called *ions*. A semiliquid solution also surrounds the outside of the cell and contains ions, too. Although both positive and negative ions are located inside and outside of the cell, the relative charge of ions inside the cell is mostly negative, and the relative charge of ions outside the cell is mostly positive. This difference in charges creates an electrical potential.

Think of the ions inside the cell as a baseball game inside a stadium (the cell walls). The sodium ions outside the cell are all the fans in the area, and they want to get inside to see the game. When the cell is resting (the electrical potential is in a state called the *resting potential*, because the cell is at rest), the fans are stuck outside. The sodium ions cannot enter when the cell is at rest between firings, because even though the cell membrane has all these channels, the *particular* channels for the sodium ions aren't open yet. But when the cell receives a strong enough stimulation from another cell (meaning that the receptor sites on the dendrites have been activated), the cell membrane opens up those *particular* channels, one after the other, all down its surface, allowing the sodium ions (the "fans") to rush into the cell. That causes the inside of the cell to become mostly positive and the outside of the cell to become mostly negative, because many of the positive sodium ions are now inside the cell—at the point where the first ion channel opened. This electrical charge reversal will proceed down the axon in a kind of chain reaction. (Picture a long hallway with many doors in which the first door opens, then the second, and so on all the way down the hall.) This electrical charge reversal (causing the axon to become depolarized) is known as the **action potential** because the electrical potential is now in action rather than at rest. Each action potential sequence takes about one-thousandth of a second. Now the action potential is traveling down the axon. When it gets to the terminal bulbs, something else happens: the message gets transmitted to another cell through the release of its chemical neurotransmitter (that step will be discussed momentarily).

Neurotransmission Once a neural signal reaches the axon terminal bulbs of a neuron, several events take place to allow neurons to communicate with each other. These events are dependent upon key structures within a neuron's terminal bulb and on the surface of adjacent neurons.

axon tube like structure of neuron that carries the neural message from the cell body to the axon terminals, for communication with other cells.

myelin fatty substances produced by certain glial cells that coat the axons of neurons to insulate, protect, and speed up the neural impulse.

action potential the release of the neural impulse, consisting of a reversal of the electrical charge within the axon.

◄ Exactly how does this "electrical message" work inside the cell?

So now that we know how the message travels within the axon of the cell, but what is that "something else" that happens when the action potential reaches the end of the axon?

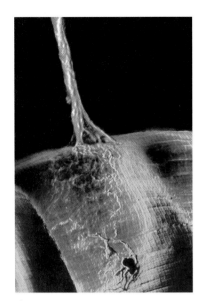

▲ *This electron micrograph shows a motor neuron making contact with muscle fibers.*

Sending the Message to Other Cells: The Synapse **Figure 4.1** shows an axon terminal enlarged to giant scale. Notice that the presynaptic terminal bulb is not empty. It has a number of little sac-like structures in it called synaptic vesicles. The word *vesicle* is Latin and means a "little blister" or "fluid-filled sac."

Inside the synaptic vesicles are chemicals suspended in fluid, which are molecules of substances called **neurotransmitters**. The name is simple enough—they are inside a neuron and they are going to transmit a message. On the other side of the space between neurons (the space is called the synaptic gap) are the dendrites with receptor sites of another neuron (see Figure 4.1). Between them is a fluid-filled space called the **synapse** or the *synaptic gap*. Instead of an electrical charge, the vesicles at the end of the axon (also called the presynaptic membrane) contain the molecules of neurotransmitters, and the surface of the next neuron's dendrite contains ion channels that have *receptor sites*, proteins that allow only particular molecules of a certain shape to fit into it, just as only a particular key will fit into a keyhole.

How do the neurotransmitters get across the gap? Recall the action potential (the actual electrical impulse) making its way down the axon after the neuron has been stimulated. When that action potential, reaches the synaptic vesicles, the synaptic vesicles release their neurotransmitters into the synaptic gap. The molecules then float across the synapse and many of them fit themselves into the receptor sites that recognize them (like a lock recognizes a particular key), opening the ion channels and allowing sodium to rush in, starting the process of transmission in that neuron.

Neurotransmitters: Messengers of the Network The first neurotransmitter to be identified was named *acetylcholine* (ACh). It is found at the synapses between neurons and muscle cells. Acetylcholine serves to stimulate the skeletal muscles to contract but actually slows contractions in the heart muscle.

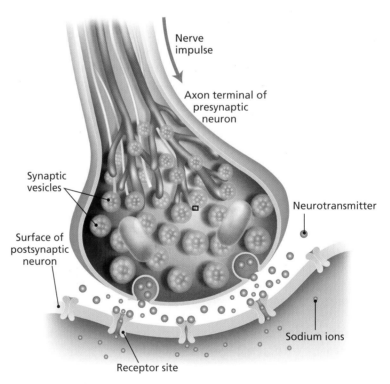

FIGURE 4.1 The Synapse
The nerve impulse reaches the axon terminal bulb, triggering the release of neurotransmitters from the synaptic vesicles. The molecules of neurotransmitter cross the synaptic gap to fit into the receptor sites that fit the shape of the molecule, opening the ion channel and allowing sodium ions to rush in.

neurotransmitter chemical found in the synaptic vesicles that, when released, has an effect on the next cell.

synapse (synaptic gap) microscopic fluid-filled space between the axon terminal of one cell and the dendrites or surface of the next cell.

If acetylcholine receptor sites on the muscle cells are blocked in some way, then the acetylcholine can't get to the site and the muscle will be incapable of contracting—paralyzed, in other words. This is exactly what happens when *curare*, a drug used by South American Indians on their blow darts, gets into the nervous system. Curare's molecules are just similar enough to fit into the receptor site without actually stimulating the cell, making curare an *antagonist* (a chemical substance that blocks or reduces the effects of a neurotransmitter) for ACh.

What would happen if the neurons released too much ACh? The bite of a black widow spider does just that. Its venom stimulates the release of excessive amounts of ACh and causes convulsions and possible death. Black widow spider venom is an *agonist* (a chemical substance that mimics or enhances the effects of a neurotransmitter) for ACh.

▲ The venom of the black widow spider causes a flood of acetylcholine to be released into the body's muscle system, causing convulsions.

Since the discovery of acetylcholine, many other neurotransmitters have been identified. These substances have a variety of roles ranging from general excitatory and inhibitory effects to influencing eating, sleeping, movement, and consciousness. Others influence cognition, memory, and mood. Refer to **Table 4.1** for an overview of various neurotransmitters and their functions.

You may have heard of *endorphins*—pain-controlling chemicals in the body. When a person is hurt, a neurotransmitter that signals pain is released. When the brain gets this message, it triggers the release of endorphins. The endorphins bind to receptors that open the ion channels on the axon. This causes the cell to be unable to fire its pain signal and the pain sensations eventually lessen. For example, you might bump your elbow and experience a lot of pain at first, but the pain will quickly subside to a much lower level. Athletes may injure themselves during an event and yet not feel the pain until after the competition is over, when the endorphin levels go down.

The name *endorphin* comes from the term *endogenous morphine*. (*Endogenous* means "native to the area"—in this case, native to the body.) Scientists studying the nervous system found receptor sites on dendrites that fit morphine molecules perfectly and decided that there must be a natural substance in the body that has the same effect as morphine.

Table 4.1	**Neurotransmitters and Their Functions**
NEUROTRANSMITTERS	FUNCTIONS
Acetylcholine (ACh)	Excitatory or inhibitory; involved in arousal, attention, memory, and controls muscle contractions
Norepinephrine (NE)	Mainly excitatory; involved in arousal and mood
Dopamine (DA)	Excitatory or inhibitory; involved in control of movement and sensations of pleasure
Serotonin (5-HT)	Excitatory or inhibitory; involved in sleep, mood, anxiety, and appetite
Gamma-aminobutyric acid (GABA)	Major inhibitory neurotransmitter; involved in sleep and inhibits movement.
Endorphins	Inhibitory neural regulators; involved in pain relief

If the neurotransmit- ▶
ters are out there in
the synaptic gap and
in the receptor sites,
what happens to them
when they aren't
needed anymore?

👁 **Watch** the **Video**, *How Drugs Affect Your Brain*, at **MyPsychLab**

Cleaning Up the Synapse: Reuptake and Enzymes The neurotransmitters have to get out of the receptor sites before the next stimulation can occur. Some just drift away through the process of diffusion, but most will end up back in the synaptic vesicles in a process called *reuptake*. (Think of a little suction tube, sucking the chemicals back into the vesicles.)

Knowing how and why drugs affect us can help us understand why a physician might prescribe a particular drug or why certain drugs are dangerous and should be avoided. Because the chemical molecules of various drugs, if similar enough in shape to the neurotransmitters, can fit into the receptor sites on the receiving neurons just like the neurotransmitters do, drugs can act as agonists or antagonists. Drugs acting as agonists, for example, can mimic* or enhance the effects of neurotransmitters on the receptor sites of the next cell

Other drugs act as antagonists, blocking or reducing a cell's response to the action of other chemicals or neurotransmitters. The video *How Drugs Affect Your Brain* includes more information about agonistic and antagonistic effects of different drugs.

This section covered the neuron and how neurons communicate. The next section looks at the bigger picture—the nervous system itself.

4.2 Describe the major divisions of the human nervous system.

Now that we have looked at the cells that make up the nervous system and ways in which they process and communicate information, take a look at **Figure 4.2**. This figure shows the organization of the various parts of the nervous system

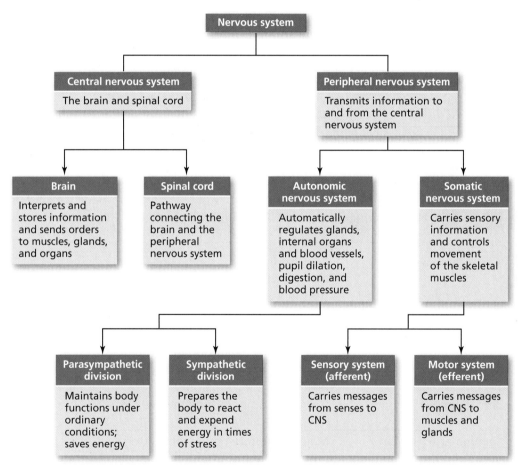

FIGURE 4.2 An Overview of the Nervous System

---

*mimic: act like.

FIGURE 4.3 The Spinal Cord Reflex

The pain from the burning heat of the candle flame stimulates the afferent nerve fibers, which carry the message up to the interneurons in the middle of the spinal cord. The interneurons then send a message out by means of the efferent nerve fibers, causing the hand to jerk away from the flame before the signal is processed by the brain.

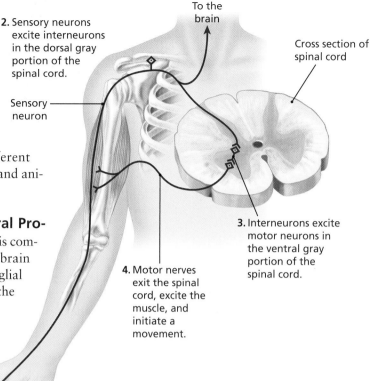

To the brain

2. Sensory neurons excite interneurons in the dorsal gray portion of the spinal cord.

Sensory neuron

Cross section of spinal cord

3. Interneurons excite motor neurons in the ventral gray portion of the spinal cord.

4. Motor nerves exit the spinal cord, excite the muscle, and initiate a movement.

1. Flame stimulates pain receptors (sensory neurons).

and will help in understanding how all the different parts work together in controlling the way people and animals think, act, and feel.

The Central Nervous System—The "Central Processing Unit" The **central nervous system (CNS)** is composed of the brain and the spinal cord. Both the brain and the spinal cord are composed of neurons and glial cells that control the life-sustaining functions of the body as well as all thought, emotion, and behavior.

The Brain The brain is the core of the nervous system; the part that makes sense of the information received from the senses, makes decisions, and sends commands out to the muscles and the rest of the body. Later parts of this chapter will cover the brain in more detail, but for now, you should know the brain is not one mass but rather is organized into different regions, each with primary functions.

The Spinal Cord The *spinal cord* is a long bundle of neurons that serves two vital functions for the nervous system. Look at the cross-sectional view of the spinal cord in **Figure 4.3**. Notice that it seems to be divided into two areas, a lighter outer section and a darker inner section. The purpose of the outer section is to carry messages from the body up to the brain and from the brain down to the body. It is simply a message "pipeline."

The inside section, which is made up of cell bodies separated by glial cells, is actually a primitive sort of "brain." This part of the spinal cord is responsible for certain reflexes—very fast, lifesaving reflexes. To understand how the spinal cord reflexes work, it is important to know there are three basic types of neurons: *afferent (sensory) neurons* that carry messages from the senses to the spinal cord, *efferent (motor) neurons* that carry messages from the spinal cord to the muscles and glands, and *interneurons* that connect the afferent neurons to the motor neurons (and make up the inside of the spinal cord and much of the brain itself). (See Figure 4.3.) Touch a flame or a hot stove with your finger, for example, and an afferent neuron will send the pain message up to the spinal column where it enters into the central area of the spinal cord. The interneuron in that central area will then receive the message and send out a response along an efferent neuron, causing your finger to pull back. This all happens very quickly. If the pain message had to go all the way up to the brain before a response could be made, the response time would be greatly increased and more damage would be done to your finger. So having this kind of *reflex arc* controlled by the spinal

▲ The look on this young woman's face clearly indicates that she has experienced pain in her finger. Pain is a warning signal that something is wrong—in this case that touching the thorns on the stem of the rose was a bad idea. What might be some of the problems encountered by a person who could feel no pain at all?

central nervous system (CNS) part of the nervous system consisting of the brain and spinal cord.

neuroplasticity the ability within the brain to constantly change both the structure and function of many cells in response to experience or trauma.

peripheral nervous system (PNS) all nerves and neurons that are not contained in the brain and spinal cord but that run through the body itself.

If the spinal cord is ▶ such an important link between the body and the brain, what happens if it is damaged?

👁 **Watch** the **Video**, *Special Topics: The Plastic Brain: Overview of Neuroplasticity*, at **MyPsychLab**

Okay, that takes care ▶ of the central nervous system, except for the detail on the brain. How does the central nervous system communicate with the rest of the body?

---

cord alone allows for very fast response times. (A good way to avoid mixing up the terms *afferent* and *efferent* is to remember "afferent neurons access the spinal cord, efferent neurons exit.") The pain message does eventually get to the brain, where other motor responses may be triggered, like saying "Ouch!" and putting the finger in your mouth.

4.3 Identify the mechanisms of, and the importance of, plasticity of the nervous system, and describe advances made in neuroscience.

Damage to the Central Nervous System Damage to the central nervous system was once thought to be permanent. Neurons in the brain and spinal cord were not seen as capable of repairing themselves. When people recovered from a stroke, for example, it was assumed that it was primarily due to healthy brain cells taking over the functions of the damaged ones. Scientists have known for a while now that some forms of central nervous system damage can be repaired by the body's systems, and in recent years great strides have been made in repairing spinal cord damage. The brain actually exhibits a great deal of **neuroplasticity**, the ability to constantly change both the structure and function of many cells in the brain in response to experience and even trauma (Neville & Bavelier, 2000; Rossini et al., 2007; Sanders et al., 2008).

The brain can change itself quite a bit by adapting neurons to serve new functions when old neurons die or are damaged. Dendrites grow and new synapses are formed in at least some areas of the brain, as people learn new things throughout life (Sanes & Jessell, 2013a, 2013b).

The video *Special Topics: The Plastic Brain: Overview of Neuroplasticity* explains neuroplasticity and some of these processes in more detail.

The Peripheral Nervous System—Nerves on the Edge The term *peripheral* refers to things that are not in the center or that are on the edges of the center. The **peripheral nervous system or PNS** (see **Figure 4.4** and also refer back to Figure 4.2) is made up of all the neurons that are not contained in the brain and spinal cord. It is this system that allows the brain and spinal cord to communicate with the sensory systems and enables the brain and spinal cord to control the muscles and glands of the body. The PNS can be divided into two major systems: the *somatic nervous system*, which consists of nerves that control the voluntary muscles of the body, and the *autonomic nervous system (ANS)*, which consists of nerves that control the involuntary muscles, organs, and glands.

The Somatic Nervous System One of the parts of a neuron is the soma, or cell body (remember that the word *soma* means "body"). The somatic nervous system is made up of the *sensory pathways*, which is all the nerves carrying messages from the senses to the central nervous system (those nerves containing afferent neurons), and the *motor pathways*, which is all the nerves carrying messages from the central nervous system to the voluntary, or skeletal,* muscles of the body— muscles that allow people to move their bodies (those nerves composed of efferent neurons). When people are walking, raising their hands in class, smelling a flower, or directing their gaze toward the person they are talking to or to look at a pretty picture, they are using the somatic nervous system. (As seen in the discussion of spinal cord reflexes, although these muscles are called the voluntary muscles, they

---

*skeletal: having to do with the bones of the body, or skeleton.

can move involuntarily when a reflex response occurs. They are called "voluntary" because they *can* be moved at will but are not limited to only that kind of movement.)

Involuntary* muscles, such as the heart, stomach, and intestines, together with glands such as the adrenal glands and the pancreas are all controlled by clumps of neurons located on or near the spinal column. (The words *on* or *near* are used quite deliberately here. The neurons *inside* the spinal column are part of the central nervous system, not the peripheral nervous system.) These large groups of neurons near the spinal column make up the *autonomic nervous system.*

The Autonomic Nervous System The word *autonomic* suggests that the functions of this system are more or less automatic, which is basically correct. Whereas the somatic division of the peripheral nervous system controls the senses and voluntary muscles, the **autonomic nervous system** controls everything else in the body—organs, glands, and involuntary muscles. The autonomic nervous system is divided into two systems, the *sympathetic division*, and the *parasympathetic division*. (See **Figure 4.5** on the next page.)

The Sympathetic Division The **sympathetic division** is usually called the "fight-or-flight system" because it allows people and animals to deal with all kinds of stressful events. Emotions during these events might be anger (hence, the term *fight*) or fear (that's the *flight* part, obviously) or even extreme joy or excitement. The sympathetic division's job is to get the body ready to deal with the stress. Many of us have experienced a fight-or-flight moment at least once in our lives. Participate in the survey *Do You Fly or Fight?* to learn more about how your body responds in certain situations.

What are the specific ways in which this division readies the body to react? (See Figure 4.5.) The pupils seem to get bigger, perhaps to let in more light and, therefore, more information. The heart starts pumping faster and harder, drawing blood away from nonessential organs such as the skin (so at first the person may turn pale) and sometimes even from the brain itself (so the person might actually faint). Blood needs lots of oxygen before it goes to the muscles, so the lungs work overtime, too (so the person may begin to breathe faster). One set of glands in particular receives special instructions. The adrenal glands will be stimulated to release certain stress-related chemicals (members of a class of chemicals released by glands called *hormones*) into the bloodstream. These stress hormones will only affect certain target organs—notably, the heart, muscles, and lungs. This further stimulates these organs to work harder.

Now, all this bodily arousal is going on during a stressful situation. If the stress ends, the activity of the sympathetic division will be replaced by the activation of the parasympathetic division. The heart slows, blood vessels open up, blood pressure in the brain drops, and if the parasympathetic division overresponds fainting can result.

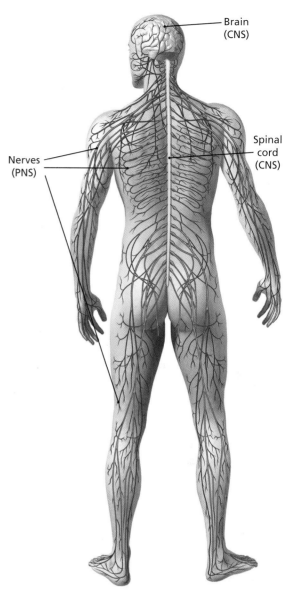

FIGURE 4.4 The Peripheral Nervous System

⚜ Complete the Survey, *Do You Fly or Fight?*, at MyPsychLab

autonomic nervous system (ANS) division of the PNS consisting of nerves that control all of the involuntary muscles, organs, and glands.

sympathetic division (fight-or-flight system) part of the ANS that is responsible for reacting to stressful events and bodily arousal.

---

*involuntary: not under deliberate control.

parasympathetic division (eat-drink-and-rest system) part of the ANS that restores the body to normal functioning after arousal and is responsible for the day-to-day functioning of the organs and glands.

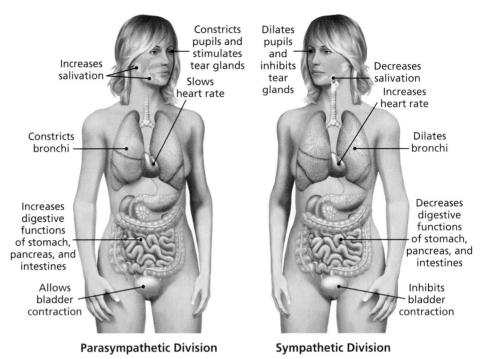

FIGURE 4.5 Functions of the Parasympathetic and Sympathetic Divisions of the Nervous System

▲ These young soccer players are using their senses and voluntary muscles, controlled by the somatic division of the peripheral nervous system. What part of the autonomic nervous system are these girls also using at this time?

How do the glands fit into all of this? How do they ▶ affect our behavior?

The Parasympathetic Division If the sympathetic division can be called the fight-or-flight system, the **parasympathetic division** might be called the "eat-drink-and-rest" system. The neurons of this division are located at the top and bottom of the spinal column on either side of the sympathetic division neurons (*para* means "beyond" or "next to" and in this sense refers to the neurons located on either side of the sympathetic division neurons).

In looking at Figure 4.5, it might seem as if the parasympathetic division does pretty much the opposite of the sympathetic division, but it's a little more complex than that. The parasympathetic division's job is to restore the body to normal functioning after a stressful situation ends. It slows the heart and breathing, constricts the pupils, and reactivates digestion and excretion. Signals to the adrenal glands stop because the parasympathetic division isn't connected to the adrenal glands. In a sense, the parasympathetic division allows the body to put back all the energy it burned—which is why people are often very hungry *after* the stress is all over.

Understand the Structure and Function of the Endocrine System

Earlier we addressed the subject of neurons and the neurotransmitters and how they release into the synapse to communicate with postsynaptic neurons. This type of chemical communication is fairly specific, primarily affecting neurons in the immediate vicinity* of the originating neuron, and also very fast (almost immediate). Other structures also use chemical communication but do so at a

---

*vicinity: near or around an area.

different rate and act in a more far-reaching manner. For example, glands are organs in the body that secrete* chemicals called hormones.

4.4 Explain how the endocrine glands interact with the nervous system.

Endocrine glands (the prefix *endo* means inside and the root word *crine* means to secrete), secrete their chemicals directly into the bloodstream thus acting rapidly to affect behavior. The chemicals secreted by this type of gland are called **hormones** (the word hormone means to excite). As mentioned earlier in the chapter when talking about the sympathetic division of the autonomic nervous system, these hormones flow into the bloodstream, which carries them to their target organs. The molecules of these hormones then fit into receptor sites on those organs to fulfill their function, affecting behavior as they do so. Endocrine communication is generally slower due to the time it takes hormones to travel to target organs; the behaviors and responses they affect may not occur until hours, weeks, or years later.

The Pituitary, Master of the Hormonal Universe The **pituitary gland** is located in the brain itself, just below the hypothalamus. The hypothalamus controls the glandular system by releasing hormones to the pituitary. That is because the pituitary gland is the *master gland*, the one that controls or influences all of the other endocrine glands. The pituitary secretes several hormones that influence the activity of the other glands. Most notable of these hormones is *growth hormone*, which controls and regulates the increase in size as children grow from infancy to adulthood.

The Pineal Gland The *pineal gland* is also located in the brain, near the back, directly above the brain stem. It plays an important role in several biological rhythms. The pineal gland secretes a hormone called *melatonin*, which helps track day length (and seasons). In humans, melatonin levels are more influential in regulating the sleep–wake cycle.

The Thyroid Gland The *thyroid gland* is located inside the neck and secretes hormones that regulate growth and metabolism. One of these, a hormone called *thyroxin*, regulates metabolism (controlling how fast the body burns its available energy). As related to growth, the thyroid plays a crucial role in body and brain development.

Pancreas The *pancreas* controls the level of blood sugar in the body by secreting *insulin*, which breaks down sugar in the bloodstream. If the pancreas secretes too little insulin, it results in *diabetes*. If it secretes too much insulin, it results in *hypoglycemia*, or low blood sugar, which causes a person to feel hungry all the time and often become overweight as a result.

The Gonads The *gonads* are the sex glands, including the *ovaries* in the female and the *testes* in the male. They secrete hormones that regulate sexual behavior and reproduction.

The Adrenal Glands Everyone has two **adrenal glands**, one on top of each kidney. Each adrenal gland releases epinephrine and norepinephrine when people are under stress and that aids in sympathetic arousal.

Overall, the interactions between the sympathetic and parasympathetic systems provide an important framework in how we respond to both internal and external events or challenges. Next we will look at how they work together to protect us, or if activated for too long, can lead to some undesirable effects.

hormones chemicals released into the bloodstream by endocrine glands.

pituitary gland gland located in the brain that secretes human growth hormone and influences all other hormone-secreting glands (also known as the master gland).

adrenal glands endocrine glands located on top of each kidney that secrete over 30 different hormones to deal with stress, regulate salt intake, and provide a secondary source of sex hormones affecting the sexual changes that occur during adolescence.

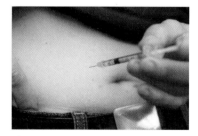

▲ *When the pancreas does not secrete enough insulin, the result is diabetes. Many diabetic people must give themselves insulin shots to supply enough of the hormone.*

---

*secrete: release or discharge.

Watch the **Video**,
The Physical Side of Stress, at
MyPsychLab

4.5 Outline how hormones influence behavior and mental processes.

The sympathetic and parasympathetic systems, and various hormones, figure prominently* in our body's physiological reactions to stress. The video *The Physical Side of Stress* includes more information on this.

The General Adaptation Syndrome Endocrinologist Hans Selye was the founder of the field of research concerning stress and its effects on the human body. He studied the sequence of physiological reactions that the body goes through when adapting to a stressor. This sequence (see **Figure 4.6**) is called the *general adaptation syndrome (GAS)* and consists of three stages (Selye, 1956).

- **Alarm:** When the body first reacts to a stressor, the sympathetic nervous system is activated. The adrenal glands release hormones that increase heart rate, blood pressure, and the supply of blood sugar, resulting in a burst of energy. Reactions such as fever, nausea, and headache are common.
- **Resistance:** As the stress continues, the body settles into sympathetic division activity, continuing to release the stress hormones that help the body fight off, or resist, the stressor. The early symptoms of alarm lessen and the person or animal may actually feel better. This stage will continue until the stressor ends or the organism has used up all of its resources.
- **Exhaustion:** When the body's resources are gone, exhaustion occurs. Exhaustion can lead to the formation of stress-related diseases (e.g., high blood pressure or a weakened immune system) or the death of the organism if outside help is unavailable (Stein-Behrens et al., 1994). Alarm and resistance are stages that people experience many times throughout life, allowing people to adapt to life's demands (Selye, 1976). It is the prolonged secretion of the stress

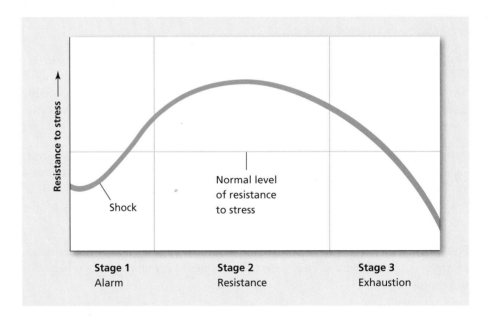

FIGURE 4.6 General Adaptation Syndrome
In the alarm stage, resistance drops at first as the sympathetic system quickly activates. But resistance then rapidly increases as the body mobilizes its defense systems. In the resistance stage, the body is working at a much increased level of resistance, using resources until the stress ends or the resources run out. In the exhaustion stage, the body is no longer able to resist as resources have been depleted, and at this point disease and even death are possible.

---

*prominently: are important to.

hormones during the exhaustion stage that can lead to the most harmful effects of stress, such as high blood pressure.

4.6 Explain how hormones interact with the immune system.

As Selye first discovered, the *immune system* (the system of cells, organs, and chemicals in the body that responds to attacks on the body from diseases and injuries) is affected by stress. The field of *psychoneuroimmunology* concerns the study of the effects of psychological factors such as stress, emotions, thinking, learning, and behavior on the immune system (Ader, 2003; Cohen & Herbert, 1996; Kiecolt-Glaser, 2009; Kiecolt-Glaser et al., 1995, 1996, 2002). Researchers in this field have found that stress triggers the same response in the immune system that infection triggers (Maier & Watkins, 1998).

Hormones also play a part in helping the immune system fight the effects of stress. Researchers (Morgan et al., 2009) have found that a hormone known to provide anti-stress benefits in animals, also aids humans in stress toleration—perhaps by regulating the effects of stress on the hippocampus (part of the limbic system).

The positive effects of stress on the immune system only seem to work when the stress is not a continual, chronic* condition. As stress continues, the body's resources begin to fail in the exhaustion phase of the general adaptation to stress (Kiecolt-Glaser et al., 1987, 1995, 1996; Prigerson et al., 1997).

Heart Disease Of course, anything that can weaken the immune system can have a negative effect on other bodily systems. Stress has been shown to put people at a higher risk of *coronary heart disease (CHD)*, the buildup of a waxy substance called plaque in the arteries of the heart. This relationship is at least in part because the liver, which is not activated while the sympathetic nervous system is aroused, does not have a chance to clear the fat and cholesterol from the bloodstream, leading to clogged arteries and eventually the possibility of heart attacks or strokes. (See **Figure 4.7**.)

Cancer Cancer is not one disease but rather a collection of diseases that can affect any part of the body. Unlike normal cells, which divide and reproduce according to genetic instructions and stop dividing according to those same instructions, cancer cells divide without stopping. The resulting tumors affect the normal functioning of the organs and systems they invade, causing them to fail, eventually killing the organism.

◀ So stress actually increases the activity of the immune system? But then how does stress end up causing those diseases, like high blood pressure?

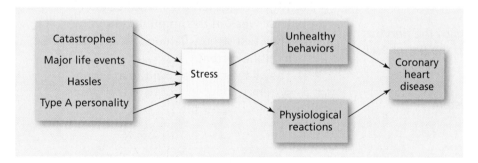

FIGURE 4.7 Stress and Coronary Heart Disease
The blue box on the left represents various sources of stress (Type A personality refers to someone who is ambitious, always working, and usually hostile). In addition to the physical reactions that accompany the stress reaction, an individual under stress may be more likely to engage in unhealthy behavior such as overeating, drinking alcohol or taking other kinds of drugs, avoiding exercise, and acting out in anger or frustration. This kind of behavior also contributes to an increased risk of coronary heart disease.

---

*chronic: ongoing for a long time.

Pick the best answer.

1. **Which part of the neuron receives messages from other cells?**

   a. axon
   b. dendrite
   c. soma
   d. myelin

2. **When the action potential reaches the end of the axon terminal, it causes the release of**

   a. an electrical spark that sets off the next cell
   b. positively charged ions that excite the next cell
   c. negatively charged ions that inhibit the next cell
   d. neurotransmitters that excite or inhibit the next cell

3. **If you burn your finger, your immediate reaction will probably involve all BUT which of the following?**

   a. the brain
   b. the spinal cord
   c. sensory neurons
   d. motor neurons

4. **If you are typing on the computer keyboard, the motions of your fingers on the keys are probably being controlled by the**

   a. autonomic nervous system
   b. somatic nervous system
   c. sympathetic division
   d. parasympathetic division

5. **Which of the following parts of the nervous system connects the brain to the peripheral nervous system?**

   a. the spinal cord
   b. the autonomic nervous system
   c. the somatic nervous system
   d. the sympathetic division

6. **The protective sheath that wraps around a neuron's axon is made of**

   a. dendrites
   b. myelin
   c. synapses
   d. hormones

7. **The hormone cortisol is produced by the**

   a. pituitary gland
   b. thyroid gland
   c. pineal gland
   d. adrenal glands

8. **The gap between two neurons is known as the**

   a. neurotransmitter
   b. receptor site
   c. axon terminal
   d. synapse

9. **What job do interneurons perform?**

   a. They carry messages from the senses to the spinal cord.
   b. They carry messages from the spinal cord to the muscles and glands.
   c. They connect the sensory neurons to the motor neurons.
   d. They connect the sympathetic division to the parasympathetic division.

10. **How do hormones produced by the thymus gland affect the immune system?**

    a. They strengthen the immune system.
    b. They weaken the immune system.
    c. They first strengthen and later weaken the immune system.
    d. They have no effect on the immune system.

5 The Brain

Module Goals

Understand how the brain is studied.

Describe the functions of parts of the brain.

Learning Objectives

5.1 Describe tools used to study the brain and nervous system.

5.2 Understand the structures and functions of the various parts of the central nervous system.

5.3 Explain how lateralization differentiates the hemispheres of the brain.

5.4 Describe various issues and advances in neuroscience and genetics.

Understand How the Brain Is Studied

Scientists can't be sure what brain tissue really looks like when it's inside the skull of a living person—nor can they be certain that it looks identical to that of a brain sitting on a dissecting table.

5.1 Describe tools used to study the brain and nervous system.

Researchers are able to learn about the brain through accidental damage, or through intentional manipulation of brain tissue. When appropriate, such manipulation can be accomplished through *lesioning* or *stimulation* methods.

◀ How can scientists find out if the brain is intact, if parts are missing or damaged, or what the various parts of the brain do?

Lesioning Studies One way to get some idea of the functions that various areas of the brain control is to study animals or people with damage in those areas. In animals, that may mean researchers will deliberately damage a part of the brain, after which, they test the animal to see what has happened to its abilities. In such an experiment, once the test animal is anesthetized and given medication for pain, a thin wire, which is insulated everywhere but at its tip, is surgically inserted into the brain. An electrical current strong enough to destroy the target neurons is sent through the tip of the wire. This procedure is called **lesioning**.

It should be obvious that researchers cannot destroy areas of brains in living human beings. One method they can use is to study and test people who already have brain damage.

Brain Stimulation In contrast to lesioning, a less harmful way to study the brain is to temporarily disrupt or enhance the normal functioning of specific brain areas through electrical stimulation, and then study the resulting changes in behavior or cognition. The procedure of stimulating a specific area of the brain is much the same as in lesioning, but the much milder current in this research does no damage to the neurons.

Invasive Techniques: Stimulating from the Inside A specific type of ESB called *deep brain stimulation (DBS)* is an invasive technique that has been shown to be very helpful in some disorders in humans. In this procedure, neurosurgeons

lesioning insertion of a thin, insulated electrode into the brain through which an electrical current is sent, destroying the brain cells at the tip of the wire.

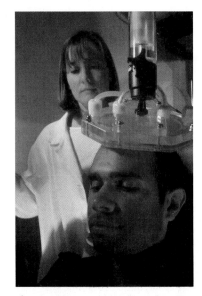

▲ *A doctor at the National Institute of Mental Health in Bethesda, Maryland, uses an electromagnet as part of an experimental treatment for depression. This treatment, called repetitive transcranial magnetic stimulation (rTMS), excites neurons in the brain, triggering activity.*

place electrodes in specific deep-brain areas and then route the electrode wires to a pacemaker-like device called an impulse generator that is surgically implanted under the collarbone or in the abdomen. The impulse generator then sends impulses to the implanted electrodes, stimulating the specific brain areas of interest.

Noninvasive Technique: Stimulating from the Outside There are also non-invasive techniques for stimulating the brain that contribute to research and our knowledge of the brain in a variety of areas. In *transcranial magnetic stimulation* (TMS), magnetic pulses are applied to the cortex using special copper wire coils that are positioned over the head. The resulting magnetic fields stimulate neurons in the targeted area of the cortex.

Neuroimaging Techniques
All of these methods of stimulation yield important information about the brain, thinking, and behavior, but they do not allow us to see what is going on with the brain as a whole. Instead, various neuroimaging techniques can do this, either by directly imaging the brain's structure (the different parts) or its function (how the parts work).

Mapping Structure
Historically, scientists and researchers would have to wait until someone died to examine the structure of their brain. Thankfully that is no longer the case. Scientists have several ways to study the parts of the human brain without causing harm to the person.

Computed Tomography (CT) One way to examine the brain of a living person is to take a series of X-rays of the brain, aided by a computer. This is accomplished during a *CT scan* (*computed tomography* involves mapping "slices" of the brain by computer). CT scans can show stroke damage, tumors, injuries, and abnormal brain structure. (See **Figure 5.1a.**)

Magnetic Resonance Imaging (MRI) As useful as a CT scan can be for imaging the skull, it doesn't show very small details within the brain. The relatively newer technique of *magnetic resonance imaging,* or *MRI*, provides much more detail (see **Figure 5.1b**), even allowing doctors to see the effects of very small strokes.

Mapping Function As important as imaging brain structure is, it is sometimes important to know how different brain areas function. And just as scientists and researchers have various options for examining the physical parts of the brain, there are also different options for studying brain function.

FIGURE 5.1 Mapping Brain Structure
(a) CT scan from a 5-year-old girl with a head injury and skull fracture, depicting the brain and swelling associated with the injury. Contrast the brain detail of (a) with the MRI scan in (b) (different, adult individual).

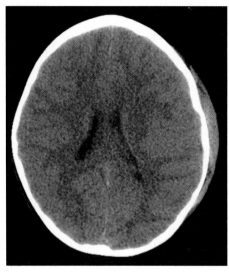

a.

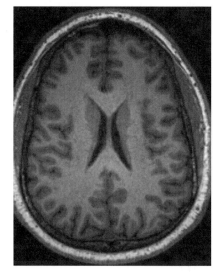

b.

The Electroencephalogram (EEG) A fairly harmless way to study the activity of the living brain is to record the electrical activity of the cortex just below the skull using a device called an **electroencephalograph**. The first *electroencephalogram (EEG)* recording in humans was accomplished in 1924 by Hans Berger (Niedermeyer, 2005). Recording the EEG involves using small metal-disk or sponge-like electrodes placed directly on the scalp, and a special solution to help conduct the electrical signals from the cortex just below. These electrodes are connected to an amplifier and then to a computer to view the information. The resulting electrical output forms waves that indicate many things, such as stages of sleep, seizures, and even the presence of tumors. The EEG can also be used to help determine which areas of the brain are active during various mental tasks that involve memory and attention. EEG activity can be classified according to appearance and frequency, and different waves are associated with different brain activity. For example, *alpha waves* in the back of the brain are one indication of relaxed wakefulness (seen in bottom two lines in **Figure 5.2a**). EEG waveforms are covered in more detail in Chapter Four. Ⓛ Ⓘ Ⓝ Ⓚ *to Chapter Four: Consciousness, pp. 126–129.*

Positron Emission Tomography (PET) The functional neuroimaging methods discussed so far rely on the electrical activity of the brain. Other techniques make use of other indicators of brain activity, including energy consumption or changes in blood oxygen levels (if areas of the brain are active, they are likely using fuel and oxygen). In *positron emission tomography (PET)*, the person is injected with a harmless type of radioactive glucose (a kind of sugar). The computer detects the activity of the brain cells by looking at which cells are using up the radioactive glucose and projecting the image of that activity onto a monitor. The computer uses colors to indicate

electroencephalograph
machine designed to record the electrical activity of the cortex below the skull.

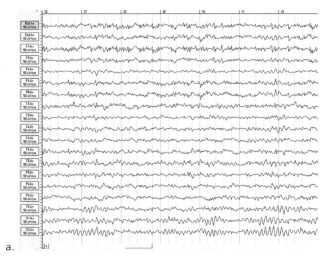
a.

FIGURE 5.2 Mapping Brain Function
Various methods for mapping brain function. An EEG record is shown in (a), a PET scan image in (b), and an image from an fMRI study in (c).

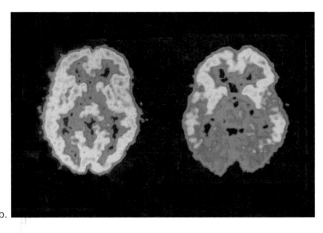
b.

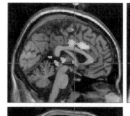
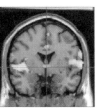
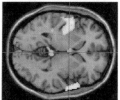

c.

different levels of brain activity, with lighter colors often indicating greater activity. (See **Figure 5.2b.**)

Functional MRI (fMRI) Although traditional MRI scans only show structure, there is a technique called *functional MRI (fMRI)* in which the computer tracks changes in the oxygen levels of the blood (see **Figure 5.2c**). By superimposing this picture of where the oxygen goes in the brain over the picture of the brain's structure, researchers can identify what areas of the brain are active. By combining such images taken over a period of time, a sort of "movie" of the brain's functioning can be made (Lin et al., 2007). Functional MRIs can give more detail, tend to be clearer than PET scans, and are an incredibly useful tool for research into the workings of the brain.

Describe the Functions of the Parts of the Brain

▶ Now it's time to look at the various structures of the brain, starting from the bottom and working up to the top. The video *Parts of the Brain* describes the major parts of the brain and their functions. Many parts of the brain also overlap in their functions, but a full understanding of the brain is not truly possible within one chapter of a high school psychology text.

5.2 Understand the structures and functions of the various parts of the central nervous system.

The Hindbrain The brain can be divided into three main divisions early in our development that later subdivide into smaller divisions. The three primary divisions are the forebrain, the midbrain, and the hindbrain. The forebrain includes the cortex, basal ganglia, and the limbic system. The midbrain is important for both sensory and motor functions, but does not contain components that will be discussed in this section. The hindbrain includes the medulla, pons, and cerebellum.

Medulla The **medulla** (which means the deep inside region or marrow, as in the "marrow" of the spinal cord) is located at the top of the spinal column. In **Figure 5.3**, it is the first "swelling" at the top of the spinal cord, just at the very bottom of the brain. This is the part of the brain that a person would least want to have damaged, as it controls life-sustaining functions such as heartbeat, breathing, and swallowing. It is in the medulla, pronounced like meh-dull-lah, that the sensory nerves coming from the left and right sides of the body crossover, so that sensory information from the left side of the body goes to the right side of the brain and vice versa.

Pons The **pons** is the larger "swelling" just above the medulla. This term means "bridge," and the pons is indeed the bridge between the lower parts of the brain and the upper sections. As in the medulla, there is a crossover of nerves, but in this case it is the motor nerves carrying messages from the brain to the body. This allows the pons to coordinate the movements of the left and right sides of the body. (It will be useful to remember these nerve crossovers when reading about the functions of the left and right sides of the brain in a later part of this chapter.) The pons also influences sleep, dreaming, and arousal.

The Reticular Formation The **reticular formation (RF)** (reticular tissue is a type of tissue in the body that "connects") is an area of neurons running through the middle of the medulla and the pons and slightly beyond. These neurons are

Okay, now I understand a little more about how we look inside the brain. What exactly IS inside the brain?

👁 **Watch** the **Video**, *Parts of the Brain*, at **MyPsychLab**

medulla the first large swelling at the top of the spinal cord, forming the lowest part of the brain, which is responsible for life-sustaining functions such as breathing, swallowing, and heart rate.

pons the larger swelling above the medulla that connects the top of the brain to the bottom and that plays a part in sleep, dreaming, left–right body coordination, and arousal.

reticular formation (RF) an area of neurons running through the middle of the medulla and the pons and slightly beyond that play a role in general arousal, alertness, and sleep.

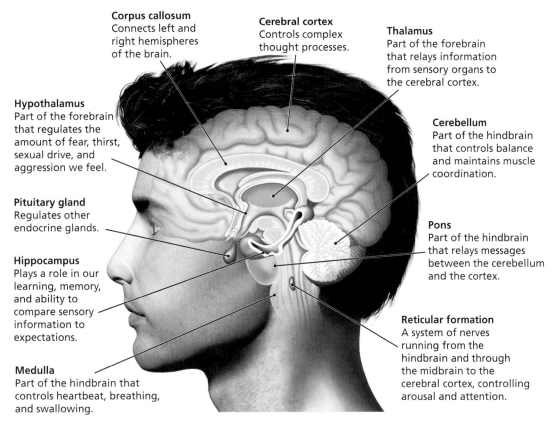

Corpus callosum
Connects left and right hemispheres of the brain.

Cerebral cortex
Controls complex thought processes.

Thalamus
Part of the forebrain that relays information from sensory organs to the cerebral cortex.

Hypothalamus
Part of the forebrain that regulates the amount of fear, thirst, sexual drive, and aggression we feel.

Cerebellum
Part of the hindbrain that controls balance and maintains muscle coordination.

Pituitary gland
Regulates other endocrine glands.

Pons
Part of the hindbrain that relays messages between the cerebellum and the cortex.

Hippocampus
Plays a role in our learning, memory, and ability to compare sensory information to expectations.

Reticular formation
A system of nerves running from the hindbrain and through the midbrain to the cerebral cortex, controlling arousal and attention.

Medulla
Part of the hindbrain that controls heartbeat, breathing, and swallowing.

FIGURE 5.3 Major Structures of the Human Brain

responsible for people's ability to selectively attend to certain kinds of information in their surroundings. Basically, the RF allows people to ignore constant, unchanging information (such as the noise of an air conditioner) and become alert to changes in information (for example, if the air conditioner stopped, most people would notice immediately). One part of the RF is called the *reticular activating system (RAS)*, and it stimulates the upper part of the brain, keeping people awake and alert. When a person is driving along and someone suddenly pulls out in front of the vehicle, it is the RAS that brings the driver to full attention.

Cerebellum At the base of the skull, behind the pons and below the main part of the brain, is a structure that looks like a small brain. (See Figure 5.3.) The **cerebellum** (meaning "little brain") is the part of the lower brain that controls all involuntary, rapid, fine motor movement. People can sit upright because the cerebellum controls all the little muscles needed to keep them from falling out of their chair. It also coordinates voluntary movements that have to happen in rapid succession, such as walking, skating, and gymnastics. Because of the cerebellum, people don't have to consciously think about their posture, muscle tone, and balance.

Other Structures under the Cortex: The Limbic System The forebrain includes the two cerebral hemispheres of the brain, including the cortex, which is discussed in detail later in this chapter, and a number of important structures located under the cortex in each hemisphere. We will focus on the subcortical structures that have been collectively referred to as the *limbic system*. (See **Figure 5.4**.)

Limbic System The *limbic system* (the word *limbic* means "marginal" or "border" and these structures are found in the inner margin of the upper brain) includes the thalamus, hypothalamus, hippocampus, amygdala, and the cingulate cortex. In general, the limbic system is involved in emotions, motivation, and learning.

▲ *This pitcher must count on his cerebellum to help him balance and coordinate the many fine motor commands that allow him to pitch the baseball accurately and swiftly.*

cerebellum part of the lower brain located behind the pons that controls and coordinates involuntary, rapid, fine motor movement, and may have some cognitive functions.

THE BIOLOGICAL PERSPECTIVE **59**

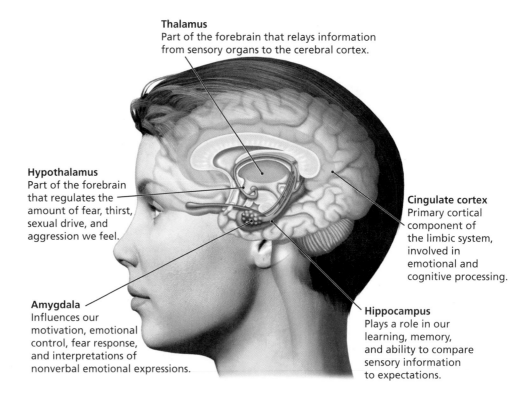

Thalamus
Part of the forebrain that relays information from sensory organs to the cerebral cortex.

Hypothalamus
Part of the forebrain that regulates the amount of fear, thirst, sexual drive, and aggression we feel.

Cingulate cortex
Primary cortical component of the limbic system, involved in emotional and cognitive processing.

Amygdala
Influences our motivation, emotional control, fear response, and interpretations of nonverbal emotional expressions.

Hippocampus
Plays a role in our learning, memory, and ability to compare sensory information to expectations.

FIGURE 5.4 The Limbic System

thalamus part of the limbic system located in the center of the brain, this structure relays sensory information from the lower part of the brain to the proper areas of the cortex and processes some sensory information before sending it to its proper area.

hypothalamus small structure in the brain located below the thalamus and directly above the pituitary gland, responsible for motivational behavior such as sleep, hunger, thirst, and sex.

homeostasis the tendency of the body to maintain a steady state.

hippocampus curved structure located within each temporal lobe, responsible for the formation of long-term declarative memories.

amygdala brain structure located near the hippocampus, responsible for fear responses and memory of fear.

Thalamus The **thalamus** ("inner chamber") is in some ways similar to a triage* nurse. This somewhat round structure in the center of the brain acts as a kind of relay station for incoming sensory information. Like a nurse, the thalamus might perform some processing of that sensory information before sending it on to the part of the cortex that deals with that kind of sensation—hearing, sight, touch, or taste. Damage to the thalamus might result in the loss or partial loss of any or all of those sensations.

Hypothalamus A very small but extremely powerful part of the brain is located just below and in front of the thalamus (see Figure 5.4). The **hypothalamus** ("below the inner chamber") regulates **homeostasis**, or keeping the body at set points, regarding body temperature, thirst, hunger, sleeping and waking.

Hippocampus Like many structures in the brain, the **hippocampus** was named based on its appearance. Hippocampus is the Greek word for "seahorse" and it was given to this brain structure because the first scientists who dissected the brain thought it looked like a seahorse. The hippocampus is located within the medial temporal lobe on each side of the brain (medial means "toward the middle"). Research has shown that the hippocampus is instrumental in forming long-term (permanent) declarative memories that are then stored elsewhere in the brain (Squire & Kandel, 2009).

Amygdala The **amygdala** (meaning "almond") is another area of the brain named for its shape and appearance. It is located near the hippocampus. The amygdala, pronounced like ah-mig- (as in big) dah-lah, is involved in fear responses and memory of fear. Information from the senses goes to the amygdala before the upper part of the brain is even involved, so that people can respond

---

*triage: a process for sorting injured people into groups based on their need for, or likely benefit from being sent on to, immediate medical treatment.

to danger very quickly, sometimes before they are consciously aware of what is happening.

The Cortex As stated earlier, the **cortex** ("rind" or outer covering) is the outermost part of the brain, which is the part of the brain most people picture when they think of what the brain looks like. It is made up of tightly packed neurons and actually is only about one-tenth of an inch thick on average (Fischl et al., 2001; MacDonald et al., 2000; Zilles, 1990). The cortex has a very recognizable surface anatomy because it is full of wrinkles.

The wrinkling of the cortex allows a much larger surface area of cortical cells to exist in the small space inside the skull. If the cortex were to be taken out, ironed flat, and measured, it would be about 2 to 3 square feet. (The owner of the cortex would also be dead, but that's fairly obvious, right?)

Cerebral Hemispheres The brain is divided into two sections called the *cerebral hemispheres*, which are connected by a thick, tough band of neural fibers (axons) called the *corpus callosum* (literally meaning "hard bodies," as calluses on the feet are hard and body as in a group or collection). (Refer back to Figure 5.4.) The corpus callosum, pronounced like core-pus-ca- (as in cat) low-sum, allows the left and right hemispheres to communicate with each other. Each hemisphere can be roughly divided into four sections or lobes by looking at the deeper wrinkles, or fissures (a valley in the cortex), in its surface. The lobes are named for the skull bones that cover them (see **Figure 5.5**).

Another organizational feature of the cortex is that for specific regions, each hemisphere is responsible for the opposite side of the body, either for control, or for receiving information. For example, the motor cortex controls the muscles on the opposite side of the body. If we are writing with our right hand, the motor cortex in the left hemisphere is responsible for controlling those movements. This feature, referred to as *contralateral organization*, plays a role in information coming from many of the sense organs to the brain, and in the motor commands originating in the brain going to the rest of the body.

cortex outermost covering of the brain consisting of densely packed neurons, responsible for higher thought processes and interpretation of sensory input.

◀ Why is the cortex so wrinkled?

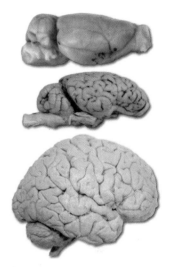

▲ *From top to bottom, a rat brain, sheep brain, and human brain (not to scale!). Note the differences in the amount of corticalization, or wrinkling, of the cortex between these three brains. Wrinkling allows for more surface area for neurons to fit.*

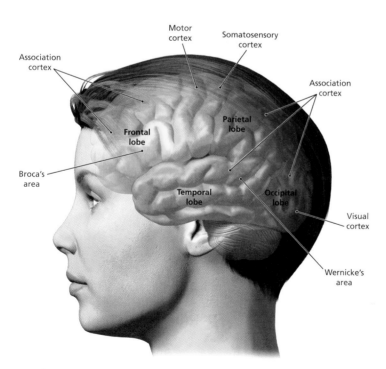

FIGURE 5.5 The Lobes of the Brain: Occipital, Parietal, Temporal, and Frontal

occipital lobe section of the brain located at the rear and bottom of each cerebral hemisphere containing the primary visual centers of the brain.

parietal lobes sections of the brain located at the top and back of each cerebral hemisphere containing the centers for touch, temperature, and body position.

somatosensory cortex area of cortex at the front of the parietal lobes responsible for processing information from the skin and internal body receptors for touch, temperature, and body position.

temporal lobes areas of the cortex located along the side of the brain, starting just behind the temples, containing the neurons responsible for the sense of hearing and meaningful speech.

frontal lobes areas of the brain located in the front and top, responsible for higher mental processes and decision making as well as the production of fluent speech.

motor cortex rear section of the frontal lobe, responsible for sending motor commands to the muscles of the somatic nervous system.

association areas areas within each lobe of the cortex responsible for the coordination and interpretation of information, as well as higher mental processing.

You've mentioned association cortex a few times. Do the other lobes of the brain contain association cortex as well? ▶

Occipital Lobes At the base of the cortex, toward the back of the brain is an area called the **occipital lobe**, pronounced like oc- (as in octave) -sip-itl. This area processes visual information from the eyes in the *primary visual cortex*. The *visual association cortex*, also in this lobe, is the part of the brain that helps identify and make sense of the visual information from the eyes. Each area of the cortex has these association areas that help people make sense of sensory information.

Parietal Lobes The **parietal lobes**, pronounced like pah-rye-itl, are at the top and back of the brain, just under the parietal bone in the skull. This area contains the **somatosensory cortex**, an area of neurons (see **Figure 5.6**) at the front of the parietal lobes on either side of the brain. This area processes information from the skin and internal body receptors for touch, temperature, and body position. The somatosensory cortex is laid out in a rather interesting way—the cells at the top of the brain receive information from the bottom of the body, and as one moves down the area, the signals come from higher and higher in the body. It's almost as if a little upside-down person were laid out along this area of cells.

Temporal Lobes The beginning of the **temporal lobes** are found just behind the temples of the head. These lobes contain the *primary auditory cortex* and the *auditory association area*. Also found in the left temporal lobe is an area that in most people is particularly involved with language.

Frontal Lobes These lobes are at the front of the brain, hence, the name **frontal lobes**. (It doesn't often get this easy in psychology; feel free to take a moment to appreciate it.) Here are found all the higher mental functions of the brain—planning, personality, memory storage, impulse control, complex decision making, and (again in the left hemisphere in most people) areas devoted to language. The frontal lobe also helps in controlling emotions by means of its connection to the limbic system. The most forward part of the frontal lobes is called the prefrontal cortex. People with damage to the frontal lobe may also experience problems with performing mental or motor tasks, such as getting stuck on one step in a process or on one wrong answer in a test and repeating it over and over again. (Asp & Tranel, 2013; Luria, 1965; Goel & Grafman, 1995).

The frontal lobes also contain the **motor cortex**, a band of neurons located at the back of each lobe. (See Figure 5.6.) These cells control the movements of the body's voluntary muscles by sending commands out to the somatic division of the peripheral nervous system. The motor cortex is laid out just like the somatosensory cortex, which is right next door in the parietal lobes.

This area of the brain has been the focus of a great deal of recent research, specifically as related to the role of a special type of neuron. These neurons are called *mirror neurons*, which fire when an animal performs an action—but they also fire when an animal observes that same action being performed by another. Previous brain-imaging studies in humans suggested that we, too, have mirror neurons in this area of the brain (Buccino et al., 2001; Buccino et al., 2004; Iacoboni et al., 1999).

The Association Areas of the Cortex **Association areas** are made up of neurons in the cortex that are devoted to making connections between the sensory information coming into the brain and stored memories, images, and knowledge. In other words, association areas help people make sense of the incoming sensory input. Although the association areas in the occipital and temporal lobes have already been mentioned, much of the brain's association cortex is in the frontal lobes. Some special association areas are worth talking about in more detail.

Broca's Area In the left frontal lobe of most people is an area of the brain devoted to the production of speech, a motor neuron activity. (In a small portion

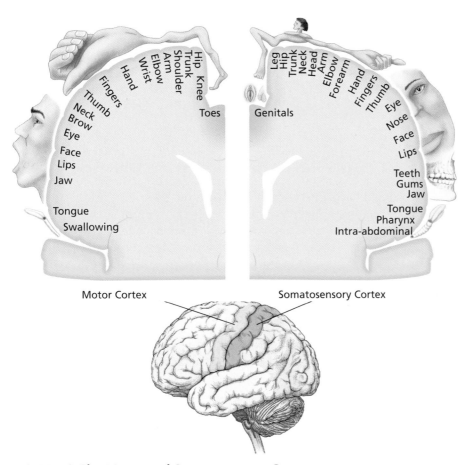

FIGURE 5.6 The Motor and Somatosensory Cortex
The motor cortex in the frontal lobe controls the voluntary muscles of the body. Cells at the top of the motor cortex control muscles at the bottom of the body, whereas cells at the bottom of the motor cortex control muscles at the top of the body. Body parts are drawn larger or smaller according to the number of cortical cells devoted to that body part. The somatosensory cortex, located in the parietal lobe just behind the motor cortex, is organized in much the same manner and receives information about the sense of touch and body position.

of the population, this area is in the right frontal lobe.) More specifically, this area allows a person to speak smoothly and fluently. It is called *Broca's area* after nineteenth-century neurologist Paul Broca, who first provided widely accepted clinical evidence that deficits in fluent and articulate speech result from damage to this area (Finger, 1994). Damage to Broca's area causes a person to be unable to get words out in a smooth, connected fashion. You can remember this by noting that damage to Broca's area causes "broken" speech. People with this condition may know exactly what they want to say and understand what they hear others say, but they cannot control the actual production of their own words. Speech is halting and words are often mispronounced, such as saying "cot" instead of "clock" or "non" instead of "nine." Some words may be left out entirely, such as "the" or "for." This is called *Broca's aphasia. Aphasia* refers to an inability to use or understand either written or spoken language (Goodglass et al., 2001).

Wernicke's Area In the left temporal lobe (again, in most people) is an area called *Wernicke's area*, named after the physiologist and Broca's contemporary, Carl Wernicke, pronounced like ver-ne- (as in necter) -ka, who first studied problems arising from damage in this location. This area of the brain appears to be involved in understanding the meaning of words (Goodglass et al., 2001). A person

Thinking Critically
Phineas Gage went from a mild-mannered railroad worker to a short-tempered and highly aggressive individual after a steel rod was driven through his frontal lobe. Discuss the extent to which his injuries and subsequent behavior change were a result of the biological changes or if they could be due to other "social" causes.

▲ As this woman brushes the right side of her hair, is she really "seeing" the left side? If she has spatial neglect, the answer is "no." While her eyes work just fine, her damaged right hemisphere refuses to notice the left side of her visual field.

◉ **Participate** in the **Experiment**, *Hemispheric Specialization*, at **MyPsychLab**

---

with *Wernicke's aphasia* would be able to speak fluently and pronounce words correctly, but the words would be the wrong ones entirely. For example, Elsie suffered a stroke to the temporal lobe, damaging this area of the brain. In the emergency room the nurse tried to take her blood pressure, and when the cuff inflated, Elsie said, "Oh, that's so Saturday hard." Elsie *thought* she was making sense. She also had trouble understanding what the people around her were saying to her.

Spatial Neglect A condition that can sometimes occur following a stroke is *spatial neglect*, or unilateral neglect, in which a person with damage to the right parietal and occipital lobes of the cortex will ignore everything in the left visual field. Unilateral refers to one side of the body, and this type of brain damage most often only affects attention to objects in the left visual field. Damage to areas of the frontal and temporal lobes may also play a part along with the parietal damage. Spatial neglect can affect the left hemisphere, but this condition occurs less frequently and in a much milder form than right-hemisphere neglect (Corbetta et al., 2005; Heilman et al., 1993; Springer & Deutsch, 1998).

5.3 Explain how lateralization differentiates the hemispheres of the brain.

Most people tend to think of the two cerebral hemispheres as identical twins. Both sides have the same four lobes and are arranged in much the same way. But language seems to be confined to the left hemisphere in about 90 percent of the population (Toga & Thompson, 2003). What other special tasks do the two halves of the *cerebrum* (the upper part of the brain consisting of the two hemispheres and the structures connecting them) engage in, and how do researchers know about such functions? Test the language abilites of the two hemispheres by completing the experiment *Hemispheric Specialization*.

Split-Brain Research Roger Sperry was a pioneer in the field of hemisphere specialization. He won a Nobel Prize for his work in demonstrating that the left and right hemispheres of the brain specialize in different activities and functions (Sperry, 1968). In looking for a way to cure epilepsy (severe muscle spasms or seizures resulting from brain damage), Sperry cut through the corpus callosum, the thick band of neural fibers that joins the two hemispheres. In early research with animals, this technique worked and seemed to have no side effects. The first people to have this procedure done also experienced relief from their severe epileptic symptoms, but testing found that (in a sense) they now had two brains in one body.

The special testing involves sending messages to only one side of the brain, which is now possible because the connecting tissue, the corpus callosum, has been cut. **Figure 5.7** shows what happens with a typical split-brain patient.

In a split-brain patient, if a picture of a ball is flashed to the right side of the screen, the image of the ball will be sent to the left occipital lobe. The person will be able to verbally say that he or she sees a ball. If a picture of a hammer is flashed to the left side of the screen, the person will not be able to *verbally* identify the object or be able to state with any certainty that something was seen. But if the *left hand* (controlled by the right hemisphere) is used, the person can point to the hammer he or she "didn't see." The right occipital lobe clearly saw the hammer, but the person could not *verbalize* that fact (Sperry, 1968). By conducting studies such as these, researchers have found that the left hemisphere specializes in language, speech, handwriting, calculation (math), sense of time and rhythm (which is mathematical in nature), and basically any kind of thought requiring analysis. The right hemisphere appears to specialize in more global (widespread) processing involving perception, visualization, spatial perception, recognition of patterns, faces, emotions, melodies, and expression of emotions. It also

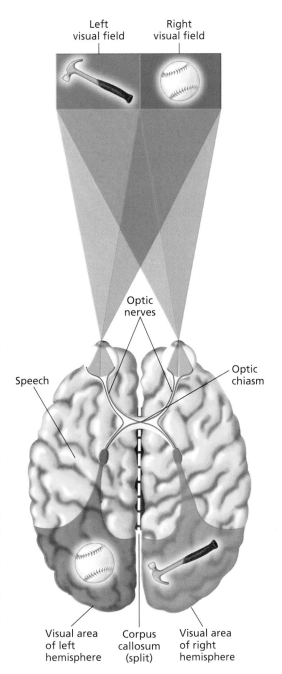

FIGURE 5.7 The Split-Brain Experiment

Roger Sperry created this experiment to demonstrate the specialization of the left and right hemispheres of the brain.

Left visual field

Right visual field

Optic nerves

Speech

Optic chiasm

Visual area of left hemisphere

Corpus callosum (split)

Visual area of right hemisphere

comprehends simple language but does not produce speech. (See **Table 5.1**.)

You may be wondering if it's true that there are left-brained or right-brained people. Actually, unless one is a split-brain patient, the two sides of the brain are always working together as an integrated whole. For example, the right side might recognize someone's face, while the left side struggles to recall the person's name. People aren't really left- or right-brained; they are "whole-brained." Michael Gazzaniga was one of Roger Sperry's students and collaborators and is a long-time researcher in the area of brain asymmetry and cognitive neuroscience. Gazzaniga's continuing work in brain lateralization has led to insights of the integrated mind, and he continues to work in related areas including human consciousness, perception, and neuroethics (Gazzaniga, 2006, 2009).

Table 5.1	**Specialization of the Two Hemispheres**
LEFT HEMISPHERE	RIGHT HEMISPHERE
Controls the right hand	Controls the left hand
Spoken language	Nonverbal
Written language	Visual-spatial perception
Mathematical calculations	Music and artistic processing
Logical thought processes	Emotional thought and recognition
Analysis of detail	Processing of the whole
Reading	Pattern recognition
	Facial recognition

5.4 Describe various issues and advances in neuroscience and genetics.

Paying Attention to the Causes of Attention-Deficit/Hyperactivity Disorder

Attention-deficit/hyperactivity disorder (ADHD) is a developmental disorder involving behavioral and cognitive aspects of inattention, impulsivity, and hyperactivity. The brain areas involved in the behavioral and cognitive characteristics of ADHD are typically divided into those responsible for regulating attention and cognitive control and those responsible for alertness and motivation (Nigg, 2010).

Since ADHD involves a variety of behaviors and cognitive aspects, research has often looked for specific markers that may lead to the actual causes of the disorder. These markers may be biological, cognitive, or behavioral measures (Nigg, 2010).

Much of the research over the past 10 years has focused on the cognitive markers for ADHD, such as attention problems, which may or may not be combined with neuroimaging. More recent research suggests that some aspects of attention are actually normal in individuals with ADHD. The aspect of attention with which individuals with ADHD do have problems is vigilance (being able to "watch out" for something important). Another cognitive area that appears to be impaired is being able to effectively control one's own cognitive processes such as staying on task, maintaining effort, or engaging in self-control (Nigg, 2010).

These findings have prompted researchers to reexamine the causes of ADHD and have highlighted the likelihood of more than one cause and more than one brain route to ADHD. Current research is looking at a variety of areas including environmental factors such as low-level lead exposure, genetic influences, the role of heredity and familial factors, and personality factors (Nigg, 2010). Furthermore, causes for the prevalence of ADHD continue to be examined, with variables ranging from the impact of sleep, circadian rhythms, and environmental light exposure (Arns et al., 2013) to the manner in which ADHD symptoms are characterized and diagnosed. Although some of these areas of investigation are not completely new and have been examined before, the possibility of multiple causes and interactions between these causes has not been studied as closely as it is at present in ADHD research.

Questions for Further Discussion

1. How might a psychology professional help parents or teachers understand the neuroimaging techniques and brain areas associated with ADHD?
2. If a college student has ADHD, what aspects of his or her school or personal life might be impacted by problems with vigilance or cognitive control?
3. What kinds of problems may arise in individuals taking ADHD medications when they do not have the actual symptoms of the disorder?

Pick the best answer.

1. Which of the following techniques uses a radioactive sugar to look at the functioning of the brain?

   a. EEG
   b. CT
   c. MRI
   d. PET

2. Which brain structure is most responsible for our balance, posture, and muscle tone?

   a. medulla
   b. cerebellum
   c. reticular formation
   d. pons

3. If you have problems storing away new memories, which area of your brain is most likely damaged?

   a. hippocampus
   b. hypothalamus
   c. cerebellum
   d. amygdala

4. In which of the following lobes of the cortex would you find the primary auditory area?

   a. frontal
   b. temporal
   c. occipital
   d. parietal

5. Which lobe controls higher mental functions such as thinking and problem solving?

   a. frontal
   b. parietal
   c. temporal
   d. corpus

6. Which of the following is true of split-brain patients?

   a. They can easily name objects in their left visual field.
   b. They cannot see objects in their left visual field.
   c. They can easily name objects in their right visual field.
   d. They cannot see objects in their right visual field.

7. Which of the following areas of the brain seems to be responsible for fear responses?

   a. thalamus
   b. amygdala
   c. corpus callosum
   d. somatosensory cortex

8. Parts of the brain that are responsible for coordinating sensory information with stored memories, images, and knowledge are called

   a. association areas
   b. peripheral locations
   c. subcortical structures
   d. cerebral hemispheres

9. Special cells that can manufacture other cell types when those cells need to be replaced are known as

   a. blood cells
   b. motor cells
   c. stem cells
   d. sensory cells

10. The brain's ability to adapt to serve new functions after it has been damaged is an example of

    a. deep lesioning
    b. action potential
    c. neuroplasticity
    d. mirroring

Heredity, Environment, and Adaptation

Module Goal

Understand the interaction between biological factors and experience.

Learning Objectives

6.1 Explain the relationship between heredity and environmental factors in determining development.

6.2 Understand the role of chromosomes and genes in determining the transmission of traits and the inheritance of disorders.

6.3 Describe the influence of evolved tendencies on behavior.

nature the influence of our inherited characteristics on our personality, physical growth, intellectual growth, and social interactions.

nurture the influence of the environment on personality, physical growth, intellectual growth, and social interactions.

👁 **Watch** the **Video**, *The Big Picture: Genes, Evolution, and Human Behavior* at **MyPsychLab**

Understand the Interaction between Biological Factors and Experience

6.1 Explain the relationship between heredity and environmental factors in determining development.

Nature versus Nurture **Nature** refers to heredity, the influence of inherited characteristics on personality, physical growth, intellectual growth, and social interactions. **Nurture** refers to the influence of the environment on all of those same things and includes parenting styles, physical surroundings, economic factors, and anything that can have an influence on development that does not come from within the person.

How much of a person's personality and behavior is determined by nature, and how much is determined by nurture? This is a key question, and the answer is quite complicated. It is also quite important: Are people like Hitler or Dzhokhar Tsarnaev (the youngest of the two brothers responsible for the bombings at the 2013 Boston Marathon) the result of bad genes? Or was it bad parenting or life-altering experiences in childhood? Or are they the unique combination of both hereditary and environmental influences? After many years of scientific research, most developmental psychologists now agree that the last possibility is the most likely explanation for most of human development: All that people are and all that people become is the product of an interaction between nature and nurture (Davis et al., 2012; Insel & Wang, 2010; Ridley, 1999; Sternberg & Grigorenko, 2006). Behavioral genetics is a relatively new field in the investigation of the origins of behavior in which researchers try to determine how much of behavior is the result of genetic inheritance and how much is because of a person's experiences. As the video *Family and Twin Studies* explains, behavioral geneticists use a variety of methods to determine this, including family, twin, and adoption studies.

👁 **Watch** the **Video**, *Family and Twin Studies Family and Twin Studies,* at **MyPsychLab**

6.2 Understand the role of chromosomes and genes in determining the transmission of traits and the inheritance of disorders.

Any study of the human life span must begin with looking at the complex material contained in the cells of the body that carries the instructions for life itself. After discussing the basic building blocks of life, we will discuss how the processes of conception and the development of the infant within the womb take place. *Genetics* is the science of heredity. Understanding how genes transmit human characteristics and traits involves defining a few basic terms.

DNA (deoxyribonucleic acid) is a very special kind of molecule (the smallest particle of a substance that still has all the properties of that substance). DNA consists of two very long sugar–phosphate strands, each linked together by certain chemical elements called *amines* or *bases* arranged in a particular pattern. The amines are organic structures that contain the genetic codes for building the proteins that make up organic life (hair coloring, muscle, and skin, for example) and that control the life of each cell. Each section of DNA containing a certain sequence (ordering) of these amines is called a **gene**. These genes are located on rod-shaped structures called **chromosomes**, which are found in the nucleus of a cell.

Humans have a total of 46 chromosomes in each cell of their bodies (with the exception of the egg and the sperm). Twenty-three of these chromosomes come from the mother's egg and the other 23 from the father's sperm. Most characteristics are determined by 22 such pairs, called the *autosomes*. The last pair determines the sex of the person. The two chromosomes of this pair are called the *sex chromosomes*. two X-shaped chromosomes indicate a female while an X and a Y indicate a male.

gene section of DNA having the same arrangement of chemical elements.

chromosome tightly wound strand of genetic material or DNA.

dominant referring to a gene that actively controls the expression of a trait

recessive referring to a gene that only influences the expression of a trait when paired with an identical gene.

Frank and Ernest

I HATE BEING A DNA MOLECULE. THERE'S SO MUCH TO REMEMBER!

©1986 Thaves. Reprinted with permission. Newspaper dist. by NEA, Inc.

Dominant and Recessive Genes The 46 chromosomes can be arranged in pairs, with one member of each pair coming from the mother and the other member from the father. Let's consider just one of these pairs for the moment. In this particular pair of chromosomes, assume that there is a gene for hair color on chromosome. The observable color of the person's hair will be determined by those two genes, one gene from each parent. If both genes are for brown hair, the person will obviously have brown hair, right? And if both are for blond hair, the person's hair will be blond.

The answer lies in the nature of each gene. Some genes that are more active in influencing the trait are called **dominant**. A dominant gene will always be expressed in the observable trait, in this case, hair color. A person with a dominant gene for brown hair color will have brown hair, no matter what the other gene is, because brown is the most dominant of all the hair colors. Some genes are less active in influencing the trait and will only be expressed in the observable trait if they are paired with another less active gene. These genes tend to recede, or fade, into the background when paired with a more dominant gene, so they are called **recessive**. Blond is the most recessive hair color and it will only show up as a trait if that person receives a blond-hair-color gene from each parent.

◄ But what if one gene is for brown hair and the other is for blond hair?

Genetic and Chromosome Problems Several genetic disorders are carried by recessive genes. Diseases carried by recessive genes are inherited when a child

Thinking Critically
The time is coming when choosing the genetic traits of your child is going to be possible. What kinds of ethical and practical problems may arise from this development?

inherits two recessive genes, one from each parent. Examples of disorders inherited in this manner are cystic fibrosis (a disease of the respiratory and digestive tracts), sickle-cell anemia (a blood disorder), Tay-Sachs disorder (a fatal neurological disorder), and phenylketonuria (PKU), in which an infant is born without the ability to break down phenylalanine, an amino acid controlling coloring of the skin and hair. If levels of phenylalanine build up, brain damage can occur; if untreated, it can result in severe intellectual disabilities. **Figure 6.1** illustrates a typical pattern of inheritance for dominant and recessive genes using the example of PKU.

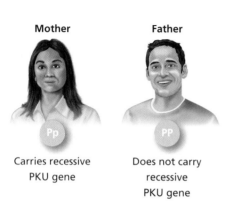

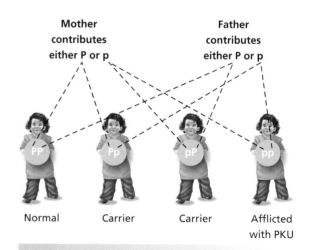

a.

b.

FIGURE 6.1 Dominant and Recessive Genes and PKU

This figure shows the variation of parents carrying zero, one, or two recessive genes and the result of this in their offspring. (a) If only one parent carries the PKU gene, the children might be carriers but will not have PKU. (b) Only if both parents are carriers of PKU will a child have the one in four possibility of having PKU.

Sometimes the chromosome itself is the problem. A chromosome can end up in the wrong cell, leaving one cell with only 22 and the other with 24. If either of these cells survives to "mate," the missing or extra chromosome can cause mild to severe problems in development (American Academy of Pediatrics, 1995; Barnes & Carey, 2002; Centers for Disease Control and Prevention, 2009c; Gardner & Sutherland, 1996). Examples of chromosome disorders include *Down syndrome*, a disorder in which there is an extra chromosome in what would normally be the 21st pair. Symptoms commonly include the physical characteristics of almond-shaped, wide-set eyes, as well as intellectual disability (Barnes & Carey, 2002; Hernandez & Fisher, 1996).

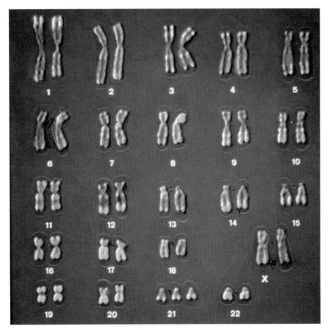

▲ *Down syndrome is a form of developmental delay caused by an extra chromosome 21.*

6.3 Describe the influence of evolved tendencies on behavior.

Many psychologists believe that human behavior is shaped not only by biology and environment but also by evolutionary forces: tendencies that have developed gradually over many generations to help humans survive. Psychologists who are interested in these tendencies study how human behavior relates to the basic evolutionary principles proposed more than 100 years ago by famous British scientist Charles Darwin.

Charles Darwin and Natural Selection Like many other 19th-century scientists, Darwin accepted the theory of *evolution*, which states that species of plants and animals change gradually over the course of many generations. But why did these changes occur? Darwin noticed that many of the changes seemed to give organisms some sort of advantage in their natural environments. For example, if dark-colored moths can hide from predators more easily than light-colored moths can, it's likely that in a few generations, there will be many more dark-colored moths than light-colored moths. Why? The moths' dark color gives them an advantage when it comes to survival. This means that, in general, dark-colored moths will live long enough to have baby dark-colored moths, whereas light-colored moths will be eaten by predators before they can reproduce. This scenario is one simple example of Darwin's groundbreaking theory of **natural selection**. Darwin argued that traits and behaviors that provide a survival advantage are more likely than other characteristics to be passed on to future generations.

natural selection traits that contribute to survival are more likely to be passed on.

Pick the best answer.

1. How many chromosomes do humans have in each cell of their bodies?

   a. 10
   b. 22
   c. 23
   d. 46

2. Which of the following is the most dominant hair color?

   a. brown
   b. blond
   c. red
   d. gray

3. Genes that tend to "fade into the background" when paired with more influential genes are called

   a. dominant
   b. recessive
   c. chromosomes
   d. autosomes

4. If a person is predisposed to burning in the sun, which of the following is true?

   a. The person will definitely experience sunburns.
   b. The person will definitely not experience sunburns.
   c. The person is unlikely to experience sunburns.
   d. The person may experience sunburns, depending on environmental factors.

5. A person who believes that our environments and experiences are entirely responsible for our personalities, skills, and behaviors believes in the power of

   a. nature over nurture
   b. nurture over nature
   c. both nature and nurture
   d. neither nature nor nurture

6. Which of the following is an example of a hereditary influence?

   a. a genetic disease
   b. parental discipline
   c. cultural values
   d. peer pressure

7. Twins who grow up with the same parents in the same environment will most likely be

   a. identical in every way
   b. similar in some ways and different in others
   c. completely different in every way
   d. identical in terms of genetics but opposite in terms of behavior

8. A culture's understood rules of behavior are

   a. beliefs
   b. guidelines
   c. norms
   d. values

9. Charles Darwin was the first to propose the theory of

   a. evolution
   b. natural selection
   c. genetics
   d. environmental influences

10. Which of the following human behaviors is most likely an evolved tendency?

    a. shopping at a mall
    b. attending school
    c. driving cars and trucks
    d. spitting out poisonous foods

Listen to an Audio File of your chapter at MyPsychLab

Module 4: The Nervous System

Understand the structure and function of the nervous system.

4.1 Describe the parts of the neuron and understand the basic process of neural transmission.
- Neurons have four primary components: dendrites that receive input, a soma or cell body, axons that carry the neural message to other cells, and axon terminals that are the site of neurotransmitter release.

4.2 Describe the major divisions of the human nervous system.
- The central nervous system consists of the brain and the spinal cord.
- There are two systems within the peripheral nervous system, the somatic nervous system, and the autonomic nervous system.

4.3 Identify the mechanisms of, and the importance of, plasticity of the nervous system, and describe advances made in neuroscience.
- Neuroplasticity refers to the brains ability to modify its structure and function as the result of experience or injury.

Understand the structure and function of the endocrine system.

4.4 Explain how the endocrine glands interact with the nervous system.
- Endocrine glands secrete chemicals called hormones directly into the bloodstream, influencing the activity of the muscles and organs.

4.5 Outline how hormones influence behavior and mental processes.
- Hormones regulate growth, sleep, metabolism, blood sugar levels, stress reactions, and other physical functions.

4.6 Explain how hormones interact with the immune system.
- As the stress continues or increases, the immune system can begin to fail.

Module 5: The Brain

Understand how the brain is studied.

5.1 Describe tools used to study the brain and nervous system.
- Early scientists examined brains of people who had died. Modern scientists perform tests on people with brain scan and imaging technology.

Describe the functions of parts of the brain.

5.2 Understand the structures and functions of the various parts of the central nervous system.
- Structures of the hindbrain control life-sustaining functions, sleep, arousal, and movement.
- The structures of the limbic system are involved in emotions, motivation, and learning.
- The cortex processes sensory information, controls voluntary muscles, and performs higher mental functions.

5.3 Explain how lateralization differentiates the hemispheres of the brain.
- Studies with split-brain patients reveal that the left side of the brain controls language, writing, logical thought, analysis, and mathematical abilities.
- The right side of the brain controls emotional expression, spatial perception, and recognition of faces.

5.4 Describe various issues and advances in neuroscience and genetics.

Applying Psychology to Everyday Life: Paying Attention to Attention-Deficit/Hyperactivity Disorder
- ADHD is often diagnosed in children. Multiple causes are possible including genetic, environmental, and several differences in brain structure and function.

Module 6: Heredity, Environment, and Adaptation

Understand the interaction between biological factors and experience.

6.1 Explain the relationship between heredity and environmental factors in determining development.
- Our thoughts and behaviors are affected not only by biological predispositions but also by the influence of our parents, our peers, and the cultures in which we participate.

6.2 Understand the role of chromosomes and genes in determining the transmission of traits and the inheritance of disorders.
- DNA molecules form genes, which interact to determine many of our physical traits and predispositions.

6.3 Describe the influence of evolved tendencies on behavior.
- Charles Darwin's theory of natural selection can explain human behaviors like avoiding dangerous animals.

Vocabulary Terms

neuron p. 42
dendrites p. 42
soma p. 42
axon p. 43
myelin p. 43
action potential p. 43
neurotransmitters p. 44
synapse p. 44
central nervous system p. 47
neuroplasticity p. 48
peripheral nervous system p. 48
autonomic nervous system p. 49

sympathetic division p. 49
parasympathetic division p. 50
hormones p. 51
pituitary gland p. 51
adrenal gland p. 51
lesioning p. 55
electroencephalograph p. 57
medulla p. 58
pons p. 58
reticular formation (RF) p. 58
cerebellum p. 59
thalamus p. 60

hypothalamus p. 60
homeostasis p. 60
hippocampus p. 60
amygdala p. 60
cortex p. 61
occipital lobe p. 62
parietal lobe p. 62
somatosensory cortex p. 62
temporal lobe p. 62
frontal lobe p. 62
motor cortex p. 62

association areas p. 62
nature p. 68
nurture p. 68
gene p. 69
chromosome p. 69
dominant p. 69
recessive p. 69
natural selection p. 71

Study and Review at **MyPsychLab**

Vocabulary Review

Match each vocabulary term to its definition.

1. soma
2. neuron
3. hypothalamus
4. hormones
5. medulla
6. neurotransmitters
7. cerebellum
8. dendrites
9. temporal lobe
10. gene

a. The basic cell that makes up the nervous system and that receives and sends messages within that system.
b. Section of DNA having the same arrangement of chemical elements.
c. The first large swelling at the top of the spinal cord, forming the lowest part of the brain, which is responsible for life-sustaining functions such as breathing, swallowing, and heart rate.
d. The area of the cortex located just behind the temples containing the neurons responsible for the sense of hearing and meaningful speech.
e. Part of the lower brain located behind the pons that controls and coordinates involuntary, rapid, fine motor movement.
f. Chemicals released into the bloodstream by endocrine glands.
g. Chemicals found in the synaptic vesicles that, when released, have an effect on the next cell.
h. The small structure in the brain located below the thalamus and directly above the pituitary gland, responsible for motivational behavior.
i. The branchlike structures that receive messages from other neurons.
j. The cell body of the neuron responsible for maintaining the life of the cell.

Psychology Project

What does it really feel like when the sympathetic division controls the body? Keep a journal and record your nervous system's responses to emotional situations.

Materials:
• small notebook   • pencil or pen

Instructions:

1. Over the course of 1 week, pay close attention to your behavior in stressful and nonstressful situations. Take the stress o meter test at: http://www.bam.gov/sub_yourlife/yourlife_stressometer.html# and see what your score is.

   At the end of each day, use a notebook to write down any emotional experiences you had that day, whether those experiences involved fear, anger, joy, or excitement.

2. For each experience you record, write a few notes about how your body responded to the experience. Did your heart beat faster before the math test? Did your stomach lurch as you waited in line for the roller coaster? Write down as many physical details as you can remember.

3. At the end of the week, analyze your findings. Take the stress o meter test again. Was there a difference in the level of stress from the beginning of the week to the end? What physical sensations did you experience in response to each event? Did you respond differently to a scary situation than you did to an exciting situation? How did your physical responses to emotional experiences differ from your normal, everyday behaviors and feelings? Based on what you know about the sympathetic and parasympathetic divisions of the autonomic nervous system, why do you think you felt the way you did? Record your responses to these questions in your notebook.

Tech Alternative

Download a stress management app to your smart phone. Use the app for a week to monitor your stress and coping choices. At the end of the week write a summary of your experiences. What was your stress like at the beginning of the week? How did the app help you with stress management? Would you recommend the app to a friend? Why? What was your stress like at the end of the week? What was the greatest benefit of using the app?

Essay Question

Briefly describe how someone might use **two** of the lobes of the cortex listed below while riding a bicycle. For **each of the lobes you choose**, include a general description of the function it performs and an example of how that function relates to riding a bicycle:

a. Occipital lobe
b. Temporal lobe
c. Frontal lobe
d. Parietal lobe

Test Yourself

Ready for your test? More quizzes and a customized plan.

Pick the best answer.

1. In the structure of the neuron, the _____ receives messages from other cells.
   - a. axon
   - b. dendrite
   - c. soma
   - d. myelin

2. A fatty substance found in the brain is known as
   - a. glial.
   - b. soma.
   - c. myelin.
   - d. neurilemma.

3. Which of the following insulates and protects a neuron's axon, as well as helps to speed along electrical impulses?
   - a. synaptic knobs
   - b. receptor sites
   - c. myelin sheath
   - d. neuromodulators

4. When a neuron is in the resting potential state, the neuron is negatively charged on the _____ and positively charged on the _____.
   - a. inside; outside
   - b. outside; inside
   - c. top; bottom
   - d. bottom; top

5. Which neurotransmitter stimulates muscle cells to contract but slows contractions in the heart?
   - a. acetylcholine
   - b. GABA
   - c. serotonin
   - d. endorphin

6. Heroin mimics the actions of endorphins, inhibiting pain signals and creating a "high" feeling. Heroin is an example of a(n)
   - a. protagonist.
   - b. antagonist.
   - c. agonist
   - d. glial cell.

7. Involuntary muscles are controlled by the _____ nervous system.
   - a. somatic
   - b. autonomic
   - c. sympathetic
   - d. parasympathetic

8. As you take notes, your heart beats at a normal rate. Your breathing is normal and your stomach slowly digests your earlier meal. What division of the autonomic nervous system is currently in action?
   - a. sympathetic
   - b. parasympathetic
   - c. peripheral
   - d. somatic

9. Robert has had difficulty sleeping for the past 6 months and his body seemingly no longer differentiates between night and day. His doctor believes the problem lies with Robert's endocrine system. What gland will Robert's physician focus on?
   - a. pituitary
   - b. adrenal
   - c. thyroid
   - d. pineal

10. Which gland(s) is/are known to influence all other glands within the endocrine system?
    - a. pineal gland
    - b. pituitary gland
    - c. thyroid gland
    - d. adrenal glands

11. In which of Selye's stages is death a possible outcome?
    - a. alarm
    - b. resistance
    - c. reaction
    - d. exhaustion

12. Bailey is a subject in a study on memory and problem solving. The researcher is applying magnetic pulses to her brain through copper wire coils positioned directly above her scalp. Bailey's study would best be described as a(n)
    - a. invasive stimulation technique.
    - b. noninvasive stimulation technique.
    - c. EEG technique.
    - d. PET technique.

13. Maria often sleeps soundly and rarely awakens to any outside noise. However, the cries of Maria's baby can awaken her immediately. What part of the brain is responsible for this reaction?
    - a. medulla
    - b. pons
    - c. reticular formation
    - d. cerebellum

14. Alexis and Theresa are synchronized swimmers for their high school swim team. They often work long hours to ensure the movements in their routine are perfectly timed. What part of their brains must Alexis and Theresa rely most upon?
    - a. medulla
    - b. pons
    - c. reticular formation
    - d. cerebellum

15. Your psychology teacher refers to this as the great relay station of the brain. What part is he or she referring to?
    - a. thalamus
    - b. hypothalamus
    - c. hippocampus
    - d. amygdala

16. Jessica has suffered a severe blow to the back of her head when she was thrown from her horse. Subsequently, her occipital lobe has been injured. Which of her senses has the highest chance of being affected?
    - a. hearing
    - b. touch
    - c. taste and smell
    - d. vision

17. Felicia is recovering from a brain injury. She is able to speak fluently but often uses incorrect words in a sentence. In one instance at a friend's birthday party, she said, "I would like something to drink. Can I have some battery?" Felicia's problem is known as
    - a. spatial neglect.
    - b. visual agnosia.
    - c. Broca's aphasia.
    - d. Wernicke's aphasia.

18. Although the brain works largely as a whole, which of the following is not a correct pairing of hemisphere and function?
    - a. left; control of right-handed motor functions
    - b. right; control of right-handed motor functions
    - c. right; recognition of faces
    - d. left; reading

19. The rod-shaped structures found in the nuclei of cells are called
    - a. DNA.
    - b. amines.
    - c. genes.
    - d. chromosomes.

20. Which of the following statements about environmental influences is most accurate?
    - a. Children's behavior is influenced mostly by their parents.
    - b. Children's behavior is influenced mostly by their peers.
    - c. Parents and peers both influence children's behavior.
    - d. Neither parents nor peers can influence children's behavior.

Concept Summary: The Biological Perspective

4.1 4.2 4.3 pp. 42–50

Understand the Structure and Function of the Nervous System

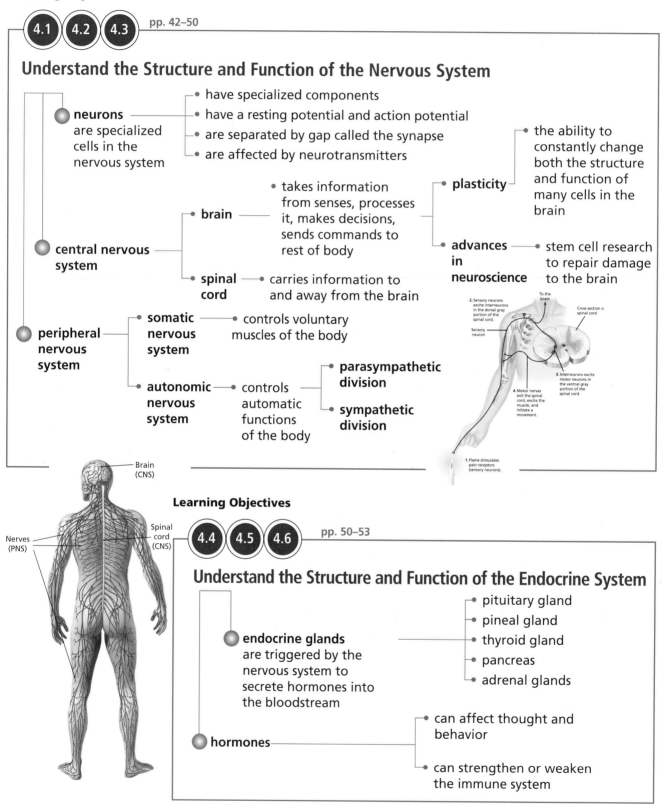

- **neurons** are specialized cells in the nervous system
  - have specialized components
  - have a resting potential and action potential
  - are separated by gap called the synapse
  - are affected by neurotransmitters

- **central nervous system**
  - **brain** — takes information from senses, processes it, makes decisions, sends commands to rest of body
  - **spinal cord** — carries information to and away from the brain

  - **plasticity** — the ability to constantly change both the structure and function of many cells in the brain
  - **advances in neuroscience** — stem cell research to repair damage to the brain

- **peripheral nervous system**
  - **somatic nervous system** — controls voluntary muscles of the body
  - **autonomic nervous system** — controls automatic functions of the body
    - **parasympathetic division**
    - **sympathetic division**

Brain (CNS)

Spinal cord (CNS)

Nerves (PNS)

2. Sensory neurons excite interneurons in the dorsal gray portion of the spinal cord.

To the brain

Cross section o spinal cord

Sensory neuron

3. Interneurons excite motor neurons in the ventral gray portion of the spinal cord.

4. Motor nerves exit the spinal cord, excite the muscle, and initiate a movement.

1. Flame stimulates pain receptors (sensory neurons).

4.4 4.5 4.6 pp. 50–53

Understand the Structure and Function of the Endocrine System

- **endocrine glands** are triggered by the nervous system to secrete hormones into the bloodstream
  - pituitary gland
  - pineal gland
  - thyroid gland
  - pancreas
  - adrenal glands

- **hormones**
  - can affect thought and behavior
  - can strengthen or weaken the immune system

Learning Objectives

5.1 pp. 55–58

🗺 Map the Concepts at MyPsychLab

Understand How the Brain Is Studied

techniques for studying brain function

- dissection of dead brains
- deep lesioning in animals
- case studies of brain-damaged individuals
- imaging techniques

structure | function

CT   MRI

- fMRI
- EEG
- PET

Learning Objectives

5.2 **5.3** **5.4** pp. 58–66

Describe the Functions of Parts of the Brain

structures of the brain

the hindbrain

- medulla
- pons
- reticular formation
- cerebellum

the limbic system

- thalamus
- hypothalamus
- hippocampus
- amygdala

the cortex

- frontal lobes
- temporal lobes
- parietal lobes
- occipital lobes

the cerebral hemispheres govern brain functions, and some brain functions are governed by one hemisphere more than the other

lateralization specialization of left and right hemispheres in the brain

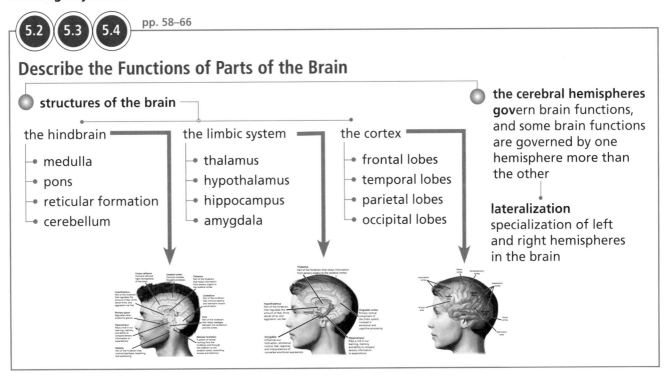

6.1 **6.2** **6.3** pp. 68–71

Understand the Interaction between Biological Factors and Experience

nature involves the influence of inherited characteristics — **genetics**

- dominant and recessive genes
- genetic predispositions

nurture involves the influence of the environment

- parent and peer influences
- cultural influences

evolved tendencies can also influence our behavior

3 Sensation and Perception

Taria Camerino is a pastry chef who experiences music, colors, shapes, and emotions as taste; Jamie Smith is a sommelier, or wine steward, who experiences smells as colors and shapes; and James Wannerton is an information technology consultant who experiences sounds, words, and colors as tastes and textures (Carlsen, 2013, March 18). All three of these individuals have a condition known as *synesthesia*, a disorder in which the signals from the various sensory organs are processed in the wrong cortical areas, resulting in the sense information being interpreted as more than one sensation. "Synesthesia" literally means "joined sensation." Recent studies suggest roughly 2%–4% of the population may experience some form of synesthesia. Although the causes of synesthesia are still being investigated, it appears in some forms that signals that come from the sensory organs, such as the eyes or the ears, go to places in the brain where they weren't originally meant to be or are processed differently. Overall, there is increased communication between sensory regions that results in synesthetes experiencing the world differently than others.

Which of your sensory abilities do you rely on most during a typical day? Are certain senses more important than others depending on the social context or setting?

Watch the **Video**, at **MyPsychLab**

*W*hy Study Sensation and Perception?

Without sensations to tell us what is outside our own mental world, we would live entirely in our own minds, separate from one another and unable to find food or any other basics that sustain life. Sensations are the mind's window to the world that exists around us. Without perception, we would be unable to understand what all those sensations mean—perception is the process of interpreting the sensations we experience so that we can act upon them.

7 Sensation

Module Goals

Understand the process of sensation.

Learn the capabilities and limitations of sensory processes.

Learning Objectives

7.1 Discuss the differences between sensation and perception.

7.2 Explain the process of sensation.

7.3 Discuss the concepts of threshold and adaptation.

7.4 Identify physical energy forms for which humans and nonhumans have sensory receptors.

7.5 Explain how the visual sensory system works.

7.6 Explain how the auditory sensory system works.

7.7 Outline other sensory systems, such as olfaction, gustation, and somesthesis.

Understand the Process of Sensation

7.1 Discuss the differences between sensation and perception.

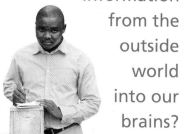

How do we get information from the outside world into our brains? ▶

Information about the world has to have a way to get into the brain, where it can be used to determine actions and responses. The way into the brain is through the sensory organs and the process of sensation. When you use your sense of sight to look around your neighborhood, or when you use your sense of hearing to listen to your favorite song at a concert, you are using sensory processes to take in information about the world around you. But that information comes in as raw data, meaningless pieces of information about the external word, captured by our senses.

The process of bringing meaning to the raw data is called *perception*. Through perception, your brain collects the data, organizes it, and interprets it to give those sensations meaning. At a concert, your ears receive sound waves, but your brain perceives those sounds as music—specifically, the opening notes of your favorite song. Sensation and perception are distinct processes, but they work together to help us make sense of ourselves and our surroundings.

7.2 Explain the process of sensation.

What Is Sensation? Sensation occurs when special neuron receptor sites in the sense organs—the eyes, ears, nose, skin, and taste buds—are activated, allowing various forms of outside stimuli to be sent as neural signals in the brain. This process of converting outside stimuli, such as light, into neural activity is called **transduction** (the prefix trans- means across or over and the root word duct means bring). Before examining these special receptors more closely, consider watching the video *How We Sense the World*.

sensation the process that occurs when special neuron receptor sites in the sense organs are activated, allowing various forms of outside stimuli to become neural signals in the brain.

transduction the process of converting outside stimuli, such as light, into neural activity.

👁 Watch the Video, *How We Sense the World*, at MyPsychLab

Sensory Receptors The *sensory receptors* are specialized forms of neurons, the cells that make up the nervous system. Instead of receiving neurotransmitters from other cells, these receptor cells are stimulated by different kinds of energy—for example, the receptors in the eyes are stimulated by light (electromagnetic energy), whereas the receptors in the ears are activated by vibrations (molecular energy). Touch receptors are stimulated by pressure or temperature, and the receptors for taste and smell are triggered by chemical substances. Each receptor type transduces the physical information into electrical information in different ways, which then affects the cell, causing it to fire more or to fire less based on the timing and intensity of information it is detecting from the environment (Gardner & Johnson, 2013).

7.3 Discuss the concepts of threshold and adaptation.

Sensory Thresholds Ernst Weber (pronounced va-ber)(1795–1878) did studies on threshold, the point at which sensations begin and end, trying to determine the smallest difference between two weights that could be detected. His research led to the formulation known as Weber's law of **just noticeable differences** (**jnd**, or the **difference threshold**). A jnd is the smallest difference between two stimuli that is detectable 50 percent of the time, and Weber's law simply means that whatever the difference between stimuli might be, it is always a *constant*. If to notice a difference the amount of sugar a person would need to add to a cup of coffee that is already sweetened with 5 teaspoons is 1 teaspoon, then the percentage of change needed to detect a just noticeable difference is one fifth, or 20 percent. So if the coffee has 10 teaspoons of sugar in it, the person would have to add another 20 percent, or 2 teaspoons, to be able to taste the difference half of the time. To see a visual example of this, complete the experiment *Weber's Law* and discover the amount of change needed to detect a just noticeable difference between two circles of light.

Gustav Fechner (pronounced feck-ner)(1801–1887) expanded on Weber's work by studying something he called the **absolute threshold** (Fechner, 1860). An absolute threshold is the lowest level of stimulation that a person can consciously detect 50 percent of the time the stimulation is present. (Remember, the jnd is detecting a difference *between two* stimuli.) For example, assuming a very quiet room and normal hearing, how far away can someone sit and you might still hear the tick of their analog watch on half of the trials? For some examples of absolute thresholds for various senses, see **Table 7.1**.

Stimuli that are below the level of conscious awareness are called *subliminal stimuli*. (The word *limin* means "threshold," so *sublimin* means "below the threshold.") These stimuli are just strong enough to activate the sensory receptors but not strong enough for people to be consciously aware of them. Many people believe that these stimuli act upon the unconscious mind, influencing behavior in a process called *subliminal perception*.

just noticeable difference (jnd, or the difference threshold) the smallest difference between two stimuli that is detectable 50 percent of the time.

absolute threshold the lowest level of stimulation that a person can consciously detect 50 percent of the time the stimulation is present.

Participate in the Experiment, *Weber's Law*, at **MyPsychLab**

I've heard about people being influenced by stuff in movies and on television, things that are just below the level of conscious awareness. Is that true?

Table 7.1	Examples of Absolute Thresholds
SENSE	THRESHOLD
Sight	A candle flame at 30 miles on a clear, dark night
Hearing	The tick of a watch 20 feet away in a quiet room
Smell	One drop of perfume diffused throughout a three-room apartment
Taste	1 teaspoon of sugar in 2 gallons of water
Touch	A bee's wing falling on the cheek from 1 centimeter above

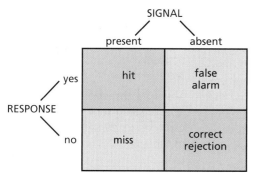

FIGURE 7.1 Signal Detection Theory
The presence or absence of a signal is followed by a response or non-response depending on our ability to detect it.

Researchers have gathered scientific evidence that subliminal perception does not work in advertising (Bargh et al., 1996; Broyles, 2006; Moore, 1988; Pratkanis & Greenwald, 1988; Trappey, 1996; Vokey & Read, 1985). This is not to say that subliminal perception does not exist—there is a growing body of evidence that we process some stimuli without conscious awareness, especially stimuli that are fearful or threatening (LeDoux & Phelps, 2008; Öhman, 2008). In this effort, researchers have used *event-related potentials* (ERPs) and functional magnetic resonance imaging (fMRI) to verify the existence of subliminal perception and associated learning in the laboratory (Babiloni et al., 2010; Bernat et al., 2001; Fazel-Rezai & Peters, 2005; Sabatini et al., 2009).

Signal Detection Theory: But What If I Don't Want to Clean My Room? Go clean your room!! is a command you've heard before and one that left you wondering why you were getting yelled at. Signal detection theory can help answer that question by factoring expectation and motivation into our sensory processes. Signal detection theory was developed in the 1950s in response to questions that arose out of the use of radar for tracking aircraft and mistakes the air traffic controllers were making. By the 1960s psychologists John A. Swets and David M. Green were examining how it applied to sensation and thresholds. They explained how motivation, biases, and expectations can influence our detection of a stimulus and described four categories that our reactions to a stimulus can fall into: hit, miss, false alarm, and correct rejection (Schonhoff & Giordano, 2006). (See **Figure 7.1**.)

When a stimulus is presented, like a directive to complete a chore, you may not be motivated to hear it because you are placing your attention on something else, like texting a friend or playing an online first person shooter game. Not sensing the stimulus that was presented, in this situation "Go clean your room!" for the third time, is a "miss" and you're going to get into trouble for not responding appropriately to the directive. However, if the stimulus breaks through your distraction and you hear the directive, and the directive is acted upon, you're not going to be grounded, and that is a "hit." Hold on, we're not done yet. What if you're in the middle of texting in your room, that could use some tidying up, and think "Did I just hear something?" and stop in the middle of what you're doing and ask to see if you were being told to clean your room? If the person you are asking looks at you like they don't know what you're talking about, the situation is a "false alarm" because you heard something that wasn't there. Finally, if you stopped your game because you thought you heard a voice, listened, then went back to playing your game and the person that you thought was speaking to you is taking a nap on the couch, the situation is a "correct rejection" and all is well.

Expectation influences the detection of a stimulus in a large number of different situations. How many times have you checked your phone thinking that you just heard the text notice signal after a friend said "I'll text you later" and found, to your disappointment, the text wasn't there? :(On the other side of the coin, how many times has something changed in your environment that you didn't notice, like a new, bright red stop sign put up by the street department on the route you always take to school? (Yikes!) Clearly signal detection theory has helped us understand how factors other than the volume of a sound, or the brightness of a light can influence our ability to detect stimuli in our daily lives.

Sometimes I can smell the odor of the garbage can in the kitchen when I first come home, but after a while the smell seems to go away—is this also habituation? ▶

Habituation and Sensory Adaptation Some of the lower centers of the brain filter sensory stimulation "ignore" or prevent conscious attention to stimuli that do not change. The brain is primarily interested in changes in information. That's why people don't really "hear" the noise of the air conditioner unless it suddenly cuts off or the noise made in some classrooms unless it gets very quiet or someone else directs their attention toward it. Although they actually are *hearing* it, they aren't paying attention to it. This is called *habituation*, and it is the way the brain deals with unchanging information from the environment.

Although different from habituation, **sensory adaptation** is another process by which constant, unchanging information from the sensory receptors is effectively ignored. In habituation, the sensory receptors are still responding to stimulation but the lower centers of the brain are not sending the signals from those receptors to the cortex. The process of sensory adaptation differs because the receptor cells *themselves* become less responsive to an unchanging stimulus—garbage odors included—and the receptors no longer send signals to the brain.

For example, when you eat, the food that you put in your mouth tastes strong at first, but as you keep eating the same thing, the taste does fade somewhat, doesn't it? Generally speaking, all of our senses are subject to sensory adaptation.

You might think, then, that if you stare at something long enough, it would also disappear, but the eyes are a little different. Even though the sensory receptors in the back of the eyes adapt to and become less responsive to a constant visual stimulus, under ordinary circumstances the eyes are never entirely still. There's a constant movement of the eyes, tiny little vibrations called "microsaccades" or "saccadic movements" that people don't consciously notice. These movements keep the eyes from adapting to what they see. (That's a good thing, because otherwise many students would no doubt go blind from staring off into space.)

sensory adaptation tendency of sensory receptor cells to become less responsive to a stimulus that is unchanging.

Learn the Capabilities and Limitations of Sensory Processes

7.4 Identify physical energy forms for which humans and nonhumans have sensory receptors.

Sensation occurs when special receptor sites on neurons in the sense organs are activated, allowing various forms of outside stimuli to become transduced into neural signals in the brain. The *sensory receptors* are specialized forms of neurons, the cells that make up the nervous system. Instead of receiving neurotransmitters from other cells, these receptor cells are stimulated by different kinds of energy— for example, the receptor neurons in the eyes are triggered by electromagnetic energy in the form of visible light, whereas molecules of air vibrating trigger the receptors in the ears. Touch receptors are triggered by pressure or temperature, and the receptors in taste and smell are activated by chemical substances. (See **Figure 7.2.**)

There are many other forms of energy—such as X-rays, radio waves, gravitational energy, and nuclear energy—that humans can't sense directly because we don't have receptor neurons sensitive to these types of energy. For example, although we can see and hear the effects of low-frequency electromagnetic waves when we turn on the TV, the radio, or the microwave oven, we can't

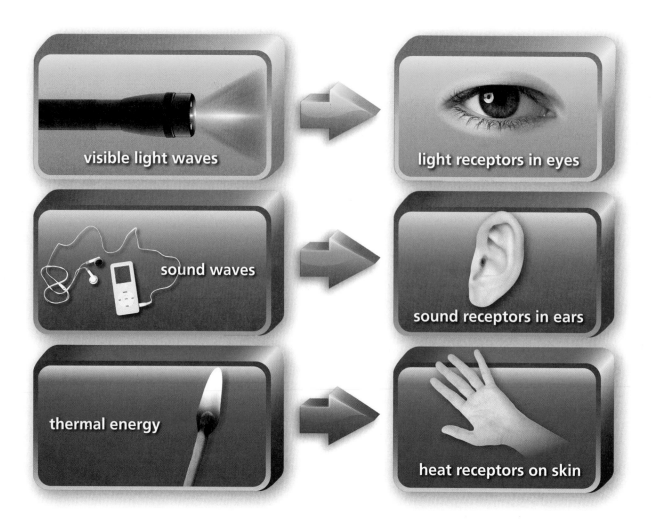

FIGURE 7.2 Some Forms of Energy We Can Sense

sense the waves themselves. Although many nonhuman animals are equipped and capable of even more acuity in their abilities to sense the world, there are a few examples of abilities that are beyond humans. Indirect evidence suggests that sharks, homing pigeons, and bees can detect the magnetic field of the earth and they use this ability for navigation (Kirschvink & Gould, 1981). In addition, the already very unusual platypus appears to be able to detect minute electrical fields, which assists them in searching out food (Pettigrew, 1999).

7.5 Explain how the visual sensory system works.

I've heard that light ▶ is waves, but I've also heard that light is made of particles— which is it?

The Science of Seeing Light is a complicated phenomenon*. Although scientists have long argued over the nature of light, they finally have agreed that light has the properties of both waves and particles. The following section gives a brief history of how scientists have tried to "shed light" on the mystery of light.

Light and the Eye It was Albert Einstein who first proposed that light is actually tiny "packets" of waves. These "wave packets" are called *photons* and have specific wavelengths associated with them (Lehnert, 2007; van der Merwe & Garuccio, 1994).

When people experience the physical properties of light, they are not really aware of its dual, wavelike and particle-like, nature. With regard to its

*phenomenon: something that is remarkable or very unusual.

psychological properties, there are three aspects to our brain's perception of light: *brightness, color,* and *saturation.*

Brightness is determined by the amplitude of the wave—how high or how low the wave actually is. The higher the wave, the brighter the light appears to be. Low waves are dimmer. *Color,* or hue, is largely determined by the length of the wave. Long wavelengths (measured in nanometers) are found at the red end of the *visible spectrum** (the portion of the whole spectrum of light that is visible to the human eye), whereas shorter wavelengths are found at the blue end. Examine how both brightness and color are related to wavelike properties in the video, *The Visible Spectrum.* (Note that when combining different colors, light behaves differently than pigments or paint. We will look at this distinction when we examine perception of color.)

Saturation refers to the purity of the color people perceive: A highly saturated red, for example, would contain only red wavelengths, whereas a less saturated red might contain a mixture of wavelengths. For example, when a child is using the red paint from a set of poster paints, the paint on the paper will look like a pure red, but if the child mixes in some white paint, the paint will look pink. The hue is still red, but it will be less of a saturated red because of the presence of white wavelengths. Mixing in black or gray would also lessen the saturation. (Note that when combining different colors, light behaves differently than pigments or paint. We will look at this distinction when we examine perception of color.)

The Structure of the Eye The best way to talk about how the eye processes light is to talk about what happens to an image being viewed as the photons of light from that image travel through the eye. Refer to **Figure 7.3** to follow the path of the image.

Watch the Video, *The Visible Spectrum*, at MyPsychLab

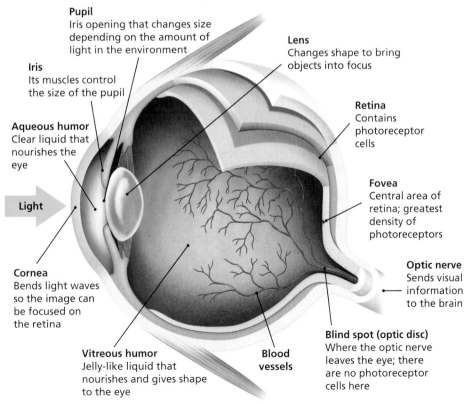

Pupil
Iris opening that changes size depending on the amount of light in the environment

Iris
Its muscles control the size of the pupil

Aqueous humor
Clear liquid that nourishes the eye

Light

Cornea
Bends light waves so the image can be focused on the retina

Vitreous humor
Jelly-like liquid that nourishes and gives shape to the eye

Lens
Changes shape to bring objects into focus

Retina
Contains photoreceptor cells

Fovea
Central area of retina; greatest density of photoreceptors

Optic nerve
Sends visual information to the brain

Blood vessels

Blind spot (optic disc)
Where the optic nerve leaves the eye; there are no photoreceptor cells here

FIGURE 7.3 Structure of the Eye
Light enters the eye through the cornea and pupil. The iris controls the size of the pupil. From the pupil, light passes through the lens to the retina, where it is transformed into nerve impulses. The nerve impulses travel to the brain along the optic nerve.

*spectrum: the band of colors that you see in the rainbow.

visual accommodation as a monocular cue of depth perception, the brain's use of information about the changing thickness of the lens of the eye in response to looking at objects that are close or far away.

▲ This photo illustrates an optical illusion caused by the refraction of light. The straw is not really broken although it appears that way.

Light enters the eye directly from a source (such as the sun) or indirectly by reflecting off of an object. To see clearly, a single point of light from a source or reflected from an object must travel through the structures of the eye and end up on the retina as a single point. Light bends as it passes through substances of different densities, through a process known as refraction, the root word *fract* means to break. For example, have you ever looked at a drinking straw in a glass of water through the side of the glass? It appears that the straw bends, or is broken, at the surface of the water. That optical illusion is due to the refraction of light.

The surface of the eye is covered in a clear membrane called the *cornea*. The cornea not only protects the eye but also is the structure that focuses most of the light coming into the eye. The cornea has a fixed curvature, like a camera that has no option to adjust the focus. However, this curvature can be changed somewhat through vision-improving techniques that change the shape of the cornea. For example, ophthalmologists, physicians who specialize in medical and surgical treatment of eye problems, can use both *photoreactive keratectomy (PRK)* and *laser-assisted in situ keratomileusis (LASIK)* procedures to remove small portions of the cornea, changing its curvature, and thus the focus in the eye.

The next visual layer is a clear, watery fluid called the *aqueous humor*. This fluid is continually replenished and supplies nourishment to the eye. The light from the visual image then enters the interior of the eye through a hole, called the *pupil*, in a round muscle called the *iris* (the colored part of the eye). The iris can change the size of the pupil, letting more or less light into the eye. That also helps focus the image; people try to do the same thing by squinting.

Behind the iris, suspended by muscles, is another clear structure that grows in layers like an onion, called the *lens*. The flexible lens finishes the focusing process begun by the cornea. In a process called **visual accommodation**, the lens changes its shape from thick to thin through the action of tiny muscles attached to each side, enabling it to focus on objects that are close or far away. The variation in thickness allows the lens to project a sharp image on the retina. People lose this ability as the lens hardens through aging (a disorder called *presbyopia*). Although people try to compensate* for their inability to focus on things that are close to them, eventually they usually need bifocals because their arms just aren't long enough anymore. In nearsightedness, or *myopia*, visual accommodation may occur but the shape of the eye causes the focal point to fall short of the retina. In farsightedness, or *hyperopia*, the focus point is behind the retina (see **Figure 7.4**). Glasses, contacts, or corrective surgery like LASIK or PRK can correct these issues.

Once past the lens, light passes through a large, open space filled with a clear, jelly-like fluid called the *vitreous humor*. This fluid, like the aqueous humor, also nourishes the eye, gives it shape, and helps keep the tissue-paper thin layers of the retina pressed firmly against the back wall of the eye.

**FIGURE 7.4
Nearsightedness
and
Farsightedness**

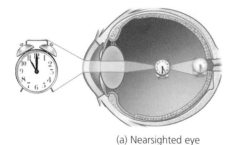

(a) Nearsighted eye

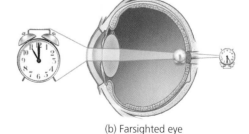

(b) Farsighted eye

---

*compensate: to correct for an error or defect

The final stop for light within the eye is the *retina*, a light-sensitive area at the back of eye containing three layers: ganglion cells, bipolar cells, and the photoreceptor neurons more commonly called the **rods** and **cones**, special receptor cells (*photoreceptors*) that respond to the various wavelengths of light. While the retina is responsible for absorbing and processing light information, the rods and the cones are the business end of the retina—the part that actually receives the photons of light and transduces them into neural signals for the brain, sending them first to the *bipolar cells* (a type of interneuron; called bipolar or "two-ended" because they have a single dendrite at one end and a single axon on the other; and then to the retinal *ganglion cells* whose axons form the optic nerve. The video *Rods and Cones* provides more detail on how they work.

The rods and cones are responsible for different aspects of vision. Although located all over the retina, cones are more concentrated at the retina's center where there are no rods (an area called the fovea). Some cones have a private line to the optic nerve (one bipolar cell for each cone). This means cones are the receptors with the greatest visual acuity, or ability, to see fine detail. Cones require a lot more light to function than rods do and work best in bright light. Cones are also sensitive to different wavelengths of light, so they are responsible for color vision.

Rods are found all over the retina except the fovea, but are concentrated in the periphery and responsible for peripheral vision, the prefix peri- means around and the root word pher means to carry. They are sensitive to changes in brightness but only a narrow band of wavelengths, so they see in black and white and shades of gray. Many rods connect to a single bipolar cell. If only one rod in a region of the retina is stimulated, the brain perceives the whole region as stimulated. But because the brain doesn't know exactly what part of the region is actually sending the message, visual acuity is quite low. That's why in low levels of light, such as twilight or a dimly lit room, things tend to be less clear and grayish.

The eyes don't adapt to constant stimuli under normal circumstances because of saccadic movements. But if people stare with one eye at one spot long enough, objects that slowly cross their visual field may at one point disappear briefly because there is a "hole" in the retina—the place where all the axons of those ganglion cells leave the retina to become the optic nerve, the optic disk or *blind spot*. There are no rods or cones here, so this is referred to as the blind spot. You can demonstrate the blind spot for yourself by following the directions in **Figure 7.5**.

rods visual sensory receptors found at the back of the retina, responsible for noncolor sensitivity to low levels of light.

cones visual sensory receptors found at the back of the retina, responsible for color vision and sharpness of vision.

👁 **Watch** the **Video**, *Rods and Cones*, at **MyPsychLab**

FIGURE 7.5 The Blind Spot Demonstration
Hold the image in front of you. Close your right eye and stare at the picture of the dog with your left eye. Slowly bring the image closer to your face. The picture of the cat will disappear at some point because the light from the picture of the cat is falling on your blind spot. If you cannot seem to find your blind spot, try moving the image more slowly.

▲ *While this deer may seem to see relatively well at night, the oncoming headlights of a car will briefly blind it. It may take only a few seconds for light adaptation to occur, but until it does, the deer is unable to fully see, so it does not move.*

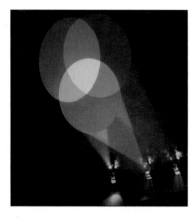

▲ *In trichromatic theory, the three types of cones combine to form different colors much as these three colored lights combine.*

trichromatic theory theory of color vision that proposes three types of cones: red, blue, and green.

opponent-process theory theory of color vision that proposes visual neurons (or groups of neurons) are stimulated by light of one color and inhibited by light of another color.

How the Eye Works Light entering the eyes can be separated into the left and right visual fields. Light from the right visual field falls on the left side of each eye's retina; light from the left visual field falls on the right side of each retina. Light travels in a straight line through the cornea and lens, resulting in the image projected on the retina actually being upside down and reversed from left to right as compared to the visual fields. Thank goodness our brains can compensate for this!

Because rods work well in low levels of light, they are also the cells that allow the eyes to adapt to low light. *Dark adaptation* occurs as the eye recovers its ability to see when going from a brightly lit state to a dark state. (The light-sensitive pigments that allow us to see are able to regenerate or "recharge" in the dark.) The brighter the light was, the longer it takes the rods to adapt to the new lower levels of light (Bartlett, 1965). When going from a darkened room to one that is brightly lit, the opposite process occurs. The cones have to adapt to the increased level of light, and they accomplish this *light adaptation* much more quickly than the rods adapt to darkness—it takes a few seconds at most (Hood, 1998).

Perception of Color Although experts in the visual system have been studying color and its nature for many years, at this point in time there is an ongoing theoretical discussion about the role the cones play in the sensation of color.

Trichromatic Theory Two theories about how people see colors were originally proposed in the 1800s. The first is called the **trichromatic ("three colors") theory**. First proposed by Thomas Young in 1802 and later modified by Hermann von Helmholtz in 1852, this theory proposed three types of cones: red cones, blue cones, and green cones, one for each of the three primary colors of light.

Most people probably think that the primary colors are red, yellow, and blue, but these are the primary colors when talking about *painting*—not when talking about *light*. Paints *reflect* light, and the way reflected light mixes is different from the way direct light mixes. For example, if an artist were to blend red, yellow, and blue paints together, the result would be a mess—a black mess. The mixing of paint (reflected light) is subtractive, removing more light as you mix in more colors. As all of the colors are mixed, more light waves are absorbed and we see black. But if the artist were to blend a red, green, and blue light together by focusing lights of those three colors on one common spot, the result would be white, not black. The mixing of direct light is additive, resulting in lighter colors, more light, and when mixing red, blue, and green, we see white, the reflection of the entire visual spectrum.

In the trichromatic theory, different shades of colors correspond to different amounts of light received by each of these three types of cones. These cones then fire their message to the brain's vision centers. It is the combination of cones and the rate at which they are firing that determine the color that will be seen. For example, if the red and green cones are firing in response to a stimulus at fast enough rates, the color the person sees is yellow. If the red and blue cones are firing fast enough, the result is magenta. If the blue and green cones are firing fast enough, a kind of cyan color (blue-green) appears.

Opponent-Process Theory The trichromatic theory would, at first glance, seem to be more than adequate to explain how people perceive color. But there's an interesting phenomenon that this theory cannot explain. If a person stares at a picture of the American flag for a little while—say, a minute—and then looks away to a blank white wall or sheet of paper, that person will see an afterimage of the flag. *Afterimages* occur when a visual sensation persists for a brief time even after the original stimulus is removed. The person would also notice rather quickly that the colors of the flag in the afterimage are all wrong—green for red, black for white, and yellow for blue. If you follow the directions for **Figure 7.6**, in which the flag is yellow, green, and black, you should see a flag with the usual red, white, and blue.

The phenomenon of the color afterimage is explained by the second theory of color perception, called the **opponent-process theory** (De Valois & De Valois, 1993; Hurvich & Jameson, 1957), and is based on an idea first suggested by Edwald Hering in 1874 (Finger, 1994). In opponent-process theory, there are four primary colors: red, green, blue, and yellow. The colors are arranged in pairs, with each member of the pair as opponents. Red is paired with its opponent green, and blue is paired with its opponent yellow. If one member of a pair is strongly stimulated, the other member is inhibited and cannot be working—so there are no reddish-greens or bluish-yellows.

So how can this kind of pairing cause a color afterimage? From the level of the bipolar and ganglion cells in the retina, all the way through the thalamus, and on to the visual cortical areas in the brain, some neurons (or groups of neurons) are stimulated by light from one part of the visual spectrum and inhibited by light from a different part of the spectrum. For example, let's say we have a red–green ganglion cell in the retina whose baseline activity is rather weak when we expose it to white light. However, the cell's activity is increased by red light, so we experience the color red. If we stimulate the cell with red light for a long enough period of time, the cell becomes fatigued. If we then swap out the red light with white light, the fatigued cell responds even less than the original baseline. Now we experience the color green because green is associated with a decrease in the responsiveness of this cell.

So which theory is the right one? Both theories play a part in color vision. Trichromatic theory can explain what is happening with the raw stimuli, the actual detection of various wavelengths of light. Opponent-process theory can explain afterimages and other aspects of visual perception that occur after the initial detection of light from our environment.

Color Blindness From the mention of red-green and yellow-blue color blindness, one might think that the opponent-process theory explains this problem. But in reality, color blindness is caused by defective cones in the retina of the eye and as a more general term, *color-deficient vision* is more accurate, as most people with color blindness have two types of cones working and can see many colors.

Color-deficient vision, or *dichromatic vision*, is caused by having one cone that does not work properly. So instead of experiencing the world with normal vision based on combinations of three cones or colors, trichromatic vision, individuals with dichromatic vision experience the world with essentially combinations

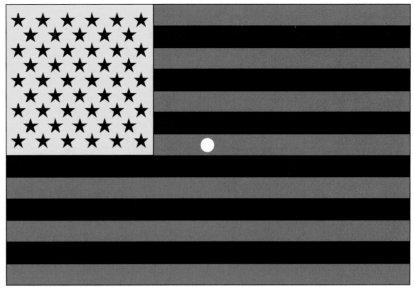

FIGURE 7.6 Color Afterimage
Stare at the white dot in the center of this oddly colored flag for about 30 seconds. Now look at a white piece of paper or a white wall. Notice that the colors are now the normal, expected colors of the American flag. They are also the primary colors that are opposites of the colors in the picture and provide evidence for the opponent-process theory of color vision.

◄ Hey, now the afterimage of the flag has normal colors! Why does this happen?

So which theory accounts for color blindness? I've heard
◄ that there are two kinds of color blindness: when you can't tell red from green and when you can't tell blue from yellow.

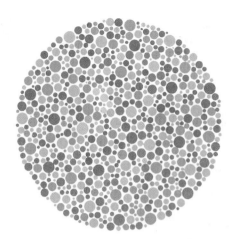
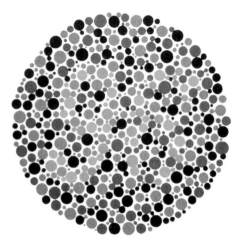

FIGURE 7.7 The Ishihara Color Test
In the circle on the left, the number 8 is visible only to those with normal color vision. In the circle on the right, people with normal vision will see the number 96, while those with red-green color blindness will see nothing but a circle of dots.

of two cones or colors. To get an idea of what a test for color-deficient vision is like, look at **Figure 7.7.**

7.6 Explain how the auditory sensory system works.

The properties of sound are indeed similar to those of light, as both senses rely on waves. But the similarity ends there, as the physical properties of sound are different from those of light.

If light works like waves, then do sound waves have similar properties?

Sound Waves and the Ear Sound waves do not come in little packets the way light comes in photons. Sound waves are simply the vibrations of the molecules of air expanding and contracting and traveling in waves that surround us. Sound waves do have the same properties of light waves though—wavelength, amplitude, and *purity*. Wavelengths are interpreted by the brain as the frequency or *pitch* (high, medium, or low). Amplitude is interpreted as *volume*, how soft or loud a sound is. (See **Figure 7.8.**) Finally, what would correspond to saturation or purity in light is called *timbre* in sound, a richness in the tone of the sound. And just as people rarely see pure colors in the world around us, they also seldom hear pure sounds. The everyday noises that surround people do not allow them to hear many pure tones.

Just as a person's vision is limited by the visible spectrum of light, a person is also limited in the range of frequencies he or she can hear. Frequency is measured in cycles (waves) per second, or *hertz (Hz)*. Human limits are between 20 and 20,000 Hz, with the most sensitivity from about 2000 to 4000 Hz, very important for conversational speech. (In comparison, dogs can hear between 50 and 60,000 Hz, and dolphins can hear up to 200,000 Hz.) To hear the higher and lower frequencies of a piece of music on their iPod® or iPhone®, for example, a person would need to increase the amplitude or volume—which explains why some people like to "crank it up."

The Structure of the Ear: Follow the Vibes The ear is a series of structures, each of which plays a part in the sense of hearing, as shown in **Figure 7.9.**

The Outer Ear The **pinna** is the visible, external part of the ear that serves as a kind of concentrator, funneling the sound waves from the outside into the

"And only you can hear this whistle?"

pinna the visible part of the ear.

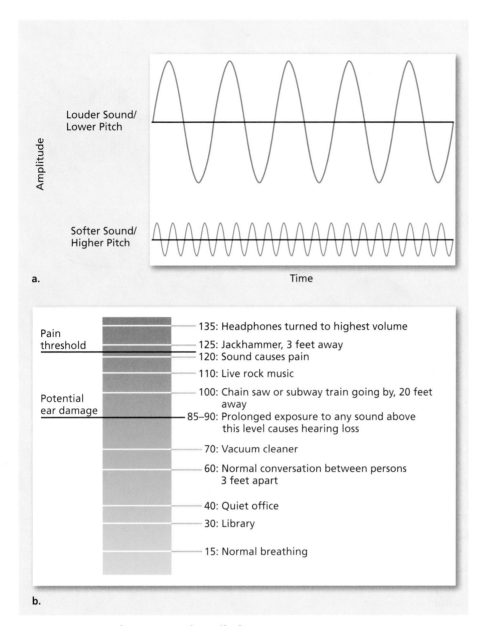

FIGURE 7.8 Sound Waves and Decibels
(a) Two sound waves. The higher the wave, the louder the sound; the lower the wave, the softer the sound. If the waves are close together in time (high frequency), the pitch will be perceived as a high pitch. Waves that are farther apart (low frequency) will be perceived as having a lower pitch. (b) Decibels of various stimuli. A *decibel* is a unit of measure for loudness. Psychologists study the effects that noise has on stress, learning, performance, aggression, and psychological and physical well-being.

structure of the ear. The pinna is also the entrance to the *auditory canal* (or ear canal), the short tunnel that runs down to the *tympanic membrane*, or eardrum. When sound waves hit the eardrum, they cause three tiny bones in the middle ear to vibrate.

The Middle Ear: Hammer, Anvil, and Stirrup The three tiny bones in the middle ear are known as the hammer (*malleus*), anvil (*incus*), and stirrup (*stapes*), each name stemming from the shape of the respective bone. The vibration of these three bones amplifies the vibrations from the eardrum. The stirrup, the

FIGURE 7.9 The Structure of the Ear
(a) This drawing shows the entire ear, beginning with the outer ear (pinna, ear canal, and eardrum). The vestibular organ includes the semicircular canals and the otolith organs (inside the round structures just above the cochlea). (b) The middle ear. Sound waves entering through the ear canal cause the eardrum to vibrate, which causes each of the three bones of the middle ear to vibrate, amplifying the sound. The stirrup rests on the oval window, which transmits its vibration to the fluid in the inner ear. (c) The inner ear. Large spaces are filled with fluid (shown in purple) that vibrates as the oval window vibrates. A thin membrane suspended in this fluid is called the basilar membrane, which contains the hairlike cells that send signals via the auditory nerve to the thalamus, which then relays information to the auditory cortex. (d) A close-up view of the basilar membrane (in dark pink) with the hair cells of the organ of Corti (in lighter pink). Notice the axons (small green lines) leaving the hair cells to form the auditory nerve.

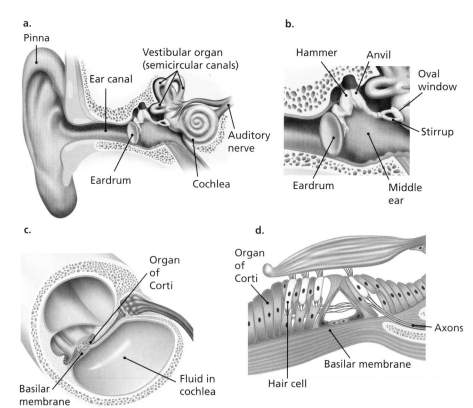

last bone in the chain, causes a membrane covering the opening of the inner ear to vibrate.

The Inner Ear This membrane is called the *oval window*, and its vibrations set off another chain reaction within the inner ear. The inner ear is a snail-shaped structure called the *cochlea*, which is filled with fluid. When the oval window vibrates, it causes the fluid in the cochlea to vibrate. This fluid surrounds a membrane running through the middle of the cochlea called the *basilar membrane*.

The *basilar membrane* contains the receptor neuron cells for the sense of hearing. When the basilar membrane vibrates, it vibrates special cells called *hair cells*, which are the receptors for sound. When these auditory receptors or hair cells are bent up against another membrane, it causes them to send a neural message through the *auditory nerve* (which contains the axons of all the receptor neurons) and into the brain, where after passing through the thalamus, the auditory cortex will interpret the sounds (the transformation of the vibrations of sound into neural messages is transduction). The louder the sound in the outside world, the stronger the vibrations that stimulate more of those hair cells—which the brain interprets as loudness.

Perceiving Pitch *Pitch* refers to how high or low a sound is. For example, the bass beats in the music pounding through the wall of your apartment from the neighbors next door are low pitch, whereas the scream of a 2-year-old child is a very high pitch. *Very* high. There are three primary theories about how the brain receives information about pitch.

The oldest of the three theories, **place theory**, is based on an idea proposed in 1863 by Hermann von Helmholtz and elaborated on and modified by Georg von Békésy, beginning with experiments first published in 1928 (Békésy, 1960).

> I think I have it straight—but all of that just explains how soft and loud sounds get to the brain from the outside. How do we hear different kinds of sounds, like high pitches and low pitches? ▶

place theory theory of pitch that states that different pitches are experienced by the stimulation of hair cells in different locations on the organ of Corti.

In this theory, the pitch a person hears depends on where the hair cells that are stimulated are located on the organ of Corti. For example, if the person is hearing a high-pitched sound, all of the hair cells near the oval window will be stimulated, but if the sound is low pitched, all of the hair cells that are stimulated will be located farther away on the organ of Corti.

Frequency theory, developed by Ernest Rutherford in 1886, states that pitch is related to how fast the basilar membrane vibrates. The faster this membrane vibrates, the higher the pitch; the slower it vibrates, the lower the pitch. (In this theory, all of the auditory neurons would be firing at the same time.)

So which of these first two theories is right? It turns out that both are right—up to a point. For place theory to be correct, the basilar membrane has to vibrate unevenly—which it does when the frequency of the sound is *above* 1000 Hz. For the frequency theory to be correct, the neurons associated with the hair cells would have to fire as fast as the basilar membrane vibrates. This only works up to 1000 Hz, because neurons don't appear to fire at exactly the same time and rate when frequencies are faster than 1000 times per second. Not to mention the maximum firing rate for neurons is approximately 1000 times per second due to the refractory period.

The frequency theory works for low pitches, and place theory works for moderate to high pitches. Is there another explanation? Yes, and it is a third theory, developed by Ernest Wever and Charles Bray, called the *volley principle* (Wever, 1949; Wever & Bray, 1930), which appears to account for pitches from about 400 Hz up to about 4000. In this explanation, groups of auditory neurons take turns firing in a process called *volleying*. If a person hears a tone of about 3000 Hz, it means that three groups of neurons have taken turns sending the message to the brain—the first group for the first 1000 Hz, the second group for the next 1000 Hz, and so on.

Types of Hearing Impairments *Hearing impairment* is the term used to refer to difficulties in hearing. A person can be partially hearing impaired or totally hearing impaired, and the treatment for hearing loss will vary according to the reason for the impairment.

Conduction hearing impairment, or conductive hearing loss, refers to problems with the mechanics of the outer or middle ear and means that sound vibrations cannot be passed from the eardrum to the cochlea. The cause might be a damaged eardrum or damage to the bones of the middle ear (usually from an infection). In this kind of impairment the causes can often be treated, for example, hearing aids may be of some use in restoring hearing.

In *nerve hearing impairment*, or sensorineural hearing loss, the problem lies either in the inner ear or in the auditory pathways and cortical areas of the brain. This is the most common type of permanent hearing loss. Normal aging causes loss of hair cells in the cochlea, and exposure to loud noises can damage hair cells. *Tinnitus* is a fancy word for an extremely annoying ringing in one's ears, and it can also be caused by infections or loud noises—including loud music in headphones. Prolonged exposure to loud noises further leads to permanent damage and hearing loss, so you might want to turn down that stereo or personal music player!

Because the damage is to the nerves or the brain, nerve hearing impairment cannot typically be helped with ordinary hearing aids, which are basically sound amplifiers, or the hearing aids are not enough. A technique for restoring some hearing to those with irreversible nerve hearing impairment makes use of an electronic device called a *cochlear implant*. This device sends signals from a microphone worn behind the ear to a sound processor worn on the belt or in a pocket, which then translates those signals into electrical stimuli that are sent to a series

frequency theory theory of pitch that states that pitch is related to the speed of vibrations in the basilar membrane.

Thinking Critically
How might someone who has had total hearing loss from birth react to being able to hear?

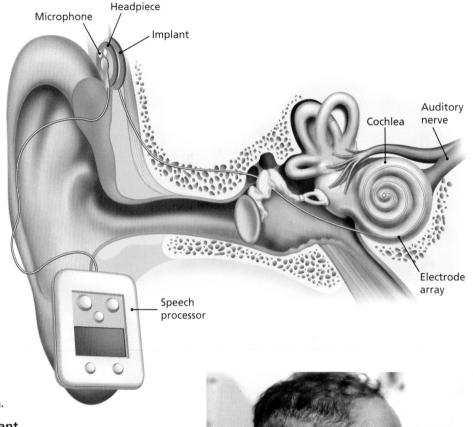

FIGURE 7.10 Cochlear Implant
(a) In a cochlear implant, a microphone implanted just behind the ear picks up sound from the surrounding environment. A speech processor, attached to the implant and worn outside the body, selects and arranges the sound picked up by the microphone. The implant itself is a transmitter and receiver, converting the signals from the speech processor into electrical impulses that are collected by the electrode array in the cochlea and then sent to the brain. (b) This child is able to hear with the help of a cochlear implant. Hearing spoken language during the early years of a child's life helps in the development of the child's own speech.

of electrodes implanted directly into the cochlea, allowing transduction to take place and stimulating the auditory nerve. (See **Figure 7.10.**) The brain then processes the electrode information as sound.

7.7 Outline other sensory systems, such as olfaction, gustation, and somesthesis.

Gustation: How We Taste the World The sense of taste (taste in food, not taste in clothing or friends) and the sense of smell are very closely related. Have you ever noticed that when your nose is all stopped up, your sense of taste is affected, too? That's because the sense of taste is really a combination of taste and smell. Without the input from the nose, there are actually only four, and possibly five, kinds of taste sensors in the mouth.

Our food preferences, or aversions, start to form very early in life, very early! **Gustation**, or taste, is one of our earliest developed senses. Research suggests developing babies are exposed to substances the mother inhales or digests and

gustation the sense of taste.

these impart flavor to the amniotic fluid, which the baby also ingests. Along with exposure to different flavors early in life after we are born, these experiences may affect food choices and nutritional status, that is, picking certain foods over others, for a long time to come (Beauchamp & Mennella, 2011; Mennella & Trabulsi, 2012).

Taste Buds *Taste buds* is the common name for the dense clusters of various taste receptor cells found within them, the special kinds of neurons that are responsible for the sense of taste, or gustation. Most taste buds are located on the tongue, but there are a few on the roof of the mouth, the cheeks, and under the tongue, and in the throat as well. How sensitive people are to various tastes depends on how many taste buds they have; some people have only around 500, whereas others have 20 times that number. The latter are called "super-tasters" and need far less seasoning in their food than those with fewer taste buds (Bartoshuk, 1993).

No, those "bumps" are called *papillae*, and the taste buds line the walls of these papillae. Each taste bud has about 20 receptors that are very similar to the receptor sites on receiving neurons at the synapse. In fact, the receptors on taste buds work exactly like receptor sites on neurons—they receive molecules of various substances that fit into the receptor like a key into a lock. Taste is often called a chemical sense because it works with the molecules of foods people eat in the same way the neural receptors work with neurotransmitters. When the molecules (dissolved in saliva) fit into the receptors, a signal is fired to the brain, which then interprets the taste sensation. The video, *Taste Buds* describes this process in more detail.

In general, the taste receptors get such a workout that they have to be replaced every 10 to 14 days (McLaughlin & Margolskee, 1994). And when the tongue is burned, the damaged cells no longer work. As time goes on, those cells get replaced and the taste sense comes back.

The Five Basic Tastes In 1916 a German psychologist named Hans Henning proposed that there are four primary tastes: sweet, sour, salty, and bitter. Lindemann (1996) supported the idea that there is a fifth kind of taste receptor that detects a pleasant "brothy" taste associated with foods like chicken soup, tuna, kelp, cheese, and soy products, among others. Lindemann proposed that this fifth taste be called *umami*, a Japanese word first coined in 1908 by Dr. Kikunae Ikeda of Tokyo Imperial University to describe the taste. Dr. Ikeda had succeeded in isolating the substance in kelp that generated the sensation of umami—glutamate (Beyreuther et al., 2007). Glutamate exists not only in the foods listed earlier but is also present in human breast milk and is the reason that the seasoning MSG—monosodium *glutamate*—adds a pleasant flavor to foods.

Although researchers used to believe that certain tastes were located on certain places on the tongue, it is now known that all of the taste sensations are processed all over the tongue (Bartoshuk, 1993). The five taste sensations work together, along with the sense of smell and the texture, temperature, and "heat" of foods, to produce thousands of taste sensations, which are further affected by our culture, personal expectations, and past learning experiences. For example, boiled peanuts are not an uncommon snack in parts of the Southern United States, but the idea of a warm, soft and mushy, slightly salty peanut may not be appealing in other parts of the country.

Just as individuals and groups can vary on their food preferences, they can also vary on level of perceived sweetness. For example, obese individuals have been found to experience less sweetness than individuals who are not obese; foods that are both sweet and high in fat tend to be especially attractive to

So taste buds are those little bumps I can see when I look closely at my ◄ tongue?

What happens to the taste buds when I burn my tongue? Do they repair them-selves? I know when I have burned my tongue, I can't taste much for a while, but the taste comes back.

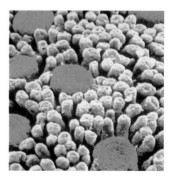

▲ *Microphotograph of the surface of the tongue, showing two different sizes of papillae. The taste buds are located under the surface of the larger red papillae, whereas the smaller and more numerous papillae form a touch-sensitive rough surface that helps in chewing and moving food around the mouth.*

olfaction the sense of smell.

individuals who are obese (Bartoshuk et al., 2006). Such differences (as well as genetic variations like the supertasters) complicate direct comparison of food preferences.

Turning our attention back to how things taste for us as individuals, have you ever noticed that when you have a cold, food tastes very bland? Everything becomes bland or muted because you can taste only sweet, salty, bitter, sour, and umami—and because your nose is stuffed up with a cold, you don't get all the enhanced variations of those tastes that come from the sense of smell.

The Sense of Scents: Olfaction Like the sense of taste, the sense of smell is a chemical sense. The ability to smell odors is called **olfaction**, or the *olfactory sense*. The outer part of the nose serves the same purpose for odors that the pinna and ear canal serve for sounds: Both are merely ways to collect the sensory information and get it to the part of the body that will translate it into neural signals. The part of the olfactory system that transduces odors—turns odors into signals the brain can understand—is located at the top of the nasal passages. This area of olfactory receptor cells is only about an inch square in each cavity, yet contains about 10 million olfactory receptors. (See **Figure 7.11**.)

Olfactory Receptor Cells The *olfactory receptor cells* each have about a half dozen to a dozen little "hairs," called *cilia*, that project into the cavity. Like taste buds, there are receptor sites on these hair cells that send signals to the brain when stimulated by the molecules of substances that are in the air moving past them.

Yes. When a person is sniffing something, the sniffing serves to move molecules of whatever the person is trying to smell into the nose and into the nasal cavities. That's okay when it's the smell of baking bread, apple pie, flowers, and the like, but when it's skunk, rotten eggs, dead animals—well, try not to think about it too much.

> Wait a minute—you mean that when I can smell something like a skunk, there are little particles of skunk ▶ odor *in* my nose?

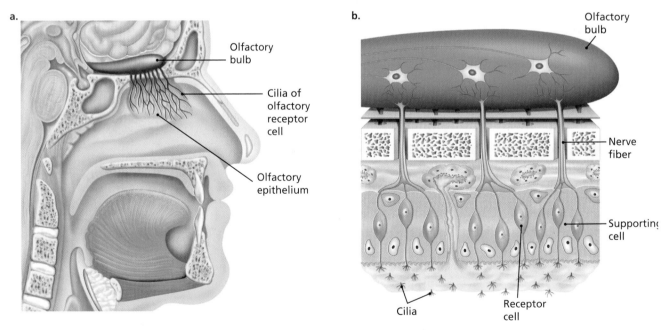

FIGURE 7.11 The Olfactory Receptors
(a) A cross section of the nose and mouth. This drawing shows the nerve fibers inside the nasal cavity that carry information about smell directly to the olfactory bulb just under the frontal lobe of the brain (shown in green). (b) A diagram of the cells in the nose that process smell. The olfactory bulb is on top. Notice the cilia, tiny hairlike cells that project into the nasal cavity. These are the receptors for the sense of smell.

Olfactory receptors are like taste buds in another way, too. Olfactory receptors also have to be replaced as they naturally die off, about every 5 to 8 weeks. Unlike the taste buds, there are many more than five types of olfactory receptors—in fact, there are at least 1,000 of them.

Signals from the olfactory receptors in the nasal cavity do not follow the same path as the signals from all the other senses. Vision, hearing, taste, and touch all pass through the thalamus and then on to the area of the cortex that processes that particular sensory information. But the sense of smell has its own special place in the brain—the olfactory bulbs, which are actually part of the brain.

The Olfactory Bulbs The *olfactory bulbs* are located right on top of the sinus cavity on each side of the brain directly beneath the frontal lobes. (Refer back to **Figure 7.11.**) The epithelium, a membrane within the nasal cavities, contains the olfactory receptor neurons that are sensitive to the chemical signals of smell. The olfactory receptors send their neural signals directly up to these bulbs, bypassing the thalamus, the relay center for all other sensory information. The olfactory information is then sent from the olfactory bulbs to higher cortical areas, including the frontal cortex, and the amygdala (remember from Chapter Two that the frontal cortex and amygdala play important roles in memory and emotion).

Somesthetic Senses: What the Body Knows So far, this chapter has covered vision, hearing, taste, and smell. That leaves touch. What is thought of as the sense of touch is really several sensations, originating in several different places in—and on—the body. It's really more accurate to refer to these as the body senses, or **somesthetic senses**. The first part of that word, *soma*, means "body," as mentioned in Chapter Two. The second part, *esthetic*, means "feeling," hence the name. We will discuss each of the three somesthetic sense systems.

Perception of Touch, Pressure, Temperature, and Pain Here's a good trivia question: What organ of the body is about 20 square feet in size? The answer is the skin. Skin is an organ. Its purposes include more than simply keeping bodily fluids in and germs out; skin also receives and transmits information from the outside world to the central nervous system (specifically, to the somatosensory cortex). Information about light touch, deeper pressure, warm cold, and even pain is collected by special receptors in the skin's layers known as the *skin senses*.

Types of Sensory Receptors in the Skin There are about half a dozen different receptors in the layers of the skin. (See **Figure 7.12.**) Some of them will respond to only one kind of sensation. For example, the *Pacinian corpuscles* are just beneath the skin and respond to changes in pressure. There are nerve endings that wrap around the ends of the hair follicles, a fact people may be well aware of when they tweeze their eyebrows, or when someone pulls their hair. These nerve endings are sensitive to both pain and touch. There are *free nerve endings* just beneath the uppermost layer of the skin that respond to changes in temperature and to pressure—and to pain.

Yes, there are pain nerve fibers in the internal organs as well as receptors for pressure. How else would people have a stomachache or intestinal* pain—or get that full feeling of pressure when they've eaten too much or their bladder is full?

---

*intestinal: having to do with the tubes in the body that digest food and process waste material.

somesthetic senses the body senses consisting of the skin senses, the kinesthetic sense, and the vestibular senses.

▲ Her sense of touch is allowing this girl with visual impairment to "read" a Braille book with her fingers. The fingertips are extremely sensitive to fine differences in texture, allowing her to distinguish between small dots representing the different letters of the alphabet.

How exactly does pain work? Why is it that sometimes I feel pain deep inside? Are there pain receptors there, too?

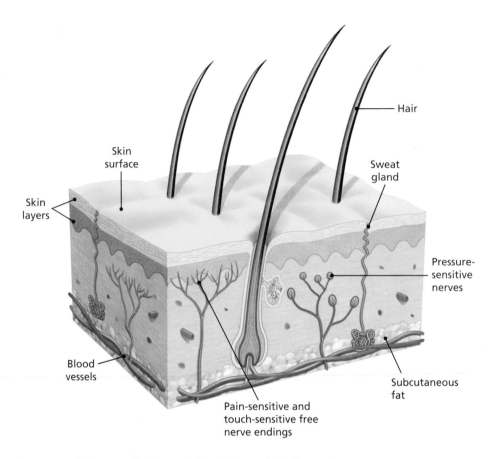

FIGURE 7.12 Cross Section of the Skin and Its Receptors
The skin is composed of several types of cells that process pain, pressure, and temperature. Some of these cells are wrapped around the ends of the hairs on the skin and are sensitive to touch on the hair itself, whereas others are located near the surface, and still others just under the top layer of tissue.

There are actually different types of pain. There are receptors that detect pain (and pressure) in the organs, a type of pain called *visceral* pain*. Pain sensations in the skin, muscles, tendons, and joints are carried on large nerve fibers and are called *somatic pain*. Somatic pain is the body's warning system that something is being, or is about to be, damaged and tends to be sharp and fast. Another type of somatic pain is carried on small nerve fibers and is slower and more of a general ache. This somatic pain acts as a kind of reminder system, keeping people from further injury by reminding them that the body has already been damaged. For example, if you hit your thumb with a hammer, the immediate pain sensation is of the first kind—sharp, fast, and bright. But later the bruised tissue simply aches, letting you know to take it easy on that thumb.

Pain Disorders People may not like pain, but its function as a warning system is vitally important. There are people who are born without the ability to feel pain, rare conditions called *congenital analgesia* and *congenital insensitivity to pain with anhidrosis (CIPA)*. Children with these disorders cannot feel pain when they cut or scrape themselves, leading to an increased risk of infection when the cut goes untreated (Mogil, 1999). They fear nothing—which can be a horrifying trial for the parents and teachers of such a child.

---

*visceral: deep internal feeling from the body.

A condition called *phantom limb pain* occurs when a person who has had an arm or leg removed sometimes "feels" pain in the missing limb (Nikolajsen & Jensen, 2001; Woodhouse, 2005). As many as 50 to 80 percent of people who have had amputations experience various sensations: burning, shooting pains, or pins-and-needles sensations where the amputated limb used to be. Once believed to be a psychological problem, some now believe that it is caused by the traumatic injury to the nerves during amputation (Ephraim et al., 2005).

Pain: Gate–Control Theory One explanation for how the sensation of pain works is called *gate-control theory*, first proposed by Ronald Melzack and Patrick Wall (1965) and later refined and expanded (Melzack & Wall, 1996). In this theory, the pain signals must pass through a "gate" located in the spinal cord. The activity of the gate can be closed by nonpain signals coming into the spinal cord from the body and by signals coming from the brain. The gate is not a physical structure but instead represents the relative balance in neural activity of cells in the spinal cord that receive information from the body and then send information to the brain. Additional research has revealed that the activity of relay centers in the brain can also be influenced and the exact locations and mechanisms are still being investigated. The video *Gate Control Theory of Pain* provides a simulation of how pain signals travel along the spinal cord.

Stimulation of the pain receptor cells releases a neuromodulator called *substance P* (for "pain," naturally). Substance P released into the spinal cord activates other neurons that send their messages through spinal gates (opened by the pain signal). From the spinal cord, the message goes to the brain, activating cells in the thalamus, somatosensory cortex, areas of the frontal lobes, and the limbic system. The brain then interprets the pain information and sends signals that either open the spinal gates farther, causing a greater experience of pain, or close them, dampening the pain. Of course, this decision by the brain is influenced by the psychological aspects of the pain-causing stimulus. Anxiety, fear, and helplessness intensify pain, whereas laughter, distraction, and a sense of control can diminish it. (This is why people might bruise themselves and not know it if they were concentrating on something else.) Pain can also be affected by competing signals from other skin senses, which is why rubbing a sore spot can reduce the feeling of pain.

Those same psychological aspects can also influence the release of the *endorphins*, the body's natural version of morphine. Endorphins can inhibit the transmission of pain signals in the brain, and in the spinal cord they can inhibit the release of substance P.

On the contrary, research has shown that women apparently feel pain more intensely than do men, and they also report pain more often than men do (Chesterton et al., 2003; Faucett et al., 1994; Norrbrink Budh et al., 2003). Men have been shown to cope better with many kinds of pain, possibly because men are often found to have a stronger belief than women that they can (or should) control their pain by their own efforts (Jackson et al., 2002).

In addition to the skin senses just covered, there are two other somesthetic senses. The *kinesthetic sense* (having to do with the location of body parts in relation to each other), and the *vestibular sense* (having to do with movement and body position).

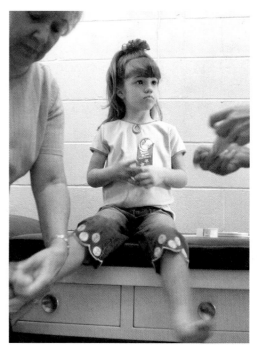

▲ Congenital insensitivity to pain with anhidrosis (CIPA) is a rare genetic disorder that makes 5-year-old Ashlyn unable to feel pain. She must be examined carefully for scrapes and cuts after recess at school because she cannot feel when she hurts herself, putting her at risk for infection. What are some of the problems that Ashlyn and her parents may face as she grows older?

👁 **Watch** the **Video**, *Gate Control Theory of Pain*, at **MyPsychLab**

Thinking Critically
What kinds of changes in your life would you have to make if you suddenly could not feel pain?

◄ I've always heard that women are able to stand more pain than men. Is that true?

▲ *This tightrope-walking violinist is performing an amazing feat of coordination and muscular control. He must not only use his vestibular organs to help maintain his balance, but also his kinesthetic sense to be aware of exactly where each foot is in relation to the rope.*

The Kinesthetic Sense Special receptors located in the muscles, tendons, and joints are part of the body's sense of movement and position in space—the movement and location of the arms, legs, and so forth in relation to one another. This sense is called *kinesthesia*, from the Greek words *kinein* ("to move") and *aesthesis* ("sensation"). When you close your eyes and raise your hand above your head, you know where your hand is because these special receptors, called proprioceptors (pro-prio means to own and receptor means to receive), tell you about joint movement or the muscles stretching or contracting.

If you have ever gotten sick from traveling in a moving vehicle, you might be tempted to blame these proprioceptors. Actually, it's not the proprioceptors in the body that make people get sick. The culprits are special structures in the ear that tell us about the position of the body in relation to the ground and movement of the head that make up the *vestibular sense*—the sense of balance.

The Vestibular Sense The name of this particular sense comes from a Latin word that means "entrance" or "chamber." The structures for this sense are located in the innermost chamber of the ear. There are two kinds of vestibular organs, the otolith organs and the semicircular canals.

The *otolith organs* are tiny sacs found just above the cochlea. These sacs contain a gelatin-like fluid within which tiny crystals are suspended (much like pieces of fruit in a bowl of Jell-O®). The head moves and the crystals cause the fluid to vibrate, setting off some tiny hairlike receptors on the inner surface of the sac, telling the person that he or she is moving forward, backward, sideways, or up and down. (It's pretty much the way the cochlea works but with movement being the stimulus instead of sound vibrations.)

The *semicircular canals* are three somewhat circular tubes that are also filled with fluid that will stimulate hairlike receptors when rotated. Having three tubes allows one to be located in each of the three planes of motion. Remember learning in geometry class about the *x*-, *y*-, and *z*-axes? Those are the three planes through which the body can rotate, and when it does, it sets off the receptors in these canals. When you spin around and then stop, the fluid in the horizontal canal is still rotating and will make you feel dizzy because your body is telling you that you are still moving, but your eyes are telling you that you have stopped.

This disagreement between what the eyes say and what the body says is pretty much what causes *motion sickness*, the tendency to get nauseated when in a moving vehicle, especially one with an irregular movement. Normally, the vestibular sense coordinates with the other senses. But for some people, the information from the eyes may conflict a little too much with the vestibular organs, and dizziness, nausea, and disorientation are the result. This explanation of motion sickness is known as *sensory conflict theory* (Oman, 1990; Reason & Brand, 1975).

One way some people overcome motion sickness is to focus on a distant point or object. This provides visual information to the person about how he or she is moving, bringing the sensory input into agreement with the visual input. This is also how ballerinas and ice skaters manage not to get sick when turning rapidly and repeatedly—they focus their eyes at least once on some fixed object every so many turns.

Pick the best answer.

1. _____ involves the detection of physical stimuli from our environment and is made possible by the activation of specific receptor cells.

   a. Perception
   b. Sublimation
   c. Adaptation
   d. Sensation

2. The lowest level of stimulation that a person can consciously detect 50 percent of the time the stimulation is present is called

   a. absolute threshold.
   b. just noticeable difference.
   c. sensation.
   d. sensory adaptation.

3. After being in class for a while, _____ is a likely explanation for not hearing the sound of the lights buzzing above you until someone says something about it.

   a. accommodation
   b. tinnitus
   c. sublimation
   d. habituation

4. The part of the ear that can be seen is also called the

   a. pinna.
   b. oval window.
   c. organ of Corti.
   d. cochlea.

5. The cochlea is found in what part of the ear?

   a. outer ear
   b. middle ear
   c. inner ear
   d. The oval window is not a structure of the ear

6. Taste is often called a _____ sense because it works with the molecules of foods that people eat.

   a. physical
   b. psychological
   c. chemical
   d. electrical

7. Research has found that a fifth taste called _____ exists.

   a. umami
   b. suprachiasm
   c. insula
   d. gustation

8. How often are olfactory receptors replaced by new olfactory receptors?

   a. every 12–24 hours
   b. every 2–3 days
   c. every 30 days
   d. every 5–8 weeks

9. Olfactory receptors project directly to the _____ and are unique in that signals do not first connect to the thalamus.

   a. occipital lobe
   b. olfactory bulbs
   c. hypothalamus
   d. gustatory cortex

10. Motion sickness often results from conflicting signals sent from the _____ and from the _____.

    a. eyes; vestibular organs
    b. brain; internal organs
    c. conscious; unconscious
    d. extremities; brain

8 Perception

Understand how we perceive the world.

Learning Objectives

8.1 Explain the nature of attention.

8.2 Discuss the importance of perceptual constancies.

8.3 Describe the Gestalt principles of perception.

8.4 Distinguish between binocular and monocular depth cues.

8.5 Describe the various types of perceptual illusions.

8.6 Outline how experiences and expectations influence perception.

Understand How We Perceive the World

Perception is the method by which the brain takes all the sensations people take in at any given moment and allows them to be interpreted in some meaningful fashion. Perception has some individuality to it. For example, two people might be looking at a cloud and while one thinks it's shaped like a horse, the other thinks it's more like a cow. They both *see* the same cloud, but they *perceive* that cloud differently.

8.1 Explain the nature of attention.

What would the world be like if you could pay constant attention to every noise, sight, feeling, and smell around you? Think about what it would be like to read this book while paying attention to all the sensations in your environment: On the page in front of you, you see words, but you also see the white spaces between the lines and in the margins. The book's cover feels smooth against your fingertips. You can hear the pages crinkling, the traffic outside, your parents talking in the next room, your own heartbeat. You are aware of each breath you take. In a world like this, you'd be so distracted that it would be hard to get any reading done!

Luckily for all of us, we are able to use our powers of attention to focus on certain stimuli in our environment and ignore the rest. Whether we focus our attention on an object or sensation willingly or unwillingly, the simple act of paying attention is the first step in the process of perception.

8.2 Discuss the importance of perceptual constancies.

How We Organize Our Perceptions As individual as perception might be, some similarities exist in how people perceive the world around them. As such, there are some circumstances during which stimuli are seemingly automatically perceived in almost the same way by various individuals.

One form of perceptual **constancy** is *size constancy*, the tendency to interpret an object as always being the same size, regardless of its distance from the viewer (or the size of the image it casts on the retina). So if an object that is normally

perception the method by which the sensations experienced at any given moment are interpreted and organized in some meaningful fashion.

constancy the tendency to interpret an object as being constant.

perceived to be about 6 feet tall appears very small on the retina, it will be interpreted as being very far away.

Another perceptual constancy is the tendency to interpret the shape of an object as constant, even when it changes on the retina. This *shape constancy* is why a person still perceives a coin as a circle even if it is held at an angle that makes it appear to be an oval on the retina. Dinner plates on a table are also seen as round, even though from the angle of viewing they are oval. (See **Figure 8.1**.)

A third form of perceptual constancy is *brightness constancy*, the tendency to perceive the apparent brightness of an object as the same even when the light conditions change. If a person is wearing black pants and a white shirt, for example, in broad daylight the shirt will appear to be much brighter than the pants. But if the sun is covered by thick clouds, even though the pants and shirt have less light to reflect than previously, the shirt will still appear to be just as much brighter than the pants as before—because the different amount of light reflected from each piece of clothing is still the same difference as before (Zeki, 2001).

8.3 Describe the Gestalt principles of perception.

The Gestalt Principles Gestalt (pronounced ge-shtault) theorists focus on human perception and the brain's tendency to group objects and perceive whole shapes.

Figure–Ground Relationships Take a look at the drawing of the cube in **Figure 8.2**. Which face of the cube is in the front? Look again—do the planes and corners of the cube seem to shift as you look at it?

This is called the "Necker cube." It has been around officially since 1832, when Louis Albert Necker, a Swiss scientist who was studying the structure of crystals, first drew it in his published papers. The problem with this cube is that there are conflicting sets of depth cues, so the viewer is never really sure which plane or edge is in the back and which is in the front—the visual presentation of the cube seems to keep reversing its planes and edges.

A similar illusion can be seen in **Figure 8.3**. In this picture, the viewer can switch perception back and forth from two faces looking at each other to the outline of a goblet in the middle. Which is the figure in front and which is the background?

Figure–ground relationships refer to the tendency to perceive objects or figures as existing on a background. People seem to have a preference for picking out figures from backgrounds even as early as birth. The illusions in Figures 8.2 and 8.3 are *reversible figures*, in which the figure and the ground seem to switch back and forth.

Proximity Another very simple rule of perception is the tendency to perceive objects that are close to one another as part of the same grouping, a principle called *proximity*, or "nearness." (See **Figure 8.4**.)

- *Similarity* refers to the tendency to perceive things that look similar as being part of the same group. When members of a sports team wear uniforms that are all the same color, it allows people viewing the game to perceive them as one group even when they are scattered around the field or court.
- *Closure* is the tendency to complete figures that are incomplete. A talented artist can give the impression of an entire face with just a few cleverly placed strokes of the pen or brush—the viewers fill in the details.

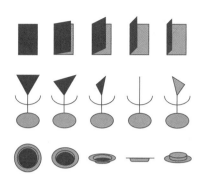

FIGURE 8.1 Shape Constancy
Three examples of shape constancy are shown here. The opening door is actually many different shapes, yet we still see it as basically a rectangular door. We do the same thing with a triangle and a circle—and, although when we look at them from different angles they cast differently shaped images on our retina, we experience them as a triangle and a circle because of shape constancy.

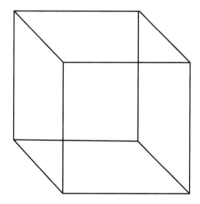

FIGURE 8.2 The Necker Cube
This is an example of a reversible figure. It can also be described as an ambiguous figure, since it is not clear which pattern should predominate.

Gestalt early perspective in psychology focusing on perception and sensation, particularly the perception of patterns and whole figures.

contiguity a Gestalt principle of perception, the tendency to perceive two things that happen close together in time as being related.

FIGURE 8.3 Figure–Ground Illusion

What do you see when you look at this picture? Is it a wine goblet? Or two faces looking at each other? This is an example in which the figure and the ground seem to "switch" each time you look at the picture.

FIGURE 8.4 Gestalt Principles of Grouping

The Gestalt principles of grouping are shown here. These are the human tendency to organize isolated stimuli into groups on the basis of five characteristics: proximity, similarity, closure, continuity, and common region. *Proximity:* The dots on the left can be seen as horizontal or vertical rows—neither organization dominates. But just by changing the proximity of certain dots, as in the other two examples, we experience the dots as vertical columns (middle) or horizontal rows (right). *Similarity:* The similarity of color here makes you perceive these dots as forming black squares and color squares rather than two rows of black and colored dots. *Closure:* Even though the lines are broken, we still see these figures as a circle and a square—an example of how we tend to "close" or "fill in" missing parts from what we know of the whole. *Continuity:* Because of continuity, we are much more likely to see the figure on the left as being made up of two lines, A to B and C to D, than we are to see it as a figure made up of lines A to D and C to B or A to C and B to D. *Common Region:* Similarity would suggest that people see two groups, stars and circles. But the colored backgrounds define a visible common region, and the tendency is to perceive three different groups.

- The principle of *continuity* is easier to see than it is to explain in words. It refers to the tendency to perceive things as simply as possible with a continuous pattern rather than with a complex, broken-up pattern. Look at Figure 8.4 for an example of continuity. Isn't it much easier to see the figure on the left as two wavy lines crossing each other than as the little sections in the diagrams to the right?
- **Contiguity** isn't shown in Figure 8.4 because it involves not just nearness in space but nearness in time also. Basically, contiguity is the tendency to perceive two things that happen close together in time as being related. Usually the first event that occurs is seen as causing the second event. Ventriloquists* make vocalizations without appearing to move their own mouths but move their dummy's mouth instead. The tendency to believe that the dummy is doing the talking is due largely to contiguity.

There is one other principle of perceptual grouping that was not one of the original principles. It was added to the list (and can be seen at the bottom of Figure 8.4) by Stephen Palmer (Palmer, 1992). In *common region*, the tendency is to perceive objects that are in a common area or region as being in a group. In Figure 8.4, people could perceive the stars as one group and the circles as another on the basis of similarity. But the colored backgrounds so visibly define common

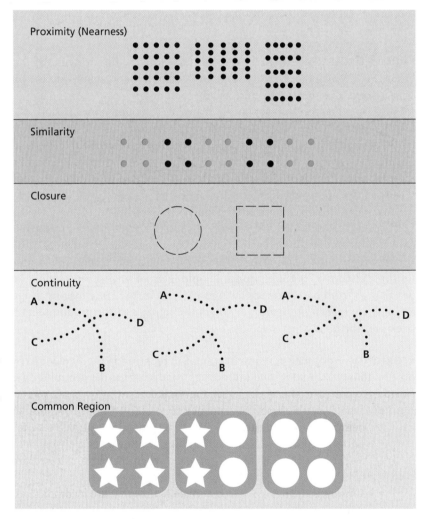

---

*ventriloquist: an entertainer who, through the use of misdirection and skill, makes other objects, such as a dummy, appear to talk.

regions that people instead perceive three groups—one of which has both stars and circles in it.

depth perception the ability to perceive the world in three dimensions.

8.4 Distinguish between binocular and monocular depth cues.

Depth Perception The capability to see the world in three dimensions is called **depth perception**. It's a handy ability because without it you would have a hard time judging how far away objects are. How early in life do humans develop depth perception? It seems to develop very early in infancy, if it is not actually present at birth. People who have had sight restored have almost no ability to perceive depth if they were blind from birth. Depth perception, like the constancies, seems to be present in infants at a very young age.

Classic Studies in Psychology

The Visual Cliff

Eleanor Gibson and her fellow researcher, Michael Walk, wondered if infants could perceive the world in three dimensions, and so they devised a way to test babies for depth perception (Gibson & Walk, 1960). They built a special table (see **Figure 8.5**) that had a big drop on one side. The surface of the table on both the top and the drop to the floor were covered in a patterned tablecloth, so that the different size of the patterns would be a cue for depth (remember, in size constancy, if something looks smaller, people assume it is farther away from them). The whole table was then covered by a clear glass top, so that a baby could safely be placed on or crawl across the "deep" side.

The infants tested in this study ranged from 6 months to 14 months in age. They were placed on the middle of the table and then encouraged

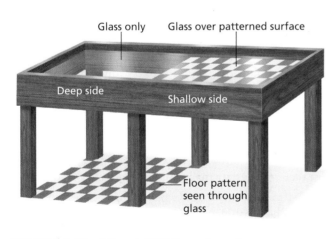

FIGURE 8.5 The Visual Cliff Experiment
In the visual cliff experiment, the table has both a shallow and a "deep" side, with glass covering the entire table. When an infant looks down at the deep-appearing side, the squares in the design on the floor look smaller than the ones on the shallow side, forming a visual cue for depth. Notice that this little girl seems to be very reluctant to cross over the deep-appearing side of the table, gesturing to be picked up, instead.

(usually by their mothers) to crawl over either the shallow side or the deep side. Most babies—81 percent—refused to crawl over the deep side, even though they could touch it with their hands and feel that it was solid. They were upset and seemed fearful when encouraged to crawl across. Gibson and Walk interpreted this as a very early sign of the concept of depth perception.

Questions for Further Discussion

1. Does the fact that 19 percent of the infants did crawl over the deep side of the visual cliff necessarily mean that those infants could not perceive the depth?
2. What other factors might explain the willingness of the 19 percent to crawl over the deep side?
3. Are there any ethical concerns in this experiment?
4. Ducks aren't bothered by the visual cliff at all—why might that be?

Various cues exist for perceiving depth in the world. Some require the use of only one eye (**monocular cues**), and some are a result of the slightly different visual patterns that exist when the visual fields of both eyes are used (**binocular cues**).

Monocular Cues Monocular cues are often referred to as *pictorial depth cues* because artists can use these cues to give the illusion of depth to paintings and drawings. Examples of these cues are discussed next and can be seen in **Figure 8.6**.

1. **Linear perspective:** When looking down a long interstate highway, the two sides of the highway appear to merge together in the distance. This tendency for lines that are actually parallel to *seem* to converge* on each other is called **linear perspective**. It works in pictures because people assume that in the picture, as in real life, the converging lines indicate that the "ends" of the lines are a great distance away from where the people are as they view them.
2. **Relative size:** The principle of size constancy is at work in *relative size*, when objects that people expect to be of a certain size appear to be small and are, therefore, assumed to be much farther away. Movie makers use this principle to make their small models seem gigantic but off in the distance.
3. **Overlap:** If one object seems to be blocking another object, people assume that the blocked object is behind the first one and, therefore, farther away. This cue is also known as *interposition*.
4. **Aerial (atmospheric) perspective:** The farther away an object is, the hazier the object will appear to be due to tiny particles of dust, dirt, and other pollutants in the air, a perceptual cue called *aerial (atmospheric) perspective*. This is why distant mountains often look fuzzy, and buildings far in the distance are blurrier than those that are close.
5. **Texture gradient:** If there are any large expanses of pebbles, rocks, or patterned roads (such as a cobblestone street) nearby, go take a look at them one day. The pebbles or bricks that are close to you are very distinctly textured, but as you look farther off into the distance, their texture becomes smaller and finer. *Texture gradient** is another trick used by artists to give the illusion of depth in a painting.

monocular cues cues for perceiving depth based on one eye only.

binocular cues cues for perceiving depth based on both eyes.

linear perspective monocular depth perception cue, the tendency for parallel lines to appear to converge on each other.

*gradient: increase or decrease in size while moving from one point to another.

a.

c.

b.

d.

FIGURE 8.6 Examples of Pictorial Depth Cues
(a) Both the lines of the trees and the sides of the road appear to come together or converge in the distance. This is an example of *linear perspective*. (b) Notice how the larger pebbles in the foreground seem to give way to smaller and smaller pebbles near the middle of the picture. *Texture gradient* causes the viewer to assume that as the texture of the pebbles gets finer, the pebbles are getting farther away. (c) In *aerial* or *atmospheric perspective*, the farther away something is the hazier it appears because of fine particles in the air between the viewer and the object. Notice that the road and farmhouse in the foreground are in sharp focus while the mountain ranges are hazy and indistinct. (d) The depth cue of *relative size* appears in this photograph. Notice that the flowers in the distance appear much smaller than those in the foreground. Relative size causes smaller objects to be perceived as farther away from the viewer.

6. **Motion parallax:** The next time you're in a car, notice how the objects outside the car window seem to zip by very fast when they are close to the car, and objects in the distance, such as mountains, seem to move more slowly. This discrepancy in motion of near and far objects is called *motion parallax**.

7. **Accommodation:** A monocular cue that is not one of the pictorial cues, *accommodation* makes use of something that happens inside the eye. The lens of the human eye is flexible and held in place by a series of muscles. The discussion of the eye earlier in this chapter mentioned the process of visual accommodation as the tendency of the lens to change its shape, or thickness, in response to objects near or far away. The brain can use this information about accommodation as a cue for distance. Accommodation is also called a "muscular cue."

Binocular Cues As the name suggests, these cues require the use of two eyes.

1. **Convergence:** Another muscular cue, *convergence*†, refers to the rotation of the two eyes in their sockets to focus on a single object. If the object is close, the convergence is pretty great (almost as great as crossing the eyes). If the object is far, the convergence is much less. Hold

---

*parallax: a change or difference in what you are looking at due to a change or difference in how you are looking at it.
†converge: come together.

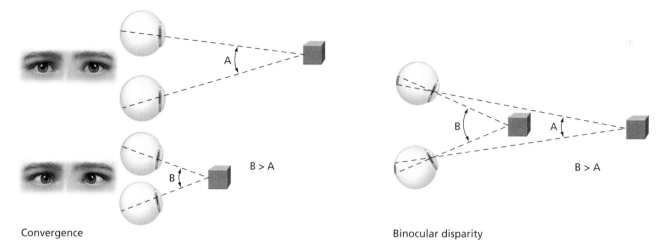

Convergence

Binocular disparity

FIGURE 8.7 Binocular Cues to Depth Perception
(left) Convergence is a depth cue that involves the muscles of the eyes. When objects are far away, the eye muscles are more relaxed; when objects are close, the eye muscles move together, or converge. (right) Binocular disparity. Because your eyes are separated by several centimeters, each eye sees a slightly different image of the object in front of you. In A, the object is far enough away that the difference is small. In B, while the object is closer, there is a greater difference between what each eye sees. The brain interprets this difference as the distance of the object.

your cell phone up in front of your nose and try to read the screen, and then move it away to read it and back again. That feeling you get in the muscles of your eyes is convergence. (See **Figure 8.7**, left.)

2. **Binocular disparity:** *Binocular disparity* is a scientific way of saying that because the eyes are a few inches apart, they don't see exactly the same image. The brain interprets the images on the retina to determine distance from the eyes. If the two images are very different, the object must be pretty close. If they are almost identical, the object is far enough away to make the retinal disparity very small. You can demonstrate this cue for yourself by holding an object in front of your nose. Close one eye, note where the object is, and then open that eye and close the other. There should be quite a difference in views. But if you do the same thing with an object that is across the room, the image doesn't seem to "jump" or move nearly as much, if at all. (See Figure 8.7, right.)

In spite of all the cues for perception that exist, even the most sophisticated* perceiver can still fail to perceive the world as it actually is, as the next section demonstrates.

You've mentioned the word *illusion* several times. Exactly what are illusions, and why is it so easy to be fooled by them?

8.5 Describe the various types of perceptual illusions.

▶ An *illusion* is a perception that does not correspond to reality: People *think* they see something when the reality is quite different. Another way of thinking of illusions is as visual stimuli that "fool" the eye. (Illusions are not hallucinations: An illusion is a distorted perception of something that is really there, but a hallucination originates in the brain, not in reality.)

Research involving illusions can be very useful for both psychologists and neuroscientists. These studies often provide valuable information about how the sensory receptors and sense organs work and how humans interpret sensory input.

---

*sophisticated: capable of grasping complexity.

Muller-Lyer Illusion One of the most famous visual illusions is the Müller–Lyer illusion. The distortion happens when the viewer tries to determine if the two lines are exactly the same length. They are identical, but one line looks longer than the other. (It's always the line with the angles on the end facing outward.) You can try to determine the length of the lines yourself in the experiment, *Müller–Lyer Illusion*.

Why is this illusion so powerful? The explanation is that most people live in a world with lots of buildings. Buildings have corners. When a person is outside a building, the corner of the building is close to that person, while the walls seem to be moving away (like the line with the angles facing inward). When the person is inside a building, the corner of the room seems to move away from the viewer while the walls are coming closer (like the line with the angles facing outward). In their minds, people "pull" the inward-facing angles toward them like the outside corners of a building, and they make the outward-facing angles "stretch" away from them like the inside corners of the room (Enns & Coren, 1995; Gregory, 1990).

Marshall Segall and colleagues (Segall et al., 1966) found that people in Western cultures, having carpentered buildings with lots of straight lines and corners (Segall and colleagues refer to this as a "carpentered world"), are far more susceptible to this illusion than people from non-Western cultures (having round huts with few corners—an "uncarpentered world"). Richard Gregory (1990) found that Zulus, for example, rarely see this illusion. They live in round huts arranged in circles, use curved tools and toys, and experience few straight lines and corners in their world.

The Moon Illusion Another common illusion is the *moon illusion*, in which the moon on the horizon appears to be much larger than the moon in the sky (Plug & Ross, 1994). One explanation for this is that the moon high in the sky is all alone, with no cues for depth surrounding it. But on the horizon, the moon appears behind trees and houses, cues for depth that make the horizon seem very far away. The moon is seen as being behind these objects and, therefore, farther away from the viewer. Because people know that objects that are farther away from them and yet still appear large are very large indeed, they "magnify" the moon in their minds—a misapplication of the principle of size constancy. This explanation of the moon illusion is called the *apparent distance hypothesis*. This explanation goes back to the second century A.D., first written about by the Greek–Egyptian astronomer Ptolemy and later further developed by an eleventh-century Arab astronomer, Al-Hazan (Ross & Ross, 1976).

Illusions of Motion Sometimes people perceive an object as moving when it is actually still. One example of this phenomenon takes place as part of a famous experiment in conformity called the *autokinetic* effect. In this effect, a small, stationary light in a darkened room will appear to move or drift because there are no surrounding cues to indicate that the light is *not* moving. Another is the *stroboscopic motion* seen in motion pictures, in which a rapid series of still pictures will seem to be in motion. Many a student has discovered that drawing little figures on the edges of a notebook and then flipping the pages quickly will also produce this same illusion of movement.

Another movement illusion related to stroboscopic motion is the *phi phenomenon*, in which lights turned on in sequence appear to move. For example, if a light is turned on in a darkened room and then turned off, and then another light a short distance away is flashed on and off, it will appear to be one light moving across that distance. This principle is used to suggest motion in many theater marquee signs—flashing arrows indicating direction that have a series of lights going on and off in a sequence, and even in strings of decorative lighting, such as the "chasing" lights seen on houses at holiday times.

Müller–Lyer illusion illusion of line length that is distorted by inward-turning or outward-turning corners on the ends of the lines, causing lines of equal length to appear to be different.

◉▸ **Participate** in the **Experiment**, *Müller–Lyer Illusion*, at **MyPsychLab**

▲ *The moon illusion. When this moon is high in the night sky, it will still be the same size to the eye as it is now. Nevertheless, it is perceived to be much larger when on the horizon. In the sky, there are no objects for comparison, but on the horizon, objects such as this tree are seen as being in front of a very large moon.*

FIGURE 8.8 "Rotating Snakes"

Notice anything as you move your eyes over this image? The image is not moving; seeing the "snakes" rotate is due at least in part to movements of your eyes.

Created by and courtesy of Dr. Akiyoshi Kitaoka, Ritsumeikan University.

What about seeing motion in static images? There are several examples, both classic and modern, of illusory movement or apparent motion being perceived in a static image. The debate about the causes for such illusions, whether they begin in the eyes or the brain, has been going on for at least 200 years (Troncoso et al., 2008).

Look at **Figure 8.8**. What do you see?

The "rotating snakes" illusion is one of many motion-illusion images designed by Dr. Akiyoshi Kitaoka. There have been a variety of explanations offered for this type of motion illusion, ranging from factors that depend on the image's luminance and/or the color arrangement, or possibly slight differences in the time it takes the brain to process this information.

Eye movements have also been found to be a primary cause for the illusory motion seen in images based on a 1981 painting by Isia Levant, *Enigma*. Look at the center of **Figure 8.9**: notice anything within the green rings? Many people will see the rings start to "sparkle" or the rings rotating. Why does this occur? By using special eye-tracking equipment that allowed them to record even the smallest of eye movements, researchers found that tiny eye movements called *microsaccades*, discussed earlier in the chapter, are directly linked to the perception of motion in *Enigma* and are at least one possible cause of the illusion (Troncoso et al., 2008).

FIGURE 8.9 "Reinterpretation of Enigma"

As in **Figure 8.8**, the motion you see in this static image is because of movements of your eyes, this time due more to tiny movements called *microsaccades*.

Created by and courtesy of Jorge Otero-Millan, Martinez-Conde Laboratory, Barrow Neurological Institute.

These two studies highlight some of the advances researchers have made in examining questions related to visual perception. For more information about the study of visual illusions as used in magic, and the study of such illusions from a neuroscientific perspective, see the Applying Psychology section at the end of the chapter.

8.6 Outline how experiences and expectations influence perception.

Other Factors That Influence Perception Human perception of the world is obviously influenced by things such as culture and misinterpretations of cues. The following are other factors that cause people to alter their perceptions.

People often misunderstand what is said to them because they were expecting to hear something else. People's tendency to perceive things a certain way because their previous experiences or expectations influence them is called **perceptual set or perceptual expectancy**. Although expectancies can be useful in interpreting certain stimuli, they can also lead people down the wrong path. The experiment *Ambiguous Figures* illustrates the way that perceptual set influences how you identify various ambiguous figures.

Inattentional blindness is another factor that can influence perception. In 1998, Dr. Arien Mack and Dr. Irvin Rock published an article that discussed their findings on how participants in their research were not observing images presented on the edges of a computer screen when concentrating on an image in the center of the screen. (Source: http://www.apa.org/monitor/apr01/blindness.aspx)

The research of Mack and Rock and the research of others has demonstrated that when we are paying attention to a stimulus, like a conversation or a basketball game, we are perceptually "blind" to other stimuli that are present. For example, when we are busy watching the action on the center of the screen when playing a video game a friend might enter the room walk in front of us and leave without us noticing. Sound hard to believe? Take a look at the videos on this web site: http://www.simonslab.com/videos.html. Watch a few of the videos and then see if you feel differently about inattentional blindness and our abilities to sense the various stimuli around us.

The way in which people *interpret* what they perceive can also influence their perception. For example, people can try to understand what they perceive by fusing information they already have (as is the case of perceptual expectancy). But if there is no existing information that relates to the new information, they can look at each feature of what they perceive and try to put it all together into one whole.

Anyone who has ever worked on a jigsaw puzzle knows that it's a lot easier to put it together if there is a picture of the finished puzzle to refer to as a guide. It also helps to have worked the puzzle before—people who have done that already know what it's going to look like when it's finished. In the field of perception, this is known as **top-down processing**—the use of preexisting knowledge to organize individual features into a unified whole. This is also a form of perceptual expectancy.

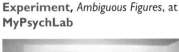
Participate in the Experiment, *Ambiguous Figures*, at MyPsychLab

The Ames Room illusion. This illusion is influenced by our past experiences and expectancies. The viewer perceives the room as a rectangle, but in reality it is a trapezoid with angled walls and floor.

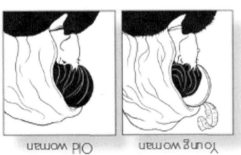

Old woman   Young woman

FIGURE 8.9 Perceptual Set
Look at the drawing on the left. What do you see? Now turn the figure upside down and look at the two smaller pictures. Would you have interpreted the original drawing differently if you had viewed these images first?
Source: Hill, "My Wife and My Mother-in- Law," Puck, p.11, 1915.

perceptual set/perceptual expectancy the tendency to perceive things a certain way because previous experiences or expectations influence those perceptions.

top-down processing the use of preexisting knowledge to organize individual features into a unified whole.

FIGURE 8.10 The Devil's Trident

At first glance, this seems to be an ordinary three-pronged figure. But a closer look reveals that the three prongs cannot be real as drawn. Follow the lines of the top prong to see what goes wrong.

bottom-up processing the analysis of the smaller features to build up to a complete perception.

If the puzzle is one the person has never worked before or if that person has lost the top of the box with the picture on it, he or she would have to start with a small section, put it together, and keep building up the sections until the recognizable picture appears. This analysis of smaller features and building up to a complete perception is called **bottom-up processing** (Cave & Kim, 1999). In this case, there is no expectancy to help organize the perception, making bottom-up processing more difficult in some respects. Fortunately, the two types of processing are often used together in perceiving the surrounding world.

Would people of different cultures perceive objects differently because of different expectancies? Some research suggests that this is true. For example, take a look at **Figure 8.10**. This figure is often called the "devil's trident." Europeans and North Americans insist on making this figure three dimensional, so they have trouble looking at it—the figure is impossible if it is perceived in three dimensions. But people in less technologically oriented cultures have little difficulty with seeing or even reproducing this figure, because they see it as a two-dimensional drawing, quite literally a collection of lines and circles rather than a solid object (Deregowski, 1969).

Applying Psychology to Everyday Life

Beyond "Smoke and Mirrors"—The Psychological Science and Neuroscience of Magic

Many people enjoy watching magic acts in person or on television. Perhaps you have been amazed by a Mindfreak® performed by Criss Angel or the performance and edgy antics of Penn & Teller. If you are one of those people, you likely witnessed a performance that included many various illusions. And like many of us, you probably wondered at some point in the performance, "How did they do that?!" Did you think the tricks were due to some type of special device (such as a fake thumb tip for hiding a scarf), or perhaps they were accomplished with "smoke and mirrors," or maybe the magician distracted the audience with one movement while actually doing something else to pull off the illusion? Magicians use many techniques to

▲ Penn & Teller have performed together for over 30 years and have joined neuroscientists in the effort to gain insights into the brain mechanisms behind magical illusions.

take advantage of, or manipulate, our actual level of awareness of what is happening right in front of us or perhaps to manipulate our attention.

Though magic is not a new topic of interest in psychology, there has been renewed interest in recent years, especially in the neuroscientific study of magic. This view suggests that researchers can work alongside magicians so we may be able to gain a better understanding of various cognitive and perceptual processes by not only examining the sensory or physical mechanics behind magic tricks, or even the psychological explanations, but to look further by examining what is happening in the brain (Macknik & Martinez-Conde, 2009).

Dr. Stephen L. Macknik and Dr. Susanna Martinez-Conde of the Barrow Neurological Institute are two neuroscientists who have teamed up with professional magicians to study their techniques and tricks in the effort to better understand the brain mechanisms underlying the illusions and how that information can be used by researchers in the laboratory. They have identified several types of illusions that can be used alone or in combination with others to serve as a basis for various magic tricks; two of these are visual illusions and cognitive illusions (Macknik et al., 2008).

As discussed earlier in the chapter, visual illusions occur when our individual perception does not match a physical stimulus. These illusions are caused by organizational or processing biases in the brain. Furthermore, our brain activity from the perception does not directly match the brain activity associated with the physical stimulus (Macknik et al., 2008). One example Dr. Macknik and Dr. Martinez-Conde point out is similar to a trick you may have performed yourself in grade school. Did you ever take a pencil or pen, grasp it in the middle, and then shake or wiggle it up and down? If you did it correctly, the pen or pencil would appear to bend or be made of rubber. Magicians use this illusion when they "bend" solid objects, such as spoons. So what is the brain explanation? We have special neurons in the visual cortex that are sensitive to both motion and edges called *end-stopped neurons*. These neurons respond differently if an object is bouncing or moving up and down quickly, causing us to perceive a solid spoon or pencil as if it is bending.

Another effect or trick that is based on the functioning of our visual system is when a magician makes an object disappear, such as a ball vanishing into the air or perhaps the outfit of an assistant changing suddenly. By showing the audience the target object, such as the ball or outfit, and then removing it very quickly from the visual field, the *persistence of vision* effect will make it appear that the object is still there. This is due to a response in vision neurons called the after-discharge, which will create an afterimage that lasts for up to 100 milliseconds after a stimulus is removed (Macknik et al., 2008). Again, you may have performed a similar trick if you have ever taken a lit sparkler or flashlight and twirled it around quickly to make a trail of light in the dark.

Questions for Further Discussion

1. The examples highlighted in this discussion are based on visual illusions; can you think of a magic trick or performance that may have been based on an illusion in a different sensory modality?
2. Of the neuroimaging methods covered in Chapter Two, which methods might be best for examining the brain activity of someone who is watching a magic performance? Why?

Pick the best answer.

1. When opening a door, the actual image on your retina changes drastically but you still perceive the door as a rectangle. This is an example of
   a. size constancy.
   b. shape constancy.
   c. color constancy.
   d. brightness constancy.

2. Hunters who wear camouflage so that they can blend in with their surroundings are relying on which principle of perception?
   a. shape constancy
   b. expectancy
   c. figure–ground relationships
   d. depth perception

3. What monocular depth cue can best explain why railroad tracks appear to come together in the distance?
   a. convergence
   b. linear perspective
   c. overlap
   d. texture gradient

4. The Müller–Lyer illusion occurs more frequently in
   a. children than adults.
   b. men than women.
   c. people living in a Western culture.
   d. individuals living in poverty.

5. Jason's uncle claimed to have seen a black panther in the trees beside the highway although no one else saw it. Knowing that his uncle has been looking for a black panther for years, Jason attributes his uncle's "sighting" to
   a. perceptual set.
   b. perceptual defense.
   c. bottom-up processing.
   d. cognitive convergence.

6. The tendency to perceive objects close to each other as part of the same group is called
   a. similarity.
   b. proximity.
   c. contiguity.
   d. continuity.

7. Which of the following is an example of motion parallax?
   a. One object appears to overlap another object.
   b. An object looks very small when it is far away.
   c. An object looks fuzzy and blurry when it is far away.
   d. Nearby objects appear to move faster than distant objects.

8. Eleanor Gibson's research using the visual cliff suggests that
   a. infants are able to perceive depth.
   b. infants are born with a fear of heights.
   c. infants use monocular cues but not binocular cues.
   d. infants understand Gestalt principles of perception.

9. A visual stimulus that fools the eye into seeing something that's not real is called a(n)
   a. illusion.
   b. hallucination.
   c. perception.
   d. false sensation.

10. A person's cultural background will most likely affect his or her
    a. binocular disparities.
    b. perceptual expectancies.
    c. ability to perceive depth.
    d. muscular cues for distance.

((• **Listen** to an **Audio File** of your chapter at **MyPsychLab**

Module 7: Sensation

Understand the process of sensation.

7.1 Discuss the differences between sensation and perception.
- Sensation is the detection of a stimulus and perception is making meaning of the stimulus.

7.2 Explain the process of sensation.
- Sensory receptors are specialized forms of neurons that are activated by different stimuli.

7.3 Discuss the concepts of threshold and adaptation.
- Absolute thresholds are the smallest amount of energy needed for conscious detection of a stimulus at least half the time it is present.
- Sensory adaptation occurs when the sensory receptors stop responding to a constant stimulus.

Learn the capabilities and limitations of sensory processes.

7.4 Identify physical energy forms for which humans and nonhumans have sensory receptors.
- Some nonhuman animals have greater acuity in their senses and rare examples of abilities to sense physical energy that humans cannot exist in the nonhuman animals.

7.5 Explain how the visual sensory system works.
- Light enters the eye, is focused on the retina, and stimulates the rods and cones.
- Rods detect changes in brightness but do not see color and function best in low levels of light.
- Cones are sensitive to colors and work best in bright light.

7.6 Explain how the auditory sensory system works.
- Sound vibrations enter the ear, are passed to the inner ear, and the vibrations stimulate auditory receptors sending signals to the brain.

7.7 Outline other sensory systems, such as olfaction, gustation, and somesthesis.
- Gustation is the sense of taste. Taste buds in the tongue receive molecules of substances, which fit into receptor sites.
- The five basic types of taste are sweet, sour, salty, bitter, and umami (brothy).
- Olfaction is the sense of smell. The olfactory receptors in the upper part of the nasal passages receive molecules of substances and create neural signals that then go to the olfactory bulbs under the frontal lobes.
- The somesthetic senses include the skin senses and the vestibular senses (touch, pain, motion, and balance).

Module 8: Perception

Understand how we perceive the world.

8.1 Explain the nature of attention.
- The ability to focus on certain stimuli and filter other stimuli out is the first step in perception.

8.2 Discuss the importance of perceptual constancies.
- Perception is the interpretation and organization of sensations.
- Size constancy is the tendency to perceive objects as always being the same size, no matter how close or far away they are. Shape constancy is the tendency to perceive objects as remaining the same shape even when the shape of the object changes on the retina of the eye. Brightness constancy is the tendency to perceive objects at a certain level of brightness, even when the light changes.

8.3 Describe the Gestalt principles of perception.
- The Gestalt psychologists developed several principles of perception that involve interpreting patterns in visual stimuli.

8.4 Distinguish between binocular and monocular depth cues.
- Depth perception is the ability to see in three dimensions. Monocular cues for depth perception include linear perspective, relative size, and overlap.

8.5 Describe the various types of perceptual illusions.
- Illusions are perceptions that do not correspond to reality or are distortions of visual stimuli.

8.6 Outline how experiences and expectations influence perception.
- Perceptual set or expectancy refers to the tendency to perceive objects and situations in a particular way because of prior experiences.

Applying Psychology to Everyday Life: Beyond "Smoke and Mirrors"—The Psychological Science and Neuroscience of Magic
- By collaborating with magicians, psychologists and neuroscientists can learn more about magic and the brain processes responsible for our perception of magic tricks.

Study and Review at **MyPsychLab**

Vocabulary Review

Match each vocabulary term to its definition.

1. sensation
2. perception
3. cones
4. pinna
5. olfaction
6. pitch
7. accommodation
8. bottom-up processing
9. contiguity
10. linear perspective

a. The method by which the sensations experienced at any given moment are interpreted and organized in some meaningful fashion.

b. As a monocular clue, the brain's use of information about the changing thickness of the lens of the eye in response to looking at objects that are close or far away.

c. The tendency for parallel lines to appear to converge on each other.

d. Visual sensory receptors found at the back of the retina, responsible for color vision and sharpness of vision.

e. The visible part of the ear.

f. The analysis of the smaller features to build up to a complete perception.

g. The sensation of smell.

h. The process that occurs when special receptors in the sense organs are activated, allowing various forms of outside stimuli to become neural signals in the brain.

i. Psychological experience of sound that corresponds to the frequency of the sound waves.

j. The tendency to perceive two things that happen close together in time as being related.

Psychology Project

How important are binocular depth cues? Perform this experiment to see what happens to your sense of depth perception when you close one eye.

Materials:
- a partner
- a beanbag or a small, soft ball
- a pencil and paper

Instructions:

1. Determine which partner will be the pitcher and which partner will be the catcher.
2. Stand several feet away from your partner in a clear area.
3. Have the pitcher throw the beanbag gently to the catcher ten times in a row. The catcher should keep both of his or her eyes open. Count how many throws are caught, and record that number on the paper.
4. Have the catcher close one eye. The pitcher should throw the beanbag gently to the catcher ten more times while the catcher's eye remains closed. Count how many throws are caught, and record that number on the paper.
5. Switch roles and repeat the experiment. Compare your results to your partner's.
6. Discuss the results. Was it easier to catch the beanbag with two eyes open or with one eye open? What monocular and binocular depth cues did you use during the activity? Which cues were not?

Tech Alternative

Go to the following web site and try the online depth perception test:

http://www.mediacollege.com/3d/depth-perception/test.html

How difficult was it to see the images that were described? Describe a situation in which depth perception would be very important. What would you say to a friend that had difficulty with the online test and found they had no depth perception?

Essay Question

Jonah, his wife Alana, and their son Rory are on a family road trip. The trip is difficult for all of them: Jonah needs to wear glasses when he drives because he cannot see objects clearly from a distance. Alana is unable to drive because she has difficulty distinguishing red traffic lights from green traffic lights. Both Jonah and Alana complain that Rory's loud music is making their ears ring. After a few hours in the car, Rory feels nauseated and dizzy. In an essay, give detailed explanations of potential biological causes for two of the following:

a. Jonah's poor eyesight
b. Alana's difficulty distinguishing red from green
c. Jonah's and Alana's ringing ears
d. Rory's nausea and dizziness

Test Yourself

Ready for your test? More quizzes and a customized plan.

☑ **Study and Review** at MyPsychLab

Pick the best answer.

1. You notice that you have to add 1 onion to your pot of chili that already has 5 onions mixed in it to notice a difference. According to Weber's law, how many onions would you have to add to notice a difference if you are making twice as much chili with 10 onions?
   a. 1
   b. 2
   c. 4
   d. 5

2. A study purportedly conducted by James Vicary teaches us what about the power of subliminal perception and its effect on advertising?
   a. Subliminal advertising can profoundly affect a consumer's decision-making process.
   b. Subliminal advertising affects a consumer's decision-making process but only when it involves comfort foods such as popcorn and soda.
   c. Subliminal advertising is effective.
   d. Subliminal advertising was never supported.

3. You detect the strong smell of cedar when you enter a furniture store. However, after a short while in the store, you no longer can detect the smell. This process is known as
   a. sensory adaptation.
   b. habituation.
   c. perceptual constancy.
   d. accommodation.

4. Which of the following terms refers to the amplitude of a light wave?
   a. color
   b. brightness
   c. pitch
   d. hue

5. Surgically correcting a patient's vision through LASIK is making adjustments to the patient's
   a. cornea.
   b. lens.
   c. retina.
   d. iris.

6. What part of the eye hardens as we age?
   a. rods
   b. cones
   c. lens
   d. vitreous humor

7. A deer's inability to quickly respond to the headlights of an approaching car is due to what sensory phenomenon?
   a. dark adaptation
   b. light adaptation
   c. afterimage
   d. opponent-process theory

8. The hammer, the anvil, and the stirrup are part of the
   a. outer ear.
   b. middle ear.
   c. inner ear.
   d. cochlea.

9. John has played his music loudly for years. Now he has a continuous ringing in both of his ears. What would John probably be diagnosed with?
   a. Tinnitus
   b. Conduction-based hearing impairment
   c. Damage to the pinna
   d. Regardless of the disorder, John will ultimately require a cochlear implant.

10. Studies show that taste preference can typically begin
    a. before a baby is born.
    b. in the first 3–6 months.
    c. by age 1.
    d. during preschool.

11. Jude's nose has been stopped up for several days. What effect, if any, might his cold have on his sense of taste?
    a. His sense of taste will be increased.
    b. His sense of taste will be dulled.
    c. His sense of taste will get better.
    d. His sense of taste will be no better or worse.

12. If a child suffers from congenital analgesia, why must he or she be careful when playing outside?
    a. The child often cannot hear sounds.
    b. The child cannot feel pain.
    c. The child cannot react to a dangerous situation.
    d. The child's sense of smell does not work properly.

13. If Tabitha closes her eyes when she rides in her parent's car, she can still tell that the car is moving. This is because of the movement of tiny crystals in the
    a. outer ear.
    b. inner ear.
    c. pinna.
    d. middle ear.

14. When a child stops spinning, he or she often feels like his or her head is still spinning. What is responsible for this sensation?
    a. fluid still rotating in the semicircular canals
    b. proprioceptors
    c. compression of the otolith organs
    d. disruption of the otolith crystals

15. Little Karla is with her mother at the docks waiting for her daddy to return from his naval deployment. While the boat is still a ways out, her mother says, "There is daddy's boat." Karla is confused. She cannot understand how her dad can be on a boat that is so small. It's safe to assume that Karla does not yet understand
    a. size constancy.
    b. shape constancy.
    c. brightness constancy.
    d. color constancy.

16. XX   XX   XX   XXXXXX
    XX   XX   XX   XXXXXX
    XX   XX   XX   XXXXXX
    Seeing three columns of Xs on the left versus three rows of Xs on the right can be explained by the Gestalt principle of _____.
    a. closure
    b. similarity
    c. proximity
    d. contiguity

17. As you watch a jet fly high overhead, it seems to slowly pass by. What monocular depth cue best explains this?
    a. motion parallax
    b. linear perspective
    c. overlap
    d. texture gradient

18. The Müller–Lyer illusion is influenced greatly by one's
    a. age.
    b. gender.
    c. level of intellect.
    d. culture.

19. Allison opened her new jigsaw puzzle but soon realized that she had the same puzzle when she was a child. With her past experience to rely upon, Allison will probably use _____ to help her reassemble the puzzle.
    a. bottom-up processing
    b. top-down processing
    c. perceptual expectancy
    d. perceptual set

20. Kip enjoys watching a friend run with a sparkler and the momentary trail of light that seems to be left behind. Which aspect of our visual system best explains this trail of light?
    a. lateral inhibition
    b. microsaccades
    c. persistence of vision
    d. achromatopsia

Concept Summary: Sensation and Perception

Learning Objectives

7.1 7.2 7.3   pp. 80–83

Understand the Process of Sensation

sensation
process by which information from the outsize world enters the brain

- **sensory thresholds** describe the extent of our sensory ability
- **habituation** the brain "ignores" unchanging information from the environment
- **sensory adaptation** sensory receptors become less responsive to unchanging stimuli

perception
process by which sensations are organized and interpreted in a meaningful fashion

Learning Objectives

7.4 7.5 7.6 7.7   pp. 83–100

Learn the Capabilities and Limitations of Sensory Processes

forms of physical energy we sense

forms of energy we can sense
- light waves
- sound waves
- thermal energy
- chemical substances

the auditory sensory system

sound
- has psychological properties
- is a physical stimulus processed by the ear
  - volume
  - frequency or pitch
  - timbre

the visual sensory system

light
- has psychological properties
  - brightness
  - color/hue
  - saturation
- is a physical stimulus processed by the eye

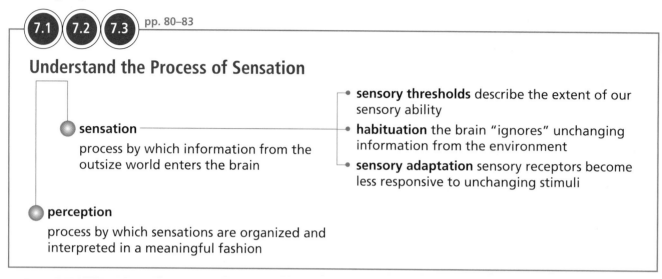

Pupil Iris opening that changes size depending on the amount of light in the environment

Iris Its muscles control the size of the pupil

Aqueous humor Clear liquid that nourishes the eye

Cornea Bends light waves so the image can be focused on the retina

Vitreous humor Jelly-like liquid that nourishes and gives shape to the eye

Lens Changes shape to bring objects into focus

Retina Contains photoreceptor cells

Fovea Central area of retina; greatest density of photoreceptors

Optic nerve Sends visual information to the brain

Blind spot (optic disc) Where the optic nerve leaves the eye; there are no photoreceptor cells here

Blood vessels

Light

seeing
- begins with the receptor sites on retinal neurons
  - rods
  - cones

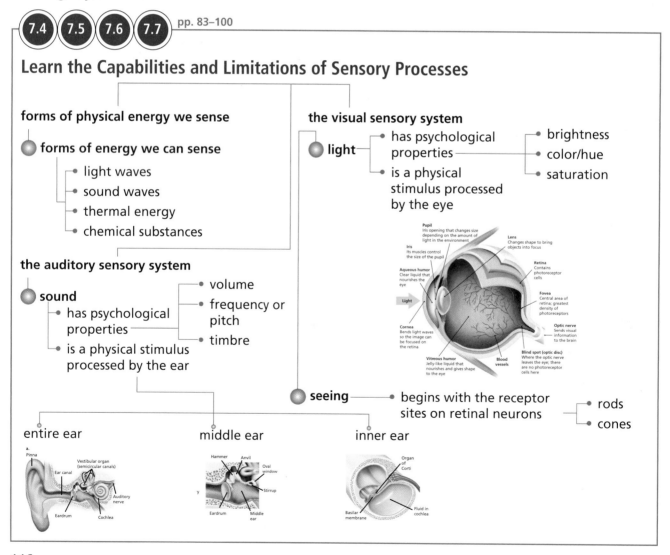

entire ear

a.
Pinna
Vestibular organ (semicircular canals)
Ear canal
Auditory nerve
Eardrum   Cochlea

middle ear

Hammer   Anvil
Oval window
y
Stirrup
Eardrum   Middle ear

inner ear

Organ of Corti
Basilar membrane
Fluid in cochlea

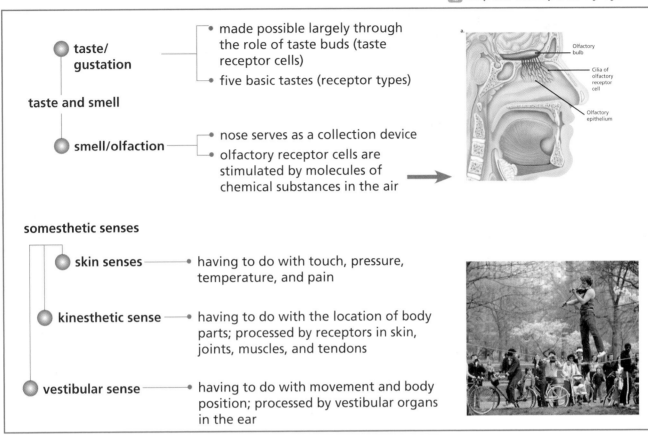

taste/gustation
- made possible largely through the role of taste buds (taste receptor cells)
- five basic tastes (receptor types)

taste and smell

smell/olfaction
- nose serves as a collection device
- olfactory receptor cells are stimulated by molecules of chemical substances in the air

somesthetic senses

skin senses
- having to do with touch, pressure, temperature, and pain

kinesthetic sense
- having to do with the location of body parts; processed by receptors in skin, joints, muscles, and tendons

vestibular sense
- having to do with movement and body position; processed by vestibular organs in the ear

Learning Objectives

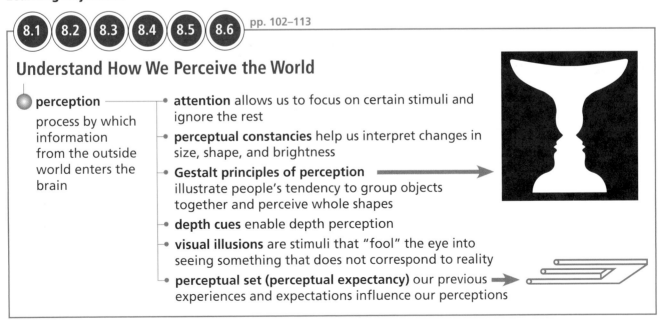

8.1 8.2 8.3 8.4 8.5 8.6 pp. 102–113

Understand How We Perceive the World

perception
process by which information from the outside world enters the brain

- **attention** allows us to focus on certain stimuli and ignore the rest
- **perceptual constancies** help us interpret changes in size, shape, and brightness
- **Gestalt principles of perception** illustrate people's tendency to group objects together and perceive whole shapes
- **depth cues** enable depth perception
- **visual illusions** are stimuli that "fool" the eye into seeing something that does not correspond to reality
- **perceptual set (perceptual expectancy)** our previous experiences and expectations influence our perceptions

CHAPTER 4 Consciousness

California police departments are cracking down on texting and talking on cell phones while driving, using a video game–like simulator to teach students just how dangerous trying to do two such demanding mental processes at once can be. AT&T has a safety campaign in which public service announcements recount the disastrous, and often fatal, consequences of texting while driving—both sending texts and receiving them. A majority of states now ban all cell phone use by new drivers and text messaging for all drivers. Why? Because contrary to common belief, the research tells us that we cannot truly multitask, and both driving and talking or texting on a phone are thought processes that make heavy demands on our conscious awareness.

What are some ways in which you multitask throughout the day? How does multitasking impact your awareness or affect the quality of your work, if at all?

Watch the **Video**, at **MyPsychLab**

*W*hy Study **Consciousness**?

In a very real sense, to understand consciousness is to understand what it means to be who we are. Waking, sleeping, dreaming, daydreaming, and other forms of conscious awareness make up the better part of the human experience. Lack of sleep may increase the likelihood of diabetes, interfere with the onset of puberty changes, decrease memory for learning, and increase weight gain. Drug use can affect consciousness as well, and not always to our benefit. Clearly, an understanding of the workings of the conscious and unconscious mind is important to both our mental and our physical well-being.

Module 9 Sleep and Dreams

Module Goals	Learning Objectives
Understand the relationship between conscious and unconscious processes.	**9.1** Describe the various states of consciousness.
	9.2 Distinguish between explicit and implicit processing.
Describe the characteristics of sleep and theories that explain why we sleep and dream.	**9.3** Understand the circadian rhythm and its relation to sleep.
	9.4 Outline theories about the functions of sleep.
	9.5 Describe the characteristics of the sleep cycle.
	9.6 Identify the types of sleep disorders.
	9.7 Compare perspectives on the functions of dreams.

consciousness a person's awareness of everything that is going on around him or her at any given time.

Understand the Relationship Between Conscious and Unconscious Processes

9.1 Describe the various states of consciousness.

Consciousness is one of those terms that most people think they understand until someone asks them to define it. Various sorts of scientists, psychologists, neuroscientists, philosophers, and even computer scientists (who have been trying to develop an artificial intelligence for some time now), have tried to define consciousness, and so there are several definitions—one for nearly every field in which consciousness is studied.

What exactly is meant by the term consciousness*? I've heard it a lot, but I'm not sure that I know* ▶ *everything it means.*

Definition of Consciousness Although early psychologist William James spoke of a "stream of consciousness" in which ideas, sensations, and thoughts flow from one into another (James, 1890), philosopher Daniel Dennett asserts that there is no single stream of consciousness but rather multiple "channels," each of which is handling its own tasks (Dennett, 1991). All of these channels operate in parallel, in a kind of chaos of consciousness. People must somehow organize all this conscious experience, and their particular social groups and culture will influence that organization.

Do animals experience consciousness in the same way as people? That is a question too complex to answer fully here, but many researchers into animal behavior, language, and cognition have some reason to propose that a kind of consciousness exists in at least some animals, although its organization would naturally not be the same as human consciousness (Block, 2005; Browne, 2004; Hurley & Nudds, 2006; Koch & Mormann, 2010).

So where does that leave us in the search for a working definition of ▶ *consciousness?*

For our purposes, a more useful definition of consciousness might be the following: Consciousness is your awareness (it literally means "with knowing") of everything that is going on around you and inside your own head at any given moment, which you use to organize your behavior (Farthing, 1992), including your thoughts, sensations, and feelings. In a cognitive neuroscience view, consciousness is generated by a set of neurons firing (the action potentials) in the communication among neurons just sufficient to produce a specific perception, memory, or experience in our awareness (Crick & Koch, 1990, 2003; Koch & Mormann, 2010). In other words, your eyes see a dog, the neurons along the optic pathway to the occipital lobe's visual cortex are activated, and the visual association cortex is activated to identify the external stimulus as a "dog." Bam!—consciousness!

Altered States of Consciousness Much of people's time awake is spent in a state called *waking consciousness* in which their thoughts, feelings, and sensations are clear and organized, and they feel alert. But there are many times in daily activities and in life when people experience states of consciousness that differ from this organized waking state. These variations are called "altered states of consciousness."

An **altered state of consciousness** occurs when a shift takes place in the quality or pattern of your mental activity. Thoughts may become fuzzy and disorganized and you may feel less alert, or your thoughts may take bizarre turns, as they so often do in dreams. Sometimes being in an altered state may mean being in a state of *increased* alertness, as when you are under the influence of a stimulant. You may also divide your conscious awareness, as when you drive to work or school and then wonder how you got there—one level of conscious awareness was driving, while the other was thinking about the day ahead, perhaps. This altered state of divided consciousness can be a dangerous thing, as many people who try to drive and talk on a cell phone at the same time have discovered. Driving and carrying on a phone conversation are both processes that should demand focused attention, and it is simply not possible to do both at once in a safe and efficient manner. Studies have shown that driving while talking on a cell phone, even a hands-free phone, puts a person at the same degree of risk as driving under the influence of alcohol (Alm & Nilsson, 1995; (Briem & Hedman, 1995; Strayer & Drews, 2007; Strayer & Johnston, 2001; Strayer et al., 2006. Texting while driving is more than risky—it can be murderous (Eastern Virginia) Medical School, 2009; Wang et al., 2012). Take the survey *What Altered States Have You Experienced?* to discover more about your own encounters with various states of consciousness.

There are many forms of altered states of consciousness, some are dangerous such as being under the influence of certain drugs, some are not such as daydreaming, being hypnotized, or achieving a meditative state. But the most common altered state people experience is the one they spend about a third of their lives in on a nightly basis—sleep.

9.2 Distinguish between explicit and implicit processing.

Are you consciously aware of every action you take in your daily life? Consider the difference between tasks that require careful thought and attention—such as presenting a report in class—and the many smaller, automatic actions that you perform in the course of a day, such as walking from place to place.

If you were to present a report in class, you would likely be consciously aware of your thought process, actions, and decisions. You would carefully consider what to say, or perhaps read from pre-written notes, and you would prepare yourself to respond to questions from the teacher or classmates. In this example, you are engaging in *explicit processing* (or *effortful processing*)—processing that is conscious. You are aware of your thought process and are focusing your full attention on the task at hand.

altered states of consciousness state in which there is a shift in the quality or pattern of mental activity as compared to waking consciousness.

▲ *The driver of this car has several competing demands on his attention: working his cell phone, listening to the passenger read to him, and driving his car. If he manages to get himself and his passenger safely to their destination— and by multitasking while driving he is certainly endangering both of their lives and others as well—it's possible that he won't even remember the trip; he may be driving in an altered state of consciousness.*

✹ **Complete** the **Survey**, *What Altered States Have You Experienced?*, at **MyPsychLab**

Walking, on the other hand, is more of an automatic action that requires little or no conscious awareness. You do not need to carefully consider your actions of putting one foot in front of the other. It is an automatic process that does not require your full focus and attention. This is an example of *implicit processing* (or *automatic processing*)—processing that happens without conscious awareness. In many cases, you can perform an action before you even become aware of it.

Describe the Characteristics of Sleep and Theories that Explain Why We Sleep and Dream

9.3 Understand the circadian rhythm and its relation to sleep.

Have you ever wondered why people have to sleep? They could get so much more work done if they didn't have to sleep, and they would have more time to play and do creative things.

The Biology of Sleep Sleep was once referred to as "the gentle tyrant" (Webb, 1992). People can try to stay awake, and sometimes they may go for a while without sleep, but eventually they *must* sleep. One reason for this fact is that sleep is one of the human body's *biological rhythms*, that is, natural cycles of activity that the body must go through. Some biological rhythms are monthly, like the cycle of a woman's menstruation, whereas others are far shorter—the beat of the heart is a biological rhythm. But many biological rhythms take place on a daily basis, like the rise and fall of blood pressure and body temperature or the production of certain body chemicals (Moore-Ede et al., 1982). The most obvious of these is the sleep–wake cycle (Baehr et al., 2000).

The Rhythms of Life: Circadian Rhythms The sleep–wake cycle is a **circadian rhythm**. The term actually comes from two Latin words, *circa* ("about") and *diem* ("day"). So a circadian rhythm is a cycle that takes "about a day" to complete.

For most people, this means that they will experience several hours of sleep at least once during every 24-hour period. The sleep–wake cycle is ultimately controlled by the brain, specifically by an area within the *hypothalamus*, the tiny section of the brain that influences the glandular system. Ever heard of melatonin? A lot of people were buying supplements of *melatonin* (a hormone normally secreted by the pineal gland) several years ago, hoping to sleep better and perhaps even slow the effects of aging (Folkard et al., 1993; Herxheimer & Petrie, 2001; Young, 1996). Sleep researcher Dr. Jerry Siegel explains the function of the SCN in the video, *Sleep and the SCN*.

How Much Sleep Do People Need? How much sleep is enough sleep? The answer varies from person to person depending on age and possibly inherited sleep needs (Feroah et al., 2004), but most young adults need about 7 to 9 hours of sleep each 24-hour period to function well. (See **Figure 9.1**.) Some people are short sleepers, needing only 4 or 5 hours, whereas others are long sleepers and require more than 9 hours of sleep (McCann & Stewin, 1988). As we age, we seem to sleep less during each night until the average length of sleep approaches only 6 hours.

▲ *Sleep, according to Webb (1992), is the "gentle tyrant." As this picture shows, when the urge to sleep comes upon a person, it can be very difficult to resist—no matter where that person is at the time. Can you think of a time or place when you fell asleep without meaning to do so? Why do you think it happened?*

👁 Watch the Video, *Sleep and the SCN*, at MyPsychLab

circadian rhythm a cycle of bodily rhythm that occurs over a 24-hour period.

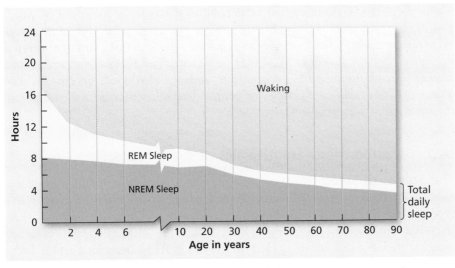

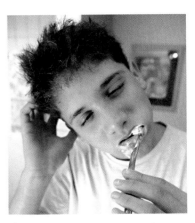

▲ *Contrary to popular belief, sleep deprivation often affects younger people more than it does older people, who need less sleep. Does this young man look well rested and able to successfully complete the task of brushing his teeth?*

FIGURE 9.1 Sleep Patterns of Infants and Adults
Infants need far more sleep than older children and adults. Both REM sleep and NREM sleep decrease dramatically in the first 10 years of life, with the greatest decrease in REM sleep. Nearly 50 percent of an infant's sleep is REM, compared to only about 20 percent for a normal, healthy adult (Roffwarg et al., 1966).

Sleep deprivation, or loss of sleep, is a serious problem, which many people have without realizing it. Students, for example, may stay up all night to study for an important test the next day. In doing so, they will lose more information than they gain. Sleep consolidates memory; that is, sleep takes what's happened during the day, like studying for the exam, and processes that into cortex storage (where you can retrieve it during the test). If you don't give the brain a chance to consolidate through at least a couple of hours of sleep, your study will be less effective. (Gillen-O'Neal et al., 2012). Even a few nights of poor sleep have serious consequences for mental and physical functioning (Van Dongen et al., 2003; Jackson et al., 2013).

9.4 Outline theories about the functions of sleep.

The Adaptive Theory of Sleep Sleep is a product of evolution (Webb, 1992) according to the **adaptive theory** of sleep. It proposes that animals and humans evolved different sleep patterns to avoid being present during their predators' normal hunting times, which typically would be at night. For example, if a human or a prey animal (one a predator will eat) is out and about at night, they are more at risk of being eaten. However, if during active hunting hours the prey is in a safe place sleeping and conserving energy, it is more likely to remain unharmed. If this theory is true, then one would expect prey animals to sleep mostly at night and for shorter periods of time than predator animals; you would also expect that predators could sleep in the daytime—virtually as much as they want. This seems to be the case for predators like lions that have very few natural predators themselves. Nocturnal animals such as the opossum can afford to sleep during the day and be active at night (when their food sources are available), because they are protected from predators by sleeping high up in trees.

The Restorative Theory of Sleep The other major theory of why organisms sleep is called **restorative theory**, which states that sleep is necessary to the physical health of the body. During sleep, chemicals that were used up during the day's activities are replenished and cellular damage is repaired (Adam, 1980;

▲ *These lionesses are predators and have no need to sleep at night to protect themselves. They sleep and hunt on and off during the day in perfect safety, whereas the animals that the lionesses prey upon sleep at night in the safety of trees, dens, or other shelter—often in very short naps.*

adaptive theory theory of sleep proposing that animals and humans evolved sleep patterns to avoid predators by sleeping when predators are most active.

restorative theory theory of sleep proposing that sleep is necessary to the physical health of the body and serves to replenish chemicals and repair cellular damage.

Moldofsky, 1995). As discussed earlier, brain plasticity is enhanced by sleep, and there is evidence that most bodily growth and repair occur during the deepest stages of sleep, when enzymes responsible for these functions are secreted in higher amounts (Saper et al., 2001). Which of these theories is correct? The answer is that both are probably needed to understand why sleep occurs the way it does. Adaptive theory explains why people sleep *when* they do, and restorative theory explains why people *need* to sleep.

9.5 Describe the characteristics of the sleep cycle.

▶ **The Stages of Sleep** There are actually two kinds of sleep: **REM (rapid eye movement) sleep** and **non-REM (NREM) sleep**. REM sleep is a relatively active type of sleep when most of a person's dreaming takes place, whereas non-REM sleep is a much deeper, more restful kind of sleep. In REM sleep, the voluntary muscles are inhibited, meaning that the person in REM sleep moves very little, whereas in non-REM sleep the person's body is free to move around (including kicking off the covers!). There are also several different stages of sleep that people go through each night in which REM sleep and non-REM sleep occur. A machine called an electroencephalograph allows scientists to record the brain-wave activity as a person passes through the various stages of sleep and to determine what type of sleep the person has entered (Aserinsky & Kleitman, 1953). See **Figure 9.2** for a look at what happens in each stage of sleep.

A person who is wide awake and mentally active will show a brain-wave pattern on the electroencephalogram (EEG) called *beta waves*. Beta waves are very small and very fast. As the person relaxes and gets drowsy, slightly larger and slower **alpha waves** appear. The alpha waves are eventually replaced by even slower and larger *theta waves*. In the deepest stages of sleep, the largest and slowest waves appear, called **delta waves**.

Much of existing sleep research is based on terminology describing sleep stages that dates back to the 1960s (Carskadon & Dement, 2011; Rechtschaffen & Kales, 1968). This terminology describes four stages (NREM) in addition to REM and wakefulness. The American Academy of Sleep Medicine (AASM) has published updated guidelines for the recording and scoring of sleep activity, which includes changes in some of the terminology. The new guidelines use R in place of REM, N instead of NREM, and W instead of wakefulness. The AASM guidelines also combine NREM Stages 3 and 4 into a single stage, now indicated by N3 (Iber et al., 2007). In looking at past research, you might encounter the sleep stages labeled as wakefulness, REM, and NREM Stages 1–4 (or simply Stages 1–4), whereas more recent studies may use W, R, N1, N2, and N3. As the area of sleep research is still in a period of transition, in the descriptions that follow, we will use the new AASM terminology as primary and the older Rechtschaffen and Kales (1968) sleep manual terminology noted in parentheses as "R&K."

N1 (R&K Stage 1): Light Sleep
As theta wave activity increases and alpha wave activity fades away, people are said to be entering N1 sleep, or light sleep. Several rather interesting things can happen in this non-REM stage of sleep. If people are awakened at this point, they will probably not believe that they were actually asleep. They may also experience vivid visual events called *hypnogogic images* or *hallucinations* (Mavromatis, 1987; Mavromatis & Richardson, 1984). (The Greek word *hypnos* means "sleep.") Some researchers believe that peoples' experiences of ghostly visits, alien abductions, and near-death experiences may be most easily explained by these hallucinations (Moody & Perry, 1993). For more about hypnogogic experiences and the role they may play in "hauntings," see the Applying Psychology section at the end of this chapter.

So are there different kinds of sleep? Do you go from being awake to being asleep and dreaming—is it instant?

---

rapid eye movement (REM) sleep stage of sleep in which the eyes move rapidly under the eyelids and the person is typically experiencing a dream.

non-REM (NREM) sleep any of the stages of sleep that do not include REM.

alpha waves brain waves that indicate a state of relaxation or light sleep (drowsing).

delta waves long, slow brain waves that indicate the deepest stage of sleep.

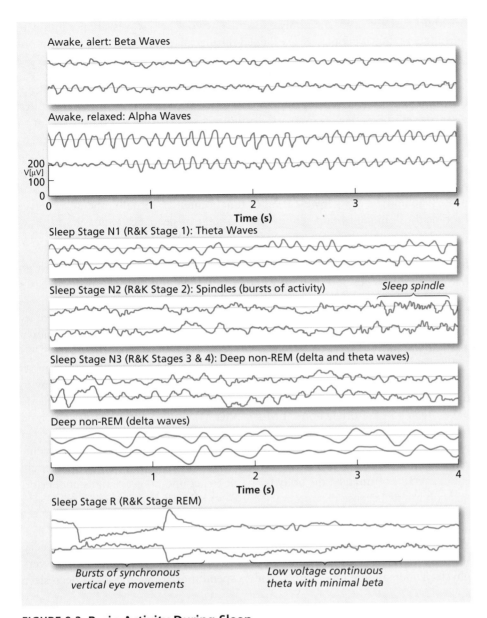

FIGURE 9.2 Brain Activity During Sleep
The EEG reflects brain activity during both waking and sleep. This activity varies according to level of alertness while awake (top two segments) and the stage of sleep. Stage N3 of sleep is characterized by the presence of delta activity, which is much slower and accounts for the larger, slower waves on these graphs. REM has activity that resembles alert wakefulness but has relatively no muscle activity except rapid eye movement. This REM activity is called "paradoxical sleep."
EEG data and images in this figure are courtesy of Dr. Leslie Sherlin.

A much more common occurrence is called the *hypnic jerk* (Mahowald & Schenck, 1996; Oswald, 1959). Have you ever been drifting off to sleep when your knees, legs, or sometimes your whole body gives a big "jerk"? Although experts have no solid proof of why this occurs, many believe that it has something to do with the possibility that the relaxation of the muscles as one drifts into sleep causes a "falling" sensation, at which point the body jerks awake, an automatic process, to prevent the "fall" (Coolidge, 2006; Sagan, 1977).

N2 (R&K Stage 2): Sleep Spindles As people drift further into sleep, the body temperature continues to drop. Heart rate slows, breathing becomes more shallow and irregular, and the EEG will show the first signs of *sleep spindles,* brief bursts of activity lasting only a second or two. Theta waves still predominate in this stage, but if people are awakened during this stage, they will be aware of having been asleep.

N3 (R&K Stages 3 and 4): Delta Waves Roll In In the third stage of sleep, the slowest and largest waves make their appearance. These waves are called **delta waves**. These waves increase during this stage from about 20 percent to more than 50 percent of total brain activity. Now the person is in the deepest stage of sleep, often referred to as slow-wave sleep (SWS) or simply, deep sleep (Carskadon & Dement, 2011). It is during this stage that growth hormones (often abbreviated as GH) are released from the pituitary gland and reach their peak. The body is at its lowest level of functioning. Eventually, the delta waves become the dominant brain activity for this stage of sleep. See **Figure 9.3** to show movement through the sleep stages throughout one night.

R (R&K REM) After spending some time in N3, the sleeping person will go back up through N2 and then into a stage in which body temperature increases to near-waking levels, the eyes move rapidly under the eyelids, the heart beats much faster, and brain waves resemble beta waves—the kind of brain activity that usually signals wakefulness. The person is still asleep but in the stage known as rapid eye movement sleep (REM).

When a person in REM sleep is awakened, he or she almost always reports being in a dream state (Shafton, 1995). REM sleep is, therefore, associated with dreaming, and 90 percent of dreams actually take place in REM sleep. People do have dreams in the other non-REM (or NREM) stages, but REM dreams tend to be more vivid, more detailed, longer, and more bizarre than the dreams of NREM sleep. NREM dreams tend to be more like thoughts about daily occurrences and far shorter than REM dreams (Foulkes & Schmidt, 1983; Takeuchi et al., 2003). Fortunately, the body is unable to act upon these dreams under normal conditions because the voluntary muscles are paralyzed during REM sleep, a condition known as sleep paralysis.

What Is the Purpose of REM Sleep? Why two kinds of sleep? REM sleep seems to serve a different purpose than does NREM, or deep sleep. After a very physically demanding day, people tend to spend more time in NREM deep sleep

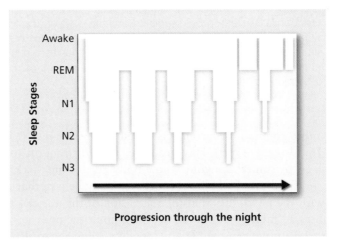

FIGURE 9.3 A Typical Night's Sleep
The graph shows the typical progression through the night of Stages N1-N2 and REM sleep. The REM periods occur about every 90 minutes throughout the night (based on Dement, 1974).

than is usual as the body recovers. But an emotionally stressful day leads to increased time in REM sleep (Horne & Staff, 1983). Perhaps the dreams people have in REM sleep are a way of dealing with the stresses and tensions of the day, whereas physical activity would demand more time for recovery of the body in NREM sleep. Also, if deprived of REM sleep (as would occur with the use of sleeping pills or other depressant drugs), a person will experience greatly increased amounts of REM sleep the next night, a phenomenon called *REM rebound* (Vogel, 1975, 1993).

An early study of REM sleep deprivation (Dement, 1960) seemed to suggest that people deprived of REM sleep would become paranoid, seemingly mentally ill from lack of this one stage of sleep. This is called the *REM myth* because later studies failed to reliably produce the same results (Dement et al., 1969).

REM sleep in early infancy differs from adult REM sleep in a couple of ways: Babies spend nearly 50 percent of their sleep in REM as compared to adults' 20 percent, the brain-wave patterns on EEG recordings are not exactly the same in infant REM when compared to adult REM recordings, and infants can and do move around quite a bit during REM sleep (Carskadon & Dement, 2005; Davis et al., 2004; Sheldon, 2002; Tucker et al., 2006). These differences can be explained: When infants are engaged in REM sleep, they are not dreaming but rather forming new connections between neurons (Carskadon & Dement, 2005; Davis et al., 2004; Sheldon, 2002).

As the infant's brain nears its adult size by age 5 or 6, the proportion of REM sleep has also decreased to a more adult like ratio of REM to non-REM. For infants, to sleep is to grow synapses. The infant brain is highly plastic, and much of brain growth and development takes place during REM sleep.

▲ While this infant is sleeping, her REM sleep (occurring about half of the time she is asleep) allows her brain to make new neural connections.

9.6 Identify the types of sleep disorders.

Sleep Disorders What happens when sleep goes wrong? Nightmares, night terrors, sleepwalking, and being unable to sleep well are all examples of sleep disorders.

Nightmares *Nightmares* are bad dreams that take place during REM sleep, and some nightmares can be utterly terrifying. Children tend to have more nightmares than adults do because they spend more of their sleep in the REM state, as discussed earlier. As they age, they have fewer nightmares because they have less opportunity to have them. But some people still suffer from nightmares as adults.

Night Terrors *Night terrors* are a rare disorder, although one that is more likely in children and also tend to disappear by puberty (Garland & Smith, 1991). A night terror is essentially a state of panic experienced while in deep non-REM sleep (distinguishing them from nightmares occurring in REM sleep). People may sit up, scream, run around the room, or flail* at some unseen attacker. It is not uncommon for people to feel unable to breathe as well. Considering that people suffering a night terror episode are in a deep stage of sleep and breathing shallowly, one can understand why breathing would seem difficult when they are suddenly active. Most people do not remember what happened during a night terror episode, although a few people can remember vividly the images and terror they experienced.

Sleep Walking True *sleepwalking*, or *somnambulism* (the prefix som- means sleep and the root word ambulism means to walk"), occurs in about 20 percent of the population and is at least partially due to heredity (Abe et al., 1984; Kales

▲ Nightmares of being chased by a monster or a similar frightening creature are common, especially in childhood.

*flail: to throw your arms wildly.

"Wait! Don't! It can be dangerous to wake them."
© The New Yorker Collection J. Dator from cartoonbank.com. All Rights Reserved.

👁 **Watch** the **Video**, *Insomnia*, at **MyPsychLab**

▲ *Tossing and turning can be a sign of someone who has trouble getting to sleep, staying asleep, or getting enough sleep—all signs of insomnia. If this woman does suffer from insomnia, how might she feel when she wakes up in the morning?*

insomnia the inability to get to sleep, stay asleep, or get a good quality of sleep.

et al., 1980). It typically occurs during N3 deep sleep, is much more common in childhood, and also occurs more frequently in boys than in girls. Although the old movies portray sleepwalkers as zombie-like and with arms outstretched, in reality a sleepwalker may do nothing more than sit up in bed. But other sleepwalking episodes may involve walking around the house, looking in the refrigerator or even eating, and getting into the car. Most sleepwalkers do not recall their nightly activities the next morning. This lack of memory is typical of most sleepwalking episodes.

Insomnia Most people think that **insomnia** is the inability to sleep. Although that is the literal meaning of the term, in reality insomnia is the inability to get to sleep, stay asleep, persistently waking too early, or get a good quality of sleep (Kryger et al., 1999). The video *Insomnia* describes some of the main causes and treatment options for this disorder and cautions against the use of sleeping pills.

In addition to these treatment options, people can take several steps to help them sleep (Kupfer & Reynolds, 1997; National Sleep Foundation, 2009):

1. Go to bed only when you are sleepy. Rather than trying too hard to go to sleep, after 20 minutes of lying there, get up and do something until you feel sleepy, and then go back to bed.

2. Don't do anything in your bed but sleep. Your bed should be a cue for sleeping, not for studying or watching television.

3. Don't try too hard to get to sleep, and especially do not look at the clock and calculate how much sleep you aren't getting.

4. Keep to a regular schedule. Go to bed at the same time and get up at the same time.

If none of these steps seems to be working, there are sleep clinics and sleep experts who can help people with insomnia. The American Academy of Sleep Medicine has an excellent Web site at **www.aasmnet.org** that provides links to locate sleep clinics in many areas.

Sleep Apnea Snoring is fairly common, occurring when the breathing passages (nose and throat) get blocked. Most people snore only when they have a cold or some other occasional problem, but some people snore every night and quite loudly. It is this type of snoring that is often associated with a condition called *sleep apnea*, in which the person stops breathing for nearly 10 seconds or more. When breathing stops, there will be a sudden silence, followed shortly by a gasping sound as the person struggles to get air into the lungs. Many people do not wake up while this is happening, but they do not get a good, restful night's sleep because of the apnea.

Apnea is a serious problem. According to the National Institutes of Health (2011), from 5 to 25 percent of adults in the United States suffer from apnea (it is difficult to be precise, as many people are unaware that they have apnea). Not only does it disturb nightly sleep, making the person excessively sleepy in the daytime, but also it can cause heart problems (Flemons, 2002). If a person suspects the presence of apnea, a visit to a physician is the first step in identifying the disorder and deciding on a treatment.

Some very young infants also experience a kind of apnea due to immaturity of the brain stem. These infants are typically placed on monitors that sound an alarm when breathing stops, allowing caregivers to help the infant begin breathing again. Although sleep apnea in infants is often associated with sudden infant death syndrome, or SIDS, it is not necessarily caused by it: Many infants who die of SIDS were never diagnosed with sleep apnea (Blackmon et al., 2003).

Table 9.1   Sleep Disorders

NAME OF DISORDER	PRIMARY SYMPTOMS
Somnambulism	Sitting, walking, or performing complex behavior while asleep
Night terrors	Extreme fear, agitation, screaming while asleep
Restless leg syndrome	Uncomfortable sensations in legs causing movement and loss of sleep
Nocturnal leg cramps	Painful cramps in calf or foot muscles
Hypersomnia	Excessive daytime sleepiness
Circadian rhythm disorders	Disturbances of the sleep–wake cycle such as jet lag and shift work
Insomnia	the inability to get to sleep, stay asleep, or get a good quality of sleep
Sleep apnea	A stop in breathing for nearly 10 seconds or more followed by difficulty breathing
Narcolepsy	Uncontrolled falling asleep; immediately into REM sleep without warning

Narcolepsy A disorder affecting one in every 2,000 persons, **narcolepsy** is a kind of "sudden sleep seizure during waking states." In narcolepsy, the person may slip suddenly into REM sleep during the day (especially when the person experiences strong emotions). Another symptom is excessive daytime sleepiness that results in the person falling asleep throughout the day at inappropriate times and in inappropriate places (Overeem et al., 2001). These sleep attacks may occur many times and without warning, making the operation of a car or other machinery very dangerous for the *narcoleptic* (person who suffers from narcolepsy). **Table 9.1** has a more detailed list of known sleep disorders.

9.7 Compare perspectives on the functions of dreams.

Dreams have long been a source of curiosity. People of ancient times tried to find meaning in dreams. Some viewed dreams as prophecy, some as messages from the spirits. But the real inquiry into the process of dreaming began with the publication of Freud's *The Interpretation of Dreams* (1900).

Freud's Interpretation: Dreams as Wish Fulfillment
Sigmund Freud (1856–1939) believed that the problems of his patients stemmed from conflicts and events that had been buried in their unconscious minds since childhood. One of the ways Freud devised to get at these early memories was to examine the dreams of his patients, believing that conflicts, events, and desires of the past would be represented in symbolic* form in the dreams. Freud believed dreams to be a kind of wish fulfillment for his patients.

"On your application it says you have narcolepsy. What is that?"

narcolepsy sleep disorder in which a person falls immediately into REM sleep during the day without warning.

---

*symbolic: having the quality of representing something other than itself.

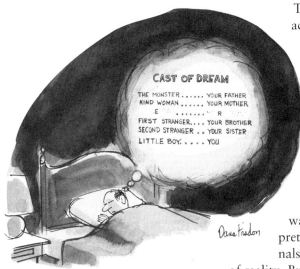

The development of techniques for looking at the structure and activity of the has led to an explanation of why people dream that is more scientific and concrete than that of Freud.

The Activation-Synthesis Hypothesis Using brain-imaging techniques such as a PET, researchers have found evidence that dreams are products of activity in the pons (Hobson, 1988; Hobson & McCarley, 1977; Hobson et al., 2000). This lower area inhibits the neurotransmitters that would allow movement of the voluntary muscles while sending random signals to the areas of the cortex that interpret vision, hearing, and so on (see **Figure 9.4**).

When signals from the pons bombard* the cortex during waking consciousness, the association areas of the cortex interpret those signals as seeing, hearing, and so on. Because those signals come from the real world, this process results in an experience of reality. But when people are asleep, the signals from the brain stem are random and not necessarily attached to actual external stimuli, yet the brain

Cerebral cortex
Controls complex thought processes.

Thalamus
Part of the forebrain that relays information from sensory organs to the cerebral cortex.

Pons
Part of the hindbrain that relays messages between the cerebellum and the cortex.

FIGURE 9.4 The Brain and Activation-Synthesis Theory
According to the activation-synthesis theory of dreaming, the pons in the brainstem sends random signals to the upper part of the brain during REM sleep. These random signals pass through the thalamus, which sends the signals to the proper sensory areas of the cortex. Once in the cortex, the association areas of the cortex respond to the random activation of these cortical cells by synthesizing (making up) a story, or dream, using bits and pieces of life experiences and memories.

---

*bombard: to attack or press.

must somehow interpret these random signals. It *synthesizes* (puts together) an explanation of the cortex's activation from memories and other stored information. (which can make for some very bizarre dreams!)

In this theory, called the activation-synthesis hypothesis, a dream is merely another kind of thinking that occurs when people sleep, as the higher centers of the cortex create a "story" to explain the cortical activation coming from the brain stem during REM. It is less realistic because it comes not from the outside world of reality but from within people's memories and experiences of the past. The frontal lobes, which people normally use in daytime thinking, are more or less shut down during dreaming, which may also account for the unrealistic and often bizarre nature of dreams (Macquet & Franck, 1996).

There are dream experts who suggest that dreams may have more meaning than Hobson and McCarley originally theorized. A survey questioning subjects about their dream content, for example, concluded that much of the content of dreams is meaningful, consistent over time, and fits in with past or present emotional concerns rather than being bizarre, meaningless, and random (Domhoff, 1996, 2005).

Hobson and colleagues have reworked the activation-synthesis hypothesis to reflect concerns about dream meaning, calling it the **activation-information-mode model, or AIM** (Hobson et al., 2000). In this newer version, information that is accessed during waking hours can have an influence on the synthesis of dreams. In other words, when the brain is "making up" a dream to explain its own activation, it uses meaningful bits and pieces of the person's experiences from the previous day or the last few days rather than just random items from memory.

What Do People Dream About? Most dreams reflect the events that occur in everyday life (Hall, 1966). People run, jump, talk, and do all of the actions that they do in normal daily life. There are gender differences in the content of dreams. In his book *Finding Meaning in Dreams*, Dr. William Domhoff (1996) concluded that across many cultures, men more often dream of other males whereas women tend to dream about males and females equally. Men across various cultures also tend to have more physical aggression in their dreams than do women, and women are more often the victims of such aggression in their own dreams. Domhoff also concluded that where there are differences in the content of dreams across cultures, the differences make sense in light of the culture's "personality." For example, there were lower levels of aggression in the dreams of those from the Netherlands when compared to the Americans' dream content.

Girls and women tend to dream about people they know, personal appearance concerns, and issues related to family and home. Boys and men tend to have more male characters in their dreams, which are also typically in outdoor or unfamiliar settings and may involve weapons, tools, cars, and roads (Domhoff, 1996; Domhoff & Schneider, 2008; Foulkes, 1982; Van de Castle, 1994). Take the survey *Are Dreams Meaningful?* to discover more about your own experiences and attitudes toward dreams.

▲ Dreams are often filled with unrealistic and imaginative events and images. A common dream is that of flying. What do you think flying might represent in a dream?

My dreams can be really weird, but sometimes they seem pretty ordinary or even seem to mean something. Can dreams be more meaningful?

activation-information-mode model AIM hypothesis (AIM) revised version of the activation-synthesis explanation of dreams in which information that is accessed during waking hours can have an influence on the synthesis of dreams.

⚙ Complete the Survey, *Are Dreams Meaningful?*, at MyPsychLab

Pick the best answer.

1. A change in the quality or pattern of mental activity, such as increased alertness or divided consciousness, is called a(n)
   a. waking consciousness.
   b. altered state of consciousness.
   c. transient state of consciousness.
   d. hallucination.

2. The sleep–wake cycle typically follows a 24-hour cycle and is regulated by the
   a. cerebellum.
   b. frontal lobe.
   c. pituitary gland.
   d. thalamus.

3. Which theory of sleep offers an explanation of why humans sleep during the nighttime?
   a. reactive theory
   b. microsleep theory
   c. REM theory
   d. adaptive theory

4. Which of the following is not a characteristic of REM sleep?
   a. paralysis of voluntary muscles
   b. increased heart rate
   c. slower, deeper breathing
   d. vivid, detailed dreaming

5. Michael finds that most of his dreams are little more than random images that seemingly have been put into a strange storyline. Which theory of dreams best explains this?
   a. Freudian dream theory
   b. dreams for survival theory
   c. Activation-information-mode model (AIM) hypothesis
   d. dreams as reflections of everyday life

6. In which disorder does breathing stop for nearly half a minute or more?
   a. sleep apnea
   b. night terrors
   c. narcolepsy
   d. REM behavior disorder

7. Which of the following is bad advice for someone suffering from insomnia?
   a. Keep a regular schedule.
   b. Do not study or watch TV in bed.
   c. Lie in bed until you fall asleep, even if it takes several hours.
   d. Avoid drugs that slow down the nervous system.

8. If you suddenly and without warning slip into REM sleep during the day, you may have the condition called
   a. sleep apnea.
   b. insomnia.
   c. narcolepsy.
   d. somnambulism.

9. Which of the following phrases best describes the purpose of dreams according to Freud?
   a. wish fulfillment
   b. memory construction
   c. problem solving
   d. activation synthesis

10. Compared to women, men across all cultures are more likely to dream about all of the following except
   a. personal appearance.
   b. male characters.
   c. the outdoors.
   d. physical aggression.

Module 10 Hypnosis and Drugs

Module Goals	Learning Objectives
Describe other states of consciousness.	**10.1** Describe hypnosis and issues surrounding its nature and use.
	10.2 Understand meditation and relaxation and their effects.
	10.3 Describe the nature of flow states.
Understand the categories of psychoactive drugs and their effects.	**10.4** Explain how psychoactive drugs act at the synaptic level.
	10.5 Evaluate the physiological and psychological effects of psychoactive drugs.
	10.6 Describe the major categories of psychoactive drugs and their effects.
	10.7 Describe how culture and expectations influence the use and experience of drugs.

Describe Other States of Consciousness

10.1 Describe hypnosis and issues surrounding its nature and use.

hypnosis state of consciousness in which the person is especially susceptible to suggestion.

Like sleep, *hypnosis* and *meditation* are other examples of states of consciousness. Although a lot of misunderstandings exist about hypnosis, it can be a useful tool when properly managed.

How Hypnosis Works Hypnosis is a state of consciousness in which a person is especially susceptible to suggestion. There are four key steps in inducing hypnosis (Druckman & Bjork, 1994):

1. The hypnotist tells the person to focus on what is being said.
2. The person is told to relax and feel tired.
3. The hypnotist tells the person to "let go" and accept suggestions easily.
4. The person is told to use vivid imagination.

The real key to hypnosis seems to be a heightened state of suggestibility.* People can be hypnotized when active and alert, but only if they are willing to be hypnotized. Only 80 percent of all people can be hypnotized, and only 40 percent are good hypnotic subjects. The ability to be hypnotized may lie in the way the brain functions. Using brain-scanning techniques, researchers found that two areas in the brains of highly hypnotizable people, areas associated with decision-making and attention, seem to be more active and connected when compared to people who cannot be hypnotized (Hoeft et al., 2012).

---

*suggestibility: being readily influenced.

Is it true that people can be hypnotized into doing things that they would never do under normal conditions?

Watch the Video, *Hypnosis and Therapy*, at MyPsychLab

Although the popular view is that the hypnotized person is acting involuntarily, the fact is that the hypnotist may only be a guide into a more relaxed state, while the subject actually hypnotizes himself or herself (Kirsch & Lynn, 1995). People cannot be hypnotized against their will. The tendency to act as though their behavior is automatic and out of their control is called the *basic suggestion effect* (Kihlstrom, 1985); it gives people an excuse to do things they might not otherwise do because the burden of responsibility for their actions falls on the hypnotist.

A more detailed discussion of the problems in using hypnosis for memory retrieval is outlined in the video, *Hypnosis and Therapy*.

In general, hypnosis is a handy way to help people relax and control pain. These subjective experiences are very much under people's mental influence. Actual physical behavior is harder to change, and that is why hypnosis is not as effective at changing eating habits or helping people to stop smoking (Druckman & Bjork, 1994). Hypnosis is sometimes used in psychological therapy to help people cope with pain, anxiety, or deal with cravings for food or drugs. For a concise look at what hypnosis can and cannot do, see **Table 10.1**.

Theories of Hypnosis There are two views of why hypnosis works. One emphasizes the role of *dissociation*, or a splitting of conscious awareness, whereas the other involves a kind of social role-playing.

Hypnosis as Dissociation: The Hidden Observer Ernest Hilgard (1991; Hilgard & Hilgard, 1994) believed that hypnosis worked only on the immediate conscious mind of a person, while a part of that person's mind (a "hidden observer") remained aware of all that was going on. It's the same kind of **dissociation** that takes place when people drive somewhere familiar and then wonder how they got there. Hilgard believes that there is a hidden part of the mind that is very much aware of the hypnotic subject's activities and sensations, even though the "hypnotized" part of the mind is blissfully unaware of these same things.

Table 10.1	Facts About Hypnosis
HYPNOSIS CAN	HYPNOSIS CANNOT
Create amnesia for whatever happens during the hypnotic session, at least for a brief time (Bowers & Woddy, 1996).	Give people superhuman strength. (People may use their full strength under hypnosis, but it is no more than they had before hypnosis.)
Relieve pain by allowing a person to remove conscious attention from the pain (Holroyd, 1996).	Reliably enhance memory. (There's an increased risk of false-memory retrieval because of the suggestible state hypnosis creates.)
Alter sensory perceptions. (Smell, hearing, vision, time sense, and the ability to see visual illusions can all be affected by hypnosis.)	Regress people back to childhood. (Although people may act like children, they do and say things children would not.)
Help people relax in situations that normally would cause them stress, such as flying on an airplane (Muhlberger et al., 2001).	Regress people to some "past life." There is no scientific evidence for past-life regression (Lilienfeld et al., 2004).

dissociation break a connection with something.

In one study (Miller & Bowers, 1993), subjects were hypnotized and told to put their arms in ice water, although they were instructed to feel no pain. There had to be pain—most people can't even get an ice cube out of the freezer without *some* pain—but subjects reported no pain at all. The subjects who were successful at denying the pain also reported that they imagined being at the beach or in some other place that allowed them to dissociate from the pain.

Hypnosis as Social Role-Playing: The Social-Cognitive Explanation The other theory of why hypnosis works began with an experiment in which participants who were *not* hypnotized were instructed to behave as if they were (Sarbin & Coe, 1972). These participants had no trouble copying many actions previously thought to require a hypnotic state, such as being rigidly suspended between two chairs. The researchers also found that participants who were not familiar with hypnosis, and had no idea what the "role" of a hypnotic subject was supposed to be, could not be hypnotized.

Add to those findings the later findings that expectancies of the hypnotized person play a big part in how the person responds and what the person does under hypnosis (Kirsch, 2000). The **social-cognitive theory of hypnosis** assumes that people who are hypnotized are not in an altered state but are merely playing the role expected of them in the situation. They might believe that they are hypnotized, but in fact it is all a very good performance, so good that even the "participants" are unaware that they are role-playing. Social roles are very powerful influences on behavior, as anyone who has ever worn a uniform can understand—the uniform stands for a particular role that becomes very easy to play (Zimbardo, 1970; Zimbardo et al., 2000).

Hypnosis is one way to relax, but there are simpler ways to reduce tension and stress. See the following *Psychology in the News* section for information about another relaxation technique: meditation.

social-cognitive theory of hypnosis theory that assumes that people who are hypnotized are not in an altered state but are merely playing the role expected of them in the situation.

meditation mental series of exercises meant to refocus attention and achieve a trancelike state of consciousness.

▲ Stage hypnotists often make use of people's willingness to believe that something ordinary is extraordinary. This woman was hypnotized and suspended between two chairs after the person supporting her middle stepped away. The hypnotist led the audience to believe that she could not do this unless hypnotized, but in reality anyone can do this while fully conscious.

10.2 Understand meditation and relaxation and their effects.

Psychology in the News

The Benefits of Meditation

Meditation is a series of mental exercises meant to refocus attention and achieve a trancelike state of consciousness. Meditation can produce a state of relaxation that can aid in coping with the physiological reactions to a stressful situation. When properly meditating, brain waves change to include more theta and alpha waves (indicating deep relaxation) but little to no delta waves, which would indicate deep sleep (Lagopoulos et al., 2009). Meditation also lowers blood pressure and increases the amounts of melatonin secreted at night (the hormone that helps induce sleep) (Benson, 1975; Benson et al., 1974a, 1974b).

Some research even suggests that practicing meditation may lead to permanent changes in the brain, as described in the video, *Meditation*.

👁 **Watch** the **Video**, *Meditation*, at **MyPsychLab**

Some studies suggest that meditation can reduce the levels of chronic pain (Brown & Jones, 2010; Kabat-Zinn et al., 1986); reduce the symptoms of anxiety, depression, and hostility (Kabat-Zinn et al., 1985); reduce the risk of heart disease (Schneider et al., 2012); and reduce stress levels in cancer patients (Speca et al., 2000). Reducing stress levels in cancer patients through meditation will increase the likelihood of recovery and reduce the incidence of recurrence.

Questions for Further Discussion

1. What might be some other advantages of meditation over other ways of relaxing?
2. Is it difficult to take meditation seriously because of its portrayal in movies and television? Why or why not?

10.3 Describe the nature of flow states.

Where Did the Time Go? Think about a time when you lost track of the clock when you were involved in an activity that was very fulfilling. Playing an online game with friends, working on a project with a classmate, practicing a piece of music for a recital, painting, and decorating are all examples of activities in which a person may experience state of flow. The theory of flow states, an outgrowth of positive psychology, are described by Dr. Mihaly Csikszentmihalyi (pronounced "Chick-sent-me-high") as events that challenge our skills enough to grow and improve in the skill, but not so difficult that the challenge creates anxiety. We lose ourselves in the activity and our sense of time is transformed in a way that fits the needs of the activity. The rewards of flow activities are intrinsic and are the product of a merging of the self and the activity so it becomes automatic and almost effortless. Athletes describe being in the zone, entertainers describe being lost in the music, artists describe their medium as an extension of themselves as they produce their works. Each of these experiences reflects the nature of flow states (Boniwell, accessed 2014).

Understand the Categories of Psychoactive Drugs and Their Effects

Whereas some people seek altered states of consciousness in sleep, daydreaming, meditation, or even hypnosis, others try to take a shortcut and use drugs. Although many such drugs have practical purposes (sedation during surgery, control of pain, or controlling anxiety, for example), there are often dangers in using these drugs.

The term **psychoactive drugs** refers to chemical substances that alter thinking, perception, memory, or some combination of those abilities. When taken for pleasure, to get "high," or to dull psychological pain, or when taken without the supervision of a qualified medical professional, these drugs can pose serious risks to one's health and may even cause death. One danger of such drugs is their potential to create either a physical or psychological dependence, both of which can lead to a lifelong pattern of abuse as well as the risk of taking increasingly larger doses, leading to one of the clearest dangers of dependence: a drug overdose.

psychoactive drugs chemical substances that alter thinking, perception, and memory.

10.4 Explain how psychoactive drugs act at the synaptic level.

Physical Dependence Drugs that people can become physically dependent on cause the user's body to crave the drug (Abadinsky, 1989; Fleming & Barry, 1992; Pratt, 1991). After using the drug for some period of time, the body becomes unable to function normally without the drug and the person is said to be dependent or addicted, a condition commonly called **physical dependence**.

One sign of physical dependence is the development of a *drug tolerance* (Pratt, 1991). As the person continues to use the drug, larger and larger doses of the drug are needed to achieve the same initial effects of the drug.

Another sign of a physical dependence is that the user experiences symptoms of **withdrawal** when deprived of the drug. Depending on the drug, these symptoms can range from headaches, nausea, and irritability to severe pain, cramping, shaking, and dangerously elevated blood pressure. These physical sensations occur because the body is trying to adjust to the absence of the drug. Many users will take more of the drug to alleviate* the symptoms of withdrawal, which makes the entire situation worse. This is actually an example of *negative reinforcement*, the tendency to continue a behavior that leads to the removal of or escape from unpleasant circumstances† or sensations. (L)(I)(N)(K) *to Chapter Six: Learning and Language Development, pp. 202–207.*

The mechanisms of dependence are not just a product of learning—the brain itself plays an important part. Drugs that can lead to dependence cause the release of dopamine in a part of the brain called the mesolimbic pathway, a neural track that begins in the midbrain area and continues to the middle of the prefrontal cortex (Hnasko et al., 2010; Schmitt & Reith, 2010). When a drug enters the body, it goes quickly to this area, known as the brain's "reward pathway," causing a release of dopamine and intense pleasure. The brain tries to adapt to this large amount of dopamine by decreasing the number of synaptic receptors for dopamine. The next time the user takes the drug, he or she needs more of it to get the same pleasure response because of the reduced number of receptors—drug tolerance has developed (Koob & Le Moal, 2005; Laviolette et al., 2008; Salamone & Correa, 2012).

10.5 Evaluate the physiological and psychological effects of psychoactive drugs.

Psychological Dependence Not all drugs cause physical dependence; some cause **psychological dependence**, or the belief that the drug is needed to continue a feeling of emotional or psychological well-being, which is a very powerful factor in continued drug use. The body may not need or crave the drug, and people may not experience the symptoms of physical withdrawal or tolerance, but they will continue to use the drug because they *think* they need it. In this case, it is the rewarding properties of using the drug that cause a dependency to develop.

Although not all drugs produce physical dependence, *any* drug can become a focus of psychological dependence. Indeed, because there is no withdrawal to go through or to recover from, psychological dependencies can last forever. Some people who gave up smoking marijuana decades ago still say that the craving returns every now and then (Roffman et al., 1988).

---

*alleviate: make something unpleasant less severe.
†circumstance: a situation or condition that a person is in.

physical dependence condition occurring when a person's body becomes unable to function normally without a particular drug.

withdrawal physical symptoms that can include nausea, pain, tremors, crankiness, and high blood pressure, resulting from a lack of an addictive drug in the body systems.

psychological dependence the feeling that a drug is needed to continue a feeling of emotional or psychological well-being.

But not all drugs produce physical dependence, right? For example, some people say that you can't get physically dependent on marijuana. If that's true, why is it so hard for some people to quit smoking pot?

stimulants drugs that increase the functioning of the nervous system.

depressants drugs that decrease the functioning of the nervous system.

hallucinogenics drugs including hallucinogens and marijuana that produce hallucinations or increased feelings of relaxation and intoxication.

10.6 Describe the major categories of psychoactive drugs and their effects.

Categories of Drugs The effect of a particular drug depends on the category to which it belongs and the particular neurotransmitter the drug affects. In this chapter we will describe several of the major drug categories, including **stimulants** (drugs that increase the functioning of the nervous system), **depressants** (drugs that decrease the functioning of the nervous system), and **hallucinogenics** (drugs that alter perceptions and may cause hallucinations).

Stimulants: Up, Up, and Away Stimulants are a class of drugs that cause either the sympathetic division or the central nervous system (or both) to increase levels of functioning, at least temporarily. In simple terms, stimulants "speed up" the neurons—the heart may beat faster or the brain may work faster, for example. Many of these drugs are called "uppers" for this reason.

Amphetamines Stimulants that are synthesized (made) in laboratories rather than being found in nature are called amphetamines. Among the amphetamines are drugs like Benzedrine, Methedrine, and Dexedrine. A related compound, *methamphetamine*, is used very rarely to treat attention-deficit/hyperactivity disorder or narcolepsy. "Crystal meth" is a crystalline form that can be smoked and is used by recreational drug users, people who do not need drugs but instead use them to gain some form of pleasure.

When the energy reserves are exhausted or the drug wears off, a "crash" is inevitable, and the tendency is to take more pills to get back "up." The person taking these pills finds that it takes more and more pills to get the same stimulant effect (drug tolerance). Nausea, vomiting, high blood pressure, and strokes are possible, as is a state called "amphetamine psychosis." This condition causes addicts to become delusional (losing contact with what is real) and paranoid. They think people are out to "get" them. Violence is a likely outcome, both against the self and others (Kratofil et al., 1996; Paparelli et al., 2011).

▼ *Far from being illegal, cocaine was once used in many health drinks and medications, such as this toothache medicine used in the late 1800s. Many patent medicines contained small traces of cocaine, including the now famous Coca-Cola TM, once marketed as a nerve tonic.*

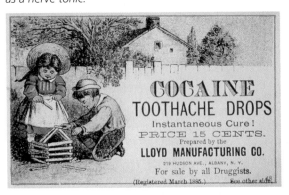

COCAINE
TOOTHACHE DROPS
Instantaneous Cure!
PRICE 15 CENTS.
Prepared by the
LLOYD MANUFACTURING CO.
219 HUDSON AVE., ALBANY, N. Y.
For sale by all Druggists.
(Registered March 1885.)   See other side.

Hasn't nicotine just been the victim of a lot of bad press? After ▶ all, it's legal, unlike cocaine and heroin.

Cocaine Unlike amphetamines, *cocaine* is a natural drug found in coca plant leaves. It produces feelings of euphoria (a feeling of great happiness), energy, power, and pleasure. It also deadens pain and suppresses the appetite. Cocaine is a highly dangerous drug, not just for its addictive properties. Some people have convulsions and may even die when using cocaine for the first time (Lacayo, 1995). It can have devastating effects on the children born to mothers who use cocaine and has been associated with increased risk of learning disabilities, delayed language development, and an inability to cope adequately* with stress, among other symptoms (Cone-Wesson, 2005; Eiden et al., 2009; Kable et al., 2008; Morrow et al., 2006). Laboratory animals have been known to press a lever to give themselves cocaine rather than eating or drinking, even to the point of starvation and death (Iwamoto & Martin, 1988; Ward et al., 1996).

As addictive as cocaine is, there is one other stimulant that is usually described as even more addictive. Most experts in addiction seem to agree that nicotine produces addiction in 99 percent of the people who use it (Benowitz, 1988; Centers for Disease Control and Prevention [CDC], 1992; Franklin, 1990; Henningfield et al., 1991; Hilts, 1998; Perrine, 1997).

—————————
*adequately: satisfactory or acceptable.

Nicotine Every year, more than 440,000 people in the United States die from illnesses related to smoking. That's more people than those who die from accidents in motor vehicles, alcohol, cocaine, heroin and other drug abuse, AIDS, suicide, and homicide *combined* (CDC, 2008a)

Nicotine is a relatively mild but nevertheless toxic stimulant, producing a slight "rush" or sense of arousal as it raises blood pressure and accelerates the heart, as well as providing a rush of sugar into the bloodstream by stimulating the release of adrenalin in addition to raising dopamine levels in the brain's reward pathway (Kovacs et al., 2010; Rezvani & Levin, 2001). As is the case with many stimulants, it also has a relaxing effect on most people and seems to reduce stress (Pormerleau & Pormerleau, 1994).Aside from the powerfully addictive nature of nicotine, the physical withdrawal symptoms can be as bad as those resulting from alcohol, cocaine, or heroin abuse (Epping-Jordan et al., 1998).

Caffeine There is one stimulant that almost everyone uses, with many using it every day. This, of course, is *caffeine*, the stimulant found in coffee, tea, most sodas, chocolate, and even many over-the-counter drugs. Caffeine is another natural substance, like cocaine and nicotine, and is found in coffee beans, tea leaves, cocoa nuts, and at least 60 other types of plants (Braun, 1996). It is a mild stimulant, helps maintain alertness, and can increase the effectiveness of some pain relievers such as aspirin. Caffeine is often added to pain relievers for that reason and is the key ingredient in medications meant to keep people awake.

▲ *Nicotine is highly addictive, and many smokers will go to great lengths to be able to smoke—including smoking right next to the "No Smoking" sign.*

Depressants: Down in the Valley Another class of psychoactive drugs is *depressants*, drugs that slow the central nervous system. Commonly known as the *tranquilizers* (drugs that have a strong depressant effect) or sleeping pills, *barbiturates* are drugs that have a sedative (sleep-inducing) effect. Overdoses can lead to death as breathing and heart action are stopped. Benzodiazepines are used to lower anxiety and reduce stress. Some of the most common are Valium, Xanax, Halcion, Ativan, and Librium.Tranquilizers can be addictive, and large doses can be dangerous, as can an interaction with alcohol or other drugs (Olin, 1993).

Alcohol The most commonly used and abused depressant is *alcohol*, the chemical resulting from fermentation or distillation of various kinds of vegetable matter. Aside from the obvious health risks to the liver, brain, and heart, alcohol is associated with loss of work time, loss of a job, and loss of economic stability.

Alcohol indirectly stimulates the release of a neurotransmitter called GABA, the brain's major depressant (Brick, 2003; Santhakumar et al., 2007). GABA slows down or stops neural activity. As more GABA is released, the brain's functioning actually becomes more and more inhibited, depressed, or slowed down. The areas of the brain that are first affected by alcohol are unfortunately the areas that control social inhibitions*, so alcohol (due to its simulation of GABA) has the effect of depressing the inhibitions. As the effects continue, motor skills, reaction time, and speech are all affected.

The dangers of abusing alcohol cannot be stressed enough. According to the Centers for Disease Control and Prevention (CDC, 2011), the number of alcohol-induced deaths in 2010 was 25,692. This figure does *not* include deaths because of accidents and homicides that may be related to abuse of alcohol—only those deaths that are caused by the body's inability to handle the alcohol. Of these deaths, 15,990 were attributed to liver disease caused by alcoholism. Alcohol was involved in nearly 22.5 percent of the fatal traffic

▲ *Sleep deprivation causes this man to struggle to wake up. Caffeine can help with alertness but may worsen his sleep deprivation when he tries to get a decent night's sleep tonight.*

---

*inhibitions: a feeling that tends to make a person feel self conscious and not act.

▲ Although many young adults see drinking as a rite of passage into adulthood, few may understand the dangers of "binge" drinking, or drinking four to five drinks within a limited amount of time. Inhibitions are lowered and poor decisions may be made, such as driving while intoxicated. Binge drinking, a popular activity on some college campuses, can also lead to alcoholism.

▲ Actor Cory Monteith struggled with addiction for several years before dying on July 13, 2013, from an accidental drug overdose. A combination of heroin and alcohol were found in his system. He was 31.

narcotics a class of opium-related drugs that suppress the sensation of pain by binding to and stimulating the nervous system's natural receptor sites for endorphins.

crashes for drivers under 21 years old and 24.8 percent of the fatal crashes for those over 21 (NIAAA, 2007).

If you are concerned about your own drinking or are worried about a friend or loved one, there is a free and very simple online assessment at this site on the Internet: **www.alcoholscreening.org.**

Narcotics: I Feel Your Pain

Narcotics are a type of depressant that suppress the sensation of pain by binding to and stimulating the nervous system's natural receptor sites for endorphins, the neurotransmitters that naturally deaden pain sensations (Olin, 1993). Because they also slow down the action of the nervous system, drug interactions with alcohol and other depressants are possible—and deadly. All narcotics are a derivative of a particular plant-based substance—opium.

Opium mimics the effects of endorphins, the nervous system's natural pain-killers. The nervous system slows or stops its production of endorphins. When the drug wears off, there is no protection against any kind of pain, causing the severe symptoms of withdrawal associated with these drugs.

Morphine was created by dissolving opium in an acid and then neutralizing the acid with ammonia. Morphine was thought to be a wonder drug, although its addictive qualities soon became a major concern to physicians and their patients. Morphine is still used today to control severe pain, but in carefully controlled doses and for very short periods of time.

Heroin—a derivative of morphine—does not have many of the disagreeable side effects of morphine. It did not take long, however, for doctors and others to realize that heroin was even more powerfully addictive than morphine or opium.

Drugs such as *methadone*, *buprenorphine*, and *naltrexone* may be used to control withdrawal symptoms and help treat opiate addictions (Kahan & Sutton, 1998; Kakko et al., 2003; Ward et al., 1999). Eventually, as the addicted person is weaned from these drugs, the natural endorphin system starts to function more normally.

Hallucinogens: Higher and Higher Hallucinogens actually cause the brain to alter its interpretation of sensations (Olin, 1993) and can produce sensory distortions very similar to *synesthesia* (LINK to *Chapter Three: Sensation and Perception, pp. 78–79*), in which sensations cross over each other—colors have sound, sounds have smells, and so on. False sensory perceptions, called *hallucinations*, are often experienced, especially with the more powerful hallucinogens. There are two basic types of hallucinogens—those that are created in a laboratory and those that are from natural sources.

Manufactured Highs There are several drugs that were developed in the laboratory instead of being found in nature. Perhaps because these drugs are manufactured, they are often more potent than drugs found in the natural world.

LSD, or *lysergic acid diethylamide*, is synthesized from a grain fungus called *ergot*. Ergot fungus commonly grows on rye grain but can be found on other grains as well. First manufactured in 1938, LSD is one of the most potent, or powerful, hallucinogens (Johnston et al., 2007; Lee & Shlain, 1986). It takes only a very tiny drop of LSD to achieve a "high."

People who take LSD usually do so to get that high feeling. Some people feel that LSD helps them expand their consciousness or awareness of the world around them. Colors seem more intense, sounds more beautiful, and so on. But the experience is not always a pleasant one, just as dreams are not always filled with positive emotions. "Bad trips" are quite common, and there is no way to control what kind of "trip" the brain is going to decide to take.

Another synthesized drug was found to be so dangerous that it remains useful only in veterinary medicine as a tranquilizer. The drug is *PCP* (which stands for *phenyl cyclohexyl piperidine*, a name which is often contracted as *phencyclidine*) and can have many different effects. Depending on the dosage, it can be a hallucinogen, stimulant, depressant, or an analgesic (painkilling) drug. As with LSD, users of PCP can experience hallucinations, distorted sensations, and very unpleasant effects. PCP can also lead to acts of violence against others or suicide (Brecher 1988; Cami et al., 2000; Johnston et al., 2007). Users may even physically injure themselves unintentionally because PCP causes them to feel no warning signal of pain.

The last synthetic drug we will address here is technically an amphetamine but it is capable of producing hallucinations as well. In fact, both *MDMA* (a "designer drug" known on the streets as *Ecstasy* or simply *X*) and PCP are now classified as *stimulatory hallucinogenics*, drugs that produce a mixture of psychomotor stimulant and hallucinogenic effects (National Institute on Drug Abuse, 2006; Shuglin, 1986). Although many users of MDMA believe that it is relatively harmless, the fact is that it—like many other substances—can be deadly when misused. MDMA causes the release of large amounts of serotonin and also blocks the reuptake of this neurotransmitter (Hall & Henry, 2006; Liechti & Vollenweider, 2001; Montgomery & Fisk, 2008).

Nonmanufactured High: Marijuana One of the best known and most commonly abused of the hallucinogenic drugs, **marijuana** (also called "pot" or "weed") comes from the leaves and flowers of the hemp plant called *cannabis sativa*. (*Hashish* is the concentrated substance made by scraping the resin from these leaves, and both marijuana and hashish contain *cannabinoids*.) The most psychoactive cannabinoid, and the active ingredient in marijuana, is *tetrahydrocannabinol* (THC). Marijuana is best known for its ability to produce a feeling of well-being, mild intoxication, and mild sensory distortions or hallucinations.

Most studies of marijuana's effects have concluded that while marijuana can create a powerful *psychological dependency*, it does not produce *physical dependency* or physical withdrawal symptoms. Recent studies have found alterations in the core reward pathways in the brains of animals suggesting more research needs to be conducted to determine marijuana's affect on the human brain (Gilman, et al.,

marijuana mild hallucinogen derived from the leaves and flowers of a particular type of hemp plant.

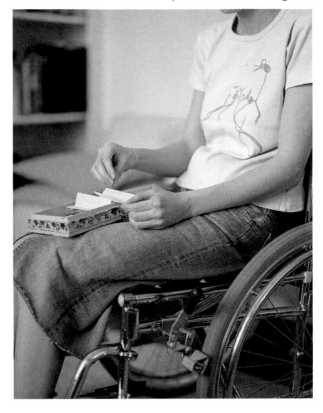
▼ *This woman is preparing a cannabis (marijuana) cigarette. Cannabis is reported to relieve pain in cases of multiple sclerosis and chronic pain from nerve damage.*

Table 10.2	How Drugs Affect Consciousness		
DRUG CLASSIFICATION	COMMON NAME	MAIN EFFECT	ADVERSE EFFECTS
Stimulants		Stimulation, excitement	
Amphetamines	Methamphet-amine, speed, Ritalin, Dexedrine		Risk of addiction, stroke, fatal heart problems, psychosis
Cocaine	Cocaine, crack		Risk of addiction, stroke, fatal heart problems, psychosis
Nicotine	Tobacco		Addiction, cancer
Caffeine	Coffee, tea		Addiction, high blood pressure
Depressants		Relaxation	
Barbiturates (major tranquilizers)	Nembutal, Seconal		Addiction, brain damage, death
Benzodiazepines (minor tranquilizers)	Valium, Xanax, Halcion, Ativan, Rohypnol		Lower risk of overdose and addiction when taken alone
Alcohol	Beer, wine, spirits		Alcoholism, health problems, depression, increased risk of accidents, death
Narcotics	Opium, Morphine, heroin	Euphoria	Addiction, death
Hallucinogens	LSD, PCP, MDMA (Ecstasy), Marijuana	Distorted Conscious-ness, altered perception	Possible permanent memory problems, bad "trips," suicide, overdose, and death

Thinking Critically
Evaluate the health risks of mari-juana, nicotine, and alcohol. Which of the drugs do you believe is the most dangerous? Explain why.

2014). However, after alcohol and nicotine, cannabis dependence is the most common form of drug dependence in the United States, Canada, and Australia (Hall & Degenhardt, 2009).

Although no one has ever been known to die from an overdose of mari-juana, smoking it is not a healthy habit. Research linking marijuana smoking and lung cancer is not definitive due to the fact that many studies have not been able to control for confounding variables, such as cigarette smoking, alcohol use, or other risk factors (Hall & Degenhardt, 2009).

Table 10.2 summarizes the various types of drugs, their common names, and their effects on human behavior.

10.7 Describe how culture and expectations influence the use and experience of drugs.

Drug use, unfortunately, remains an all-too-common problem in today's society. In many cases, people use drugs partly to deal with pressures from the outside world.

Some of these pressures are psychological. People who feel depressed often turn to drugs because they feel that their lives are meaningless, hopeless, and directionless. This can occur especially among school dropouts and the unemployed (Newcomb & Harlow, 1986). Others who are at risk for drug use include people who have recently left home (Bachman et al., 1997), or who suffer from anger, anxiety, or insomnia.

External forces can play a role in drug use as well. Among teenagers in particular, peer pressure can lead to experimentation with drugs. If a teen's friends are using drugs, that teen will be more likely to end up using them, too. They may use drugs because they think it will make them more popular with their peers. Alcohol and other drugs are often found at parties and other social gatherings, which increases the pressure on teenagers to "fit in with the crowd."

By the same token, if a teen's friends stop using drugs, that teen will be more likely to stop using them, too. Alcohol and drug use also decreases when people marry and have children. They no longer want to take part in such risky behavior now that they have a responsibility to their family.

Culture also plays a role in substance use and abuse. For example, in some areas of the United States, the use of medical marijuana is permitted, and two states allow marijuana for recreational use, as well. In Scotland, drinking whiskey is considered socially acceptable and a national pastime, whereas drinking is forbidden in Islamic cultures such as Pakistan, Qatar, and Sudan. Some cultures may incorporate the use of drugs into religious rituals and ceremonies, whereas others strictly forbid the use of any such substance.

As you have learned in this section, psychoactive drugs can have a very harmful impact on people's health and well-being. Although peer influence may sometimes seem intimidating, it is important to make an extra effort to resist these social pressures. The negative consequences of drug use can be devastating—and even deadly.

▲ *Peer pressure is one of the key reasons that teens experiment with drugs and alcohol. However, no one can make you participate in unsafe behavior.*

Pick the best answer.

1. The primary key to hypnosis is finding someone who
   a. accepts suggestions easily.
   b. has a vivid imagination.
   c. is already very tired.
   d. is easily distracted.

2. "Hey, I couldn't help it. I was hypnotized." What theory best explains this rationale for one's behavior while hypnotized?
   a. dissociative theory
   b. expectancy theory
   c. social-cognitive theory
   d. biological theory

3. Your friend tells you she is seeing a therapist who wishes to use hypnosis as part of her therapy. However, your friend is concerned that she might be hypnotized without knowing it. What might you tell her?
   a. Be careful. Hypnotists are in control of you while hypnotized.
   b. Not to worry. Hypnotists can only control their patient's behavior about 40 percent of the time.
   c. That you actually hypnotize yourself and you cannot be hypnotized against your will.
   d. Don't worry. Hypnosis is just an illusion and doesn't really work.

4. What is the role of a hypnotist during a hypnotic therapy session?
   a. They are in complete control.
   b. They are partially in control.
   c. They create the illusion that the patient is in control.
   d. They are little more than a guide.

5. As consequences to stopping drug use, headaches, nausea, shaking, and elevated blood pressure are all signs of
   a. withdrawal.
   b. overdose.
   c. psychological dependency.
   d. amphetamine toxicity.

6. What drug's physical withdrawal symptoms include severe mood swings (crash), paranoia, extreme fatigue, and an inability to feel pleasure?
   a. heroin
   b. caffeine
   c. alcohol
   d. cocaine

7. Which of the following statements about nicotine are true?
   a. In terms of addictive power, nicotine is more powerful than heroin or alcohol.
   b. Nicotine can slow the heart and therefore create a sense of relaxation.
   c. Overall, the number of Americans smoking is on the increase.
   d. Overall, the number of women and teenagers smoking is on the decrease.

8. _____ is a tranquilizer that is also known as the "date rape" drug.
   a. Halcion
   b. Librium
   c. Rohypnol
   d. Xanax

9. Typically, narcotics have the ability to
   a. cause intense hallucinations.
   b. suppress the sensation of pain.
   c. stimulate the user.
   d. cause deep levels of depression.

10. Most studies of marijuana's effects have found that
    a. it creates a powerful psychological dependency.
    b. it creates a strong physical dependency.
    c. it produces intense withdrawal symptoms.
    d. it is easy to overdose on the substance.

((Listen to an **Audio File** of your chapter at **MyPsychLab**

Module 9: Sleep and Dreams

Understand the relationship between conscious and unconscious processes.

9.1 Describe the various states of consciousness.
- Consciousness is a person's awareness of everything that is going on at any given moment.
- Altered states of consciousness are shifts in the quality or pattern of mental activity.

9.2 Distinguish between explicit and implicit processing.
- Explicit processing is that which you are aware of and requires your attention, while implicit processing is "automatic."

Describe the characteristics of sleep and theories that explain why we sleep and dream.

9.3 Understand the circadian rhythm and its relation to sleep.
- The sleep–wake cycle is a circadian rhythm that occurs over a 24-hour period.

9.4 Outline theories about the functions of sleep.
- The theories of the function of sleep include adaptive theory to explain when we sleep and restorative theory to explain why we sleep.

9.5 Describe the characteristics of the sleep cycle.
- N1 (NREM Stage 1) sleep is light sleep.
- N2 (NREM Stage 2) sleep is indicated by the presence of sleep spindles, bursts of activity on the EEG.
- N3 (NREM Stages 3 and 4) is highlighted by the first appearance of delta waves.
- REM sleep occurs four or five times a night, replacing N1 after a full cycle.

9.6 Identify the types of sleep disorders.
- Sleep disorders and problems include: nightmares, night terrors, sleepwalking, insomnia, sleep apnea, and narcolepsy.

9.7 Compare perspectives on the functions of dreams.
- Freud believed dreams to be a form of wish fulfillment.
- The (AIM) Model states that information experienced during waking hours can influence the synthesis of dreams.

Module 10: Hypnosis and Drugs

Describe other states of consciousness.

10.1 Describe hypnosis and issues surrounding its nature and use.
- Hypnosis is a state of consciousness in which a person is especially susceptible to suggestion.
- Social-cognitive theory states that the hypnotized subject is merely playing a social role.

10.2 Understand meditation and relaxation and their effects.
- Meditation can produce a state of relaxation and reduce the physical reactions common to stressful situations.

10.3 Describe the nature of flow states.
- Flow states are peak experiences that include a shift in the perception of time and are intrinsically fulfilling.

Understand the categories of psychoactive drugs and their effects.

10.4 Explain how psychoactive drugs act at the synaptic level.
- Drugs that are physically addictive cause the user's body to crave the drug. When deprived of the drug, the user will go through physical withdrawal.

10.5 Evaluate the physiological and psychological effects of psychoactive drugs.
- Drug tolerance occurs as the user's body becomes conditioned to the level of the drug.
- In psychological dependence, the user believes that he or she needs the drug to function well and maintain a sense of well-being.

10.6 Characterize the major categories of psychoactive drugs and their effects.
- The major categories of drugs are stimulants, depressants, hallucinogens, and narcotics.

10.7 Describe how culture and expectations influence the use and experience of drugs.
- Cultural expectations through social sources like peers can have a positive or negative influence on the use of drugs and cultural forces can foster an open or prohibitive attitude toward the use of drugs.

Vocabulary Terms

consciousness p. 122
altered states of consciousness p. 123
circadian rhythm p. 124
adaptive theory p. 125
restorative theory p. 125
REM p. 126
non-REM p. 126

alpha waves p. 126
delta waves p. 126
insomnia p. 130
narcolepsy p. 131
activation-information-mode model (AIM) hypothesis p. 133
hypnosis p. 135

dissociation p. 136
social-cognitive theory of hypnosis p. 137
meditation p. 137
psychoactive drugs p. 138
physical dependence p. 139
withdrawal p. 139
psychological dependence p. 139

stimulants p. 140
depressants p. 140
hallucinogenics p. 140
narcotics p. 142
marijuana p. 143

Study and Review at **MyPsychLab**

Vocabulary Review

Match each vocabulary term to its definition.

1. altered state of consciousness
2. rapid eye movement (REM)
3. meditation
4. hypnosis
5. stimulants
6. depressants
7. narcotics
8. hallucinogenics
9. physical dependence
10. psychological dependence

a. Mental series of exercises meant to refocus attention and achieve a trancelike state of consciousness.

b. A class of opium-related drugs that suppress the sensation of pain by binding to and stimulating the nervous system's natural receptor sites for endorphins.

c. Stage of sleep in which the eyes move rapidly under the eyelids and the person is typically experiencing a dream.

d. The feeling that a drug is needed to continue a feeling of emotional or psychological well-being.

e. State of consciousness in which the person is especially susceptible to suggestion.

f. Drugs that increase the functioning of the nervous system.

g. State in which there is a shift in the quality or pattern of mental activity as compared to waking consciousness.

h. Drugs including marijuana that produce hallucinations or increased feelings of relaxation and intoxication.

i. Condition occurring when a person's body becomes unable to function normally without a particular drug.

j. Drugs that decrease the functioning of the nervous system.

Psychology Project

Meditation or resting peacefully can calm your mind, but can these practices also calm your body? Find out how sitting peacefully affects your heart rate.

Materials:
- a stopwatch or clock
- a quiet, comfortable place to sit
- meditation audio instructions or calming music (optional)

Instructions:

1. Plan a time to perform your experiment. Choose a time just after you have been engaging in normal activities like going to school or taking a walk. Do not perform the experiment immediately after sleeping or exercising.

2. Find your pulse on your neck or wrist (you may need someone to help you) and count how many heartbeats you feel in a 10-second period. Multiply this number by six to find your heart rate in beats per minute. This is your starting heart rate.

3. Sit in a quiet, comfortable place and meditate or rest peacefully for at least 20 minutes. You may wish to listen to calming music or follow instructions for guided meditation. Avoid thinking about anything that makes you feel stressed or excited.

4. After at least 20 minutes have passed, calculate your heart rate again, following the instructions in step 2. Has your heart rate changed? How do you think activities like meditation or resting peacefully affect the body?

Tech Alternative

Search an app store and find a hypnosis app (if a "hypnosis" app is not for you, perhaps a "meditation" app or a "mindfulness" app or a "relaxation" app will do). A typical hypnosis app contains a large number of files associated with various scenarios that people might be looking for help with in improving their well-being. Play through three to five of the files and pay attention not to the content of the files but instead pay attention to the presentation of the content.

Based on your observations, describe the approach that is being taken by the makers of the app files to create a product that engages with the app user's expectations of what hypnosis is and what hypnosis can do. Based on your understanding of hypnosis, describe what you think the benefit of such an app may or may not be and explain why you would or would not recommend such an app to a friend.

Essay Question

Alpa's friends believe that Alpa has developed a drug dependence. In an essay, using *one* term from each group, explain the effects and risks of a drug dependence, and the signs Alpa's friends may have noticed:

Group One
a. cocaine   **c.** heroin
b. alcohol   **d.** LSD

Group Two
a. Physical dependence
b. Physiological dependence

Group Three
a. Psychological pressures
b. Social pressures
c. Cultural pressures

Test Yourself

Ready for your test? More quizzes and a customized plan.

Pick the best answer.

✓ Study and Review at MyPsychLab

1. If Jane is aware of what is going on around her and what is going on within her, then it is safe to say that she is in a(n)
   a. state of waking consciousness.
   b. altered state of consciousness.
   c. unconscious state.
   d. preconscious state.

2. What part of the brain is influential in determining when to sleep?
   a. hippocampus
   b. hypothalamus
   c. thalamus
   d. frontal lobe

3. It might be best to say that adaptive theory explains _____, whereas restorative theory explains _____.
   a. when we sleep; why we need to sleep
   b. where we sleep; why we need to sleep
   c. why we need to sleep; where we sleep
   d. when we sleep; where we sleep

4. What is the result on Carlos's memory if he deprives himself of sleep the night prior to his exam?
   a. Carlos will retain information from staying up all night.
   b. Carlos will remember more if it is a cloudy day.
   c. Carlos will remember less if he deprives himself of sleep.
   d. Carlos's memory will not be affected in any way.

5. In REM sleep
   a. voluntary muscles are inhibited.
   b. the body sleeps deeply.
   c. brain wave activity is very slow.
   d. people are rarely dreaming.

6. Hypnogogic images are experienced in ___ sleep.
   a. N1
   b. N2
   c. N3
   d. REM

7. In N3 sleep
   a. people are seldom aware they were asleep if awakened.
   b. people typically experience hypnic jerks of the muscles.
   c. the EEG will show the first signs of sleep spindles.
   d. people experience the deepest stage of sleep.

8. Nightmares are often more common in childhood, most likely because children
   a. spend more time in deep sleep.
   b. are so easily awakened in deep sleep stage.
   c. spend more time in REM sleep than adults.
   d. need less sleep than adults.

9. In which stage of sleep are dreams most likely to occur?
   a. N1 (NREM Stage 1)
   b. N2 (NREM Stage 2)
   c. N3 (NREM Stage
   d. REM

10. What is another name for somnambulism?
    a. insomnia
    b. sleepwalking
    c. sleep apnea
    d. narcolepsy

11. Though Josef's work is not physically challenging, it tends to mentally drain him. What type of sleep will Josef require more of?
    a. N1 (NREM Stage 1)
    b. N2 (NREM Stage 2)
    c. N3 (NREM Stage 3)
    d. REM sleep

12. Gerald has difficulty falling to sleep. Harley falls a sleep but often wakes up early. Dale typically sleeps for 10 hours. All three are not rested upon rising. Who seems to be experiencing insomnia?
    a. Gerald
    b. Harley
    c. Dale
    d. All three suffer from insomnia.

13. Bill suddenly and without warning slips into REM sleep during the day. Bill may have a condition called
    a. sleep apnea.
    b. insomnia.
    c. narcolepsy.
    d. epilepsy.

14. Why might some very young infants have difficulty breathing?
    a. Many of these infants are obese and therefore their airways are obstructed.
    b. The brain stem is not yet fully mature.
    c. The tissue lining in the nasal passageway may be obstructing their airflow.
    d. No medical explanation has been determined.

15. Tawny is bothered by the fact that her dreams often seem to jump randomly from scene to scene with little meaning. What theory best explains her dreams?
    a. activation-synthesis
    b. dreams-for-survival
    c. sociocultural theory
    d. Freudian

16. Anthony's therapist is using hypnosis to help him recall difficult memories. Danny's therapist is using hypnosis to help him prepare for the pain of dental surgery. Patrick's therapist is using hypnosis to help him quit drinking. Which client has the highest chance for success?
    a. Anthony
    b. Danny
    c. Patrick
    d. All three can benefit from hypnosis.

17. While hypnotized, Bobby stood on his chair and crowed like a rooster. Bobby said later that he had to do those things because he was hypnotized. What theory best explains his behavior?
    a. the hidden observer theory of hypnosis
    b. the social-cognitive explanation of hypnosis
    c. the biological theory of hypnosis
    d. the behavioral theory of hypnosis

18. Which of the following is *not* one of the effects of meditation?
    a. reduced chronic pain
    b. reduced anxiety
    c. reduced need for sleep
    d. lower blood pressure

19. Jackie has found that when she tries to quit drinking, she shakes uncontrollably. Such a reaction is an example of
    a. psychological dependence.
    b. overdose.
    c. withdrawal.
    d. learned behavior.

20. What is the most commonly used and abused depressant?
    a. alcohol
    b. Prozac
    c. tranquilizers
    d. caffeine

Learning Objectives

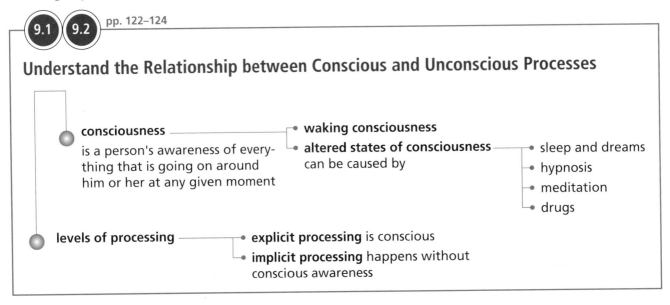

9.1 9.2 pp. 122–124

Understand the Relationship between Conscious and Unconscious Processes

consciousness ————————— • **waking consciousness**
is a person's awareness of every- | • **altered states of consciousness** ——— • sleep and dreams
thing that is going on around | can be caused by | • hypnosis
him or her at any given moment | | • meditation
| | • drugs

levels of processing ————— • **explicit processing** is conscious
• **implicit processing** happens without
  conscious awareness

Learning Objectives

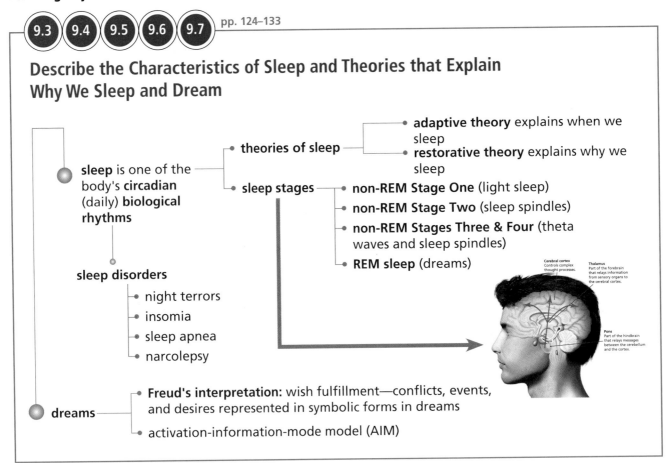

9.3 9.4 9.5 9.6 9.7 pp. 124–133

Describe the Characteristics of Sleep and Theories that Explain Why We Sleep and Dream

theories of sleep ——— • **adaptive theory** explains when we
sleep
sleep is one of the | • **restorative theory** explains why we
body's **circadian** | sleep
(daily) biological ——— • **sleep stages** ——— • **non-REM Stage One** (light sleep)
rhythms | • **non-REM Stage Two** (sleep spindles)
| • **non-REM Stages Three & Four** (theta
| waves and sleep spindles)
| • **REM sleep** (dreams)

sleep disorders
• night terrors
• insomia
• sleep apnea
• narcolepsy

Cerebral cortex
Controls complex
thought processes.

Thalamus
Part of the forebrain
that relays information
from sensory organs to
the cerebral cortex.

Pons
Part of the hindbrain
that relays messages
between the cerebellum
and the cortex.

dreams ——— • **Freud's interpretation:** wish fulfillment—conflicts, events,
and desires represented in symbolic forms in dreams
• activation-information-mode model (AIM)

Learning Objectives

10.1 10.2 10.3 pp. 135–138

Map the Concepts at MyPsychLab

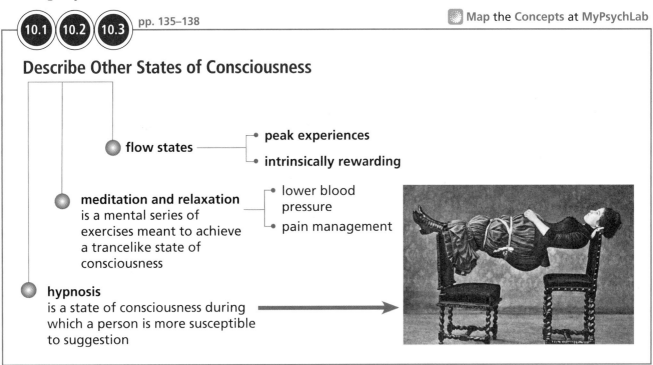

Describe Other States of Consciousness

flow states — • **peak experiences**
— • **intrinsically rewarding**

meditation and relaxation is a mental series of exercises meant to achieve a trancelike state of consciousness — • lower blood pressure
— • pain management

hypnosis is a state of consciousness during which a person is more susceptible to suggestion

Learning Objectives

10.4 10.5 10.6 10.7 pp. 138–145

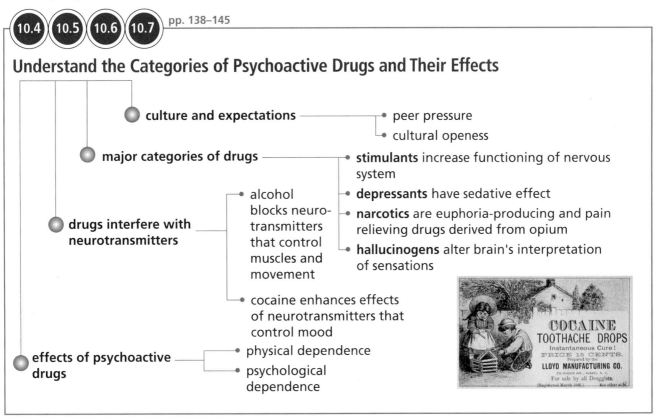

Understand the Categories of Psychoactive Drugs and Their Effects

culture and expectations — • peer pressure
— • cultural openess

major categories of drugs — • **stimulants** increase functioning of nervous system
— • **depressants** have sedative effect
— • **narcotics** are euphoria-producing and pain relieving drugs derived from opium
— • **hallucinogens** alter brain's interpretation of sensations

drugs interfere with neurotransmitters — • alcohol blocks neuro-transmitters that control muscles and movement
— • cocaine enhances effects of neurotransmitters that control mood

effects of psychoactive drugs — • physical dependence
— • psychological dependence

COCAINE TOOTHACHE DROPS
Instantaneous Cure!
PRICE 15 CENTS.
Prepared by the
LLOYD MANUFACTURING CO.
For sale by all Druggists.

CHAPTER

5 Development Across the Life Span

At a time when many teenagers are hanging out at the mall with friends, 16-year-old Jessica Watson was on a mission to become the youngest individual to sail nonstop and unassisted around the world. She left Sydney, Australia, on October 18, 2009, and returned seven months later, on May 15, 2010, unofficially breaking the previous record (Marks, 2010; Munoz, 2010). Watson's record will remain unrecognized, however. The World Speed Sailing Record Council did away with its "youngest" category to discourage what it considers dangerous and foolhardy attempts by those who are too young. Adolescence is one among many stages of life that we will explore in this chapter. Although we will focus on several of the common features of human development in all of those stages, the story of Jessica Watson should be a reminder that each of us is an individual, with different motivations, goals, and desires.

How have you changed since your childhood years? In what ways are you similar to other individuals of your age and in what ways are you different and unique?

Watch the **Video**, at **MyPsychLab**

*W*hy Study **Human Development**?

Beginning to understand how we come to be the people we are is a critical step in understanding ourselves as we are today and who we may become as we grow older. From the moment of conception, each of us is headed down a pathway of change, influenced by our biology, environment, and social interactions, to a final destination that is the same for all of us. The twists and turns of the pathway are what make each of us unique individuals. In this chapter, we'll look at the influences that help determine our developmental pathway through life.

11 Topics in Development

Learning Objectives

11.1 Understand methods used to study development.

11.2 Describe the issues of continuity/discontinuity and stability/change.

11.3 Describe how environmental and biological factors interact in development.

Describe Methods and Issues in Life Span Development

What is development? In the context of life, **human development** is the scientific study of the changes that occur in people as they age, from conception until death. This chapter will touch on almost all of the topics covered in the other chapters of this text, such as personality, cognition, biological processes, and social interactions. Yet, in this chapter, all of those topics will be studied in the context of changes that occur as a result of the process of human development.

11.1 Understand methods used to study development.

Research Designs Research in development is affected by the problem of age. In any experiment, the participants who are exposed to the independent variable (the variable in an experiment that is deliberately manipulated by the experimenter) should be randomly assigned to the different experimental conditions. The problem in developmental research is that the age of the people in the study should always be an independent variable, but people cannot be randomly assigned to different age groups.

Special designs used in researching age-related changes are the **longitudinal design**, in which one group of people is followed and assessed at different times as the group ages; the **cross-sectional design**, in which several different age-groups are studied at one time; and the **cross-sequential design**, which is a combination of the longitudinal and cross-sectional designs (Baltes et al., 1988; Schaie & Willis, 2010).

The longitudinal design has the advantage of looking at real age-related changes as those changes occur in the same individuals. The disadvantages of this method are the lengthy amount of time, money, and effort involved in following participants over the years as well as the loss of participants when they move away, lose interest, or die. The cross-sectional design has the advantages of being quick, relatively inexpensive, and easier to accomplish than the longitudinal design. The main disadvantage is that one is no longer comparing changes in the same individuals as they age; instead, individuals of different ages are being compared to one another. Differences between age groups are often a problem in developmental research. For example, in comparing the IQ scores of 30-year-olds to 80-year-olds to see how aging affects intelligence, questions arise concerning the differing experiences those two age-groups have had in educational

human development the scientific study of the changes that occur in people as they age from conception until death.

longitudinal design research design in which one participant or group of participants is studied over a long period of time.

cross-sectional design research design in which several different age-groups of participants are studied at one particular point in time.

cross-sequential design research design in which participants are first studied by means of a cross-sectional design but are also followed and assessed for a period of no more than six years.

Table 11.1	A Comparison of Three Developmental Research Designs		
Cross-Sectional Design			
Different participants of various ages are compared at one point in time to determine age-related *differences*.	**Group One:** 20-year-old participants **Group Two:** 40-year-old participants **Group Three:** 60-year-old participants		Research done in 2012
Longitudinal Design			
The **same** participants are studied at various ages to determine age-related changes.	**Study One:** 20-year-old participants		Research done in 1972
	Study Two: Same participants are 40 years old		Research done in 1992
	Study Three: Same participants are now 60 years old		Research done in 2012
Cross-Sequential Design			
Different participants of various ages are compared at several points in time, for a period of no more than six years, to determine both age-related differences and age-related changes.	**Study One:** **Group One:** 20-year-old participants **Group Two:** 40-year-old participants		Research done in 2012
	Study Two: **Group One:** participants will be 25 years old **Group Two:** participants will be 45 years old		Research to be done in 2017

opportunities that might affect IQ scores in addition to any effects of aging. This is known as the *cohort effect*, the particular impact on development that occurs when a group of people share a common time period or common life experience (for example, having been born in the same time period or having gone through a specific historical event together). **Table 11.1** shows a comparison of a longitudinal design, a cross-sectional design, and a cross-sequential design.

In studying human development, developmental psychologists have outlined many theories of how these age-related changes occur. There are some areas of controversy, however, and one of these is the issue of nature versus nurture.

11.2 Describe the issues of continuity/discontinuity and stability/change.

As a field of research, developmental psychology is particularly concerned with two big questions:

- **Continuity or discontinuity:** Does development happen in a smooth, continuous progression, or in a series of clear-cut stages?
- **Stability or change:** What remains stable over the course of human development, and what changes?

Neither question has a simple answer; it depends largely on which aspect of development is under discussion. The characteristics psychologists examine fall into three broad areas: physical, cognitive, and psychosocial development. *Physical development*, or development of the body, is fairly discontinuous, occurring in clearly defined stages that are distinct from each other. *Cognitive development*, or development of thinking and reasoning skills, is fairly continuous, and it

dominant referring to a gene that actively controls the expression of a trait.

recessive referring to a gene that influences the expression of a trait only when paired with an identical gene.

changes over time. *Psychosocial development* encompasses our emotional and social lives. Aspects that are studied include *temperament*, a child's innate personality and emotional characteristics; *attachment*, the first emotional bond a child forms with its primary caretaker; and finally, the psychological characteristics and social relationships a person has throughout childhood, adolescence, and adulthood. Research suggests that temperament is somewhat influenced by the environment but, like attachment style, remains fairly stable over time.

11.3 Describe how environmental and biological factors interact in development.

Nature Versus Nurture For years, psychologists have tried to understand what influences our behavior more—biological or environmental factors. Nature refers to heredity, the influence of inherited characteristics on personality, physical growth, intellectual growth, and social interactions. Nurture refers to the influence of the environment on all of those same things and includes parenting styles, physical surroundings, economic factors, and anything that can have an influence on development that does not come from within the person.

How much of a person's personality and behavior is determined by nature, and how much is determined by nurture? This is a key question, and the answer is quite complicated. After many years of scientific research, most developmental psychologists now agree that the most likely explanation for most of human development is this: All that people are and all that people become is the product of an interaction between nature and nurture (Davis et al., 2012; Insel & Wang, 2010; Ridley, 1999; Sternberg & Grigorenko, 2006). For instance, a girl's genes may determine that she will grow up to be tall and have swift reflexes. However, genetics alone will not make her a star basketball player. (L)(I)(N)(K) *to Chapter Two: The Biological Perspective, pp. 68–71.*

So, are people like Gandhi or Mother Theresa born that way, or did something happen to make them the people they were? ▶

FIGURE 11.1 DNA Molecule
In this model of a DNA molecule, the two strands making up the sides of the "twisted ladder" are composed of sugars and phosphates. The "rungs" of the ladder that link the two strands are amines. Amines contain the genetic codes for building the proteins that make up organic life.

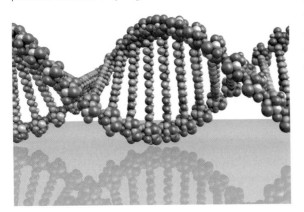

Genetic Influences Any study of the human life span must begin with looking at the complex material contained in the cells of the body that carries the instructions for life itself. After discussing the basic building blocks of life, we will discuss how the processes of conception and the development of the infant within the womb take place.

The basic building blocks of life are special DNA molecules that contain the instructions for all of an organism's traits (see **Figure 11.1**). These "instructions" known as genes are sections of the DNA molecules. Genes that are more active in influencing a trait are called **dominant**. A dominant gene will always be expressed in the observable trait. Some disorders, such as Huntington's disease (a genetic disorder that affects muscle coordination) and Marfan's syndrome (genetic disorder that affects the body's connective tissue), are carried by dominant genes. In these disorders, only one parent needs to have the gene for the disorder to be passed on to offspring. More often genetic disorders are carried by recessive genes. **Recessive** genes tend to recede, or fade, into the background when paired with a dominant gene. Diseases carried by recessive genes are only inherited when a child receives two recessive genes, one from each parent. Examples of disorders inherited in this manner are cystic fibrosis (a disease of the respiratory and digestive tracts), sickle-cell anemia (a blood disorder), Tay-Sachs disorder (a fatal neurological disorder), and phenylketonuria or PKU (a problem with digesting the amino acid phenylalanine, which can lead to brain damage).

Chromosomes are rod-shaped structures found in the nucleus of each cell and are nothing more than tightly wound strands of genes. Sometimes the chromosome itself is the problem. Although each egg and each sperm (the sex cells for females and males, respectively) is only supposed to have 23 chromosomes, in the division of these cells a chromosome can end up in the wrong cell, leaving one cell with only 22 and the other with 24. If either of these cells survives to "mate," the missing or extra chromosome can cause mild to severe problems in development (American Academy of Pediatrics, 1995; Barnes & Carey, 2002; Centers for Disease Control, 2009; Gardner & Sutherland, 1996).

Examples of chromosome disorders include Trisomy-21, also called Down syndrome (LINK *to Chapter Two: The Biological Perspective, pp. 69–71*), and Fragile X syndrome, a genetic disorder caused by an abnormality of an overabundance of a DNA segment within a particular gene on the X chromosome. Symptoms of Fragile X tend to be more subtle than those of Down syndrome, and include large ears, a prominent chin and/or forehead, unusually flexible fingers, and in boys, large testes. Persons with Fragile X syndrome may also have intellectual disabilities. Symptoms are typically more severe in males than in females.

▲ *Fragile X symptoms, though subtle, can include a prominent chin and forehead and large, protruding ears.*

Environmental Influences The environmental influences that surround us before birth and during our lives significantly affect our development. These influences include our immediate environment, such as family and friends, as well as the larger culture in which we participate. Parents or other caretakers influence children's behavior, knowledge and skills, and values. In early childhood, caretakers model the most basic human behaviors, such as talking and eating. Later, children encounter a wider circle of influences. They may participate in a sport or develop academic interests because of a friend or teacher. Finally, the culture at large influences personality and behavior. For instance, in many parts of the United States, most people learn to drive in their mid- to late-teens. A teenager from a culture that places less importance on driving might not learn this skill until much later, if ever.

▲ *Do you participate in team sports, or plan to someday? The decision to to do so (or not) is impacted by your cultural values.*

Pick the best answer.

1. In what type of research design are several different age groups of participants studied at one point in time?

   a. case study
   b. longitudinal
   c. cross-sectional
   d. cross-sequential

2. Which of these is generally true of recessive genes?

   a. They are not located on the chromosome.
   b. They are not expressed unless paired with a similar gene.
   c. They are the cause of genetic defects.
   d. They do not determine specific traits.

3. Which of the following affects the human brain's development?

   a. genetic influences
   b. environmental influences
   c. both genetic and environmental influences
   d. neither genetic nor environmental influences

4. Which aspect of development is the least continuous?

   a. physical development
   b. cognitive development
   c. emotional development
   d. social development

5. Which of these is an example of nature affecting development?

   a. a class taken in school
   b. an inherited mental illness
   c. peer pressure from other children
   d. imitation of a parent's actions

6. If a woman's diet in the first weeks of pregnancy does not include enough folic acid, it may permanently harm the baby's brain development. This period could be described as

   a. temperamental.
   b. insensitive.
   c. critical.
   d. continuous.

7. Which of the following is the most stable over time?

   a. one's body
   b. one's temperament
   c. one's moral reasoning
   d. one's social relationships

8. Studying the same group of people as they age and assessing them at a different time is using the:

   a. sequential design.
   b. discontinuity design.
   c. longitudinal design.
   d. environmental design.

9. A group of people sharing a common time period or common life experience that gives them unique characteristics is called:

   a. a cohort effect.
   b. a biological effect.
   c. a stability effect.
   d. recessive effect.

10. Which of the following areas is fairly continuous?

    a. physical development
    b. cognitive development
    c. biological development
    d. sensitive development

12 Prenatal, Infant and Childhood Development

Module Goals	Learning Objectives
Learn about prenatal and newborn development.	**12.1** Trace physical development from conception through birth and identify influences on prenatal development.
	12.2 Explain the role of sensitive and critical periods in development.
Describe development during infancy and childhood.	**12.3** Learn about childhood physical and motor development.
	12.4 Explain how cognitive abilities develop during childhood.
	12.5 Outline the development of communication and language.
	12.6 Explain temperament, the development of attachment, and the role of the caregiver.
	12.7 Discuss social, cultural, and emotional development through childhood.

Learn about Prenatal and Newborn Development

From conception to the actual birth of the baby is a period of approximately 9 months, during which a single fertilized egg cell, which carries all the genetic information needed, will develop into a complete infant. It is also during this time that many things can have a positive or negative influence on the developing infant.

12.1 Trace physical development from conception through birth and identify influences on prenatal development.

Fertilization, the Zygote, and Twinning When an egg (also called an *ovum*) and a sperm unite in the process of *fertilization*, the resulting single cell will have a total of 46 chromosomes and is called a *zygote*. Normally, the zygote will begin to divide, first into two cells, then four, then eight, and so on, with each new cell also having 46 chromosomes because the DNA molecules produce duplicates of themselves before each division. (This division process is called mitosis.) Eventually, the mass of cells becomes a baby. When this division process doesn't work exactly this way, twins or multiples are sometimes the result.

There are actually two main types of twins. Twins who are commonly referred to as "identical" are **monozygotic twins**, meaning that the two babies come from one (mono) fertilized egg (zygote). Early in the division process, the

monozygotic twins identical twins formed when one zygote splits into two separate masses of cells, each of which develops into a separate embryo.

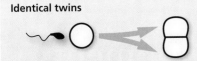

Identical twins

1 Accounting for about 1 in 250 births, these are created when a single egg is fertilized by one sperm.

2 The egg splits into halves. Each develops into a fetus with the same genetic composition.

Fraternal twins

1 Twice as common as identicals, fraternals arise when two eggs are released at once.

2 If both are fertilized by separate sperm, two fetuses form. Genetically, they are just ordinary siblings.

FIGURE 12.1 Monozygotic and Dizygotic Twins
Because identical twins come from one fertilized egg (zygote), they are called monozygotic. Fraternal twins, who come from two different fertilized eggs, are called dizygotic.

How does a mass of cells become a baby with eyes, nose, hands, feet, and so on? How do all those different things come from the same original single cell?

dizygotic twins often called fraternal twins, occurring when two eggs each get fertilized by two different sperm, resulting in two zygotes in the uterus at the same time.

germinal period first two weeks after fertilization, during which the zygote moves down to the uterus and begins to implant in the lining.

mass of cells splits completely—no one knows exactly why—into two separate masses, each of which will develop into a separate infant. The infants will be the same sex and have identical features because they each possess the same set of 46 chromosomes. Nonidentical twins are more an accident of timing and are more common in women who are older and who are from certain ethnic groups (Allen & Parisi, 1990; Bonnelykke, 1990; Imaizumi, 1998). A woman's body may release more than one egg at a time or release an egg after she has already conceived once. If two eggs are fertilized, the woman may give birth to fraternal or **dizygotic twins** (two zygotes) or possibly triplets or some other multiple number of babies (Bryan & Hallett, 2001). This is also more likely to happen to women who are taking fertility drugs to help them get pregnant. (See **Figure 12.1.**)

Twins are important because they provide developmental psychologists with another way to look at the contribution of nature and nurture to human development. Researchers may seek out genetically identical twins who have been separated at birth and adopted into different families, looking at all the ways those twins are alike in spite of being raised in different environments, as well as comparing adopted children to their adoptive parents and to their biological parents.

Sometimes in the twinning process, the mass of cells does not completely split apart. When this occurs, the resulting conjoined twins will be joined at the point where the two cell masses remained "stuck." Sometimes this joining may involve only soft tissues. It may also involve the sharing of certain body parts. It is estimated that conjoined twins are born only one in 100,000 births, and the survival of both is rare (Martínez-Frías et al., 2009).

The Three Stages of Development There are three stages of prenatal development: the germinal period, the embryonic period, and the fetal period.

▶ **The Germinal Period** Once fertilization has taken place, the zygote begins dividing and moving down to the uterus, the muscular organ that will contain and protect the developing organism. This process takes about a week, followed by about a week during which the mass of cells, now forming a hollow ball, firmly attaches itself to the wall of the uterus. This two-week period is called the **germinal period** of pregnancy.

During the germinal period, the cells begin to differentiate, which means they are developing into specialized cells, in preparation for becoming all the various kinds of cells that make up the human body—skin cells, heart cells, and so on. Perhaps the most important of these cells are the stem cells, which stay in a somewhat immature state until needed to produce more cells. Researchers are currently looking into ways to use stem cells found in the umbilical cord to grow new organs and tissues for transplant or to repair neurological damage (Chen & Ende, 2000; Holden & Vogel, 2002; Lu & Ende, 1997; Moreno-Manzano et al., 2009).

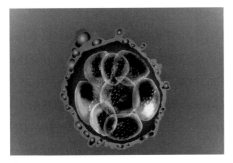 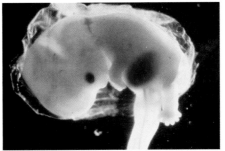 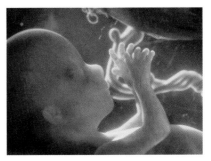

▲ The three periods of pregnancy are the germinal period, lasting about two weeks, the embryonic period, from about two to eight weeks, and fetal period, which lasts from eight weeks until the end of pregnancy.

The Embryonic Period Once firmly attached to the uterus, the developing organism is called an *embryo*. The **embryonic period** will last from two weeks after conception to eight weeks, and during this time the cells will continue to specialize and become the various organs and structures of a human infant. By the end of eight weeks after conception, the embryo is about 1 inch long and has primitive* eyes, nose, lips, teeth, little arms and legs, and a beating heart. Although no organ is fully developed or completely functional at this time, nearly all are "there."

The Fetal Period: Grow, Baby, Grow The **fetal period** is a period of tremendous growth lasting from about eight weeks after conception until birth. The length of the developing organism (now referred to as a *fetus*) increases by about 20 times, and its weight increases from about 1 ounce at 2 months to a little over 7 pounds. The organs, while accomplishing most of their differentiation in the embryonic period, continue to develop and become functional. At this time, teratogens, discussed in the following section, will more likely affect the physical functioning (physiology) of the organs rather than their structure.

12.2 Explain the role of sensitive and critical periods in development.

Critical Periods As soon as the embryo begins to receive nourishment from the mother through the placenta, it becomes vulnerable† to hazards such as diseases of the mother, drugs, and other toxins that can pass from the mother through the placenta to the developing infant. Because of the direct connection between mother and embryo and the fact that all major organs are in the process of forming, we can most clearly see the effects of **critical periods** (also referred to as *sensitive periods*), times during which some environmental influence can have an impact—often devastating—on the development of the infant.

Prenatal Hazards: Teratogens Any substance such as a drug, chemical, virus, or other factor that can cause a birth defect is called a **teratogen** (the word terato literally means monster and the suffix –gen means to produce). **Table 12.1** shows some common teratogens and their possible negative effects on the developing embryo.

One of the more common teratogens is alcohol. Consumption of alcohol during pregnancy, particularly during the critical embryonic period, can lead to *fetal alcohol syndrome (FAS)*, a series of physical and mental defects including stunted growth, facial deformities, and brain damage (Ethen et al., 2008; Guerri, 2002). Exposure to alcohol in early pregnancy is the leading known cause of

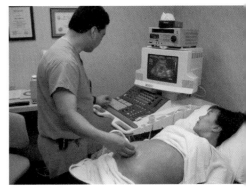

▲ This pregnant woman is getting a sonogram. Sonograms allow doctors to see any physical deformities and make accurate measurements of gestational age without risk to the mother or the fetus.

embryonic period the period from two to eight weeks after fertilization, during which the major organs and structures of the organism develop.

fetal period the time from about eight weeks after conception until the birth of the child.

critical periods times during which certain environmental influences can have an impact on the development of the infant.

teratogen any factor that can cause a birth defect.

---

*primitive: having the characteristics of an early stage of development.
†vulnerable: susceptible to harm.

Table 12.1	Common Teratogens
TERATOGENIC AGENT	EFFECT ON DEVELOPMENT
Measles, Mumps, and Rubella	Blindness, deafness, heart defects, brain damage
Marijuana	Irritability, nervousness, tremors; infant is easily disturbed, startled
Cocaine	Decreased height, low birth weight, respiratory problems, seizures, learning difficulties; infant is difficult to soothe
Alcohol	Fetal alcohol syndrome (intellectual disability, delayed growth, facial malformation), learning difficulties, smaller than normal heads
Nicotine	Miscarriage, low birth weight, stillbirth, short stature, intellectual disability, learning disabilities
Mercury	Intellectual disability, blindness
Vitamin A (high doses)	Facial, ear, central nervous system, and heart defects
Caffeine	Miscarriage, low birth weight
Toxoplasmosis	Brain swelling, spinal abnormalities, deafness, blindness, intellectual disability
High Water Temperatures	Increased chance of neural tube defects

Sources: March of Dimes Foundation (2009); Organization of Teratology Information Specialists (2011); Shepard, T. H. (2001)

intellectual disability (previously called mental retardation) in the Western hemisphere (Abel & Sokol, 1987; Caley et al., 2005). So how much alcohol is safe to drink while pregnant? The answer is clearly "none!"

Describe Development During Infancy and Childhood

Surprisingly, babies can do a lot more than researchers used to believe they could. Since those early days, researchers have developed ways of studying what infants cannot tell us in words.

12.3 Learn about childhood physical and motor development.

Physical Development Immediately after birth, several things start to happen. The respiratory system begins to function, filling the lungs with air and putting oxygen into the blood. The blood now circulates only within the infant's system because the umbilical cord has been cut. Body temperature is now regulated by the infant's own activity and body fat (which acts as insulation) rather than by the amniotic fluid.

Reflexes Babies come into this world able to interact with it. Infants have a set of innate (existing from birth) involuntary behavior patterns called reflexes. Until an infant is capable of learning more complex means of interaction, reflexes help the infant to survive. **Figure 12.2** shows five infant reflexes. Pediatricians use

a.

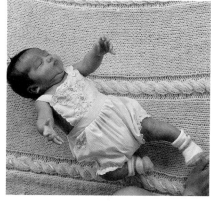
b.

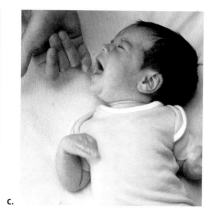
c.

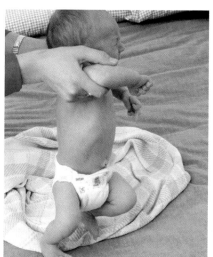
d.

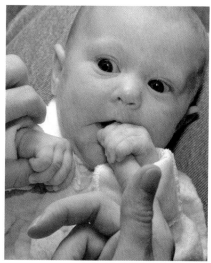
e.

FIGURE 12.2 Five Infant Reflexes
Shown here are (a) grasping reflex, (b) startle reflex (also known as the Moro reflex), (c) rooting reflex (when you touch a baby's cheek it will turn toward your hand, open its mouth, and search for the nipple), (d) stepping reflex, and (e) sucking reflex. These infant reflexes can be used to check on the health of an infant's nervous system. If a reflex is absent or abnormal, it may indicate brain damage or some other neurological problem.

these and other reflexes to determine whether or not an infant's nervous system is working properly.

Motor Development From crawling to a blur of motion, infants manage a tremendous amount of development in motor skills from birth to about 2 years of age. **Figure 12.3** shows some of the major physical milestones of infancy. When looking at the age ranges listed, remember that even these ranges are averages based on large samples of infants. An infant may reach these milestones earlier or later than the average and still be considered to be developing normally.

Brain Development At birth, an infant's brain consists of over 100 billion neurons. Rapid and extensive growth of these neurons occurs as the brain triples in weight from birth to age 3 years, with much of the increase caused by growth of new dendrites, axon terminals, and increasing numbers of synaptic connections (Nelson, 2011). This is a natural process and exceedingly stimulating "smart baby" toys will not enhance the development of the neural network. Normal experiences, and plenty of them, like different tastes, smells, touches, sounds, and stimulating visuals are all a baby needs to have optimum brain development. Surprisingly, the development of the infant brain after birth involves a necessary loss of neurons called *synaptic pruning*, as unused synaptic connections and nerve cells are cleared away to make way for functioning connections and cells (Couperus & Nelson, 2006; Graven & Browne, 2008; Kozberg et al., 2013). This process is similar to weeding your garden—you take out the weeds to make room for the plants that you want.

◀ What can babies do? Aren't they pretty much unaware of what's going on around them at first?

FIGURE 12.3 Six Motor Milestones

Shown here are (a) raising head and chest—2 to 4 months, (b) rolling over—2 to 5 months, (c) sitting up with support—4 to 6 months, (d) sitting up without support—6 to 7 months, (e) crawling—7 to 8 months, and (f) walking—8 to 18 months. The motor milestones develop as the infant gains greater voluntary control over the muscles in his or her body, typically from the top of the body downward. This pattern is seen in the early control of the neck muscles and the much later development of control of the legs and feet.

I've heard that babies can't see or hear very much at birth. Is that true? ▶

Baby, Can You See Me? Baby, Can You Hear Me? Sensory Development

Researchers have developed a couple of methods to help gauge infant's abilities. Two common methods are the use of *preferential looking* and *habituation*. Preferential looking assumes that the longer an infant spends looking at a stimulus, the more the infant prefers that stimulus over others (Fantz, 1961). Habituation is the tendency for infants (and adults) to stop paying attention to a stimulus that does not change. By exposing the infant to an unchanging sound or picture, for example, researchers can wait for the infant to habituate (look away) and then change the stimulus. If the infant reacts (dishabituates), the infant is capable of detecting that change (Columbo & Mitchell, 2009).

Although most infant sensory abilities are fairly well developed at birth, some require a bit more time to reach "full power." By using techniques such as the habituation method researchers have found that the sense of touch is the most well developed, which makes perfect sense when one realizes how much skin-to-womb contact the baby has had in the last months of pregnancy. The sense of smell is also highly developed. Breast-fed babies can actually tell the difference between their own mother's milk scent and another woman's milk scent within a few days after birth.

Taste is also nearly fully developed. At birth, infants show a preference for sweets (and human breast milk is very sweet) and by four months have developed a preference for salty tastes (which may come from exposure to the salty taste of their mother's skin). Sour and bitter, two other taste sensations, produce spitting up and the making of horrible faces (Ganchrow et al., 1983).

Hearing is functional before birth but may take a little while to reach its full potential after birth. The fluids of the womb must clear out completely. From birth, newborns seem most responsive to high pitches, as in a woman's voice, and low pitches, as in a male's voice.

The least functional sense at birth is vision. The eye is quite a complex organ. The rods, which see in black and white and have little visual acuity, are fairly well developed at birth, but the cones, which see color and provide sharpness of vision, will take about another six months to fully develop.

So the newborn has relatively poor color perception when compared to sharply contrasting lights and darks until about two months of age (Adams, 1987) and has fairly "fuzzy" vision, much as a nearsighted person would have. The lens of the newborn stays fixed until the muscles that hold it in place mature. Until then the newborn is unable to shift what little focus it has from close to far. Thus, newborns actually have a fixed distance for clear vision of about 7 to 10 inches, which is the distance from the baby's face to the mother's face while nursing (Slater, 2000).

12.4 Explain how cognitive abilities develop during childhood.

By the time the average infant has reached the age of 1 year, it has tripled its birth weight and added about another foot to its height. The brain triples its weight in the first two years, reaching about 75 percent of its adult weight. By age 5, the brain is at 90 percent of its adult weight. This increase makes possible a tremendous amount of major advances in *cognitive development*, including the development of thinking, problem solving, and memory.

Piaget's Theory: Four Stages of Cognitive Development One way of examining the development of cognition is found in the work of Jean Piaget. Piaget believed, based on observations of his own children and others, that children form mental concepts or **schema** as they experience new situations and events. For example, if Sandy points to a picture of an apple and tells her child, "that's an apple," the child forms a schema for "apple" that looks something like that picture. Children first try to understand new things in terms of schemata (plural for schema) they already possess in a process called assimilation. The child might see an orange and say "apple" because both objects are round. When corrected, the child might alter the schema for apple to include "round" and "red" in a process called accommodation (Piaget, 1952, 1962, 1983).

Piaget also proposed that there are four distinct stages of cognitive development that occur from infancy to adolescence, as shown in the video *Piaget's Stages* and in **Table 12.2** (Piaget, 1952, 1962, 1983).

The Sensorimotor Stage The **sensorimotor stage** is the first of Piaget's stages. It concerns infants from birth to age 2. In this stage, infants use their senses and motor abilities to learn about the world around them. At first, infants only have the involuntary reflexes present at birth to interact with objects and people. As their sensory and motor development progresses, they begin to interact deliberately with objects by grasping, pushing, tasting, and so on. Infants move from simple repetitive actions, such as grabbing their toes, to complex patterns, such as trying to put a shape into a sorting box.

By the end of the sensorimotor stage, infants have fully developed a sense of **object permanence**, the knowledge that an object exists even when it is not in sight. For example, the game of "peek-a-boo" is important in teaching infants that Mommy's smiling face is always going to be behind her hands. This is a critical step in developing language (and eventually abstract thought), as words themselves are symbols of things that may not be present. Symbolic thought,

schema in this case, a mental concept formed through experiences with objects and events.

sensorimotor stage Piaget's first stage of cognitive development in which the infant uses its senses and motor abilities to interact with objects in the environment.

object permanence the knowledge that an object exists even when it is not in sight.

👁 **Watch** the **Video**, *Piaget's Stages*, at **MyPsychLab**

Table 12.2	Piaget's Stages of Cognitive Development	
STAGE		COGNITIVE DEVELOPMENT
Sensorimotor	Birth to 2 years old	Children explore the world using their senses and ability to move. They develop object permanence and the understanding that concepts and mental images represent objects, people, and events.
Preoperational	2 to 7 years old	Young children can mentally represent and refer to objects and events with words or pictures, and they can pretend. However, they can't conserve, logically reason, or simultaneously consider many characteristics of an object.
Concrete Operations	7 to 12 years old	Children at this stage are able to conserve, reverse their thinking, and classify objects in terms of their many characteristics. They can also think logically and understand analogies but only about concrete events.
Formal Operations	12 years old to adulthood	People at this stage can use abstract reasoning about hypothetical events or situations, think about logical possibilities, use abstract analogies, and systematically examine and test hypotheses. Not everyone can eventually reason in all these ways.

Why is it so easy for children to believe in Santa Claus and the Tooth Fairy when they're little? ▶

preoperational stage Piaget's second stage of cognitive development in which the preschool child learns to use language as a means of exploring the world.

egocentrism the inability to see the world through anyone else's eyes.

which is the ability to represent objects in one's thoughts with symbols such as words, becomes possible by the end of this stage, with children at 2 years old capable of thinking in simple symbols and planning out actions.

The Preoperational Stage The **preoperational stage** (ages 2–7) is a time of developing language and concepts. Children, who can now move freely about in their world, no longer have to rely only on senses and motor skills but now can ask questions and explore their surroundings more fully. Pretending and make-believe play become possible because children at this stage can understand, through symbolic thinking, that a line of wooden blocks can "stand in" for a train. They are limited, however, in several ways. They are not yet capable of logical thought—they can use simple mental concepts but are not able to use those concepts in a more rational, logical sense. They believe that anything that moves is alive, a quality called animism. They tend to believe that what they see is literally true, so when children of this age see Santa Claus in a book, on television, or at the mall, Santa Claus becomes real to them. It doesn't occur to them to think about how Santa might get to every child's house in one night or why those toys are the same ones they saw in the store just last week.

Another limitation is **egocentrism**, the inability to see the world through anyone else's eyes except one's own. For the preoperational child, everyone else must see what the child sees, and what is important to the child must be important to everyone else. For example, 2-year-old Hiba, after climbing out of her crib for the third time, was told by her mother, "I don't want to see you in that living room again tonight!" So Hiba's next appearance was made with her hands over her eyes—if she couldn't see her mother, her mother couldn't see her.

Type of conservation	Initial presentation	Transformation	Question	Preoperational child's answer
Liquids	Two equal glasses of liquid	Pour one into a taller, narrower glass.	Which glass contains more?	The taller one.
Number	Two equal lines of pennies	Increase spacing of pennies in one line.	Which line has more pennies?	The longer one.

FIGURE 12.4 Conservation Experiment
In this conservation task, pennies are laid out in two equal lines. When the pennies in the top line are spaced out, the child who cannot yet conserve will centrate on the top line and assume that there are actually more pennies in that line.

Remember that children in this stage are also overwhelmed by appearances. A child who complains that his piece of pie is smaller than his brother's may be quite happy once his original piece is cut into two pieces—now he thinks he has "more" than his brother. He has focused only on the number of pieces, not the actual amount of the pie. Focusing only on one feature of some object rather than taking all features into consideration is called *centration*. In the pennies example in **Figure 12.4**, children of this stage will focus (or center) on the length of the top line of pennies only and ignore the number of pennies. Centration is one of the reasons that children in this stage often fail to understand that changing the way something looks does not change its substance. The ability to understand that altering the appearance of something does not change its amount (as in the pennies example), its volume, or its mass is called **conservation**.

Concrete Operations In the **concrete operations stage** (ages 7–12), children finally become capable of conservation and reversible thinking. Centration no longer occurs, as children become capable of considering all the relevant features of any given object. They begin to think more logically about beliefs such as Santa Claus, and they ask questions, eventually coming to their own more rational conclusions about the fantasies of early childhood. They are in school, learning all sorts of science and math, and are convinced that they know more than their parents at this point.

The major limitation of this stage is the inability to deal effectively with abstract concepts. Abstract concepts are those that do not have some physical, concrete, touchable reality. For example, "freedom" is an abstract concept. People can define it, they can get a good sense of what it means, but there is no "thing" that they can point to and say, "This is freedom." Concrete concepts, which are the kind of concepts understood by children of this age, are about objects, written rules, and real things. Children need to be able to see it, touch it, or at least see it in their heads to be able to understand it.

Formal Operations In the last of Piaget's stages, **formal operations** (age 12 to adulthood), abstract thinking becomes possible. Teenagers not only understand

▲ These concrete operational children, seen in a science class, have begun to think logically and are able to solve many kinds of problems that were not possible for them to solve while in the preoperational stage.

conservation in Piaget's theory, the ability to understand that simply changing the appearance of an object does not change the object's nature.

concrete operations stage Piaget's third stage of cognitive development in which the school-age child becomes capable of logical thought processes but is not yet capable of abstract thinking.

formal operations stage Piaget's last stage of cognitive development, in which the adolescent becomes capable of abstract thinking.

▲ *This boy is helping his younger sister learn to read a book. Vygotsky's view of cognitive development states that the help of skilled others aids in making cognitive advances such as this one.*

concepts that have no physical reality, but also they get deeply involved in hypothetical thinking, or thinking about possibilities and even impossibilities. "What if everyone just got along?" "If women were in charge of countries, would there be fewer wars?"

Piaget's theory has been criticized on several points. Some researchers believe that the idea of distinct stages of cognitive development is not completely correct and that changes in thought are continuous and gradual rather than reached by jumping from one stage to another (Courage & Howe, 2002; Feldman, 2003; Schwitzgebel, 1999; Siegler, 1996). Others point out that preschoolers are not as egocentric as Piaget seemed to believe (Flavell, 1999) and that object permanence exists much earlier than Piaget thought (Aguiar & Baillargeon, 2003; Baillargeon, 1986).

Vygotsky's Theory: The Importance of Being There Russian psychologist Lev Vygotsky's pioneering work in developmental psychology has had a profound influence on school education in Russia, and interest in his theories continues to grow throughout the world (Bodrova & Leong, 1996; Duncan, 1995). Vygotsky wrote about children's cognitive development but differed from Piaget in his emphasis on the role of others in cognitive development (Vygotsky, 1934/1962, 1978, 1987). Whereas Piaget stressed the importance of the child's interaction with objects as a primary factor in cognitive development, Vygotsky stressed the importance of social and cultural interactions with other people, typically more highly skilled children and adults. Vygotsky believed that children develop cognitively when someone else helps them by asking leading questions and providing examples of concepts in a process called *scaffolding*. In scaffolding, the more highly skilled person gives the learner more help at the beginning of the learning process and then begins to withdraw help as the learner's skills improve (Rogoff, 1994).

Vygotsky also proposed that each developing child has a **zone of proximal development (ZPD)**, which is the difference between what a child can do alone versus what that child can do with the help of a teacher. For example, if little Jenny can do math problems up to the fourth-grade level on her own but with the help of a teacher can successfully work problems at a sixth-grade level, her ZPD is two years.

12.5 Outline the development of communication and language.

Stages of Language Development The development of language is a very important milestone in the cognitive development of a child because language allows children to think in words rather than just images, to ask questions, to communicate their needs and wants to others, and to form concepts (L. Bloom, 1974; P. Bloom, 2000).

Language development in infancy is influenced by the language they hear, a style of speaking known as child-directed speech (the way adults and older children talk to infants and very young children, with higher pitched, repetitive, sing-song speech patterns). Infants and toddlers attend more closely to this kind of speech, which creates a learning opportunity in the dialogue between caregiver and infant (Dominey & Dodane, 2004; Fernald, 1984, 1992; Küntay & Slobin, 2002).

There are several stages of language development that all children experience, no matter what culture they live in or what language they will learn to speak (Brown, 1973):

1. *Cooing*: At around two months of age, babies begin to make vowel-like sounds. (Note that prelinguistic vocalizations include crying as well as cooing and babbling.)

zone of proximal development (ZPD) Vygotsky's concept of the difference between what a child can do alone versus what that child can do with the help of a teacher.

2. *Babbling*: At about 6 months, infants add consonant sounds to the vowels to make a babbling sound, which at times can almost sound like real speech.

3. *One-word speech*: Somewhere just before or around age 1, most children begin to say actual words. These words are typically nouns and may seem to represent an entire phrase of meaning. They are called holophrases (whole phrases in one word) for that reason. For example, a child might say "Milk!" and mean "I want some milk!" or "I drank my milk!"

4. *Telegraphic speech*: At around a year and a half, toddlers begin to string words together to form short, simple sentences using nouns, verbs, and adjectives. "Baby eat," "Mommy go," "Doggie go bye-bye" are examples of telegraphic speech. Only the words that carry the meaning of the sentence are used.

5. *Whole sentences*: As children move through the preschool years, they learn to use grammatical terms and increase the number of words in their sentences, until by age 6 or so they are nearly as fluent as an adult, although the number of words they know is still limited when compared to adult vocabulary.

▲ This infant has already learned some of the basics of language, including the use of gestures to indicate meaning and enhance communication.

Autism Spectrum Disorder

Before leaving the topic of cognitive development in infancy, let's briefly discuss a topic that has been making the news for a number of years: the causes underlying autism spectrum disorder. In recent years the rate of diagnosis of autism has increased, from 1 in 110 in 2006 to 1 in 88 at the present time. This increase does not necessarily mean a rise in actual autism cases, however. Methods of diagnosing autism have become far more efficient and the definition of what is labeled as autism has been expanded, accounting for much of the increase (Centers for Disease Control and Prevention, 2013).

Autism spectrum disorder (ASD) is actually a whole range of disorders (with what may be an equally broad range of causes), which cause problems in thinking, feeling, language, and social skills in relating to others (Atladóttir et al., 2009; Johnson & Myers, 2007). Rumors and misinformation about the causes of autism have been circulating on the Internet for many years.

The major source of misinformation began in 1998, when British gastroenterologist Dr. Andrew Wakefield published the results of two studies that seemed to link the MMR (measles, mumps, and rubella) vaccine to autism and bowel disease in children (Wakefield et al., 1998). With a sample size of only 12 children, no control groups, and with neither study being blind—single or double—the studies were quickly denounced as inadequate and

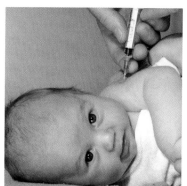

▲ One of the most important things parents can do for the continued health and safety of their infant is to have the baby immunized, following an approved schedule for each type of vaccine. Immunizations today are safe and effective and prevent dangerous and often deadly childhood diseases, such as rubella.

dangerous by autism specialists and others (Fitzpatrick, 2004; Judelsohn, 2007; Matthew & Dallery, 2007; Novella, 2007; Stratton et al., 2001a, 2001b). As a result of the British Medical Council's investigation into Wakefield's actions, Wakefield's medical license was revoked in May 2010 after the council found him guilty of "serious professional misconduct" (Meikle & Boseley, 2010).

Questions for Further Discussion

1. What more could be done to convince parents that infant immunization is safe?
2. The Internet allows the speedy spread of the results of studies such as Wakefield's. What are the pros and cons of this kind of access?

12.6 Explain temperament, the development of attachment, and the role of the caregiver.

The psychological and social development of infants and children involves the development of personality, relationships, and a sense of being male or female. Although these processes begin in infancy, they will continue in many respects well into adulthood.

Why are some children negative and whiny while others are sweet and good-natured?

Temperament One of the first ways in which infants demonstrate that they have different personalities (long-lasting characteristics that make each person different from others) is in their **temperament**, the behavioral and emotional characteristics that are fairly well established at birth. Researchers (Chess & Thomas, 1986; Thomas & Chess, 1977) have been able to identify three basic temperament styles of infants:

1. *Easy*: "Easy" babies are regular in their schedules of waking, sleeping, and eating and are adaptable to change. Easy babies are happy babies and when distressed are easily soothed.
2. *Difficult*: "Difficult" babies are almost the opposite of easy ones. Difficult babies tend to be irregular in their schedules and are very unhappy about change of any kind. They are loud, active, and tend to be crabby rather than happy.
3. *Slow to warm up*: This kind of temperament is associated with infants who are less grumpy, quieter, and more regular than difficult children but who are slow to adapt to change. If change is introduced gradually, these babies will "warm up" to new people and new situations.

Of course, not all babies will fall neatly into one of these three patterns—some children may be a mix of two or even all three patterns of behavior, as Chess and Thomas (1986) discovered. Even so, longitudinal research strongly suggests that these temperament styles last well into adulthood and are strongly influenced by heredity (Kagan, 1998; Kagan et al., 2007; Korn, 1984; Scarpa et al., 1995; Schwartz et al., 2010), although they are somewhat influenced by the environment in which the infant is raised. For example, a "difficult" infant who is raised by parents who are themselves very loud and active may not be perceived as difficult by the parents, whereas a child who is slow to warm up might be perceived as difficult if the parents themselves like lots of change and noise. The first infant is in a situation in which the "goodness of fit" of the infant's temperament to the parents' temperament is very close, but the parents of the second infant are a poor fit in temperament for that less active child (Chess & Thomas,

temperament the behavioral characteristics that are fairly well established at birth, such as easy, difficult, and slow to warm up.

1986). A poor fit can make it difficult to form an attachment, the important psychosocial–emotional bond we will discuss next.

Attachment The emotional bond that forms between an infant and a primary caregiver is called **attachment**. Attachment is a very important development in the social and emotional life of the infant, usually forming within the first 6 months of the infant's life and showing up in a number of ways during the second 6 months, such as *stranger anxiety* (wariness of strangers) and *separation anxiety* (fear of being separated from the caregiver). Although attachment to the mother is usually the primary attachment, infants can attach to fathers and to other caregivers as well. Take the survey *What Has Your Father Done for You?* to reflect back on the relationship you had with your father while you were growing up.

attachment the emotional bond between an infant and the primary caregiver.

✳ **Complete** the **Survey**, *What Has Your Father Done for You?*, at **MyPsychLab**

Attachment Styles Mary Ainsworth (Ainsworth, 1985; Ainsworth et al., 1978) came up with a special experimental design to measure the attachment of an infant to the caregiver called the Strange Situation (exposing an infant to a series of leave-takings and returns of the mother and a stranger). Through this measurement technique, Ainsworth and another colleague identified four attachment styles:

1. *Secure*: Infants labeled as secure were willing to get down from their mother's lap when they first entered the room with their mothers. They explored happily, looking back at their mothers and returning to them every now and then (sort of like "touching base"). When the stranger came in, these infants were wary but calm as long as their mother was nearby. When the mother left, the infants got upset. When the mother returned, the infants approached her, were easily soothed, and were glad to have her back.

2. *Avoidant*: In contrast, avoidant babies, though somewhat willing to explore, did not "touch base." They did not look at the stranger or the mother and reacted very little to her absence or her return, seeming to have no interest or concern.

3. *Ambivalent*: The word *ambivalent* means to have mixed feelings about something. Ambivalent babies in Ainsworth's study were clinging and unwilling to explore, very upset by the stranger regardless of the mother's presence, protested mightily when the mother left, and were hard to soothe. When the mother returned, these babies would demand to be picked up but at the same time push the mother in a mixed reaction to her return.

4. *Disorganized-disoriented*: In subsequent studies, other researchers (Main & Hesse, 1990; Main & Solomon, 1990) found that some babies seemed unable to decide just how they should react to the mother's return. These disorganized-disoriented infants would approach her but with their eyes turned away from her, as if afraid to make eye contact.

▲ *This toddler shows reluctance to explore his environment, instead clinging to his father's leg. Such clinging behavior, if common, can be a sign of an ambivalent attachment.*

Critics of Ainsworth's Strange Situation research focus on the artificial nature of the design and wonder if infants and mothers would behave differently in the more familiar surroundings of home, even though Ainsworth's experimental observers also observed the infants and mothers in the home prior to the Strange Situation (Ainsworth, 1985).

Influences of Culture on Attachment Although there are some cultural differences in attachment, such as the finding that mothers in the United States tend to wait for a child to express a need before trying to fulfill that need, whereas Japanese mothers prefer to anticipate the child's needs (Rothbaum et al., 2000), attachment does not seem to suffer in spite of the differences in sensitivity. Evidence that similar attachment styles are found in other cultures demonstrates the need to consider attachment as an important first step in forming relationships with others. It may set the stage for all relationships that follow (Hu & Meng, 1996; Juffer & Rosenboom, 1997; Keromoian & Leiderman, 1986; Rothbaum et al., 2010).

Before leaving the topic of attachment, let's take a look at one of the first studies that examined the key factors necessary for attachment.

Harlow and Contact Comfort

As psychologists began to study the development of attachment, they at first assumed that attachment to the mother occurred because the mother was associated with satisfaction of primary drives such as hunger and thirst. The mother is always present when the food (a primary reinforcer) is presented, so the mother becomes a secondary reinforcer capable of producing pleasurable feelings.

Psychologist Harry Harlow felt that attachment had to be influenced by more than just the provision of food. He conducted a number of studies of attachment using infant Rhesus monkeys (Harlow, 1958). Noticing that the monkeys in his lab liked to cling to the soft cloth pad used to line their cages, Harlow designed a study to examine the importance of what he termed *contact comfort*, the seeming attachment of the monkeys to something soft to the touch.

He isolated eight baby Rhesus monkeys shortly after their birth, placing each in a cage with two surrogate (substitute) "mothers." The surrogates were actually a block of wood covered in soft padding and terry cloth and a wire form, both heated from within. For half of the monkeys, the wire "mother" held the bottle from which they fed, while for the other half the soft "mother" held the bottle. Harlow then recorded the time each monkey spent with each "mother." If time spent with the surrogate is taken as an indicator of attachment, then learning theory would predict that the monkeys would spend more time with whichever surrogate was being used to feed them.

The results? Regardless of which surrogate was feeding them, the monkeys all spent significantly more time with the soft, cloth-covered surrogate. In fact, all monkeys spent very little time with the wire surrogate, even if this was the one with the bottle. Harlow and his colleagues concluded that "contact comfort was an important basic affectional or love variable" (Harlow, 1958, p. 574).

Harlow's work represents one of the earliest investigations into the importance of touch in the attachment process and remains an important study in human development.

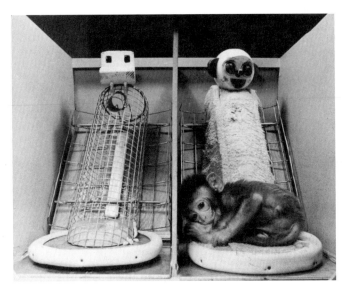

▲ *The wire surrogate "mother" provides the food for this infant Rhesus monkey. But the infant spends all its time with the soft, cloth-covered surrogate. According to Harlow, this demonstrates the importance of contact comfort in attachment.*

Questions for Further Discussion

1. Even though the cloth surrogate was warm and soft and seemed to provide contact comfort, do you think that the monkeys raised

in this way would behave normally when placed into contact with other monkeys? How might they react?

2. What might be the implications of Harlow's work for human mothers who feed their infants with bottles rather than breast-feeding?

12.7 Discuss social, cultural, and emotional development through childhood.

Who Am I?: The Development of the Self-Concept Infants begin life without understanding that they are separate from their surroundings, and also from the other people in their social world. The *self-concept* is the image you have of yourself, and it is based on your interactions with the important people in your life. As infants experience the world around them, they slowly learn to separate "me" from both physical surroundings and the other people in their world.

One way to demonstrate a child's growing awareness of self is known as the *rouge test*. A spot of red rouge or lipstick is put on the end of the child's nose and the child is then placed in front of a mirror. Infants from about six months to a little over a year will reach out to touch the image of the baby in the mirror, reacting as if to another child (Amsterdam, 1972; Courage & Howe, 2002). In fact, some infants crawl or walk to the other side of the mirror to look for the "other." But at about 15 to 18 months of age, the infant begins to touch his or her own nose when seeing the image in the mirror, indicating an awareness that the image in the mirror is the infant's own (Nielsen et al., 2006).

Erikson's Theory Erik Erikson trained as a Freudian psychoanalyst but became convinced that social interactions were more important in development than Freud's emphasis on psychosexual development. Erikson believed that development occurred in a series of eight stages, with the first four of these stages occurring in infancy and childhood (Erikson, 1950; Erikson & Erikson, 1997). (Freud's stages of psychosexual development are covered in detail in a later chapter). Each stage is an emotional crisis, or a turning point, in personality, and the crisis in each stage must be successfully met for normal, healthy psychological development.

Erikson focused on the relationship of the infant and the child to significant others in the immediate surroundings—parents and then later teachers and even peers. Keep in mind that the stages are not an "either or" experience and are better thought of in terms of "more like or less like." **Table 12.3** summarizes the conflict in each of Erikson's eight stages and some of the implications for future development (Erikson, 1950; Erikson & Erikson, 1997). For now, look at the first four stages in particular.

Table 12.3	Erikson's Psychosocial Stages of Development		
STAGE	DEVELOPMENTAL CRISIS	SUCCESSFUL DEALING WITH CRISIS	UNSUCCESSFUL DEALING WITH CRISIS
1. **Infant** Birth to 1 year old	**Trust versus Mistrust** Infants learn a basic sense of trust dependent upon how their needs are met	If babies' needs for food, comfort, and affection are met, they develop a sense of trust in people and expect those needs to be met in future.	If babies' needs for food, comfort, and affection are not met, they develop a sense of mistrust and do not expect their needs to be met in future.

(Continued on next page)

Table 12.3   (Continued)

STAGE	DEVELOPMENTAL CRISIS	SUCCESSFUL DEALING WITH CRISIS	UNSUCCESSFUL DEALING WITH CRISIS
2. **Toddler** 1 to 3 years old	**Autonomy versus Shame and Doubt** Toddlers begin to understand that they can control their own actions.	Toddlers who are successful in controlling their own actions develop independence.	Toddlers whose attempts at being independent are blocked develop a sense of self-doubt and shame for failing.
3. **Preschool Age** 3 to 5 years old	**Initiative versus Guilt** Preschool children learn to take responsibility for their own behavior as they develop self-control.	If preschoolers succeed in controlling their reactions and behavior, they feel capable and develop a sense of initiative.	If preschoolers fail in controlling their reactions and behavior, they feel irresponsible, anxious, and develop a sense of guilt.
4. **Elementary School Age** 5 to 12 years old	**Industry versus Inferiority** The school-aged child must learn new skills in both the academic world and the social world. They compare themselves to others to measure their success or failure.	When children feel they have succeeded at learning these skills, they develop a sense of industry, making them feel competent and improving their self-esteem.	When children fail, or feel that they have failed in learning these skills, they feel inferior when compared to others.
5. **Adolescence** 13 to early 20s	**Identity versus Role Confusion** Adolescents must decide who they are, what they believe, and what they want to be as an adult.	Adolescents who are able to define their values, goals, and beliefs will develop a stable sense of identity.	Adolescents who are unable to define themselves remain confused and may isolate themselves from others or try to be like everyone else instead of themselves.
6. **Early Adulthood** 20s and 30s	**Intimacy versus Isolation** Young adults face the task of finding a person with whom they can share their identity in an ongoing, close personal relationship.	Young adults who successfully find someone and share their identities will have a fulfilling relationship founded on psychological intimacy.	Young adults who are unable to find someone (often because they do not yet have a stable identity to share) will isolate themselves and may experience loneliness, even when involved in shallow relationships with others.
7. **Middle Adulthood** 40s and 50s	**Generativity versus Stagnation** The focus of this task is to find a way to be a creative, productive person who is nurturing the next generation.	Adults who are able to focus on the next generation will be productive and creative, leaving a legacy for the future.	Adults who are unable to focus outside themselves will remain stagnated, self-centered, and feeling that they have not made a difference.
8. **Late Adulthood** 60s and beyond	**Ego Integrity versus Despair** The task in this stage involves coming to terms with the end of life, reaching a sense of wholeness and acceptance of life as it has been.	Older adults who are able to come to terms with their lives, things they have done and left undone, and able to "let go" of regrets will have a sense of completion and will see death as simply the last stage of a full life.	Older adults who have not been able to achieve identity or intimacy or generativity, who cannot let go of their regrets, will feel a sense of having left things too late and see death as coming too soon.

Pick the best answer.

1. **The first 2 weeks of pregnancy are called the**
   a. gestational period
   b. germinal period
   c. embryonic period
   d. fetal period

2. **Which of the following does not happen during the germinal period?**
   a. A dividing mass of cells travels to the uterus
   b. Cells begin to differentiate into specialized human cells
   c. The zygote attaches itself to the uterus
   d. Toxins passing through the placenta can affect developing organs

3. **Which sense is least functional at birth?**
   a. touch
   b. taste
   c. hearing
   d. vision

4. **Which motor milestone occurs first in infants?**
   a. standing
   b. raising the head and chest
   c. rolling over
   d. sitting with support

5. **A child who has not developed object permanence is in which of Piaget's stages?**
   a. sensorimotor
   b. preoperational
   c. concrete operational
   d. formal operational

6. **The fertilized egg is called a(n)**
   a. zygote
   b. ovum
   c. sperm
   d. gene

7. **"I play cars" is an example of which stage of language development?**
   a. babbling
   b. holophrases
   c. telegraphic speech
   d. whole sentences

8. **According to Ainsworth, which kind of attachment is shown by a baby who demands to be picked up when the mother returns, but then pushes her away?**
   a. secure
   b. avoidant
   c. ambivalent
   d. disorganized-disoriented

9. **According to Harlow's research, which of the following surrogate mothers would infant monkeys most likely prefer?**
   a. a cold wire surrogate with a milk bottle
   b. a warm wire surrogate with a milk bottle
   c. a warm wire surrogate without a milk bottle
   d. a warm cloth surrogate without a milk bottle

10. **In which of Erikson's stages does a child learn self-control and begin to feel more capable?**
   a. autonomy versus shame and doubt
   b. initiative versus guilt
   c. industry versus inferiority
   d. identity versus role confusion

13 Adolescence and Adulthood

Module Goals	Learning Objectives
Describe development during adolescence.	**13.1** Trace major physical changes. **13.2** Outline the development of cognition and morality. **13.3** Consider the role of family and peers in adolescent development. **13.4** Explain identity formation.
Understand development during adulthood and aging.	**13.5** Describe major physical changes associated with adulthood and aging. **13.6** Understand cognitive changes in adulthood and aging. **13.7** Learn about social, cultural, and emotional issues in aging. **13.8** Discuss issues related to the end of life.

Describe Development During Adolescence

Adolescence is the period of life from about age 13 to the early 20s during which a young person is no longer physically a child but is not yet an independent, self-supporting adult. Adolescence has been defined as the "teens," from ages 13 to 19, but adolescence also concerns how a person deals with life issues such as work, family, and relationships. So although we can agree there is a clear age of onset, the end of adolescence may come earlier or later for different individuals.

13.1 Trace major physical changes.

Isn't adolescence just ▶ the physical changes that happen to your body?

Physical Development The clearest sign of the beginning of adolescence is the onset of *puberty*, the physical changes in both primary sex characteristics (growth and maturation of the actual sex organs) and secondary sex characteristics (changes in the body such as the development of breasts and body hair) that occur in the body as sexual development reaches its peak. Puberty occurs as the result of a complex series of glandular activities, stimulated by the "master gland" or the pituitary gland, when the proper genetically determined age is reached. Certain psychosocial and environmental factors such as stress, exercise, and nutrition may also have an impact on the timing of puberty (Ellis et al., 1999; Graber et al., 1995). Puberty often begins about two years after the beginning of the growth spurt, the rapid period of growth that takes place at around age 10 for girls and around age 12 for boys.

After about 4 years, the changes of puberty are relatively complete. The development of the brain, however, continues well into the early 20s. In particular, the prefrontal cortex of the brain, which is responsible in part for impulse control, judgment and decision making, and the organization and understanding of information, does not complete its development until about age 25 years (Somerville et al., 2013). It is easy to understand, then, why adolescents may engage in risky

adolescence the period of life from about age 13 to the early 20s, during which a young person is no longer physically a child but is not yet an independent, self-supporting adult.

behavior even when they know better, as the video *Risky Behavior and the Developing Brain*, explains.

👁 **Watch** the **Video**, *Risky Behavior and the Developing Brain*, at **MyPsychLab**

13.2 Outline the development of cognition and morality.

The physical development of adolescents has not changed radically in its pattern over the last century, even though aspects of physical development such as puberty do happen earlier than in the past. Cognitive and psychosocial development, however, have changed quite in bit—the adolescent of the early nineteen hundreds was a far different being than the adolescent of the same physical age in the early twenty-first century.

Cognitive Development The cognitive development of adolescents is less visible than the physical development but still represents a major change in the way adolescents think about themselves, their peers and relationships, and the world around them. Adolescents, especially those who receive a formal high school education, move into Piaget's final stage of formal operations, in which abstract thinking becomes possible. Teenagers begin to think about hypothetical situations, leading to a picture of what an "ideal" world would be like.

◄ If I'm remembering correctly, teenagers should be in Piaget's formal operations stage. So why don't many teenagers think just like adults?

Although headed into an adult style of thinking the brain cortex neurons are not finished developing and this affects abstract thinking and decision making, as a result adolescents are not yet completely free of egocentric thought. At this time in life, however, their egocentrism shows up in their preoccupation with their own thoughts. They do a lot of introspection (turning inward) and may become convinced that their thoughts are as important to others as they are to themselves. Two ways in which this adolescent egocentrism emerges are the personal fable and the imaginary audience (Elkind, 1985; Lapsley et al., 1986; Vartanian, 2000).

In the **personal fable**, adolescents have spent so much time thinking about their own thoughts and feelings that they become convinced that they are special, one of a kind, and that no one else has ever had these thoughts and feelings before them. "You just don't understand me; I'm different from you" is a common feeling of teens. The personal fable is not without a dangerous side. Because they feel unique, teenagers may feel that they are somehow protected from the dangers of the world and so do not take the precautions that they should. This may result in an unwanted pregnancy, severe injury or death while racing in a car, drinking and driving, and drug use, to name a few possibilities. "It can't happen to me" is a risky but common thought.

The **imaginary audience** shows up as extreme self-consciousness in adolescents. They become convinced that everyone is looking at them and that they are always the center of everyone else's world, just as they are the center of their own. This explains the intense self-consciousness that many adolescents experience concerning what others think about how the adolescent looks or behaves.

personal fable type of thought common to adolescents in which young people believe themselves to be unique and protected from harm.

imaginary audience type of thought common to adolescents in which young people believe that other people are just as concerned about the adolescent's thoughts and characteristics as they themselves are.

Moral Development Another important aspect in the cognitive advances that occur in adolescence concerns the teenager's understanding of "right" and "wrong." Harvard University professor Lawrence Kohlberg was a developmental psychologist who, influenced by Piaget and others, outlined a theory of the development of moral thinking through looking at how people of various ages responded to stories about people caught up in moral dilemmas* (see **Figure 13.1** for an example of a dilemma). Kohlberg (1973) proposed three

---

*dilemmas: when you have to choose between two possibilities and neither possibility is desirable.

Example of a Moral Dilemma

The ant worked long and hard over the summer to gather food for himself and his family. The grasshopper, who preferred to play and be lazy all summer, laughed at the ant for working so hard. The ant said, "you will be sorry this winter when you have no food." Sure enough, when winter came the very sorry grasshopper, cold and hungry, came to the ant and begged for food and shelter. Should the ant give food and shelter to the grasshopper?

FIGURE 13.1 Example of a Moral Dilemma

Thinking Critically
Have you ever had a decision to make that challenged your moral thinking? In which of Kohlberg's three levels would you classify your decision?

levels of moral development, or the knowledge of right and wrong behavior. These levels are summarized in **Table 13.1**, along with an example of each type of thinking.

Kohlberg's theory has been criticized as being male-oriented and biased toward Western cultures, especially since he used only males in his studies (Gilligan, 1982; Snarey, 1985). Carol Gilligan (1982) proposed that men and women have different perspectives on morality: Men tend to judge as moral the actions that lead to a fair or just end, whereas women tend to judge as moral the actions that are nonviolent and hurt the fewest people. Researchers, however, have not found consistent support for gender differences in moral thinking (Walker, 1991). Another criticism is that Kohlberg's assessment of moral development involves

Table 13.1 Kohlberg's Three Levels of Morality

LEVEL OF MORALITY	HOW RULES ARE UNDERSTOOD	EXAMPLE
Preconventional morality (typically very young children)	The consequences determine morality; behavior that is rewarded is right; that which is punished is wrong.	A child who steals a toy from another child and does not get caught does not see that action as wrong.
Conventional* morality (older children, adolescents, and most adults)	Conformity to social norms is right; nonconformity is wrong.	A child criticizes his or her parent for speeding because speeding is against the posted laws.
Postconventional morality (about 20 percent of the adult population)	Moral principles determined by the person are used to determine right and wrong and may disagree with societal norms.	A reporter who wrote a controversial story goes to jail rather than reveal the source's identity.

*The term *conventional* refers to general standards or norms of behavior for a particular society, which will differ from one social group or culture to another.

asking people what they think should be done in hypothetical moral dilemmas. What people say they will do and what people actually do when faced with a real dilemma are often two different things.

13.3 Consider the role of family and peers in adolescent development.

The development of personality and social relationships in adolescence primarily concerns the search for a consistent sense of self or personal identity.

▲ The comedy movie Mean Girls portrays the ins and outs of peer pressure and the desire to fit in that many adolescents face.

Parent/Teen Conflict Even for the majority of adolescents who end up successfully finding a consistent sense of self, there will be conflicts with parents. Many researchers believe that a certain amount of "rebellion" and conflict is a necessary step in breaking away from childhood dependence on the parents and becoming a self-sufficient* adult (Bengston, 1970; Lynott & Roberts, 1997). Although many people think that these conflicts are intense and concern very serious behavior, the reality is that most parent/teen conflict is over trivial issues—hair, clothing, taste in music, and so on. On the really big moral issues, most parents and teens would be quite surprised to realize that they are in agreement (Giancola, 2006).

What kind of parent is the best parent— one who's really strict or one who's pretty ◀ easygoing?

Parenting Styles Relationships between parents and children can be challenging during adolescence. Diana Baumrind (1967) outlined three basic styles of parenting, each of which may be related to certain personality traits in the child raised by that style of parenting. The video *Impact of Parenting Styles* explains why goodness-of-fit, or matching the parenting style to the child's needs, may be most important.

👁 Watch the Video, *Impact of Parenting Styles*, at MyPsychLab

Authoritarian parenting tends to be overly concerned with rules. This type of parent is stern, rigid, demanding perfection, controlling, uncompromising,† and has a tendency to use physical punishment. Children raised in this way are often insecure, timid, withdrawn, and resentful. As teenagers, they will very often rebel against parental authority in very negative and self-destructive ways, such as delinquency (criminal acts committed by minor children), drug use, or premarital sex (Baumrind, 1991, 2005; Sleddens et al., 2011).

Permissive parenting occurs when parents put very few demands on their children for behavior. *Permissive neglectful* parents simply aren't involved with their children, ignoring them and allowing them to do whatever they want until it interferes with what the parent wants. At that point, this relationship may become an abusive one. *Permissive indulgent* parents seem to be too involved with their children, allowing their "little angels" to behave in any way they wish, refusing to set limits on the child's behavior or to require any kind of obedience. Children from both kinds of permissive parenting tend to be selfish, immature, dependent, lacking in social skills, and unpopular with peers (Baumrind, 1991, 2005; Dwairy, 2004; Sledden et al., 2011).

---

*self-sufficient: able to function without outside aid; capable of providing for one's own needs.

†uncompromising: not making or accepting any viewpoint other than one's own, allowing no other viewpoints.

authoritative parenting style of parenting in which parents combine warmth and affection with firm limits on a child's behavior.

identity versus role confusion fifth stage of personality development in which the adolescent must find a consistent sense of self.

Authoritative parenting involves combining firm limits on behavior with love, warmth, affection, respect, and a willingness to listen to the child's point of view. Authoritative parents are more democratic, allowing the child to have some input into the formation of rules but still maintaining the role of final decision maker. Punishment tends to be nonphysical, such as restrictions, time-out, or loss of privileges. Authoritative parents set limits that are clear and understandable, and when a child crosses the limits, they allow an explanation and then agree on the right way to handle the situation. Children raised in this style of parenting tend to be self-reliant and independent (Baumrind, 1991, 2005; Dwairy, 2004; Sledden et al., 2011; Sorkhabi, 2005; Underwood et al., 2009).

13.4 Explain identity formation.

Erikson's Identity versus Role Confusion The psychosocial crisis that must be faced by the adolescent, according to Erikson, is that of **identity versus role confusion** (see **Table 12.3**). In this stage, the teenager must choose from among many options for values in life and beliefs concerning things such as political issues, career options, and marriage (Feldman, 2003). From those options, a consistent sense of self must be found. Erikson believed that teens who have successfully resolved the conflicts of the earlier four stages are much better "equipped" to resist peer pressure to engage in unhealthy or illegal activities and find their own identity during the adolescent years. Those teens who are not as successful come into the adolescent years with a lack of trust in others, feelings of guilt and shame, low self-esteem, and dependency on others.

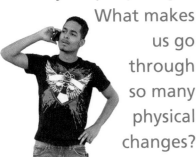

When exactly does adulthood begin? ▶

Understand Development during Adulthood and Aging

Adulthood can be thought of as the period of life from the early 20s until old age and death. Exactly when adulthood begins is not always easy to determine. In some cultures, adulthood is reached soon after puberty (Bledsoe & Cohen, 1993; Ocholla-Ayayo et al., 1993), while in other cultures events such as high school graduation or having a job and home separate from one's parents mark entry into adulthood.

13.5 Describe major physical changes associated with adulthood and aging.

Why do people age? ▶
What makes us go through so many physical changes?

There are a number of theories of why people physically age. Some theories of physical aging point to biological changes in cellular structure, whereas others focus on the influence of external stresses on body tissues and functioning.

Cellular Clock Theory One of the biologically based theories is the *cellular clock theory* (Hayflick, 1977). In this theory, cells are limited in the number of times they can reproduce to repair damage. Evidence for this theory is the existence of telomeres, structures on the ends of chromosomes that shorten each time a cell reproduces (Martin & Buckwalter, 2001). Stress speeds the destruction of telomeres.

Free Radical Theory One older theory points to outside influences such as stress, physical exertion, and bodily damage and is known as the *wear-and-tear theory of aging*. In this theory, the body's organs and cell tissues simply wear out with repeated use and abuse. The *free radical theory* is actually the latest version of the wear-and-tear theory in that it gives a biological explanation for the damage done to cells over time. Free radicals are oxygen molecules that have an unstable electron (negative particle). They bounce around the cell, stealing electrons from other molecules and increasing the damage to structures inside the cell. As people get older, more and more free radicals do more and more damage, producing the effects of aging (Hauck & Bartke, 2001; Knight, 1998).

Activity Theory Activity theory (Havighurst et al., 1968) proposes that an elderly person adjusts more positively to aging when remaining active in some way. Elderly people who volunteer at hospitals or schools, those who take up new hobbies or throw themselves full time into old ones, and those who maintain their friendships with others and continue to have social activities have been shown to be happier and live longer than those who withdraw themselves from activity.

▲ *One way to age successfully and maintain psychological health is to remain active and involved in life. This woman is volunteering in a grade school classroom as a teacher's aide. This not only allows her to feel useful but also helps her to stay mentally alert and socially involved.*

Physical Development Adulthood can also be divided into at least three periods: young adulthood, middle age, and late adulthood. Many developmental psychologists now talk about "emerging adulthood" as a time from late adolescence through the 20s and referring to mainly those in developed countries who are childless, do not live in their own home, and are not earning enough money to be independent (Arnett, 2000; Azmitia et al., 2008; Nelson et al., 2008).

Physical changes in young adulthood are relatively minimal. The good news is that the 20s are a time of peak physical health, sharp senses, fewer insecurities, and mature cognitive abilities. The bad news is that even in the early 20s, the signs of aging are already beginning. Vision and hearing are beginning to decline and by around age 40, bifocal lenses may become necessary as the lens of the eye hardens, becoming unable to change its shape to shift focus. Hearing loss becomes noticeable by the 60s or 70s, when hearing aids may become necessary.

In the 40s, when most adults are able to experience some security and stability without the worries and concerns of adolescence and young adulthood, physical aging continues: Skin begins to show more wrinkles, hair turns gray (or falls out), vision and hearing decline further, and physical strength may begin to decline (Frontera et al., 1991). In the 50s, these changes continue. Throughout middle age, weight may increase as the rate at which the body functions slows down but eating increases and less time is spent exercising. Height begins to decrease, with about half an inch of height lost for every 10 years past age 40, although people with the bone-loss disease osteoporosis (*osteo-* means bone and *porosis* means porous) may lose up to 8 inches or more (Cummings & Melton, 2002).

In a woman's 40s, the levels of the female hormone estrogen decline as the body's reproductive system prepares to cease that function. Some women begin to experience "hot flashes," a sudden sensation of heat and sweating that may keep them awake at night. Interestingly, in some cultures, particularly those in which the diet contains high amounts of soy products, hot flashes are almost nonexistent (Cassidy et al., 1994; Lock, 1994). At an average age of 51, most women will cease

activity theory theory of adjustment to aging that assumes older people are happier if they remain active in some way, such as volunteering or developing a hobby.

ovulation altogether, ending their reproductive years. The cessation of ovulation and the menstrual cycle is called *menopause* (Mishell, 2001).

Effects of Aging on Health It is in middle age that many health problems first occur, although their true cause may have begun in the young adulthood years. Young adults may smoke, drink heavily, stay up late, and get dark tans, and the wear and tear that this lifestyle causes on their bodies will not become obvious until their 40s and 50s.

Some of the common health problems that may show up in middle age are high blood pressure, skin cancer, heart problems, arthritis, and obesity. The most common causes of death in middle age are heart disease, cancer, and stroke—in that order (McGinnis & Foege, 1993).

13.6 Understand cognitive changes in adulthood and aging.

Intellectual abilities do not decline overall, although speed of processing (or reaction time) does slow down. Compared to a younger adult, a middle-aged person may take a little longer to solve a problem. However, a middle-aged person also has more life experience and knowledge to bring to bear on a problem, which counters the lack of speed.

Changes in memory ability are probably the most noticeable changes in middle-aged cognition. People find themselves having a hard time recalling a particular word or someone's name. This difficulty in retrieval is probably not evidence of a cognitive decline but is more likely caused by the stresses a middle-aged person experiences and the sheer amount of information that a person of middle years must try to keep straight (Craik, 1994; Launer et al., 1995; Sands & Meredith, 1992).

How to Keep Your Brain Young People who exercise their mental abilities have been found to be far less likely to develop memory problems and even senile dementias such as Alzheimer's in old age (Ball et al., 2002; Colcombe et al., 2003; Fiatarone, 1996). "Use it or lose it" is the phrase to remember. Working challenging crossword puzzles, for example, can be a major factor in maintaining a healthy level of cognitive functioning. Reading, having an active social life, going to plays, taking classes, and staying physically active can all have a positive impact on the continued well-being of the brain (Bosworth & Schaie, 1997; Cabeza et al., 2002; Singh-Manoux et al., 2003).

▲ *This middle-aged woman works on a crossword puzzle. Mental exercises such as this are one way to keep the brain healthy and fit. What might be some other ways to exercise one's brain?*

13.7 Learn about social, cultural, and emotional issues in aging.

Psychosocial Development In adulthood, concerns involve career, relationships, family, and approaching old age. The late teens and early 20s may be college years for many, although other young people go to work directly from high school. Choosing and entering a career is a very serious task that many young adults have difficulty accomplishing. College students may change majors more than once during the first few years of college. Those who are working may also change careers several times (perhaps as many as five to seven times) and may experience periods of unemployment while between jobs.

Erikson's Intimacy versus Isolation: Forming Relationships In young adulthood, Erikson saw the primary task to be finding a mate. True *intimacy* is an emotional and psychological closeness that is based on the ability to trust, share, and care (an ability developed during the earlier stages such as trust versus mistrust), while still maintaining one's sense of self. Young adults who have difficulty trusting others and who are unsure of their own identities may find isolation instead of intimacy—loneliness, shallow relationships with others, and even a fear of real intimacy. For example, many marriages end in divorce within a few years, with one partner leaving the relationship—and even the responsibilities of parenting—to explore personal concerns and those unfinished issues of identity. (See Table 12.3.)

generativity providing guidance to one's children or the next generation, or contributing to the well-being of the next generation through career or volunteer work.

Erikson's Generativity versus Stagnation: Parenting the Next Generation In middle adulthood, persons who have found intimacy can now focus outward on others (Table 12.3). Erikson saw this as parenting the next generation and helping them through their crises, a process he called **generativity**. Educators, supervisors, health care professionals, doctors, and community volunteers might be examples of positions that allow a person to be generative. Other ways of being generative include engaging in careers or some major life work that can become one's legacy* to the generations to come.

13.8 Discuss issues related to the end of life.

Erikson's Ego Integrity versus Despair: Dealing with Mortality As people enter the stage known as late adulthood, life becomes more urgent as the realities of physical aging and the approaching end of life become harder and harder to ignore. (See Table 12.3.) Erikson (1980) believed that at this time people look back on the life they have lived in a process called a life review. In the life review people must deal with mistakes, regrets, and unfinished business. If people can look back and feel that their lives were relatively full and come to terms with regrets and losses, then a feeling of *integrity* or wholeness results. Integrity is the final completion of the identity, or ego. If people have many regrets and lots of unfinished business, they feel despair, a sense of deep regret over things that will never be accomplished because time has run out.

Death and Dying There are several ways of looking at the process of dying. One of the more well-known theories is that of Elisabeth Kübler-Ross (Kübler-Ross, 1997), who conducted extensive interviews with dying persons and their caregivers.

Elisabeth Kübler-Ross theorized that people go through five stages of reaction when faced with death (Backer et al., 1994; Kübler-Ross, 1997). These stages are denial, in which people refuse to believe that the diagnosis of death is real; anger, which is really anger at death itself and the feelings of helplessness to change things; bargaining, in which the dying person tries to make a deal with doctors or even with God; depression, which is sadness from losses already experienced (e.g., loss of a job or one's dignity) and those yet to come (e.g., not being able to see a child grow up); and finally acceptance, when the person has accepted the inevitable* and quietly awaits death.

Obviously, some people do not have time to go through all of these stages or even go through them in the listed order (Schneidman, 1983, 1994). Some theorists do not agree with the stage idea, seeing the process of dying as a series of ups and downs, with hope on the rise at times and then falling, to be replaced by a rise in despair or disbelief (Corr, 1993; Maciejewski et al., 2007; Schneidman, 1983, 1994; Weisman, 1972). The danger in holding too strictly to a stage theory is that people may feel there is a "right" way to face death and a "wrong" way when in fact each person's dying process is unique.

---

*legacy: something handed down or passed on to others.

Kübler-Ross's theory is also strongly tied to Western cultural values and norms. For a look at how other cultures view death, see the Applying Psychology feature that follows.

Applying Psychology to Everyday Life

Cross-Cultural Views on Death

While Westerners see a person as either dead or alive, in some cultures a person who by Western standards is clearly alive is mourned as already dead—as is the case in many Native American cultures. Let's take a look at two diverse cultures and their views on death and dying, remembering to contrast them with what you know of death and funeral rites common in your own culture.

- In a wealthy Hindu family in India, the dying person is surrounded by family members, even while in the hospital. In addition, many visitors will attend to the dying person, creating a nearly constant flow of visitors in and out of the room. Once the person has passed away, preparations for the funeral period—which can take nearly two weeks—are begun. The body is not sent to a funeral home but rather is taken into the family home until the actual day of the funeral, where a cremation will take place. During the funeral preparation period, visitors and family stream in and out of the deceased's home and an abundance of food—all vegetarian at this time—are prepared and eaten. Until the day of the funeral, mattresses are placed on the floor, and all but the very old and infirm are expected to sleep there; the body of the deceased is also placed on the floor. The family members themselves will eventually wash the body in preparation for wrapping and the trip to the crematorium (Laungani, 1997). In Hinduism, it is believed that the dead person's soul will be reincarnated at either a higher level or a lower level of status, depending upon how the person lived his or her life.

- In the culture of the Northern Cheyenne Native American tribe, death is considered only the end of the physical body, while the self and one's Cheyenne nature will persist. The very old and the very young are said to be "close to the spirit," meaning that the infant has just come from the nonphysical world and the aged person is close to returning to it. The Cheyenne, like the Hindu, also believe in reincarnation, so many infants are seen to be the living embodiment of ancestors. Death itself is a long process, with various aspects of one's spirit leaving at different times. The first such "leaving" results in changes in the behavior and the mental activity of the dying person, but the person may still be able to walk and communicate. The second leads to loss of the senses, then consciousness, and finally, breathing. The very last essence to leave is the life principle, the first life given into an infant but the last to leave. This life principle stays in the skeleton until the bones begin to crumble into dust. Thus some Cheyenne believe that bones can become alive again (Strauss, 2004).

Questions for Further Discussion

1. How has your own experience with death, if any, affected you and your outlook on life? What were the cultural trappings of the days leading up to the death and/or the funeral arrangements?

2. How do the customs of the wealthy Hindu family differ from those of the Cheyenne, and how are they alike?

Practice Quiz

Pick the best answer.

1. **Which of the following refers to the feeling of being unique and protected from harm?**
   a. personal fable
   b. moral dilemma
   c. imaginary audience
   d. adolescent rebellion

2. **According to Kohlberg, most adolescents are at which level of morality?**
   a. overly conventional
   b. preconventional
   c. conventional
   d. postconventional

3. **According to Erikson, the adolescent's primary challenge is to**
   a. learn to feel successful at new tasks.
   b. develop a consistent sense of self.
   c. form relationships based on true intimacy.
   d. resist peer pressure successfully.

4. **Conflicts between adolescents and their parents or caregivers usually focus on**
   a. issues of morality.
   b. issues of little real importance.
   c. issues of personal responsibility.
   d. issues of academic success.

5. **According to Baumrind, which type of parent would most likely say, "Because I said so" or "It's my way or the highway!"**
   a. authoritarian
   b. authoritative
   c. permissive neglectful
   d. permissive indulgent

6. **According to Erikson, the primary task of early adulthood is**
   a. completing your education.
   b. finding a mate.
   c. starting a career.
   d. taking care of aging parents.

7. **The period of 5 or 10 years during which a woman's reproductive system begins to decline is called**
   a. ovulation.
   b. andropause.
   c. perimenopause.
   d. menopause.

8. **Adam, a middle-aged man, might outperform a younger person on a cognitive task because**
   a. his reaction time has improved over the years.
   b. his stressful life makes his mind sharper.
   c. he has more life experience to draw upon.
   d. his sense of generativity makes him more confident.

9. **Which of these is most likely to help Joanne, a 65-year-old woman, adjust positively to aging?**
   a. staying active in her community
   b. withdrawing from social demands
   c. giving up her career
   d. accepting that her life will end soon

10. **According to this theory of aging, shortened telomeres cause cells to age.**
    a. cellular clock theory
    b. wear-and-tear theory
    c. free radical theory
    d. activity theory

((Listen to an Audio File of your chapter at MyPsychLab

Module 11: Topics in Development

Describe methods and issues in life span development.

11.1 Understand methods used to study development.

- Three special research methods used in developmental research are the longitudinal design, the cross-sectional design, and the cross-sequential design.

11.2 Describe the issues of continuity/discontinuity and stability/change.

- Physical development, or development of the body, is fairly discontinuous occurring in clearly defined stages.
- Cognitive development, or development of thinking and reasoning skills, is fairly continuous, and it changes over time.

11.3 Explain how environmental and biological factors interact in development.

- Behavioral genetics is a field investigating the relative contributions to development of heredity (nature) and environment (nurture).
- Dominant genes control the expression of a trait, whereas recessive gene traits are only expressed when paired with another recessive gene for the same trait.
- Chromosome disorders includes Down syndrome, whereas genetic disorders include PKU, cystic fibrosis, sickle-cell anemia, and Tay-Sachs disease.

Module 12: Prenatal, Infant and Childhood Development

Learn about prenatal and newborn development.

12.1 Trace physical development from conception through birth and identify influences on prenatal development.

- The fertilized egg cell is called a zygote and divides into many cells, eventually forming the baby.
- Monozygotic twins are formed when the zygote splits into two separate masses of cells, each of which will develop into a baby identical to the other. When the two masses do not fully separate, conjoined twins occur.
- Dizygotic twins are formed when the mother's body releases multiple eggs and at least two are fertilized.
- The germinal period is the first two weeks of pregnancy in which the dividing mass of cells (blastocyst) moves down the fallopian tube into the uterus.

12.2 Explain the role of sensitive and critical periods in development.

- The embryonic period begins at two weeks after conception and ends at eight weeks.
- The fetal period is from the beginning of the ninth week until the birth of the baby.

Describe development during infancy and childhood.

12.3 Learn about childhood physical and motor development.

- Four critical areas of adjustment for the newborn are respiration, digestion, circulation, and temperature regulation.

- Infants are born with reflexes that help the infant survive until more complex learning is possible.
- The senses, except for vision, are fairly well developed at birth.

12.4 Explain how cognitive abilities develop during childhood.

- Piaget's stages include the sensorimotor stage of sensory and physical interaction with the world, preoperational thought in which language becomes a tool of exploration, concrete operations in which logical thought becomes possible, and formal operations in which abstract concepts are understood and hypothetical thinking develops.
- Vygotsky believed that children learn best when being helped by a more highly skilled peer or adult in a process called scaffolding.

12.5 Outline the development of communication and language.

- The stages of language development are cooing, babbling, one-word speech (holophrases), and telegraphic speech.

Issues in Psychology: Autism Spectrum Disorder

- Autism spectrum disorder (ASD) is a range of disorders that cause problems in thinking, feeling, language, and social skills in relating to others.
- Dr. Andrew Wakefield falsified data that led to parents refusing to have their children immunized against measles, mumps, and rubella, leading to epidemic outbreaks of these diseases.

12.6 Explain temperament, the development of attachment, and the role of the caregiver.

- The three basic infant temperaments are easy (regular, adaptable, and happy), difficult (irregular, nonadaptable, and irritable), and slow to warm up (need to adjust gradually to change).
- The four types of attachment are secure, avoidant (unattached), ambivalent (insecurely attached), and disorganized-disoriented (insecurely attached and sometimes abused or neglected).
- Harlow's classic research with infant Rhesus monkeys demonstrated the importance of contact comfort in the attachment process.

12.7 Discuss social, cultural, and emotional development through childhood.

- In trust versus mistrust, the infant must gain a sense of predictability and trust in caregivers or risk developing a mistrustful nature; in autonomy versus shame and doubt, the toddler needs to become physically independent.
- In initiative versus guilt, the preschool child is developing emotional and psychological independence; in industry versus inferiority, school-age children are gaining competence and developing self-esteem.

Module 13: Adolescence and Adulthood

Describe development during adolescence.

13.1 Trace major physical changes.
- Adolescence is the period of life from about age 13 to the early 20s during which physical development reaches completion.
- Puberty is a period of about four years during which the sexual organs and systems fully mature.

13.2 Outline the development of cognition and morality.
- Adolescents engage in two kinds of egocentric thinking called the imaginary audience and the personal fable.
- Kohlberg proposed three levels of moral development: preconventional morality, conventional morality, and postconventional morality.

13.3 Consider the role of family and peers in adolescent development.
- Baumrind proposed three parenting styles: authoritarian (rigid and uncompromising), authoritative (consistent and strict but warm and flexible), and permissive (either indifferent and unconcerned with the daily activities of the child or indulgent and unwilling to set limits on the child).

13.4 Explain identity formation.
- In Erikson's identity versus role confusion crisis the job of the adolescent is to achieve a consistent sense of self from among all the roles, values, and futures open to him or her.

Understand development during adulthood and aging.

13.5 Describe major physical changes associated with adulthood and aging.
- Adulthood begins in the early 20s and ends with death in old age. It can be divided into young adulthood, middle adulthood, and late adulthood.
- Research strongly indicates that remaining active and involved results in the most positive adjustment to aging; this is a component of activity theory.
- The cellular clock theory is based on the idea that cells only have so many times that they can reproduce; once that limit is reached, damaged cells begin to accumulate.
- The free radical theory states that oxygen molecules with an unstable electron move around the cell, damaging cell structures as they go.
- The 20s are the peak of physical health; in the 30s the signs of aging become more visible, and in the 40s visual problems may occur, weight may increase, strength may decrease, and height begins to decrease.
- Women experience a physical decline in the reproductive system called the climacteric, ending at about age 50 with menopause.
- Many health problems such as high blood pressure, skin cancers, and arthritis begin in middle age, with the most common causes of death in middle age being heart disease, cancer, and stroke.

13.6 Understand cognitive changes in adulthood and aging.
- Reaction times slow down, but intelligence and memory remain relatively stable.

13.7 Learn about social, cultural, and emotional issues in aging.
- Erikson's crisis of young adulthood is intimacy versus isolation, in which the young adult must establish an intimate relationship, usually with a mate.
- The crisis of middle adulthood is generativity versus stagnation, in which the task of the middle-aged adult is to help the next generation through its crises, either by parenting, mentoring, or a career that leaves some legacy to the next generation.
- Erikson's final crisis is integrity versus despair, in which an older adult must come to terms with mortality.

13.8 Discuss issues related to the end of life.
- The five stages of reaction to death and dying are denial, anger, bargaining, depression, and acceptance.

Applying Psychology to EveryDay Life:
Cross-Cultural Views on Death
- In wealthy Hindu families, a dying person is surrounded by family and friends and then honored with a funeral process of nearly two weeks.
- In Northern Cheyenne culture, death is seen as part of the process of the life cycle and takes place in three stages.

Vocabulary Terms

cross-sectional design p. 154
cross-sequential design p. 154
human development p. 154
longitudinal design p. 154
dominant p. 156
recessive p. 156
monozygotic twins p. 159
germinal period p. 160
dizygotic twins p. 160

critical periods p. 161
embryonic period p. 161
fetal period p. 161
teratogen p. 161
schema p. 165
sensorimotor stage p. 165
object permanence p. 165
preoperational stage p. 166
egocentrism p. 166

formal operations p. 167
concrete operations stage p. 167
conservation p. 167
zone of proximal development (ZPD) p. 168
temperament p. 170
attachment p. 171
adolescence p. 176

imaginary audience p. 177
personal fable p. 177
identity versus role confusion p. 180
authoritative parenting p. 180
activity theory p. 181
generativity p. 183

Study and Review at **MyPsychLab**

Vocabulary Review
Match each vocabulary term to its definition.

1. critical period
2. longitudinal design
3. conservation
4. activity theory
5. generativity
6. attachment
7. personal fable
8. teratogen
9. sensitive period
10. zone of proximal development (ZPD)

a. A time when a child is needs the presence or absence of particular stimuli in the environment.

b. Theory of adjustment to aging that assumes older people are happier if they remain active.

c. Thought common to adolescents in which they believe themselves to be unique and protected from harm.

d. The first emotional bond a child forms with its primary caretaker.

e. A time when a child is susceptible to stimuli and receptive to learning from particular types of experiences.

f. The difference between what a child can do alone versus what that child can do with the help of a teacher.

g. In Piaget's theory, the ability to understand that simply changing the appearance of an object does not change the object's nature.

h. Any factor that can cause a birth defect.

i. Research design in which one group is assessed at different times as the group ages.

j. Providing guidance to one's children, or contributing to the well-being of the next generation.

Psychology Project
Conduct observations or interviews to help you understand Erikson's theories.

Materials: a notebook, an audio/video recorder, pen, and paper

Instructions:

1. Choose a person of a different age group to study. You may choose to *observe* a child you know who is between the ages of 2 and 10 or to *interview* an adult who is at least 30.

2. Based on the age of the person you are observing or interviewing, determine which of Erikson's stages is most appropriate to focus on.

3. Plan your interview/observation session in advance.

4. Identify related questions you might ask your interviewee, or related behaviors you might expect to see in the child you are observing.

5. Conduct and record your observation or interview.

6. Write a one-page report summing up what you learned from the observation or interview. Are your findings consistent with Erikson's theory? If so, how? If not, what was different?

Tech Alternative

1. Log in to your favorite social networking site.

2. Select three friends (one child, one adolescent, and one adult).

3. Look at the content of their pages carefully.

   a. Identify their current Erikson Psychosocial stage. Provide three examples of evidence for each friend from their social networking site that support your choice.

   b. Describe how you think their pages would change if they successfully move to the next stage.

   c. Describe how you think their pages would change if they move to the next stage with unsuccessful experiences in the current stage.

4. Write a one-page report summing up what you learned from your observations.

Essay Question

Tisha and Ken are preparing for their first child. They are wondering to what degree their child's physical and mental characteristics will be determined by biology or by environmental factors such as parenting styles and cultural expectations. Discuss two ways in which the child's development will likely be influenced by biological factors and two ways in which the child's development will likely be influenced by environmental factors. Select **two** factors from each group.

a. Biological
Recessive genes
Dominant genes
Monozygotic twins

b. Environmental
Teratogens
Cultural expectations
Parenting styles

Test Yourself

Ready for your test? More quizzes and a customized plan.

✅ Study and Review at MyPsychLab

Pick the best answer.

1. The thinking and attitudes of many who survived the Depression of the 1930s changed them for the rest of their lives. This would be an example of a
   a. cohort effect.
   b. cultural group.
   c. longitudinal group.
   d. cross-sequential group.

2. If a person has one gene for blue eyes but actually has brown eyes, blue eyes must be a _____ trait.
   a. dominant
   b. recessive
   c. sex-linked
   d. polygenic

3. Which of the following is a disorder caused by a transmission through recessive genes?
   a. PKU
   b. Down
   c. Klinefelter's
   d. Turner's

4. Which of the following represents the fertilization process for monozygotic twins?
   a. One egg is fertilized by two different sperm.
   b. One egg splits and is then fertilized by two different sperm.
   c. One egg is fertilized by one sperm and then splits.
   d. Two eggs are fertilized by the same sperm.

5. Which of the following is said to stay in an immature state until needed to produce more cells?
   a. uterus
   b. stem cells
   c. umbilical cord
   d. placenta

6. Which of the following best describes the relationship between age and task performance?
   a. The older you are, the faster you will complete a task.
   b. The younger you are, the better you will complete a task.
   c. Old age negatively impacts performance but experience positively impacts performance.
   d. Old age positively impacts performance but experience negatively impacts performance.

7. Dr. Kahn measures how long baby Lydia looks at a particular stimulus. The technique is known as
   a. preferential looking.
   b. dishabituation.
   c. habituation.
   d. stimulus discrimination.

8. At what age can the typical infant roll over?
   a. 2 months
   b. 5 weeks
   c. 8 months
   d. 12 months

9. What occurs during the process of synaptic pruning?
   a. The brain creates additional neural connections by removing parts of the surrounding bone.
   b. Unused synaptic connections and nerve cells are cleared out to make way for new cells.
   c. New cells work to "rewrite" old cells.
   d. New cells will not develop until the body makes sufficient physical space within the brain.

10. In which of Piaget's stages does the child become capable of understanding conservation?
    a. sensorimotor
    b. preoperational
    c. formal operations
    d. concrete operations

11. Monique says "milk" when she wants her milk from the kitchen counter. Subsequently, she says "milk" after she has had a drink. Using a single phrase to mean different things is an example of
    a. telephrase.
    b. private speech.
    c. holophrase.
    d. public speech.

12. Which of the following is a myth regarding immunizations?
    a. Most immunizations are made up of dead viruses.
    b. If all the other children in a school are immunized, there is really no harm in not immunizing one's own child.
    c. Vaccines work in up to 99 percent of cases.
    d. Only in rare cases do immunizations trigger seizures.

13. In the Strange Situation, _____ babies would cry when their mother left the room but were happy upon her return.
    a. secure
    b. avoidant
    c. ambivalent
    d. disorganized-disoriented

14. What is a new explanation as to why teenagers and young adults may engage in risky and dangerous behavior?
    a. Such behavior is due to peer pressure.
    b. Such behavior is actually hereditary.
    c. Such behavior may be due to unbalanced hormones.
    d. Such behavior may be due to incomplete development of the prefrontal cortex.

15. When Sami enters a room, two students stop their discussion. That Sami thinks they were talking about her is an example of
    a. the imaginary audience.
    b. the personal fable.
    c. abstract egocentrism.
    d. formal operations.

16. What cognitive changes occurring during middle adulthood are the most noticeable?
    a. Changes in memory begin to occur.
    b. Problem-solving skills diminish.
    c. Hearing begins to decline.
    d. Hair begins to turn gray.

17. Independence and self-reliance in the teenage years is the most likely due to _____ parenting.
    a. authoritarian
    b. authoritative
    c. permissive neglectful
    d. permissive indulgent

18. According to Erikson, late adulthood focuses on
    a. identity.
    b. generativity.
    c. intimacy.
    d. integrity.

19. Which theory of aging states that unstable oxygen molecules cause damage to surrounding cells?
    a. cellular-clock theory
    b. wear-and-tear theory
    c. free-radical theory
    d. activity theory

20. Kip thinks he is losing his mind because he is angry at a friend who died in an accident. Based on Kübler-Ross's research, what might you tell him?
    a. Anger of this type is self-destructive and unhealthy.
    b. Anger is usually a mask to your true feelings.
    c. Anger towards a deceased individual is not normal.
    d. Anger is a normal reaction to death.

Learning Objectives

11.1 **11.2** **11.3**   pp. 154–157

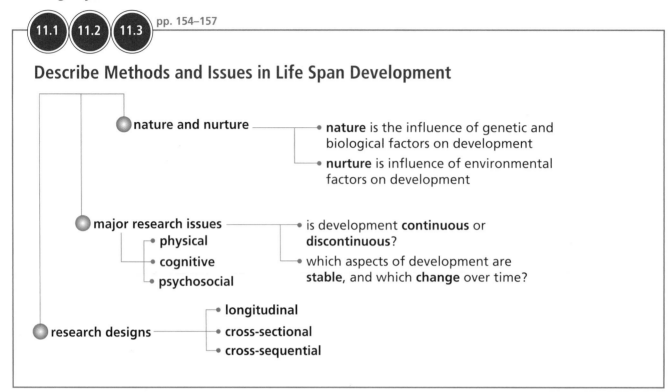

Describe Methods and Issues in Life Span Development

nature and nurture
- **nature** is the influence of genetic and biological factors on development
- **nurture** is influence of environmental factors on development

major research issues
- **physical**
- **cognitive**
- **psychosocial**
- is development **continuous** or **discontinuous**?
- which aspects of development are **stable**, and which **change** over time?

research designs
- **longitudinal**
- **cross-sectional**
- **cross-sequential**

Learning Objectives

12.1 **12.2**   pp. 159–162

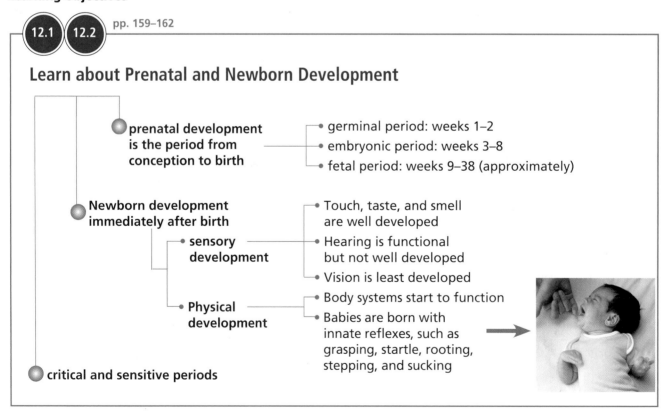

Learn about Prenatal and Newborn Development

prenatal development is the period from conception to birth
- germinal period: weeks 1–2
- embryonic period: weeks 3–8
- fetal period: weeks 9–38 (approximately)

Newborn development immediately after birth
- **sensory development**
- **Physical development**
- Touch, taste, and smell are well developed
- Hearing is functional but not well developed
- Vision is least developed
- Body systems start to function
- Babies are born with innate reflexes, such as grasping, startle, rooting, stepping, and sucking

critical and sensitive periods

the Life Span

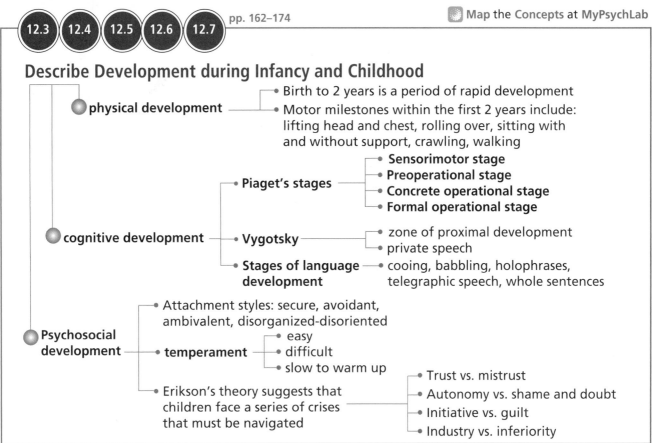

12.3 12.4 12.5 12.6 12.7 pp. 162–174

Map the Concepts at MyPsychLab

Describe Development during Infancy and Childhood

physical development
- Birth to 2 years is a period of rapid development
- Motor milestones within the first 2 years include: lifting head and chest, rolling over, sitting with and without support, crawling, walking

cognitive development
- **Piaget's stages**
  - **Sensorimotor stage**
  - **Preoperational stage**
  - **Concrete operational stage**
  - **Formal operational stage**
- **Vygotsky**
  - zone of proximal development
  - private speech
- **Stages of language development**
  - cooing, babbling, holophrases, telegraphic speech, whole sentences

Psychosocial development
- Attachment styles: secure, avoidant, ambivalent, disorganized-disoriented
- **temperament**
  - easy
  - difficult
  - slow to warm up
- Erikson's theory suggests that children face a series of crises that must be navigated
  - Trust vs. mistrust
  - Autonomy vs. shame and doubt
  - Initiative vs. guilt
  - Industry vs. inferiority

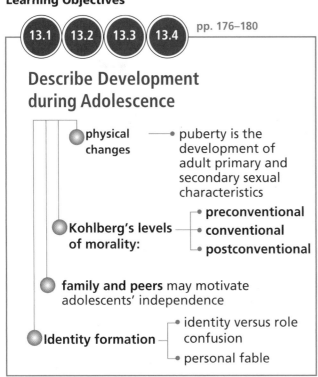

13.1 13.2 13.3 13.4 pp. 176–180

Describe Development during Adolescence

physical changes
- puberty is the development of adult primary and secondary sexual characteristics

Kohlberg's levels of morality:
- **preconventional**
- **conventional**
- **postconventional**

family and peers may motivate adolescents' independence

Identity formation
- identity versus role confusion
- personal fable

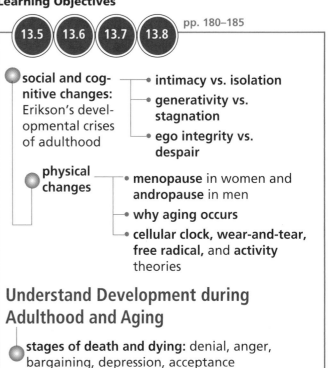

13.5 13.6 13.7 13.8 pp. 180–185

social and cognitive changes: Erikson's developmental crises of adulthood
- **intimacy vs. isolation**
- **generativity vs. stagnation**
- **ego integrity vs. despair**

physical changes
- **menopause** in women and **andropause** in men
- **why aging occurs**
- **cellular clock, wear-and-tear, free radical,** and **activity** theories

Understand Development during Adulthood and Aging

stages of death and dying: denial, anger, bargaining, depression, acceptance

6 Learning and Language Development

Yoshiko's first-grade teacher started a reading contest. For every book read, a child would get a gold star on the reading chart, and at the end of one month the child with the most stars would get a prize. Yoshiko went to the library and checked out several books each week. At the end of the month, Yoshiko had the most gold stars and got to stand in front of her classmates to receive her prize. Would it be candy? A toy? She was so excited! Imagine her delight when the big prize turned out to be another book! Through Yoshiko's love of books and reading, Yoshiko's teacher had made use of a key technique of learning called *reinforcement*. Reinforcement is anything that, when following a response, increases the likelihood that the response will occur again. The reinforcers of gold stars and a prize caused Yoshiko's reading to increase.

How have you used reinforcement to modify your own behavior or the behavior of others?

MODULE 14 ▸ CLASSICAL CONDITIONING
MODULE 15 ▸ OPERANT CONDITIONING
MODULE 16 ▸ OBSERVATIONAL LEARNING AND COGNITIVE LEARNING
MODULE 17 ▸ LANGUAGE

👁 **Watch** the **Video**, at **MyPsychLab**

Why Study Learning?

If we had not been able to learn, we would have died out as a species long ago. Learning is the process that allows us to adapt to the changing conditions of the world around us. We can alter our actions until we find the behavior that leads us to survival and rewards, and we can eliminate actions that have been unsuccessful in the past. Without learning, there would be no buildings, no agriculture, no lifesaving medicines, and no human civilization.

Learning Objectives

14.1 Outline the principles of classical conditioning.

14.2 Understand clinical and experimental examples of classical conditioning.

14.3 Explain how classical conditioning applies to everyday life.

Learn about the Process of Classical Conditioning

14.1 Outline the principles of classical conditioning.

The term *learning* is one of those concepts whose meaning is crystal clear until one has to put it into actual words. "Learning is when you learn something." "Learning is learning how to do something." A more useful definition is as follows: **Learning** is any relatively permanent change in behavior brought about by experience or practice.

The "relatively permanent" part of the definition refers to the fact that when people learn anything, some part of their brain is physically changed to record what they've learned. This is actually a process of memory, for without the ability to remember what happens, there is no evidence that learning took place. Although there is no conclusive proof as yet, research suggests strongly that once people learn something, it is always present somewhere in memory (Barsalou, 1992; Smolen et al., 2008). They may be unable to "get" to it, but it's there.

Not all change is accomplished through learning. Changes like an increase in height or the size of the brain are another kind of change controlled by a genetic blueprint. This kind of change is called *maturation* and is due to biology, not experience. For example, children learn to walk *when* they do because their nervous systems, muscle strength, and sense of balance have reached the point where walking is possible for them—all factors controlled by maturation, not by how much practice those children have had in trying to walk. No amount of experience or practice will help that child walk before maturation makes it possible—in spite of what some eager parents might wish.

It Makes Your Mouth Water: Classical Conditioning In the early 1900s, research scientists were unhappy with psychology's focus on mental activity. Many were looking for a way to bring some kind of objectivity and scientific research to the field. It was a Russian *physiologist* (a person who studies the workings of the body) named Ivan Pavlov (1849–1936) who pioneered the empirical study of the basic principles of a particular kind of learning (Pavlov, 1906, 1926).

Studying the digestive system in his dogs, Pavlov had built a device that would accurately measure the amount of saliva produced by the dogs when they were fed a measured amount of food. Normally, when food is placed in

What does "relatively permanent" mean? And how does experience change ▶ what we do?

the neighborhood. Jerry Van Amerongen

▲ *An instantaneous learning experience.*

learning any relatively permanent change in behavior brought about by experience and or practice.

the mouth of any animal, the salivary glands automatically start releasing saliva to help with chewing and digestion. This is a normal *reflex*—an unlearned, involuntary* response that is not under personal control or choice—one of many that occur in both animals and humans. The food causes the particular reaction of salivation. A *stimulus* can be defined as any object, event, or experience that causes a *response*, the reaction of an organism. In the case of Pavlov's dogs, the food is the stimulus and salivation is the response.

Pavlov soon discovered that his dogs began salivating when they weren't supposed to be salivating. Some dogs would start salivating when they saw the lab assistant bringing their food, others when they heard the clatter of the food bowl from the kitchen, and still others when it was the time of day they were usually fed. Pavlov spent the rest of his career studying what eventually he termed **classical conditioning**, learning to elicit† an involuntary, reflex-like response to a stimulus other than the original, natural stimulus that normally produces it.

The original, naturally occurring stimulus mentioned in the preceding paragraph is called the **unconditioned stimulus (UCS)**. The term *unconditioned* means "unlearned" or "naturally occurring." In the case of Pavlov's dogs, the food is the unconditioned stimulus.

The automatic and involuntary response to the unconditioned stimulus is called the **unconditioned response (UCR)** for much the same reason. It is unlearned and occurs because of genetic "wiring" in the nervous system. For example, in Pavlov's experiment, the salivation to that food is the UCR (unconditioned response).

After being paired with the food so many times, the dish came to produce the same salivation response, although a somewhat weaker one, as did the food itself. When a previously neutral stimulus (NS), through repeated pairing with the unconditioned stimulus, begins to cause the same kind of involuntary response, learning has occurred. The neutral stimulus can now be called a **conditioned stimulus (CS)**. (*Unconditioned* means "unlearned," and *conditioned* means "learned.")

The response that is given to the CS (conditioned stimulus) is not usually quite as strong as the original unconditioned response (UCR), but it is essentially the same response. However, because it comes as a response to the conditioned stimulus (CS), it is called the **conditioned response (CR)**.

Pavlov did a classic experiment in which he paired the ticking sound of a metronome (a simple device that produces a rhythmic ticking sound) with the presentation of food to see if the dogs would eventually salivate at the sound of the metronome (Pavlov, 1927). Because the metronome's ticking did not normally produce salivation, it was a neutral stimulus (NS) before any conditioning took place. The repeated pairing of a NS and the UCS (unconditioned stimulus) is usually called *acquisition*, because the organism is in the process of acquiring learning. **Figure 14.1** is a chart of how each element of the conditioning relationship worked in Pavlov's experiment.

Notice that the responses, CR (conditioned response) and UCR (unconditioned response), are the same—salivation. They simply differ in what they are the response *to*. An *unconditioned* stimulus (UCS) is always followed by an *unconditioned* response (UCR), and a *conditioned* stimulus (CS) is always followed by a *conditioned* response (CR).

Is this rocket science? No, not really. Classical conditioning is actually one of the simplest forms of learning. It's so simple that it happens to people all the time without them even being aware of it. Does your mouth water when you merely *see* an advertisement for your favorite food on television? Does your stomach get

classical conditioning learning to elicit an involuntary response to a stimulus other than the original, natural stimulus that normally produces the response.

unconditioned stimulus (UCS) a naturally occurring stimulus that leads to an involuntary response.

unconditioned response (UCR) an involuntary response to a naturally occurring or unconditioned stimulus.

conditioned stimulus (CS) stimulus that becomes able to produce a learned response by being paired with the original unconditioned stimulus.

conditioned response (CR) learned response to a conditioned stimulus.

---

*involuntary: not under personal control or choice.
†elicit: to draw forth reflexively.

FIGURE 14.1 Classical Conditioning

Before conditioning takes place, the sound of the metronome does not cause salivation and is a neutral stimulus, or NS. During conditioning, the sound of the metronome occurs just before the presentation of the food, the UCS. The food causes salivation, the UCR. When conditioning has occurred after several pairings of the metronome with the food, the metronome will begin to elicit a salivation response from the dog without any food. This is learning, and the sound of the metronome is now a CS and the salivation to the ticking is the CR.

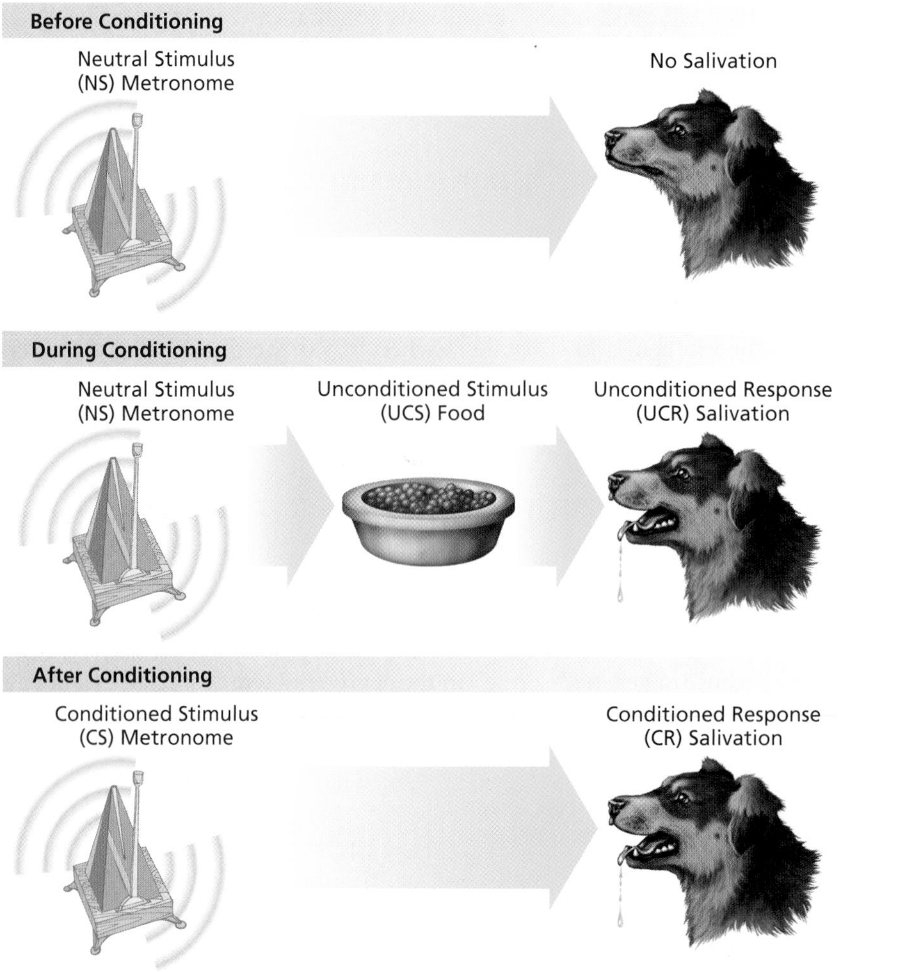

Before Conditioning

Neutral Stimulus (NS) Metronome → No Salivation

During Conditioning

Neutral Stimulus (NS) Metronome → Unconditioned Stimulus (UCS) Food → Unconditioned Response (UCR) Salivation

After Conditioning

Conditioned Stimulus (CS) Metronome → Conditioned Response (CR) Salivation

---

stimulus generalization the tendency to respond to a stimulus similar to the original conditioned stimulus with the conditioned response.

stimulus discrimination a distinction is made between the conditioned stimulus and a similar stimulus and an unconditioned response is not elicited.

upset every time you hear the high-pitched whine of the dentist's drill? These are both examples of classical conditioning.

After all the dog stories, the salivation to the TV ad probably needs no explanation, but what about the dentist's drill? Over the course of many visits, the body comes to associate that sound (CS) with the anxiety or fear (UCR) the person has felt while receiving a painful dental treatment (UCS), and so the sound produces a feeling of anxiety (CR) whether that person is in the chair or just in the outer waiting area.

Pavlov did find that similar sounds would produce the same conditioned response from his dogs. He and other researchers found that the strength of the response to the similar sounds was not as strong as to the original one, but the more similar the other sound was to the original sound (be it a metronome or any other kind of sound), the more similar the strength of the response was as well (Siegel, 1969). (See **Figure 14.2.**) The tendency to respond to a stimulus that is only similar to the original conditioned stimulus is called **stimulus generalization**. Of course, Pavlov did not give the dogs any food after the similar ticking sound. It didn't take long for the dogs to stop responding (generalizing) to the "fake" ticking sounds altogether. Because only the real CS was followed with food, they learned to tell the difference, or *discriminate*, between the "fake" ticking and the CS ticking, a process called **stimulus discrimination**. Stimulus discrimination occurs when an organism learns to respond to different stimuli in different ways.

Extinction and Spontaneous Recovery What would have happened if Pavlov had stopped giving the dogs food after the real CS? Would they

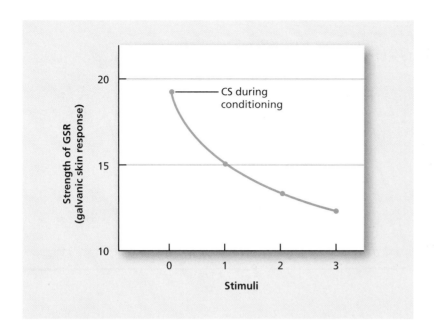

FIGURE 14.2 Strength of the Generalized Response
An example of stimulus generalization. The UCS was an electric shock and the UCR was the galvanic skin response (GSR), a measure associated with anxiety. The subjects had been conditioned originally to a CS tone (0) of a given frequency. When tested with the original tone, and with tones 1, 2, and 3 of differing frequencies, a clear generalization effect appeared. The closer the frequency of the test tone to the frequency of tone 0, the greater was the magnitude of the galvanic skin response to the tone (Hovland, 1937).

"unlearn" the association between the CS and UCS? Pavlov did just that, and the dogs gradually stopped salivating to the sound of the ticking. When the metronome's ticking (CS or conditioned stimulus) was repeatedly presented in the absence of the UCS (unconditioned stimulus or food, in this case), the salivation (CR or conditioned response) "weakened" in a process called **extinction**.

Why does the removal of an unconditioned stimulus lead to extinction of the conditioned response? One theory is that the presentation of the CS alone leads to new learning. During extinction, the CS–UCS association that was learned is weakened, as the CS no longer predicts the UCS. In the case of Pavlov's dogs, through extinction they learned to not salivate to the metronome's ticking, as it no longer predicted that food was on its way.

Look back at Figure 14.1. Once conditioning is acquired, the conditioned stimulus (CS) and conditioned response (CR) will always come *before* the original unconditioned stimulus (UCS). The UCS, which comes after the CS and CR link, now serves as a strengthener, or reinforcer, of the CS–CR association. Remove that reinforcer, and the CR it strengthens will weaken and disappear—at least for a while.

After extinguishing the conditioned salivation response in his dogs, Pavlov waited a few weeks, putting the conditioned stimulus (e.g., the metronome) away. There were no more training sessions, and the dogs were not exposed to the metronome's ticking in that time at all. But when Pavlov took the metronome back out and set it ticking, the dogs all began to salivate, although it was a fairly weak response and didn't last very long. This brief recovery of the conditioned response proves that the CR is "still in there" somewhere (remember, learning is *relatively permanent*). It is just suppressed or inhibited by the lack of an association with the unconditioned stimulus of food (which is no longer reinforcing or strengthening the CR). As time passes, this inhibition weakens, especially if the original conditioned stimulus has not been present for a while. In **spontaneous recovery**, the conditioned response can briefly reappear when the original CS returns, although the response is usually weak and short-lived. See **Figure 14.3** for a graph showing both extinction and spontaneous recovery. People experience classical conditioning in many ways. People who are allergic to cats sometimes sneeze when they see a *picture* of a cat.

extinction the disappearance or weakening of a learned response following the removal or absence of the unconditioned stimulus (in classical conditioning) or the removal of a reinforcer (in operant conditioning).

spontaneous recovery the reappearance of a learned response after extinction has occurred.

FIGURE 14.3 Extinction and Spontaneous Recovery
This graph shows the acquisition, extinction, spontaneous recovery, and reacquisition of a conditioned salivary response. Typically, the measure of conditioning is the number of drops of saliva elicited by the CS on each trial. Note that on the day following extinction, the first presentation of the CS elicits quite a large response. This response is due to spontaneous recovery.

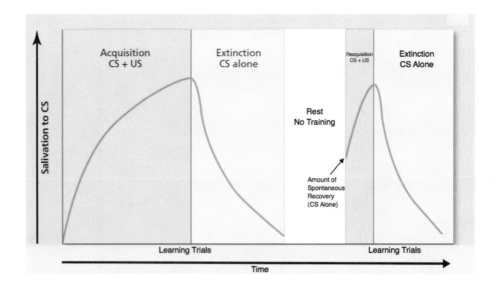

14.2 Understand clinical and experimental examples of classical conditioning.

Later scientists took Pavlov's concepts and expanded them to explain not only animal behavior but also human behavior. One of the earliest of these studies showed that even an emotional response could be conditioned.

Conditioned Emotional Responses: Rats! In the first chapter of this text, John B. Watson's classic experiment with "Little Albert" and the white rat was discussed. This study was a demonstration of the classical conditioning of a phobia—an irrational fear response (Watson & Rayner, 1920).

Watson, and graduate student Rosalie Rayner, paired the presentation of the white rat to the baby with a loud, scary noise. Although the baby was not initially afraid of the rat, he was naturally afraid of the loud noise and started to cry. Soon, every time the baby saw the rat, he started to cry. In conditioning terms, the loud noise was the UCS, the fear of the noise the UCR, the white rat became the CS, and the fear of the rat (the phobia) was the CR. (It should be pointed out that Watson didn't really "torture" the baby—Albert's fright was temporary. Of course, no ethics committee today would approve an experiment in which an infant experiences such psychological distress.)

The learning of phobias is a very good example of a certain type of classical conditioning, the *conditioned emotional response (CER)*. Conditioned emotional responses are some of the easiest forms of classical conditioning to accomplish and our lives are full of them. It's easy to think of fears people might have that are conditioned or learned: a child's fear of the dentist's chair, a puppy's fear of a rolled-up newspaper, or the fear of dogs that is often shown by a person who has been attacked by a dog in the past. But other emotions can be conditioned, too.

The next time you watch television, watch the commercials closely. Advertisers often use certain objects or certain types of people in their ads to

▲ *After "Little Albert" had been conditioned to fear a white rat, he later demonstrated fear of a rabbit, a dog, a fur coat, and this mask worn by Watson. Can you think of any emotional reactions you experience that might be classically conditioned emotional responses? Do you have any such reactions to similar situations or stimuli?*

generate a specific emotional response in viewers, hoping that the emotional response will become associated with their product. Sexy models, cute little babies, and adorable puppies are some of the examples of stimuli the advertising world uses to tug at our heartstrings, so to speak.

It is even possible to become classically conditioned by simply watching someone else respond to a stimulus in a process called *vicarious conditioning* (Bandura & Rosenthal, 1966; Hygge & Öhman, 1976; Jones & Menzies, 1995). Many years ago, children received vaccination shots in school. The nurse lined the children up, and one by one they had to go forward to get a needle in the arm. When some children received their shots, they cried quite a bit. By the time the nurse got near the end of the line of children, they were all crying—many of them before she ever touched needle to skin. They had learned their fear response from watching the reactions of the other children.

14.3 Explain how classical conditioning applies to everyday life.

Conditioned Taste Aversions and Biological Preparedness Are there any foods that you just can't eat anymore because of a bad experience with them? Believe it or not, your reaction to that food is a kind of classical conditioning.

Many experiments, including the research by Dr. John Garcia, have shown that laboratory rats will develop a *conditioned taste aversion* for any liquid or food they swallow up to 6 hours before becoming nauseated. Researchers (Garcia & Koelling, 1966; Garcia et al., 1989) found that rats that were given a sweetened liquid and then several hours later were injected with a drug or exposed to radiation that caused nausea would not touch the liquid again. In a similar manner, alcoholics who are given a drug to make them violently nauseated when they drink alcohol may learn to avoid drinking any alcoholic beverage. The chemotherapy drugs that cancer patients receive also can create severe nausea, which causes those people to develop a taste aversion for any food they have eaten before going in for the chemotherapy treatment (Berteretche et al., 2004).

It's interesting to note that birds, which find their food by sight, will avoid any object or insect that simply looks like the one that made them sick. There is a certain species of moth with coloring that mimics the monarch butterfly. That particular butterfly is poisonous to birds, but the moth isn't. The moth's mimicry causes birds to avoid eating it, even though it is quite edible. Whereas mammals are *biologically prepared* to associate taste with illness, birds are biologically prepared to associate visual characteristics with illness (Shapiro et al., 1980).

◀ But I thought that it took several pairings of these stimuli to bring about conditioning. How can classical conditioning happen so fast?

Thinking Critically
Do you think that humans are as controlled by their biology as other animals? Why or why not?

◀ *Conditioned taste aversions in nature. This moth is not poisonous to birds, but the monarch butterfly whose coloring the moth imitates is quite poisonous. Birds find their food by vision and will not eat anything that resembles the monarch. In evolutionary terms, how is this an evolved "adaptive trait" for the moth?*

Pick the best answer.

1. Learning can best be described as
   a. a relatively permanent change in behavior.
   b. a permanent change in behavior.
   c. due primarily to unconscious motives.
   d. momentary changes in behavior.

2. Which of the following statements is most characteristic of effective classical conditioning?
   a. The CS and UCS are paired close together in time.
   b. The CS must come immediately after the CR.
   c. The neutral stimulus and UCR must be paired several times before conditioning takes place.
   d. The CS should be something highly unusual.

3. Ed noticed that whenever he used his electric can opener, his cat would come into the kitchen. The sound of the can opener has become a(n)
   a. unconditioned stimulus.
   b. conditioned stimulus.
   c. conditioned response.
   d. neutral stimulus.

4. Stephanie developed a fear of white coats as a result of painful shots given to her by doctors dressed in white coats. Now she is also afraid of photographers in white coats. This is an example of
   a. extinction.   c. spontaneous recovery.
   b. reinforcement.   d. stimulus generalization.

5. A dog, whose conditioned response to a bell has been extinguished, briefly displays the conditioned response to the bell. This is an example of
   a. extinction.
   b. association.
   c. spontaneous recovery.
   d. generalization.

6. Which of the following is a concern about Watson's "Little Albert" experiment?
   a. the use of a child in an experiment
   b. positive reinforcement was used
   c. negative reinforcement was used
   d. the ethics of the experiment

7. What did Watson's classic experiment with "Little Albert" demonstrate?
   a. the learning of a phobia
   b. the biological basis of fear
   c. the existence of vicarious conditioning
   d. the extinction of a conditioned response

8. If Cindy had scrambled eggs for breakfast and then took a chemotherapy treatment that caused nausea later that same morning, which of the following responses is most likely to occur?
   a. Cindy will develop a strong liking for scrambled eggs.
   b. Cindy will be able to eat scrambled eggs with no nausea at all.
   c. Cindy will get nauseated the next time she tries to eat scrambled eggs.
   d. Cindy will get nauseated the next time she tries to eat any sort of food.

9. What must be removed in order for extinction of the association made between a conditioned stimulus and a conditioned response to occur?
   a. unconditioned stimulus
   b. conditioned stimulus
   c. generalized stimulus
   d. neutral stimulus

10. Companies who use popular actors and actresses in their ad campaigns are trying to create a(n) _____ in people who look at their advertisements.
    a. neutral response
    b. higher order response
    c. vicarious response
    d. emotional response that are conditioned

15 Operant Conditioning

Module Goal	Learning Objectives
Learn about the process of operant conditioning	**15.1** Understand the Law of Effect.
	15.2 Explain the principles of operant conditioning.
	15.3 Describe specialized examples of operant conditioning.
	15.4 Describe how operant conditioning applies to everyday life.

Learn about the Process of Operant Conditioning

All organisms are capable of two kinds of behavior: involuntary and voluntary. If Inez blinks her eyes because a gnat flies close to them, that's a reflex and totally involuntary. But if she then swats at the gnat to frighten it, that's a voluntary choice. She *had* to blink, but she *chose* to swat.

Classical conditioning is the kind of learning that occurs with automatic, involuntary behavior. The kind of learning that applies to voluntary behavior is called **operant conditioning**, which is both different from and similar to classical conditioning.

15.1 Understand the Law of Effect.

Frustrating Cats: Thorndike's Puzzle Box and the Law of Effect

Edward L. Thorndike (1874–1949) was one of the first researchers to explore and attempt to outline the laws of learning voluntary responses, although the field was not yet called operant conditioning. Thorndike placed a hungry cat inside a "puzzle box" from which the only escape was to press a lever located on the floor of the box. Thorndike placed a dish of food *outside* the box, so that the hungry cat would be highly motivated to get out. Thorndike observed that the cat would move around the box, pushing and rubbing up against the walls in an effort to escape. Eventually, the cat would accidentally push the lever, opening the door. Upon escaping, the cat was fed from a dish placed just outside the box. The lever is the stimulus, the pushing of the lever is the response, and the consequence is both escape (good) and food (even better).

The cat did not learn to push the lever and escape right away. After a number of trials (and many errors) in a box like this one, the cat took less and less time to push the lever that would open the door. It's important not to assume that the cat had "figured out" the connection between the lever and freedom—Thorndike kept moving the lever to a different position, and the cat had to learn the whole process over again. The cat would simply continue to rub and push in the same general area that led to food and freedom the last time, each time getting out and fed a little more quickly.

Based on this research, Thorndike developed the **law of effect**: If an action is followed by a pleasurable consequence, it will tend to be repeated. If an

◀ So far, all learning seems to involve involuntary behavior, but I know that I am more than just automatic responses. People do things on purpose, so is that kind of behavior also learned?

law of effect law stating that if an action is followed by a pleasurable consequence, it will tend to be repeated, and if followed by an unpleasant consequence, it will tend not to be repeated.

action is followed by an unpleasant consequence, it will tend not to be repeated (Thorndike, 1911). This is the basic principle behind learning voluntary behavior. In the case of the cat in the box, pushing the lever was followed by a pleasurable consequence (getting out and getting fed), so pushing the lever became a repeated response. Thorndike's important and groundbreaking work began the study of what would eventually become *operant conditioning*.

15.2 Explain the principles of operant conditioning.

B. F. Skinner (1904–1990) was the behaviorist who assumed leadership of the field after John Watson. He was even more determined than Watson that psychologists should study only measurable, observable behavior. In addition to his knowledge of Pavlovian classical conditioning, Skinner found in the work of Thorndike a way to explain all behavior as the product of learning. He even gave the learning of voluntary behavior a special name: **operant conditioning** (Skinner, 1938). Voluntary behavior is what people and animals do to *operate* in the world. When people perform a voluntary action, it is to get something they want or avoid something they don't want, right? So a voluntary behavior (an "operant"), for Skinner, is *operant* behavior, and the learning of such behavior is operant conditioning.

The heart of operant conditioning is the effect of consequences on behavior. Thinking back to the section on classical conditioning, learning an involuntary behavior really depends on what comes *before* the response—the unconditioned stimulus and what will become the conditioned stimulus. These two stimuli are the *antecedent* stimuli (antecedent means something that comes before another thing). But in operant conditioning, learning depends on what happens *after* the response—the consequence (think of this as the "ABCs" of behavior: **A**ntecedent, **B**ehavior, **C**onsequence). In a way, operant conditioning could be summed up as this: "If I do this, what's in it for me?"

The Concept of Reinforcement "What's in it for me?" represents the concept of *reinforcement*, one of Skinner's major contributions to behaviorism. The word itself means "to strengthen," and Skinner defined reinforcement as anything that, when following a response, causes that response to be more likely to happen again. Typically, this means that reinforcement is a consequence that is in some way pleasurable to the organism, which relates back to Thorndike's law of effect. The "pleasurable consequence" is what's in it for the organism. (Keep in mind that a "pleasurable consequence" might be something like getting food or money when you need it, but it might also mean *avoiding* a tiresome chore, like doing the dishes or taking out the garbage. I'll do almost anything to get out of doing the dishes, myself!)

Skinner had his own version of a puzzle box called a "Skinner box" or "operant conditioning chamber." His early research often involved placing a rat into one of these chambers and training it to push down on a bar to get food.

Primary and Secondary Reinforcers The events or items that can be used to reinforce behavior are not all alike. Let's say that a friend of yours asks you to help her move some books from the trunk of her car to her apartment on the second floor. She offers you a choice of $25 or a candy bar. Unless you've suffered recent brain damage, you'll most likely choose the money, right? With $25, you could buy more than one candy bar. (At today's prices, you might even be able to afford three.)

Now pretend that your friend offers the same deal to a 3-year-old child who lives downstairs for carrying up some of the paperback books: $25 or a candy bar. Which reward will the child more likely choose? Most children at that age

operant conditioning the learning of voluntary behavior through the effects of pleasant and unpleasant consequences to responses.

primary reinforcer any reinforcer that is naturally reinforcing by meeting a basic biological need, such as hunger, thirst, or touch.

secondary reinforcer any reinforcer that becomes reinforcing after being paired with a primary reinforcer, such as praise, tokens, or gold stars.

have no real idea of the value of money, so the child will probably choose the candy bar. The money and the candy bar represent two basic kinds of *reinforcers*, items or events that when following a response will strengthen it. The reinforcing properties of money must be learned, but candy gives immediate reward in the form of taste and satisfying hunger.

A reinforcer such as a candy bar that satisfies a basic need like hunger is called a **primary reinforcer**. Examples would be any kind of food (hunger drive), liquid (thirst drive), or touch (pleasure drive). Infants, toddlers, preschool-age children, and animals can be easily reinforced by using primary reinforcers.

A **secondary reinforcer** such as money, however, gets its reinforcing properties from being associated with primary reinforcers in the past. A child who is given money to spend soon realizes that the ugly green paper can be traded for candy and treats—primary reinforcers—and so money becomes reinforcing in and of itself.

Secondary reinforcers do indeed get their reinforcing power from the process of classical conditioning. After all, the pleasure people feel when they eat, drink, or get a back rub is an automatic response, and any automatic response can be classically conditioned to occur to a new stimulus. In the case of money, the candy is a UCS for pleasure (the UCR), and the money is present just before the candy is obtained. The money becomes a CS for pleasure, and people certainly do feel pleasure when they have a lot of that green stuff, don't they?

Positive and Negative Reinforcement Reinforcers can also differ in the way they are used. Most people have no trouble at all understanding that following a response with some kind of pleasurable consequence (like a reward) will lead to an increase in the likelihood of that response being repeated. This is called **positive reinforcement**, the reinforcement of a response by the *addition* or experience of a pleasurable consequence, such as a reward or a pat on the back. But many people have trouble understanding that the opposite is also true: Following a response with *the removal or escape* from something *unpleasant* will also increase the likelihood of that response being repeated—a process called **negative reinforcement**. If a person's behavior gets pain to stop, the person is much more likely to do that same thing again.

We've discussed what reinforcement is and how it affects the behavior that follows the reinforcement. In the next section we'll discuss the different ways in which reinforcement can be administered as well as the difference between reinforcement and punishment. We'll also look at the role of the stimuli that come *before* the behavior that is to be reinforced and a few other operant conditioning concepts.

15.3 Describe specialized examples of operant conditioning.

Schedules of Reinforcement: Why the One-Armed Bandit Is So Seductive
The timing of reinforcement can make a tremendous difference in the speed at which learning occurs and the strength of the learned response. However, Skinner (1956) found that reinforcing every response was not necessarily the best schedule of reinforcement for long-lasting learning as we'll see in the video, *Schedules of Reinforcement*.

The Partial Reinforcement Effect Alicia's mother gives her a quarter every night she remembers to put her dirty clothes in the clothes hamper. Bianca's mother gives her a dollar at the end of the week, but only if Bianca has put her

positive reinforcement the reinforcement (strengthening) of a response by the addition or experience of a pleasurable stimulus.

negative reinforcement the reinforcement (strengthening) of a response by the removal, escape from, or avoidance of an unpleasant stimulus.

That sounds very familiar. ◄ Isn't this related to classical conditioning?

Thinking Critically
What type of reinforcement worked best for you when you were in grade school? Positive or negative? Did this change in high school?

👁 **Watch** the **Video**, *Schedules of Reinforcement*, at **MyPsychLab**

clothes in the hamper every night. Alicia learns more quickly than does Bianca because responses that are reinforced each time they occur are more easily and quickly learned.

As soon as the reinforcers stop, the behavior extinguishes. Bianca has expected to get a reinforcer only after *seven correct responses*. When the reinforcers stop, Bianca might continue to put the clothes in the hamper for several more days or even another whole week, hoping that the reinforcer will eventually come anyway. Bianca may have learned more slowly than Alicia, but once she learned the connection between putting her clothes in the hamper and getting that dollar, she was less likely to stop doing it.

Bianca's behavior illustrates the *partial reinforcement effect* (Skinner, 1956): A response that is reinforced after some, but not all, correct responses will be more resistant to extinction than a response that receives *continuous reinforcement* (a reinforcer for each and every correct response). Imagine being paid for every hamburger you make or every report you turn in. In the real world, people tend to receive partial reinforcement rather than continuous reinforcement for their work.

Partial reinforcement can be accomplished according to different patterns or schedules. For example, it might be a certain interval of time that's important, such as an office safe that can only be opened at a certain time of day. It wouldn't matter how many times one tried to open the safe if the effort didn't come at the right *time*. On the other hand, it may be the number of responses that is important, as it would be if one had to sell a certain number of raffle tickets in order to get a prize. When the timing of the response is more important, it is called an *interval schedule*. When it is the number of responses that is important, the schedule is called a *ratio schedule* because a certain number of responses is required for each reinforcer (e.g., 50 raffle tickets for each prize). The other way in which schedules of reinforcement can differ is in whether the number of responses or interval of time is *fixed* (the same in each case) or *variable* (a different number or interval is required in each case). So it is possible to have a fixed interval schedule, a variable interval schedule, a fixed ratio schedule, and a variable ratio schedule (Skinner, 1961).

Fixed Interval Schedule of Reinforcement The kind of reinforcement schedule most people are more familiar with is called a **fixed interval schedule of reinforcement**, in which a reinforcer is received after a certain, fixed interval of time has passed. If a researcher was teaching a rat to press a lever to get food pellets, she might require it to push the lever for 2 minutes to get a pellet. It wouldn't matter how many times the rat pushed the bar press, it would only get the pellet after 2 minutes had passed. If people receive a paycheck once every two weeks (provided that they show up to work in those two weeks), they are being reinforced on this kind of schedule.

So what would be ▶ a variable interval schedule?

Variable Interval Schedule of Reinforcement Social networking sites like Facebook create a variable interval schedule when you have to "log in" to check for a friend request message (a reinforce). Facebook friend requests are good examples of a **variable interval schedule of reinforcement**. The interval of time after which the organism must respond in order to receive a reinforcer changes from one time to the next. In a more basic example, a rat might receive a food pellet when it pushes a lever, every 5 minutes on average. Sometimes the interval might be 2 minutes, sometimes 10, but the rat must push the lever at least once *during* that interval to get the pellet. Because the rat can't predict how long the interval is going to be, it pushes the bar more or less continuously. Once again, speed is not important, so the rate of responding is slow but steady.

Fixed Ratio Schedule of Reinforcement In ratio schedules, it is the number of responses that counts. In a **fixed ratio schedule of reinforcement**, the number of responses required to receive each reinforcer will always be the same number.

In human terms, anyone who does piecework, in which a certain number of items have to be completed before payment is given, is reinforced on a fixed ratio schedule. Some sandwich shops give out punch cards that get punched one time for each sandwich purchased. When the card has 10 punches, for example, the person would get a free sandwich.

Variable Ratio Schedule of Reinforcement A **variable ratio schedule of reinforcement** is one in which the number of responses changes from one trial to the next. In the rat example, the rat might be expected to push the bar an average of 20 times to get reinforcement. That means that sometimes the rat would push the lever only 10 times before a reinforcer comes, but at other times it might take 30 lever pushes or more.

In human terms, people who shove money into the one-armed bandit, or slot machine, are being reinforced on a variable ratio schedule of reinforcement (they hope). They put their coins in (response), but they don't know how many "pulls" they will have to make before reinforcement (the jackpot) comes. People who do this may sit there until they either win or run out of money. They may not stop and continue playing, even while they are losing their money, because the "next one" might hit that jackpot. Buying lottery tickets is much the same thing, as is any kind of gambling. People don't know how many tickets they will have to buy, and they have a notion that if they don't buy the next one, that will be the ticket that would have won, so they keep buying and buying.

Regardless of the schedule of reinforcement one uses, there are some things that can be done to make using reinforcement of a behavior as effective as possible. One thing also concerns timing: A reinforcer should be given as immediately as possible after the desired behavior. Delaying reinforcement tends not to work well, especially when dealing with animals and small children. (Older children and adults can think about future reinforcements, such as saving up one's money to buy a highly desired item, so delayed reinforcement can work with them.) Care should also be taken to reinforce *only* the desired behavior—for example, many parents make the mistake of giving a child who has not done some chore the promised treat anyway, which completely undermines the child's learning of that chore or task.

The Role of Punishment in Operant Conditioning Let's go back to the discussion of positive and negative reinforcement. These strategies are important for *increasing* the likelihood that the targeted behavior will occur again. But what about behavior that we do not want to reoccur?

Defining Punishment People experience two kinds of things as consequences in the world: things they like (food, money, candy, sex, praise, and so on) and things they don't like (spankings, being yelled at, and experiencing any kind of pain, to name a few). In addition, people experience these two kinds of consequences in one of two ways: Either people experience them directly (such as getting money for working or getting yelled at for misbehaving) or they don't experience them, such as losing an allowance for misbehaving or avoiding a scolding by lying about misbehavior. These four consequences are named and described in **Table 15.1**.

First, take a look at the left column of Table 15.1, the one labeled "Reinforcement." Getting money for working is an example of *positive reinforcement*,

fixed ratio schedule of reinforcement schedule of reinforcement in which the number of responses required for reinforcement is always the same.

variable ratio schedule of reinforcement schedule of reinforcement in which the number of responses required for reinforcement is different for each trial or event.

◀ So I think I get reinforcement now, but what about punishment? How does punishment fit into the big picture?

Table 15.1   **Four Ways to Modify Behavior**

	REINFORCEMENT		PUNISHMENT	
Positive (Adding)	**Positive Reinforcement** Something valued or desirable	Example: getting a gold star for good behavior in school	**Punishment by Application** Something unpleasant	Example: getting a spanking for disobeying
Negative (Removing or Avoiding)	**Negative Reinforcement** Something unpleasant	Example: fastening a seat belt to stop the alarm from sounding	**Punishment by Removal** Something valued or desirable	Example: losing a privilege such as going out with friends

the reinforcement of a response by the *addition* or experience of a *pleasurable* consequence, as mentioned earlier. That one everyone understands. But what about avoiding a penalty by turning one's income tax return in on time? That is an example of *negative reinforcement,* the reinforcement of a response by the *removal or escape* from an *unpleasant* consequence. Because the behavior (submitting the return before the deadline) results in *avoiding* an unpleasant stimulus (a penalty), the likelihood that the person will behave that way again (turn it in on time in the future) is *increased*—just as positive reinforcement will increase a behavior's likelihood.

I'm confused. I thought taking something away was a kind of punishment? ▶

Two Kinds of Punishment People get confused because "negative" sounds like it ought to be something bad, like a kind of punishment. *Punishment* is actually the opposite of reinforcement. It is any event or stimulus that, when following a response, causes that response to be less likely to happen again. Punishment *weakens* responses, whereas reinforcement (no matter whether it is positive or negative) *strengthens* responses. There are two ways in which punishment can happen, just as there are two ways in which reinforcement can happen.

Now take a look at the right column of Table 15.1, labeled "Punishment." **Punishment by application** occurs when something unpleasant (such as a spanking, scolding, or other unpleasant stimulus) is added to the situation or *applied.* This is the kind of punishment that most people think of when they hear the word *punishment.* This is also the kind of punishment that many child development specialists strongly recommend parents avoid using with their children because it can easily escalate into abuse (Dubowitz & Bennett, 2007; Straus, 2000; Trocmé et al., 2001). A spanking might be *physically* harmless if it is only two or three swats with a hand, but if done in anger or with a belt or other instrument, it becomes abuse, both physical and emotional.

Punishment by removal, on the other hand, is the kind of punishment most often confused with negative reinforcement. In this type of punishment, behavior is punished by the removal of something pleasurable or desired after the behavior occurs. "Grounding" a teenager is removing the freedom to do what the teenager wants to do and is an example of this kind of punishment. This type of punishment is far more acceptable to child development specialists because it involves no physical aggression and avoids many of the problems caused by more aggressive punishments.

punishment by application the punishment of a response by the addition or experience of an unpleasant stimulus.

punishment by removal the punishment of a response by the removal of a pleasurable stimulus.

The confusion over the difference between negative reinforcement and punishment by removal of a pleasant or desirable thing makes it worth examining the difference just a bit more. The difference between them lies in *what* is taken away: In the case of negative reinforcement, it is an *unpleasant* thing; in the case of this particular form of punishment, it is a *pleasant* or desirable thing.

shaping the reinforcement of simple steps in behavior that lead to a desired, more complex behavior.

15.4 Describe how operant conditioning applies to everyday life.

Applications of Operant Conditioning: Shaping and Behavior Modification Operant conditioning is more than just the reinforcement of simple responses. It can be used to modify the behavior of both animals and humans.

Shaping When you see an animal in a circus or in a show at a zoo perform tricks, you are seeing the result of applying the rules of conditioning—both classical and operant—to animals. But the more complex tricks are a process in operant conditioning called **shaping**, in which small steps toward some ultimate goal are reinforced until the goal itself is reached.

◀ How do the circus trainers get their animals to do all those complicated tricks?

For example, if Jody wanted to train his dog Rover to jump through a hoop, he would have to start with some behavior that the dog is already capable of doing on its own. Then he would gradually "mold" that starting behavior into the jump—something the dog is capable of doing but not likely to do on its own. The goal is achieved by reinforcing each *successive approximation* (small steps one after the other that get closer and closer to the goal). This process is called shaping (Skinner, 1974). Through pairing of a sound such as a whistle or clicker with the primary reinforcer of food, animal trainers can use the sound as a secondary reinforcer and avoid having an overfed learner.

Although animals can learn many types of behavior through the use of operant conditioning, it seems that not every animal can be taught *anything*. For more on this topic, see the following section on biological constraints.

Classic Studies in Psychology

Biological Constraints on Operant Conditioning

Raccoons are fairly intelligent animals and are sometimes used in learning experiments. In a typical experiment, a behaviorist would use shaping and reinforcement to teach a raccoon a trick. The goal might be to get the raccoon to pick up several coins and drop them into a metal container, for which the raccoon would be rewarded with food. The behaviorist starts by reinforcing the raccoon for picking up a single coin. Then the metal container is introduced, and the raccoon is now required to drop the coin into the slot on the container in order to get reinforcement.

It is at this point that operant conditioning seems to fail. Instead of dropping the coin in the slot, the raccoon puts the coin in and out of the slot and rubs it against the inside of the container, then holds it firmly for a few seconds before finally letting it go. When the requirement is upped to two coins, the raccoon spends several minutes rubbing them against each other and dipping them into the container, without actually dropping them in. In spite of the fact that this dipping and rubbing

▲ *Raccoons commonly dunk their food in and out of water before eating. This "washing" behavior is controlled by instinct and is difficult to change even using operant techniques.*

behavior is not reinforced, it gets worse and worse until conditioning becomes impossible.

Keller and Marian Breland, in their attempt to train a raccoon, found that this problem was not limited to the raccoon (Breland & Breland, 1961). They ran into a similar difficulty with a pig that was being trained to pick up a total of five large wooden coins and put them into a "piggy bank." Although at first successful, the pig became slower and slower at the task over a period of weeks, dropping the coin, rooting (pushing) it around with its nose, picking it up, dropping it again, and rooting some more. This behavior became so persistent that the pig actually did not get enough to eat for the day.

The Brelands concluded that the raccoon and the pig were reverting* to behavior that was instinctual for them. Instinctual behavior is genetically determined and not under the influence of learning. Apparently, even though the animals were at first able to learn the tricks, as the coins became more and more associated with food, the animals began to drift back into the instinctual patterns of behavior that they used with real food. Raccoons rub their food between their paws and dip it in and out of water. Pigs root and throw their food around before eating it. The Brelands called this tendency to revert to genetically controlled patterns *instinctive drift*.

In their 1961 paper describing these and other examples of instinctive drift, the Brelands (both trained by Skinner himself) determined that, contrary to Skinner's original ideas:

1. The animal does NOT come to the laboratory a *tabula rasa*, or "blank slate," and cannot be taught just any behavior.
2. Differences between species of animals matter in determining what behavior can or cannot be conditioned.
3. Not all responses are equally able to be conditioned to any stimulus.

As became quickly obvious in their studies with these animals, each animal comes into the world (and the laboratory) with certain genetically determined instinctive patterns of behavior already in place. These instincts differ from species to species, with the result that there are some responses that simply cannot be trained into an animal regardless of conditioning.

Questions for Further Discussion

1. What other kinds of limitations do animals have in learning?
2. What kinds of behavior might people do that would be resistant to conditioning?
3. How can these research findings about animal behavior be generalized to human behavior?

Behavior Modification Operant conditioning principles such as reinforcement and the process of shaping have been used for many years to change undesirable behavior and create desirable responses in animals and humans—particularly in schoolchildren. The term **behavior modification** refers to the application of operant conditioning (and sometimes classical conditioning) to bring about such changes. The video *Behavior Modification Plan for Improving Heath* describes a sample behavior modification plan for someone who wants to watch less television and exercise more.

Watch the Video, *Behavior Modification Plan for Improving Heath*, at **MyPsychLab**

---

*reverting: to go back in action, thought, speech, and so on.

As another example, if a teacher wants to use behavior modification to help a child learn to be more attentive during the teacher's lectures, the teacher may do the following:

1. Select a target behavior, such as making eye contact with the teacher.

2. Choose a reinforcer. This may be a gold star applied to the child's chart on the wall, for example.

3. Put the plan in action. Every time the child makes eye contact, the teacher gives the child a gold star. Inappropriate behavior (such as looking out of the window) is not reinforced with gold stars.

4. At the end of the day, the teacher gives the child a special treat or reward for having a certain number of gold stars. This special reward is decided on ahead of time and discussed with the child.

Gold stars can be considered *tokens*, secondary reinforcers that can be traded in for other kinds of reinforcers. The use of tokens to modify behavior is called a *token economy*. In the example, the child is collecting gold stars to "buy" the special treat at the end of the day.

Another tool that behaviorists can use to modify behavior is the process of *time-out*. Time-out is a form of mild punishment by removal in which a misbehaving animal, child, or adult is placed in a special area away from the attention of others. Essentially, the organism is being "removed" from any possibility of positive reinforcement in the form of attention. When used with children, time-out should be limited to 1 minute for each year of age with a maximum time-out of 10 minutes (longer than that and the child can forget why the time-out occurred).

Other techniques for modifying behavior have been developed so that even behavior that is normally considered involuntary such as blood pressure and muscle tension can be brought under conscious control. For nearly 60 years, scientists have known how to use feedback of a person's biological information (such as heart rate) to create a state of relaxation (Margolin & Kubic, 1944). *Biofeedback* is the traditional term used to describe this kind of biological feedback of information, and through its use many problems can be relieved or controlled.

Pick the best answer.

1. Bennie is afraid of birds. When he sees a bird in his back yard, he screams and causes the bird to fly away. Bennie's screaming behavior is an example of

   a. positive reinforcement.
   b. punishment by application.
   c. punishment by removal.
   d. negative reinforcement.

2. Little Jimmie's mother was upset to find that Jimmie had not picked up his building blocks after repeated requests to do so. The next morning, Jimmie found all his blocks had been picked up and put into a bag on the top of the refrigerator. Jimmie's mother told him that he couldn't play with his blocks for the next two days. Which type of discipline did she use?

   a. negative reinforcement
   b. punishment by application
   c. punishment by removal
   d. positive reinforcement

3. Elizabeth's parents want her to put her clothes in the hamper. At first, they praise her for putting the clothes together in one pile. Then they praise her for getting the clothes on the same side of the room as the hamper. When she gets the clothes on top of the hamper, she gets praise. Finally, her parents praise her when she puts her clothes in the hamper. This process is an example of

   a. shaping.
   b. punishment.
   c. negative reinforcement.
   d. a discriminative stimulus.

4. Ella is teaching her parrot a new word. Every time the parrot says a sound that is close to the new word, she gives it a treat. But the parrot keeps repeating other words it has learned in the past, trying to get a treat that way. The parrot is exhibiting

   a. extinction.
   b. discrimination.
   c. generalization.
   d. spontaneous recovery.

5. Which of the following is an example of Thorndike's law of effect?

   a. John, a teenager, gets compliments from Carla for wearing a nice shirt. Subsequently, John wears the shirt whenever he thinks he will be seeing Carla.
   b. James always cleans his room or he knows he will be punished.

   c. Josh tries to complete his homework even though he hates having to do it.
   d. Jeremy often sits around inside hoping that someone will call him to go do something.

6. Joe owned a small repair shop. Each day, he would check the mail to see if any of his customers mailed in a payment for the work he had done for them. Some days, he would receive a check or two. At other times, he would have to wait days before getting another payment. What schedule of reinforcement is evident here?

   a. fixed interval
   b. variable interval
   c. fixed ratio
   d. variable ratio

7. An elementary school teacher gives students a sticker each time the students raise their hands before speaking in class. When a student has earned 10 stickers, he or she is given an extra 5 minutes of recess. What process is the teacher using?

   a. behavior modification and/or a token economy
   b. neurofeedback
   c. partial reinforcement
   d. applied behavior analysis

8. Alex works at a local bookstore. He receives his paycheck every 2 weeks. What schedule of reinforcement is illustrated in this scenario?

   a. fixed interval
   b. variable interval
   c. fixed ratio
   d. variable ratio

9. Which of the following is an example of punishment by application?

   a. putting a child in time-out
   b. taking away a toy or treat
   c. ignoring a tantrum
   d. giving a spanking or a scolding

10. To ensure that his students are studying, Mr. Wagner will give them occasional pop quizzes. Through what type of schedule are his students being reinforced?

    a. A fixed interval schedule
    b. A fixed ratio schedule
    c. A variable interval schedule
    d. A variable ratio schedule

16 Cognitive Learning and Observational Learning

Module Goal

Identify the aspects of cognitive and observational learning.

Learning Objectives

16.1 Understand the principles of cognitive learning.
16.2 Learn how cognitive learning applies to everyday life.
16.3 Understand the principles of observational learning.
16.4 Learn how observational learning applies to everyday life.

Identify the Aspects of Cognitive and Observational Learning

16.1 Understand the principles of cognitive learning.

In the early days of behaviorism, the original focus of Watson, Skinner, and many of their followers was on observable, measurable behavior. Anything that might be occurring inside a person or animal's head during learning was considered to be of no interest to the behaviorist because it could not be seen or directly measured. Other psychologists, however, were still interested in the mind's influence over behavior. This continued interest in the mind was followed, in the 1950s and 1960s, by the comparison of the human mind to the workings of those fascinating "thinking machines," computers. Many behavioral psychologists could no longer ignore the thoughts, feelings, and expectations that clearly existed in the mind and that seemed to influence observable behavior and eventually began to develop a cognitive learning theory to supplement the more traditional theories of learning (Kendler, 1985). Three important figures often cited as key theorists in the early days of the development of cognitive learning theory were the Gestalt psychologists Edward Tolman and Wolfgang Köhler and modern psychologist Martin Seligman.

Tolman's Maze-Running Rats: Latent Learning One of Gestalt psychologist Edward Tolman's best-known experiments in learning involved teaching three groups of rats the same maze, one at a time (Tolman & Honzik, 1930). In the first group, each rat was placed in the maze and reinforced with food for making its way out the other side. The rat was then placed back in the maze, reinforced, and so on until the rat could successfully solve the maze with no errors—the typical maze-learning experiment.

The second group of rats was treated exactly like the first, except that they never received any reinforcement upon exiting the maze. They were simply put back in again and again, until the tenth day of the experiment. On that day, the rats in the second group began to receive reinforcement for getting out of the maze. The third group of rats, serving as a control group, was also not reinforced and was not given reinforcement for the entire duration of the experiment.

A strict Skinnerian behaviorist would predict that only the first group of rats would learn the maze successfully because learning depends on reinforcing consequences. At first, this seemed to be the case. The first group of rats did indeed

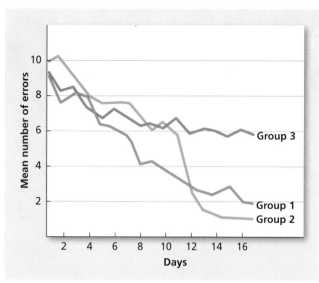

FIGURE 16.1 Learning Curves for Three Groups of Rats
In the results of the classic study of latent learning, Group 1 was rewarded on each day, while Group 2 was rewarded for the first time on Day 10. Group 3 was never rewarded. Note the immediate change in the behavior of Group 2 on Day 12 (Tolman & Honzik, 1930).

Participate in the Experiment, *Learning*, at **MyPsychLab**

▲ Another of Köhler's chimpanzees, Grande, has just solved the problem of how to get to the banana by stacking boxes. Does this meet the criteria for insight, or was it simple trial-and-error learning?

latent learning learning that remains hidden until its application becomes useful.

insight the sudden perception of relationships among various parts of a problem, allowing the solution to the problem to come quickly.

solve the maze after a certain number of trials, whereas the second and third groups seemed to wander aimlessly around the maze until accidentally finding their way out.

On the tenth day, however, something happened that would be difficult to explain using only Skinner's basic principles. The second group of rats, upon receiving the reinforcement for the first time, *should* have then taken as long as the first group to solve the maze. Instead, they began to solve the maze almost immediately (see **Figure 16.1**).

Tolman concluded that the rats in the second group, while wandering around in the first nine days of the experiment, had indeed learned where all the blind alleys, wrong turns, and correct paths were and stored this knowledge away as a kind of "mental map," or *cognitive map*, of the physical layout of the maze. Tolman called this **latent learning**. The idea that learning could happen without reinforcement, and then later affect behavior, was not something traditional operant conditioning could explain. To see a real-life example of latent learning, participate in the experiment *Learning*.

Köhler's Smart Chimp: Insight Learning In one of his more famous studies, Wolfgang Köhler (1887–1967) (Köhler (1925) set up a problem for one of the chimpanzees in the primate lab at which he was researching at during World War I. Sultan the chimp was faced with the problem of how to get to a banana that was placed just out of his reach outside his cage. Sultan solved this problem relatively easily, first trying to reach through the bars with his arm, then using a stick that was lying in the cage to rake the banana into the cage. As chimpanzees are natural tool users, this behavior is not surprising and is still nothing more than simple trial-and-error learning.

Köhler called Sultan's rapid "perception of relationships" **insight** and determined that insight could not be gained through trial-and-error learning alone (Köhler, 1925). Although Thorndike and other early learning theorists believed that animals could not demonstrate insight, Köhler's work seems to demonstrate that insight requires a sudden "coming together" of all the elements of a problem in a kind of "aha!" moment that is not predicted by traditional animal learning studies. More recent research has also found support for the concept of animal insight (Heinrich, 2000; Heyes, 1998; Zentall, 2000), but there is still controversy over how to interpret the results of those studies (Wynne, 1999).

Seligman's Depressed Dogs: Learned Helplessness In the mid- to late 1960s, Martin Seligman, a learning theorist, and his colleagues accidentally discovered an unexpected phenomenon while doing experiments on dogs using classical conditioning (Seligman, 1975). Their original intention was to study escape and avoidance learning. Seligman and colleagues presented a tone followed by a harmless but painful electric shock to one group of dogs (Overmier & Seligman, 1967; Seligman & Maier, 1967). The dogs in this group were harnessed so that they could not escape the shock. The researchers assumed that the dogs would learn to fear the sound of the tone and later try to escape from the tone before being shocked.

These dogs, along with another group of dogs that had not been conditioned to fear the tone, were placed into a special box consisting of a low fence that divided the box into two compartments. The dogs, which were now unharnessed, could easily see over the fence and jump over if they wished—which is precisely what the dogs that had not been conditioned did as soon as the shock occurred. Imagine the researchers' surprise when, instead of jumping over the fence when the tone sounded, the previously conditioned dogs just sat there. In fact, these dogs showed distress but didn't try to jump over the fence *even when the shock itself began.*

Why would the conditioned dogs refuse to move when shocked? The dogs that had been harnessed while being conditioned had apparently **learned helplessness** in the original tone/shock situation and behaved as though there was nothing they could do to escape the shock. So when placed in a situation in which escape was possible, the dogs still did nothing because they had learned to be "helpless." They believed they could not escape, so they did not try.

16.2 Learn how cognitive learning applies to everyday life.

Seligman extended this theory of learned helplessness, to explain *depression*. Depressed people seem to lack normal emotions and become somewhat apathetic, often staying in unpleasant work environments or bad marriages or relationships rather than trying to escape or better their situation. Seligman proposed that this depressive behavior is a form of learned helplessness. Depressed people may have learned in the past that they seem to have no control over what happens to them (Alloy & Clements, 1998). A sense of powerlessness and hopelessness is common to depressed people, and certainly this would seem to apply to Seligman's dogs as well.

Cognitive learning is also an important part of a fairly well-known form of learning, often simplified as "monkey see, monkey do." Let's take a look at learning through watching the actions of others.

◄ I know some people who seem to act just like those dogs—they live in a horrible situation but won't leave. Is this the same thing?

16.3 Understand the principles of observational learning.

Observational learning is the learning of new behavior through watching the actions of a model (someone else who is doing that behavior). Sometimes that behavior is desirable, and sometimes it is not, as the next section describes.

Bandura and the Bobo Doll Bandura's classic study in observational learning involved having a preschool child in a room in which the experimenter and a model interacted with toys in the room in front of the child (Bandura et al., 1961). In one condition, the model interacted with the toys in a nonaggressive manner, completely ignoring the presence of a "Bobo" doll (a punch-bag doll in the shape of a clown). In another condition, the model became very aggressive with the doll, kicking it and yelling at it, throwing it in the air and hitting it with a hammer.

When each child was left alone in the room and had the opportunity to play with the toys, a camera filming through a one-way mirror caught the children who were exposed to the aggressive model beating up the Bobo doll in exact imitation of the model (see **Figure 16.2**). The children who saw the model ignore the doll did not act aggressively toward the toy. Obviously, the aggressive children had learned their aggressive actions from merely watching the model—with no reinforcement necessary. The fact that learning can take place without actual performance (a kind of latent learning) is called the *learning/performance distinction.*

In later studies, Bandura showed a film of a model beating up the Bobo doll. In one condition, the children saw the model rewarded afterward. In another, the model was punished. When placed in the room with toys, the children in the first group beat up the doll, but the children in the second group did not. But when Bandura told the children in the second group that he would give them a reward

◄ Ah, but would that child have imitated the model if the model had been punished? Wouldn't the *consequences* of the model's behavior make a difference?

FIGURE 16.2 Bandura's Bobo Doll Experiment
In Albert Bandura's famous Bobo doll experiment, the doll was used to demonstrate the impact of observing an adult model performing aggressive behavior on the later aggressive behavior of children. The children in these photos are imitating the adult model's behavior even though they believe they are alone and are not being watched.

if they could show him what the model in the film did, each child duplicated the model's actions. Both groups had learned from watching the model, but only the children watching the successful (rewarded) model imitated the aggression with no prompting (Bandura, 1965). Apparently, consequences do matter in motivating a child (or an adult) to imitate a particular model. The tendency for some movies and television programs to make "heroes" out of violent, aggressive "bad guys" is particularly disturbing in light of these findings. In fact, Bandura began this research to investigate possible links between children's exposure to violence on television and aggressive behavior toward others.

Correlational research stretching over nearly two decades suggests that a link exists between viewing violent television and an increased level of aggression in children (Bushman & Huesmann, 2001; Engelhardt et al., in press; Huesmann & Eron, 1986; Sacks et al., 2011). Although correlations do not prove that viewing violence on TV is the *cause* of increased violence, one cannot help but be curious as to the effects, especially given the continuing rise of media consumption in young people, coupled with the multiple ways young people interact with media.

16.4 Learn how observational learning applies to everyday life.

The Four Elements of Observational Learning Bandura (1986) concluded, from these studies and others, that observational learning required the presence of four elements: attention, memory, imitation, and desire. To learn anything through observation, the learner must first pay *attention* to the model. For example, people pay more attention to those people they perceive as similar to them and to people whom they perceive as attractive.

The learner must also be able to retain the *memory* of what was done, such as remembering the steps in preparing a dish that was first seen on a cooking show.

The learner must be capable of reproducing, or *imitating*, the actions of the model. A person with extremely weak ankles might be able to watch and remember how some ballet move was accomplished but will not be able to reproduce it.

Finally, the learner must have the motivation or *desire* to perform the action. A person at the fancy dinner, for example, might not care which fork or which knife is the "proper" one to use.

Pick the best answer.

1. Attention, memory, imitation, and motivation are the four elements required for the process of

    a. insight.
    b. latent learning.
    c. observational learning.
    d. spontaneous recovery.

2. In Edward Tolman's maze study, the fact that the group of rats receiving reinforcement only after the 10th day of the study solved the maze far more quickly than did the rats who had been reinforced from the first day can be interpreted to mean that these particular rats

    a. were much smarter than the other rats.
    b. had already learned the maze in the first 9 days.
    c. had the opportunity to cheat by watching the other rats.
    d. were able to learn only because they had not received much reinforcement.

3. Martin Seligman found many similarities between his "helpless" dogs and people suffering from

    a. depression.
    b. agoraphobia.
    c. schizophrenia.
    d. aggressive behavior syndrome.

4. Which theory is commonly referred to as the "aha!" phenomenon?

    a. Tolman's latent learning theory
    b. Köhler's insight theory
    c. Seligman's learned helplessness theory
    d. Bandura's observational learning

5. In Albert Bandura's study with the Bobo doll, the children in the group that saw the model punished did not imitate the model at first. They would only imitate the model if given a reward for doing so. The fact that these children had obviously learned the behavior without actually performing it is an example of

    a. observational learning.
    b. insight learning.
    c. operant conditioning.
    d. classical conditioning.

6. In _____, a person will learn something but will not display this learned behavior because there is no incentive to show what they have learned.

    a. depression
    b. latent learning
    c. vicarious learning
    d. learned helplessness

7. A teacher tells her students that they will have recess as soon as they put their art supplies away. This is an example of

    a. attention.
    b. motivation.
    c. imitation.
    d. memory.

8. People who study what goes on in a person's mind as he or she learns are interested in

    a. latent learning theory.
    b. cognitive learning theory.
    c. observational learning theory.
    d. motivational learning theory.

9. Fatimah decides to run in a 5k race. However, she does not join a race immediately. She trains for 3 months before signing up. Which of the following elements best describes why she waits to run?

    a. attention: she wants to see someone else run a race before she tries herself
    b. memory: she has to be able to remember how to pace herself throughout the race
    c. imitation: she has to be physically able to run a 5k race before she can succeed
    d. motivation: she has to find a race that best fits her interests and her busy schedule

10. A jar with a small purse of seeds and a long piece of wire is placed in a room with a crow. The crow attempts to use the wire to push the seed purse out of the jar. When this fails, the crow examines the jar, then takes out the piece of wire. The crow bends the wire into a hook, and uses this hook to pull the purse out of the jar. Which of the following did this crow display?

    a. insight
    b. attention
    c. memory
    d. aggression

Module 17 Language

Module Goals	Learning Objectives	
Identify the structural features of language.	**17.1**	Learn about the structure and function of language.
	17.2	Understand the relationship between language and thought.
Explain the process and theories of language acquisition.	**17.3**	Describe the process of language acquisition.
	17.4	Consider the theories of language acquisition.
Learn about language and the brain.	**17.5**	Describe the brain structures associated with language and understand how damage to the brain may affect language.

Identify the Structural Features of Language

17.1 Learn about the structure and function of language.

Language can possibly affect our memory. For example, being asked "Did you see the car bump into the truck?" may prompt a slightly different memory than "Did you see the car smash into the truck?" In this section, we will examine language and how cognition can be affected by language.

The Levels of Language Analysis *Language* is a system for combining symbols (such as words) so that an infinite* number of meaningful statements can be made for the purpose of communicating with others. Language allows people not only to communicate with one another but also to represent their own internal mental activity. In other words, language is a very important part of how people think.

The structures of languages all over the world share common characteristics. They consist of the sounds that exist within a language, word meanings, word order, the rules for making words into other words, the meanings of sentences and phrases, and the rules for practical communication with others.

Phonemes Phonemes are the basic units of sound in a language. The *a* in the word *car* is a very different phoneme from the *a* in the word *day*, even though it is the same letter of the alphabet. The difference is in how we say the sound of the *a* in each word. Phonemes are more than just the different ways in which we pronounce single letters, too. *Th, sh,* and *au* are also phonemes. Phonemes for different languages are also different, and one of the biggest problems for people who are trying to learn another language is the inability to both hear and pronounce

phonemes the basic units of sound in a language.

---

*infinite: unlimited, without end.

the phonemes of that other language. Although infants are born with the ability to recognize all phonemes (Werker & Lalonde, 1988), after about 9 months that ability has deteriorated and the infant recognizes only the phonemes of the language to which the infant is exposed (Boyson-Bardies et al., 1989).

Morphemes **Morphemes** are the smallest units of meaning within a language. For example, the word *playing* consists of two morphemes, *play* and *ing*.

Grammar *Grammar* is the system of rules governing the structure and use of a language. Grammar includes phonemes (the basic sounds of language), morphology (the study of the formation of words, the prefix *morph* means form or shape), rules for the order of words known as syntax, and pragmatics (the practical social expectations and uses of language).

Syntax *Syntax* is a system of rules for combining words and phrases to form grammatically correct sentences. Syntax is quite important, as just a simple mix-up can cause sentences to be completely misunderstood. For example, "John kidnapped the boy" has a different meaning from "John, the kidnapped boy," although all four words are the same (Lasnik, 1990).

Semantics *Semantics* are rules for determining the meaning of words and sentences. Sentences, for example, can have the same semantic meaning while having different syntax: "Johnny hit the ball" and "the ball was hit by Johnny."

Pragmatics The **pragmatics** of language has to do with the practical aspects of communicating with others, or the social "niceties" of language. Simply put, pragmatics involves knowing things like how to take turns in a conversation, the use of gestures to emphasize a point or indicate a need for more information, and the different ways in which one speaks to different people (Yule, 1996).

morphemes the smallest units of meaning within a language

pragmatics aspects of language involving the practical ways of communicating with others, or the social "niceties" of language.

▲ *Pragmatics involves the practical aspects of communicating. This young mother is talking and then pausing for the infant's response. In this way, the infant is learning about taking turns, an important aspect of language development. What kinds of games do adults play with infants that also aid the development of language?*

17.2 Understand the relationship between language and thought.

Two very influential developmental psychologists, Jean Piaget and Lev Vygotsky, often debated the relationship of language and thought (Duncan, 1995). Piaget (1926, 1962) theorized that concepts preceded and aided the development of language. For example, a child would have to have a concept or mental schema for "mother" before being able to learn the word "mama." In a sense, concepts become the "pegs" upon which words are "hung." Piaget also noticed that preschool children seemed to spend a great deal of time talking to themselves—even when playing with another child. Each child would be talking about something totally unrelated to the speech of the other, in a process Piaget called *collective monologue**. Piaget believed that this kind of nonsocial speech was very egocentric (from the child's point of view only, with no regard for the listener) and that as the child became more socially involved and less egocentric, these nonsocial speech patterns would reduce.

Vygotsky, however, believed almost the opposite. He theorized that language actually helped develop concepts and that language could also help the child learn to control behavior—including social behavior (Vygotsky, 1962, 1978, 1987). For Vygotsky, the word helped form the concept: Once a child had learned the word "mama," the various elements of "mama-ness"—*warm,*

---

*monologue: a long speech or statement by one person.

soft, *food*, *safety*, and so on—could come together around that word. Vygotsky also believed that the "egocentric" speech of the preschool child was actually a way for the child to form thoughts and control actions. This "private speech" was a way for children to plan their behavior and organize actions so that their goals could be obtained. Because socializing with other children would demand much more self-control and behavioral regulation on the part of the preschool child, Vygotsky believed that private speech would actually increase as children became more socially active in the preschool years. This was, of course, the opposite of Piaget's assumption, and the evidence seems to bear out Vygotsky's view: Children, especially bright children, do tend to use more private speech when learning how to socialize with other children or when working on a difficult task (Berk, 1992; Berk & Spuhl, 1995; Bivens & Berk, 1990).

The hypothesis that language shapes and influences thoughts was accepted by many theorists, with a few notable exceptions, such as Piaget. One of the best-known versions of this view is the Sapir–Whorf hypothesis (named for the two theorists who developed it, Edward Sapir and his student, Benjamin Lee Whorf). This hypothesis assumes that the thought processes and concepts within any culture are determined by the words of the culture (Sapir, 1921; Whorf, 1956). It has come to be known as the *linguistic relativity hypothesis*, meaning that thought processes and concepts are controlled by (relative to) language. That is, the words people use determine much of the way in which they think about the world around them.

Is there evidence for the linguistic relativity hypothesis? Neither Sapir nor Whorf provided any scientific studies that would support their proposition. There have been numerous studies by other researchers, however. For example, in one study researchers assumed that a language's color names would influence the ability of the people who grew up with that language to distinguish among and perceive colors. The study found that basic color terms did directly influence color recognition memory (Lucy & Shweder, 1979). But an earlier series of studies of the perception of colors by Eleanor Rosch-Heider and others (Rosch-Heider, 1972; Rosch-Heider & Olivier, 1972) had already found just the opposite effect: Members of the Dani tribe, who have only two names for colors, were no different in their ability to perceive all of the colors than were the English speakers in the study. More recent studies (Davies et al., 1998a, 1998b; Laws et al., 1995; Pinker & Bloom, 1990) support Rosch-Heider's findings and the idea of a cognitive universalism (concepts are universal and influence the development of language) rather than linguistic relativity.

I've heard that chimpanzees can be taught to use sign language. Is this for real, or are the chimps just performing tricks like the animals in the circus or the zoo?

▶ **Animal Studies in Language** Can animals be taught to use symbols that are abstract? There have been attempts to teach animals (primates and dolphins) how to use sign language (as animals lack the vocal structure to form spoken words), but many of these attempts were simply not "good science." The most successful of these experiments (which is not without its critics as well) has been with Kanzi, a bonobo chimpanzee trained to press abstract symbols on a computer keyboard (Savage-Rumbaugh & Lewin, 1994). Kanzi actually was not the original subject of the study—his mother, Matata, was the chimp being trained. She did not learn many of the symbols, but Kanzi watched his mother use the keyboard and appeared to learn how to use the symbols through that observation. At last count, Kanzi could understand about 150 spoken English words. Trainers who speak to him are not in his view, so he is not responding to physical cues or symbols. He has managed to follow correctly complex instructions up to the level of a 2-year-old child (Savage-Rumbaugh et al., 1998).

▲ *Kanzi looks at the keyboard used in teaching language to chimpanzees. Kanzi's language abilities were learned through watching researchers train his mother rather than directly—much as a human infant learns through listening to the speech of adults.*

Understand the Process and the Theories of Language Acquisition

17.3 Describe the process of language acquisition.

We acquire language through a stepped learning process. Initially, 2-month-old infants are only capable of producing vowel sounds, a stage known as *cooing*. They begin *babbling*, or creating consonant sounds, at about 6 months old, but do not begin speaking actual words until about 1 year. At this age, most children speak in *holophrases*, single words meant to represent entire phrases of meaning. Children begin to group words together in short sentences at around 18 months of age, gaining more complexity and more understanding of grammar and syntax as they mature. By the time they are 6 years old, children are as fluent in the language as an adult; they simply have a limited vocabulary.

17.4 Consider the theories of language acquisition.

The earliest theories of language development were based on Skinnerian principles of reinforcement. However, Chomsky (Chomsky, 2006; Chomsky et al., 2002) argued that language was an innate part of human nature. He claimed that all humans are born with a **language acquisition device (LAD)** schema that allows them to learn and use language. The LAD "listens" to the language input of the infant's world and then begins to produce language sounds and eventually words and sentences in a pattern found across cultures. According to Chomsky, children use this innate language "program" to analyze and comprehend the language they hear. They use this schema to reproduce the language sounds and eventually speak the language.

New theories in language concentrate on the environmental factors that go into language acquisition. The way adults speak to babies is one factor; adults

language acquisition device (LAD) inborn schema that allows humans to learn and use language.

use a higher pitched, repetitive sing-song voice, to which infants and toddlers are very responsive (Dominey & Dodane, 2004; Fernald, 1984, 1992; Küntay & Slobin, 2002). Studies have also shown a phenomenon called *expressive language delay* in infants, where children understand much more than they can reproduce (Stevenson et al., 1988). Until they learn how to utilize the language they hear, infants use gestures and signs to communicate.

Learning a second language poses challenges to many foreign language students. While the difficulties of learning a second language grow as one ages, research findings are mixed regarding the idea that the hard wiring of the brain's language centers close a language learning window over time. Motivational factors and the opportunity to be immersed in a second language environment can also contribute to the difficulty of learning a second language at a later age. Like learning a new musical instrument, practice makes perfect (or at least better) when learning a second language. Oui?

Learn about Language and the Brain

17.5 Describe the brain structures associated with language and understand how damage to the brain may affect language.

Broca's Area In the left frontal lobe of most people is an area of the brain devoted to the production of speech. (In a small portion of the population, this area is in the right frontal lobe.) More specifically, this area allows a person to speak smoothly and fluently. It is called *Broca's area* after nineteenth-century neurologist Paul Broca, who first provided widely accepted clinical evidence that deficits in fluent and articulate speech result from damage to this area (Finger, 1994). Damage to Broca's area causes a person to be unable to get words out in a smooth, connected fashion. You can remember this by noting that damage to Broca's area causes "broken" speech. People with this condition may know exactly what they want to say and understand what they hear others say, but they cannot control the actual production of their own words. Speech is halting and words are often mispronounced, such as saying "cot" instead of "clock" or "non" instead of "nine." Some words may be left out entirely, such as "the" or "for." This is called *Broca's aphasia*. *Aphasia* refers to an inability to use or understand either written or spoken language (Goodglass et al., 2001). (Stuttering is a somewhat different problem in getting words *started*, rather than mispronouncing them or leaving them out, but may also be related to Broca's area.)

Wernicke's Area In the left temporal lobe (again, in most people) is an area called *Wernicke's area*, named after the physiologist and Broca's contemporary, Carl Wernicke, pronounced like ver-ne- (as in necter) -ka, who first studied problems arising from damage in this location. This area of the brain appears to be involved in understanding the meaning of words (Goodglass et al., 2001). A person with *Wernicke's aphasia* would be able to speak fluently and pronounce words correctly, but the words would be the wrong ones entirely. For example, Elsie suffered a stroke to the temporal lobe, damaging this area of the brain. In the emergency room the nurse tried to take her blood pressure, and when the cuff inflated, Elsie said, "Oh, that's so Saturday hard." Elsie *thought* she was making sense. She also had trouble understanding what the people around her were saying to her.

Pick the best answer.

1. **The system of rules for combining words and phrases to make meaningful sentences is called**

   a. syntax.
   b. phonics.
   c. pragmatics.
   d. grammar.

2. **Grammar includes all but which of the following aspects of language?**

   a. tone of spoken words
   b. order of words
   c. formation of words
   d. structure of language

3. **Which of the following is an English phoneme?**

   a. the word *ball*
   b. the word *play*
   c. the suffix *ing*
   d. the sound *sh*

4. **_____ believed that language helps to develop concepts, whereas _____ believed that concepts must be developed first if language is to follow.**

   a. Vygotsky; Piaget
   b. Chomsky; Sapir and Whorf
   c. Piaget; Rosch-Heider
   d. Sapir and Whorf; Vygotsky

5. **According to Chomsky, grammar is**

   a. impossible for older children and adults to learn.
   b. innately understood by the developing human brain.
   c. identical in content across all languages and cultures.
   d. not a requirement for any relatively simple language.

6. **The first language sounds infants begin to make are**

   a. vowels.
   b. consonants.
   c. animal sounds.
   d. partial words.

7. **Which of the following best describes Chomsky's LAD theory?**

   a. A child will talk to itself as a way to determine actions and organize thoughts.
   b. A child is as fluent as an adult in a language by the age of 5.
   c. A child is able to understand what is said to it, even if it is unable to respond.
   d. A child is born with the ability to recognize any language, although it loses that ability as it matures.

8. **Henry's speech is halting, and many of his words are mispronounced. Henry most likely has**

   a. Broca's aphasia.
   b. Wernicke's aphasia.
   c. Rosch-Heider disorder.
   d. Seligman's disorder.

9. **Knowing how to take turns in a conversation is an example of**

   a. syntax.
   b. pragmatics.
   c. accelerated aphasia.
   d. cognitive universalism.

10. **For most people, which portion of the brain is associated with comprehending the meanings of words?**

    a. right parietal lobe
    b. cerebellum
    c. left temporal lobe
    d. left frontal lobe

((Listen to an Audio File of your chapter at MyPsychLab

Module 14: Classical Conditioning

Learn about the process of classical conditioning.

14.1 Outline the principles of classical conditioning.

- Learning is any relatively permanent change in behavior brought about by experience or practice and is different from maturation that is genetically controlled.
- In classical conditioning, one stimulus can, through pairing with another stimulus, come to produce a similar response.
- The unconditioned stimulus (UCS) is a naturally occurring stimulus that produces the innate, or involuntary unconditioned response (UCR).
- When paired with the UCR, a neutral stimulus eventually begins to elicit an involuntary, and automatic behavior called the conditioned response (CR).
- The neutral stimulus (NS) and UCS must be paired several times and the CS must precede the UCS by only a few seconds.
- Other important aspects of classical conditioning include stimulus generalization, stimulus discrimination, extinction, and spontaneous recovery.

14.2 Understand clinical and experimental examples of classical conditioning.

- Watson demonstrated that a phobia could be learned through classical conditioning by exposing a baby to a white rat and a loud noise, producing conditioned fear of the rat in the baby.

14.3 Explain how classical conditioning applies to everyday life.

- Conditioned taste aversions occur when an organism becomes nauseated some time after eating a certain food, which then becomes aversive to the organism.
- Some kinds of conditioned responses are more easily learned than others because of biological preparedness.

Module 15: Operant Conditioning

Learn about the process of operant conditioning.

15.1 Understand the law of effect.

- Thorndike developed the law of effect: A response followed by a pleasurable consequence will be repeated, but a response followed by an unpleasant consequence will not be repeated.

15.2 Explain the principles of operant conditioning.

- B. F. Skinner named the learning of voluntary responses operant conditioning because voluntary responses are what we use to operate in the world around us.
- Reinforcement is the process of strengthening a response by following it with a pleasurable, rewarding consequence.
- A primary reinforcer is a stimulus that satisfies a basic, natural drive, whereas a secondary reinforcer is a stimulus that becomes reinforcing only after being paired with a primary reinforcer.
- In positive reinforcement, a response is followed by the presentation of a pleasurable stimulus, whereas in negative reinforcement, a response is followed by the

removal or avoidance of an unpleasant stimulus.

15.3 Describe specialized examples of operant conditioning.

- Continuous reinforcement occurs when each and every correct response is followed by a reinforcer.
- Partial reinforcement, in which only some correct responses are followed by reinforcement, is much more resistant to extinction. This is called the partial reinforcement effect.
- In a fixed interval schedule of reinforcement, at least one correct response must be made within a set interval of time to obtain reinforcement.
- In a variable interval schedule of reinforcement, reinforcement follows the first correct response made after an interval of time that changes for each reinforcement opportunity.
- In a fixed ratio schedule of reinforcement, a certain number of responses are required before reinforcement is given.
- In a variable ratio schedule of reinforcement, a varying number of responses are required to obtain reinforcement.
- Punishment is any event or stimulus that, when following a response, makes that response less likely to happen again.
- In punishment by application, a response is followed by the application or experiencing of an unpleasant stimulus, such as a spanking.
- In punishment by removal, a response is followed by the removal of some pleasurable stimulus, such as taking away a child's toy for misbehavior.

15.4 Describe how operant conditioning applies to everyday life.

- Operant conditioning can be used in many settings on both animals and people to change, or modify, behavior. This use is termed *behavior modification* and includes the use of reinforcement and shaping to alter behavior.
- Token economies are a type of behavior modification in which secondary reinforcers, or tokens, are used.

Module 16: Cognitive Learning and Observational Learning

Identify the aspects of cognitive and observational learning.

16.1 Understand the principles of cognitive learning.

- Tolman found that rats that were allowed to wander in a maze but were not reinforced still showed evidence of having learned the maze once reinforcement became possible. He termed this hidden learning latent learning, a form of cognitive learning.
- Köhler found evidence of insight, the sudden perception of the relationships among elements of a problem, in chimpanzees.

16.2 Learn how cognitive learning applies to everyday life.

- Seligman found that dogs that had been placed in an inescapable situation failed to try to escape when it became possible to do so; he called this phenomenon learned helplessness.

16.3 Understand the principles of observational learning.
- Observational learning is learning by watching others perform, or model, certain actions.
- Bandura's famous Bobo doll experiment demonstrated that young children will imitate the aggressive actions of a model even when there is no reinforcement for doing so.

16.2 Learn how observational learning applies to everyday life.
- Bandura determined that four elements needed to be present for observational learning to occur: attention, memory, imitation, and motivation.

Module 17: Language

Identify the structural features of language.

17.1 Learn about the structure and function of language.
- Language is a system for combining symbols so that an infinite number of meaningful statements can be created and communicated to others.
- Grammar is the system of rules by which language is governed and includes the rules for using phonemes, morphemes, and syntax. Pragmatics refers to practical aspects of language.

17.2 Understand the relationship between language and thought.
- Sapir and Whorf originally proposed that language controls and helps the development of thought processes and concepts, an idea that is known as the linguistic relativity hypothesis.
- Other researchers have found evidence that concepts are universal and directly influence the development of language, called the cognitive universalism viewpoint.

- Studies with chimpanzees, parrots, and dolphins have been somewhat successful in demonstrating that animals can develop a basic kind of language.
- Controversy exists over the lack of evidence that animals can learn syntax, which some feel means that animals are not truly learning and using language.

Explain the process and theories of language acquisition.

17.3 Describe the process of language acquisition.
- Language is acquired through a series of stages: cooing, babbling, one-word speech, telegraphic speech, and whole sentences.

17.4 Consider the theories of language acquisition.
- Chomsky believed that humans are born with an ability to understand and learn how to speak language.

Learn about language and the brain.

17.5 Describe the brain structures associated with language and understand how damage to the brain may affect language.
- A region called Broca's area in the left frontal lobe is responsible for producing fluent, understandable speech. If damaged, the person has Broca's aphasia, in which words will be halting and pronounced incorrectly.
- An area called Wernicke's area in the left temporal lobe is responsible for the understanding of language. If damaged, the person has Wernicke's aphasia, in which speech is fluent but nonsensical. The wrong words are used.

Vocabulary Terms

☑ **Study and Review** at **MyPsychLab**

Vocabulary Review

Match each vocabulary term to its definition.

1. pragmatics
2. conditioned stimulus
3. negative reinforcement
4. latent learning
5. operant conditioning
6. classical conditioning
7. punishment by removal
8. morpheme
9. extinction
10. unconditioned stimulus

a. Learning in which one learns an involuntary response when a stimulus that normally causes a particular response is paired with a new, neutral stimulus.
b. The smallest units of meaning within a language.
c. Aspects of language involving the practical ways of communicating with others.
d. The learning of voluntary behavior through the effects of pleasant and unpleasant consequences to responses.
e. The disappearance or weakening of a learned response following the removal or absence of the unconditioned stimulus (in classical conditioning).
f. A naturally occurring stimulus that leads to an involuntary (reflex) response.
g. Stimulus that becomes able to produce a learned reflex response by being paired with the original unconditioned stimulus.
h. The punishment of a response by the removal of a pleasurable stimulus.
i. The reinforcement of a response by the removal or escape from an unpleasant stimulus.
j. Learning that remains hidden until its application becomes useful.

Psychology Project

Explore techniques that advertisers use to evoke conditioned emotional responses in their audience.

Materials: a print advertisement OR a screen capture of a commercial with brief description OR a transcript of a radio advertisement

Instructions:

1. Select an advertisement or commercial that you think is designed to evoke an emotional response.
2. Write a brief visual analysis of this advertisement. Use the following questions as a guide as you write:
   - What conditioned emotional response is the advertisement designed to evoke in the viewer?
   - What visual or audio features are used to bring about this emotion?
   - Is the advertisement successful? Why or why not?
3. Share your advertisement and analysis with a classmate.

Tech Alternative

Video gaming uses very powerful elements of learning theory in their design.

1. Select a video game that you enjoy and are familiar with.
2. Analyze the game through the eyes of a psychologist thinking about what we just read about learning theory.

3. What aspects of the game use classical conditioning?
4. What aspects of the game use operant conditioning?
5. How does observational learning apply to the video gaming experience?
6. Find two or three examples of each type of learning, describe your examples using terms from learning theory, and write up a summary of your findings.

Essay Question

Owen is a 6-year-old child who frequently misbehaves at home. Owen's parents would like to use fundamental principles of learning to curb Owen's inappropriate behavior. Describe three of the concepts that follow, and explain how Owen's parents could use the concepts you choose to improve Owen's behavior:

a. The Law of Effect
b. Negative punishment
c. Fixed interval schedule of reinforcement
d. Applied behavior analysis
e. Token economy
f. Observational learning

Test Yourself

Ready for your test? More quizzes and a customized plan.

☑ **Study and Review** at **MyPsychLab**

Pick the best answer.

1. Sheila got hit by a car at a street corner because she was too busy gossiping about her coworkers with a friend on her phone and did not pay attention to the traffic before she entered the crosswalk. From that day on, Sheila looks before she reaches the street corner. Her change in behavior is a result of
   a. learning.
   b. memory.
   c. motivation.
   d. both sensation and perception.

2. Your dog comes running at the rattle of the chain on his leash when you get ready to take him for a walk. In this example, what is the conditioned stimulus?
   a. going for a walk
   b. the sound of the leash
   c. the front door
   d. the dog runs to the door

3. A child has been classically conditioned to fear a white rat. If the child does not show fear when shown a black rat, this is called
   a. stimulus generalization.
   b. stimulus discrimination.
   c. spontaneous recovery.
   d. extinction.

4. You have stopped taking your dog for walks and now he doesn't come running when he hears the rattle the rattle of his leash. What has occurred?
   a. stimulus generalization
   b. stimulus discrimination
   c. spontaneous recovery
   d. extinction

5. Rhonda had tartar sauce with her fish and suddenly became nauseated. The next morning she was nauseated and sick for much of the day. Now the thought of fish with tartar sauce makes her queasy. Her queasiness is probably due to
   a. higher-order conditioning.
   b. a conditioned taste aversion.
   c. stimulus substitution.
   d. stimulus generalization.

6. Caitlin found that many of her lab rats would develop a conditioned taste aversion to certain foods after as little as one trial. This is a classic example of
   a. biological preparedness.
   b. psychological preparedness.
   c. instinctive drift.
   d. stimulus drift

7. Blake washes his car because then his friends will ride with him. What theory best explains why he washes his car?
   a. the law of reflex
   b. operant conditioning
   c. classical conditioning
   d. insight learning theory

8. In classical conditioning, behavior typically is _____, whereas with operant conditioning, behavior is _____.
   a. rewarded; punished
   b. biological; internal
   c. voluntary; involuntary
   d. involuntary; voluntary

9. Where do secondary reinforcers get their power from?
   a. classical conditioning
   b. the law of effect
   c. observational theory
   d. insight theory

10. Positive reinforcement results in _____ in the target behavior and negative reinforcement results in _____ in the target behavior.
    a. an increase; a decrease
    b. an increase; an increase
    c. a decrease; a decrease
    d. a decrease; an increase

11. Belinda takes some aspirin to make her headache go away. This is an example of
    a. positive reinforcement.
    b. negative reinforcement.
    c. punishment.
    d. generalization.

12. Ben gets paid every 2 weeks. Regardless of the total number of hours he works each week, he is paid every 2 weeks. What schedule of reinforcement is being used?
    a. fixed ratio
    b. variable ratio
    c. fixed interval
    d. variable interval

13. Denise came home after curfew. Her parents have taken away her cell phone for a month. Losing her cell phone privileges is an example of
    a. negative reinforcement.
    b. punishment by application.
    c. punishment by removal.
    d. learned helplessness.

14. Which of the following strengthens a response?
    a. negative punishment
    b. positive punishment
    c. negative reinforcement
    d. neutral stimului

15. A mother ignores her child's temper tantrum so that the behavior ultimately goes away. This is an example of
    a. extinction.
    b. positive reinforcement.
    c. generalized punishment.
    d. instinctive drift.

16. Keller and Breland found that the animals they studied would learn skills through reinforcement but eventually revert to their genetically controlled patterns of behavior. This phenomenon is know as
    a. instinct revival.
    b. instinctive drift.
    c. instinctive maturation.
    d. survival instinct.

17. Jose was lying in bed when it suddenly came to him out of nowhere how he might deal with a fast approaching deadline at work. Psychologists would refer to this as
    a. latent learning.
    b. learned helplessness.
    c. insight learning.
    d. observational learning.

18. Jody failed repeatedly in college algebra. Finally, she gave up and refused to try again even though her best friend offered to help her. What concept might explain her reluctance?
    a. latent learning
    b. learned helplessness
    c. insight learning
    d. observational learning

19. What does AMID stand for?
    a. Attention, Memory, Intention, Detention
    b. Attention, Memory, Imitation, Desire
    c. Ask, Memory, Imitate, Develop
    d. Association, Memory, Imitation, Desires

20. What component of the observational learning model explains why Darla doesn't want to exercise even though she sees her friends exercising?
    a. Darla does not believe she can achieve the goal.
    b. Darla is not motivated to lose weight.
    c. Darla's self-esteem must first be addressed.
    d. Darla's unwillingness may be a sign of mental disorder.

Learning Objectives

14.1 14.2 14.3 pp. 194–199

Learn about the process of classical conditioning

- **key elements**
  - unconditioned stimulus (UCS)
  - unconditioned response (UCR)
  - conditioned stimulus (CS)
  - conditioned response (CR)
- **key features**
  - stimulus generalization
  - stimulus discrimination
  - extinction
  - spontaneous recovery

Learning Objectives

15.1 15.2 15.3 15.4 pp. 201–209

Learn about the process of operant conditioning

- **reinforcement** is any event or stimulus that, when following a response, increases the probability that the response will occur again
- **punishment** is any event or stimulus that, when following a response, decreases the probability that the response will occur again

Learning Objectives

16.1 16.2 16.3 16.4 pp. 211–214

Identify the aspects of cognitive and observational learning

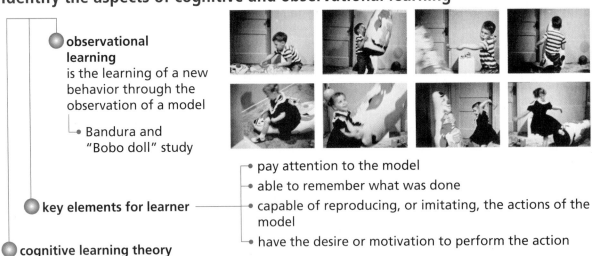

- **observational learning** is the learning of a new behavior through the observation of a model
  - Bandura and "Bobo doll" study
- **key elements for learner**
  - pay attention to the model
  - able to remember what was done
  - capable of reproducing, or imitating, the actions of the model
  - have the desire or motivation to perform the action
- **cognitive learning theory** focuses on role of thought processes on learning
  - latent learning
  - insight learning
  - learned helplessness

Language Development

Map the Concepts at MyPsychLab

Learning Objectives

17.1 17.2 pp. 216–218

Identify the structural features of language

- **language**
  is a system of combining symbols to communicate
  - **grammar**
  - **syntax**
  - **morphemes**
  - **phonemes**
  - **semantics**
  - **pragmatics**

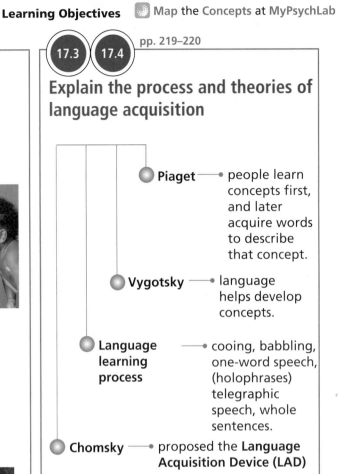

- **the relationship between language and thought**
  - does language influence thought or does thinking influence language?
  - animal studies in language

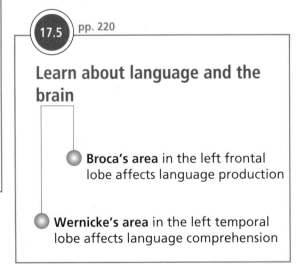

Learning Objectives

17.3 17.4 pp. 219–220

Explain the process and theories of language acquisition

- **Piaget** — people learn concepts first, and later acquire words to describe that concept.
- **Vygotsky** — language helps develop concepts.
- **Language learning process** — cooing, babbling, one-word speech, (holophrases) telegraphic speech, whole sentences.
- **Chomsky** — proposed the **Language Acquisition Device (LAD)**

Learning Objectives

17.5 pp. 220

Learn about language and the brain

- **Broca's area** in the left frontal lobe affects language production
- **Wernicke's area** in the left temporal lobe affects language comprehension

CHAPTER 7

Social Psychology

Early in May of 2013, a man helped three young women escape from a decade of captivity. Amanda Berry, Gina DeJesus, and Michelle Knight had been kidnapped as young girls and held captive in a house in Cleveland, Ohio. Charles Ramsey, who lived next door, had been eating dinner one night when he heard Amanda's cries for help. Instead of turning back to his dinner, he went to the aid of the young woman, helping her and the other victims escape. Ramsey's actions may not seem heroic at first—it's what anyone should, and would, do, right? But psychologists have long known that just the opposite is often true. A well-known principle in social psychology is the *bystander effect*: The likelihood of someone who is in trouble being helped decreases as the number of witnesses, or bystanders, increases. As we'll learn, there are many aspects of how people influence the actions and even the thinking of others.

How are your actions influenced by others, including your friends, family, and coworkers? Are there certain actions or personal beliefs that you feel are consistent regardless of your social surroundings?

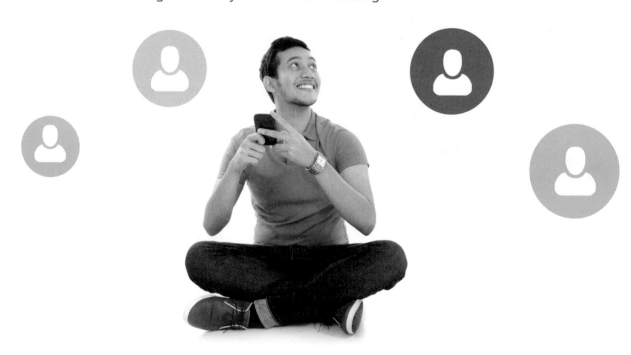

👁 **Watch** the **Video**, at **MyPsychLab**

*W*hy Study **Social Psychology**?

If people lived in total isolation from other people, there would be no reason to study the effect that other people have on the behavior of individuals and groups. But human beings are social creatures—we live with others, work with others, and play with others. The people who surround us all of our lives have an impact on our beliefs and values, decisions and assumptions, and the way we think about other people in general. Why are some people prejudiced toward certain other people? Why do we obey some people but not others? What causes us to like, to love, or to hate others? The answers to all these questions and many more can be found in the study of social psychology.

18 Social Influence

Learning Objectives

18.1 Understand the power of the situation.

18.2 Explain how the presence of others affects conformity in an individual's behavior.

18.3 Trace how group dynamics influence an individual's behavior.

18.4 Describe how an individual influences group behavior.

18.5 Explain how the presence of others affects compliance in an individual's behavior.

18.6 Explain how the presence of others affects obedience in an individual's behavior.

Explore How Social Influence Affects Behavior

18.1 Understand the power of the situation.

Chapter One defined psychology as the scientific study of behavior and mental processes, including how people think and feel. The field of **social psychology** also looks at behavior and mental processes but includes as well, the social world in which we exist, as we are surrounded by others to whom we are connected and by whom we are influenced in so many ways. It is the scientific study of how a person's behavior, thoughts, and feelings influence and are influenced by social groups.

People live in a world filled with other people. An infant is born into a world with adults who have an impact on the infant's actions, personality, and growth. Adults must interact with others on a daily basis. Such interactions provide ample opportunity for the presence of other people to directly or indirectly influence the behavior, feelings, and thoughts of each individual in a process called *social influence*. (This influence exists even if the presence of others is merely implied.) There are many forms of social influence. People can influence others to follow along with their own actions or thoughts, to agree to do things even when the person might prefer to do otherwise, and to be obedient to authorities.

18.2 Explain how the presence of others affects conformity in an individual's behavior.

Conformity Have you ever noticed someone looking up at something? Did the urge to look up to see what that person was looking at become so strong that you actually found yourself looking up? This common practical joke always works, even when people suspect that it's a joke. It clearly demonstrates the power of **conformity**: changing one's own behavior to more closely match the actions of others.

social psychology the scientific study of how a person's thoughts, feelings, and behavior influence and are influenced by other people and groups.

conformity changing one's own behavior to match that of other people.

In 1936, social psychologist Muzafer Sherif conducted a study in which participants were shown into a darkened room and exposed to a single point of light. Under those conditions, a point of light will seem to move because of tiny, involuntary movements of the eye. The participants were not told of this effect and reported the light moved anywhere from a few inches to several feet. When a confederate (a person chosen by the experimenter to deliberately manipulate the situation) also gave estimates, the original participants began to make estimates of motion that were more and more similar to those of the confederate (Sherif, 1936).

Asch's Classic Study on Conformity Solomon Asch (1951) conducted the first of his classic studies on conformity by having seven participants gather in a room. They were told that they were participating in an experiment on visual judgment. They were then shown a white card with only one line on it followed by another white card with three lines of varying lengths. The task was to determine which line on the second card was most similar to the line on the first card (see **Figure 18.1**).

In reality, only the next-to-the-last person in the group was a real participant. The others were all confederates (people following special directions from the experimenter) who were instructed to pick the same incorrect line from the comparison lines. Would the real participant, having heard the others pick what seemed to be the wrong answer, change to conform to the group's opinion? Surprisingly, the participants conformed to the group answer

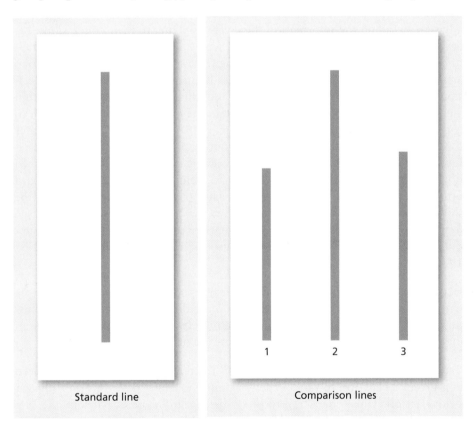

Standard line   Comparison lines

FIGURE 18.1 Stimuli Used in Asch's Study
Participants in Asch's famous study on conformity were first shown the standard line. They were then shown the three comparison lines and asked to determine to which of the three was the standard line most similar. Which line would you pick? What if you were one of several people, and everyone who answered ahead of you chose line 3? How would that affect your answer?

Source: Adapted from Asch (1956).

a little over one-third of the time. Asch also found that the number of confederates mattered: Conformity increased with each new confederate until there were four confederates; more than that did not increase the participants' tendency to conform (Asch, 1951). In a later experiment, Asch (1956) found that conformity decreased if there was just one confederate who gave the correct answer—apparently, if participants knew that there was at least one other person whose answer agreed with their own, the evidence of their own eyes won out over the pressure to conform to the group. (L)(I)(N)(K) to *Chapter Eight: Sociocultural Diversity and Gender, p. 267.*

Research shows that gender differences are practically nonexistent unless the situation involves behavior that is not private. If it is possible to give responses in private, conformity is no greater for women than for men, but if a public response is required, women do tend to show more conformity than men (Eagly, 1987; Eagly & Carly, 2007; Eagly et al., 2000). This effect may be due to the socialization that women receive in being agreeable and supportive; however, the difference in conformity is quite small.

18.3 Trace how group dynamics influence an individual's behavior.

The Hazards of Groupthink Shortly after the terrorist attack on the World Trade Center in New York, President George W. Bush and his administration made the decision to invade Iraq, find Saddam Hussein, and stop him before he could use his "weapons of mass destruction" that the administration and its advisers, based on the information they were applying to their conclusions, believed were hidden in Iraq. Although there were advisers who thought the action to be a mistake, no one person was willing to stand up to the rest of the group and challenge the group's decision and assumptions. Many now see this decision as a prime example of **groupthink**. Groupthink occurs when people within a group feel it is more important to maintain the group's cohesiveness* than to consider the facts realistically (Hogg & Hains, 1998; Janis, 1972, 1982; Schafer & Crichlow, 1996). Other examples of Groupthink include the sinking of the *Titanic* in 1912 (the group responsible for designing and building the ship assumed it was unsinkable and did not even bother to include enough lifeboats on board for all the passengers), the *Challenger* disaster of 1986 in which a part on the shuttle was known by a few to be faulty, and the Bay of Pigs disaster during the Kennedy administration. **Table 18.1** summarizes several "symptoms" of groupthink devised by social psychologist and groupthink expert Irving Janis (1972, 1982).

Group Behavior Social influence is clearly seen in the behavior of people within a group, as Asch's classic study and the discussion of groupthink illustrated. But conformity and groupthink are only two ways in which a group can influence the behavior of an individual. Here are just a few others.

Group Polarization **Group polarization** is the tendency for members involved in a group discussion to take somewhat more extreme positions and suggest riskier actions when compared to individuals who have not participated in a group discussion (Bossert & Schworm, 2008; Moscovici & Zavalloni, 1969). A good example of group polarization can occur when a jury tries to decide on punitive damages during a civil trial: Studies have found that if members of a jury individually favored a relatively low amount of punitive damages before

What about ▶ gender—are men or women more conforming?

groupthink kind of thinking that occurs when people place more importance on maintaining group cohesiveness than on assessing the facts of the problem with which the group is concerned.

group polarization the tendency for members involved in a group discussion to take somewhat more extreme positions and suggest riskier actions when compared to individuals who have not participated in a group discussion.

---

*cohesiveness: sticking together.

Table 18.1	Characteristics of Groupthink
CHARACTERISTIC	DESCRIPTION
Invulnerability[†]	Members feel they cannot fail.
Rationalization	Members explain away warning signs and help each other justify their decision.
Lack of introspection	Members do not examine the ethical implications of their decision because they believe that they cannot make immoral choices.
Stereotyping	Members label their enemies as weak, stupid, or unreasonable.
Pressure	Members push each other not to question the prevailing opinion.
Lack of disagreement	Members do not express opinions that differ from the group consensus.
Self-deception	Members share in the illusion that they all agree with the decision.
Insularity	Members prevent the group from hearing disruptive but potentially useful information from people who are outside the group.

[†]invulnerability: quality of being unable to be attacked or harmed.
Source: Janis (1972, 1982).

deliberation, after deliberation the amount usually lessened further. Similarly, if the individual jurors favored stiffer penalties, the deliberation process resulted in even higher penalties (MacCoun & Kerr, 1988). Group polarization is thought to be because of both normative social influence and informational social influence.

Social Facilitation and Social Loafing Social influence can affect the success or failure of an individual's task performance within a group. The perceived difficulty of the task seems to determine the particular effect of the presence of others as well: If a task is perceived as easy, the presence of other people seems to improve performance. If the task is perceived as difficult, the presence of others actually has a negative effect on performance. The positive influence of others on performance is called **social facilitation**, whereas the negative influence is called **social impairment** (Aiello & Douthitt, 2001; Michaels et al., 1982; Zajonc, 1965).

Interestingly, people who are lazy tend not to do as well when other people are also working on the same task, but they can do quite well when working on their own. This phenomenon is called **social loafing** (Karau & Williams, 1993, 1997; Latané et al., 1979; Suleiman & Watson, 2008). The reason for this is that it is easier for a lazy person (a "loafer") to hide laziness when working in a group of people, because it is less likely that the individual will be evaluated alone. But when the social loafer is working alone, the focus of evaluation will be on that person only. In that case, the loafer works harder because there is no one else to whom the work can be shifted. Social loafing depends heavily on the assumption that personal responsibility for a task is severely lessened when working with a

social facilitation the tendency for the presence of other people to have a positive impact on the performance of an easy task.

social impairment the tendency for the presence of other people to have a negative impact on the performance of a difficult task.

social loafing the tendency for people to put less effort into a simple task when working with others on that task.

group of other people. One study suggests that although Americans may readily make that assumption, Chinese people, who come from a more interdependent cultural viewpoint, tend to assume that each individual within the group is still nearly as responsible for the group's outcome as the group at large (Menon et al., 1999). Chinese people may, therefore, be less likely to exhibit social loafing than are people in the United States.

18.4 Describe how an individual influences group behavior.

Leadership in Groups Several things can be done to minimize the possibility of groupthink (Hart, 1998; McCauley, 1998; Moorhead et al., 1998). For example, leaders should remain impartial, and the entire group should seek the opinions of people outside the group. Any voting should be done on secret ballots rather than by a show of hands, and it should be made clear that group members will be held responsible for decisions made by the group.

18.5 Explain how the presence of others affects compliance in an individual's behavior.

Compliance Compliance occurs when people change their behavior as a result of another person or group asking or directing them to change. The person or group asking for the change in behavior typically doesn't have any real authority or power to command a change; when that authority does exist and behavior is changed as a result, it is called obedience, which is the topic of the next major section of this chapter.

A number of techniques that people use to get the compliance of others clearly show the relationship of compliance to the world of marketing, as they refer to techniques that door-to-door salespersons would commonly use. Think of the times you've seen students and others go door to door trying to make sales for fundraising projects. Do you feel more compelled to buy from a classmate doing fundraising that you would for a similar product in the store?

A neighbor asks you to keep an eye on his house while he is on vacation. You agree, thinking that it's a rather small request. Later that day, the neighbor asks if you would kindly water his plants while he's gone. This is a little bit more involved and requires more of your time and energy—will you do it? If you are like most people, you probably will comply with this second larger request. In the **foot-in-the-door technique,** the first small request acts as an opener. When compliance with a smaller request is followed by a larger request, people are quite likely to comply because they have already agreed to the smaller one and they want to behave consistently with their previous response (Cialdini et al., 1995; Dillard, 1990, 1991; Freedman & Fraser, 1966; Meineri & Guéguen, 2008).

Another compliance technique, also common in the world of sales, is called the **lowball technique** (Bator & Cialdini, 2006; Burger & Petty, 1981; Weyant, 1996). In this technique, once a commitment is made, the cost of that commitment is increased. (In the sense used here, cost does not necessarily mean money; cost can also mean time, effort, or other kinds of sacrifices.) For example, let's say that as a member of a student organization you agreed to volunteer for one hour on Saturday morning to clean up litter in a park near your school. Once committed to that process you discover that the task involves not only picking up litter but also raking the leaves, pulling weeds around the sidewalks, and painting the swing sets. What began as a one-hour commitment has now turned into a task that takes all of your Saturday to complete. A common example of

Thinking Critically
Can you think of a time when you conformed with the actions of a group of friends, even though you disagreed with their actions? Based on Asch's studies and studies on groupthink, why do you think you conformed?

I have a friend who ▶ watches infomercials on the shopping channels and buys stuff that isn't worth the money or that doesn't work like it's supposed to work. Why do people fall for pitches like that?

compliance changing one's behavior as a result of other people directing or asking for the change.

foot-in-the-door technique asking for a small commitment and, after gaining compliance, asking for a bigger commitment.

lowball technique getting a commitment from a person and then raising the cost of that commitment.

these techniques will occur to anyone who has ever bought a car, as the video *Compliance Techniques* explains.

Watch the Video, *Compliance Techniques,* at MyPsychLab

Cultural differences exist in people's susceptibility to these techniques. For the foot-in-the-door technique in particular, research has shown that people in individualist cultures (such as the United States) are more likely to comply with the second request than are people in collectivist cultures (such as Japan). The research suggests that people in collectivist cultures are not as concerned with being consistent with previous behavior because they are less focused on their inner motivation than are people in individualist cultures, who are more concerned with their inner motives and consistency (Cialdini et al., 1999; Petrova et al., 2007).

18.6 Explain how the presence of others affects obedience in an individual's behavior.

Obedience There is a difference between the concepts of compliance, which is agreeing to change one's behavior because someone else asks for the change, and **obedience**, which is changing one's behavior at the direct order of an authority figure. A salesperson who wants a person to buy a car has no real power to force that person to buy, but an authority figure is a person with social power—such as a police officer, a teacher, or a work supervisor—who has the right to demand certain behavior from the people under the authority figure's command or supervision.

How far will people go in obeying the commands of an authority figure? What factors make obedience more or less likely? These are some of the questions that researchers have been investigating for many years. The answers to these questions became very important not only to researchers but also to people everywhere after the atrocities committed by the soldiers in Nazi Germany—soldiers who were "just following orders."

Milgram's Shocking Research Social psychologist Stanley Milgram set out to find answers to these questions. He was aware of Asch's studies of conformity and wondered how much impact social influence could have on a behavior that was more meaningful than judging the length of lines on cards. He designed what has become one of the most famous (even notorious*) experiments in the history of psychology.

Through ads placed in the local newspaper, Milgram recruited people who were told that they would be participating in an experiment to test the effects of punishment on learning behavior (Milgram, 1963, 1974). The participants believed that they had randomly been assigned to either the "teacher" role or the "learner" role, when in fact the "learner" was a confederate already aware of the situation. The task for the learner was a simple memory test for paired words.

The "teacher" was seated in front of a machine through which the shocks would be administered and the level of the shocks changed. (See **Figure 18.2.**) For each mistake made by the "learner," the "teacher" was instructed to increase the level of shock by 15 volts. The learner (who was not actually shocked) followed a carefully arranged script by pounding on the wall and playing a series of prerecorded audio responses (sounds of discomfort, asking for the experiment to end, screaming) or remained silent as if unconscious—or dead. As the "teachers" became reluctant to continue administering the shocks, the experimenter in his white lab coat, which signified authority, said, for example, "The experiment requires you to continue" or "You must continue," and reminded the "teacher" that the experimenter would take full responsibility for the safety of the "learner."

obedience changing one's behavior at the command of an authority figure.

---

*notorious: widely and unfavorably known.

FIGURE 18.2 Control Panel in Milgram's Experiment
In Stanley Milgram's classic study on obedience, the participants were presented with a control panel like this one. Each participant ("teacher") was instructed to give electric shocks to another person (the "learner," who only pretended to be shocked by pounding on the wall and playing a prerecorded audio tape of grunts, protests, and screams). At what point do you think you would have refused to continue the experiment?

So what happened? Were those people sadists? Why would they keep shocking someone like that?

It was predicted by a group of people that Milgram surveyed that the participants would all refuse to go on at some point, with most believing that the majority of the participants would start refusing as soon as the "learner" protested—150 volts. None of those he surveyed believed that any participant would go all the way to the highest voltage.

So were they right? Far from it—in the first set of experiments, 65 percent of the "teachers" went all the way through the experiment's final 450-volt shock level, although many were obviously uncomfortable and begged to be allowed to stop. Of those "teachers" who did protest and finally stop, not one of them stopped before reaching 300 volts!

No one was more stunned than Milgram himself. He had not believed that his experiments would show such a huge effect of obedience to authority. These results do not appear to be some random "fluke" resulting from a large population of cruel people residing in the area. These experiments have been repeated at various times, in the United States and in other countries, and the percentage of participants who went all the way consistently remained between 61 and 66 percent (Blass, 1999; Slater et al., 2006).

That's incredible—I just don't believe that I could do something like that to someone else.

Evaluation of Milgram's Research Researchers have looked for particular personality traits that might be associated with high levels of obedience but have not found any one trait or group of traits that consistently predicts who will obey and who will not in experiments similar to Milgram's original studies (Blass, 1991). The people who "went all the way" were not necessarily more dependent or susceptible to being controlled by others; they were simply people like most other people, caught in a situation of "obey or disobey" the authority.

Milgram's research also raised a serious ethical question: How far should researchers be willing to go to answer a question of interest? Some have argued that the participants in Milgram's studies may have suffered damaged self-esteem and serious psychological stress from the realization that they were willing to administer shocks great enough to kill another person, just on the say-so of an experimenter (Baumrind, 1964). Milgram (1964b) responded to the criticism by citing his follow-up study of the participants, in which he found that 84 percent of the participants were glad to have been a part of the experiment. Even so, most psychologists do agree that under the current ethical rules that exist for such research, this study would never be allowed to happen today.

Pick the best answer.

1. Solomon Asch's 1951 study with a standard line and comparison lines showed the influence of
   a. compliance.
   b. obedience.
   c. persuasion.
   d. conformity.

2. Which of the following is not a characteristic of groupthink?
   a. pressure
   b. objectivity
   c. invulnerability
   d. rationalization

3. Francisco wants to buy a new laptop. He sees a laptop being sold for what he thinks is a reasonable price, so he commits to buying it. After he makes this commitment, however, he is forced to spend even more money on a warranty, an anti-theft plan, and required software for the laptop. Which technique has Francisco been manipulated by?
   a. lowball technique
   b. that's-not-all technique
   c. foot-in-the-door technique
   d. door-in-the-face technique

4. Conner needs just $20 more to go out with his friends. He asks his mother for $50 but she tells him he can have $30 instead. In the end, Conner ended up with $10 more than he originally planned. What technique did Connor use?
   a. foot-in-the-door technique
   b. door-in-the-face technique
   c. lowball technique
   d. planned obedience

5. Milgram's classic 1964 experiment found that
   a. the foot-in-the-door technique is rarely effective.
   b. most people are surprisingly obedient to authority.
   c. the presence of others improves the performance of easy tasks.
   d. women and men are equally likely to conform in group situations.

6. Jenna always did well in during group projects because she allowed the rest of the group to do most of the work, but she shared in the good grade. Her new teacher requires each student to complete a different section of a project to prevent students like Jenna from
   a. social loafing.
   b. deindividuation.
   c. rationalization.
   d. invulnerability.

7. Which has the greatest effect on conformity?
   a. one's gender
   b. testosterone levels
   c. one's hair color
   d. whether one's culture is collectivist

8. Sandy plays tennis very well. Lately she seems to play even better when other people watch her. The difference in Sandy's playing is most likely due to
   a. social loafing.
   b. social identity.
   c. social facilitation.
   d. social comparison.

9. Emily refuses to eat her dinner. Her father tells her she cannot go play until she eats all the food on her plate. She folds her arms and refuses. Her father then tells her to eat half her Brussels sprouts and take three bites of salad. Emily happily gobbles up the limited amount of food and rushes outside to play. Which technique did Emily's father use?
   a. lowball
   b. that's not all
   c. door-in-the-face
   d. foot-in-the-door

10. Which of the following studies is most questionable regarding research ethics in psychology today?
    a. Asch's experiment on conformity
    b. Milgram's experiment on conformity
    c. Milgram's experiment on obedience
    d. Asch's experiment on obedience

19 Social Cognition

Module Goal

Understand the effects of social cognition.

Learning Objectives

19.1 Explain the relationship between attitudes and behavior.

19.2 Discuss persuasive methods used to change attitudes.

19.3 Explain attributional explanations of behavior.

Understand the Effects of Social Cognition

Social cognition focuses on the ways in which people *think* about other people and how those cognitions influence behavior toward those other people. In this section, we'll concentrate on how we perceive others and form our first impressions of them, as well as how we explain the behavior of others and ourselves.

19.1 Explain the relationship between attitudes and behavior.

One area of social cognition concerns the formation and influence of attitudes on the behavior and perceptions of others. An **attitude** can be defined as a tendency to respond positively or negatively to a certain idea, person, object, or situation (Triandis, 1971). This tendency, developed through people's experiences as they live and work with others, can affect the way they behave toward those ideas, people, objects, and situations and can include opinions, beliefs, and biases. In fact, attitudes can influence the way people view these things before they've actually been exposed to them (Petty et al., 2003).

Attitudes are not something people have when they are born. They are learned through experiences and contact with others and even through direct instruction from parents, teachers, and other important people in a person's life. Because attitudes involve a positive or negative evaluation of things, it's possible to go into a new situation, meet a new person, or be exposed to a new idea with one's "mind already made up" to like or dislike, agree or disagree, and so on (Eagly & Chaiken, 1993; Petty et al., 2003). For example, children are known for making up their minds about certain foods before ever tasting them, simply because the foods are "green." Those children may have tried a green food in the past and disliked it and now are predisposed* to dislike any green food whether they've tasted it or not.

The ABC Model of Attitudes Attitudes are actually made of up to three different parts, or components, as shown in **Figure 19.1**. These components should not come as a surprise to anyone who has been reading the other chapters in this text because, throughout the text, references have been made to

What do you mean—▶ how can an attitude have an effect on something that hasn't happened yet?

attitude a tendency to respond positively or negatively toward a certain person, object, idea, or situation.

---

*predisposed: referring to a tendency to respond in a particular way based on previous experience.

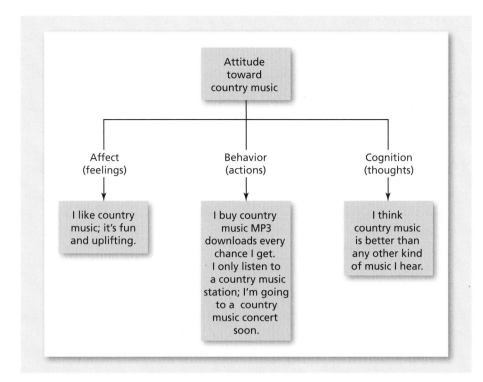

FIGURE 19.1 Three Components of an Attitude
Attitudes consist of the way a person feels and thinks about something, as well as the way the person chooses to behave. If you like country music, you are also likely to think that country music is good music. You are also more likely to listen to this style of music, buy this type of music, and even go to a performance. Each of the three components influences the other two.

personality and traits being composed of the ways people think, feel, and act. By using certain terms to describe these three things, psychologists have come up with a handy way to describe the three components of attitudes (Eagly & Chaiken, 1993, 1998; Fazio & Olsen, 2003).

- **Affective Component:** The affective component of an attitude is the way a person feels toward the object, person, or situation. *Affect* is used in psychology to mean "emotions" or "feelings," so the affective component is the emotional component. For example, some people might feel that country music is fun and uplifting.
- **Behavior Component:** The behavior component of an attitude is the action that a person takes in regard to the person, object, or situation. For example, a person who feels that country music is fun is likely to listen to country music, buy country music MP3s, or go to a country music concert.
- **Cognitive Component:** Finally, the cognitive component of an attitude is the way a person thinks about the person, object, or situation. These thoughts, or cognitions, include beliefs and ideas about the focus of the attitude. For example, the country music lover might believe that country music is superior to other forms of music.

Some attitudes are stronger than others, and strong attitudes are more likely to predict behavior than weak ones. A person who quit smoking because of failing health might have a stronger attitude toward secondhand smoke than someone who quit smoking on a dare, for example.

Attitude Formation Attitude formation is the result of a number of different influences with only one thing in common: They are all forms of learning.

- **Direct Contact:** One way in which attitudes are formed is by direct contact with the person, idea, situation, or object that is the focus of the attitude.
- **Direct Instruction:** Another way attitudes are formed is through direct instruction, either by parents or some other individual.
- **Interaction with Others:** Sometimes attitudes are formed because the person is around other people with that attitude.

◄ So if you know what someone thinks or feels about something, you can predict what that person will do, right?

- **Observational Learning:** Many attitudes are learned through the observation of other people's actions and reactions to various objects, people, or situations.

Attitudes are not only influenced by other people in a person's immediate world but also by the larger world of mass media (magazines, television, the internet, and the movie) a fact of which advertisers and marketing experts are well aware (Gresham & Shimp, 1985; MacKenzie et al., 1986).

19.2 Discuss persuasive methods used to change attitudes.

Sometimes people learn attitudes that aren't necessarily good ones, right? So can attitudes change?

Attitude Change: The Art of Persuasion Because attitudes are learned, they are also subject to change with new learning. The world is full of people, companies, and other organizations that want to change people's attitudes. It's all about the art of *persuasion*, the process by which one person tries to change the belief, opinion, position, or course of action of another person through argument, pleading, or explanation.

Persuasion is not a simple matter. Several factors become important in predicting how successful any persuasive effort at attitude change might be. These factors include the following:

- **Source:** The communicator is the person delivering the message. There is a strong tendency to give more weight to people who are perceived as experts, as well as those who seem trustworthy, attractive, and similar to the person receiving the message (Eagly & Chaiken, 1975; Petty & Cacioppo, 1986, 1996; Priester & Petty, 1995).
- **Message:** The actual message should be clear and well organized (Booth-Butterfield, 1996). It is usually more effective to present both sides of an argument to an audience that has not yet committed to one side or the other (Crowley & Hoyer, 1994; Petty & Cacioppo, 1996; Petty et al., 2003).
- **Target Audience:** The characteristics of the people who are the intended target of the message of persuasion are also important in determining the effectiveness of the message. The age of the audience members can be a factor, for example.
- **Medium:** The form through which a person receives a message is also important. For example, seeing and hearing a politician's speech on television or on Facebook or Twitter may have a very different effect than simply reading about it in the newspaper or online.

Thinking Critically
Imagine that you are asked to create a television commercial to sell a new product. Given what you know of the factors that effectively influence persuasion, how might you persuade a customer?

How easily influenced a person is will also be related to the way people tend to process information. In the **elaboration likelihood model** of persuasion (Petty & Cacioppo, 1986), it is assumed that people either elaborate (add details and information) based on what they hear (the facts of the message), or they do not elaborate at all, preferring to pay attention to the surface characteristics of the message (length, who delivers it, how attractive the message deliverer is, etc.). Two types of processing are hypothesized in this model: **central-route processing,** in which people attend to the content of the message, and **peripheral-route processing,** a style of information processing that relies on peripheral cues (cues outside of the message content itself) such as the expertise of the message source, the length of the message, and other factors that have nothing to do with the message content. This style of processing causes people not to pay attention to the message itself but instead to base their decisions on those peripheral factors (Petty & Cacioppo, 1986; Stiff & Mongeau, 2002).

elaboration likelihood model model of persuasion stating that people will either elaborate (give second thought) on the persuasive message or fail to elaborate on it and that the future actions of those who do elaborate are more predictable than those who do not.

central-route processing type of information processing that involves attending to the content of the message itself.

peripheral-route processing type of information processing that involves attending to factors not involved in the message, such as the appearance of the source of the message, the length of the message, and other noncontent factors.

Cognitive Dissonance: When Attitudes and Behavior Clash When people find themselves doing things or saying things that don't match their idea of themselves as smart, nice, or moral, for example, they experience an emotional discomfort (and physiological arousal) known as **cognitive dissonance** (Aronson, 1997; Festinger, 1957; Kelly et al., 1997). (*Dissonance* is a term referring to an inconsistency or lack of agreement.)

When people experience cognitive dissonance, the resulting tension and arousal are unpleasant, and their motivation is to change something so that the unpleasant feelings and tension are reduced or eliminated. There are three basic things that people can do to reduce cognitive dissonance:

1. Change their conflicting behavior to make it match their attitude.
2. Change their current conflicting cognition to justify their behavior.
3. Form new cognitions to justify their behavior.

In a classic experiment conducted at Stanford University by psychologist Leon Festinger and colleague James Carlsmith (Festinger & Carlsmith, 1959), each male student volunteer was given an hour-long, very boring task of sorting wooden spools and turning wooden pegs. After the hour, the experimenters asked the participant to tell the female volunteer in the waiting room that the task was enjoyable. Whereas half of the participants were paid only $1 to try to convince the waiting woman, the other participants were paid $20. (In the late 1950s, $20 was a considerable sum of money—the average income was $5,000, the average car cost $3,000, and gas was only 25 cents a gallon.)

At the time of this study, many researchers would have predicted that the more the participants were paid to lie, the more they would come to like the task, because they were getting more reinforcement ($20) for doing so. But what actually happened was that those participants who were paid only $1 for lying actually convinced themselves that the task was interesting and fun. The reason is cognitive dissonance: Participants who were paid only $1 experienced discomfort at thinking that they would lie to someone for only a dollar. Therefore, they must not be lying—the task really was pretty interesting, after all, and fun, too! Those who were paid more experienced no dissonance because they knew exactly why they were lying—for lots of money—and the money was a sufficient amount to explain their behavior to their satisfaction. Although most people don't want to be thought of as liars, back then, getting paid enough money to fill the gas tank of one's car three or four times over was incentive enough to tell what probably seemed to be a harmless fib. Those who were paid only $1 had to change their attitude toward the task so that they would not really be lying and could maintain their self-image of honesty. (See **Figure 19.2**.)

19.3 Explain attributional explanations of behavior.

Attribution Another aspect of social cognition is the need people seem to have to explain the behavior of other people. Have you ever watched someone who was doing something you didn't understand? Chances are you were going through a number of possible explanations in your head: "Maybe he's sick, or maybe he sees something I can't see," and so on. It seems to be human nature to want to know why people do the things they do so that we know how to behave toward them and decide whom we might want to use as role models. If no obvious answer is available, people tend to come up with their own reasons. People also need an explanation for their own behavior. This need is so great that if an explanation isn't obvious, it causes the distress known as cognitive dissonance. The process of explaining both one's own behavior and the behavior of other people is called **attribution**, or to what do you attribute that attitude.

Causes of Behavior *Attribution theory* was originally developed by social psychologist Fritz Heider (1958) as a way of explaining not only why things

Inducement	Attitude
$1	+1.35
$20	− 0.5
Control	− .45

*Based on a –5 to +5 scale, where –5 means "extremely boring" and +5 means "extremely interesting"

FIGURE 19.2 Cognitive Dissonance: Attitude Toward a Task

After completing a boring task, some participants were paid $1 and some $20 to convince others waiting to do the same task that the task was interesting and fun. Surprisingly, the participants who were paid only $1 seemed to change their own attitude toward the task, rating it as interesting, whereas those who were paid $20 rated the task no differently than a control group did.

Source: Adapted from Festinger and Carlsmith (1959).

cognitive dissonance sense of discomfort or distress that occurs when a person's behavior does not correspond to that person's attitudes.

attribution the process of explaining one's own behavior and the behavior of others.

fundamental attribution error the tendency to over estimate the influence of internal factors in determining behavior while underestimating situational factors.

happen but also why people choose the particular explanations of behavior that they do. There are basically two kinds of explanations—those that involve an external cause and those that assume that causes are internal.

When the cause of behavior is assumed to be from external sources, such as the weather, traffic, educational opportunities, and so on, it is said to be a *situational cause*. The observed behavior is assumed to be caused by whatever situation exists for the person at that time. For example, if John is late, his lateness might be explained by heavy traffic or car problems.

On the other hand, if the cause of behavior is assumed to come from within the individual, it is called a *dispositional cause*. In this case, it is the person's disposition (internal personality characteristics) that is seen as the cause of the observed behavior. Someone attributing John's behavior to a dispositional cause, for example, might assume that John was late because his personality includes being careless of his and other people's time.

These kinds of attributions also have an emotional component. When people are happy in a marriage, for example, researchers have found that when a spouse's behavior has a positive effect, the tendency is to attribute it to an internal cause ("he did it because he wanted me to feel good"). When the effect is negative, the behavior is attributed to an external cause ("she must have had a difficult day"). But if the marriage is an unhappy one, the opposite attributions occur: "He is only being nice because he wants something from me" or "She's being mean because it's her nature to be crabby" (Fincham et al., 2000; Karney & Bradbury, 2000).

But what else determines which type of cause a person will use? For example, what determines how people explain the behavior of someone they don't already know or like?

But why do we do that? Why not assume an external cause for everyone?

▶ **Fundamental Attribution Error** The most well-known attributional bias is the **fundamental attribution error**, which is the tendency for people observing someone else's actions to overestimate the influence of that person's internal characteristics on behavior and underestimate the influence of the situation (whereas in explaining our own behavior, the tendency to use situational attributions instead of personal is called the *actor–observer bias* because we are the actor, not the observer). In other words, people tend to explain the actions of others based on what "kind" of person they are rather than looking for outside causes such as social influences or situations (Blanchard-Fields et al., 2007; Harman, 1999; Jones & Harris, 1967; Leclerc & Hess, 2007; Weiner, 1985). For example, people hearing about Milgram's "shock" study tend to assume that something is wrong with the "teachers" in the study rather than explaining their behavior within the circumstances of the situation.

When people are the actors, they are very aware of the situational influences on their own behavior. For example, tardy John was actually the one driving to school, and he knows that heavy traffic and a small accident made him late to school—he was there, after all. But an outside observer of John's behavior doesn't have the opportunity to see all of the possible situational influences and has only John himself in focus and, thus, assumes that John's tardiness is caused by some internal personality flaw and commits the fundamental attribution error.

Although the fundamental attribution error has been found in American culture (Jones & Harris, 1967), would the same error occur in a culture that is very different from American culture, such as in Japan? This is the question asked by researchers Masuda and Kitayama (2004), who had both American and Japanese participants ask a target person to read a prewritten attitudinal statement. The participants were then asked to give their opinion on the target's real attitude. American participants made the classic error, assuming that the target's attitude matched the reading. The Japanese participants, however, assumed that the person's attitude might be different from the statement—the person might have been under social obligation to write the piece. Japanese society is a collectivistic culture, and a Japanese person might expect to write a paper to please a teacher or employer, even though the paper's contents do not necessarily express the writer's attitudes (Peng et al., 2000).

Pick the best answer.

1. On Paul's birthday, his girlfriend Beth doesn't treat him specially. Paul assumes that Beth simply doesn't care about him because she didn't recognize his special day. When he complains, she seems shocked and explains that her family never celebrated birthdays, and asks him if he'd like to go out to celebrate. Paul has possibly made the

   a. assumption error.
   b. false consensus error.
   c. social categorization error.
   d. fundamental attribution error.

2. Studies have found that attitudes are primarily the result of

   a. heredity.
   b. hormonal chemistry.
   c. traumatic incidents.
   d. learned behavior.

3. Elizabeth's room is almost always a mess. Her parents attribute this to Elizabeth's laziness, which is an example of a

   a. situational cause.
   b. superficial cause.
   c. fundamental cause.
   d. dispositional cause.

4. Which of the following represents the affective component of an attitude?

   a. "I love to go to the clubs—it makes me so happy!"
   b. "Tonight, we're going to that new club downtown."
   c. "It is interesting to watch people when I'm out at a club."
   d. "I'm going to wear a new outfit to the club tonight."

5. Which of the following represents the cognitive component of an attitude?

   a. "I just love Italian food!"
   b. "I'm going to bake lasagna tonight."
   c. "Italian food is the best of the European cuisines."
   d. "Tonight we're going to a new Italian restaurant."

6. Lilly's mother always listens to the classic rock radio station, so Lilly has grown up hearing classic rock and noticing how much her mother enjoys it. Now Lilly says that classic rock is her favorite. Lilly's attitude toward classic rock was most likely acquired through

   a. indirect contact.
   b. direct instruction.
   c. observational learning.
   d. interaction with others.

7. Physical attractiveness is most involved in which of the following aspects of persuasion?

   a. the target
   b. the message
   c. the source
   d. the audience

8. Pamela hates when people use their cell phones during class. One day Pamela gets an urgent call during class, and she answers the call. She tells herself that answering a phone in class isn't so bad after all. Pamela is reducing her sense of

   a. attitude formation.
   b. cognitive dissonance.
   c. social impairment.
   d. justified conformity.

9. Many times, food companies will market their products to young children by putting images of popular cartoon characters on cereal boxes, egg cartons, snack packs, and yogurt lids. These companies hope that which of the following will influence their target audience?

   a. central-route processing
   b. fundamental attribution error
   c. peripheral-route processing
   d. the elaboration likelihood model

10. In the famous Festinger experiment, participants were paid either $1 or $20 to lie to a woman in the waiting room about how interesting the task really was. The participants who convinced themselves that the task really was fun were the ones who were

    a. paid immediately.
    b. paid after one day.
    c. paid only $1.
    d. paid $20.

20 Social Interaction

Module Goal

Describe different kinds of social relations.

Learning Objectives

20.1 Describe the nature and effects of stereotyping, prejudice, and discrimination.

20.2 Explain factors that influence attraction and relationships.

20.3 Explain influences upon aggression and conflict.

20.4 Discuss determinants of prosocial behavior.

▲ On September 6, 1957, this high school in Little Rock, Arkansas, became integrated, allowing African American students to attend school with White students. The desegregation laws were aimed at stopping discrimination but attitudes of prejudice persisted then, and to some degree still exist today. The courts can make laws against discrimination, but changing prejudicial attitudes is much more difficult.

It sounds as though we'd be better ▶ off if people didn't use social categorization.

Describe Different Kinds of Social Relations

Social influence and social cognition are two of three main areas included in the field of social psychology. The third major area has to do with social interactions with others, or the relationships between people, both casual and intimate. Social interactions include the influence of stereotyping, prejudice, and discrimination, liking and loving, and aggression and prosocial behavior.

20.1 Describe the nature and effects of stereotyping, prejudice, and discrimination.

Stereotypes One of the processes that occur when people meet someone new is the assignment of that person to some kind of category or group. This assignment is usually based on characteristics the new person has in common with other people or groups with whom the perceiver has had prior experience. This *social categorization* is mostly automatic and occurs without conscious awareness of the process (Macrae & Bodenhausen, 2000). Although this is a natural process (human beings are just born categorizers, sometimes it can cause problems. When the characteristics used to categorize the person are superficial* ones that have become improperly attached to certain ideas, such as "red hair equals a bad temper," social categorization can result in a **stereotype**, a set of characteristics that people believe is shared by all members of a particular social category (Fiske, 1998). Stereotypes (though not always negative) are very limiting, causing people to misjudge what others are like and often to treat them differently as a result.

Social categorization does have an important place in the perception of others. It allows people to access a great deal of information that can be useful about others, as well as helping people to remember and organize information about the characteristics of others (Macrae & Bodenhausen, 2000). The way to avoid falling into the trap of negatively stereotyping someone is to be aware of existing stereotypes and apply a little critical thinking: "Okay, so he's a guy on the street living out of a shopping cart. That doesn't mean that he's lazy—it just means he needs help."

---

*superficial: on the surface.

Prejudice and Discrimination When a person holds an unsupported and often negative stereotyped attitude about the members of a particular social group, it is called **prejudice**. When prejudicial attitudes cause members of a particular social group to be treated differently than others in situations that call for equal treatment, it is called **discrimination**. Although laws can be made to minimize discriminatory behavior, it is not possible to have laws against holding certain attitudes. In other words, discrimination can be controlled and in some cases eliminated, but the prejudicial attitude that is responsible for the discrimination cannot be so easily controlled or eliminated.

Types of Prejudice and Discrimination There are many kinds of prejudice. There are also many kinds of discrimination that occur as a result of prejudice, notably: ageism, or prejudicial attitudes toward the elderly or teenagers (among others); sexism; racism, or prejudice toward those from different ethnic groups; prejudice toward those from different religions, those from different economic levels, those who are overweight, those who are too thin, or who have a different sexual orientation. Prejudice can also vary in terms of what type of people or groups make the most likely targets. In any society, there will always be **in-groups** and **out-groups**, or "us" versus "them." The in-group is all the people with whom a particular person identifies, and the out-groups are everyone else (Brewer, 2001; Hewstone et al., 2002; Tajfel & Turner, 1986).

Once an in-group is established, prejudice toward and discriminatory treatment of the out-group or groups soon follow (Brewer, 2001). Members of the out-groups are usually going to become stereotyped according to some superficial characteristic, such as skin color or hair color, and getting rid of a stereotype once formed is difficult at best (Cameron et al., 2001; Hamilton & Gifford, 1976).

Conflicts between groups are usually greater when there are other pressures or stresses going on, such as war, economic difficulties, or other misfortunes. When such pressures exist, the need to find a scapegoat becomes stronger. A scapegoat is a person or a group, typically a member or members of an out-group, who serves as the target for the frustrations and negative emotions of members of the in-group.

Scapegoats are going to be the group of people with the least power, and the newest immigrants to any area are typically those who have the least power at that time. That is why many social psychologists believe that the rioting that took place in Los Angeles, California, in the spring of 1992 occurred in the areas it did. This was the time of the infamous Rodney King beating. Rodney King was an African American man who was dragged out of his car onto the street and severely beaten by four police officers. The beating was caught on tape by a bystander. At the trial, the officers were found not guilty of assault with a deadly weapon. This decision was followed by a series of violent riots (Knight, 1996).

The puzzling thing about these riots is that the greatest amount of rioting was greatest in the neighborhoods of the Asian Americans and Asians who were the most recent immigrants to the area. When a group has only recently moved into an area, as the Asians had, that group has the least social power and influence in that new area. So the rioters took out their frustrations not on the people seen as directly responsible for those frustrations but on the group of people with the least power to resist.

How People Learn Prejudice As we will see in the Classic Studies in Psychology section, even children are, under the right circumstances, prone to developing prejudiced attitudes. Is all prejudice simply a matter of learning, or are there other factors at work? Several theories have been proposed to explain

stereotype a set of characteristics that people believe is shared by all members of a particular social category.

prejudice negative attitude held by a person about the members of a particular social group.

discrimination treating people differently because of prejudice toward the social group to which they belong.

in-groups social groups with whom a person identifies; "us."

out-groups social groups with whom a person does not identify; "them."

▼ *These Korean demonstrators were protesting the riots that followed the 1992 not guilty verdict in the beating of Rodney King. The riots lasted six days, killing 42 people and damaging 700 buildings in mainly Korean and other Asian American neighborhoods. The Asian American population of Los Angeles, California, became scapegoats for aggression.*

the origins and the persistence* of prejudice. In *social cognitive theory*, prejudice is seen as an attitude that is formed as other attitudes are formed, through direct instruction, modeling, and other social influences on learning.

Classic Studies in Psychology

Brown Eyes, Blue Eyes

In a small town in Iowa in 1968, a few days after the assassination of Dr. Martin Luther King, Jr., a third-grade teacher named Jane Elliot tried to teach her students a lesson in prejudice and discrimination. She divided her students into two groups, those with blue eyes and those with brown eyes.

On the first day of the lesson, the blue-eyed children were given special privileges, such as extra time at recess and getting to leave first for lunch. She also told the blue-eyed children that they were superior to the brown-eyed children, telling the brown-eyed children not to bother taking seconds at lunch because it would be wasted. She kept the blue-eyed children and the brown-eyed children apart (Peters, 1971).

When Elliot became critical of the brown-eyed out-group, she soon found that the blue-eyed children also began to criticize, belittle, and viciously attack the brown-eyed children. By the end of the day, the blue-eyed children felt and acted superior, and the brown-eyed children were miserable, and even scored lower on tests. Two days later, the brown-eyed children became the favored group and the effects from the first two days appeared again but in reverse this time: The blue-eyed children began to feel inferior and their test scores dropped.

The fact that test scores reflected the treatment received by the out-group is a stunning one, raising questions about the effects of prejudice and discrimination on the education of children who are members of stereotyped out-groups. That the children were so willing to discriminate against their own classmates, some of whom were their close friends before the experiment, is also telling. In his book about this classroom experiment, *A Class Divided*, Peters (1971) reported that the students who were part of the original experiment, when reunited 15 years later to talk about the experience, said that they believed that this early experience with prejudice and discrimination helped them to become less prejudiced as young adults.

Questions for Further Discussion

1. Is there anything about this experiment that you find disturbing?
2. How do you think adults might react in a similar experiment?
3. Are there any ethical concerns with what Elliot did in her classroom?

---

social identity theory theory in which the formation of a person's identity within a particular social group is explained by social categorization, social identity, and social comparison.

social categorization the assignment of a person one has just met to a category based on characteristics the new person has in common with other people with whom one has had experience in the past.

In **social identity theory**, three processes are responsible for the formation of a person's identity within a particular social group and the attitudes, concepts, and behavior that go along with identification with that group (Tajfel & Turner, 1986). The first process is **social categorization**, as discussed earlier in this chapter. Just as people assign categories to others (such as black, white, student, teacher) to help organize information about those others, people also assign themselves to social categories to help determine how they should behave. The second element of social identity theory is identification, or the formation

---

*persistence: continuing an action or thought even though it is difficult.

of one's *social identity*. A social identity is the part of one's self-concept that includes the view of oneself as a member of a particular social group within the social category—typically, the in-group. The third aspect of social identity theory is **social comparison**, Festinger's (1954) concept in which people compare themselves favorably to others to improve their own self-esteem: "Well, at least I'm better off than that person." (Members of the out-group make handy comparisons.)

With respect to prejudice, social identity theory helps to explain why people feel the need to categorize or stereotype others, producing the in-group sense of "us versus them" that people adopt toward out-groups. Prejudice may result, at least in part, from the need to increase one's own self-esteem by looking down on others.

social comparison the comparison of oneself to others in ways that raise one's self-esteem.

stereotype vulnerability the effect that people's awareness of the stereotypes associated with their social group has on their behavior.

Stereotype Vulnerability As discussed previously, stereotypes are the widespread beliefs a person has about members of another group. Not only do stereotypes affect the way people perceive other people, but also stereotypes can affect the way people see themselves and their performance (Snyder et al., 1977). **Stereotype vulnerability** refers to the effect that a person's knowledge of another's stereotyped opinions can have on that person's behavior (Steele, 1992, 1997). Research has shown that when people are aware of stereotypes that are normally applied to their own group by others, they feel anxious about behaving in ways that might support that stereotype. This fear results in anxiety and self-consciousness that have negative effects on their performance in a kind of *self-fulfilling prophecy*, or the effect that expectations can have on outcomes.

Stereotype vulnerability is highly related to *stereotype threat*, in which members of a stereotyped group are made anxious and wary of any situation in which their behavior might confirm a stereotype (Hyde & Kling, 2001; Steele, 1999). In one study, researchers administered a difficult verbal test to both Caucasian and African American participants (Steele & Aronson, 1995). Half of the African American participants were asked to record their race on a demographic* question before the test, making them very aware of their minority status. Those participants showed a significant decrease in scores on the test when compared to the other participants, both African American and Caucasian, who did not answer such a demographic question. They had more incorrect answers, had slower response times, answered fewer questions, and demonstrated more anxiety when compared to the other participants (Steele & Aronson, 1995).

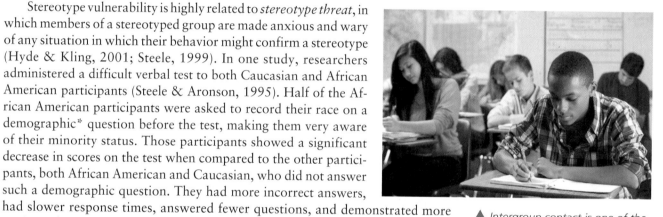

▲ Intergroup contact is one of the best ways to combat prejudice. When people have an opportunity to work together, as the students in this diverse classroom do, they get to know each other on common ground. Can you think of the first time you had direct contact with someone who was different from you? How did that contact change your viewpoint?

The best weapon against prejudice is education: learning about people who are different from you in many ways. The best way to learn about others is to have direct contact with them and learn to see them as people rather than as outsiders or strangers.

Equal Status Contact Contact between social groups can backfire under certain circumstances, however, as seen in a famous study (Sherif et al., 1961) called the "Robber's Cave." In this experiment conducted at a summer camp called Robber's Cave, 22 white, well-adjusted 11- and 12-year-old boys were divided into two groups. The groups each lived in separate housing and were kept apart from each other for daily activities. During the second week, after in-group relationships had formed, the researchers scheduled highly competitive events pitting one group against the other. Intergroup conflict quickly occurred, with name-calling, fights, and hostility emerging between the two groups.

The third week involved making the two groups come together for pleasant, noncompetitive activities, in the hopes that cooperation would be the result. Instead, the groups used the activities of the third week as opportunities for more hostility. It was only after several weeks of being forced to work together to

---

*demographic: having to do with the statistical characteristics of a population.

mere exposure effect idea that repeated presentation of novel stimuli increases liking the stimuli.

resolve a series of crises (created deliberately by the experimenters) that the boys lost the hostility and formed friendships between the groups. When dealing with the crises, the boys were forced into a situation of *equal status contact*, in which they were all in the same situation with neither group holding power over the other. Equal status contact has been shown to reduce prejudice and discrimination, along with ongoing, positive cooperation. It appears that personal involvement with people from another group must be cooperative and occur when all groups are equal in terms of power or status to have a positive effect on reducing prejudice (Pettigrew & Tropp, 2000; Robinson & Preston, 1976).

20.2 Explain factors that influence attraction and relationships.

Prejudice pretty much explains why people don't like each other. What does psychology say about why people like someone else? There are some "rules" for those whom people like and find attractive. Liking or having the desire for a relationship with someone else is called *interpersonal attraction*, and there's a great deal of research on the subject. (Who wouldn't want to know the rules?)

Several factors are involved in the attraction of one person to another, including both superficial physical characteristics, such as physical beauty and proximity, as well as elements of personality.

Physical Attractiveness When people think about what attracts them to other people, one of the topics that usually arises is the physical attractiveness of the other person. Some research suggests that physical beauty is one of the main factors that influence people's choices for selecting people they want to know better, although other factors may become more important in the later stages of relationships (Eagly et al., 1991; Feingold, 1992; White, 1980).

Proximity—Close to You The closer together people are physically, such as working in the same office building or living in the same dorm, the more likely they are to form a relationship. *Proximity* refers to being physically near someone else. People choose friends and lovers from the pool of people available to them, and availability depends heavily on proximity.

One theory about why proximity is so important involves the idea of repeated exposure to new stimuli, sometimes called the **mere exposure effect**. The more people experience something, whether it is a song, a picture, or a person, the more they tend to like it. The phrase "it grew on me" refers to this reaction. When people are in physical proximity to each other, repeated exposure may increase their attraction to each other.

Isn't there a saying that "opposites attract"? Aren't people sometimes attracted to people who are different instead of similar? ▶

Birds of a Feather—Similarity People tend to like being around others who are similar to them in some way. The more people find they have in common with others—such as attitudes, beliefs, and interests—the more they tend to be attracted to those others (Hartfield & Rapson, 1992; Moreland & Zajonc, 1982; Neimeyer & Mitchell, 1998). When other people hold the same attitudes and beliefs and do the same kinds of actions, it makes a person's own concepts seem more correct or valid.

There is often a "grain* of truth" in many old sayings. "Opposites attract" is no exception. Some people find that forming a relationship with another person who has complementary qualities (characteristics in one person that fill a need in the other) can be very rewarding. Research does not support this view of attraction, however. It is similarity, not complementarity, that draws people together and helps them stay together (Berscheid & Reis, 1998; McPherson et al., 2001).

*grain: in this sense, an old unit of measurement equal to 1/10,000th of a pound. (That's not very much truth!)

Reciprocity of Liking Finally, people have a very strong tendency to like people who like them, a simple but powerful concept referred to as *reciprocity of liking*. In one experiment, researchers paired college students with other students (Curtis & Miller, 1986). Neither student in any of the pairs knew the other member. One member of each pair was randomly chosen to receive some information from the experimenters about how the other student in the pair felt about the first member. In some cases, target students were led to believe that the other students liked them and, in other cases, that the targets disliked them.

When the pairs of students were allowed to meet and talk with each other again, they were friendlier, disclosed more information about themselves, agreed with the other person more, and behaved in a warmer manner if they had been told that the other student liked them. The other students came to like these students better as well, so liking produced more liking.

Psychology in the News

Facing Facebook—The Social Nature of Online Networking

There are some interesting research findings concerning the online networking phenomenon. For example, people using particular sites seem to have certain things in common. The findings of one study suggest that the student's choice of social network sites is related to racial identity, ethnic identity, and the education level of the student's parents (Hargittai, 2007). White students prefer Facebook, and Hispanic students prefer MySpace; and although Asian and Asian American students use Facebook more than MySpace, they use less popular sites like Xanga and Friendster more than any other ethnic group does. The more education the parents have, the more likely the student is to use Facebook and Xanga, and the less likely to use MySpace.

In China, the popular social networking site is Ozone, but Chinese users of this site spend less time on it, have fewer contacts, and seem to consider its use as less important when compared to users of Facebook in the United States (Jackson & Wang, 2013). When you consider the self-promotion focus of such social networking sites, it doesn't seem surprising that Chinese users, coming from a collectivistic cultural background that promotes connections with others over individual independence, would be less likely to use such a resource.

There may also be gender differences in how people organize their social networking. In a recent study, researchers found that females have more "friends," do more buying and selling, and are more likely to "friend" people who make the request than are males (Szell & Thurner, 2013). The study also found that females take fewer risks online than do males. Males talk to larger groups of contacts, are less likely to "friend" other males than females. They respond very quickly to females requesting a friendship.

Finally, one study's findings suggest that users of social networking sites spend a lot more time on "social searching," which is defined as searching a site for specific information about a certain person, group, or event, than they do on "social browsing," defined as surveying the site without any specific target in mind (Wise et al., 2010). Users were also found to be more emotionally and positively engaged when searching rather than browsing. Again, this runs counter to the complaints of some who feel that such sites encourage time-wasting browsing. Instead, people are actively searching for information they desire.

1. Why might certain networking sites be more attractive to one ethnicity over another?
2. How do you find yourself using networking sites, and how does that relate to the findings of these studies?

We use the word love to describe many things. I love my family and I love my friends, but in different ways. But those aren't all the same kind of relationships.

👁 **Watch** the **Video**, *Sternberg's Triangular Theory of Love,* at **MyPsychLab**

Love Is a Triangle—Robert Sternberg's Triangular Theory of Love

Dictionary definitions of love refer to a strong affection for another person due to kinship, personal ties, physical attraction, admiration, or common interests. Psychologists generally agree that there are different kinds of love.

One psychologist, Robert Sternberg, outlined a theory of what he determined were the three main components of love and the different types of love that combinations of these three components can produce (Sternberg, 1986, 1988b, 1997a). According to Sternberg, love consists of three basic components: intimacy, passion, and commitment. *Intimacy*, in Sternberg's view, refers to the feelings of closeness that one has for another person or the sense of having close emotional ties to another. Intimacy in this sense is not physical but psychological. Friends have an intimate relationship because they disclose things to each other that most people might not know, they feel strong emotional ties to each other, and they enjoy the presence of the other person.

Passion is the physical aspect of love. Passion refers to the emotions and physical arousal a person feels toward the other person. Holding hands, loving looks, and hugs can all be forms of passion.

Commitment involves the decisions one makes about a relationship. A short-term decision might be, "I think I'm in love." An example of a more long-term decision is, "I want to be with this person for the rest of my life."

A love relationship between two people can involve one, two, or all three of these components in various combinations. The combinations can produce seven different forms of love, as can be seen in **Figure 20.1**, and in the video *Sternberg's Triangular Theory of Love.*

Two of the more familiar and more heavily researched forms of love from Sternberg's theory are romantic love and companionate love. When intimacy and passion are combined, the result is the more familiar **romantic love**, which is

FIGURE 20.1 Sternberg's Triangular Theory of Love
This diagram represents the seven different kinds of love that can result from combining the three components of love: intimacy, passion, and commitment. Notice that some of these types of love sound less desirable or positive than others. What is the one key element missing from the less positive types of love?

Source: Adapted from Sternberg (1986).

sometimes called passionate love by other researchers (Bartels & Zeki, 2000; Diamond, 2003; Hartfield, 1987). Romantic love is often the basis for a more lasting relationship. In many Western cultures, the ideal relationship begins with liking, then becomes romantic love as passion is added to the mix, and finally becomes a more enduring form of love as a commitment is made. In other cultures, marriages are arranged and romance is not the basis upon which a marriage is constructed.

When intimacy and commitment are the main components of a relationship, it is called **companionate love.** In companionate love, people who like each other, feel emotionally close to each other, and understand one another's motives have made a commitment to live together, usually in a marriage relationship. Companionate love is often the binding tie that holds a marriage together through the years of parenting, paying bills, and lessening physical passion (Gottman & Krokoff, 1989; Steinberg & Silverberg, 1987). In many non-Western cultures, companionate love is seen as more sensible. Choices for a mate on the basis of compatibility are often made by parents or matchmakers rather than the couple themselves (Duben & Behar, 1991; Hortaçsu, 1999; Jones, 1997; Thornton & Hui-Sheng, 1994).

Finally, when all three components of love are present, the couple has achieved consummate love, the ideal form of love that many people see as the ultimate goal. This is also the kind of love that may evolve into companionate love when the passion lessens during the middle years of a relationship's commitment.

20.3 Explain influences upon aggression and conflict.

People have a tendency to either behave negatively or positively toward other people. When behavior is negative, it can become violent. But sometimes the choice is to act to help others rather than hurt them, and the next section discusses the differences between those two extremes.

Aggression Unfortunately, violence toward others is another form of social interaction. When one person hurts or tries to destroy another person deliberately, either with words or with physical behavior, psychologists call it **aggression.** One common cause of aggressive behavior is frustration, which occurs when a person is prevented from reaching some desired goal. The concept of aggression as a reaction to frustration is known as the *frustration–aggression hypothesis* (Berkowitz, 1993; Miller et al., 1941). Many sources of frustration can lead to aggressive behavior. Pain, for example, produces negative sensations that are often intense and uncontrollable, leading to frustration and often aggressive acts against the nearest available target (Berkowitz, 1993). Loud noises, excessive heat, the irritation of someone else's cigarette smoke, and even awful smells can lead people to act out in an aggressive manner (Anderson, 1987; Rotton & Frey, 1985; Rotton et al., 1979; Zillmann et al., 1981).

Alcohol does have an impact on aggressive behavior. Psychologically, alcohol acts to release inhibitions, making people less likely to control their behavior even if they are not yet intoxicated. Biologically, alcohol affects the functioning of many neurotransmitters and in particular is associated with a decrease in serotonin (Virkkunen & Linnoila, 1996). In one study, volunteers were asked to administer electric shocks to an unseen "opponent" in a study reminiscent of Milgram's shock experiment. The actual responses to the shock were simulated by a computer, although the volunteers believed that the responses were coming from a real person. The volunteers were told it was a test of reaction time and learning (Bushman, 1997). Volunteers participated both before consuming

romantic love type of love consisting of intimacy and passion.

companionate love type of love consisting of intimacy and commitment.

aggression behavior intended to hurt or destroy another person.

Don't some people get pretty violent after ◄ drinking too much? Does alcohol do something to those brain chemicals?

social role the pattern of behavior that is expected of a person who is in a particular social position.

deindividuation the lessening of a person's sense of personal identity and responsibility.

alcohol and after consuming alcohol. Participants were much more aggressive in administering stronger shocks after drinking.

The Power of Social Roles Although frustration, genetics, body chemicals, and even the effects of drugs can be blamed for aggressive behavior to some degree, much of human aggression is also influenced by learning. The social learning theory explanation for aggression states that aggressive behavior is learned (in a process called observational learning) by watching aggressive models get reinforced for their aggressive behavior (Bandura, 1980; Bandura et al., 1961). Aggressive models can be parents, siblings, friends, or people on television.

There is some evidence to suggest that even taking on a particular social role, such as that of a soldier, can lead to an increase in aggressive behavior. A **social role** is the pattern of behavior that is expected of a person who is in a particular social position. For example, "doctor" is a social role that implies wearing a white coat, asking certain types of questions, and writing prescriptions, among other things.

A deeply disturbing experiment was conducted by famed social psychologist Philip Zimbardo at Stanford University in 1971. About 70 young men, most of whom were college students, volunteered to participate for two weeks. They were told that they would be randomly assigned the social role of either a guard or a prisoner in the experiment. The "guards" were given uniforms and instructions not to use violence but to maintain control of the "prison." The "prisoners" were booked at a real jail, blindfolded, and transported to the campus "prison," actually the basement of one of the campus buildings. On day 2, the prisoners staged a revolt (not planned as part of the experiment), which was quickly crushed by the guards. The guards then became increasingly more aggressive, using humiliation to control and punish the prisoners. For example, prisoners were forced to clean out toilet bowls with their bare hands. The staff observing the experiment had to release five of the prisoners who became so upset that they were physically ill. The entire experiment was canceled on the fifth day, after one of the prisoners reported to Zimbardo that what the experimenters were doing to the young men was terrible (Zimbardo, 1971).

The conclusions of Zimbardo and his colleagues highlighted the influence that a social role, such as that of "guard," can have on perfectly ordinary people. Also, when people are gathered in a group there is often a tendency for each individual in the group to experience **deindividuation**, the lessening of their sense of personal identity and personal responsibility (Diener et al., 1980). One only has to think about behavior of people in a riot or even the actions of groups like the Ku Klux Klan to see examples of deindividuation. The Stanford prison experiment is an excellent study of deindividuation in action (Zimbardo, 1970, 1971; Zimbardo et al., 2000).

During the war in Iraq in 2003, an army reserve general was suspended from duty while an investigation into reported prisoner abuses was conducted. Between October and December 2003, investigators found numerous cases of cruel, humiliating, and other startling abuses of the Iraqi prisoners by the army military police stationed at the prison of Abu Ghraib (Hersh, 2004).

The "guards" in the Stanford prison study were normal people, but the effect of putting on the uniform and taking on the social role of guard changed

▲ This photograph shows a "guard" searching a "prisoner" in Zimbardo's famous Stanford prison experiment. The students in the experiment became so deeply involved in their assigned roles that Zimbardo had to cancel the experiment after only five days—less than half the time originally scheduled for the study.

their behavior radically. Is it possible that a similar factor was at work at Abu Ghraib? The behavior of the guards at Abu Ghraib was not part of a formal, controlled study, so further research will be needed to determine to what degree the social roles at work in situations like this influence the kind of behavior seen in this real-life example.

Violence in the Media and Aggression Bandura's early study in which small children viewed a video of an aggressive model was one of the first attempts to investigate the effect of violence in the media on children's aggressive behavior (Bandura et al., 1963). Since then, many researchers have examined the impact of television and other media violence on the aggressive behavior of children of various ages. The earliest conclusions were similar: Children who are exposed to high levels of violent media are more aggressive than children who are not (Baron & Reiss, 1985; Bushman & Huesmann, 2001; Centerwall, 1989; Geen & Thomas, 1986; Huesmann & Miller, 1994; Huesmann et al., 1997, 2003; Villani, 2001). Other research has suggested strongly that these earlier studies have been seriously flawed in several ways, and often subject to a bias held by the general population: Violent video games are bad for you.

Recent research now strongly suggests that linking video games to school shooters is a mistake. There are many other factors left out or otherwise skipped over when conducting this type of research. One meta-analysis (a careful statistical analysis of a large number of studies on a particular topic, able to more accurately measure the sizes of research effects than any one smaller study can measure) of 26 studies examining the relationship between exposure to media violence and violent aggressive behavior concluded that size effects were too small to provide evidence for a correlational relationship between the two variables (Savage & Yancey, 2008). The authors of the study stress that variables such as socioeconomic status, parent's education level, parental violence, conditions of neglect, and intelligence levels of the participants would need to be methodically controlled in any study of aggression and media effects. It is important to realize that the bulk of research examining the effects of media violence on aggressive behavior is correlational, not experimental. Remember, correlation does *not* prove causation—no study has yet shown that playing violent video games causes increased aggression!

I've heard that violent television programs can cause children to become more aggressive. How true is that?

20.4 Discuss determinants of prosocial behavior.

Another and far more pleasant form of human social interaction is *prosocial behavior*, or socially desirable behavior that benefits others rather than brings them harm.

One form of prosocial behavior that almost always makes people feel good about other people is **altruism**, or helping someone in trouble with no expectation of reward and often without fear for one's own safety. Although no one is surprised by the behavior of a mother who enters a burning house to save her child, some people are often surprised when total strangers step in to help, risking their own lives for people they do not know.

But why do people risk their own lives to help total strangers? One answer may lie in the structure of the brain. Using brain imaging techniques, researchers have found evidence that a brain region known as the temporoparietal junction (TPJ) is larger in individuals who make altruistic choices, particularly in the right hemisphere (Marishima et al., 2012). This area was also more active during decision making that involved a greater cost of helping to the individual.

More important, why do people sometimes refuse to help when their own lives are not at risk?

altruism prosocial behavior that is done with no expectation of reward and may involve the risk of harm to oneself.

Why People Won't Help On March 13, 1964, at about 3:15 in the morning, Winston Mosely saw Catherine "Kitty" Genovese in the parking lot of her

bystander effect referring to the effect that the presence of other people has on the decision to help or not help, with help becoming less likely as the number of bystanders increases.

diffusion of responsibility occurs when a person fails to take responsibility for actions or for inaction because of the presence of other people who are seen to share the responsibility.

apartment complex, stabbed her, left, and then came back nearly half an hour later to rape and stab her to death in the entryway of the complex. Upon learning of the crime, a reporter for the *New York Times* wrote a story in which he claimed that at least 38 people heard or watched some part of the fatal attack from their apartment windows, and that not one of these people called the police until after the attack was over (Delfiner, 2001; Gado, 2004; Rosenthal, 1964). This story outraged the public and has since become a symbol of bystander apathy.

In recent years, the truth of that fateful event has come to light, and the details may be more complex than originally reported. According to trial records, the two attacks occurred much closer in time than originally believed. At the first attack, a man shouted out his window "Leave that girl alone!" and Moseley fled. Another man supposedly called the police after that first attack, although there is no record of the call. The second attack took place in the entryway to the apartment complex—a far more sheltered area in which there could have been only a few witnesses. At this point, another witness, Sophia Farrar, told a friend to call the police while she went to Kitty Genovese's aid and held her until an ambulance arrived (Cook, 2014; Manning et al., 2007). Even though some did call for help and at least one came to Kitty's aid, there were several witnesses who still stood by and did nothing. One man, whose apartment door opened onto the entryway where the second attack occurred, cracked open his apartment door, saw the attack—and closed the door (Cook, 2014).

People were outraged by the apparent indifference and lack of sympathy for the poor woman's plight. Why did those people simply stand by and watch or listen? Social psychologists would explain that the lack of response to Kitty Genovese's screams for help was not due to indifference or a lack of sympathy but instead to the presence of other people.

The **bystander effect** refers to the finding that the likelihood of a bystander (someone observing an event and close enough to offer help) to help someone in trouble decreases as the number of bystanders increases. If only one person is standing by, that person is far more likely to help than if there is another person, and the addition of each new bystander decreases the possibility of helping behavior even more (Darley & Latané, 1968; Eagly & Crowley, 1986; Latané & Darley, 1969).

Diffusion of responsibility is the phenomenon in which a person fails to take responsibility for either action or inaction because of the presence of other people who are seen to share the responsibility (Leary & Forsyth, 1987). Diffusion of responsibility is a form of attribution in which people explain why they acted (or failed to act) as they did because of others. "I was just following orders," "Other people were doing it," and "There were a lot of people there, and I thought one of them would do something" are all examples of statements made in such situations. Kitty Genovese received no help because there were too many potential "helpers," and not one of the people listening to her cries for help took the responsibility to intervene—they thought surely someone else was doing something about it.

> But why does the ▶
> number of bystanders
> matter?

Five Decision Points in Helping Behavior In all of the experiments reported in the preceding section, there were people who did try to help in every condition. What kind of decision-making process might they have gone through before deciding to help? What are the requirements for deciding when help is needed? Darley and Latané (1968) identified several decision points that a bystander must face before helping someone in trouble: noticing the situation, defining it as an emergency, taking responsibility for acting, planning a course of action, and finally taking that action. These decision points, which are discussed in the video *The Bystander Effect*, are still considered valid over 40 years later.

👁 **Watch** the **Video**, *The Bystander Effect*, at **MyPsychLab**

Pick the best answer.

1. **Mental patterns that represent what a person believes about certain types of people are called**
   a. schemas.
   b. attitudes.
   c. attributions.
   d. stereotypes.

2. **Which of the following is best classified as an altruistic act?**
   a. saving a loved one from danger
   b. making a living teaching children
   c. protecting a stranger from an attack
   d. using aggression only in self-defense

3. **In the classic Stanford prison experiment, participants succumbed to the power of**
   a. altruism.
   b. social roles.
   c. compliance.
   d. self-fulfilling prophecy.

4. **Once a situation has been defined as an emergency, the next step in the decision-making process is**
   a. noticing.
   b. taking action.
   c. requesting assistance.
   d. taking responsibility.

5. **Research based on the bystander effect suggests that a victim is MOST likely to get help from a bystander if**
   a. no one else is around.
   b. the person is overweight.
   c. the person seems unconscious.
   d. several other people are passing by.

6. **The more you see someone, the more likely you are to like that person. Such a phenomenon is often due to**
   a. reciprocity of liking.
   b. similarity.
   c. mere exposure.
   d. proximity.

7. **Which of the following is not a major cause of interpersonal attraction?**
   a. similarity
   b. reciprocity of liking
   c. physical attractiveness
   d. complementary qualities

8. **A person who has very low self-worth is less likely to be affected by the**
   a. primacy effect.
   b. proximity effect.
   c. reciprocity of liking effect.
   d. opposites attract effect.

9. **According to Sternberg, which of the following describes the feelings of emotional closeness between two people?**
   a. passion
   b. intimacy
   c. infatuation
   d. commitment

10. **When people are unable to reach a goal, frustration may result, which can ultimately turn into**
    a. aggression.
    b. pain.
    c. confusion.
    d. depression.

(((Listen to an Audio File of your chapter at MyPsychLab

Module 18: Social Influence
Explore how social influence affects behavior.

18.1 Understand the power of the situation.
- Social psychology is the scientific study of how a person's thoughts, feelings, and behavior are influenced by the real, imagined, or implied presence of other people.

18.2 Explain how the presence of others affects conformity in an individual's behavior.
- In Asch's experiment, subjects conformed to group opinion about one-third of the time, and conformity decreased if just one confederate gave the correct answer.
- Cross-cultural research has found that collectivistic cultures show more conformity than individualistic cultures.
- Gender differences do not exist in conformity unless the response is not private, in which case women are more conforming than men.

18.3 Trace how group dynamics influence an individual's behavior.
- Groupthink occurs when a decision-making group feels that it is more important to maintain group unanimity and cohesiveness than to consider the facts realistically.
- Group polarization occurs when members take somewhat more extreme positions and take greater risks as compared to those made by individuals.
- When the performance of an individual on a relatively easy task is improved by the presence of others, it is called social facilitation. When the performance of an individual on a relatively difficult task is negatively affected by the presence of others, it is called social impairment.
- When a person who is lazy is able to work in a group of people, that person often performs less well than if the person were working alone, in a phenomenon called social loafing.

18.4 Describe how an individual influences group behavior.
- To minimize the possibility of groupthink, leaders should remain impartial, and the entire group should seek the opinions of people outside the group.

18.5 Explain how the presence of others affects compliance in an individual's behavior.
- Compliance occurs when a person changes behavior as a result of another person asking or directing that person to change.
- Cults use love-bombing, isolation, rituals, and activities to keep new recruits from questioning and critical thinking. Cults also use the foot-in-the-door technique.
- Common ways of getting compliance from others are the foot-in-the-door technique, the door-in-the-face technique, and the lowball technique.

18.6 Explain how the presence of others affects obedience in an individual's behavior.
- Milgram found that 65 percent of people obeyed the authority figure of an experimenter in his classic shock study.

Module 19: Social Cognition
Understand the effects of social cognition.

19.1 Explain the relationship between attitudes and behavior.
- Attitudes are tendencies to respond positively or negatively to ideas, persons, objects, or situations.
- The three components of an attitude are the affective (emotional) component, the behavioral component, and the cognitive component.
- Attitudes are often poor predictors of behavior unless the attitude is very specific or very strong.
- Attitudes can be formed through direct instruction, interaction with others, and observation of others.

19.2 Discuss persuasive methods used to change attitudes.
- Persuasion is the process by which one person tries to change the attitudes of others through argument, pleading, or explanation.
- The key elements in persuasion are the source of the message, the message itself, and the target audience.
- In the elaboration likelihood model, central-route processing involves attending to the content of the message itself, whereas peripheral-route processing involves attending to factors not involved in the message.
- Cognitive dissonance is discomfort or distress that occurs when a person's actions do not match the person's attitudes.

19.3 Explain attributional explanations of behavior.
- Attribution is the process of explaining the behavior of others as well as one's own behavior.
- A situational cause is an explanation of behavior based on factors in the surrounding environment or situation.
- A dispositional cause is an explanation of behavior based on the internal personality characteristics of the person being observed.
- The fundamental attribution error is the tendency to overestimate the influence of internal factors on behavior while underestimating the influence of the situation.

Module 20: Social Interaction
Describe different kinds of social relations.

20.1 Describe the nature and effects of stereotyping, prejudice, and discrimination.
- A stereotype is a superficial categorization of an individual. Prejudice is a negative attitude that a person holds about the members of a particular social group. Discrimination occurs when members of a social group are treated differently because of prejudice toward that group.
- In-groups are the people with whom a person identifies, whereas out-groups are everyone else at whom prejudice tends to be directed.
- Scapegoating refers to the tendency to direct prejudice and discrimination at out-group members who have little social power or influence. New immigrants are often the scapegoats for the frustration and anger of the in-group.

- Conflict between groups increases prejudice and discrimination according to realistic conflict theory.
- In the blue-eyed brown-eyed experiment, children quickly began to discriminate against whichever group was the out-group during a certain time period.
- Social cognitive theory views prejudice as an attitude acquired through direct instruction, modeling, and other social influences.
- Social identity theory sees a person's formation of a social sense of self within a particular group as being due to three things: social categorization, social identity, and social comparison.
- Stereotype vulnerability refers to the effect that a person's knowledge of the stereotypes that exist against his or her social group can have on that person's behavior.
- People who are aware of stereotypes may unintentionally come to behave in a way that makes the stereotype real in a self-fulfilling prophecy.
- Intergroup contact is more effective in reducing prejudice if the groups have equal status.
- Prejudice and discrimination can also be reduced when a superordinate goal that is large enough to override all other goals needs to be achieved by all groups.
- Prejudice and discrimination are reduced when people must work together to solve a problem because each person has an important key to solving the problem, creating a mutual interdependence. This technique used in education is called the "jigsaw classroom."

20.2 Explain factors that influence attraction and relationships.
- Interpersonal attraction refers to liking or having the desire for a relationship with another person.
- People tend to form relationships with people who are in physical proximity to them, similar to them, or who complement them in areas they themselves may be lacking.
- Because of the mere exposure effect the more people experience something the more they tend to like it.

- Love is a strong affection for another person due to kinship, personal ties, physical attraction, admiration, or common interests.
- Sternberg states that the three components of love are intimacy, passion, and commitment.
- Romantic love is intimacy with passion, companionate love is intimacy with commitment, and consummate love contains all three components.

20.3 Explain influences upon aggression and conflict.
- Aggression is behavior intended to hurt or destroy another person and may be physical or verbal. Frustration is a major source of aggression.
- Social roles are powerful influences on the expression of aggression. Social learning theory states that aggression can be learned through direct reinforcement and through the imitation of successful aggression by a model.
- Deindividuation occurs when group members feel anonymous and personally less responsible for their actions.
- Studies of the connection between violent media exposure and increased levels of aggression find little evidence of a connection between the two variables.

20.4 Discuss determinants of prosocial behavior.
- Prosocial behavior is behavior that is socially desirable and benefits others.
- Altruism is prosocial behavior in which a person helps someone else without expectation of reward or recognition, often without fear for his or her own safety.
- The bystander effect means that people are more likely to get help from others if there are one or only a few people nearby rather than a larger number because of diffusion of responsibility.
- The five steps in making a decision to help are noticing, defining an emergency, taking responsibility, planning a course of action, and taking action.

Vocabulary Terms

conformity p. 230
social psychology p. 230
group polarization p. 232
groupthink p. 232
social facilitation p. 233
social impairment p. 233
social loafing p. 233
lowball technique p. 234
compliance p. 234
foot-in-the-door technique p. 234
obedience p. 235

attitude p. 238
central-route processing
  p. 240
elaboration likelihood model
  p. 240
peripheral-route processing
  p. 240
attribution p. 241
cognitive dissonance p. 241
fundamental attribution error
  p. 242

out-groups p. 245
in-groups p. 245
prejudice p. 245
discrimination p. 245
stereotype p. 245
social categorization p. 246
social identity theory p. 246
social comparison p. 247
stereotype vulnerability p. 247
mere exposure effect p. 248
aggression p. 251

romantic love p. 251
companionate love p. 251
social role p. 252
deindividuation p. 252
altruism p. 253
bystander effect p. 254
diffusion of responsibility
  p. 254

Vocabulary Review

Match each vocabulary term to its definition.

1. dispositional cause
2. attitude
3. stereotype vulnerability
4. bystander effect
5. cognitive dissonance
6. companionate love
7. conformity
8. central-route processing
9. obedience
10. prejudice

a. The sense of discomfort or distress that occurs when a person's behavior does not correspond to that person's attitudes.
b. Changing one's own behavior to be similar to that of other people.
c. Changing one's behavior at the command of an authority figure.
d. Involves attending to the content of the message instead of noncontent behaviors.
e. A cause of behavior attributed to internal factors such as personality or character.
f. The impact that the presence of other people has on the decision to help or not help, with help becoming less likely as the number of bystanders increases.
g. The effect that people's awareness of the stereotypes associated with their social group has on their behavior.
h. Negative attitude held by a person about the members of a particular social group.
i. Consists of intimacy and commitment.
j. A tendency to respond positively or negatively toward a certain person, object, idea, or situation.

Psychology Project

How do people use compliance techniques in everyday life? Try to identify the use of compliance techniques in real-life advertisements.

Materials:
- magazines or newspapers with advertisements
- a television (optional)

Instructions:

1. Review the compliance techniques discussed in this chapter: the door-in-the-face technique, the foot-in-the-door technique, and the lowball technique.

2. Find several advertisements in magazines or newspapers, or watch several commercials on television. Identify one advertisement or commercial that uses one of the compliance techniques you've studied.

3. Give a short presentation to your class in which you describe the advertisement, identify the compliance technique it used, and explain how the technique was used. Finally, explain whether or not you think the advertisement's use of the technique was effective.

Tech Alternative

Go to your favorite Internet video site and take a look at what you see through the eyes of a social psychologist. Videos are uploaded to Internet sites for various reasons including entertainment, education, marketing a product, and making money by getting people to watch videos so advertisers will want to post ads on a person's "video channel." Internet videos that "go viral" are rare, but many video channels have become popular with the general Internet audience.

When browsing videos think about what is being done to attract viewers. Are the video creators using methods that were discussed in this chapter to enhance the possibility that a viewer will click on their video? Explain your thoughts in a paragraph and use three specific examples to support your idea.

Think about the ads that are placed on the Web site when you select a video. Is there a reason that certain ads appear with certain videos? Explain your thoughts in a paragraph and use three specific examples to support your idea.

After conducting your analysis of a number of Internet videos, write a paragraph explaining how you would use three concepts you learned in this chapter to attract viewers to your "video channel."

Essay Question

In a well-organized essay, describe how each of the following elements could cause or perpetuate prejudiced attitudes and behaviors. Give examples to support your claims:

a. Groupthink
b. Cognitive dissonance
c. Fundamental attribution error
d. Stereotype vulnerability

Test Yourself

Ready for your test? More quizzes and a customized plan

✓ Study and Review at MyPsychLab

Pick the best answer.

1. Saul admits that he conforms so as to be liked by others. This is known as
   a. compliance.
   b. obedience.
   c. informational social influence.
   d. normative social influence.

2. According to the text, in which of the following has groupthink been known to occur?
   a. presidential elections
   b. the fall of communism
   c. mass suicides by cults
   d. the sinking of the *Titanic*

3. Maria was asked by her neighbor to adopt two or three kittens that were abandoned by their mother. Although Maria refused to take in three kittens, she did agree to adopt just one. What compliance technique did her neighbor use on Maria?
   a. foot-in-the-door
   b. door-in-the-face
   c. lowball
   d. double foot-in-the-door

4. Follow-up studies to Stanley Milgram's research have suggested that a "teacher's" willingness to deliver potentially lethal shocks may be more a product of _____ than of obedience.
   a. conformity
   b. compliance
   c. social identity
   d. groupthink

5. The public service messages that encourage parents to sit down with their children and talk frankly about drugs are promoting which method of attitude formation?
   a. direct contact
   b. direct instruction
   c. vicarious conditioning
   d. observational learning

6. Researchers have found that a _____ degree of fear in a message makes it more effective, particularly when it is combined with _____.
   a. maximum; information about how to prevent the fearful consequences
   b. minimum; threats
   c. moderate; threats
   d. moderate; information to prevent the consequences

7. Sandy was a juror in the trial for a man accused of stealing guns. The defendant was not very well spoken and came from a very poor background, but Sandy listened carefully and made her decision based on the evidence. Sandy was using _____ processing.
   a. central-route
   b. peripheral-route
   c. cognitive-route
   d. visual-route

8. If LaShonda was experiencing cognitive dissonance between her attitude and behavior, which of the following would help her reduce that sensation?
   a. thinking constantly about the mismatch
   b. maintaining her existing attitude
   c. discussing the inconsistency with others
   d. changing her behavior

9. The behavioral component of prejudice is
   a. attitude.
   b. aggression.
   c. stereotyping.
   d. discrimination.

10. If behavior is assumed to be caused by external characteristics, this is known as
    a. a situational cause.
    b. a dispositional cause.
    c. a fundamental attribution error.
    d. actor–observer bias.

11. Thomas likes to "hang with the guys." These people with whom Thomas identifies most strongly with are called a(n)
    a. referent group.
    b. in-group.
    c. out-group.
    d. "them" group.

12. The "Robber's Cave" experiment showed the value of _____ in combating prejudice.
    a. "jigsaw classrooms"
    b. equal status contact
    c. subordinate goals
    d. stereotyping vulnerability

13. Carla loves to play pool and has become quite good at the game. Lately, she has noticed that she seems to play better when there are people watching her than when she is playing alone. This difference in Carla's playing is most likely the result of _____.
    a. social loafing
    b. social identity
    c. social facilitation
    d. social comparison

14. Alexei misses a soccer practice. Which of the following explanations for Alexei's absence is dispositional?
    a. He is irresponsible.
    b. He is stuck in traffic.
    c. He has injured himself.
    d. He has a prior commitment.

15. Vivian met Steve at work and become friends. Over time, they found themselves falling in love—or as Vivian tells her friends, "Steve just grew on me!" According to research in interpersonal attraction, the most likely explanation for their attraction is
    a. mere exposure.
    b. personal attractiveness.
    c. fate.
    d. reciprocity of liking.

16. A couple whose love is based off of intimacy and passion but who are not yet committed to a long-term relationship are in the form of love called _____ love.
    a. companionate
    b. romantic
    c. affectionate
    d. consummate

17. The concept that aggression results from a social role is based on what psychological theory?
    a. humanistic
    b. learning
    c. psychoanalytical
    d. cognitive

18. To which two processes do most social psychologists attribute the failure of those around Kitty Genovese to help her?
    a. bystander effect and altruism
    b. aggression and diffusion of responsibility
    c. altruism and diffusion of responsibility
    d. bystander effect and diffusion of responsibility

19. Gladys knows that she can help people simply by dialing 9-1-1 on her cell phone if an emergency arises. Which step in the decision process for helping would Gladys be at?
    a. noticing
    b. taking action
    c. taking responsibility
    d. planning a course of action

20. Helping someone in trouble with no expectation of reward describes the prosocial behavior _____.
    a. altruism
    b. positive reinforcement
    c. diffusion of responsibility
    d. bystander effect

Learning Objectives

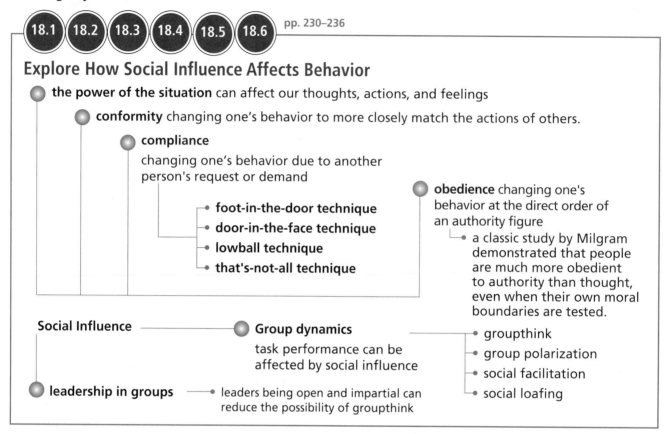

(18.1)(18.2)(18.3)(18.4)(18.5)(18.6) pp. 230–236

Explore How Social Influence Affects Behavior

- **the power of the situation** can affect our thoughts, actions, and feelings
  - **conformity** changing one's behavior to more closely match the actions of others.
    - **compliance**
      changing one's behavior due to another person's request or demand
      - **foot-in-the-door technique**
      - **door-in-the-face technique**
      - **lowball technique**
      - **that's-not-all technique**
    - **obedience** changing one's behavior at the direct order of an authority figure
      - a classic study by Milgram demonstrated that people are much more obedient to authority than thought, even when their own moral boundaries are tested.

Social Influence ———— **Group dynamics**
task performance can be affected by social influence

- groupthink
- group polarization
- social facilitation
- social loafing

leadership in groups ——— leaders being open and impartial can reduce the possibility of groupthink

Learning Objectives

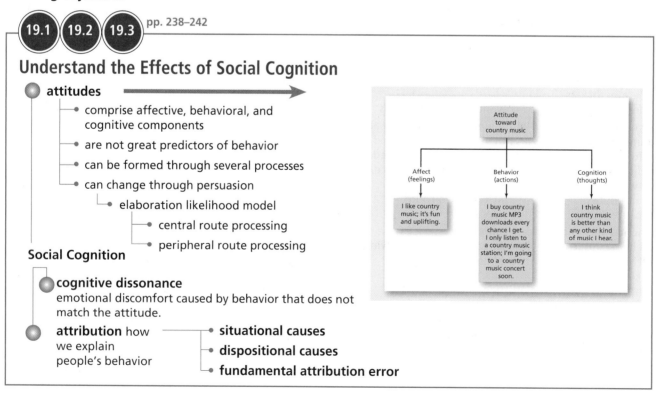

(19.1)(19.2)(19.3) pp. 238–242

Understand the Effects of Social Cognition

- **attitudes** →
  - comprise affective, behavioral, and cognitive components
  - are not great predictors of behavior
  - can be formed through several processes
  - can change through persuasion
    - elaboration likelihood model
      - central route processing
      - peripheral route processing

Social Cognition

- **cognitive dissonance**
  emotional discomfort caused by behavior that does not match the attitude.
- **attribution** how we explain people's behavior
  - **situational causes**
  - **dispositional causes**
  - **fundamental attribution error**

Attitude toward country music

Affect (feelings)	Behavior (actions)	Cognition (thoughts)
I like country music; it's fun and uplifting.	I buy country music MP3 downloads every chance I get. I only listen to a country music station; I'm going to a country music concert soon.	I think country music is better than any other kind of music I hear.

20.1 20.2 20.3 20.4   pp. 244–254

Map the Concepts at MyPsychLab

Describe Different Kinds of Social Relations

interpersonal attraction
liking or having the desire for a relationship with someone else. Influenced by

- **physical attractiveness**
- **proximity**
- **similarity**
- **complementary qualities**
- **reciprocity of liking**

Sternberg's triangular theory of love

Liking
Intimacy
Consumate Love
Intimacy + Passion + Commitment
Romantic Love
Passion
Commitment
Companionate
Infatuation
Fatuous Love
Empty Love

love is strong affection for another person due to kinship, personal ties, sexual attraction, admiration, or common interests.

→ **Sternberg's triangular theory** suggests different components of love

Social Interaction —

stereotyping, prejudice and discrimination

- rely on negative **stereotypes**
- cause members of a social group to be treated differently
- vary based on in-groups and out-groups

prosocial or socially desirable behavior benefits others

- **altruism**
- can be influenced by helper's mood and victim's gender, attractiveness, or "just rewards"; racial and ethnic differences can decrease probability of helping
- can be negatively affected by presence of others

aggression occurs when one person verbally or physically hurts or tries to destroy another person; often the result of frustration

- may be partly attributed to genetics
- can be triggered by variations in brain function and by internal or external chemical influences
- is influenced by learning

8 Sociocultural Diversity and Gender

Social networking sites have grown in popularity since their inception and are bringing people from around the world together in new and unprecedented* ways. Sports fans join social network groups to discuss their favorite team's last competition. Online video game players discuss in chat rooms better strategies and game updates. Adventure seekers coordinate events and timing schedules for flash mob dances and dazzle spectators with their performances. The impact of social networking technology is large and growing as new and innovative ways to benefit from the globalized culture that is emerging are developed and implemented. Psychologists are forced to rethink their beliefs on the nature of human behavior as cross-cultural research expands and brings to light previously unknown differences in how humans think and behave because of their cultural environment.

In what ways has cultural diversity changed your thinking about others from around the world? In what ways have the roles and behaviors of men and women within your culture changed as a result of globalization?

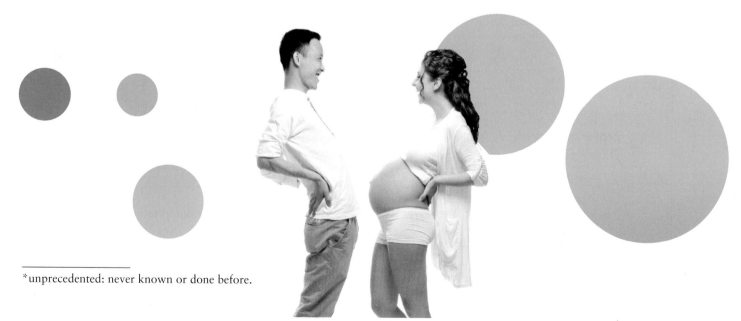

*unprecedented: never known or done before.

MODULE 21 ▸ SOCIOCULTURAL DIVERSITY
MODULE 22 ▸ GENDER

Watch the Video, at MyPsychLab

*W*hy Study Sociocultural Diversity and Gender?

We are all affected by the social influences that shape our lives and determine our identities. Sociocultural diversity and gender are two of these influences that particularly affect how we perceive ourselves and how we perceive the world around us. By studying psychology from cross-cultural and gender-based perspectives, we can gain a broader, more diverse, and more thorough understanding of human thought and behavior.

Module Goal

Understand culture's role in psychology.

Learning Objectives

21.1 Describe culture and diversity.

21.2 Explain how culture varies across time and place.

21.3 Outline how culture influences our conceptions of self and identity.

21.4 Describe the major areas of cross-cultural psychology research.

21.5 Explain psychological research that examines socioeconomic status.

21.6 Explain how privilege and social power structures relate to stereotypes, prejudice, and discrimination.

Understand Culture's Role in Psychology

21.1 Describe culture and diversity.

Psychology is devoted to the examination of human thought and behavior—but does everyone around the world think and act in the same way? As a matter of fact, they don't. No matter how independent we may think we are, our thoughts and behaviors are partially influenced by the beliefs and values of our culture. Every day, these cultural forces affect the decisions we make, the values we hold, and even the way in which we see ourselves.

In the field of psychology, the term **culture** refers to a shared set of beliefs, behaviors, values, and attitudes held by a group of people or a society. The culture in which we live can have an enormous effect on our thoughts and actions. A culture's understood rules, or **norms**, tell us what behavior is acceptable or unacceptable. Cultural norms can influence a wide variety of beliefs and behaviors, from what we eat to how we worship. In many cases, cultural norms help us decide what behaviors are "normal" or "abnormal." For example, despite what your mother may have told you when you were younger, there is no biological basis for saying "please" and "thank you" at the dinner table. However, in many cultures, using polite language is an important example of "normal" behavior.

Common Characteristics of Culture Although no two cultures are exactly alike, all cultures do share a few common characteristics. Here are a few of the most important qualities that all cultures share:

Culture is learned. It is not a biological or genetic phenomenon; children learn cultural norms and values from their parents or guardians, or from the society in which they grow up.

Culture is shared. Culture is a social phenomenon that connects humans and helps them work together. According to psychologist David Matsumoto, a prominent researcher in the field of cross-cultural psychology, the rules established by a culture actually help to ensure that culture's survival (1999). For example the tendency of humans to form "social groups" has been passed down, as opposed to humans being "loners," to best meet their survival needs.

culture a shared set of beliefs, behaviors, values, and attitudes held by a group of people or a society.

norms a culture's understood rules for expected behavior, values, beliefs, and attitudes.

Culture changes over time. For example, in the not-so-distant past, American fathers rarely stayed home to take care of their children. Instead, they were expected to provide financial support. Over the past several years, however, more and more American men have taken on childcare duties, and the idea of being a stay-at-home dad is far less unusual than it once was (Shaver, 2007). Cultural norms create an environment that shapes our behavior, but norms—like other environmental influences in our lives—can change drastically over time.

Have you ever shaken someone's hand or given a high five? What do those gestures mean to you? In many cultures within the United States, a handshake is a common form of greeting and a high five means "Good job!" If you tried to give a person from another culture a handshake or a high five, however, he or she might not understand what you were doing, because those gestures do not have the same meanings in different cultures. In Japan, for example, people traditionally greet each other by bowing rather than by shaking hands.

The language you speak, the spiritual beliefs you hold, and the moral values to which you adhere are also important parts of your culture that most likely impact you every day. When you chat with your friends, attend a religious service, or volunteer for a cause you believe in, you are acting under the influence of culture.

21.2 Explain how culture varies across time and place.

Although all cultures have certain general characteristics in common, there is a huge amount of variation from one culture to the next. Approaches to studying cultures can focus on their similarities, examined objectively from outside the cultures "looking in" for comparisons (**etic**) or their uniqueness, gained by observing a culture subjectively from within "up close and personal" (**emic**). By combining the results of such studies a new and more broad understanding of human behavior can be gained. Around the world, cultures are shaped by geographic factors like climate and the availability of natural resources, as well as by human factors like population density, increased exposure to other cultures, and technological development (Matsumoto, 1993).

All of these factors, for example, affect life in the Lahaul Valley, a region nestled in the Himalayas in northern India. Currently, the valley can only be reached by traveling through one of the highest mountain passes in the world, the Rohtang Pass. This road is covered with snow for 6 months of the year, and many people have lost their lives trying to travel along the Rohtang Pass during the winter. As a result, the people of the Lahaul Valley generally cannot leave their homes for months at a time. During the cold winter months, there is no light, no mail delivery, and no fresh vegetables (Polgreen, 2010). Life in the Lahaul Valley is obviously very different from life in a major metropolitan area like Beijing or Los Angeles where the climate is milder, natural resources are more accessible, the population is larger and denser, and advanced technologies are easier to come by. In June 2010, however, work began on a tunnel that will bypass the Rohtang Pass and connect the Lahaul Valley to the rest of India year-round. This technological development will almost certainly lead to cultural changes as the people who live in the valley gain greater access to resources and become more able to interact with people outside their geographic area.

If you have traveled to another country—or even to another part of your own country—you have probably already seen the effects of cultural diversity in the real world. Even within the United States, there is a wealth of cultural variety: Ford and Toyota drivers in Lancaster County, Pennsylvania share the road with horses and buggies driven by their Amish neighbors. Some road signs in Texas give instructions in both Spanish and English, while some road signs in northern Maine feature both French and English phrases. If we tried to list all the

> I think I get the big picture, but how are the things I do every day affected by my culture?

▲ *People come from a variety of ethnic and cultural backgrounds, which influence how they think and behave. How might learning more about a person's cultural background help you understand his or her thoughts and behaviors?*

etic studying the similarities between cultures objectively from the outside.

emic studying the differences between cultures subjectively from the inside.

differences and similarities among all the world's cultures, our list would take up the rest of this book (and it still wouldn't be complete!). Instead, we will take a look at differences and similarities between the cultures in two countries—the collectivist culture of China and the individualist culture of the United States.

Cultural Differences and Similarities: China and the United States

Many Chinese cultural traditions might seem unusual or surprising to an American audience, but keep in mind that many American cultural traditions would seem equally strange to a Chinese audience. Differences between cultures do not imply that one culture is better or worse than another. When we study how cultures vary, we gain a greater understanding of other lifestyles and other points of view, and we begin to appreciate the diversity that makes our world so interesting. We are also likely to find ways in which other cultures are not so different from our own.

In both China and the United States, celebrations and rituals that mark family events such as births, marriages, and deaths are important, but these events are celebrated differently in each culture. In the United States, for example, a baby shower is usually held a few weeks before the baby's birth, but in China, the baby shower is held after the baby arrives. In Western culture, it is traditional to wear black clothing to a funeral, but at traditional Chinese funerals, the dress code is slightly different: The immediate family of the deceased person wears black, but the grandchildren of the deceased wear blue, and the great-grandchildren wear light blue.

Brides in the United States often wear white gowns, but in China, the color white is associated with mourning and is generally avoided at traditional weddings. Red, on the other hand, symbolizes happiness in Chinese culture, and many Chinese brides wear red dresses. In China, it is traditional to give a newly married couple a check or cash in a red envelope as a wedding gift, whereas in the United States, couples often create "wedding registries" on which they list the silverware, kitchen appliances, and other gifts they hope to receive from their guests. At many weddings in the United States, the bride and groom hug and shake hands with their guests after the ceremony, whereas at the end of a Chinese wedding reception, the bride and groom are joined by their parents and other relatives. The entire family thanks the guests for attending, a tradition that highlights the importance of the family in Chinese culture.

▲ Sometimes, a couple will choose to incorporate traditions from both cultures into their wedding. This couple has decided to have western attire for the bride and groom, while the room's decorations are traditional.

Despite the differences between traditional Chinese and traditional American weddings, it should be clear by now that in both cultures, weddings are important celebrations of family and friendship, involving quite a lot of planning, budgeting, feasting, and gift-giving. In addition, many modern wedding ceremonies in both China and America are marked by cross-cultural influences. For example, although many Chinese brides still wear red gowns, white wedding gowns have become more popular in China in recent years, likely due to Western influences. And a popular American wedding planning Web site offers brides and grooms-to-be "Five ways to feng shui* your wedding," suggesting tips for

*feng shui: favorable flow characteristics applied to design of space.

incorporating ancient Chinese traditions into Western-style celebrations. This type of cross-cultural communication and inspiration is currently thriving as people around the world become familiar with cultures outside their own.

Conformity and Culture In the 1950s, Solomon Asch studied conformity and found that there was a strong tendency for Americans at that time to **conform**, the tendency of a person to change their own behavior to match the behavior of others, under the experimental conditions he applied. ⓛⓘⓝⓚ *to Chapter Seven: Social Psychology, pp. 231–232.* More recent research in the United States has found less conformity among participants, perhaps suggesting that the Asch conformity effect was due to the more conforming nature of people in the era he studied and culture of the United States in the 1950s (Lalancette & Standing, 1990; Nicholson et al., 1985; Perrin & Spencer, 1980, 1981). In other cultures, however, studies have found conformity effects similar to those in Asch's study (Neto, 1995). Still others have found even greater effects of conformity in collectivist cultures such as Hong Kong, Japan, and Zimbabwe (Bond & Smith, 1996; Kim & Markus, 1999). This cultural difference may exist only when face-to-face contact is a part of the task, however. One study found that when the Asch judgment task is presented in an online format (participants were in communication but not able to see each other), the cultural difference disappears (Cinnirella & Green, 2007).

Variations in Immigration and Acculturation Another variation in experience based on culture is when a person from one culture must live in another culture, how that person acculturates, which can cause that person to experience a great deal of stress. **Acculturation** means the process of adapting to a new or different culture, often the dominant culture (Sodowsky et al., 1991). The stress resulting from the need to change and adapt to the dominant or majority culture is called *acculturative stress* (Berry & Kim, 1998; Berry & Sam, 1997).

Integration into Culture The method by which a minority person enters into the majority culture can also have an impact on the degree of stress that person will experience (Berry & Kim, 1988).

Integration involves maintaining one's original cultural identity while still forming positive relationships with dominant culture members. For people who choose integration, acculturative stress is usually low (Ward & Rana-Deuba, 1999).

In *assimilation*, the minority person gives up the old cultural identity and completely adopts the ways of the majority culture. Assimilation leads to moderate levels of stress, most likely owing to the loss of cultural patterns and rejection by other members of the minority culture who have not chosen assimilation (LaFromboise et al., 1993; Lay & Nguyen, 1998).

Separation is a pattern in which the minority person rejects the majority culture's ways and tries to maintain the original cultural identity. Members of the minority culture refuse to learn the language of the dominant culture, and they live where others from their culture live, socializing only with others from their original culture.

The greatest acculturative stress will most likely be experienced by people who have chosen to be *marginalized*; that is, they neither maintain contact with the original culture nor join the majority culture. Marginalized individuals do not have the security of the familiar culture of origin or the acceptance of the majority culture and may suffer a loss of identity and feel alienated from others (Roysircai-Sodowsky & Maestas, 2000).

conformity changing one's own behavior to match that of other people.

acculturation the process of adapting to a new or different culture.

21.3 Outline how culture influences our conceptions of self and identity.

Which is more important to you, your independence or your role as a member of your family? Do you think of yourself as an individual, or do you see yourself as the "third child" of a family? Is it more important for you to meet your own personal goals or to help your friends and family meet their goals?

Whatever your answers to these questions are, it is likely that your answers have been shaped by cultural influences. Some cultures value **individualism**, meaning that they prioritize individual rights and responsibilities, independence, personal needs and goals, and accepting consequences of personal choices. Other cultures, however, value **collectivism**. These cultures emphasize the interdependence of all people in a group, and they tend to value group goals and needs more highly than individual goals and needs.

Most cultures are not 100 percent individualist or 100 percent collectivist. It makes sense to think about a scale with pure individualism on one end and pure collectivism on the other end, and most cultures falling somewhere in the middle. It is evident that Western cultures tend to be more individualist, and Eastern (and some developing cultures) tend to be more collectivist.

Individualism, Collectivism, and Self-Concept Psychologists have found that the degree to which a culture is individualist or collectivist can influence how people in that culture think of themselves. Two prominent researchers in cross-cultural psychology, Hazel Markus and Shinobu Kitayama, have spent years comparing how people think and act in individualist countries like the United States and in collectivist countries like Japan. Their research (1991) strongly supports the idea that people in the United States have an **independent self-concept**, meaning that Americans view themselves as generally independent from their friends, family members, classmates, and coworkers. They are more likely to describe themselves through references to their individual goals or desires; for example, an American might say, "I am a scientist" or "I am creative." In contrast, people in Japan have an **interdependent self-concept**, meaning that Japanese people view themselves in terms of their social roles and relationships. They see themselves as fundamentally connected to their friends, family members, classmates, and coworkers, and they are more likely to describe themselves through references to their social roles. Although an American might say, "I am a scientist," a Japanese person might say, "I am a daughter and a sister."

Being brought up in an individualist or collectivist culture can also influence how people think of others. In the United States, we tend to attribute other people's behavior to their personalities and other internal characteristics rather than to their social positions and other external situations. (Remember the fundamental attribution error Westerners tend to make.) ⓛⓘⓝⓚ *to Chapter Seven: Social Psychology, p.242.* But people raised in more collectivist cultures are more likely to attribute others' behavior to situational factors (Miller, 1984). For example, imagine that a man is walking quickly down the sidewalk, pushing aside people who stand in his way and not pausing to excuse himself or apologize. How would you explain this behavior? People from individualist cultures might say that the man is a rude, thoughtless person, whereas people from collectivist cultures would be more likely to consider external reasons for the man's behavior: They may think that he is late for an important meeting, or he is about to miss his train, or his wife is giving birth and he is trying to get to the hospital before the baby arrives.

Which cultures are ▶ individualist, and which are collectivist?

individualism emphasis on individuality, independence, and personal needs.

collectivism emphasis on the interdependence of all people in a group.

independent self-concept an individual's perception of self as entirely independent from others.

interdependent self-concept an individual's perception of self as fundamentally connected to others.

21.4 Describe the major areas of cross-cultural psychology research.

Culture and Personality Although five personality factors have been found across several cultures ((L)(I)(N)(K) *to Chapter Twelve: Theories of Personality , pp. 374–393.*), this does not mean that different cultures do not have an impact on personality. For more on this topic, see the Classic Studies in Psychology section that follows.

Classic Studies in Psychology

Geert Hofstede's Four Dimensions of Cultural Personality

In the early 1980s, organizational management specialist Geert Hofstede conducted a massive study into the work-related values of employees of IBM, a multinational corporation, to help them understand differing cultural mores so as to serve IBM's goals better (Hofstede, 1980; Hofstede et al., 2002). The study surveyed workers in 64 countries across the world. Hofstede analyzed the data collected from this survey and found four basic dimensions of personality along which cultures differed.

1. **Individualism/collectivism:** *Individualistic cultures* tend to have loose ties between individuals, with people tending to look after themselves and their immediate families only. In contrast, in a *collectivistic culture*, people are from birth deeply tied into very strong in-groups.

2. **Power distance:** This dimension refers to the degree to which the less-powerful members of a culture accept and even expect that the power within the culture is held in the hands of a select few rather than being more evenly distributed. Countries such as the Philippines, Mexico, many Arab countries, and India were found to be high in such expectations, whereas countries such as Austria, Sweden, Australia, Great Britain, and the United States were low in power distance.

3. **Masculinity/femininity:** Referring to how a culture distributes the roles played by men and women within the culture, this dimension varies more for the men within a culture than for the women. "Masculine" cultures are assertive and competitive, although more so for men than for women, and "feminine" cultures are more modest and caring. Japan, Austria, Venezuela, Italy, Switzerland, Mexico, Ireland, Jamaica, the United States, Great Britain, and Germany were found to be masculine countries, whereas Sweden, Norway, the Netherlands, Denmark, Costa Rica, Yugoslavia, Finland, Chile, Portugal, Thailand, and Guatemala were ranked as more feminine.

4. **Uncertainty avoidance:** Some cultures are more tolerant of uncertainty, ambiguity, and unstructured situations. Cultures that do not tolerate such uncertainty and lack of structure tend to have strict rules and laws with lots of security and safety measures and tend toward a philosophical/religious belief of One Truth (and "we have it!"). Cultures that are more accepting of uncertainty are more tolerant of different opinions and have fewer rules. Uncertainty-avoiding countries include Greece, Portugal, Guatemala, Uruguay, Belgium, El Salvador, Japan, Yugoslavia, and Peru, whereas those that are more tolerant of uncertainty include Singapore, Jamaica, Denmark, Sweden, Hong

Kong, Ireland, Great Britain, Malaysia, India, Philippines, the United States, Canada, and Indonesia.

Questions for Further Discussion

1. Was your own culture listed for any of these dimensions? If so, do you agree with the personality dimension assigned to your culture?
2. If your culture was not listed for a personality dimension, where do you think your culture would fall on that dimension?

Culture and Creativity Creativity is promoted in many cultures and valued for the innovative contributions creative people make to their society. However, not all cultures place the same value on the creative process.

Cross-cultural research (Basadur et al., 2002; Colligan, 1983) has found that divergent thinking and problem-solving skills cannot be easily taught in the Japanese or Omaha Native American cultures, for example. In these cultures, creativity in many areas is not normally prized and the preference is to hold to well-established, cultural traditions, such as traditional dances that have not varied for centuries. See Table 21.1 for some ways to become a more divergent thinker.

Table 21.1	Stimulating Divergent Thinking
Brainstorming	Generate as many ideas as possible in a short period of time, without judging each idea's merits until all ideas are recorded.
Keeping a Journal	Carry a journal to write down ideas they occur or a recorder to capture those same ideas and thoughts.
Freewriting	Write down or record everything that comes to mind about a topic without revising or proofreading until all of the information is recorded. Organize it later.
Mind or Subject Mapping	Start with a central idea and draw lines from the center to related ideas, forming a visual map of the concepts and their connections.

What about people who live in a tropical area? Would their prototype for fruit be different? And would people's prototypes vary in ▶ other cultures?

Culture and Cognition In Western cultures, when someone says "fruit," what's the first image that comes to mind? More than likely, it's a specific kind of fruit like an apple, pear, or orange. It's less likely that someone's first impulse will be to say "guava" or "papaya," or even "banana," unless that person comes from a tropical area. In the United States, apples are a good example of a **prototype**, a concept that closely matches the defining characteristics of the concept (Mervis & Rosch, 1981; Rosch, 1977). Prototypes and other cognitive process are influenced by the culture a person is exposed to while the concepts they possess are emerging.

Culture and IQ Testing The problem with trying to measure intelligence with a test that is based on an understanding of the world and its resources is that not everyone comes from the same "world." People raised in a different culture, or

prototype a concept that closely matches the defining characteristics of the concept.

even a different economic situation from the one in which the designer of an IQ test is raised, are not likely to perform well on such a test—not to mention the difficulties of taking a test that is written in an unfamiliar language or dialect. In the early days of immigration, people from non–English-speaking countries would score very poorly on intelligence tests, in some cases being denied entry to the United States on the basis of such tests (Allen, 2006).

It is very difficult to design an intelligence test that is completely free of **cultural bias**, a term referring to the tendency of IQ tests to reflect, in language, dialect, and content, the culture of the person or persons who designed the test. A person who comes from the same culture (or even socioeconomic background) as the test designer may have an unfair advantage over a person who is from a different cultural or socioeconomic background (Helms, 1992). If people raised in an Asian culture are given a test designed within a traditional Western culture, many items on the test might make no sense to them. For example, one kind of question might be: Which one of the five is least like the other four?

DOG—CAR—CAT—BIRD—FISH

The answer is supposed to be "car," which is the only one of the five that is not alive. But a Japanese child, living in a culture that relies on the sea for so much of its food and culture, might choose "fish," because none of the others are found in the ocean. That child's test score would be lower but not because the child is not intelligent.

Attempts have been made to create intelligence tests that are as free of cultural influences as is humanly possible. Many test designers have come to the conclusion that it may be impossible to create a test that is completely free of cultural bias (Carpenter et al., 1990). Instead, they are striving to create tests that are at least culturally fair. These tests use questions that do not create a disadvantage for people whose culture differs from that of the majority. Many items on a "culture-fair" test require the use of nonverbal abilities, such as rotating objects, rather than items about verbal knowledge that might be culturally specific.

Culture and Emotion People in different cultures may share many of the same emotions, but the degree of individualism or collectivism in our culture can affect how we label and express those emotions. According to researcher Phoebe Ellsworth, we interpret experiences differently based on our cultural backgrounds, and those different interpretations of experiences lead to different emotional reactions. To illustrate her point, Ellsworth used fish—computer-animated fish, to be exact.

She showed Chinese and American subjects animations of fish interacting with each other and then asked the subjects to label the fish's emotions. For example, one animation showed a blue fish being approached from both sides by a lot of other different-colored fish. When they saw this animation, most of the Chinese participants said that the blue fish was feeling happy, but most of the American participants said that the blue fish was feeling afraid. Ellsworth believes that this difference in responses is due in part to China's more collectivist culture and the United States' more individualist culture: It makes sense that the approach of a large group would seem like a happy event to collectivists and a potentially frightening event to individualists (Swanbrow, 1998).

Although the emotions and the related facial expressions appear to be universal, exactly when, where, and how an emotion is expressed may be determined by the culture. **Display rules** that can vary from culture to culture (Ekman, 1973; Ekman & Friesen, 1969) are learned ways of controlling displays of emotion in social settings. For example, Japanese people have strict

▲ *How might these two women, apparently from different cultures, come to an agreement on what best defines intelligence? A cross-cultural psychologist studies the similarities and differences between cultures. As the world is becoming more globalized and diversity increases opportunities for a career in cross-cultural psychology are growing.*

Thinking Critically
What kind of questions would you include on an intelligence test to minimize cultural bias?

cultural bias the tendency of IQ tests to reflect, in language, dialect, and content, the culture of the person or persons who designed the test.

display rules learned ways of controlling displays of emotion in social settings.

social rules about showing emotion in public situations—they simply do not show emotion, remaining cool, calm, and collected, at least on the outside. But in a more private situation, such as a parent scolding a child within the home, the adult's facial expression would easily be recognized as "angry" by people of any culture. The emotion is universal, and the way it is expressed on the face is universal; whether it is expressed or displayed, however, depends on the learned cultural rules for displaying emotion.

Display rules are different between cultures that are individualistic and those that are collectivistic. Because the United States is individualistic and Japan is collectivistic, the display rules are different between the two cultures (Edelmann & Iwawaki, 1987; Hofstede, 1980; Hofstede et al., 2002).

The label a person applies to a subjective feeling is at least in part a learned response influenced by that person's language and culture. Such labels may differ among people of different cultural backgrounds. For example, researchers in one study (Tsai et al., 2004) found that Chinese Americans who were still firmly rooted in their original Chinese culture were far more likely to use labels to describe their emotions that referred to bodily sensations (such as "dizzy") or social relationships (such as "friendship") than were more "Americanized" Chinese Americans and European Americans, who tended to use more directly emotional words (such as "liking" or "love").

In another study, even the subjective feeling of happiness showed cultural differences (Kitayama & Markus, 1994). In this study, Japanese and U.S. students were found to associate a general positive emotional state with entirely different circumstances. In the case of the Japanese students, the positive state was more associated with friendly or socially engaged feelings. The students from the United States associated their positive emotional state more with feelings that were socially disengaged, such as pride.

Culture and Abnormal Behavior In the *sociocultural perspective* of abnormality, abnormal thinking or behavior (as well as normal) is seen as the product of behavioral shaping within the context of family influences, the social group to which one belongs, and the culture within which the family and social group exist. In particular, cultural differences in abnormal thoughts or actions must be addressed when psychological professionals are attempting to assess and treat members of a culture different from that of the professional.

Cultural relativity is a term that refers to the need to consider the unique characteristics of the culture in which the person with a disorder was nurtured to be able to correctly diagnose and treat the disorder (Castillo, 1997). For example, in most traditional Asian cultures, mental illness is often seen as a shameful thing that brings disgrace to one's family. This leads many Asian people suffering from disorders that would be labeled as depression or even schizophrenia to report bodily symptoms rather than emotional or mental ones, because bodily ailments are more socially acceptable (Fedoroff & McFarlane, 1998; Lee, 1995; Ritts, 1999).

Disorders unique to specific cultures have previously been referred to as *culture-bound syndromes*. For example, anorexia nervosa and bulimia nervosa have traditionally been most often found in Western societies. The conceptualization of culture and its influences on psychological function and disorders has been expanded in the most recent publication of the *Diagnostic and Statistical Manual of Mental Disorders,* the *DSM-5.*

The idea of "culture-bound" has been replaced by three concepts: *cultural syndromes, cultural idioms of distress,* and *cultural explanations or perceived cause* (American Psychiatric Association, 2013). Cultural syndromes may or may not be recognized as an illness within the culture but are

cultural relativity the need to consider the unique characteristics of the culture in which the person with a disorder was nurtured to be able to correctly diagnose and treat the disorder.

nonetheless recognizable as a distinct set of symptoms or characteristics of distress. Cultural idioms* of distress refer to terms or phrases used to describe suffering or distress within a given cultural context. And cultural explanations or perceived cause are culturally defined ways of explaining the source or cause of symptoms or illness (American Psychiatric Association, 2013).

Culture and Anxiety Anxiety disorders are found around the world, although the particular form the disorder takes might be different in various cultures. For example, in some Latin American cultures anxiety can take the form of *ataque de nervios*, or "attack of nerves," in which the person may have fits of crying, shout uncontrollably, experience sensations of heat, and become very aggressive, either verbally or physically. These attacks usually come after some stressful event such as the death of a loved one (American Psychiatric Association, 2013). Several syndromes that are essentially types of phobias are specific to certain cultures. For example, *taijin kyofusho* (TKS), found primarily in Japan, involves excessive fear and anxiety, but in this case it is the fear that one will do something in public that is socially inappropriate or embarrassing, such as blushing, staring, or having an offensive body odor (Kirmayer, 1991). Panic disorder occurs at similar rates in adolescents and adults in the United States and parts of Europe, but found less often in Asian, African, and Latin American countries. Within the United States, American Indians have significantly higher rates whereas Latinos, African Americans, Caribbean blacks, and Asian Americans have significantly lower rates as compared to non-Latino whites (American Psychiatric Association, 2013).

Eating Disorders and Culture Although many researchers have believed eating disorders, especially anorexia, are cultural syndromes that only show up in cultures obsessed with being thin (as many Western cultures are), eating disorders are also found in non-Western cultures (Miller & Pumariega, 1999). What differs between Western and non-Western cultures is the rate at which such disorders appear. For example, Chinese and Chinese American women are far less likely to suffer from eating disorders than are non-Hispanic White women (Pan, 2000). Why wouldn't Chinese American women be more likely to have eating disorders after being exposed to the Western cultural obsession with thinness? Pan (2000) assumes that whatever Chinese cultural factors "protect" Chinese women from developing eating disorders may also still have a powerful influence on Chinese American women.

One problem with studying anorexia and bulimia in other cultures is that the behavior of starving oneself may be seen in other cultures as having an entirely different purpose than in Western cultures. One key component of anorexia, for example, is a fear of being fat, a fear that is missing in many other cultures. Yet women in those cultures have starved themselves for other socially recognized reasons: religious fasting or unusual ideas about nutrition (Castillo, 1997).

Anorexia and bulimia have also been thought to occur only rarely in African American women, but that characterization seems to be changing. Researchers are seeing an increase in anorexia and bulimia among young African American women of all socioeconomic levels (Crago et al., 1996; Mintz & Betz, 1998; Pumariega & Gustavson, 1994).

Thinking Critically
How might the proliferation† of various media and the Internet affect the development of eating disorders in cultures not previously impacted by them?

---

*idiom: a phrase that has a meaning that is not literal; for example, "between a rock and a hard place."
†proliferation: rapid growth in numbers or size.

21.5 Explain psychological research that examines socioeconomic status.

▲ *A migrant farming background has been found to be related to increased symptoms of anxiety and depression among college students of Mexican heritage when compared to those without a migrant background.*

It is important to take into account other background and culturally influential factors such as socioeconomic status and education level. Another area of awareness should be primary language and, if applicable, degree of acculturation (adapting to or merging with another culture). Psychosocial functioning has been part of the diagnostic process for some time now, but traditionally, greater attention has been paid to specifically identifying symptoms of pathology* rather than focusing on the environmental factors that influence an individual's overall level of functioning (Ro & Clark, 2009). For example, in one recent study, college students of Mexican heritage with migrant farming backgrounds reported more symptoms of anxiety and depression as compared to nonmigrant college students of Mexican heritage (Mejía & McCarthy, 2010). A migrant farming background has been found to be related to increased symptoms of anxiety and depression among college students of Mexican heritage when compared to those without a migrant background.

21.6 Explain how privilege and social power structures relate to stereotypes, prejudice, and discrimination.

We've seen how **stereotypes**, a set of characteristics that people believe is shared by all members of a particular social category or group, can be formed by using only superficial information about that person or group of people. When a person holds an unsupported and often negative stereotyped *attitude* about the members of a particular social group, it is called **prejudice**. The video *In the Real World: Are Stereotypes and Prejudices Inevitable?: Defining Prejudice* explains the connection between stereotypes and prejudice.

When prejudicial attitudes cause members of a particular social group to be treated differently than others in situations that call for equal treatment, it is called **discrimination**. Prejudice is the attitude and discrimination is the behavior that can result from that attitude.

While laws exist to prevent discriminatory behavior, the laws do not prevent some people from holding discriminatory attitudes. Efforts to control or, even eliminate, discrimination have been effective, but what cannot be so easily addressed are the prejudicial attitudes that are the basis of the discrimination.

Types of Prejudice and Discrimination Prejudice and discrimination come in many forms. There's bullying, negative racial or ethnic attitudes, prejudice against different faith-based perspectives, even against those who don't have the ideal body weight or shape.

Groups vary in the likelihood that they will be prejudiced against. *Outgroups* (people you don't identify with) versus *in-groups* (people you do identify with) and beliefs about "our team" versus "their team" put others in a position of being a likely target for prejudice (Brewer, 2001; Hewstone et al., 2002; Tajfel & Turner, 1986).

◉ **Watch** the **Video**, *In the Real World: Are Stereotypes and Prejudices Inevitable?: Defining Prejudice*, at **MyPsychLab**

stereotype a set of characteristics that people believe is shared by all members of a particular social category; a concept held about a person or group of people that is based on superficial, irrelevant characteristics.

prejudice negative attitude held by a person about the members of a particular social group.

discrimination treating people differently because of prejudice toward the social group to which they belong.

---

*pathology: the causes of diseases and disorders.

In-groups and out-groups are formed at very young ages (Ruble et al., 2004) and remain well into adulthood. After the formation of in-groups, prejudice and discrimination toward the out group are likely to emerge (Brewer, 2001). Superficial features of the out-groups (for example, skin tone, eye color, height) grow into stereotypes, are resistant to change, and tend to endure over time (Cameron et al., 2001; Hamilton & Gifford, 1976).

▲ *"First, can we agree that it's a big backyard?"*

© *The New Yorker Collection 2002 Charles Barsotti from cartoonbank. com. All Rights Reserved.*

Scapegoating External pressures often contribute toward tensions between groups. A downward turn in the economy, natural disasters, famine, and other difficult circumstances fuel the need to direct anger, hurt, and suffering toward something or someone, and often leads to directing it at a scapegoat (a person or group to blame one's troubles on) with less power and status. One example of this is the rioting in Los Angeles, California, in the spring of 1992 as a result of the now infamous Rodney King beating by police officers. (L)(I)(N)(K) *to Chapter Seven: Social Psychology, p. 245.* Surprisingly, the rioting took place in the neighborhoods of recent Asian American immigrants. Like the Asian American immigrants in this case, it is common for the group with the least social power to bear the brunt of the more powerful group's frustrations.

An example of scapegoating that occurs often in schools is when a sports team loses a close competition. It is easy for team members to direct their sad feelings and frustrations toward the one person on the team (with lesser abilities than the others) that didn't come through successfully in a crucial moment of the game. The team blames the loss on a single event of the competition instead of looking at their play overall during the rest of the event and recognizing that there is plenty of blame for the loss to go around.

More recently, there is increased attention on bullying and bullying behavior in schools and on social network sites. The ease of logging into a Facebook page and having access to an audience is too tempting to some "friends" and they feel compelled to vent their anger and sadness to a cyber-audience. Cyber-bullying can lead to embarrassment and even conflict back at school when individuals are feeling very hurt.

▲ *Blaming an individual for a team loss is an example of scapegoating and often results in hurt feelings from the poor sportsmanship of the other team members.*

Pick the best answer.

1. **Which of the following statements about culture is true?**

   a. It is possible to identify with more than one culture.

   b. It is not difficult to move from one culture to another.

   c. Cultural factors do not affect most aspects of people's daily lives.

   d. No country can contain more than one culture.

2. **A culture may have certain rules, traditions, or beliefs that people are expected to follow. These rules are known as**

   a. norms.

   b. roles.

   c. display rules.

   d. self-concepts.

3. _____**thoughts and behaviors are those which are unique from culture to culture.**

   a. Normal

   b. Universal

   c. Collective

   d. Culture-bound

4. **Which of the following people is likely to make the fastest transition from an old culture to a new culture?**

   a. a 10-year-old girl

   b. a 30-year-old man

   c. a 50-year-old woman

   d. an 80-year-old man

5. **A man who thinks of himself in terms of his relationship to his family and coworkers is most likely from a(n) _____ culture.**

   a. individualist

   b. collectivist

   c. developing

   d. industrialized

6. **IQ tests are not a preferred measure of intelligence in cross-cultural psychology because**

   a. The tests are outdated and do not analyze modern skills.

   b. IQ changes too quickly to be measured accurately.

   c. Intelligence takes different forms in different cultures.

   d. Psychologists cannot write tests in languages other than English.

7. **Which of the following statements is the best illustration of an independent self-concept?**

   a. "I am a friendly and considerate person."

   b. "I am a mother to three small boys."

   c. "I am a teacher in a public high school."

   d. "I am a member of the basketball team."

8. **Which of the following is NOT a culture-bound action?**

   a. smiling

   b. shaking hands

   c. giving a thumbs-up

   d. making a victory "V" sign with two fingers

9. **In which of the following scenarios does display rules play a part?**

   a. A girl moves to a new country with her family. She makes friends with people from her new culture but still feels like she is part of her old culture.

   b. A girl brings food and decorations from her home culture to school to share her cultural background with her friends.

   c. A girl watches a sad movie with friends. She wants to cry, but because she is with other people, she keeps her emotions to herself.

   d. A girl takes an IQ test designed in a culture different from her own, and she is not familiar with many of the terms and concepts used in the test.

10. **Which of the following research questions would a cross-cultural psychologist most likely ask?**

    a. Is there a biological basis for depression?

    b. Can moving to a new country cause depression?

    c. Are symptoms of depression different now than they were in the past?

    d. Do people in different countries experience depression in the same way?

Module Goal

Learn about gender identity development.

Learning Objectives

22.1 Define gender and discuss the development of gender roles.

22.2 Compare and contrast two theories of gender-role development.

22.3 Describe gender differences.

22.4 Discuss how the roles of women and men in societies are perceived.

Learn about Gender Identity Development

22.1 Define gender and discuss the development of gender roles.

One important aspect of development that encompasses both physical and psychological changes is gender development, the growing sense of being male or female.

Gender Roles Whereas sex can be defined as the physical characteristics (the body) of being male or female, **gender** is defined as the psychological aspects (the mind) of being male or female. The expectations of one's culture, the development of one's personality, and one's sense of identity are all affected by the concept of gender.

Gender roles are the culture's expectations for behavior of a person who is perceived as male or female, including attitudes, actions, and personality traits associated with a particular gender within that culture (Tobach, 2001; Unger, 1979). The process of developing a person's **gender identity** (a sense of being male or female) is influenced by both biological and environmental factors (in the form of parenting and other child-rearing behaviors), although which type of factor has greater influence is still controversial. Most researchers today would agree that biology has an important role in gender identity, at least in certain aspects of gender identity and behavior (Diamond & Sigmundson, 1997; Money, 1994; Reiner, 1999, 2000).

22.2 Describe theories of gender role development.

How do children acquire the knowledge of their society or culture's gender-role expectations? How does that knowledge lead to the development of a gender identity? Many modern theorists focus on learning and cognitive processes for the development of gender identity and behavior.

gender the behavior associated with being male or female.

gender roles the culture's expectations for masculine or feminine behavior, including attitudes, actions, and personality traits associated with being male or female in that culture.

gender identity the individual's sense of being male or female.

social learning theory learning through observation and imitation of models, attributes gender-role development to those processes.

gender schema theory theory of gender identity acquisition in which a child develops a mental pattern, or schema, for being male or female and then organizes observed and learned behavior around that schema.

androgyny a gender role characteristic of people whose personalities reflect the characteristics of both males and females, regardless of gender.

When do little kids ▶ learn the difference between girls and boys?

Social learning theory, which emphasizes learning through observation and imitation of models, attributes gender-role development to those processes. Children observe their same-sex parents behaving in certain ways and imitate that behavior. When the children imitate the appropriate gender behavior, they are reinforced with positive attention. Inappropriate gender behavior is either ignored or actively discouraged (Fagot & Hagan, 1991; Mischel, 1966).

A theory of gender-role development that combines social learning theory with cognitive development is called **gender schema theory** (Bem, 1987, 1993). In this theory based on the Piagetian concept of schemas, children develop a schema, or mental pattern, for being male or female in much the same way that they develop schemas for other concepts such as "dog," "bird," and "big." As their brains mature, they become capable of distinguishing among various concepts. For example, a "dog" might at first be anything with four legs and a tail, but as children encounter dogs and other kinds of animals and are given instruction, "dog" becomes more specific and the schema for "dog" becomes well defined.

In a similar manner, children develop a concept for "boy" and "girl." Once that schema is in place, children can identify themselves as "boy" or "girl" and will notice other members of that schema. They notice the behavior of other "boys" or "girls" and imitate that behavior. Rather than being simple imitation and reinforcement, as in social learning theory, children acquire their gender role behavior by organizing that behavior around the schema of "boy" or "girl." Evidence for this theory includes the finding that children can discriminate between male and female faces and voices before age 1 (Martin, 2000), a sign that the world is already being organized into those two concepts. The concept of **androgyny** (Bem, 1975, 1981) describes a gender role characteristic of people whose personalities reflect the characteristics of both males and females, regardless of gender. Androgynous people can make decisions based on the situation's demands rather than being masculine or feminine, which allows them to be more flexible in everyday behavior and career choices.

22.3 Describe gender differences.

How do men and women differ in thinking, social behavior, and personality? Although there are clear biological differences in males and females, even to the point of affecting the size of certain structures in the brain (Swaab et al., 2012; Zilles & Amunts, 2012), what sort of differences exist in the behavior of males and females? Are those differences due to biology, socialization, or a combination of the two influences?

Cognitive Differences Researchers have long held that females score higher on tests of verbal abilities than do males, but that males score higher on tests of mathematical skills and spatial skills (Diamond, 1991; Voyer et al., 1995). Early explanations of these differences in cognitive functioning involved physical differences in the way each sex used the two hemispheres of the brain as well as hormonal differences (Witelson, 1991). Other research, however, strongly suggests that psychological and social issues may be more responsible for these differences, as these differences have become less and less obvious (Hyde & Plant, 1995; Kimura, 1999; Voyer et al., 1995; Watt, 2000). In particular, the supposed differences in math abilities between boys and girls have now been shown to be more the effect of girls' lack of confidence rather than any biological difference in the working of the brain (American Association of University Women, 1992,

▲ *"It's a guy thing."*

1998; Else-Quest et al., 2010; Sadker & Sadker, 1994). That the disparities (which are actually quite small) seem to be disappearing as society has begun to view the two genders as more equal in ability.

Social and Personality Differences The differences normally cited between men and women in the ways they interact with others and in their personality traits are often the result of stereotyped thinking about the sexes. It is difficult to demonstrate differences that are not caused by the way boys and girls are socialized as they grow up. Boys are taught to hold in their emotions, not to cry, to be "strong" and "manly." Girls are encouraged to form emotional attachments, be emotional, and be open about their feelings with others.

▲ It was long believed that the difference between girls and boys in math skills was a function of biology, but research now shows that psychological and social issues are the more likely causes.

In communication, research suggests that when men talk to each other, they tend to talk about current events, sports, and other events. This has been called a "report" style of communication and seems to involve switching topics frequently, with attempts to dominate the conversation by certain members of the group. In contrast, women tend to use a "relate" style of communication with each other, revealing a lot about their private lives and showing concern and sympathy. They tend to interrupt each other less and let everyone participate in the conversation (Argamon et al., 2003; Coates, 1986; Pilkington, 1998; Swann, 1998). Another study, using fMRI technology, found that men listen with the left hemisphere only, whereas women listen with both hemispheres, suggesting that women pay attention to the tone and emotion of statements as well as the content (Lurito et al., 2000).

22.4 Discuss how the roles of women and men in societies are perceived.

Environment must also play its part. In most cultures, there are certain roles that males and females are expected to play (gender roles, in other words), and the pressure that can be brought to bear on a person who does not conform to these expectations can be tremendous. In most Western cultures, the pressure to be masculine is even greater for males than the pressure to be feminine is for girls. And although studies of parents' influence on their children's gender typing show that both parents have an impact, they also show that the fathers are almost always more concerned about their sons showing male gender behavior than their daughters showing female gender behavior (Lytton & Romney, 1991). Cultures that are more individualistic (those stressing independence and with loose ties among individuals) and have fairly high standards of living are becoming more nontraditional, especially for women in those cultures, whereas the more traditional views seem to be held by collectivistic cultures (those stressing interdependence and with strong ties among individuals, especially familial ties) that have less wealth, although even in the latter, women were more likely to be less traditional than men (Forbes et al., 2009; Gibbons et al., 1991).

Pick the best answer.

1. **The term for the psychological aspect of being male or female is**

   a. sex.
   b. sexual orientation.
   c. gender.
   d. gender role.

2. **What is gender typing?**

   a. a biological predisposition for behavior
   b. an environmental factor that affects one sex
   c. a physical differentiation between male and female
   d. a cultural perception of what is masculine and feminine

3. **In many Western cultures, boys are expected to play with trucks while girls are expected to play with dolls. This is an example of**

   a. gender roles.
   b. gender identity.
   c. gender typing.
   d. gender discrimination.

4. **Which of the following statements about gender is true?**

   a. A person's gender has absolutely nothing to do with his or her biological sex.
   b. A person's gender is entirely determined by his or her biological sex.
   c. A person's gender is influenced by biological characteristics but is not always determined by those characteristics.
   d. A person's gender is generally determined by cultural influences rather than by biological characteristics.

5. **The ideas that a man works out of the house and a woman stays at home are examples of**

   a. cultural gender stereotypes.
   b. alternative gender identities.

   c. transcultural gender roles.
   d. environmental gender influences.

6. **Which of the following statements is true?**

   a. Cultural and social factors have little influence over brain activities.
   b. Women use both brain hemispheres, while men use one hemisphere at a time.
   c. Men are always more analytical, while women are always more emotional.
   d. Gender-based differences in brain activity disappear with equal educational exposure.

7. **Which of the following factors are MOST influential in the development of gender identity?**

   a. economic and social factors
   b. physical and hormonal factors
   c. ethical and moral factors
   d. biological and environmental factors

8. **A set of cultural expectations based on a person's sex is a**

   a. gender role.
   b. gender typing.
   c. gender bias.
   d. gender discrimination.

9. **In which of the following types of cultures are nontraditional gender roles most likely to thrive?**

   a. conservative cultures
   b. historic cultures
   c. collectivist cultures
   d. individualist cultures

10. **In the United States and in many other cultures, boys are generally taught to**

   a. keep their feelings to themselves.
   b. relate to others through conversation.
   c. seek help from friends in tough times.
   d. express their emotions freely.

(((**Listen** to an **Audio File** of your chapter at **MyPsychLab**

Module 21: Sociocultural Diversity
Understand culture's role in psychology.

21.1 Describe culture and diversity.
- Culture is a shared set of beliefs, behaviors, values and attitudes held by a group of people or society. Culture is learned, shared, and changes over time.
- A culture's norms tell us what behavior is acceptable or unacceptable.

21.2 Explain how culture varies across time and place.
- Cultures are shaped by geographic factors like climate and the availability of natural resources as well as by human factors like population density and technological advancement.
- Conformity is the tendency to change one's own behavior to math of others. The effects of conformity can vary depending on culture.
- The degree of stress a person will experience when attempting to enter into a new culture can vary.

21.3 Outline how culture influences our conceptions of self and identity.
- Cultures may be individualist or collectivist. People living in individualist cultures tend to have an independent self-concept, while people who live in collectivist cultures tend to have an interdependent self-concept.

21.4 Describe the major areas of cross-cultural psychology research.
- Geert Hofstede described four basic dimensions of personality along which cultures differ: individualism/collectivism, power distance, masculinity/femininity, and uncertainty avoidance.
- Creativity is not valued equally in all cultures.
- Prototypes and other cognitive processes are influenced by the culture a person is exposed.
- Intelligence does not have a universal definition, and takes different forms in different cultures.
- People in different cultures may share many of the same emotions, but our culture can affect how we label and express those emotions.
- What is considered "normal" and accepted within a culture is variable. Cultural relativity refers to the need to consider the unique culture of a person with a disorder when attempting to diagnose and treat the disorder itself.

21.5 Explain psychological research that examines socioeconomic status.
- It is important to take into account other background and culturally influential factors such as socioeconomic status and education level.

21.6 Explain how privilege and social power structures relate to stereotypes, prejudice, and discrimination.
- Stereotypes can be formed by using only superficial information about that person or group of people.
- Prejudice is an unsupported and often negative stereotyped attitude about the members of a particular social group. There are many types of prejudice.

Module 22: Gender
Learn about gender identity development.

22.1 Define gender and discuss the development of gender roles.
- Gender is defined as the psychological aspects of being male or female. Gender roles are the culture's expectations for behavior of a person who is perceived as male or female.
- The process of developing a gender identity is influenced by both biological and environmental factors.

22.2 Describe theories of gender role development.
- Social learning theory emphasizes learning through observation and imitation of models and attributes gender-role development to those processes.
- Gender schema theory combines social learning theory with cognitive development. Children develop a schema for being male or female.

22.3 Describe gender differences.
- Females score higher on tests of verbal abilities and males score higher on tests of mathematical skills and spatial skills. These differences seem to be disappearing as society has begun to view the two genders as more equal in ability.
- Males and females are socialized differently, which influences personality. However, males tend to "report" when in conversation, while females tent to "relate" when conversing.

22.4 Discuss how the roles of women and men in societies are perceived.
- In most cultures, there are certain roles that males and females are expected to play (gender roles, in other words). Gender roles are impacted by a number of factors, including type of culture, environment, and parental influence.

Vocabulary Terms

✓ **Study and Review** at **MyPsychLab**

Vocabulary Review

Match each vocabulary term to its definition.

1. culture
2. norms
3. individualism
4. collectivism
5. acculturation
6. gender
7. culture-bound
8. etic
9. display rules
10. gender roles

a. The process of adapting to a new culture by adopting the new culture's beliefs and behaviors.

b. A culture's understood rules for expected behavior, values, beliefs, and attitudes.

c. The psychological aspects of being male or female.

d. A shared set of beliefs, behaviors, values, and attitudes held by a group of people or a society.

e. A way of studying cultures to look for their similarities objectively from the outside.

f. Found only in particular cultures.

g. Learned ways of controlling displays of emotion in social settings.

h. A culture's expectations for masculine or feminine behavior, including attitudes, actions, and personality traits associated with being male or female in that culture.

i. A cultural style that emphasizes the importance of interdependence, group goals, and group needs.

j. A cultural style that emphasizes the importance of individuality, independence, and personal needs.

Psychology Project

What cultural and individual traits do you share with your classmates? Interview your peers to learn about your similarities and differences.

Materials:
- three partners
- a pencil and paper

Instructions:

1. Answer the following questions about your culture and your own personal identity:
   - What are some of your values?
   - How does your family history affect your values?
   - How would you describe yourself?
   - Are you similar to or different from others in your community?
   - How does the area you live in affect your personal identity and your cultures?
   - What culture(s) would you say you belong to?

2. Choose a partner to "interview" and discuss these questions. Write down any responses your partner says.

3. Interview a second and third partner and write down their responses.

4. Review your partners' responses. What are the similarities? Where are there differences? Circle the similarities you share, and underline the differences.

5. Discuss the results. Were all responses similar? How were they different? As a group, talk about what role culture plays in your everyday life, as well as how it affects how you view yourself.

Tech Alternative

Think of ways that sociocultural diversity has grown in your school. In what ways has technology contributed to the increase in sociocultural diversity at your school? Write a response that identifies three ways technology has contributed to the increase in sociocultural diversity at your school. Include an example to support each idea.

Essay Question

Briefly describe how someone might use two of the concepts listed below when explaining differences between cultures. For each concept you choose, include a general description of the concept and an example of how the concept applies to a specific difference between two cultures:

a. collectivism and individualism

b. culture bound syndromes

c. gender roles

d. display rules

Test Yourself

Ready for your test? More quizzes and a customized plan.

✔ Study and Review at MyPsychLab

Pick the best answer.

1. A shared set of beliefs, behaviors, values, and attitudes held by a group of people or a society is known as
   a. civilization.
   c. culture.
   b. society.
   d. ethnicity.

2. Gender is defined as
   a. the psychological aspect of being male or female.
   b. a biological distinction between males and females.
   c. a cultural role defined by social standards and rules.
   d. identification with a person's physical aspects.

3. Which of the following questions might a psychologist using the etic approach to studying cultures ask?
   a. How are Western cultures different than Eastern cultures?
   b. How are Western cultures the same as Eastern cultures?
   c. How do perceptions of love vary in different countries?
   d. How many generations of immigrant families are bilingual?

4. Research has shown that men tend to talk to each other about
   a. private concerns.
   b. their feelings.
   c. relationships.
   d. current events.

5. Cross-cultural psychology is the study of
   a. cultures from around the world.
   b. human thought and behavior across cultures.
   c. human thought and behavior in a multicultural country.
   d. the spread of culture through technology.

6. A cultural pressure to work together and be part of the group is most common in cultures that have a high degree of
   a. universalism.
   b. collectivism.
   c. ethnocentrism.
   d. individualism.

7. Which of the following cultures was found to value creativity to a lesser degree than in Western cultures?
   a. French
   b. Brazilian
   c. Japanese
   d. Belgian

8. A young child moves and adapts to a new culture. This is an example of
   a. acculturation.
   c. integration.
   b. naturalization.
   d. assimilation.

9. The differences between males and females in math and verbal skills may be caused by psychological and social issues because
   a. these differences have increased in recent years.
   b. these differences have decreased in recent years.
   c. these differences have remained constant.
   d. females now score higher than males in math.

10. In China, some brides now wear white gowns instead of traditional red gowns. This example demonstrates that
    a. cultures cannot change over time.
    b. one culture can influence another.
    c. cultural norms are not powerful.
    d. individualism is more popular than collectivism.

11. A gender role characteristic of people whose personalities reflect the characteristics of both males and females, regardless of gender, is best known as
    a. homogeneity.
    c. androgyny.
    b. heterogeneity.
    d. pandrogyny.

12. Gender roles are created by a(n)
    a. biological need and response.
    b. individual's personal identity.
    c. society's strengthening of stereotypes.
    d. culture's expectations for male and female behavior.

13. Studies have shown that _____ are more concerned about appropriate gender behavior in their children, particularly their _____ children.
    a. fathers; male
    b. fathers; female
    c. mothers; male
    d. mothers; female

14. Each culture has its own or learned ways of controlling displays of emotion in social settings.
    a. base feelings
    b. display rules
    c. emotive expressions
    d. social interactions

15. The development of a person's sense of being male or female is called
    a. gender role.
    b. gender identity.
    c. gender typing.
    d. gender stereotyping.

16. Which of the following conclusions does Phoebe Ellsworth's study of emotions suggest?
    a. Our culture helps us determine how to display our emotions physically.
    b. Our culture gives us a context for interpreting actions and assigning emotions to those actions.
    c. Emotions are not universal, and most emotions are not present in more than one culture.
    d. Cross-cultural studies of emotion do not reveal significant differences between cultures.

17. Alex sees his father hammering some nails into a board. Later Alex pretends to hammer in some imaginary nails. Of which theory of gender development would this be a good example?
    a. gender schema theory
    c. psychoanalytic theory
    b. gender-role theory
    d. social learning theory

18. In _____ cultures, gender roles are seen as more traditional, whereas in _____ cultures they may be more nontraditional, especially for women.
    a. individualistic; collectivistic
    c. European; Asian
    b. collectivistic; individualistic
    d. affluent; poor

19. Which of the following would be a prototype fruit in the United States?
    a. mango
    c. breadfruit
    b. guava
    d. apple

20. Which of the following is not a quality associated with culture?
    a. culture is learned
    b. culture is shared
    c. culture is biologically based
    d. culture changes over time

Learning Objectives

    21.1 21.2 21.3 21.4 21.5 21.6 pp. 264–275

Understand Culture's Role in Psychology

- **culture** is a shared set of beliefs, behaviors, values and attitudes held by a group of people or a society

  - cultures have **norms**, understood rules dictating what behavior is acceptable or unacceptable
  - common characteristics of culture
    - culture is learned
    - culture is shared
    - culture changes over time

- **cultural variation** across place and time
  - cultures can be shaped by
  - **acculturation** is the process of adapting to a new culture by adopting the new culture's beliefs and behaviors
    - **geographic factors**
      - climate
      - natural resources
    - **human factors**
      - population density
      - technological development

- **individualism and collectivism**
  - **individualism** is a cultural style that emphasizes the importance of individuality, independence, personal consequences and personal needs
    - independent self-concept
  - **collectivism** is a cultural style that emphasizes the importance of interdependence, group goals, and group needs
    - interdependent self-concept

- **privilege and social power**
  - prejudice is the attitude that can result from that attitude
  - discrimination is the behavior that can result from that attitude.

- **cross-cultural psychology** the study of human thought and behavior across cultures
  - there are many areas of cross-cultural psychology research, including
  - **culture-bound** thought and behavior is found only in particular cultures
  - **universal** thought and behavior is found across all cultures
    - emotion
    - intelligence
    - development across the life span
    - abnormal behavior

Diversity and Gender

22.1 **22.2** **22.3** **22.4**   pp. 277–279

Map the Concepts at MyPsychLab

Learn About Gender Identity Development

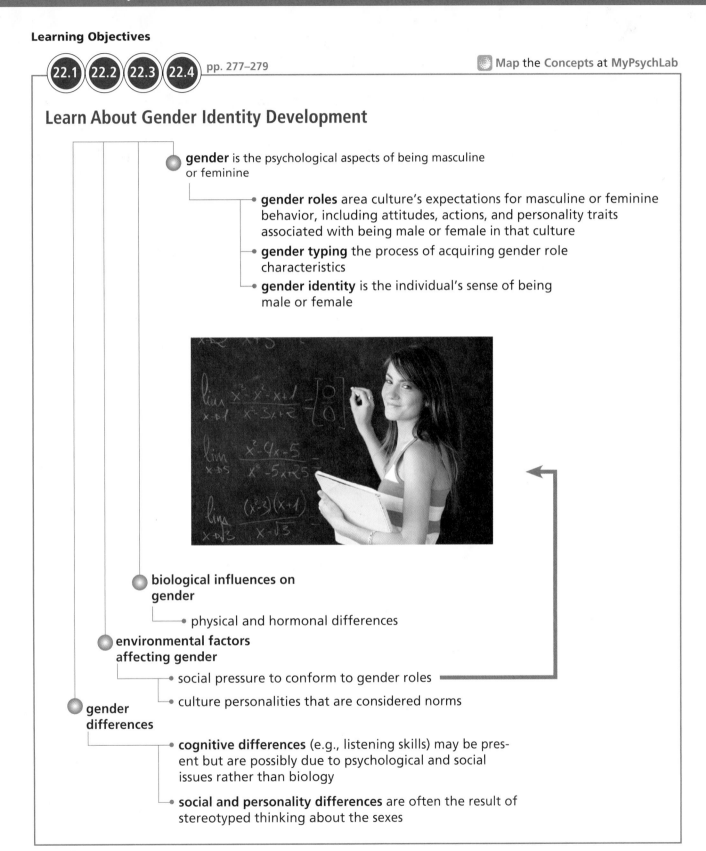

gender is the psychological aspects of being masculine or feminine

gender roles area culture's expectations for masculine or feminine behavior, including attitudes, actions, and personality traits associated with being male or female in that culture

gender typing the process of acquiring gender role characteristics

gender identity is the individual's sense of being male or female

biological influences on gender

physical and hormonal differences

environmental factors affecting gender

social pressure to conform to gender roles

culture personalities that are considered norms

gender differences

cognitive differences (e.g., listening skills) may be present but are possibly due to psychological and social issues rather than biology

social and personality differences are often the result of stereotyped thinking about the sexes

CHAPTER 9 Memory

Most of us, at some point in our busy lives, have trouble remembering things, especially events from the distant past. What if you could remember nearly every day of your life? This rare ability is possessed by Brad Williams, who is known as the "Human Google." Brad is one of a small group of individuals with a syndrome called *hyperthymesia* (hī-pr-thī-mē-sē-uh). A person with hyperthymesia not only has an astonishing and rare ability to recall specific events from his or her personal past but also spends an unusually large amount of time thinking about that personal past. Brad can recall almost any news event or personal event he himself has experienced, particularly specific dates—and even the weather on those dates.

How is your memory of events? Do you find that you remember events from your past differently than others who were also present at that time?

MODULE 23 ▸ ENCODING AND STORAGE
MODULE 24 ▸ RETRIEVAL AND RETRIEVAL FAILURE

Watch the Video, at MyPsychLab

*W*hy Study Memory?

Without memory, how would we be able to learn anything? The ability to learn is the key to our very survival, and we cannot learn unless we can remember what happened the last time a particular situation arose. Why study forgetting? If we can learn about the ways in which we forget information, we can apply that learning so that forgetting occurs less frequently.

 23 Encoding and Storage

Module Goals	Learning Objectives
Explain how the brain encodes memories.	**23.1** Explain how memories are encoded. **23.2** Characterize the different levels of processing. **23.3** Understand strategies for improving the encoding of memory.
Understand how memories are stored in the brain.	**23.4** Describe the roles of working memory and long-term memory. **23.5** Explain how memory is stored. **23.6** Learn strategies for improving the storage of memories.

Explain How the Brain Encodes Memories

In reading through this chapter, it becomes clear that memory is a process but that it also has a "place" in the brain. Perhaps the best definition of **memory** is an active system that receives information from the senses, puts that information into a usable form, organizes it as it stores it away, and then retrieves the information from storage (Baddeley, 1996, 2003).

23.1 Explain how memories are encoded.

Although there are several different models of how memory works, all of them involve the same three processes: getting the information into the memory system, storing it there, and getting it back out.

Putting it in: Encoding The first stage in the memory system is to get sensory information (sight, sound, etc.) into a form that the brain can use in a process called **encoding**. Encoding is a variety of mental operations that the brain performs on sensory information that processes raw data into something meaningful that can be stored in the cortex. For example, when people hear a sound, their ears turn the vibrations in the air into neural messages from the auditory nerve (*transduction*), which makes it possible for the brain to interpret that sound.

Keeping it in: Storage The next step in memory is to hold on to the information for some period of time in a process called **storage**. This period of time will vary depending on the storage system being used. For example, in one system people hold on to information just long enough to work with it, about 20 seconds or so. In another system, people hold on to information more or less permanently.

Getting it out: Retrieval The biggest problem many people have is **retrieval**, getting the information they know they have out of storage. Have you ever handed in an essay test and *then* remembered several other things you could have said? Retrieval problems are discussed in a major section of this chapter.

memory an active system that receives information from the senses, puts that information into a usable form, organizes it as it stores it away, and then retrieves the information from storage.

encoding the set of mental operations that people perform on sensory information to process that information into a form that is usable in the brain's storage systems.

storage holding onto information for some period of time.

retrieval getting information that is in storage into a form that can be used.

23.2 Characterize the different levels of processing.

Three Models of Memory Memory experts have proposed several different ways of looking at memory. The model that many researchers feel is the most comprehensive* and has perhaps been the most influential over the last several decades is the **information-processing model**. This approach focuses on the way information is handled, or processed, through three different systems of memory. The processes of encoding, storage, and retrieval are seen as part of this model.

The Information-Processing Model: Three Stages of Memory

Information-processing theory looks at how thought processes such as memory work and uses as its model for human thought the way that a computer functions (Massaro & Cowan, 1993). It was information-processing theorists who first proposed that there are three stages or types of memory systems (see **Figure 23.1**): sensory memory, short-term memory, and long-term memory (Atkinson & Shiffrin, 1968). The first two of these, sensory memory and short-term memory, will be discussed here, whereas long-term memory will be covered later in the chapter.

Sensory Memory: Messages from the Nervous System Sensory **memory** is the first stage of memory, the point at which information enters the nervous system through the sensory systems—eyes, ears, and so on. Information is encoded into sensory memory as neural (neuron) messages in the nervous system. As long as those neural messages are traveling through the system, it can be said that people have a "memory" for that information that can be accessed if needed.

Two kinds of sensory memory that have been studied extensively are iconic (visual) and echoic (auditory) sensory memories. In this and the sections that follow, these and other types of memories as well as several of the experiments that have added a great deal of information to the understanding of memory will be discussed.

information-processing model model of memory put forth by Atkinson & Shiffrin that assumes the processing of information for memory storage is similar to the way a computer processes memory in a series of three stages.

sensory memory the very first stage of memory; the point at which information enters the nervous system through the sensory systems.

▲ *Like Brad Williams, the man with the amazing memory described in the opening pages of this chapter, Aurelian Hayman has been diagnosed with hyperthymesia.*

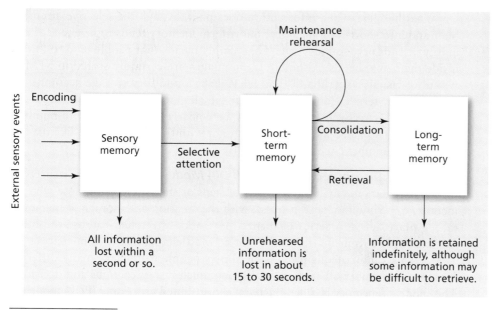

FIGURE 23.1 Three-Stage Process of Memory
Information enters through the sensory system, briefly registering in sensory memory. Selective attention moves the information into short-term memory, where it is held while attention (rehearsal) continues. If the information receives enough rehearsal, it will enter and be stored in long-term memory.

*comprehensive: all inclusive, covering everything.

**What happens if ▶
the lower brain
centers send the
information on to
the higher centers?**

iconic memory visual sensory memory, lasting only a fraction of a second.

echoic memory the brief memory of something a person has just heard.

short-term memory (STM) the memory system in which information is held for brief periods of time while being used.

selective attention the ability to focus on only one stimulus from among all sensory input.

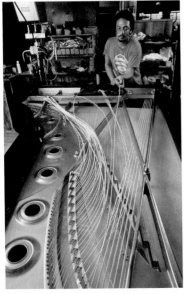

▲ Once these piano strings have been attached to the tuning pins, the piano can be tuned. Tuning a piano requires the use of echoic sensory memory. What other occupations might find a good echoic memory to be an asset?

Icon is the Greek word for "image." When we take in images through the sense of sight, we are using **iconic memory**. Unless we encode an image and move it into our short-term memory, however, iconic memory does not last very long. The capacity of iconic memory is everything that can be seen at one time.

The other type of sensory memory is **echoic memory**, or the brief memory of something a person has heard. A good example of echoic memory is the "What?" phenomenon. You might be reading or concentrating on the television, and your parent, classmate, or friend walks up and says something to you. You sit there for a second or two and then say "What? Oh—yes, I'm ready to eat now," or whatever comment is appropriate. You didn't really process the statement from the other person as he or she said it. You heard it, but your brain didn't interpret it immediately. Echoic memory's capacity is limited to what can be heard at any one moment and is smaller than the capacity of iconic memory, although it lasts longer—about 2 to 4 seconds (Schweickert, 1993).

Short-Term Memory If an incoming sensory message is important enough to enter consciousness, that message will move from sensory memory to the next stage of memory, called **short-term memory (STM)**. Unlike sensory memory, short-term memories are held for up to 30 seconds.

Selective attention is the ability to focus on only one stimulus from among all sensory input (Broadbent, 1958). It is through selective attention that information enters our STM system. A stimulus that is "important" enough (determined by a kind of "pre-analysis" accomplished by the attention centers in the brain stem) will be selected from all of the information in sensory memory to be consciously analyzed for meaning in STM.

It is somewhat difficult to use the selective-attention filter to explain the "*cocktail party effect*" that has been long established in studies of perception and attention (Bronkhorst, 2000; Cherry, 1953; Handel, 1989). If you've ever been at a party where there's a lot of noise and conversations going on in the background but you are able to notice when someone says your name, you have experienced this effect. The areas of the brain that are involved in selective attention were working even though you were not consciously aware of it, and when that important bit of information (your name) appeared, those areas somehow filtered the information to your conscious awareness—in spite of the fact that you were not paying conscious attention to the other background noise (Hopfinger et al., 2000; Mesgarani & Chang, 2012; Stuss et al., 2002).

What happens when information does pass through the selective attention filter and into short-term memory? Short-term memory tends to be encoded primarily in auditory (sound) form. That simply means that people tend to "talk" inside their own heads. Although some images are certainly stored in STM in a kind of visual "sketchpad" (Baddeley, 1986), auditory storage accounts for much of short-term encoding. Research in which participants were asked to recall numbers and letters showed that errors were nearly always made with numbers or letters that sounded like the target but not with those that looked like the target word or number (Acheson et al., 2010; Conrad & Hull, 1964).

The Parallel Distributed Processing (PDP) Model Although many aspects of memory formation may follow a series of steps or stages, there are those who see memory as a simultaneous* process, with the creation and storage of memories taking place across a series of mental networks "stretched" across the brain (McClelland & Rumelhart, 1988; Plaut & McClelland, 2010; Rumelhart et al., 1986). This simultaneous processing allows people to retrieve many different aspects of a memory all at once, facilitating much faster reactions and decisions. This model of memory is called the **parallel distributed processing (PDP) model**.

---

*simultaneous: all at the same time.

The Levels-of-Processing Model The information-processing model assumes that the length of time that a memory will be remembered depends on the stage of memory in which it is stored. Other researchers have proposed that a memory's duration depends on the depth (i.e., the effort made to understand the meaning) to which the information is processed or encoded (Cermak & Craik, 1979; Craik & Lockhart, 1972). If the word *BALL* is flashed on a screen, for example, and people are asked to report whether the word was in capital letters or lowercase, the word itself does not have to be processed very much at all—only its visual characteristics need enter into conscious attention. But if those people were to be asked to use that word in a sentence, they would have to think about what a ball is and how it can be used. This model of memory is called the **levels-of-processing model**.

23.3 Understand strategies for improving the encoding of memory.

Capacity: The Magical Number Seven George Miller (1956) wanted to know how much information humans can hold in short-term memory at any one time (or how many "files" will fit on the "desk"). He reviewed several memory studies, including some using a memory test called the digit-span test, in which a series of numbers is read to subjects in the study who are then asked to recall the numbers in order. Each series gets longer and longer, until the subjects cannot recall any of the numbers in order.

Miller reported that the capacity of STM is about seven chunks or pieces of information, plus or minus two, or from five to nine bits of information. Miller called this the "magical number seven, plus or minus two." So the "desk" isn't really very big and can hold only so many "files." Current research suggests that younger adults can only hold three to five items at a time without using a memory strategy, and if the information consists of long, confusing, or unfamiliar words the capacity is further reduced (Cowan, 2001; Cowan et al., 2005; Palva et al., 2010).

There is a way to "fool" STM into holding more information than is usual. (Think of it as "stacking" related files on the desk.) If the bits of information are combined into meaningful units, or chunks, more information can be held in STM. For instance, if someone were to recode the sequence of numbers "6547893217" as "654-789-3217," instead of 10 bits of information, there would only be three "chunks" that read like a phone number. This process of recoding, or reorganizing, the information is called chunking. To see how well you do at remembering numbers, participate in the *Digit Span* experiment.

Why Do You Think They Call It Short Term? How long is the "short" of short-term memory? Research has shown that short-term memory lasts from about 12 to 30 seconds without rehearsal (Atkinson & Shiffrin, 1968; Brown, 1958; Peterson & Peterson, 1959). After that, the memory seems to rapidly "decay" or disappear.

Most people learn that saying something they want to remember over and over again in their heads, such as repeating a phone number they need just long enough to dial it, can help them remember longer, a process called **maintenance rehearsal**. With maintenance rehearsal, a person is simply continuing to pay attention to the information to be held in memory, and since attention is how that information got into STM in the first place, it works quite well (Atkinson & Shiffrin, 1968; Rundus, 1971). With this type of rehearsal, information will stay in short-term memory until rehearsal stops.

Parallel Distributed Processing (PDP) model a model of memory in which memory processes are proposed to take place at the same time over a large network of neural connections.

levels-of-processing model model of memory that assumes information that is more "deeply processed," or processed according to its meaning rather than just the sound or physical characteristics of the word or words, will be remembered more efficiently and for a longer period of time.

▲ *Each student in the cafeteria is involved in a conversation with others, with dozens of such conversations going on at the same time all around. Yet if a person in another conversation says the name of one of the student in the crowd, that person in the crowd will be able to selectively attend to his or her name. This is known as the "cocktail party effect."*

⊚→ **Participate** in the **Experiment**, *Digit Span*, at **MyPsychLab**

◄ What do you mean by rehearsal? How long can short-term memories last if rehearsal is a factor?

Understand How Memories Are Stored in the Brain

23.4 Describe the roles of working memory and long-term memory.

▲ *It is very important for this pharmacist to count out the number of pills in the prescription accurately. Short-term memory allows her to remember the last number she counted, but if she is interrupted, she will have to start all over again. Short-term memory is very susceptible to interference.*

Working Memory Working memory is an active system that processes the information present in short-term memory. Working memory is thought to consist of three interrelated systems: a central executive (a kind of "CEO" or "Big Boss") that controls and coordinates the other two systems, a visual "sketchpad" of sorts, and a kind of auditory "recorder" (Baddeley, 1986; Baddeley & Hitch, 1974; Baddeley & Larsen, 2007; Engle & Kane, 2004). The central executive acts as interpreter for both the visual and auditory information, and the visual and auditory information are themselves contained in short-term memory. For example, when a person is reading a book, the sketchpad will contain images of the people and events of the particular passage being read, while the recorder "plays" the dialogue in the person's head. The central executive helps interpret the information from both systems and pulls it all together. In a sense, then, short-term memory can be seen as being a part of the working memory system (Acheson et al., 2010; Bayliss et al., 2005; Colom et al., 2006; Kail & Hall, 2001).

Long-Term Memory Long-term memory (LTM) is the system into which all the information is placed to be kept more or less permanently. In terms of capacity, LTM is unlimited (Bahrick, 1984; Barnyard & Grayson, 1996). Think about it: Would there ever really come a time when you could not fit one more piece of information into your head? When you could learn nothing more? There is always room for more information (in spite of what some students may believe).

As for duration, the name *long term* says it all. There is a relatively permanent physical change in the brain itself when a long-term memory is formed. That means that many of the memories people have stored away for a long, long time—even since childhood—may still be there.

23.5 Explain how memory is stored.

Information that is rehearsed long enough may actually find its way into long-term memory. After all, it's how most people learned their Social Security number and the letters of the alphabet (although people cheated a little on the latter by putting the alphabet to music, which makes it easier to retrieve).

Although many long-term memories are encoded as images (think of the *Mona Lisa*), sounds, smells, and tastes (Cowan, 1988), in general LTM is encoded in meaningful form, a kind of mental storehouse of the meanings of words, concepts, and all the events that people want to keep in mind. Even the images, sounds, smells, and tastes involved in these events have some sort of meaning attached to them that gives them

maintenance rehearsal practice of saying information to be remembered over and over in one's head in order to maintain it in short-term memory.

working memory an active system that processes the information in short-term memory.

long-term memory (LTM) the system of memory into which all the information is placed to be kept more or less permanently.

▲ *These students are rehearsing for a concert. They will use maintenance rehearsal (repeating the musical passages over and over) until they can play their parts perfectly. The movements of their fingers upon their instruments will be stored in long-term memory. How is this kind of long-term memory different from something like the memorized lines of one's part in a play?*

enough importance to be stored long term. If STM can be thought of as a working "surface" or desk, then LTM can be thought of as a huge series of filing cabinets behind the desk, in which files are stored in an organized fashion according to meaning. The best way to encode information into LTM in an organized fashion is to make it meaningful through *elaborative rehearsal.*

23.6 Learn strategies for improving the storage of memories.

Elaborative Rehearsal **Elaborative rehearsal** is a way of transferring information from STM into LTM by making that information meaningful in some way (Postman, 1975). The easiest way to do this is to connect new information with something that is already well known (Craik & Lockhart, 1972; Harris & Qualls, 2000; Postman, 1975). For example, the French word *maison* means "house." "*Maison* sounds like masons, and masons build houses." That makes the meaning of the word tie in with something the person already knows (masons, who lay stone or bricks to build houses) and helps in remembering the French term.

Types of Long-Term Information Long-term memories include general facts and knowledge, personal facts, and even skills that can be performed. Memory for skills is called *nondeclarative (implicit) memory* (also called procedural memory) because it usually involves a series of steps or procedures; memory for facts is called *declarative (explicit) memory* because facts are things that are known and can be declared (stated outright). These two types of long-term memory are quite different, as the following sections will explain.

Nondeclarative (Implicit) LTM Memories for skills that people know how to do, like tying shoes and riding a bicycle, are a kind of LTM called **nondeclarative (implicit) memory.** Nondeclarative memories also include emotional associations, habits, and simple conditioned reflexes that may or may not be in conscious awareness, which are often very strong memories. Referring back to Chapter Two, we will recall that the amygdala is the most probable location for emotional associations, such as fear, and the cerebellum in the hindbrain is responsible for storage of memories of conditioned responses, skills, and habits (Debiec et al., 2010; Squire et al., 1993).

Nondeclarative memories are not easily retrieved into conscious awareness. Have you ever tried to tell someone how to tie shoes without using your hands to show them? Such knowledge is in people's memories because they use this information, but they are often not consciously aware of this knowledge (Roediger, 1990). Conscious memories for events in childhood, on the other hand, are usually considered to be a different kind of long-term memory called declarative memory.

Declarative (Explicit) LTM Nondeclarative memory is about the things that people can *do,* but **declarative (explicit) memory** is about all the things that people can *know*—the facts and information that make up knowledge. People know things such as the names of the planets in the solar system, that adding two and two makes four, and that a noun is the name of a person, place, or thing— all facts that are readily available to anyone who wants to learn them. People can also know more personal facts and other facts that are not readily available to others. Therefore, there are two types of declarative long-term memories, *semantic* and *episodic* (Nyberg & Tulving, 1996).

General knowledge that anyone has the ability to know and that is often learned in school or by reading is called **semantic memory.** The word *semantic* refers to meaning, so this kind of knowledge is the awareness of the meanings of words, concepts, and terms as well as names of objects, math skills, and so on. This is also the type of knowledge that is used on game shows such as *Jeopardy.*

elaborative rehearsal a method of transferring information from STM into LTM by making that information meaningful in some way.

nondeclarative (implicit) memory type of long-term memory including memory for skills, procedures, habits, and conditioned responses. These memories are not conscious but are implied to exist because they affect conscious behavior.

declarative (explicit) memory type of long-term memory containing information that is conscious and known.

◄ I can remember a lot of stuff from my childhood. Some of it I learned in school and some of it is more personal, like the first day of school. Are these two different kinds of long-term memories?

▲ *This woman must hold the phone number she is reading in short-term memory long enough to dial it on her phone.*

semantic memory type of declarative memory containing general knowledge, such as knowledge of language and information learned in formal education.

episodic memory type of declarative memory containing personal information not readily available to others, such as daily activities and events.

semantic network model model of memory organization that assumes information is stored in the brain in a connected fashion, with concepts that are related stored physically closer to each other than concepts that are not highly related.

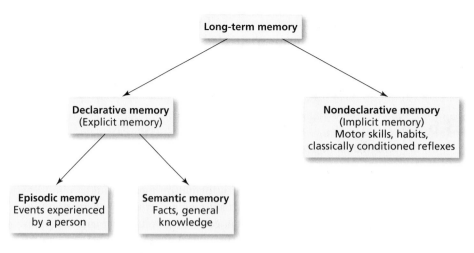

FIGURE 23.2 Types of Long-Term Memories
Long-term memory can be divided into declarative memories, which are factual and typically conscious (explicit) memories, and nondeclarative memories, which are skills, habits, and conditioned responses that are typically unconscious (implicit). Declarative memories are further divided into episodic memories (personal experiences) and semantic memories (general knowledge).

▲ Nondeclarative knowledge, such as tying one's shoes, often must be learned by doing, as it is difficult to put into words. Once this child learns how to tie shoes, the knowledge will always be there to retrieve.

Semantic memories, like nondeclarative memories, are relatively permanent. But it is possible to "lose the way to" this kind of memory, as discussed in the section on forgetting.

The other kind of factual memory is the personal knowledge that each person has of his or her daily life and personal history, a kind of autobiographical* memory (LePort et al., 2012). Memories of what has happened to people each day, certain birthdays, anniversaries that were particularly special, childhood events, and so on are called **episodic memory** because they represent episodes from their lives. Unlike nondeclarative and semantic long-term memories, episodic memories tend to be updated and revised more or less constantly. You can probably remember what you had for breakfast today, but what you had for breakfast two years ago on this date is most likely a mystery. Episodic memories that are especially *meaningful*, such as the memory of the first day of school or your first date, are more likely to be kept in LTM (although they may not be as exact as people sometimes assume they are).

Episodic and semantic memories are *explicit memories* because they are easily made conscious and brought from long-term storage into short-term memory. For a look at the connections among all these types of LTM, see **Figure 23.2**.

Long-Term Memory Organization As stated before, LTM has to be fairly well organized for retrieval to be so quick. Can you remember the name of your first-grade teacher? If you can, how long did it take you to pull that name out of LTM and "put it on the desk" of STM? It probably took hardly any time at all. One way to look at how LTM is organized it to think of it as network with nodes (focal points) of related information linked to each other in a hierarchy. To verify the statement "a canary is a bird" requires moving to only one node, but "a canary is an animal" would require moving through two nodes (first birds and then animals) and should take longer. This difference in the length of time to process the information led to the development of the **semantic network model**, which assumes that information is stored in the brain in a connected fashion (Collins & Quillian, 1969).

---

*autobiographical: the story of a person's life as told by that person.

Pick the best answer.

1. Tayvyn has just finished his essay test and handed it in. As he walks out of the classroom, he realizes that there were a few more things he should have included in the essay. Tayvyn's problem is in the memory process of
   a. encoding.
   b. storage.
   c. retrieval
   d. retention

2. Which type of memory is most likely used to remember names of people whom you have just met at a social gathering?
   a. procedural memory
   b. implicit memory
   c. short-term memory
   d. long-term memory

3. Azaylee learned her multiplication tables by repeating them over and over until she had them memorized. Azaylee was using which kind of rehearsal?
   a. repetitive
   b. imagery
   c. elaborative
   d. maintenance

4. Of the following, which is the most similar to the concept of long-term memory?
   a. a revolving door
   b. a filing cabinet
   c. a desk top
   d. a computer keyboard

5. Long-term memories are encoded in terms of
   a. sounds.
   b. visual images.
   c. meanings of words and concepts.
   d. all of the above.

6. Which type of LTM is seldom, if ever, lost by people with Alzheimer's disease?
   a. procedural
   b. semantic
   c. episodic
   d. state dependent

7. In the game show *Who Wants to Be a Millionaire?* contestants are asked an increasingly difficult series of questions about general information. The type of memory needed to access the answers to these kinds of questions is
   a. procedural.
   b. semantic.
   c. episodic.
   d. working.

8. The Internet, with its series of links from one site to many others, is a good analogy for the organization of
   a. short-term memory.
   b. episodic memory.
   c. long-term memory.
   d. procedural memory.

9. When Lux studies her psychology terms, she tries to tie each concept into something she already knows. She thinks about the meaning of the concept rather than just saying the words over and over. Which of the following best explains Lux's approach to encoding memories?
   a. information-processing model
   b. levels-of-processing model
   c. selective attention
   d. maintenance rehearsal

10. Which of the following is responsible for the "cocktail party effect," in which Zade was able to hear someone say his name, even when there was a lot of background noise?
    a. working memory
    b. episodic memory
    c. selective attention
    d. elaborative rehearsal

Module Goal

Learn how memories are retrieved from the brain.

Learning Objectives

24.1 Explain the importance of retrieval cues in memory.

24.2 Explain how memories can change.

24.3 Explain why we forget and how we can improve memory retrieval.

24.4 Discuss interference and other factors that influence how memories are retrieved.

24.5 Describe types of memory and memory disorders.

---

retrieval cue a stimulus for remembering.

encoding specificity the tendency for memory of information to be improved if related information (such as surroundings or physiological state) available when the memory is first formed is also available when the memory is being retrieved.

▲ When this bride and groom dance together later on in their marriage, they will be able to recall this moment at their wedding and the happiness they felt at that time. State-dependent learning makes it easier for people to recall information stored while in a particular emotional state (such as the happiness of this couple) if the recall occurs in a similar emotional state.

Learn How Memories Are Retrieved from the Brain

24.1 Explain the importance of retrieval cues in memory.

Oddly enough, most people's problems with getting information stored in LTM back out again has to do with *how* they put that information *into* LTM.

Retrieval Cues Remember the previous discussions about maintenance rehearsal and elaborative rehearsal? One of the main reasons that maintenance rehearsal is not a very good way to get information into LTM is that saying something over and over only gives one kind of **retrieval cue** (a stimulus for remembering), the sound of the word or phrase. When people try to remember a piece of information by thinking of what it means and how it fits in with what they already know, they are giving themselves cues for meaning in addition to sound. The more cues stored with a piece of information, the easier the retrieval of that information will be (Roediger, 2000; Roediger & Guynn, 1996).

Although most people would assume that cues for retrieval would have to be directly related to the concepts being studied, the fact is that almost anything in one's surroundings is capable of becoming a cue. Researchers have found strong evidence for the concept of **encoding specificity**, the tendency for memory of any kind of information to be improved if retrieval conditions are similar to the conditions under which the information was encoded (Tulving & Thomson, 1973). These conditions, or cues, can be internal or external. *Context-dependent learning* may refer to the physical surroundings a person is in when they are learning specific information. For example, encoding specificity would predict that the best place to take one's chemistry test is in the same room in which you learned the material.

Physical surroundings at the time of encoding a memory are not the only kinds of cues that can help in retrieval. In another form of encoding specificity called *state-dependent learning*, memories formed during a particular physiological or psychological state will be easier to remember while in a similar state. For example, when you are arguing with someone, it's much easier to remember all of the bad things that person has done than to remember the good times.

Improving Memory Retrieval When we store information in LTM, there's no guarantee that we'll be able to retrieve that information again easily through either recognition or recall. We can, however, use strategies and memory "tricks" to help us remember information more effectively. These strategies are called *mnemonic devices,* or simply **mnemonics**, from the Greek word for memory. Examples of mnemonic devices include the following:

▲ *The results of the Godden and Baddeley (1975) study indicated the retrieval of words learned while underwater was higher when the retrieval also took place underwater. Similarly, words learned while out of the water (on land) were retrieved at a higher rate out of the water.*

- *Acronyms* are easy-to-remember words that abbreviate a longer term; for example, NASA is an acronym for the <u>N</u>ational <u>A</u>eronautical and <u>S</u>pace <u>A</u>dministration.
- *Acrostics* are sentences used to remember something. For example, to remember the oceans, you could use the acrostic "<u>I</u> <u>A</u>m <u>A</u> <u>P</u>erson," with each letter standing for the first letter of the corresponding oceans: <u>I</u>ndian, <u>A</u>rctic, <u>A</u>tlantic, and <u>P</u>acific.
- *Linking*, also sometimes called the Story Method, involves making a list to remember items that are linked together. For example, if you are trying to remember that you need to pick up milk, bread, and cat food on the way home from school, you might make up a story about "the hungry cat who drank the milk and ate the bread, because she had no food."
- *Rhythmic devices* organize information in a rhyming or rhythmic song or pattern. Remember when you learned to your ABCs by singing the alphabet song? Little did you know you were using a mnemonic device!

24.2 Explain how memories can change.

Recall and Recognition There are two kinds of retrieval of memories, *recall* and *recognition*. It is the difference between these two retrieval methods that makes some kinds of exams seem harder than others. In **recall**, memories are retrieved with few or no external cues, such as filling in the blanks on an application form. **Recognition**, on the other hand, involves looking at or hearing information and matching it to what is already in memory. A word-search puzzle, in which the words are already written down in the grid and simply need to be circled, is an example of recognition. The following section takes a closer look at these two important processes.

Recall: Hmm...Let Me Think When someone is asked a question such as "Where were you born?" the question acts as the cue for retrieval of the answer. This is an example of recall, as are essay question, short-answer, and fill-in-the-blank tests that are used to measure a person's memory for information (Borges et al., 1977; Gillund & Shiffrin, 1984; Raaijmakers & Shiffrin, 1992).

Whenever people find themselves struggling for an answer, recall has failed (at least temporarily). Sometimes the answer seems so very close to the surface of conscious thought that it feels like it's "on the tip of the tongue." (If people could just get their tongues out there far enough, they could read it.) This is

Why do multiple-choice tests seem so much easier than essay tests?

mnemonics strategies and memory "tricks" to help us remember information more effectively.

recall type of memory retrieval in which the information to be retrieved must be "pulled" from memory with very few external cues.

recognition the ability to match a piece of information or a stimulus to a stored image or fact.

sometimes called the *tip of the tongue (TOT)* phenomenon (Brown & McNeill, 1966; Burke et al., 1991). Although people may be able to say how long the word is or name letters that start or even end the word, they cannot retrieve the sound or actual spelling of the word. Another interesting feature of recall is that it is often subject to a kind of "prejudice" of memory retrieval, in which information at the beginning and the end of a list, such as a poem or song, tends to be remembered more easily and accurately. This is called the **serial position effect** (Murdock, 1962).

A good demonstration of this phenomenon involves instructing people to listen to and try to remember words that are read to them that are spaced about 4 or 5 seconds apart. People typically use maintenance rehearsal by repeating each word in their heads. They are then asked to write as many of the words down as they can remember. If the frequency of recall for each word in the list is graphed, it will nearly always look like the graph in **Figure 24.1**. To try this demonstration for yourself, participate in the *Serial Position Effect* experiment.

Words at the very beginning of the list tend to be remembered better than those in the middle of the list. This effect is called the **primacy effect** and is due to the fact that the first few words, when the listener has nothing already in STM to interfere with their rehearsal, will receive far more rehearsal time than the words in the middle, which are constantly being replaced by the next word on the list (Craik, 1970; Murdock, 1962).

@ Participate in the **Experiment,** *Serial Position Effect,* at **MyPsychLab**

▲ *These people are waiting to audition for a play. The person who auditioned first and the one who auditioned last have the greatest chance of being remembered when the time comes for the director to choose. The serial position effect will cause the impression made by the actors who come in the "middle" to be less memorable.*

serial position effect tendency of information at the beginning and end of a body of information to be remembered more accurately than information in the middle of the body of information.

primacy effect tendency to remember information at the beginning of a body of information better than the information that follows.

recency effect tendency to remember information at the end of a body of information better than the information at the beginning of it.

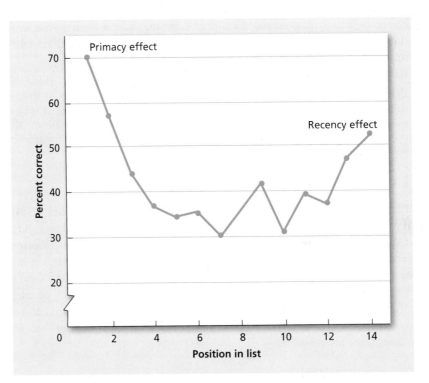

FIGURE 24.1 Serial Position Effect
In the serial position effect, information at the beginning of a list will be recalled at a higher rate than information in the middle of the list (primacy effect), because the beginning information receives more rehearsal and may enter LTM. Information at the end of a list is also retrieved at a higher rate (recency effect) because the end of the list is still in STM, with no information coming after it to interfere with retrieval.

At the end of the graph there is another increase in recall. This is the **recency effect**; it is usually attributed to the fact that the last word or two was *just heard* and is still in short-term memory for easy retrieval, with no new words entering to "push" the most recent word or words out of memory (Bjork & Whitten, 1974; Murdock, 1962).

Recognition: Hey, Don't I Know You from Somewhere?

The other form of memory retrieval is *recognition*, the ability to match a piece of information or a stimulus to a stored image or fact (Borges et al., 1977; Gillund & Shiffrin, 1984; Raaijmakers & Shiffrin, 1992). Recognition is usually much easier than recall because the cue is the actual object, word, sound, and so on that one is simply trying to detect as familiar and known. Examples of tests that use recognition are multiple-choice, matching, and true–false tests. The answer is right there and simply has to be matched to the information already in memory.

Recognition tends to be very accurate for images, especially human faces. Recognition isn't foolproof, however. Sometimes there is just enough similarity between a stimulus that is not already in memory and one that is in memory so that a *false positive* occurs (Muter, 1978). Eyewitness recognition can be especially prone to false positives, although most people seem to think that "seeing is believing." For more about the problems with eyewitnesses, see the following Classic Studies in Psychology feature.

Classic Studies in Psychology

Elizabeth Loftus and Eyewitnesses

▲ *Dr. Elizabeth Loftus is an internationally known expert on the accuracy of eyewitness testimony. She is often called on to testify in court cases.*

Elizabeth Loftus is a Distinguished Professor of Social Ecology, a Professor of Law, and a Professor of Cognitive Science at the University of California in Irvine. One of the world's leading memory researchers, her focus has been on the accuracy of recall of memories—or rather, the inaccuracies of memory retrieval. She has been an expert witness at more than 200 trials, including that of Ted Bundy, the serial killer who was finally executed in Florida (Neimark, 1996).

Loftus and many others have demonstrated time and again that memory is not an unchanging, stable process but rather is a constantly changing one. People continually update and revise their memories of events without being aware that they are doing so, and they incorporate information gained after the actual event, whether correct or incorrect.

flashbulb memories type of automatic encoding that occurs because an unexpected event has strong emotional associations for the person remembering it.

In one classic experiment, Loftus (1975) showed subjects a 3-minute video clip taken from the movie *Diary of a Student Revolution*. In this clip, eight demonstrators run into a classroom and eventually leave after interrupting the professor's lecture in a noisy confrontation. At the end of the video, two questionnaires were distributed containing one key question and 90 "filler" questions. The key question for half of the subjects was, "Was the leader of the four demonstrators who entered the classroom a male?" The other half was asked, "Was the leader of the twelve demonstrators who entered the classroom a male?" One week later, a new set of questions was given to all subjects in which the key question was, "How many demonstrators did you see entering the classroom?" Subjects who were previously asked the question incorrectly giving the number as "four" stated an average recall of 6.4 people, whereas those who read the question incorrectly giving the number as "twelve" recalled an average of 8.9 people. Loftus concluded that subjects were trying to compromise the memory of what they had actually seen—eight demonstrators—with later information. This study, along with many others, clearly demonstrates the heart of Loftus's research: What people see and hear about an event after the fact can easily affect the accuracy of their memories of that event.

Questions for Further Discussion

1. How might police officers taking statements about a crime avoid getting inaccurate information from eyewitnesses?
2. The Innocence Project (www.innocenceproject.org) helps prisoners prove their innocence through DNA testing. More than 300 people in the United States have been freed by this testing, and the average time they served in prison before release is 13 years. Is eyewitness testimony enough, or should DNA evidence be required for sending someone to prison?

Automatic Encoding: Flashbulb Memories Although some long-term memories need extensive maintenance rehearsal or effortful encoding in the form of elaborative rehearsal to enter from STM into LTM, many other kinds of long-term memories seem to enter permanent storage with little or no effort at all, in a kind of *automatic encoding* (Kvavilashvili et al., 2009; Mandler, 1967; Schneider et al., 1984).

A special kind of automatic encoding takes place when an unexpected event or episode in a person's life has strong emotional associations, such as fear, horror, or joy. Memories of highly emotional events can often seem vivid and detailed, as if the person's mind took a "flash picture" of the moment in time. These kinds of memories are called **flashbulb memories** (Neisser, 1982; Neisser & Harsch, 1992; Winningham et al., 2000).

While there is evidence for a high degree of accuracy in flashbulb memories of *major events*, research reveals that flashbulb memories are just as subject to decay and alterations over time as other kinds of memories (Neisser & Harsch, 1992). In fact, memory of highly stressful events such as experiencing a crime have been shown to be less accurate than other memories, as the video *How Stress Affects Memory* explains.

Watch the **Video**, *How Stress Affects Memory*, at **MyPsychLab**

How Reliable Are Our Memories? People tend to assume that their memories are accurate when actually memories are revised, edited, and altered on an almost continuous basis. The reason for the changes that occur in memory has to do with the way in which memories are formed as well as how they are retrieved.

Constructive Processing of Memories Many people have the idea that when they recall a memory, they are recalling it as if it were an "instant replay." As new memories are created in LTM, old memories can get "lost," but they are more likely to be changed or altered in some way (Baddeley, 1988). In reality, memories (including those very vivid flashbulb memories) are never quite accurate, and the more time that passes, the more inaccuracies creep in.

Loftus, along with other researchers (Hyman, 1993; Hyman & Loftus, 1998, 2002), has provided ample evidence for the **constructive processing** view of memory retrieval. In this view, memories are literally "built" from the pieces stored away at encoding. Each time a memory is retrieved, it may be altered or revised in some way to include new information, or details that were there at encoding may be left out of the new retrieval.

An example of how memories are reconstructed occurs when people, on learning the details of a particular event, revise their memories to reflect their feeling that they "knew it all along." They will discard any incorrect information they actually had and replace it with more accurate information gained after the fact. This tendency of people to falsely believe that they would have accurately predicted an outcome without having been told about it in advance is called **hindsight bias** (Bahrick et al., 1996; Hoffrage et al., 2000).

Memory Retrieval Problems Some people may say that they have "total recall." What they usually mean is that they feel that their memories are more accurate than those of other people. As should be obvious by now, true total recall is not a very likely ability for anyone to have. Here are some reasons why people have trouble recalling information accurately.

The Misinformation Effect Elizabeth Loftus, in addition to her studies concerning eyewitness testimony, has also done several similar studies that demonstrate the **misinformation effect**. In one study, subjects viewed a slide presentation of a traffic accident. The actual slide presentation contained a stop sign, but in a written summary of the presentation, the sign was referred to as a yield sign. Subjects who were given this misleading information after viewing the slides were far less accurate in their memories for the kind of sign present than were subjects given no such information. One of the interesting points to be made by this study is that information that comes not only after the original event but also in an entirely different format (i.e., written instead of visual) can cause memories of the event to be incorrectly reconstructed.

24.3 Explain why we forget and how we can improve memory retrieval.

Brad Williams, the Human Google of the opening story, seems to have a fairly ◄ normal life despite his unusual memory abilities. But the same has not been true of other people with not only the ability to remember nearly everything, but also the inability to *forget*.

constructive processing referring to the retrieval of memories in which those memories are altered, revised, or influenced by newer information.

hindsight bias the tendency to falsely believe, through revision of older memories to include newer information, that one could have correctly predicted the outcome of an event.

misinformation effect the tendency of misleading information presented after an event to alter the memories of the event itself.

Thinking Critically
Think about the last time you argued with a family member about something that happened when you were younger. How might hindsight bias have played a part in your differing memories of the event?

▲ These teens may engage in "Monday morning quarterbacking" as they apply hindsight to their memories of this game. Their memories of the game may be altered by information they get afterward from the television, newspapers, or their friends.

Why do we forget things? And why do we forget some things but not others?

Ebbinghaus and the Forgetting Curve The video *Jill Price: The Woman Who Cannot Forget* describes the case of a woman who remembers every detail of her life, both the good and the bad.

That is exactly the problem experienced in the case of A. R. Luria's (1968) famous *mnemonist*, Mr. S. (A mnemonist is a memory expert or someone with exceptional memory ability.) He could not easily separate important memories from trivial ones and eventually invented a way to "forget" things—by writing them on a piece of paper and then burning the paper (Luria, 1968).

Hermann Ebbinghaus (1913) was one of the first researchers to study forgetting. Because he did not want any verbal associations to aid him in remembering, he created several lists of "nonsense syllables," pronounceable but meaningless (such as GEX and WOL). He memorized a list, waited a specific amount of time, and then tried to retrieve the list, graphing his results each time. The result has become a familiar graph: the **curve of forgetting**. This graph clearly shows that forgetting happens quickly within the first hour after learning the lists and then tapers off gradually. (See **Figure 24.2**.) In other words, forgetting is greatest just after learning. This curve can be applied to other types of information as well. Although meaningful material is forgotten much more slowly and much less completely, the pattern obtained when testing for forgetting is similar (Conway et al., 1992).

In his early studies, Ebbinghaus (1885) found that it is also important not to try to "cram" information you want to remember into your brain. Research has found that spacing out one's study sessions, or **distributed practice**, will produce far better retrieval of information studied in this way than does *massed practice*, or the attempt to study a body of material all at once (Cepeda et al., 2006; Dempster & Farris, 1990; Donovan & Radosevich, 1999; Simon & Bjork, 2001).

▲ As this young woman observes the activity outside the window, she is storing some of the things she sees into memory while ignoring others. If she were to witness a crime, how would investigators know if her memories of the events were accurate or not? Would hypnotizing her help her remember more effective? Why or why not?

👁 **Watch** the **Video**, *Jill Price: The Woman Who Cannot Forget*, at **MyPsychLab**

curve of forgetting a graph showing a distinct pattern in which forgetting is very fast within the first hour after learning a list and then tapers off gradually.

distributed practice spacing the study of material to be remembered by including breaks between study periods.

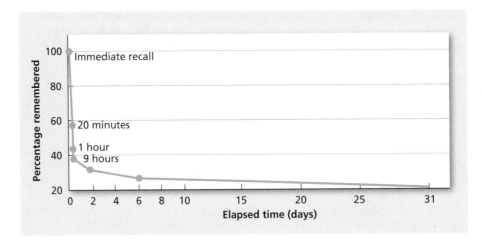

FIGURE 24.2 Curve of Forgetting
Ebbinghaus found that his recall of words from his memorized word lists was greatest immediately after learning the list but rapidly decreased within the first hour. After the first hour, forgetting leveled off.

24.4 Discuss interference and other factors that influence how memories are retrieved.

There are several reasons why people forget things. We'll examine three theories here.

Encoding Failure One of the simplest reasons that people forget is that some things never get encoded in the first place. Your friend, for example, may have said something to you as he walked out the door, and you may have heard him, but if you weren't paying attention to what he said, it would not get past sensory memory. This isn't forgetting so much as it is **encoding failure**, the failure to process information into memory. Researchers (Nickerson & Adams, 1979) developed a test of long-term memory using images of a common object for many people, a stop sign. Look at **Figure 24.3**. Which view of a stop sign is the correct one? People see stop signs every day, but how many people actually look at them that closely so the information is encoded into long-term memory?

Memory Trace Decay Theory One of the older theories of forgetting involves the concept of a **memory trace**. A memory trace is some physical change in the brain, perhaps in a neuron or in the activity between neurons, which occurs when a memory is formed (Brown, 1958; Peterson & Peterson, 1959). Over time, if these traces are not used, they may **decay**, fading into nothing. It would be similar to what happens when a number of people walk across a particular patch of grass, causing a path to appear in which the grass is trampled down and perhaps turning brown. But if people stop using the path, the grass grows back and the path disappears.

▲ The fact that this woman can remember the things shown in the pictures even after many years makes it unlikely that disuse of memory can explain all forgetting in long-term memory.

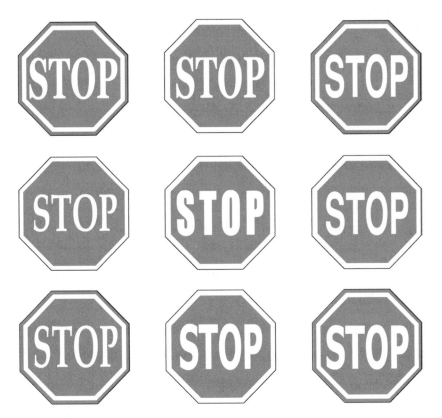

FIGURE 24.3 Stop!
Many people look at stop signs multiple times a day. Which of these stop signs is closest to an actual stop sign? The answer can be found on the next page.

encoding failure failure to process information into memory.

memory trace physical change in the brain that occurs when a memory is formed.

decay loss of memory due to the passage of time, during which the memory trace is not used.

proactive interference memory problem that occurs when older information prevents or interferes with the learning or retrieval of newer information.

Forgetting in sensory memory (decay) and short-term memory (displacement) seems easy to explain: Information that is not brought to attention in sensory memory or continuously rehearsed in STM will fade away. But are these a good explanation for forgetting from long-term memory? When referring to LTM, forgetting (retrieval failure) is usually called *disuse*, and the phrase "use it or lose it" takes on great meaning (Bjork & Bjork, 1992). Although the fading of information from LTM through disuse sounds logical, often people can recall memories they had assumed were long forgotten. There must be other factors involved in the forgetting of long-term memories.

Interference Theory A possible explanation of LTM forgetting is that although most long-term memories may be stored more or less permanently in the brain, those memories may not always be accessible to attempted retrieval because other information interferes (Anderson & Neely, 1995). An analogy might be this: The can of paint that Phillip wants may very well be on some shelf in his storeroom, but there's so much other junk in its way that he can't see it and can't get to it. In the case of LTM, interference can come from two different "directions."

The answer to Figure 24.3 is the middle right image.

Proactive Interference Have you ever switched from driving a car with the gearshift on the steering wheel to one with the gearshift on the floor of the car? If the answer is yes, you probably found that you had some trouble when you first got into the new car. You may have grabbed at the wheel instead of reaching to the gearshift on the floor. The reason you reached for the gearshift in the "old" place is called **proactive interference**: the tendency for older or previously learned material to interfere with the learning (and subsequent retrieval) of new material. (See **Figure 24.4**.)

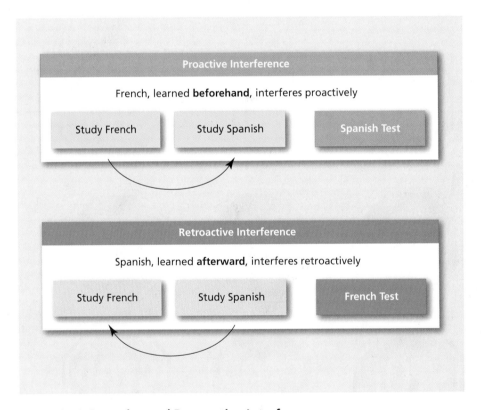

FIGURE 24.4 Proactive and Retroactive Interference
If a student were to study for a French exam and then a Spanish exam, interference could occur in two directions. When taking the Spanish exam, the French information studied first may proactively interfere with learning of the Spanish information. But when taking the French exam, the more recently studied Spanish information may retroactively interfere with the retrieval of the French information.

Retroactive Interference When newer information interferes with the retrieval of older information, this is called **retroactive interference**. (See Figure 24.4.) What happens when you change back from the car with the gearshift on the floor to the older car with the gearshift on the wheel? You'll probably reach down to the floor at least once or twice because the newer skill retroactively interferes with remembering the old way of doing it.

How might interference work in each of the following cases?

1. Moving from the United States to England, where people drive on the left instead of the right side of the road.

2. Trying to remember your old cell phone number after having the new one for a year.

24.5 Describe types of memory and memory disorders.

When Memory Fails: Organic Amnesia Problems in the functioning of the memory areas of the brain cause two forms of severe loss of memory disorders. These problems can result from concussions, brain injuries brought about by trauma, alcoholism (Korsakoff's syndrome), or disorders of the aging brain.

Retrograde Amnesia If the hippocampus is that important to the formation of memories, what would happen if it got temporarily "disconnected"? People who are in accidents in which they received a head injury often are unable to recall the accident itself. Sometimes they cannot remember the last several hours or even days before the accident. This type of amnesia (literally, "without memory") is called **retrograde amnesia**, which is loss of memory from the point of injury backward (Hodges, 1994). What apparently happens in this kind of memory loss is that the consolidation process, which was busy making the physical changes to allow new memories to be stored, gets disrupted and loses everything that was not already nearly "finished." It's similar to what happens when a computer's power goes out: Whatever you were working on that was not yet saved is gone.

Anterograde Amnesia Concussions can also cause a more temporary version of the kind of amnesia experienced by H. M. This kind of amnesia is called **anterograde amnesia**, or the loss of memories from the point of injury or illness forward (Squire & Slater, 1978). People with this kind of amnesia, like H. M., have difficulty remembering anything new. This is also the kind of amnesia most often seen in people with *senile dementia*, a mental disorder in which severe forgetfulness, mental confusion, and mood swings are the primary symptoms. (Dementia patients also may suffer from retrograde amnesia in addition to anterograde amnesia.) If retrograde amnesia is like losing a document in the computer because of a power loss, anterograde amnesia is like discovering that your hard drive has become defective—you can read data that are already on the hard drive, but you can't store any new information.

▲ *Major league baseball outfielder Johnny Damon (seen here colliding with player Damian Jackson) suffered a concussion after this injury. Concussions such as this can "wipe out" whatever was in the process of being consolidated into long-term memory. Which type of amnesia would you expect Johnny Damon to have, retrograde or anterograde?*

retroactive interference memory retrieval problem that occurs when newer information prevents or interferes with the retrieval of older information.

retrograde amnesia loss of memory from the point of some injury or trauma backward, or loss of memory for the past.

anterograde amnesia loss of memory from the point of injury or trauma forward, or the inability to form new long-term memories.

Pick the best answer.

1. Collin is asked to repeat what his dad just told him. He says he "forgot" but in reality Collin wasn't paying attention to his dad at all. This is an example of the _____ explanation of forgetting.

    a. interference
    b. memory trace
    c. encoding failure
    d. repression

2. McKenya can remember the name of the first person she was introduced to at Cody's party, and she can remember the names of the last two people she met, but the names of the dozen or so people in between are gone. This is an example of the

    a. encoding specificity effect.
    b. serial position effect.
    c. tip-of-the-tongue effect.
    d. primacy effect.

3. This quiz question, as well as the other quiz questions, makes use of which form of retrieval of memories?

    a. rehearsal
    b. recency
    c. recall
    d. recognition

4. Alisha has just finished learning a list of nonsense words given to her by her psychology instructor as part of a class activity. She had 100 percent recall at the end of class. According to Ebbinghaus's curve of forgetting, how quickly will Alisha likely forget about 40 percent of the information she has just learned?

    a. within the first 20 minutes after leaving the class
    b. within the first day after leaving the class
    c. nearly a week after the class
    d. nearly a month after the class

5. Which of the following statements about flashbulb memories is FALSE?

    a. They may be formed by the hormones released during emotional moments.
    b. They are usually vivid and detailed.
    c. They are unusually accurate.
    d. They can be of a personal nature or concern world events.

6. The phenomenon of hindsight bias is an example of the _____ view of long-term memory retrieval.

    a. instant replay
    b. constructive processing
    c. levels-of-processing
    d. curve of forgetting

7. In Loftus's 1978 study, subjects viewed a slide presentation of an accident. Later, some of the subjects were asked a question about a yield sign when the actual slides contained pictures of a stop sign. When these same subjects were later asked about what kind of sign was at the accident, they were very likely to be confused. This is an example of

    a. constructive processing.
    b. encoding failure.
    c. the serial position effect.
    d. the misinformation effect.

8. Lexi spent a year living abroad in Spain. During that time, her ability to read and speak Spanish grew tremendously. However, now, two years later, Lexi feels she can no longer travel there because she can barely remember a thing. Her problem is most likely due to

    a. encoding failure.
    b. retroactive interference.
    c. proactive interference.
    d. decay theory.

9. Noah went from the United States, where he grew up, to England. The first week he was there, he had a terrible time remembering to drive on the left side of the road. His problem was most likely due to

    a. encoding failure.
    b. retroactive interference.
    c. proactive interference.
    d. the curve of forgetting.

10. Taylor was in a car accident and suffered a concussion. After he recovered, he found that he could not remember the accident itself or the events of the morning leading up to the accident. Taylor had

    a. retrograde amnesia.
    b. anterograde amnesia.
    c. Alzheimer's disease.
    d. encoding failure.

Listen to an **Audio File** of your chapter at **MyPsychLab**

Module 23: Encoding and Storage

Explain how the brain encodes memories.

23.1 Explain how memories are encoded.
- Memory can be defined as an active system that receives information from the senses, organizes and alters it as it stores it away, and then retrieves the information from storage.
- The three processes are encoding, storage, and retrieval.

23.2 Characterize the different levels of processing.
- In the levels-of-processing model of memory, information that gets more deeply processed is more likely to be remembered.
- In the parallel distributed processing model of memory, information is simultaneously stored across an interconnected neural network that stretches across the brain.
- Iconic memory is the visual sensory memory in which an afterimage or icon will be held in neural form for about one-fourth to one-half second.
- Echoic memory is the auditory form of sensory memory and takes the form of an echo that lasts up to 4 seconds.

23.3 Understand strategies for improving the encoding of memory.
- Short-term memory is where information is held while it is conscious and being used. It holds about seven plus or minus two chunks of information and lasts about 30 seconds without rehearsal.

Understand how memories are stored in the brain.

23.4 Describe the roles of working memory and long-term memory.
- Working memory is an active system responsible for processing the information in STM.

23.5 Explain how memory is stored.
- Information is stored in LTM as implicit and explicit memories. Implicit memories include skills, habits, and emotional associations. Explicit memories include facts and experiences.

23.6 Learn strategies for improving the storage of memories.
- Mnemonic devices like acronyms can be used it improve memory recall.

Module 24: Retrieval and Retrieval Failure

Learn how memories are retrieved from the brain.

24.1 Explain the importance of retrieval cues in memory.
- Recall is a type of memory retrieval in which the information to be retrieved must be "pulled" out of memory with few or no cues, whereas recognition involves matching information with stored images or facts.
- The serial position effect, or primacy or recency effect, occurs when the first items and the last items in a list of information are recalled more efficiently than items in the middle of the list.

24.2 Explain how memories can change.

Classic Studies in Psychology: Elizabeth Loftus and Eyewitnesses
- Loftus and others have found that people constantly update and revise their memories of events.

24.3 Explain why we forget and how we can improve memory retrieval.
- Information that is not brought to attention in sensory memory or rehearsed in STM will fade away. Over time, memory traces that are not used may decay. Other information can interfere with the retrieval of information from LTM.

24.4 Discuss interference and other factors that influence how memories are retrieved.
- Some "forgetting" is actually a failure to encode information.
- Memory trace decay theory assumes the presence of a physical memory trace that decays with disuse over time.
- Forgetting in LTM is most likely due to proactive or retroactive interference.

24.5 Describe types of memory and memory disorders.
- In retrograde amnesia, memory for the past (prior to the injury) is lost, which can be a loss of only minutes or a loss of several years.
- In anterograde amnesia, memory for anything new becomes impossible, although old memories may still be retrievable.

Vocabulary Terms

encoding p. 288
memory p. 288
retrieval p. 288
storage p. 288
sensory memory p. 289
information processing model p. 289
short term memory p. 290
echoic memory p. 290
selective attention p. 290
iconic memory p. 290
parallel distributed processing (PDP) p. 291

levels-of-processing model p. 291
long term memory p. 292
maintenance rehearsal p. 292
working memory p. 292
declarative (explicit) memory p. 293
nondeclarative (implicit) memory p. 293
elaborative rehearsal p. 293
episodic memory p. 294
semantic memory p. 294
semantic network model p. 294

encoding specificity p. 296
retrieval cue p. 296
recall p. 297
recognition p. 297
mnemonics p. 297
serial position effect p. 298
recency effect p. 298
primacy effect p. 298
flashbulb memories p. 300
constructive processing p. 301
misinformation effect p. 301
hindsight bias p. 301

distributed practice p. 302
curve of forgetting p. 302
decay p. 303
encoding failure p. 303
memory trace p. 303
proactive interference p. 304
anterograde amnesia p. 305
retroactive interference p. 305
retrograde amnesia p. 305

Study and Review at **MyPsychLab**

Vocabulary Review

Match each vocabulary term to its definition.

1. memory
2. sensory memory
3. declarative memory
4. serial position effect
5. flashbulb memory
6. primacy effect
7. curve of forgetting
8. retroactive interference
9. retrograde amnesia
10. autobiographical memory

a. The point at which information enters the nervous system through the sensory systems.
b. Memory that seems to enter permanent storage with little or no effort at all.
c. A graph showing a distinct pattern in which forgetting is very fast within the first hour after learning a list and then tapers off gradually.
d. Type of long-term memory containing information that is conscious and known.
e. A system that receives information from the senses, puts that information into a usable form, and organizes it as it stores it away, and then retrieves the information from storage.
f. The memory for events and facts related to one's personal life story.
g. Tendency of information at the beginning and end of a body of information to be remembered more accurately than information in the middle of the body of information.
h. Memory retrieval problem that occurs when newer information prevents or interferes with the retrieval of older information.
i. Loss of memory for the past.
j. Remembering words at the very beginning of the list better than those in the middle of the list.

Psychology Project

Is it easier to remember information that is only seen, only heard, or seen and heard?

Materials:
- a group of five or more subjects
- a list of 20 random words
- an audio recording of an additional 20 random words
- an audiovisual presentation (such as a PowerPoint) of an additional 20 random words
- pencils and paper

Instructions:
1. Distribute paper and pencils to subjects.
2. Distribute the list of 20 words to subjects. Lists should be typed in a column so that the words are clearly legible. Allow subjects to study the words for 2 minutes and then ask subjects to write down all of the words they remember from the list.
3. After 5 minutes or so, play the audio recording of 20 words. After subjects have heard the list, ask them to write down the words they remember.
4. After a second 5-minute break, play the audiovisual presentation and then ask subjects to write down the words that they remember.
5. Analyze the results and look for patterns. Were subjects able to remember more words in visual (written), audio, or audiovisual format? Did subjects experience proactive interference by the time they were exposed to the third list? Write a summary of your findings, and create a graph of your results.

Tech Alternative

You and a partner will each write a list of the names of ten people that you have on your cell phone's call list. (Make sure there are no duplicate names between the lists.) Without checking your phone, write as much as you can remember of the phone numbers for the ten people on your list.

Trade phones and read ten phone numbers of people on your partner's cell phone call list that they did not write down on the list of ten names. Try to guess the names of the people that go with the numbers and keep track of how many you get correct.

Now go back and check the numbers that you wrote down on your first list. Which method of identifying phone numbers did you do better on? Write a summary of your phone number quizzing applying the memory concepts of recognition and recall to explain your findings.

Essay Question

Lisa is studying for her U.S. history test. To do well on the test, she will need to memorize dates of important events, answer multiple-choice questions about historical figures, and write an essay about the Civil War. If you were Lisa's tutor, what advice would you give her to help her study for the test? Describe your advice in a detailed, well-organized essay that addresses *three* of the following topics:
a. Levels of processing
b. Maintenance rehearsal versus elaborative rehearsal
c. Retrieval cues
d. Recognition versus recall
e. Serial position effect

Test Yourself

Ready for your test? More quizzes and a customized plan.

✅ **Study and Review** at **MyPsychLab**

Pick the best answer.

1. The steps to memory can best be described as follows:
   a. finding it, using it, storing it, using it again.
   b. putting it in, keeping it in, getting it out.
   c. sensing it, perceiving it, remembering it, forgetting it.
   d. a series of passive data files.

2. Everything that can be seen at one time is best known as
   a. iconic memory.
   b. echoic memory.
   c. semantic memory.
   d. episodic memory.

3. Which type of memory best explains the "What?" phenomenon?
   a. iconic sensory memory
   b. echoic sensory memory
   c. short-term memory
   d. tactile sensory memory

4. For information to travel from sensory memory to short-term memory, it must first be _____ and then encoded primarily into _____ form.
   a. unconsciously chosen; auditory
   b. selectively attended to; visual
   c. biologically chosen; visual
   d. selectively attended to; auditory

5. While talking with a person you just met, you realize that you have already forgotten the person's name. What amount of time does it typically take before such information is lost from short-term memory?
   a. 1 second
   b. 5 minutes
   c. 12 to 30 seconds
   d. 10 to 20 minutes

6. Early studies of short-term memory suggested that most people could remember about _____ bits of information.
   a. two
   b. three
   c. seven
   d. ten

7. Carla has just met a man named will and wants to remember his name. What should she do?
   a. Repeat Will's name continuously.
   b. Write Will's name five times.
   c. Remind herself that Will has the same name as her uncle.
   d. Create a song to help her remember Will's name.

8. _____ memory includes what people can do or demonstrate, whereas _____ memory is about what people know and can report.
   a. Nondeclarative; declarative
   b. Declarative; nondeclarative
   c. Semantic; nondeclarative
   d. Episodic; semantic

9. The semantic network model of memory suggests that the _____ nodes you must pass through to access information, the longer it will take for you to recall information.
   a. fewer
   b. more
   c. bigger the
   d. more complex the

10. Phineas walked into the conference room from his office and forgot what he went there for. According to the encoding specificity hypothesis, what should Phineas do to regain his lost memory?
    a. Phineas should return to his office.
    b. Phineas should ask "What did I come in here for?"
    c. Phineas should remain in the conference room.
    d. Phineas should consider seeing a doctor.

11. A true false test is an example of using
    a. recall.
    b. encoding.
    c. chunking.
    d. recognition.

12. When creating a presentation, develop a strong opening as well as a good summary and finish. What aspect of memory best explains these suggestions?
    a. recency effect
    b. flashbulb memory
    c. elaborative rehearsal theory
    d. chunking

13. When your mother tells you to dress for success at your interview, she is telling you that people often remember what they see first. This belief is in line with what element of memory?
    a. the primacy effect
    b. interference effect
    c. the recency effect
    d. echoic effect

14. Research by Elizabeth Loftus shows that eyewitness recognition is very prone to what psychologists call
    a. automatic encoding.
    b. a false positive.
    c. a flashbulb memory.
    d. a recency effect.

15. The tendency of certain elements to enter long-term memory with little or no effort to encode and organize them is what defines
    a. encoding specificity.
    b. flashbulb memory.
    c. context cues.
    d. eidetic imagery.

16. The ability of a person to remember what they were doing when the United States was attacked on September 11, 2001, is an example of
    a. eyewitness testimony.
    b. encoding specificity hypothesis.
    c. false-memory syndrome.
    d. flashbulb memory.

17. In Hermann Ebbinghaus's classic study on memory and the forgetting curve, how long after learning the lists does most forgetting happen?
    a. Forgetting started immediately.
    b. one hour
    c. five hours
    d. nine hours

18. You are surprised by the fact that you cannot remember if Abraham Lincoln's head faces the left or the right on a penny. What would best explain such an inability to recall this information?
    a. encoding failure
    b. decay theory
    c. interference theory
    d. distributed practice effect

19. H. M. was unable to form new declarative memories. He suffered from what psychologists call
    a. psychogenic amnesia.
    b. retrograde amnesia.
    c. retroactive amnesia.
    d. anterograde amnesia.

20. Brenda knows how to tie her shoes but finds it difficult to explain to her brother how to tie his shoes—but she can easily demonstrate it for him. Brenda's memory for shoe-tying is best characterized as a(n) _____ memory.
    a. declarative (explicit)
    b. semantic
    c. episodic
    d. nondeclarative (implicit)

Learning Objectives

23.1 **23.2** **23.3**   pp. 288–291

Explain How the Brain Encodes Memories

- **memory** is an active system that receives, organizes, stores, and retrieves information

- **three basic steps**
  - encoding
  - storage
  - retrieval

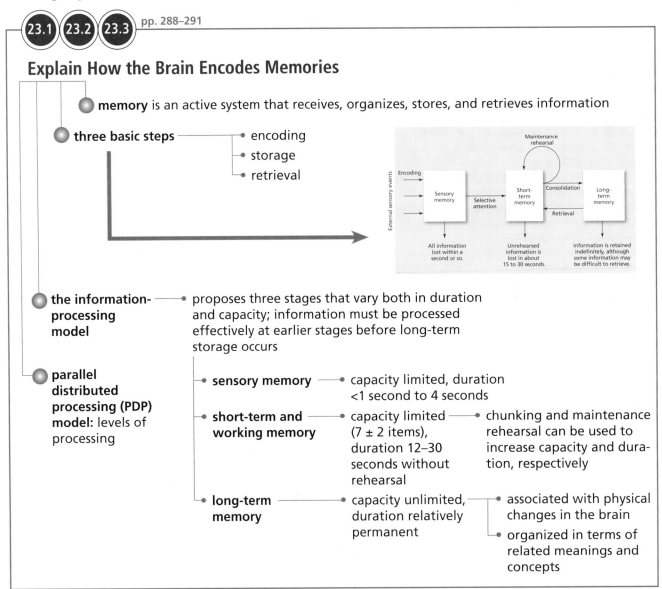

- **the information-processing model** — proposes three stages that vary both in duration and capacity; information must be processed effectively at earlier stages before long-term storage occurs

- **parallel distributed processing (PDP) model:** levels of processing
  - **sensory memory** — capacity limited, duration <1 second to 4 seconds
  - **short-term and working memory** — capacity limited (7 ± 2 items), duration 12–30 seconds without rehearsal — chunking and maintenance rehearsal can be used to increase capacity and duration, respectively
  - **long-term memory** — capacity unlimited, duration relatively permanent
    - associated with physical changes in the brain
    - organized in terms of related meanings and concepts

Learning Objectives

23.4 **23.5** **23.6**   pp. 292–294

Understand How Memories Are Stored in the Brain

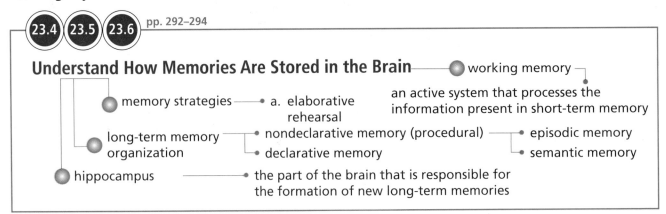

- working memory — an active system that processes the information present in short-term memory

- memory strategies — a. elaborative rehearsal

- long-term memory organization
  - nondeclarative memory (procedural) — episodic memory / semantic memory
  - declarative memory

- hippocampus — the part of the brain that is responsible for the formation of new long-term memories

24.1 24.2 24.3 24.4 24.5   pp. 296–305

Map the Concepts at MyPsychLab

Learn How Memories Are Retrieved from the Brain

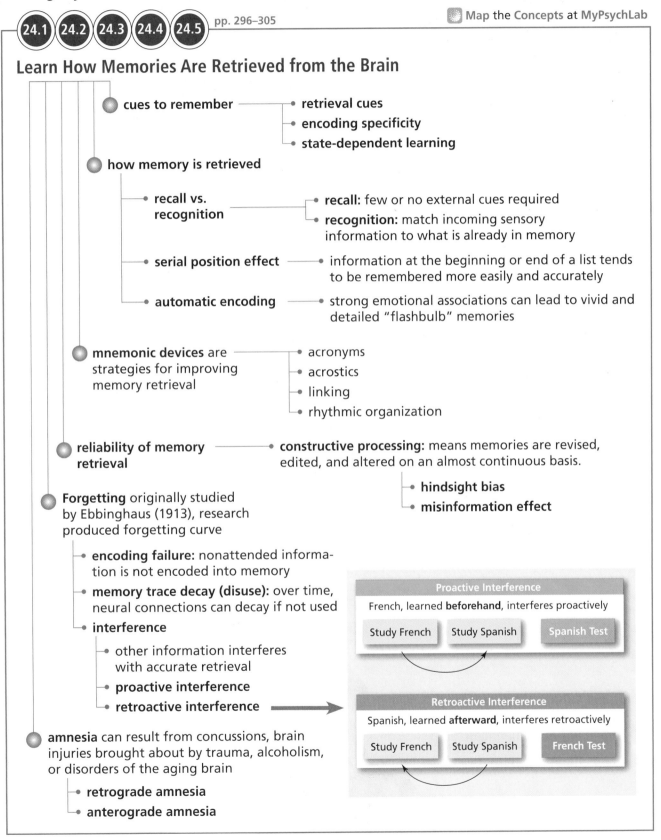

cues to remember
- **retrieval cues**
- **encoding specificity**
- **state-dependent learning**

how memory is retrieved

- **recall vs. recognition**
  - **recall:** few or no external cues required
  - **recognition:** match incoming sensory information to what is already in memory

- **serial position effect** — information at the beginning or end of a list tends to be remembered more easily and accurately

- **automatic encoding** — strong emotional associations can lead to vivid and detailed "flashbulb" memories

mnemonic devices are strategies for improving memory retrieval
- acronyms
- acrostics
- linking
- rhythmic organization

reliability of memory retrieval — **constructive processing:** means memories are revised, edited, and altered on an almost continuous basis.
- **hindsight bias**
- **misinformation effect**

Forgetting originally studied by Ebbinghaus (1913), research produced forgetting curve

- **encoding failure:** nonattended information is not encoded into memory
- **memory trace decay (disuse):** over time, neural connections can decay if not used
- **interference**
  - other information interferes with accurate retrieval
  - **proactive interference**
  - **retroactive interference**

Proactive Interference

French, learned **beforehand**, interferes proactively

| Study French | Study Spanish | Spanish Test |

Retroactive Interference

Spanish, learned **afterward**, interferes retroactively

| Study French | Study Spanish | French Test |

amnesia can result from concussions, brain injuries brought about by trauma, alcoholism, or disorders of the aging brain
- **retrograde amnesia**
- **anterograde amnesia**

Cognition: Thinking and Intelligence

Think about how you interact with the world around you. How often do you simply respond without knowing how or why you do the things you do, say, or think? How much of your conscious experience involves effortful, mindful attention and decision making? These two types of thinking, sometimes referred to as System 1 and System 2, characterize much of how we think and process information (Kahneman, 2011; Stanovich & West, 2000). System 1, which involves making quick decisions and using cognitive shortcuts, is guided by our innate abilities and personal experiences. System 2, which is relatively slow, analytical, and rule based, is dependent more on our formal educational experiences. System 2 takes effort and we must learn to develop the ability to think in this way—like learning to study productively. Overall, our thinking has to be governed by the interplay between the two.

Do you tend to rely more on instinctual (System 1) or deliberate (System 2) thought processes? How do your thought processes and decision-making strategies vary depending on the situation?

Watch the Video, at MyPsychLab

Why Study the Nature of Thought?

To fully understand how we do any of the things we do (such as learning, remembering, and behaving), we need to understand how we think. How do we organize our thoughts? What do we mean by intelligence? Why are some people able to learn so much faster than others?

25 Thinking

Module Goals	Learning Objectives
Understand the basic elements of thought.	**25.1** Explain cognitive processes involved in understanding information.
	25.2 Explain processes involved in problem solving and decision making.
	25.3 Explain nonhuman problem-solving abilities.
Learn about obstacles related to thought.	**25.4** Describe obstacles to problem solving, making good judgments, and making good decisions.

thinking (cognition) mental activity that goes on in the brain when a person is organizing and attempting information processing and communicating information to others.

mental images mental representations that stand for objects or events and have a picture-like quality.

So more windows means more time to count them in your head? I guess mentally "walking" through a bigger house in your head would take longer than "walking" through a smaller one. ▶

Understand the Basic Elements of Thought

What does it mean to think? People are thinking all the time and talking about thinking as well: "What do you think?" "Let me think about that." "I don't think so." So, what does it mean to think?

25.1 Explain cognitive processes involved in understanding information.

How People Think: Mental Imagery and Concepts Thinking, or cognition (from a Latin word meaning "to know"), can be defined as mental activity that goes on in the brain when a person is processing information—organizing it, understanding it, and communicating it to others. Thinking includes memory, but it is much more. When people think, they are not only aware of the information in the brain but also are making decisions about it, comparing it to other information, and using it to solve problems.

Thinking also includes more than just a kind of verbal "stream of consciousness." When people think, they often have images as well as words in their minds.

Mental Imagery As stated in Chapter Nine, short-term memories are encoded in the form of sounds and also as visual images, forming a mental picture of the world. Thus, **mental images** (representations that stand in for objects or events and have a picture like quality) are one of several tools used in the thought process.

Here's an interesting demonstration of the use of mental images. Get several people together and ask them to tell you *as fast as they can* how many windows are in the place where they live. Usually you'll find that the first people to shout out an answer have fewer windows in their houses than the ones who take longer to respond. You'll also notice that most of them look up, as if looking at some image that only they can see. If asked, they'll say that to determine the number of windows, they pictured where they live and simply counted windows as they "walked through" the image they created in their mind.

That's what researchers think, too. They have found that it does take longer to view a mental image that is larger or covers more distance than a smaller, more compact one (Kosslyn et al., 2001; Ochsner & Kosslyn, 1994). In one study (Kosslyn et al., 1978), participants were asked to look at a map of an imaginary island (see **Figure 25.1**). On this map were several landmarks, such as a hut, a lake, and a grassy area. After viewing the map and memorizing it, participants were asked to imagine a specific place on the island, such as the hut, and then to "look" for another place, like the lake. When they mentally "reached" the second place, they pushed a button that recorded reaction time. The greater the physical distance on the map between the two locations, the longer it took participants to scan the image for the second location. The participants were apparently looking at their mental image and scanning it just as if it were a real, physical map.

People are even able to mentally rotate, or turn, images (Shepherd & Metzler, 1971). Kosslyn (1983) asked participants questions such as the following: "Do frogs have lips and a stubby tail?" He found that most participants reported visualizing a frog, starting with the face ("no lips"), then mentally rotating the image so it was facing away from them, and then "zooming in" to look for the stubby tail ("hmmm, I don't think I see one").

A very important aspect of the research on mental rotation is that we tend to engage *mental* images in our mind much like we engage or interact with *physical* objects. When we rotate an object in our minds (or in other ways interact with or manipulate mental images), it is not instantaneous—it takes time, just as it would if we were rotating a physical object with our hands. To see how well you are able to mentally rotate images, try the *Mental Rotation* experiment.

In the brain, creating a mental image is almost the opposite of seeing an actual image. With an actual image, the information goes from the eyes to the visual cortex of the occipital lobe and is processed, or interpreted, by other areas of the cortex that compare the new information to information already in memory. In creating a mental image, areas of the cortex associated with stored knowledge send information to the visual cortex, where the image is perceived in the "mind's eye" (Kosslyn et al., 1993; Sparing et al., 2002). PET scans show areas of the visual cortex being activated during the process of forming an image, providing evidence for the role of the visual cortex in mental imagery (Kosslyn et al., 1993, 1999, 2001).

Concepts and Prototypes Mental images are only one form of mental representation. Another aspect of thought processes is the use of concepts. **Concepts** are ideas that represent a class or category of objects, events, or activities. People use concepts to think about objects or events without having to think about all the specific examples of the category. For example, a person can think about "fruit" without thinking about every kind of fruit there is in the world, which would take far more effort and time. This ability to think in terms of concepts allows us to communicate with each other: If I mention a bird to you, you know what I am referring to, even if we aren't actually thinking of the same *type* of bird.

Concepts not only contain the important features of the objects or events people want to think about, but also they allow the identification of new objects and events that may fit the concept. For example, dogs come in all shapes, sizes, colors, and lengths of fur. Yet most people have no trouble recognizing dogs as dogs, even though they may never before have seen that particular breed of dog. Friends of the author have a dog called a Briard, which is a kind of sheepdog. In spite of the fact that this dog is easily the size of a small pony, the author had no trouble recognizing it as a dog, albeit a huge and extremely shaggy one.

concepts ideas that represent a class or category of objects, events, or activities.

Participate in the **Experiment**, *Mental Rotation*, at **MyPsychLab**

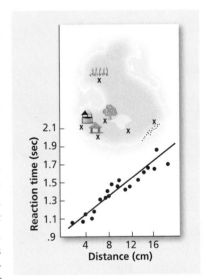

FIGURE 25.1 Kosslyn's Fictional Island
In Kosslyn's 1978 study, participants were asked to push a button when they had imagined themselves moving from one place on the island to another. As the graph below the picture shows, participants took longer times to complete the task when the locations on the image were farther apart. *Source*: Kosslyn et al. (1978).

prototype an example of a concept that closely matches the defining characteristics of the concept.

But what about ▶ things that don't easily fit the rules or features? What if a thing has some, but not all, features of a concept?

Concepts can have very strict definitions, such as the concept of a square as a shape with four equal sides. Concepts defined by specific rules or features are called *formal concepts* and are quite rigid. To be a square, for example, an object must be a two-dimensional figure with four equal sides and four angles adding up to 360 degrees. Mathematics is full of formal concepts. For example, in geometry there are triangles, squares, rectangles, polygons, and lines. In psychology, there are double-blind experiments, sleep stages, and conditioned stimuli, to name a few. Each of these concepts must fit very specific features to be considered true examples.

People are surrounded by objects, events, and activities that are not as clearly defined as formal concepts. What is a vehicle? Cars and trucks leap immediately to mind, but what about a bobsled or a raft? Those last two objects aren't quite as easy to classify as vehicles immediately, but they fit some of the rules for "vehicle." These are examples of *natural concepts*, concepts people form not as a result of a strict set of rules but rather as the result of experiences with these concepts in the real world (Ahn, 1998; Barton & Komatsu, 1989; Rosch, 1973). Formal concepts are well defined, but natural concepts are "fuzzy" (Hampton, 1998). Natural concepts are important in helping people understand their surroundings in a less structured manner than school-taught formal concepts, and they form the basis for interpreting those surroundings and the events that may occur in everyday life.

When someone says "fruit," what's the first image that comes to mind? More than likely, it's a specific kind of fruit like an apple, pear, or orange. It's less likely that someone's first impulse will be to say "guava" or "papaya," or even "banana," unless that person comes from a tropical area. In the United States, apples are a good example of a **prototype**, a concept that closely matches the defining characteristics of the concept, dependent upon the culture and area in which he or she lives (Mervis & Rosch, 1981; Rosch, 1977). Fruit is sweet, grows on trees, has seeds, and is usually round—all very apple-like qualities. Coconuts are sweet and they also grow on trees, but many people in the Northern Hemisphere have never actually seen a coconut tree. They have more likely seen countless apple trees. So people who do have very different experiences

▲ Both of these animals are dogs. They both have fur, four legs, a tail—but the similarities end there. With so many variations in the animals we call "dogs," what is the prototype for "dog"?

with fruit, for instance, will have different prototypes, which are the most basic examples of concepts.

More than likely, prototypes develop according to the exposure a person has to objects in that category. So someone who grew up in an area where there are many coconut trees might think of coconuts as more prototypical than apples, whereas someone growing up in the northwestern United States would more likely see apples as a prototypical fruit (Aitchison, 1992). Culture also matters in the formation of prototypes. Research on concept prototypes across various cultures found greater differences and variations in prototypes between cultures that were dissimilar, such as Taiwan and America, than between cultures that are more similar, such as Hispanic Americans and non–Hispanic Americans living in Florida (Lin et al., 1990; Lin & Schwanenflugel, 1995; Schwanenflugel & Rey, 1986).

How do prototypes affect thinking? People tend to look at potential examples of a concept and compare them to the prototype to see how well they match—which is why it takes most people much longer to think about olives and tomatoes as fruit because they aren't sweet, one of the major characteristics of the prototype of fruit (Rosch & Mervis, 1975).

No matter what type, concepts are one of the ways people deal with all the information that bombards* their senses every day, allowing them to organize their perceptions of the world around them. This organization may take the form of **schemas**, mental generalizations about objects, places, events, and people (for example, one's schema for "library" would no doubt include books and bookshelves), or *scripts*, a kind of schema that involves a familiar sequence of activities (for example, "going to a movie" would include traveling there, getting the ticket, buying snacks, finding the right theater, etc.). Concepts not only help people think, but also they are an important tool in *problem solving*, a type of thinking that people engage in every day and in many different situations.

25.2 Explain processes involved in problem solving and decision making.

Think about it as you read on and solve the following: Put a coin in a bottle and then cork the opening. How can you get the coin out of the bottle without pulling out the cork or breaking the bottle? (For the solution, see the section on Insight.)

As stated earlier, images and concepts are mental tools that can be used to solve problems and make decisions. For the preceding problem, you are probably trying to create an image of the bottle with a coin in it. *Problem solving* occurs when a goal must be reached by thinking and behaving in certain ways. Problems range from figuring out how to cut a recipe in half to understanding complex mathematical proofs to deciding what to major in at college. Problem solving is one aspect of *decision making*, or identifying, evaluating, and choosing among several alternatives. There are several different ways in which people can think to solve problems.

Trial and Error (Mechanical Solutions) One method is to use **trial and error, also known as a mechanical solution**. Trial and error refers to trying one solution after another until finding one that works. For example, if Shelana has forgotten the PIN for her online banking Web site, she can try one combination after another until she finds the one that works, if she has only a few such PINs

◀ What about people who live in a tropical area? Would their prototype for fruit be different? Also, would people's prototypes vary in other cultures?

◀ Problem solving is certainly a big part of any high school student's life. Is there any one "best" way to go about solving a problem?

schema the concept or framework that organizes the information.

trial and error (mechanical solution) problem-solving method in which one possible solution after another is tried until a successful one is found.

---

*bombards: attacks again and again.

▲ *This child may try one piece after another until finding the piece that fits. This is an example of trial-and-error learning.*

that she normally uses. Mechanical solutions can also involve solving by *rote*, or a learned set of rules. This is how word problems were solved in grade school, for example. One type of rote solution is to use an algorithm.

Using Algorithms: Step by Step Algorithms are specific, step-by-step procedures for solving certain types of problems. Algorithms will always result in a correct solution, if there is a correct solution to be found, and you have enough time to find it. Mathematical formulas are algorithms. When librarians organize books on bookshelves, they also use an algorithm: Place books in alphabetical order within each category, for example. Many puzzles, like a Rubik's Cube®, have a set of steps that, if followed exactly, will always result in solving the puzzle. But algorithms aren't always practical to use. For example, if Shelana didn't have a clue what those four numbers might be, she *might* be able to figure out her forgotten PIN by trying *all possible combinations* of four digits, 0 through 9. She would eventually find the right four-digit combination—but it might take a very long while! Computers, however, can run searches like this one very quickly, so the systematic search algorithm is a useful part of some computer programs.

Heuristics Unfortunately, humans aren't as fast as computers and need some other way to narrow down the possible solutions to only a few. One way to do this is to use a heuristic. A **heuristic**, or "rule of thumb," is a simple rule that is intended to apply to many situations. Whereas an algorithm is very specific and will always lead to a solution, a heuristic is an educated guess based on prior experiences that helps narrow down the possible solutions for a problem. For example, if a student is typing a paper in a word-processing program and wants to know how to format the page, he or she could try to read an entire manual on the word-processing program. That would take a while. Instead, the student could use an Internet search engine or type "format" into the help feature's search program. Doing either action greatly reduces the amount of information the student will have to look at to get an answer. Using the help feature or clicking on the appropriate toolbar word will also work for similar problems. The human tendency to "gestalt"—to take a few pieces of information and create a "whole"—illustrates our natural tendency to seek FAST ways to problem solve.
ⓁⒾⓃⓀ to *Chapter Six: Learning and Language Development, pp. 192–227.* Heuristics are faster, not surer, and humans like to do things fast—even if we are sometimes wrong.

Representativeness Heuristic Will using a rule of thumb always work, like algorithms do? Using a heuristic is faster than using an algorithm in many cases, but unlike algorithms, heuristics will *not* always lead to the correct solution. What you gain in speed is sometimes lost in accuracy. For example, a **representativeness heuristic** is used for categorizing objects and simply assumes that any object (or person) that shares characteristics with the members of a particular category is also a member of that category. This is a handy tool when it comes to classifying plants but doesn't work as well when applied to people. The representativeness heuristic can cause errors due to ignoring base rates, the actual probability of a given event. Are all people with dark skin from Africa? Does everyone with red hair also have a bad temper? Are all blue-eyed blondes from Sweden? See the point? The representativeness heuristic can be used—or misused—to create and sustain stereotypes (Kahneman & Tversky, 1973; Kahneman et al., 1982).

Availability Heuristic Another heuristic that can have undesired outcomes is the **availability heuristic**, which is based on our estimation of the frequency or likelihood of an event based on how easy it is to recall relevant information from memory or how easy it is for us to think of related examples (Tversky &

algorithms very specific, step-by-step procedures for solving certain types of problems.

heuristic mental shortcut based on prior experiences that helps narrow down the possible solutions for a problem. Also known as a "rule of thumb."

representativeness heuristic assumption that any object (or person) sharing characteristics with the members of a particular category is also a member of that category.

availability heuristic estimating the frequency or likelihood of an event based on how easy it is to recall (often associated with a vivid, emotional memory) relevant information from memory or how easy it is for us to think of related examples.

Kahneman, 1973). Imagine, for example, that after you have already read this entire textbook (it could happen!) you are asked to estimate how many words in the book start with the letter *K* and how many have the letter *K* as the third letter in the word. Which place do you think is more frequent, the first letter or as the third letter? Next, what do you think the ratio of the more frequent placement is to the less frequent placement? What is easier to think of, words that begin with the letter *K* or words that have *K* as the third letter? Tversky & Kahneman (1973) asked this same question of 152 participants for five consonants (*K, N, L, R, V*) that appear more frequently in the third position as compared to the first in a typical text. Sixty-nine percent of the participants indicated that the first position was the more frequent placement and the median estimated ratio was 2:1 for the letter *K*—however, there are typically twice as many words with *K* as the third letter as compared to the first. Can you think of an example where you may have used the availability heuristic and it did not work in your favor?

Working Backward A useful heuristic that *does* work much of the time is to *work backward from the goal*. For example, if you want to know the shortest way to get to the new coffee shop in town, you already know the goal, which is finding the coffee shop. There are probably several ways to get there from your house, and some are shorter than others. Assuming you have the address of the store, for many the best way to determine the shortest route is to look up the location of the store on an Internet map, a GPS, or a smartphone, and compare the different routes by the means of travel (walking versus driving). People actually used to do this with a physical map and compare the routes manually! Think about it, does technology help or hinder some aspects of problem solving? What are, if any, the benefits to using technology for solving some problems as compared to actively engaging in problem solving as a mental challenge?

▲ Smartphones and other portable devices provide tools for easy navigation. How might the use or overuse of these tools affect our ability to navigate when we do not have access to them?

Subgoals Sometimes it's better to break a goal down into *subgoals*, so that as ◄ each subgoal is achieved, the final solution is that much closer. Writing a term paper, for example, can seem overwhelming until it is broken down into steps: Choose a topic, research the topic, organize what has been gathered, write one section at a time, and so on. Other examples of heuristics include making diagrams to help organize the information concerning the problem or testing possible solutions to the problem one by one and eliminating those that do not work.

What if my problem is writing a term paper? Starting at the end isn't ◄ going to help me much!

Insight When the solution to a problem seems to come suddenly to mind, it is ◄ called insight. Chapter Five contained a discussion of Köhler's (1925) work with Sultan the chimpanzee, which demonstrated that even some animals can solve problems by means of a sudden insight. In humans, insight often takes the form of an "aha!" moment—the solution seems to come in a flash. A person may realize that this problem is similar to another one that he or she already knows how to solve or might see that an object can be used for a different purpose than its original one, like using a dime as a screwdriver.

Remember the problem of the bottle discussed earlier in this chapter? The task was to get the coin out of the bottle without removing the cork or breaking the bottle. The answer is simple: *Push the cork into the bottle and shake out the coin. Aha!*

Insight is not really a magical process, although it can seem like magic. What usually happens is that the mind simply reorganizes a problem, sometimes while the person is thinking about something else, or even sleeping! (Durso et al., 1994).

Sometimes I have to find answers to problems one step at a time, but in other cases the answer seems to just "pop" into my head all of a sudden. Why do some answers come so easily to mind?

So far, we've only talked about logic and pretty straightforward thinking. How do people come up with totally new ideas, things no one has thought of before?

✳ Complete the Survey, *What Is Creativity?*, at MyPsychLab

creativity the process of solving problems by combining ideas or behavior in new ways.

convergent thinking type of thinking in which a problem is seen as having only one answer, and all lines of thinking will eventually lead to that single answer, using previous knowledge and logic.

divergent thinking type of thinking in which a person starts from one point and comes up with many different ideas or possibilities based on that point.

functional fixedness a block to problem solving that comes from thinking about objects in terms of only their typical functions.

Here's a problem that can be solved with insight: Marsha and Marjorie were born on the same day of the same month of the same year to the same mother and the same father, yet they are not twins. How is that possible? Think about it and then look for the answer in the section on Mental Sets.

▶ **Creativity** Not every problem can be answered by using information already at hand and the rules of logic in applying that information. Sometimes a problem requires coming up with entirely new ways of looking at the problem or unusual, inventive solutions. This kind of thinking is called **creativity**: solving problems by combining ideas or behavior in new ways (Csikszentmihalyi, 1996; pronounced chĭck-sĕnt-mē-HĬ-ē). Before we learn more, take the survey *What Is Creativity?* to examine your own beliefs about creativity.

The logical method for problem solving that has been discussed so far is based on a type of thinking called **convergent thinking**. In convergent thinking, a problem is seen as having only one answer and all lines of thinking will eventually lead to (converge on) that single answer by using previous knowledge and logic (Ciardiello, 1998). For example, the question "In what ways are a pencil and a pen alike?" can be answered by listing the features that the two items have in common: Both can be used to write, have similar shapes, and so on, in a simple comparison process. Convergent thinking works well for routine problem solving but may be of little use when a more creative solution is needed.

Divergent thinking is the reverse of convergent thinking. Here a person starts at one point and comes up with many different, or divergent, ideas or possibilities based on that point (Finke, 1995). For example, if someone were to ask the question, "What is a pencil used for?" the convergent answer would be "to write." But if the question is put this way: "How many different uses can you think of for a pencil?" the answers multiply: "writing, poking holes, a weight for the tail of a kite, a weapon." Divergent thinking has been attributed not only to creativity but also to intelligence (Guilford, 1967).

What are the characteristics of a creative, divergent thinker? Theorists in the field of creative thinking have found through examining the habits of highly creative people that the most productive periods of divergent thinking for those people tend to occur when they are doing some task or activity that is more or less automatic, such as walking or swimming (Csikszentmihalyi, 1996; Gardner, 1993a; Goleman, 1995). These automatic tasks take up some attention processes, leaving the remainder to devote to creative thinking. The fact that all of one's attention is not focused on the problem is actually a benefit, because divergent thinkers often make links and connections at a level of consciousness just below alert awareness, so that ideas can flow freely without being censored* by the higher mental processes (Goleman, 1995). In other words, having part of one's attention devoted to walking, for example, allows the rest of the mind to "sneak up on" more creative solutions and ideas.

Divergent thinkers will obviously be less prone to some of the barriers to problem solving, such as **functional fixedness**. For example, what would most people do if it suddenly started to rain and they were stuck in their office with no umbrella? How many people would think of using a see-through vinyl tote bag as a makeshift umbrella?

Creative, divergent thinking is often a neglected topic in the education of young people. Although some people are naturally more creative, it is possible to develop one's creative ability. The ability to be creative is important—coming up with topics for a research paper, for example, is something that many students have trouble doing. Cross-cultural research (Basadur et al., 2002; Colligan, 1983) has found that divergent thinking and problem-solving skills cannot be

---

*censored: blocked from conscious awareness as unacceptable thoughts.

easily taught in the Japanese or Omaha Native American cultures, for example. In these cultures, creativity in many areas is not normally prized and the preference is to hold to well-established cultural traditions such as traditional dances that have not varied for centuries.

insight the sudden perception of relationships among various parts of a problem, allowing the solution to the problem to come quickly.

25.3 Explain nonhuman problem-solving abilities.

Köhler's Smart Chimp: Insight Learning Another exploration of the cognitive elements of learning came about almost by accident. Wolfgang Köhler (1887–1967) was a Gestalt psychologist who became marooned on an island in the Canaries (a series of islands off the coast of North Africa) when World War I broke out. Stuck at the primate research lab that had first drawn him to the island, he turned to studies of animal learning.

In a famous study, Köhler (1925) gave Sultan the chimp a problem of how to reach a banana that was placed outside his cage just beyond his grasp. Sultan tried to reach the banana but soon figured out that he needed to use a stick that was placed inside his cage to "rake" the banana toward him in order to be rewarded with the banana as a snack. This trial-and-error learning was not a surprise because chimpanzees are tools users and the stick was readily available.

But then the problem was made more difficult. The banana was placed just out of reach of Sultan's extended arm with the stick in his hand. At this point there were two sticks lying around in the cage, which could be fitted together to make a single pole that would be long enough to reach the banana. Sultan first tried one stick, then the other (simple trial and error). After about an hour of trying, Sultan seemed to have a sudden flash of inspiration. He pushed one stick out of the cage as far as it would go toward the banana and then pushed the other stick behind the first one. Of course, when he tried to draw the sticks back, only the one in his hand came. He jumped up and down and was very excited, and when Köhler gave him the second stick, he sat on the floor of the cage and looked at them carefully. He then fitted one stick into the other and retrieved his banana. Sultan's "perception of relationships" was called **insight** by Köhler because he claimed that Sultan's solution to the more difficult banana problem could not be achieved through trial-and-error alone (Köhler, 1925). Though other researchers, like Thorndike, held that animals could not demonstrate insight, Köhler's work with Sultan seemed to show that a sudden "coming together" of a solution led to an "aha" event that traditional animal learning studies would not have predicted. While recent research has also offered support for the idea that animals possess insight (Heinrich, 2000; Heyes, 1998; Zentall, 2000), there is still controversy surrounding how the results of animal insight studies are being interpreted (Wynne, 1999).

In summary, thinking is a complex process involving the use of mental imagery and various types of concepts to organize the events of daily life. Problem solving is a special type of thinking that involves the use of many tools, such as trial-and-error thinking, algorithms, heuristics, and creativity, to solve different types of problems for humans and nonhuman animals.

▲ Another of Köhler's chimpanzees, Grande, has just solved the problem of how to get to the banana by stacking boxes. Does this meet the criteria for insight, or was it simple trial-and-error learning?

mental set the tendency for people to persist in using problem-solving patterns that have worked for them in the past.

Learn about Obstacles Related to Thought

25.4 Describe obstacles to problem solving, making good judgments, and making good decisions.

Problems with Problem Solving and Decision Making Using insight to solve a problem is not always foolproof. Sometimes a solution to a problem remains just "out of reach" because the elements of the problem are not arranged properly or because people get stuck in certain ways of thinking that act as barriers* to solving problems. Such ways of thinking occur more or less automatically, influencing attempts to solve problems without any conscious awareness of that influence. Here's a classic example:

Two strings are hanging from a ceiling but are too far apart to allow a person to hold one and walk to the other. (See **Figure 25.2.**) Nearby is a table with a pair of pliers on it. The goal is to tie the two pieces of string together. How?

People can become aware of automatic tendencies to try to solve problems in ways that are not going to lead to solutions and in becoming aware can abandon the "old" ways for more appropriate problem-solving methods. Three of the most common barriers to successful problem solving are functional fixedness, mental sets, and confirmation bias.

Functional Fixedness One problem-solving difficulty involves thinking about objects only in terms of their typical uses, which is a phenomenon called **functional fixedness** (literally, "fixed on the function"). Have you ever searched high and low for a screwdriver to fix something around the house? All the while there are several objects close at hand that could be used to tighten a screw: a butter knife, a key, or even a dime in your pocket. Because the tendency is to think of those objects in terms of cooking, unlocking, and spending, we sometimes ignore the less obvious possible uses. The string problem introduced before is an example of functional fixedness. The pair of pliers is often seen as useless until the person realizes it can be used as a weight.

Mental Sets Functional fixedness is actually a kind of **mental set**, which is defined as the tendency of people to persist in using problem-solving patterns that have worked for them in the past. Solutions that have worked in the past tend to be the ones people try first, and people are often hesitant or even unable to think of other possibilities. Look at **Figure 25.3** and see if you can solve the dot problem.

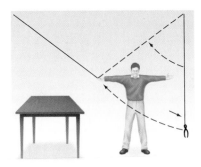

FIGURE 25.2 The String Problem
How do you tie the two strings together if you cannot reach them both at the same time?

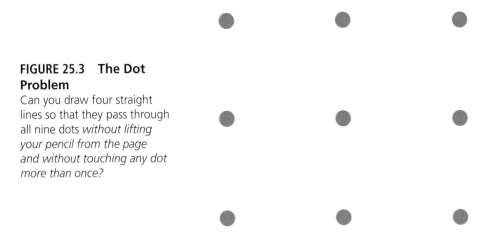

FIGURE 25.3 The Dot Problem
Can you draw four straight lines so that they pass through all nine dots *without lifting your pencil from the page and without touching any dot more than once?*

---

*barrier: something that blocks one's path; an obstacle preventing a solution.

People are taught from the earliest grades to stay within the lines, right? That tried-and-true method will not help in solving the dot problem. The solution involves drawing the lines beyond the actual dots.

Answer to insight problem: *Marsha and Marjorie are two of a set of triplets. Gotcha!*

Confirmation Bias Another barrier to effective decision making or problem solving is **confirmation bias**, the tendency to search for evidence that fits one's beliefs while ignoring any evidence to the contrary. This is similar to a mental set, except that what is "set" is a belief rather than a method of solving problems. Believers in ESP tend to remember the few studies that seem to support their beliefs and psychic predictions that worked out while at the same time "forgetting" the cases in which studies found no proof or psychics made predictions that failed to come true. They remember only that which confirms their bias toward a belief in the existence of ESP. Another example is that people who believe that they are good multitaskers and can safely drive a motor vehicle while talking or texting on their cell phones may tend to remember their own personal experiences, which may not include any vehicle accidents or "near-misses" (that they are aware of). While it might be tempting to think of one's self as a "super-tasker," recent research suggests otherwise. When tested on driving simulators while having to perform successfully on two attention-demanding tasks, over 97 percent of individuals are unable to do so without significant impacts on their performance. During the dual-task condition, only 2.5 percent of individuals were able to perform without problems (Watson & Strayer, 2010). This specific example can be quite dangerous, as it is estimated that at least 28 percent of all traffic crashes are caused by drivers using their cell phone and or texting (National Safety Council, 2010).

confirmation bias the tendency to search for evidence that fits one's beliefs while ignoring any evidence that does not fit those beliefs.

▲ *The driver of this train was texting from his cell phone immediately before this crash that killed 25 people and injured more than 130 others.*

Pick the best answer.

1. Assuming that the correct solution is available, which problem-solving strategy will always result in a correct solution?
   a. means-end analysis
   b. heuristic
   c. algorithm
   d. trial and error

2. A "rule of thumb" is another name for a(n)
   a. anchoring effect.
   b. heuristic.
   c. formal concept.
   d. prototype.

3. Laticia has been instructed to write an analysis of the Bolshevik revolution for her 11th-grade world history class. The paper is to be between 15 and 20 pages, and is due in 1 month. Laticia is feeling very overwhelmed by such a huge assignment. What shortcut would be most useful as she attempts to conquer this very large task?
   a. the representative heuristic
   b. the availability heuristic
   c. trial and error
   d. the use of subgoals

4. Miguel was struggling with the answer to one of the questions on his psychology midterm. Seeing that the answer was not going to come easily, he went on to answer some of the other easier questions. Then, suddenly, the answer to the problematic question just seemed to "pop" into his head. Miguel's experience is an example of
   a. insight.
   b. a mechanical solution.
   c. convergent thinking.
   d. a natural concept.

5. Al goes out one frosty morning to find that his car is covered with a layer of thick frost. He needs to get to work and looks for his ice scraper. Unable to find it, he thinks a moment, goes into the house, and returns with a hard plastic spatula from the kitchen. In using the spatula as a makeshift ice scraper, what has Al overcome?
   a. confirmation bias
   b. functional fixedness
   c. loss aversion
   d. the anchoring effect

6. Randall believes that aliens crashed in the western United States in the 1950s. When looking for information about this on the Internet, he ignores any sites that are skeptical of his belief and visits and talks only with his friends about the sites that support his belief. What is this an example of?
   a. confirmation bias
   b. a mental set
   c. the gambler's fallacy
   d. divergent thinking

7. What type of thinking occurs when a problem is seen as having only one answer, with all lines of thinking leading to that answer?
   a. convergent
   b. divergent
   c. formal
   d. natural

8. Which of the following statements about creative people is true?
   a. They are unconventional in most aspects of their lives.
   b. They tend to focus exclusively on one field of knowledge.
   c. They are more open to new experiences than other people.
   d. They can solve almost any type of problem easily.

9. If you ask someone to give you as many uses as possible for a piece of paper, what type of thinking is being used?
   a. divergent
   b. functional fixedness
   c. convergent
   d. mentalset

10. People in the United States often think of a sports car when asked to envision a fun, fast form of travel. In this example, a sports car would be considered a
    a. prototype.
    b. natural concept.
    c. formal concept.
    d. mental image.

Module 26 Intelligence

Module Goals	Learning Objectives	
Compare and contrast perspectives on intelligence.	**26.1**	Explain intelligence as a general factor.
	26.2	Describe alternative conceptualizations of intelligence.
	26.3	Discuss the extremes of intelligence.
Learn how intelligence is measured.	**26.4**	Explain the history of intelligence testing, including historical use and misuse in the context of fairness.
	26.5	Describe current methods of assessing human abilities.
	26.6	Explain measures of and data on reliability and validity for intelligence test scores.
Consider key issues in intelligence.	**26.7**	Describe the influences of biological, cultural, and environmental factors on intelligence.
	26.8	Explain issues related to the consequences of intelligence testing.

Compare and Contrast Perspectives on Intelligence

What does it mean to be "smart"? Is this the same as being intelligent? It is likely the answer depends on the immediate task or context. What exactly do we mean by the term *intelligence*?

26.1 Explain intelligence as a general factor.

Is intelligence merely a score on some test, or is it practical knowledge of how to get along in the world? Is it making good grades or being a financial success or a social success? Ask a dozen people and you will probably get a dozen different answers. Before we attempt to answer these questions, take the survey *What Is Intelligence?* to discover more about your own notions of intelligence.

Psychologists have come up with a workable definition that combines many of the ideas just mentioned: They define **intelligence** (which literally means "choose between") as the ability to learn from one's experiences, acquire knowledge, and use resources effectively in adapting to new situations or solving problems (Sternberg & Kaufman, 1998; Wechsler, 1975). These are the characteristics that individuals need in order to survive in their culture.

Although we have defined intelligence in a general way, there are differing opinions of the specific knowledge and abilities that make up the concept of intelligence. Charles Spearman (1904) defined intelligence as two primary abilities: the wider ability to reason and solve problems was labeled as **g factor**, for *general intelligence*, whereas task-specific abilities in certain areas such as music, business, or art are labeled as *s factor* for *specific intelligence*.

❄ Complete the Survey, *What Is Intelligence?*, at MyPsychLab

intelligence the ability to learn from one's experiences, acquire knowledge, and use resources effectively in adapting to new situations or solving problems.

g factor the ability to reason and solve problems, or general intelligence.

emotional intelligence the awareness of and ability to manage one's own emotions to facilitate thinking and attain goals, as well as the ability to understand emotions in others.

👁 **Watch** the **Video,** *Gardner's Theory of Intelligence,* at **MyPsychLab**

▲ *Sternberg's practical intelligence is a form of "street smarts" that includes the ability to adapt to one's environment and solve practical problems. These girls are giving their younger brother a drink of water by using a folded leaf as an impromptu cup.*

▲ *Emotional intelligence includes empathy, which is the ability to feel what others are feeling. This doctor is not only able to listen to her patient's problems but also is able to show by her facial expression, body language, and gestures that she understands how the patient feels.*

26.2 Describe alternative conceptualizations of intelligence.

Multiple Intelligences Some later theorists have suggested that intelligence cannot be defined so simply and have therefore proposed different aspects and abilities. The idea of multiple intelligences was proposed by Howard Gardner (1993b, 1999a), and his theory originally listed seven different kinds of intelligence but later added an eighth and a ninth (Gardner, 1998, 1999b). The nine types of intelligence are described in the video *Gardner's Theory of Intelligence.* Yet another theory suggests that there are three kinds of intelligence. Robert Sternberg's (1988a, 1997b, 2005) triarchic theory of intelligence suggests that intelligence comprises analytical, creative, and practical aspects.

Emotional Intelligence What about people who have a lot of "book smarts" but not much common sense? There are some people like that, who never seem to get ahead in life, in spite of having all that so-called intelligence. It is true that not everyone who is intellectually able is going to be a success in life (Mehrabian, 2000). Sometimes the people who are most successful are those who didn't do all that well in the regular academic setting.

One explanation for why some people who do poorly in school succeed in life and why some who do well in school don't do so well in the "real" world is that success relies on a certain degree of **emotional intelligence**, the accurate awareness of and ability to manage one's own emotions to facilitate* thinking and attain specific goals, and the ability to understand what others feel (Mayer & Salovey, 1997; Mayer & Salovery et al., 2008).

The concept of emotional intelligence was first introduced by Peter Salovey and John Mayer (1990) and later popularized by Dan Goleman (1995). And although Goleman originally suggested emotional intelligence was a more powerful influence on success in life than more traditional views of intelligence, his work and the work of others used the term in a variety of different ways than originally proposed, and claims by some were not backed by scientific evidence. For example, emotional intelligence is not the same as having high self-esteem or being optimistic. One who is emotionally intelligent possesses self-control of emotions such as anger, impulsiveness, and anxiety. Empathy, the ability to understand what others feel, is also a component, as are an awareness of one's own emotions, sensitivity, persistence even in the face of frustrations, and the ability to motivate oneself (Salovey & Mayer, 1990; Mayer & Salovey, 1997).

26.3 Describe the extremes of intelligence.

Individual Differences In Intelligence IQ tests are used to help identify people who differ from those of average intelligence by a great degree. Although one such group is composed of those who are sometimes called "geniuses" (who fall at the extreme high end of the normal curve for intelligence), the other group is made up of people who, for various reasons, are considered intellectually disabled and whose IQ scores fall well below the mean on the normal curve (see **Figure 26.1**).

---

*facilitate: make something easier.

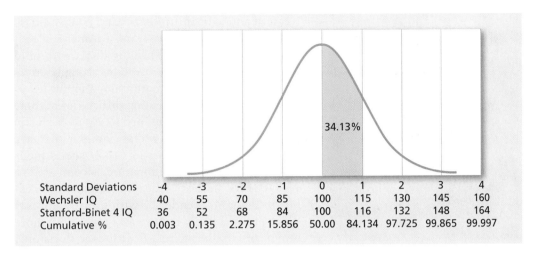

Standard Deviations	-4	-3	-2	-1	0	1	2	3	4
Wechsler IQ	40	55	70	85	100	115	130	145	160
Stanford-Binet 4 IQ	36	52	68	84	100	116	132	148	164
Cumulative %	0.003	0.135	2.275	15.856	50.00	84.134	97.725	99.865	99.997

FIGURE 26.1 The Normal Curve
The percentages under each section of the normal curve represent the percentage of scores falling within that section for each standard deviation (SD) from the mean. Scores on intelligence tests are typically represented by the normal curve. The dotted vertical lines each represent one standard deviation from the mean, which is always set at 100. For example, an IQ of 115 on the Wechsler represents one standard deviation above the mean, and the area under the curve indicates that 34.13 percent of the population falls between 100 and 115 on this test. Note: The figure shows the mean and standard deviation for the Stanford-Binet Fourth Edition (Stanford-Binet 4). The Stanford-Binet Fifth Edition was published in 2003 and now has a mean of 100 and a standard deviation of 15 for composite scores.

Intellectual Disability Intellectual disability (intellectual developmental disorder) (formerly *mental retardation* or *developmentally delayed*) is a neurodevelopmental disorder and is defined in several ways. First, the person exhibits deficits in mental abilities, which is typically associated with an IQ score approximately two standard deviations below the mean on the normal curve, such as below 70 on a test with a mean of 100 and standard deviation of 15. Second, the person's *adaptive behavior* (skills that allow people to live independently, such as being able to work at a job, communicate well with others, and grooming skills such as being able to get dressed, eat, and bathe with little or no help) is severely below a level appropriate for the person's age. Finally, these limitations must begin in the developmental period. Intellectual disability occurs in about 1 percent of the population (American Psychiatric Association, 2013).

Diagnosis Recognizing tests of IQ are less valid as one approaches the lower end of the IQ range, and the importance of adaptive living skills in multiple life areas, levels of severity (mild, moderate, severe, and profound) are now based on level of adaptive functioning and level of support the individual requires (American Psychiatric Association, 2013). Thus, a *DSM-5* diagnosis of intellectual disability is based on deficits in intellectual functioning, determined by standardized tests of intelligence and clinical assessment, which impact adaptive functioning across three domains. The domains include: conceptual (memory, reasoning, language, reading, writing, math, and other academic skills), social (empathy, social judgment, interpersonal communication, and other skills that impact the ability to make and maintain friendships), and practical (self-management skills that affect personal care, job responsibilities, school, money management, and other areas) (American Psychiatric Association, 2013). Previous editions indicated these deficits must occur prior to 18 years of age, but the *DSM-5* removes the specific age criteria, specifying symptoms must begin during the developmental period.

◄ So how would a professional go about deciding whether or not a child has an intellectual disability? Is the IQ test the primary method?

intellectual disability (intellectual developmental disorder) condition in which a person's behavioral and cognitive skills exist at an earlier developmental stage than the skills of others who are the same chronological age; may also be referred to as developmentally delayed. This condition was formerly known as mental retardation.

▲ This middle-aged man, named Jack, lives in a small town in Arkansas and serves as a deacon in the local church. He is loved and respected and leads what, for him, is a full and happy life. Jack also has Down syndrome, but he has managed to find his place in the world.

Intellectual disability can vary from mild to profound. According to the *DSM-5* (American Psychiatric Association, 2013), individuals with mild intellectual disability may not be recognized as having deficits in the conceptual domain until they reach school age where learning difficulties become apparent; as an adult, they are likely to be fairly concrete thinkers. In the social domain, they are at risk of being manipulated as their social judgment and interactions are immature as compared to same-age peers. In the practical domain, they are capable of living independently with proper supports in place but will likely require assistance with more complex life skills such as health care decisions, legal issues, or raising a family (American Psychiatric Association, 2013). This category makes up the vast majority of those with intellectual disabilities. Other classifications in order of severity are moderate, severe, and profound. Conceptually, individuals with profound intellectual disability have a very limited ability to learn beyond simple matching and sorting tasks and socially, have very poor communication skills, although they may recognize and interact nonverbally with well-known family members and other caretakers. In the practical domain, they may be able to participate by watching or assisting but are likely totally dependent upon others for all areas of their care (American Psychiatric Association, 2013). All of these skill deficits are likely compounded by multiple physical or sensory impairments.

Causes What causes intellectual disability? Unhealthy living conditions can affect brain development. Examples of such conditions are lead poisoning from eating paint flakes (Lanphear et al., 2000)), as well as other toxicants (Ericksson et al., 2001; Eskenazi et al., 1999; Schroeder, 2000). Deficits may also be attributed to factors resulting in inadequate brain development or other health risks associated with poverty. Examples include malnutrition, health consequences as the result of not having adequate access to health care, or lack of mental stimulation through typical cultural and educational experiences.

Some of the biological causes of intellectual disability include Down, fetal alcohol syndrome, and fragile X syndrome. *Fetal alcohol syndrome* is a condition that results from exposing a developing embryo to alcohol, and intelligence levels can range from below average to levels associated with intellectual disability (Olson & Burgess, 1997). In *fragile X syndrome*, an individual (more frequently a male) has a defect in a gene on the X chromosome of the 23rd pair, leading to a deficiency in a protein needed for brain development. Depending on the severity of the damage to this gene, symptoms of fragile X syndrome can range from mild to severe or profound intellectual disability (Dykens et al., 1994; Valverde et al., 2007).

There are many other causes of intellectual disability (Murphy et al., 1998). Lack of oxygen at birth, damage to the fetus in the womb from diseases, infections, or drug use by the mother, and even diseases and accidents during childhood can lead to intellectual disability.

One thing should always be remembered: Intellectual disability affects only a person's intellectual capabilities and adaptive behaviors. Individuals with an intellectual disability are just as responsive to love and affection as anyone else and need to be loved and to have friends just as all people do. Intelligence is only one characteristic; warmth, friendliness, caring, and compassion also count for a great deal and should not be underrated.

Giftedness At the other end of the intelligence scale* are those who fall on the upper end of the normal curve (see Figure 26.1), above an IQ of 130 (about 2 percent of the population). The term applied to these individuals is **gifted**, and if their IQ falls above 140 to 145 (less than half of 1 percent of the population), they are often referred to as highly advanced or *geniuses*.

People have long held many false beliefs about people who are very, very intelligent. Such beliefs have included that gifted people are weird and socially awkward, physically weak, and more likely to suffer from mental illnesses. From these beliefs come the "mad scientist" of the cinema and the "evil geniuses" of literature.

These beliefs were shattered by a groundbreaking study that was initiated in 1921 by Lewis M. Terman, the same individual responsible for the development of the Stanford-Binet Test. Terman (1925) selected 1,528 children to participate in a longitudinal study. These children, 857 boys and 671 girls, had IQs (as measured by the Stanford-Binet) ranging from 130 to 200. The early findings of this major study (Terman & Oden, 1947) demonstrated that the gifted were socially well adjusted and often skilled leaders. They were also above average in height, weight, and physical attractiveness, putting an end to the myth of the weakling genius. Terman was able to demonstrate not only that his gifted children were not more susceptible to mental illness than the general population, but he was also able to show that they were actually more resistant to mental illnesses than those of average intelligence. Only those with the highest IQs (180 and above) were found to have some social and behavioral adjustment problems *as children* (Janos, 1987).

Terman's "Termites," as they came to be called, were also typically successful as adults. They earned more academic degrees and had higher occupational and financial success than their average peers (at least, the men in the study had occupational success—women at this time did not typically have careers outside the home). Researchers Zuo and Cramond (2001) examined some of Terman's gifted people to see if their identity formation as adolescents was related to later occupational success. They found that most of the more successful "Termites" had in fact successfully achieved a consistent sense of self, whereas those who were less successful had not done so.

A book by Joan Freeman called *Gifted Children Grown Up* (Freeman, 2001) describes the results of a similar longitudinal study of 210 gifted and nongifted children in Great Britain. One of the more interesting findings from this study is that gifted children who are "pushed" to achieve at younger and younger ages, sitting for exams long before their peers would do so, often grow up to be disappointed, somewhat unhappy adults. Freeman points to differing life conditions for the gifted as a major factor in their success, adjustment, and well-being: Some lived in poverty and some in wealth, for example. A final note, there are many examples of people that have not been recognized as "gifted" in their early years who have gone on to become Supreme Court justices, Nobel Prize winners, and novelists by working hard and persisting in their efforts to achieve their goals in life.

gifted the 2 percent of the population falling on the upper end of the normal curve and typically possessing an IQ of 130 or above.

I've heard that geniuses are sometimes a little "nutty" and odd. Are geniuses, especially the really high-IQ ones, " not playing with a full deck," as the saying goes?

▲ Stanford University psychologist Lewis Terman is pictured at his desk in 1942. Terman spent a good portion of his career researching children with high IQ scores and was the first to use the term gifted to describe these children.

---

*scale: a graded series of tests or performances used in rating individual intelligence or achievement.

Learn How Intelligence Is Measured

26.4 Explain the history of intelligence testing, including historical use and misuse in the context of fairness.

Watch the Video, *The History of Intelligence Testing: Binet and Terman,* at MyPsychLab

The history of intelligence testing spans the twentieth century and has at times been marked by controversies and misuse. A full history of how intelligence testing developed would take at least an entire chapter, so this section will discuss only some of the better known forms of testing and how they came to be. For some additional detail, watch the video, *The History of Intelligence Testing: Binet and Terman.*

Intelligence Tests The measurement of intelligence by some kind of test is a concept that is less than a century old. It began when educators in France realized that some students needed more help with learning than others did. They thought that if a way could be found to identify these students more in need, they could be given a different kind of education than the more capable students.

Binet's Mental Ability Test In those early days, a French psychologist named Alfred Binet was asked by the French Ministry of Education to design a formal test of intelligence that would help identify children who were unable to learn as quickly or as well as others, so that they could be given remedial education. Eventually, he and colleague Théodore Simon came up with a test that not only distinguished between fast and slow learners but also between children of different age groups as well (Binet & Simon, 1916). They noticed that the fast learners seemed to give answers to questions that older children might give, whereas the slow learners gave answers that were more typical of a younger child. Binet decided that the key element to be tested was a child's *mental age*, or the average age at which children could successfully answer a particular level of questions.

> It doesn't sound like intelligence would be easy to measure on a test—how do IQ tests work, anyway?

Stanford-Binet and IQ Lewis Terman (1916), a researcher at Stanford University, adopted German psychologist William Stern's method for comparing mental age and *chronological age* (number of years since birth) for use with the translated and revised Binet test. Stern's (1912) formula was to divide the mental age (MA) by the chronological age (CA) and multiply the result by 100 to get rid of any decimal points. The resulting score is called an **intelligence quotient, or IQ.** (A *quotient* is a number that results from dividing one number by another.)

$$IQ \times 1MA/CA = 100$$

For example, if a child who is 10 years old takes the test and scores a mental age of 15 (is able to answer the level of questions typical of a 15-year-old), the IQ would look like this:

$$IQ \times 115/10 \times 100 = 150$$

The quotient has the advantage of allowing testers to compare the intelligence levels of people of different age groups. While this method works well for children, it produces IQ scores that start to become meaningless as the person's chronological age passes 16 years. (Once a person becomes an adult, the idea of questions that are geared for a particular age group loses its power. For example, what kind of differences would there be between questions designed for a 30-year-old versus a 40-year-old?) Most intelligence tests today, such as the *Stanford-Binet Intelligence Scales, Fifth Edition (SB5)* (Roid, 2003) and the Wechsler tests (see the following section), use age-group comparison norms instead. The SB5 is often used by educators to make decisions about the placement of students into special educational programs, both for those with disabilities and for those with exceptionalities. See **Table 26.1** for descriptions of some items similar to those from the SB5.

intelligence quotient (IQ) a number representing a measure of intelligence, resulting from the division of one's mental age by one's chronological age and then multiplying that quotient by 100.

Table 26.1	Paraphrased Sample Items from the Stanford-Binet Intelligence Test	
AGE*	TYPE OF ITEM	PARAPHRASED SAMPLE ITEM
2	Board with three differently shaped holes	Child can place correct shape into matching hole on board.
4	Building block bridge	Child can build a simple bridge out of blocks after being shown a model.
7	Similarities	Child can answer such questions as "In what way are a ship and a car alike?"
9	Digit reversal	Child can repeat four digits backward.
Average adult	Vocabulary	Child can define 20 words from a list.

*Age at which item typically is successfully completed.
Source: Roid, G. H. (2003).

26.5 Describe current methods of assessing human abilities.

The Wechsler Tests Although the original Stanford-Binet Test is now in its fifth edition and includes different questions for people of different age groups, it is not the only IQ test that is popular today. David Wechsler (Wechsler, 2002, 2003, 2008) was the first to devise a series of tests designed for specific age groups. Originally dissatisfied with the fact that the Stanford-Binet was designed for children but being administered to adults, he developed an IQ test specifically for adults. He later designed tests specifically for older school-age children and preschool children, as well as those in the early grades. The Wechsler Adult Intelligence Scale (WAIS-IV), Wechsler Intelligence Scale for Children (WISC-IV), and the Wechsler Preschool and Primary Scale of Intelligence (WPPSI-IV) are the three versions of this test, and in the United States these tests are now used more frequently than the Stanford-Binet. In earlier editions, another way these tests differed from the Stanford-Binet was by having both a verbal and performance (nonverbal) scale, as well as providing an overall score of intelligence (the original Stanford-Binet was composed predominantly of verbal items). **Table 26.2** has sample items for each of the four index scales from the WAIS-IV.

26.6 Identify measures of and data on reliability and validity for intelligence test scores.

Test Construction: Good Test, Bad Test? All tests are not equally good tests. Some tests may fail to give the same results on different occasions for the same person when that person has not changed—making the test useless. These would be considered unreliable tests. **Reliability** of a test refers to the test producing consistent results each time it is given to the same individual or group of people. For example, if Nicholas takes a personality test today and then again in a month or so, the results should be very similar if the personality test is reliable. Other tests might be easy to use and even reliable, but

reliability the tendency of a test to produce the same scores again and again each time it is given to the same people.

Table 26.2	Simulated Sample Items from the Wechsler Adult Intelligence Scale (WAIS-IV)
	SIMULATED SAMPLE TEST ITEMS
Verbal Comprehension Index	
Vocabulary	What is a hippopotamus? What does "resemble" mean?
Perceptual Reasoning Index	
Visual Puzzles	Look at a completed puzzle and select three components from a set of options that would re-create the puzzle, all within a specified time limit.
Working Memory Index	
Digit Span	Recall lists of numbers, some lists forward and some lists in reverse order, and recall a mixed list of numbers in correct ascending order.
Processing Speed Index	
Symbol Search	Visually scan a group of symbols to identify specific target symbols, within a specified time limit.

Simulated items and descriptions similar to those in the *Wechsler Adult Intelligence Scale—Fourth Edition* (2008).

if they don't actually measure what they are supposed to measure, they are also useless. These tests are thought of as "invalid" (untrue) tests. **Validity** is the degree to which a test actually measures what it's supposed to measure. Another aspect of validity is the extent that an obtained score accurately reflects the intended skill or outcome in real-life situations, or *ecological validity*, not just validity for the testing or assessment situation. For example, we hope that someone who passes his or her test for a driver's license will also be able to safely operate a motor vehicle when they are actually on the road. When evaluating a test, consider what a specific test score means and to what, or to whom, it is compared.

Take the hypothetical example of Mr. Stumpwater, who believes that intelligence is related to a person's golf scores. Let's say that he develops an adult intelligence test based on golf scores. What do we need to look at to determine if his test is a good one?

Standardization of Tests First of all, we would want to look at how he tried to standardize his test. *Standardization* refers to the process of giving the test to a large group of people that represents the kind of people for whom the test is designed. One aspect of standardization is in the establishment of consistent and standard methods of test administration. All test subjects would take the test under the same conditions. In Mr. Stumpwater's case, this would mean that he would have his sample members play the same number of rounds of golf on the same course under the same weather conditions, and so on. Another aspect addresses the comparison group whose scores will be used to compare individual test results. Standardization groups are chosen randomly from the population for whom the test is intended and, like all samples, must be representative of that population. If a test is designed for children, for example, then a large sample of randomly selected children would be given the test.

validity the degree to which a test actually measures what it's supposed to measure.

The scores from the standardization group would be called the *norms*, the standards against which all others who take the test would be compared. Most tests of intelligence follow a *normal curve*, or a distribution in which the scores are the most frequent around the *mean*, or average, and become less and less frequent the further from the mean they occur (see Figure 26.1).

On the Wechsler IQ test, the percentages under each section of the normal curve represent the percentage of scores falling within that section for each *standard deviation (SD)* from the mean on the test. The standard deviation is the average variation of scores from the mean.

In the case of the Mr. Stumpwater's golf test, he might find that a certain golf score is the average, which he would interpret as average intelligence. People who scored extremely well on the golf test would be compared to the average, as well as people with unusually poor scores.

The normal curve allows IQ scores to be more accurately estimated than the old IQ scoring method formula devised by Stern. Test designers replaced the old ratio IQ of the earlier versions of IQ tests with *deviation IQ scores*, which are based on the normal curve distribution (Eysenck, 1994): IQ is assumed to be normally distributed with a mean IQ of 100 and a typical standard deviation of about 15 (the standard deviation can vary according to the particular test). An IQ of 130, for example, would be two standard deviations above the mean, whereas an IQ of 70 would be two standard deviations below the mean, and in each case the person's score is being compared to the population's average score.

With respect to validity and reliability, Mr. Stumpwater's test fares poorly. If the results of his test were compared with other established intelligence tests, there would probably be no relationship at all. Golf scores have nothing to do with intelligence, so the test is not a valid, or true, measure of intelligence.

On the other hand, his test might work well for some people and poorly for others on the question of reliability. Some people who are good and regular golfers tend to score about the same for each game that they play, so for them, the golf score IQ would be fairly reliable. But others, especially those who do not play golf or play infrequently, would have widely varying scores from game to game. For those people, the test would be very unreliable, and if a test is unreliable for some, it's not a good test.

Usefulness of IQ Tests IQ tests are generally valid for predicting academic success and job performance (Sackett et al., 2008). This may be truer for those who score at the higher and lower ends of the normal curve, as the predictive value is less clear for those who score in the average range of IQ. The kinds of tests students are given in school are often similar to intelligence tests, and so people who do well on IQ tests typically do well on other kinds of academically oriented tests as well, such as the Scholastic Assessment Test (SAT), the American College Test (ACT), the Graduate Record Examinations (GRE), and actual college examinations. These achievement tests are very similar to IQ tests but are administered to groups of people rather than to individuals. However, recent research suggests skills in self-regulation or levels of motivation may impact IQ measures and raises concerns about situations or circumstances where IQ scores may not be unbiased predictors of academic or job success (Duckworth et al., 2011; Duckworth & Seligman, 2005; Nisbett et al., 2012).

Intelligence testing also plays an important role in neuropsychology, where specially trained psychologists use intelligence tests and other forms of cognitive and behavioral testing to assess neurobehavioral disorders in which cognition

◀ If intelligence tests are so flawed, why do people still use them?

and behavior are impaired as the result of brain injury or brain malfunction (National Academy of Neuropsychology, 2001). As part of their profession, neuropsychologists use intelligence testing in diagnosis (e.g., head injury, learning disabilities, neuropsychological disorders), tracking progress of individuals with such disorders, and in monitoring possible recovery.

Consider Key Issues in Intelligence

26.7 Describe the influences of biological, cultural, and environmental factors on intelligence.

The Nature/Nurture Controversy Regarding Intelligence Are people born with all of the "smarts" they will ever have, or does experience and learning count for something in the development of intellect? The influence of *nature* (heredity or genes) and *nurture* (environment) on personality traits has long been debated in the field of human development, and intelligence is one of the traits that has been examined closely.

Twin and Adoption Studies The problem with trying to separate the role of genes from that of environment is that controlled, perfect experiments are neither practical nor ethical. Instead, researchers find out what they can from *natural experiments*, circumstances existing in nature that can be examined to understand some phenomenon. *Twin studies* are an example of such circumstances.

Identical twins are those who originally came from one fertilized egg and, therefore, share the same genetic inheritance (called DNA). Any differences between them on a certain trait, then, should be caused by environmental factors. Fraternal twins come from two different eggs, each fertilized by a different sperm,

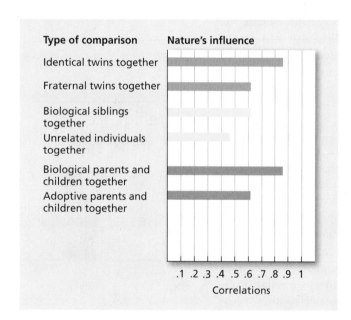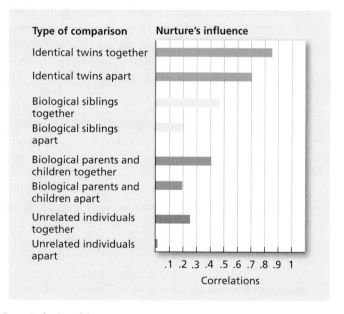

FIGURE 26.2 Correlations between IQ Scores of Persons with Various Relationships
In the graph on the left, the degree of genetic relatedness seems to determine the agreement (correlation) between IQ scores of the various comparisons. For example, identical twins, who share 100 percent of their genes, are more similar in IQ than fraternal twins, who share only about 50 percent of their genes, even when raised in the same environment. In the graph on the right, identical twins are still more similar to each other in IQ than are other types of comparisons, but being raised in the same environment increases the similarity considerably.

and share only the amount of genetic material that any two siblings would share. By comparing the IQs of these two types of twins reared together (similar environments) and reared apart (different environments), as well as persons of other degrees of relatedness, researchers can get a general, if not exact, idea of how much influence heredity has over the trait of intelligence (see **Figure 26.2**). As can be easily seen from the chart, the greater the degree of genetic relatedness, the stronger the correlation is between the IQ scores of those persons. The fact that genetically identical twins show a correlation of .86 means that the environment must play a part in determining some aspects of intelligence as measured by IQ tests. If heredity alone were responsible, the correlation between genetically identical twins should be 1.00. At this time, researchers have determined that the estimated *heritability* (proportion of change in IQ across a whole population that is caused by hereditary factors) for intelligence is about .50 or 50 percent (Plomin & DeFries, 1998; Plomin & Spinath, 2004).

Although the correlation between identical twins is higher than the estimated heritability of .50, that similarity is not entirely because of the twins' genetic similarity. Twins who are raised in the same household obviously share very similar environments as well. Even twins who are reared apart, as seen in adoption studies, are usually placed in homes that are similar in socioeconomic and ethnic background—more similar than one might think. So when twins who are genetically similar are raised in similar environments, their IQ scores are also going to be similar. However, similar environmental influences become less important over time (where genetic influences increase over time), accounting for only about 20 percent of the variance in intelligence by age 11 or 12 (Posthuma et al., 2009). In turn, environmental influences tend not to be a factor by adolescence, and with the increasing impact of genetic factors, it has been suggested that the heritability of intelligence might be as high as .91 or 91 percent by the age of 65 (Posthuma et al., 2009).

One of the things that people need to understand about heritability is that estimates of heritability apply only to changes in IQ within a *group* of people, *not to the individual people themselves*. Each individual is far too different in experiences, education, and other nongenetic factors to predict exactly how a particular set of genes will interact with those factors in that one person. Only differences among people *in general* can be investigated for the influence of genes (Dickens & Flynn, 2001). Genes always interact with environmental factors, and in some cases extreme environments can modify even very heritable traits, as would happen in the case of a severely malnourished child's growth pattern. Enrichment, on the other hand, could have improved outcomes. Some observations suggest IQ scores are steadily increasing over time, from generation to generation, in modernized countries, a phenomenon called the *Flynn effect* (Flynn, 2009).

◀ Wait a minute—if identical twins have a correlation of .86, wouldn't that mean that intelligence is 86 percent inherited?

26.8 Explain issues related to the consequences of intelligence testing.

IQ Tests and Cultural Bias The problem with trying to measure intelligence with a test that is based on an understanding of the world and its resources is that not everyone comes from the same "world." People raised in a different culture, or even a different economic situation, from the one in which the designer of an IQ test is raised are not likely to perform well on such a test—not to mention the difficulties of taking a test that is written in an unfamiliar language or dialect. In the early days of immigration, people from non–English-speaking countries would score very poorly on intelligence tests, in some cases being denied entry to the United States on the basis of such tests (Allen, 2006).

Intelligence tests free of cultural bias are difficult to design. If the test designer comes from the same cultural and socioeconomic background as the person that is taking the test, the person taking the test may have an unfair advantage over a person from a different cultural or socioeconomic background (Helms, 1992). A test designed by a person from a Western culture may put a person from an Eastern culture at a disadvantage because items on the test may make no sense to them. For example, one kind of question might be: Which one of these words is least like the others?

LION—HOUSE—BEAR—EAGLE—TUNA

A person from an Eastern culture that relies on the ocean for food resources might select TUNA instead of the "correct" answer HOUSE, as was the intention of the question's author who comes from an urban background.

Efforts to create culture-bias-free intelligence tests have led test designers to conclude that it may be impossible to create a test that is completely with cultural bias (Carpenter et al., 1990). A "culture-fair" test requires the use of nonverbal abilities like object rotation, instead of items about culturally-specific verbal knowledge. These tests are more culturally fair; however, they do not measure other important mental abilities, like verbal knowledge, that are associated with intelligence.

The Bell Curve and Misinterpretation of Statistics One of the other factors that has been examined for possible heritable differences in performance on IQ tests is the concept of race. (The term *race* is used in most of these investigations as a way to group people with common skin colors or facial features, and one should always be mindful of how suspect that kind of classification is. Cultural background, educational experiences, and socioeconomic factors typically have far more to do with similarities in group performances than does the color of one's skin.) In 1994, Herrnstein and Murray published the controversial book *The Bell Curve*, in which they cite large numbers of statistical studies (never published in scientific journals prior to the book) that led them to make the claim that IQ is largely inherited. These authors go further by also implying that people from lower economic levels are poor because they are unintelligent.

In their book, Herrnstein and Murray made several statistical errors and ignored the effects of environment and culture. First, they assumed that IQ tests actually do measure intelligence; that is, they are truly valid. As discussed earlier, IQ tests are not free of cultural or socioeconomic bias. Furthermore, just being aware of negative stereotypes can result in an individual scoring poorly on intelligence tests or other tasks, a response called **stereotype threat** (Steele & Aronson, 1995; Jameson et al., 2007). So all they really found was a correlation between race and *IQ score*, not *intelligence*. They also assumed that intelligence itself is very heavily influenced by genetics, with a heritability factor of about .80. The current estimate of the heritability of intelligence is actually about .50 (Plomin & DeFries, 1998).

Thinking Critically
What kind of questions would you include on an intelligence test to minimize cultural bias?

stereotype threat condition in which being made aware of a negative performance stereotype interferes with the performance of someone that considers himself or herself part of that group.

Mental and Physical Exercises Combine for Better Cognitive Health?

You may have heard the saying "use it or lose it" and likely think of it in terms of maintaining physical fitness. But it is not limited to that; in many regards, the saying applies as well to our ability to maintain cognitive fitness. However, just as there is a difference between physical activity and physical exercise, there is a difference in mental *activity* and mental *exercise*.

Quite a few computerized brain-training programs and devices have hit the market in the last few years. In addition, a lot of attention in the media has focused on the benefits of specific computer-based brain exercises you can do to improve your cognitive fitness. Although some are more scientifically grounded and offer the possibility of real benefits, many more appear to be riding the current wave of interest and may not be useful. For some individuals, practicing certain mental skills through cognitive exercises appears to help with those same skills when tested later. In general, however, research has not identified any benefits that transfer to untrained areas (Owen et al., 2010). Just as being physically active in general will not make you an Olympic athlete, to tune up your cognitive fitness you have to perform proper, focused cognitive exercises.

What else can you do more generally to benefit your cognitive health? Exercise! And this time, we are referring to physical exercise. Physical activity and specifically aerobic fitness has repeatedly been demonstrated to be associated with improved cognitive function across the life span. A physically active lifestyle and greater aerobic fitness has been implicated with better executive control and memory processes in preadolescent children (Chaddock et al., 2010; Hillman et al., 2009), better educational outcomes later in life and improved affect and visual spatial memory in young adults (Åberg et al., 2009; Stroth et al., 2009), increased hippocampal volume (associated with better memory) in elderly adults (Erickson et al., 2009), and as a useful intervention in a group of individuals at high risk of cognitive decline or impairment, especially for females in the group (Baker et al., 2010).

So instead of "use it or lose it," perhaps a better saying to keep in mind is "what is good for the heart or body is also good for the mind." If you want to learn more, an interesting overview of research related to exercise and brain health can be found in the book *Spark: The Revolutionary New Science of Exercise and the Brain* by John Ratey and Eric Hagerman (2008).

Questions for Further Discussion

1. Aside from those involving working memory, what other kinds of focused mental exercises might help to keep the brain fit?
2. Should doctors suggest aerobic exercise for their patients interested in maintaining or improving their cognitive functions? What about psychologists working with individuals who have mood or anxiety disorders, or clients with attention problems?

Pick the best answer.

1. According to Spearman, what would a traditional IQ test most likely measure?

   a. general intelligence
   b. emotional intelligence
   c. specific intelligence
   d. practical intelligence

2. In Gardner's view, astronauts, navigators, and artists would have high levels of which type of intelligence?

   a. naturalist   c. interpersonal
   b. visual/spatial   d. kinesthetic

3. What does it mean for an IQ test to be culturally fair?

   a. The test is completely free of cultural bias.
   b. The test does not put people from minority cultures at a disadvantage.
   c. The test assesses how a subject would perform in a different culture.
   d. The test is created by a member of the subjects' own culture.

4. Darla is 4 years old. The intelligence test that would most likely be used to measure her intelligence is the

   a. Binet's Mental Ability Test.
   b. Wechsler Intelligence Scale for Children.
   c. Wechsler Adult Intelligence Scale.
   d. Dove Counterbalance General Intelligence Test.

5. Mr. Beckett designed an IQ test. He hopes to use it in high schools throughout the county. Which of the following would be a problem for him if he wanted to standardize the test?

   a. He always administers the test in the same conditions.
   b. He can only give the test to his class of 10 students.
   c. He asks similar questions on the test every time.
   d. He finds that people tend to get similar scores each time they take the test.

6. Jared, age 13, has an intellectual disability complicated by multiple physical and sensory impairments that significantly impact his skills of daily living and ability to communicate. He is unable to take care of himself in any area of life. Jared would most likely be classified with _____ intellectual disability.

   a. mild
   b. moderate
   c. severe
   d. profound

7. A male with a defective chromosome from his mother leading to severe protein deficiency and poor brain development probably suffers from

   a. Down syndrome.
   b. fetal alcohol syndrome.
   c. hydrocephaly.
   d. fragile X syndrome.

8. Elizabeth was tested while in grade school and found to have an IQ of 134. Elizabeth's intelligence level can be labeled as

   a. average.
   b. slightly above average.
   c. gifted.
   d. genius.

9. Current estimates place the heritability of IQ at about

   a. 30 percent.
   b. 50 percent.
   c. 70 percent.
   d. 90 percent.

10. According to Sternberg, a person who has "street smarts" and can easily manage situations has what kind of intelligence?

    a. intrapersonal
    b. analytical
    c. creative
    d. practical

((Listen to an **Audio File** of your chapter at **MyPsychLab**

Module 25: Thinking

Understand the basic elements of thought.

25.1 Explain cognitive processes involved in understanding information.
- Thinking (cognition) is mental activity that occurs in the brain when information is being organized, stored, communicated, or processed.

25.2 Explain processes involved in problem solving and decision making.
- Problem solving consists of thinking and behaving in certain ways to reach a goal.
- A heuristic or "rule of thumb" is a strategy that narrows down the possible solutions for a problem.
- Creative people are usually good at mental imagery, have knowledge on a wide range of topics, and are often unconventional in their work.
- Insight is the sudden perception of a solution to a problem.

25.3 Explain nonhuman problem-solving abilities.
- Köhler found evidence of insight in chimpanzees.

Learn about obstacles related to thought.

25.4 Describe obstacles to problem solving, making good judgments, and making good decisions.
- Functional fixedness is the tendency to perceive objects as having only the use for which they were originally intended.
- Confirmation bias is the tendency to search for evidence that confirms one's beliefs.

Module 26: Intelligence

Compare and contrast perspectives on intelligence.

26.1 Explain intelligence as a general factor.
- Spearman proposed general intelligence, or g factor, as the ability to reason and solve problems, whereas specific intelligence, or s factor, includes task-specific abilities in certain areas such as music, business, or art.

26.2 Describe alternative conceptualizations of intelligence.
- Gardner proposed nine different types of intelligence.
- Sternberg proposed three types of intelligence: analytical, creative, and practical.

26.3 Discuss the extremes of intelligence.
- Intellectual disability is a neurodevelopmental condition in which IQ falls below 70 and adaptive behavior across conceptual, social, and practical domains of life is severely deficient for a person of a particular chronological age.
- The four levels of intellectual disability are mild, moderate, severe, and profound.

Learn how intelligence is measured.

26.4 Explain the history of intelligence testing, including historical use and misuse in the context of fairness.
- The Stanford-Binet Intelligence Test yields an IQ score that was once determined by dividing mental age by chronological age and multiplying that quotient by 100.

26.5 Describe current methods of assessing human abilities.
- The Wechsler Intelligence Tests yield four scores derived from verbal and nonverbal subtests.

26.6 Explain measures of and data on reliability and validity for intelligence test scores.
- Standardization, validity, and reliability are all important factors in the construction of an intelligence test.

Consider key issues in intelligence.

26.7 Describe the influences of biological, cultural, and environmental factors on intelligence.
- Stronger correlations are found between IQ scores as genetic relatedness increases.

26.8 Explain issues related to the consequences of intelligence testing.
- In 1994, Herrnstein and Murray published *The Bell Curve*, in which they made widely criticized claims about the heritability of intelligence.

Applying Psychology to Everyday Life: Mental and Physical Exercises Combine for Better Cognitive Health
- Both specific mental exercises and physical exercise are important for optimal cognitive functioning.

Vocabulary Terms

thinking (cognition) p. 314
mental images p. 314
concept p. 315
prototype p. 316
schema p. 317
trial and error (mechanical solution) p. 317
algorithms p. 318

heuristic p. 318
representativeness heuristic p. 318
availability heuristic p. 318
convergent thinking p. 320
creativity p. 320
divergent thinking p. 320
functional fixedness p. 320
insight p. 321

mental set p. 322
confirmation bias p. 323
intelligence p. 325
g factor p. 325
emotional intelligence p. 326
intellectual disability (intellectual developmental disorder) p. 327

gifted p. 329
intelligence quotient (IQ) p. 330
reliability p. 331
validity p. 332
stereotype threat p. 336

✓ **Study and Review** at **MyPsychLab**

Vocabulary Review

Match each vocabulary term to its definition.

1. validity
2. mental set
3. g factor
4. creativity
5. algorithm
6. availability heuristic
7. cultural bias
8. convergent thinking
9. emotional intelligence
10. prototype

a. An example of a concept that closely matches the defining characteristics of a concept.

b. The awareness of and ability to manage one's own emotions as well as the ability to be self-motivated, empathetic, and socially skilled.

c. The tendency for people to persist in using problem-solving patterns that have worked for them in the past.

d. The degree to which a test actually measures what it's supposed to measure.

e. Type of thinking in which a problem is seen as having only one answer, and all lines of thinking will eventually lead to that single answer, using previous knowledge and logic.

f. The tendency to estimate the probability of a certain condition or event based on how many similar instances we can recall.

g. A very specific, step-by-step procedure for solving a certain type of problem.

h. The tendency of IQ tests to reflect, in language, dialect, and content, the culture of the test designer(s).

i. The ability to reason and solve problems, or general intelligence.

j. The ability to solve problems by combining ideas or behavior in new ways.

Psychology Project

How do cultural biases affect the way we assess intelligence? Complete this project to examine how intelligence tests may be culturally biased.

Materials:
- a partner
- a computer with an Internet connection
- a pencil and paper

Instructions:

1. With your partner, use an Internet search engine to locate 1–2 intelligence or IQ tests online. You do not need to use the tests named in this chapter, but do find tests that are substantial enough so that you are looking at least 20 test questions total. You might try the Web site of Mensa International or use other online intelligence tests.

2. Working separately, read through the test(s). Note any test items that could be considered to have a bias that might cause a person from another culture, or from a subculture within the United States, to miss the item even if he or she spoke reasonably fluent English. For example, one online test asks people to determine what words the letters stand for in this sentence: *32 is the T in D, F at which W F* A person raised in the United States, where temperature is commonly measured in degrees Fahrenheit, will probably find the answer fairly easily: 32 is the temperature in degrees Fahrenheit at which water freezes. Someone from a country where temperature is usually measured in degrees Celsius might have a harder time.

3. In evaluating test items, keep in mind that cultural biases can exist even when people are from the same large cultural group but belong to different subgroups. Consider the possible effect of socioeconomic status, geographical location, and so forth.

4. Mark any items that you think are culturally biased and jot down why. Then compare notes with your partner. Did you flag the same items? Why or why not?

Tech Alternative

Download an AI (artificial intelligence) app onto your smartphone. (There are a number of free ones available.) Experiment by asking different types of questions and seeing what questions are answered by the app. Determine which types of questions get the best answers from the app and which types of questions get less helpful answers. Write about your findings and describe how working with AI has benefits and limitations.

Essay Question

Prashant, a student who has recently moved to the United States from India, takes an IQ test. In a well-organized essay, explain how two of the following factors could potentially contribute to Prashant's score on the test:

a. Mental sets
b. Divergent thinking
c. Test validity

d. Cultural bias
e. Fragile X syndrome

Test Yourself

Ready for your test? More quizzes and a customized plan.

✅ **Study and Review** at **MyPsychLab**

Pick the best answer.

1. It takes _____ to view a mental image that covers more distance than a more compact one.
   a. longer
   b. less time
   c. the same amount of time
   d. half the time

2. Research suggests we engage mental images in our mind _____ the way we engage or interact with physical objects.
   a. a little like
   b. much like
   c. not at all like
   d. randomly and completely different than

3. The fact that a circle typically fits a specific and rigid set of rules is an example of a
   a. formal concept.
   b. natural concept.
   c. fuzzy concept.
   d. prototype.

4. Trial and error is sometimes referred to as a(n)
   a. algorithm.
   b. heuristic.
   c. rule of thumb.
   d. mechanical solution.

5. John, while searching the garage for his basketball, applies a rule to only look in places big enough for a basket ball to fit in. This process of problem solving is known as using a(n)
   a. heuristic.
   b. trial and error method.
   c. working backward method.
   d. algorithm.

6. Using a pencil eraser to replace a lost earing back is an example of overcoming
   a. a mental set.
   b. functional fixedness.
   c. confirmation bias.
   d. transformation bias.

7. Which of the following questions would be more likely to produce divergent thinking?
   a. "What is a clothes hanger?"
   b. "How do you spell clothes hanger?"
   c. "How many uses can you think of for a clothes hanger?"
   d. "What does a clothes hanger typically look like?"

8. Which type of intelligence, according to Howard Gardner, would most likely be present in farmers, landscapers, and biologists?
   a. naturalist
   b. visual/spatial
   c. existentialist
   d. movement

9. According to Sternberg, "book smarts" is another way of talking about which kind of intelligence?
   a. analytical
   b. creative
   c. practical
   d. emotional

10. Which of the following tests came first?
    a. The Wechsler tests
    b. The Stanford–Binet
    c. The ACT
    d. Binet's mental ability test

11. Ms. Davenport gives all her classes 45 minutes to complete their psychology test regardless of whether the class meets for 50 minutes, 75 minutes, or even 3 hours. Such a technique ensures test
    a. reliability.
    b. validity.
    c. norms.
    d. standardization.

12. In contrast to comparing mental age to chronological age, most modern tests of intelligence use _____.
    a. Stern's formula.
    b. age-group comparison norms.
    c. creativity assessments.
    d. emotional assessments.

13. The goal of all test developers is to _____ cultural bias in their intelligence tests.
    a. maximize
    b. eliminate
    c. minimize
    d. hide

14. Dr. Miller works with children who have grown up in poor socioeconomic conditions. Many are malnourished, have been exposed to a variety of environmental toxins, and have multiple infections without adequate or timely health care. What might these children be at risk for?
    a. intellectual disability
    b. genetic inhibition
    c. organically induced deprivation
    d. increased emotional intelligence

15. Dr. Thomas has found that William, her patient, has a defect in a gene on the X chromosome of his 23rd pair. William most likely suffers from
    a. Down syndrome.
    b. cretinism.
    c. fragile X syndrome.
    d. fetal alcohol syndrome.

16. In Terman's study of gifted children, mental health issues and relationship problems only occurred in those with IQs of
    a. 150 or higher.
    b. 180 or higher.
    c. 100 or lower.
    d. 45 or lower.

17. What may be the best predictor of why some people do not excel in school but essentially succeed in their life and career choices?
    a. cretinism
    b. phonemes
    c. one's intelligence quotient
    d. emotional intelligence

18. What does the Flynn effect theorize?
    a. Intelligence scores are steadily increasing in modernized countries.
    b. Intelligence scores are decreasing due to an overreliance on technology.
    c. Intelligence scores are relatively stable in contrast to improvement in our educational system.
    d. Intelligence scores are meaningless and should be abandoned.

19. Jane grew up in an isolated rural area of the United States, with very little exposure to popular culture. Jane does not know the common slang meanings of words like "cool" and "awesome." What problem might Jane encounter if she took an intelligence test?
    a. the conjunction fallacy
    b. lack of reliability
    c. cultural bias
    d. lack of standardization

20. Which heuristic can be used to create and maintain stereotypes?
    a. representative
    b. means-end analysis
    c. availability
    d. convergent thinking

Learning Objectives

25.1 **25.2** **25.3** pp. 314–321

Understand the Basic Elements of Thought

● **thinking (cognition)**
is mental activity that goes on in the brain when a person is organizing and attempting to understand information and communicating information.

● **mental images**
are picture-like mental representations that stand in for objects or events.

● **concepts**
are ideas that represent a class or category of objects, events, or activities.

● **problem solving**
- creativity: divergent thinking
- a **mechanical solution** relies on trial-and-error and may involve solving by rote, or a learned set of rules.
- a **heuristic** is a simple "rule of thumb" that is intended to apply to many situations
- **insight** is an instance when the solution to a problem seems to come to mind suddenly.
- to human and to an extent nonhuman animals

Learning Objectives

25.4 pp. 322–323

Learn about Obstacles Related to Thought

● **obstacles to problem solving**
- functional fixedness
- mental set
- confirmation bias

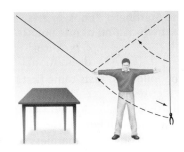

Thinking and Intelligence

Learning Objectives

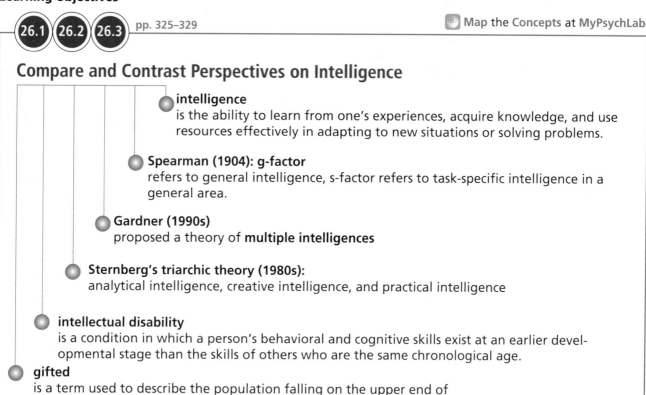

26.1 26.2 26.3   pp. 325–329

🔵 Map the Concepts at MyPsychLab

Compare and Contrast Perspectives on Intelligence

intelligence
is the ability to learn from one's experiences, acquire knowledge, and use resources effectively in adapting to new situations or solving problems.

Spearman (1904): g-factor
refers to general intelligence, s-factor refers to task-specific intelligence in a general area.

Gardner (1990s)
proposed a theory of **multiple intelligences**

Sternberg's triarchic theory (1980s):
analytical intelligence, creative intelligence, and practical intelligence

intellectual disability
is a condition in which a person's behavioral and cognitive skills exist at an earlier developmental stage than the skills of others who are the same chronological age.

gifted
is a term used to describe the population falling on the upper end of the normal curve and typically possessing an IQ of 130 or above.

Learning Objectives

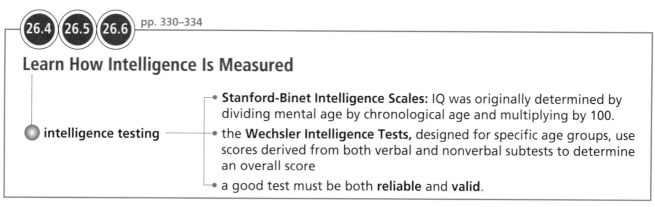

26.4 26.5 26.6   pp. 330–334

Learn How Intelligence Is Measured

intelligence testing
- **Stanford-Binet Intelligence Scales:** IQ was originally determined by dividing mental age by chronological age and multiplying by 100.
- the **Wechsler Intelligence Tests,** designed for specific age groups, use scores derived from both verbal and nonverbal subtests to determine an overall score
- a good test must be both **reliable** and **valid**.

Learning Objectives

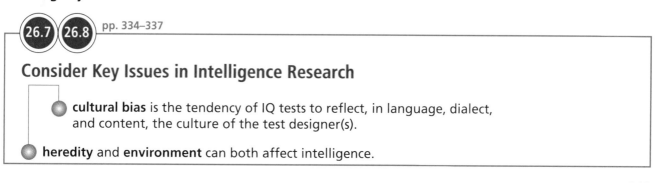

26.7 26.8   pp. 334–337

Consider Key Issues in Intelligence Research

cultural bias is the tendency of IQ tests to reflect, in language, dialect, and content, the culture of the test designer(s).

heredity and **environment** can both affect intelligence.

CHAPTER 11

Motivation and Emotion

Jennifer got excellent grades in high school. She was involved in a variety of activities, but her classes always came first, and she earned an academic scholarship to college. The scholarship required her to maintain a 3.0 GPA—something that she didn't think would be too difficult. Jennifer really enjoyed her college courses as well as the newfound freedoms of college life. With the abundance of social opportunities, she found several new activities to pursue and devoted less time to studying. She was shocked when she got a D on her first exam. She vowed to do better but finished the semester with only a 2.0 GPA and lost her scholarship.

With the help of her academic advisor, Jennifer was able to identify lack of time-management and study strategies as preventing her progress, and she learned to balance her academic and social lives. Her renewed focus enabled her to raise her GPA, later regain and maintain her scholarship, and ultimately graduate.

As a busy high school student, how do you stay motivated to succeed?

Watch the Video, at MyPsychLab

*W*hy Study Motivation and Emotion*?*

The study of motivation not only helps us understand why some people are more driven to achieve than others but also why we experience certain drives such as hunger. Emotions are a part of everything we do, affecting our relationships with others and our own health, as well as influencing important decisions. In this chapter, we will explore the motives behind our actions and the origins and influences of emotions.

27 Motivation

Module Goals	Learning Objectives
Explain major theories of motivation.	**27.1** Understand biologically based theories of motivation.
	27.2 Learn about cognitively based theories of motivation.
	27.3 Discuss humanistic theories of motivation.
Describe motivated behaviors.	**27.4** Understand eating behavior and the influence of culture.
	27.5 Learn about sexual behavior and orientation.
	27.6 Understand achievement motivation.
	27.7 Describe other ways in which humans and nonhuman animals are motivated.

Explain Major Theories of Motivation

Some people are content to sit and watch life pass them by, while others seem to need far more out of life. Some people want to do great things, while others are happy with more ordinary lives. What motivates people to do the things they do? What exactly is motivation?

27.1 Understand biologically based theories of motivation.

Motivation is the process by which activities are started, directed, and continued so that physical or psychological needs or wants are met (Petri, 1996). The word itself comes from the Latin word *movere*, which means "to move." Motivation is what "moves" people to do the things they do. For example, when a person is relaxing in front of the television and begins to feel hungry, the physical need for food might cause the person to get up, go into the kitchen, and search for something to eat. The physical need of hunger caused the action (getting up), directed it (going to the kitchen), and sustained the search (finding or preparing something to eat). Hunger is only one example, of course. Loneliness may lead to calling a friend or going to a place where there are people. The desire to get ahead in life motivates many people to go to college. Just getting out of bed in the morning is motivated by the need to keep a roof over one's head and food on the table by going to work.

Extrinsic and Intrinsic Motivation There are different types of motivation. Sometimes people are driven to do something because of an external reward (or the avoidance of an unpleasant consequence), as when someone goes to work at a job to make money and avoid losing possessions such as a house or a car. In **extrinsic motivation**, a person performs an action because it leads to an outcome that is separate from or external to the person (Ryan & Deci, 2000). Other examples would be giving money to a child for every "A" on a report card, offering a bonus to an employee for increased performance, or tipping a server in a restaurant for good service. The child, employee, and server are motivated to work for the

motivation the process by which activities are started, directed, and continued so that physical or psychological needs or wants are met.

extrinsic motivation type of motivation in which a person performs an action because it leads to an outcome that is separate from or external to the person.

external or extrinsic rewards. In contrast, **intrinsic motivation** is the type of motivation in which a person performs an action because the act itself is rewarding or satisfying in some internal manner. Psychologist Teresa Amabile (Amabile et al., 1976) found that children's creativity was affected by the kind of motivation for which they worked: Extrinsic motivation decreased the degree of creativity shown in the experimental group's artwork when compared to the creativity levels of the children in the intrinsically motivated control group. To learn more about the factors motivating your behavior, take the survey *What Motivates You?*

✳ Complete the Survey, *What Motivates You?*, at MyPsychLab

Instincts and the Evolutionary Approach Early attempts to understand motivation focused on the biologically determined and innate patterns of behavior called **instincts** that exist in both people and animals. Just as animals are governed by their instincts to migrate, build a nest, mate, and protect their territory, evolutionary theorists proposed that human beings may also be governed by similar instincts (James, 1890; McDougall, 1908). For instance, according to these theorists, the human instinct to reproduce is responsible for sexual behavior, and the human instinct for territorial protection may be related to aggressive behavior.

William McDougall (1908) proposed a total of 18 instincts for humans, including curiosity, flight (running away), pugnacity (aggressiveness), and acquisition (gathering possessions). As the years progressed, psychologists added more and more instincts to the list until there were thousands of proposed instincts. However, none of these early theorists did much more than give names to these instincts. Although there were plenty of descriptions, such as "submissive* people possess the instinct of submission," there was no attempt to explain why these instincts exist in humans, if they exist at all (Petri, 1996).

Instinct approaches have faded away because, although they could describe human behavior, they could not explain it. But these approaches did force psychologists to realize that some human behavior is controlled by hereditary factors.

Drive-Reduction Theory The next approach to gain support involved the concepts of needs and drives. A **need** is a requirement for some material (such as food or water) that is essential for survival of the organism. When an organism has a need, it leads to a psychological tension as well as a physical arousal that motivates the organism to act to fulfill the need and reduce the tension. This tension is called a **drive** (Hull, 1943). Therefore, think of it as a need gives rise to a drive (to satisfy the need).

Drive-reduction theory proposes just this connection between internal physiological states and outward behavior. In this theory, there are two kinds of drives. **Primary drives** involve the survival needs of the body such as hunger and thirst, whereas **acquired (secondary) drives** are learned through experience or conditioning, such as the need for money or social approval, or the need of recent former smokers to have something to put in their mouths. If this sounds familiar, it should. The concepts of primary and secondary reinforcers from Chapter Six are related to these drives. Primary reinforcers satisfy primary drives, and secondary reinforcers satisfy acquired, or secondary, drives.

This theory also includes the concept of **homeostasis**, or the tendency of the body to maintain a steady state. One could think of homeostasis as the body's version of a thermostat—thermostats keep the temperature of a house at a constant level, and homeostasis does the same for the body's functions. When there is a primary drive need, the body is in a state of imbalance. This stimulates the behavior that brings the body back into balance, or homeostasis. For example, if

intrinsic motivation type of motivation in which a person performs an action because the act itself is rewarding or satisfying in some internal manner.

instincts the biologically determined and innate patterns of behavior that exist in both people and animals.

need a requirement of some material (such as food or water) that is essential for survival of the organism.

drive a psychological tension and physical arousal arising when there is a need that motivates the organism to act in order to fulfill the need and reduce the tension.

drive-reduction theory approach to motivation that assumes behavior arises from physiological needs that cause internal drives to push the organism to satisfy the need and reduce tension and arousal.

primary drives those drives that involve needs of the body such as hunger and thirst.

acquired (secondary) drives those drives that are learned through experience or conditioning, such as the need for money or social approval.

homeostasis the tendency of the body to maintain a steady state.

---

*submissive: conforming to authority.

▲ *(left) The human body needs water, especially when a person is working hard or under stress, as this man appears to be. Thirst is a survival need of the body, making it a primary drive, according to drive-reduction theory. What other kinds of needs might be primary drives?*
(right) Some people are driven to do strenuous, challenging activities even when there is no physical need to do so. When a drive is acquired through learning, it is called an acquired or secondary drive. Fulfilling an acquired drive provides secondary reinforcement. What might this rock climber find reinforcing about scaling this steep cliff?

Jarrod's body needs food, he feels hunger and the state of tension/arousal associated with that need. He will then seek to restore his homeostasis by eating something. (See **Figure 27.1.**)

Although drive-reduction theory works well to explain the actions people take to reduce tension created by needs, it does not explain all human motivation.

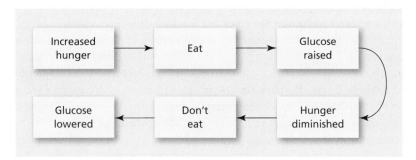

FIGURE 27.1 Homeostasis
In homeostasis, the body maintains balance in the body's physical states. For example, this diagram shows how increased hunger (a state of imbalance) prompts a person to eat. Eating increases the level of glucose (blood sugar), causing the feelings of hunger to decrease. After a period without eating, the glucose levels become low enough to stimulate the hunger drive once again, and the entire cycle is repeated.

27.2 Learn about cognitively based theories of motivation.

Thinking Critically
How might the three types of needs discussed in this section relate to the goals of many politicians? Would some needs be more important than others?

Obviously, motivation is about needs. Drive-reduction theory talks about needs, and other theories of motivation include the concept of needs. In many of these theories, most needs are the result of some inner physical drive (such as hunger or sex) that demands to be satisfied, but other theories examine our psychological needs.

McClelland's Theory: Affiliation, Power, and Achievement Needs

Harvard University psychologist David C. McClelland (1961, 1987) proposed a theory of motivation that highlights the importance of three psychological needs not typically considered by the other theories: affiliation, power, and achievement.

According to McClelland, human beings have a psychological need for friendly social interactions and relationships with others. Called the **need for affiliation** (abbreviated as nAff in McClelland's writings), people high in this need seek to be liked by others and to be held in high regard by those around them. This makes high-affiliation people good team players.

A second psychological need proposed by McClelland is the **need for power** (nPow). Power is not about reaching a goal but about having control over other people. People high in this need would want to have influence over others and make an impact on them. They want their ideas to be the ones that are used, regardless of whether or not their ideas will lead to success. Status and prestige are important, so these people wear expensive clothes, live in expensive houses, drive fancy cars, and dine in the best restaurants. Someone who is high in the need for power typically sees the money (and cars, houses, jewelry, and other "toys") as the achievement.

The **need for achievement** (nAch) involves a strong desire to succeed in attaining goals, not only realistic ones but also challenging ones. People who are high in nAch look for careers and hobbies that allow others to evaluate them because these high achievers also need to have feedback about their performance in addition to the achievement of reaching the goal. Although many of these people do become wealthy, famous, and publicly successful, others fulfill their need to achieve in ways that lead only to their own personal success, not material riches—they just want the challenge. Achievement motivation appears to be strongly related to success in school, occupational success, and the quality and amount of what a person produces (Collins et al., 2004; Gillespie et al., 2002; Spangler, 1992).

▲ *Sean Combs at the Cannes International Film Festival. Many people who are as wealthy as Combs continue to buy new houses, businesses, clothing, and cars (among other things) even though they do not need them. Such actions are examples of the need for power. How might this need for power be expressed in a person's relationships with others, such as a spouse, employee, or friend?*

Arousal and Incentive Approaches

Another explanation for human motivation involves the recognition of yet another type of need, the need for stimulation. A *stimulus motive* is one that appears to be unlearned but causes an increase in stimulation. Examples would be curiosity, playing, and exploration. On the

need for affiliation (nAff) the need for friendly social interactions and relationships with others.

need for power (nPow) the need to have control or influence over others.

need for achievement (nAch) the need that involves a strong desire to succeed in attaining goals, not only realistic ones but also challenging ones.

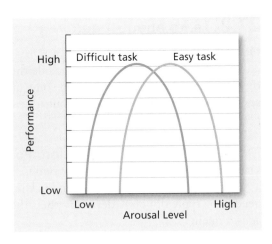

FIGURE 27.2 Arousal and Performance
The optimal level of arousal for task performance depends on the difficulty of the task. We generally perform easy tasks well if we are at a high-moderate level of arousal (green) and accomplish difficult tasks well if we are at a low-moderate level (red).

▲ *Does this look fun? If so, you may score relatively higher in sensation seeking.*

arousal theory theory of motivation in which people are said to have an optimal (best or ideal) level of tension that they seek to maintain by increasing or decreasing stimulation.

Yerkes–Dodson law law stating performance is related to arousal; moderate levels of arousal lead to better performance than do levels of arousal that are too low or too high. This effect varies with the difficulty of the task: Easy tasks require a high-moderate level, whereas more difficult tasks require a low-moderate level.

sensation seeker someone who needs more arousal than the average person.

incentives things that attract or lure people into action.

incentive approaches theories of motivation in which behavior is explained as a response to the external stimulus and its rewarding properties.

other hand, sometimes our motives for doing things involve the rewards or *incentives* we get when we act, such as eating food even when we are not hungry just because it tastes so good—an example of learned behavior.

Arousal Theory In **arousal theory**, people are said to have an optimal (best or ideal) level of tension. Task performances, for example, may suffer if the level of arousal is too high (such as severe test anxiety) or even if the level of arousal is too low (such as boredom). For many kinds of tasks, a moderate level of arousal seems to be best. This relationship between task performance and arousal has been explained by the **Yerkes–Dodson law** (Teigen, 1994; Yerkes & Dodson, 1908), although Yerkes and Dodson formulated the law referring to stimulus intensity, not arousal level (Winton, 1987).

Of special interest to both sports psychologists and social psychologists, this effect is modified by the difficulty level of the task: Easy tasks demand a somewhat "high-moderate" level for optimal performance, whereas difficult tasks require a "low-moderate" level. **Figure 27.2** shows this relationship in graphic form.

Even though the average person might require a moderate level of arousal to feel content, some people need less arousal and some need more. The person who needs more arousal is called a **sensation seeker** (Zuckerman, 1979, 1994). Sensation seekers seem to need more complex and varied sensory experiences than do other people. The need does not always have to involve danger. For example, students who travel to other countries to study tend to score higher on scales of sensation seeking than do students who stay at home (Schroth & McCormack, 2000).

Incentive Approaches **Incentives** are things that attract or lure people into action. In **incentive approaches**, behavior is explained in terms of the external stimulus and its rewarding properties. These rewarding properties exist independently of any need or level of arousal and can cause people to act only upon the incentive. Thus, incentive theory is actually based, at least in part, on the principles of learning that were discussed in Chapter Five.

27.3 Discuss humanistic theories of motivation.

Some final approaches to the study of motivation are humanistic in nature. One of the classic humanistic approaches is that of Maslow, whereas a more modern approach is represented by self-determination theory.

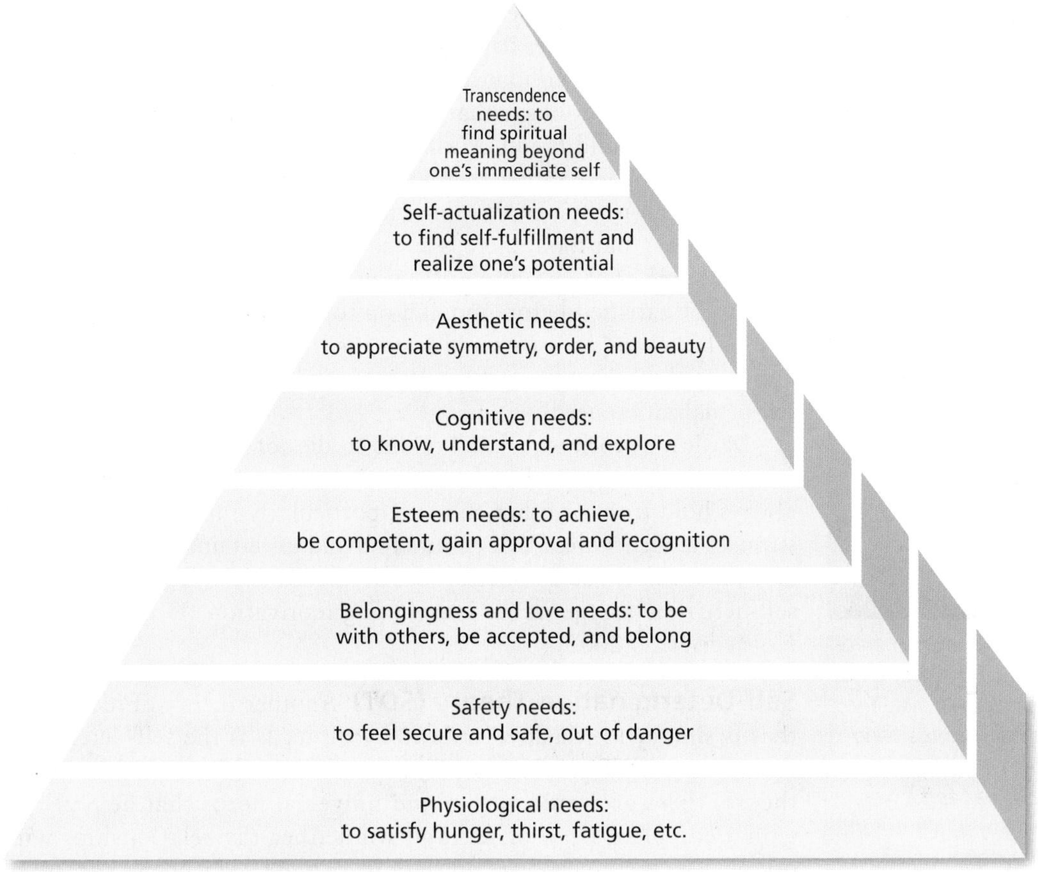

FIGURE 27.3 Maslow's Hierarchy of Needs
Maslow proposed that human beings must fulfill the more basic needs, such as physical and security needs, before being able to fulfill the higher needs of self-actualization.

Maslow's Hierarchy of Needs The first humanistic theory is based on the work of Abraham Maslow (1943, 1987). As explained in the video *Maslow's Hierarchy of Needs*, Maslow proposed that there are several levels of needs that a person must strive to meet before achieving the highest level of personality fulfillment.

According to Maslow, **self-actualization** is the point that is seldom reached at which people have satisfied the lower needs and achieved their full human potential.

These needs include both fundamental deficiency needs, such as the need for food or water, and growth needs, such as the desire for having friends or feeling good about oneself (Maslow, 1971; Maslow & Lowery, 1998). For a person to achieve self-actualization, which is one of the highest levels of growth needs, the primary, fundamental needs must first be fulfilled. The only need higher than self-actualization is transcendence, a search for spiritual meaning beyond one's immediate self, which Maslow added many years after his original hierarchy was formulated. **Figure 27.3** shows the typical way to represent Maslow's series of needs as a pyramid, with the most basic needs for survival at the bottom and the highest needs at the top. This type of ranking is called a hierarchy.

People move up the pyramid as they go through life, gaining wisdom and the knowledge of how to handle many different situations. But a shift in life's circumstances can result in a shift down to a lower need. Moving up and down and then back up can occur frequently—even from one hour to the next. The times in a person's life in which self-actualization is achieved, at least temporarily, are called

○ **Watch** the **Video,** *Maslow's Hierarchy of Needs,* at **MyPsychLab**

self-actualization according to Maslow, the point that is seldom reached at which people have sufficiently satisfied the lower needs and achieved their full human potential.

Does this ▶
theory apply
universally?

▲ *In the movie Castaway, Tom Hanks's character is stranded on a deserted island. Once he has his needs for food, water, and shelter met, he gets lonely. He finds a volleyball, paints a hand-print and then a crude face on it, and names it "Wilson." He talks to the volleyball as if it were a person, at first as a kind of way to talk out the things he needs to do and later as a way of staying relatively sane. The need for companionship is that strong.*

But don't we some-
times do things for ▶
both kinds of motives?

peak experiences according to Maslow, times in a person's life during which self-actualization is temporarily achieved.

self-determination theory (SDT) theory of human motivation in which the social context of an action has an effect on the type of motivation existing for the action.

peak experiences. For Maslow, the process of growth and self-actualization is the striving to make peak experiences happen again and again.

Maslow's theory is not without its critics. There are several problems with his theory, and the most serious is that there is little scientific support (Drenth et al., 1984). Like Sigmund Freud, Maslow developed his theory based on his own observations of people rather than any empirically gathered observations or research. Although many people report that while they were starving, they could think of nothing but food, there is anecdotal evidence in the lives of many people, some of them quite well known, that the lower needs do not have to be satisfied before moving on to a higher need (Drenth et al., 1984). For example, artists and scientists throughout history have been known to deny their own physical needs while producing great works (a self-actualization need).

Maslow's work was based on his studies of Americans. Cross-cultural research suggests that the order of needs on the hierarchy does not always hold true for other cultures, particularly those cultures with a stronger tendency than U.S. culture to avoid uncertainty, such as Greece and Japan. In those countries, security needs are much stronger than self-actualization needs in determining motivation (Hofstede, 1980; Hofstede et al., 2002)

Self-Determination Theory (SDT) Another theory of motivation that is similar to Maslow's hierarchy of needs is the **self-determination theory (SDT)** of Richard Ryan and Edward Deci (2000). In this theory, there are three inborn and universal needs that help people gain a complete sense of self and whole, healthy relationships with others. The three needs are autonomy, or the need to be in control of one's own behavior and goals (i.e., self-determination); competence, or the need to be able to master the challenging tasks of one's life; and relatedness, or the need to feel a sense of belonging, intimacy, and security in relationships with others. These needs are common in several theories of personality; the relatedness need is, of course, similar to Maslow's belongingness and love needs, and both autonomy and competence are important aspects of Erikson's theory of psychosocial personality development (Erikson, 1950, 1980). ⓛⓘⓝⓚ *to Chapter Twelve: Theories of Personality, p. 380.*

There are usually elements of both intrinsic and extrinsic motives in many of the things people do. Most teachers, for example, work for money to pay bills (the extrinsic motive) but may also feel that they are helping young children to become better adults in the future, which makes the teachers feel good about themselves (the intrinsic motive).

Describe Motivated Behaviors

How do basic motivations drive and determine our behaviors every day? Whenever we sit down for a meal, go on a date, or study for an exam, we are performing motivated behaviors. In the following pages, we will explore the physiological and psychological components of a few motivated behaviors in detail.

27.4 Understand eating behavior and the influence of culture.

Eating is not only a basic survival behavior that reduces a primary drive; it is also a form of entertainment for many and the attractive presentations and social environment of many eating experiences are a powerful incentive.

The Physiological and Social Components of Hunger The physical hunger drive involves several factors. If the stomach is empty and contracted, hunger usually occurs. Another factor is the insulin response. **Insulin** and **glucagon** are hormones that are secreted by the pancreas to control the levels of fats, proteins, and carbohydrates in the whole body, including glucose (blood sugar). Insulin, normally released in greater amounts after eating has begun, causes a feeling of more hunger because of a drop in blood sugar levels. High blood sugar (which is more likely when one eats sugary foods and white breads, rice, and pasta) leads to more insulin released, which leads to a low blood sugar level, increased appetite, and the tendency to overeat.

When released into the bloodstream, the hormone *leptin* signals the hypothalamus that the body has had enough food, reducing appetite. Also, part of the hypothalamus stops the eating response as blood sugar increases, while another part controls the beginning of eating as insulin levels go up (Neary et al., 2004). In one study, rats whose ventromedial hypothalamus (VMH) areas (located toward the bottom and center of the hypothalamus) were damaged would no longer stop eating—they ate and ate until they were quite overweight (Hetherington & Ranson, 1940). (See **Figure 27.4** for a picture of a rat with this kind of damage.)

The physical controls of hunger are not enough to explain all eating behavior. People often eat when they are not really hungry or just because the food looks so good or smells so good. Social cues also tell people to eat, such as the convention of eating breakfast, lunch, and dinner at certain times. A large part of that convention is actually the result of classical conditioning. The body becomes conditioned to respond with the hunger reflex at certain times of the day; through association with the act of eating, those times of the day have become conditioned stimuli for hunger. Classical conditioning may cause insulin levels to increase even before food is eaten, just as Pavlov's dogs salivated before getting food (Rodin, 1981, 1985). **LINK** to *Chapter Six: Learning and Language Development, pp. 194–199.*

Cultural factors and gender also play a part in determining hunger and eating habits. In one study, a questionnaire about eating habits was given to both men and women from the United States and Japan. Although no significant differences in what initiates eating existed for men in either culture, women in the United States were found to be much more likely to start eating for emotional reasons, such as depression. Japanese women were more likely to eat because of hunger signals or social demands (Hawks et al., 2003). In this same study, both men and women from the United States were more likely to eat while watching television or movies than were Japanese men and women. Both culture and gender must be taken into account when studying why and under what circumstances people eat.

Obesity Several factors contribute to obesity, a condition in which the body weight of a person is 20 percent or more over the ideal body weight for that person's height. A significant factor in obesity is heredity. There appear to be several sets of genes, some on different chromosomes, that influence a person's likelihood of becoming obese (Barsh et al., 2000). If there is a history of obesity in a particular family, each family member has a risk of becoming obese that is double or triple the risk of people who do not have a family history of obesity (Bouchard, 1997). Hormones also play a part, particularly leptin. When released into the bloodstream, the hormone leptin signals the hypothalamus that the body has had enough food, reducing appetite. Problems with leptin production or detection can lead to overeating (Friedman & Halaas, 1998).

FIGURE 27.4 Obese Laboratory Rat
The rat on the left has reached a high level of obesity because its ventromedial hypothalamus has been deliberately damaged in the laboratory. The result is a rat that no longer receives signals of being satiated, and so the rat continues to eat and eat and eat.

▲ *Cultural factors play an important part in why people eat. Women in Japan have been found to be motivated to eat by hunger and social demands, illustrated by the interaction during a meal at this family gathering.*

insulin a hormone secreted by the pancreas to control the levels of fats, proteins, and carbohydrates in the body by lowering or raising the level of glucose in the bloodstream.

glucagon hormone that is secreted by the pancreas to control the levels of fats, proteins, and carbohydrates in the body by increasing the level of glucose in the bloodstream.

▲ *Women in the United States may eat because they are depressed or for other emotional reasons, rather than just to appease hunger or as part of a social situation. Obviously, this woman does not need the social trappings of a bowl, dining table, and the company of others to motivate her eating habits—unless you count the cat.*

Another factor is certainly overeating. Around the world, as developing countries get stronger economies and their food supplies become stable, the rates of obesity increase dramatically and quickly (Barsh et al., 2000). Foods become more varied and enticing* as well, and an increase in variety is associated with an increase in eating beyond the physiological need to eat (Raynor & Epstein, 2001). In industrialized societies when workers spend more hours in the workplace, there is less time available for preparing meals at home and more incentive to dine out (Chou et al., 2004). When the "dining out" choices include fast food and soft drinks, as is so often the case, obesity rates increase. At about 31 percent (nearly a third of its population), the United States has the highest rate of obesity in the world (Flegal et al., 2010, Friedman, 2000, 2003; Marik, 2000; Mokdad et al., 2001). Over the last 20 years, rates of obesity in developing countries have tripled. Of children from developing countries such as China, the Middle East, Southeast Asia, and the Pacific Islands, 10 to 25 percent are overweight and another 2 to 10 percent are obese (Hossain et al., 2007). Metabolism slows down as people age. Aside from not changing the eating habits of their youth and lowering their intake, as they earn more income people also often increase the amount of food they consume, thereby assuring a weight gain that may lead to obesity.

27.5 Learn about sexual behavior and orientation.

Yet another motivating factor that is hard to ignore and often causes stress is our sexual behavior. The study of sexual behavior is not the study of the sex act but rather when, with whom, and under what circumstances sexual acts take place.

What were the findings of the report? ▶ **Sexual Behavior** Although other attempts were made to study human sexual behavior before the mid-twentieth-century studies of Alfred Kinsey (Kinsey et al., 1948; 1953), his original work remains an important source of information concerning sexual behavior.

The Kinsey Study In 1948, Alfred Kinsey published a controversial report on the results of a massive survey of sexual behavior he had collected over 10 years (Kinsey et al., 1948). His findings rocked many people, who were apparently not ready to believe that so many people had tried alternative sexual behaviors. Kinsey believed that sexual orientation was not an either/or situation but instead that sexual orientation is on a continuum† with some people falling at either extreme and some falling closer to the middle.

Although Kinsey's data are still quoted in many discussions of sexual behavior, his original surveys were far from perfect. As stated earlier, the participants were almost exclusively white, middle class, and college educated. Older people, those who lived in rural regions, and less educated people were not well represented. Some critics claimed that Kinsey gave far more attention to sexual behavior that was considered unusual or abnormal than he did to "normal" sexual behavior (Geddes, 1954). Also, Kinsey's surveys were no less susceptible to the exaggerations, falsifications, and errors of any method using self-report techniques. Finally, a face-to-face interview might cause some

---

*enticing: attractive; desirable.
†continuum: a sequence of values, elements, or behavior that varies by small degrees.

people being interviewed to be inhibited about admitting to certain kinds of sexual behavior, or others might exaggerate wildly, increasing the likelihood of inaccurate data.

Sexual Orientation The term **sexual orientation** refers to a person's sexual attraction and affection for members of either the opposite or the same sex. One of the more important questions that researchers are trying to answer is whether sexual orientation is the product of learning and experience or whether it is biological in origin. As the video *Categories of Sexual Orientation* shows, there are a variety of sexual orientation categories that individuals may identify with and getting reliable data can be challenging. The most common sexual orientation is **heterosexual**, in which people are sexually attracted to members of the opposite physical sex, as in a man being attracted to a woman or vice versa. (The Greek word *hetero* means "other," so heterosexual means "other sexual" or attraction for the other sex.) Heterosexuality is a socially acceptable form of sexual behavior in all cultures. A national survey estimates that about 2.3 percent of men and 1.3 percent of women aged 15 to 44 years consider themselves to be homosexuals, meaning that their sexual orientations are exclusively or predominantly **homosexual** (Mosher et al., 2005). A person who is **bisexual** may be either male or female and is attracted to both sexes. In the same national survey, only 1.8 percent of the men and 2.8 percent of the women considered themselves to be bisexual (Mosher et al., 2005).

This is a very controversial issue for both heterosexuals and homosexuals (Diamond, 1995). If homosexuality is a product of upbringing and environmental experiences, it can be assumed to be a behavior that can be changed, placing a burden of choice to be "normal" or "abnormal" squarely on the shoulders of the person. If it is biological, either through genetic influences or hormonal influences during pregnancy, then it can be seen as a behavior that is no more a choice than whether the infant is born a male or a female, or with brown eyes or blue eyes. Human sexual orientation is a complex issue with no single, easy answer. There are multiple factors of development, environment, and an interaction of both that continues to be studied scientifically.

◀ **Is sexual orientation a product of environment, biology, or both?**

27.6 Understand achievement motivation.

Personality and nAch: Carol Dweck's Self-Theory of Motivation

According to motivation and personality psychologist Carol Dweck (1999), the need for achievement is closely linked to personality factors, including a person's view of how *self* (the beliefs a person holds about his or her own abilities and relationships with others) can affect the individual's perception of the success or failure of his or her actions. This concept is related to the much older notion of locus of control, in which people who assume that they have control over what happens in their lives are considered to have an internal locus of control, and those who feel that their lives are controlled by powerful others, luck, or fate are considered to have an external locus of control (MacDonald, 1970; Rotter, 1966).

Dweck has amassed a large body of empirical research, particularly in the field of education, to support the idea that people's "theories" about their own selves can affect their level of achievement motivation and their willingness to keep trying to achieve success in the face of failure (Dweck, 1986; Dweck & Elliott, 1983; Dweck & Leggett, 1988; Elliott & Dweck, 1988). According to this research, people can form one of two belief systems about intelligence, which in turn affects their motivation to achieve. Those who believe

sexual orientation a person's sexual attraction and affection for members of either the opposite or the same sex.

heterosexual person attracted to the opposite sex.

homosexual person attracted to the same sex.

bisexual person attracted to both men and women.

▲ Many people are driven by a need to attain both realistic and challenging goals. This young girl seems eager to provide an answer to the teacher's question, and the teacher's positive feedback will help foster the girl's need for achievement.

intelligence is fixed and unchangeable often demonstrate an external locus of control, leading them to give up easily or avoid situations in which they might fail—often ensuring their own failure in the process (Dweck & Molden, 2008). They are prone to developing learned helplessness, the tendency to stop trying to achieve a goal because past failure has led them to believe that they cannot succeed.

Their goals involve trying to "look smart" and outperform others ("See, at least I did better than she did"). For example, a student faced with a big exam may avoid coming to class that day, even though that might mean getting an even lower score on a makeup exam.

This does not mean that students with this view of intelligence are always unsuccessful. In fact, Dweck's research (1999) suggests that students who have had a long history of successes may be most at risk for developing a learned helplessness after a big failure precisely because their previous successes have led them to believe in their own fixed intelligence. For example, a child who had never earned anything less than an A in school who then receives his first C might become depressed and refuse to do any more homework, ensuring future failure.

The other type of person believes that intelligence is changeable and can be shaped by experiences and effort in small increases, or increments. These people tend to show an internal locus of control, believing that their own actions and efforts will improve their intelligence (Dweck & Molden, 2008). They work at developing new strategies and get involved in new tasks with the goal of increasing their "smarts." They are motivated to master tasks, and they don't allow failure to destroy their confidence in themselves or prevent them from trying again and again, using new strategies each time.

Based on this and other research, Dweck recommends that parents and teachers praise efforts and the methods that children use to make those efforts, not just successes or ability. Instead of saying, "You're right, how smart you are," the parent or teacher should say something such as, "You are really thinking hard," or "That was a very clever way to think about this problem." In the past, teachers and parents have been told that praise is good and criticism is bad because it might damage a child's self-esteem. Dweck believes that constructive criticism, when linked with praise of effort and the use of strategies, will be a positive influence on the child's self-esteem and willingness to challenge themselves (Gunderson et al., 2013).

27.7 Describe other ways in which humans and nonhuman animals are motivated.

The Motivation to Love *Romantic love* encompasses several different feelings: the initial attraction to another person; *passionate love*, or the intense emotions and physical passion experienced at the beginning of a romantic relationship; and *companionate love*, or the deep intimacy, affection, and trust enjoyed by longtime partners. These feelings are influenced by both biological and environmental factors.

Although the idea of romantic love is, in part, a modern Western cultural construction, there is an evolutionary advantage to romantic love: It may lead to sexual reproduction, ensuring the survival of the species. Interestingly, some of the same hormones involved in romantic love are involved in the bonds between infants and their caretakers. This also makes sense from an evolutionary standpoint. A human infant is quite helpless, and humans remain dependent on their caretakers for a relatively long time. Close family bonds are essential for children's survival.

Both infant–caretaker attachments and romantic attraction are experienced as pleasurable. The hormone *oxytocin*—released by women during labor and breastfeeding, and by both sexes during sexual activity—plays a role in these feelings. Administering oxytocin to research subjects can increase feelings of trust (Kosfeld et al., 2005) and expressions of romantic affection (Gonzaga et al., 2006).

Endorphins—the brain's "natural painkillers" that produce feelings of euphoria—also seem to be involved. Animal research suggests that endorphins play a role in responding to the distress we feel when separated from a caregiver or partner, as well as the joy we feel upon reuniting (Diamond, 2004; Panksepp et al., 1980). Researchers using functional MRI have found that the same parts of the brain light up when people look at photographs of their romantic partners and when mothers look at photographs of their children (Bartels and Zeki, 2004).

Of course, environmental factors also influence love. Again, there are parallels between caretaker attachments and romantic attachments. Attachment style in infancy—that is, the nature of the connection between infant and caretaker ((L)(I)(N)(K) to *Chapter Five: Development Across the Lifespan, pp. 170–173.*) affects our family relationships as children, which in turn is correlated with how we form close relationships as adults. Children who experience close, secure family relationships are more likely to form secure romantic relationships as adults (Mickelson et al., 1997).

Other environmental influences include proximity—who's nearby—and similarity. We tend to become close with people whom we see regularly and who are like us in terms of looks, interests, attitudes, and so on. Broader social and cultural factors also influence our expression of romantic love and sexual feelings.

The Motivation to Belong Of course, we form many relationships besides family and romantic relationships. Human beings also feel a strong need for friendships and a sense of belonging within a group. Again, this has an evolutionary basis. Early humans were more likely to survive—by finding or producing food and evading dangerous predators—if they traveled in groups, cooperated, and worked toward common goals.

Naturally, then, we want to belong. Feeling connected and accepted makes us happy, whereas isolation makes us anxious and depressed. Studies of ostracism—being deliberately excluded by a group—have shown that being ostracized causes increased activity in a region of the brain that is also active when we respond to physical pain (Eisenberger et al., 2003). Being left out hurts.

Our need to belong can motivate positive behaviors such as cooperating, helping others, and striving to make a good impression. Unfortunately, it can also motivate us to stay in destructive or even abusive relationships to avoid being alone.

Pick the best answer.

1. Liz picked out "her" desk on the first day of class. But in the second class period, someone else was sitting in her chosen seat. Liz's territorial attitude about that desk and her negative feelings toward the "interloper" sitting there is best explained by which of the following?

   a. instinct approach
   b. drive-reduction theory
   c. extrinsic motivation
   d. homeostasis

2. Which of these needs is an example of a primary drive?

   a. the need for love
   b. the need for food
   c. the need for creative expression
   d. the need to belong to a group

3. Ronnie believes that people are just born smart or not smart, and he thinks of himself as "not smart." As a result, Ronnie doesn't try all that hard to succeed in school. Dweck would say that Ronnie's achievement motivation is being affected by his

   a. acquired secondary drives.
   b. internal locus of control.
   c. primary drives.
   d. external locus of control.

4. Which approach to motivation claims that people have an optimal level of tension?

   a. arousal
   b. incentive
   c. humanistic
   d. self-determination

5. Which of the following is not one of the physiological factors involved in hunger?

   a. the release of insulin
   b. sensory receptors in the stomach
   c. changes in the corpus collosum
   d. activity in the hypothalamus

6. Which of these is an example of fulfilling an esteem need?

   a. eating a hamburger
   b. graduating from college
   c. purchasing a smoke detector
   d. looking at a work of art

7. Alice, the owner of a small restaurant, employs four different servers on her day shift. All of them try to do a good job, but for different reasons. Which one is motivated by an intrinsic reward?

   a. Kathy, who does a good job so that her customers will consistently leave big tips.
   b. Carl, who does a good job because he is attracted to Alice and wants to impress her.
   c. Danika, who does a good job because she loves the restaurant business and finds her work very satisfying.
   d. Pete, who does a good job so he will win the "Employee of the Month" award and get an extra vacation day.

8. The hormone that is secreted by the pancreas to control the levels of fats is

   a. thyroxine.
   b. adrenaline.
   c. epinephrine.
   d. insulin.

9. What motivational theory relies heavily on the concept of homeostasis?

   a. instinctual theory
   b. need for affiliation theory
   c. drive-reduction theory
   d. need for achievement theory

10. Which of the following terms describes sexual attraction to members of the opposite sex?

    a. sexuality
    b. bisexuality
    c. homosexuality
    d. heterosexuality

28 Emotion

Module Goal

Understand perspectives on emotion and emotional behavior.

Learning Objectives

28.1 Identify the biological and cognitive components of emotion.

28.2 Explain how culture, environment, and gender influence emotional expression, interpretation, and behavior.

28.3 Describe research and theories of emotional experience.

Understand Perspectives on Emotion and Emotional Behavior

This chapter began with an overview of the motives that drive human behavior. But people do more than just behave—they experience feelings during every human action. Human beings are full of feelings, or emotions, and although emotions may be internal processes, there are outward physical signs of what people are feeling. This section of the chapter explores the world of human emotions and how those emotions are connected to both thinking and actions.

28.1 Identify the biological and cognitive components of emotion.

The Latin word meaning "to move" is the source of both words used in this chapter over and over again—motive and emotion. **Emotion** can be defined as the "feeling" aspect of consciousness, characterized by three elements: a certain physical arousal, a certain behavior that reveals the feeling to the outside world, and an inner awareness of feelings.

The Physiology of Emotion Physically, when a person experiences an emotion, an arousal is created by the sympathetic nervous system. The heart rate increases, breathing becomes more rapid, the pupils dilate, and the mouth may become dry. Think about the last time you were angry and then about the last time you were frightened. Weren't the physical symptoms pretty similar? Although facial expressions do differ among various emotional responses (Ekman, 1980; Ekman & Friesen, 1978; Ekman et al., 1969), emotions are difficult to distinguish from one another on the basis of inward and outward physical reactions alone. For example, it is quite easy to mistake a person who is actually afraid or angry as being aroused if the person's face is not clearly visible, which can lead to much miscommunication and misunderstanding. However, in the laboratory using devices to measure the heart rate, blood pressure, and skin temperature, researchers have found that different emotions may be associated with different physiological reactions: Fear is associated with a decrease in skin temperature, whereas anger is associated with an increase in skin temperature and a greater increase in blood pressure (Larsen et al., 2008; Levenson, 1992; Levenson et al., 1992).

emotion the "feeling" aspect of consciousness, characterized by a certain physical arousal, a certain behavior that reveals the emotion to the outside world, and an inner awareness of feelings.

Which parts of the brain are involved in various aspects of emotion? As discussed in Chapter Two, the amygdala, a small area located within the limbic system on each side of the brain, is associated with emotions such as fear and pleasure in both humans and animals (Breiter et al., 1997; Davis & Whalen, 2001; Fanselow & Gale, 2003; Hurlemann et al., 2010; Ritchey et al., 2011) and is also involved in the facial expressions of human emotions (Morris et al., 1998). In humans, damage to the amygdala has been associated with similar effects (LaBar et al., 1995) and with impairment of the ability to determine emotions from looking at the facial expressions of others (Adolphs & Tranel, 2003).

The ability to interpret the facial expressions of others as a particular emotion also seems to be a function of one side of the brain more than the other. Researchers have found that when people are asked to identify the emotion on another person's face, the right hemisphere is more active than the left, particularly in women (Voyer & Rodgers, 2002). This difference begins weakly in childhood but increases in adulthood, with children being less able to identify negative emotions as well as positive emotions when compared to adults (Barth & Boles, 1999; Lane et al., 1995). This finding is consistent with early research that assigns the recognition of faces to the right hemisphere (Berent, 1977; Ellis, 1983).

28.2 Explain how culture, environment, and gender influence emotional expression, interpretation, and behavior.

The Behavior of Emotion: Emotional Expression Facial expressions can vary across different cultures, although some aspects of facial expression seem to be universal. (See **Figure 28.1** for some examples of universal facial expressions.) Charles Darwin (1898) was one of the first to theorize that emotions were a product of evolution and, therefore, universal: All human beings, no matter what their culture, would show the same facial expression because the facial muscles evolved to communicate specific information to onlookers. For example, an angry face would signal to onlookers that they should act submissively or expect a fight. Darwin's ideas were not in line with the behaviorist movement of the early- and mid-twentieth-century, which promoted environment rather than heredity as the cause of behavior. Nonetheless, other researchers have since found evidence of a universal nature in at least seven basic emotions that are instantly recognized in the absence of language or other communication, giving more support to the evolutionary perspective within psychology (Ekman, 1973; Ekman & Friesen, 1969, 1971). Ⓛ Ⓘ Ⓝ Ⓚ *to Chapter One: The Science of Psychology, p. 12*. Even children who are blind from birth can produce the appropriate facial expressions for any given situation without ever having witnessed those expressions on others. This finding strongly supports the idea that emotional expressions have their basis in biology rather than in learning (Charlesworth & Kreutzer, 1973; Fulcher, 1942).

In their research, Paul Ekman and Wallace Friesen found that people of many different cultures (Japanese, Europeans, Americans, and even the Fore tribe of New Guinea) can consistently recognize at least seven facial expressions: anger, fear, disgust, happiness, surprise, sadness, and contempt (Ekman & Friesen, 1969, 1971). Although the emotions and the related facial expressions appear to be universal, exactly when, where, and how an emotion is expressed may be determined by the culture. **Display rules** that can vary from culture to culture (Ekman, 1973; Ekman & Friesen, 1969) are learned ways of controlling displays of emotion in social settings. For example, Japanese people have strict social rules about showing emotion in public situations—they simply do not show emotion, remaining cool, calm, and collected, at least on the outside. But in a more private situation, such as a parent scolding a child within the home, the adult's facial expression would easily be recognized as "angry" by people of any culture.

display rules learned ways of controlling displays of emotion in social settings.

FIGURE 28.1 Facial Expressions of Emotion
Facial expressions appear to be universal. For example, these faces are interpreted as showing (a) anger, (b) fear, (c) disgust, (d) happiness, (e) surprise, and (f) sadness by people of
cultures all over the world. Although the situations that cause these emotions may differ
from culture to culture, the expression of particular emotions remains strikingly the same.

Subjective Experience: Labeling Emotion The third element of emotion
is interpreting the subjective feeling by giving it a label: anger, fear, disgust,
happiness, sadness, shame, interest, and so on. Another way of labeling this
element is to call it the "cognitive element" because the labeling process is a
matter of retrieving memories of previous similar experiences, perceiving the
context of the emotion, and coming up with a solution—a label.

The label a person applies to a subjective feeling is at least in part a learned
response influenced by that person's language and culture. Such labels may differ among people of different cultural backgrounds. For example, researchers in
one study (Tsai et al., 2004) found that Chinese Americans who were still firmly
rooted in their original Chinese culture were far more likely to use labels to describe their emotions that referred to bodily sensations (such as "dizzy") or social relationships (such as "friendship") than were more "Americanized" Chinese
Americans and European Americans, who tended to use more directly emotional
words (such as "liking" or "love").

28.3 Describe research and theories of emotional experience.

In the early days of psychology, it was assumed that feeling a particular emotion
led first to a physical reaction and then to a behavioral one. This is known as the
common-sense theory of emotion. Seeing a snarling dog in one's path causes the
feeling of fear, which stimulates the body to arousal, followed by the behavioral
act of running. People are aroused because they are afraid. (See **Figure 28.2**.)

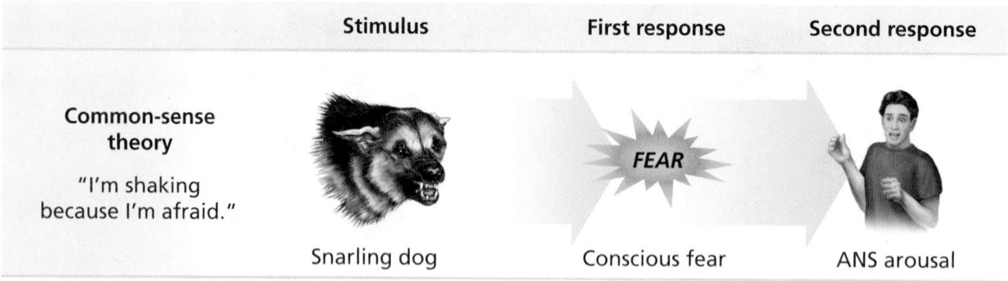

FIGURE 28.2 Common-Sense Theory of Emotion
In the common-sense theory of emotion, a stimulus (snarling dog) leads to an emotion of fear, which then leads to bodily arousal (in this case, indicated by shaking) through the autonomic nervous system (ANS).

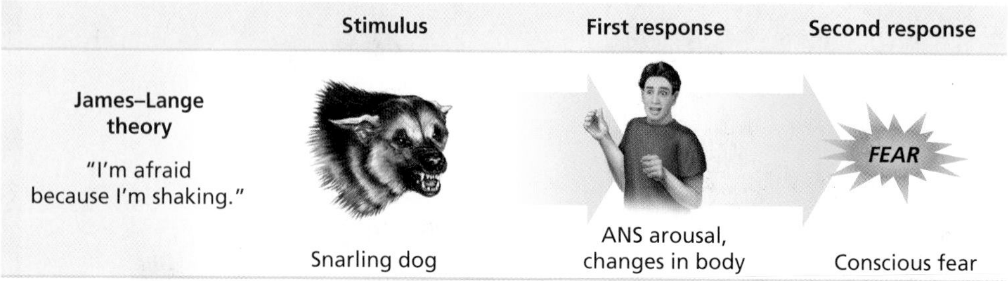

FIGURE 28.3 James–Lange Theory of Emotion
In the James–Lange theory of emotion, a stimulus leads to bodily arousal first, which is then interpreted as an emotion.

James–Lange Theory of Emotion William James (1884, 1890, 1894), who was also the founder of the functionalist perspective in the early history of psychology, (Ⓛ Ⓘ Ⓝ Ⓚ to *Chapter One: The Science of Psychology, pp. 6–8.*) , disagreed with the idea that emotion led to bodily arousal which then led to action. He believed that the order of the components of emotions was quite different. At nearly the same time, a physiologist and psychologist in Denmark, Carl Lange (1885), came up with an explanation of emotion so similar to James's that the two names are used together to refer to the theory—the **James–Lange theory of emotion**. (See **Figure 28.3.**)

In this theory, a stimulus of some sort (e.g., the large snarling dog) produces a physiological reaction. This reaction, which is the arousal of the "fight-or-flight" sympathetic nervous system (wanting to run), produces bodily sensations such as increased heart rate, dry mouth, and rapid breathing. James and Lange believed that the physical arousal led to the labeling of the emotion (fear). Simply put, "I am afraid because I am aroused," "I am embarrassed because my face is red," "I am nervous because my stomach is fluttering," and "I am in love because my heart rate increases when I look at her or him."

What about people who have spinal cord injuries that prevent the sympathetic nervous system from functioning? Although James–Lange would predict that these people should show decreased emotion because the arousal that causes emotion is no longer there, this does not in fact happen. Several studies of people with spinal cord injuries report that these people are capable of experiencing the same emotions after their injury as before, and sometimes even more intensely (Bermond et al., 1991; Chwalisz et al., 1988).

Cannon–Bard Theory of Emotion Physiologists Walter Cannon (1927) and Philip Bard (1934) theorized that the emotion and the physiological arousal occur more or less at the same time. Cannon, an expert in sympathetic arousal mechanisms, did not feel that the physical changes caused by different emotions were distinct enough to allow them to be perceived as different emotions. Bard expanded on this idea by

James–Lange theory of emotion theory in which a physiological reaction leads to the labeling of an emotion.

362 CHAPTER 11

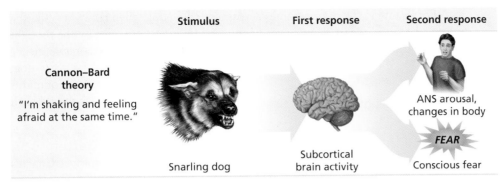

Stimulus **First response** **Second response**

Cannon–Bard theory

"I'm shaking and feeling afraid at the same time."

Snarling dog

Subcortical brain activity

ANS arousal, changes in body

FEAR

Conscious fear

FIGURE 28.4 Cannon–Bard Theory of Emotion
In the Cannon–Bard theory of emotion, a stimulus leads to activity in the brain, which then sends signals to arouse the body and interpret the emotion at the same time.

stating that the sensory information that comes into the brain is sent simultaneously (by the thalamus) to both the cortex and the organs of the sympathetic nervous system. The fear and the bodily reactions are, therefore, experienced at the same time—not one after the other. "I'm afraid and running and aroused!" (See **Figure 28.4**.)

This theory, known as the **Cannon–Bard theory of emotion**, also had its critics. K. S. Lashley (1938) stated that the thalamus would have to be very sophisticated to make sense of all the possible human emotions and relay them to the proper areas of the cortex and body. It would seem that other areas of the brain must be involved in processing emotional reactions. Studies of people with spinal cord injuries appear to suggest that emotions can be experienced without feedback from the sympathetic organs to the cortex; these studies were cited as a criticism of the James–Lange theory. At first these investigations seem to support the Cannon–Bard version of emotions: People do not need feedback from those organs to experience emotion. However, there is an alternate pathway that does provide feedback from these organs to the cortex; this is the vagus nerve, one of the cranial nerves (LeDoux, 1994). The existence of this feedback pathway makes the case for Cannon–Bard a little less convincing.

Schachter–Singer and Cognitive Arousal Theory of Emotion In their **cognitive arousal theory (two-factor theory)**, Schachter and Singer (1962) proposed that two things have to happen before emotion occurs: the physical arousal and a labeling of the arousal based on cues from the surrounding environment. These two events happen at the same time, resulting in the labeling of the emotion. (See **Figure 28.5**.)

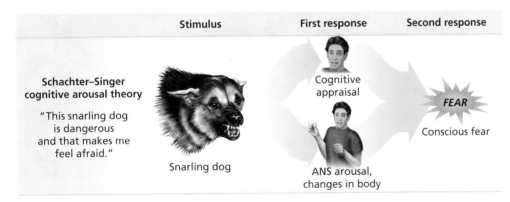

Stimulus **First response** **Second response**

Schachter–Singer cognitive arousal theory

"This snarling dog is dangerous and that makes me feel afraid."

Snarling dog

Cognitive appraisal

ANS arousal, changes in body

FEAR

Conscious fear

FIGURE 28.5 Schachter–Singer's Cognitive Arousal Theory of Emotion
Schachter–Singer's cognitive arousal theory is similar to the James–Lange theory but adds the element of cognitive labeling of the arousal. In this theory, a stimulus leads to both bodily arousal and the labeling of that arousal (based on the surrounding context), which leads to the experience and labeling of the emotional reaction.

Cannon–Bard theory of emotion theory in which the physiological reaction and the emotion are assumed to occur at the same time.

cognitive arousal theory (two-factor theory) theory of emotion in which both the physical arousal and the labeling of that arousal based on cues from the environment must occur before the emotion is experienced.

Watch the Video, *Three Theories of Emotion*, at MyPsychLab

For example, if a person comes across a snarling dog when taking a walk, the physical arousal (heart racing, eyes opening wide) is accompanied by the thought (cognition) that this must be fear. Then and only then will the person experience the fear emotion. In other words, "I am aroused in the presence of a scary dog; therefore, I must be afraid." The video *Three Theories of Emotion*, compares how the James–Lange, Cannon–Bard, and cognitive arousal theory would each explain the emotion of fear.

The Facial Feedback Hypothesis: Smile, You'll Feel Better In his (1898) book *The Expression of the Emotions in Man and Animals*, Charles Darwin stated that facial expressions evolved as a way of communicating intentions, such as threat or fear, and that these expressions are universal within a species rather than specific to a culture. He also believed (as in the James–Lange theory) that when such emotions are expressed freely on the face, the emotion itself intensifies—meaning that the more one smiles, the happier one feels.

Modern psychologists have proposed a theory of emotion that is consistent with much of Darwin's original thinking. Called the **facial feedback hypothesis**, this explanation assumes that facial expressions provide feedback to the brain concerning the emotion being expressed, which in turn not only intensifies the emotion but also actually causes the emotion (Buck, 1980; Ekman, 1980; Ekman & Friesen, 1978; Keillor et al., 2002). (See **Figure 28.6**.)

As the old song goes, "put on a happy face," and yes, you'll feel happier, according to the facial feedback hypothesis. One fairly recent study does cast some doubt on the validity of this hypothesis, however. If the facial feedback hypothesis is correct, then wouldn't people who have facial paralysis on both sides of the face be unable to experience emotions in a normal way? A case study conducted on just such a person revealed that although she was unable to express emotions on her paralyzed face, she could respond emotionally to slides meant to stimulate emotional reactions, just as anyone else would (Keillor et al., 2002). Clearly, the answer to the question of how much the actual facial expression determines the emotional experience is complex and more needs to be learned before conclusions can be drawn.

Does that mean that I ▶ don't smile because I'm happy —I'm happy because I smile?

facial feedback hypothesis theory of emotion that assumes that facial expressions provide feedback to the brain concerning the emotion being expressed, which in turn causes and intensifies the emotion.

▲ *The facial feedback hypothesis assumes that changing your own facial expression can change the way you feel. Smiling makes people feel happy, and frowning makes people feel sad. This effect seems to have an impact on the people around us as well. Is it hard for you to stay in a bad mood when the people around you are smiling and laughing?*

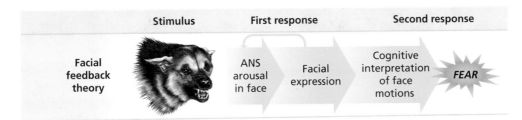

Stimulus	First response	Second response
Facial feedback theory	ANS arousal in face → Facial expression	Cognitive interpretation of face motions → **FEAR**

FIGURE 28.6 Facial Feedback Theory of Emotion
In the facial feedback theory of emotion, a stimulus such as this snarling dog causes arousal and a facial expression. The facial expression then provides feedback to the brain about the emotion. The brain then interprets the emotion and may also intensify it.

Stimulus	First response	Second response
Lazarus's cognitive-mediational theory	Appraisal of threat **FEAR**	Bodily response

FIGURE 28.7 Lazarus's Theory of Emotion
In Lazarus's cognitive-mediational theory of emotion, a stimulus causes an immediate appraisal (e.g., "The dog is snarling and not behind a fence, so this is dangerous"). The cognitive appraisal results in an emotional response, which is then followed by the appropriate bodily response.

Lazarus and the Cognitive-Mediational Theory of Emotion As mentioned in the Classic Studies in Psychology feature, Schachter and Singer's (1962) study stressed the importance of cognition, or thinking, in the determination of emotions. One of the more modern versions of cognitive emotion theories is Lazarus's **cognitive-mediational theory** (1991). In this theory, the most important aspect of any emotional experience is how the person interprets, or appraises, the stimulus that causes the emotional reaction. To mediate means to "come between," and in this theory, the cognitive appraisal mediates by coming between the stimulus and the emotional response to that stimulus (See **Figure 28.7**.)

Human emotions are so incredibly complex that it might not be out of place to say that all of the theories are correct to at least some degree. In certain situations, the cognitive appraisal might have time to mediate the emotion that is experienced (such as falling in love), whereas in other situations, the need to act first and think and feel later is more important.

cognitive-mediational theory theory of emotion in which a stimulus must be interpreted (appraised) by a person in order to result in a physical response and an emotional reaction.

Which theory is ◀ right?

Thinking Critically
Which of these theories of emotion do you feel is most correct? Why?

Pick the best answer.

1. What are the three elements of emotion?

   a. attention, behavior, and cognition
   b. attention, behavior, and motivation
   c. physical arousal, behavior, and cognition
   d. physical arousal, cognition, and motivation

2. Which theory of emotion is based on the assumption that the thalamus sends sensory information to the cortex and the organs of the sympathetic nervous system at the same time?

   a. Cannon–Bard
   b. Schachter–Singer
   c. Facial feedback
   d. Cognitive-mediational

3. Giuliana, a generally happy person, is enrolled in a psychology experiment. She is injected with epinephrine and then shown a movie clip of two people fighting. Immediately after watching the clip, Giuliana is most likely to feel

   a. angry.   c. scared.
   b. happy.   d. relaxed.

4. Ming comes home from school one day in a very bad mood, due to a fight he had with his girlfriend. His mother, hoping to improve his mood, starts telling him jokes. Ming resists laughing, but he can't help but smile at the jokes his mother is telling him, and soon his mood begins to improve. Which theory of emotion best explains the change?

   a. James–Lange   c. Schachter–Singer
   b. Cannon–Bard   d. facial feedback

5. In which theory of emotion is the most important aspect of an emotional experience, the interpretation or appraisal of the stimulus?

   a. James–Lange
   b. Cannon–Bard
   c. facial feedback
   d. cognitive-mediational

6. Suppose a research team conducts an experiment with teenagers from two different countries, Rebelland and Obedia. The two groups sit in different rooms and watch the same video, in which parents argue with their teenage daughter about her grades and eventually tell her she is grounded. From a distance, the experimenters secretly observe both groups reacting to the video with annoyance. When it's just the teenagers in the room, both groups angrily say things like, "Her parents are so unfair! She should sneak out anyway!" However, when the experimenter comes in and asks them about the video, only the teens from Rebelland openly express these feelings. The teens from Obedia politely say things like, "Well, her parents were a little strict, but it's for her own good." What best explains the difference?

   a. display rules
   b. innate temperamental differences
   c. the adaptation-level phenomenon
   d. cognitive-mediational theory

7. One day at school, someone collides with you in the hall and knocks you down, causing you to be angry. However, when playing football with friends, if you get knocked down, you do not express anger. What theory best explains how we label each situation and choose the appropriate emotion to show?

   a. James–Lange   c. Schachter–Singer
   b. Cannon–Bard   d. facial feedback

8. The ability to learn to fear a particular situation is impaired by damage to the

   a. amygdala.
   b. lateral hypothalamus.
   c. nucleus accumbens.
   d. anterior cingulate cortex.

9. Which of the following is not a universal emotion?

   a. fear   c. surprise
   b. disgust   d. indignation

10. According to research on gender and emotions

   a. women are less likely to express negative emotions.
   b. women have more emotions than men.
   c. men have more emotions that women.
   d. men are less likely to express negative emotions.

((Listen to an **Audio File** of your chapter at **MyPsychLab**

Module 27: Motivation
Explain major theories of motivation.

27.1 Understand biologically based theories of motivation.
- Instinct approaches proposed that some human actions may be motivated by instincts.
- Drive-reduction approaches state that when an organism has a need (such as hunger), the need leads to psychological tension that motivates the organism to act.
- Primary drives involve the needs of the body, whereas acquired (secondary) drives are those learned through experience.

27.2 Learn about cognitively based theories of motivation.
- The self-theory of emotion links the need for achievement to the concept of locus of control.
- The need for affiliation is the desire to have friendly social interactions and relationships with others.
- The need for power concerns having control over others, influencing them, and having an impact on them.
- In the incentive approach, an external stimulus may be so rewarding that it motivates a person to act.

27.3 Discuss humanistic theories of motivation.
- Self-determination theory (SDT) is a model of motivation in which three basic needs are seen as necessary to an individual's successful development: autonomy, competence, and relatedness.
- Intrinsic motivation occurs when people act because the act itself is satisfying or rewarding.

Describe motivated behaviors.

27.4 Understand eating behavior and the influence of culture.
- The physiological components of hunger include signals from the stomach and the hypothalamus, and the increased secretion of insulin.
- The social components of hunger include social cues for when meals are to be eaten, cultural customs and food preferences.

27.5 Learn about sexual behavior and orientation.
- Alfred Kinsey conducted a series of sexual behavior surveys revealing some highly controversial findings.

27.6 Understand achievement motivation.
- The need for achievement is a strong desire to succeed in achieving one's goals, both realistic and challenging.

27.7 Describe other ways in which humans and nonhuman animals are motivated.
- The motivation to love has an evolutionary basis and is influenced by biological and environmental factors.

Module 28: Emotion
Understand perspectives on emotion and emotional behavior.

28.1 Identify the biological and cognitive components of emotion.
- Emotion is the "feeling" aspect of consciousness and includes physical, behavioral, and subjective (cognitive) elements.

28.2 Explain how culture, environment, and gender influence emotional expression, interpretation, and behavior.
- Display rules influence the expression of emotion in public based on cultural values and expectations.

28.3 Describe research and theories of emotional experience.
- The James–Lange theory states that a stimulus creates a physiological response, which then leads to the labeling of the emotion.
- The Cannon–Bard theory asserts that the physiological reaction and the emotion are simultaneous.
- In Schachter–Singer's cognitive arousal theory, both the physiological arousal and the actual interpretation of that arousal must occur before the emotion itself is experienced.
- In the facial feedback hypothesis, facial expressions provide feedback to the brain about the emotion being expressed on the face, intensifying the emotion.
- In the cognitive-mediational theory of emotion, the cognitive component of emotion (the interpretation) precedes both the physiological reaction and the emotion itself.

Vocabulary Terms

motivation p. 346
extrinsic motivation p. 346
intrinsic motivation p. 347
instincts p. 347
need p. 347
drive p. 347
drive-reduction theory p. 347
primary drives p. 347
acquired (secondary) drives p. 347
homeostasis p. 347

need for affiliation (nAff) p. 349
need for power (nPow) p. 349
need for achievement (nAch) p. 349
arousal theory p. 350
Yerkes--Dodson law p. 350
sensation seeker p. 350
incentives p.350
incentive approaches p. 350
self-actualization p. 351

peak experiences p. 352
self-determination theory (SDT) p. 352
insulin p. 353
glucagon p. 353
sexual orientation p. 355
heterosexual p. 355
homosexual p. 355
bisexual p. 355
emotion p. 359
display rules p. 360

James–Lange theory of emotion p. 362
Cannon–Bard theory of emotion p. 363
cognitive arousal theory (two-factor theory) p. 363
facial feedback hypothesis p. 364
cognitive-mediational theory p. 365

✔ Study and Review at MyPsychLab

Vocabulary Review

Match each vocabulary term to its definition.

1. self-actualization
2. heterosexual
3. sensation seeker
4. display rules
5. two-factor theory
6. homosexual
7. emotion
8. extrinsic motivation
9. drive
10. drive-reduction theory

a. Approach to motivation that assumes behavior arises from physiological needs that cause internal drives to push an organism to satisfy the needs, reducing tension and arousal.

b. A psychological tension and physical arousal arising when there is a need that motivates the organism to act.

c. Type of motivation in which a person performs an action because it leads to an outcome that is separate from or external to the person.

d. The point that is seldom reached at which people have achieved their full human potential.

e. Learned ways of controlling displays of emotion in social settings.

f. Person attracted to the same sex.

g. Person attracted to the opposite sex.

h. Someone who needs more arousal than the average person.

i. Theory of emotion in which both physical arousal and the labeling of that arousal based on cues from the environment must occur before the emotion is experienced.

j. The "feeling" aspect of consciousness.

Psychology Project

What do Maslow's needs look like in real life? Does his hierarchy make sense—or would you organize these needs differently? Complete this project to examine how people meet their needs and to comment on Maslow's theory.

Materials: posterboard, markers, magazines and newspapers

Instructions:

1. Work with a partner to create a poster that visually represents the physical and psychological needs Abraham Maslow identified.

2. With your partner, examine Maslow's hierarchy and discuss how it might be modified. You and your partner may have some differences of opinion. The important thing is to discuss these needs based on your own understanding of the world and find some points you definitely agree on.

3. Now, work with your partner to plan your poster. Find and cut out photographs, illustrations, or brief text clippings that you can use to illustrate the different needs.

4. Create your poster. Make sure each need is clearly labeled.

Tech Alternative

Selfie Analysis

Log in to your favorite social networking site and take a look at your friends selfies. See if you can locate selfies that show five or six of the universal emotional expressions. When you find a selfie that fits one of the universal emotional expressions, write down three facial details that go with the expression. After you have identified five or six expressions and their characteristics, think back on what you observed as you were looking at the selfies. Which emotions were most popular in the selfies? Why do you think these emotions were popular? Which emotions were least popular in the selfies? Why do you think these emotions were less popular? Write four paragraphs describing your findings to complete your assignment.

Essay Question

You are hiking in the desert when you see a large, poisonous snake poised to attack you, and you feel afraid. In a well-organized essay, describe how *two* of the following theories would explain your emotional response to this situation:

a. Common-sense theory
b. James–Lange theory
c. Cannon–Bard theory
d. Schacter–Singer cognitive arousal theory
e. Cognitive-mediational theory

Test Yourself

Ready for your test? More quizzes and a customized plan.

☑ **Study and Review** at MyPsychLab

Pick the best answer.

1. Jasmine often requires her friends' approval when she buys new outfits. Her need is an example of a(n) _____ drive.
   - a. primary
   - b. acquired (secondary)
   - c. innate
   - d. instinctive

2. Eli enjoys woodcarving. His enjoyment of the task is all his own. Many would call his motivation _____ in nature.
   - a. instinctual
   - b. arousal
   - c. extrinsic
   - d. intrinsic

3. The approach to motivation that forced psychologists to consider the value of homeostasis in motivation was the _____ approach.
   - a. arousal
   - b. drive-reduction
   - c. instinct
   - d. incentive

4. Motivational theories such as _____ are physical in terms of their needs.
   - a. drive theory
   - b. biological theory
   - c. need theory
   - d. power theory

5. Dodi constantly asks for feedback from customers so he can know what he needs to do to be the best. Dodi is high in the need for
   - a. achievement.
   - b. affiliation.
   - c. power.
   - d. attention.

6. An important component to Carol Dweck's theory of motivation is
   - a. one's view of self.
   - b. an understanding of classical conditioning.
   - c. an understanding of heredity.
   - d. an understanding of emotions.

7. According to the arousal theory, people are typically motivated toward _____ point of arousal.
   - a. the highest
   - b. the optimal
   - c. the easiest
   - d. the quickest

8. A point, even for a moment, when someone reaches a state of self-actualization is a(n) _____ experience.
   - a. peak
   - b. extrinsic
   - c. power
   - d. affiliation

9. Jacob believes he is in control of his own destiny; however, he still feels the need to master many of the challenges in his life. According to self-determination theory, which stage is Jacob still working to complete?
   - a. autonomy
   - b. competence
   - c. relatedness
   - d. affiliation

10. According to Maslow's hierarchy, our lowest-level needs are
    - a. cognitive.
    - b. social.
    - c. physiological.
    - d. aesthetic.

11. According to Maslow's hierarchy, our highest-level need is
    - a. affiliation.
    - b. belonging.
    - c. self-actualization.
    - d. shelter.

12. A person that seems to need more complex and varied sensory experiences than do other people is best described as a(n) _____ person.
    - a. attention seeking
    - b. self actualized
    - c. conflict avoidant
    - d. sensation seeking

13. Studies indicate that women from _____ are more likely to eat because their body tells them they are hungry.
    - a. Hungary
    - b. the United States
    - c. Italy
    - d. Japan

14. The research on human sexuality that is criticized for putting more emphasis on "abnormal" behavior is the _____ report.
    - a. James
    - b. Yerkes
    - c. Kinsey
    - d. Bard

15. LeDoux's work on the physiology involving emotions has focused on what part of the brain?
    - a. thalamus
    - b. hippocampus
    - c. prefrontal cortex
    - d. amygdala

16. Research on facial expressions has taught us that facial expressions are
    - a. inherent to a region.
    - b. inherent to a culture.
    - c. learned.
    - d. universal.

17. An understanding of when and under what conditions emotions and feelings may be displayed within a culture is a
    - a. display rule.
    - b. feedback rule.
    - c. biological need.
    - d. power need.

18. What theory of emotion states that the emotion typically occurs before arousal and behavior?
    - a. the original, or common-sense, theory
    - b. Schachter and Singer's theory
    - c. Cannon and Bard's theory
    - d. James and Lange's theory

19. Schachter and Singer's theory of emotion relies heavily on
    - a. physical arousal.
    - b. labeling.
    - c. facial expressions.
    - d. heredity.

20. According to Lazarus, _____.
    - a. an emotion is biologically based
    - b. an emotion is situationally based
    - c. appraisal of a situation precedes both physical arousal and the experience of emotion
    - d. physical arousal precedes appraisal of the situation and the experience of emotion

Learning Objectives

27.1 27.2 27.3 pp. 346–352

motivation is the process by which activities are started, directed, and continued to meet physical or psychological needs or wants

Increased hunger	→	Eat	→	Glucose raised
Glucose lowered	←	Don't eat	←	Hunger diminished

extrinsic motivation causes a person to act to obtain an external reward

intrinsic motivation causes a person to act to feel internal satisfaction

early instinct approaches focused on innate, biologically determined patterns of behavior, such as the need to eat, drink, or reproduce

drive-reduction approaches focus on an organism's need to reduce tension and maintain homeostasis

Explain Major Theories of Motivation

arousal theory emphasizes people's need to maintain an optimal level of tension

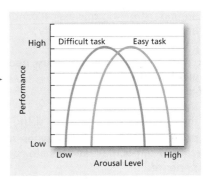

achievement, affiliation, and power need theory

incentive approaches explain behavior in terms of the external stimulus and its rewarding properties

humanist theories address physical, social, and emotional needs.

Transcendence needs: to find spiritual meaning beyond one's immediate self

Self-actualization needs: to find self-fulfillment and realize one's potential

Aesthetic needs: to appreciate symmetry, order, and beauty

Cognitive needs: to know, understand, and explore

Esteem needs: to achieve, be competent, gain approval and recognition

Belongingness and love needs: to be with others, be accepted, and belong

Safety needs: to feel secure and safe, out of danger

Physiological needs: to satisfy hunger, thirst, fatigue, etc.

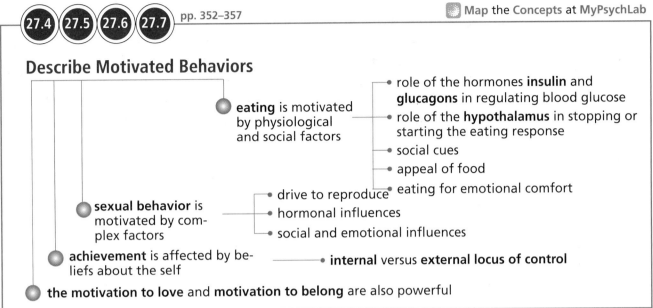

Learning Objectives

27.4 27.5 27.6 27.7   pp. 352–357

Describe Motivated Behaviors

eating is motivated by physiological and social factors
- role of the hormones **insulin** and **glucagons** in regulating blood glucose
- role of the **hypothalamus** in stopping or starting the eating response
- social cues
- appeal of food
- eating for emotional comfort

sexual behavior is motivated by complex factors
- drive to reproduce
- hormonal influences
- social and emotional influences

achievement is affected by beliefs about the self
- **internal** versus **external locus of control**

the motivation to love and **motivation to belong** are also powerful

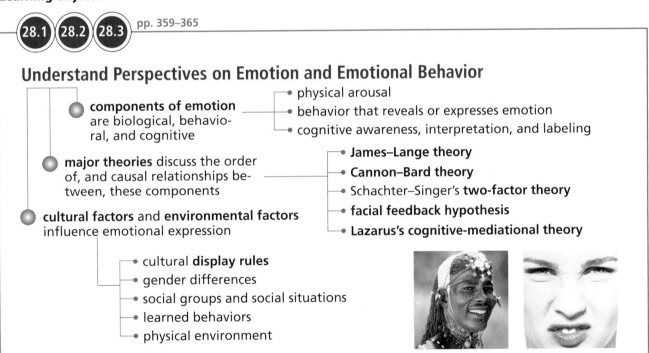

Learning Objectives

28.1 28.2 28.3   pp. 359–365

Understand Perspectives on Emotion and Emotional Behavior

components of emotion are biological, behavioral, and cognitive
- physical arousal
- behavior that reveals or expresses emotion
- cognitive awareness, interpretation, and labeling

major theories discuss the order of, and causal relationships between, these components
- **James–Lange theory**
- **Cannon–Bard theory**
- Schachter–Singer's **two-factor theory**
- **facial feedback hypothesis**
- **Lazarus's cognitive-mediational theory**

cultural factors and **environmental factors** influence emotional expression
- cultural **display rules**
- gender differences
- social groups and social situations
- learned behaviors
- physical environment

CHAPTER 12

Theories of Personality

Many people have heard the story of the "Jim" twins, James Arthur Springer and James Edward Lewis, identical twins separated just after birth. At age 39 Springer and Lewis were the first set of twins studied by University of Minnesota psychologist Thomas Bouchard, who examined the differences and similarities between identical and fraternal twins raised apart from each other (Bouchard et al., 1990).

The two "Jims" were remarkably similar. They shared interests in mechanical drawing and carpentry, they smoked and drank the same amount, and they even both divorced women named Linda before marrying women named Betty. It is easy to attribute these similarities to their shared genetics. But Springer and Lewis were both raised in Ohio by parents from relatively similar socioeconomic backgrounds—how much of their similarity to each other might be due to those environmental conditions?

In what ways are you similar to and different from your siblings?
How has your personality been shaped by your environment?

👁 **Watch** the **Video**, at **MyPsychLab**

*W*hy Study **Personality?**

Personality is the sum total of who you are—your attitudes and reactions, both physical and emotional. It's what makes each person different from every other person in the world. How can any study of human behavior not include the study of who we are and how we got to be that way?

29 Perspectives on Personality

Module Goal	Learning Objectives
Understand personality perspectives and issues.	**29.1** Explain stability and change.
	29.2 Discuss psychodynamic theories.
	29.3 Describe social-cognitive theories.
	29.4 Explore self-concept.
	29.5 Learn about humanistic theories.
	29.6 Understand trait theories.
	29.7 Describe biological and situational influences.
	29.8 Consider how individualistic and collectivistic cultural perspectives relate to personality.
	29.9 Trace connections to health and work.

Understand Personality Perspectives and Issues

Personality is the unique way in which each individual thinks, acts, and feels throughout life. Personality should not be confused with *character*, which refers to value judgments made about a person's morals or ethical behavior, nor should it be confused with *temperament*, the enduring characteristics with which each person is born, such as irritability or adaptability. Temperament is based in one's biology, either through genetic influences, prenatal influences, or a combination of those influences, and forms the basis upon which one's larger personality is built. Both character and temperament are vital parts of personality, however.

Personality is an area of the still relatively young field of psychology in which there are several ways in which the characteristic behavior of human beings can be explained. However, the investigation of personality goes back quite some time. For example, physiological roots of personality were suggested as early as the fourth century B.C.E. by Empedocles and later by Hippocrates, with Hippocrates's work later influencing Galen in the second century C.E. (Dumont, 2010). Hippocrates and Galen believed that temperament or personality was related to the relative balance of the four physical humors ("fluids") of the body: blood, black bile, yellow bile, and phlegm.

29.1 Explain stability and change.

Researchers have long wondered if the elements of personality change over a person's life. The *plaster hypothesis*, based on a metaphor written by William James, suggests that personality develops until people hit maturity at about age 30. Personality then firms up and sets, similar to plaster, throughout middle age, and begins to crack and crumble as cognitive declines appear with old age. A different take on this theory, the *soft plaster hypothesis*, suggests that there may be some changes after age 30, but the changes between 21 and 30 are much more dramatic than changes between 30 and 60.

personality the unique and relatively stable ways in which people think, feel, and behave.

Newer research on how some traits (personality characteristics) change over time shows more complexity than the plaster hypothesis suggests. A large research study on participants younger and older than 30 demonstrates some interesting changes in major personality traits throughout adulthood. These findings reject both the plaster hypothesis and the soft plaster hypothesis, demonstrating that personalities can change throughout our lives (Srivastava et al., 2003).

One reason no single explanation of personality exists is because personality is still difficult to measure precisely and scientifically, and different perspectives of personality have arisen. Overall, these tend to examine the source of personality, such as individual behavioral dispositions or situational processes, mediating factors that may be conscious or unconscious (Mischel & Shoda, 1995). From a foundational aspect, we will focus on several traditional perspectives in personality theory:

- The *psychodynamic perspective* had its beginnings with the founding of psychoanalysis by Sigmund Freud and still exists today. It focuses on the role of the unconscious mind in the development of personality. This perspective is also heavily focused on biological causes of personality.
- The *behaviorist and social-cognitive perspectives* based on the theories of learning and observation as discussed in Chapter Five. This approach focuses on the effect of the environment on behavior.
- The *humanistic perspective* first arose as a reaction against the psychoanalytic and behaviorist perspectives and focuses on the role of each person's conscious life experiences and choices in personality development.
- The *trait perspective* differs from the other three in its basic goals: The psychodynamic, behaviorist, and humanistic perspectives all seek to explain the process that causes personality to form into its unique characteristics, whereas trait theorists are more concerned with the end result—the characteristics themselves. Early trait theorists (Allport, Cattell) assumed that traits are biologically determined, others make no such assumption.

Before we begin our study of the various personality perspectives, take a moment to complete the survey, *What Has Shaped Your Personality?* to learn more about what factors may have influenced your own personality.

Complete the Survey, *What Has Shaped Your Personality?*, at MyPsychLab

29.2 Discuss psychodynamic theories.

It's hard to understand how Freud developed his ideas about personality unless we have some knowledge of the world in which he and his patients lived. He was born and raised in Europe during the Victorian Age, a time of sexual repression. To enjoy sexual intercourse was considered a sin. Men and women were understood to be unable to control their sexual desires. Freud's "obsession" with sexual explanations for abnormal behavior seems more understandable in light of his cultural background and that of his patients.

Freud came to believe that there were layers of consciousness in the mind. His belief in the influence of the unconscious mind on conscious behavior, published in *The Psychopathology of Everyday Life* (Freud, 1901), shocked the Victorian world.

The Man and the Couch: Sigmund Freud and the Origins of the Psychodynamic Perspective Freud believed that the mind was divided into three parts: the conscious, preconscious, and unconscious minds (Freud, 1900). (See **Figure 29.1**.) Although no one really disagreed with the idea of a conscious mind in which one's current awareness exists, or even of a preconscious mind containing memories, information, and events of which one can easily become aware, the **unconscious mind** (also called "the unconscious") was the real departure for the professionals of Freud's day. Freud theorized that there is a part

unconscious mind level of the mind in which thoughts, feelings, memories, and other information are kept that are not easily or voluntarily brought into consciousness.

FIGURE 29.1 Freud's Conception of the Personality

This iceberg represents the three levels of the mind. The part of the iceberg visible above the surface is the conscious mind. Just below the surface is the preconscious mind, everything that is not yet part of the conscious mind. Hidden deep below the surface is the unconscious mind, feelings, memories, thoughts, and urges that cannot be voluntarily brought into consciousness. While two of the three parts of the personality (ego and superego) exist at all three levels of awareness, the id is completely in the unconscious mind.

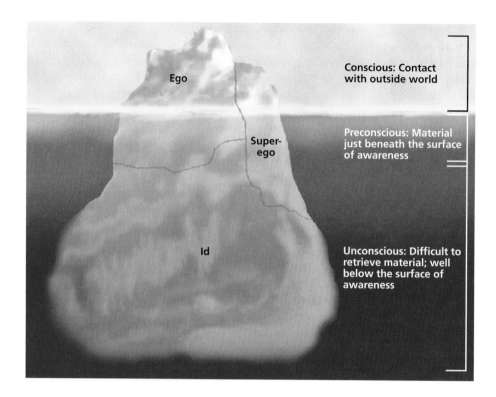

Ego

Super-ego

Id

Conscious: Contact with outside world

Preconscious: Material just beneath the surface of awareness

Unconscious: Difficult to retrieve material; well below the surface of awareness

of the mind that remains hidden at all times, surfacing only in symbolic form in dreams and in some of the behavior people engage in without knowing why they have done so. Freud believed that the unconscious mind was the most important determining factor in human behavior and personality.

Freud's Divisions of the Personality Freud believed, based on observations of his patients, that personality itself could be divided into three parts, each existing at one or more levels of conscious awareness (see Figure 29.1). The way these three parts of the personality develop and interact with one another became the heart of his theory (Freud, 1923, 1933, 1940).

Id: If It Feels Good, Do It The first and most primitive part of the personality, present in the infant, is the **id**. *Id* is a Latin word that means "it." The id is a completely unconscious, pleasure-seeking, amoral part of the personality that exists at birth, containing all of the basic biological drives.

Yes, Freud thought babies have sex drives. By "sex drive" he really meant "pleasure drive," the need to seek out pleasurable sensations. People do seem to be pleasure-seeking creatures, and even infants seek pleasure from sucking and chewing on anything they can get into their mouths. In fact, thinking about what infants are like when they are just born provides a good picture of the id. Infants are demanding, irrational, illogical, and impulsive. They want their needs satisfied immediately, and they don't care about anyone else's needs or desires.

Freud called this id need for immediate satisfaction the *pleasure principle*, which can be defined as the desire for immediate gratification of needs with no regard for the consequences. The id is completely out of touch with reality and the pleasure principle can be summed up simply as "if it feels good, do it."

Ego: The Executive Director People normally try to satisfy an infant's needs as quickly as possible. But as infants begin to grow, adults start denying them their every wish, and they must learn to wait for certain things, such as food. Freud would say that the id simply cannot deal with the reality of having to wait or not getting what it wants.

Wait a minute—▶ Freud thought babies have sex drives?

id part of the personality present at birth and completely unconscious.

According to Freud, to deal with reality, a second part of the personality develops called the **ego**. The ego works within the *reality principle*, which is the need to satisfy the demands of the id only within the confines of reality that will not lead to negative consequences. This means that sometimes the ego decides to deny the id its desires because the consequences would be painful or too unpleasant.

For example, although an infant might reach out and take an object despite a parent's protests, a toddler with the developing ego will avoid taking the object when the parent says, "No!" to avoid punishment—but may go back for the object when the parent is not looking. The ego works for both the id and reality and is completely in touch with reality. A simpler way of stating the reality principle, then, is "if it feels good, do it, but only if you can get away with it."

Superego: The Moral Watchdog Freud called the third and final part of the personality, the moral center of personality, the **superego**. The superego (also Latin, meaning "over the self") develops as a preschool-aged child learns the rules, customs, and expectations of society. The superego contains the *conscience*, the part of the personality that makes people feel guilt, or *moral anxiety*, when they do the wrong thing. Remember, the superego is out of touch with reality and absolute. It is not until the conscience develops, within the moral expectations of their culture, that children have a sense of right and wrong. (Note that the term *conscience* is a different word from *conscious*. They may look and sound similar, but they represent totally different concepts.)

How the Three Parts of the Personality Work Together Anyone who has ever watched cartoons while growing up has probably seen these three parts of the personality shown in animated form—the id is usually a little devil, the superego an angel, and the ego is the person or animal caught in the middle, trying to decide what action to take. So, the id makes demands, the superego puts restrictions on how those demands can be met, and the ego has to come up with a plan that will quiet the id but satisfy the superego. Sometimes the id or the superego does not get its way, resulting in a great deal of anxiety for the ego itself. This constant state of conflict is Freud's view of how personality works; it is only when the anxiety created by this conflict gets out of hand that disordered behavior arises.

The **psychological defense mechanisms** are ways of dealing with anxiety through unconsciously distorting one's perception of reality. These defense mechanisms, productions of the ego to handle the demands of the id and superego and lessen anxiety were mainly outlined and studied by Freud's daughter, Anna Freud, who was a psychoanalyst (Benjafield, 1996; A. Freud, 1946). In order for the three parts of the personality to function, the constant conflict among them must be managed, and Freud assumed that the defense mechanisms were one of the most important tools for dealing with the anxiety caused by this conflict. A partial list of the defense mechanisms, their definitions, and examples of each appears in **Table 29.1**.

Stages of Personality Development

Freud believed that personality development occurs in a series of **psychosexual stages** that are determined by the developing sexuality of the child. At each stage, a different *erogenous zone*, or area of the body that produces pleasurable feelings, becomes important and can become the source of conflicts. Conflicts that are not fully resolved can result in **fixation**, or getting "stuck" to some degree in a stage of development. The child may grow into an adult but will still carry emotional and psychological "baggage" from that earlier fixated stage.

Oral Stage (first 18 months) The first stage is called the **oral stage** because the erogenous zone is the mouth. The conflict that can arise here, according to Freud, will be over weaning (taking the mother's breast away from the child,

If everyone acted on the pleasure principle, the world would be pretty scary. How does knowing right from wrong come into Freud's theory?

ego part of the personality that develops out of a need to deal with reality; mostly conscious, rational, and logical.

superego part of the personality that acts as a moral center.

psychological defense mechanisms unconscious distortions of a person's perception of reality that reduce stress and anxiety.

psychosexual stages five stages of personality development proposed by Freud and tied to the sexual development of the child.

fixation disorder in which the person does not fully resolve the conflict in a particular psychosexual stage, resulting in personality traits and behavior associated with that earlier stage.

oral stage the first stage in Freud's psychosexual stages, occurring in the first 18 months of life in which the mouth is the erogenous zone and weaning is the primary conflict.

| Table 29.1 | The Psychological Defense Mechanisms |

DEFENSE MECHANISM AND DEFINITION	EXAMPLE
Denial: refusal to recognize or acknowledge a threatening situation.	Pat is a bully who denies being a bully.
Repression: "pushing" threatening or conflicting events or situations out of conscious memory.	Regan, who was emotionally traumatized as a child, cannot remember the cause of the emotional trauma.
Rationalization: making up acceptable excuses for unacceptable behavior.	"If I don't have breakfast, I can have that piece of cake later on without hurting my diet."
Displacement: expressing feelings that would be threatening if directed at the real target onto a less threatening substitute target.	Sandra gets reprimanded by her teacher and goes in the hall and kicks her locker.
Identification: trying to become like someone else to deal with one's anxiety.	Samantha really admires Emily, the most popular girl in school, and tries to copy her behavior and dress.
Compensation (substitution): trying to make up for areas in which a lack is perceived by becoming superior in some other area.	Ethan is not good at athletics, so he puts all of his energies into becoming an academic scholar.

who will now drink from a cup). Weaning that occurs too soon or too late can result in too little or too much satisfaction of the child's oral needs, resulting in the activities and personality traits associated with an orally fixated adult personality: overeating, , talking too much, nail biting, and gum chewing.

Anal Stage (18 to 36 months) As the child becomes a toddler, Freud believed that the erogenous zone moves from the mouth to the anus, because he also believed that children obtain a great deal of pleasure from both withholding and releasing their feces at will. This stage, where "control" over one's life is the main issue, is called the **anal stage**.

Obviously, Freud thought that the main area of conflict here is toilet training, the demand that the child, unlike an animal in the wild, use the toilet at a particular time and in a particular way. This invasion of reality is part of the process that stimulates the development of the ego during this stage. Fixation in the anal stage, from toilet training that is too harsh, can take one of two forms. The child who rebels openly will refuse to go in the toilet and, according to Freud, translate in the adult as an *anal expulsive personality*, someone who sees messiness as a statement of personal control. Some children, however, are terrified of making a mess and rebel passively—refusing to go at all. As adults, they are stingy, stubborn, and excessively neat. This type is called the *anal retentive personality*.

Phallic Stage (3 to 6 years) As the child grows older, the erogenous zone shifts to the genitals. Children have discovered the differences between the sexes by now.

anal stage the second stage in Freud's psychosexual stages, occurring from about 18 to 36 months of age, in which the anus is the erogenous zone and toilet training is the source of conflict.

This awakening of sexual curiosity and interest in the genitals is the beginning of what Freud termed the **phallic stage**. (The word *phallic* comes from the Greek word *phallos* and means "penis.") The conflict in the phallic stage centers on the awakening sexual feelings of the child. Freud essentially believed that boys develop both sexual attraction to their mothers and jealousy of their fathers during this stage, a phenomenon called the *Oedipus complex*. (Oedipus was a king in a Greek tragedy (a type of play) who unknowingly killed his father and married his mother.)

The sexual attraction is not that of an adult male for a female but more of a sexual curiosity that becomes mixed up with the boy's feelings of love and affection for his mother. Of course, his jealousy of his father leads to feelings of anxiety and fears that his father, a powerful authority figure, might get angry and do something terrible—remember that castration anxiety? To deal with this anxiety, two things must occur by the time the phallic stage ends. The boy will *repress* his sexual feelings for his mother and *identify* with his father. (*Identification* is one of the defense mechanisms used to combat anxiety.) Girls go through a similar process called the *Electra complex* with their father as the target of their affections and their mother as the rival. The result of identification is the development of the superego, the internalized moral values of the same-sex parent.

Latency Stage (6 years to puberty) Remember that by the end of the phallic stage, children have pushed their sexual feelings for the opposite sex into the unconscious in another defensive reaction, repression. From age 6 to the onset of puberty, children will remain in this stage of hidden, or *latent*, sexual feelings, so this stage is called **latency**. In this stage, children grow and develop intellectually, physically, and socially but not sexually. This is the age at which boys play only with boys, girls play only with girls, and each thinks the opposite sex is pretty awful.

Genital Stage (puberty on) When puberty does begin, the sexual feelings that were once repressed can no longer be ignored. Bodies are changing and sexual urges are once more allowed into consciousness, but these urges will no longer have the parents as their targets. Instead, the focus of sexual curiosity and attraction will become other adolescents, celebrities, and other objects of adoration (a form of displacement). Because Freud tied personality development into sexual development, the genital stage represented the final process in Freud's personality theory, as well as the entry into adult social and sexual behavior.

The Neo-Freudians and the Psychodynamic Perspective
At first Freud's ideas were met with resistance and ridicule by the growing community of doctors and psychologists. Eventually, a number of early psychoanalysts, objecting to Freud's emphasis on biology and particularly on sexuality, broke away from a strict interpretation of psychoanalytic theory, instead altering the focus of *psychoanalysis* (the term Freud applied to both his explanation of the workings of the unconscious mind and the development of personality and the therapy he based on that theory) to the impact of the social environment. At the same time they retained many of Freud's original concepts such as the id, ego, superego, and defense mechanisms. These early psychoanalysts became the *neo-Freudians*, or "new" Freudian psychoanalysts. This section briefly covers some of the more famous neo-Freudians.

Jung Carl Gustav Jung ("YOONG") disagreed with Freud about the nature of the unconscious mind. Jung believed that the unconscious held much more than personal fears, urges, and memories. He believed that there was not only a *personal unconscious,* as described by Freud, but a **collective unconscious** as well (Jung, 1933).

phallic stage the third stage in Freud's psychosexual stages, occurring from about 3 to 6 years of age, in which the child discovers sexual feelings.

latency the fourth stage in Freud's psychosexual stages, occurring during the school years, in which the sexual feelings of the child are repressed while the child develops in other ways.

genital stage the final stage in Freud's psychosexual stages, from puberty on, sexual urges are allowed back into consciousness and the individual moves toward adult social and sexual behavior.

collective unconscious Jung's name for the memories shared by all members of the human species.

archetypes Jung's collective, universal human memories.

According to Jung, the collective unconscious contains a kind of "species" memory, memories of ancient fears and themes that seem to occur in many folktales and cultures. These collective, universal human memories were called **archetypes** by Jung. There are many archetypes, but two of the more well known are the *anima/animus* (the feminine and masculine sides of all human beings) and the *shadow* (the dark side of personality). The side of one's personality that is shown to the world, like a "mask," is termed the *persona*.

Adler Alfred Adler was also in disagreement with Freud over the importance of sexuality in personality development. Adler (1954) developed the theory that as young, helpless children, people all develop feelings of inferiority when comparing themselves to the more powerful, superior adults in their world. The driving force behind all human endeavors, emotions, and thoughts for Adler was not the seeking of pleasure but the seeking of superiority. The defense mechanism of *compensation*, in which people try to overcome feelings of inferiority (an inferiority complex) in one area of life by striving to be superior in another area, figured prominently in Adler's theory (see Table 29.1).

Horney Karen Horney (horn-EYE) disagreed with Freudian views about the differences between males and females and most notably with the concept of penis envy. She countered with her own concept of "womb envy," stating that men felt the need to compensate for their lack of child-bearing ability by striving for success in other areas (Burger, 1997).

Horney focused on the *basic anxiety* created in a child born into a world that is so much bigger and more powerful than the child. Although people whose parents gave them love, affection, and security would overcome this anxiety, others with less secure upbringings would develop *neurotic personalities* and maladaptive ways of dealing with relationships. Some children, according to Horney, try to deal with their anxiety by moving toward people, becoming dependent and clingy. Others move against people, becoming aggressive, demanding, and cruel. A third way of coping would be to move away from people by withdrawing from personal relationships.

Erikson Erik Erikson (1950, 1959, 1982) was an art teacher who became a psychoanalyst by studying with Anna Freud. He also broke away from Freud's emphasis on sex, preferring instead to emphasize the social relationships that are important at every stage of life. Erikson's eight psychosocial stages are discussed in detail in Chapter Five.

> It sounds as if all of these theorists became famous by ditching some of Freud's original ideas. Is Freud even worth studying anymore?

▶ ### Current Thoughts on Freud and the Psychodynamic Perspective

Although Freud's original psychoanalytic theory seems less relevant in today's sexually saturated world, many of his concepts have remained useful and still form a basis for many modern personality theories, and the psychodynamic perspective. The idea of the defense mechanisms has had some research support and has remained useful in clinical psychology as a way of describing people's defensive behavior and irrational thinking. The concept of an unconscious mind also has some research support.

This might be a good time to point out a very important fact about Freud's theory is based on his own observations (case studies) research methods of patients. (L)(I)(N)(K) *to Chapter One: The Science of Psychology, p. 19.* He felt free to interpret what his patients told him of their childhoods as fantasy or fact, depending on how well those memories fit in with his developing theory.

Freud based much of his diagnoses of patients' problems on the interpretations of dreams and the results of the patient's free association (talking about anything without fear of negative feedback). These "sources" of information are often criticized as being too ambiguous and without scientific support for the validity of his interpretations.

Another criticism of Freud's theory concerns the people on whose dreams, recollections, and comments the theory of psychoanalysis was based. Critics state that basing his theory on observations made with such a limited group of clients promoted his emphasis on sexuality as the root of all problems in personality.

Although most professionals today view Freud's theory with a great deal of skepticism, his influence on the modern world cannot be ignored. Freudian concepts have had an impact on literature, movies, and even children's cartoons. People who have never taken a course in psychology are familiar with some of Freud's most basic concepts, such as the defense mechanisms. He was also one of the first theorists to emphasize the importance of childhood experiences on personality development—in spite of the fact that he did not work extensively with children.

It has only been in the last several decades that people have had the necessary tools to examine the concepts of the unconscious mind. One can only wonder how Freud's ideas will be supported as our understanding of the inner workings of the brain increase through advances in neuroscience.

Thinking Critically
What aspects of psychodynamic theory do you think still have relevance in today's world? Was there one neo-Freudian whose theory appealed to you, and if so, why?

29.3 Describe social-cognitive theories.

At the time that Freud's theory was shocking the Western world, another psychological perspective was also making its influence known. In Chapter Six the theories of classical and operant conditioning were discussed in some detail. *Behaviorists* (researchers who use the principles of conditioning to explain the actions and reactions of both animals and humans) and *social cognitive theorists* (researchers who emphasize the influence of social-environmental, cognitive-problem solving, and thoughtful strategies on learning) have a very different view of personality.

Learning Theories For the radical behaviorist, personality is nothing more than a set of learned responses or *habits* (DeGrandpre, 2000; Dollard & Miller, 1950). In the strictest traditional view of Watson and Skinner, everything a person or animal does is a response to some environmental stimulus that has been reinforced or strengthened by a reward in some way.

Think about how a traditional behaviorist might explain a shy personality. Beginning in childhood, a person might be exposed to a parent with a rather harsh discipline style (stimulus). Avoiding the attention of that parent would result in fewer punishments and scoldings, so that avoidance response is negatively reinforced—the "bad thing" or punishment is avoided by keeping out of sight and quiet. Later, that child might generalize that avoidance response to other authority figures and adults, such as teachers. In this way, a pattern (habit) of shyness would develop.

Of course, many learning theorists today do not use only classical and operant conditioning to explain the development of the behavior patterns referred to as personality. *Social cognitive learning theorists*, who emphasize the importance of both the influences of other people's behavior and of a person's own expectancies on learning, hold that observational learning, modeling, and other cognitive learning techniques can lead to the formation of patterns of personality.

One of the more well-researched learning theories that includes the concept of cognitive processes as influences on behavior is the social cognitive theory of Albert Bandura. In the *social cognitive view*, behavior is governed not just by the influence of external stimuli and response patterns but also by cognitive processes such as anticipating, judging, and memory, as well as learning through the imitation of models. In fact, you might remember Bandura's work with observation learning and imitation of models from his Bobo doll study. Ⓛ Ⓘ Ⓝ Ⓚ *to Chapter Six: Learning and Language Development, pp. 213–214.*

◄ So how does a pattern of rewarding certain behavior end up becoming part of some kind of personality pattern?

Bandura's Reciprocal Determinism Bandura (1989) believes that three factors influence one another in determining the patterns of behavior that make up personality: the environment, the behavior itself, and personal or cognitive factors that the person brings into the situation from earlier experiences. These three factors each affect the other two in a reciprocal, or give-and-take, relationship. Bandura calls this relationship **reciprocal determinism**.

The environment includes the actual physical surroundings, the other people who may or may not be present, and the potential for reinforcement in those surroundings. The intensity and frequency of the behavior will not only be influenced by the environment but will also have an impact on that environment. The person brings into the situation previously reinforced responses (personality, in other words) and mental processes such as thinking and anticipating.

Here's how this might work: Richard walks into a classroom filled with other students, but no teacher is present at this time. (This is the *environment*.) Part of Richard's *personal* characteristics includes the desire to have attention from other people by talking loudly and telling jokes, which has been very rewarding to him in the past (past reinforcements are part of his cognitive processes, or expectancies of future rewards for his behavior). Also in the past, he has found that he gets more attention when an authority figure is not present. His *behavior* will most likely be to start talking and telling jokes, which will continue if he gets the reaction he expects from his fellow students. If the teacher walks in (the *environment* changes), his behavior will change. If the other students don't laugh, his behavior will change. In the future Richard might be less likely to behave in the same way because his expectations for reward (a cognitive element of his *personal* variables) are different.

29.4 Explore self-concept.

One of the more important personal variables that Bandura talks about is **self-efficacy**, a person's expectancy of how effective his or her efforts to accomplish a goal will be in any particular circumstance (Bandura, 1998). (Self-efficacy is not the same concept as *self-esteem*, which is the positive values a person places on his or her sense of worth.)

People's sense of self-efficacy can be high or low, depending on what has happened in similar circumstances in the past (success or failure), what other people tell them about their competence, and their own assessment of their abilities. For example, if Fiona has an opportunity to write an extra-credit paper to improve her grade in psychology, she will be more likely to do so if her self-efficacy is high: She has gotten good grades on such papers in the past, her teachers have told her that she writes well, and she knows she can write a good paper. According to Bandura, people high in self-efficacy are more persistent and expect to succeed, whereas people low in self-efficacy expect to fail and tend to avoid challenges (Bandura, 1998).

Rotter's Social Learning Theory: Expectancies Julian Rotter (1966, 1978, 1981, 1990) devised a theory based on a basic principle of motivation derived from Thorndike's law of effect: People are motivated to seek reinforcement and avoid punishment. He viewed personality as a relatively stable set of *potential* responses to various situations. If in the past, a certain way of responding led to a reinforcing or pleasurable consequence, that way of responding would become a pattern of responding, or part of the "personality" as learning theorists see it.

One very important pattern of responding in Rotter's view became his concept of **locus of control**, the tendency for people to assume that they either

reciprocal determinism Bandura's explanation of how the factors of environment, personal characteristics, and behavior can interact to determine future behavior.

self-efficacy individual's expectancy of how effective his or her efforts to accomplish a goal will be in any particular circumstance.

locus of control the tendency for people to assume that they either have control or do not have control over events and consequences in their lives.

have control or do not have control over events and consequences in their lives. (LINK) to *Chapter Eleven: Motivation and Emotion, p. 355.* People who assume that their own actions and decisions directly affect the consequences they experience are said to be *internal* in locus of control, whereas people who assume that their lives are more controlled by powerful others, luck, or fate are *external* in locus of control (MacDonald, 1970; Rotter, 1966). Rotter associated people high in internal locus of control with the personality characteristics of high achievement motivation (the will to succeed in any attempted task).

▲ *According to Rotter, what would be the most likely form of locus of control experienced by this young woman?*

Those who give up too quickly or who attribute events in their lives to external causes can fall into patterns of learned helplessness and depression (Abramson et al., 1978, 1980; Gong-Guy & Hammen, 1980).

Rotter (1978, 1981) also believed that an interaction of factors would determine the behavioral patterns that become personality for an individual. For Rotter, there are two key factors influencing a person's decision to act in a certain way given a particular situation: expectancy and reinforcement value. **Expectancy** is fairly similar to Bandura's concept of self-efficacy in that it refers to the person's subjective feeling that a particular behavior will lead to a reinforcing consequence. A high expectancy for success is similar to a high sense of self-efficacy and is also based on past experiences with successes and failures. *Reinforcement value* refers to an individual's preference for a particular reinforcer over all other possible reinforcing consequences. Things or circumstances that are particularly appealing to us have a higher reinforcement value than other possible reinforcers.

Current Thoughts on the Social Cognitive View of Personality

Behaviorism as an explanation of the formation of personality has its limitations. The classic theory does not take mental processes into account when explaining behavior, nor does it give weight to social influences on learning. The social cognitive view of personality, unlike traditional behaviorism, does include social and mental processes and their influence on behavior. Unlike psychoanalysis, the concepts in this theory can and have been tested under scientific conditions (Backenstrass et al., 2008; Bandura, 1965; Catanzaro et al., 2000; DeGrandpre, 2000; Domjan et al., 2000; Skinner, 1989).

29.5 Learn about humanistic theories.

As first discussed in Chapter One, in the middle of the twentieth century the pessimism of Freudian psychodynamic theory with its emphasis on conflict and animalistic needs, together with the emphasis of behaviorism on external control of behavior, gave rise to a third force in psychology: the *humanistic perspective.*

Carl Rogers and the Humanistic Perspective The **humanistic perspective**, led by psychologists such as Carl Rogers and Abraham Maslow, wanted

expectancy a person's subjective feeling that a particular behavior will lead to a reinforcing consequence.

self-actualizing tendency
the striving to fulfill one's innate capacities and capabilities.

 **Watch** the **Video**, *Humanistic Perspective on Personality*, at **MyPsychLab**

psychology to focus on the things that make people uniquely human, such as subjective emotions and the freedom to choose one's own destiny. As Maslow's theory was discussed more fully in Chapter Eleven, in this chapter the discussion of the humanistic view of personality will focus on the theory of Carl Rogers. A brief overview of the humanistic perspective is also offered in the video, *Humanistic Perspective on Personality.*

Both Maslow and Rogers (1961) believed that human beings are always striving to fulfill their innate capacities and capabilities and to become everything that their genetic potential will allow them to become. This striving for fulfillment is called the **self-actualizing tendency.** An important tool in human self-actualization is the development of an image of oneself, or the *self-concept.* The self-concept is based on what people are told by others and how the sense of *self* is reflected in the words and actions of important people in one's life, such as parents, siblings, coworkers, friends, and teachers.

Real and Ideal Self Two important components of the self-concept are the *real self* (one's actual perception of characteristics, traits, and abilities that form the basis of the striving for self-actualization) and the *ideal self* (the perception of what one should be or would like to be). The ideal self primarily comes from important, significant others in a person's life, especially our parents when we are children. Rogers believed that when the real self and the ideal self are very close or similar to each other, people feel competent and capable, but when there is a mismatch between the real self and ideal self, anxiety and dysfunctional behavior can be the result. (See **Figure 29.2.**)

The two halves of the self are more likely to match if they aren't that far apart at the start. When a person has a realistic view of the real self, and the ideal self is something that is actually attainable, there usually isn't a problem of a mismatch. It is when a person's view of self is distorted or the ideal self is impossible to attain that problems, as a product of this incongruence, arise. Once again, how the important people (who can be either good or bad influences) in a person's life react to the person can greatly impact the degree of

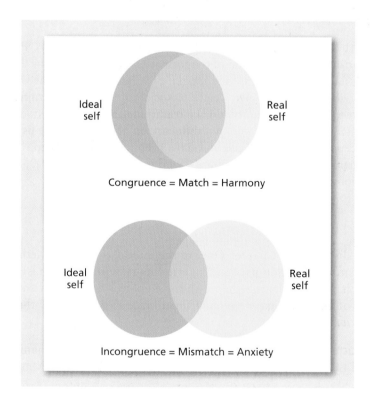

FIGURE 29.2 Real and Ideal Selves
According to Rogers, the self-concept includes the real self and the ideal self. The real self is a person's actual perception of traits and abilities, whereas the ideal self is the perception of what a person would like to be or thinks he or she should be. When the ideal self and the real self are very similar (matching), the person experiences harmony and contentment. When there is a mismatch between the two selves, the person experiences anxiety and may engage in neurotic behavior.

agreement, or congruence, between real and ideal selves. However, as an individual develops, they look less to others for approval and disapproval, and more within themselves to decide if they are living in a way that is satisfying to them (Rogers, 1951, 1961).

Conditional and Unconditional Positive Regard Rogers defined *positive regard* as warmth, affection, love, and respect that come from the significant others (parents, admired adults, friends, and teachers) in people's experience. Positive regard is vital to people's ability to cope with stress and to strive to achieve self-actualization. Rogers believed that **unconditional positive regard**, or love, affection, and respect with no strings attached, is necessary for people to be able to explore fully all that they can achieve and become. Unfortunately, some parents, spouses, and friends give *conditional positive regard*, which is love, affection, respect, and warmth that depend, or seem to depend, on doing what those people want.

Here is an example: As a freshman, Sasha was thinking about becoming a math teacher, a computer programmer, or an elementary school teacher. Karen, also a freshman, already knew that she was going to be a doctor. Whereas Sasha's parents had told her that what she wanted to become was up to her and that they would love her no matter what, Karen's parents had made it very clear to her as a small child that they expected her to become a doctor. She was under the very strong impression that if she tried to choose any other career, she would lose her parents' love and respect. Sasha's parents were giving her unconditional positive regard, but Karen's parents (whether they intended to do so or not) were giving her conditional positive regard. Karen was obviously not as free as Sasha to explore her potential and abilities.

For Rogers, a person who is in the process of self-actualizing, actively exploring potentials and abilities and experiencing a match between the real self and ideal self, is a **fully functioning person**. Fully functioning people are in touch with their own feelings and abilities and are able to trust their innermost urges and intuitions (Rogers, 1961). To become fully functioning, a person needs unconditional positive regard. In Rogers's view, Karen would not have been a fully functioning person.

Current Thoughts on the Humanistic View of Personality Humanistic views of personality paint a very rosy picture. Some critics believe that the picture is a little too rosy, ignoring the more negative aspects of human nature. Humanistic theory is also very difficult to test scientifically, like Freud's theories. Little research support exists for this viewpoint, which could be considered more a philosophical view of human behavior than it is a psychological explanation. Its greatest impact has been in the development of therapies designed to promote self-growth and help people better understand themselves and others.

29.6 Understand trait theories.

The theories discussed so far attempt to explain how personality develops or how factors within or external to the individual influence personality. These theories may also provide psychologists and other professionals with hints as to how personality may be changed. However, not all personality theories have the same goals.

Trait theories are less concerned with the explanation for personality development and changing personality than they are with describing personality and predicting behavior based on that description. A **trait** is a consistent, enduring way of thinking, feeling, or behaving, and trait theories attempt to describe

unconditional positive regard referring to the warmth, respect, and accepting atmosphere created by the therapist for the client in person-centered therapy; or with any other person where positive regard is given without conditions or strings attached.

fully functioning person a person who is in touch with and trusting of the deepest, innermost urges and feelings.

trait a consistent, enduring way of thinking, feeling, or behaving.

⊙ Watch the **Video**, *Trait Theories of Personality*, at **MyPsychLab**

personality in terms of a person's traits. The video, *Trait Theories of Personality*, describes this perspective in more detail.

Allport and Cattell: Early Attempts to List and Describe Traits One of the earliest attempts to list and describe the traits that make up personality can be found in the work of Gordon Allport (Allport & Odbert, 1936). Allport and his colleague H. S. Odbert literally scanned the dictionary for words that could be traits, finding about 18,000, then paring that down to 200 traits after eliminating synonyms. Allport believed (with no scientific evidence, however) that these traits were literally wired into the nervous system to guide one's behavior across many different situations and that each person's "constellation" of traits was unique. (In spite of Allport's lack of evidence, behavioral geneticists have found support for the heritability of personality traits, and these findings are discussed in the next section of this chapter.)

Two hundred traits is still a very large number of descriptors. How might an employer be able to judge the personality of a potential employee by looking at a list of 200 traits? A more compact way of describing personality was needed. Raymond Cattell (1990) defined two types of traits as *surface traits* and *source traits*. *Surface traits* are like those found by Allport, representing the personality characteristics easily seen by other people. *Source traits* are those more basic traits that underlie the surface traits. For example, shyness, being quiet, and disliking crowds might all be surface traits related to the more basic source trait of **introversion**, a tendency to withdraw from excessive stimulation.

Cattell identified 16 source traits (Cattell, 1950, 1966), and although he later determined that there might be another 7 source traits to make a total of 23 (Cattell & Kline, 1977), he developed his assessment questionnaire, *The Sixteen Personality Factor (16PF) Questionnaire* (Cattell, 1995), based on just 16 source traits.

Modern Trait Theory Sixteen factors are still quite a lot to discuss when talking about someone's personality. Later researchers attempted to reduce the number of trait dimensions to a more manageable number, with several groups of researchers arriving at more or less the same five trait dimensions (Botwin & Buss, 1989; Jang et al., 1998; McCrae & Costa, 1996).

The Big Five: OCEAN, or the Five-Factor Model of Personality The five trait dimensions have become known as the **five-factor model**, or the **Big Five** (see **Table 29.2**), and represent the core description of human personality—that is, the only dimensions necessary to understand what makes us tick.

As shown in the table, these five trait dimensions can be remembered by using the acronym OCEAN, in which each of the letters is the first letter of one of the five dimensions of personality.

- *Openness* can best be described as a person's willingness to try new things and be open to new experiences.
- *Conscientiousness* refers to a person's organization and motivation, with people who score high in this dimension being those who are careful about being places on time and careful with belongings as well.
- *Extraversion** is a term first used by Carl Jung (1933), who believed that all people could be divided into two personality types: *extraverts* and

introversion dimension of personality in which people tend to withdraw from excessive stimulation.

five-factor model (Big Five) model of personality traits that describes five basic trait dimensions.

---

*Extraversion: dimension of personality referring to one's need to be with other people.

Table 29.2	The Big Five	
HIGH SCORER CHARACTERISTICS	FACTOR (OCEAN)	LOW SCORER CHARACTERISTICS
Creative, artistic, curious, imaginative	Openness (O)	Conventional, down-to-earth, uncreative nonconforming
Organized, reliable, neat, ambitious	Conscientiousness (C)	Unreliable, lazy, careless, negligent, spontaneous
Talkative, optimistic, sociable, affectionate	Extraversion (E)	Reserved, comfortable being alone, stays in the background
Good-natured, trusting, helpful	Agreeableness (A)	Rude, uncooperative, irritable, aggressive, competitive
Worrying, insecure, anxious, temperamental	Neuroticism (N)	Calm, secure, relaxed, stable

Source: Adapted from McCrae & Costa (1990).

introverts. Extraverts are outgoing and sociable, whereas introverts are more solitary and dislike being the center of attention.

- *Agreeableness* refers to the basic emotional style of a person, who may be easygoing, friendly, and pleasant (at the high end of the scale) or grumpy, crabby, and hard to get along with (at the low end).
- *Neuroticism* refers to emotional instability or stability. People who are excessive worriers, overanxious, and moody would score high on this dimension.

Robert McCrae and Paul Costa proposed that these five traits are not interdependent. In other words, knowing someone's score on extraversion would not give any information about scores on the other four dimensions, allowing for a tremendous amount of variety in personality descriptions.

Current Thoughts on the Trait Perspective Some theorists have cautioned that personality traits will not always be expressed in the same way across different situations. Walter Mischel, a social cognitive theorist, has emphasized that there is a **trait–situation interaction** in which the particular circumstances of any given situation are assumed to influence the way in which a trait is expressed (Mischel & Shoda, 1995). An outgoing extravert, for example, might laugh, talk to strangers, and tell jokes at a party. That same person, if at a funeral, would still talk and be open, but the jokes and laughter would be less likely to occur. However, the five-factor model provides a dimensional approach to classifying personality structure (as opposed to a categorical approach), which is consistent with possible alternative approaches to diagnosing personality disorders discussed in the most recent edition of the *Diagnostic and Statistical Manual of Mental Disorders* (DSM-5; American Psychiatric Association, 2013). Ⓛ Ⓘ Ⓝ Ⓚ *to Chapter Thirteen: Psychological Disorders, pp. 416–429.*

trait–situation interaction the assumption that the particular circumstances of any given situation will influence the way in which a trait is expressed.

But what about people from different cultures? Although regional variations exist, cross-cultural research from 56 countries has found evidence of these five trait dimensions in all primary cultural regions of the world (Schmitt et al., 2007). Furthermore, it appears these dimensions are evident or recognizable not only in most languages and cultures; they are also consistent when assessed by either self-ratings or observers (Allik et al., 2013; McCrae & Terracciano, 2005). This cultural commonality raises the question of the origins of the Big Five trait dimensions: Are child-rearing practices across all those cultures similar enough to result in these five aspects of personality, or could these five dimensions have a genetic component that transcends cultural differences? The next section will discuss the evidence for a genetic basis of the Big Five.

What about ▶ genetics? How much of our personality is inherited?

29.7 Describe biological and situational influences.

When was the last time you were around a lot of family members other than your own? Was it a reunion? Or maybe when meeting your special friend's family for the first time? Did you notice any commonalities in the way different family members interacted, spoke, or behaved? This section will explore the "nature" side of personality, or the degree that some of our personality is linked to our parents and close relations.

Behavioral Genetics The field of **behavioral genetics** is devoted to the study of just how much of an individual's personality is because of inherited traits. Animal breeders have known for a long time that selective breeding of certain animals with specific desirable traits can produce changes not only in size, fur color, and other physical characteristics but also in the temperament of the animals (Isabel, 2003; Trut, 1999). As stated earlier in this chapter, temperament consists of the characteristics with which each person is born and is, therefore, determined by biology to a great degree. If the temperaments of animals can be influenced by manipulating patterns of genetic inheritance, then it is only one small step to assume that at least those personality characteristics related to temperament in human beings may also be influenced by heredity.

Twin Studies The difference between monozygotic (identical) and dizygotic (fraternal) twins was discussed in Chapter Five. As discussed previously, identical twins share 100 percent of their genetic material, having come from one fertilized egg originally, whereas fraternal twins share only about 50 percent of their genetic material, as any other pair of siblings would. By comparing identical twins to fraternal twins, especially when twins can be found who were not raised in the same environment, researchers can begin to find evidence of possible genetic influences on various traits, including personality. (See **Figure 29.3**.)

The results of the Minnesota twin study have revealed that identical twins are more similar than fraternal twins or unrelated people in intelligence, leadership abilities, the tendency to follow rules, and the tendency to uphold traditional cultural expectations (Bouchard, 1997; Finkel & McGue, 1997). They are also more alike with regard to nurturance,* empathy,† and assertiveness (Neale et al., 1986); and aggressiveness (Miles & Carey, 1997). This similarity holds even if the twins are raised in separate environments.

Adoption Studies Another tool of behavioral geneticists is to study adopted children and their adoptive and birth families. If studying genetically identical twins raised in different environments can help investigators understand the

---

*nurturance: affectionate care and attention.
†empathy: the ability to understand the feelings of others.

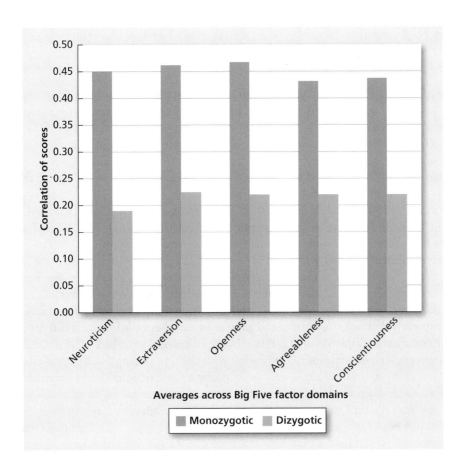

FIGURE 29.3 Personalities of Identical and Fraternal Twins Identical and fraternal twins differ in the way they express the Big Five personality factors. In a recent study, data from 696 twin pairs suggest identical twins have a correlation of about 45 percent for self-ratings across each of the Big Five factor domains, whereas fraternal twins have a correlation of about 22 percent. These findings support the idea that some aspects of personality are genetically based. *Based on: Kandler et al. (2010).*

genetic influences on personality, then studying *unrelated* people who are raised in the *same* environment should help investigators discover the influence of environment. By comparing adopted children to their adoptive parents and siblings and, if possible, to their biological parents who have not raised them, researchers can uncover some of the shared and non-shared environmental and genetic influences on personality.

Adoption studies have confirmed what twin studies have shown: Genetic influences account for a great deal of personality development, regardless of shared or non-shared environments (Hershberger et al., 1995; Loehlin et al., 1985; Loehlin et al., 1998). Through this kind of study, for example, a genetic basis has been suggested for shyness (Plomin et al., 1988) and aggressiveness (Brennan et al., 1997).

Current Findings on the Heritability of Personality One important aspect of genetic studies is the concept of **heritability**, or how much some trait within a total population can be attributed to genetic influences, and the extent individual genetic variation impacts differences in observed behavior. Several studies have found that the five personality factors of the five-factor model have nearly a 50 percent rate of heritability across several cultures (Bouchard, 1994; Herbst et al., 2000; Jang et al., 1996; Loehlin, 1992; Loehlin et al., 1998). The studies of genetics and personality seem to indicate that variations in personality traits are about 25 to 50 percent inherited (Jang et al., 1998). This also means that environmental influences apparently account for about half of the variation in personality traits as well. Although the five factors have been found across several cultures, this does not mean that different cultures do not have an impact on personality. For more on this topic, see the Classic Studies in Psychology section that follows.

heritability degree to which the changes in some trait within a population can be considered to be due to genetic influences; the extent individual genetic differences affect individual differences in observed behavior; in IQ, proportion of change in IQ within a population that is caused by hereditary factors.

29.8 Consider how individualistic and collectivistic cultural perspectives relate to personality.

Culture and Personality Although five personality factors have been found across several cultures, this does not mean that different cultures do not have an impact on personality.

Geert Hofstede conducted a study of IBM employees to gain an understanding of how cultures differed in their cultural mores. In the 1980s IBM, a multinational corporation, wanted to better understand the work-related values of their employees from different cultures and worked with Hofstede to achieve this goal (Hofstede, 1980; Hofstede et al., 2002). Hofstede's study investigated employees from over 60 different countries around the world. His analysis of the survey data he collected led him to conclude that there are four dimensions of personality that cultures differed within.

According to Hofstede's findings *individualistic cultures* have more distance in the ties between individuals. People are independent, take care of their close family members, and are less connected with their extended family. Sharing activities with friends that hold like interests and being a member of informal social groups is characteristic of members of individualistic cultures. The values of individualistic cultures include autonomy*, engaging with change, prizing youth, establishing one's security as an individual, and maintaining a sense of equality, as it applies to different situations in life. Members of collectivist cultures belong to very strong-in groups from the time that they are born as well as throughout the rest of their lives. Close ties between members of extended families are typical and grandparents, cousins, aunts, and uncles play important roles in the lives of individuals. Cultural values focus on the importance of traditions, being respectful toward to elderly, following a sense of duty, ensuring the security of groups, and recognizing an individual's role in a group as it applies to the group's higher and lower status positions.

The dimension of *power* is a concept that describes the distribution of power in a culture. Power held in the hands of an elite few or "high power distance" is characterized by a number of Arab countries as well as, India, the Philippines, and Mexico. The general expectations by members of these cultures are higher that a small group of people would exercise power over the population. However, countries like Great Britain, the United States, Austria, and Sweden expect a much different level in the distance of power. A low power distance is characteristic in countries that have a representative government, and the political system is designed for the power to be in the hands of the governing body that is closest to the citizens in that country. Democratically elected members of this type of a governing body are responsible to their electors and, because they are "of the people," they must work to meet the needs of the county's population. Additionally, there are countries that are led by dictatorships, such as North Korea, but the connection between the citizens and their government is reduced by the difficult situation created when a government is ruling "over the people."

How the roles of men and women are distributed in a culture is a third dimension identified by Hofstede, which he labeled *masculinity/femininity*. This dimension does not vary as much inside a culture for women as it does for men. Cultures that are "masculine" display an assertive and competitive nature, more so for men than for women, while the modest and caring cultures show a "feminine" or nurturing characteristic. The value placed on caring within "feminine" cultures is similar between men and women; however, a greater difference is found in "masculine" countries because women are not as outgoing and remain less competitive than men. This results in the difference between men and women

---

*autonomy: existing and acting separately from a larger group of others.

being smaller in feminine cultures than it is in masculine cultures. According to Hofstede's research, "masculine" countries included Germany, Mexico, Switzerland, Great Britain, Jamaica, Ireland, and the United States. The group of more "feminine" countries consisted of Costa Rica, Norway, the Netherlands, Yugoslavia, Chile, Thailand, and Guatemala.

The final dimension, as described by Hostede, is *uncertainty avoidance*. Ambiguity, unstructured situations, and uncertainty is not well accepted by members of some cultures. Strict rules and laws combined with safety and security measures are found in cultures that are less tolerant of a lack of structure and the "unknown." Instead, they promote the idea that their religious/philosophical beliefs are the single path toward an acceptable society, and they possess the true approach that members of their culture should aspire to achieve in their lives. Less rules, divergent opinions, and greater acceptance of uncertainty are the aspects of cultures that allow different religious perspectives to co-exist and are considered less "uncertainty avoidant." Levels of anxiety and emotional behavior are lower in these countries that include Sweden, Denmark, Canada, Indonesia, Malaysia, the United States, India, and Great Britain. Countries that are considered uncertainty-avoidant are Peru, El Salvador, Guatemala, Greece, Japan, and Portugal.

Though the idea of universal emotions that cross cultural boundaries is supported by the research of Costa and McCrae (2000), it is not a direct contradiction to Hofstede's dimensions. Cultural personality traits exist and have been identified, but they apply to the culture as a whole. It is the traits at an individual level, like the Big Five dimensions, that have been shown to cross cultural boundaries.

29.9 Trace connections to health and work.

It should be no surprise that personality influences all aspects of our day-to-day lives. From the clothes we wear, the people we hang out with, and even the food we eat, personality can play a role. But what about everyday challenges such as finding a parking place before school starts, finding out you have to work the night before having a research paper due, or perhaps more serious life issues such as finding out you just lost a job, or that a loved one has fallen ill? The way an individual interprets a given situation or stressful event, the methods they choose to address the stressor, and the actual impact of the event, vary through differences in individual cognitive factors and other aspects of our personality. In this section we will discuss some of the ways personality and associated factors can influence the way we face such challenges and the way we cope or manage stress.

Cognitive Factors in Stress: Lazarus's Cognitive Appraisal Approach Cognitive psychologist Richard Lazarus developed a cognitive view of stress called the *cognitive–mediational* theory of emotions, in which the way people think about and appraise a stressor is a major factor in how stressful that particular stressor becomes (Lazarus, 1991, 1999; Lazarus & Folkman, 1984). To Lazarus, there is a two-step process in assessing the degree of threat or harm of a stressor and how one should react to that stressor.

Primary Appraisal The first step in appraising a stressor is called **primary appraisal**, which involves estimating the severity of the stressor and classifying it as a threat (something that could be harmful in the future), a challenge (something to be met and defeated), or a harm or loss that has already occurred. If the stressor is appraised as a threat, negative emotions may arise that inhibit the person's ability to cope with the threat. If the stressor is seen as a challenge, it is possible to plan to meet that challenge, which is a more positive and less stressful approach.

primary appraisal estimating the severity of the stressor and classifying it as a threat.

secondary appraisal estimating the resources that they have available for coping with the stressor.

Type A personality a person who is ambitious, time conscious, extremely hardworking, and tends to have high levels of hostility and anger as well as being easily annoyed.

Type B personality a person who is relaxed and laid-back, less driven and competitive than Type A, and slow to anger.

Perceiving a stressor as a challenge instead of a threat makes coping with the stressor (or the harm it may already have caused) more likely to be successful. Whereas perceiving the stressor as an embarrassment, or imagining future failure or rejection, is more likely to lead to increased stress reactions, negative emotions, and an inability to cope well (Folkman, 1997; Lazarus, 1993). Think positive!

Secondary Appraisal In **secondary appraisal**, people who have identified a threat or harmful effect must estimate the resources that they have available for coping with the stressor. Resources might include social support, money, time, energy, ability, or any number of potential resources, depending on the threat. If resources are perceived as adequate or abundant, the degree of stress will be considerably less than if resources are missing or lacking.

Personality Factors in Stress Of course, how one cognitively assesses a stressor has a lot to do with one's personality. People with certain kinds of personality traits—such as aggressiveness or a naturally high level of anxiety, for example—seem to create more stress for themselves than may exist in the actual stressor. Even as long ago as the early 1930s, psychologists have had evidence that personality characteristics are a major factor in predicting health. A longitudinal study begun in 1932 (Lehr & Thomae, 1987) found that personality was almost as important to longevity* as were genetic, physical, or lifestyle factors. Other researchers have found that people who live to be very old—into their 90s and even over 100 years—tend to be relaxed, easygoing, cheerful, and active. People who have the opposite personality traits, such as aggressiveness, stubbornness, inflexibility, and tenseness, typically do not live as long as the *average* life expectancy (Levy et al., 2002).

Those positive and negative personality traits are some of the factors associated with two personality types that have been related to how people deal with stress and the influence of certain personality characteristics on coronary heart disease.

Type A and Type B In 1974, medical doctors Meyer Freidman and Ray Rosenman published a book titled *Type A Behavior and Your Heart*. The book was the result of studies spanning three decades of research into the influence of certain personality characteristics on coronary heart disease (Friedman & Kasanin, 1943; Friedman & Rosenman, 1959; Rosenman et al., 1975). Since then, numerous researchers have explored the link between what Friedman called **Type A** and **Type B personalities.**

People that are more Type A are workaholics—they are very competitive, ambitious, hate to waste time, and are easily annoyed. They feel a constant sense of pressure and have a strong tendency to try to do several things at once. Often successful but frequently unsatisfied, they always seem to want to go faster and do more, and they get easily upset over small things. A typical Type A finds it difficult to relax and do nothing—Type A people take work with them on vacation, a laptop to the beach, and do business over the phone in the car.

In contrast, people that are more Type B are not that competitive or driven, tend to be easygoing and slow to anger, and seem relaxed and at peace. Type B people are more likely to take a book to the beach to cover up their face than to actually read the book.

In 1961, the Western Collaborative Group Study (Rosenman et al., 1975) assessed 3,500 men and followed them for 8 years. For example, participants were asked to agree or disagree with statements such as "I can relax without

---

*longevity: how long people live.

guilt," in which strong agreement indicates a Type B personality. The results were that Type A men were 3 times more likely to develop heart disease than were Type B men. The Framingham Heart Study found that the risk of coronary heart disease for women who work and are also Type A is four times that of Type B working women (Eaker & Castelli, 1988). Other research has narrowed the key factors in Type A personality and heart disease to one characteristic: hostility (Frederickson et al., 1999; Matthews et al., 2004; Williams, 1999; Williams et al., 1980).

Type C A third personality type was identified by researchers Temoshok and Dreher (1992) as being associated with a higher incidence of cancer. People with a **Type C personality** tend to be very pleasant and try to keep the peace but find it difficult to express emotions, especially negative ones. They tend to internalize their anger and often experience a sense of despair over the loss of a loved one or a loss of hope. They are often lonely. These personality characteristics are strongly associated with cancer, and people who have cancer and this personality type often have thicker cancerous tumors as well (Eysenck, 1994; Temoshok & Dreher, 1992). Just as the stress of hostility puts the cardiovascular systems of Type A people at greater risk, the internalized negative emotions of the Type C personality may increase the levels of the harmful stress hormone cortisol thus weakening the immune system, and slowing recovery.

The Hardy Personality Not all Type A people are prone to heart disease. Some people actually seem to thrive on stress instead of letting stress wear them down. These people have what is called the *hardy personality*, a term first coined by psychologist Suzanne Kobasa (1979) Kobasa, 1979. Hardy people (call them "Type H") differ from ordinary, hostile Type A people and others who suffer more ill effects owing to stress in three ways:

- Hardy people have a deep sense of *commitment to their values, beliefs, sense of identity, work, and family life.*
- Hardy people also feel that they are in *control* of their lives and what happens to them.
- Hardy people tend to interpret events in primary appraisal differently than people who are not hardy. When things go wrong, they do not see a frightening problem to be avoided but instead a *challenge* to be met and answered.

Explanatory Style: Optimists and Pessimists
In addition to personality type, there are other personal factors that have an influence on people's reactions to stressors. One of these factors is the attitude that people have toward the things that happen to them in life.

Optimists are people who always tend to look for positive outcomes. **Pessimists** seem to expect the worst to happen. For an optimist, a glass is half full, whereas for a pessimist, the glass is half empty. Researchers have found that optimism is associated with longer life and increased immune-system functioning (Maruta et al., 2002). The results for pessimists were not good: They had a much higher death rate than did the optimists, more problems with physical and emotional health, more pain, less ability to take part in social activities, and less energy than optimists. Other studies link being optimistic to higher levels of helper T cells (immune system cells that direct and increase the functioning of the immune system) and higher levels of natural killer cells, the body's antivirus, and anticancer cells (Segerstrom et al., 1998; Segerstrom & Sephton, 2010). For some advice on how to become more optimistic, see the Applying Psychology feature at the end of the chapter.

◄ What about people who don't blow their top but try to keep everything "in" instead? Wouldn't that be bad for a person's health?

Type C personality a pleasant but repressed person, who tends to internalize his or her anger and anxiety and who finds expressing emotions difficult.

hardy personality a person who seems to thrive on stress but lacks the anger and hostility of the Type A personality.

optimists people who expect positive outcomes.

pessimists seem to expect the worst to happen.

Pick the best answer.

1. If you are asked to describe your best friends by explaining how they act, typically feel, and what they think about, you would be describing their
   a. temperament.
   b. character.
   c. personality.
   d. mood.

2. According to Freud, the _____ mind was the most important determining factor in human behavior and personality.
   a. preconscious
   b. conscious
   c. conscience
   d. unconscious

3. According to Freud, which part of the personality is totally buried within each individual?
   a. ego
   b. superego
   c. id
   d. conscience

4. According to the behavioral theory, personality primarily consists of
   a. unconscious forces.
   b. learned responses.
   c. biologically driven traits.
   d. personal choices.

5. Albert Bandura considers _____ as a person's expectancy of how effective his or her efforts to accomplish a goal will be in any particular circumstance.
   a. self-image
   b. self-esteem
   c. self-awareness
   d. self-efficacy

6. Nina appreciates compliments about her new photography business but really values constructive criticism, as she can then address particular issues. According to Julian Rotter, Nina has a(n)
   a. strong self-concept.
   b. real self.
   c. internal locus of control.
   d. external locus of control.

7. What did Carl Rogers mean by the term "fully functioning person"?
   a. Someone who is working to discover his or her real self.
   b. Someone who is working to discover his or her ideal self.
   c. Someone who is experiencing a match between his or her real and ideal self, and who is also trusting of their innermost intuitions and urges.
   d. Someone who has discovered his or her self-efficacy.

8. Trait theories are less concerned with _____ and more concerned with _____.
   a. changing personality; predicting personality
   b. describing personality; explaining personality development
   c. predicting personality; changing personality
   d. predicting behavior; changing personality

9. Cattell's research and use of factor analysis essentially scaled down many, many different ways of describing aspects of personality into _____ source traits.
   a. 10
   b. 16
   c. 5
   d. 2

10. In the Big Five theory of personality, "E" stands for
    a. empathy.
    b. energy.
    c. external.
    d. extraversion.

Assessment and Issues in Personality

Module Goal

Learn about personality assessment.

Learning Objective

30.1 Describe different personality assessment techniques and evaluate their reliability and validity.

Learn about Personality Assessment

30.1 Describe different personality assessment techniques and evaluate their reliability and validity.

The methods for measuring or assessing personality vary according to the theory of personality used to develop those methods, as one might expect. However, most psychological professionals doing a personality assessment on a client do not necessarily tie themselves down to one theoretical viewpoint only, preferring to take a more *eclectic* view of personality. The eclectic view is a way of choosing the parts of different theories that seem to best fit a particular situation, rather than using only one theory to explain a phenomenon. In fact, looking at behavior from multiple perspectives can often bring insights into a person's behavior that would not easily come from taking only one perspective. Many professionals will not only use several different perspectives but also several of the assessment techniques that follow. Even so, certain methods are more commonly used by certain kinds of theorists, as can be seen in **Table 30.1**.

◀ With all the different theories of personality, how do people find out what kind of personality they have?

Table 30.1	Who Uses What Method?
TYPE OF ASSESSMENT	MOST LIKELY USED BY . . .
Interviews	Psychoanalysts, humanistic therapists

Projective Tests
  Rorschach
  Thematic Apperception Test
	Psychoanalysts

Behavioral Assessments
  Direct observation
  Rating scales
  Frequency counts
	Behavioral and social cognitive therapists

Personality Inventories
  Sixteen Personality Factor
  Questionnaire (16PF)
	Trait theorists

(*Continued*)

Table 30.1 (Continued)

TYPE OF ASSESSMENT	MOST LIKELY USED BY . . .
Revised Neuroticism/Extraversion/Openness Personality Inventory (NEO-PI-R) Myers-Briggs Type Indicator (MBTI) Eysenck Personality Questionnaire (EPQ) Keirsey Temperament Sorter II California Psychological Inventory (CPI) Minnesota Multiphasic Personality Inventory, Version II (MMPI-2)	

Personality assessments may also differ in the purposes for which they are conducted. For example, sometimes a researcher may administer a personality test of some sort to participants in a research study so that the participants may be classified according to certain personality traits. There are tests available to people who simply want to learn more about their own personalities. Finally, clinical and counseling psychologists, psychiatrists, and other psychological professionals use these personality assessment tools in the diagnosis of disorders of personality.

Interviews, Behavioral Assessments, and Personality Inventories As covered in the last section, the methods for measuring or assessing personality vary according to the theory of personality used to develop those methods. They also vary according to the type of data that is desired. We will first examine a variety of methods aimed at providing more objective data.

Interviews Some therapists ask questions and note down the answers in a survey process called an *interview*. This type of interview, unlike a job interview, is likely to be *unstructured* and flow naturally from the beginning dialogue between the client and the psychologist.

Yes, when psychologists interview clients, clients must report on their innermost feelings, urges, and concerns—all things that only they can directly know.

 *So an interview is a kind of self-report process?*

Behavioral Assessments Behaviorists do not typically want to "look into the mind." Because behaviorists assume that personality is merely habitually learned responses to stimuli in the environment, the preferred method for a behaviorist would be to watch that behavior unfold in the real world.

In **direct observation**, the psychologist observes the client engaging in ordinary, everyday behavior, preferably in the natural setting of home, school, or workplace, for example. A therapist who goes to the classroom and observes that tantrum behavior only happens when a child is asked to do something involving fine motor abilities (like drawing or writing) might be able to conclude that the child has difficulty with those skills and throws a tantrum to avoid the task.

Personality Inventories Trait theorists are typically more interested in personality descriptions. They tend to use an assessment known as a **personality inventory**, a questionnaire that has a standard list of questions and only requires certain specific answers, such as "yes," "no," and "can't decide." The standard nature of the questions (everyone gets the same list) and the lack of open-ended answers make these assessments far more objective and

direct observation assessment in which the professional observes the client engaged in ordinary, day-to-day behavior in either a clinical or natural setting.

personality inventory paper-and-pencil or computerized test that consists of statements that require a specific, standardized response from the person taking the test.

reliable than projective tests (Garb et al., 1998), although they are still a form of self-report. One such personality inventory is Cattell's 16PF, described earlier in this chapter. Costa and McCrae have recently revised their *Revised Neuroticism/Extraversion/Openness Personality Inventory (NEO-PI-R)*, which is based on the five-factor model of personality traits and is still being published. The newer version is the NEO-PI-3, which has been made easier to read for use with adolescents and has new norms (McCrae et al., 2005; McCrae, Martin et al., 2005). You can answer select questions from the NEO-PI for yourself by completing the experiment, *IPIP Neo Personality Inventory.*

Other common personality tests include the Eysenck Personality Questionnaire (Eysenck & Eysenck, 1993), the Keirsey Temperament Sorter II (Keirsey, 1998), the California Psychological Inventory (Gough, 1995), and the Sixteen Personality Factor Questionnaire (Cattell, 1994).

Another inventory in common use is the *Myers-Briggs Type Indicator (MBTI)*. This inventory is based on the ideas of Carl Jung and looks at four personality dimensions. The *sensing/intuition* (S/N) dimension includes people who prefer to rely on what they can see, hear, and so on through their own physical senses (sensing) and, on its opposite end, those who look for patterns and trust their hunches (intuition). Sensing people are very detail oriented, preferring to work only with the known facts, whereas intuitive people are more willing to use metaphors, analogies, and look for possibilities. The *thinking/feeling* (T/F) dimension runs from those who prefer to use logic, analysis, and experiences that can be verified as facts (thinkers) to those who tend to make decisions based on their personal values and emotional reactions (feeling). *Introversion/extraversion* (I/E) is the same classic dimension that began with Jung and is represented in nearly every personality theory, including the Big Five. *Perceiving/judging* (P/J) describes those who are willing to adapt and modify decisions, be spontaneous, and who are naturally curious and tend to put off making a final decision so that all possibilities are covered (perceiving) as well as those who are the opposite: the action-oriented, decisive, get-the-task-done-and-don't-look-back type (judging). These four dimensions can differ for each individual, resulting in 16 (4 × 4) possible personality types: ISTJ, ISTP, ISFP, ISFJ, and so on (Briggs & Myers, 1998).

By far the most common personality inventory is the *Minnesota Multiphasic Personality Inventory, Version II*, or *MMPI-2*, which specifically tests for abnormal behavior and thinking patterns in personality (Butcher & Rouse, 1996; Butcher et al., 2000, 2001). This questionnaire consists of 567 statements such as "I am often very tense" or "I believe I am being plotted against." The person taking the test must answer "true," "false," or "cannot say." The MMPI has 10 clinical scales and 8 validity scales in addition to numerous subscales. Each scale tests for a particular kind of behavior. The thinking and behavior patterns assessed include those associated with relatively mild personality problems such as excessive worrying and shyness as well as patterns representative of disorders such as schizophrenia and depression

Validity scales, which are built into any well-designed psychological inventory, are intended to indicate whether or not a person taking the inventory is responding honestly. Responses to certain items on the test will indicate if people are trying to make themselves look better or worse than they are, for example, and certain items are repeated throughout the test in a slightly different form, so that anyone trying to "fake" the test will have difficulty responding to those items consistently (Butcher et al., 2001). For example, if one of the statements is "I am always happy" and a person responds "true" to that statement, the suspicion would be that this person is trying to look better than he or she really is.

How can you tell ◄ if a person is telling the truth on a personality inventory?

If several of the validity scale questions are answered in this way, the conclusion is that the person is not being honest.

Evaluating Interviews, Behavioral Assessments, and Personality Inventories In this section we have discussed a variety of assessment techniques aimed at providing objective data. Each of these has advantages and disadvantages. For example, the same problems that exist with self-report data (such as surveys) exist with interviews. Clients can lie, distort the truth, misremember, or give what they think is a socially acceptable answer instead of true information. Interviewers themselves can be biased, interpreting what the client says in light of their own belief systems or prejudices. Freud certainly did this when he refused to believe that his patients had actually been sexually molested as children, preferring to interpret that information as a fantasy instead of reality (Russell, 1986).

Another problem with interviews is something called the **halo effect**, which is a tendency to form a favorable or unfavorable impression of someone at the first meeting, so that all of a person's comments and behavior after that first impression will be interpreted to agree with the impression—positively or negatively. The halo effect can happen in any social situation, including interviews between a psychological professional and a client. First impressions really do count, and people who make a good first impression because of clothing, personal appearance, or some other irrelevant* characteristic will seem to have a "halo" hanging over their heads—they can do no wrong after that (Lance et al., 1994; Thorndike, 1920). And of course, as we will discuss in this chapter, negative first impressions are hard to change.

Problems with behavioral assessments can include the observer effect (when a person's behavior is affected by being watched) and observer bias, which can be controlled by having multiple observers and correlating their observations with each other. Ⓛ Ⓘ Ⓝ Ⓚ *to Chapter One: The Science of Psychology, pp. 18–25.*

The advantage of personality inventories over projective tests (which we will cover shortly) and interviews is that inventories are standardized (i.e., everyone gets exactly the same questions and the answers are scored in exactly the same way). In fact, responses to inventories are often scored on a computer. Observer bias and bias of interpretation are simply not possible, because this kind of assessment is objective rather than subjective. The validity and reliability of personality inventories are generally recognized as being greatly superior to those of projective tests (Anastasi & Urbina, 1997).

There are some problems, however. The validity scales, for example, are a good check against cheating, but they are not perfect. Some people are still able to fake their answers and respond in what they feel are the socially appropriate ways (Anastasi & Urbina, 1997; Hicklin & Widiger, 2000). Despite the best intentions of the test creators, individual responses to specific questions may also vary as they may be interpreted in different ways by different individuals, and are very likely to be subject to cultural influences (Kagan, 2010).

Projective Tests Have you ever tried to see "shapes" in the clouds? You might see a house where another person might see the same cloud as a horse. The cloud isn't really either of those things but can be *interpreted* as one or the other, depending on the person doing the interpretation. That makes a cloud an ambiguous stimulus—one that is capable of being interpreted in more than one way.

In just this way, psychoanalysts (and a few other psychologists) show their clients ambiguous visual stimuli and ask the clients to tell them what they see. The hope is that the client will project unconscious concerns onto the visual

halo effect tendency of an interviewer to allow positive characteristics of a client to influence the assessments of the client's behavior and statements.

---

*irrelevant: not applying to the case or example at hand.

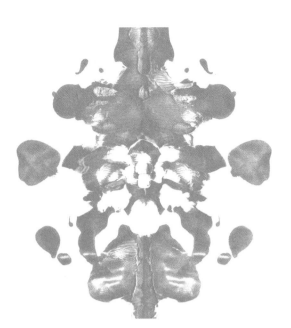

FIGURE 30.1 Rorschach Inkblot Example
A facsimile of a Rorschach inkblot. A person being tested is asked to tell the interviewer what he or she sees in an inkblot similar to the one shown. Answers are neither right nor wrong but may reveal unconscious concerns. What do you see in this inkblot?

stimulus, revealing them to the examiner. Tests using this method are called **projective tests**. In psychodynamic psychology such tests can be used to explore a client's personality or used as a diagnostic tool to uncover problems in personality.

The Rorschach Inkblots One of the more well-known projective tests is the *Rorschach inkblot test*, developed in 1921 by Swiss psychiatrist Hermann Rorschach (ROR-shok). There are 10 inkblots, 5 in black ink on a white background and 5 in colored inks on a white background. (See **Figure 30.1** for an image similar to a Rorschach-type inkblot.)

People being tested are asked to look at each inkblot and simply say whatever it might look like to them. Using predetermined categories and responses commonly given by people to each picture (Exner, 1980), psychologists score responses on key factors, such as reference to color, shape, figures seen in the blot, and response to the whole or to details.

Rorschach tested thousands of inkblots until he narrowed them down to the 10 in use today. They are still used to describe personality, diagnose mental disorders, and predict behavior (Watkins et al., 1995; Weiner, 1997). However, along with the use of other projective techniques in general, their use is controversial given questions about some scoring methods and overall validity (Lilienfeld et al., 2000).

The TAT First developed in 1935 by psychologist Henry Murray and his colleagues (Morgan & Murray, 1935), the *Thematic Apperception Test (TAT)* consists of 20 pictures, all black and white, that are shown to a client. The client is asked to tell a story about the person or people in the picture, who are all deliberately drawn in ambiguous situations (see **Figure 30.2**). Again, the story developed by the client is interpreted by the psychoanalyst, who looks for revealing statements and projection of the client's own problems onto the people in the pictures.

Evaluating Projective Tests Projective tests are by their nature very *subjective* (valid only within the person's own perception), and interpreting the answers of clients is almost an art. It is certainly not a science and is not known for its accuracy. Problems lie in the areas of reliability and validity. A person's answers to the Rorschach, for example, might be quite different from one day to the next, depending on the person's mood and what scary movie might have been on television the previous night.

projective tests personality assessments that present ambiguous visual stimuli to the client and ask the client to respond with whatever comes to mind.

FIGURE 30.2 Thematic Apperception Test Example
A sample from the Thematic Apperception Test (TAT). When you look at this picture, what story does it suggest to you? Who is the person? Why is he climbing a rope?

Becoming More Optimistic

Martin Seligman is a social learning psychologist who developed the concept of *learned helplessness*, and began the positive psychology movement. He has outlined four ways in which optimism may affect how long a person lives Seligman (2002):

- Optimists are less likely to develop learned helplessness, the tendency to stop trying to achieve a goal that has been blocked in the past.
- Optimists are more likely than pessimists to take care of their health by preventive measures because they believe that their actions make a difference in what happens to them.
- Optimists are far less likely than pessimists to become depressed, and depression is associated with mortality because of the effect of depression on the immune system.
- Optimists have more effectively functioning immune systems than pessimists do, perhaps because they experience less psychological stress.

Seligman (1998) has also found that optimists are more successful in their life endeavors than pessimists are. Optimistic politicians win more elections, optimistic students get better grades, and optimistic athletes win more contests.

How can you become more optimistic? The way to become an optimist is to monitor one's own thinking. Recognition of negative thoughts is the first step, followed by disputing those same negative thoughts (Seligman, 2002). Here's a plan to follow to become an optimistic thinker:

1. When a bad mood strikes, stop and think about what just went through your head.
2. When you've recognized the negative statements, treat them as if they came from someone else—someone who is trying to make your life miserable.
3. Argue with those thoughts. Challenge each negative statement and replace it with a more positive statement.

Essentially, the last step in becoming a more optimistic thinker is to learn to argue with yourself and correct distorted or faulty thinking. Recognizing faulty thinking can be difficult at first. The following questions may help people to home in on negative thinking:

1. In thinking about the thoughts you have had in the last few hours, how many of them were negative thoughts? How could you change those thoughts to be more positive?
2. When thinking about people you know who make a lot of negative self-statements or who are always minimizing their efforts or putting themselves down, how does their behavior make you feel? How do you think their behavior makes them feel?

Questions for Further Discussion

1. Do you think you are an optimist, a pessimist, or somewhere in between?
2. What are some things you can do in your own life to become more optimistic?

Thinking Critically

Should employers require prospective employees to take a personality test? Why or why not? Would such a requirement make more sense in certain professions, and, if so, what professions might those be?

Pick the best answer.

1. **What, if anything, have adoption studies taught us regarding the relationship between heredity and personality?**

   a. Adoption studies are a new area of study and have yet to offer any information on the effects of heredity on personality.

   b. Adoption studies have confirmed that personality can be strongly influenced by genetics.

   c. Adoption studies have not supported many behavioral genetics studies, thus questioning the idea that personality can be influenced by genetics.

   d. Adoption studies have resulted in conflicting findings, with some strongly supporting the influence of heredity on personality while others suggest that heredity has no influence whatsoever.

2. **According to Richard Lazarus, when someone asks themselves, "How can I deal with this potentially harmful stressor?" the individual is focused on a _____ appraisal.**

   a. primary
   b. secondary
   c. tertiary
   d. minimal

3. **Greg rushes to an appointment, arriving 20 minutes early, whereas Aaron arrives with only minutes to spare. Slightly annoyed when Greg points this out, Aaron replies very casually, "Hey, I'm here." We might assume Greg has more of a _____ personality whereas Aaron is more _____.**

   a. Type A; Type B
   b. Type A; Type C
   c. Type B; Type C
   d. Type C; Type A

4. **What is the function of a validity scale?**

   a. To determine if a person is giving an accurate response

   b. To determine how a subject really feels

   c. To help better explain the results of a personality test

   d. To offer both a diagnosis of abnormal behavior plus a positive therapeutic treatment

5. **Which of the following personality assessment methods is most likely to be reliable?**

   a. Projective test
   b. Subjective interview
   c. Personality inventory
   d. Rorschach inkblot test

6. **Mr. Phillips is constantly late for his classes, leaving students waiting in the hallway outside his door for nearly five minutes at times. Which dimension of the five-factor model would show a very low score for Mr. Phillips?**

   a. Openness
   b. Conscientiousness
   c. Extraversion
   d. Agreeableness

7. **Which of the following personality inventories is based on the five-factor model?**

   a. CPI
   b. 16PF
   c. MBTI
   d. NEO-PI

8. **Monik is a generally calm person who stays relaxed even in stressful situations. He does not have a history of mental health problems. On the Big Five inventory, Monik would probably score very low on**

   a. openness.
   b. neuroticism.
   c. extraversion.
   d. agreeableness.

9. **Jake was adopted as an infant and raised by his adoptive family. Jake has always been an extravert, but his adoptive parents are both quite introverted. A researcher discovers that Jake's twin brother, who was adopted by another family as an infant and whom Jake has never met, is also very extraverted. Which of the following concepts seems most related to Jake's extraversion?**

   a. Extraversion as a heritable trait
   b. Extraversion as a learned trait
   c. Extraversion as a habitual trait
   d. Extraversion as a psychosexual trait

10. **Which of the following personality assessment methods would most likely be used by a psychoanalyst?**

    a. MMPI-2
    b. Myers-Briggs
    c. Frequency counts
    d. Rorschach inkblot test

(((**Listen** to an **Audio File** of your chapter at **MyPsychLab**

Module 29: Perspectives on Personality

Understand personality perspectives and issues.

29.1 Explain stability and change.
- Personality is the unique way individuals think, feel, and act. It is different from character and temperament but includes those aspects.
- Although once thought to be stable it is understood that personalities are subject to change throughout adulthood.
- The four traditional perspectives in the study of personality are the psychodynamic, behavioristic (including social cognitive theory), humanistic, and trait perspectives.

29.2 Discuss psychodynamic theories.
- The three divisions of the mind are the conscious, preconscious, and unconscious. The unconscious can be revealed in dreams.
- The three parts of the personality are the id, ego, and superego.
- The id works on the pleasure principle and the ego works on the reality principle; the superego is the moral center of personality, containing the conscience, and is the source of moral anxiety.
- The conflicts between the demands of the id and the rules and restrictions of the superego lead to anxiety for the ego, which uses defense mechanisms to deal with that anxiety.
- The personality develops in a series of psychosexual stages: oral (id dominates), anal (ego develops), phallic (superego develops), latency (period of sexual repression), and genital (sexual feelings reawaken with appropriate targets).
- The Oedipus and Electra complexes (sexual "crushes" on the opposite-sex parent) create anxiety in the phallic stage, which is resolved through identification with the same-sex parent.
- Fixation occurs when conflicts are not fully resolved during a stage, resulting in adult personality characteristics reflecting childhood inadequacies.
- The neo-Freudians changed the focus of psychoanalysis to fit their own interpretation of the personality, leading to the more modern version known as the psychodynamic perspective.

29.3 Describe social-cognitive theories.
- Behaviorists define personality as a set of learned responses or habits.
- The social cognitive view of personality includes the concept of reciprocal determinism, in which the environment, characteristics of the person, and the behavior itself all interact.

29.4 Explore self-concept.
- Self-efficacy is a characteristic in which a person perceives a behavior as more or less effective based on previous experiences, the opinions of others, and perceived personal competencies.

- Locus of control is a determinant of personality in which one either assumes that one's actions directly affect events and reinforcements one experiences or that such events and reinforcements are the result of luck, fate, or powerful others.
- Personality, in the form of potential behavior patterns, is also determined by an interaction between one's expectancies for success and the perceived value of the potential reinforcement.
- Behaviorist personality theory has scientific support but is criticized as being too simplistic.

29.5 Learn about humanistic theories.
- Humanism developed as a reaction against the negativity of psychoanalysis and the deterministic nature of behaviorism.
- Carl Rogers proposed that self-actualization depends on proper development of the self-concept.
- The self-concept includes the real self and the ideal self. When these two components do not match or agree, anxiety and disordered behavior result.
- Unconditional positive regard from important others in a person's life helps the formation of the self-concept and the congruity of the real and ideal selves, leading to a fully functioning person.
- Humanistic theory is not scientifically researched but has been effective in therapy situations.

29.6 Understand trait theories.
- Trait theorists describe personality traits to predict behavior.
- Allport first developed a list of about 200 traits and believed that these traits were part of the nervous system.
- Cattell reduced the number of traits to between 16 and 23 with a computer method called factor analysis.
- Several researchers have arrived at five trait dimensions that have research support across cultures, called the Big Five or five-factor model. The five factors are openness, conscientiousness, extraversion, agreeableness, and neuroticism.
- Personality neuroscience is a growing area of research, and brain structure differences associated with some aspects of the Big Five dimensions of personality have been identified using structural MRI.
- Cross-cultural research has found support for the five-factor model of personality traits in a number of different cultures; future research will explore the degree to which child-rearing practices and heredity may influence the five personality factors.

29.7 Describe biological and situational influences.
- Behavioral genetics is a field of study of the relationship between heredity and personality.
- Studies of twins and adopted children have found support for a genetic influence on many personality traits, including intelligence, leadership abilities,

traditionalism, nurturance, empathy, assertiveness, neuroticism, and extraversion.
- Heritability of personality, or how much some trait within a population can be attributed to genetic influences, ranges from about 25 to 50%.

29.8 Consider how individualistic and collectivistic cultural perspectives relate to personality.
- Geert Hofstede's research has suggested there may be four dimensions of cultural personality, including individualism/collectivism, power distance, masculinity/femininity, and uncertainty avoidance.
- Hofstede's dimensions are cultural personality traits, whereas those of the Big Five refer to individuals.

29.9 Trace connections to health and work.
- The cognitive appraisal approach states that how people think about a stressor determines, at least in part, how stressful that stressor will become.
- The first step in appraising a stressor is called primary appraisal, in which the person determines whether an event is threatening, challenging, or of no consequence. Threatening events are more stressful than those seen as challenging.
- The second step is secondary appraisal, in which the person assesses the resources available to deal with the stressor, such as time, money, and social support.
- Type A personalities are ambitious, time conscious, hostile, and angry workaholics who are at increased risk of coronary heart disease, primarily due to their anger and hostility.
- Type B personalities are relaxed and easygoing and have one-third the risk of coronary heart disease as do Type A personalities if male, and one-fourth the risk if female and working outside the home.
- Type C personalities are pleasant but repressed, internalizing their negative emotions.
- Hardy people are hard workers who lack the anger and hostility of the Type A personality, instead seeming to thrive on stress.
- Optimists look for positive outcomes and experience far less stress than pessimists, who take a more negative view.

Module 30: Assessment and Issues in Personality

Learn about personality assessment.

30.1 Describe different personality assessment techniques and evaluate their reliability and validity.
- Interviews are used primarily by psychoanalysts and humanists and can include structured or unstructured interviews; disadvantages of interviews can include the halo effect and bias of the interpretation on the part of the interviewer.
- Behavioral assessments are primarily used by behaviorists and include direct observation of behavior, rating scales of specific behavior, and frequency counts of behavior. Behavioral assessments have the disadvantage of the observer effect, which causes an observed person's behavior to change, and observer bias on the part of the person doing the assessment.
- Personality inventories are typically developed by trait theorists and provide a detailed description of certain personality traits. They are objective tests rather than subjective.
- The NEO-PI-R is based on the five-factor model, whereas the Myers-Briggs Type Indicator is based on Jung's theory of personality types. The MMPI-2 is designed to detect social issues in personality.
- Personality inventories include validity scales to prevent cheating, but such measures are not perfect and cheating is sometimes possible.
- Projective tests are based on the defense mechanism of projection and are used by psychoanalysts. Projective tests include the Rorschach inkblot test and the Thematic Apperception Test.
- A projective tests has been useful in finding starting points to open a dialogue between therapist and client but have been criticized for being low in reliability and validity.

Applying Psychology to Everyday Life: Becoming More Optimistic
- The best way to become more optimistic is to recognize negative thoughts and change them to more helpful positive thoughts.

Vocabulary Terms

Vocabulary Review

Match each vocabulary term to its definition

1. reciprocal determinism
2. personality
3. self-efficacy
4. superego
5. temperament
6. trait
7. locus of control
8. projection
9. Type A
10. identification

a. The unique and relatively stable ways in which people think, feel, and behave.

b. Individual's expectancy of how effective his or her efforts to accomplish a goal will be in any particular circumstance.

c. Person who is ambitious, time conscious, extremely hardworking, and tends to have high levels of hostility and anger as well as being easily annoyed.

d. Defense mechanism in which a person tries to become like someone else to deal with anxiety.

e. Part of the personality that acts as a moral center.

f. Defense mechanism involving placing one's own unacceptable thoughts onto others, as if the thoughts actually belonged to those others and not to oneself.

g. A consistent, enduring way of thinking, feeling, or behaving.

h. A child's innate personality and emotional characteristics, observable in infancy; the enduring characteristics with which each person is born.

i. The tendency for people to assume that they either have control or do not have control over events and consequences in their lives.

j. Bandura's explanation of how the factors of environment, personal characteristics, and behavior can interact to determine future behavior.

Psychology Project

How reliable are online personality tests? Perform this experiment to see how your perception of your personality measures up to the results of an online test.

Materials:
- a computer with Internet access
- a pencil and paper

Instructions:

1. First, review the Big Five model of personality. For each trait, think about your own personality and decide whether you are a "high scorer" or a "low scorer" in terms of that trait.

2. Next, take an online personality test based on the five-factor model, such as the one located at **http://www.personalitytest.org.uk/**

3. Review the results of the online personality test. Are the test results similar or different to the conclusions you drew about yourself?

4. After comparing your test results to your own self-assessment, take a few minutes to think about factors that could have affected your results. Is the online test reliable and valid? Is your self-assessment reliable and valid? What are the benefits and drawbacks of each testing method? What methods might give you a more accurate picture of your own personality?

Tech Alternative

Design a personality test app.

If you look on various app sites you can find a number of personality test apps. Browse the different apps to see what is out there. As an app developer it is a challenge to be innovative and unique. Describe the types of personality test apps you see available. Describe an app that you would design to test personality that is innovative and unique. Consider the following questions:

How is personality measured on your app?

How could a biological basis for personality be used in your app?

How can the person using your app influence the results?

How can your app be user friendly?

How reliable and valid are the results of your app test?

Write your responses in paragraph form to complete the assignment.

Essay Question

In a well-organized essay, contrast *two* of the approaches to personality listed below. Describe each approach you choose, including advantages and disadvantages, and discuss at least one prominent individual associated with each approach.

a. Psychodynamic theory of personality

b. Behavioral and social cognitive theories of personality

c. Humanistic theories of personality

d. Trait theories of personality

Test Yourself

Pick the best answer.

1. Irritability or adaptability are examples of
   a. character.
   b. consciousness.
   c. mood.
   d. temperament.

2. According to Freud, the _____ works off of the pleasure principle.
   a. id
   b. ego
   c. superego
   d. collective unconscious

3. You are shocked to hear that two of your friends who seemingly hated one another are now getting married. According to Freud, what defense mechanism best explains their prior behavior?
   a. projection
   b. reaction formation
   c. repression
   d. regression

4. Resolving the Oedipal conflict results in
   a. compensation.
   b. identification.
   c. sublimation.
   d. denial.

5. Your teacher explains how all females have an inner masculine side that adds to their personality. This concept is known as a(n)
   a. anima.
   b. animus.
   c. shadow.
   d. source trait.

6. Which of the following is a way in which Jung's beliefs differed from Freud's?
   a. Jung did not believe in archetypes.
   b. Jung did not believe in defense mechanisms.
   c. Jung believed in the collective unconscious.
   d. Jung did not believe in the id, ego, and superego.

7. Karen Horney's study of one's personality focused on
   a. anxiety during childhood.
   b. biological changes during adolescence.
   c. trait-based characteristics that were present in infancy.
   d. environmental influences through adulthood.

8. Candice believes that fate will help her find the right man with whom to live her life. She likely has an external
   a. locus of control.
   b. oral fixation.
   c. Oedipal complex.
   d. defense mechanism.

9. Keisha works hard at her job because she believes it will increase her chances for a promotion. According to Julian Rotter's theory, her effort is an example of what he calls
   a. reinforcement value.
   b. expectancy.
   c. archetypes.
   d. latency stage.

10. That it can be tested scientifically is an advantage of the _____ view over the psychodynamic view.
    a. behavioral
    b. projective
    c. Jungian
    d. social cognitive

11. Which perspective of psychology focuses on the role of each person's conscious life experiences and choices in personality development?
    a. trait
    b. behavior
    c. humanistic
    d. psychodynamic

12. An old motto of the U.S. Army was, "Be all you can be." This concept fits well with Carl Rogers's theory of
    a. unconditional positive regard.
    b. empathy.
    c. self-actualizing tendency.
    d. real versus the ideal self.

13. According to Rogers, a mismatch between the real and ideal self
    a. typically motivates individuals to close the gap.
    b. can result in anxiety and neurotic behavior.
    c. causes one to better understand their unconscious motives.
    d. causes an increase in unconditional positive regard.

14. To explain an individual's personality, trait theorists would look to
    a. early childhood emotional traumas.
    b. the kind of love, warmth, and affection given to the person by his or her parents.
    c. the early experiences of rewards and punishments for certain behavior.
    d. the constellation of personality characteristics possessed by the person.

15. Studies of the hereditability of personality traits have found
    a. little evidence to support the belief that personality can be passed by genetics.
    b. evidence to support the belief that personality can be passed by genetics but only in highly developed countries.
    c. strong evidence to support some personality traits can be passed by genetics.
    d. strong evidence that personality is passed exclusively by genetics.

16. Jolene carefree and not as ambitious as some of the other women in her office. Instead, Jolene likes to have a lot of leisure time whenever possible. Jolene is most likely a
    a. Type A personality.
    b. Type B personality.
    c. Type C personality.
    d. Hardy personality.

17. Azriel thrives on stress and feels in control of his life. His personality would be labeled a
    a. Type A.
    b. Type B.
    c. Type C.
    d. hardy.

18. Which type of assessment would be the most reliable?
    a. subjective test
    b. projective test
    c. personality inventory
    d. observational study

19. The _____ is based on the five-factor model.
    a. NEO-PI-R
    b. MBTI
    c. MMPI-2
    d. 16PF

20. Personality neuroscience is an emerging field offering evidence of a possible relationship between various aspects of personality with
    a. brain structure and function.
    b. the structure of neurons.
    c. skull shape.
    d. neuroticism.

Learning Objectives

29.1 29.2 29.3 29.4 29.5 29.6 29.7 29.8 29.9 pp. 374–393

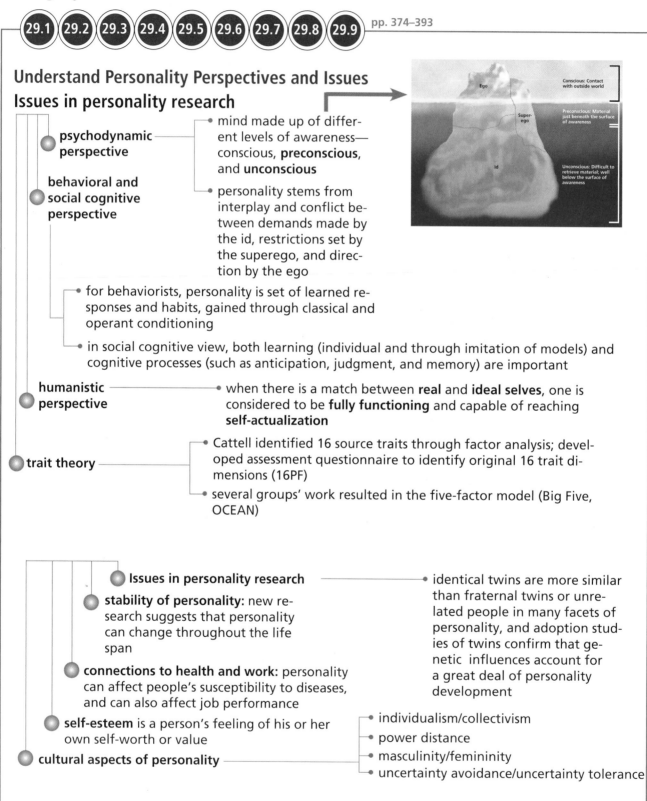

Understand Personality Perspectives and Issues
Issues in personality research

- **psychodynamic perspective**
  - mind made up of different levels of awareness—conscious, **preconscious**, and **unconscious**
  - personality stems from interplay and conflict between demands made by the id, restrictions set by the superego, and direction by the ego

- **behavioral and social cognitive perspective**
  - for behaviorists, personality is set of learned responses and habits, gained through classical and operant conditioning
  - in social cognitive view, both learning (individual and through imitation of models) and cognitive processes (such as anticipation, judgment, and memory) are important

- **humanistic perspective**
  - when there is a match between **real** and **ideal selves**, one is considered to be **fully functioning** and capable of reaching **self-actualization**

- **trait theory**
  - Cattell identified 16 source traits through factor analysis; developed assessment questionnaire to identify original 16 trait dimensions (16PF)
  - several groups' work resulted in the five-factor model (Big Five, OCEAN)

- **Issues in personality research**
  - identical twins are more similar than fraternal twins or unrelated people in many facets of personality, and adoption studies of twins confirm that genetic influences account for a great deal of personality development
  - **stability of personality:** new research suggests that personality can change throughout the life span
  - **connections to health and work:** personality can affect people's susceptibility to diseases, and can also affect job performance
  - **self-esteem** is a person's feeling of his or her own self-worth or value

- **cultural aspects of personality**
  - individualism/collectivism
  - power distance
  - masculinity/femininity
  - uncertainty avoidance/uncertainty tolerance

Map the Concepts at MyPsychLab

Learn about Personality Assessment

- interviews
- projective tests
  - Rorschach inkblots
  - TAT
- behavioral assessments
- personality inventories

Table 30.1	Who Uses What Method?
TYPE OF ASSESSMENT	MOST LIKELY USED BY...
Interviews	Psychoanalysts, Humanistic Therapists

Projective Tests
  Rorschach
  Thematic Apperception Test
	Psychoanalysts

Behavioral Assessments
  Direct observation
  Rating scales
  Frequency counts
	Behavioral and social cognitive therapists

Personality Inventories
  Sixteen Personality Factor Questionnaire (16PF)
  Revised Neuroticism/Extraversion/Openness Personality Inventory (NEO-PI-R)
  Myers-Briggs Type Indicator (MBTI)
  Eysenck Personality Questionnaire (EPQ)
  Keirsey Temperament Sorter II
  California Psychological Inventory (CPI)
  Minnesota Multiphasic Personality Inventory, Version II (MMPI-2)
	Trait theorists

Psychological Disorders

Do you or someone you know have any quirky beliefs or behaviors? Have you ever been sad for more than a day? What about being very energetic or extremely happy for the better part of a week? Maybe you are a "checker." Have you ever double- or triple-checked a door to see if you locked it? Today it may not be that uncommon to observe someone walking down the street and apparently talking to herself or himself, only then to observe they are actually wearing a Bluetooth headset. It also may mean one thing to see someone lying on the sidewalk outside a local restaurant, and something slightly different if you see someone lying on the sidewalk outside your school building, and yet still different meanings if it is a student versus a faculty member.

Have you ever questioned if someone's way of thinking or acting was normal? How do you know if a behavior is normal or abnormal?

👁 **Watch** the **Video**, at **MyPsychLab**

*W*hy Study **Abnormal Behavior** and Mental Processes?

Because abnormal behavior is all around us, it raises many questions: How should one react? What should be done to help? What kind of person develops a mental illness? Could this happen to someone close to you? The key to answering these questions is to develop an understanding of just what is meant by abnormal behavior and thinking, and the different ways in which thinking and behavior can depart from the "normal" path.

Module Goal

Learning Objectives

Module Goal

Learn about perspectives on abnormal behavior.

Learning Objectives

31.1 Discuss historical and cross-cultural views of abnormality.

31.2 Explain psychologically abnormal behavior.

31.3 Describe the challenges associated with diagnosis.

31.4 Explain major models of abnormality.

31.5 Explain the classification of psychological disorders.

31.6 Explain how stigma relates to abnormal behavior.

31.7 Describe the impact of psychological disorders on the individual, family, and society.

Learn About Perspectives on Abnormal Behavior

31.1 Discuss historical and cross-cultural views of abnormality.

Exactly what is meant by the term *abnormal behavior*? When is thinking, or any mental process *maladaptive*? Abnormal or maladaptive as compared to what? Who gets to decide what is normal and what is not? Has the term always meant what it means now? We'll explore these questions and others in this section.

A Very Brief History of Psychological Disorders The study of abnormal behavior and psychological dysfunction is called **psychopathology**. Defining abnormality is a complicated process, and our view of what is abnormal has changed significantly over time.

Dating from as early as 3000 B.C.E., archaeologists have found human skulls with small holes cut into them, and close examination indicates that the holes were made while the person was still alive. Many of the holes show evidence of healing, meaning that the person survived the process. Although *trephining*, or cutting holes into the skull of a living person, is still done today to relieve pressure of fluids on the brain, in ancient times the reason may have had more to do with releasing the "demons" possessing the poor victim (Gross, 1999).

Hippocrates (460–377 B.C.E.), a Greek physician, considered the "Father of Medicine," during the time in which the rest of the world and even many Greeks believed in the demonic possession explanation of mental illness, challenged that belief with his assertion that illnesses of both the body and the mind were the result of imbalances in the body's vital fluids, or *humors*. Although Hippocrates was not correct in his assumptions about the humors of the body (phlegm, black bile, blood, and yellow bile), his was the first recorded attempt to explain abnormal thinking or behavior as due to some biological process. ⓛⓘⓝⓚ *to Chapter Twelve: Theories of Personality, p. 374.*

Moving forward in time, people of the Middle Ages believed in spirit possession (a belief influenced by the teachings of religious/cultural systems) as one cause of abnormality. The treatment of choice for such maladies was a religious

psychopathology the study of abnormal behavior and psychological dysfunction.

one: *exorcism*, or the formal casting out of the demon through a religious ritual (Lewis, 1995). During the Renaissance, belief in demonic possession (in which the possessed person was seen as a victim) gave way to a belief in witchcraft, and mentally ill persons were most likely called witches and put to death.

Fast forward to the present day, psychological disorders are often viewed from a *medical model* in that they can be diagnosed according to various symptoms and have an *etiology,** *course*, and *prognosis*† (Kihlstrom, 2002). In turn, psychological disorders can be treated, and like many physical ailments, some may be "cured" whereas other psychological disorders will require lifelong attention. And although numerous perspectives in psychology are not medical in nature, the idea of diagnosis and treatment of symptoms bridges many of them. This chapter will focus on the types of psychological disorders and some of their possible causes. We will focus more on psychological treatment and therapies in the next chapter.

31.2 Explain psychologically abnormal behavior.

Defining abnormal behavior, abnormal thinking, or abnormality is not as simple as it might seem at first. The easy way out is to say that abnormal behavior is behavior that is not normal, abnormal thinking is thinking that is not normal, but what does that mean? It's complicated, as you'll see by considering different criteria for determining abnormality. Before we explore different criteria for identifying abnormality and mental illness, take a moment to reflect on your own beliefs in the survey, *Are You Normal?*

Complete the Survey, *Are You Normal?*, at MyPsychLab

Statistical or Social Norm Deviance One way to define *normal* and *abnormal* is to use a statistical definition. Frequently occurring behavior would be considered normal, and behavior that is rare would be abnormal. Or how much behavior or thinking deviates from the norms of a society. For example, refusing to wear clothing in a society that does not permit nudity would likely be rare and be seen as abnormal. But deviance (variation) from social norms is not always labeled as negative or abnormal. For instance, a person who decides to become a monk and live in a monastery in the United States would be exhibiting unusual behavior, and certainly not what the society considers a standard behavior, but it wouldn't be a sign of abnormality.

The *situational context* (the social or environmental setting of a person's behavior) can also make a difference in how behavior or thinking is labeled. For example, if a man comes to a therapist complaining of people listening in on his phone conversations and spying on all his activities, the therapist's first thought might be that the man is suffering from thoughts of persecution. But if the man then explains that he is in a witness protection program, the complaints take on an entirely different and quite understandable tone.

Subjective Discomfort One sign of abnormality is when the person experiences a great deal of *subjective discomfort*, or emotional distress while engaging in a particular behavior or thought process. A woman who suffers from a fear of going outside her house, for example, would experience a great deal of anxiety when trying to leave home and distress over being unable to leave. However, all thoughts or behavior that might be considered abnormal do not necessarily create subjective discomfort in the person having them or committing the act—a serial killer, for example, does not experience emotional distress after taking someone's life, and some forms of disordered behavior involve showing no emotions at all.

Inability to Function Normally Thinking or behavior that does not allow a person to fit into society or function normally can also be labeled abnormal. These may be termed *maladaptive*, meaning that the person finds it hard

Thinking Critically
In today's growing technological age, can you think of any new criteria that should be considered in defining abnormal behavior or thinking?

---

*etiology: the origin, cause, or set of causes for a disorder
†prognosis: the course an illness will take with or without treatment

to adapt to the demands of day-to-day living. Maladaptive thinking or behavior may initially help a person cope but has harmful or damaging effects. For example, a woman who cuts herself to relieve anxiety does experience initial relief but is harmed by the action. Maladaptive thinking or behaviors are key elements in the definition of abnormality.

I've heard people call the different things other people do "crazy" or "weird." How do psychologists decide when people are really mentally ill and not just a little odd?

31.3 Describe the challenges associated with diagnosis.

▶ **A Working Definition of Abnormality**   To get a clear picture of abnormality, it is often necessary to take all of the factors just discussed into account. Psychologists and other psychological professionals must consider several different criteria when determining whether or not psychological functioning or behavior is abnormal (at least two of these criteria must be met to form a diagnosis of abnormality):

1. Is the thinking or behavior unusual, such as experiencing severe panic when faced with a stranger or being severely depressed in the absence of any stressful life situations?
2. Does the thinking or behavior go against social norms?
3. Does the behavior or psychological function cause the person significant subjective discomfort?
4. Is the thought process or behavior maladaptive, or does it result in an inability to function?
5. Does the thought process or behavior cause the person to be dangerous to self or others, as in the case of someone who tries to commit suicide or who attacks other people without reason?

Abnormal thinking or behavior that includes at least two of these five criteria are perhaps best classified by the term **psychological disorder**, which is defined as any pattern of behavior or psychological functioning that causes people significant distress, causes them to harm themselves or others, or harms their ability to function in daily life.

Before moving on, it is important to clarify how the term *abnormality* is different from the term *insanity*. Only psychological professionals can diagnose disorders and determine the best course of treatment for someone who suffers from mental illness. Lawyers and judges are sometimes charged with determining how the law should address crimes committed under the influence of mental illness. In the United States, *insanity* is a legal term used to argue that a mentally ill person who has committed a crime should not be held responsible for his or her actions because that person was unable to understand the difference between right and wrong at the time of the offense. This argument is called the *insanity defense*.

31.4 Explain major models of abnormality.

What causes psychological disorders? ▶ Recognition of abnormal behavior and thinking depends on the "lens," or perspective, from which it is viewed. Different perspectives determine how the disordered behavior or thinking is explained. And as we will see in *Chapter Fourteen: Psychological Therapies and Treatments*, those same perspectives influence how psychological disorders are treated.

The Biological Model: Medical Causes for Psychological Disorders   The **biological model** proposes that psychological disorders have a biological or medical cause (Gamwell & Tomes, 1995). This model explains disorders such as anxiety, depression, and schizophrenia as caused by faulty neurotransmitter systems, genetic problems, brain damage and dysfunction, or some combination of those causes. For example, as you may recall from the discussion of trait theory and the five-factor theory of personality traits, a growing body of evidence suggests

psychological disorder any pattern of behavior or thinking that causes people significant distress, causes them to harm others, or harms their ability to function in daily life.

biological model model of explaining behavior as caused by biological changes in the chemical, structural, or genetic systems of the body.

that basic personality traits are as much influenced by genetic inheritance as they are by experience and upbringing, even across cultures (Bouchard, 1994; Herbst et al., 2000; Jang et al., 1996; Loehlin, 1992; Loehlin et al., 1998).

The Psychological Models Although biological explanations of psychological disorders are influential, they are not the only ways or even the first ways in which disorders are explained. Several different theories of personality were discussed in *Chapter Twelve*. These theories of personality can be used to describe and explain the formation of not only personality but disordered thinking, behavior, and abnormal personality as well.

The Psychodynamic View: Hiding Problems The psychodynamic model, based on the work of Freud and his followers, explains disordered thinking and behavior as the result of repressing one's threatening thoughts, memories, and concerns in the unconscious mind (Carducci, 1998). These repressed thoughts and urges try to resurface, and disordered functioning develops as a way of keeping the thoughts repressed. According to this view, a woman who has unacceptable thoughts of having an affair with her brother-in-law might feel "dirty" and be compelled to wash her hands every time those thoughts threaten to become conscious, ridding herself symbolically of the "dirty" thoughts.

Behaviorism: Learning Problems Behaviorists, who define personality as a set of learned responses, have no trouble explaining disordered behavior as being learned just like normal behavior (Skinner, 1971; Watson, 1913). For example, when Emma was a small child, a spider dropped onto her leg, causing her to scream and react with fear. Her mother made a big fuss over her, giving her lots of attention. Each time Emma saw a spider after this, she screamed again, drawing attention to herself. Behaviorists would say that Emma's fear of the spider was classically conditioned, and her screaming reaction was positively reinforced by all the attention.

Cognitive Perspective: Thinking Problems Cognitive psychologists study the way people think, remember, and mentally organize information; they see maladaptive functioning as resulting from illogical thinking patterns (Mora, 1985). A cognitive psychologist might explain Emma's fear of spiders as distorted thinking: "All spiders are vicious and will bite me, and I will die!" Emma's particular thinking patterns put her at a higher risk of depression and anxiety than those of a person who thinks more logically.

The Sociocultural Perspective In the sociocultural perspective of abnormality, abnormal thinking or behavior (as well as normal) is seen as the product of behavioral shaping within the context of family influences, the social group to which one belongs, and the culture within which the family and social group exist. In particular, cultural differences in abnormal thoughts or actions must be addressed when psychological professionals are attempting to assess and treat members of a culture different from that of the professional. **Cultural relativity** is a term that refers to the need to consider the unique characteristics of the culture in which the person with a disorder was nurtured to be able to correctly diagnose and treat the disorder (Castillo, 1997). Disorders unique to specific cultures have previously been referred to as *culture-bound syndromes*. For example, anorexia nervosa and bulimia nervosa have traditionally been most often found in Western societies.

The conceptualization of culture and its influences on psychological function and disorders has been expanded in the most recent publication of the *Diagnostic and Statistical Manual of Mental Disorders*, the *DSM-5*. The idea of "culture-bound" has been replaced by three concepts: *cultural syndromes*, *cultural idioms of distress*, and *cultural explanations or perceived cause* (American Psychiatric Association, 2013). Cultural syndromes may or may not be recognized as an illness

cultural relativity the need to consider the unique characteristics of the culture in which behavior takes place.

within the culture but are nonetheless recognizable as a distinct set of symptoms or characteristics of distress. Cultural idioms of distress refer to terms or phrases used to describe suffering or distress within a given cultural context. And cultural explanations or perceived cause are culturally defined ways of explaining the source or cause of symptoms or illness (American Psychiatric Association, 2013).

It is important to take into account other background and influential factors such as socioeconomic status and education level. College students of Mexican heritage with migrant farming backgrounds reported more symptoms of anxiety and depression as compared to nonmigrant college students of Mexican heritage (Mejía & McCarthy, 2010). The nature of migrant farming poses different stressors than those faced by nonmigrant families. ⓛⓘⓝⓚ to *Chapter Eight: Sociocultural Diversity and Gender, p. 274.*

Biopsychosocial Perspective: All of the Above The biological, psychological, and sociocultural influences on abnormality are no longer seen as independent causes. Instead, these influences interact with one another to cause the various forms of disorders. For example, a person may have a genetically inherited tendency for a type of disorder, such as anxiety, but may not develop a full-blown disorder unless the family and social environments produce the right stressors at the right time in development. We will see later how this idea specifically applies to a theory of schizophrenia. How accepting a particular culture is of a specific disorder will also play a part in determining the exact degree and form that disorder might take. This is known as the **biopsychosocial perspective** of disorder, which has become a very influential way to view the connection between mind and body.

31.5 Explain the classification of psychological disorders.

Have you ever asked a young child, or remember from being one yourself, "what's wrong?" when they reported not feeling well? If so, you likely received a variety of answers describing their tummy ache, ouchie, or boo boo. And in turn, you may have not known exactly what was wrong due to differences in their descriptive language and yours, especially when you could not see where or why they were hurting. The same applies to understanding and treating psychological disorders. Having a common set of terms and systematic way of describing psychological and behavioral symptoms is vital not only to correct identification and diagnosis but also in communication among and between psychological professionals and other health-care providers.

◉ **Watch** the **Video**, *The DSM*, at **MyPsychLab**

The *DSM-5* In the United States, the prevalent resource to help psychological professionals diagnose psychological disorders has been the *Diagnostic and Statistical Manual of Mental Disorders (DSM)*, first published in 1952. The DSM has been revised multiple times as our knowledge and ways of thinking about psychological disorders has changed. The most recent version, which was released in 2013, is the *Diagnostic and Statistical Manual of Mental Disorders, Fifth Edition (DSM-5)* (American Psychiatric Association, 2013). It includes changes in organization of disorders and modifications in terminology used to describe disorders and their symptoms. The DSM has been useful in providing clinicians with descriptions and criteria for diagnosing mental disorders but it has not been without its share of controversy as the video *The DSM* explains.

The *DSM-5* describes about 250 different psychological disorders. It does not address the causes of disorders. Each disorder is described in terms of its symptoms, the typical path the disorder takes as it progresses, and a checklist of specific criteria that must be met in order for the diagnosis of that disorder to be made. Whereas previous editions of the manual divided disorders and relevant facts about the person being diagnosed along five different categories, or axes, the *DSM-5* combines all disorders and diagnoses into a single list, therefore eliminating the multiaxis system (American Psychiatric Association, 2013).

A few of the 20 categories of disorders that can be diagnosed include depressive disorders, anxiety disorders, schizophrenia spectrum and other psychotic disorders, feeding and eating disorders, and neurodevelopmental disorders such as ADHD (American Psychiatric Association, 2013). Other categories include personality disorders, intellectual disability, trauma- and stressor-related disorders, and obsessive-compulsive and related disorders.

How Common are Psychological Disorders? Actually, psychological disorders are more common than most people might think. In any given year, about 26.2 percent of American adults over age 18 suffer from a mental disorder (National Institute of Mental Health, 2010); that comes to about 61.5 million people in the United States using 2010 census data. Fortunately, only about 5.8 percent of the U.S. population, or 1 in 17 adults, suffers from a severe mental disorder. Statistically, mental disorders are the leading cause of disability in the United States and Canada (National Institute of Mental Health, 2010). It is quite common for people to suffer from more than one mental disorder at a time, such as a person with depression who also has a substance-abuse disorder. Approximately 45 percent of individuals with a mental disorder meet criteria for two or more disorders (National Institute of Mental Health, 2010). **Table 31.1** has percentages of selected psychological disorders in the United States. (Note that this table does not include all of the disorders that occur in the 61.5 million adults in the United States mentioned earlier in this paragraph.)

◀ That sounds like a lot of possible disorders, but most people don't get these problems, right?

Table 31.1	Yearly Occurrence of Psychological Disorders in the United States	
CATEGORY OF DISORDER	SPECIFIC DISORDER	PERCENTAGE OF U.S. POPULATION AND NUMBER AFFECTED*
Bipolar and Depressive Disorders	All types	9.5% or 22.3 million
	Major depressive disorder	6.7% or 15.7 million
	Persistent depressive disorder (dysthymia)	1.5% or 3.5 million
	Bipolar disorder	2.6% or 6.1 million
Anxiety, Obsessive-Compulsive, and Trauma-Related Disorders	All types	18.1% or 42.5 million
	Specific phobia	8.7% or 20.4 million
	Social anxiety disorder (social phobia)	6.8% or 16 million
	Panic disorder	2.7% or 6.3 million
	Agoraphobia	0.8% or 1.9 million
	Generalized anxiety disorder	3.1% or 7.3 million
	Obsessive-compulsive disorder	1% or 2.3 million
	Posttraumatic stress disorder	3.5% or 8.2 million
Schizophrenia	All types	1.1% or 2.6 million

*Percentage of adults over age 18 affected annually and approximate number within the population based on 2010 United States Census data.

Adapted from National Institute of Mental Health (2013). Table uses terminology from both the *DSM-IV* and *DSM-5* (American Psychiatric Association, 2000, 2013).

31.6 Explain how stigma relates to abnormal behavior.

With its lists of disorders and their corresponding symptoms, the *DSM-5* helps psychological professionals diagnose patients and provide those patients with labels that explain their conditions. In the world of psychological diagnosis and treatment, labels like *depression*, *anxiety*, and *schizophrenia* can be very helpful: They make up a common language in the mental health community, allowing psychological professionals to communicate with each other clearly and efficiently.

Labels establish distinct diagnostic categories that all professionals recognize and understand, and they help patients receive effective treatment.

However, labels can also be dangerous—or, at the very least, overly prejudicial. In 1972, researcher David Rosenhan asked healthy participants to enter psychiatric hospitals and complain that they were hearing voices. All of the participants, whom Rosenhan called "pseudopatients," were admitted into the hospitals and diagnosed with either schizophrenia or manic depression (now called bipolar disorder). Once the pseudopatients were admitted, they stopped pretending to be ill and acted as they normally would, but the hospital staff's interpretation of the pseudopatients' normal behavior was skewed by the label of mental illness. For example, one pseudopatient's note-taking habits were considered to be a pathological behavior. The pseudopatients had been diagnosed and labeled, and those labels stuck, even when actual symptoms of mental illness disappeared. Rosenhan concluded that psychological labels are long-lasting and powerful, affecting not only how other people see mental patients but how patients see themselves (Rosenhan, 1973).

Before describing the various categories and types of disorders, here is a word of caution: It's very easy to see oneself in these disorders. Medical students often become convinced that they have every one of the symptoms for some rare, exotic disease they have been studying. Psychology students studying abnormal behavior can also become convinced that they have some mental disorder, a problem that can be called "psychology student's syndrome." The problem is that so many psychological disorders are really ordinary variations in human behavior taken to an extreme. So if you start "seeing" yourself or even your friends and family in any of the following discussions, don't panic—all of you are *probably* okay.

31.7 Describe the impact of psychological disorders on the individual, family, and society.

Like other forms of illness, psychological disorders disrupt a person's day-to-day life and come with their own physical and mental challenges. As we've discussed, abnormal behavior is still stigmatized in many societies, and people diagnosed with psychological disorders may feel judged or labeled by others around them, even their friends and family members. The stigmas associated with mental illness, along with the challenging health problems that can occur as a result of certain disorders, may lead to a loss of friendships, family support, and even employment, depending on the severity of the illness. Also, individuals who are treated for psychological disorders may have to cope with the side effects of treatment: Some drugs that effectively treat psychological disorders also result in weight loss, weight gain, or other health problems. Additionally, many health insurance plans severely limit coverage of the treatment of mental illnesses.

The individual diagnosed with a psychological disorder is not the only person affected by the disorder. It can be extremely stressful for families and friends to care for a loved one with a mental illness. Caring for a person with a mental illness is often time-consuming, and drugs and therapy sessions can be expensive. The stress of caretaking can actually put family members at greater risk to develop certain types of mental illnesses if they are genetically predisposed to do so. Children of parents with mental disorders are also at an increased risk of developing mental illnesses—partly as a result of genetic factors, and partly due to environmental factors.

Because psychological disorders can and do affect millions of people's lives, it is increasingly important that societies devote resources and funding to the effective treatment of mental illness. In addition to effective and accessible treatment, educational programs that share the facts of mental illness with all members of society can help people with mental illnesses—along with their friends and families—better understand the challenges they face and learn how to meet those challenges. Taking a psychology class is just one way in which you can educate yourself about the facts of mental illness.

Pick the best answer.

1. **Who would be the most likely to assume that psychological disorders are caused by an imbalance in the fluids (humors) of the body?**
   a. an ancient Egyptian physician
   b. a modern psychiatrist
   c. an ancient Greek physician
   d. a physician of the Middle Ages

2. **In Japan, the disorder that is called _____ centers around a fear of doing something embarrassing or socially inappropriate.**
   a. anxiety
   b. taijin kyofusho
   c. susto
   d. amok

3. **Which model of abnormality explains abnormal behavior as caused by illogical thinking?**
   a. psychodynamic
   b. cognitive
   c. behavioral
   d. biopsychosocial

4. **A biopsychologist might explain the occurrence of a major depressive episode as being the result of**
   a. unresolved unconscious conflicts that are left over from a difficult childhood.
   b. maladaptive automatic thoughts that lead a person to think negatively about his or her world.
   c. chemical imbalances, brain damage or dysfunction, or some combination of the two.
   d. a combination of biological, social, and psychological factors.

5. **Which is NOT one of the criteria that psychological professionals consider when determining whether a behavior is abnormal?**
   a. Is the behavior maladaptive?
   b. Does the behavior cause the person to be dangerous to self or others?
   c. Does the behavior cause the person significant subjective discomfort?
   d. Is the behavior a genetically inherited trait?

6. **What was the most likely reason that ancient people performed trephining to others?**
   a. to relieve fluid pressure on the brain
   b. to look into the brain to see what was wrong
   c. to release evil spirits that were in the person's head
   d. to restore balance to the body's humors

7. **Which model of abnormality talks about reinforcement and imitation as ways of developing abnormal behavior?**
   a. psychodynamic
   b. behavioral
   c. cognitive
   d. biological

8. **Lisa has started having feelings of fearfulness about going to school. She has begun to suffer from headaches and stomachaches and has missed several days of school already. Lisa's condition is abnormal from the _____ definition.**
   a. statistical
   b. situational context
   c. social deviance
   d. subjective discomfort

9. **The term _____ can refer to society's disapproval of people with mental illnesses.**
   a. stigma
   b. psychopathology
   c. cultural relativity
   d. social nonconformity

10. **Which of the following concepts is not specifically associated with the *DSM-5* examination of culture-related disorders?**
    a. cultural syndrome
    b. cultural idioms of distress
    c. cultural explanations or perceived cause
    d. cultural binding

Module Goal

Learn about the types of psychological disorders.

Learning Objectives

32.1 Describe symptoms and causes of anxiety disorders.

32.2 Describe symptoms and causes of dissociative disorders.

32.3 Describe symptoms and causes of mood disorders.

32.4 Describe symptoms and causes of eating disorders.

32.5 Describe symptoms and causes of schizophrenia.

32.6 Describe symptoms and causes of personality disorders.

32.7 Discuss how different factors influence an individual's experience of psychological disorders.

Learn About the Types of Psychological Disorders

32.1 Describe symptoms and causes of anxiety disorders.

In this section we will examine disorders in which the most dominant symptom is excessive or unrealistic anxiety. In addition to anxiety disorders, we will also address disorders that many people associate with anxiety symptoms, including *obsessive-compulsive disorder*, *posttraumatic stress disorder*, and *acute stress disorders*. These were classified as anxiety disorders in previous editions of the *DSM*. However, they now fall under different categories in the *DSM-5*. *Obsessive-compulsive disorder* now falls in the category of "Obsessive-Compulsive and Related Disorders," whereas *posttraumatic stress disorder* and *acute stress disorder* are found under "Trauma- and Stressor-Related Disorders" (American Psychiatric Association, 2013).

The *DSM-5* category of **anxiety disorders** includes disorders in which the most dominant symptom is excessive or unrealistic anxiety. Anxiety can take very specific forms, such as a fear of a specific object, or it can be a very general emotion, such as that experienced by someone who is worried and doesn't know why.

Everyone does have anxiety, and some people have a great deal of anxiety at times. When talking about anxiety disorders, the anxiety is either excessive—greater than it should be given the circumstances—or unrealistic. If final exams are coming up and a student hasn't studied enough, that student's anxiety is understandable and realistic. But a student who has studied, has done well in all the exams, and is very prepared and still worries *excessively* about passing is showing an unrealistic amount of anxiety. People who are in danger of losing their job might experience quite a bit of anxiety, but its source is obvious and understandable. But someone whose life is going well and for whom nothing bad is looming in the future, and who still feels extremely anxious may be experiencing an anxiety disorder. **Free-floating anxiety** is the term given to anxiety that seems to be

> But doesn't everybody have anxiety sometimes? What makes it a disorder? ▶

anxiety disorders class of disorders in which the primary symptom is excessive or unrealistic anxiety.

free-floating anxiety anxiety that is unrelated to any specific and known cause.

unrelated to any realistic and specific, known factor, and it is often a symptom of an anxiety disorder (Freud, 1977).

Phobic Disorders: When Fears Get Out of Hand

One of the more specific anxiety disorders is a **phobia**, an irrational, persistent fear of something. The "something" might be an object or a situation or may involve social interactions. For example, many people would feel fear if they suddenly came upon a live snake as they were walking and would take steps to avoid the snake. Although those same people would not necessarily avoid a *picture* of a snake in a book, a person with a phobia of snakes would. Consider the degree to which the phobia interferes with daily living. Avoiding a live snake is rational; avoiding a picture of a snake is not.

Social Anxiety Disorder (Social Phobia) **Social anxiety disorder** (also called *social phobia*) involves a fear of interacting with others or being in a social situation and is one of the most common phobias people experience (Kessler et al., 2012). People with social anxiety disorder are apprehensive of being evaluated in some negative way by others, so they tend to avoid situations that could lead to something embarrassing or humiliating. They are very self-conscious as a result. Common types of social phobia are stage fright, fear of public speaking, and fear of urinating in a public restroom. Not surprisingly, people with social phobias often have a history of being shy as children (Sternberger et al., 1995).

Specific Phobias A **specific phobia** is an irrational fear that is way out of proportion to the threat of some object or specific situation, such as a fear of dogs, or a fear of being in small, enclosed spaces (**claustrophobia**). Some examples of other specific phobias include a fear of spiders (*arachnophobia*), darkness (*nyctophobia*), injections (*trypanophobia*), fear of dental work (*odontophobia*), fear of blood (*hematophobia*), and fear of heights (**acrophobia**).

Agoraphobia A third type of phobia is **agoraphobia**, a Greek name that literally means "fear of the marketplace." It is the fear of being in a place or situation from which escape is difficult or impossible if something should go wrong (American Psychiatric Association, 2013). Furthermore, the anxiety is present in more than one situation. Someone is diagnosed with agoraphobia if they feel anxiety in at least two of five possible situations such as using public transportation like a bus or plane, being out in an open space such as on a bridge or in a parking lot, being in an enclosed space such as a grocery store or movie theater, standing in line or being in a crowd like at a concert, or being out of the home alone (American Psychiatric Association, 2013).

Exactly. People with specific phobias can usually avoid the object or situation without too much difficulty and people with social phobias may simply avoid jobs and situations that involve meeting people face to face. But people with agoraphobia cannot avoid their phobia's source because it is simply being outside in the real world. A severe case of agoraphobia can make a person's home a prison, leaving the person trapped inside unable to go to work, shop, or engage in any kind of activity that requires going out of the home.

Panic Disorder

Fourteen-year-old Dariya was sitting in science class watching a film. All of a sudden, she started feeling really strange. Her ears seemed to be stuffed with cotton and her vision was very dim. She was cold, had broken out in a sweat, and felt extremely afraid for no good reason. Her heart was racing, and she immediately became convinced that she was dying. A friend sitting behind her saw how pale she had become and tried to ask her

---

phobia an irrational, persistent fear of an object, situation, or social activity.

social anxiety disorder (social phobia) fear of interacting with others or being in social situations that might lead to a negative evaluation.

specific phobia fear of objects or specific situations or events.

agoraphobia fear of being in a place or situation from which escape is difficult or impossible.

◀ If a person has agoraphobia, it might be difficult to even go to work or to the store, right?

panic attack sudden onset of intense panic in which multiple physical symptoms of stress occur, often with feelings that one is dying.

panic disorder disorder in which panic attacks occur more than once or repeatedly, and cause persistent worry or changes in behavior.

generalized anxiety disorder disorder in which a person has feelings of dread and impending doom along with physical symptoms of stress, which lasts 6 months or more.

obsessive-compulsive disorder disorder in which intruding, recurring thoughts, or obsessions create anxiety that is relieved by performing a repetitive, ritualistic behavior or mental act (compulsion).

What about people ▶ who are just worriers? Can that become a disorder?

I knew someone who had just had a baby, and she spent the first few nights home with the baby checking it to see if it was breathing—is that an obsessive-compulsive ▶ disorder?

what was wrong, but Dariya couldn't speak. She was in a state of panic and couldn't move.

Dariya's symptoms are the classic symptoms of a **panic attack**, a sudden onset of extreme panic with various physical symptoms: racing heart, rapid breathing, a sensation of being "out of one's body," dulled hearing and vision, sweating, and dry mouth (Kumar & Oakley-Browne, 2002). Many people who have a panic attack think that they are having a heart attack and can experience pain as well as panic, but the symptoms are caused by the panic, not by any actual physical disorder. Psychologically, the person having a panic attack is in a state of terror, thinking that this is it, death is happening, and many people may feel a need to escape. The attack happens without warning and quite suddenly. Although some panic attacks can last as long as half an hour, some last only a few minutes, with most attacks peaking within 10 to 15 minutes.

Having a panic attack is not that unusual, especially for adolescent girls and young adult women (Eaton et al., 1994; Hayward et al., 1989, 2000). Researchers have also found evidence that cigarette smoking greatly increases the risk of panic attacks in adolescents and young adults (Johnson, 2000; Zvolensky et al., 2003). Regardless, it is only when panic attacks occur more than once or repeatedly, and cause persistent worry or changes in behavior, that they become a **panic disorder**. Many people try to figure out what triggers a panic attack and then do their best to avoid the situation if possible. If driving a car sets off an attack, they don't drive. If being in a crowd sets off an attack, they don't go where crowds are.

Generalized Anxiety Disorder Remember free-floating anxiety? That's the kind of anxiety that has no known specific source and may be experienced by people with **generalized anxiety disorder**, in which excessive anxiety and worries (apprehensive expectations) occur more days than not for at least 6 months. People with this disorder may also experience anxiety about a number of events or activities (such as work or school performance). These feelings of anxiety have no particular source that can be pinpointed, nor can the person control the feelings even if an effort is made to do so.

Other Disorders Related to Anxiety As discussed earlier, despite anxiety being a common symptom, the following disorders are not classified as anxiety disorders in the *DSM-5*.

Obsessive-Compulsive Disorder Sometimes people get a thought running through their head that just won't go away, like when a song gets stuck in one's mind. If that particular thought causes a lot of anxiety, it can become the basis for an **obsessive-compulsive disorder**, or OCD. OCD is a disorder in which intruding* thoughts that occur repeatedly (obsessions, such as a fear that germs are on one's hands) are followed by some repetitive, ritualistic behavior or mental acts (compulsions, such as repeated hand washing, counting, etc.). The compulsions are meant to lower the anxiety caused by the thought (Soomro, 2001).

No, many parents check their baby's breathing often at first. Everyone has a little obsessive thinking on occasion or some small ritual that makes them feel better. The difference is whether a person *likes* to perform the ritual (but doesn't *have* to) or feels *compelled* to perform the ritual and feels extreme anxiety if

---

*intruding: forcing one's way in; referring to something undesirable that enters awareness.

unable to do so. The distress caused by a failure or an inability to successfully complete the compulsion is a defining feature of OCD.

Acute Stress Disorder (ASD) and Posttraumatic Stress Disorder (PTSD)

Both general and specific stressors were discussed in Chapter Eleven: Motivation, stress, and emotion. Two trauma- and stressor-related disorders—*acute stress disorder* and *posttraumatic stress disorder*—are related to exposure to significant and traumatic stressors. The trauma, severe stress, and anxiety experienced by people after 9/11, Hurricane Katrina, the East Japan Earthquake, and the April 2013 Boston Marathon bombings can lead to **acute stress disorder (ASD)**. The symptoms of ASD often occur immediately after the traumatic event and include anxiety, dissociative symptoms (such as emotional numbness/lack of responsiveness, not being aware of surroundings, dissociative amnesia), recurring nightmares, sleep disturbances, problems in concentration, and moments in which people seem to "relive" the event in dreams and flashbacks for as long as 1 month following the event. One study gathered survey information from Katrina evacuees at a major emergency shelter and found that 62 percent of those sampled met the criteria for having acute stress disorder (Mills et al., 2007).

When the symptoms associated with ASD last for more than 1 month, the disorder is then called **posttraumatic stress disorder (PTSD)**. In the same study (Mills et al., 2007), researchers concluded that it was likely that anywhere from 38 to 49 percent of all the evacuees sampled were at risk of developing PTSD that would still be present 2 years after the disaster. Furthermore, whereas the onset of ASD often occurs immediately after the traumatic event, the symptoms of PTSD may not occur until 6 months or later after the event (American Psychiatric Association, 2013). Treatment of these stress disorders may involve psychotherapy and the use of drugs to control anxiety.

▲ *After the BP oil spill in April of 2010, anywhere from 35 to 45 percent of people living around or near the Gulf of Mexico reported suffering symptoms of stress (Abramson et al., 2010).*

Causes of Anxiety, Trauma, and Stress Disorders

Different perspectives on how personality develops offer different explanations for these disorders. For example, the psychodynamic model sees anxiety as a kind of danger signal that repressed urges or conflicts are threatening to surface (Freud, 1977). A phobia is seen as a kind of displacement, in which the phobic object is actually only a symbol of whatever the person has buried deep in his or her unconscious mind—the true source of the fear. A fear of knives might mean a fear of one's own aggressive tendencies, or a fear of heights may hide a suicidal desire to jump.

Behavioral and Cognitive Factors Behaviorists believe that anxious behavioral reactions are learned. They see phobias, for example, as nothing more than classically conditioned fear responses, as was the case with "Little Albert" (Rachman, 1990; Watson & Rayner, 1920). Cognitive psychologists see anxiety disorders as the result of illogical, irrational thought processes. One way in which people with anxiety disorders show irrational thinking (Beck, 1976, 1984) is through *magnification*, or the tendency to "make mountains out of molehills" by interpreting situations as being far more harmful, dangerous, or embarrassing

acute stress disorder (ASD) a disorder resulting from exposure to a major stressor, with symptoms of anxiety, dissociation, recurring nightmares, sleep disturbances, problems in concentration, and moments in which people seem to "relive" the event in dreams and flashbacks for as long as 1 month following the event.

posttraumatic stress disorder (PTSD) a disorder resulting from exposure to a major stressor, with symptoms of anxiety, dissociation, nightmares, poor sleep, reliving the event, and concentration problems, lasting for more than 1 month; symptoms may appear immediately, or not occur until 6 months or later after the traumatic event.

▲ *Anxiety disorders affect children as well as adults.*

than they actually are. In panic disorder, for example, a person might interpret a racing heartbeat as a sign of a heart attack instead of just a momentary arousal.

Cognitive-behavioral psychologists may see anxiety as related to another distorted thought process called *all-or-nothing thinking*, in which a person believes that his or her performance must be perfect or the result will be a total failure. *Overgeneralization* (a single negative event interpreted as a never-ending pattern of defeat), jumping to conclusions without facts to support that conclusion, and *minimization* (giving little or no emphasis to one's successes or positive events and traits) are other examples of irrational thinking.

Biological Factors Growing evidence exists that biological factors contribute to anxiety disorders. Several disorders, including generalized anxiety disorder, panic disorders, phobias, and OCD, tend to run in families, pointing to a genetic basis for these disorders. Furthermore, genetic factors in PTSD seem to influence both the risk of developing the disorder and the likelihood individuals may be involved in potentially dangerous situations (Hyman & Cohen, 2013).

Cultural Variations Anxiety disorders are found around the world, although the particular form the disorder takes might be different in various cultures. For example, in some Latin American cultures anxiety can take the form of *ataque de nervios*, or "attack of nerves," in which the person may have fits of crying, shout uncontrollably, experience sensations of heat, and become very aggressive, either verbally or physically. These attacks usually come after some stressful event such as the death of a loved one (American Psychiatric Association, 2013). Several syndromes that are essentially types of phobias are specific to certain cultures. For example, *taijin kyofusho* (TKS), found primarily in Japan, involves excessive fear and anxiety, but in this case it is the fear that one will do something in public that is socially inappropriate or embarrassing, such as blushing, staring, or having an offensive body odor (Kirmayer, 1991).

32.2 Describe symptoms and causes of dissociative disorders.

Just as there is sometimes overlap of symptoms between different diagnoses, various disorders can be related to similar circumstances or phenomena. As already discussed, exposure to trauma is a key component to ASD and PTSD, and both may include symptoms of dissociation. Dissociation plays a more prominent role in the dissociative disorders, where the dissociative symptoms encompass many aspects of everyday life, and not just memories of the traumatic events themselves or the time around them (American Psychiatric Association, 2013).

Dissociative disorders involve a break, or dissociation, in consciousness, memory, or a person's sense of identity. They are found in individuals that have experienced trauma and may include feelings of detachment, or alterations in emotion, perception, or behavior.

Dissociative Amnesia and Fugue: Who Am I and How Did I Get Here? In *dissociative amnesia*, the individual cannot remember personal information such as one's own name or specific personal events—the kind of information contained in episodic long-term memory. Dissociative amnesia may sound like retrograde amnesia, but it differs in its cause. In retrograde amnesia,

dissociative disorders disorders in which there is a break in conscious awareness, memory, the sense of identity, or some combination.

the memory loss is typically caused by a physical injury, such as a blow to the head. In dissociative amnesia, the cause is psychological rather than physical. The reported memory loss is usually associated with a stressful or emotionally traumatic experience, and may be a loss of memory for only one small segment of time, or it involve a total loss of one's personal memories. For example, a soldier might remember being in combat but unable to recall the death of a friend he witnessed, or a person might forget his or her entire life. These memories usually resurface, sometimes quickly, and sometimes after a long delay. Dissociative amnesia can occur with or without *fugue*. The Latin word *fugere* means "flight" and is the word from which the term *fugue* is taken. A *dissociative fugue* occurs when a person suddenly travels away from home (the flight) and afterward cannot remember the trip or even personal information such as identity. The individual may become confused about identity, sometimes even taking on a whole new identity in the new place (Nijenhuis, 2000). Such flights usually take place after an emotional trauma and are more common in times of disasters or war.

Dissociative Identity Disorder: How Many Am I? Perhaps the most controversial dissociative disorder is **dissociative identity disorder (DID)**, formerly known as multiple personality disorder. In this disorder, a person seems to experience at least two or more distinct personalities existing in one body. There may be a "core" personality, who usually knows nothing about the other personalities and is the one who experiences "blackouts" or losses of memory and time.

Causes of Dissociative Disorders Psychodynamic theory sees the repression of threatening or unacceptable thoughts and behavior as a defense mechanism at the heart of all disorders, and the dissociative disorders in particular seem to have a large element of repression—motivated forgetting—in them. In the psychodynamic view, loss of memory or disconnecting one's awareness from a stressful or traumatic event is adaptive in that it reduces the emotional pain (Dorahy, 2001).

Cognitive and behavioral explanations for dissociative disorders are connected: The person may feel guilt, shame, or anxiety when thinking about disturbing experiences or thoughts and start to avoid thinking about them. This "thought avoidance" is negatively reinforced by the reduction of the anxiety and unpleasant feelings and eventually will become a habit of "not thinking about" these things. This is similar to what many people do when faced with something unpleasant, such as an injection or a painful procedure such as having a root canal. They "think about something else."

There are possible biological sources for dissociations, as well. Researchers have found that people with *depersonalization/derealization disorder* (a dissociative disorder in which people feel detached and disconnected from themselves, their bodies, and their surroundings) have lower brain activity in the areas responsible for their sense of body awareness than do people without the disorder (Simeon et al., 2000). Other research has provided evidence that people with DID show significant differences in PET scan activity taken when different "personalities" are present (Reinders et al., 2001; Tsai et al., 1999).

32.3 Describe symptoms and causes of mood disorders.

When was the last time you felt down and sad? Or maybe a period of excitement or jubilation? Did these come about as the result of normal, day-to-day events or circumstances and change accordingly? Imagine how the experience of such

dissociative identity disorder (DID) disorder occurring when a person seems to have two or more distinct personalities within one body.

affect in psychology, a term indicating "emotion" or "mood."

mood disorders disorders in which mood is severely disturbed.

major depressive disorder severe depression that comes on suddenly and seems to have no external cause or is too severe for current circumstances.

manic having the quality of excessive excitement, energy, and elation or irritability.

bipolar disorder periods of mood that may range from normal to manic, with or without episodes of depression (bipolar I disorder), or spans of normal mood interspersed with episodes of major depression and episodes of hypomania (bipolar II disorder).

feelings would impact your life if they lasted for much longer periods of time, were much more persistent across life events, and if you were unable to identify the source or cause for such emotions. That is often the case when someone experiences a disordered mood.

Major Depressive Disorder and Bipolar Disorders

In psychological terms, the word **affect** is used to mean "emotion" or "mood." **Mood disorders** are disturbances in emotion and are also referred to as affective disorders. Although the range of human emotions runs from deep, intense sadness, and despair to extreme happiness and elation, under normal circumstances people stay in between those extremes—neither too sad nor too happy, but content. It is when stress or some other factor pushes a person to one extreme or the other that mood disorders can result. Mood disorders can be relatively mild or moderate (straying only a short distance from the "average") or they can be extreme (existing at either end of the full range). Another major change in the *DSM-5* was to separate disorders previously and collectively classified as "mood disorders" into different categories. As such, in the *DSM-5*, disorders of mood can be found under "Bipolar and Related Disorders" or "Depressive Disorders." Given disordered mood is still a common feature, these disorders will be examined together here.

Major Depressive Disorder

When a deeply depressed mood comes on fairly suddenly and either seems to be too severe for the circumstances or exists without any external cause for sadness, it is called **major depressive disorder**. People suffering from major depressive disorder are depressed for most of every day, take little or no pleasure in any activities, feel tired, have trouble sleeping or sleep too much, experience changes in appetite and significant weight changes, experience excessive guilt or feelings of worthlessness, and have trouble concentrating. Some people with this disorder also suffer from delusional thinking and may experience hallucinations. Some people with depression may have thoughts of death or suicide, including suicide attempts.

Major depressive disorder is the most common of the diagnosed disorders of mood and is 1.5 to 3 times more likely in women as it is in men (American Psychiatric Association, 2013). This is true even across various cultures (Kessler et al., 2012; Seedat et al., 2009). Many possible explanations have been proposed for this gender difference, including the different hormonal structure of the female system (menstruation, hormonal changes during and after pregnancy, menopause, etc.) and different social roles played by women in the culture (Blehar & Oren, 1997). Women also tend to ruminate, or repeatedly focus more on negative emotions, more than men, and this may also be a contributing factor for reported gender differences in prevalence rates for both depression and anxiety (Nolen-Hoeksema, 2012).

Bipolar Disorders

Major depressive disorder is sometimes referred to as a *unipolar disorder* because the emotional problem exists at only one end, or "pole," of the emotional range. When a person experiences periods of mood that can range from severe depression to **manic** episodes (excessive excitement, energy, and elation), that person is said to suffer from a type of **bipolar disorder** (American Psychiatric Association, 2013). However, although an individual may experience periods of mood at the two extremes, in some instances the individual may only experience mood that spans from normal to manic, and may or may not experience episodes of depression, called *bipolar I disorder*. In the manic episodes, the person is extremely happy or euphoric* without any real cause to

---

*euphoric: having a feeling of vigor, well-being, or high spirits.

be so happy. Restlessness, irritability, an inability to sit still or remain inactive, and seemingly unlimited energy are also common. The person may seem silly to others and can become aggressive when not allowed to carry out the grand (and sometimes delusional) plans that may occur in mania. Speech may be rapid and jump from one topic to another. Oddly, people in the manic state are often very creative until their lack of organization renders their attempts at being creative useless (Blumer, 2002; McDermott, 2001; Rothenberg, 2001). In *bipolar II disorder*, spans of normal mood are interspersed with episodes of major depression and episodes of *hypomania*, a level of mood that is elevated but at a level below or less severe than full mania (American Psychiatric Association, 2013).

Causes of Disordered Mood Explanations of depression and other disorders of mood today come from the perspectives of behavioral, social cognitive, and biological theories as well as genetics. Behavioral theorists link depression to learned helplessness (Seligman, 1975, 1989), whereas social cognitive theorists point to distortions of thinking such as blowing negative events out of proportion and minimizing positive, good events (Beck, 1976, 1984). In the social cognitive view, depressed people continually have negative, self-defeating thoughts about themselves, which depress them further in a downward spiral of despair. Learned helplessness has been linked to an increase in such self-defeating thinking and depression in studies with people who have experienced uncontrollable, painful events (Abramson et al., 1978, 1980). A recent study has also found that when therapists focus on helping clients to change their way of thinking, depression improves significantly when compared to therapy that focuses only on changing behavior; these results lend support to the cognitive explanation of distorted thinking as the source of depression (Strunk et al., 2010).

Biological explanations of disordered mood focus on the effects of brain chemicals such as serotonin, norepinephrine, and dopamine; drugs used to treat depression and mania typically affect the levels of these three neurotransmitters, either alone or in combination (Cohen, 1997; Cummings & Coffey, 1994; Ruhe et al., 2007).

Genes also play a part in these disorders. The fact that the more severe mood disorders are not a reaction to some outside source of stress or anxiety but rather seem to come from within the person's own body, together with the tendency of mood disorders to appear in genetically related individuals at a higher rate, suggests rather strongly that inheritance may play a significant part in these disorders (Barondes, 1998; Farmer, 1996). More than 65 percent of people with bipolar disorder have at least one close relative with either bipolar disorder or major depression (Craddock et al., 2005; National Institute of Mental Health Genetics Workgroup, 1998; Sullivan et al., 2000).

32.4 Describe symptoms and causes of eating disorders.

Thus far we have talked about disorders that have primarily focused on mood, anxiety, stress, and trauma. We will now shift to disorders of a slightly different type: eating disorders.

Types of Eating Disorders There are a variety of disorders that relate to the intake of food, or in some cases non-nutritive substances, or in the elimination of bodily waste. These are found in the *DSM-5* under "Feeding and Eating Disorders." We will specifically examine three eating disorders: *anorexia nervosa*, *bulimia nervosa*, and *binge-eating disorder*.

Anorexia nervosa, often called *anorexia* (which literally means "without appetite"), is a condition in which a person (typically young and female) reduces

anorexia nervosa (anorexia) a condition in which a person reduces eating to the point that their body weight is significantly lower or less than minimally expected. In adults, this is likely associated with a BMI < 18.5.

▲ *This young model is not merely thin; by medical standards she is probably at a weight that would allow her to be labeled as having anorexia. The "thin is in" mentality that dominates the field of fashion design models is a major contributor to the Western cultural concept of very thin women as beautiful and desirable. The model pictured here is a far cry from the days of sex symbol Marilyn Monroe, who was rumored to be a size 12.*

bulimia nervosa (bulimia)
a condition in which a person develops a cycle of "binging," or overeating enormous amounts of food at one sitting, and then using unhealthy methods to avoid weight gain.

But wait a minute—▶ if individuals with bulimia are so concerned about gaining weight, why do they binge at all?

Thinking Critically
How might the proliferation of various media and the Internet affect the development of eating disorders in cultures not previously impacted by them?

eating to the point that their body weight is significantly low, or less than minimally expected. For adults, this is likely a body mass index (BMI; weight in kilograms/height in meters^2) less than 18.5 (American Psychiatric Association, 2013). Hormone secretion becomes abnormal, especially in the thyroid and adrenal glands. The heart muscles become weak and heart rhythms may alter. Other physical effects of anorexia may include diarrhea, loss of muscle tissue, loss of sleep, low blood pressure, and lack of menstruation in females.

Bulimia nervosa, often called *bulimia* (which literally means "ravenous appetite"), is a condition in which a person develops a cycle of "binging," or overeating enormous amounts of food at one sitting, and then using inappropriate methods for avoiding weight gain (American Psychiatric Association, 2013). Most individuals with bulimia engage in "purging" behaviors, such as deliberately vomiting after the binge or misuse of laxatives, but some may not, using other inappropriate methods to avoid weight gain such as fasting the day or two after the binge or engaging in excessive exercise (American Psychiatric Association, 2013). There are some similarities to anorexia: The victims are usually female, are obsessed with their appearance, diet excessively, and believe themselves to be fat even when they are quite obviously not fat.

Binge-eating disorder also involves uncontrolled binge eating but differs from bulimia primarily in that individuals with binge-eating disorder do not purge or use other inappropriate methods for avoiding weight gain (American Psychiatric Association, 2013). Treatment of binge-eating disorder may use some of the same strategies used for anorexia and bulimia, with the added issue of weight loss management in those with obesity.

Causes of Eating Disorders The causes of anorexia, bulimia, and binge-eating disorder are not yet fully understood, but the greatest risk factor appears to be someone being an adolescent or young adult female (Keel & Forney, 2013). Increased sensitivity to food and its reward value may play a role in bulimia and binge-eating disorder while fear and anxiety may become associated with food in anorexia nervosa, with altered activity or functioning of associated brain structures in each (Friedrich et al., 2013; Kaye et al., 2009; Kaye et al., 2013). Research continues to investigate genetic components for eating disorders, as they account for 40 to 60 percent of the risk for anorexia, bulimia, and binge-eating disorder, and although several genes have been implicated, the exact ones to focus on have not yet been identified (Trace et al., 2013; Wade et al., 2013). Although many researchers have believed eating disorders, especially anorexia, are cultural syndromes that show up only in cultures obsessed with being thin (as many Western cultures are), eating disorders are also found in non-Western cultures (Miller & Pumariega, 1999). What differs between Western and non-Western cultures is the rate at which such disorders appear. For example, Chinese and Chinese American women are far less likely to suffer from eating disorders than are non-Hispanic White women (Pan, 2000). Why wouldn't Chinese American women be more likely to have eating disorders after being exposed to the Western cultural obsession with thinness? Pan (2000) assumes that whatever Chinese cultural factors "protect" Chinese women from developing eating disorders may also still have a powerful influence on Chinese American women.

Anorexia and bulimia have also been thought to occur only rarely in African American women, but that characterization seems to be changing. Researchers are seeing an increase in anorexia and bulimia among young African American women of all socioeconomic levels (Crago et al., 1996; Mintz & Betz, 1998; Pumariega & Gustavson, 1994). If clinicians and doctors are not aware that these disorders can affect more than the typical White, young, middle-class to upper-middle-class woman, important signs and symptoms of eating disorders in non-White or non-Western people may allow these disorders to go untreated until it is too late.

32.5 Describe symptoms and causes of schizophrenia.

Once known as *dementia praecox*, a Latin-based term meaning "out of one's mind before one's time," *schizophrenia* was renamed by Eugen Bleuler, a Swiss psychiatrist, to better illustrate the division (*schizo-*) within the brain (*phren*) among thoughts, feelings, and behavior that seems to take place in people with this disorder (Bleuler, 1911; Möller & Hell, 2002). Because the term literally means "split mind," it has often been confused with dissociative identity disorder, which was at one time erroneously called "split personality." To be clear, schizophrenia is a splitting from rational thinking and break with reality, whereas DID is a splitting or fragmenting of a person's identity. So you can see by the different characteristics that these two disorders are *not* synonymous.

Symptoms of Schizophrenia Today, **schizophrenia** is described as a long-lasting **psychotic** disorder (involving a severe break with reality), in which there is an inability to distinguish what is real from fantasy as well as disturbances in thinking, emotions, behavior, and perception. The disorder typically arises in the late teens or early twenties, affects both males and females, and is consistent across cultures.

Schizophrenia includes several different kinds of symptoms. Disorders in thinking are a common symptom and are called **delusions**. Although delusions are not prominent in everyone with schizophrenia, they are the symptom that most people associate with this disorder. Delusions are false beliefs about the world that the person holds and that tend to remain fixed and unshakable even in the face of evidence that disproves the delusions. Common schizophrenic delusions include *delusions of persecution*, in which people believe that others are trying to hurt them in some way; *delusions of reference*, in which people believe that other people, television characters, and even books are specifically talking to them; *delusions of influence*, in which people believe that they are being controlled by external forces, such as the devil, aliens, or cosmic forces; and *delusions of grandeur* (or *grandiose delusions*), in which people are convinced that they are powerful people who can save the world or have a special mission (American Psychiatric Association, 2013).

Delusional thinking alone is not enough to merit a diagnosis of schizophrenia, as other symptoms must be present (American Psychiatric Association, 2013). Speech disturbances are common: People with schizophrenia will make up words, repeat words or sentences persistently, string words together on the basis of sounds (called *clanging*, such as "come into house, louse, mouse, mouse and cheese, please, sneeze"), and experience sudden interruptions in speech or thought. Thoughts are significantly disturbed as well, with individuals with schizophrenia having a hard time linking their thoughts together in a logical fashion and, in advanced schizophrenia, possibly

schizophrenia severe disorder in which the person suffers from disordered thinking, bizarre behavior, hallucinations, and inability to distinguish between fantasy and reality.

psychotic refers to an individual's inability to separate what is real and what is fantasy.

delusions false beliefs held by a person who refuses to accept evidence of their falseness.

▲ *Dr. John Nash is a famous mathematician who won the Nobel Prize for economics in 1994. His fame, however, is more due to the fact that Nash once suffered from a form of schizophrenia in which he experienced delusions of persecution. He at one time believed that aliens were trying to contact him through the newspaper (delusions of reference). His life story and remarkable recovery from schizophrenia are portrayed in the 2001 movie* A Beautiful Mind, *which starred Russell Crowe as Nash.*

hallucinations false sensory perceptions, such as hearing voices that do not really exist.

flat affect a lack of emotional responsiveness.

catatonia disturbed behavior ranging from statue-like immobility to bursts of energetic, frantic movement, and talking.

positive symptoms symptoms of schizophrenia that are excesses of behavior or occur in addition to normal behavior; hallucinations, delusions, and distorted thinking.

negative symptoms symptoms of schizophrenia that are less than normal behavior or an absence of normal behavior; poor attention, flat affect, and poor speech production.

▲ *Nathaniel Ayers, a homeless musician, is pictured in 2003 in front of the Midnight Mission shelter in Los Angeles, California. Mr. Ayers's life is the subject of the 2009 movie* The Soloist *starring Jamie Foxx. Mr. Ayers was a Julliard-trained musician who developed schizophrenia.*

expressing themselves in a meaningless and jumbled mixture of words and phrases sometimes referred to as a *word salad*. Attention is also a problem for many people with schizophrenia. They seem to have trouble "screening out" information and stimulation that they don't really need, causing them to be unable to focus on information that is relevant (Asarnow et al., 1991; Luck & Gold, 2008).

People with schizophrenia may also have **hallucinations**, in which they hear voices or see things or people that are not really there. Hearing voices is actually more common and one of the key symptoms in making a diagnosis of schizophrenia (Kuhn & Nasar, 2001; Nasar, 1998). Hallucinations involving touch, smell, and taste are less common but also possible. Emotional disturbances are also a key feature of schizophrenia. **Flat affect** is a condition in which the person shows little or no emotion. Emotions can also be excessive and/or inappropriate—a person might laugh when it would be more appropriate to cry or show sorrow, for example. The person's behavior may also become disorganized and extremely odd. The person may not respond to the outside world and either doesn't move at all, maintaining often odd-looking postures for hours on end, or moves about wildly in great agitation. Both extremes, either wildly excessive movement or total lack thereof are referred to as **catatonia**.

Another way of describing symptoms in schizophrenia is to group them by the way they relate to normal functioning. **Positive symptoms** appear to reflect an excess or distortion of normal functions, such as hallucinations and delusions. **Negative symptoms** appear to reflect a decrease of normal functions, such as poor attention or lack of affect (American Psychiatric Association, 2013). According to the American Psychiatric Association (2013), at least two or more of the following symptoms must be present frequently for at least one month to diagnose schizophrenia: delusions, hallucinations, disorganized speech, negative symptoms, and grossly disorganized or catatonic behavior, and at least one of the two symptoms has to be delusions, hallucinations, or disorganized speech. The video, *Schizophrenia*, summarizes the key biological, psychological, and social components of the disorder.

Causes of Schizophrenia When trying to explain the cause or causes of schizophrenia, biological models and theories prevail, as it appears to be most likely caused by a combination of genetic and environmental factors. This is captured by the neurodevelopmental model, or neurodevelopmental hypothesis, of schizophrenia (Rapoport et al., 2005; Rapoport et al., 2012). Biological explanations of schizophrenia have generated a significant amount of research pointing to genetic origins, prenatal influences such as the mother experiencing viral infections during pregnancy, inflammation in the brain, chemical influences (dopamine, GABA, glutamate, and other neurotransmitters), and brain structural defects (frontal lobe defects, deterioration of neurons, and reduction in white matter integrity) as the causes of schizophrenia (Brown & Derkits, 2010; Cardno & Gottesman, 2000; Gottesman & Shields, 1982; Harrison, 1999; Kety et al., 1994; Nestor et al., 2008; Rijsdijk et al., 2011; Söderlund et al., 2009). Dopamine was first suspected when amphetamine users began to show schizophrenia-like psychotic symptoms. One of the side effects of amphetamine usage is to increase the release of dopamine in the brain. Drugs used to treat schizophrenia decrease the activity of dopamine in areas of the brain responsible for some of the positive symptoms. However, it is not that simple, the prefrontal cortex (an area of the brain involved

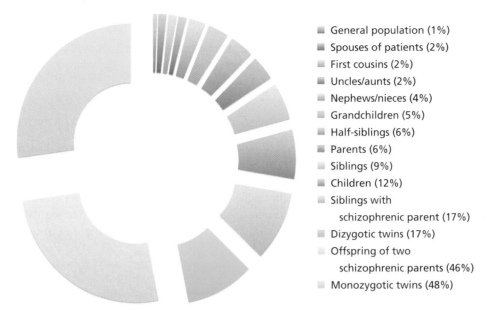

FIGURE 32.1 Genetics and Schizophrenia
This chart shows a definite pattern: The greater the degree of genetic relatedness, the higher the risk of schizophrenia in individuals related to each other. The only individual to carry a risk even close to that of identical twins (who share 100 percent of their genes) is a person who is the child of two parents with schizophrenia.
Source: Based on Gottesman (1991).

Legend for chart:
- General population (1%)
- Spouses of patients (2%)
- First cousins (2%)
- Uncles/aunts (2%)
- Nephews/nieces (4%)
- Grandchildren (5%)
- Half-siblings (6%)
- Parents (6%)
- Siblings (9%)
- Children (12%)
- Siblings with schizophrenic parent (17%)
- Dizygotic twins (17%)
- Offspring of two schizophrenic parents (46%)
- Monozygotic twins (48%)

in planning and organization of information) of people with schizophrenia has been shown to produce lower levels of dopamine than normal (Harrison, 1999), resulting in attention deficits (Luck, & Gold, 2008) and poor organization of thought, negative symptoms of the disorder.

Further support for a biological explanation of schizophrenia comes from studies of the incidence of the disorder across different cultures. If schizophrenia were caused mainly by environmental factors, the expectation would be that rates of schizophrenia would vary widely from culture to culture. There is some variation for immigrants and children of immigrants, but about 7 to 8 individuals out of 1,000 will develop schizophrenia in their lifetime, regardless of the culture (Saha et al., 2005).

Family, twin, and adoption studies have provided strong evidence that genes are a major means of transmitting schizophrenia. The highest risk for developing schizophrenia if one has a blood relative with the disorder is faced by monozygotic (identical) twins, who share 100 percent of their genetic material, with a risk factor of about 50 percent (Cardno & Gottesman, 2000; Gottesman & Shields, 1976, 1982; Gottesman et al., 1987). Dizygotic twins, who share about 50 percent of their genetic material, have about a 17 percent risk, the same as a child with one parent with schizophrenia. As genetic relatedness decreases, so does the risk (see **Figure 32.1**).

If schizophrenia were entirely controlled by genes, identical twins would indeed both have the disorder at a risk of 100 percent, not merely 50 percent. Obviously, there is some influence of environment on the development of schizophrenia. One model that has been proposed is the **stress-vulnerability model**, which assumes that persons with the genetic "markers" for schizophrenia have a physical vulnerability to the disorder but will not develop schizophrenia unless they are exposed to environmental or emotional stress at

stress-vulnerability model
explanation of disorder that assumes a biological sensitivity, or vulnerability, to a certain disorder will result in the development of that disorder under the right conditions of environmental or emotional stress.

There's something I don't understand. If one identical twin has the gene and the disorder, shouldn't the other one always have it, too? Why is the rate only 50 percent?

critical times in development, such as puberty (Harrison, 1999; Weinberger, 1987). That would explain why only one twin out of a pair might develop the disorder when both carry the genetic markers for schizophrenia—the life stresses for the affected twin were different from those of the one who remained healthy.

32.6 Describe symptoms and causes of personality disorders.

Personality disorders are a little different from other psychological disorders in that the disorder does not affect merely one aspect of the person's life, such as a higher than normal level of anxiety or a set of distorted beliefs, but instead affects the entire life adjustment of the person. The disorder is the personality itself, not one aspect of it. However, despite personality disorders affecting the entire person, the current research suggests they are not always lifelong in nature as once believed.

Categories of Personality Disorder In personality disorder, a person has an excessively rigid, maladaptive pattern of behavior and ways of relating to others (American Psychiatric Association, 2013). This rigidity and the inability to adapt to social demands and life changes make it very difficult for the individual with a personality disorder to fit in with others or have relatively normal social relationships. The *DSM-5* lists 10 primary types of personality disorder across three basic categories (American Psychiatric Association, 2013): those in which the people are seen as odd or eccentric by others (Paranoid, Schizoid, Schizotypal), those in which the behavior of the person is very dramatic, emotional, or erratic (Antisocial, Borderline, Histrionic, Narcissistic), and those in which the main emotion is anxiety or fearfulness (Avoidant, Dependent, Obsessive-Compulsive). These categories are labeled Cluster A, Cluster B, and Cluster C, respectively.

Antisocial Personality Disorder One of the most well researched of the personality disorders is **antisocial personality disorder (ASPD)**. People with ASPD are literally "against society." The antisocial person may habitually break the law, disobey rules, tell lies, and use other people without worrying about their rights or feelings. The person with ASPD may be irritable or aggressive. These individuals may not keep promises or other obligations and are consistently irresponsible. They may also seem indifferent, or able to rationalize taking advantage of or hurting others. Typically they borrow money or belongings and don't bother to repay the debt or return the items, they are impulsive, they don't keep their commitments either socially or in their jobs, and they tend to be very selfish, self-centered, and manipulative. There is a definite gender difference in ASPD with many more males diagnosed with this disorder than females (American Psychiatric Association, 2013). The habitual disregard for both the law and rights of others may be confused with the terms *sociopath* or *psychopath* (these terms mean the same thing according to most experts). Although some people with psychopathic personality may be diagnosed with ASPD, the majority of individuals with ASPD are not psychopathic.

Borderline Personality Disorder People with **borderline personality disorder (BLPD)** have relationships with other people that are intense and relatively unstable. They are impulsive, have an unstable sense of self, and are intensely fearful of abandonment. Life goals, career choices, friendships, and even sexual behavior may change quickly and dramatically. Close personal and romantic relationships are marked by extreme swings from idealization to

personality disorders disorders in which a person adopts a persistent, rigid, and maladaptive pattern of behavior that interferes with normal social interactions.

antisocial personality disorder (ASPD) disorder in which a person uses other people without worrying about their rights or feelings and often behaves in an impulsive or reckless manner without regard for the consequences of that behavior.

borderline personality disorder (BLPD) maladaptive personality pattern in which the person is moody, unstable, lacks a clear sense of identity, and often clings to others with a pattern of self-destructiveness, chronic loneliness, and disruptive anger in close relationships.

demonization. Periods of depression are not unusual, and some may engage in excessive spending, drug abuse, or suicidal behavior (suicide attempts may be part of the manipulation used against others in a relationship). Emotions are often inappropriate and excessive, leading to confusion with *histrionic personality disorder*. What makes the individual with BLPD different is the pattern of self-destructiveness, chronic loneliness, and disruptive anger in close relationships (American Psychiatric Association, 2013). The frequency of this disorder in women is nearly three times greater than in men (American Psychiatric Association, 2013).

Causes of Personality Disorders Cognitive-behavioral theorists talk about how specific behavior can be learned over time through the processes of reinforcement, shaping, and modeling. More cognitive explanations involve the belief systems formed by the personality-disordered persons, such as the paranoia, extreme self-importance, and fear of being unable to cope by oneself of the paranoid, narcissistic, and dependent personalities, for example.

There is some evidence of genetic factors in personality disorders (Reichborn-Kjennerud, 2008). Close biological relatives of people with disorders such as antisocial, schizotypal, and borderline are more likely to have these disorders than those who are not related (American Psychiatric Association, 2013; Kendler et al., 2006; Reichborn-Kjennerud et al., 2007; Torgersen et al., 2008). Adoption studies of children whose biological parents had antisocial personality disorder show an increased risk for that disorder in those children, even though raised in a different environment by different people (American Psychiatric Association, 2013).

Disturbances in family relationships and communication have also been linked to personality disorders and, in particular, to antisocial personality disorder (Benjamin, 1996; Livesley, 1995). Childhood abuse, neglect, overly strict parenting, overprotective parenting, and parental rejection have all been put forth as possible causes, making the picture of the development of personality disorders a complicated one. It is safe to say that many of the same factors (genetics, social relationships, and parenting) that help to create ordinary personalities also create disordered personalities.

32.7 Discuss how different factors influence an individual's experience of psychological disorders.

Although environmental influences such as parenting and social relationships do not generally cause mental illness, these factors can cause a person who is genetically predisposed toward an illness to develop the illness. For example, unsupportive or abusive family relationships can aggravate mental illness, as can low socioeconomic status and lack of community support. There is a strong correlation between poverty and mental illness: The stress and negativity experienced as a result of poverty can lead to disorders such as anxiety, depression, and substance abuse (Dohrenwend et al., 1992). Other factors that can negatively influence those with a tendency toward psychological disorders are academic failure, family conflict, personal tragedies, child abuse, and neglect. However, positive family and social influences, such as a healthy parent–child relationship and economic independence, can protect those at risk of mental illnesses by offering stability, support, and security. This isn't to say that if a person comes from a supportive family or community, they won't develop a mental illness; it's just less likely.

Pick the best answer.

1. **Who is most likely to be diagnosed with a phobic disorder?**

   a. Brianne, who is afraid of snakes after nearly being bitten while running.
   b. Calista, who is afraid of snakes after watching a documentary on poisonous snakes found in her region.
   c. Jennifer, who is morbidly afraid of snakes and refuses to even look a picture of a snake.
   d. Both Calista and Jennifer's behavior would qualify as a phobic disorder.

2. **Aunt Amelia has recently given birth to her first child. She mentions that she often goes into her baby's bedroom to check if he is still breathing. Would this qualify as an obsessive-compulsive disorder (OCD)?**

   a. If Amelia continues to carry out this behavior for more than one or two days, this would qualify as an OCD.
   b. If Amelia and her husband both carry out this behavior, then it would qualify as an OCD.
   c. If Amelia enjoys frequently checking to see that her baby is breathing, then this would qualify as an OCD.
   d. As long as Amelia is not compelled to check on her baby and does not suffer from severe anxiety if she is unable to do so, then this is not an OCD.

3. **Sandy took part in the April 2013 Boston Marathon, where two bombs were detonated near the finish line killing three spectators. For approximately two weeks after the marathon, Sandy was unable to sleep or concentrate and often found herself reliving the moment she heard the bombs explode. What disorder might Sandy be diagnosed with?**

   a. acute stress disorder
   b. posttraumatic stress disorder
   c. phobic disorder
   d. panic disorder

4. **What is the major difference between dissociative amnesia and retrograde amnesia?**

   a. Retrograde amnesia patients often suffer from some form of physical brain trauma.
   b. Individuals suffering from dissociative amnesia often have a history of memory loss that seems to be hereditary.

   c. Those suffering from dissociative amnesia have prior damage to the brain, which in turn causes memory loss.
   d. Retrograde amnesia patients often have suffered from painful psychological trauma.

5. **David believes that characters in a popular science fiction show are secretly sending him messages. This would be an example of a**

   a. delusion.
   b. phobia.
   c. flat affect.
   d. hallucination.

6. **Dr. Hannover has several patients with schizophrenia who appear to exhibit excessive or distorted characteristics in relation to what one might consider normal functioning. Specific symptoms include varied hallucinations and multiple delusions. According to the *DSM-5*, these are referred to as**

   a. flat affect.
   b. positive symptoms.
   c. negative symptoms.
   d. catatonia.

7. **Which of the following is not an accurate portrayal of antisocial personality disorder?**

   a. Most people with this disorder are female.
   b. Most people with this disorder are male.
   c. People with this disorder suffer little or no guilt for their criminal acts.
   d. People with this disorder are consistently irresponsible and don't keep commitments.

8. **Studies show that _____ personality disorders occur more frequently in women while _____ personality disorders happen more often in men.**

   a. antisocial; borderline
   b. borderline; schizotypal
   c. schizotypal; antisocial
   d. borderline; antisocial

9. **Which disorder is characterized by severe mood swings, intense energy, and intense sadness?**

   a. dysthymia
   b. bipolar disorder
   c. cyclothymia
   d. major depression

10. **The controversial condition formerly known as multiple personality disorder is now called**

    a. panic disorder.
    b. depersonalization disorder.
    c. generalized anxiety disorder.
    d. dissociative identity disorder.

Learn about perspectives on abnormal behavior.

31.1 Discuss historical and cross-cultural views of abnormality.
- In ancient times holes were cut in an ill person's head to let out evil spirits in a process called trephining. Hippocrates believed that mental illness came from an imbalance in the body's four humors, whereas in the early Renaissance period the mentally ill were labeled as witches.

31.2 Explain psychologically abnormal behavior.
- Abnormality can be characterized as thinking or behavior that is statistically rare, deviant from social norms, causes subjective discomfort, does not allow day-to-day functioning, or causes a person to be dangerous to self or others.

31.3 Describe the challenges associated with diagnosis.
- In the United States, *insanity* is a legal term, not a psychological term.

31.4 Explain major models of abnormality.
- Biological models propose that psychological disorders have a biological cause. Psychological models explain disordered behavior as the result of thought-related malfunctioning. The biopsychosocial model proposes that biological, psychological, and sociological factors interact to cause abnormal behavior.

31.5 Explain the classification of psychological disorders.
- *The Diagnostic and Statistical Manual of Mental Disorders, Fifth Edition (DSM-5)* is a manual of psychological disorders and their symptoms.

31.6 Explain how stigma relates to abnormal behavior.
- Over one-fifth of all adults over age 18 suffer from a mental disorder in any given year.

31.7 Describe the impact of psychological disorders on the individual, family, and society.
- Individuals must cope with stigma and labels. Friends and family members must cope with the stress of caring for a loved one.

Module 32: Types of Psychological Disorders

Learn about the types of psychological disorders.

32.1 Describe symptoms and causes of anxiety disorders.
- Anxiety disorders are all disorders in which the most dominant symptom is excessive and unrealistic anxiety.

- Disorders may be caused by repressed desires, conditioning, illogical thought processes, chemical imbalances in the nervous system, or genetic factors.

32.2 Describe symptoms and causes of dissociative disorders.
- Dissociative disorders involve a break in consciousness, memory, or both. These disorders include dissociative amnesia, with or without fugue, and dissociative identity disorder.
- They may be caused by repression, avoidance learning, or abnormal brain activity.

32.3 Describe symptoms and causes of mood disorders.
- Major depressive disorder has a fairly sudden onset and is extreme sadness and despair, typically with no obvious external cause. It is the most common of the mood disorders and is more common in women than in men.
- Mood disorders may be caused by learned helplessness, disordered thinking, or chemical imbalances in the brain.

32.4 Describe symptoms and causes of eating disorders.
- Maladaptive eating problems include anorexia nervosa, bulimia nervosa, and binge-eating disorder.
- Genetics, increased sensitivity to the rewarding value of food, or food-related anxiety, altered brain function, and being female contribute to risk of being diagnosed with an eating disorder.

32.5 Describe symptoms and causes of schizophrenia.
- Symptoms of schizophrenia include delusions (false beliefs about the world), hallucinations, emotional disturbances, attentional difficulties, disturbed speech, and disordered thinking. Biological factors are linked to causes of schizophrenia.

32.6 Describe symptoms and causes of personality disorders.
- Personality disorders are extremely rigid, maladaptive patterns of behavior that prevent a person from normal social interactions and relationships. There is some evidence of genetic factors in personality disorders.

32.7 Discuss how different factors influence an individual's experience of psychological disorders.
- Factors that can negatively influence those with a tendency toward psychological disorders are poverty, academic failure, family conflict, personal tragedies, child abuse, and neglect. Positive social influences can protect those at risk.

Vocabulary Terms

psychopathology p. 410
psychological disorder p. 412
biological model p. 412
cultural relativity p. 413
biopsychosocial model p. 414
anxiety disorders p. 418
free-floating anxiety p. 418
phobia p. 419
social anxiety disorder p. 419
specific phobia p. 419
agoraphobia p. 419
panic attack p. 420

panic disorder p. 420
generalized anxiety disorder p. 420
obsessive-compulsive disorder p. 420
acute stress disorder (ASD) p. 421
posttraumatic stress disorder (PTSD) p. 421
dissociative disorders p. 422
dissociative identity disorder (DID) p. 423

affect p. 424
mood disorders p. 424
major depressive disorder p. 424
manic p. 424
bipolar disorder p. 424
anorexia nervosa p. 425
bulimia nervosa p. 426
schizophrenia p. 427
psychotic p. 427
delusions p. 427
hallucinations p. 428

flat affect p. 428
catatonia p. 428
positive symptoms p. 428
negative symptoms p. 428
stress-vulnerability model p. 429
personality disorder p. 430
antisocial personality disorder p. 430
borderline personality disorder (BLPD) p. 430

Study and Review at MyPsychLab

Vocabulary Review

Match each vocabulary term to its definition.

1. borderline personality disorder
2. bipolar
3. delusions
4. dissociative disorders
5. phobia
6. schizophrenia
7. affective disorders
8. subjective discomfort
9. catatonic
10. dysthymia

a. A type of schizophrenia in which the person experiences periods of statue-like immobility mixed with occasional bursts of energetic, frantic movement and talking.
b. A moderate depression that lasts for 2 years or more and is typically a reaction to some external stressors.
c. False beliefs held by a person who refuses to accept evidence of his or her falseness.
d. Disorders that take the form of a split with memory or personality.
e. An intense fear of a specific object or situation, which may or may not be typically considered frightening.
f. A disorder that consists of mood swings from depressive to manic states.
g. Emotional distress or emotional pain.
h. Maladaptive personality pattern in which the person is moody, unstable, lacks a clear sense of identity, and often clings to others.
i. Disorders in which there is a break in conscious awareness, memory, the sense of identity, or some combination.
j. disorders involving mood

Psychology Project

This project will give you a chance to study one disorder in depth.

Materials:
- access to print or electronic reference resources
- a pencil and paper, or other note-taking materials
- poster board, markers, and craft supplies (optional)

Instructions:
1. Choose one of the psychological disorders discussed in this chapter to research in more detail.
2. Use print or electronic resources to learn about the history of the disorder you have chosen. Ask yourself, "How long has this disorder been recognized as a mental illness? How were people treated for this disorder in the past? Is the disorder different today than it was in the past? Does this disorder exist in other cultures? Has this disorder become rarer or more common?" Take notes as you gather information.
3. Share what you've learned with your classmates by delivering a short oral presentation or creating a poster filled with the information you've collected.

Tech Alternative

Using Technology to Raise Awareness

QR codes are fast becoming a mainstream way to communicate with others. You'll need a computer with Internet access and a printer for this project. Search the Web for a site that provides a free QR code generator. After you found a QR code generator, select five disorders from the reading. Open up a document in your word processer and for each of the five disorders, using separate pages for each disorder, type on to each page the name of the disorder, the major characteristics of the disorder, and describe how it can affect the lives of students in high school.

- Now, using the QR code generator create one QR code for each disorder.
- Once you have the QR codes generated paste them into the document you have created and print it out.
- Be sure to get permission for this part: Post the pages around the classroom or around your school building.
- Students with QR code scanners on their smartphones can scan the codes to access the "hidden" content in the strange looking squares.

Raising awareness can help inform others about the disorders we studied in this chapter.

Essay Question

Two psychologists, Dr. Hashimoto and Dr. Ward, have differing views about the basis of schizophrenia. Dr. Hashimoto believes that schizophrenia has a biological basis, whereas Dr. Ward believes that schizophrenia is caused primarily by environmental factors. Chose a side and in a well-organized essay, first describe the types and symptoms of schizophrenia. Then, explain why the psychologist you chose is more correct. Provide detailed evidence to support your position.

Test Yourself

Ready for your test? More quizzes and a customized plan.

✔ Study and Review at MyPsychLab

Pick the best answer.

1. If you believed an evil spirit was causing a mental disorder, you might perform
   a. trepanning.
   b. an inquisition.
   c. an exorcism.
   d. a lobotomy.

2. You are eating frogs because you are hopelessly lost in a forest and starving. By what definition might your behavior best be classified?
   a. statistical
   b. subjective discomfort
   c. maladaptive
   d. situational context

3. Although Dr. Akido knows that his patient, Aki, believes her anxiety has a biological explanation, in learning more about her family of origin, he suspects it has a psychological cause. This is an example of
   a. agoraphobia.
   b. dissociative amnesia.
   c. cultural relativitiy.
   d. PTSD.

4. How many axes does the *DSM-5* use to aid mental health professionals in making a diagnosis?
   a. it does not use the axis system
   b. two
   c. four
   d. five

5. *Trypanophobia*, also known as a fear of receiving an injection, is an example of
   a. obsession.
   b. social phobia.
   c. anxiety attack.
   d. specific phobia.

6. Aaron hates to go to restaurants for fear that he will be seated in the far back of the restaurant and be unable to get out in case of an emergency. This may be a symptom of
   a. acrophobia.
   b. psychophobia.
   c. agoraphobia.
   d. claustrophobia.

7. Ria experienced a sudden intense fear when she was boarding a plane. Ria's heart raced and she became dizzy. Ria experienced
   a. a depressive episode.
   b. a panic attack.
   c. panic disorder.
   d. agoraphobia.

8. When the symptoms associated with acute stress disorder last for more than one month, the disorder is then called
   a. PTSD.
   b. anxiety disorder.
   c. schizophrenia.
   d. depression.

9. Survivors of natural disasters like Hurricane Sandy in 2012 may experience higher incidences of
   a. depression.
   b. PTSD.
   c. anxiety disorders.
   d. schizophrenia.

10. Calvin had a poor job interview and believes he ruined his future. He says to himself, "I had to ace the interview. It had to be perfect, and it wasn't!" How might a cognitive-behavioral psychologist classify this distorted thought process?
    a. magnification
    b. overgeneralization
    c. all-or-nothing thinking
    d. minimization

11. A type of amnesia caused by physical trauma is _____ amnesia.
    a. retrograde
    b. dissociative
    c. anterograde
    d. fugue

12. Depersonalization/derealization disorder is a type of dissociative disorder that has been found to have possible _____ foundations for the experience of detachment.
    a. biological
    b. psychodynamic
    c. behavioral
    d. cognitive

13. The most common type of mood disorder is _____ disorder.
    a. bipolar
    b. manic
    c. seasonal affective
    d. major depressive

14. Behavioral theorists link depression to _____.
    a. distortions in thinking
    b. biological abnormalities
    c. unconscious forces
    d. learned helplessness

15. A person who rationalizes that since they have had a single treat, their diet is ruined and therefore they might as well go ahead and eat excessively may be suffering from
    a. bulimia.
    b. anorexia.
    c. mania.
    d. agoraphobia.

16. An eating disorder associated with overeating but not purging is called
    a. anorexia.
    b. binge eating.
    c. bulimia.
    d. nervosa.

17. Which model of abnormality talks about reinforcement and imitation as ways of developing abnormal behavior?
    a. Biological
    b. Cognitive
    c. Behavioral
    d. Psychodynamic

18. Rodney has been diagnosed with schizophrenia. He shows little emotion to any situation. Psychologists refer to this characteristic as
    a. catatonia.
    b. flat affect.
    c. positive symptoms.
    d. negative symptoms.

19. What neurotransmitter was first believed to be the cause of schizophrenia?
    a. GABA
    b. serotonin
    c. epinephrine
    d. dopamine

20. Colleen found herself attracted to her psychology instructor. When he didn't respond to her advances, Colleen eventually told him that she had thoughts of killing herself so that he would spend time trying to counsel her. What personality disorder best describes Colleen's thinking and behavior?
    a. borderline
    b. schizoid
    c. schizotypal
    d. antisocial

Learning Objectives

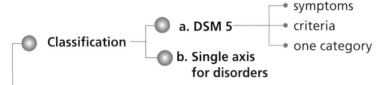
(31.1)(31.2)(31.3)(31.4)(31.5)(31.6)(31.7) pp. 410–416

Perspectives on Abnormal Behavior

Classification
— a. **DSM 5**
  - symptoms
  - criteria
  - one category
— b. **Single axis for disorders**

definition of abnormal behavior any pattern of behavior that causes significant distress, causes people to harm themselves or others, or harms their ability to function in daily life

cultural factors: *cultural syndromes, cultural idioms of distress,* and *cultural explanations or perceived cause*

models of abnormality
- **biological model**
- **psychological models**
- **biopsychosocial perspective**

stigma refers, in psychology, to social disapproval of conditions or characteristics that are considered abnormal

impact of mental illness may include stigma, labeling, expense, side effects of treatment, stress, and guilt

Learning Objectives

(32.1)(32.2)(32.3)(32.4)(32.5)(32.6)(32.7) pp. 418–431

Learn About Psychological Disorders, Their Symptoms, and Their Causes

anxiety disorders
most dominant symptom is excessive or unrealistic anxiety; can be free-floating or more specific

- **obsessive compulsive disorder (OCD)**
  - obsessive thoughts
  - compulsive behaviors
- panic disorder
- generalized anxiety disorder

dissociative disorders
involve a dissociation in consciousness, memory, or sense of identity, often associated with extreme stress or trauma

- dissociative amnesia
- dissociative fugue
- dissociative identity disorder

32.1 32.2 32.3 32.4 32.5 32.6 32.7   pp. 418–431   Map the Concepts at MyPsychLab

Learn About Psychological Disorders, Their Symptoms, and Their Causes *(continued)*

mood disorders
involve a disturbance in mood or
emotion; can be mild or severe

- major depression deeply depressed mood
- bipolar disorder extreme mood swings, severe
  depression and mania

eating disorders
disorders that relate to the intake
of food

- anorexia nervosa
- bulimia nervosa
- binge-eating disorder

schizophrenia
psychotic disorder involving a break
with reality and disturbances in
thinking, emotions, behavior, and
perceptions

- positive symptoms
  - delusions
  - hallucinations
- negative symptoms
  - distorted language
  - disordered thinking

personality disorders
involve excessively rigid and maladaptive patterns of
behavior and ways of relating to others

- **antisocial personality disorder**
- **borderline personality disorder**

family and social influences

- negative influences can make predisposed individuals more likely to
  develop a psychological disorder
- positive influences can protect
  against psychological disorders

CHAPTER 14

Psychological Therapies and Treatments

A set of films were made in the mid-1960s, *Three Approaches to Psychotherapy*, that focused on three pioneering therapists working with a single client, "Gloria." Often referred to as the "Gloria tapes" or "Gloria films," this collection provided many students of psychology and professionals in training their first look into what actually may occur during a therapy session.

Each of the therapists worked with Gloria to address concerns she was experiencing as a recently divorced mother. In doing so, each demonstrated aspects of their respective techniques and theories. The therapists were none other than Carl Rogers demonstrating his *person-centered therapy*, Fritz Perls demonstrating his *Gestalt therapy*, and Albert Ellis demonstrating his *rational therapy* or *rational emotive therapy* (later developed into *rational emotive behavior therapy*).

The field of psychology has grown a great deal since the Gloria films were made, and potential clients now have many more sources of information available to them regarding therapy options.

What information might be most useful for someone interested in pursuing a particular therapy or treatment for a psychological disorder?

MODULE 33 ▸ PSYCHOLOGICAL TREATMENTS
MODULE 34 ▸ BIOMEDICAL TREATMENTS AND ISSUES IN TREATMENTS

Watch the **Video**, at **MyPsychLab**

*W*hy Study Therapies for Psychological Disorders?

There are almost as many therapy methods as there are disorders. Correctly matching the type of therapy to the disorder can mean the difference between a cure and a crisis. It is important to know the choices available for treatment and how they relate to the different kinds of disorders so that an informed decision can be made and the best possible outcome can be achieved for mental health and wellness.

33 Psychological Treatments

Module Goals	Learning Objectives
Understand perspectives on treating psychological disorders.	**33.1** Discuss how psychological treatments have changed over time and among cultures.
	33.2 Discuss why psychologists use a variety of treatment options.
	33.3 Discuss treatment providers for psychological disorders and the training required for each.
Identify psychological treatments and evaluate their effectiveness.	**33.4** Understand approaches to psychological treatments.
	33.5 Evaluate the effectiveness of psychological treatments.
	33.6 Identify other factors that improve the effectiveness of treatment.

Understand Perspectives on Treating Psychological Disorders

33.1 Discuss how psychological treatments have changed over time and among cultures.

As discussed in *Chapter Thirteen: Psychological Disorders*, although psychological or social causes might have been identified for some disorders, until the late 1700s, people suffering severe mental illnesses were sometimes thought to be possessed by demons or evil spirits, and the "treatments" to rid the person of these spirits were severe and deadly. Even within the last 200 years, a period of supposedly more "enlightened" awareness, the mentally ill did not always receive humane treatment.

I've seen movies ▶ about mental hospitals, and they didn't look like great places to be in even now— how bad was it back then? What did people do with relatives who were ill that way?

The first truly organized effort to do something with mentally ill persons began in England in the middle of the sixteenth century. Bethlehem Hospital in London (later known as "Bedlam") was converted into an asylum (a word meaning "place of safety") for the mentally ill. In reality, the first asylums were little more than prisons where the mentally ill were chained to their beds. "Treatments" consisted of bloodletting (which more often than not led to death or the need for lifelong care for the patient), beatings, ice baths in which the person was submerged until passing out or suffering a seizure, and induced vomiting in a kind of spiritual cleansing (Hunt, 1993). This cleansing or purging was meant to rid the body of physical impurities so that the person's mind and soul could function more perfectly.

It was not until 1793 that efforts were made to treat the mentally ill with kindness and guidance—known as "moral treatment"—rather than beating them or subjecting them to the harsh physical purging that had been commonplace. It was at this time that Philippe Pinel personally unchained the inmates at La Bicêtre Asylum in Paris, France, beginning the movement of humane treatment of the mentally ill (Brigham, 1844; Curtis, 1993).

Today, we can group the primary approaches to **therapy** (treatment methods aimed at making people feel better and function more effectively) into two broad categories. One category is based primarily in psychological theory and techniques; people tell the therapist about their problems, and the therapist listens and tries to help them understand those problems or assists them in changing the behaviors related to the problem. The other category uses medical interventions to bring the symptoms under control. Although we can separate treatments into these two larger categories, in actual practice, many effective treatment strategies or treatment plans combine facets of both. Just as there is no one single "cause" of a disorder (Maxmen et al., 2009), different psychological treatments are often used in tandem or combined with biomedical interventions.

▲ In this famous painting by French artist Robert Fleury, French physician Dr. Philippe Pinel orders the chains removed from patients at a Paris asylum for insane women. Pinel was one of the first reformers to recommend humane treatment of the mentally ill.

33.2 Discuss why psychologists use a variety of treatment options.

Many psychology professionals do not limit themselves to a single technique and are **eclectic**, using more than one treatment approach or technique to best meet the needs of the people they are working with. The fields of clinical psychology and counseling psychology are diverse, and professionals have a wide variety of educational and training experiences. Before we discuss the various types of therapy and treatments in more detail, take a moment to evaluate your views and experiences with, therapy in the survey, *How Do You Take Care of Your Mental Health?*

Psychotherapy typically involves an individual, couple, or small group of individuals working directly with a therapist and discussing their concerns or problems. The goal of most psychotherapy is to help both mentally healthy and psychologically disordered persons understand themselves better (Goin, 2005; Wolberg, 1977). Because understanding of one's motives and actions is called *insight*, therapies aimed mainly at this goal are called **insight therapies**. A therapy that is directed more at changing behavior than providing insights into the reasons for that behavior is called **action therapy**. Many psychological professionals use a combination of insight and action therapeutic*methods.

Biomedical therapy, the other main type of therapy, uses some biological treatment in the form of a medical procedure to bring about changes in the person's disordered behavior. **Biomedical therapies** include the use of drugs, surgical methods, electroconvulsive therapy (ECT), and noninvasive stimulation techniques. It is important to understand that biomedical therapy often eliminates or alleviates the symptoms of a disorder, whereas psychotherapy addresses issues associated with the disorder, and when used together, these two types of therapy facilitate each other (Maxmen et al., 2009).

33.3 Discuss treatment providers for psychological disorders and the training required for each.

Several types of professionals can treat psychological problems. These professionals have different training with different focuses, and they may have different goals.

※ Complete the Survey, *How Do You Take Care of Your Mental Health?*, at MyPsychLab

therapy treatment methods aimed at making people feel better and function more effectively.

eclectic using more than one treatment approach or technique.

psychotherapy therapy for mental disorders in which a person with a problem talks with a psychological professional.

insight therapies therapies in which the main goal is helping people to gain personal understanding with respect to their behavior, thoughts, and feelings.

action therapy therapy in which the main goal is to change disordered or inappropriate behavior directly.

biomedical therapies therapies that directly affect the biological functioning of the body and brain; therapies for mental disorders in which a person with a problem is treated with biological or medical methods to relieve symptoms.

---

*therapeutic: providing or assisting in a cure.

psychiatrist a physician who specializes in the diagnosis and treatment of psychological disorders.

psychologist a professional with a Doctorate degree and specialized training in one or more areas of psychology.

counselor Masters-level professional trained in offering psychological services.

psychoanalysis an insight therapy based on the theory of Freud, emphasizing the revealing of unconscious conflicts; Freud's term for both the theory of personality and the therapy based on it.

Psychiatrists A psychiatrist is a medical doctor who specializes in diagnosing and treating psychological disorders, such as schizophrenia or depression. Like other doctors, psychiatrists have a Medical Doctor (M.D.) degree and are qualified to write prescriptions and perform medical procedures. They have special training in mental health. As medical doctors, they tend to have a *biopsychological* perspective.

Psychiatric Social Workers A *psychiatric social worker* is trained in social work, usually possesses a master of social work (M.S.W.) degree, and may be licensed by his or her state of employment as a licensed clinical social worker (L.C.S.W.). These professionals focus more on environmental conditions that can affect mental health, such as poverty, overcrowding, stress, and drug abuse.

Psychologists A psychologist has no medical degree but instead undergoes intense academic and practical training, learning about many areas of psychology before choosing one in which to specialize. According to the American Psychological Association, psychologists must hold either a doctor of philosophy (Ph.D.) or a doctor of psychology (Psy.D.) degree. Unlike psychiatrists, clinical psychologists typically cannot prescribe medicines or perform medical procedures. However, some states now allow psychologists to prescribe medication if they have received special training.

Although some psychologists are trained as a psychodynamic therapist, most are not. **Counselors** or therapists today typically use techniques that emphasize creating a safe environment in which clients can talk about their experiences.

Identify Psychological Treatments and Evaluate Their Effectiveness

33.4 Understand approaches to psychological treatments.

We'll begin our discussion of psychotherapy with two types of insight therapies: psychodynamic therapy and humanistic therapy. Although these approaches use different methods, they both strive to gain an understanding of one's motives and actions.

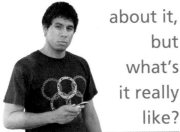

So what exactly ▶ happens in psychoanalysis? I've heard lots of stories about it, but what's it really like?

Psychotherapy Begins: Freud's Psychoanalysis In a sense, Freud took the sixteenth-century method of physical cleansing to a different level. Instead of a physical purge, cleansing for Freud meant removing all the "impurities" of the unconscious mind that he believed were responsible for his patients' psychological and nervous disorders. (Freud was a medical doctor, a specialist in neurology, and referred to the people who came to him for help as "patients.") The impurities of the unconscious mind were considered to be disturbing thoughts, socially unacceptable desires, and immoral urges that originated in the id.

Psychoanalysis Freud believed that his patients used these unconscious thoughts to prevent anxiety, and as such, the thoughts would not be easily brought into conscious awareness. Freud designed a therapy technique to help his patients feel more relaxed, open, and able to explore their innermost feelings without fear of embarrassment or rejection. This method was called **psychoanalysis**, and it is an insight therapy that emphasizes revealing the unconscious conflicts, urges, and desires that are assumed to cause disordered emotions and behavior (Freud, 1904; Mitchell & Black, 1996). This is the original reason for the couch in Freud's version of psychoanalysis; people lying on the couch were more relaxed.

Freud also made use of two techniques to try to reveal the repressed information in his patients' unconscious minds. These techniques were the interpretation of dreams and allowing patients to talk freely about anything that came to mind.

Dream Interpretation *Dream interpretation*, or the analysis of the elements within a patient's reported dream, formed a large part of Freud's psychoanalytic method. Freud believed that repressed material often surfaced in dreams, although in symbolic form. The *manifest content* of the dream was the actual dream and its events, but the **latent content** was the hidden, symbolic meaning of those events that would, if correctly interpreted, reveal the unconscious conflicts that were creating the nervous disorder (Freud, 1900).

Free Association The other technique for revealing the unconscious mind was a method originally devised by Freud's coworker, Josef Breuer (Breuer & Freud, 1895). Breuer encouraged his patients to say freely whatever came into their minds without fear of being negatively evaluated or condemned. As the patients talked, they began to reveal things that were loosely associated with their flow of ideas, often revealing what Breuer felt were hidden, unconscious concerns. Freud adopted this method of **free association**, believing that repressed impulses and other materials were trying to "break free" into consciousness and would eventually surface using this technique.

Resistance and Transference Other components of Freud's original psychoanalytic method were *resistance* (the point at which the patient becomes unwilling to talk about certain topics) and *transference* (when the therapist becomes a symbol of a parental authority figure from the past). As in all of the therapeutic approaches, peer and professional supervision helps therapists recognize potential issues in providing effective therapy.

Evaluation of Psychoanalysis and Psychodynamic Approaches Freud's original theory, on which he based his interpretations of his patients' revelations, has been criticized as having several flaws, which were discussed in Chapter Twelve. These included the lack of scientific research to support his claims, his unwillingness to believe some of the things revealed by his patients when those revelations did not fit into his view of the world, and his assumption that problems with sex and sexuality were at the heart of nearly every nervous disorder.

Few psychodynamic therapists today still use Freud's original methods, which could take years to produce results. Rather than remaining quiet until the client says something revealing, the modern psychodynamic therapist is far more **directive**, asking questions, suggesting helpful behavior, and giving opinions and interpretations earlier in the relationship, which helps speed up the therapeutic process. Today's psychodynamic therapists also focus less on the id as the motivator of behavior, instead looking more at the ego or sense of self as the motivating force behind all actions (Prochaska & Norcross, 2003).

Humanistic Therapy: To Err Is Human Humanistic psychologists focus on conscious, subjective experiences of emotion and people's sense of self, as well as the more immediate experiences in their daily lives rather than early childhood experiences of the distant past (Cain & Seeman, 2001; Rowan, 2001; Schneider et al., 2001. Humanistic therapy emphasizes the importance of the choices made by individuals and the potential to change one's behavior. A therapy based on humanistic theory is Carl Rogers's person-centered therapy, which is primarily an insight therapy.

Tell Me More: Rogers's Person-Centered Therapy Rogers proposed that everyone has a *real self* (how people see their actual traits and abilities) and an *ideal self* (how people think they should be). The closer the real and ideal selves

latent content the symbolic or hidden meaning of dreams.

free association psychoanalytic technique in which a patient was encouraged to talk about anything that came to mind without fear of negative evaluations.

directive therapy in which the therapist actively gives interpretations of a client's statements and may suggest certain behavior or actions.

▲ *Psychotherapy often takes place one-on-one, with a client and therapist exploring various issues together to achieve deeper insights or to change undesirable behavior.*

So the key to getting over unhappiness would be to get the real and ideal selves closer together? How does a therapist do that?

▲ A Rogerian person-centered therapist listens with calm acceptance to anything the client says. A sense of empathy with the client's feelings is also important.

nondirective therapy style in which the therapist remains relatively neutral and does not interpret or take direct actions with regard to the client, instead remaining a calm, nonjudgmental listener while the client talks.

person-centered therapy a nondirective insight therapy based on the work of Carl Rogers in which the client does all the talking and the therapist listens.

reflection therapy technique in which the therapist restates what the client says rather than interpreting those statements.

match up, the happier and more well-adjusted the person. To have these two self-concepts be congruent, people need to receive *unconditional positive regard*, which is love, warmth, respect, and affection without any conditions attached. If people think that there are conditions put on the love and affection they receive, their ideal selves will be determined by those conditions and become more difficult to achieve, resulting in a mismatch of selves and incongruence.

Rogers believed that the goal of the therapist should be to provide the unconditional positive regard that has been absent from the troubled person's life and to help the person recognize the discrepancies between the real and ideal selves. He also believed that the person would actually have to do most of the work, talking out problems and concerns in an atmosphere of warmth and acceptance from the therapist, so he originally called the people in this therapy relationship "clients" instead of "patients," to put the therapeutic relationship on a more equal footing. As a result, Rogers's therapy is very **nondirective** because the person actually does all the real work, with the therapist merely acting as a sounding board. However, therapists may help individuals redirect or reallocate their attention to focus on feelings not fully processed previously (Prochaska & Norcross, 2009). His therapy is now called **person-centered therapy** because the person is truly the center of the process.

Rogers (1961) saw three key elements as being necessary in any successful person–therapist relationship:

- **Authenticity** The therapist must show *authenticity* in a genuine, open, and honest response to the individual. In person-centered therapy, the therapist has to be able to tolerate a person's differences without being judgmental.
- **Unconditional Positive Regard** Another key element of person-centered therapy is the warm, accepting, completely uncritical atmosphere that the therapist must create for the people they work with called *unconditional positive regard*.
- **Empathy** The third key element of person-centered therapy is that the therapist needs to be able to see the world through the eyes of the person they are working with. The therapist has to be able to acknowledge what people are feeling and experiencing by using a kind of understanding called *empathy*. This involves listening carefully and closely to what individuals are saying and trying to feel what they feel.

A person-centered therapist typically responds in a way that seeks clarification and demonstrates attempts to understand the experience of the individual. **Reflection** refers to a technique therapists use to allow clients to continue to talk and have insights without the interference of the therapist's interpretations and possible biases. Reflection is literally a kind of mirroring of clients' statements. Here's an example from one of Rogers's own therapy sessions with a client (Meador & Rogers, 1984, p. 143):

CLIENT: I just ain't no good to nobody, never was, and never will be.
ROGERS: Feeling that now, hm? That you're just no good to yourself, no good to anybody. Never will be any good to anybody. Just that you're completely worthless, huh?—Those really are lousy feelings. Just feel that you're no good at all, hm?
CLIENT: Yeah.

Evaluation of the Humanistic Therapies Humanistic therapies have been used to treat psychological disorders, help people make career choices, deal with workplace problems, and counsel married couples. Person-centered therapy in particular can be a very "hands-off" form of therapy because it is so nondirective: Most often, there's nothing that the therapist says that the client has not already said, so the therapist runs a lower risk of misinterpretation.

Unfortunately, there is little experimental research to support the basic ideas on which this type of therapy is founded, but humanistic psychologists have always preferred to use case studies to build their theories. People must be intelligent, verbal, and able to express their thoughts, feelings, and experiences in a logical manner.

Action Therapies: Behavior Therapies and Cognitive Therapies

Whereas insight therapies strive to understand the motives behind one's behavior, action therapies are focused on changing the behavior itself. In behavior therapies, the goal is to change behavior through the use of learning techniques, whereas cognitive therapies strive to change maladaptive thoughts.

Behavior Therapies: Learning One's Way to Better Behavior That's right—the basic concept behind behaviorism is that all behavior, whether "normal" or "abnormal," is learned through the same processes of classical and operant conditioning. **Behavior therapies** aim to change behavior through the use of the same kinds of learning techniques that people (and animals) use to learn any new responses. The abnormal or undesirable behavior is not seen as a symptom of anything else but rather is the problem itself. Learning created the problem, and new learning can correct it (Onken et al., 1997; Skinner, 1974; Sloan & Mizes, 1999). The video *Behavior Therapies* provides an overview of these therapies.

Therapies Based on Classical Conditioning Through classical conditioning, old and undesirable automatic responses can be replaced by desirable ones. There are several techniques that have been developed using this type of learning to treat disorders such as phobias, anxiety disorders, and obsessive-compulsive disorder.

Using learning techniques to change undesirable behavior and increase desirable behavior has a long history (Hughes, 1993; Lovaas, 1987; Lovaas et al., 1966). Originally called *behavior modification*, the more recent adaptation of these techniques is **applied behavior analysis (ABA)**. The newer term better highlights the need for a functional analysis of the behavior to be modified, which is then followed by the use of conditioning techniques to modify the behavior.

Systematic desensitization, in which a therapist guides the client through a series of steps meant to reduce fear and anxiety, is normally used to treat phobic disorders and consists of a three-step process. First, the client must learn to relax through deep muscle relaxation training. Next, the client and the therapist construct a list, known as a hierarchy of fears, beginning with the object or situation that causes the least fear to the client, eventually working up to the object or situation that produces the greatest degree of fear. Finally, under the guidance of the therapist the client begins at the first item on the list that causes minimal fear and looks at it, thinks about it, or actually confronts it, all while remaining in a relaxed state. By pairing the old conditioned stimulus (the fear object) with a new relaxation response that is incompatible with the emotions and physical arousal associated with fear, the person's fear is reduced and relieved. The person then proceeds to the next item on the list of the *hierarchy of fears* until the phobia is gone. It is even possible to use a computer-generated virtual reality technique for desensitization (Rothbaum et al., 1995).

Another way to use classical conditioning is to reduce the frequency of undesirable behaviors, such as smoking or overeating, by teaching the client to pair an aversive (unpleasant) stimulus with the stimulus that results in the undesirable response, in a process called **aversion therapy**. For example, someone who wants to stop smoking might go to a therapist who uses a *rapid-smoking* technique, in which the client is allowed to smoke but must take a puff on the cigarette every 5 or 6 seconds. As nicotine is a poison, such rapid smoking produces nausea and dizziness, both unpleasant effects.

Because phobias are already very unpleasant, aversive conditioning is not the most useful nor effective method of therapy. But although desensitization

The last chapter talked about how behaviorists have a very different way of looking at abnormality—it's all learned. So do behaviorists do any kind of therapy?

Watch the **Video**, *Behavior Therapies*, at **MyPsychLab**

behavior therapies action therapies based on the principles of classical and operant conditioning and aimed at changing disordered behavior without concern for the original causes of such behavior.

applied behavior analysis (ABA) modern term for a form of functional analysis and behavior modification that uses a variety of behavioral techniques to mold a desired behavior or response.

systematic desensitization behavior technique used to treat phobias, in which a client is asked to make a list of ordered fears and taught to relax while concentrating on those fears.

aversion therapy form of behavioral therapy in which an undesirable behavior is paired with an aversive stimulus to reduce the frequency of the behavior.

exposure therapies behavioral techniques that expose individuals to anxiety- or fear-related stimuli, under carefully controlled conditions, to promote new learning.

flooding technique for treating phobias and other stress disorders in which the person is rapidly and intensely exposed to the fear-provoking situation or object and prevented from making the usual avoidance or escape response.

modeling learning through the observation and imitation of others.

token economy the use of objects called tokens to reinforce behavior in which the tokens can be accumulated and exchanged for desired items or privileges.

remains one of the more common therapies for phobias, it does not always bring quick results.

Behavioral techniques that introduce the client to situations, under carefully controlled conditions, which are related to their anxieties or fears are called **exposure therapies**. Exposure can be accomplished through a variety of routes and is intended to promote new learning. It can be *in vivo* ("in life"), where the client is exposed to the actual anxiety-related stimulus; *imaginal*, where the client visualizes or imagines the stimulus; and even *virtual*, where virtual reality (VR) technology is used (Najavits, 2007). (For more on virtual reality in psychology, see the Applying Psychology to Everyday Life section at the end of this chapter.)

For example, if Chang-sun has social anxiety disorder, for in vivo exposure he might have to attend a social event; for imaginal exposure he might be asked to visualize himself attending a social event; and for virtual exposure, Chang-sun might experience a social event, such as attending a dinner party, through VR technology.

Exposure methods can introduce the feared stimulus gradually, or quite suddenly. A gradual, or *graded*, exposure involves the client and therapist developing a fear hierarchy as in systematic desensitization: Exposure begins at the least feared event and progresses through to the most feared, similar to desensitization. If the exposure is rapid and intense, it begins with the most feared event and is called **flooding** (Gelder, 1976; Olsen, 1975).

Therapies Based on Operant Conditioning Operant conditioning techniques include reinforcement, extinction, shaping, and modeling to change the frequency of voluntary behavior. In the treatment of psychological disorders, the goal is to reduce the frequency of undesirable behavior and increase the frequency of desirable responses.

One of the advantages of using operant conditioning to treat a problem behavior is that results are usually quickly obtained. When bringing the behavior under control is the goal, operant and other behavioral techniques are very practical.

Learning through the observation and imitation of others (**modeling**) is discussed in *Chapter Six: Learning and Language*. The use of modeling as a therapy is based on the work of Albert Bandura, which states that a person with specific fears or someone who needs to develop social skills can learn to do so by watching someone else (the model) confront those fears or demonstrate the needed social skills (Bandura et al., 1969). In *participant modeling*, a model demonstrates the desired behavior in a step-by-step gradual process. The client is encouraged by the therapist to imitate the model in the same gradual, step-by-step manner (Bandura, 1986; Bandura et al., 1974).

Reinforcement is the strengthening of a response by following it with some pleasurable consequence (positive reinforcement) or the removal of an unpleasant stimulus (negative reinforcement). Reinforcement of both types can form the basis for treatment of people with behavioral problems.

In a **token economy**, objects known as *tokens* (secondary reinforcements) can be traded for food, candy, treats, or special privileges. Clients earn tokens for behaving correctly or accomplishing behavioral goals or may also lose tokens for inappropriate behavior. Token economies have also been used successfully in modifying the behavior of relatively disturbed persons in mental institutions,

▲ This boy is sitting in the "time-out" corner at his school. By removing the attention that he found rewarding, the teacher is attempting to extinguish the behavior that earned the boy a time-out. Do you see anything in this time-out corner that might make it less effective?

such as people with schizophrenia or depressed persons (Dickerson et al., 1994; Glynn, 1990; McMonagle & Sultana, 2002).

Extinction involves the removal of a reinforcer to reduce the frequency of a particular response. In modifying behavior, operant extinction often involves removing one's attention from the person when that person is engaging in an inappropriate or undesirable behavior. With children, this removal of attention may be a form of *time-out*, in which the child is removed from the situation that provides reinforcement (Kazdin, 1980).

cognitive therapy therapy in which the focus is on helping clients recognize distortions in their thinking and replacing distorted, unrealistic beliefs with more realistic, helpful thoughts.

Evaluation of Behavior Therapies Behavior therapies may be more effective than other forms of therapy in treating specific behavioral problems, such as bedwetting, overeating, drug addictions, and phobic reactions (Burgio, 1998; Wetherell, 2002). More serious psychological disorders, such as severe depression or schizophrenia, do not respond as well overall to behavioral treatments, although improvement of specific symptoms can be achieved (Glynn, 1990; McMonagle & Sultana, 2002).

Cognitive Therapies: Thinking Is Believing Cognitive therapy (Beck, 1979; Freeman et al., 1989) was developed by Aaron T. Beck and is focused on helping people change their ways of thinking. Rather than focusing on the behavior itself, the cognitive therapist focuses on the distorted thinking and unrealistic beliefs that lead to maladaptive behavior (Hollon & Beck, 1994), especially those distortions relating to depression (Abela & D'Allesandro, 2002; McGinn, 2000). The goal is to help clients test, in a more objective, scientific way, the truth of their beliefs and assumptions, as well as their attributions concerning both their own behavior and the behavior of others in their lives. Then they can recognize thoughts that are distorted and negative and replace them with more positive, helpful thoughts. Because the focus is on changing thoughts rather than gaining deep insights into their causes, this kind of therapy is primarily an action therapy.

Beck's Cognitive Therapy Cognitive therapy focuses on the distortions of thinking. Here are some of the more common distortions in thought that can create negative feelings and unrealistic beliefs in people:

◄ What are these unrealistic beliefs?

- **Arbitrary inference:** This refers to "jumping to conclusions" without any evidence. Arbitrary means to decide something based on nothing more than personal whims. Example: "Suzy canceled our lunch date—I'll bet she's seeing someone else!"
- **Selective thinking:** In selective thinking, the person focuses only on one aspect of a situation, leaving out other relevant facts that might make things seem less negative. Example: Peter's teacher praised his paper but made one comment about needing to check his punctuation. Peter assumes that his paper is lousy and that the teacher really didn't like it, ignoring the other praise and positive comments.
- **Overgeneralization:** Here a person draws a sweeping conclusion from one incident and then assumes that the conclusion applies to areas of life that have nothing to do with the original event. Example: "I got yelled at by my boss. My boyfriend is going to break up with me and kick me out of the apartment—I'll end up living in a van down by the river."
- **Magnification and minimization:** Here a person blows bad things out of proportion while not emphasizing good things. Example: A student who has received good grades on every other exam believes that the C she got on the last quiz means she's not going to succeed in college.
- **Personalization:** In personalization, an individual takes responsibility or blame for events that are not really connected to the individual.

cognitive–behavioral therapy (CBT) action therapy in which the goal is to help clients overcome problems by learning to think more rationally and logically, which in turn will impact their behavior.

rational emotive behavior therapy (REBT) cognitive–behavioral in which clients are directly challenged in their irrational beliefs and helped to restructure their thinking into more rational belief statements.

Example: When Sandy's husband comes home in a bad mood because of something that happened at work, she immediately assumes that he is angry with her.

A cognitive therapist tries to get clients to look at their beliefs and test them to see how accurate they really are. The first step is to identify an illogical or unrealistic belief, which the therapist and client do in their initial talks. Then the client is guided by the therapist through a process of asking questions about that belief, such as "When did this belief of mine begin?" or "What is the evidence for this belief?"

Cognitive–Behavioral Therapy Cognitive therapy really is critical thinking applied to one's own thoughts and beliefs. Just as cognitive psychology emerged as a reaction to behaviorism, therapies using cognitive methods have behavioral elements within them as well, leading to the term **cognitive–behavioral therapy (CBT)**.

CBT focuses on the present rather than the past (like behaviorism) but also assumes that people interact with the world with more than simple, automatic reactions to external stimuli. People observe the world and the people in the world around them, make assumptions and inferences* based on those observations or cognitions, and then decide how to respond (Rachman & Hodgson, 1980). As a form of cognitive therapy, CBT also assumes that disorders come from illogical, irrational cognitions and that changing the thinking patterns to more rational, logical ones will relieve the symptoms of the disorder, making it an action therapy. CBT has three basic elements: cognitions affect behavior, cognitions can be changed, and behavior change can result from cognitive change (Dobson & Block, 1988). Cognitive–behavioral therapists may also use any of the tools that behavioral therapists use to help clients alter their actions. The three basic goals of any cognitive–behavioral therapy are as follows:

1. Relieve the symptoms and help clients resolve the problems.
2. Help clients develop strategies that can be used to cope with future problems.
3. Help clients change the way they think from irrational, self-defeating thoughts to more rational, self-helping, positive thoughts.

Ellis and Rational Emotive Behavior Therapy (REBT) Albert Ellis proposed a version of CBT called **rational emotive behavior therapy (REBT)**, in which clients are taught a way to challenge their own irrational beliefs with more rational, helpful statements (Ellis, 1997, 1998). Here are some examples of irrational beliefs:

- Everyone should love and approve of me (if they don't, I am awful and unlovable). (In the words of Ellis, saying something like this is to "*awfulize*.")
- When things do not go the way I wanted and planned, it is terrible and I am, of course, going to get very disturbed. I can't stand it! (Ellis used the word "*catastrophize*" to describe this type of thinking.)

Notice that these statements have one thing in common: It's either all or nothing. Can a person really expect the love and affection of every single person? Is it realistic to expect things to work as planned every time? Rational emotive behavioral therapy is about challenging these types of "my way or nothing"

But I've felt that way at times. Why are these statements so irrational?

---

*inferences: conclusions drawn from observations and facts.

statements, helping people to realize that life can be good without being "perfect." In REBT, therapists take a very directive role, challenging the client when the client makes statements like those listed earlier, assigning homework, using behavioral techniques to modify behavior, and arguing with clients about the rationality of their statements.

Evaluation of Cognitive and Cognitive–Behavioral Therapies Cognitive and cognitive–behavioral therapies are less expensive than the typical insight therapy because they are comparatively short-term therapies. As in behavior therapy, clients do not have to dig too deep for the hidden sources of their problems. Instead, cognitive-based therapies get right to the problems themselves, helping clients deal with their symptoms more directly. In fact, one of the criticisms of these therapies as well as behavior therapies is that they treat the symptom, not the cause. However, it should be noted that in the cognitive viewpoint, the maladaptive thoughts are seen as the cause of the problems, not merely the symptoms. There is also an element of potential bias because of the therapist's opinions as to which thoughts are rational and which are not (Westen, 2005). For a summary of the various types of psychotherapies discussed up to this point, see **Table 33.1**.

Group Therapies: Not Just for the Shy Not everyone that receives psychological treatment does so individually with a therapist. There are conditions and situations where psychological professionals work with more than one client at a time, and circumstances when individuals benefit by seeing how others address

Table 33.1	Characteristics of Psychotherapies	
TYPE OF THERAPY (KEY PEOPLE)	GOAL	METHODS
Psychodynamic therapy (Freud)	Insight	Aims to reveal unconscious conflicts through dream interpretation, free association, resistance, and transference
Humanistic therapy Person-centered therapy (Rogers)	Insight	Nondirective therapy; client does most of the talking; key elements are authenticity, unconditional positive regard, and empathy
Behavior therapy (Watson, Jones, Skinner, Bandura)	Action	Based on principles of classical and operant conditioning; aimed at changing behavior without concern for causes of behavior
Cognitive therapy (Beck) CBT (various professionals) REBT (Ellis)	Action	Aims to help clients overcome problems by learning to think more rationally and logically Clients are challenged in their irrational beliefs and helped to restructure their thinking

group therapy form of therapy or treatment during which a small group of clients with similar concerns meet together with a therapist to address their issues.

support groups (self-help groups) a group composed of people who have similar problems and who meet together without a therapist or counselor for the purpose of discussion, problem solving, and social and emotional support.

concerns and challenges. People can work with other individuals in group therapy, family therapy, and in self-help groups.

Types of Group Therapies An alternative to individual therapy, in which the client and the therapist have a private, one-on-one session, is **group therapy**, in which a group of clients with similar problems gather together to discuss their problems under the guidance of a single therapist (Yalom, 1995).

Group therapy can be accomplished in several ways. The therapist may use either an insight or cognitive–behavioral style, although person-centered, and behavior therapies seem to work better in group settings than psychodynamic and cognitive–behavioral therapies (Andrews, 1989).

In addition to the variations in the style of therapy, the group structure can also vary. There may be small groups formed of related persons or other groups of unrelated persons that meet without the benefit of a therapist. Their goal is to share their problems and provide social and emotional support for each other.

One form of group therapy is *family counseling* or *family therapy*, in which all of the members of a family who are experiencing some type of problem—marital problems, problems in child discipline, or sibling rivalry, for example—are seen by the therapist as a group. The therapist may also meet with one or more family members individually at times, but the real work in opening the lines of communication among family members is accomplished in the group setting (Frankel & Piercy, 1990; Pinsoff & Wynne, 1995). The family members may include grandparents, aunts and uncles, and in-laws as well as the core family. This is because family therapy focuses on the family as a whole unit or system of interacting "parts." The goal in family therapy, then, is to discover the unhealthy ways in which family members interact and communicate with one another and change those ways to healthier, more productive means of interaction.

Many people may feel that a therapist who has never had, for example, a drug problem would be unable to truly understand their situation; and they may also feel that someone who has experienced addiction and beaten it is more capable of providing real help. Therapists are also often in short supply, and they charge a fee for leading group-therapy sessions. These are reasons some people choose to meet with others who have problems similar to their own, with no therapist in charge. Called **support groups** or **self-help groups**, these groups are usually formed around a particular problem. Some examples of support groups are Alcoholics Anonymous, Overeaters Anonymous, and Narcotics Anonymous, all of which have groups meeting all over the country at almost any time of the day or night. The advantages of self-help groups are that they are free and provide the social and emotional support that a group session can provide (Bussa & Kaufman, 2000).

▼ *In group therapy, several people who share similar problems gather with a therapist to discuss their feelings and concerns. The presence of others who are going through the same kind of emotional difficulties can be comforting as well as provide the opportunity for insights into one's own problems by hearing about the problems of others.*

Evaluation of Group Therapy

There are many advantages to using group therapy over other forms of therapy. Group therapy can provide help to people who might be unable to afford individual psychotherapy. Because the therapist can see several clients at one time, this type of therapy is usually less expensive than individual therapy. It also offers social and emotional support from people who have problems that are similar or nearly identical to one's own. This advantage is an important one; studies have shown that breast cancer patients who were part of a group-therapy process had much higher survival and recovery rates than those who received only individual therapy or no psychotherapy (Fawzy et al., 1993; Spiegel et al., 1989).

33.5 Evaluate the effectiveness of psychological treatments.

Does Psychotherapy Really Work? In the 1950s, Hans Eysenck did one of the earliest studies of the effectiveness of therapy. His conclusion was that the people receiving psychotherapy did not recover at any higher rate than those who had no psychotherapy and that the passage of time alone could account for all recovery.

> ◀ There sure are a lot of psychotherapies, but do any of them really work?

Eysenck's classic survey created a major controversy within the world of clinical and counseling psychology. Other researchers began their own studies to see if Eysenck's findings would be upheld. One such effort reviewed studies that the researchers considered to be well controlled and concluded that the psychotherapies did not differ from one another in effectiveness (Luborsky et al., 1975).

There are numerous problems with studying the effectiveness of psychotherapy. Controlled studies can be done using an experimental group of people who receive a particular psychotherapy and a control group of people who are put on a waiting list, but this is less than ideal. The control group is not getting the attention from the therapist, for one thing, and so there would be no placebo-effect expectations about getting better because of therapy (Shapiro & Shapiro, 1997).

Recent surveys have shown that people who have received psychotherapy believe that they have been helped more often than not (*Consumer Reports*, 1995; Kotkin et al., 1996). The *Consumer Reports* research was a survey of the magazine's readers in which those who had been or were currently clients in psychotherapy rated the effectiveness of the therapy they received. Here are the findings from a summary of this and several other similar surveys (Lambert & Ogles, 2004; Seligman, 1995; Thase, 1999):

- An estimated 75–90 percent of people feel that psychotherapy has helped them.
- The longer a person stays in therapy, the greater the improvement.

Although psychotherapy usually occurs face to face with a therapist, a new type of therapy known as **cybertherapy** is offered via the Internet. This method of delivery may have the advantages of lower or no cost, availability of therapy opportunities for those unable to get to a therapist easily, access to support groups online, and relative anonymity. However, there is no guarantee that the cybertherapist has any credentials or training in psychotherapy. Although some cybertherapists use voice or video conferencing, some only use text-based chat. When there is no face-to-face or voice-to-voice contact, the therapist has no access to body language or vocal tones in trying to assess a client's emotional and psychological state.

What have studies shown regarding the effectiveness of cybertherapy? A group of researchers in Germany found that people who were treated as inpatients and then allowed to "meet" with a group therapist in an Internet chat room showed a significantly lower risk of negative changes in their mental status than a control group (Golkaramnay et al., 2007).

cybertherapy psychotherapy that is offered on the Internet. Also called online, Internet, or Web therapy or counseling.

So how does a person with a problem know what kind of therapist to go to? How do you pick a good one?

👁 **Watch** the **Video**, *What's In It For Me?: Finding a Therapist if You Need One: Resources for Students*, at **MyPsychLab**

It can sometimes be hard to know where to turn for professional help, and how to determine which type of therapy is a good fit for you. The video, *What's In It For Me?: Finding a Therapist if You Need One: Resources for Students*, offers some advice.

As discussed before, many psychological professionals today take an eclectic view of psychotherapy, using a combination of methods or switching methods to fit the particular client's needs or specific problems. The *common factors approach* in psychotherapy is a modern approach to eclecticism and focuses on those factors common to successful outcomes from different forms of therapy (Norcross, 2005). These factors are seen as the source of the success rather than specific differences among therapies. The most important common factor of a successful psychotherapy may be the relationship between the client and the therapist, known as the *therapeutic alliance*. This relationship should be caring, warm, and accepting, and be characterized by empathy, mutual respect, and understanding. Therapy should also offer clients a *protected setting* in which to release emotions and reveal private thoughts and concerns and should help clients understand why they feel the way they do and provide them with ways to feel better. Other common factors in therapy effectiveness are *opportunity for catharsis* (relieving pent-up emotions), *learning and practice of new behaviors*, and *positive experiences* for the client (Norcross, 2005).

33.6 Identify other factors that improve the effectiveness of treatment.

Cultural, Ethnic, and Gender Concerns in Psychotherapy Consider the following situation (adapted from Wedding, 2004).

> K. is a 24-year-old Korean American. She lived with her parents, who were both born and reared in Korea before moving to the United States as adults. She came to a therapist because she was depressed and unhappy with her lack of independence. Her father was angry about her plans to marry a non-Korean. Her therapist immediately began assertiveness training and role-playing to prepare K. to deal with her father. The therapist was disappointed when K. failed to keep her second appointment.

This example of an actual case demonstrates a problem that exists in the therapist–client relationship for many clients when the ethnicity or culture of the client is different from that of the therapist. This cultural difference makes it difficult for therapists to understand the exact nature of their clients' problems and for clients to benefit from therapies that do not match their needs (Matsumoto, 1994; Moffic, 2003; Wedding, 2004). The values of different cultures and ethnic groups are not universally the same. How, for example, could a well-educated White female therapist from an upper-middle-class family understand the problems of a Hispanic adolescent boy from a poor family living in substandard housing if she did not acknowledge the differences between them? In this case, the gender, ethnicity, and economic background of the client and therapist are all vastly different.

In the case of K., for example, the therapist mistakenly assumed that the key to improving K.'s situation was to make her more assertive and independent from her family, particularly her father. This Western idea runs counter to Korean cultural values. Korean culture stresses interdependence, not independence. K.'s real problem may have been her feelings of guilt about her situation and her father's anger. She may have wanted help in dealing with her family situation and her feelings about that situation, not help in becoming more independent.

For therapy to be effective, the client must continue in treatment until a successful outcome is reached. K. never came back after the first session. One of the problems that can occur when the culture or ethnic backgrounds of the client and therapist are mismatched, as in K.'s case, is that the therapist may project his or her values onto the client, failing to achieve true empathy with the client's feelings or even to realize what the client's true feelings are, thus causing the client to drop out of therapy. Studies of such situations have found that members of minority racial or ethnic groups drop out of therapy at a significantly higher rate than the majority of group clients (Brown et al., 2003; Cooper et al., 2003; Flaherty & Adams, 1998; Fortuna et al., 2010; Sue, 1977, 1992; Sue et al., 1994; Vail, 1976; Vernon & Roberts, 1982).

Research on gender and therapist–client relationships varies. When talking about White, middle-class clients, it seems that both men and women prefer a female therapist (Jones et al., 1987). But African American clients were more likely to drop out of therapy if the therapist was the *same* sex as the client (Vail, 1976); male Asian clients seemed to prefer a male therapist; and female Asian clients stayed in therapy equally long with either male or female therapists (Flaherty & Adams, 1998; Flaskerud, 1991).

◀ Are differences in gender that important? For example, do women prefer female therapists, but men would rather talk to another man?

Four barriers to effective psychotherapy exist when the culture or ethnic backgrounds of client and therapist are different (Sue & Sue, 2008):

1. **Culture-bound values.** Including individual centered versus other (or others) centered, verbal/emotional/behavioral expressiveness, communication patterns from client to counselor, nuclear family, and so forth (Sue & Sue, 2008). Differing cultural values can cause therapists to fail at forming an empathetic relationship (Sattler, 1977; Wedding, 2004).

2. **Class-bound values.** Adherence to time schedules, ambiguous approach to problems, looking for long-range goals (Sue & Sue, 2008). Clients from impoverished backgrounds may have values and experiences that the therapist cannot understand (Wedding, 2004).

3. **Language.** Use of standard English, emphasis on verbal communication (Sue & Sue, 2008). Speaking different languages becomes a problem in understanding what both client and therapist are saying and in psychological testing (Betancourt & Jacobs, 2000; Lewis, 1996).

4. **Nonverbal communication.** Body language, or nonverbal communication, can also differ between cultures and ethnicities. The physical distance between the client and therapist, the use of gestures, and eye contact, for example, can cause misunderstandings during the session and in interpretation of the client's moods and intentions (Galanti, 1997; Like et al., 1996). People in some cultures are content with long periods of silence whereas others are not, direct eye contact is desirable in some cultures and offensive in others, and even facial expressions of emotion vary from very expressive (as with many Hispanic people) to nonexpressive (as with many Asian people).

The American Psychiatric Association (2013) has included information for psychology professionals concerning cultural issues and culture syndromes. All therapists need to make an effort to become aware of cultural differences, syndromes, and possible gender issues. Sociopolitical issues should also be examined (Sue & Sue, 2008). ⓛⓘⓝⓚ *to Chapter Thirteen: Psychological Disorders*, pp. 408–437.

Thinking Critically
Which of the forms of psychotherapy discussed so far would probably work best for a client who has commitment issues in relationships? Why?

Pick the best answer.

1. Psychotherapies that attempt to change inappropriate or disordered behavior directly are known as
   a. action therapies.
   b. insight therapies.
   c. biomedical therapies.
   d. psychoanalytic therapies.

2. The process during which a psychodynamic therapist encourages a patient to talk about whatever comes to mind without fear of negative evaluation is called
   a. resistance.
   b. transference.
   c. free association.
   d. dream interpretation.

3. Compared to traditional psychoanalysis, modern psychodynamic therapy is
   a. more directive.
   b. more time consuming.
   c. more action oriented.
   d. more focused on the id.

4. Humanistic therapies are different from psychoanalysis because they focus more on
   a. personal insights.
   b. childhood events.
   c. biomedical approaches.
   d. conscious experiences.

5. Which of the following is not one of the four basic elements of Roger's person-centered therapy?
   a. empathy
   b. authenticity
   c. reflection
   d. reinforcement

6. Which of the following would most likely not be a person-centered therapist's response to the client's claim, "I feel like a failure"?
   a. "I don't think you're a failure."
   b. "Why do you feel like a failure?"

   c. "Have you always felt like a failure?"
   d. "You feel that you're failing in some way?"

7. Jeremy is trying to stop biting his fingernails. He wears a rubber band around each of his wrists, and whenever he finds himself biting his nails, he snaps the band. Jeremy is using a form of
   a. flooding.
   b. extinction.
   c. aversion therapy.
   d. systematic desensitization.

8. Maya is upset because her tutor teased her about turning in her assignment several hours late. Although her tutor was quite pleased with the report itself and told Maya that her work was excellent, Maya remains unhappy. Which type of distorted thinking is Maya engaging in?
   a. minimization
   b. personalization
   c. arbitrary inference
   d. selective thinking

9. Annelina is frightened of water. Her therapist first shows her pictures of an ocean, then takes her to the ocean front, then asks her to wade in the water, and finally asks Annelina to go swimming. This therapeutic technique is called
   a. flooding.
   b. modeling.
   c. reinforcement.
   d. systematic desensitization.

10. Which of the following is not a potential barrier to effective therapy when therapists and clients come from different cultural backgrounds?
    a. age
    b. language
    c. social class
    d. nonverbal communication

Biomedical Treatments and Issues in Treatments

Module Goals	Learning Objectives
Identify biomedical treatments and evaluate their effectiveness.	**34.1** Understand approaches to biomedical treatments and evaluate their effectiveness.
	34.2 Consider appropriate treatments for different age groups.
Consider legal, ethical, and professional challenges in the treatment of psychological disorders.	**34.3** Learn about ethical challenges involved in delivery of treatment.
	34.4 Describe national and local resources available to support individuals with psychological disorders and their families.

Identify Biomedical Treatments and Evaluate their Effectiveness

34.1 Understand approaches to biomedical treatments and evaluate their effectiveness.

Just as a therapist trained in psychoanalysis is more likely to use that technique, a therapist whose perspective on personality and behavior is biological will most likely turn to medical techniques to manage disordered behavior. Even psychotherapists who are not primarily biological in orientation may combine psychotherapy with medical treatments that are supervised by a medical doctor working with the psychologist. As medical doctors, psychiatrists are almost inevitably biological in perspective and, thus, use **biomedical therapies** (directly affecting the biological functioning of the body and brain) in addition to any psychotherapy technique they may favor. The biomedical therapies fall into several approaches and may consist of drug therapy, shock therapy, surgical treatments, or noninvasive stimulation techniques.

Psychopharmacology The use of drugs to control or relieve the symptoms of a psychological disorder is called **psychopharmacology**. Although these drugs are sometimes used alone, they are more often combined with some form of psychotherapy and are more effective as a result (Kearney & Silverman, 1998; Keller et al., 2000). There are four basic categories of drugs used to treat psychotic disorders, anxiety disorders, the manic phase of mood disorders, and depression.

Antipsychotic Drugs Drugs used to treat psychotic symptoms, such as hallucinations, delusions, and bizarre behavior, are called *antipsychotic drugs*. These

biomedical therapies therapies that directly affect the biological functioning of the body and brain; therapies for mental disorders in which a person with a problem is treated with biological or medical methods to relieve symptoms.

psychopharmacology the use of drugs to control or relieve the symptoms of psychological disorders.

drugs can be classified into two categories, the classical, or *typical antipsychotics*, and newer *atypical antipsychotics*. The first of the typical antipsychotics to be developed was *chlorpromazine*. The first-generation antipsychotics caused "neurolepsis," or psychomotor slowing and reduced emotionality, and thus were referred to as *neuroleptics*, due to the neurological side effects they produced (Julien et al., 2011; Preston et al., 2008; Stahl, 2013). **Table 34.1** lists several typical and atypical antipsychotic drugs and their side effects.

Typical antipsychotic drugs work by blocking certain dopamine receptors in the brain, namely the D2 receptor, thereby reducing the effect of dopamine in synaptic transmission (Julien et al., 2011; Preston et al., 2008; Stahl, 2013). However, because they block more pathways in the dopamine system than are involved in psychosis, with prolonged use they tend to cause problems. Such problems include movement disorders such as *tardive dyskinesia*. The syndrome

Table 34.1	Types of Drugs Used in Psychopharmacology		
CLASSIFICATION	TREATMENT AREAS	SIDE EFFECTS	EXAMPLES
Antipsychotic: Typical antipsychotic	Positive (excessive) symptoms such as delusions or hallucinations	Motor problems, tardive dyskinesia	chlorpromazine, droperidol, haloperidol
Antipsychotic: Atypical antipsychotic	Positive and some negative symptoms of psychoses	Fewer than typical antipsychotic; clozapine may cause serious blood disorder	risperidone, clozapine, aripiprazole
Antianxiety: Minor Tranquilizers	Symptoms of anxiety and phobic reactions	Slight sedative effect; potential for physical dependence	alprazolam, lorazepam, diazepam
Antimanic	Manic behavior	Potential for toxic buildup	lithium, anticonvulsant drugs
Antidepressants: MAOIs	Depression	Weight gain, constipation, dry mouth, dizziness, headache, drowsiness, insomnia, some sexual arousal disorders	iproniazid, isocarboxazid, phenelzine sulfite, tranylcypromine sulfate
Antidepressants: Tricyclics	Depression	Skin rashes, blurred vision, lowered blood pressure, weight loss	imipramine, desipramine, amitriptyline, doxepin
Antidepressants: SSRIs	Depression	Nausea, nervousness, insomnia, diarrhea, rash, agitation, some sexual arousal problems	fluoxetine, sertraline, paroxetine

is characterized by the person making facial and tongue movements such as repeatedly sticking their tongue out, grimacing, or constant chewing, or causing repetitive involuntary jerks or dance-like movements of the arms and legs (Julien et al., 2011; Preston et al., 2008; Stahl, 2013).

The atypical antipsychotics may also suppress dopamine but to a much greater degree in the one dopamine pathway that seems to cause psychotic problems. These drugs also block or partially block certain serotonin receptors, resulting in fewer negative side effects and occasionally some improvement in the negative symptoms of schizophrenia (Julien et al., 2011; Preston et al., 2008; Stahl, 2013). Despite their effectiveness, the atypical antipsychotics may also have unwanted side effects, such as weight gain, diabetes, blood lipid level changes, or changes in the electrical rhythms of the heart (Julien et al., 2011).

Antianxiety Drugs The traditional *antianxiety drugs* are the minor tranquilizers or *benzodiazepines* such as Xanax, Ativan, and Valium. All of these drugs have a sedative effect and in the right dose can start to relieve symptoms of anxiety within 20 to 30 minutes of taking the drug by mouth (Preston et al., 2008). Although many side effects are possible, the main concern in using these drugs is their potential for addiction as well as abuse in the form of taking larger doses to "escape" (National Institute on Drug Abuse [NIDA]).

Mood-Stabilizing Drugs For many years, the treatment of choice for bipolar disorder and episodes of mania has been *lithium*, a metallic chemical element that in its salt form (lithium carbonate) evens out both the highs and the lows of bipolar disorder. It is generally recommended that treatment with lithium continue at maintenance levels in people with recurring bipolar disorder. Lithium affects the way sodium ions in neuron and muscle cells are transported, although it is not clear exactly how this affects mood. Side effects typically disappear quickly, although the use of lithium has been associated with weight gain. Diet needs to be controlled when taking lithium because lowered levels of sodium in the diet can cause lithium to build up to toxic levels, as can any substance that removes water from the body such as the caffeine in sodas, tea, and coffee.

Antidepressant Drugs As is so often the case in scientific discoveries, the first types of drugs used in the treatment of depression were originally developed to treat other disorders. Iproniazid, for example, was used to treat tuberculosis symptoms in the early 1950s and was found to have a positive effect on mood, becoming the first modern *antidepressant* (Trujillo & Chinn, 1996). This drug became the first of the *monoamine oxidase inhibitors* (MAOIs), a class of antidepressants that blocks the activity of an enzyme called monoamine oxidase. Monoamine oxidase is the brain's "cleanup worker" because its primary function is to break down the neurotransmitters norepinephrine, serotonin, and dopamine—the three neurotransmitters most involved in control of mood. Under normal circumstances, the excess neurotransmitters are broken down *after* they have done their "job" in mood control. In depression, these neurotransmitters need more time to do their job, and the MAOIs allow them that time by inhibiting the enzyme's action.

Some common MAOIs in use today are isocarboxazid (Marplan), phenelzine sulfate (Nardil), and tranylcypromine sulfate (Parnate). These drugs can produce some unwanted side effects, although in most cases the side effects decrease or disappear with continued treatment: weight gain, constipation, dry mouth, dizziness, headache, drowsiness or insomnia, and sexual arousal disorders are possible.

The second category of antidepressant drug to be developed is called the *tricyclic antidepressants*. These drugs were discovered in the course of developing

electroconvulsive therapy (ECT) form of biomedical therapy to treat severe depression in which electrodes are placed on either one or both sides of a person's head, and an electric current is passed through the electrodes that is strong enough to cause a seizure or convulsion.

treatments for schizophrenia (Trujillo & Chinn, 1996). Tricyclics, so called because of their molecular structure consisting of three rings (cycles), increase the activity of serotonin and norepinephrine in the nervous system by inhibiting their reuptake into the synaptic vesicles of the neurons. Some common tricyclics are imipramine (Tofranil), desipramine (Norpramin, Pertofrane), amitriptyline (Elavil), and doxepin (Sinequan, Adapin). Side effects of these drugs, which may also decrease over the course of treatment, are very similar to those of the MAOIs but can also include skin rashes, blurred vision, lowered blood pressure, and weight gain (Julien et al., 2011; Preston et al., 2008; Stahl, 2013).

The effect of the MAOIs and the tricyclics on the action of the three critical neurotransmitters led researchers to try to develop drugs that would more specifically target the critical neural activity involved in depression with fewer negative side effects. This led to the development of the *selective serotonin reuptake inhibitors* (SSRIs), drugs that inhibit the reuptake process of only serotonin. This causes fewer side effects while still providing effective antidepressant action, making these drugs relatively safe when compared to the older antidepressants. But like the other two classes of antidepressants, the SSRIs may take from 2 to 6 weeks to produce effects. Some of the better-known SSRIs are fluoxetine (Prozac), sertraline (Zoloft), and paroxetine (Paxil).

Other Biomedical Treatments: ECT, Psychosurgery, and Emerging Techniques

As addressed at the beginning of the chapter, psychological disorders have been treated in a variety of ways, via a variety of medical means, and some treatments have been better options than others. Unfortunately, some methods were used indiscriminately, were ineffective, or caused more harm than good. That has changed and current alternative biomedical options are effective options when other strategies have not been successful, and sometimes the best option.

How are electroconvulsive therapy and psychosurgery used to treat psychological disorders today? ▶

▼ Electroconvulsive therapy consists of applying an electric shock to one or both sides of the head. The result is rapid improvement in mood. It has been shown to be most effective in treating severe depression that has not responded to medication or where medication side effects cannot be tolerated.

Electroconvulsive Therapy Many people are—well—*shocked* to discover that **electroconvulsive therapy (ECT)** is still in use to treat cases of severe depression. ECT involves the delivery of an electric shock to either one side or both sides of a person's head, resulting in a seizure or convulsion of the body and the release of a flood of neurotransmitters in the brain (American Psychiatric Association [APA] Committee on Electroconvulsive Therapy, 2001). The result is an almost immediate improvement in mood, and ECT is used not only in severe cases of depression that have not responded to drug treatments or psychotherapy, or where the side effects of medication are not acceptable, but also in the treatment of several other severe disorders, such as schizophrenia and severe mania, that are not responding to alternate treatments (APA Committee on Electroconvulsive Therapy, 2001; Pompili et al., 2013).

In the 1930s, doctors actually were researching the possible uses of inducing seizures in treating schizophrenia, although the seizures were induced through means of a drug (camphor) in those early experiments. It was Italian researchers Cerletti and Bini who first used electricity to induce a seizure in a man with schizophrenia, who fully recovered after only 11 such treatments (Endler, 1988; Fink, 1984; Shorter, 1997). Soon doctors were using ECT on every kind of severe mental disorder. In those early days, no anesthesia was used because the shock was severe enough to result in a

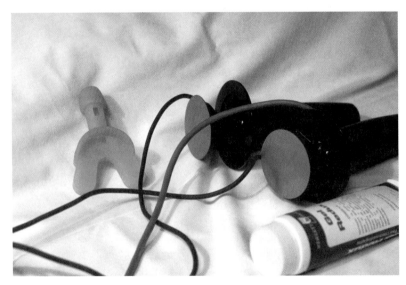

loss of consciousness (most of the time). Broken bones, bitten tongues, and fractured teeth were not untypical "side effects."

Today's ECT is far more controlled and humane. It is only used to treat severe disorders, and written and informed consent is required in most states. ECT has been found to be most useful for severe depression that has not responded to medications or psychotherapy and in cases where suicide is a real possibility or has already been attempted. ECT works more quickly than antidepressant medications, so it can play an important role in helping to prevent suicide attempts (APA Committee on Electroconvulsive Therapy, 2001). However, ECT should not be considered a "cure." It is a way to get a person suffering from severe depression into a state of mind that is more receptive to other forms of therapy or psychotherapy. Relapse is very possible in individuals receiving ECT, and maintenance or continuation therapies are an important treatment strategy to pursue (Nordenskjold et al., 2011; Petrides et al., 2011).

ECT does have several negative side effects, some of which last longer than others. Memory is definitely affected, as ECT disrupts the consolidation process and prevents the formation of long-term memories. This causes both retrograde amnesia, the loss of memories for events that happen close to the time of the treatment, and anterograde amnesia, the rapid forgetting of new material (APA Committee on Electroconvulsive Therapy, 2001; Lisanby et al., 2000; Weiner, 2000). The retrograde effects can extend to several months before and a few weeks after treatment and the older memories may return with time, whereas the anterograde amnesia is more temporary, clearing up in a few weeks after treatment. Only a very few patients suffer more severe and long-lasting cognitive difficulties, and it is not easy to determine whether these difficulties originate with the treatment or the disorder the person exhibits (Smith, 2001). When ECT is used today, an effort is made to reduce as many side effects as possible. The modern patient is given muscle relaxants to reduce the effects of the convulsion as well as a very short-term anesthetic. Despite its efficacy, the utilization of ECT in general is not uniform. In the United States, racial differences in the use of ECT appear to be present, with Black Americans with depression less likely to pursue or receive ECT treatment as compared to White Americans, and the overall use of ECT in general appears to be declining (Case et al., 2013; Case et al., 2012).

Psychosurgery Just as surgery involves cutting into the body, **psychosurgery** involves cutting into the brain to remove or destroy brain tissue for the purpose of relieving symptoms of mental disorders. One of the earliest and best-known psychosurgical techniques is the **prefrontal lobotomy**, in which the connections of the prefrontal cortex to other areas of the brain are severed. The lobotomy was developed in 1935 by Portuguese neurologist Dr. Antonio Egas Moniz, who was awarded the Nobel Prize in medicine for his contribution to psychosurgery (Cosgrove & Rauch, 1995; Freeman & Watts, 1937). Walter Freeman and James W. Watts modified Moniz's technique and developed a procedure called the *transorbital lobotomy*, during which an instrument resembling an ice pick, called a leucotome, was inserted through the back of the eye socket and into the brain to sever the brain fibers. It was this technique that became widely used, and unfortunately sometimes overused, in the pursuit of relief for so many people suffering from mental illness.

Although it is true that some of the early lobotomy patients did seem less agitated, anxious, and delusional, it is also true that some early patients did not survive the surgery (about 6 percent died, in fact) and others were left with negative changes in personality: apathy, lack of emotional response, intellectual dullness, and childishness, to name a few. Fortunately, the development of antipsychotic drugs, beginning with chlorpromazine, together with the results of long-term studies that highlighted serious side effects of lobotomies, led to the discontinuation of lobotomies as a psychosurgical technique (Cosgrove & Rauch, 1995;

psychosurgery surgery performed on brain tissue to relieve or control severe psychological disorders.

prefrontal lobotomy psychosurgery in which the connections of the prefrontal cortex to other areas of the brain are severed.

◄ What are some of the side effects? Wasn't there something from an earlier chapter about this therapy affecting memory?

But I thought lobotomies left most people ◄ worse off than before—didn't it take away their emotions or something?

Swayze, 1995). Some famous recipients of the last decades of lobotomies (and the disorders for which the procedure was performed) were Rosemary Kennedy, sister of John F. Kennedy (mild intellectual disability), and Rose Williams, sister of playwright Tennessee Williams (schizophrenia).

The lobotomy is gone, but there is a different and more modern technique called *bilateral anterior cingulotomy*, in which magnetic resonance imaging, is used to guide an electrode to a specific area of the brain called the cingulate gyrus. This area connects the frontal lobes to the limbic system, which controls emotional reactions. By running a current through the electrode, a very small and specific area of brain cells can be destroyed. This process is called *lesioning*. *Cingulotomies* have been shown to be effective in about one-third to one half of cases of major depression, bipolar disorder, and certain forms of obsessive-compulsive disorder that have not responded to any other therapy techniques (Dougherty et al., 2002; Kuhn et al., 2010; Spangler et al., 1996). Because this is deliberate brain damage and quite permanent, all other possible treatments must be exhausted before a bilateral cingulotomy will be performed and, unlike the early days of lobotomies, it can be performed only with the patient's full and informed consent (Rodgers, 1992; Spangler et al., 1996). In fact, because of the ethical, social, and legal implications of psychosurgery in general, today only a very small number of such surgeries are carried out in a few medical centers across the world (Cosgrove & Rauch, 1995).

▲ The woman on the left is Rosemary Kennedy, sister of President John F. Kennedy. The man on the right is her father, U.S. Ambassador to Great Britain Joseph Kennedy. About 6 years after this photograph was taken, Rosemary, who had mild intellectual disability and whose behavior had become difficult to control, was subjected to a transorbital lobotomy. The results were disastrous, and she remained institutionalized until her death on January 7, 2005.

Emerging Techniques Some new noninvasive techniques for effecting changes in the brain were discussed in *Chapter Two: The Biological Perspective* including repetitive transcranial magnetic stimulation (rTMS), where magnetic pulses are applied to the cortex, and transcranial direct current stimulation (tDCS), which uses scalp electrodes to pass very low amplitude direct currents to the brain. These new and exciting strategies are being evaluated as possible treatment options for a variety of psychological disorders or in assisting researchers to better understand the brain mechanisms underlying them, including PTSD, depression, stroke, spinal cord injuries, and ADHD, along with many others (Adeyemo et al., 2012; Benito et al., 2012; Boggio et al., 2009; Cristancho et al., 2013; Helfrich et al., 2012; Nitsche et al., 2009). Another technique highlighted in Chapter Two is deep brain stimulation (DBS), and it is being evaluated as a treatment modality for both depression and OCD (Harvard Mental Health Letter, 2010; Huff et al., 2010). Exciting research is also investigating the use of DBS for individuals with chronic anorexia nervosa who have not responded well to other treatments, with initial results suggesting some individuals have improved body mass index (BMI), mood, and anxiety symptoms after DBS treatment (Lipsman et al., 2013).

▲ Repetitive transcranial magnetic stimulation (rTMS) uses a pulsating magnetic field to activate specific parts of the brain's surface. As seen above, by placing an electromagnet on the scalp, rTMS can be used to stimulate small areas of the cortex and is being evaluated as a way to control some psychological symptoms, such as those related to depression and PTSD.

34.2 Consider appropriate treatments for different age groups.

Concerns have arisen that children and teenagers taking newer antidepressant medications may have an increased risk of suicide versus those not receiving treatment. Recent meta-analyses have provided conflicting information, with some data suggesting an increased risk for suicide while other data does not support an increased risk (Gibbons et al., 2012; Hetrick et al., 2012). Where there is an increased risk, it is possible depressive symptoms are being addressed while suicidal thoughts and behavior are not reduced. Regardless, caution is urged, especially in children and teens being treated with newer antidepressant medications.

Thinking Critically
At what age do you think children and/or teenagers should be able to decide if they will take medications to treat abnormal psychological functioning or behavior?

Consider Legal, Ethical, and Professional Challenges in the Treatment of Psychological Disorders

34.3 Learn about ethical challenges involved in delivery of treatment.

Consider the following scenarios:

- Dr. A. is a social worker. One day, a client of hers admits to feeling out of control around his two children and regularly hitting them with a belt. Dr A. knows the importance of maintaining confidentiality but fears for the children's safety.
- Dr. B., a marriage counselor, is treating Mr. and Mrs. Smith. When Dr. B. occasionally sees Mrs. Smith alone, she flirts with him. During one such session, Mrs. Smith announces her plans to leave her husband. She confesses her attraction to Dr. B., who admits the feeling is mutual.
- Dr. C., a psychiatrist, has experience providing psychodynamic and humanistic therapy. A new client explains that he would like help in overcoming his social phobia using behavioral therapy. Dr. C has no formal training in this method.
- Dr. D., a psychologist, copies some patient files onto a laptop computer so he can catch up on work over the weekend. He stops at the supermarket on his way home. Upon returning to his car, he discovers that it has been broken into. The briefcase containing his laptop has been stolen.

These scenarios illustrate ethical issues that therapists face. By the nature of their work, they have access to great deal of personal information and may have a powerful influence over their clients' lives and well-being. With such power comes great responsibility. Good therapists take their ethical responsibilities to clients, other psychological professionals, and the community very seriously. Ethical issues fall into four broad categories:

- commitment to the client's well-being
- confidentiality and privacy
- professional boundaries and conflicts of interest
- competence and professionalism

Commitment to the Client's Well-Being Good therapists commit wholeheartedly to the therapeutic relationship and work to ensure that the client has an active, empowered role. When a client first seeks treatment, the therapist will determine whether he or she can meet the client's needs. A therapist who cannot take on a new client for some reason (such as a too-full schedule or lack of expertise with a certain problem) will attempt to refer the client elsewhere for treatment. In treatment, the therapist keeps the client informed—about what to expect; the therapist's and client's responsibilities; various treatments' purpose, risks, and benefits; and any other relevant issues. The principle here is "informed consent."

Before prescribing a new medication, a psychiatrist must inform the client about potential side effects. If a client is not fluent in English, the therapist must still ensure that treatment decisions are communicated clearly. Self-determination is also important. The therapist's role is to help the client—not to direct every aspect of his or her life. Therapists must be careful not to exert excessive or unhealthy influence.

Finally, therapists stay committed until the client no longer needs them. Termination of the relationship should occur by mutual consent. If circumstances make it impossible to continue treatment—for instance, if the therapist is moving to another state—the therapist will help the client transition to another qualified provider. Simply not liking a patient isn't grounds for ending the relationship; however, if interpersonal issues are so great that they interfere with treatment, the therapist may refer the patent elsewhere. (Good therapists also won't let therapy drag out for years if the client clearly doesn't need it or isn't improving. In those cases, the ethical thing to do would be to suggest termination or to help the client find someone who could better help them.)

Confidentiality and Its Limits To build trust, therapists must be able to assure the client that personal disclosures will remain confidential and privacy will be protected. Obviously, an ethical therapist would never gossip about clients or reveal information shared in confidence to the client's spouse, employer, or other connections. Although therapists treating minors may update parents or guardians about the client's progress, they should not disclose information shared in therapy sessions.

Additionally, therapists must exercise discretion and omit potentially identifying details when discussing cases with colleagues and publishing articles or books. If the therapist wishes to record a session on audio or video, or have colleagues observe a session, it must be done with the client's consent. Finally, therapists follow strict guidelines for ensuring confidentiality of records, including destroying those records when appropriate. In the hypothetical scenario described above, Dr. D's carelessness grossly endangered clients' right to privacy.

What about Dr. A's dilemma? In situations where clients are clearly a danger to themselves or others, a therapist must break confidentiality and alert appropriate medical or legal professionals. (Behaviors that are illegal but do not endanger anyone, such as shoplifting, do not meet this criterion.) For instance, if a client revealed detailed plans to commit suicide, the therapist would be professionally obligated to seek emergency inpatient care. In many states, psychological professionals are among the people legally required to report suspected child abuse or neglect, so Dr. A should contact her local child protective services agency.

Professional Boundaries and Conflicts of Interest Ethical therapists must maintain appropriate professional boundaries and avoid conflicts of interest—that is, situations where the therapist's personal interests or motives might interfere with his or her professional obligations. To fulfill this responsibility, therapists avoid forming other types of relationships with the client—personal friendships, romantic relationships, business partnerships, and so on. Therapist also do not treat clients with whom they have a preexisting relationship, including family relationships.

In Dr. B's case, acting on or even revealing his attraction to Mrs. Smith would violate professional boundaries. It would also place his own interests above his obligations to both Mr. and Mrs. Smith. Therapists are prohibited from having romantic or sexual relationships with clients, and professional organizations also stipulate that, even if therapy is terminated, the therapist cannot enter into such a relationship for a period of years afterward. (It is also unacceptable to terminate therapy for the sake of pursuing a romantic or other personal relationship.)

Less dramatic, but still important, conflicts of interest include accepting gifts from a client, socializing together, and the like. While it is important for therapists and clients to relate to each other as people, their relationship must have clearly defined limits.

Competence and Professionalism Finally, good therapists fulfill a high standard of competence and behave professionally not only with clients, but also with colleagues and with the psychology community as a whole. This responsibility encompasses a wide range of day-to-day actions. Good therapists are continually learning. They keep informed about new research, new therapeutic practices, and medical, social, or legal developments that affect the treatment they provide. They also represent themselves honestly—in person, in publications, and in any form of advertising or business promotion. They do not claim expertise they don't possess. In Dr. C's case, if she knows behavioral therapy would be the best treatment for her potential new client but she herself isn't qualified to provide it, the ethical choice would be to help the client find someone who is.

Many treatment professionals also have other responsibilities such as research, writing, or teaching. Just as they are expected to be thoughtful, ethical, and honest when treating clients, they must also bring these qualities to other aspects of their work, including their interactions with students, colleagues, employees they supervise, and others. This doesn't mean therapists never have a bad day or make a mistake—just that they hold themselves to a high standard.

34.4 Describe national and local resources available to support individuals with psychological disorders and their families.

Given the many different forms of therapy and the importance of choosing the best treatment, seeking help might seem like an overwhelming task. A person who needs a mental health specialist but isn't sure where to begin finding one might start by talking with another healthcare provider (such as a family doctor), a social services agency, or a student or employee assistance program. Additionally, numerous national and local resources are dedicated to helping people locate the services they need.

Several national organizations provide information about mental health services. One of the best known is the National Alliance on Mental Illness (NAMI; see more at www.nami.org). This grassroots organization advocates for patients and clients in several ways: through educating people about mental illness (and combating stigma), working to improve national policies, sponsoring initiatives such as walk-a-thons to raise money and awareness, and maintaining connections to more specialized support groups. NAMI has branches in all 50 states, and affiliated organizations also exist in many communities. Some affiliates provide support to specific groups, such as veterans, children, and adolescents.

Additionally, several other national organizations can help put people in touch with local treatment resources and support groups. These groups include Mental Health America (www.nmha.org), the American Self-Help Clearinghouse (www.mentalhelp.net/selfhelp/), the National Mental Health Consumers' Self-Help Clearinghouse (www.mhselfhelp.org/), and Network of Care (networkofcare.org/). Other national resources provide information and support for people coping with a specific problem or disorder. These include groups like the Depression and Bipolar Support Alliance (www.dbsalliance.org/) the National

Eating Disorders Association (www.nationaleatingdisorders.org), and the Anxiety Disorders Association of America (www.adaa.org/), to name just a few.

Local support groups exist to help people cope with many challenging situations—not only clinical psychological disorders but also specific life situations that can cause psychological symptoms. (For example, many adults experience profound grief and show signs of clinical depression after the death of a parent; support groups can help them cope.) Information about local support groups can be found in the phone book or online. Many support groups help people struggling with substance-abuse problems or addictive behaviors. These include 12-step groups with numerous local chapters, such as Alcoholics Anonymous and Gamblers Anonymous.

What mental health resources are available to students? Primary care doctors and school counselors can provide some basic services, and they can give students information about additional services and resources available in the community. A teacher or adult you trust can help you get in touch with your doctor or school counselor if you are looking for help, advice, or information.

▲ *Virtual reality can be used to expose patients to phobic objects and situations. Dr. JoAnn Difede, director of the Anxiety and Traumatic Stress Studies Program at Weill Cornell Medical College, left, has adapted virtual reality therapy to treat World Trade Center survivors.*

▲ *A soldier injured in the Lebanon war undergoes therapy with an Israeli-developed virtual reality "Computer Assisted Rehabilitation Environment" (CAREN) system.*

Applying Psychology to Everyday Life

Virtual Reality Therapies

Virtual reality is a software-generated three-dimensional simulated environment. Imagine yourself playing a video game, but instead of viewing your character on the screen in front of you, you are immersed in the visual and auditory world created by the game designers, seeing and hearing through the eyes and ears of your character. Although playing a video game in this manner might be a lot of fun, there are some very practical uses of virtual reality (VR) for treating psychological disorders.

One of the main uses of VR as a therapy incorporates exposure therapy of some form. Exposure therapy involves preventing a person with a phobia, for example, from avoiding the presentation of the phobic object—preventing the typical avoidance response and eventually resulting in extinction of the conditioned fear. Using VR ensures that the person being treated cannot avoid exposure, as the sight and sound of the animal, open spaces, or whatever the phobia involves is always right in front of him or her.

Posttraumatic stress disorder (PTSD) is another mental health issue benefiting from the use of VR psychotherapy. Cases of this disorder are rising and traditional treatments are not always effective. Although still a relatively new area of research, evidence suggests virtual reality psychotherapy may be as effective as traditional exposure methods in the treatment of PTSD and may especially be appealing for clients that do not want to pursue traditional exposure methods or techniques (Goncalves et al., 2012; Motraghi et al., 2013). Another advantage is the more vivid and realistic imagery possible with VR, especially for patients who are asked to "imagine" the scenarios that disturb them who may not be highly skilled in visualization. Think also of the portability of VR: There are currently handheld VR devices that eventually could be used to deliver therapy for PTSD, for example, to survivors of earthquakes, tsunamis, hurricanes, and other massive disasters around the world.

Questions for Further Discussion

1. What other disorders can you think of that might benefit from virtual reality psychotherapy?
2. Can you think of any disadvantages to this method of therapy?

Pick the best answer.

1. A class of drugs used to treat psychotic symptoms is called
   a. anticonvulsants.
   b. dopamine selectors.
   c. neuroleptics.
   d. selective serotonin reuptake inhibitors.

2. Which of the following treatments involves running a current through an electrode to destroy a small, specific area of brain cells?
   a. bilateral cingulotomy
   b. prefrontal lobotomy
   c. electroconvulsive therapy
   d. psychopharmacology

3. The main disadvantage of the benzodiazepines traditionally used to treat anxiety disorders is that benzodiazepines
   a. can be addictive.
   b. are slow to take effect.
   c. have many unpleasant side effects.
   d. cannot be combined with certain foods and beverages.

4. Tricyclic antidepressants treat depression by
   a. producing a sedative effect.
   b. suppressing dopamine receptors in the brain.
   c. affecting the transportation of sodium ions in cells.
   d. inhibiting the reuptake of serotonin and norepinephrine.

5. Drugs in the newest class of antidepressants, which includes Prozac and Paxil, have fewer side effects because
   a. these drugs inhibit serotonin reuptake, but not reuptake of norepinephrine and dopamine.
   b. these drugs inhibit the reuptake of norepinephrine, dopamine, and serotonin.
   c. these drugs inhibit norepinephrine and serotonin reuptake, but not reuptake of dopamine.
   d. these drugs inhibit dopamine and serotonin reuptake but have a limited effect on norepinephrine.

6. Which of the following is most commonly used to treat manic episodes and bipolar disorder?
   a. ECT
   b. MAOIs
   c. lithium
   d. psychosurgery

7. ECT, or electroconvulsive therapy, is most strongly associated with which of the following?
   a. temporary loss of memory
   b. apathy and lack of emotional response
   c. increased risk of suicidal behavior
   d. potentially dangerous increases in blood pressure

8. Which of the following statements about psychosurgery is true?
   a. Psychosurgery is a popular treatment for mental illness today.
   b. Psychosurgery is no longer performed in the United States.
   c. Psychosurgery is still performed today, but only as a last resort.
   d. Psychosurgery is never an ethical course of treatment.

9. Which of the following situations would most clearly create a conflict of interest for a therapist?
   a. discussing a client's problems with the therapist's colleagues
   b. forming a business partnership with a current client
   c. working with a client to set a mutually agreed-upon target end-date for therapy
   d. providing a teenage client's parents with a general update on the client's progress

10. Which of the following is a 12-step group designed to help people suffering from substance abuse?
    a. Alcoholics Anonymous
    b. Mental Health America
    c. Network of Care
    d. the National Alliance on Mental Illness (NAMI)

Listen to an Audio File of your chapter at MyPsychLab

Module 33: Psychological Treatments

Understand Perspectives on Treating Psychological Disorders

33.1 Discuss how psychological treatments have changed over time and among cultures.

- Mentally ill people began to be confined to institutions called asylums in the mid-1500s. Treatments were harsh and often damaging.
- Philippe Pinel became famous for demanding that the mentally ill be treated with kindness, personally unlocking the chains of inmates at Bicêtre Asylum in Paris, France.
- Psychotherapy today involves a person talking to a psychological professional about the person's problems.

33.2 Discuss why psychologists use a variety of treatment options.

- Today therapists largely use an eclectic approach and draw from a number of approaches to fit the client's need.
- Psychotherapy for the purpose of gaining understanding into one's motives and actions is called insight therapy, whereas psychotherapy aimed at changing disordered behavior directly is called action therapy.
- Biomedical therapy uses a medical procedure to bring about changes in behavior.

33.3 Discuss treatment providers for psychological disorders and the training required for each.

- Treatment providers include psychiatrists, psychologists, and psychiatric social workers.

Identify Psychological Treatments and Evaluate Their Effectiveness

33.4 Understand approaches to psychological treatments.

- Sigmund Freud developed a treatment called psychoanalysis that focused on releasing a person's hidden, repressed urges and concerns from the unconscious mind.
- Psychoanalysis helps patients reveal their unconscious concerns. Modern psychodynamic therapists take less time and are much more direct.
- Freud's original therapy technique is criticized for its lack of scientific research and his own personal biases that caused him to misinterpret much of what his patients revealed.
- Modern psychodynamic therapists have modified the technique so that it takes less time and is much more direct, and they do not focus on the id and sexuality as Freud did. Humanistic therapies focus on the conscious mind and subjective experiences to help clients gain insights.
- Person-centered therapy is very nondirective, allowing the client to talk through problems and concerns while the therapist provides a supportive background.
- The three basic elements of person-centered therapy are authenticity of the therapist in the client's perception, unconditional positive regard given to the client by the therapist, and the empathy of the therapist for the client.
- Humanistic therapies are also not based on experimental research and work best with intelligent, highly verbal persons.
- Behavior therapies are action therapies that do not look at thought processes but instead focus on changing the abnormal or disordered behavior itself through classical or operant conditioning.
- Classical conditioning techniques for changing behavior include systematic desensitization, aversion therapy, and exposure therapy.
- Therapies based on operant conditioning include modeling, reinforcement and the use of token economies, and extinction.
- Behavior therapies can be effective in treating specific problems, such as bed-wetting, drug addictions, and phobias, and can help improve some of the more troubling behavioral symptoms associated with more severe disorders.
- Cognitive therapy is oriented toward teaching clients how their thinking may be distorted and helping clients to see how inaccurate some of their beliefs may be.
- Some of the cognitive distortions in thinking include arbitrary inference, selective thinking, overgeneralization, magnification and minimization, and personalization.
- Cognitive–behavioral therapies are action therapies that work at changing a person's illogical or distorted thinking.
- The three goals of cognitive–behavioral therapies are to relieve the symptoms and solve the problems, to develop strategies for solving future problems, and to help change irrational, distorted thinking.
- Rational emotive behavior therapy is a directive therapy in which the therapist challenges clients' irrational beliefs, often arguing with clients and even assigning them homework.
- Although CBT has seemed successful in treating depression, stress disorders, and anxiety, it is criticized for focusing on the symptoms and not the causes of disordered behavior.
- Group therapy can be accomplished using many styles of psychotherapy and may involve treating people who are all part of the same family, as in family counseling.
- Group therapy can also be accomplished without the aid of a trained therapist in the form of self-help or support groups composed of other people who have the same or similar problems.
- Group therapy is most useful to persons who cannot afford individual therapy and who may obtain a great deal of social and emotional support from other group members.
- Group therapy has the advantages of low cost, exposure to other people with similar problems, social interaction with others, and social and emotional support from people with similar disorders or problems. It has also been demonstrated to be very effective for people with social anxiety.
- Disadvantages of group therapy can include the need to share the therapist's time with others in the group, the lack of a private setting in which to reveal concerns, and the inability of people with severe disorders to tolerate being in a group.

33.5 Evaluate the effectiveness of psychological treatments.

- Eysenck's early survey of client improvement seemed to suggest that clients would improve as time passed, with or without therapy.

- Surveys of people who have received therapy suggest that psychotherapy is more effective than no treatment at all.
- Surveys reveal that 75 to 90 percent of people who receive therapy report improvement, the longer a person stays in therapy the better the improvement, and psychotherapy works as well alone as with drugs.

33.6 Identify other factors that improve the effectiveness of treatment.
- Effective therapy should be matched to the particular client and the particular problem, there should exist a therapeutic alliance between therapist and client, and a protected setting in which clients can release emotions and reveal private thoughts is essential.
- When the culture, ethnic group, or gender of the therapist and the client differs, misunderstandings and misinterpretations can occur due to differences in cultural/ethnic values, socioeconomic differences, gender roles, and beliefs.
- The four barriers to effective psychotherapy that exist when the backgrounds of client and therapist differ are language, cultural values, social class, and nonverbal communication.
- Cybertherapy is therapy that is offered on the Internet. Cybertherapists may or may not be trained in psychotherapy, but cybertherapy offers the advantages of anonymity and therapy for people who cannot otherwise get to a therapist.

Module 34: Biomedical Treatments and Issues in Treatments

Identify Biomedical Treatments and Evaluate their Effectiveness.

34.1 Understand approaches to biomedical treatments and evaluate their effectiveness.
- Biomedical therapies include the use of drugs, induced convulsions, and surgery to relieve or control the symptoms of mental disorders.
- Antipsychotic drugs are used to control delusions, hallucinations, and bizarre behavior and include the typical antipsychotics, atypical antipsychotics, and partial dopamine agonists.
- Antianxiety drugs are used to treat anxiety and related disorders and include the benzodiazepines and certain antidepressant drugs.
- Antimanic drugs are used to treat bipolar disorder and include lithium and certain anticonvulsant drugs.
- Antidepressant drugs are used in the treatment of depression and include monoamine oxidase inhibitors

(MAOIs), tricyclic antidepressants, and selective serotonin reuptake inhibitors (SSRIs).
- Electroconvulsive therapy, or ECT, is used to treat severe depression, bipolar disorder, and schizophrenia and involves the use of a muscle relaxant, a short-term anesthetic, and induction of a seizure under controlled conditions.
- One of the earliest psychosurgeries was the prefrontal lobotomy, in which the front part of the frontal lobe was cut away from the back part of the brain, producing effects ranging from a disappearance of symptoms to a lack of emotional response and dulling of mental abilities.
- Modern psychosurgery includes the bilateral cingulotomy, used to treat major depression, bipolar disorders, and certain forms of obsessive-compulsive disorder that have not responded to other forms of treatment.

34.2 Consider appropriate treatments for different age groups.
- Currently researchers are examining the effects of psychoactive prescription drugs and the effects on the behavior of young people.

Consider Legal, Ethical, and Professional Challenges in the Treatment of Psychological Disorders

34.3 Learn about ethical challenges involved in delivery of treatment.
- Therapists' ethical challenges include the responsibility of maintaining a relationship with the client; the need to maintain confidentiality; the need to maintain professional boundaries; and the need to be professional in dealing with clients.

34.4 Describe national and local resources available to support individuals with psychological disorders and their families.
- Resources include national advocacy organizations, organizations that provide support for people with a specific disorder, local support groups, and community health centers.

Applying Psychology to Everyday Life: Virtual Realities
- Virtual reality therapy is a computer-based simulation of environments that can be used to treat disorders such as phobias and PTSD with less risk than that of actual exposure to anxiety-provoking stimuli.
- Virtual reality therapy is particularly useful as a delivery system for exposure therapy.

Vocabulary Terms

action therapy p. 441
biomedical therapies p. 441
eclectic p. 441
insight therapy p. 441
psychotherapy p. 441
therapy p. 441
counselor p. 442
psychiatrist p. 442
psychoanalysis p. 442
psychologist p. 442
directive p. 443

free association p. 443
latent content p. 443
nondirective p. 444
person-centered therapy p. 444
reflection p. 444
applied behavior analysis (ABA) p. 445
aversion therapy p. 445
behavior therapies p. 445
biomedical therapies p. 445
systematic desensitization p. 445

exposure therapy p. 446
flooding p. 446
modeling p. 446
token economy p. 446
cognitive therapy p. 447
cognitive–behavioral therapy (CBT) p. 448
rational emotive behavior therapy (REBT) p. 448
group therapy p. 450

support groups (self-help groups) p. 450
cybertherapy p. 451
psychopharmacology p. 455
biomedical therapies p. 455
electroconvulsive therapy (ECT) p. 458
prefrontal lobotomy p. 459
psychosurgery p. 459

Vocabulary Review

Match each vocabulary term to its definition.

1. insight therapies
2. cognitive–behavioral therapy (CBT)
3. nondirective
4. eclectic therapies
5. benzodiazepines
6. contingency contracting
7. reflection
8. action therapy
9. token economy
10. psychopharmacology

a. Term used to describe a therapy style in which the therapist remains relatively neutral and does not interpret or take direct actions with regard to the client, instead remaining a calm, nonjudgmental listener while the client talks.

b. Therapy in which the goal is to help clients overcome problems by learning to think more rationally and logically.

c. Drugs that lower anxiety and reduce stress.

d. Therapy in which the main goal is to change disordered or inappropriate behavior directly.

e. The use of drugs to control or relieve the symptoms of psychological disorders.

f. Therapies that strive to help clients understand their thoughts, feelings, and behaviors.

g. A therapy that uses secondary reinforcements to change behavior.

h. Therapy style that results from combining elements of several different therapy techniques.

i. A kind of mirroring of clients' statements.

j. The use of a formal, written agreement between the therapist and client (or other parties) that clearly states behavioral goals, reinforcements, and penalties.

Psychology Project

How do psychological professionals collaborate on treatment approaches? Complete this project to improve your understanding of different therapeutic approaches.

Materials:
- three partners (to form a group of four)
- access to print or electronic reference resources
- a pencil and paper, or other note-taking materials

Instructions:

1. Assign the following roles to the four members of your group: Case Manager, Action-oriented Therapist, Insight-oriented Therapist, Biomedically-oriented Therapist.

2. Have the Case Manager complete a one- to two-paragraph description of a client suffering from a common psychological disorder. You may wish to consult *Chapter Thirteen: Psychological Disorders*, or other references. Include specific details.

3. Have each of the therapists review the available methods in his or her assigned treatment category and choose the most appropriate method to treat the client's particular problem.

4. Have each of the therapists complete a one- to two-paragraph description of how and why you would use your chosen method to treat the client's problem. Include advantages and possible disadvantages of using this method.

5. As a group, come to an agreement about the best treatment plan for this client. Is there any one method that clearly stands out as the best for this particular problem, or would it make sense to combine methods? If so, why? Based on the group discussion, have the Case Manager write a paragraph summarizing which treatment method(s) will be used and why.

Tech Alternative

Open your favorite Web browser and do a search for "computer therapist." You will quickly find a number of links to ELIZA. ELIZA is a keyboard-based software interface that emulates a Rogerian psychotherapist. Experiment with ELIZA by typing in comments and reading the responses. What type of questions work well? What type of questions do not work well? How convincing is ELIZA as a therapist? What improvements could be made to ELIZA to help people seeking therapy?

Write your responses to the question prompts and a paragraph describing your experience to complete your assignment.

Essay Question

Matilda becomes anxious whenever she has to speak in public, and she has developed a phobia of public speaking. In a well-organized essay, describe how Matilda's anxiety and phobia would be treated in the context of *two* of the following therapies:

a. Psychodynamic therapy
b. Behavior therapy
c. Cognitive therapy
d. Biomedical therapy

Test Yourself

Ready for your test? More quizzes and a customized plan.

✓ **Study and Review** at **MyPsychLab**

Pick the best answer.

1. Clara is going to a therapist to gain a better understanding of why she has self-destructive relationships with all her friends. This type of therapy is known as _____ therapy.
   - a. insight
   - b. action
   - c. behavioral
   - d. biomedical

2. Through the use of _____, a person-centered therapist conveys they are trying to understand the experience of the person they are working with.
   - a. reflection
   - b. unconditional positive regard
   - c. empathy
   - d. authenticity

3. Ioana is seeing a psychodynamic therapist. She begins to feel safe and protected by the psychodynamic therapist, the same way she feels about her parents. Freud would most likely argue that Ioana is experiencing
   - a. latency.
   - b. resistance.
   - c. transference.
   - d. free association.

4. Which of the following clients would probably get the least benefit from a humanistic therapy?
   - a. Corbin, who is bright but confused about self-image
   - b. Cole, who is very talkative and open in discussing feelings
   - c. Colleen, who enjoys exploring the inner workings of the mind
   - d. Cody, who has a hard time putting thoughts and feelings into words in a logical manner

5. To overcome her fear of balloons, because of the loud sound they might suddenly make should they pop, Bella must sit in a room filled with balloons while the therapist continuously pops each one. After a while, Bella realizes that her fear is unjustified and even begins to pop balloons herself. This technique is known as
   - a. systematic desensitization.
   - b. aversion therapy.
   - c. flooding.
   - d. extinction.

6. Maria sat down with her daughter, Zoe, and together wrote out a list of things that Zoe was expected to do each day and the rewards she would get if she accomplished them, as well as the penalties she would face if she did not do them. This is most like which technique?
   - a. token economy
   - b. time-out
   - c. extinction
   - d. contingency contracting

7. For both children and adults, and for many undesirable behaviors, the use of _____ or some form of "time-out" can be quite effective.
   - a. arbitrary inference
   - b. extinction
   - c. positive reinforcement
   - d. negative reinforcement

8. Stephan gets a text message from his girlfriend saying that she will have to work overtime tonight. Stephan immediately assumes his girlfriend is seeing someone else at work. Beck would say that Stephan has engaged in what type of distorted thinking?
   - a. arbitrary inference
   - b. selective thinking
   - c. overgeneralization
   - d. personalization

9. Devin's wife comes home angry from her job, and he immediately assumes that he has done something wrong. Such irrational thinking is an example of
   - a. overgeneralization.
   - b. personalization.
   - c. arbitrary inference.
   - d. selective thinking.

10. Which therapy style requires the therapist to actively confront a client's irrational beliefs?
    - a. person-centered
    - b. frontal lobotomy
    - c. rational emotive behavior therapy (REBT)
    - d. cognitive restructuring

11. Family therapy is a form of group therapy in which
    - a. nonprofessionals lead a group of family members.
    - b. the entire family participates as no one person is seen as the problem.
    - c. family members meet to single out an individual.
    - d. psychology professionals treat their own family.

12. Using one, or a combination, of any number of therapeutic treatments depending on the situation is an example of a(n)_____ approach.
    - a. behavioral
    - b. retroactive
    - c. medical
    - d. eclectic

13. Typical antipsychotic drugs work by blocking what neurotransmitter?
    - a. norepinephrine
    - b. serotonin
    - c. dopamine
    - d. epinephrine

14. Antipsychotic drug side effects like repetitive, involuntary jerks and movements of the face, lips, legs, and body make up a syndrome known as
    - a. agoraphobia.
    - b. neurolepsis.
    - c. tardive dyskinesia.
    - d. psychotic syndrome.

15. Which of the following is not an ethical principle of mental health treatment?
    - a. The therapist must permit the client to give informed consent before starting treatment.
    - b. The therapist must direct as many aspects of the client's life as possible to help the client fully recover.
    - c. The therapist and the client should end their relationship through mutual consent.
    - d. The therapist should not gossip about clients.

Learning Objectives

 33.1 33.2 33.3 pp. 440–442

Understand Perspectives on Treating Psychological Disorders

psychotherapy involves having the person with a psychological problem talk with a psychological professional

biomedical therapy involves treating the person with a psychological problem using biological or medical methods

Learning Objectives

  33.4 33.5 33.6 pp. 442–453

Identify Psychological Treatments and Evaluate Their Effectiveness

Freudian psychoanalysis (Sigmund Freud)
- uses **dream interpretation** and **free association** to uncover unconscious conflicts
- modern **psychodynamic therapy** is shorter, more direct, and more focused on transference

humanistic therapies
- **person-centered therapy** (Carl Rogers) emphasizes sense of self and reconciling one's real self and ideal self

cognitive therapies
- **common thinking distortions**
- **cognitive–behavioral therapies (CBT)** address distorted thinking and the resulting behavioral responses; may involve behavioral techniques

effectiveness of therapy
- Eysenck (1957) found psychotherapy made no difference in improvement
- recent surveys find that many people feel psychotherapy has helped them

behavior therapies

classical conditioning techniques:
- systematic desensitization
- aversion therapy
- flooding

operant conditioning techniques:
- **reinforcement** techniques
- modeling
- shaping
- extinction

group therapies involve gathering a group of people with similar problems; may or may not involve a trained therapist

factors influencing effectiveness of therapy
- length of therapy
- **therapeutic alliance** between patient and therapist
- differences in cultural or ethnic background
- gender differences

Treatments

34.1 **34.2**   pp. 455–461

Map the Concepts at MyPsychLab

Identify Biomedical Treatments and Evaluate their Effectiveness

psychopharmacology is the use of drugs to control or relieve the symptoms of a psychological disorder

- **antipsychotic drugs**
- **antidepressant drugs**
- **antianxiety drugs**
- **antimanic drugs**

electroconvulsive therapy involves delivering an electric shock to one side (**unilateral ECT**) or both sides (**bilateral ECT**) of a person's head

psychosurgery involves cutting into the brain to remove or destroy brain tissue and thereby relieve psychiatric symptoms

34.3 **34.4**   pp. 461–464

Consider Legal, Ethical, and Professional Challenges in the Treatment of Psychological Disorders

ethical issues in therapy

- requires intense commitment to clients' well-being
- confidentiality and privacy issues
- boundaries and conflicts of interest
- competence and professionalism

resources and support

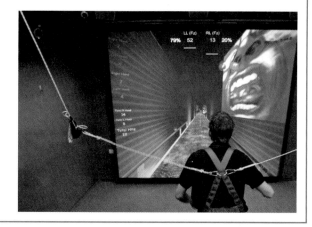

- national organizations (e.g., NAMI) that provide information about mental health services
- national organizations that address specific disorders
- local support groups
- community mental health centers

CHAPTER

15 Stress and Health

Secretary to psychologist: "Doctor, there is a patient here who thinks he is invisible."
Psychologist: "Tell him I can't see him right now."
Why begin a chapter on stress and health with a joke? Researchers have long known that humor is a great stress reliever and have recently found two possible reasons for the stress-reducing benefits of laughter. In one study, researchers found that laughing cannot only significantly increase levels of health-protecting hormones, but also just looking forward to a positive and humorous laughing experience can significantly decrease levels of potentially damaging hormones (Berk et al., 2008). Another study found that repetitive, joyous laughter causes the body to respond as if receiving moderate exercise, which enhances mood and immune system activity, lowers both bad cholesterol and blood pressure, raises good cholesterol, and decreases stress hormones (Berk et al., 2009). The moral of the story: Laugh it up!

What are some common sources of stress in your life? How do you cope with or relieve stress?

Watch the **Video**, at **MyPsychLab**

$\mathcal{W}$hy Study Stress and Health?

How are they related? Stress, good and bad, is not a rare experience but something that all people experience in varying degrees every day. This chapter will explore the sources of stress in daily life, the factors that can make the experience of stress easier or more difficult, and the ways that stress influences our physical and mental health. We'll finish by discussing various ways to cope with the stresses of everyday life as well as with the extraordinary experiences that arise in life that have the potential to induce stress.

35 Stress and Stressors

Module Goal

Understand the causes
and consequences of
stress.

Learning Objectives

35.1 Define stress.

35.2 Identify and explain sources of stress.

35.3 Discuss psychological and physiological
consequences of stress.

Understand the Causes and Consequences of Stress

Life is really about change. Every day, each person faces some kind of challenge, big or small. Just deciding what to wear to school can be a challenge for some people, whereas others find the morning commute the most challenging part of the day. There are decisions to be made and changes that will require adapting plans already made. Sometimes there are actual threats to well-being—an accident, a fight with friends, a failed exam, or a parent's job loss, to name a few. All of these challenges, threats, and changes require people to respond in some way.

35.1 Define stress.

Stress is the term used to describe the physical, emotional, cognitive, and behavioral responses to events that are judged to be threatening or challenging.

Stress can show itself in many ways. Physical problems can include unusual fatigue, sleeping problems, frequent colds, and even chest pains and nausea. People under stress may behave differently, too: pacing, eating too much, crying a lot, or physically striking out at others. Emotionally, people under stress experience anxiety, depression, fear, and irritability, as well as anger and frustration. Mental symptoms of stress include problems in concentration, memory, and decision making, and people under stress often lose their sense of humor.

Most people experience some degree of stress on a daily basis, and students are even more likely to face situations and events that require them to make changes and adapt their behavior: Assigned readings, papers, studying for tests, juggling part-time jobs, relationships, and dealing with deadlines are all examples of things that can cause a person to experience stress. Some people feel the effects of stress more than others because what is appraised as a threat by one person might be appraised as an opportunity by another. (For example, think of how you and your friends might respond differently to the opportunity to write a 10-page paper for extra credit in the last 3 weeks of the semester.) Stress causing events are called *stressors*; they can come from within a person or from an external source and range from relatively mild to severe.

Stressors can range from the deadly serious (hurricanes, fires, crashes, combat) to the merely irritating and annoying (delays, rude people, losing your house keys). Stressors can even be imaginary, as when a student puts off opening a report card, imagining that it will be full of failing grades, or when a parent imagines the worst happening to a teenage child who hasn't come home from an evening out.

I feel like ▶
that
most
of the
time!

stress the term used to describe the physical, emotional, cognitive, and behavioral responses to events that are appraised as threatening or challenging.

Actually, there are two kinds of stressors: those that cause **distress**, which occur when people experience unpleasant stressors, and those that cause *eustress*, which occurs when people experience stress from positive events. Hans Selye (ZEL-yeh) coined the term *eustress* to describe the stress experienced when positive events require the body to adapt or change (1936). Starting college, getting married, and earning a job promotion may all be positive events for most people, but they all require a great deal of adaptation or change in people's habits, duties, and even lifestyle, thereby creating stress.

In an update of Selye's original definition, researchers now define **eustress** as the optimal amount of stress that people need to promote health and well-being. The arousal theory is based on the idea that a certain level of stress, or arousal, is actually necessary for people to feel content (Zuckerman, 1994). Ⓛⓘⓝⓚ to *Chapter Eleven: Motivation and Emotion, p. 350.* That is, that arousal can be viewed in terms of eustress. For example, many students are aware that experiencing a little anxiety or stress is helpful to them because it motivates them to study. Without the eustress created by the impending exam, many students might not study very much or at all.

What about the student who is so stressed out that everything he's studied just flies right out of his head? Obviously, a high level of anxiety concerning an impending exam that actually interferes with the ability to study or to retrieve the information at exam time is not eustress but is, in fact, distress. The difference is not only in the degree of anxiety but also in how the person *interprets* the exam situation. A number of events, great and small, good and bad, can cause us to feel "stressed out."

▲ *Taking a test is just one of many possible stressors in a high school student's life. What aspects of high school life have you found to be stressful? Do other students experience the same degree of stress in response to the same stressors?*

35.2 Identify and explain sources of stress.

Environmental Factors: Life's Ups and Downs

Losing one's home in a tornado is an example of a stressor called a catastrophe, an unpredictable event that happens on a large scale and creates tremendous amounts of stress and feelings of threat. Wars, hurricanes, floods, fires, airplane crashes, and other disasters are catastrophes. The terrorist-driven destruction of the World Trade Center in New York City on September 11, 2001, is a prime example of a catastrophe. In one study, nearly 8 percent of the people living in the area near the attacks developed a severe stress disorder, and nearly 10 percent reported symptoms of depression even as late as 2 months after the attack (Galea et al., 2002). Another example of a catastrophe was the devastation caused by Hurricane Katrina on August 29, 2005. A Category 3 hurricane when it made landfall in Louisiana, Katrina laid waste to the north-central coastal area of the Gulf of Mexico. In New Orleans, the damage from Katrina was increased by the failure of the levees to hold back flood waters. Eighty percent of the city and many neighboring areas were flooded for weeks (Swenson & Marshall, 2005).

Thankfully, most people do not have to face the extreme stress of a catastrophe. But stress is present even in relatively ordinary life experiences and does not have to come from only negative events, such as job loss. Sometimes there are big events, such as going to college, getting married, or having a baby, that also require a person to make adjustments and changes—and adjustments and changes are really the core of stress, according to early researchers in the field (Holmes & Rahe, 1967).

distress the effect of unpleasant and undesirable stressors.

eustress the effect of positive events, or the optimal amount of stress that people need to promote health and well-being.

Holmes and Rahe (1967) believed that any life event that required people to change, adapt, or adjust their lifestyles would result in stress. Like Selye, they assume that both negative events (such as getting fired) and positive events (such as getting a promotion) demand that a person adjust in some way, and so both kinds of events are associated with stress. Holmes and Rahe devised a way to measure the amount of stress in a person's life by having that person add up the total "life change units" associated with each major event in their Social Readjustment Rating Scale (SRRS) (see **Table 35.1**).

Table 35.1	Items from the Social Readjustment Rating Scale (SRRS)
MAJOR LIFE EVENT	LIFE CHANGE UNITS
Death of spouse	100
Divorce	75
Marital separation	65
Jail term	63
Death of a close family member	63
Personal injury or illness	53
Marriage	50
Dismissal from work	47
Marital reconciliation	45
Pregnancy	40
Death of close friend	37
Change to different line of work	36
Change in number of arguments with spouse	36
Major mortgage	31
Foreclosure of mortgage or loan	30
Begin or end school	26
Change in living conditions	25
Change in work hours or conditions	20
Change in residence/schools/recreation	19
Change in social activities	18
Small mortgage or loan	17
Vacation	13
Christmas	12
Minor violations of the law	11

Source: Adapted and abridged from Holmes & Rahe (1967).

When an individual adds up the points for each event that has happened to him or her within the past 12 months (and counting points for repeat events as well), the resulting score can provide a good estimate of the degree of stress being experienced by that person. The researchers found that certain ranges of scores on the SRRS could be associated with increased risk of illness or accidents. (Warning: Table 35.1 is *not* a complete listing of the original 43 events and associated life change units and should not be used to calculate a stress "score"! If you would like to calculate your SRRS score, try this free site: **http://www. stresstips.com/lifeevents.htm**).

Scores of 150 or below were not associated with any significant problems, but scores between 150 and 199 were considered a "mild life crisis" and associated with a 33 percent increase in the risk of that person experiencing an illness or accident in the near future (when compared to persons not experiencing any crisis). Scores between 200 and 299 were labeled "moderate life crisis" and associated with a 50 percent increase in risk, whereas scores over 300 were considered a "major life crisis" and represented an 80 percent increase in risk (Holmes & Masuda, 1973). Simply put, if a person's score is 300 or above, that person has a very high chance of becoming physically or mentally ill or having an accident (caused by stress-related distractions) in the near future.

The SRRS as it was originally designed seems more appropriate for adults who are already established in their careers. There are variations of the SRRS that use as life events some of those things more likely to be experienced by teenagers and young adults. One of these variations is the College Undergraduate Stress Scale (CUSS) (Renner & Mackin, 1998). This scale looks quite different from Holmes and Rahe's original scale because the stressful events listed and rated include those that would be more common or more likely to happen to a college student. Some of the higher stress items on the CUSS include rape, a close friend's death, contracting a sexually transmitted disease also final exam week and flunking a class. Some of the lower stress items include peer pressure, homesickness, falling asleep in class, pressure to make high grades, and dating concerns.

Ah, but if you fall asleep in class, even if the teacher doesn't catch on, you'll miss everything that happened in class that day. You might then have to borrow a friend's notes, copy out the notes yourself, try to read your friend's handwriting, and so on—all of which can be stressful situations. Actually, all the events listed on both the SRRS and the CUSS are stressful not just because some of them are emotionally intense but also because there are so many little details, changes, adjustments, adaptations, frustrations, and delays that are caused by the events themselves. The death of a spouse, for example, rates 100 life change units because it requires the greatest amount of adjustment in a person's life. A lot of those adjustments are the little details: planning the funeral, getting the notice in the obituaries, and eventually deciding what to do with the spouse's belongings. Although it's easy to think about big disasters and major changes in life as sources of stress, the bulk of the stress we experience daily actually comes from little frustrations, delays, irritations, minor disagreements, and similar annoyances. These daily annoyances are called **hassles** (Lazarus, 1993; Lazarus & Folkman, 1984).

Lazarus and Folkman (1984) developed a "hassles" scale that has items such as "misplacing or losing things" and "troublesome neighbors." A person taking the test for hassles would rate each item in the scale in terms of how much of a hassle that particular item was for the person. The ratings range from 0 (no hassle or didn't occur) to 3 (extremely severe hassle). Whereas the major life events of Holmes and Rahe's scale (1967) may have a long-term effect on a person's chronic physical and mental health, the day-to-day minor annoyances, delays, and irritations that affect immediate health and well-being are far better predictors of short-term illnesses such as headaches, colds, backaches, and similar symptoms (Burks & Martin, 1985; DeLongis et al., 1988; Dunn et al., 2006).

A recent study has indicated that hassles may also come from quite different sources depending on a person's developmental stage (Ellis et al., 2001). In this study, researchers surveyed 270 randomly selected people from ages 3 to 75. The participants were asked to check off a list of daily hassles and pleasures associated

hassles the daily annoyances of everyday life.

Wait, how can falling asleep in class be ◄ stressful? It's what happens when the teacher catches you that's stressful, isn't it?

▼ *Children in the preschool-age range find teasing by their peers to be the biggest daily hassle they experience. This boy may be upset because he has been teased by the other children. What other hassles might a child in this age range experience?*

burnout negative changes in thoughts, emotions, and behavior as a result of prolonged stress or frustration, leading to feelings of exhaustion.

acculturative stress stress resulting from the need to change and adapt a person's ways to the majority culture.

with having "bad days" and "good days," respectively, as well as ranking the hassles in terms of frequency and severity of impact. For children ages 3–5, getting teased was the biggest daily hassle. For children in the 6–10 age group, the biggest hassle was getting bad grades. Children 11–15 years old reported feeling pressured to use drugs, whereas older adolescents (ages 16–22) cited trouble at school or work. Adults found fighting among family members the greatest source of stress, whereas the elderly people in the study cited a lack of money. No matter how old you are, however, chances are extremely good that you will have to put up with day-to-day annoyances and frustrations that can increase your levels of stress.

Social Factors: Poverty, Job Stress, and Culture Sometimes, a source of stress is social: Much of the stress in everyday life comes from our interactions with other people and our own place in society. Two of the more prominent social factors that contribute to stress are poverty and job stress.

Living in poverty is stressful for many reasons. Lack of sufficient money to provide the basic necessities of life can lead to many stressors for both adults and children: overcrowding, lack of medical care, increased rates of disabilities due to poor prenatal care, noisy environments, increased rates of illness (such as asthma in childhood) and violence, and substance abuse (Aligne et al., 2000; Bracey, 1997; Leroy & Symes, 2001; Park et al., 2002; Renchler, 1993; Rouse, 1998; Schmitz et al., 2001).

Even if a person has a job and is making an adequate salary, there are stresses associated with the workplace that add to daily stressors. Some of the typical sources of stress in the workplace include the workload, a lack of variety or meaningfulness in work, lack of control over decisions, long hours, poor physical work conditions, and lack of job security (Murphy, 1995).

▲ Poverty can lead to many conditions that increase the degree of stress experienced by both adults and children. These children, for example, may face an increased risk of malnutrition, illness, and exposure to violence because of the conditions under which they must live.

One of the more serious effects of workplace stress is a condition called burnout. **Burnout** can be defined as negative changes in thoughts, emotions, and behavior as a result of prolonged stress or frustration (Miller & Smith, 1993). Symptoms of burnout are extreme dissatisfaction, pessimism, lowered job satisfaction, and a desire to quit. Although burnout is most commonly associated with job stress, students can also suffer from burnout when the stresses of school life—term papers, exams, assignments, and the like—become overwhelming.

The emotional exhaustion associated with burnout can be lessened when a person at risk of burnout is a member of a social group within the work environment that provides support and the motivation to continue to perform despite being exhausted (Halbesleben & Bowler, 2007).

When a person from one culture must live in another culture, that person may experience a great deal of stress. *Acculturation* means the process of adapting to a new or different (often dominant) culture (Sodowsky et al., 1991). The stress resulting from the need to change and adapt to the dominant or majority culture is called **acculturative stress** (Berry & Kim, 1998; Berry & Sam, 1997). Ⓛ Ⓘ Ⓝ Ⓚ to Chapter Eight: Sociocultural Diversity and Gender, p. 267.

The method that a minority person chooses to enter into the majority culture can also have an impact on the degree of stress that person will experience (Berry & Kim, 1988). One method is *integration*, in which the individual tries to maintain a sense of the original cultural identity while also trying to form a positive relationship with members of the dominant culture. For example, an integrated person will maintain a lot of original cultural traditions within the home and with immediate family members but will dress like the majority culture and adopt some of those characteristics as well. Some research has suggested that acculturative stress because of integration is usually low (Ward & Rana-Deuba, 1999). However, other researchers have suggested that this interpretation has been affected by confounding factors, and we may not truly understand the effect—if any—that integration has on mental health (Rudmin, 2010).

In *assimilation*, the minority person gives up the old cultural identity and completely adopts the majority culture's ways. In the early days of the United States, many immigrants were assimilated into the mainstream American culture, even changing their names to sound more "American." Assimilation leads to moderate levels of stress, most likely because of the loss of cultural patterns and rejection by other members of the minority culture who have not chosen assimilation (LaFromboise et al., 1993; Lay & Nguyen, 1998).

Separation is a pattern in which the minority person rejects the majority culture's ways and tries to maintain the original cultural identity. Members of the minority culture refuse to learn the language of the dominant culture, and they live where others from their culture live, socializing only with others from their original culture. Separation can result in a fairly high degree of stress.

The greatest acculturative stress will most likely be experienced by people who have chosen to be *marginalized*, neither maintaining contact with the original culture nor joining the majority culture. They essentially live on the "margins" of both cultures without feeling or becoming part of either culture. Marginalized individuals do not have the security of the familiar culture of origin or the acceptance of the majority culture and may suffer a loss of identity and feel alienated from others (Roysircai-Sodowsky & Maestas, 2000). Obviously, marginalized people have little in the way of a social-support system to help them deal with both everyday stresses and major life changes.

35.3 Discuss psychological and physiological consequences of stress.

Psychological Factors: Pressure, Lack of Control, and Frustration

Although many factors that contribute to stress come from the world around us, some stressful situations are caused or intensified by our thoughts and perceptions. **Pressure**, which occurs when people feel that they must work harder, work faster, or do more, is one of these psychological factors. Although some people claim to "work well under pressure," the truth is that pressure can have a negative impact on a person's ability to be creative. Psychologist Teresa Amabile has gathered research within actual work settings strongly indicating that when time pressure is applied to workers who are trying to come up with creative, innovative ideas, creativity levels decrease dramatically—even though the workers may think they have been quite productive because of the effort they have made (Amabile et al., 2002).

Another factor that increases a person's experience of stress is the degree of control that the person has over a particular event or situation. The less control a person has, the greater the degree of stress. In two studies carried out in a nursing home with the elderly residents as the participants, researchers Rodin and Langer (Langer & Rodin, 1976; Rodin & Langer, 1977) gave each of the residents a houseplant. Decisions about watering and how much sun each plant should have were up to each resident. These residents, who comprised the experimental group, were also given choices such as whether they wanted to see a weekly movie, on which of the two evenings that the movie was shown did they want to attend, and in what area or room they would like to see their visitors.

Participants in the control group, although also given plants, were told that the nurses would take care of the plants and were not encouraged to make decisions for themselves. The follow-up study took place a year and a half later. Using participation in activities, measures of happiness, and other assessments, the researchers found that those who had more control over their lives and who

▲ This Buddhist group is celebrating Songkran, the new year, by performing their cultural ritual of pouring water over their elder's palms. Although they are wearing clothing typical of people living in Los Angeles, California, where the ceremony is taking place, they still maintain some of their former cultural traditions. This is a good example of integration.

pressure the psychological experience produced by urgent demands or expectations for a person's behavior that come from an outside source.

frustration the psychological experience produced by the blocking of a desired goal or fulfillment of a perceived need.

general adaptation syndrome (GAS) the three stages of the body's physiological reaction to stress, including alarm, resistance, and exhaustion.

👁 **Watch** the **Video,**
The Physical Side of Stress, at
MyPsychLab

had been given more responsibility were more vigorous, active, and sociable than those in the control group.

Frustration occurs when people are blocked or prevented from achieving a desired goal or fulfilling a perceived need. As a stressor, frustration can be *external*, as when you're stuck in traffic on the way to an important event, you're cut from a sports team or a musical group, or your wallet is stolen. Losses, rejections, failures, and delays are all sources of external frustration. *Internal frustrations*, also known as *personal frustrations*, occur when a person's goal or need cannot be attained because of his or her internal or personal characteristics. A person who wants to be an engineer but has no math skills would find it difficult to attain that goal.

Obviously, some frustrations are minor and others are more serious. The seriousness of a frustration is affected by how important the goal or need actually is. A person who is delayed in traffic while driving to the mall to do some shopping just for fun will be less frustrated than a person who is trying to get to the mall before it closes to get that last-minute forgotten and important birthday gift.

Effects on Physical Health No matter where stress comes from—whether from major life events or daily hassles, from social conditions, or from a person's own pressures and frustrations—it can take a serious toll on our health. Even though stress is not a physical illness, it can actually damage the body, weaken the immune system, and make people more likely to develop a variety of health problems. The sympathetic and parasympathetic systems, and various hormones, figure prominently in our body's physiological reactions to stress. See the video, *The Physical Side of Stress,* for more information on this.

The General Adaptation Syndrome Endocrinologist Hans Selye was the founder of the field of research concerning stress and its effects on the human body. He studied the sequence of physiological reactions that the body goes through when adapting to a stressor. This sequence (see **Figure 35.1**) is called the **general adaptation syndrome (GAS)** and consists of three stages (Selye, 1956).

- **Alarm:** When the body first reacts to a stressor, the sympathetic nervous system is activated. The adrenal glands release hormones that increase heart rate, blood pressure, and the supply of blood sugar, resulting in a burst of energy. Reactions such as fever, nausea, and headache are common.
- **Resistance:** As the stress continues, the body settles into sympathetic division activity, continuing to release the stress hormones that help the body fight off, or resist, the stressor. The early symptoms of alarm lessen and the person or animal may actually feel better. This stage will continue until the stressor ends or the organism has used up all of its resources. Researchers have found that one of the hormones released under stress actually seems to affect the brain's processing of pain, so that when under stress a person may experience a kind of analgesia (insensitivity to pain) if, for example, the person hits their arm or shin (Delaney et al., 2007).
- **Exhaustion:** When the body's resources are gone, exhaustion occurs. Exhaustion can lead to the formation of stress-related diseases (e.g., high blood pressure or a weakened immune system) or the death of the organism if outside help is unavailable (Stein-Behrens et al., 1994). When the stressor ends, the parasympathetic division activates and the body attempts to replenish its resources.

Alarm and resistance are stages that people experience many times throughout life, allowing people to adapt to life's demands (Selye, 1976). It is the prolonged secretion of the stress hormones during the exhaustion stage that can lead to the most harmful effects of stress. It was this aspect of Selye's work that convinced

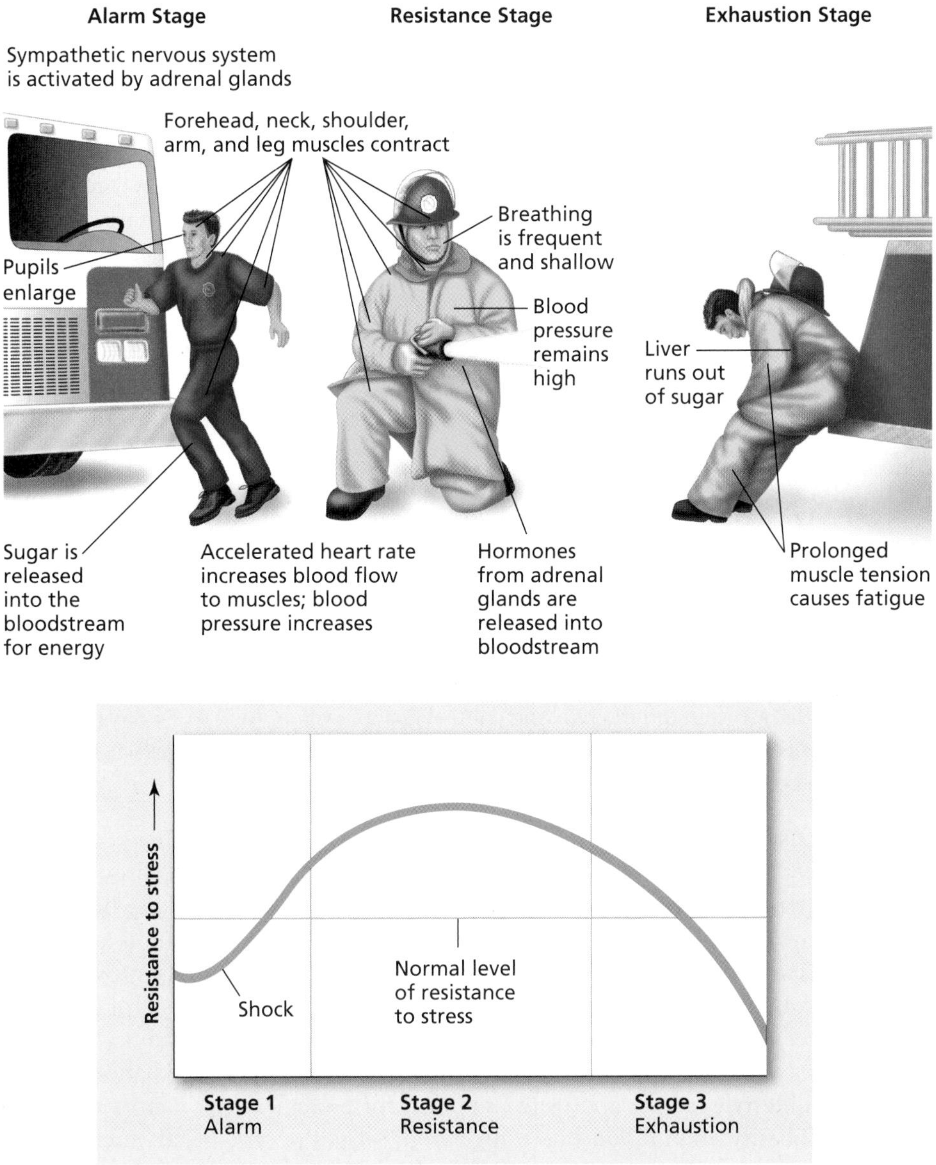

Alarm Stage

Sympathetic nervous system is activated by adrenal glands

Forehead, neck, shoulder, arm, and leg muscles contract

Pupils enlarge

Sugar is released into the bloodstream for energy

Accelerated heart rate increases blood flow to muscles; blood pressure increases

Resistance Stage

Breathing is frequent and shallow

Blood pressure remains high

Hormones from adrenal glands are released into bloodstream

Exhaustion Stage

Liver runs out of sugar

Prolonged muscle tension causes fatigue

Stage 1 Alarm · Stage 2 Resistance · Stage 3 Exhaustion — Resistance to stress — Shock — Normal level of resistance to stress

FIGURE 35.1 General Adaptation Syndrome

The diagram at the top shows some of the physical reactions to stress in each of the three stages of the general adaptation syndrome. The graph at the bottom shows the relationship of each of the three stages to the individual's ability to resist a stressor. In the alarm stage, resistance drops at first as the sympathetic system quickly activates. But resistance then rapidly increases as the body mobilizes its defense systems. In the resistance stage, the body is working at a much increased level of resistance, using resources until the stress ends or the resources run out. In the exhaustion stage, the body is no longer able to resist as resources have been depleted, and at this point disease and even death are possible.

other researchers of the connection between stress and certain *diseases of adaptation* as Selye termed them, such as high blood pressure.

Immune System and Stress As Selye first discovered, the *immune system* (the system of cells, organs, and chemicals in the body that responds to attacks on the body from diseases and injuries) is affected by stress. The field of *psychoneuroimmunology* concerns the study of the effects of psychological factors such as stress, emotions, thinking, learning, and behavior on the immune system (Ader, 2003; Cohen & Herbert, 1996; Kiecolt-Glaser, 2009; Kiecolt-Glaser et al., 1995, 1996, 2002). Researchers in this field have found that stress triggers the same response in the immune system that infection triggers (Maier & Watkins, 1998). Certain enzymes and other chemicals (including antibodies) are created by immune cells when the immune cells or white blood cells encounter an infection in the body. The white blood cells surround the bacteria or other infectious material and release the chemicals and enzymes into the bloodstream. From there, these chemicals activate receptor sites on the *vagus nerve*, the longest nerve that connects the body to the brain. It is the activation of these receptor sites that signals the brain that the body is sick, causing the brain to respond by further activation of the immune system.

Stress activates this same system but starts in the brain rather than in the bloodstream. The same chemical changes that occur in the brain when it has been alerted by the vagus nerve to infection in the body occurred in laboratory animals when they were kept isolated from other animals or given electric shocks (Maier & Watkins, 1998). This has the effect of "priming" the immune system, allowing it to more successfully resist the effects of the stress, as in Selye's resistance stage of the GAS.

Hormones also play a part in helping the immune system fight the effects of stress. Researchers (Morgan et al., 2009) have found that a hormone known to provide antistress benefits in animals, also aids humans in stress toleration—perhaps by regulating the effects of stress on the hippocampus (part of the limbic system).

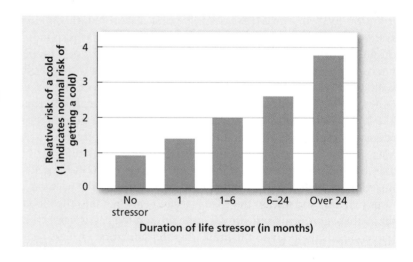

So stress actually ▶ increases the activity of the immune system? But then how does stress end up causing those diseases, like high blood pressure?

The positive effects of stress on the immune system only seem to work when the stress is not a continual, chronic condition. As stress continues, the body's resources begin to fail in the exhaustion phase of the general adaptation to stress (Kiecolt-Glaser et al., 1987, 1995, 1996; Prigerson et al., 1997). In one study, college students who were undergoing a stressful series of exams were compared to a group of similar students relaxing during a time of no classes and no exams (Deinzer et al., 2000). The exam group tested significantly lower for immune system chemicals that help fight off disease than did the relaxing control group, even as long as 14 days after the exams were over. The suppression of immune system functioning by stress apparently can continue even after the stress itself is over (**Figure 35.2**).

Heart Disease Of course, anything that can weaken the immune system can have a negative effect on other bodily systems. Stress has been shown to put people at a higher risk of *coronary heart disease (CHD)*, the buildup of a waxy substance called plaque in the arteries of the heart. This relationship is at least in part because the liver, which is not activated while the sympathetic nervous system is aroused, does not have a chance to clear the fat and cholesterol from the bloodstream, leading to clogged arteries and eventually the possibility of heart attacks or strokes. In one study, middle-aged men were questioned about stress, diet, and lifestyle factors and were examined for biological risk factors for heart disease: obesity, high blood sugar, high triglycerides (a type of fatty acid found in the blood), and low levels of HDL or "good" cholesterol. (The production of stress hormones were found to be strongly linked to all four biological risk factors. The more stress the men were exposed to in their work environment and home life, the more likely they were to exhibit these risk factors (Brunner et al., 2002).

FIGURE 35.2 Stress Duration and Illness
In this graph, the risk of getting a cold virus increases greatly as the months of exposure to a stressor increase. Although a stress reaction can be useful in its early phase, prolonged stress has a negative impact on the immune system, leaving the body vulnerable to illnesses such as a cold.
Source: Cohen et al. (1998).

Cancer Cancer is not one disease but rather a collection of diseases that can affect any part of the body. Unlike normal cells, which divide and reproduce according to genetic instructions and stop dividing according to those same instructions, cancer cells divide without stopping. The resulting tumors affect the normal functioning of the organs and systems they invade, causing them to fail, eventually killing the organism.

Although stress itself cannot directly give a person cancer, stress can have a suppressing effect on the immune system, making the unchecked growth of cancer more likely. In particular, an immune-system cell called a *natural killer (NK) cell* has as its main functions the suppression of viruses and the destruction of tumor cells (Herberman & Ortaldo, 1981). Stress has been shown to depress the release of natural killer cells, making it more difficult for the body's systems to fight cancerous growths (Zorilla et al., 2001). Stress may impact the effectiveness of cancer treatments as well. In one study of mice implanted with human prostate cancer cells, treatment with a drug to destroy the cancer cells and prevent growth of tumors was effective when the mice were kept calm and stress-free, but failed miserably when the mice were stressed (Hassan et al., 2013).

Other Health Issues Heart disease and cancer are not the only diseases affected by stress. As indicated earlier, weight problems may also become associated with stress. One chronic illness sometimes associated with excessive weight gain is *diabetes*, specifically *Type 2 diabetes* (Type 1 diabetes is associated with failure of the pancreas to secrete enough insulin, necessitating medication, and is usually diagnosed before the age of 40). Type 2 diabetes is associated with excessive weight gain and occurs when pancreas insulin levels become less efficient as the body size increases. Type 2 diabetes can respond favorably to proper diet, exercise, and weight loss, but may also require medication. Typically, it is associated with older adults, but with the rise in obesity among children, more cases of Type 2 diabetes in children are now occurring.

Studies have shown that children in families experiencing ongoing stress are more likely to develop fevers with illness than are other children (Wyman et al., 2007). (Oddly enough, this same study showed that in children, stress actually seems to improve the function of their natural killer cells, just the opposite effect that is seen in adults.)

Issues in Psychology

Health Psychology and Stress

In the last three decades, people have become more aware of health issues and their relationship to what we do, what we eat, who we see, and how we think. A relatively new branch of psychology has begun to explore these relationships. Health psychology focuses on how our physical activities, psychological traits, and social relationships affect our overall health and rate of illnesses. Psychologists who specialize in this field are typically clinical or counseling psychologists and may work with medical doctors in a hospital or clinic setting, although there are health psychologists who are primarily engaged in teaching and research. Some health psychologists focus on health and wellness issues in the workplace or public health issues such as disease prevention through immunizations or nutrition education. Others are more concerned with health-care programs that service all levels of the socioeconomic layers of society (Marks et al., 2005) as seen in the video, *The Big Picture: Health Psychology.*

Health psychologists seek to understand how behavior (such as use of drugs, optimism, personality, or the type of food one eats) can affect a

Watch the Video, *The Big Picture: Health Psychology*, at MyPsychLab

Watch the Video, *Special Topics: Health Disparities*, at **MyPsychLab**

person's ability to fight off illnesses—or increase the likelihood of getting sick. They want to know how to prevent illness, and how factors like poverty, wealth, religion, social support, personality, and even one's ethnicity can affect health. In this age of a new focus on health care, health psychology is destined to become a more important force in future research, as indicated in the video, *Special Topics: Health Disparities.*

Questions for Further Discussion

1. How have some of the factors studied by health psychologists affected you in recent months?
2. What health issues might arise in the high school setting that could have a positive or negative impact on your psychological and physical well-being?

Effects on Psychological Health People who experience high levels of stress are at risk not only for physical illnesses but also for mental illnesses, particularly a type of anxiety disorder called *acute stress disorder (ASD)*. ASD is a severe stress disorder suffered by people who experience a traumatic event, particularly a traumatic event that most humans don't experience in their lifetimes (like a natural disaster, a combat experience, or the death of a child). Symptoms of ASD occur within 4 weeks of the traumatic event and include anxiety, dissociative symptoms (such as emotional numbness/lack of responsiveness, not being aware of surroundings, and dissociative amnesia), recurring nightmares, sleep disturbances, problems in concentration, and moments in which people seem to "relive" the event in dreams and flashbacks for as long as 1 month following the event. One recently published study gathered survey information from Hurricane Katrina evacuees at a major emergency shelter and found that 62 percent of those sampled met the criteria for having ASD (Mills et al., 2007).

When the symptoms associated with ASD last for more than 1 month, the disorder is then called *post-traumatic stress disorder (PTSD)*. In that same study, researchers concluded that it was likely that anywhere from 38 to 49 percent of all the evacuees sampled were at risk of developing PTSD that would still be present 2 years after the disaster. Furthermore, whereas the onset of ASD occurs within 4 weeks of the traumatic event, the symptoms of PTSD may not occur until 6 months or later after the event (American Psychiatric Association, 2000). Treatment of these stress disorders may involve psychotherapy and the use of drugs to control anxiety. **LINK** to *Chapter Fourteen: Psychological Therapies and Treatments, pp. 438–471.*

Women seem to be more vulnerable to PTSD than men. Researchers have found that women have almost twice the risk of developing PTSD than do men and that the likelihood increases if the traumatic experience took place before the woman was 15 years old (Breslau et al., 1997, 1999). Children may also suffer different effects from stress than do adults. Severe PTSD has been linked to a decrease in the size of the hippocampus in children with the disorder (Carrion et al., 2007). The hippocampus is important in the formation of new long-term declarative memories and this may have a detrimental effect on learning and the effectiveness of treatments for these children. The rate of PTSD (self-reported) among combat-exposed military personnel has tripled since 2001 (Smith et al., 2008), so the problems associated with this long-term stress disorder are not going away any time soon.

Pick the best answer.

1. The optimal amount of stress that people need to promote their health and sense of well-being is called
   a. intensity.
   b. distress.
   c. eustress.
   d. acute stress.

2. Research has shown that _____have a long-term effect on physical and mental health, but _____ have a greater impact on short-term health.
   a. hassles; major life events
   b. major life events; hassles
   c. major life events; catastrophes
   d. hassles; catastrophes

3. Eduardo is on his way to an important job interview when his car breaks down on the highway. Eduardo is likely to experience what kind of frustration?
   a. external
   b. internal
   c. personal
   d. uncontrollable

4. In the _____ stage of the GAS, the person may actually start to feel better.
   a. alarm
   b. resistance
   c. exhaustion
   d. termination

5. The activation of the immune system response by stress differs from the activation of that system by illness in that
   a. illness activates areas in the brain first.
   b. stress increases the release of natural killer cells.
   c. illness increases the release of natural killer cells.
   d. stress activates areas in the brain first.

6. Which of the following is NOT a typical source of stress in the workplace?
   a. heavy workload
   b. lack of variety
   c. lack of shift work
   d. lack of job security

7. Larysa moved from Ukraine to the United States. She learned to speak and write English, changed her last name so that it would sound more "American," and no longer maintains any of her old culture's styles of dress or customs. Larysa has used which method of entering the majority culture?
   a. assimilation
   b. integration
   c. separation
   d. acute stress

8. Which of the following experiences is a better predictor of stress-related headaches?
   a. having a parent die
   b. becoming pregnant
   c. living through an earthquake
   d. misplacing important documents

9. Anxiety, recurring nightmares, sleep disturbances, and concentration problems that occur for more than 1 month after a major stressor are symptoms of
   a. acute stress disorder.
   b. post-traumatic stress disorder.
   c. general adaptation syndrome.
   d. general stress disorder.

10. Which of the following events is considered the most stressful, according to the Social Readjustment Rating Scale (SRRS)?
    a. death of a spouse
    b. divorce
    c. pregnancy
    d. dismissal from work

Coping with Stress and Promoting Wellness

Module Goal

Learn behaviors and attitudes that promote health.

Learning Objectives

36.1 Explain ways to promote mental health and physical fitness.

36.2 Discuss the characteristics of and factors that promote resilience and optimism.

36.3 Explain the differences between effective and ineffective means of dealing with stressors and other health issues.

---

coping strategies actions that people can take to master, tolerate, reduce, or minimize the effects of stressors.

problem-focused coping coping strategies that try to eliminate the source of a stress or reduce its impact through direct actions.

emotion-focused coping coping strategies that change the impact of a stressor by changing the emotional reaction to the stressor.

Learn Behaviors and Attitudes That Promote Health

36.1 Explain ways to promote mental health and physical fitness.

Coping strategies are actions that people can take to master, tolerate, reduce, or minimize the effects of stressors, and they can include both behavioral strategies and psychological strategies.

Problem-Focused Coping One type of coping strategy is to work on eliminating or changing the stressor itself. When people try to eliminate the source of a stress or reduce its impact through their own actions, it is called problem-focused coping (Folkman & Lazarus, 1980; Lazarus, 1993). For example, a student might have a problem understanding a particular teacher. The teacher is knowledgeable but has trouble explaining the concepts of the course in a way that this student can understand. **Problem-focused coping** might include talking to the teacher after class, asking fellow students to clarify the concepts, getting a tutor, or forming a study group with other students who are also having difficulty to pool the group's resources.

Emotion-Focused Coping Problem-focused coping can work quite well but is not the only method people can use. Most people use both problem-focused coping and emotion-focused coping to successfully deal with controllable stressful events (Eschenbeck et al., 2008; Folkman & Lazarus, 1980; Lazarus, 1993; Stowell et al., 2001). **Emotion-focused coping** is a strategy that involves changing the way a person feels or emotionally reacts to a stressor. This reduces the emotional impact of the stressor and makes it possible to deal with the problem more effectively. For example, the student who is faced with a professor who isn't easy to understand might share his or her concerns with a friend, talking it through until calm enough to tackle the problem in a more direct manner. Emotion-focused coping also works for stressors that are uncontrollable and for which problem-focused coping is not possible. Someone using emotion-focused coping may decide to view the stressor as a challenge rather than a threat, decide that the problem is a minor one, write down concerns in a journal, or even ignore the problem altogether.

True, ignoring a problem is not a good strategy when there is something a person can actively do about solving the problem. But when it is not possible to change or eliminate the stressor, or when worrying about the stressor can be a problem itself, ignoring the problem is not a bad idea. Researchers working with people who had suffered heart attacks found that those people who worried about a future attack were more likely to suffer from symptoms of severe stress, such as nightmares and poor sleep (both factors that increase the risk of a future heart attack), than were the people who tried to ignore their worries (Ginzburg et al., 2003).

Using humor can also be a form of emotion-focused coping, as the opening story to this chapter suggests. A study on the effects of laughter found that laughter actually boosted the action of the immune system by increasing the work of natural killer cells (cells that attack viruses in the body). In this study, participants were shown a humor video for 1 hour. Blood samples were taken 10 minutes before the viewing, 30 minutes into the viewing, 30 minutes after viewing, and 12 hours after viewing the humor video. There were significant increases in natural killer cell activity and nearly half a dozen other immune-system cells and systems, with some effects lasting the full 12 hours after the video ended (Berk et al., 2001).

Meditation and Relaxation as a Coping Mechanism Meditation is a series of mental exercises meant to refocus attention and achieve a trancelike state of consciousness. Meditation can produce a state of relaxation that can aid in coping with the physiological reactions to a stressful situation. When properly meditating, brain waves change to include more theta and alpha waves (indicating deep relaxation), but little to no delta waves, which would indicate deep sleep (Lagopoulos et al., 2009).

Have you ever found yourself staring out into space, or at some little spot on the wall or table, only to realize that your mind has been a complete blank for the last several minutes? The state just described is really nothing more than concentrative meditation, the form of meditation best known to the general public. In concentrative meditation, the goal is to focus the mind on some repetitive or unchanging stimulus (such as a spot or the sound of one's own heart beating) so that the mind can forget daily hassles and problems and the body can relax. In fact, Herbert Benson (Benson, 1975; Benson et al., 1974a, 1974b) found that meditation produces a state of relaxation in which blood pressure is lowered, alpha waves (brain waves associated with relaxation) are increased, and the amounts of melatonin secreted at night (the hormone that helps induce sleep) are increased.

Research shows that meditation is a good way to relax and lower blood pressure in adolescents and adults, men and women, and both Whites and African Americans (Barnes et al., 1997; Rainforth et al., 2007; Schneider et al., 1995; Wenneberg et al., 1997). It isn't the only way, as reading a good book or taking a warm bath also produces relaxation. Even simply resting for the same amount of time as one might meditate can be just as relaxing. The advantage of meditation is that people can do it almost anywhere, even in the classroom just before a big test. (It would be a little difficult to take a warm bath then.) Other research has suggested that meditation can reduce the levels of chronic pain (Brown & Jones, 2010; Kabat-Zinn et al., 1986), reduce the symptoms of anxiety, depression, and hostility (Kabat-Zinn et al., 1985), reduce the risk of heart disease (Schneider et al., 2010), and reduce stress levels in cancer patients (Speca et al., 2000). Reducing stress levels in cancer patients through meditation will increase the likelihood of recovery and reduce the incidence of recurrence.

Meditation for only 20 minutes can produce lowered blood pressure in people with hypertension (high blood pressure). It can calm anxiety, help people get to sleep, and help people deal with stress.

As mentioned above, meditation is only one way to relax. In addition to warm baths and reading a good book, there are a few techniques recommended

◄ Ignore it? But won't that just make matters worse?

▲ An audience watches what is obviously a funny movie, one of the more popular choices for filmgoers. A large part of the success of such comedies can be attributed to the human need to laugh—laughter helps us cope with many of life's stresses.

▲ This man is practicing Zen yoga meditation. Meditation increases relaxation and helps to lower blood pressure and muscle tension.

by experts to promote stress relief. One method is progressive muscle relaxation, in which you focus on tensing and then relaxing each of your muscle groups, usually beginning with the feet and working your way up the body. The purpose of this exercise is to help people recognize the difference between tense muscles and relaxed ones—we are often tensed up without realizing it. Another method is visualization, in which you use your imagination to "go" to a calm, peaceful place or situation, using as many of your senses as you can.

How Culture Affects Coping Imagine this scene: You are driving out in the country when you come upon an elderly man working on a large wooden box, polishing it with great care. You stop to talk to the man and find out that the box is his own coffin, and he spends his days getting it ready, tending to it with great care. He isn't frightened of dying and doesn't feel strange about polishing his own coffin. How would you react?

If you were from the same rural area of Vietnam as the elderly man, you would probably think nothing strange is going on. For elderly people in the Vietnamese culture, thoughts of death and the things that go along with dying, such as a coffin, are not as stressful as they are to people from Western cultures. In fact, stress isn't all that common a term in Vietnamese society compared to Western societies (Phan & Silove, 1999).

Coping with stress in Vietnamese culture may include rituals, consulting a fortune-teller, or eating certain foods (Phan & Silove, 1999). In many Asian cultures, meditation is a common stress-relief tool, including the art of tai chi, a form of meditational exercise (Yip, 2002).

Other examples of cultural differences in coping: Thai children are twice as likely to use emotion-focused coping methods when facing powerful adults (doctors giving shots, angry teachers, etc.) than are children in the United States (McCarty et al., 1999). Adolescents in Northern Ireland, when compared to those in Colombia and Australia, tend to blame themselves when experiencing stress over social issues (e.g., fear of war, community violence) but also use more social/emotional support (Frydenberg et al., 2001). The Colombian youth used more problem-focused coping, as well as spiritual support and taking social action. Even within subcultures, there are different forms of coping: In interviews with Asian American, African American, and Hispanic American people living in New York after the September 11 terrorist attacks, researchers found that while both African American and Hispanic American people reported using church attendance and other forms of religious coping, Asian Americans reported using acceptance of the event as something out of their control (Constantine et al., 2005; Kuo, 2011). Cultures also vary in how much they engage their social network to help them cope.

Obviously, culture is an important factor in the kinds of coping strategies an individual may adopt and even in determining the degree of stress that is experienced. Mental health professionals should make an effort to include an assessment of a person's cultural background as well as immediate circumstances when dealing with adjustment problems due to stress.

How Religion Affects Coping A belief in a higher power can also be a source of great comfort in times of stress. There are several ways that religious beliefs can affect the degree of stress people experience and the ability to cope with that stress (Hill & Butter, 1995; Pargament, 1997).

First, most people who hold strong religious beliefs belong to a religious organization and attend regular religious functions, such as services at a synagogue, mosque, temple, or

▼ These Peruvian villagers in a cemetery are honoring their loved ones who have passed away. The Day of the Dead is not only a celebration of the lives of those who have passed on but also a celebration for the living, who use this holiday to gain a sense of control over one of life's most uncontrollable events—death itself. What rituals or ceremonies do people of other cultures use to cope with death?

church. This membership can be a vital part of a person's social-support system. People do not feel alone in their struggle, both literally because of the people who surround them in their religious community and spiritually because of the intangible presence of their deity (Koenig et al., 1999).

Another way that religion helps people cope involves the rituals and rites that help people feel better about personal weaknesses, failures, or feelings of inadequacy (Koenig et al., 2001). These include rituals such as confession of sins or prayer services during times of stress. Religion can also increase the likelihood that a person will volunteer to help others, and feel stronger and better in many ways. Finally, religious beliefs can give meaning to things that otherwise seem to have no meaning or purpose, such as viewing death as a pathway to a paradise, or the destruction of one's home in a natural disaster as a reminder to place less attachment on material things.

Many religions also encourage healthy behavior and eating habits—eating wisely; limiting or forgoing the use of alcohol, tobacco, and other drugs; and sanctioning monogamous relationships. Some research even suggests that people with religious commitments live longer than those who have no such beliefs, although this is correlational research, and should not be interpreted as concluding that religious belief causes longer life expectancies (Hummer et al., 1999; Koenig et al., 1999; Lambert et al., 2013; Strawbridge et al., 1997; Thoresen & Harris, 2002).

36.2 Discuss the characteristics of and factors that promote resilience and optimism.

optimists people who expect positive outcomes.

Optimists are people who always tend to look for positive outcomes. *Pessimists* seem to expect the worst to happen. For an optimist, a glass is half full, whereas for a pessimist, the glass is half empty. Researchers have found that optimism is associated with longer life and increased immune-system functioning. Mayo Clinic researchers conducted a longitudinal study of optimists and pessimists (as assessed by a scale) over a period of 30 years (Maruta et al., 2002). The results for pessimists were not good: They had a much higher death rate than did the optimists, more problems with physical and emotional health, more pain, less ability to take part in social activities, and less energy than optimists. The optimists had a 50 percent lower risk of premature death and were more calm, peaceful, and happy than the pessimists (Maruta et al., 2002). Other studies link being optimistic to higher levels of helper T cells (immune system cells that direct and increase the functioning of the immune system) and higher levels of natural killer cells, the body's antivirus, and anticancer cells (Segerstrom & Sephton, 2010; Segerstrom et al., 1998). Martin Seligman is a social learning psychologist who developed the concept of *learned helplessness*, and began the positive psychology movement.

Seligman (2002) has outlined four ways in which optimism may affect how long a person lives:

1. Optimists are less likely to develop learned helplessness, the tendency to stop trying to achieve a goal that has been blocked in the past.

2. Optimists are more likely than pessimists to take care of their health by preventive measures (such as going to the doctor regularly, eating right, and exercising) because they believe that their actions make a difference in what happens to them. (Remember, this is a characteristic of hardy people as well.)

3. Optimists are far less likely than pessimists to become depressed, and depression is associated with mortality because of the effect of depression on the immune system.

4. Optimists have more effectively functioning immune systems than pessimists do, perhaps because they experience less psychological stress.

▲ *Type Z behavior*

Seligman (1998) has also found that optimists are more successful in their life endeavors than pessimists are. Optimistic politicians win more elections, optimistic students get better grades, and optimistic athletes win more contests. For some advice on how to become more optimistic, see the Applying Psychology feature below.

Optimism is associated with a person's belief that he or she can control moods or emotional reactions to situations. According to psychiatrist Dr. Susan Vaughan (2000), optimists tend to engage in *alternative thinking*, coming up with alternative explanations for why the bad thing happened. For example, optimists tend to attribute poor exam grades to the difficulty of that particular material or to not having enough time to study. They appraise it as a challenge and assume that they will perform more successfully in the future. Optimists also use *downward social comparison* frequently, comparing their performance to that of less competent others, which makes them feel better and protects their self-esteem. Finally, some optimists improve their mood through relaxation techniques such as exercising, meditating, or reading a good book.

Applying Psychology to Everyday Life

Put on a Happy Face: Thinking Like An Optimist

Keeping on the brighter side of life is positive and mentally healthy. Martin Seligman, along with others, has focused his research on finding out and explaining how a positive approach to psychology can help people experience a better quality of life. According to their research, learning to monitor one's thoughts, and controlling mood along with emotional reactions to the events in life are a few ways a person can become more optimistic. Part of the process is learning to pay attention to negative thoughts and then considering how they are pessimistic, so a person can look for alternative ways to process the events (Seligman, 2002). Unfortunately, thinking about thoughts is not something most people do, let alone examining them to decide if they are negative or pessimistic. Consequently, the effects of negative thinking go unchecked, and that leaves a person dealing with pessimism and unfulfilling results of negative thinking.

However, there are a number of approaches to negative thoughts that can help a person become more optimistic. An important first step is to take a moment to think about why you are feeling so down when you get in a bad mood. Listen to your thoughts and consider how they would sound if they were from someone else, as if that person wanted you to be unhappy and negative. What kind of effects would statements that are so negative have on you if they were coming from another person?

Now that you have identified your negative thoughts it is important not to let them pass without scrutinizing them, challenging their accuracy, and before moving on, creating a positive alternative the initial thought that can replace the negative thought and improve your mood. For example, if you are thinking, "I don't have a friend to call for a ride to school because I am not a popular person." Consider what is negative about your thought. Are you sure you are not popular, or are you comparing yourself to the most popular person in your school? Are you sure you don't have a friend you can call for a ride, or are you just worried that the first person you call might say no and make you feel bad because they didn't help you when you needed them? A negative thought like "I don't have a friend" can make a difficult situation feel even worse, so instead, now that you recognized it and challenged it, replace your negative thought with a positive one. Examples of positive statements include: "I will call five people and see if one of them can pick me up on their way to school." or " In the future, instead of staying in my room and watching TV tonight, I am going to spend some time with a couple new students I met at school and make a few more friends."

By challenging your negative thoughts you are finding ways around the barrier they created to more positive thinking and being hopeful. Your last step toward becoming a more positive thinker is to practice arguing with yourself and making the necessary adjustments to see events in a more objective perspective. Because your negative thoughts can be a habit they may be hard to recognize, so remember a few good questions to ask about your thoughts so you can focus on them.

1. What types of thoughts have been in your mind recently? Were most of the thoughts negative? What alternatives to the negative thoughts could be more positive?

2. Think about other people that you know. Do they make negative comments about themselves? Do they put themselves in a bad mood by seeing only the negative side of a situation? When you see them being negative toward themselves, how does it make you feel?

Questions for Further Discussion

1. Where to think you fit on a line between optimism and pessimism? Are you neutral, more optimistic, or more pessimistic?

2. How can you make changes in your life to be more optimistic and "put on a happy face?"

36.3 Explain the differences between effective and ineffective means of dealing with stressors and other health issues.

You know by now that people deal with stress in a variety of different ways: Some of us go out and take action to fix the problem; others stay at home and punch a pillow. Unfortunately, some of the most typical responses to stressors are not the most practical, helpful, or healthy responses.

A typical first response to a frustrating situation is *persistence*, or the continuation of efforts to get around whatever is causing the frustration. Persistence may involve making more intense efforts or changing the style of response. For example, anyone who has ever put coins into a drink machine only to find that the drink does not come out has probably (1) pushed the button again, more forcefully, and (2) pushed several other buttons in an effort to get some kind of response from the machine. If neither of these strategies works, many people may hit or kick the machine itself in an act of aggression.

Aggression, or actions meant to harm or destroy, is unfortunately another typical reaction to frustration. Early psychologists in the field of behaviorism proposed a connection between frustration and aggression, calling it the *frustration–aggression hypothesis* (Dollard et al., 1939; Miller et al., 1941). Although they believed that some form of frustration nearly always precedes aggression, that does not mean that frustration *always* leads to aggression. In fact, aggression is a frequent and persistent response to frustration, but it is

◄ I understand that people with different personality types react to stressors differently, but are some reactions more helpful than others?

aggression actions meant to harm or destroy; behavior intended to hurt or destroy another person.

seldom the first response. In a reformulation of the frustration–aggression hypothesis, Berkowitz (1993) stated that frustration creates an internal "readiness to aggress" but that aggression will not follow unless certain external cues are also present. For example, if the human source of a person's frustration is far larger and stronger in appearance than the frustrated person, aggression is an unlikely outcome!

Okay, so if the person who ticked you off is ▶ bigger than you—if aggression isn't possible— what can you do?

One could try to reason with the person who is the source of frustration. Reasoning with someone is a form of persistence. Trying to "get around" the problem is another way in which people can deal with frustration. Another possibility is to take out one's frustrations on less threatening, more available targets, in a process called **displaced aggression**. Anyone who has ever been frustrated by things that occurred at work or school and then later yelled at another person (such as a spouse, parent, child, etc.) has experienced displaced aggression. The person one really wants to strike out at is one's boss, the teacher, or whoever or whatever caused the frustration in the first place. That could be dangerous, so the aggression is reserved for another less threatening or weaker target. For example, unemployment and financial difficulties are extremely frustrating, as they block a person's ability to maintain a certain standard of living and acquire desired possessions. In one study, male unemployment and single parenthood were the two factors most highly correlated to rates of child abuse (Gillham et al., 1998). Unemployment is also one of the factors correlated most highly with the murder of abused women, creating four times the risk of murder for women in abusive relationships (Campbell & Wolf, 2003). Both studies are examples of displaced aggression toward the weaker targets of children and women. Such targets often become *scapegoats*, or habitual targets of displaced aggression. Scapegoats are often pets, children, spouses, and even minority groups (who are seen as having less power).

Another possible reaction to frustration is **escape or withdrawal**. Escape or withdrawal can take the form of leaving, dropping out of school, quitting a job, or ending a relationship. Some people manage a psychological escape or withdrawal into apathy (ceasing to care about or act upon the situation), fantasy (which is only a temporary escape), or the use of drugs. Obviously the latter

displaced aggression taking out one's frustrations on some less threatening or more available target.

escape or **withdrawal** leaving the presence of a stressor, either literally or by a psychological withdrawal into fantasy, drug abuse, or apathy.

▲ *These parents are fighting in front of their obviously distressed daughter. In some instances, a child who experiences this kind of frustration might act out aggressively toward a sibling or a pet in a form of displaced aggression.*

reaction can lead to even more problems. Others resort to what they see as the final escape: suicide.

What are some ways to promote wellness? *Wellness* can be defined as the practice of behaviors and lifestyle choices that promote both physical and mental health. Here are some helpful hints on how to promote wellness in your own life:

- **Exercise.** No one likes to admit it, but exercise is the best way to become healthier. Exercise makes the heart healthier, raises the body's metabolic rate to help maintain a healthy weight, raises good cholesterol and lowers bad cholesterol, strengthens bones, improves sleep quality, reduces tiredness, increases natural killer cell activity to help ward off viruses and cancer, and is a great way to reduce the effects of stress (Fiatarone found to reduce feelings of tiredness and increase energy in young adults who, because of a sedentary lifestyle, have been diagnosed with persistent fatigue. Puetz et al., 2008).

▲ *Regular exercise—whether alone or in the company of family and friends—increases the functioning of the immune system and helps give people a sense of control over their health. Having a sense of control decreases feelings of stress, which also helps the immune system to function well.*

- **Get involved with others.** Make some new friends, join a club, or perform community service. Make it a point to do things with other people. Ask friends over to watch a movie, or work on a service project with a group of classmates or other people in your community.
- **Get some sleep.** Sleep serves to restore the body physically and provides a way to manage stress during dreaming. L I N K *to Chapter Four: Consciousness, p. 130.* Try to get at least 7–8 hours of sleep each night, including weekends. Try to go to bed and get up at the same time every day to maintain your sleep–wake cycle. Sleep deprivation can lead to a lower production of natural killer cells, which are a necessary and vital part of the immune system (Irwin et al., 1994, 1996).
- **Eat healthy foods.** Eat breakfast every day, making sure to include a good amount of protein in that meal. Protein in the morning helps improve concentration and alertness, and eating breakfast helps you to avoid overeating at lunch or dinner. Eating breakfast has even been shown to decrease the risk of stroke, obesity, and diabetes (Pereira et al., 2003). Be sure to include some healthy snacks at least twice a day.
- **Have some fun.** Playing is important! Schedule some time to just relax, play a game with a friend, read a book, or do something fun. Playing helps prevent burnout.
- **Manage your time.** One of the things that can create a lot of stress is feeling overwhelmed when there are lots of tasks to do. Make a list of the tasks you need to accomplish, and check each item off the list as you finish it. This gives you a sense of control over your day's activities and rewards you with a sense of accomplishment each time you can check off an item.
- **Take a deep breath.** When you feel stressed, take a moment to cope. When you are feeling "stressed" one of the hardest things is to actually do what you know is the healthy choice. Take some deep breaths to help calm yourself and relax tension. If you're so stressed that you feel like crying, find a quiet, private place and cry—crying can relieve stress.

Pick the best answer.

1. **What does the research tell us about the effects of laughter on alleviating stress?**

   a. Laughter can alleviate immediate stress but the effects last only a few minutes.
   b. Laughter has been shown to help the immune system.
   c. Laughter in reality has little to no effect on one's overall stress level.
   d. Laughter can actually have a negative effect on the body.

2. **Meditation, progressive muscle relaxation, and guided visualization are _____ coping strategies for stress.**

   a. very effective
   b. basically ineffective
   c. emotion-focused
   d. problem-focused

3. **Which of the following statements about optimists is true?**

   a. Optimists are more likely than pessimists to develop coronary heart disease.
   b. Optimists are less likely than pessimists to go to the doctor regularly.
   c. Optimists are more likely than pessimists to develop learned helplessness.
   d. Optimists are less likely than pessimists to experience premature death.

4. **Mima is knitting a scarf, but she keeps making mistakes, and she becomes frustrated. Which of the following is most likely Mima's first response to frustration?**

   a. deciding to make a hat instead
   b. yelling and tearing the scarf apart
   c. taking out the frustration on a friend
   d. continuing to attempt to fix the scarf

5. **Which of the following is an example of problem-focused coping?**

   a. ignoring an argument with a friend and focusing on other things
   b. venting to mutual acquaintances about an argument with a friend
   c. making excuses for behavior that led to an argument with a friend
   d. attempting to settle an argument with a friend by apologizing

6. **Clarissa feels anxious because she is having trouble making in math class. Clarissa begins skipping math class. Clarissa is engaging in**

   a. repression.
   b. projection.
   c. displacement.
   d. escape.

7. **Ellie yells at her plants when she is under stress. Ellie is engaging in**

   a. reaction formation.
   b. displacement.
   c. regression.
   d. projection.

8. **When a person tries to cope by eliminating or changing the stressor directly, it is known as**

   a. a defense mechanism.
   b. problem-focused coping.
   c. self-focused coping.
   d. emotion-focused coping.

9. **Which of the following is NOT an effective way to promote wellness?**

   a. exercising
   b. getting enough sleep
   c. holding back tears
   d. playing with friends

10. **Which of the following statements about aggression is true?**

    a. Aggression is rarely the first response to frustration.
    b. Aggression will always follow frustration.
    c. Aggression is not a typical response to frustration.
    d. Aggression is not affected by external cues.

Listen to an Audio File of your chapter at MyPsychLab

Module 35: Stress and Stressors

Understand the causes and consequences of stress.

35.1 Define stress.
- Stress is the physical, emotional, and behavioral responses that occur when events are identified as threatening or challenging.
- Stress that has a negative impact is called "distress." Eustress is the optimal amount of stress that people need to function well.

35.2 Identify and explain sources of stress.
- Catastrophes are events such as floods or crashes that can result in high levels of stress.
- Major life changes create stress by requiring adjustments. Major life changes have an impact on chronic health problems and risk of accidents.
- Hassles are the daily frustrations and irritations that have an impact on day-to-day health.
- Several social factors can be a source of stress or increase the effects of stress: poverty, stresses on the job or in the workplace, and entering a majority culture that is different from one's culture of origin.
- Burnout is a condition that occurs when job stress is so great that the person develops negative thoughts, emotions, and behavior as well as an extreme dissatisfaction with the job and a desire to quit.
- The four methods of acculturation are integration, assimilation, separation, and marginalization.
- Social-support systems are important in helping people cope with stress.

35.3 Discuss psychological and physiological consequences of stress.
- Four sources of stress are pressure, degree of control, external frustrations, and internal frustrations.
- The autonomic nervous system consists of the sympathetic system, which responds to stressful events, and the parasympathetic system, which restores the body to normal functioning after the stress has ceased.
- The general adaptation syndrome is the body's reaction to stress and includes three stages of reaction: alarm, resistance, and exhaustion.
- Stress causes the immune system to react as though an illness or invading organism has been detected, increasing the functioning of the immune system.
- As the stress continues or increases, the immune system can begin to fail.

Module 36: Coping with stress and promoting wellness

Learn behaviors and attitudes that promote health.

36.1 Explain ways to promote mental health and physical fitness.
- Problem-focused coping is used when the problem can be eliminated or changed so that it is no longer stressful or so that the impact of the stressor is reduced.
- Emotion-focused coping is often used with problem-focused coping and involves changing one's emotional reactions to a stressor.
- Meditation can produce a state of relaxation and reduce the physical reactions common to stressful situations.
- Concentrative meditation involves focusing inward on some repetitive stimulus, such as one's breathing.
- Different cultures perceive stressors differently, and coping strategies will also vary from culture to culture.
- People with religious beliefs also have been found to cope better with stressful events.

36.2 Discuss the characteristics of and factors that promote resilience and optimism.
- Optimists are people who tend to look for positive outcomes. People can become more optimistic by engaging in alternative thinking, making downward social comparisons, and improving mood through relaxation techniques.

Applying Psychology to Everyday Life: Put on a Happy Face: Thinking Like an Optimist
- The best way to become more optimistic is to recognize negative thoughts and change them to more helpful positive thoughts.

36.3 Explain the differences between effective and ineffective means of dealing with stressors and other health issues.
- Typical responses to frustration include persistence, aggression, displaced aggression, and escape or withdrawal. Most of these responses are not effective ways to minimize stressors, and aggression and withdrawal can be dangerous strategies.
- Behaviors and lifestyle choices that promote physical and mental health include exercising, socializing, sleeping enough, eating healthy foods, having fun, managing time effectively, and taking deep breaths to release tension.

Vocabulary Terms

stress p. 474
distress p. 475
eustress p. 475
hassles p. 477
acculturative stress p. 478

burnout p. 478
pressure p. 479
frustration p. 480
general adaptation syndrome (GAS) p. 480

coping strategies p. 486
emotion-focused coping p. 486
problem-focused coping p. 486
optimist p. 489
aggression p. 491

displaced aggression p. 492
escape or withdrawal p. 492

✓ Study and Review at MyPsychLab

Vocabulary Review

Match each vocabulary term to its definition

1. eustress
2. catastrophe
3. problem-focused coping
4. escape or withdrawal
5. aggression
6. displaced aggression
7. hassles
8. general adaptation syndrome
9. emotion-focused coping
10. pressure

a. The effect of positive events, or the optimal amount of stress that people need to promote health and well-being.

b. The daily annoyances of everyday life.

c. Actions meant to harm or destroy.

d. The psychological experience produced by urgent demands or expectations for a person's behavior that come from an outside source.

e. An unpredictable, large-scale event that creates a tremendous need to adapt and adjust as well as overwhelming feelings of threat.

f. Taking out one's frustrations on some less threatening or more available target.

g. Leaving the presence of a stressor.

h. Coping strategies that try to eliminate the source of a stress or reduce its impact through direct actions.

i. Coping strategies that change the impact of a stressor by changing the emotional reaction to the stressor.

j. The three stages of the body's physiological reaction to stress, including alarm, resistance, and exhaustion.

Psychology Project

Can simple lifestyle changes really affect your physical and psychological health? Perform this activity to find out.

Materials: a notebook and pencil

Instructions:

1. You've learned that some ways to promote physical and mental health include exercising more, joining a club or organization, getting more sleep, eating healthier foods, spending some time relaxing or playing each day, making to-do lists, and taking deep breaths to calm yourself and relax tension. Now, choose one of these activities that you think you can realistically incorporate into your daily life for at least 2 weeks.

2. On the first page of your notebook, write down the lifestyle change that you plan to make for the next 2 weeks. For example, you might plan to eat more vegetables, make a to-do list of your homework assignments every day, or get at least 8 hours of sleep each night. Then, write down how you plan to meet this goal.

3. Put your plan into action. Over the next 2 weeks, spend some time every day participating in the activity that you have chosen. Record a brief summary of your daily experiences in your notebook at the end of every day. If you notice changes in your physical health or the amount of stress in your life, record those changes in your notebook, too.

4. At the end of the 2-week period, evaluate your notes. Has your life changed at all since you put your plan into action? Do you feel more physically healthy or less stressed out? Remember that 2 weeks is not a very long time, and consider continuing the changes you have made for a longer period of time if you feel that they are helping you become healthier.

Tech Alternative

One factor that can contribute to stress is inefficient time management. Search your favorite app site and download a time management app that looks like a good fit for you. (There are a lot of free ones!) Use the app for a week and track your use of time. After using the app for a week report on your findings: How did the app best apply to your daily needs for time management? How did using the app affect the way you were spending your time? What are three suggestions you would make to the app developer to improve the app? What are three suggestions you would make to a friend that was looking for a time management app?

Essay Question

Briefly describe how someone might use **two** of the following concepts listed below when dealing with the stress of starting a new job. For **each of the concepts you choose**, include a general description of the concept and an example of how that concept will apply to stress and coping when starting a new job:

a. optimism
b. displacement of aggression
c. escape or withdrawal
d. emotion-focused coping

Test Yourself

Ready for your test? More quizzes and a customized plan.

Pick the best answer.

✔️ Study and Review at **MyPsychLab**

1. Which of the following is a cognitive symptom of stress?
   a. frequent colds
   b. anxiety
   c. overeating
   d. memory problems

2. The term used to describe the stress from positive events is
   a. distress.
   b. hassles.
   c. eustress.
   d. frustration.

3. Unpredictable, large-scale events that create a great deal of stress and feelings of threat are called
   a. major life events.
   b. catastrophes.
   c. hassles.
   d. frustrations.

4. After the car accident, Yoshiko suffered from nightmares and other sleeping problems, and she could not concentrate on her work. After about 2 weeks, these symptoms disappeared and she was able to work and sleep normally again. Yoshiko was suffering from
   a. acute stress disorder.
   b. PSTD.
   c. mild stress reaction.
   d. shell shock.

5. For which of the following groups of people would a lack of money be more stressful than for the other groups, according to Ellis et al. (2001)?
   a. children
   b. adolescents
   c. young adults
   d. elderly people

6. After getting yelled at by her boss, Rachel goes home and yells at her cat. Rachel is displaying
   a. aggression.
   b. withdrawal.
   c. persistence.
   d. displaced aggression.

7. In which stage of the general adaptation syndrome is death a possible outcome?
   a. alarm
   b. resistance
   c. reaction
   d. exhaustion

8. Mike told his friends he was cut from the basketball team because the coach did not like him, but his friends know Michael was cut because he hardly ever practiced. In this situation, Michael's excuse is an example of a(n) _____ frustration, while the fact he despises practicing is an example of a(n) _____ frustration.
   a. personal; external
   b. external; personal
   c. internal; external
   d. personal; internal

9. Which of the following is a psychological factor in stress?
   a. poverty
   b. prejudice
   c. uncontrollability
   d. hassles

10. Which of the following is NOT one of the three methods suggested by Vaughan to promote a positive, optimistic mood?
    a. alternative thinking
    b. relaxation
    c. using a scapegoat
    d. downward social comparison

11. Shauna goes to the school's academic help center for tutoring and spends extra time working algebra problems at home. Shawna's method of coping is
    a. problem-focused.
    b. emotion-focused.
    c. a defense mechanism.
    d. meditative.

12. Expressing feelings that would be threatening if directed at the real target onto a less threatening substitute target is the psychological defense mechanism known as
    a. displacement.
    b. projection.
    c. repression.
    d. denial.

13. Which of the following is one of the ways to promote wellness in one's life?
    a. Get enough sleep.
    b. Eat whatever you want, as long as it tastes good.
    c. Don't worry about managing your time.
    d. Avoid getting too involved with other people.

14. Who among the following probably has the least ability to cope effectively with stress?
    a. Marian, who is a very religious person
    b. Mei Ling, who comes from a culture that emphasizes the family
    c. Jackie, who has few friends and whose family lives far away from her
    d. Lenora, who has recently gotten married

15. Which of the following people is most likely to experience job stress?
    a. a worker who must handle a variety of tasks each day
    b. a worker who controls his or her own daily schedule
    c. a worker who is well compensated for any overtime
    d. a worker who has no contract and may be fired at any time

16. Negative changes in thoughts, emotions, and behavior as a result of prolonged stress and frustration are known as
    a. burnout.
    b. job stress.
    c. exhaustion.
    d. marginalization.

17. An increased rate of PTSD in a population would most likely be a result of which of the following factors?
    a. an ongoing, large-scale military conflict
    b. an increase in technological hassles
    c. a sustained economic recession
    d. a lack of highly trained psychology professionals

18. Which of the following is the most valid criticism of the Social Readjustment Rating Scale (SRRS)?
    a. The SRRS includes events that most people don't experience.
    b. The SRRS is inaccurate because it includes positive events.
    c. The SRRS may not be effective across cultures.
    d. The 1997 revision is only relevant to adults who were working in 1997.

19. Although she dresses and acts like her American friends, Huong has still retained much of her cultural heritage and attends traditional Chinese dance classes on the weekends. This is an example of
    a. assimilation.
    b. integration.
    c. separation.
    d. marginalization.

20. Jenny often closes her eyes and envisions herself on a quiet beach during sunset. This vision often helps her to relax. Such an approach is known as
    a. relaxation.
    b. concentrative meditation.
    c. muscle relaxation.
    d. visualization.

Learning Objectives

35.1 **35.2** **35.3** pp. 474–484

Understand the Causes and Consequences of Stress

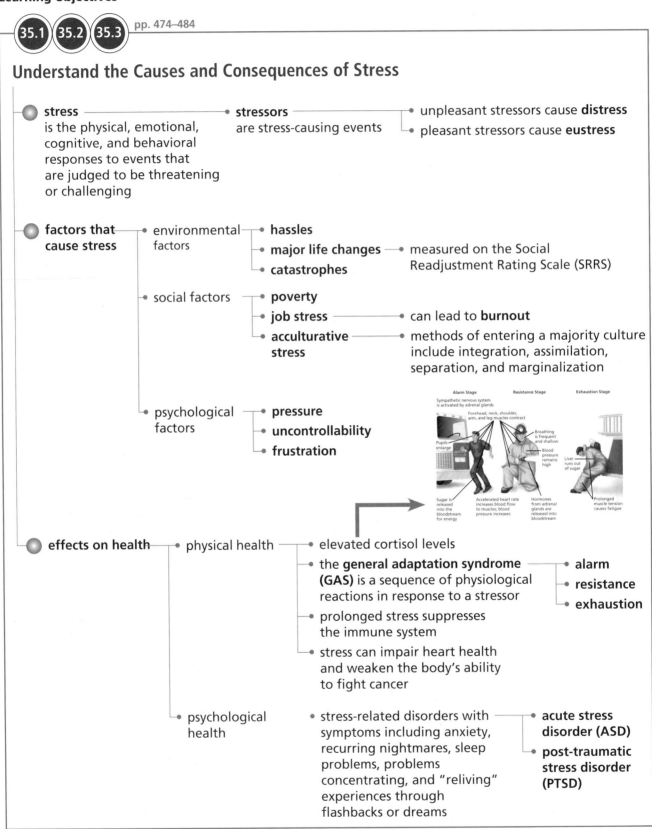

- **stress** ──────► **stressors** ──────► unpleasant stressors cause **distress**
  is the physical, emotional, cognitive, and behavioral responses to events that are judged to be threatening or challenging
  are stress-causing events
  pleasant stressors cause **eustress**

- **factors that cause stress**
  - environmental factors
    - **hassles**
    - **major life changes** ──► measured on the Social Readjustment Rating Scale (SRRS)
    - **catastrophes**
  - social factors
    - **poverty**
    - **job stress** ──► can lead to **burnout**
    - **acculturative stress** ──► methods of entering a majority culture include integration, assimilation, separation, and marginalization
  - psychological factors
    - **pressure**
    - **uncontrollability**
    - **frustration**

- **effects on health**
  - physical health
    - elevated cortisol levels
    - the **general adaptation syndrome (GAS)** is a sequence of physiological reactions in response to a stressor
      - **alarm**
      - **resistance**
      - **exhaustion**
    - prolonged stress suppresses the immune system
    - stress can impair heart health and weaken the body's ability to fight cancer
  - psychological health
    - stress-related disorders with symptoms including anxiety, recurring nightmares, sleep problems, problems concentrating, and "reliving" experiences through flashbacks or dreams
      - **acute stress disorder (ASD)**
      - **post-traumatic stress disorder (PTSD)**

Learning Objectives

(36.1) (36.2) (36.3) pp. 486–493

 Map the Concepts at MyPsychLab

Learn Behaviors and Attitudes That Promote Health

● **coping strategies** are behavioral and psychological actions taken to master, tolerate, reduce, or minimize the effects of stressors

- **problem-focused coping** involves working to change or eliminate the stressor itself

- **emotion-focused coping** involves changing the way a person feels or emotionally reacts to a stressor

  - **psychological defense mechanisms**

- religious beliefs, culture, and social-support systems can influence coping strategies

● **optimism** is associated with controlling mood or emotional reactions; can be a learned skill through alternative thinking, downward social comparison, relaxation, and correcting faulty thinking

● **typical reactions to stressors**
- **persistence**
- **aggression** — **displaced aggression**
- **withdrawal or escape**

● **strategies for promoting wellness**
- exercise
- social involvement
- adequate sleep
- healthy diet
- having fun
- time management
- relaxation

CHAPTER 16

Applied Psychology and Psychology Careers

Professor John Gambon of Ozarks Technical and Community College in Springfield, Missouri, begins his class like any other. After a few minutes two students rush in and each throw two water balloons at the professor. As they run out, they yell something about fried eggs. Professor Gambon, soaked from the balloons, asks his students to write down everything they just saw, including what was said. After a few minutes, he gathers up the paperwork and invites his two balloon-throwing accomplices back into the room.

As he reads the papers of his students, many realize that they made mistakes in identifying the perpetrators. Quite often, students mismatch hair color, height, facial features, and even the clothes that each was wearing. What's more, nearly 90 percent claim that they heard the two men yell, "That was for last Friday!" When students are shown the truth, many are shocked at their overall inaccuracy at identifying the two men.

Work such as this is not new to Professor Gambon. He has worked as a consultant in several trials where the issue of accurately identifying someone has been brought into question. His cases include several homicides, assault, breaking and entering, and armed robbery.

His demonstrations show the overall unreliability of eyewitness identification, as outlined by psychologist Elizabeth Loftus. The kind of issues that influence an eyewitness's accuracy include the presence of a weapon (people tend to look at a weapon more than the physical attributes of the assailant), time of day, fatigue, and the amount of time between the crime and when they are required to recall it. Clearly, there are flaws inherent in eyewitness identification.

Forensic psychology is just one of many areas in which psychological principles can be applied to issues and concerns of everyday life. This chapter will look at several areas of applied psychology as well as the types of careers that are open to someone who studies psychology today.

*W*hy Study Applied Psychology and Psychology Careers?

Many different kinds of psychologists study or work in many different fields. Whereas early psychologists were still discovering the processes that govern the human mind, today's psychologists are more often applying information and principles gained from research to people in the real world. Why study careers in psychology? With so many different areas of focus, a career in psychology can be varied and exciting. There is much more to psychology than helping people who have mental health problems.

Module Goals	Learning Objectives	
Identify educational requirements for careers in psychology.	**37.1**	Explain degree requirements for psychologists and psychology-related careers.
	37.2	Identify resources to help programs for further study in psychology.
Explore psychology career options in a global world.	**37.3**	Identify careers in psychology and psychology-related fields.
Learn about vocational applications of psychological science.	**37.4**	Explain ways in which psychological science addresses domestic and global issues.

applied psychology the use of psychological concepts in solving real-world problems.

It seems to me that ▶ psychology could be useful in a lot of different areas, not just education. In fact, wasn't that what all those "Applying Psychology" sections at the end of each chapter were about?

Identify Educational Requirements for Careers in Psychology

The term **applied psychology** refers to using findings from psychological research to solve real-world problems. The psychological professional, who might be a psychiatrist, a psychologist, or even a psychiatric social worker (as described later in this chapter), may do testing or use some other type of assessment and then describe a plan of action intended to solve whatever problem is of concern. As is evident in the opening comments about John Gambon, you can see that his training in psychology and his specialized knowledge enabled him to testify in court as an expert witness. This is a practical application of psychological tools to a real problem—the professional literally "applies" psychology.

The chapters in this text (including this chapter) do include some application of psychology to the real world. The field of applied psychology isn't just one field but rather a lot of different areas that all share the common goal of using psychology in a practical way. A large number of areas can be considered applied psychology, including one of the broadest areas of psychology: clinical and counseling psychology. For example, health psychologists examine the effects of stress on physical as well as mental health; educational and school psychologists look for ways to improve student learning and apply the findings to the classroom; sports psychologists help athletes prepare themselves mentally for competition; human-factors psychologists deal with the way people and machines interact; forensic psychologists deal with psychological issues within the legal system; and industrial/organizational (I/O) psychologists deal with the work environment. In addition, environmental psychologists examine the interaction of people with their surroundings at work, in social settings, and in schools, homes, and other buildings. Those surroundings include not just the physical structures but also the particular population of people who live, work, and play in those surroundings. Other psychologists look at the factors that influence people to buy certain products, analyze the best ways to market a product, and examine the buying habits of the typical consumer.

This chapter includes information on the different roles of psychological professionals and the type of education required for many professions, along with a brief overview of many of the specialized areas in psychology. The remainder of this chapter briefly explores how psychology can be used in practical ways in several different areas of life: the environment, law, education, the military, sports, and the world of work.

When most people think of psychology as a potential career, they assume certain things about the profession that are not true. For example, many people assume that to help people with their problems one has to be a psychologist, or that all psychologists are medical doctors, and that all psychologists counsel mentally ill people. In fact, none of these assumptions are completely true.

37.1 Explain degree requirements for psychologists and psychology-related careers.

Types of Psychological Professionals There are several types of professionals who work in psychology. These professionals have different training with different focuses and may have different goals.

A **psychiatric social worker** is trained in the area of social work and usually possesses a master of social work (M.S.W.) degree and may be licensed in the state he or she works as a licensed clinical social worker (LCSW). These professionals focus more on the social conditions that can have an impact on mental disorders, such as poverty, overcrowding, stress, and drug abuse. They may administer psychotherapy (talking with clients about their problems) and often work in a clinical setting where other types of psychological professionals are available.

A **psychiatrist** has a medical doctorate (M.D. or D.O.) degree and is a physician who specializes in the diagnosis and treatment of psychological disorders. Like any other medical doctor who may specialize in emergency medicine, treating the diseases of the elderly, treating infants and children, or any other special area of medicine, psychiatrists are able to write prescriptions and perform medical procedures on their patients. They simply have special training in the diagnosis and treatment of disorders that are considered to be mental disorders, such as schizophrenia, depression, or extreme anxiety. Because they are medical doctors, they tend to have a biopsychological perspective on the causes of and treatments for such disorders.

A **psychologist** doesn't have a medical degree but instead undergoes intense academic training, learning about many different areas of psychology before choosing an area in which to specialize. Psychologists typically have either a doctor of philosophy (Ph.D.) or doctor of psychology (Psy.D.) degree. People who hold a Master of Science (M.S.) degree or a Master of Arts (M.A.) are not usually called psychologists except in a few states. They can be called therapists or counselors, or they may be teachers or researchers.

The Ph.D. is a type of degree that usually indicates the highest degree of learning available in almost any subject area—psychology, the study of languages, education, philosophy, the sciences, and many others. It is typically very research oriented, and earning the degree usually requires a previous master's degree in addition to course work for the doctorate itself, as well as a dissertation—a scholarly work of research in the area of focus that is as long as a book and may even be published as a book.

The Psy.D. is a type of degree developed in the late 1970s that is focused less on research and more on the practical application of psychological principles (Peterson, 1976, 1982). In addition to academic course work such as that required for the Ph.D., this degree may require a major paper instead of a dissertation, with the difference being that the paper is not a report of research

psychiatric social worker a social worker with some training in therapy methods who focuses on the environmental conditions that can have an impact on mental disorders, such as poverty, overcrowding, stress, and drug abuse.

psychiatrist a physician who specializes in the diagnosis and treatment of psychological disorders

psychologist a professional with an academic degree and specialized training in one or more areas of psychology.

◀ What's the difference between a Ph.D. and a Psy.D.?

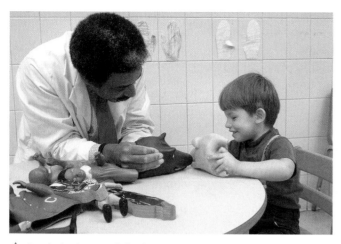

▲ Psychologists specialize in many different areas and work in many different settings. This child psychologist is evaluating the young boy by using puppets and dolls to encourage the boy to talk about his feelings.

designed and conducted by the student but is rather a large-scale term paper. Each year of a Psy.D. program will also require the student to participate in a *practicum*, an actual experience with observing and eventually conducting therapy and treatments under supervision.

Unlike psychiatrists, psychologists typically cannot prescribe medicines or perform medical procedures. Some states are seeking legislative changes to allow psychologists to prescribe psychoactive drugs if they receive special education in the use of prescription drugs. Such privileges were first pursued by the U.S. military. The reasoning behind this move, for which the American Psychological Association has been lobbying since 1984, involves both cost and the delay in receiving mental health services. If a person sees a psychologist and then has to go to a psychiatrist for medical prescriptions, the cost can be prohibitive. There are also fewer psychiatrists in some states than in others, causing long waits for mental health services from those doctors—delays that can sometimes lead to an increase in suicide rates for patients who are not getting the help they need. Although some psychologists in the military or Indian Health Service can already prescribe, as of May 2013, only two states and one territory (New Mexico, Louisiana, and Guam) have successfully afforded prescription privileges to psychologists.

Some psychologists provide counseling or therapy and use a variety of techniques and approaches. However, many psychologists do no counseling at all. There are psychologists who only engage in assessment, those who teach at colleges or universities, those who do only research in those same institutions or for industries, and those who do a combination of teaching and research (and some that do a combination of teaching, research, and counseling or clinical practice). Other psychologists are involved in designing equipment and workplaces, developing educational methods, or working as consultants to businesses and the court system.

Although becoming a psychologist requires a doctorate degree of some kind, many career fields can benefit from a four-year college degree in psychology as the basis of that career or going on to obtain a master's degree in psychology.

Careers Available to Someone with a Master's Degree in Psychology

Although individuals earning a master's degree in psychology are not typically able to engage in the same level of independent research or practice of psychology as someone with a doctoral degree, they can still work in a variety of areas, both within and beyond the field of psychology. They may work directly under the supervision of a doctoral psychologist if engaged in clinical, counseling, or school psychology, or engaged in assessment. Others work outside of the field in jobs requiring research or analysis skills and work in health, industry, or government areas.

For those interested in counseling or providing therapy, many states allow individuals with master's degrees and prerequisite training and supervision experiences to become licensed to provide unsupervised counseling and therapy. Titles may vary by state, but some of the areas and titles associated with licensed master's level work include licensed marriage and family therapist (LMFT), licensed professional counselor (LPC), licensed mental health counselor (LMHC), or licensed clinical social worker (LCSW). These individuals may work in a larger organization or work independently in private practice. Beyond these areas, some individuals with a master's degree in psychology become certified or licensed to serve as school counselors at various levels and may work in an elementary, middle, or high school.

Careers Available to Someone with a Bachelor's Degree in Psychology

Although people earning only the baccalaureate (bachelor's) degree in psychology cannot be called psychologists or provide therapy in a private practice, there are many career fields open to such a person. More than 1 million bachelor's degrees in psychology have been awarded since 1970, and since 2000 the number has increased each year (Landrum, 2009; Snyder & Dillow, 2010). A bachelor's degree in psychology can be highly flexible and adaptable to many different kinds of careers (Landrum, 2009; Landrum & Davis, 2007; Schwartz, 2000). Although surveys, both by the American Psychological Association and others, reveal many may work in health-related or social fields, individuals with a bachelor's degree in psychology may be employed in research development or research management, administration, business, education and teaching, professional services, sales, or management (Grocer & Kohout, 1997; Landrum, 2009).

Other possible careers include marketing researcher, social worker, and communications specialist (Landrum & Davis, 2007; Schwartz, 2000). With its emphasis on critical thinking and empirical observation, psychology trains people for a variety of potential workplace environments and requirements. Psychology is an excellent major even if you intend to do graduate work in some other career: Business, medicine, law, childcare, teaching, and management are only a few of the areas that relate to psychology.

Areas of Specialization in Psychology There are many different areas in which psychologists may focus their energies. They conduct experiments, surveys, observations, and so on to gather more information for their particular field of interest, to find support for current theories, or to develop new ones. Let's look at some of the areas in which psychologists may specialize.

Clinical Psychology Even though not all psychologists do counseling or therapy, many psychologists do provide therapy. **Clinical psychology** is the most similar of the areas to psychiatry in that professionals with this focus traditionally work with individuals with more serious forms of mental illness. It is also the area of specialization with the largest number of psychologists. Clinical psychologists, like psychiatrists, diagnose and treat psychological disorders in people. However, the clinical psychologist cannot prescribe drugs or medical therapies (with the exceptions discussed earlier, of course) but instead relies on listening or observing the client's problems, possibly administering psychological tests, and then providing explanations for the client's behavior and feelings or directing the client in specific actions to make positive changes in his or her life.

Counseling Psychology **Counseling psychology** is similar to clinical psychology in that this type of psychologist diagnoses and treats problems. The difference is that a counseling psychologist usually works with relatively healthy people who have less severe forms of mental illness or problems, such as adjustment to college, marriage, family life, work problems, and so on. As of 2008, nearly 73 percent of surveyed psychologists currently providing health services identified themselves as clinical psychologists or counseling psychologists (Michalski et al., 2010).

Developmental Psychology **Developmental psychology** is an area that focuses on the study of change or development. Developmental psychologists are interested in changes in the way people think, in how people relate to others, and in the ways people feel over the entire span of life. These psychologists work in academic settings such as colleges and universities and may do research in various areas of development. They do not provide therapy.

▲ *Many people with a bachelor's degree in psychology work in health-related or social fields, such as this social worker who is working with a mother and child.*

◀ You said that some psychologists teach or do research. What kind of research do they do?

clinical psychology area of psychology in which the psychologists diagnose and treat people with psychological disorders that may range from mild to severe.

counseling psychology area of psychology in which the psychologists help people with problems of adjustment.

developmental psychology area of psychology in which the psychologists study the changes in the way people think, relate to others, and feel as they age.

experimental psychology
area of psychology in which
the psychologists primarily do
research and experiments in the
areas of learning, memory,
thinking, perception, motivation,
and language.

social psychology the scientific study of how a person's
thoughts, feelings, and behavior
influence and are influenced by
social groups; area of psychology
in which psychologists focus on
how human behavior is affected
by the presence of other people.

personality psychology area of
psychology in which the psychologists study the differences
in personality among people.

physiological psychology area
of psychology in which the psychologists study the biological
bases of behavior.

neuropsychology area of psychology in which psychologists
specialize in the research or clinical implications of brain-behavior
relationships.

comparative psychology area
of psychology in which the psychologists study animals and
their behavior for the purpose of
comparing and contrasting it to
human behavior.

Experimental Psychology Experimental psychology encompasses several different areas such as learning, memory, thinking, perception, motivation, and
language. The focus of these psychologists, however, is on doing research and
conducting studies and experiments with both people and animals in various areas. They tend to work in academic settings, especially in large universities.

Social Psychology Social psychology is an area that focuses on how human
behavior is affected by the presence of other people. For example, social psychologists explore areas such as prejudice, attitude change, aggressive behavior,
and interpersonal attraction. Although most social psychologists work in academic settings teaching and doing research, some work in federal agencies and
big business doing practical (applied) research. In fact, many social psychologists are experimental psychologists who perform their experiments in real-world
settings rather than the laboratory to preserve the natural reactions of people.
When people are in an artificial setting, they often behave in self-conscious ways,
which is not the behavior the researcher wishes to study.

Personality Psychology Personality psychology focuses on the differences in
personality among people. These psychologists may look at the influence of heredity on personality. They study the ways in which people are both alike and
different. They look at the development of personality and do personality assessment. They may be involved in forming new theories of how personality works
or develops. Personality psychologists work in academic settings, doing research
and teaching.

Physiological Psychology Physiological psychology is an area that focuses on
the study of the biological bases of behavior. Many professionals now refer to
this area as *behavioral neuroscience* or *biopsychology*. Physiological psychologists study the brain, nervous system, and the influence of the body's chemicals,
such as hormones and the chemicals in the brain, on human behavior. They
study the effects of drug use and possible genetic influences on some kinds of
abnormal and normal human behavior, such as schizophrenia or aspects of intelligence. Most physiological psychologists, like experimental psychologists, work
in an academic setting.

Neuropsychology Neuropsychology is an area within the field of psychology
in which professionals explore the relationships between the brain systems and
behavior. Neuropsychologists may be engaged in research or more focused on
the assessment, diagnosis, treatment, and/or rehabilitation of individuals with
various neurological, medical, neurodevelopmental, or psychiatric conditions
(National Academy of Neuropsychology, 2001).

Comparative Psychology Comparative psychology is an area that focuses exclusively on animals and animal behavior. By comparing and contrasting animal
behavior with what is already known about human behavior, comparative psychologists can contribute to the understanding of human behavior by studying
animals. Research in animal behavior also helps people to learn how to treat animals more humanely and to coexist with the animals in a common environment.
Comparative psychologists might work in animal laboratories in a university or
may do observation and studies of animals in the animals' natural habitats.

    Psychologists in these areas may do research that is directed at discover-
ing basic principles of human behavior (basic research) or they may engage in
research designed to find solutions to practical problems of the here and now
(applied research). There are many other areas in which psychologists may specialize that focus almost exclusively on applied research. These areas are those
most often associated with applied psychology.

37.2 Identify resources to help programs for further study in psychology.

If you're interested in studying psychology in the future, your head might be spinning by now. There are so many different branches of psychology, and so many possible careers in the field, that you might not be sure where to begin. Your school guidance counselor (and perhaps your psychology teacher as well) can help you get started; a number of print and online resources can also help you.

For an extensive collection of resources specific to psychology, visit the Web site of the APA at http://www.apa.org. Its Education section (http://www.apa .org/education/index.aspx) can help you determine whether to major in psychology in college and, later, how to get into a graduate program and get the most out of it. It also provides information about careers in psychology, including brief articles written by people who use psychology in various nonacademic careers (see http://www.apa.org/careers/resources/profiles/index.aspx). Much of the information on this site is geared toward people who are already working as psychology professionals, but it is still a valuable resource, and students can also obtain affiliate membership status from the APA.

In addition to online information, the APA site also provides links for various print publications. Specific books you might find helpful as a high school or college student include:

- *The Insider's Guide to the Psychology Major: Everything You Need to Know About the Degree and Profession* (Wegenek & Buskist, 2010)
- *Career Paths in Psychology: Where Your Degree Can Take You,* 2nd edition (Sternberg, 2006)
- *What Psychology Majors Could (and Should) Be Doing: An Informal Guide to Research Experience and Professional Skills* (Silvia, Delaney, & Marcovitch, 2009)

Another resource to consult is the *Occupational Outlook Handbook* (OOH), which is published and regularly updated by the Bureau of Labor Statistics. This publication provides detailed information about hundreds of different occupations, including the education and training required, typical job responsibilities and working conditions, average salaries, and the prospects for growth in that field.

Explore Psychology Career Options in a Global World

Individuals working in psychology can serve an important role in many different fields. Some are extensions of the areas of specialization just covered. Other fields are well suited due to the general, and sometimes specific, skills psychology professionals can provide.

37.3 Identify careers in psychology and psychology-related fields.

Psychology and Health Health psychology focuses on the relationship of human behavior patterns and stress reactions to physical health with the goal of improving and helping to maintain good health while preventing and treating illness. For example, a health psychologist might design a program to help people

health psychology area of psychology focusing on how physical activities, psychological traits, stress reactions, and social relationships affect overall health and rate of illnesses.

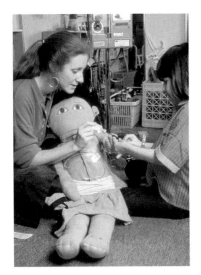

▲ This woman is a health psychologist. She is helping this girl to control her fear of receiving an injection by letting her act out giving an injection to a special doll.

educational psychology area of psychology in which the psychologists are concerned with the study of human learning and development of new learning techniques.

school psychology area of psychology in which the psychologists work directly in the schools, doing assessments, educational placement, and diagnosing educational problems.

sports psychology area of psychology in which the psychologists help athletes and others to prepare themselves mentally for participation in sports activities.

▲ School psychologists often administer tests to assess a child's level of achievement, intelligence, or psychological well-being.

lose weight or stop smoking. Stress management techniques are also a major focus of this area. Health psychologists may work in hospitals, clinics, medical schools, health agencies, academic settings, or private practice.

In one study (Kerwin et al., 2010), researchers found an association between obesity in older women and a decline in memory functioning in those women. This finding was particularly true for women carrying the excess weight around their hips (pear shapes) and less so for women carrying the excess weight around their waists (apple shapes). The study controlled for other health variables, such as diabetes, heart disease, and stroke. This is a good example of the kind of research that health psychologists conduct. Other areas studied by health psychologists include the influence of optimistic attitudes on the progress of disease, the link between mental distress and health, and the promotion of wellness and hope in an effort to prevent illness.

Psychology and Education Educational psychology is concerned with the study of human learning. As educational psychologists come to understand some of the basic aspects of learning, they develop methods and materials for aiding the process of learning. For example, educational psychologists helped to design the phonics method of teaching children to read. This type of psychologist may have a doctorate of education (Ed.D.) rather than a Ph.D. and typically works in academic settings.

What types of research might an educational psychologist conduct? The August 2013 issue of *Journal of Educational Psychology* included articles on teacher self-efficacy and instructional quality, stereotype threat in girls' math performance motivation, and effects of teacher's professional competence on both instruction and student development—just to name a few.

School psychology is related to, but not at all the same as, educational psychology. Whereas educational psychologists may do research and develop new learning techniques, school psychologists may take the results of that research or those methods and apply them in the actual school system. School psychologists work directly with children in the school setting. They do testing and other forms of assessment to place children in special programs or to diagnose educational problems such as dyslexia or attention-deficit/hyperactivity disorder. They may act as consultants to teachers, parents, and educational administrators. Counseling students is actually a relatively small part of the job of a school psychologist, although counseling takes a much bigger role when tragedies strike a school. When traumatic events such as the unexpected and tragic death of a classmate or even larger-scale tragedies such as the numerous school shootings of the past decade take place, school psychologists are often called on to offer help and counseling to students.

Psychology and Sports Sports psychology is a relatively new and fast-growing field in which the main focus is on helping athletes and others involved in sports activities prepare mentally, rather than just physically, for participation in sports. The idea behind this field is that a superior physical performance is not enough to guarantee success; rather, the mind must be prepared for the activity by setting clear short-term goals, holding positive thoughts, using visualization of the goal, stopping negative thoughts, and other techniques based primarily in the cognitive perspective. For example, a sports psychologist might have a golfer, who has been having trouble with the accuracy of his drives, perform visualization exercises, mentally seeing himself hit the ball down the fairway again and again. Sports psychologists work in athletic organizations and may have a private practice or do consulting work. (For more on the techniques used in sports psychology, see the Applying Psychology to Everyday Life section at the end of this chapter.)

Psychology and the Military Within the military, psychologists work in a variety of areas ranging from assessment, teaching, management, research, and the provision of mental health services. The variety of psychologists in this field may include clinical, counseling, experimental, I/O, or human factors, among others, and may reflect any specialty area in the field of psychology. In short, they apply psychological skills to human issues in military environments, working with both military personnel and their families (American Psychological Association, Division 19, 2010). One poignant example, the rise of suicides in the armed forces associated with the conflicts in Iraq and Afghanistan have placed demands on both the military and military families at a level not seen before (Berman et al., 2010). For more on the work of psychologists (specifically neuropsychologists) in the military, see the Psychology in the News section of Chapter Seven .

▲ A Fort Lewis Army psychologist demonstrates a headset from the "Virtual Reality Iraq" therapy program on April 18, 2007, in Spanaway, Washington. The virtual reality program, which simulates the sights, sounds, and smells of combat, will be used in working with soldiers suffering from posttraumatic stress disorder.

Psychology and the Law Psychologists have often been involved in the world of legal matters in various ways. Social psychologists often do research in the areas of criminal behavior and may consult with attorneys or other agents of the court system on such topics as witness credibility, jury selection, and the kind of influences that exist for decision-making processes. Developmental psychologists may become involved in determining the accuracy of and influences on the testimony of children and adolescents, as well as the needs of children caught up in a custody battle between divorced or divorcing parents. Cognitive psychologists may become expert witnesses on the accuracy of memory and eyewitness testimony or ways to determine the truth or falsehood of statements made by witnesses or defendants. Clinical psychologists may deliver their services directly to incarcerated prisoners or may conduct assessments of intelligence and/or mental status to determine whether or not a person charged with a crime should stand trial.

All of the forms of psychological involvement in legal matters mentioned here can be considered as part of the growing field of **forensic psychology**. Forensic psychology is the practice of psychology related to the legal system and it involves examining criminal evidence and aiding law enforcement investigations into criminal activities. Some forensic psychologists provide information and advice to officials in the legal system, such as lawyers or judges; some act as expert witnesses (like Professor John Gambon in the opening story); some actually diagnose and treat criminals within the prison system; and others may administer psychological tests to criminal defendants. Forensic psychologists may aid either the prosecution or the defense in a trial by helping determine which potential jurors would be the best or worst choices. This type of professional may do consulting work in addition to maintaining a regular

forensic psychology area of psychology concerned with people in the legal system, including psychological assessment of criminals, jury selection, and expert witnessing.

community psychology area of psychology in which psychologists serve at various levels including individual, group, and community, focusing on promoting social welfare and preventing social problems.

environmental psychology area of psychology in which the focus is on how people interact with and are affected by their physical environments.

industrial/organizational (I/O) psychology area of psychology concerned with the relationships between people and their work environment.

private practice in clinical or counseling psychology, or may work entirely within the justice system as a police psychologist or a full-time jury expert, for example.

Psychology and the Community Community psychology is an area that focuses on both individuals and their community. This field is often concerned with issues at various levels, including individual, group, neighborhood, and organizational. It is an area that focuses on promoting health and preventing common societal issues across all levels. Community psychology aims to understand human behavior in context, and recognizes the role of human diversity in promoting change. Advocacy is a key role for individuals in this area as they work to promote social justice, or practices and policies that directly impact aspects of life such as equal opportunity for all people, prevention of violence, and active citizenship. Community psychologists are involved in a variety of life activities and may be engaged in promoting mental health, physical health, educational interventions, or work policies.

Psychology and the Environment Another broad area in which psychological principles can be applied to solve practical problems is the area of managing the environment. **Environmental psychology** is an area that focuses on the relationship between human behavior and the environment in which the behavior takes place, such as an office, store, school, dormitory, or hospital. Because the concern of researchers in this field deals directly with behavior in a particular setting, research is always conducted in that setting rather than in a laboratory. Environmental psychologists may work with other professionals such as urban or city planners, economists, engineers, and architects, helping those professionals to plan the most efficient buildings, parks, housing developments, or plants.

Learn About Vocational Applications of Psychological Science

37.4 Explain ways in which psychological science addresses domestic and global issues.

▼ Human factors psychologists design machines that are more practical and comfortable for people to use. For example, this keyboard is designed to reduce the risk of pain in the wrists and increase accuracy in typing.

Work is a tremendous part of many people's lives. People often spend more time at work than they do with their families or in social activities. One of the largest branches of applied psychology focuses on how psychology can help people in management, productivity, morale, and many other areas of the world of work.

Industrial/organizational (I/O) psychology is concerned with the relationships between people and their work environments. I/O psychologists may help in personnel selection, administer job performance assessments, design work schedules that help workers adjust to new work hours with less difficulty, or design new work areas to increase morale and productivity. Psychologists in this field may study the behavior of entire organizations. They are often hired by corporations and businesses to deal with the hiring and assessment of employees. They may research and

Table 37.1	Areas in I/O Psychology
AREAS IN INDUSTRY	AREAS IN ORGANIZATIONS
Job analysis	Social behavior of work teams
Job evaluation and compensation	Job satisfaction
Characteristics critical to effective management	Personality characteristics critical to job performance
Personnel recruiting, selection, and placement	Relationships between management and workers
Occupational training	Leadership characteristics and training
Examination of working conditions	Consumer psychology
Interviewing and testing	Motivational concerns
Performance appraisal and feedback	Conflict management

develop ways for workers to be more efficient and productive. They may work in business, government agencies, and academic settings. Table 37.1 briefly lists some of the areas of specialization.

A specific kind of I/O specialist, called a *human factors engineer*, focuses on ergonomics, or designing machines, furniture, and other devices that people have to use so that those devices are the most practical, comfortable, and logical for human use. **Human factors psychology** consists of these researchers and designers who study the way humans and machines interact with each other. They may work directly in the companies involved in the design of appliances, airplane controls, and the operation of computers or other mechanical devices. For example, recall a recent iPhone® commercial about how your thumb can reach all parts of the screen. Or have you ever seen an ergonomic chair? Most likely a human factors engineer was involved in the design or testing of these products.

Psychologists working in I/O settings apply psychological principles and theories to the workplace. For example, Maslow's humanistic theory and hierarchy of needs has had a powerful influence on the field of management (Heil et al., 1998). Douglas McGregor, in his explanations of two different styles of management (McGregor, 1960), relates the older and less productive "Theory X" (workers are unmotivated and need to be managed and directed) to Maslow's lower needs and the newer, more productive style of management called "Theory Y" (workers want to work and want that work to be meaningful) to the higher needs.

▲ These women were participants in one of the early industrial/organizational psychology experiments conducted by Elton Mayo for the Western Electric Company.

human factors psychology
area of industrial/organizational psychology concerned with the study of the way humans and machines interact with each other.

Acts of violence in the workplace have increased dramatically in the past few decades—nearly tripling in the 1980s alone (Baron, 1993). Psychologists are devoting time and energy to studying the reasons for this violence and are looking for ways to recognize and prevent future incidents. Some highlights from research in workplace violence show that people in some types of jobs face a higher probability of becoming a victim of a crime because of the characteristics of the job. For example, three of the most likely occupations are police officers, corrections officers, and taxi drivers (Centers for Disease Control and Prevention, 2009). For taxi drivers (along with convenience-store clerks), it is the availability of cash and the solitary nature of the job that entices many criminals to attempt robbery. In the case of police and correctional officers, violence is part of the very nature of their job. Consider the following statistics:

- Between 1992 and 2006, there were 11,613 workplace homicide victims reported.
- Of those homicides, 11.6 police officers out of every 100,000 were killed on the job compared to the national average for all occupations of 4.0 out of every 100,000.
- From 2004 to 2008 there was an average of 564 work-related homicides each year—10 percent of all fatal work injuries.
- Four out of every 5 homicide victims in 2008 were male.
- Men were more likely to be killed by a stranger, whereas women were more likely to be killed by a relative or personal acquaintance.

▲ *The aftermath of workplace violence: A somber crowd gathers at a candlelight vigil Sunday, August 8, 2010, in honor of the victims of a workplace shooting at a Connecticut beer distribution company, which took place on August 3, 2010. Less than one week prior to this vigil, Omar Thornton killed eight coworkers and wounded two others before killing himself at the Hartford Distributors building.*

- In 2008, there were 30 multiple-fatality workplace homicide incidents, with an average of two people dying in each incident. Most were shot, and in 12 percent of the shootings the assailants were coworkers or former coworkers (Bureau of Labor Statistics, 2010).

Industrial/organizational psychologists have developed a term for the employee who becomes highly violent and commits violent crimes resulting in serious injury or death to other employees: the berserker. What are the characteristics of persons who "go berserk" in the workplace? Typically, they have at least a high school diploma or some college. Their self-esteem, or sense of worth as a person, is intimately tied to their job. They tend to like watching violent television or movies. Prevention of violence in the workplace can include some simple, commonsense steps as well as more complicated training and preparation (Arbury, 2005; Harvey & Keashly, 2003; Security Director's Report, 2008; VandenBos & Bulatao, 1996):

- entrances and exits that are well lighted
- presence of video cameras or security guards, especially at night
- criminal background checks performed on all potential new employees
- training managers and supervisors to identify signs of potential workplace violence, including such things as employees (1) who have a tendency to use verbal threats or who use low-grade acts of violence, such as pushing or shoving; (2) who are fascinated with and have access to firearms; or (3) who appear desensitized to television and movie violence and show a preference for watching such media.

Questions for Further Discussion

1. Refer back to the Learning and Social Psychology chapters. ⓁⒾⓃⓀ *to Chapter Six: Learning and Language Development, pp. 192–227, to Chapter Seven: Social Psychology, pp. 228–261.* What might be some other reasons for workplace violence?
2. In what ways might a psychologist serve as a resource for individuals working in an occupation with higher risks of violence?

Applying Psychology to Everyday Life

Techniques Used by Sports Psychologists

Many athletes become frustrated when their performance seems to be less than it could be or when they reach some "roadblock" on their way to achieving new goals. The techniques that follow are designed to help athletes get around the roadblocks and get the most out of their performance. The same techniques are also helpful in the careers of acting, musical performance, professional speaking, teaching, or any career in which there is an element of performance in front of others.

1. *Visualization.* In this technique, athletes try to "see" their performance in their minds as if watching from the sidelines before actually doing it.
2. *Imagery/mental rehearsal.* Similar to visualization, imagery can be used to mentally rehearse the desired performance. Instead of

▲ The sports psychologist on the right is helping Red Sox player David Ortiz work through his frustration at being injured during the game.

visualizing oneself as if from the sidelines, however, imagery/mental rehearsal involves actually "seeing" and "feeling" the performance in one's mind from one's own viewpoint. This helps prepare the muscles that will be used for action.

3. *Distraction desensitization.* Athletes can be trained to ignore distractions, such as the shouts of spectators.

4. *Thought stopping.* People often have negative thoughts about things that might happen: "I'm going to miss it, I just know it!" is a good example of a negative, self-defeating thought. Sports psychologists train athletes to stop such thoughts in the making, replacing them with more positive thoughts: "I can do this. I've done it before and it was easy."

5. *Confidence training.* Another thing that sports psychologists do is try to build confidence and self-esteem in the athletes who come to them for help. Lack of confidence in one's own abilities is a major roadblock.

6. *Focus training.* Athletes can also be trained to focus attention, often through the use of hypnosis, concentrative meditation, or similar psychological techniques.

7. *Relaxation training.* Athletes can be trained to use special breathing methods, tension and relaxation of muscles, and other strategies for relaxation to reduce anxiety and tension before a performance.

8. *Autogenic training.* Autogenic essentially means "from within the self." In the sense used here, autogenic training involves helping athletes learn about their physiological responses to stress. Once learned, athletes can gain control over these responses, such as learning to slow one's heart rate or to lower anxiety.

9. *Fostering realistic goals and expectations.* Sports psychologists try to teach athletes that although setting goals is important, setting unrealistic goals can lead to burnout, frustration, and feelings of failure. Sports psychologists try to help athletes modify their expectations and goals to be more realistic.

10. *Fostering team unity.* Sports psychologists may also work with entire teams of athletes, helping them to become a unit that works as one single "organism" while still providing support for each individual athlete.

Questions for Further Discussion

1. What are some other occupations in which people might benefit from using some of these techniques?

2. Are there factors outside of the game itself that might interfere with fostering team unity?

((•)) Listen to an Audio File of your chapter at MyPsychLab

Module 37: Careers In Psychology

Identify educational requirements for careers in psychology.

- Applied psychology refers to using psychological principles and research to solve problems in the real world.

37.1 Explain degree requirements for psychologists and psychology-related careers.

- Different types of psychological professionals vary by level of education and training. Examples include psychiatrists, psychiatric social workers, and psychologists.
- Psychologists hold either a Ph.D. or Psy.D. degree.
- Individuals with a master's degree may work under the supervision of a doctoral-level psychology professional, practice independently if licensed, or work in private or educational settings.
- Education, statistical consulting, administration and other business occupations, as well as health services are examples of careers that a person with a bachelor's degree in psychology might enter.

37.2 Identify resources to help programs for further study in psychology.

- Web sites and publications from professional associations are helpful sources for high school students to find more information on careers in psychology.

Explore psychology career options in a global world.

37.3 Identify careers in psychology and psychology-related fields.

- Areas of specialization include clinical and counseling psychology, developmental, experimental, social, personality, and physiological psychology, neuropsychology, and comparative psychology.
- Health psychology is an area in which the goal is to discover relationships between human behavior, including stress factors and physical health, with the intention of preventing and treating ill health.
- Educational psychologists study the processes of human learning to develop new techniques and methods, whereas school psychologists apply those methods

in the school, administer assessments, recommend placement, and provide counseling and diagnosis of educational problems.

- Sports psychologists help athletes prepare themselves mentally for participation in sports.
- Psychologists working in the military represent almost all subfields of psychology and work with both military personnel and their families in military environments.
- Psychologists may act as expert witnesses for legal matters, help in jury selection, provide clinical services to defendants or prisoners, or produce personality profiles of various types of criminals in the field of forensic psychology.
- Community psychologists help solve social issues and work to promote health for individuals and for the larger community in which people live.
- Environmental psychology looks at the relationship between human behavior and the physical environment in which that behavior takes place.

Learn about vocational applications of psychological science.

37.4 Explain ways in which psychological science addresses domestic and global issues.

- Industrial/organizational psychology is concerned with how people function in and are affected by their work environments.
- Human factors is a type of I/O psychology in which the focus is on the way humans and machines interact with each other, designing or helping to design the machines used by people in various science and industrial settings.

Applying Psychology to Everyday Life: Techniques Used by Sports Psychologists

- Sports psychologists use many techniques to help athletes better their performances, including visualization, imagery, thought stopping, confidence training, relaxation training, and fostering team unity.

Vocabulary Terms

applied psychology p. 502
psychologist p. 503
psychiatrist p. 503
psychiatric social worker p. 503
counseling psychology p. 505
clinical psychology p. 505
developmental psychology
   p. 505

comparative psychology p. 506
experimental psychology p. 506
neuropsychology p. 506
personality psychology p. 506
physiological psychology p. 506
social psychology p. 506
health psychology p. 507
school psychology p. 508

educational psychology p. 508
sports psychology p. 508
forensic psychology p. 509
community psychology p. 510
environmental psychology
   p. 510

industrial/organizational (I/O)
   psychology p. 510
human factors psychology
   p. 511

✓ **Study and Review** at **MyPsychLab**

Vocabulary Review

Match each vocabulary term to its definition.

1. applied psychology
2. master's degree
3. school psychology
4. forensic psychology
5. doctor of philosophy (Ph.D.)
6. educational psychology
7. industrial/organizational (I/O) psychology
8. doctor of psychology (Psy.D.)
9. human factors psychology
10. sports psychology

a. A graduate degree students may pursue after completing a 4-year college degree, generally taking 2 to 3 years to complete and providing more specialized knowledge, training, and experience than students typically receive as undergraduates.

b. Area of psychology in which the psychologists are concerned with the study of human learning and development of new learning techniques.

c. Area of psychology concerned with people in the legal system, including profiling of criminals, jury selection, and expert witnessing.

d. Area of psychology concerned with relationships between people and their work environment.

e. A doctorate that is research oriented and culminates in a dissertation based on original research.

f. A doctorate that focuses on applying psychological principles and provides extensive hands-on experience working in a clinical or counseling setting.

g. Area of industrial/organizational psychology concerned with the study of the way humans and machines interact with each other.

h. Area of psychology in which the psychologists work directly in the schools, doing assessments, educational placement, and diagnosing educational problems.

i. The use of psychological concepts in solving real-world problems.

j. Area of psychology in which the psychologists help athletes and others to prepare themselves mentally for participation in sports activities.

Psychology Project

What do different types of psychological professionals do in their day-to-day work? Complete this project to improve your understanding of careers in psychology.

Materials: access to print or electronic reference resources; a pencil and paper or other note-taking materials; poster board; markers or other drawing materials

Instructions:

1. With a partner, choose one career in psychology to research. (You may also choose a career in a related field, such as social work, but it must be a field that requires an understanding of psychology.) Work with your partner to create an informational poster about this career.

2. Review the information in this chapter about the career you selected.

3. Conduct additional research about this career. Take notes on important details. To guide your research, you may want to start with a few key questions, such as: What are the educational training and licensing requirements for this career? Why do people choose this career? What kinds of day-to-day responsibilities are associated with this career? What is the typical working environment for people who pursue this career? (For example, do they work independently or within an organization? With laboratory rats or with people?) Where could someone learn more about how to pursue this career?

4. Prepare a poster that provides information about the career you chose. Include text that answers questions like the ones listed above. Use Internet sources and/or magazines to find images related to this career and include them in your poster.

Tech Alternative

Swiping and gestures are becoming common in how humans interact with their personal electronic devices. Think about the "human factors" that go into designing a feature like swiping text or using gestures to access different areas on your phone. What interactive features do you like about your phone or a phone you would like to upgrade to? What interactive features do you not like about your phone or a phone you had in the past? How would you improve the design of your phone to make a more user-friendly version of your phone? What do you predict will be the next major advance in mobile phone technology? Write your answers in paragraph form to complete your assignment.

Essay Question

Link and Zelda are meeting with their school guidance counselor to discuss career plans. The students enjoyed their psychology class so much they are both thinking about going into a field of psychology. Link is outgoing, action oriented, and likes to solve clever and challenging problems. Zelda is very intelligent, likes to read, and enjoys staying after school and helping students in the tutoring center.

Select from the list below one field of psychology for each student as a possible career choice; describe the career field and how it would be a good choice for Link or Zelda.

a. Human factors psychology
b. Education psychology
c. Clinical psychology
d. Environmental psychology
e. Experimental psychology
f. Forensic psychology

Test Yourself

Ready for your test? More quizzes and a customized plan.

☑ Study and Review at MyPsychLab

Pick the best answer.

1. Which of the following professionals has a medical degree?
   a. clinical psychologist
   b. psychiatrist
   c. psychiatric social worker
   d. counseling psychologist

2. Elaine has always wanted to be a psychologist. She dreams of helping people with their problems and wants to become "Dr. Elaine." However, she is not interested in conducting scientific research or in becoming a medical doctor. What type of degree would be best for Elaine to pursue?
   a. a master's degree in psychology
   b. a Ph.D.
   c. a Psy.D.
   d. a master's degree in social work

3. Dr. Troxell conducts scientific studies on topics such as the power of prejudice, attitude change, aggressive behavior, and interpersonal attraction in teenagers. Dr. Troxell's area of specialization is most likely in _____ psychology.
   a. social
   b. personality
   c. comparative
   d. developmental

4. Dr. Cavendish is a _____ psychologist who conducts experiments using animals as her subjects. Her focus of study includes animal learning, memory, and even language.
   a. experimental
   b. comparative
   c. developmental
   d. social

5. What type of psychologist would be most likely to put together an anti-bullying program for middle school students?
   a. experimental
   b. clinical
   c. forensic
   d. educational

6. In working with a professional athlete, what aspects of performance might a sports psychologist likely focus on?
   a. strength and agility training
   b. focus and relaxation
   c. memory and motivation
   d. perceptual and problem solving

7. Dr. Lewis studies the topic of crowding. She often wonders why people can feel crowded in an elevator that has 8–10 people in it but not at a large sporting event where over 2,000 people are present. What is Dr. Lewis's specialty?
   a. developmental
   b. physiological
   c. social
   d. environmental

8. Which type of psychologist is most concerned with maximizing job satisfaction in night-shift employees?
   a. industrial/organizational
   b. clinical
   c. forensic
   d. environmental

9. Suzanne is working to redesign the controls for a new type of plane so that pilots can tell the difference between instruments in the dark just by the way each control feels. Suzanne is probably a(n) _____ psychologist.
   a. industrial/organizational
   b. human factors
   c. experimental
   d. military

10. Thought stopping, mental rehearsal, and focus training are some of the tools of the _____ psychologist.
    a. experimental
    b. clinical
    c. sports
    d. military

Learning Objectives

37.1 **37.2** pp. 502–507

Identify Educational Requirements for Careers in Psychology

● **graduate degrees**
are often required for professional positions

    ● a **master's degree** is required to work as a counselor, therapist, or social worker

    ● a **medical degree (M.D.)** is required to work as a psychiatrist

    ● a **doctorate** is required to work as a psychologist

        ● **Ph.D. (doctor of philosophy)** has a research focus

        ● **Psy.D. (doctor of psychology)** has a clinical focus

● **print, electronic, and in-person resources**
provide detailed information about studying psychology and pursuing psychology careers

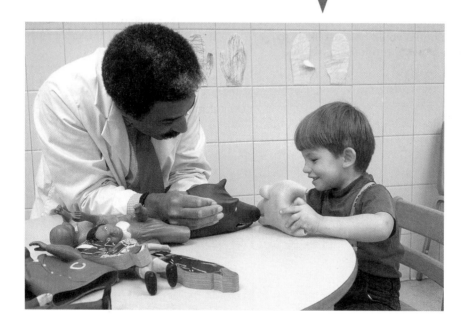

Psychology Careers

37.3 **37.4** pp. 507–514

Map the Concepts at MyPsychLab

Explore Psychology Career Options in Psychology in a Global World

- **a bachelor's degree** in psychology can be used in many career fields.
  - education and teaching
  - consulting and statistical analysis
  - administration or clerical services
  - professional services
  - sales and marketing
  - health and health-related services
  - research and development
  - market research
  - social work
  - communications

- **areas that interact with other career fields**
  - **health psychologists** study the relationship between behavior patterns, stress reactions, and physical health
  - **educational psychology** focuses on the nature of human learning
    - **educational psychologists** conduct research to help people understand and improve learning processes
    - **school psychologists** apply research through working directly with students and school personnel
  - **sports psychologists** help athletes prepare mentally for sports using a variety of specialized techniques such as relaxation training
  - **forensic psychology** helps people in the legal system by examining criminal evidence and aiding law enforcement investigations
  - **environmental psychologists** study the relationship between human behavior and the environment where the behavior takes place
  - **industrial/organizational (I/O) psychologists** study the relationship between people and their work environments.
  - **human factors psychologists** study the way humans and machines interact with each other.

Glossary/Glosario

A

absolute threshold: the lowest level of stimulation that a person can consciously detect 50 percent of the time the stimulation is present. 81
umbral absoluto: nivel más bajo de estimulación que puede percibir la persona de manera consciente el 50 por ciento de las veces que la estimulación está presente.

acculturation: the process of adapting to a new or different culture. 267
aculturación: proceso de adaptación a una cultura nueva o diferente.

acculturative stress: stress resulting from the need to change and adapt a person's ways to the majority culture. 478
estrés cultural: estrés que resulta de la necesidad de cambiar y adaptar la manera de ser de una persona a la cultura mayoritaria.

acquired (secondary) drives: those drives that are learned through experience or conditioning, such as the need for money or social approval. 347
impulsos adquiridos (secundarios): impulsos que se aprenden mediante la experiencia o el condicionamiento como, por ejemplo, la necesidad de tener dinero o la aprobación social.

action potential: the release of the neural impulse, consisting of a reversal of the electrical charge within the axon. 43
potencial de acción: liberación del impulso neural consistente en la inversión de la carga eléctrica dentro del axón.

action therapy: therapy in which the main goal is to change disordered or inappropriate behavior directly. 441
terapia activa: tipo de terapia cuyo fin principal es cambiar directamente una conducta desordenada o inapropiada.

activation-information-mode model AIM hypothesis (AIM): revised version of the activation-synthesis explanation of dreams in which information that is accessed during waking hours can have an influence on the synthesis of dreams. 133
modelo activación-información-modulación: versión revisada de la explicación de los sueños "activación-síntesis", según la cual la información que se recibe durante las horas de vigilia puede tener influencia en la síntesis de los sueños.

activity theory: theory of adjustment to aging that assumes older people are happier if they remain active in some way, such as volunteering or developing a hobby. 181
teoría de la actividad: teoría de adaptación al envejecimiento que supone que las personas mayores son más felices si permanecen activas de alguna manera, como, por ejemplo, haciendo servicios de voluntariado o desarrollando algún pasatiempo.

acute stress disorder (ASD): a disorder resulting from exposure to a major stressor, with symptoms of anxiety, dissociation, recurring nightmares, sleep disturbances, problems in concentration, and moments in which people seem to "relive" the event in dreams and flashbacks for as long as one month following the event. 421
trastorno de estrés agudo: trastorno que se produce tras someterse a un factor estresante mayor, y que produce síntomas de ansiedad, disociación, pesadillas recurrentes, perturbaciones del sueño, problemas de concentración y momentos en los que la persona parece "revivir" el suceso en sueños y reviviscencias durante periodos de hasta un mes después de ocurrido el evento.

adaptive theory: theory of sleep proposing that animals and humans evolved sleep patterns to avoid predators by sleeping when predators are most active. 125
teoría de adaptación: teoría del sueño que propone que los animales y los seres humanos desarrollaron patrones de sueño para evitar a los depredadores, al dormir cuando los depredadores están más activos.

adolescence: the period of life from about age 13 to the early 20s, during which a young person is no longer physically a child but is not yet an independent, self-supporting adult. 176
adolescencia: periodo de la vida comprendido, más o menos, entre los 13 y pasados los 20 años de edad, en el que la persona deja de ser físicamente un niño, pero no se ha convertido aún en un adulto independiente que se mantiene a sí misma.

adrenal gland: endocrine glands located on top of each kidney that secrete over 30 different hormones to deal with stress, regulate salt intake, and provide a secondary source of sex hormones affecting the sexual changes that occur during adolescence. 51
glándulas suprarrenales: glándulas endocrinas ubicadas en la parte superior de cada riñón y que secretan más de 30 hormonas distintas para afrontar el estrés, regular la ingesta de sal y suministrar una fuente secundaria de hormonas sexuales que intervienen en los cambios sexuales que se producen en la adolescencia.

affect: in psychology, a term indicating "emotion" or "mood." 424
afecto: en psicología, término que indica "emoción" o "estado de ánimo".

aggression: behavior intended to hurt or destroy another person. 251, 491
agresión: acciones destinadas a dañar o destruir a otra persona.

agoraphobia: fear of being in a place or situation from which escape is difficult or impossible. 419
agorafobia: temor a estar en un lugar o en una situación de la cual es imposible o muy difícil escapar.

algorithms: very specific, step-by-step procedures for solving certain types of problems. 318
algoritmos: procedimientos muy específicos, paso a paso, para resolver determinados tipos de problemas.

alpha waves: brain waves that indicate a state of relaxation or light sleep (drowsing). 126
ondas alfa: ondas cerebrales que indican un estado de relajación o sueño ligero (somnolencia).

altered states of consciousness: state in which there is a shift in the quality or pattern of mental activity as compared to waking consciousness. 123
estado alterado de conciencia: estado en el cual hay un cambio en la calidad o el patrón de la actividad mental, en comparación con la conciencia activa.

altruism: prosocial behavior that is done with no expectation of reward and may involve the risk of harm to oneself. 253
altruismo: conducta prosocial que se realiza sin esperar gratificación y que puede implicar el riesgo de dañarse a sí mismo.

amygdala: brain structure located near the hippocampus, responsible for fear responses and memory of fear. 60
amígdala: estructura encefálica ubicada cerca del hipocampo, responsable de las respuestas al miedo y del recuerdo del miedo.

anal stage: the second stage in Freud's psychosexual stages, occurring from about 18 to 36 months of age, in which the anus is the erogenous zone and toilet training is the source of conflict. 378
fase anal: segunda de las etapas psicosexuales de Freud que tiene lugar aproximadamente entre los 18 y los 36 meses de edad, en la cual el ano es la zona erógena, y aprender a defecar en el baño es una fuente de conflicto.

androgyny: a gender role characteristic of people whose personalities reflect the characteristics of both males and females, regardless of gender. 278
androginia: rol de género propio de aquellas personas cuyas personalidades reflejan características tanto masculinas como femeninas, con indepedencia de su sexo.

anorexia nervosa (anorexia): condition in which a person reduces eating to the point that their body weight is significantly lower or less than minimally expected. In adults, this is likely associated with a BMI < 18.5. 425
anorexia nerviosa: afección en la cual se reduce la ingesta hasta el extremo de llegar a un peso significativamente menor al mínimo esperado. En adultos, esta afección se asocia a un índice de masa corporal < 18.5.

anterograde amnesia: loss of memory from the point of injury or trauma forward, or the inability to form new long-term memories. 305
amnesia anterógrada: pérdida de la memoria desde el punto de lesión o trauma hacia adelante o incapacidad de formar nuevos recuerdos a largo plazo.

antisocial personality disorder (ASPD): disorder in which a person uses other people without worrying about their rights or feelings and often behaves in an impulsive or reckless manner without regard for the consequences of that behavior. 430
trastorno de personalidad antisocial: trastorno en el cual la persona usa a los demás sin ninguna consideración por sus derechos y sentimientos, y que suele actuar de forma impulsiva o temeraria sin tener en cuenta las consecuencias de ese comportamiento.

anxiety disorders: class of disorders in which the primary symptom is excessive or unrealistic anxiety. 418
trastornos de ansiedad: trastornos en los cuales el síntoma principal es la ansiedad y el temor excesivo o injustificado.

applied behavior analysis (ABA): modern term for a form of functional analysis and behavior modification that uses a variety of behavioral techniques to mold a desired behavior or response. 445
análisis conductual aplicado (ACA): término moderno que describe una forma de modificación de la conducta mediante técnicas de modelado para obtener una conducta o respuesta deseada.

applied psychology: the use of psychological concepts in solving real-world problems. 502
psicología aplicada: uso de conceptos de psicología para resolver problemas de la vida real.

archetypes: Jung's collective, universal human memories. 380
arquetipos: recuerdos humanos universales y colectivos de Jung.

arousal theory: theory of motivation in which people are said to have an optimal (best or ideal) level of tension that they seek to maintain by increasing or decreasing stimulation. 350
teoría del "arousal": teoría de la motivación según la cual las personas tienen un nivel de tensión óptimo (mejor o ideal) que tratan de mantener mediante un aumento o una reducción de la estimulación.

association areas: areas within each lobe of the cortex responsible for the coordination and interpretation of information, as well as higher mental processing. 62
áreas de asociación: áreas internas de cada lóbulo de la corteza cerebral responsables de la coordinación e interpretación de la información, y de los procesos mentales superiores.

attachment: the emotional bond between an infant and the primary caregiver. 171
apego: vínculo emocional que se establece entre un niño con su cuidador(a) principal.

attitude: a tendency to respond positively or negatively toward a certain person, object, idea, or situation. 238
actitud: tendencia a responder de manera positiva o negativa a cierta persona, objeto, idea o situación.'

attribution: the process of explaining one's own behavior and the behavior of others. 241
atribución: proceso de explicar el propio comportamiento y el de los demás.

authoritative parenting: style of parenting in which parents combine warmth and affection with firm limits on a child's behavior. 180
crianza autoritaria de los hijos: estilo de crianza en el que los padres combinan la calidez y el afecto hacia los hijos con unos límites estrictos en su comportamiento.

autonomic nervous system: division of the PNS consisting of nerves that control all of the involuntary muscles, organs, and glands. 49
sistema nervioso autónomo: división del sistema nervioso periférico formado por los nervios que controlan todos los músculos involuntarios, los órganos y las glándulas.

availability heuristic: estimating the frequency or likelihood of an event based on how easy it is to recall (often associated with a vivid, emotional memory) relevant information from memory or how easy it is for us to think of related examples. 318
disponibilidad heurística: tendencia a estimar la frecuencia o probabilidad de un suceso a partir de lo fácil que resulte recordar información relevante (por lo general relacionado con un recuerdo vívido y emotivo) de una memoria, o por lo fácil que resulte acordarse de ejemplos relacionados.

aversion therapy: form of behavioral therapy in which an undesirable behavior is paired with an aversive stimulus to reduce the frequency of the behavior. 445
terapia de aversión: tipo de terapia conductual en la que una conducta indeseable se empareja con un estímulo desagradable para reducir la frecuencia de dicha conducta.

axon: tube like structure of neuron that carries the neural message from the cell body to the axon terminals, for communication with other cells. 43
axón: estructura tubular que transporta el mensaje neural desde el cuerpo celular de los axones terminales para comunicarse con otras células.

B

behavior modification: the use of operant conditioning techniques to bring about desired changes in behavior. 208
modificación de conducta: uso de técnicas de condicionamiento operante para producir cambios de conducta deseados.

behavior therapies: action therapies based on the principles of classical and operant conditioning and aimed at changing disordered behavior without concern for the original causes of such behavior. 445
terapias de conducta: terapias de acción que se basan en principios de condicionamiento clásico y operante, cuyo fin es cambiar conductas alteradas sin considerar las causas originales de tal conducta.

behavioral genetics: field of study devoted to discovering the genetic bases for personality characteristics. 388
genética conductual: ciencia que estudia cómo se forma la personalidad mediante los rasgos heredados que se expresan en un ambiente particular.

behaviorism: the science of behavior that focuses on observable behavior only. 9
conductismo: ciencia de la conducta que sólo se centra en la conducta observable.

behaviorist perspective: the science of behavior that focuses on observable behavior only. 10
perspectiva conductivista: rama de la ciencia de la conducta que sólo se centra en la conducta observable.

binocular cues: cues for perceiving depth based on both eyes. 106
señales binoculares: señales para percibir la profundidad con ambos ojos.

biological model: model of explaining behavior as caused by biological changes in the chemical, structural, or genetic systems of the body. 412
modelo biológico: modelo que sostiene que la conducta está causada por cambios biológicos en el sistema químico, estructural o genético del cuerpo.

biomedical therapies: therapies that directly affect the biological functioning of the body and brain; therapies for mental disorders in which a person with a problem is treated with biological or medical methods to relieve symptoms. 441, 455
terapias biomédicas: terapias que afectan directamente el funcionamiento biológico del cuerpo y del cerebro; terapias para para aliviar los síntomas de trastornos mentales con métodos biológicos o médicos.

biopsychological perspective: perspective that attributes human and animal behavior to biological events occurring in the body, such as genetic influences, hormones, and the activity of the nervous system. 11
perspectiva biopsicológica: perspectiva que atribuye conductas humanas y animales a los fenómenos biológicos del cuerpo, tales como influencias genéticas, hormonales y la actividad del sistema nervioso.

biopsychosocial perspective: perspective in which disorders are seen as the result of the combined and interacting forces of biological, psychological, social, and cultural influences. 12, 414
perspectiva biopsicosocial: perspectiva según la cual los trastornos se entienden como el resultado de una serie de fuerzas biológicas, psicológicas, sociales y culturales combinadas y relacionadas entre sí .

bipolar disorder: periods of mood that may range from normal to manic, with or without episodes of depression (bipolar I disorder), or spans of normal mood interspersed with episodes of major depression and episodes of hypomania (bipolar II disorder). 424
trastorno bipolar: periodos de estado de ánimo que van de normal a maníaco, con o sin episodios de depresión (trastorno bipolar I), o periodos de estado de ánimo normal salpicados de episodios de depresión profunda o episodios de hipomanía (trastorno bipolar II).

bisexual: person attracted to both men and women. 355
bisexual: persona que se siente atraída tanto a hombres como a mujeres.

borderline personality disorder (BLPD): maladaptive personality pattern in which the person is moody, unstable, lacks a clear sense of identity, and often clings to others with a pattern of self-destructiveness, chronic loneliness, and disruptive anger in close relationships. 430
trastorno límite de la personalidad: esquema de personalidad inadaptiva en el cual la persona es temperamental, inestable, carece de un sentido definido de la identidad y con frecuencia se aferra a otros; además presenta un cuadro autodestructivo, de soledad crónica y de ira disruptiva en relaciones estrechas.

bottom up processing: the analysis of the smaller features to build up to a complete perception. 112
procesamiento del fondo hacia arriba: análisis de los rasgos más pequeños hasta desarrollar una percepción completa.

bulimia nervosa (bulimia): a condition in which a person develops a cycle of "binging," or overeating enormous amounts of food at one sitting, and then using unhealthy methods to avoid weight gain. 426
bulimia nerviosa (bulimia): afección en la cual una persona desarrolla un ciclo de "atracones" o ingesta descontrolada de grandes cantidades de alimentos de una sentada, y luego usa métodos no saludables para evitar ganar peso.

burnout: negative changes in thoughts, emotions, and behavior as a result of prolonged stress or frustration, leading to feelings of exhaustion. 478
agotamiento: cambios negativos en los pensamientos, las emociones y la conducta como resultado del estrés o de una frustración prolongada, y que conducen a un estado de extenuación mental.

bystander effect: referring to the effect that the presence of other people has on the decision to help or not help, with help becoming less likely as the number of bystanders increases. 254
efecto espectador: efecto que tiene la presencia de otras personas sobre la decisión de ayudar o no ayudar, donde la probabilidad de ayudar disminuye a medida que la cantidad de espectadores aumenta.

C

Cannon–Bard theory of emotion: theory in which the physiological reaction and the emotion are assumed to occur at the same time. 363
teoría de la emoción de Cannon–Bard: teoría que supone que la reacción fisiológica y la emoción ocurren al mismo tiempo.

case study: study of one individual in great detail. 19
estudio de caso: estudio minucioso de una persona.

catatonia: disturbed behavior ranging from statue-like immobility to bursts of energetic, frantic movement, and talking. 428
catatonia: perturbación de la conducta que va desde una inmovilidad pétrea a episodios de movimientos y habla frenéticos.

central nervous system: part of the nervous system consisting of the brain and spinal cord. 47
sistema nervioso central: parte del sistema nervioso que consta del encéfalo y la médula espinal.

central-route processing: type of information processing that involves attending to the content of the message itself. 240
procesamiento a través de ruta central: tipo de procesamiento de la información que implica prestar atención al contenido mismo del mensaje.

cerebellum: part of the lower brain located behind the pons that controls and coordinates involuntary, rapid, fine motor movement, and may have some cognitive functions. 59
cerebelo: parte del encéfalo inferior ubicada detrás del puente de Varolio que controla y coordina el movimiento involuntario, rápido y de motricidad fina, y que podría tener funciones cognitivas.

chromosome: tightly wound strand of genetic material or DNA. 69
cromosoma: filamento enrollado de material genético o ADN.

circadian rhythm: a cycle of bodily rhythm that occurs over a 24-hour period. 124
ritmo circadiano: ciclo de ritmo corporal que transcurre en un periodo de 24 horas.

classical conditioning: learning to elicit an involuntary response to a stimulus other than the original, natural stimulus that normally produces the response. 195
condicionamiento clásico: aprender a suscitar una respuesta involuntaria a un estímulo que no sea el estímulo inicial y original que suele generar dicha respuesta.

clinical psychology: area of psychology in which the psychologists diagnose and treat people with psychological disorders that may range from mild to severe. 505
psicología clínica: ámbito de la psicología que diagnostica y trata a las personas con trastornos psicológicos que van de moderados a severos.

cognitive arousal theory (two-factor theory): theory of emotion in which both the physical arousal and the labeling of that arousal based on cues from the environment must occur before the emotion is experienced. 363
teoría de los dos factores: teoría de la emoción según la cual tanto la excitación física como la identificación de dicha excitación basada en señales del entorno, deben producirse antes de que se experimente la emoción.

cognitive dissonance: sense of discomfort or distress that occurs when a person's behavior does not correspond to that person's attitudes. 241

disonancia cognitiva: sensación de incomodidad o angustia que ocurre cuando la conducta de una persona no se corresponde con sus actitudes.

cognitive perspective: modern perspective in psychology that focuses on memory, intelligence, perception, problem solving, and learning. 11
perspectiva cognitiva: perspectiva moderna de la psicología que se centra en la memoria, la inteligencia, la percepción, la resolución de problemas y el aprendizaje.

cognitive therapy: therapy in which the focus is on helping clients recognize distortions in their thinking and replacing distorted, unrealistic beliefs with more realistic, helpful thoughts. 447
terapia cognitiva: terapia que se centra en ayudar a los clientes a reconocer las distorsiones en su razonamiento y en sustituir creencias distorsionadas y poco realistas con pensamientos más realistas y útiles.

cognitive–mediational theory: theory of emotion in which a stimulus must be interpreted (appraised) by a person in order to result in a physical response and an emotional reaction. 365
teoría de mediación cognitiva: teoría de la emoción en la cual el estímulo debe ser interpretado (evaluado) por alguien para que resulte en una respuesta física y una reacción emocional.

cognitive–behavioral therapy (CBT): action therapy in which the goal is to help clients overcome problems by learning to think more rationally and logically, which in turn will impact their behavior. 448
terapia cognitivo–conductual: terapia activa diseñada para ayudar a los clientes a superar problemas enseñándoles a pensar de una manera más racional y lógica lo cual, a su vez, tendrá un efecto positivo en su conducta.

collective unconscious: Jung's name for the memories shared by all members of the human species. 379
inconsciente colectivo: nombre dado por Jung a los recuerdos compartidos por todos los miembros de la especie humana.

collectivism: emphasis on the interdependence of all people in a group. 268
colectivismo: interdependencia de todos los integrantes de un grupo.

community psychology: area of psychology in which psychologists serve at various levels including individual, group, and community, focusing on promoting social welfare and preventing social problems. 510
psicología comunitaria: ámbito de la psicología en la que los psicólogos participan a nivel individual, grupal y comunitario, y se centran en fomentar tanto el bienestar social como en la prevención de problemas sociales.

companionate love: type of love consisting of intimacy and commitment. 251
amor de compañía o sociable: tipo de amor consistente en la intimidad y el compromiso.

comparative psychology: area of psychology in which the psychologists study animals and their behavior for the purpose of comparing and contrasting it to human behavior. 506
psicología comparada: ámbito de la psicología que estudia a los animales y su conducta con el propósito de compararla y contrastarla con la conducta humana.

compliance: changing one's behavior as a result of other people directing or asking for the change. 234

sumisión: cambio en la conducta personal propia como resultado de que otras personas le hayan ordenado o pedido que cambie.

concepts: ideas that represent a class or category of objects, events, or activities. 315

conceptos: ideas que representan una clase o categoría de objetos, sucesos o actividades.

concrete operations stage: Piaget's third stage of cognitive development in which the school-age child becomes capable of logical thought processes but is not yet capable of abstract thinking. 167

etapa de las operaciones concretas: tercera etapa del desarrollo cognitivo de Piaget en la cual el niño en edad escolar desarrolla la capacidad de razonar lógicamente, aunque aún no puede tener pensamientos abstractos.

conditioned response (CR): learned response to a conditioned stimulus. 195

respuesta condicionada: respuesta refleja aprendida a un estímulo condicionado.

conditioned stimulus (CS): stimulus that becomes able to produce a learned response by being paired with the original unconditioned stimulus. 195

estímulo condicionado: estímulo capaz de producir una respuesta refleja aprendida al unirse con el estímulo original no condicionado.

cones: visual sensory receptors found at the back of the retina, responsible for color vision and sharpness of vision. 87

conos: receptores sensoriales visuales que se encuentran en la parte posterior de la retina y que son responsables de la visión de los colores y de la agudeza visual.

confirmation bias: the tendency to search for evidence that fits one's beliefs while ignoring any evidence that does not fit those beliefs. 323

sesgo de confirmación: tendencia a buscar pruebas que satisfagan las propias creencias y a ignorar toda otra evidencia que no se ajuste a esas creencias.

conformity: changing one's own behavior to match that of other people. 230, 267

conformidad: cambiar la conducta personal para adecuarse a la de otras personas.

consciousness: a person's awareness of everything that is going on around him or her at any given time. 122

consciencia: percepción que tiene una persona de todo lo que le rodea en un momento determinado.

conservation: in Piaget's theory, the ability to understand that simply changing the appearance of an object does not change the object's nature. 167

conservación: en la teoría de Piaget, capacidad para comprender que cambiar la mera apariencia de un objeto no hace que cambie su naturaleza.

constancy: the tendency to interpret an object as being constant. 102

constancia: tendencia a interpretar un objeto como algo constante.

constructive processing: referring to the retrieval of memories in which those memories are altered, revised, or influenced by newer information. 301

procesamiento constructivo: se refiere a una recuperación de recuerdos en la que tales recuerdos se ven alterados, revisados o influidos por información nueva.

contiguity: a Gestalt principle of perception, the tendency to perceive two things that happen close together in time as being related. 104

contigu"idad: principio de percepción Gestalt que describe la tendencia a relacionar dos sucesos si estos están cercanos en el tiempo .

convergent thinking: type of thinking in which a problem is seen as having only one answer, and all lines of thinking will eventually lead to that single answer, using previous knowledge and logic. 320

pensamiento convergente: tipo de pensamiento en el cual se considera que un problema tiene una sola solución, y que todas las líneas de pensamiento basadas en la lógica y en el conocimiento previo confluirán finalmente hacia dicha solución.

coping strategies: actions that people can take to master, tolerate, reduce, or minimize the effects of stressors. 486

estrategias de afrontamiento: acciones que inician las personas para controlar, tolerar, reducir o minimizar los efectos de un factor de estrés.

correlation: a measure of the relationship between two variables. 20

correlación: medida de la relación entre dos variables.

cortex: outermost covering of the brain consisting of densely packed neurons, responsible for higher thought processes and interpretation of sensory input. 61

corteza cerebral: cubierta exterior del cerebro formado por una densa masa de neuronas, y que es responsable de los procesos de razonamiento superior y de la interpretación de las percepciones sensoriales.

counseling psychology: area of psychology in which the psychologists help people with problems of adjustment. 505

orientación psicológica: ámbito de la psicología que ayuda a las personas con problemas de adaptación.

counselor: Masters-level professional trained in offering psychological services. 442

psicólogo: profesional con un título de maestría y capacitado para ofrecer servicios psicológicos.

creativity: the process of solving problems by combining ideas or behavior in new ways. 320

creatividad: proceso de resolver problemas de maneras nuevas mediante la combinación de ideas o conductas.

critical periods: times during which certain environmental influences can have an impact on the development of the infant. 161

periodos críticos: periodos durante los cuales ciertas influencias ambientales pueden afectar al desarrollo de un niño.

cross-sectional design: research design in which several different age-groups of participants are studied at one particular point in time. 154

diseño transversal: diseño de investigación en el cual se estudian participantes de distintos grupos de edad en un momento determinado.

cross-sequential design: research design in which participants are first studied by means of a cross-sectional design but are also followed and assessed for a period of no more than six years. 154

diseño transversal secuencial: diseño de investigación en el que, primero, los participantes son estudiados mediante un diseño transversal, y que luego se someten a un periodo de seguimiento y evaluación de no más de seis años.

cultural bias: the tendency of IQ tests to reflect, in language, dialect, and content, the culture of the person or persons who designed the test. 271

sesgo cultural: tendencia de las pruebas de coeficiente intelectual a reflejar, en lenguaje, dialecto y contenido, la cultura de la persona o personas que diseñaron la prueba.

cultural relativity: the need to consider the unique characteristics of the culture in which behavior takes place. 272, 413

relatividad cultural: necesidad de considerar las características únicas de la cultura en la cual ocurre determinada conducta.

culture: a shared set of beliefs, behaviors, values, and attitudes held by a group of people or a society. 264

cultura: conjunto de creencias, conductas, valores y actitudes compartidas por un grupo de personas o por una sociedad.

curve of forgetting: a graph showing a distinct pattern in which forgetting is very fast within the first hour after learning a list and then tapers off gradually. 302

curva del olvido: gráfica que muestra un patrón distintivo en el cual el olvido es muy rápido durante la primera hora después de aprender una lista y luego disminuye gradualmente.

cybertherapy: psychotherapy that is offered on the Internet. Also called online, Internet, or Web therapy or counseling. 451

ciberterapia: psicoterapia que se administra por Internet. También se conoce como terapia online, web o por Internet.

D

decay: loss of memory due to the passage of time, during which the memory trace is not used. 303

deterioro: pérdida de la memoria debido al paso del tiempo, durante el cual no se usa el rastro de la memoria.

declarative (explicit) memory: type of long-term memory containing information that is conscious and known. 293

memoria declarativa: tipo de memoria a largo plazo que contiene información consciente y conocida.

deindividuation: the lessening of a person's sense of personal identity and responsibility. 252

desindividualización: disminución del sentido de identidad personal y de responsabilidad de un individuo.

delta waves: long, slow brain waves that indicate the deepest stage of sleep. 126

ondas delta: ondas largas y lentas que indican un estado profundo de sueño.

delusions: false beliefs held by a person who refuses to accept evidence of their falseness. 427

delirios: creencias falsas de una persona que se niega a aceptar la evidencia de su falsedad.

dendrites: branchlike structures of a neuron that receive messages from other neurons. 42

dendritas: estructuras similares a ramas que reciben mensajes de otras neuronas.

dependent variable: variable in an experiment that represents the measurable response or behavior of the subjects in the experiment. 23

variable dependiente: en un experimento, variable que representa la respuesta o conducta mensurable de los sujetos del experimento.

depressants: drugs that decrease the functioning of the nervous system. 140

depresor: fármacos que reducen la actividad del sistema nervioso.

depth perception: the ability to perceive the world in three dimensions. 105

percepción de profundidad: capacidad de percibir el mundo en tres dimensiones.

descriptive statistics: a way of organizing numbers and summarizing them so that patterns can be determined. 28

estadística descriptiva: manera de organizar números y sintetizarlos para hallar patrones.

developmental psychology: area of psychology in which the psychologists study the changes in the way people think, relate to others, and feel as they age. 505, 506

psicología del desarrollo: ámbito de la psicología que estudia los cambios en la manera de pensar, de relacionarse y de sentir de las personas a medida que envejecen.

diffusion of responsibility: occurs when a person fails to take responsibility for actions or for inaction because of the presence of other people who are seen to share the responsibility. 254

difusión de la responsabilidad: ocurre cuando una persona no asume la responsabilidad de sus acciones o inacciones debido a la presencia de otras personas consideradas corresponsables.

direct observation: assessment in which the professional observes the client engaged in ordinary, day-to-day behavior in either a clinical or natural setting. 396

observación directa: evaluación en la cual el profesional observa al cliente mientras está ocupado en actividades cotidianas tanto en un entorno clínico como en un entorno natural.

directive: therapy in which the therapist actively gives interpretations of a client's statements and may suggest certain behavior or actions. 443

directiva: tratamiento en el que el terapeuta interpreta activamente las palabras de un cliente y sugiere ciertos comportamientos y acciones.

discrimination: treating people differently because of prejudice toward the social group to which they belong. 245, 274

discriminación: acto de tratar a una persona de forma diferente por prejuicios hacia el grupo social al cual pertenecen.

displaced aggression: taking out one's frustrations on some less threatening or more available target. 492

agresión desplazada: descargar las frustraciones personales en un objetivo menos amenazante o más accesible.

display rules: learned ways of controlling displays of emotion in social settings. 271, 360

reglas de exhibición: maneras aprendidas para controlar la manifestación de las emociones en entornos sociales.

dissociation: break a connection with something. 136

disociación: interrumpir la conexión con algo.

dissociative disorders: disorders in which there is a break in conscious awareness, memory, the sense of identity, or some combination. 422

trastornos disociativos: trastornos en los cuales hay una ruptura de la percepción consciente, la memoria, el sentido de la identidad o alguna combinación de ellos.

dissociative identity disorder (DID): disorder occurring when a person seems to have two or more distinct personalities within one body. 423
trastorno de identidad disociativo: trastorno que ocurre cuando una persona parece tener dos o más personalidades distintas dentro de sí.

distress: the effect of unpleasant and undesirable stressors. 475
angustia: efecto producido por factores estresantes desagradables y no deseados.

distributed practice: spacing the study of material to be remembered by including breaks between study periods. 302
práctica distribuida: separar el material de estudio para memorizar mediante la inserción de pausas entre los periodos de estudio.

divergent thinking: type of thinking in which a person starts from one point and comes up with many different ideas or possibilities based on that point. 320
pensamiento divergente: tipo de pensamiento en el cual la persona comienza desde un punto a partir del cual surgen muchas ideas o posibilidades distintas .

dizygotic twins: often called fraternal twins, occurring when two eggs each get fertilized by two different sperm, resulting in two zygotes in the uterus at the same time. 160
gemelos dicigóticos: los llamados mellizos o gemelos fraternos tienen lugar cuando dos óvulos resultan fecundados por dos espermatozoides diferentes, dando lugar a la presencia de dos cigotos en el útero.

dominant: referring to a gene that actively controls the expression of a trait. 69, 156
dominante: hace referencia al gen que controla activamente la expresión de un rasgo.

drive: a psychological tension and physical arousal arising when there is a need that motivates the organism to act in order to fulfill the need and reduce the tension. 347
impulso: tensión psicológica y excitación física que surgen cuando hay una necesidad que motiva al organismo a actuar para satisfacer dicha necesidad y reducir la tensión.

drive-reduction theory: approach to motivation that assumes behavior arises from physiological needs that cause internal drives to push the organism to satisfy the need and reduce tension and arousal. 347
teoría de reducción del impulso: perspectiva de la motivación según la cual el comportamiento surge de necesidades fisiológicas que, a su vez, causan impulsos internos que llevan al organismo a satisfacer dicha necesidad y a reducir la tensión.

E

echoic memory: the brief memory of something a person has just heard. 290
memoria ecoica: recuerdo breve que se tiene de una cosa que se ha oído decir a otra persona.

eclectic: using more than one treatment approach or technique. 441
ecléctico (tratamiento): estilo de terapia basado en más de una perspectiva o técnica de tratamiento.

educational psychology: area of psychology in which the psychologists are concerned with the study of human learning and development of new learning techniques. 508
psicología educacional: ámbito de la psicología que estudia el aprendizaje humano y el desarrollo de nuevas técnicas de aprendizaje.

ego: part of the personality that develops out of a need to deal with reality; mostly conscious, rational, and logical. 377
ego: parte de la personalidad que se desarrolla a partir de la necesidad de enfrentar la realidad; mayormente consciente, racional y lógico.

egocentrism: the inability to see the world through anyone else's eyes. 166
egocentrismo: incapacidad de ver el mundo a través de los ojos de otra persona.

elaboration likelihood model: model of persuasion stating that people will either elaborate (give second thought) on the persuasive message or fail to elaborate on it and that the future actions of those who do elaborate are more predictable than those who do not. 240
modelo de la probabilidad de la elaboración: modelo de persuasión según el cual las personas que reciben un mensaje persuasivo, o bien lo elaboran (se lo piensan dos veces) o no lo elaboran; según este modelo las acciones futuras de aquellos que sí lo elaboran son más predecibles que las de aquellos que no.

elaborative rehearsal: a method of transferring information from STM into LTM by making that information meaningful in some way. 293
ensayo elaborativo: método por el que se transfiere la información de la memoria a corto plazo (MCP) a la memoria a largo plazo (MLP) al otorgar a la primera una relevancia que antes no tenía.

electroconvulsive therapy (ECT): form of biomedical therapy to treat severe depression in which electrodes are placed on either one or both sides of a person's head, and an electric current is passed through the electrodes that is strong enough to cause a seizure or convulsion. 458
terapia electroconvulsiva (TEC): forma de terapia biomédica para tratar depresiones graves, en la cual se colocan electrodos en uno o ambos lados de la cabeza del paciente; estos electrodos dan una corriente eléctrica lo suficientemente fuerte como para causar un ataque o una convulsión.

electroencephalograph: machine designed to record the electrical activity of the cortex below the skull. 55
electroencefalógrafo: equipo diseñado para grabar a través del cráneo la actividad eléctrica de la corteza cerebral.

embryonic period: the period from two to eight weeks after fertilization, during which the major organs and structures of the organism develop. 161
periodo embrionario: periodo comprendido entre las dos y las ocho semanas posteriores a la fecundación durante el cual se desarrollan los principales órganos y estructuras del organismo.

emic: studying the differences between cultures subjectively from the inside. 265
emic: relativo al estudio de las diferencias entre culturas de manera subjetivam y desde dentro de la propia cultura.

emotion: the "feeling" aspect of consciousness, characterized by a certain physical arousal, a certain behavior that reveals the emotion to the outside world, and an inner awareness of feelings. 359
emoción: aspecto "sensible" de la conciencia caracterizado por una cierta excitación física, y una cierta conducta que exterioriza la emoción y genera una conciencia interior de ciertos sentimientos.

emotion-focused coping: coping strategies that change the impact of a stressor by changing the emotional reaction to the stressor. 486

afrontamiento focalizado en las emociones: estrategias de afrontamiento que cambian el impacto del factor estresante al cambiar la reacción emocional a dicho factor estresante.

emotional intelligence: the awareness of and ability to manage one's own emotions to facilitate thinking and attain goals, as well as the ability to understand emotions in others. 326

inteligencia emocional: percepción y capacidad para gestionar las propias emociones con el fin de facilitar el razonamiento y conseguir objetivos, y para comprender las emociones de los demás.

encoding: the set of mental operations that people perform on sensory information to process that information into a form that is usable in the brain's storage systems. 288

codificación: conjunto de operaciones mentales que realizan las personas a partir de la información sensorial para procesar esa información, de manera que sea utilizable en los sistemas de almacenamiento del cerebro.

encoding failure: failure to process information into memory. 303

falla de codificación: incapacidad de procesar la información para convertirla en memoria.

encoding specificity: the tendency for memory of information to be improved if related information (such as surroundings or physiological state) available when the memory is first formed is also available when the memory is being retrieved. 296

especificidad de codificación: tendencia a mejorar la memoria de la información si la información relacionada (como el entorno o el estado fisiológico) disponible en el momento de formación del recuerdo también está disponible en el momento en que se recupera ese recuerdo.

environmental psychology: area of psychology in which the focus is on how people interact with and are affected by their physical environments. 510

psicología ambiental: ámbito de la psicología centrado en la interrelación de las personas con su entorno físico y en como las personas se ven afectadas por dicho entorno.

episodic memory: type of declarative memory containing personal information not readily available to others, such as daily activities and events. 294

memoria episódica: tipo de memoria declarativa que contiene información personal que no está disponible para los demás, como actividades y eventos diarios.

escape or withdrawal: leaving the presence of a stressor, either literally or by a psychological withdrawal into fantasy, drug abuse, or apathy. 492

escape o repliegue: abandonar el lugar en presencia de un factor estresante, ya sea de manera literal o mediante un repliegue psicológico en la fantasía, las drogas o la apatía.

etic: studying the similarities between cultures objectively from the outside. 265

etic: relativo al estudio de las semejanzas entre culturas observadas objetivamente y desde fuera.

eustress: the effect of positive events, or the optimal amount of stress that people need to promote health and well-being. 475

eustrés: efecto de los sucesos positivos o cantidad de estrés óptima de una persona para alentar su salud y bienestar.

evolutionary perspective: perspective that focuses on the biological bases of universal mental characteristics that all humans share. 12

psicología evolutiva: perspectiva centrada en las bases biológicas de las características mentales universales compartidas por todos los seres humanos.

expectancy: a person's subjective feeling that a particular behavior will lead to a reinforcing consequence. 383

expectativa: sentimiento subjetivo de la persona de que una conducta particular dará como resultado una consecuencia de refuerzo.

experiment: a deliberate manipulation of a variable to see if corresponding changes in behavior result, allowing the determination of cause-and-effect relationships. 22

experimento: manipulación deliberada de una variable para ver si hay cambios correspondientes en la conducta, y establecer así relaciones de causa y efecto.

exposure therapies: behavioral techniques that expose individuals to anxiety- or fear-related stimuli, under carefully controlled conditions, to promote new learning. 446

terapias de exposición: técnicas de comportamiento para fomentar el aprendizaje basadas en someter al individio a estimulos de ansiedad, o miedo, bajo condiciones minuciosamente controladas.

extinction: the disappearance or weakening of a learned response following the removal or absence of the unconditioned stimulus (in classical conditioning) or the removal of a reinforcer (in operant conditioning). 197

extinción: desaparición o debilitamiento de una respuesta aprendida después de quitar el estímulo no condicionado o ante la ausencia de este (en el condicionamiento clásico) o después de quitar el refuerzo (en el condicionamiento operante).

extrinsic motivation: type of motivation in which a person performs an action because it leads to an outcome that is separate from or external to the person. 346

motivación extrínseca: tipo de motivación en la cual la persona realiza una acción porque dicha acción llega a un resultado separado o externo a la persona.

F

facial feedback hypothesis: theory of emotion that assumes that facial expressions provide feedback to the brain concerning the emotion being expressed, which in turn causes and intensifies the emotion. 364

hipótesis de la retroalimentación facial: teoría de la emoción que supone que las expresiones faciales brindan retroalimentación al cerebro con respecto a la emoción que expresan, que a su vez causa e intensifica la emoción.

fetal period: the period from two to eight weeks after fertilization, during which the major organs and structures of the organism develop. 161

periodo fetal: periodo comprendido entre las dos y las ocho semanas después de la fecundación, durante las cuales se desarrollan los principales órganos y estructuras del organismo.

five-factor model (Big Five): model of personality traits that describes five basic trait dimensions. 386

modelo de los cinco factores: modelo de rasgos de la personalidad que describe cinco dimensiones de rasgos básicos.

fixation: disorder in which the person does not fully resolve the conflict in a particular psychosexual stage, resulting in

personality traits and behavior associated with that earlier stage. 377

fijación: trastorno en el cual la persona no resuelve totalmente el conflicto en una etapa psicosexual particular, que causa atributos de personalidad y conducta asociados con esa etapa anterior.

fixed interval schedule of reinforcement: schedule of reinforcement in which the interval of time that must pass before reinforcement becomes possible is always the same. 204

programa de refuerzo de intervalo fijo: programa de refuerzo en el cual el intervalo de tiempo que debe transcurrir antes de que pueda ocurrir el refuerzo es siempre el mismo.

fixed ratio schedule of reinforcement: schedule of reinforcement in which the number of responses required for reinforcement is always the same. 205

programa de refuerzo de razón fija: programa de refuerzo en el cual el número de respuestas necesarias para el refuerzo es siempre el mismo.

flashbulb memories: type of automatic encoding that occurs because an unexpected event has strong emotional associations for the person remembering it. 300

destellos de memoria: tipo de codificación automática que ocurre porque un suceso inesperado tiene fuertes asociaciones emocionales para la persona que lo recuerda.

flat affect: a lack of emotional responsiveness. 428

afecto plano: falta de respuesta emocional.

flooding: technique for treating phobias and other stress disorders in which the person is rapidly and intensely exposed to the fearprovoking situation or object and prevented from making the usual avoidance or escape response. 446

inundación: técnica para el tratamiento de fobias y otros trastornos de estrés en la cual se expone a la persona de manera rápida e intensa a la situación u objeto que provoca temor y se impide que pueda eludirlo o escapar.

foot-in-the-door technique: asking for a small commitment and, after gaining compliance, asking for a bigger commitment. 234

técnica del pie en la puerta: procedimiento que consiste en solicitar un compromiso pequeño y, una vez obtenido, solicitar un compromiso mayor.

forensic psychology: area of psychology concerned with people in the legal system, including psychological assessment of criminals, jury selection, and expert witnessing. 509

psicología forense: ámbito de la psicología que ocupa a las personas en el sistema legal y que consta de perfiles psicológicos de criminales, selección de jurados y testigos expertos.

formal operations stage: Piaget's last stage of cognitive development, in which the adolescent becomes capable of abstract thinking. 167

etapa de las operaciones formales: última etapa del desarrollo cognitivo de Piaget, en la cual el adolescente desarrolla la capacidad de razonar de manera abstracta.

free association: psychoanalytic technique in which a patient was encouraged to talk about anything that came to mind without fear of negative evaluations. 443

asociación libre: técnica psicoanalítica en la cual se anima al paciente a que hable de cualquier cosa sin miedo a ser juzgado negativamente.

free-floating anxiety: anxiety that is unrelated to any specific and known cause. 418

ansiedad flotante: ansiedad que no está relacionada con una causa específica o conocida.

frequency theory: theory of pitch that states that pitch is related to the speed of vibrations in the basilar membrane. 93

teoría de la frecuencia: teoría según la cual el tono está relacionado con la velocidad de las vibraciones en la membrana basilar.

frontal lobe: areas of the brain located in the front and top, responsible for higher mental processes and decision making as well as the production of fluent speech. 62

lóbulo frontal: área de la corteza cerebral ubicada en la zona frontal y superior del cerebro, responsable de los procesos mentales superiores, de la toma de decisiones y de la fluidez del habla.

frustration: the psychological experience produced by the blocking of a desired goal or fulfillment of a perceived need. 480

frustración: experiencia psicológica que se produce por el bloqueo de un objetivo deseado o por no satisfacer una necesidad percibida.

fully functioning person: a person who is in touch with and trusting of the deepest, innermost urges and feelings. 385

persona completamente funcional: persona que está en contacto con sus necesidades y sentimientos más profundos.

functional fixedness: a block to problem solving that comes from thinking about objects in terms of only their typical functions. 320

fijación funcional: incapacidad de resolver problemas derivada de pensar en los objetos solo en términos de sus funciones típicas.

functionalism: early perspective in psychology associated with William James, in which the focus of study is how the mind allows people to adapt, live, work, and play. 8

funcionalismo: perspectiva temprana de la psicología asociada con William James, centrada en la manera en que la mente permite a las personas adaptarse, vivir, trabajar y jugar.

fundamental attribution error: the tendency to overestimate the influence of internal factors in determining behavior while underestimating situational factors. 242

error fundamental de atribución: tendencia a sobrestimar la influencia de factores internos en la determinación de la conducta de otros y subestimar los factores situacionales.

G

g factor: the ability to reason and solve problems, or general intelligence. 325

factor g: capacidad de una persona para razonar y resolver problemas; inteligencia general.

gender: the behavior associated with being male or female. 277

género: comportamientos asociados a ser hombre o mujer.

gender identity: the individual's sense of being male or female. 277

identidad de género: percepción de ser masculino o femenino que cada individuo tiene de sí mismo.

gender roles: the culture's expectations for masculine or feminine behavior, including attitudes, actions, and personality traits associated with being male or female in that culture. 277

roles de género: expectativas de la cultura con respecto a las conductas masculinas y femeninas, que incluyen actitudes, acciones y atributos de personalidad asociados con ser hombre o mujer en esa cultura.

gender schema theory: theory of gender identity acquisition in which a child develops a mental pattern, or schema, for being male or female and then organizes observed and learned behavior around that schema. 278

teoría del esquema de género: teoría de la adquisición de identidad de género según la cual un niño desarrolla el esquema mental de ser varón o hembra, y posteriormente organiza el comportamiento observado y aprendido en torno a dicho esquema.

gene: section of DNA having the same arrangement of chemical elements. 69

gen: sección de ADN que tiene la misma disposición de elementos químicos.

general adaptation syndrome (GAS): the three stages of the body's physiological reaction to stress, including alarm, resistance, and exhaustion. 480

síndrome general de adaptación: las tres etapas de la reacción fisiológica del cuerpo al estrés, que incluyen alarma, resistencia y agotamiento.

generalized anxiety disorder: disorder in which a person has feelings of dread and impending doom along with physical symptoms of stress, which lasts 6 months or more. 420

trastorno de ansiedad generalizada: trastorno en el cual la persona tiene sentimientos de temor y desastre inminente, junto con síntomas físicos de estrés, y que dura seis meses o más.

generativity: providing guidance to one's children or the next generation, or contributing to the well-being of the next generation through career or volunteer work. 183

generatividad: brindar guía a los hijos o a la siguiente generación o contribuir al bienestar de la siguiente generación mediante trabajo voluntario o profesional.

genital stage: the final stage in Freud's psychosexual stages, from puberty on, sexual urges are allowed back into consciousness and the individual moves toward adult social and sexual behavior. 379

fase genital: última de las fases psicosexuales de Freud; a partir de la pubertad, se permite que los deseos sexuales afloren en la consciencia y el individuo progresa hacia comportamientos sociales y sexuales adultos.

germinal period: first two weeks after fertilization, during which the zygote moves down to the uterus and begins to implant in the lining. 160

periodo germinal: primeras dos semanas después de la fecundación, durante las cuales el cigoto se traslada al útero y comienza a implantarse en el revestimiento de éste.

Gestalt: early perspective in psychology focusing on perception and sensation, particularly the perception of patterns and whole figures. 103

Gestalt: escuela temprana de la psicología que se centra en la percepción y la sensación, particularmente en la percepción de patrones y figuras completas.

gifted: the 2 percent of the population falling on the upper end of the normal curve and typically possessing an IQ of 130 or above. 329

superdotado: término que se usa para describir al dos por ciento de la población que se encuentra dentro del extremo superior de la curva normal, y que típicamente posee un coeficiente intelectual de 130 o mayor.

glucagon: hormone that is secreted by the pancreas to control the levels of fats, proteins, and carbohydrates in the body by increasing the level of glucose in the bloodstream. 353

glucagón: hormona que secreta el páncreas para controlar los niveles de grasas, proteínas y carbohidratos del cuerpo mediante un aumento del nivel de glucosa en el torrente sanguíneo.

group polarization: the tendency for members involved in a group discussion to take somewhat more extreme positions and suggest riskier actions when compared to individuals who have not participated in a group discussion. 232

polarización del grupo: tendencia de los miembros que participan en un debate a tomar posiciones más extremas y a sugerir acciones más arriesgadas, que aquellos individuos que no participaron en el debate.

group therapy: form of therapy or treatment during which a small group of clients with similar concerns meet together with a therapist to address their issues. 450

terapia de grupo: forma de terapia o tratamiento en el que un pequeño grupo de clientes con problemas similares se reunen con un terapeuta para hablar de sus problemas.

groupthink: kind of thinking that occurs when people place more importance on maintaining group cohesiveness than on assessing the facts of the problem with which the group is concerned. 232

pensamiento de grupo: tipo de pensamiento que ocurre cuando los miembros de un grupo le dan más importancia a mantener la cohesión del grupo que a evaluar los hechos del problema que enfrenta el grupo.

gustation: the sense of taste. 94

gustación: sentido del sabor.

H

hallucinations: false sensory perceptions, such as hearing voices that do not really exist. 428

alucinaciones: falsas percepciones sensoriales, como oír voces que realmente no existen.

hallucinogenics: drugs including hallucinogens and marijuana that produce hallucinations or increased feelings of relaxation and intoxication. 140

alucinógenos: drogas como la marihuana que producen alucinaciones o sensaciones de mayor relajación e intoxicación.

halo effect: tendency of an interviewer to allow positive characteristics of a client to influence the assessments of the client's behavior and statements. 398

efecto de halo: tendencia del entrevistador a permitir que las características positivas del cliente influyan en la evaluación de su conducta y en sus declaraciones.

hardy personality: a person who seems to thrive on stress but lacks the anger and hostility of the Type A personality. 393

personalidad resistente: persona que parece funcionar muy bien en condiciones de estrés pero que no tiene la ira ni la hostilidad propias de las personas con personalidad tipo A.

hassles: the daily annoyances of everyday life. 477

complicaciones: molestias de la vida cotidiana.

health psychology: area of psychology focusing on how physical activities, psychological traits, stress reactions, and social relationships affect overall health and rate of illnesses. 507

psicología de la salud: ámbito de la psicología que se centra en los efectos que tienen las actividades físicas, las reacciones al estrés y las relaciones sociales, en la salud general y en las probabilidades de contraer enfermedades.

heritability: degree to which the changes in some trait within a population can be considered to be due to genetic influences; the extent individual genetic differences affect individual differences in observed behavior; in IQ, proportion of change in IQ within a population that is caused by hereditary factors. 389
heredabilidad: grado en el cual los cambios en algún rasgo dentro de una población pueden atribuirse a influencias genéticas; hasta qué punto las diferencias genéticas individuales afectan a las diferencias individuales observadas en el comportamiento; en términos de coeficiente intelectual (CI), la proporción de cambio de CI en una población provocada por factores hereditarios.

heterosexual: person attracted to the opposite sex. 355
heterosexual: persona que siente atracción hacia el sexo opuesto.

heuristic: mental shortcut based on prior experiences that helps narrow down the possible solutions for a problem. Also known as a "rule of thumb." 318
heurística: atajo mental basado en experiencias previas y que ayuda a limitar las posibles soluciones a un problema. También se conoce como "regla general".

hindsight bias: the tendency to falsely believe, through revision of older memories to include newer information, that one could have correctly predicted the outcome of an event. 301
sesgo retrospectivo: tendencia a creer, erróneamente, que es posible predecir el resultado de un suceso haciendo modificaciones en viejos recuerdos, de manera que estos contengan información reciente.

hippocampus: curved structure located within each temporal lobe, responsible for the formation of long-term declarative memories. 60
hipocampo: estructura curva ubicada dentro de cada lóbulo temporal y que es responsable de la formación de recuerdos a largo plazo.

homeostasis: the tendency of the body to maintain a steady state. 60, 347
homeostasis: tendencia del cuerpo a mantener un estado estable.

homosexual: person attracted to the same sex. 355
homosexual: que siente atracción hacia personas del mismo sexo.

hormones: chemicals released into the bloodstream by endocrine glands. 51
hormonas: compuestos químicos que las glándulas endocrinas liberan en el torrente sanguíneo.

human development: the scientific study of the changes that occur in people as they age from conception until death. 154
desarrollo humano: estudio científico de los cambios que operan en las personas a medida que envejecen, desde la concepción hasta la muerte.

human factors psychology: area of industrial/organizational psychology concerned with the study of the way humans and machines interact with each other. 511
psicología de los factores humanos: ámbito de la psicología industrial u organizacional que se ocupa de las interacciones entre los seres humanos y las máquinas.

humanistic perspective: the "third force" in psychology that focuses on those aspects of personality that make people uniquely human, such as subjective feelings and freedom of choice. 10
perspectiva humanista: "tercera fuerza" de la psicología que se centra en aquellos aspectos de la personalidad que hacen a las personas esencialmente humanas, como los sentimientos subjetivos y la libertad de elección.

hypnosis: state of consciousness in which the person is especially susceptible to suggestion. 135
hipnosis: estado de conciencia en el cual la persona es especialmente susceptible a la sugestión.

hypothalamus: small structure in the brain located below the thalamus and directly above the pituitary gland, responsible for motivational behavior such as sleep, hunger, thirst, and sex. 60
hipotálamo: pequeña estructura del cerebro ubicada debajo del tálamo y justo encima de la glándula pituitaria; es responsable de conductas motivacionales como el sueño, el hambre, la sed y el sexo.

hypothesis: tentative explanation of a phenomenon based on observations. 17
hipótesis: explicación aproximada de un fenómeno sobre la base de la observación.

I

iconic memory: visual sensory memory, lasting only a fraction of a second. 290
memoria icónica: memorial visual sensorial que dura entre una fracción de segundo y un segundo.

id: part of the personality present at birth and completely unconscious. 376
id o ello: parte de la personalidad que está presente en el nacimiento y que es completamente inconsciente.

identity versus role confusion: fifth stage of personality development in which the adolescent must find a consistent sense of self. 180
identidad ante confusión de roles: quinta fase del desarrollo de la personalidad en la que el adolescente debe encontrar un sentido sólido de sí mismo.

imaginary audience: type of thought common to adolescents in which young people believe that other people are just as concerned about the adolescent's thoughts and characteristics as they themselves are. 177
audiencia imaginaria: tipo de pensamiento común en los adolescentes, que consiste en creer que los demás están tan preocupados por sus pensamientos y características como sí mismos.

in-groups: social groups with whom a person identifies; "us." 245
grupos exclusivos: grupos sociales con los que se identifica la persona; "nosotros".

incentive approaches: theories of motivation in which behavior is explained as a response to the external stimulus and its rewarding properties. 350
método de incentivos: teorías de la motivación en las cuales se explica la conducta como una respuesta al estímulo externo y a sus propiedades gratificantes.

incentives: things that attract or lure people into action. 350
incentivos: cosas que atraen o tientan a las personas para ponerse en acción.

independent self-concept: an individual's perception of self as entirely independent from others. 268
autoconcepto independiente: percepción que un individuo tiene de sí mismo y que consiste en creerse totalmente independiente de los demás.

independent variable: variable in an experiment that is manipulated by the experimenter. 23
variable independiente: variable de un experimento que es manipulada por el experimentador.

individualism: emphasis on individuality, independence, and personal needs. 268
individualismo: énfasis en la individualidad, la independencia y las necesidades personales.

industrial/organizational (I/O) psychology: area of psychology concerned with the relationships between people and their work environment. 510
psicología industrial/organizacional (I/O): ámbito de la psicología que se ocupa de la relación entre las personas y su entorno de trabajo.

inferential statistics: statistical analysis of two or more sets of numerical data to reduce the possibility of error in measurement and to determine if the differences between the data sets are greater than chance variation would predict. 28
estadística inferencial: análisis estadístico de dos o más grupos de datos numéricos para reducir la probabilidad de un error de medida y determinar si las diferencias entre los conjuntos de datos son mayores que lo que predice la variación accidental.

information-processing model: model of memory put forth by Atkinson & Shiffrin that assumes the processing of information for memory storage is similar to the way a computer processes memory in a series of three stages. 289
modelo de procesamiento de la información: modelo de memoria propuesto por Atkinson y Shiffrin que supone que el procesamiento de la información para su almacenamiento de memoria es similar al procesamiento de memoria en tres fases de las computadoras .

insight: the sudden perception of relationships among various parts of a problem, allowing the solution to the problem to come quickly. 212, 321
perspicacia o penetración: súbita percepción de las relaciones entre las distintas partes de un problema que permite su pronta resolución.

insight therapies: therapies in which the main goal is helping people to gain personal understanding with respect to their behavior, thoughts, and feelings. 441
terapias de penetración: terapias en las cuales el objetivo principal es ayudar a las personas a conocer en profundidad su conducta, pensamientos y sentimientos.

insomnia: the inability to get to sleep, stay asleep, or get a good quality of sleep. 130
insomnio: incapacidad de conciliar el sueño, mantenerlo o lograr un sueño de buena calidad.

instincts: the biologically determined and innate patterns of behavior that exist in both people and animals. 347
instintos: patrones de conducta biológicamente determinados e innatos que existen tanto en las personas como en los animales.

insulin: a hormone secreted by the pancreas to control the levels of fats, proteins, and carbohydrates in the body by lowering or raising the level of glucose in the bloodstream. 353
insulina: hormona secretada por el páncreas para controlar los niveles de grasas, proteínas y carbohidratos del cuerpo mediante la reducción de los niveles de glucosa en el torrente sanguíneo.

intellectual disability (intellectual developmental disorder): condition in which a person's behavioral and cognitive skills exist at an earlier developmental stage than the skills of others who are the same chronological age; may also be referred to as developmentally delayed. This condition was formerly known as mental retardation. 327
discapacidad intelectual (trastorno de desarrollo intelectual): afección definida por unas condiciones conductuales y cognitivas que se presentan en una fase de desarrollo anterior a la otras personas de la misma edad cronológica; también se conoce como desarrollo intelectual tardío. Esta afección solía conocerse como retraso mental.

intelligence: the ability to learn from one's experiences, acquire knowledge, and use resources effectively in adapting to new situations or solving problems. 325
inteligencia: capacidad de aprender de las propias experiencias, adquirir conocimientos y usar los recursos de manera efectiva para adaptarse a nuevas situaciones o para resolver problemas.

intelligence quotient (IQ): a number representing a measure of intelligence, resulting from the division of one's mental age by one's chronological age and then multiplying that quotient by 100. 330
coeficiente intelectual: número que representa una medida de la inteligencia, que es el resultado de dividir la edad mental de un individuo entre su edad cronológica y luego multiplicar ese cociente por 100.

interdependent self-concept: an individual's perception of self as fundamentally connected to others. 268
autoconcepto interdependiente: percepción de un individuo de sí mismo como fundamentalmente conectado a otros.

intrinsic motivation: type of motivation in which a person performs an action because the act itself is rewarding or satisfying in some internal manner. 347
motivación intrínseca: tipo de motivación en el cual una persona realiza una acción porque el acto en sí es gratificante o satisfactorio.

introversion: dimension of personality in which people tend to withdraw from excessive stimulation. 386
introversión: dimensión de la personalidad en la cual las personas tienden a distanciarse de la estimulación excesiva.

J

James–Lange theory of emotion: theory in which a physiological reaction leads to the labeling of an emotion. 362
teoría de la emoción de James-Lange: teoría según la cual una emoción va precedida de una reacción fisiológica.

just noticeable difference: the smallest difference between two stimuli that is detectable 50 percent of the time. 81
umbral diferencial: diferencia más pequeña entre dos estímulos que se detecta el 50 por ciento de las veces.

L

language acquisition device (LAD): inborn schema that allows humans to learn and use language. 219
dispositivo de adquisición del lenguaje (DAL): esquema innato que permite aprender y usar el lenguaje a los humanos.

latency: the fourth stage in Freud's psychosexual stages, occurring during the school years, in which the sexual feelings of the child are repressed while the child develops in other ways. 379

latencia: cuarta de las etapas psicosexuales de Freud que se manifiesta durante los años escolares y en la cual los sentimientos sexuales del niño son reprimidos mientras éste se desarrolla en otros aspectos.

latent content: the symbolic or hidden meaning of dreams. 443

contenido latente: significado oculto y simbólico de los sueños.

latent learning: learning that remains hidden until its application becomes useful. 212

enseñanza latente: enseñanza que permanece oculta hasta que su aplicación resulta útil.

Law of Effect: law stating that if an action is followed by a pleasurable consequence, it will tend to be repeated, and if followed by an unpleasant consequence, it will tend not to be repeated. 201

Ley del efecto: ley que sostiene que si a una acción le sigue una consecuencia agradable, tenderá a repetirse, mientras que si es seguida por una consecuencia desagradable, tenderá a no repetirse.

learned helplessness: the tendency to fail to act to escape from a situation because of a history of repeated failures in the past. 213

incapacidad aprendida: tendencia a dejar de actuar para escapar de una situación debido a una historia de fracasos repetidos en el pasado.

learning: any relatively permanent change in behavior brought about by experience and or practice. 194

aprendizaje: todo cambio relativamente permanente en la conducta causado por la experiencia o la práctica.

lesioning: insertion of a thin, insulated electrode into the brain through which an electrical current is sent, destroying the brain cells at the tip of the wire. 55

lesión por radiofrecuencia: inserción en el encéfalo de un electrodo aislado y fino, a través del cual se envia una corriente eléctrica que destruye las células encefálicas que tocan el extremo del cable.

levels-of-processing model: model of memory that assumes information that is more "deeply processed," or processed according to its meaning rather than just the sound or physical characteristics of the word or words, will be remembered more efficiently and for a longer period of time. 291

modelo de niveles de procesamiento: modelo de memoria que supone que aquella información que se "procesa profundamente", o que se procesa de acuerdo con el significado en lugar de solo el sonido o las características físicas de las palabras, será recordada de manera más eficiente y durante un periodo de tiempo mayor.

linear perspective: monocular depth perception cue, the tendency for parallel lines to appear to converge on each other. 106

perspectiva lineal: señal de percepción de profundidad monocular; tendencia a que las líneas paralelas parezcan converger hacia sí.

locus of control: the tendency for people to assume that they either have control or do not have control over events and consequences in their lives. 382

locus de control: tendencia de las personas a suponer que ellas tienen o no tienen control sobre los sucesos y consecuencias de su vida.

long-term memory (LTM): the system of memory into which all the information is placed to be kept more or less permanently. 292

memoria a largo plazo (MLP): sistema de memoria en el que toda la información se guarda para su mantenimiento de manera más o menos permanente.

longitudinal design: research design in which one participant or group of participants is studied over a long period of time. 154

diseño longitudinal: diseño de investaci el que un participante o grupo de participantes es estudiado durante un largo periodo de tiempo. ón en el que un participante o grupo de participantes es estudiado durante un largo periodo de tiempo.

lowball technique: getting a commitment from a person and then raising the cost of that commitment. 234

técnica del engaño: obtener un compromiso de una persona y luego elevar el costo de tal compromiso.

M

maintenance rehearsal: practice of saying information to be remembered over and over in one's head in order to maintain it in short-term memory. 292

ensayo de mantenimiento: práctica de repetir una información una y otra vez para mantenerla en la memoria a corto plazo.

major depressive disorder: severe depression that comes on suddenly and seems to have no external cause or is too severe for current circumstances. 424

trastorno depresivo grave: depresión grave que aparece de forma repentina sin causa externa aparente o que cuya severidad no está justificada por las circunstancias en que aparece.

manic: having the quality of excessive excitement, energy, and elation or irritability. 424

maníaco: que tiene excitación, energía y euforia o irritabilidad excesivas.

marijuana: mild hallucinogen derived from the leaves and flowers of a particular type of hemp plant. 143

marihuana: alucinógeno moderado derivado de las hojas y las flores de un tipo particular de planta de cáñamo.

mean: the arithmetic average of a distribution of numbers. 29

media: promedio aritmético de una distribución de números.

median: the middle score in an ordered distribution of scores, or the mean of the two middle numbers; the 50th percentile. 29

mediana: valor intermedio en una distribución de valores, o la media de los dos números centrales; el percentil 50.

meditation: mental series of exercises meant to refocus attention and achieve a trancelike state of consciousness. 137

meditación: serie de ejercicios mentales diseñados para centrar la atención y lograr un estado de conciencia similar al trance.

medulla: the first large swelling at the top of the spinal cord, forming the lowest part of the brain, which is responsible for life-sustaining functions such as breathing, swallowing, and heart rate. 58

bulbo raquídeo o médula oblonga: primera gran protuberancia que se encuentra en la parte superior de la médula espinal y forma la parte inferior del encéfalo; es responsable de funciones vitales como la respiración, la deglución y la frecuencia cardíaca.

memory: an active system that receives information from the senses, puts that information into a usable form, organizes it as it stores it away, and then retrieves the information from storage. 288

memoria: sistema activo que recibe información de los sentidos, la hace utilizable, la guarda de manera organizada y luego la extrae de su lugar de almacenamiento.

memory trace: physical change in the brain that occurs when a memory is formed. 303

rastro de memoria: cambio físico en el cerebro que ocurre cuando se forma un recuerdo.

mental images: mental representations that stand for objects or events and have a picture-like quality. 314

imágenes mentales: representaciones similares a dibujos que representan objetos o eventos.

mental set: the tendency for people to persist in using problem- solving patterns that have worked for them in the past. 322

predisposición mental: tendencia de las personas a persistir en el uso de aquellos patrones de resolución de problemas que usaron con éxito en el pasado.

mere exposure: effect idea that repeated presentation of novel stimuli increases liking the stimuli. 248

mera exposición: efecto de que la mera repetición de nuevos estímulos aumenta nuestra predilección por tales estímulos.

misinformation effect: the tendency of misleading information presented after an event to alter the memories of the event itself. 301

efecto equívoco: tendencia a presentar información engañosa después de un suceso para alterar los recuerdos de dicho suceso.

mnemonics: strategies and memory "tricks" to help us remember information more effectively. 297

nemotécnia: estrategias y "trucos" de memoria que nos ayudan a recordar información de manera más efectiva.

mode: the most frequent score in a distribution of scores. 29

moda: resultado más frecuente en una distribución de valores.

modeling: learning through the observation and imitation of others. 446

modelado: aprendizaje que se da a través de la observación e imitación de otros.

monocular cues: cues for perceiving depth based on one eye only. 106

señales monoculares: indicadores para percibir la profundidad con un solo ojo.

monozygotic twins: identical twins formed when one zygote splits into two separate masses of cells, each of which develops into a separate embryo. 159

gemelos monocigóticos: gemelos idénticos que se forman cuando un cigoto se divide en dos masas celulares independientes, cada una de las cuales se desarrolla para formar un embrión diferente.

mood disorders: disorders in which mood is severely disturbed. 424

trastornos del estado de ánimo: trastornos en los que se perturba gravemente el estado de ánimo.

morphemes: the smallest units of meaning within a language. 216

morfemas: unidades más pequeñas de significado dentro de un lenguaje.

motivation: the process by which activities are started, directed, and continued so that physical or psychological needs or wants are met. 346

motivación: proceso por el cual se comienza, controla y continúa una actividad para satisfacer una necesidad o un deseo físico o psicológico.

motor cortex: rear section of the frontal lobe, responsible for sending motor commands to the muscles of the somatic nervous system. 62

corteza motora: sección del lóbulo frontal ubicada en la parte posterior, responsable de enviar órdenes motoras a los músculos del sistema nervioso somático.

Müller–Lyer illusion: illusion of line length that is distorted by inward-turning or outward-turning corners on the ends of the lines, causing lines of equal length to appear to be different. 109

ilusión de Mu"ller-Lyer: ilusión óptica en la cual las líneas rectas parecen más largas o más cortas según si las puntas de flecha añadidas en sus extremos apuntan hacia adentro o hacia afuera; esto causa que líneas rectas de la misma longitud parezcan diferentes.

myelin: fatty substances produced by certain glial cells that coat the axons of neurons to insulate, protect, and speed up the neural impulse. 43

mielina: sustancia grasa que recubre los axones de las neuronas para aislar, proteger y acelerar el impulso neural.

N

narcolepsy: sleep disorder in which a person falls immediately into REM sleep during the day without warning. 131

narcolepsia: trastorno del sueño en el cual la persona cae inmediatamente en sueño REM durante el día, sin previo aviso.

narcotics: a class of opium-related drugs that suppress the sensation of pain by binding to and stimulating the nervous system's natural receptor sites for endorphins. 142

narcóticos: clase de drogas derivadas del opio que anulan la sensación de dolor al unirse y estimular los receptores naturales de endorfinas del sistema nervioso.

natural selection: traits that contribute to survival are more likely to be passed on. 71

selección natural: principio que sostiene que las características heredadas que brindan una ventaja de supervivencia son más propensas a pasar a las futuras generaciones.

nature: the influence of our inherited characteristics on our personality, physical growth, intellectual growth, and social interactions. 68

naturaleza: influencia de nuestros rasgos heredadas en nuestra personalidad, crecimiento físico, crecimiento intelectual e interacciones sociales.

need: a requirement of some material (such as food or water) that is essential for survival of the organism. 347

necesidad: requerimiento de algún material (como alimentos o agua) esencial para la supervivencia del organismo.

need for achievement (nAch): a need that involves a strong desire to succeed in attaining goals, not only realistic ones but also challenging ones. 349

necesidad de logro (nLog): necesidad que implica un fuerte deseo de triunfar en la obtención de logros, no solo realistas sino también los que implican un desafío.

need for affiliation (nAff): the need for friendly social interactions and relationships with others. 349

necesidad de afiliación (nAfi): necesidad de interacciones sociales amistosas y relaciones con otros.

need for power (nPow): the need to have control or influence over others. 349

necesidad de poder (nPod): necesidad de tener control o influencia sobre otros.

negative reinforcement: the reinforcement (strengthening) of a response by the removal, escape from, or avoidance of an unpleasant stimulus. 203

refuerzo negativo: refuerzo (fortalecimiento) de una respuesta mediante la eliminación, escapatoria o evitación de un estímulo negativo.

negative symptoms: symptoms of schizophrenia that are less than normal behavior or an absence of normal behavior; poor attention, flat affect, and poor speech production. 428

síntomas negativos: síntomas de esquizofrenia que representan una conducta poco normal o una ausencia de conducta normal; poca atención, afecto plano y una producción insuficiente de habla.

neuron: the basic cell that makes up the nervous system and that receives and sends messages within that system. 42

neurona: célula básica que conforma el sistema nervioso y que recibe y envía mensajes dentro de ese sistema.

neuroplasticity: the ability within the brain to constantly change both the structure and function of many cells in response to experience or trauma. 48

neuroplasticidad: capacidad del cerebro de cambiar constantemente tanto la estructura como la función de muchas de sus células en respuesta a experiencias o traumas.

neuropsychology: area of psychology in which psychologists specialize in the research or clinical implications of brain-behavior relationships. 506

neuropsicología: ámbito de la psicología especializada en la investigación o en las consecuencias clínicas de las relaciones entre el cerebro y la conducta.

neurotransmitters: neurotransmitter chemical found in the synaptic vesicles that, when released, has an effect on the next cell. 44

neurotransmisor: compuesto químico que se encuentra en las vesículas sinápticas y que, cuando se libera, tiene un efecto en la célula adyacente.

non-REM (NREM) sleep: any of the stages of sleep that do not include REM. 126

sueño no REM: cualquiera de las etapas del sueño que no incluyen el sueño REM.

nondeclarative (implicit) memory: type of long-term memory including memory for skills, procedures, habits, and conditioned responses. These memories are not conscious but are implied to exist because they affect conscious behavior. 293

memoria procedimental (implícita): tipo de memoria a largo plazo que incluye la memoria de las destrezas, procedimientos, hábitos y respuestas condicionadas. Estas memorias no son conscientes pero existen de manera implícita ya que afectan al comportamiento consciente.

nondirective: therapy style in which the therapist remains relatively neutral and does not interpret or take direct actions with regard to the client, instead remaining a calm, nonjudgmental listener while the client talks. 444

no directiva: estilo de terapia en el cual el terapeuta permanece relativamente neutral y no interpreta o inicia acciones directas con respecto al cliente, sino que le deja hablar y lo escucha permaneciendo en calma y sin hacer ningún juicio.

norms: a culture's understood rules for expected behavior, values, beliefs, and attitudes. 264

normas: reglas implícitas de una cultura sobre conducta esperada, valores, creencias y actitudes.

nurture: the influence of the environment on personality, physical growth, intellectual growth, and social interactions. 68

crianza: influencia del medio ambiente en la personalidad, el crecimiento físico, el desarrollo intelectual y las interacciones sociales.

O

obedience: changing one's behavior at the command of an authority figure. 235

obediencia: cambiar la propia conducta bajo las órdenes de una figura de autoridad.

object permanence: the knowledge that an object exists even when it is not in sight. 165

permanencia del objeto: conocimiento de que el objeto existe incluso cuando no está a la vista.

observational learning: learning new behavior by watching someone else, called a "model," perform that behavior. 213

aprendizaje observacional: aprendizaje de nuevas conductas observando a otra persona, llamada "modelo", realizar dichas conductas.

obsessive-compulsive disorder: disorder in which intruding, recurring thoughts, or obsessions create anxiety that is relieved by performing a repetitive, ritualistic behavior or mental act (compulsion). 420

trastorno obsesivo-compulsivo: trastorno en el cual pensamientos y obsesiones recurrentes e invasivos causan una ansiedad que se alivia mediante la realización de una conducta o de un acto mental repetitivo y ritual (compulsión).

occipital lobe: section of the brain located at the rear and bottom of each cerebral hemisphere containing the primary visual centers of the brain. 62

lóbulo occipital: sección del cerebro ubicada en la parte posterior e inferior de cada hemisferio cerebral, y que contiene los centros visuales del cerebro.

olfaction: the sense of smell. 96

olfato: sentido del olfato.

operant conditioning: the learning of voluntary behavior through the effects of pleasant and unpleasant consequences to responses. 202

condicionamiento operante: aprendizaje de conductas voluntarias a través de los efectos agradables y desagradables de las respuestas.

operational definition: definition of a variable of interest that allows it to be measured. 22

definición operacional: definición de una variable de interés que permite su cuantificación o medida.

opponent-process theory: theory of color vision that proposes visual neurons (or groups of neurons) are stimulated by light of one color and inhibited by light of another color. 88

teoría oponente-proceso: teoría de la visión de los colores según la cual las neuronas (o grupo de neuronas) visuales se estimulan ante la luz de un color determinado y se inhiben ante otro color.

optimists: people who expect positive outcomes. 393, 489

optimistas: personas que esperan resultados positivos.

oral stage: the first stage in Freud's psychosexual stages, occurring in the first 18 months of life in which the mouth is the erogenous zone and weaning is the primary conflict. 377

fase oral: primera de las etapas psicosexuales de Freud que se produce durante los primeros 18 meses de vida, en la que la boca es la zona erógena y en la que el destete es un conflicto primario.

out-groups: social groups with whom a person does not identify; "them." 245

grupos externos: grupos sociales con los que la persona no se identifica; "ellos".

P

panic attack: sudden onset of intense panic in which multiple physical symptoms of stress occur, often with feelings that one is dying. 420

ataque de pánico: aparición repentina de un pánico intenso que suscita múltiples síntomas físicos de estrés, y que suele llevar a sentir a quien lo sufre que se está muriendo.

panic disorder: disorder in which panic attacks occur more than once or repeatedly, and cause persistent worry or changes in behavior. 420

trastorno de pánico: trastorno que da lugar a más de un ataque de pánico o episodios repetidos, y que causa un estado de preocupación persistente o cambios de comportamiento.

Parallel Distributed Processing (PDP) model: a model of memory in which memory processes are proposed to take place at the same time over a large network of neural connections. 291

modelo de procesamiento distribuido en paralelo (PDP): modelo de memoria en el que se propone que los procesos de memoria se producen simultáneamente a lo largo de una amplia red de conexiones neuronales.

parasympathetic division: part of the ANS that restores the body to normal functioning after arousal and is responsible for the day-to-day functioning of the organs and glands. 50

división parasimpática: parte del sistema nervioso autónomo que restablece la función normal del cuerpo al despertar y que es responsable del funcionamiento diario de órganos y glándulas.

parietal lobe: sections of the brain located at the top and back of each cerebral hemisphere containing the centers for touch, temperature, and body position. 62

lóbulos parietales: secciones del cerebro ubicadas en la parte superior y posterior de cada hemisferio cerebral, y que contienen los centros del tacto, el gusto, las sensaciones de temperatura y la posición corporal.

peak experiences: according to Maslow, times in a person's life during which self-actualization is temporarily achieved. 352

momentos pico: según Maslow, momentos en la vida de una persona durante los cuales se consigue temporalmente la autorrealización.

perception: the method by which the sensations experienced at any given moment are interpreted and organized in some meaningful fashion. 102

percepción: método mediante el cual las sensaciones que se experimentan en un momento dado se interpretan y adquieren una organización significativa.

perceptual set: the tendency to perceive things a certain way because previous experiences or expectations influence those perceptions. 111

expectativa perceptiva: tendencia a percibir las cosas de determinada manera debido a que las experiencias o expectativas previas influyen en esas percepciones.

peripheral nervous system: all nerves and neurons that are not contained in the brain and spinal cord but that run through the body itself. 48

sistema nervioso periférico: todos los nervios y las neuronas que no están contenidas en el cerebro y la médula espinal sino en el cuerpo en sí.

peripheral-route processing: type of information processing that involves attending to factors not involved in the message, such as the appearance of the source of the message, the length of the message, and other noncontent factors. 240

procesamiento por ruta periférica: tipo de procesamiento de la información que implica atender a factores ajenos al mensaje, como la apariencia de la fuente del mensaje, la longitud del mensaje y otros factores ajenos el contenido.

person-centered therapy: a nondirective insight therapy based on the work of Carl Rogers in which the client does all the talking and the therapist listens. 444

psicoterapia centrada en el cliente: terapia no directiva de penetración basada en los estudios de Carl Rogers, en los que el cliente habla y el terapeuta se limita a escuchar.

personal fable: type of thought common to adolescents in which young people believe themselves to be unique and protected from harm. 177

fábula personal: tipo de pensamiento común en los adolescentes en el cual creen ser únicos y estar protegidos de todo mal.

personality: the unique and relatively stable ways in which people think, feel, and behave. 374

personalidad: manera singular y relativamente estable en el cual las personas piensan, sienten y se comportan.

personality disorders: disorders in which a person adopts a persistent, rigid, and maladaptive pattern of behavior that interferes with normal social interactions. 430

trastornos de la personalidad: trastornos en los que la persona adopta patrones de conducta persistentes, rígidos e inadaptivos que interfieren en sus interacciones sociales normales.

personality inventory: paper-and-pencil or computerized test that consists of statements that require a specific, standardized response from the person taking the test. 396

inventario de personalidad: prueba en papel y lápiz o computarizada que consta de de enunciados que requieren una respuesta específica y estandarizada por parte del examinado.

personality psychology: area of psychology in which the psychologists study the differences in personality among people. 506

psicología de la personalidad: ámbito de la psicología que estudia las diferencias de personalidad entre las personas.

pessimists: seem to expect the worst to happen. 393

pesimistas: personas que esperan resultados negativos.

phallic stage: the third stage in Freud's psychosexual stages, occurring from about 3 to 6 years of age, in which the child discovers sexual feelings. 379

fase fálica: tercera de las etapas psicosexuales de Freud, que se da entre los tres y los seis años de edad aproximadamente, en la que el niño descubre sus sentimientos sexuales.

phobia: an irrational, persistent fear of an object, situation, or social activity. 419

fobia: miedo irracional y persistente a un objeto, situación o actividad social.

phonemes: the basic units of sound in a language. 216

fonemas: unidades básicas de sonido del lenguaje.

physical dependence: condition occurring when a person's body becomes unable to function normally without a particular drug. 139

dependencia física: afección que ocurre cuando el cuerpo de una persona deja de funcionar normalmente sin la ayuda de un medicamento específico.

physiological psychology: area of psychology in which the psychologists study the biological bases of behavior. 506

psicología fisiológica: ámbito de la psicología que estudia las bases biológicas de la conducta.

pinna: the visible part of the ear. 90

pabellón auricular: parte visible del aparato auditivo.

pituitary gland: gland located in the brain that secretes human growth hormone and influences all other hormone-secreting glands (also known as the master gland). 51

glándula pituitaria: glándula ubicada en el cerebro que secreta la hormona del crecimiento humano e influye en todas las otras glándulas secretoras de hormonas (también se conoce como glándula maestra).

place theory: theory of pitch that states that different pitches are experienced by the stimulation of hair cells in different locations on the organ of Corti. 92

teoría del lugar: teoría del tono según la cual los distintos tonos se experimentan debido a la estimulación de las células pilosas situadas en diversos lugares del órgano de Corti.

pons: the larger swelling above the medulla that connects the top of the brain to the bottom and that plays a part in sleep, dreaming, left–right body coordination, and arousal. 58

puente de Varolio: gran protuberancia situada sobre el bulbo raquídeo que conecta la parte superior del cerebro con la inferior, y que tiene un papel importante en el sueño, la actividad onírica, la coordinación izquierda-derecha del cuerpo y el despertar.

positive perspective: perspective in psychology that shifts focus away from the negative and instead focuses on well-being. 12

psicología positiva: perspectiva de la psicología que se aparta de lo negativo para centrarse en el bienestar.

positive reinforcement: the reinforcement (strengthening) of a response by the addition or experience of a pleasurable stimulus. 203

refuerzo positivo: refuerzo (fortalecimiento) de una respuesta por la suma o experimentación de un estímulo placentero.

positive symptoms: symptoms of schizophrenia that are excesses of behavior or occur in addition to normal behavior; hallucinations, delusions, and distorted thinking. 428

síntomas positivos: síntomas de esquizofrenia que son excesos de conducta o que ocurren además de la conducta normal; alucinaciones, delirios y pensamiento distorsionado.

posttraumatic stress disorder (PTSD): a disorder resulting from exposure to a major stressor, with symptoms of anxiety, dissociation, nightmares, poor sleep, reliving the event, and concentration problems, lasting for more than 1 month; symptoms may appear immediately, or not occur until 6 months or later after the traumatic event. 421

trastorno de estrés postraumático (TEPT): trastorno que se produce por haber estado sometido a un factor estresante severo, que genera síntomas de ansiedad, pesadillas, insomnio, reviviscencias del suceso y problemas de concentración y que dura más de un mes; los síntomas pueden aparecer de inmediato o no producirse hasta después de los seis meses, o más, del episodio traumático

pragmatics: aspects of language involving the practical ways of communicating with others, or the social "niceties" of language. 216

pragmática: aspectos del lenguaje que implican las maneras prácticas de comunicarse con otros, o las "sutilezas" sociales del lenguaje.

prefrontal lobotomy: psychosurgery in which the connections of the prefrontal cortex to other areas of the brain are severed. 459

lobotomía prefrontal: psicocirugía en la cual se cortan las conexiones de la corteza prefrontal con otras partes del cerebro.

prejudice: negative attitude held by a person about the members of a particular social group. 245, 274

prejuicio: actitud negativa que tiene una persona hacia los miembros de un grupo social particular.

preoperational stage: Piaget's second stage of cognitive development in which the preschool child learns to use language as a means of exploring the world. 166

etapa preoperacional: segunda etapa del desarrollo cognitivo de Piaget, en la cual el niño en edad preescolar aprende a usar el lenguaje como un medio de explorar el mundo.

pressure: the psychological experience produced by urgent demands or expectations for a person's behavior that come from an outside source. 479

presión: experiencia psicológica producida por exigencias o expectativas urgentes de la conducta de la persona y que provienen de una fuente externa.

primacy effect: tendency to remember information at the beginning of a body of information better than the information that follows. 298

efecto de primacía: tendencia a recordar mejor lo que aparece al comienzo de una información que aquello que aparece después.

primary appraisal: estimating the severity of the stressor and classifying it as a threat. 391

apreciación primaria: estimación de la gravedad del factor estresante y clasificarlo después como una amenaza.

primary drives: those drives that involve needs of the body such as hunger and thirst. 347

instintos primarios: aquellos instintos relacionados con las necesidades corporales, como el hambre y la sed.

primary reinforcer: any reinforcer that is naturally reinforcing by meeting a basic biological need, such as hunger, thirst, or touch. 202

reforzador primario: todo reforzador que actúa de manera natural y que cubre una necesidad biológica básica como el hambre, la sed o el contacto.

proactive interference: memory problem that occurs when older information prevents or interferes with the learning or retrieval of newer information. 304

interferencia proactiva: problema que ocurre en la recuperación de la memoria cuando la información más antigua impide o interfiere en la recuperación de la información más reciente.

problem-focused coping: coping strategies that try to eliminate the source of a stress or reduce its impact through direct actions. 486

afrontamiento centrado en el problema: estrategias de afrontamiento que tratan de eliminar la fuente de estrés o de reducir su impacto mediante acciones directas.

projective tests: personality assessments that present ambiguous visual stimuli to the client and ask the client to respond with whatever comes to mind. 399

pruebas proyectivas: evaluaciones de la personalidad que consisten en presentar al cliente estímulos visuales ambiguos y en pedirle después que responda lo que le venga a la mente.

prototype: an example of a concept that closely matches the defining characteristics of the concept. 270, 316

prototipo: ejemplo de un concepto que concuerda estrechamente con las características definitorias de dicho concepto.

psychiatric social worker: a social worker with some training in therapy methods who focuses on the environmental conditions that can have an impact on mental disorders, such as poverty, overcrowding, stress, and drug abuse. 503

trabajador social psiquiátrico: trabajador social con formación en métodos de terapia que se centra en las condiciones ambientales (como la pobreza, el hacinamiento, el estrés y el uso de drogas) susceptibles de tener un impacto en los trastornos mentales del cliente.

psychiatrist: a physician who specializes in the diagnosis and treatment of psychological disorders. 442, 503

psiquiatra: médico que se especializa en el diagnóstico y tratamiento de trastornos psicológicos.

psychoactive drugs: chemical substances that alter thinking, perception, and memory. 138

drogas psicoactivas: drogas que alteran el pensamiento, la percepción y la memoria.

psychoanalysis: an insight therapy based on the theory of Freud, emphasizing the revealing of unconscious conflicts; Freud's term for both the theory of personality and the therapy based on it. 442

psicoanálisis: terapia de penetración basada en la teoría de Freud, que hace hincapié en la revelación de conflictos inconscientes; término acuñado por Freud tanto para su teoría de la personalidad como para la terapia en ella basada.

psychodynamic perspective: modern version of psychoanalysis that is more focused on the development of a sense of self and the discovery of motivations behind a person's behavior other than sexual motivations. 10

perspectiva psicodinámica: visión moderna del psicoanálisis que está más centrada en el desarrollo de un sentido del yo y en el descubrimiento de otras motivaciones de la conducta de la persona que en los deseos reprimidos.

psychological defense mechanisms: unconscious distortions of a person's perception of reality that reduce stress and anxiety. 377

mecanismos psicológicos de defensa: distorsiones inconscientes de la percepción de la realidad de la persona que reducen el estrés y la ansiedad.

psychological dependence: the feeling that a drug is needed to continue a feeling of emotional or psychological well-being. 139

dependencia psicológica: sensación de que una droga es necesaria para mantener el bienestar emocional o psicológico.

psychological disorder: any pattern of behavior or thinking that causes people significant distress, causes them to harm others, or harms their ability to function in daily life. 412

trastorno psicológico: todo patrón de conducta o de pensamiento que causa en las personas una angustia importante, que les lleva a dañar a otras personas o que les incapacita para funcionar en la vida cotidiana.

psychologist: a professional with an academic degree and specialized training in one or more areas of psychology. 442, 503

psicólogo: profesional con un título académico y con formación en una o más especialidades de psicología.

psychology: scientific study of behavior and mental processes. 4

psicología: estudio científico de la conducta y los procesos mentales.

psychopathology: the study of abnormal behavior and psychological dysfunction. 410

psicopatología: estudio de las conductas anormales y de las disfunciones psicológicas.

psychopharmacology: the use of drugs to control or relieve the symptoms of psychological disorders. 455

psicofarmacología: uso de medicamentos para controlar o aliviar los síntomas de los trastornos psicológicos.

psychosexual stages: five stages of personality development proposed by Freud and tied to the sexual development of the child. 377

fases psicosexuales: las cinco etapas del desarrollo de la personalidad propuestas por Freud y ligadas al desarrollo sexual del niño.

psychotherapy: therapy for mental disorders in which a person with a problem talks with a psychological professional. 441

psicoterapia: terapia para los trastornos mentales en la cual la persona con problemas conversa con un psicólogo profesional.

psychotic: refers to an individual's inability to separate what is real and what is fantasy. 427

psicótica: término que se aplica a la persona que ya no es capaz de percibir qué es real y qué es fantasía.

punishment by application: the punishment of a response by the addition or experience of an unpleasant stimulus. 206

castigo por aplicación: castigo de una respuesta mediante la aplicación o experimentación de un estímulo desagradable.

punishment by removal: the punishment of a response by the removal of a pleasurable stimulus. 206

castigo por supresión: castigo de una respuesta mediante la eliminación de un estímulo agradable.

R

rapid eye movement (REM) sleep: stage of sleep in which the eyes move rapidly under the eyelids and the person is typically experiencing a dream. 126

sueño de movimientos oculares rápidos (MOR): etapa del sueño en la que los ojos se mueven rápidamente debajo de los párpados y la persona por lo general sueña.

rational emotive behavior therapy (REBT): cognitive behavioral therapy in which clients are directly challenged in their irrational beliefs and helped to restructure their thinking into more rational belief statements. 448

terapia racional emotiva conductual: terapia cognitiva del comportamiento en la cual se expone al cliente directamente a sus propias creencias irracionales y se le ayuda a reestructurar su pensamiento en enunciados más racionales.

recall: type of memory retrieval in which the information to be retrieved must be "pulled" from memory with very few external cues. 297

recuerdo: tipo de rememoración en el que la información debe ser "extraída" de la memoria con muy pocas señales exteriores.

recency effect: tendency to remember information at the end of a body of information better than the information at the beginning of it. 298

efecto de lo más reciente: tendencia a recordar mejor la parte final de una información que la parte inicial.

recessive: referring to a gene that only influences the expression of a trait when paired with an identical gene. 69, 156

recesivo: gen que solo influye en la expresión de un rasgo cuando se empareja con un gen idéntico a él.

reciprocal determinism: Bandura's explanation of how the factors of environment, personal characteristics, and behavior can interact to determine future behavior. 382

determinismo recíproco: explicación de Bandura de cómo interactúan los factores del entorno, los rasgos personales y la conducta para determinar conductas futuras.

recognition: the ability to match a piece of information or a stimulus to a stored image or fact. 297

reconocimiento: capacidad de unir una información o un estímulo a una imagen o un hecho almacenado.

reflection: therapy technique in which the therapist restates what the client says rather than interpreting those statements. 444

reflexión: técnica de tratamiento en la cual el terapeuta repite en voz alta lo que dice el cliente en lugar de interpretar sus palabras.

reliability: the tendency of a test to produce the same scores again and again each time it is given to the same people. 33, 331

confiabilidad: tendencia de una prueba a producir los mismos resultados una y otra vez cuando se le administra a las mismas personas.

representative sample: randomly selected sample of subjects from a larger population of subjects. 19

muestra representativa: muestra de sujetos seleccionada aleatoriamente de una población más grande.

representativeness heuristic: assumption that any object (or person) sharing characteristics with the members of a particular category is also a member of that category. 318

representatividad heurística: suposición de que un objeto (o una persona) que comparte características con los miembros de una categoría en particular también pertenece a esa categoría.

restorative theory: theory of sleep proposing that sleep is necessary to the physical health of the body and serves to replenish chemicals and repair cellular damage. 125

teoría del sueño reparador: teoría según la cual el sueño es necesario para la salud física del cuerpo y sirve para reponer sustancias químicas y para reparar el daño celular.

reticular formation (RF): an area of neurons running through the middle of the medulla and the pons and slightly beyond that play a role in general arousal, alertness, and sleep. 58

formación reticular: área de neuronas que se extiende a través de una zona que comprende y trasciende el centro del bulbo raquídeo y el puente de Varolio, y que interviene en el despertar general, la vigilia y el sueño.

retrieval: getting information that is in storage into a form that can be used. 288

recuperación: obtener información que está almacenada y darle una forma que se pueda usar.

retrieval cue: a stimulus for remembering. 296

señal de recuperación: estímulo para recordar.

retroactive interference: memory retrieval problem that occurs when newer information prevents or interferes with the retrieval of older information. 305

interferencia retroactiva: problema de recuperación de la memoria cuando la información más reciente evita o interfiere en la recuperación de la información más antigua.

retrograde amnesia: loss of memory from the point of some injury or trauma backward, or loss of memory for the past. 305

amnesia retrógrada: pérdida de memoria desde el momento de la lesión que la produce hacia atrás o pérdida de la memoria del pasado.

rods: visual sensory receptors found at the back of the retina, responsible for noncolor sensitivity to low levels of light. 87

bastoncillos: receptores sensoriales visuales que se encuentran en la parte posterior de la retina y que son responsables de la percepción visual sin color en bajos niveles de luz.

romantic love: type of love consisting of intimacy and passion. 251

amor romántico: tipo de amor que consta de intimidad y pasión.

S

schema: (1) the concept or framework that organizes the information. 317 (2) in this case, a mental concept formed through experiences with objects and events. 165

esquema: (1) idea de estructura sobre la cual se organiza la información. (2) en este caso, concepto mental que se forma a través de experiencias con objetos y sucesos.

schizophrenia: severe disorder in which the person suffers from disordered thinking, bizarre behavior, hallucinations, and inability to distinguish between fantasy and reality. 427

esquizofrenia: trastorno grave en el cual la persona sufre de pensamiento desordenado, conducta extravagante, alucinaciones e incapacidad de distinguir entre fantasía y realidad.

school psychology: area of psychology in which the psychologists work directly in the schools, doing assessments, educational placement, and diagnosing educational problems. 508

psicología escolar: ámbito de la psicología que se desarrolla en las escuelas mediante la realización de evaluaciones, asignaciones de clases y recursos, y diagnósticos de problemas educativos.

scientific method: system of gathering data so that bias and error in measurement are reduced. 16

método científico: sistema de recolección de datos que reduce el sesgo y los errores de medida.

secondary appraisal: estimating the resources that they have available for coping with the stressor. 392

apreciación secundaria: estimación de los recursos disponibles para afrontar un factor estresante.

secondary reinforcer: any reinforcer that becomes reinforcing after being paired with a primary reinforcer, such as praise, tokens, or gold stars. 202

reforzador secundario: elogios, fichas, estrellas doradas y cualquier otro reforzador que actúa como tal al emparejarlo con un reforzador primario.

selective attention: the ability to focus on only one stimulus from among all sensory input. 290

atención selectiva: capacidad de centrarse en un solo estímulo de entre todas las entradas sensoriales.

self-actualization: according to Maslow, the point that is seldom reached at which people have sufficiently satisfied the lower needs and achieved their full human potential. 351

autorrealización: según Maslow, punto que casi nunca se alcanza en el cual las personas tienen suficientemente cubiertas las necesidades menores y han alcanzado su potencial humano completo.

self-actualizing tendency: the striving to fulfill one's innate capacities and capabilities. 384

tendencia a la autorrealización: esfuerzo por desarrollar las propias capacidades innatas.

self-determination theory (SDT): theory of human motivation in which the social context of an action has an effect on the type of motivation existing for the action. 352

teoría de la autodeterminación (TAD): teoría de la motivación humana en la cual el contexto social de una acción tiene un efecto en el tipo de motivación previa a dicha acción.

self-efficacy: individual's expectancy of how effective his or her efforts to accomplish a goal will be in any particular circumstance. 382

autoeficacia: expectativa del individuo de lo efectivos que son sus esfuerzos para alcanzar una meta en una circunstancia concreta.

semantic memory: type of declarative memory containing general knowledge, such as knowledge of language and information learned in formal education. 294

memoria semántica: tipo de memoria declarativa que contiene conocimientos generales, tales como el conocimiento del lenguaje materno y la información aprendida durante la educación formal.

semantic network model: model of memory organization that assumes information is stored in the brain in a connected fashion, with concepts that are related stored physically closer to each other than concepts that are not highly related. 294

modelo de red semántica: modelo de organización de la memoria que representa la memoria almacenada en el cerebro mediante conexiones; los conceptos relacionados se guardan físicamente más cerca que los conceptos cuya relación no es tan estrecha.

sensation: the process that occurs when special neuron receptor sites in the sense organs are activated, allowing various forms of outside stimuli to become neural signals in the brain. 80

sensación: proceso que ocurre cuando se activan neurorreceptores especiales en los órganos sensoriales permitiendo la transformación de diversos tipos de estímulos externos en señales neurales del cerebro.

sensation seeker: someone who needs more arousal than the average person. 350

buscador de emociones: alguien que necesita más excitación que las personas promedio.

sensorimotor stage: Piaget's first stage of cognitive development in which the infant uses its senses and motor abilities to interact with objects in the environment. 165

etapa sensoriomotriz: primera etapa del desarrollo cognitivo de Piaget, en la cual el niño pequeño usa sus sentidos y capacidades motrices para interactuar con los objetos del entorno.

sensory adaptation: tendency of sensory receptor cells to become less responsive to a stimulus that is unchanging. 83

adaptación sensorial: tendencia de las células sensoriales receptoras a responder menos ante un estímulo que no cambia.

sensory memory: the very first stage of memory; the point at which information enters the nervous system through the sensory systems. 289

memoria sensorial: primera etapa de la memoria; punto en el que la información entra en el sistema nervioso a través de los sistemas sensoriales.

serial position effect: tendency of information at the beginning and end of a body of information to be remembered more accurately than information in the middle of the body of information. 298

efecto de posición serial: tendencia a recordar con mayor precisión el principio y el final de una información, que aquella que se encuentra en el medio.

sexual orientation: a person's sexual attraction and affection for members of either the opposite or the same sex. 354

orientación sexual: atracción sexual y afecto de una persona hacia miembros de su mismo sexo o del sexo contrario.

shaping: the reinforcement of simple steps in behavior that lead to a desired, more complex behavior. 207

modelado: refuerzo de pasos simples de la conducta que conducen a una conducta deseada más compleja.

short-term memory (STM): the memory system in which information is held for brief periods of time while being used. 290

memoria a corto plazo (MCP): sistema de memoria en el cual la información se mantiene durante periodos cortos de tiempo mientras se usa.

social anxiety disorder (social phobia): fear of interacting with others or being in social situations that might lead to a negative evaluation. 419

trastorno de ansiedad social (fobia social): miedo a interactuar con otras personas o a estar en situaciones sociales por temor a ser evaluado de forma negativa.

social categorization: the assignment of a person one has just met to a category based on characteristics the new person has in common with other people with whom one has had experience in the past. 246

categorización social: asignar una categoría a una persona a la que se acaba de conocer basándose en las características que dicha persona comparte con personas conocidas.

social comparison: the comparison of oneself to others in ways that raise one's self-esteem. 247

comparación social: compararse a sí mismo con otros individuos de manera que se mejore la autoestima.

social facilitation: the tendency for the presence of other people to have a positive impact on the performance of an easy task. 233

facilitación social: tendencia a que la presencia de otras personas tenga un impacto positivo en la realización de tareas sencillas.

social identity theory: theory in which the formation of a person's identity within a particular social group is explained by social categorization, social identity, and social comparison. 246

teoría de la identidad social: teoría según la cual la formación de la identidad individual de una persona dentro de un grupo social concreto se explica mediante la categorización social, la identificación social y la comparación social.

social impairment: the tendency for the presence of other people to have a negative impact on the performance of a difficult task. 233

menoscabo social: tendencia a que la presencia de otras personas tenga un impacto negativo en la realización de una tarea compleja.

social learning theory: learning through observation and imitation of models, attributes gender-role development to those processes. 278

teoría del aprendizaje social: aprendizaje mediante la observación e imitación de modelos, en una serie de procesos en los que se desarrollan los roles sexuales.

social loafing: the tendency for people to put less effort into a simple task when working with others on that task. 233

pereza social: tendencia de las personas a poner menos esfuerzo en una tarea simple cuando se trabaja con otras personas.

social psychology: the scientific study of how a person's thoughts, feelings, and behavior influence and are influenced by social groups; area of psychology in which psychologists focus on how human behavior is affected by the presence of other people. 230, 506

psicología social: estudio científico de cómo influyen los grupos sociales en los pensamientos, sentimientos y conductas del individuo; ámbito de la psicología que se centra en el efecto que tienen los demás en la conducta individual.

social role: the pattern of behavior that is expected of a person who is in a particular social position. 252

rol social: patrón de conducta que se espera de una persona que está en determinada posición social.

social-cognitive theory of hypnosis: theory that assumes that people who are hypnotized are not in an altered state but are merely playing the role expected of them in the situation. 137

teoría sociocognitiva de la hipnosis: teoría según la cual las personas hipnotizadas no están en un estado alterado sino que simplemente representan el papel que se espera de ellas en esa situación.

soma: the cell body of the neuron responsible for maintaining the life of the cell. 42

soma: cuerpo celular de la neurona; parte responsable de mantener la vida de la célula.

somatosensory cortex: area of cortex at the front of the parietal lobes responsible for processing information from the skin and internal body receptors for touch, temperature, and body position. 62

corteza somatosensorial: área de la corteza cerebral de la región anterior de los lóbulos parietales, encargada de procesar la información de la piel y de los receptores internos del cuerpo que controlan el tacto, la temperatura y la posición corporal.

somesthetic senses: the body senses consisting of the skin senses, the kinesthetic sense, and the vestibular senses. 97

sentidos somestésicos: conjunto de los sentidos cutáneo, cinestésico y vestibular.

specific phobia: fear of objects or specific situations or events. 419

fobia específica: temor a objetos, situaciones o eventos específicos.

spontaneous recovery: the reappearance of a learned response after extinction has occurred. 197

recuperación espontánea: reaparición de una respuesta aprendida después de haberla eliminado.

sports psychology: area of psychology in which the psychologists help athletes and others to prepare themselves mentally for participation in sports activities. 508

psicología deportiva: ámbito de la psicología que ayuda a los deportistas y a otras personas a prepararse mentalmente para participar en actividades deportivas.

standard deviation: the square root of the average squared deviations from the mean of scores in a distribution; a measure of variability. 29

desviación estándar: raíz cuadrada del promedio de las desviaciones de la media de una distribución al cuadrado; medida de variabilidad.

statistically significant: referring to differences in data sets that are larger than chance variation would predict. 33

estadísticamente relevante: referido a las diferencias entre grupos de datos cuando estas diferencias son mayores que las predicciones de variación accidental.

statistics: branch of mathematics concerned with the collection and interpretation of numerical data. 28

estadística: rama de las matemáticas que se ocupa de la recolección e interpretación de datos numéricos.

stereotype: a set of characteristics that people believe is shared by all members of a particular social category; a concept held about a person or group of people that is based on superficial, irrelevant characteristics. 245, 274
estereotipo: conjunto de características que se cree que comparten todos los miembros de una categoría social particular; concepto que se tiene de una persona o grupo de personas basado en características superficiales e irrelevantes.

stereotype threat: condition in which being made aware of a negative performance stereotype interferes with the performance of someone that considers himself or herself part of that group. 336
amenaza de estereotipo: condición por la cual al informar a una persona de un estereotipo de rendimiento negativo, el rendimiento de esa persona se ve afectado si se considera a sí misma parte de ese grupo.

stereotype vulnerability: the effect that people's awareness of the stereotypes associated with their social group has on their behavior. 247
vulnerabilidad de los estereotipos: efecto que tiene en el comportamiento de las personas conocer los estereotipos asociados al grupo social al que pertenecen.

stimulants: drugs that increase the functioning of the nervous system. 140
estimulantes: sustancias que aceleran el funcionamiento del sistema nervioso.

stimulus discrimination: a distinction is made between the conditioned stimulus and a similar stimulus and an unconditioned response is not elicited. 196
discriminación de estímulo: se produce cuando un estímulo condicionado da lugar a una respuesta condicionada y otro estímulo similar suscita otra respuesta condicionada diferente o ninguna respuesta en absoluto.

stimulus generalization: the tendency to respond to a stimulus similar to the original conditioned stimulus with the conditioned response. 196
generalización de estímulo: tendencia a dar una respuesta condicionada, a un estímulo similar al estímulo condicionado original.

storage: holding onto information for some period of time. 288
almacenar: mantener información durante algún tiempo.

stress: the term used to describe the physical, emotional, cognitive, and behavioral responses to events that are appraised as threatening or challenging. 474
estrés: término que se usa para describir las respuestas físicas, emocionales, cognitivas y conductuales a sucesos que se perciben como amenazantes o desafiantes.

stress-vulnerability model: explanation of disorder that assumes a biological sensitivity, or vulnerability, to a certain disorder will result in the development of that disorder under the right conditions of environmental or emotional stress. 429
modelo estrés vulnerabilidad: explicación de un trastorno según la cual una sensibilidad biológica o vulnerabilidad a cierto trastorno dará como resultado el desarrollo de ese trastorno en unas condiciones determinadas de estrés emocional y ambiental.

superego: part of the personality that acts as a moral center. 377
superego: parte de la personalidad que actúa como centro moral.

support groups (self-help groups): a group composed of people who have similar problems and who meet together without a therapist or counselor for the purpose of discussion, problem solving, and social and emotional support. 450
grupos de apoyo (grupos de autoayuda): grupo compuesto por personas con problemas similares y que se reúnen, sin ningún terapeuta o psicólogo, con el fin de comentar y resolver problemas, y para darse apoyo social y emocional mutuo.

sympathetic division: part of the ANS that is responsible for reacting to stressful events and bodily arousal. 49
división simpática: parte del sistema nervioso autónomo responsable de reaccionar ante sucesos estresantes y de la excitación corporal.

synapse: microscopic fluid-filled space between the axon terminal of one cell and the dendrites or surface of the next cell. 44
espacio sináptico: espacio microscópico y lleno de fluidos entre el axón terminal de una célula y las dendritas o superficie de la célula siguiente.

systematic desensitization: behavior technique used to treat phobias, in which a client is asked to make a list of ordered fears and taught to relax while concentrating on those fears. 445
desensibilización sistemática: técnica de conducta que se usa para tratar fobias; consiste en que el cliente haga una lista ordenada de sus miedos y en relajarse mientras se concentra en esos miedos.

T

temperament: the behavioral characteristics that are fairly well established at birth, such as easy, difficult, and slow to warm up. 170
temperamento: características del comportamiento bastante bien definidas al nacer como, por ejemplo, la capacidad de socializar fácilmente, con dificultad o con lentitud.

temporal lobe: areas of the cortex located along the side of the brain, starting just behind the temples, containing the neurons responsible for the sense of hearing and meaningful speech. 62
lóbulos temporales: áreas de la corteza cerebral ubicadas justo detrás de las sienes y que contienen las neuronas responsables del sentido del oído y del lenguaje.

teratogen: any factor that can cause a birth defect. 161
teratógeno: todo factor que puede causar un defecto congénito.

thalamus: part of the limbic system located in the center of the brain, this structure relays sensory information from the lower part of the brain to the proper areas of the cortex and processes some sensory information before sending it to its proper area. 60
tálamo: parte del sistema límbico ubicado en el centro del cerebro. Esta estructura transmite información sensorial desde la parte inferior del cerebro a las áreas correspondientes de la corteza cerebral, y procesa parte de la información sensorial antes de enviarla al área correspondiente.

theory: a general explanation of a set of observations or facts. 5
teoría: explicación general de un conjunto de observaciones o datos.

therapy: treatment methods aimed at making people feel better and function more effectively. 441

terapia: métodos de tratamiento diseñados para que las personas se sientan mejor y sean más funcionales.

thinking (cognition): mental activity that goes on in the brain when a person is organizing and attempting information processing and communicating information to others. 314

razonamiento (cognición): actividad mental que ocurre en el cerebro cuando una persona está procesando información (organizando y tratando de comprender la información y comunicándola a otros).

token economy: the use of objects called tokens to reinforce behavior in which the tokens can be accumulated and exchanged for desired items or privileges. 446

economía de fichas: uso de objetos que se denominan "fichas" para reforzar la conducta; las fichas pueden acumularse y cambiarse por artículos o privilegios deseados.

top down processing: the use of preexisting knowledge to organize individual features into a unified whole. 111

procesamiento de arriba hacia abajo: uso de conocimientos previos para organizar elementos individuales en un todo unificado.

trait: a consistent, enduring way of thinking, feeling, or behaving. 385

rasgo: forma consistente y perdurable de pensar, sentir y comportarse.

trait–situation interaction: the assumption that the particular circumstances of any given situation will influence the way in which a trait is expressed. 387

interacción rasgo-situación: suposición de que las circunstancias particulares de una situación dada influirán en el modo en que se expresa un rasgo.

transduction: the process of converting outside stimuli, such as light, into neural activity. 80

transducción: proceso de conversión de un estímulo externo, como la luz, en actividad neural.

trial and error (mechanical solution): problem-solving method in which one possible solution after another is tried until a successful one is found. 317

ensayo y error (solución mecánica): método de resolución de problemas en el cual se tratan varias soluciones sucesivamente hasta que se halla una solución exitosa.

trichromatic theory: theory of color vision that proposes three types of cones: red, blue, and green. 88

teoría tricromática: teoría de la visión de los colores que propone tres tipos de conos: rojos, azules y verdes.

Type A personality: person who is ambitious, time conscious, extremely hardworking, and tends to have high levels of hostility and anger as well as being easily annoyed. 392

personalidad tipo A: persona ambiciosa, consciente del tiempo, extremadamente trabajadora, que tiende a presentar altos niveles de hostilidad y agresividad, y que se enoja fácilmente.

Type B personality: person who is relaxed and laid-back, less driven and competitive than Type A, and slow to anger. 392

personalidad tipo B: persona relajada y flexible, menos impulsiva y competitiva que el tipo A y que no se enoja fácilmente.

Type C personality: pleasant but repressed person, who tends to internalize his or her anger and anxiety and who finds expressing emotions difficult. 393

personalidad tipo C: persona agradable pero reprimida, que tiende a internalizar su enojo y ansiedad y a la que no le resulta fácil expresar sus emociones.

U

unconditional positive regard: referring to the warmth, respect, and accepting atmosphere created by the therapist for the client in person-centered therapy; or with any other person where positive regard is given without conditions or strings attached. 385

aprecio positivo incondicional: atmósfera cálida, y de respeto y aceptación que crea el terapeuta durante las sesiones centradas en la persona; también referido a cualquier persona a la que se ofrece aprecio sin ningún tipo de condición.

unconditioned response (UCR): an involuntary response to a naturally occurring or unconditioned stimulus. 195

respuesta no condicionada: respuesta involuntaria (refleja) a un estímulo natural o no condicionado.

unconditioned stimulus (UCS): a naturally occurring stimulus that leads to an involuntary response. 195

estímulo no condicionado: estímulo que ocurre naturalmente y lleva a una respuesta involuntaria (refleja).

unconscious mind: level of the mind in which thoughts, feelings, memories, and other information are kept that are not easily or voluntarily brought into consciousness. 375

mente inconsciente: nivel de la mente desde el cual no se pueden hacer aflorar fácilmente a la consciencia los pensamientos, los sentimientos, los recuerdos u otra información.

V

validity: the degree to which a test actually measures what it's supposed to measure. 33, 332

validez: grado en el cual una prueba mide en realidad lo que se supone que mide.

variable interval schedule of reinforcement: schedule of reinforcement in which the interval of time that must pass before reinforcement becomes possible is different for each trial or event. 204

programa de refuerzo de intervalo variable: patrón de refuerzo en el cual el intervalo de tiempo que debe pasar antes de que sea posible el refuerzo es diferente en cada prueba o evento.

variable ratio schedule of reinforcement: schedule of reinforcement in which the number of responses required for reinforcement is different for each trial or event. 205

programa de refuerzo de razón variable: programa de refuerzo en el cual el número de respuestas que se requieren para el refuerzo es diferente en cada prueba o evento.

visual accommodation: as a monocular cue of depth perception, the brain's use of information about the changing thickness of the lens of the eye in response to looking at objects that are close or far away. 86

adaptación visual: referido a la percepción de profundidad monocular: utilización de la información del cerebro sobre la variación del grosor del cristalino al fijar la mirada en objetos situados cerca o lejos.

W

withdrawal: physical symptoms that can include nausea, pain, tremors, crankiness, and high blood pressure, resulting from a lack of an addictive drug in the body systems. 139
síndrome de abstinencia: síntomas físicos tales como náuseas, dolor, temblores, irritabilidad y tensión arterial alta producidos por la ausencia de una droga adictiva en los sistemas del cuerpo.

working memory: an active system that processes the information in short-term memory. 292
memoria de trabajo: sistema activo que procesa la información de la memoria a corto plazo.

Y

Yerkes–Dodson law: law stating performance is related to arousal; moderate levels of arousal lead to better performance than do levels of arousal that are too low or too high. This effect varies with the difficulty of the task: Easy tasks require a high-moderate level, whereas more difficult tasks require a low-moderate level. 350
Ley de Yerkes-Dodson: ley que establece que el rendimiento está relacionado con la activación (*arousal*); un nivel moderado de activación da mejor rendimiento que un nivel demasiado bajo o demasiado alto. Este efecto varía según la dificultad de la tarea: las tareas fáciles requieren un nivel alto-moderado, mientras que las más difíciles requieren un nivel bajo-moderado.

Z

zone of proximal development (ZPD): Vygotsky's concept of the difference between what a child can do alone versus what that child can do with the help of a teacher. 168
zona de desarrollo próximo (ZDP): idea de Vygotsky sobre la diferencia entre lo que puede hacer un niño por sí solo y lo que puede hacer con la ayuda de su maestro(a).

References

Abadinsky, H. (1989). *Drug abuse: An introduction*. Chicago: Nelson-Hall Series in Law, Crime, and Justice.

Abe, K., Amatomi, M., & Oda, N. (1984). Sleepwalking and recurrent sleep talking in children of childhood sleepwalkers. *American Journal of Psychiatry, 141*, 800–801.

Abel, E. L., & Sokol, R. J. (1987). Incidence of fetal alcohol syndrome and economic impact of FAS-related anomalies: Drug alcohol syndrome and economic impact of FAS-related anomalies. *Drug and Alcohol Dependency, 19*(1), 51–70.

Abela, J. R. Z., & D'Allesandro, D. U. (2002). Beck's cognitive theory of depression: The diathesis-stress and causal mediation components. *British Journal of Clinical Psychology, 41*, 111–128.

Åberg, M. A., Pedersen, N. L., Torén, K., Svartengren, M., Bäckstrand, B., Johnsson, T., et al. (2009). Cardiovascular fitness is associated with cognition in young adulthood. *Proceedings of the National Academy of Sciences, 106*(49), 20906–20911.

Abramson, D., Redlener, I., Stehling-Ariza, T., Sury, J., Banister, A., & Soo Park, Y. (2010). Impact on children and families of the Deepwater Horizon oil spill: Preliminary findings of the Coastal Population Impact Study. National Center for Disaster Preparedness, Mailman School of Public Health at Columbia University, August 3, 2010. Retrieved December 15, 2013, from http://www.eoearth.org/article/Impact_on_children_and_families_of_the_Deepwater_Horizon_oil_spill?topic=50364

Abramson, L. Y., Garber, J., & Seligman, M. E. P. (1980). Learned helplessness in humans: An attributional analysis. In J. Garber & M. E. P. Seligman (Eds.), *Human helplessness* (pp. 3–34). New York: Academic Press.

Abramson, L. Y., Seligman, M. E. P., & Teasdale, J. D. (1978). Learned helplessness in humans: Critique and reformulation. *Journal of Abnormal Psychology, 87*, 49–74.

Acheson, D. J., MacDonald, M. C., & Postle, B. R. (2010). The interaction of concreteness and phonological similarity in verbal working memory. *Journal of Experimental Psychology: Learning, Memory and Cognition, 36*(1), 17–36.

Adachi, P. J. C., & Willoughby, T. (2011a). The effect of violent video games on aggression: Is it more than just the violence? *Aggression and Violent Behavior, 16*, 55–62. doi:10.1016/j.avb.2010.12.002

Adachi, P. J. C., & Willoughby, T. (2011b). The effect of video game competition and violence on aggressive behavior: Which characteristic has the greatest influence? *Psychology of Violence, 1*(4), 259–274. doi:10.1037/a0024908

Adam, K. (1980). Sleep as a restorative process and a theory to explain why. *Progressive Brain Research, 53*, 289–305.

Adams, R. J. (1987). An evaluation of colour preferences in early infancy. *Infant Behaviour and Development, 10*, 143–150.

Ader, R. (2003). Conditioned immunomodulation: Research needs and directions. *Brain, Behavior, and Immunity, 17*(1), 51–57.

Adeyemo, B. O., Simis, M., Macea, D. D., & Fregni, F. (2012). Systematic review of parameters of stimulation, clinical trial design characteristics, and motor outcomes in non-invasive brain stimulation in stroke. *Frontiers in Psychiatry, 3*, 88. doi:10.3389/fpsyt.2012.00088

Adler, A. (1954). *Understanding human nature*. New York: Greenburg Publisher.

Adolphs, R. (2010). Conceptual challenges and directions for social neuroscience. *Neuron, 65*(6), 752–767.

Adolphs, R., & Tranel, D. (2003). Amygdala damage impairs emotion recognition from scenes only when they contain facial expressions. *Neuropsychologia, 41*, 1281–1289.

Agresti, A., & Finlay, B. (1997). *Statistical methods for the social sciences*. Upper Saddle River, NJ: Prentice Hall.

Aguiar, A., & Baillargeon, R. (2003). Perseverative responding in a violation-of-expectation task in 6.5-month-old infants. *Cognition, 88*(3), 277–316.

Ahn, W. (1998). Why are different features central for natural kinds and artifacts? The role of causal status in determining feature centrality. *Cognition, 69*, 135–178.

Aiello, J. R., & Douthitt, E. A. (2001). Social facilitation from Triplett to electronic performance monitoring. *Group Dynamics: Theory, Research, and Practice, 5*(3), 163–180.

Ainsworth, M. D. S. (1985). Attachments across the life span. *Bulletin of the New York Academy of Medicine, 61*, 792–812.

Ainsworth, M. D. S., Blehar, M. C., Waters, E., & Wall, S. (1978). *Patterns of attachment: A study of the strange situation*. Hillsdale, NJ: Erlbaum.

Aitchison, J. (1992). Good birds, better birds, and amazing birds: The development of prototypes. In P. J. Arnaud & H. Béjoint (Eds.), *Vocabulary and applied linguistics* (pp. 71–84). London: Macmillan.

Ajzen, I. (2001). Nature and operation of attitudes. *Annual Review of Psychology, 52*, 27–58.

Ajzen, I., & Fishbein, M. (2000). Attitudes and the attitude-behavior relation: Reasoned and automatic processes. In W. Stroebe & M. Hewstone (Eds.), *European review of social psychology* (pp. 1–33). New York: Wiley.

Aldridge-Morris, R. (1989). *Multiple personality: An exercise in deception*. Hillsdale, NJ: Erlbaum.

Aligne, C. A., Auinger, P., Byrd, R. S., & Weitzman, M. (2000). Risk factors for pediatric asthma contributions of poverty, race, and urban residence. *American Journal of Respiratory Critical Care Medicine, 162*(3), 873–877.

Allen, D. (2001). *Getting things done: The art of stress-free productivity*. New York: Viking Adult.

Allen, D. (2008). *Making it all work*. New York: Viking Adult.

Allen, F. (1994). *Secret formula*. New York: HarperCollins.

Allen, G. E. (2006). *Intelligence tests and immigration to the United States, 1900–1940*. Hoboken, NJ: Wiley.

Allen, G., & Parisi, P. (1990). Trends in monozygotic and dizygotic twinning rates by maternal age and parity. Further analysis of Italian data, 1949–1985, and rediscussion of U.S. Data, 1964–1985. *Acta Genetic Medicine and Gemellology, 39*, 317–328.

Allik, J., Realo, A., & McCrae, R. R. (2013). Universality of the five-factor model of personality. In T. A. Widiger & P. T. Costa (Eds.), *Personality disorders and the five-factor model of personality* (3rd ed., pp. 61–74). Washington, DC: American Psychological Association.

Alloy, L. B., & Clements, C. M. (1998). Hopelessness theory of depression: Tests of the symptom component. *Cognitive Therapy and Research, 22*, 303–335.

Allport, G. W., & Odbert, H. S. (1936). Trait names: A psycho-lexical study. *Psychological Monographs, 47*(211).

Alm, H., & Nilsson, L. (1995). The effects of a mobile telephone conversation on driver behaviour in a car following situation. *Accident Analysis and Prevention, 27*(5), 707–715.

Alzheimer's Association. (2010). Alzheimer's disease facts and figures. *Alzheimer's and Dementia, 6*, 4–54.

Amabile, T. M., DeJong, W., & Lepper, M. R. (1976). Effects of externally imposed deadlines on subsequent intrinsic motivation. *Journal of Personality and Social Psychology, 34*, 92–98.

Amabile, T., Hadley, C. N., & Kramer, S. J. (2002). Creativity under the gun. *Harvard Business Review, 80*(8), 52–60.

Amaral, D. G., & Strick, P. L. (2013). The organization of the central nervous system. In E. R. Kandel, J. H. Schwartz, T. M. Jessell, S. A. Siegelbaum, & A. J. Hudspeth (Eds.), *Principles of neural science* (5th ed., pp. 337–355). USA: McGraw-Hill.

American Academy of Pediatrics. (1995). Health supervision for children with turner syndrome. *Pediatrics, 96*(6), 1166–1173.

American Association of University Women. (1992). *How schools shortchange girls.* Washington, DC: Author.

American Association of University Women. (1998). *Separated by sex: A critical look at singlesex education for girls.* Washington, DC: Author.

American Association on Intellectual and Developmental Disabilities [AAIDD]. (2009). *FAQ on intellectual disability.* Retrieved June 8, 2010, from www.aamr.org/content_104.cfm

American College Counseling Association's (ACCA) Community College Task Force. (2010). *2009–2010 Community college counselors survey.* Retrieved August 12, 2010, from http://www.collegecounseling.org/community-college-survey-09-10

American Psychiatric Association. (2013). *Diagnostic and statistical manual of mental disorders* (5th ed.). Washington, DC: Author.

American Psychiatric Association Committee on Electroconvulsive Therapy. (2001). *The practice of electroconvulsive therapy: Recommendations for treatment, training, and privileging* (2nd ed.). Washington, DC: American Psychiatric Association.

American Psychological Association Division 19. (2010). *Society for military psychology.* Retrieved from http://www.apadivisions.org/division-19/about/index.aspx

American Psychological Association. (2002). Ethical principles of psychologists and code of conduct. *American Psychologist, 57,* 1060–1073.

Amsterdam, B. (1972). Mirror self-image reactions before age two. *Developmental Psychobiology, 5*(4), 297–305. doi:10.1002/dev.420050403

Anastasi, A., & Urbina, S. (1997). *Psychological testing* (7th ed.). Upper Saddle River, NJ: Prentice-Hall.

Anderson, C. A. (1987). Temperature and aggression: Effects on quarterly, yearly, and city rates of violent and nonviolent crime. *Journal of Personality and Social Psychology, 52*(6), 1161–1173.

Anderson, C. A., Berkowitz, L., Donnerstein, E., Huesmann, L. R., Johnson, J. D., Linz, D., et al. (2003). The influence of media violence on youth. *Psychological Science in the Public Interest, 4*(3), 81–110.

Anderson, M. C., & Neely, J. H. (1995). Interference and inhibition in memory retrieval. In E. L. Bjork & R. A. Bjork (Eds.), *Handbook of perception and cognition, Vol. 10: Memory.* San Diego, CA: Academic Press.

Andrews, J. D. W. (1989). Integrating visions of reality: Interpersonal diagnosis and the existential vision. *American Psychologist, 44,* 803–817.

Antuono, P. G., Jones, J. L., Wang, Y., & Li, S. (2001). Decreased glutamate [plus] glutamine in Alzheimer's disease detected in vivo with (1)H-MRS at 0.5 T. *Neurology, 56*(6), 737–742.

Arbury, S. (2005, March 4). *Workplace violence: Training young workers in preventative strategies.* Washington, DC: NFIB Business Toolbox.

Arcelus, J., Mitchell, A. J., Wales, J., & Nielsen, S. (2011). Mortality rates in patients with anorexia nervosa and other eating disorders: A meta-analysis of 36 studies. *Archives of General Psychiatry, 68*(7), 724–731. doi:10.1001/archgenpsychiatry.2011.74

Argamon, S., Koppel, M., Fine, J., & Shimoni, A. (2003, August). Gender, genre, and writing style in formal written texts. *Text, 23*(3).

Armstrong, R. (1997). When drugs are used for rape. *Journal of Emergency Nursing, 23*(4), 378–381.

Arnett, J. J. (2000). Emerging adulthood: A theory of development from the late teens through the twenties. *American Psychologist, 55*(5), 469–480.

Arnett, P. A., Smith, S. S., & Newman, J. P. (1997). Approach and avoidance motivation in psychopathic criminal offenders during passive avoidance. *Journal of Personality and Social Psychology, 72*(6), 1413–1428.

Arns, M., de Ridder, S., Strehl, U., Breteler, M., & Coenen, A. (2009). Efficacy of neurofeedback treatment in ADHD: The effects on inattention, impulsivity and hyperactivity: A meta-analysis. *Clinical EEG and Neuroscience, 40*(3), 180–189.

Arns, M., van der Heijden, K. B., Arnold, L. E., & Kenemans, J. L. (2013). Geographic variation in the prevalence of attention-deficit/hyperactivity disorder: The sunny perspective. *Biological Psychiatry.* doi:10.1016/j.biopsych.2013.02.010

Aron, A., Aron, E., & Coups, E. (2005). *Statistics for the behavioral and social sciences: Brief course* (4th ed.). Upper Saddle River, NJ: Prentice-Hall.

Aronson, E., Blaney, N., Stephan, C., Sikes, J., & Snapp, M. (1978). *The jigsaw classroom.* Beverly Hills, CA: Sage.

Asarnow, R. F., Granholm, E., & Sherman, T. (1991). Span of apprehension in schizophrenia. In H. A. Nasrallah, S. R. Steinhauer, J. H. Gruzelie, & J. Zubin (Eds.), *Handbook of Schizophrenia, Vol. 5: Neuropsychology, psychophysiology and information processing* (pp. 335–370). Amsterdam: Elsevier.

Asch, S. E. (1951). Effects of group pressure upon the modification and distortion of judgement. In H. Guetzkow (Ed.), *Groups, leadership and men.* Pittsburgh: Carnegie Press.

Asch, S. E. (1956). Studies of independence and conformity: A minority of one against a unanimous majority. *Psychological Monographs, 70*(Whole no. 416).

Aserinsky, E., & Kleitman, N. (1953). Regularly occurring periods of eye motility, and concomitant phenomena, during sleep. *Science, 118,* 273–274.

Ash, M. G. (1998). *Gestalt psychology in German culture, 1890–1967: Holism and the quest for objectivity.* Cambridge: Cambridge University Press.

Asp, E., & Tranel, D. (2013). False tagging theory. In D. T. Stuss & R. T. Knight (Eds.), *Principles of frontal lobe function* (pp. 383–416). New York: Oxford University Press.

Atkinson, R. C., & Shiffrin, R. M. (1968). Human memory: A proposed system and its control processes. In K. W. Spence & J. T. Spence (Eds.), *The psychology of learning and motivation* (Vol. 2, pp. 89–105). New York: Academic Press.

Atladóttir, H. O., Pedersen, M. G., Thorsen, C., Mortensen, P. B., Deleuran, B., Eaton, W. W., et al. (2009). Association of family history of autoimmune diseases and autism spectrum disorders. *Pediatrics, 124*(2), 687–694.

Azmitia, M., Syed, M., & Radmacher, K. (2008). On the intersection of personal and social identities: Introduction and evidence from a longitudinal study of emerging adults. In M. Azmitia, M. Syed, & K. Radmacher (Eds.), *The intersections of personal and social identities: New Directions for Child and Adolescent Development* (Vol. 120, pp. 1–16). San Francisco: Jossey-Bass.

Babiloni, C., Vecchio, F., Buffo, P., Buttiglione, M., Cibelli, G., & Rossini, P. M. (2010). Cortical responses to consciousness of schematic emotional facial expressions: A high resolution EEG study. *Human Brain Mapping, 8,* 8.

Bachman, J., Wadsworth, K., O'Malley, P., Johnston, L., & Schulenberg, J. (1997). *Smoking, drinking, and drug use in young adulthood: The impact of new freedoms and new responsibilities.* Mahwah, NJ: Erlbaum.

Backenstraß, M., Pfeiffer, N., Schwarz, T., Catanzaro, S. J., & Mearns, J. (2008). Reliability and validity of the German version of the generalized expectancies for Negative Mood Regulation (NMR) scale. *Diagnostica, 54,* 43–51.

Backer, B., Hannon, R., & Russell, N. (1994). *Death and dying: Understanding and care* (2nd ed.). Albany, NY: Delmar.

Baddeley, A. D. (1986). *Working memory.* London: Oxford University Press.

Baddeley, A. D. (1988). Cognitive psychology and human memory. *Trends in Neurosciences, 11,* 176–181.

Baddeley, A. D. (1996). Exploring the central executive. *Quarterly Journal of Experimental Psychology, 49A,* 5–28.

Baddeley, A. D. (2003). Working memory: Looking back and looking visual forward. *Nature Reviews Neuroscience, 4*(10), 829–839.

Baddeley, A. D., & Hitch, G. (1974). Working memory. In G. A. Bower (Ed.), *The psychology of learning and motivation* (Vol. 8, pp. 47–89). New York: Academic Press.

Baddeley, A. D., & Larsen, J. D. (2007). The phonological loop unmasked? A comment on the evidence for a "perceptual-gestural" alternative. *Quarterly Journal of Experimental Psychology, 60*(4), 497–504.

Baehr, E. K., Revelle, W., & Eastman, C. I. (2000). Individual difference in the phase amplitude of the human circadian temperature rhythm: With an emphasis on morningness-eveningness. *Journal of Sleep Research, 9,* 117–127.

Bahrick, H. (1984). Fifty years of second language attrition: Implications for programmatic research. *Modern Language Journal, 68,* 105–118.

Bahrick, H. P., Hall, L. K., & Berger, S. A. (1996, September). Accuracy and distortion in memory for high school grades. *Psychological Science, 7,* 265–271.

Ball, K., Berch, D. B., Helmers, K. F., Jobe, J. B., Leveck, M. D., Marsiske, M., et al. (2002). Advanced cognitive training for independent and vital elderly study group. Effects of cognitive training interventions with older adults: A randomized controlled trial. *Journal of the American Medical Association, 288,* 2271–2281.

Baltes, P. B., Reese, H. W., & Nesselroade, J. R. (1988). *Introduction to research methods, life-span developmental psychology*. Hillsdale, NJ: Erlbaum.

Bandura, A. (1965). Influence of models' reinforcement contingencies on the acquisition of imitative responses. *Journal of Social Psychology, 1,* 589–595.

Bandura, A. (1980). The social learning theory of aggression. In R. A. Falk & S. S. Kim (Eds.), *The war system: An interdisciplinary approach* (p. 146). Boulder, CO: Westview Press.

Bandura, A. (1986). *Social foundations of thought and action: A social cognitive theory*. Englewood Cliffs, NJ: Prentice Hall.

Bandura, A. (1989). Human agency in social cognitive theory. *American Psychologist, 44,* 1175–1184.

Bandura, A. (1998). Exploration of fortuitous determinants of life paths. *Psychological Inquiry, 9,* 95–99.

Bandura, A., & Rosenthal, T. L. (1966). Vicarious classical conditioning as a functioning of arousal level. *Journal of Personality and Social Psychology, 3,* 54–62.

Bandura, A., Blanchard, E. B., & Ritter, B. (1969). Relative efficacy of desensitization and modeling approaches for inducing behavioral, affective, and attitudinal changes. *Journal of Personality and Social Psychology, 13,* 173–199.

Bandura, A., Jeffrey, R. W., & Wright, C. L. (1974). Efficacy of participant modeling as a function of response induction aids. *Journal of Abnormal Psychology, 83,* 56–64.

Bandura, A., Ross, D., & Ross, S. A. (1961). Transmission of aggression through imitation of aggressive models. *Journal of Abnormal and Social Psychology, 63,* 575–582.

Bandura, A., Ross, D., & Ross, S. A. (1963). Imitation of film-mediated aggressive models. *Journal of Abnormal and Social Psychology, 66,* 3–11.

Bard, P. (1934). On emotional expression after decortication with some remark on certain theoretical views. *Psychological Review, 41,* 309–329, 424–449.

Bargh, J. A., Chen, M., & Burrows, C. (1996). Automaticity of social behavior: Direct effects of trait construct and stereotype activation on action. *Journal of Personality and Social Psychology, 71*(2), 230–244.

Barker, E. (1983). The ones who got away: People who attend unification church workshops and do not become Moonies. In E. Barker (Ed.), *Of gods and men: New religious movements in the West*. Macon, GA: Mercer University Press.

Barker, E. (2007). Religious movements: Cult and anticult since Jonestown. In M. Hamilton (Ed.), *Sociology of religion. Critical concepts in sociology* (Vol. 5, pp. 157–177). Abingdon, UK: Routledge.

Barkley, R. A., Murphy, K. R., & Fischer, M. (2008). *ADHD in adults: What the science says*. New York: Guilford Press.

Barlow, D. H., Allen, L. B., & Basden, S. L. (2007). Psychological treatments for panic disorders, phobias, and generalized anxiety disorder. In P. E. Nathan & J. M. Gorman (Eds.), *A guide to treatments that work* (3rd ed., pp. 351–394). New York, NY: Oxford University Press.

Barlow, D. H., Bullis, J. R., Comer, J. S., & Ametaj, A. A. (2013). Evidence-based psychological treatments: An update and a way forward. *Annual Review of Clinical Psychology, 9,* 1–27. doi:10.1146/annurev-clinpsy-050212-185629

Barnes, A. M., & Carey, J. C. (2002, January 11). *Common problems of babies with trisomy 18 or 13*. Rochester, NY: Support Organization for Trisomy 18, 13, and Related Disorders.

Barnes, V., Schneider, R., Alexander, C., & Staggers, F. (1997). Stress, stress reduction, and hypertension in African Americans: An updated review. *Journal of the National Medical Association, 89*(7), 464–476.

Barnyard, P., & Grayson, A. (1996). *Introducing psychological research*. London: Macmillan Press.

Baron, J. N., & Reiss, P. C. (1985). Same time, next year: Aggregate analyses of the mass media and violent behavior. *American Sociological Review, 50,* 347–363.

Baron, S. A. (1993). *Violence in the workplace*. Ventura, CA: Pathfinder Publishing of California.

Barondes, S. H. (1998). *Mood genes: Hunting for origins of mania and depression*. New York: W. H. Freeman.

Barsalou, L. W. (1992). *Cognitive psychology: An overview for cognitive scientists*. Hillsdale, NJ: Lawrence Erlbaum.

Barsh, G. S., Farooqi, I. S., & O'Rahilly, S. (2000). Genetics of body-weight regulation. *Nature, 404,* 644–651.

Bartels, A., & Zeki, S. (2000). The neural basis of romantic love. *NeuroReport, 11,* 3829–3834.

Bartels, A., & Zeki, S. (2004). The neural correlates of material and romantic love. *NeuroImage, 21,* 1155–1166.

Barth, J. M., & Boles, D. B. (1999, September). *Positive relations between emotion recognition skills and right hemisphere processing*. Paper presented at the 11th Annual Convention of the American Psychological Society, Denver, CO.

Bartholomew, K. (1990). Avoidance of intimacy: An attachment perspective. *Journal of Social and Personal Relationships, 7,* 147–178.

Bartlett, F. C. (1932). *Remembering: A study in experimental ad social psychology*. Cambridge, U.K.: Cambridge University Press.

Bartlett, N. R. (1965). Dark and light adaptation. In C. H. Graham (Ed.), *Vision and visual perception*. New York: Wiley.

Barton, M. E., & Komatsu, L. K. (1989). Defining features of natural kinds and artifacts. *Journal of Psycholinguistic Research, 18,* 433–447.

Bartoshuk, L. M. (1993). The biological basis for food perception and acceptance. *Food Quality and Preference, 4*(1–2), 21–32.

Bartoshuk, L. M., Duffy, V. B., Hayes, J. E., Moskowitz, H. R., & Snyder, D. J. (2006). Psychophysics of sweet and fat perception in obesity: Problems, solutions and new perspectives. *Philosophical Transactions of the Royal Society of London. Series B, Biological Sciences, 361*(1471), 1137–1148.

Basadur, M., Pringle, P., & Kirkland, D. (2002). Crossing cultures: Training effects on the divergent thinking attitudes of Spanish-speaking South American managers. *Creativity Research Journal, 14*(3, 4), 395–408.

Bator, R. J., & Cialdini, R. B. (2006). The nature of consistency motivation: Consistency, aconsistency, and anticonsistency in a dissonance paradigm. *Social Influence, 1,* 208–233.

Baumrind, D. (1964). Some thoughts on ethics of research: After reading Milgram's "behavioral study of obedience." *American Psychologist, 19,* 421–423.

Baumrind, D. (1967). Child care practices anteceding three patterns of preschool behavior. *Genetic Psychology Monograph, 75,* 43–88.

Baumrind, D. (1991). The influence of parenting style on adolescent competence and substance abuse. *Journal of Early Adolescence, 11*(1), 56–95.

Baumrind, D. (1997). Necessary distinctions. *Psychological Inquiry, 8,* 176–182.

Baumrind, D. (2005). Patterns of parental authority and adolescent autonomy. In J. Smetana (Ed.), *New directions for child development: Changes in parental authority during adolescence* (pp. 61–69). San Francisco: Jossey-Bass.

Bayliss, D. M., Baddeley, J. C., & Gunn, D. M. (2005). The relationship between short-term memory and working memory: Complex span made simple? *Memory, 13*(3–4), 414–421.

Beauchamp, G. K., & Mennella, J. A. (2011). Flavor perception in human infants: Development and functional significance. *Digestion, 83*(Suppl. 1), 1–6. doi:10.1159/000323397

Beck, A. T. (1976). *Cognitive therapy and the emotional disorders*. New York: International Universities Press.

Beck, A. T. (1979). *Cognitive therapy and the emotional disorders*. New York: Penguin Books.

Beck, A. T. (1984). Cognitive approaches to stress. In C. Lehrer & R. L. Woolfolk (Eds.), *Clinical guide to stress management*. New York: Guilford Press.

Beck, H. P., & Irons, G. (2011). Finding Little Albert: A seven-year search for psychology's lost boy. *The Psychologist, 25,* 180–181.

Beck, H. P., Levinson, S., & Irons, G. (2009). Finding Little Albert: A journey to John B. Watson's infant laboratory. *American Psychologist, 64*(7), 605–614. doi:10.1037/a0017234

Beck, J. S. (2007). *Cognitive therapy for personality disorders*. Retrieved November 17, 2010, from http://www.academyofct.org

Beckman, M., & Pierrehumbert, J. (1986). Intonational structure in English and Japanese. *Phonology Year Book III,* 15–70.

Behne, T., Carpenter, M., & Tomasello, M. (2005). One-year-olds comprehend the communicative intentions behind gestures in a hiding game. *Developmental Science, 8*, 492–499.

Békésy, G. V. (1960). *Experiments in hearing* (E. G. Wever, Trans.). New York: McGraw-Hill.

Belsky, J. (2005). Differential susceptibility to rearing influence: An evolutionary hypothesis and some evidence. In B. Ellis & D. Bjorklund (Eds.), *Origins of the social mind: Evolutionary psychology and child development* (pp. 139–163). New York: Guilford Press.

Belsky, J., & Johnson, C. D. (2005). Developmental outcome of children in day care. In J. Murph, S. D. Palmer, & D. Glassy (Eds.), *Health in child care: A manual for health professionals* (4th ed., pp. 81–95). Elks Grove Village, IL: American Academy of Pediatrics.

Belsky, J., Vandell, D., Burchinal, M., Clarke-Stewart, K. A., McCartney, K., Owen, M., et al. (2007). Are there long-term effects of early child care? *Child Development, 78*, 681–701.

Bem, S. L. (1975). Sex role adaptability: The consequence of psychological androgyny. *Journal of Personality and Social Psychology, 31*, 634–643.

Bem, S. L. (1981). Gender schema theory: A cognitive account of sex typing. *Psychological Review, 88*, 354–364.

Bem, S. L. (1987). Gender schema theory and the romantic tradition. In P. Shaver & C. Hendrick (Eds.), *Review of personality and social psychology* (Vol. 7, pp. 251–271). Newbury Park, CA: Sage.

Bem, S. L. (1993). Is there a place in psychology for a feminist analysis of the social context? *Feminism and Psychology, 3*, 247–251.

Bengston, V. L. (1970). The generation gap. *Youth and Society, 2*, 7–32.

Benito, J. M., Kumru, H. P., Murillo, N. P., Costa, U. P., Medina, J. P., Tormos, J. M. P., et al. (2012). Motor and gait improvement in patients with incomplete spinal cord injury induced by high-frequency repetitive transcranial magnetic stimulation. *Topics in Spinal Cord Injury Rehabilitation, 18*(2), 106–112. doi:10.1310/sci1802-106

Benjafield, J. J. G. (1996). *A history of psychology*. Boston: Allyn & Bacon.

Benjamin, S. L. (1996). An interpersonal theory of personality disorders. In J. F. Clarkin & M. F. Lenzenweger (Eds.), *Major theories of personality disorder*. New York: Guilford Press.

Benowitz, N. L. (1988). Pharmacologic aspects of cigarette smoking and nicotine addiction. *New England Journal of Medicine, 319*, 1318–1330.

Ben-Shakhar, G., Bar-Hillel, M., Bliu, Y., Ben-Abba, E., & Flug, A. (1986). Can graphology predict occupational success? Two empirical studies and some methodological ruminations. *Journal of Applied Psychology, 71*, 645–653.

Benson, H. (1975). *The relaxation response*. New York: Morrow.

Benson, H., Beary, J., & Carol, M. (1974a). The relaxation response. *Psychiatry, 37*, 37–46.

Benson, H., Rosner, B. A., Marzetta, B. R., & Klemchuk, H. M. (1974b). Decreased blood pressure in pharmacologically treated hypertensive patients who regularly elicited the relaxation response. *Lancet, 1*(7852), 289–291.

Berent, S. (1977). Functional asymmetry of the human brain in the recognition of faces. *Neuropsychologia, 15*, 829–831.

Berg, F. (1999). Health risks associated with weight loss and obesity treatment programs. *Journal of Social Issues, 55*(2), 277–297.

Berk, L. E. (1992). Children's private speech: An overview of theory and the status of research. In R. M. Diaz & L. E. Berk (Eds.), *Private speech: From social interaction to self-regulation* (pp. 17–53). Hillsdale, NJ: Erlbaum.

Berk, L. E., & Spuhl, S. T. (1995). Maternal interaction, private speech, and task performance in preschool children. *Early Childhood Research Quarterly, 10*, 145–169.

Berk, L. S., Felten, D. L., Tan, S. A., Bittman, B. B., & Westengard, J. (2001, March). Modulation of neuroimmune parameters during the eustress of humor-associated mirthful laughter. *Alternative Therapy Health Medicines, 7*(2), 62–72, 74–76.

Berk, L., Prowse, M., Petrofsky, J. S., Batt, J., Laymon, M., Bains, G., Daher, N., Tan, S., & Berk, D. (2009, May). *Laughercise: Health benefits similar of exercise lowers cholesterol and systolic blood pressure*. Presented at the Association for Psychological Science 21st Annual Convention, San Francisco, California.

Berk, L., Tan, S. A., & Berk, D. (2008, April). *Cortisol and catecholamine stress hormone decrease is associated with the behavior of perceptual anticipation of mirthful laughter*. Presented at the 121st Annual Meeting of the American Physiological Society, San Diego, California.

Berkowitz, L. (1993). *Aggression: Its causes, consequences and control*. New York: McGraw-Hill.

Berman, A., Bradley, J. C., Carroll, B., Certain, R. D., Gabrelcik, J. C., Green, R., et al. (2010). *The challenge and the promise: Strengthening the force, preventing suicide and saving lives. Final report of the Department of Defense task force on the prevention of suicide by members of the armed forces*. Washington, DC: U.S. Government.

Bermond, B., Nieuwenhuyse, B., Fasotti, L., & Schuerman, J. (1991). Spinal cord lesions, peripheral feedback, and intensities of emotional feelings. *Cognition and Emotion, 5*, 201–220.

Bernat, E., Shevrin, H., & Snodgrass, M. (2001). Subliminal visual oddball stimuli evoke a P300 component. *Clinical Neurophysiology, 112*, 159–171.

Berry, J. W., & Kim, U. (1998). Acculturation and mental health. In P. R. Dasen, J. W. Berry, & N. Sartorius (Eds.), *Health and cross-cultural psychology: Toward applications* (pp. 207–236). Newbury Park, CA: Sage.

Berry, J. W., & Sam, D. L. (1997). Acculturation and adaptation. In J. W. Berry, M. H. Segall, & C. Kagitcibasi (Eds.), *Handbook of cross-cultural psychology, Vol. 3: Social behaviour and applications* (2nd ed., pp. 291–326). Boston: Allyn & Bacon.

Berscheid, E., & Reis, H. T. (1998). Attraction and close relationships. In D. T. Gilbert, S. T. Fiske, & G. Lindzey (Eds.), *The handbook of social psychology, Vol. 2* (4th ed., pp. 193–281). New York: McGraw-Hill.

Berteretche, M. V., Dalix, A. M., Cesar d'Ornano, A. M., Bellisle, F., Khayat, D., & Faurion, A. (2004). Decreased taste sensitivity in cancer patients under chemotherapy. *Supportive Care in Cancer, 12*(8), 571–576.

Bertram, L., & Tanzi, R. E. (2005). The genetic epidemiology of neurodegenerative disease. *The Journal of Clinical Investigation, 115*(6), 1449–1457.

Best, D. L., & Williams, J. E. (2001). Gender and culture. In D. Matsumoto (Ed.), *The handbook of culture and psychology* (pp. 195–212). New York: Oxford University Press.

Betancourt, J. R., & Jacobs, E. A. (2000). Language barriers to informed consent and confidentiality: The impact on women's health. *Journal of American Medical Women's Association, 55*, 294–295.

Beyer, B. K. (1995). *Critical thinking*. Bloomington, IN: Phi Delta Kappa Educational Foundation.

Beyreuther, K., Biesalski, H. K., Fernstrom, J. D., Grimm, P., Hammes, W. P., Heinemann, U., et al. (2007). Consensus meeting: Monosodium glutamate, an update. *European Journal of Clinical Nutrition, 61*, 304–313.

Binet, A., & Simon, T. (1916). *The development of intelligence in children*. Baltimore: Williams & Wilkins.

Bivens, J. A., & Berk, L. E. (1990). A longitudinal study of the development of elementary school children's private speech. *Merill-Palmer Quarterly, 36*, 443–463.

Bjork, R. A., & Bjork, E. L. (1992). A new theory of disuse and an old theory of stimulus fluctuation. In A. Healy, S. Kosslyn, & R. Shiffrin (Eds.), *From learning processes to cognitive processes: Essays in honor of William K. Estes* (Vol. 2, pp. 35–67). Hillsdale, NJ: Erlbaum.

Bjork, R. A., & Whitten, W. B. (1974). Recency-sensitive retrieval processes in long-term free recall. *Cognitive Psychology, 6*, 173–189.

Blackmon, L. R., Batton, D. G., Bell, E. F., Engle, W. A., Kanto, W. P., Martin, G. I., et al. (2003). Apnea, sudden infant death syndrome, and home monitoring. *Pediatrics, 111*(4), 914–917.

Blair, R. J. R., Sellars, C., Strickland, I., Clark, F., Williams, A. O., Smith, M., et al. (1995). Emotion attributions in the psychopath. *Personality and Individual Differences, 19*(4), 431–437.

Blanchard-Fields, F., Chen, Y., Horhota, M., & Wang, M. (2007). Cultural differences in the relationship between aging and the correspondence bias. *Journals of Gerontology Series B: Psychological Sciences and Social Sciences, 62*(6), 362–365.

Blass, T. (1991). Understanding behavior in the Milgram obedience experiment: The role of personality, situations, and their interactions. *Journal of Personality and Social Psychology, 60*, 398–413.

Blass, T. (1999). The Milgram paradigm after 35 years: Some things we now know about obedience to authority. *Journal of Applied Social Psychology, 25*, 955–978.

Bledsoe, C. H., & Cohen, B. (1993). *Social dynamics of adolescent fertility in sub-Saharan Africa*. Washington, DC: National Academy Press.

Blehar, M. C., & Oren, D. A. (1997, June 27). Gender differences in depression. *Medscape General Medicine, 1*(2). Retrieved June 27, 2004, from http://www.medscape.com/viewarticle/719236

Bleuler, E. (1911, reissued 1950). *Dementia praecox or the group of schizophrenias*. New York: International Universities Press.

Block, N. (2005). Two neural correlates of consciousness. *Trends in Cognitive Sciences, 9*, 41–89.

Bloom, B. S. (Ed.). (1956). *Taxonomy of educational objectives, the classification of educational goals—Handbook I: Cognitive domain*. New York: McKay.

Bloom, L. (1974). Talking, understanding and thinking. In R. Schiefelbusch & L. L. Lloyd (Eds.), *Language perspectives: Acquisition, retardation and intervention*. New York: Macmillan.

Bloom, P. (2000). *How children learn the meaning of words*. Cambridge, MA: MIT Press.

Blumer, D. (2002). The illness of Vincent van Gogh. *American Journal of Psychiatry, 159*(4), 519–526.

Bodrova, E., & Leong, D. J. (1996). *Tools of the mind: The Vygotskian approach to early childhood education*. Englewood Cliffs, NJ: Prentice Hall.

Boggio, P. S., Fregni, F., Valasek, C., Ellwood, S., Chi, R., Gallate, J., et al. (2009). Temporal lobe cortical electrical stimulation during the encoding and retrieval phase reduces false memories. *PLoS One, 4*(3), e4959.

Boggio, P. S., Rocha, M., Oliveira, M. O., Fecteau, S., Cohen, R. B., Campanha, C., et al. (2009). Noninvasive brain stimulation with high-frequency and low-intensity repetitive transcranial magnetic stimulation treatment for posttraumatic stress disorder. *The Journal of Clinical Psychiatry, 29,* 29.

Bogle, K. D. (2000). Effect of perspective, type of student, and gender on the attribution of cheating. *Proceedings of the Oklahoma Academy of Science, 80,* 91–97.

Bond, R. A., & Smith, P. B. (1996). Culture and conformity: A meta-analysis of studies using Asch's (1952, 1956) line judgment task. *Psychological Bulletin, 119,* 111–137.

Bonnelykke, B. (1990). Maternal age and parity as predictors of human twinning. *Acta Genetic Medicine and Gemellology, 39,* 329–334.

Boor, M. (1982). The multiple personality epidemic: Additional cases and inferences regarding diagnosis, etiology, dynamics, and treatment. *Journal of Nervous and Mental Disease, 170,* 302–304.

Booth-Butterfield, S. (1996). Message characteristics. *Steve's Primer of Practical Persuasion and Influence*. Retrieved August 2, 2004, from http://www.as.wvu.edu/~sbb/comm221/primer.htm

Borgeat, F., & Goulet, J. (1983, June). Psychophysiological changes following auditory subliminal suggestions for activation and deactivation. *Perceptual and Motor Skills, 56*(3), 759–766.

Borges, M. A., Stepnowsky, M. A., & Holt, L. H. (1977). Recall and recognition of words and pictures by adults and children. *Bulletin of the Psychonomic Society, 9,* 113–114.

Boroditsky, L. (2001). Does language shape thought? Mandarin and English speakers' conceptions of time. *Cognitive Psychology, 43*(1), 1–22.

Boroditsky, L. (2009). How does our language shape the way we think? In M. Brockman (Ed.), *What's next? Dispatches on the future of science* (pp. 116–129). New York: Vintage.

Bossert, W., & Schworm, W. (2008). A class of two-group polarization measures. *Journal of Public Economic Theory, Association for Public Economic Theory, 10*(6): 1169–1187.

Bosworth, H. B., & Schaie, K. W. (1997). The relationship of social environment, social networks, and health outcomes in the Seattle Longitudinal Study: Two analytical approaches. *Journals of Gerontology Series B: Psychological Sciences and Social Sciences, 52*(5), 197–205.

Botwin, M. D., & Buss, D. M. (1989). The structure of act data: Is the Five-Factor Model of personality recaptured? *Journal of Personality and Social Psychology, 56,* 988–1001.

Bouchard T.J., et al. (1990). "Sources of human psychological differences: The Minnesota Study of Twins Reared Apart." *Science, 250*(4978): 223–228. doi:10.1126/science.2218526. PMID 2218526.

Bouchard, C., Tremblay, A., Nadeau, A., Dussault, J., Despres, J. P., Theriault, G., et al. (1990). Long-term exercise training with constant energy intake. 1: Effect on body composition and selected metabolic variables. *International Journal on Obesity, 14*(1), 57–73.

Bouchard, T. (1994). Genes, environment, and personality. *Science, 264,* 1700–1701.

Bouchard, T. J., Jr. (1997). Whenever the twain shall meet. *The Science, 37*(5), 52–57.

Bouchard, T. J., Jr., & Segal, N. L. (1985). Environment and IQ. In B. B. Wolman (Ed.), *Handbook of intelligence: Theories, measurements, and applications* (pp. 391–464). New York: Wiley.

Bowman, E. S. (1996). Delayed memories of child abuse: Part II: An overview of research findings relevant to understanding their reliability and suggestibility. *Dissociation: Progress in the Dissociative Disorders, 9,* 232–243.

Boyson-Bardies, B., deHalle, P., Sagart, L., & Durand, C. (1989). A cross-linguistic investigation of vowel formats in babbling. *Journal of Child Language, 16,* 1–17.

Bracey, G. (1997). A few facts about poverty. *Phi Delta Kappan, 79,* 163–164.

Braun, S. R. (1996). *Buzz: The science and lore of alcohol and caffeine* (pp. 137–169). New York: Oxford University Press.

Brazelton, T. B. (1992). *Touchpoints: Your child's emotional and behavioral development*. Reading, MA: Addison-Wesley.

Brecher, M., Wang, B. W., Wong, H., & Morgan, J. P. (1988). Phencyclidine and violence: Clinical and legal issues. *Journal of Clinical Psychopharmacology, 8,* 397–401.

Breiter, H. C., Gollub, R. L., Weisskoff, R. M., Kennedy, D. N., Makris, N., Berke, J. D., et al. (1997). Acute effects of cocaine on human brain activity and emotion. *Neuron, 19*(3), 591–611.

Breland, K., & Breland, M. (1961). The misbehavior of organisms. *American Psychologist, 16,* 681–684.

Brennan, J. F. (2002). *History and systems of psychology* (6th ed.). Upper Saddle River, NJ: Prentice Hall.

Brennan, P. A., Raine, A., Schulsinger, F., Kirkegaard-Sorensen, L., Knop, J., Hutchings, B., et al. (1997). Psychophysiological protective factors for male subjects at high risk for criminal behavior. *American Journal of Psychiatry, 154,* 853–855.

Breslau, N., Chilcoat, H. D., Kessler, R. C., Peterson, E. L., & Lucia, V. C. (1999). Vulnerability to assaultive violence: Further specification of the sex difference in posttraumatic stress disorder. *Psychological Medicine, 29,* 813–821.

Breslau, N., Davis, G. C., Andreski, P., & Peterson, E. L. (1997). Sex differences in posttraumatic stress disorder. *Archives of General Psychiatry, 54*(11), 1044–1048.

Breuer, J., & Freud, S. (1895). *Studies on hysteria (cathartic method)*. *Special Edition, 2,* 1–309.

Brewer, M. B. (2001). Ingroup identification and intergroup conflict: When does in-group love become outgroup hate? In R. D. Ashmore, L. Jussim, & D. Wilder (Eds.), *Social identity, intergroup conflict, and conflict reduction*. New York: Oxford University Press.

Brick, J. (2003). The characteristics of alcohol: Chemistry, use and abuse. In J. Brick (Ed.), *Handbook of the medical consequences of alcohol and drug abuse* (pp. 1–11). New York: Haworth Medical Press.

Briem, V., & Hedman, L. R. (1995). Behavioural effects of mobile telephone use during simulated driving. *Ergonomics, 38,* 2536–2562.

Briggs, K. C., & Myers, I. B. (1998). *The Myers-Briggs Type Indicator-Form M*. Palo Alto, CA: Consulting Psychologists Press.

Brigham, A. (1844). Asylums exclusively for the incurably insane. *Classic article in the American Journal of Psychiatry, 151,* 50–70.

Broadbent, D. (1958). *Perception and communication*. Elmsford, NY: Pergamon.

Brondolo, E., Rieppi, R., Ericksson, S. A., Bagiella, E., Shapiro, P. A., McKinley, P., et al. (2003). Hostility, interpersonal interactions, and ambulatory blood pressure. *Psychosomatic Medicine, 65,* 1003–1011.

Bronkhorst, A. W. (2000). The cocktail party phenomenon: A review on speech intelligibility in multiple-talker conditions. *Acta Acustica United with Acustica, 86,* 117–128. Retrieved from http://www.ingentaconnect.com/content/dav/aaua/2000/00000086/00000001/art00016

Brooks, J. G., & Brooks, M. G. (1993). *In search of understanding: The case for constructivist classrooms.* Alexandria, VA: The Association for Supervision and Curriculum Development.

Brown, A. S., & Derkits, E. J. (2010). Prenatal infection and schizophrenia: A review of epidemiologic and translational studies. *The American Journal of Psychiatry, 167*(3), 261–280. doi:10.1176/appi.ajp.2009.09030361

Brown, C. A., & Jones, A. K. P. (2010). Meditation experience predicts less negative appraisal of pain: Electrophysiological evidence for the involvement of anticipatory neural responses. *Pain.* doi:10.1016/j.pain.2010.04.017

Brown, C., Taylor, J., Green, A., Lee, B. E., Thomas, S. B., & Ford, A. (2003). *Managing depression in African Americans: Consumer and provider perspectives* [Final Report to Funders]. Pittsburgh: Mental Health Association of Allegheny County.

Brown, E. (2012, September 2). Sun Myung Moon dies at 92; Washington Times owner led the Unification Church. *The Washington Post.* Retrieved May 24, 2013, from http://www.washingtonpost.com/world/asia_pacific/sun-myungmoon-dies-at-92-washington-times-owner-led-the-unification-church/2012/09/02/001b747a-f531-11e1-aab7-f199a16396cf_story.html

Brown, G., Lawrence, T. B., & Robinson, S. L. (2005). Territoriality in management organizations. *Academy of Management Review, 30*(3), 577–594.

Brown, J. (1958). Some tests of the decay theory of immediate memory. *Quarterly Journal of Experimental Psychology, 10,* 12–21.

Brown, R. (1973). *A first language: The early stages.* Cambridge, MA: Harvard University Press.

Brown, R., & McNeill, D. (1966). The "tip of the tongue" phenomenon. *Journal of Verbal Learning and Verbal Behavior, 5*(4), 325–337.

Browne, D. (2004). Do dolphins know their own minds? *Biology and Philosophy, 19,* 633–653.

Browne, M. N., & Keeley, S. M. (2009). *Asking the right questions: A guide to critical thinking* (9th ed., pp. 37–129). Upper Saddle River, NJ: Pearson Prentice-Hall.

Broyles, S. (2006). Subliminal advertising and the perpetual popularity of playing to people's paranoia. *Journal of Consumer Affairs, 40*(2), 392–406.

Brubaker, D. A., & Leddy, J. J. (2003). Behavioral contracting in the treatment of eating disorders. *The Physician and Sportsmedicine, 31*(9).

Brunner, E. J., Hemingway, H., Walker, B., Page, M., Clarke, P., Juneja, M., et al. (2002). Adrenocortical, autonomic and inflammatory causes of the metabolic syndrome: Nested case-control study. *Circulation, 106,* 2659–2665.

Bryan, E. B., & Hallett, F. (2001). *Guidelines for professionals. Twins and triplets: The first five years and beyond.* London: Multiple Births Foundation.

Bryan, J., & Freed, F. (1982). Corporal punishment: Normative data and sociological and psychological correlates in a community college population. *Journal of Youth and Adolescence, 11*(2), 77–87.

Bryant, R. A., & McConkey, K. M. (1989). Hypnotic blindness: A behavioral and experimental analysis. *Journal of Abnormal Psychology, 98,* 71–77.

Brzustowicz, L. M., Simone, J., Mohseni, P., Hayter, J. E., Hodgkinson, K. A., Chow, E. W., et al. (2004). Linkage disequilibrium mapping of schizophrenia susceptibility to the CAPON region of chromosome 1q22. *American Journal of Human Genetics, 74*(5), 1057–1063.

Buccino, G., Binkofski, F., & Riggio, L. (2004). The mirror neuron system and action recognition. *Brain and Language, 89*(2), 370–376.

Buccino, G., Binkofski, F., Fink, G. R., Fadiga, L., Fogassi, L., Gallese, V., et al. (2001). Action observation activates premotor and parietal areas in a somatotopic manner: An fMRI study. *European Journal of Neuroscience, 13*(2), 400–404.

Bucher, B. D., & Lovaas, O. I. (1967). Use of aversive stimulation in behavior modification. In M. R. Jones (Ed.), *Miami symposium on the prediction of behavior 1967: Aversive stimulation* (pp. 77–145). Coral Gables: University of Miami Press.

Buck, R. (1980). Nonverbal behavior and the theory of emotion: The facial feedback hypothesis. *Journal of Personality and Social Psychology, 38,* 811–824.

Bullock, T. H., Bennett, M. V., Johnston, D., Josephson, R., Marder, E., & Fields, R. D. (2005). Neuroscience. The neuron doctrine, redux. *Science, 310*(5749), 791–793.

Bunge, M. (1984). What is pseudoscience? *The Skeptical Inquirer, 9*(1), 36–46.

Bureau of Labor Statistics. (2010). *Census of fatal occupational injuries.* Retrieved August 9, 2010, from http://www.bls.gov/iif/oshcfoi1.htm

Burger, J. M. (1997). The psychoanalytic approach: Neo-Freudian theory, application, and assessment. In *Personality* (4th ed.). Pacific Grove, CA: Brooks/Cole.

Burger, J. M. (2009). Replicating Milgram: Would people still obey today? *American Psychologist, 64,* 1–11.

Burger, J. M., & Petty, R. E. (1981). The low-ball compliance technique: Task or person commitment? *Journal of Personality and Social Psychology, 40,* 492–500.

Burgio, K. L. (1998). Behavioral vs. drug treatment for urge urinary incontinence in older women: A randomized controlled trial. *Journal of the American Medical Association, 280,* 1995–2000.

Burke, D. M., MacKay, D. G., Worthley, J. S., & Wade, E. (1991). On the tip of the tongue: What causes word finding failures in young and older adults. *Journal of Memory and Language, 30,* 542–579.

Burks, N., & Martin, B. (1985). Everyday problems and life change events: Ongoing versus acute sources of stress. *Journal of Human Stress, 11,* 27–35.

Burns, J. F. (2010, May 24). British medical council bars doctor who linked vaccine with autism. *New York Times.* Retrieved from http://www.nytimes.com

Bush, G., Spencer, T. J., Holmes, J., Shin, L. M., Valera, E. M., Seidman, L. J., et al. (2008). Functional magnetic resonance imaging of methylphenidate and placebo in Attention-Deficit/Hyperactivity Disorder during the Multi-Source Interference Task. *Archives of General Psychiatry, 65*(1), 102–114.

Bushman, B. J. (1997). Effects of alcohol on human aggression: Validity of proposed explanations. In M. Galanter (Ed.), *Recent developments in alcoholism. Vol. 1: Alcohol and violence—Epidemiology, neurobiology, psychology, family issues* (pp. 227–243). New York: Plenum Press.

Bushman, B. J., & Huesmann, L. R. (2001). Effects of televised violence on aggression. In D. G. Singer & J. L. Singer (Eds.), *Handbook of children and the media* (Chapter 11, pp. 223–254). Thousand Oaks, CA: Sage.

Buss, D. M. (2009). The multiple adaptive problems solved by human aggression. *Behavioral and Brain Sciences, 32,* 271–272.

Buss, D. M. (2011). Personality and the adaptive landscape: The role of individual differences in creating and solving social adaptive problems. In D. M. Buss & P. H. Hawley (Eds.), *The evolution of personality and individual differences* (pp. 29–60). New York: Oxford University Press.

Bussa, B., & Kaufman, C. (2000). What can self-help do? *The Journal of the California Alliance of the Mentally Ill, 2*(2), 34–45.

Butcher, J. N., & Rouse, S. V. (1996). Personality: Individual differences and clinical assessment. *Annual Review of Psychology, 47,* 87–111.

Butcher, J. N., Graham, J. R., Ben-Poarth, Y. S., Tellegen, A., Dahlstrom, W. G., & Kaemmer, B. (2001). *Minnesota Multiphasic Personality Inventory-2. Manual for administration, scoring, and interpretation* (Rev. ed.). Minneapolis: University of Minnesota Press.

Butcher, J. N., Rouse, S. V., & Perry, J. N. (2000). Empirical description of psychopathology in therapy clients: Correlates of MMPI-2 scales. In J. N. Butcher (Ed.), *Basic sources on the MMPI-2* (pp. 487–500). Minneapolis: University of Minnesota Press.

Cabeza, R., Anderson, N. D., Locantore, J. K., & McIntosh, A. R. (2002). Aging gracefully: Compensatory brain activity in high-performing older adults. *NeuroImage, 17*(3), 1394–1402.

Cacioppo, J. T., Berntson, G. G. (1992). Social psychological contributions to the decade of the brain: Doctrine of multilevel analysis. *American Psychologist, 47,* 1019–1028.

Cain, D., & Seeman, J. (Eds.). (2001). *Humanistic psychotherapies: Handbook of research and practice.* Washington, DC: APA Publications.

Caley, L. M., Kramer, C., & Robinson, L. K. (2005). Fetal alcohol spectrum disorder. *The Journal of School Nursing, 21*(3), 139–146.

Camacho, M. (2012). Abby and Brittany. *Common Sense Media*. Retrieved April 26, 2013, from http://www.commonsensemedia.org/tv-reviews/abby-and-brittany

Cameron, J., Banko, K. M., & Pierce, W. D. (2001). Pervasive negative effects of rewards on intrinsic motivation: The myth continues. *The Behavior Analyst, 24,* 1–44.

Cami, J., Farre, M., Mas, M., Roset, P. N., Poudevida, S., Mas, A., et al. (2000). Human pharmacology of 3,4-methylenedioxymethamphetamine ("ecstasy"): Psychomotor performance and subjective effects. *Journal of Clinical Psychopharmacology, 20,* 455–466.

Campbell, J. C., & Wolf, A. D. (2003). Risk factors for femicide in abusive relationships: Results from a multisite case control study. *American Journal of Public Health, 93*(7).

Cannon, W. B. (1927). The James-Lange theory of emotion: A critical examination and an alternative theory. *American Journal of Psychology, 39,* 10–124.

Cardno, A. G., & Gottesman, I. I. (2000). Twin studies of schizophrenia: From bow-and-arrow concordances to star wars Mx and functional genomics. *American Journal of Medical Genetics, 97*(1), 12–17.

Carducci, B. (1998). *The psychology of personality*. Pacific Grove, CA: Brooks/Cole Publishing Co.

Carlson, G. A., Jensen, P. S., & Nottelmann, E. D. (Eds.). (1998). Current issues in childhood bipolarity [Special issue]. *Journal of Affective Disorders, 51.*

Carpenter, P. A., Just, M. A., & Shell, P. (1990). What one intelligence test measures: A theoretical account of the processing in the Raven Progressive Matrices test. *Psychological Review, 97*(3), 404–431.

Carpenter, S. (2001). Sights unseen. *APA Monitor, 32*(4), 54.

Carr, E. G., & Lovaas, O. I. (1983). Contingent electric shock as a treatment for severe behavior problems. In S. Axelrod & J. Apsche (Eds.), *The effects of punishment on human behavior* (pp. 221–245). New York: Academic Press.

Carruthers, M. (2001). A multifactorial approach to understanding andropause. *Journal of Sexual and Reproductive Medicine, 1,* 69–74.

Carskadon, M. A., & Dement, W. C. (2005). Normal human sleep overview. In M. H. Kryger, T. Roth, & W. C. Dement (Eds.), *Principles and practice of sleep medicine* (4th ed., pp. 13–23). Philadelphia: Elsevier/Saunders.

Carskadon, M. A., & Dement, W. C. (2011). Normal human sleep: An overview. In M. H. Kryger, T. Roth, & W. C. Dement (Eds.), *Principles and practice of sleep medicine*. St. Louis, MO: Elsevier Saunders.

Carson, R. C. (1969). *Interaction concepts of personality*. Chicago: Aldine.

Carter, R. M., Bowling, D. L., Reeck, C., & Huettel, S. (2012). A distinct role of the temporal-parietal junction in predicting socially guided decisions. *Science, 337*(6090), 109–111.

Case, B. G., Bertollo, D. N., Laska, E. M., Price, L. H., Siegel, C. E., Olfson, M., et al. (2013). Declining use of electroconvulsive therapy in United States general hospitals. *Biological Psychiatry, 73*(2), 119–126. doi:10.1016/j.biopsych.2012.09.005

Case, B. G., Bertollo, D. N., Laska, E. M., Siegel, C. E., Wanderling, J. A., & Olfson, M. (2012). Racial differences in the availability and use of electroconvulsive therapy for recurrent major depression. *Journal of Affective Disorders, 136*(3), 359–365.

Cassidy, A., Bingham, S., & Setchell, K. D. R. (1994). Biological effects of a diet of soy protein rich in isoflavones on the menstrual cycle of premenopausal women. *American Journal of Clinical Nutrition, 60,* 333–340.

Castillo, R. J. (1997). Eating disorders. In R. J. Castillo (Ed.), *Culture and mental illness: A client-centered approach* (p. 152). Pacific Grove, CA: Brooks/Cole.

Catanzaro, S. J., Wasch, H. H., Kirsch, I., & Mearns, J. (2000). Coping-related expectancies and dispositions as prospective predictors of coping responses and symptoms: Distinguishing mood regulation expectancies, dispositional coping, and optimism. *Journal of Personality, 68,* 757–788.

Cattell, R. B. (1990). Advances in Cattellian personality theory. In L. A. Pervin (Ed.), *Handbook of personality: Theory and research* (pp. 101–110). New York: Guilford Press.

Cattell, R. B. (1994). *Sixteen personality factor questionnaire* (5th ed.). Champaign, IL: Institute for Personality and Ability Testing.

Cattell, R. B. (1995). Personality structure and the new fifth edition of the 16PF. *Educational and Psychological Measurement, 55*(6), 926–937.

Cattell, R. B. (Ed.). (1966). *Handbook of multivariate experimental psychology*. Chicago: Rand McNally.

Cattell, R. B., & Kline, P. (1977). *The scientific analysis of personality and motivation*. New York: Academic Press.

Cave, K. R., & Kim, M. (1999). Top-down and bottom-up attentional control: On the nature of interference from a salient distractor. *Perception and Psychophysics, 61,* 1009–1023.

Centers for Disease Control and Prevention (CDC). (1992). *Smoking and health in the Americas: The Surgeon General's report*. Atlanta, GA: National Center for Chronic Disease Prevention and Health Promotion.

Centers for Disease Control and Prevention (CDC). (2008). Annual smoking-attributable mortality, years of potential life lost, and economic costs—United States, 2000–2004. *Morbidity and Mortality Weekly Report, 57*(45), 1226–1228.

Centers for Disease Control and Prevention (CDC). (2008a). Annual smoking-attributable mortality, years of potential life lost, and economic costs—United States, 2000–2004. *Morbidity and Mortality Weekly Report, 57*(45), 1226–1228.

Centers for Disease Control and Prevention (CDC). (2009a). *HIV/AIDS surveillance report 2007* (Vol. 19). Atlanta, GA: National Center for Chronic Disease Prevention and Health Promotion.

Centers for Disease Control and Prevention (CDC). (2009b). *Health effects of cigarette smoking*. Retrieved January 13, 2010, from http://www.cdc.gov/tobacco/data_statistics/fact_sheets/health_effects/effects_cig_smoking/index.htm

Centers for Disease Control and Prevention (CDC). (2009c). Down syndrome. Retrieved June 19, 2010, from http://www.cdc.gov/ncbddd/birthdefects/downsyndrome.html

Centers for Disease Control and Prevention (CDC). (2010). *How tobacco smoke causes disease: The biology and behavioral basis for smoking-attributable disease: A report of the Surgeon General*. Retrieved March 27, 2013, from http://www.cdc.gov/tobacco/data_statistics/sgr/2010/index.htm

Centers for Disease Control and Prevention (CDC). (2013). *Vaccine safety: Addressing common concerns*. Retrieved April 26, 2013, from http://www.cdc.gov/vaccinesafety/Concerns/Index.html

Centers for Disease Control and Prevention (CDC), 2013. Autism Spectrum Disorders (ASDs): Data & Statistics. Retrieved from the Internet on March 6, 2013 at http://www.cdc.gov/ncbddd/autism/data.html

Centerwall, B. S. (1989). Exposure to television as a risk factor for violence. *American Journal of Epidemiology, 129,* 643–652.

Cepeda, N. J., Pashler, H., Vul, E., Wixted, J. T., & Rohrer, D. (2006). Distributed practice in verbal recall tasks: A review and quantitative synthesis. *Psychological Bulletin, 132,* 354–380.

Cermak, L., & Craik, F. (1979). *Levels of processing in human memory*. Hillsdale, NJ: Erlbaum.

Cha, J. H., & Nam, K. D. (1985). A test of Kelley's cube theory of attribution: A crosscultural replication of McArthur's study. *Korean Social Science Journal, 12,* 151–180.

Chaddock, L., Hillman, C. H., Buck, S. M., & Cohen, N. J. (2010). Aerobic fitness and executive control of relational memory in preadolescent children. *Medicine and Science in Sports and Exercise*. doi:10.1249/MSS.0b013e3181e9af48

Chang, P. P., Ford, D. E., Meoni, L. A., Wang, N., & Klag, M. J. (2002). Anger in young men and subsequent premature cardiovascular disease: The precursors study. *Archives of Internal Medicine, 162,* 901–906.

Chang, S. W., Gariepy, J. F., & Platt, M. L. (2013). Neuronal reference frames for social decisions in primate frontal cortex. *Nature Neuroscience, 16,* 243–250.

Charlesworth, W. R., & Kreutzer, M. A. (1973). Facial expression of infants and children. In P. Ekman (Ed.), *Darwin and facial expression: A century of research in review*. New York: Academic.

Chen, J. Y. (2007). Do Chinese and English speakers think about time differently? Failure of replicating Boroditsky (2001). *Cognition, 104*(2), 427–436.

Chen, L. Y., Rex, C. S., Sanaiha, Y., Lynch, G., & Gall, C. M. (2010). Learning induces neurotrophin signaling at hippocampal synapses. *Proceedings of the National Academy of Sciences, 107*(15), 7030–7035.

Chen, R., & Ende, N. (2000). The potential for the use of mononuclear cells from human umbilical cord blood in the treatment of amyotrophic lateral sclerosis in SOD1 mice. *Journal of Medicine, 31,* 21–31.

Chen, Y., Huang, X., Zhang, Y.-W., Rockenstein, E., Bu, G., Golde, T. E., Masliah, E., & Xu, H. (2012). Alzheimer's β-Secretase (BACE1) regulates the cAMP/PKA/ CREB pathway independently of β-Amyloid. *Journal of Neuroscience, 32*(33), 11390. doi: 10.1523/JNEUROSCI.0757-12.2012

Cherry, E. C. (1953). Some experiments on the recognition of speech, with one and with two ears. *Journal of the Acoustical Society of America, 25*(5), 975–979.

Cheryan, S., Plaut, V., Davis, P., & Steele, C. (2009). Ambient belonging: How stereotypical cues impact gender participation in computer science. *Journal of Personality and Social Psychology, 97*(6), 1045–1060.

Chess, S., & Thomas, A. (1986). *Temperament in clinical practice.* New York: Guilford Press.

Chesterton, L. S., Barlas, P., Foster, N. E., Baxter, G. D., & Wright, C. C. (2003). Gender differences in pressure pain threshold in healthy humans. *Pain, 101,* 259–266.

Cheyne, J. A. (2003). Sleep paralysis and the structure of waking-nightmare hallucinations. *Dreaming, 13*(3), 163–179.

Chidester, D. (2003). *Salvation and suicide: Jim Jones, the peoples temple, and Jonestown* (Rev. ed., pp. 1–51). Bloomington: Indiana University Press.

Chirkov, V. I. (2009). A cross-cultural analysis of autonomy in education: A self-determination theory perspective. *Theory and Research in Education, 7*(2), 253–262.

Chirkov, V. I., Lebedeva, N. M., Molodtsova, I., & Tatarko, A. (2011). Social capital, motivational autonomy, and health behavior: A comparative study of Canadian and Russian youth. In D. Chadee & A. Kosti (Eds.), *Social psychological dynamics* (pp. 211–241). Trinidad: University of West Indies Press.

Choca, J. P. (2013). *The Rorschach inkblot test: An interpretive guide for clinicians.* Washington, DC: American Psychological Association.

Choi, I., & Nisbett, R. E. (1998). Situational salience and cultural differences in the correspondence bias and in the actor–observer bias. *Personality and Social Psychology Bulletin, 24,* 949–960.

Choi, I., Nisbett, R. E., & Norenzayan, A. (1999). Causal attribution across cultures: Variation and universality. *Psychological Bulletin, 125,* 47–63.

Chomsky, N. (2006). *Language and mind* (3rd ed.). New York: Cambridge University Press.

Chomsky, N., Belletti, A., & Rizzi, L. (2002). *On nature and language.* New York: Cambridge University Press.

Chou, S. Y., Grossman, M., & Saffer, H. (2004). An economic analysis of adult obesity: Results from the behavioral risk factor surveillance system. *Journal of Health Economics, 23,* 565–587.

Christensen, A., Jacobson, N. S., & Babcock, J. C. (1995). Integrative behavioral couple therapy. In N. S. Jacobson & A. S. Gurman (Eds.), *Clinical handbook of couple therapy* (pp. 31–64). New York: Norton.

Chwalisz, K., Diener, E., & Gallagher, D. (1988). Autonomic arousal feedback and emotional experience: Evidence from the spinal cord injured. *Journal of Personality and Social Psychology, 54,* 820–828.

Cialdini, R. B., Trost, M. R., & Newsom, J. T. (1995). Preference for consistency: The development of a valid measure and the discovery of surprising behavioral implications. *Journal of Personality and Social Psychology, 69,* 318–328.

Cialdini, R. B., Vincent, J., Lewis, S., Catalan, J., Wheeler, D., & Darby, B. (1975). Reciprocal concessions procedure for inducing compliance: The door-in-the-face technique. *Journal of Personality and Social Psychology, 31,* 206–215.

Cialdini, R. B., Wosinska, W., Barrett, D., Butner, J., & Gornik-Durose, M. (1999). Compliance with a request in two cultures: The differential influence of social proof and commitment/consistency on collectivists and individualists. *Personality and Social Psychology Bulletin, 25,* 1242–1253.

Ciardiello, A. (1998). Did you ask a good question today? Alternative cognitive and metacognitive strategies. *Journal of Adolescent and Adult Literacy, 42,* 210–219.

Cinnirella, M., & Green, B. (2007). Does "cyber-conformity" vary cross-culturally? Exploring the effect of culture and communication medium on social conformity. *Computers in Human Behavior, 23*(4), 2011–2025.

Clarke, A. R., Barry, R. J., McCarthy, R., Selikowitz, M., Johnstone, S. J., Hsu, C. I., et al. (2007). Coherence in children with Attention-Deficit/Hyperactivity Disorder and excess beta activity in their EEG. *Clinical Neurophysiology, 118*(7), 1472–1479.

Clarke, J. (1994). Pieces of the puzzle: The jigsaw method. In S. Sharan (Ed.), *Handbook of cooperative learning methods* (pp. 34–50). Westport, CT: Greenwood Press.

Clarkin, J. F., Levy, K. N., Lenzenweger, M. F., & Kernberg, O. F. (2007). Evaluating three treatments for borderline personality disorder: A multiwave study. *American Journal of Psychiatry, 164*(6), 922–928.

Coates, J. (1986). *Women, men, and language.* New York: Longman.

Cohen, N. J., Eichenbaum, R., Decedo, J. C., & Corkin, S. (1985). Preserved learning capacity in amnesia: Evidence for multiple memory systems. In L. S. Squire & N. Butters (Eds.), *Neuropsychology of memory.* New York: Guilford Press.

Cohen, S., & Herbert, T. B. (1996). Health psychology: Psychological factors and physical disease from the perspective of human psychoneuroimmunology. *Annual Review of Psychology, 47,* 113–142.

Colcombe, S. J., Erickson, K. I., Raz, N., Webb, A. G., Cohen, N. J., McAuley, E., et al. (2003). Aerobic fitness reduces brain tissue loss in aging humans. *Journal of Gerontology Series A: Biological Sciences and Medical Sciences, 58,* 176–180.

Cole, S. W., Arevalo, J. M. G., Takahashi, R., Sloan, E. K., Lutgendorf, S. K., Sood, A. K., et al. (2010). Computational identification of gene-social environment interaction oat the human IL6 locus. *Proceedings of the National Academy of Sciences of the United States of America.* Retrieved September 27, 2010, from http://www.pnas.org/content/107/12/5681.full

Colligan, J. (1983). Musical creativity and social rules in four cultures. *Creative Child and Adult Quarterly, 8,* 39–44.

Collins, A. M., & Loftus, E. F. (1975). A spreading activation theory of semantic processing. *Psychological Review, 82,* 407–428.

Collins, A. M., & Quillian, M. R. (1969). Retrieval time from semantic memory. *Journal of Verbal Learning and Verbal Behaviour, 8,* 240–247.

Collins, C. J., Hanges, P. J., & Locke, E. A. (2004). The relationship of achievement motivation to entrepreneurial behavior: A meta-analysis. *Human Performance, 17*(1), 95–117.

Colom, R., Shih, P. C., Flores-Mendoza, C., & Quiroga, M. A. (2006). The real relationship between short-term memory and working memory. *Memory, 14*(7), 804–813.

Columbo, J., & Mitchell, D. W. (2009). Infant visual habituation. *Neurobiology of Learning and Memory, 92*(2), 225–234.

Committee on Animal Research and Ethics. (2004). *Research with animals in psychology.* Retrieved October 12, 2004, from www.apa.org/science/animal2.html

Cone-Wesson, B. (2005). Prenatal alcohol and cocaine exposure: Influences on cognition, speech, language, and hearing. *Journal of Communication Disorders, 38*(4), 279–302.

Conrad, R., & Hull, A. J. (1964). Information, acoustic confusion, and memory span. *British Journal of Psychology, 55,* 429–432.

Constantine, M. G., Alleyne, V. L., Caldwell, L. D., McRae, M. B., & Suzuki, M. B. (2005). Coping responses of Asian, Black, and Latino/Latina New York City residents following the September 11, 2001 terrorist attacks against the United States. *Cultural Diversity & Ethnic Minority, 11,* 293–308.

Consumer Reports. (1995, November). Mental health: Does psychotherapy help? 734–739.

Conway, M. A., Cohen, G., & Stanhope, N. (1992). Very long-term memory for knowledge acquired at school and university. *Applied Cognitive Psychology, 6,* 467–482.

Cook, K (2014). *Kitty Genovese: The murder, the bystander, the crime, the crime that changed America.* New York, W.W. Norton & Company, Inc.

Cook, M., & Mineka, S. (1989). Observational conditioning of fear to fear-relevant versus fear-irrelevant stimuli in rhesus monkeys. *Journal of Abnormal Psychology, 98*(4), 448–459.

Coolidge, F. L. (2006). *Dream interpretation as a psychotherapeutic technique.* London: Radcliffe.

Cooper, L. A., Gonzales, J. J., Gallo, J. J., Rost, K. M., Meredith, L. S., Rubenstein, L. V., et al. (2003). The acceptability of treatment for depression among African-American, Hispanic, and White primary care patients. *Medical Care, 41*(4), 479–489.

Corbetta, M., Kincade, M. J., Lewis, C., Snyder, A. Z., & Sapir, A. (2005). Neural basis and recovery of spatial attention deficits in spatial neglect. *Nature Neuroscience, 8*, 1603–1610.

Cormier, J. F., & Thelen, M. H. (1998). Professional skepticism of multiple personality disorder. *Professional Psychology: Research and Practice, 29*, 163–167.

Corr, C. A. (1993). Coping with dying: Lessons that we should and should not learn from the work of Elisabeth Kubler-Ross. *Death Studies, 17*, 69–83.

Cosgrove, G. R., & Rauch, S. L. (1995). Psychosurgery. *Neurosurgery Clinics of North America, 6*, 167–176.

Costa, P. T., Jr., & McCrae, R. R. (2000). The Revised NEO Personality Inventory (NEO PI-R). In J. Cheek & E. M. Donahue (Eds.), *Handbook of personality inventories.* New York: Plenum.

Costello, D. M., Swendsen, J., Rose, J. S., & Dierker, L. C. (2008). Risk and protective factors associated with trajectories of depressed mood from adolescence to early adulthood. *Journal of Consulting and Clinical Psychology, 76*(2), 173–183.

Couperus, J. W., & Nelson, C. A. (2006). Early brain development and plasticity. In K. McCartney & D. Phillips (Eds.), *The Blackwell handbook of early childhood development* (pp. 85–105). Oxford, UK: Blackwell Press.

Courage, M. L., & Howe, M. L. (2002). From infant to child: The dynamics of cognitive change in the second year of life. *Psychological Bulletin, 128*, 250–277.

Cowan, N. (1988). Evolving conceptions of memory storage, selective attention, and their mutual constraints within the human information processing system. *Psychological Bulletin, 104*, 163–191.

Cowan, N. (1995). *Attention and memory: An integrated framework* (Oxford Psychology Series, No. 26). Oxford, NY: Oxford University Press.

Cowan, N. (2001). The magical number 4 in short-term memory: A reconsideration of mental storage capacity. *Behavioral and Brain Sciences, 24*, 97–185.

Cowan, N., Elliott, E. M., Saults, J. S., Morey, C. C., Mattox, S., Hismjatullina, A., & Conway, A. R. A. (2005). On the capacity of attention: Its estimation and its role in working memory and cognitive aptitudes. *Cognitive Psychology, 51*(1), 42–100.

Craddock, N., O'Donovan, M. C., & Owen, M. J. (2005). The genetics of schizophrenia and bipolar disorder: Dissecting psychosis. *Journal of Medical Genetics, 42*, 288–299.

Crago, M. B., Shisslak, C. M., & Estes, L. S. (1996). Eating disturbances among American minority groups: A review. *International Journal of Eating Disorders, 19*, 239–248.

Craik, F. I. M. (1970). The fate of primary memory items in free recall. *Journal of Verbal Learning and Verbal Behavior, 9*, 143–148.

Craik, F. I. M. (1994). Memory changes in normal aging. *Current Directions in Psychological Science, 3*(5), 155–158.

Craik, F. I. M., & Lockhart, R. S. (1972). Levels of processing. A framework for memory research. *Journal of Verbal Learning and Verbal Behaviour, 11*, 671–684.

Craik, F. I. M., & Tulving, E. (1975). Depth of processing and the retention of words in episodic memory. *Journal of Experimental Psychology: General, 104*, 268–294.

Craske, M. G., & Barlow, D. H. (2014). Panic disorder and agoraphobia. In D. H. Barlow (Ed.), *Clinical handbook of psychological disorders: A step-by-step treatment manual* (5th ed., pp. 1–61). New York: Guilford Press.

Crick, F., & Koch, C. (1990). Towards a neurobiological theory of consciousness. *Seminars in the Neurosciences, 2*, 263–275.

Cristancho, M. A., Helmer, A., Connolly, R., Cristancho, P., & O'Reardon, J. P. (2013). Transcranial magnetic stimulation maintenance as a substitute for maintenance electroconvulsive therapy: A case series. *J ECT, 29*(2), 106–108. doi:10.1097/YCT.0b013e31827a70ba

Critchfield, T. S., Haley, R., Sabo, B., Colbert, J., & Macropoulis, G. (2003). A half century of scalloping in the work habits of the United States congress. *Journal of Applied Behavior Analysis, 36*(4), 465–486.

Crowley, A. E., & Hoyer, W. D. (1994). An integrative framework for understanding two-sided persuasion. *Journal of Consumer Research, 20*, 561–574.

Csikszentmihalyi, M. (1996). *Creativity: Flow and the psychology of discovery and invention.* New York: Harper Perennial.

Cummings, J. L., & Coffey, C. E. (1994). Neurobiological basis of behavior. In C. E. Coffey & J. L. Cummings (Eds.), *Textbook of geriatric neuropsychiatry* (pp. 72–96). Washington, DC: American Psychiatric Press.

Cummings, S. R., & Melton, L. J., III. (2002). Epidemiology and outcomes of osteoporotic fractures. *Lancet, 359*(9319), 1761–1767.

Curtis, R. C., & Miller, K. (1986). Believing another likes or dislikes you: Behaviors making the beliefs come true. *Journal of Personality and Social Psychology, 51*, 284–290.

Curtis, R. H. (1993). *Great lives: Medicine.* New York: Charles Scribner's Sons Books for Young Readers.

Damasio, H., Grabowski, T., Frank, R., Galaburda, A. M., & Damasion, A. R. (1994). The return of Phineas Gage: Clues about the brain from the skull of a famous patient. *Science, 264*, 1102–1105.

Darley, J. M., & Latané, B. (1968). Bystander intervention in emergencies: Diffusion of responsibility. *Journal of Personality and Social Psychology, 8*, 377–383.

Darvill, T., Lonky, E., Reihman, J., Stewart, P., & Pagano, J. (2000). Prenatal exposure to PCBs and infant performance on the Fagan test of infant intelligence. *Neurotoxicology, 21*(6), 1029–1038.

Darwin, C. (1859). *The origin of species by means of natural selection.* London: John Murray.

Darwin, C. (1898). *The expression of the emotions in man and animals.* New York: D. Appleton.

Davidson, R. J. (2003). Affective neuroscience and psychophysiology: Toward a synthesis. *Psychophysiology, 40*(5), 655–665.

Davidson, R. J., Kabat-Zinn, J., Schumacher, J., Rosenkranz, M., Muller, D., Santorelli, S., et al. (2003). Alterations in brain and immune function produced by mindfulness meditation. *Psychosomatic Medicine, 65*, 564–570.

Davidson, R. J., Putman, K. M., & Larson, C. L. (2000). Dysfunction in the neural circuitry of emotion regulation—a possible prelude to violence. *Science, 289*, 591–594.

Davies, I. R. L., Laws, G., Corbett, G. G., & Jerrett, D. J. (1998a). Cross-cultural differences in colour vision: Acquired "colour blindness" in Africa. *Personality and Individual Differences, 25*, 1153–1162.

Davies, I. R. L., Sowden, P., Jerrett, D. T., Jerrett, T., & Corbett, G. G. (1998b). A crosscultural study of English and Setswana speakers on a colour triads task: A test of the Sapir-Whorf hypothesis. *British Journal of Psychology, 89*, 1–15.

Davis, H. A., DiStefano, C., & Schutz, P. A. (2008). Identifying patterns of appraising tests in first-year college students: Implications for anxiety and emotion regulation during test taking. *Journal of Educational Psychology, 100*(4), 942–960. doi:10.1037/a0013096

Davis, J. O., Phelps, J. A., & Bracha, H. S. (1995). Prenatal development of monozygotic twins and concordance for schizophrenia. *Schizophrenia Bulletin, 21*, 357–366.

Davis, K. F., Parker, K. P., & Montgomery, G. (2004). Sleep in infants and young children: Part 1: Normal sleep. *Journal of Pediatric Healthcare, 18*(2), 65–71.

Davis, M., & Whalen, P. J. (2001). The amygdala: Vigilance and emotion. *Molecular Psychiatry, 6*, 13–34.

Davis, O. S. P., Haworth, C. M. A., Lewis, C. M., & Plomin, R. (2012). Visual analysis of geocoded twin data puts nature and nurture on the map. *Molecular Psychiatry, 17*, 867–874. doi:10.1038/mp.2012.68

De Valois, R. L., & De Valois, K. K. (1993). A multi-stage color model. *Vision Research, 33*(8), 1053–1065.

Dean, G., & Kelly, I. W. (2000). Does astrology work? Astrology and skepticism 1975–2000. In P. Kurtz (Ed.), *Skepticism: A 25 year retrospective* (pp. 191–207). Amherst, NY: Prometheus Books.

Dean, G., Kelly, I. W., Sakolfske, D. H., & Furnham, A. (1992). Graphology and human judgment. In B. L. Beyerstein & D. F. Beyerstein (Eds.), *The write stuff: Evaluations of graphology—The study of handwriting analysis* (pp. 342–396). Amherst, NY: Prometheus Books.

Debiec, J., Diaz-Mataix, L., Bush, D. E. A., Doyere, V., & LeDoux, J. E. (2010). The amygdala encodes specific sensory features of an aversive reinforcer. *Nature Neuroscience, 13,* 536–537.

deCharms, R. (1968). *Personal causation.* New York: Academic Press.

Deci, E. L., Eghrari, H., Patrick, B. C., & Leone, D. R. (1994). Facilitating internalization: The self-determination theory perspective. *Journal of Personality, 62,* 119–142.

Deci, E. L., Koestner, R., & Ryan, R. M. (1999). A meta-analytic review of experiments examining the effects of extrinsic rewards on intrinsic motivation. *Psychological Bulletin, 125,* 627–668.

DeGrandpre, R. J. (2000). A science of meaning: Can behaviorism bring meaning to psychological science? *American Psychologist, 55,* 721–739.

Deinzer, R., Kleineidam, C. H., Winkler, R., Idel, H., & Bachg, D. (2000). Prolonged reduction of salivary immunoglobulin A (slgA) after a major academic exam. *International Journal of Psychophysiology, 37,* 219–232.

Delaney, A. J., Crane, J. W., & Sah, P. (2007). Noradrenaline modulates transmission at a central synapse by a presynaptic mechanism. *Neuron, 56*(6), 880–892.

Delfiner, R. (2001, November 16). Kitty left at death's door. *New York Post.* Retrieved from http://www.nypost.com

DeLongis, A., Lazarus, R. S., & Folkman, S. (1988). The impact of daily stress on health and mood: Psychological and social resources as mediators. *Journal of Personality and Social Psychology, 54*(3), 486–495.

Demers, R. A. (1988). Linguistics and animal communication. In F. J. Newmeyer (Ed.), *Language form and language function* (pp. 314–335). Cambridge, MA: MIT Press.

Dempster, F. N., & Farris, R. (1990). The spacing effect: Research and practice. *Journal of Research and Development in Education, 23*(2), 97–101.

Deng, L. X., Deng, P., Ruan, Y., Xu, Z. C., Liu, N. K., Wen, X., et al. (2013). A novel growth-promoting pathway formed by gdnf-overexpressing Schwann cells promotes propriospinal axonal regeneration, synapse formation, and partial recovery of function after spinal cord injury. *The Journal of Neuroscience, 33*(13), 5655–5667. doi:10.1523/jneurosci.2973-12.2013

Dennett, D. C. (1991). *Consciousness explained.* New York: Little, Brown.

Deregowski, J. B. (1969). Perception of the two-pronged trident by two- and three-dimensional perceivers. *Journal of Experimental Psychology, 82,* 9–13.

Dew, M. A., Whyte, E. M., Lenze, E. J., Houck, P. R., Mulsant, B. H., Pollock, B. G., et al. (2007). Recovery from major depression in older adults receiving augmentation of antidepressant pharmacotherapy. *American Journal of Psychiatry, 164*(6), 892–899.

DeYoung, C. G., Hirsh, J. B., Shane, M. S., Papademetris, X., Rajeevan, N., & Gray, J. R. (2010). Testing predictions from personality neuroscience: Brain structure and the Big Five. *Psychological Science, 21*(6), 820–828.

Diamond, L. M. (2003). What does sexual orientation orient? A biobehavioral model distinguishing romantic love and sexual desire. *Psychological Review, 110,* 173–192.

Diamond, L. M. (2004). Emerging perspectives on distinctions between romantic love and sexual desire. *Current Directions in Psychological Science, 13,* 116–119.

Diamond, M. (1995). Biological aspects of sexual orientation and identity. In L. Diamant & R. McAnulty (Eds.), *The psychology of sexual orientation, behavior, and identity: A handbook* (pp. 45–80). Westport, CT: Greenwood Press.

Diamond, M. C. (1991). Hormonal effects on the development of cerebral lateralization. *Psychoneuroendocrinology, 16,* 121–129.

Diamond, M., & Sigmundson, H. K. (1997). Sex reassignment at birth. Long-term review and clinical implications. *Archives of Pediatric Adolescent Medicine, 151*(3), 298–304.

Dickens, W. T., & Flynn, J. R. (2001, April). Heritability estimates vs. large environmental effects: The IQ paradox resolved. *Psychological Review, 108*(2), 346–369.

Dickerson, F., Ringel, N., Parente, F., & Boronow, J. (1994). Seclusion and restraint, assaultiveness, and patient performance in a token economy. *Hospital and Community Psychiatry, 45,* 168–170.

Diener, E., Lusk, R., DeFour, D., & Flax, R. (1980). Deindividuation: Effects of group size, density, number of observers, and group member similarity on self-consciousness and disinhibited behavior. *Journal of Personality and Social Psychology, 39,* 449–459.

Dillard, J. (1990). Self-inference and the foot-in-the-door technique: Quantity of behavior and attitudinal mediation. *Human Communication Research, 16,* 422–447.

Dillard, J. (1991). The current status of research on sequential-request compliance techniques. *Personality and Social Psychology Bulletin, 17,* 282–288.

Dobson, K. S., & Block, L. (1988). Historical and philosophical bases of the cognitive behavioral therapies. In K. S. Dobson (Ed.), *Handbook of cognitive-behavioral therapies* (pp. 3–38). New York: Guilford Press.

Dodge, K. A., Bates, J. E., & Pettit, G. S. (1990). Mechanisms in the cycle of violence. *Science, 250,* 1678–1683.

Dohrenwend, B. P., Levav, I. Shrout, P. E., Schwartz, S., Naveh, G., Link, B. G., et al. (1992). Socioeconomic status and psychiatric disorders: The causation-selection issue. *Science, 313,* 979–982.

Dolcos, F., LaBar, K. S., Cabeza, R., & Purves, D. (2005). Remembering one year later: Role of the amygdala and the medial temporal lobe memory system in retrieving emotional memories. *Proceedings of the National Academy of Sciences, USA.* doi:10.1073/ pnas.0409848102

Dollard, J., & Miller, N. F. (1950). *Personality and psychotherapy.* New York: McGraw-Hill.

Dollard, J., Doob, L. W., Miller, N. E., Mowrer, O. H., & Sears, R. R. (1939). *Frustration and aggression.* New Haven, CT: Yale University Press.

Domagalski, T. A., & Steelman, L. A. (2007). The impact of gender and organizational status on workplace anger expression. *Management Communication Quarterly, 20*(3), 297–315.

Domhoff, G. W. (1996). *Finding meaning in dreams: A quantitative approach.* New York: Plenum Publishing.

Domhoff, G. W. (2005). The content of dreams: Methodologic and theoretical implications. In M. Kryger, T. Roth, & W. Dement (Eds.), *Principles and practices of sleep medicine* (4th ed., pp. 522–534). Philadelphia: Saunders.

Domhoff, G. W., & Schneider, A. (2008). Similarities and differences in dream content at the cross-cultural, gender, and individual levels. *Consciousness and Cognition, 17,* 1257–1265.

Dominey, P. F., & Dodane, C. (2004). Indeterminacy in language acquisition: The role of child-directed speech and joint attention. *Journal of Neurolinguistics, 17*(2–3), 121–145.

Domjan, M., Cusato, B., & Villarreal, R. (2000). Pavlovian feed-forward mechanisms in the control of social behavior. *Behavioral and Brain Sciences, 23,* 235–282.

Donovan, J. J., & Radosevich, D. R. (1999). A meta-analytic review of the distribution of practice effect: Now you see it, now you don't. *Journal of Applied Psychology, 84,* 795–805.

Dorahy, M. J. (2001). Dissociative identity disorder and memory dysfunction: The current state of experimental research and its future directions. *Clinical Psychology Review, 21*(5), 771–795.

Dougherty, D. D., Baer, L., Cosgrove, G. R., Cassem, E. H., Price, B. H., Nierenberg, A. A., et al. (2002). Prospective long-term follow-up of 44 patients who received cingulotomy for treatment-refractory obsessive-compulsive disorder. *The American Journal of Psychiatry, 159*(2), 269–275.

Drenth, P. J., Thierry, H., Willems, P. J., & de Wolff, C. J. (1984). *Handbook of work and organizational psychology.* Chichester, UK: Wiley.

Druckman, D., & Bjork, R. A. (Eds.). (1994). *Learning, remembering, believing: Enhancing human performance* (Study conducted by the National Research Council). Washington, DC: National Academy Press.

Duben, A., & Behar, C. (1991). *Istanbul households: Marriage, family and fertility 1880–1940.* Cambridge, NY: Cambridge University Press.

Dubowitz, H., & Bennett, S. (2007). Physical abuse and neglect of children. *Lancet, 369*(9576), 1891–1899.

Duckworth, A. L., & Seligman, M. E. P. (2005). Self-discipline outdoes IQ in predicting academic performance of adolescents. *Psychological Science, 16*(12), 939–944. doi:10.1111/j.1467-9280.2005.01641.x

Duckworth, A. L., Quinn, P. D., Lynam, D. R., Loeber, R., & Stouthamer-Loeber, M. (2011). Role of test motivation in intelligence testing. *Proceedings of the National Academy of Sciences, 108*(19), 7716–7720. doi:10.1073/pnas.1018601108

Duker, P. C., & Seys, D. M. (1996). Long-term use of electrical aversion treatment with self-injurious behaviors. *Research in Developmental Disabilities, 17,* 293–301.

Dumont, F. (2010). *A history of personality psychology.* New York, NY: Cambridge University Press.

Duncan, R. M. (1995). Piaget and Vygotsky revisited: Dialogue or assimilation? *Developmental Review, 15,* 458–472.

Dundas, I., Wormnes, B. R., & Hauge, H. (2009). Making exams a manageable task. *Nordic Psychology, 61*(1), 26–41.

Dunn, J. C., Whelton, W. J., & Sharpe, D. (2006). Maladaptive perfectionism, hassles, coping, and psychological distress in university professors. *Journal of Counseling Psychology, 53*(4), 511–523.

Durrant, M. (Ed.). (1993). *Aristotle's De anima in focus.* London: Routledge.

Durso, F., Rea, C., & Dayton, T. (1994). Graph-theoretic confirmation of restructuring during insight. *Psychological Science, 5,* 94–98.

Dwairy, M. (2004). Parenting styles and mental health of Palestinian-Arab adolescents in Israel. *Transcultural Psychiatry, 41*(2), 233–252.

Dweck, C. S. (1986). Motivational processes affecting learning. *American Psychologist, 41*(10), 1040–1048.

Dweck, C. S. (1999). *Self-theories: Their role in motivation, personality and development.* Philadelphia: Psychology Press.

Dweck, C. S., & Elliott, E. (1983). Achievement motivation. In P. Mussen (Ed.), *Handbook of child psychology: Vol. 4. Socialization, personality, and social development* (pp. 643–691). New York: Wiley.

Dweck, C. S., & Leggett, E. L. (1988). A social-cognitive approach to motivation and personality. *Psychological Review, 95,* 256–273.

Dweck, C. S., & Molden, D. C. (2008). Self-theories: The construction of free will. In J. Baer, J. C. Kaufman, & R. F. Baumeister (Eds.), *Are we free? Psychology and free will* (pp. 44–64). New York: Oxford University Press.

Dykens, E. M., Hodapp, R. M., & Leckman, J. F. (1994). *Behavior and development in fragile X syndrome.* Thousand Oaks, CA: Sage.

Eagly, A. H., & Carli, L. L. (2007). *Through the labyrinth: The truth about how women become leaders* (pp. 119–136). Boston: Harvard Business School Press.

Eagly, A. H., & Chaiken, S. (1975). An attribution analysis of the effect of communicator characteristics on opinion change: The case of communicator attractiveness. *Journal of Personality and Social Psychology, 37,* 136–144.

Eagly, A. H., & Chaiken, S. (1993). *The psychology of attitudes.* Fort Worth, TX: Harcourt Brace.

Eagly, A. H., & Chaiken, S. (1998). Attitude structure and function. In D. T. Gilbert, S. T. Fiske, & G. Lindzey (Eds.), *The handbook of social psychology* (4th ed., pp. 269–322). New York: McGraw-Hill.

Eagly, A. H., & Crowley, M. (1986). Gender and helping behavior: A meta-analytic review of the social psychological literature. *Psychological Bulletin, 100,* 283–308.

Eagly, A. H., Ashmore, R. D., Makhijani, M. G., & Longo, L. C. (1991). What is beautiful is good, but ... : A meta-analytic review of the physical attractiveness stereotype. *Psychological Bulletin, 110,* 109–128.

Eagly, A. H., Wood, W., & Diekman, A. B. (2000). Social role theory of sex differences and similarities: A current appraisal. In T. Eckes & H. M. Trautner (Eds.), *The developmental social psychology of gender* (pp. 123–174). Mahwah, NJ: Erlbaum.

Eaker, E. D., & Castelli, W. P. (1988). Type A behavior and mortality from coronary disease in the Framingham Study. *New England Journal of Medicine, 319,* 1480–1481.

Eastern Virginia Medical School. (2009, May 5). Texting while driving can be deadly, study shows. *ScienceDaily.* Retrieved May 5, 2010, from http://www.sciencedaily.com/releases/2009/05/090504094434.htm

Eaton, W. W., Kessler, R. C., Wittchen, H. U., & Magee, W. J. (1994). Panic and panic disorder in the United States. *American Journal of Psychiatry, 151*(3), 413–420.

Ebbinghaus, H. (1885). *Memory: A contribution to experimental psychology.* New York: Dover Publications.

Ebbinghaus, H. (1913). *Memory: A contribution to experimental psychology.* New York: Teachers College Press. (Translated from the 1885 German original.)

Eddy, J., Fitzhugh, E., & Wang, M. (2000). Smoking acquisition: Peer influence and self-selection. *Psychological Reports, 86,* 1241–1246.

Edelmann, R. J., & Iwawaki, S. (1987). Self-reported expression of embarrassment in five European cultures. *Psychologia: An International Journal of Psychology, 30,* 205–216.

Eich, E., & Metcalfe, J. (1989). Mood dependent memory for internal vs. external events. *Journal of Experimental Psychology: Learning, Memory and Cognition, 15,* 443–455.

Eiden, R. D., McAuliffe, S., Kachadourian, L., Coles, C., Colder, C., & Schuetze, P. (2009). Effects of prenatal cocaine exposure on infant reactivity and regulation. *Neurotoxicology and Teratology, 31,* 60–68.

Eisenberger, N. I., Lieberman, M. D., & Williams, K. D. (2003). Does rejection hurt? An fMRI study of social exclusion. *Science, 302,* 290–292.

Ekman, P. (1973). Darwin and cross-cultural studies of facial expression. In P. Ekman (Ed.), *Darwin and facial expression: A century of research in review.* New York: Academic Press.

Ekman, P. (1980). Asymmetry in facial expression. *Science, 209,* 833–834.

Ekman, P., & Friesen, W. (1969). The repertoire of nonverbal behavior: Categories, origins, usage, and coding. *Semiotica, 1,* 49–98.

Ekman, P., & Friesen, W. V. (1971). Constants across cultures in the face and emotion. *Journal of Personality and Social Psychology, 17*(2), 124–129.

Ekman, P., & Friesen, W. V. (1978). *The facial action coding system.* Palo Alto, CA: Consulting Psychologists Press.

Ekman, P., Sorensen, E. R., & Friesen, W. V. (1969). Pan-cultural elements in facial displays of emotion. *Science, 164,* 86–88.

Elkind, D. (1985). Egocentrism redux. *Developmental Review, 5,* 218–226.

Elliott, E., & Dweck, C. (1988). Goals: An approach to motivation and achievement. *Journal of Personality and Social Psychology, 54,* 5–12.

Ellis, A. (1997). *The practice of rational emotive behavior therapy.* New York: Springer.

Ellis, A. (1998). *The Albert Ellis reader: A guide to well-being using rational emotive behavior therapy.* Secaucus, NJ: Carol Publishing Group.

Ellis, B. J., McFayden-Ketchum, S. A., Dodge, K. A., Pettit, G. S., & Bates, J. E. (1999). Quality of early family relationships and individual differences in the timing of pubertal maturation in girls: A longitudinal test on an evolutionary model. *Journal of Personality and Social Psychology, 77,* 387–401.

Ellis, H. D. (1983). The role of the right hemisphere in face perception. In A. W. Young (Ed.), *Functions of the right cerebral hemisphere* (pp. 33–64). London: Academic Press.

Ellis, L. K., Gay, P. E., & Paige, E. (2001). Daily pleasures and hassles across the lifespan. Poster presented at the annual meeting of the American Psychological Association, San Francisco, CA.

Else-Quest, N., Shibley Hyde, J., Linn, M. C. (2010). Cross-national patterns of gender differences in mathematics: A meta-analysis. *Psychological Bulletin, 136*(1), 103–127.

Endler, N. S. (1988). The origins of electroconvulsive therapy (ECT). *Convulsive Therapy, 4,* 5–23.

Engelhardt, C. R., & Bartholow, B. D. (2013). Aggression, Risk Factors of (pp. 14–17). In Matthew S. Eastin's (Ed.), *Encyclopedia of media violence.* Sage Publications.

Engle, R. W., & Kane, M. J. (2004). Executive attention, working memory capacity, and a two-factor theory of cognitive control. *The Psychology of Learning and Motivation, 44,* 145–199.

Enns, J. T., & Coren, S. (1995). The box alignment illusion: An orientation illusion induced by pictorial depth. *Perception and Psychophysics, 57,* 1163–1174.

Ephraim, P. L., Wegener, S. T., MacKenzie, E. J., Dillingham, T. R., & Pezzin, L. E. (2005). Phantom pain, residual limb pain and back pain in persons with limb loss: Results of a national survey. *Archives of Physical Medicine and Rehabilitation, 86,* 1910–1919.

Epping-Jordan, M., Waltkins, S. S., Koob, G. F., & Markou, A. (1998). Dramatic decreases in brain reward function during nicotine withdrawal. *Nature, 393*, 76–79.

Erickson, K. I., Prakash, R. S., Voss, M. W., Chaddock, L., Hu, L., Morris, K. S., et al. (2009). Aerobic fitness is associated with hippocampal volume in elderly humans. *Hippocampus, 19*(10), 1030–1039.

Erikson, E. H. (1950). *Childhood and society.* New York: Norton.

Erikson, E. H. (1959). Growth and crises of the healthy personality. *Psychological Issues, 1,* 50–100.

Erikson, E. H. (1980). Elements of a psychoanalytic theory of psychosocial development. In S. Greenspan & G. Pollock (Eds.), *The course of life,* (Vol. 1, pp. 11–61). Washington, DC: U.S. Department of Health and Human Services.

Erikson, E. H. (1982). *The life cycle completed.* New York: Norton.

Erikson, E. H., & Erikson, J. M. (1997). *The life cycle completed.* New York: Norton.

Eriksson, P., Ankarberg, E., Viberg, H., & Fredriksson, A. (2001). The developing cholinergic system as target for environmental toxicants, nicotine and polychlorinated biphenyls (PCBs): Implications for neurotoxicological processes in mice. *Neurotoxicity Research, 3*(1), 37–51.

Escandon, A., Al-Hammadi, N., & Galvin, J. E. (2010). Effect of cognitive fluctuation on neuropsychological performance in aging and dementia. *Neurology, 74,* 210–217.

Eschenbeck, H., Kohlmann, C. W., & Lohaus, A. (2008). Gender differences in coping strategies in children and adolescents. *Journal of Individual Differences, 28*(1), 18–26.

Eskenazi, B., Bradman, A., & Castorina, R. (1999). Exposures of children to organophosphate pesticides and their potential adverse health effects. *Environmental Health Perspectives, 107*(Suppl. 3), 409–419.

Ethen, M. K., Ramadhani, T. A., Scheuerle, A. E., Canfield, M. A., Wyszynski, D. F., Druschel, C. M., et al. (2008). Alcohol consumption by women before and during pregnancy. *Maternal and Child Health Journal, 13*(2), 274–285. doi:10.1007/s10995-008-0328-2

Evans, I. M., & Meyer, L. H. (1985). *An educative approach to behavior problems: A practical decision model for interventions with severely handicapped learners.* Baltimore: Paul H. Brookes.

Everson, S. (1995). Psychology. In J. Barnes (Ed.), *The Cambridge companion to Aristotle* (pp. 168–194). Cambridge, UK: Cambridge University Press.

Exner, J. E. (1980). But it's only an inkblot. *Journal of Personality Assessment, 44,* 562–577.

Experts urge caution in using deep brain stimulation. (2010). *Harvard Mental Health Letter, 26*(8), 6–7.

Eysenck, H. J. (1994a). *Test your IQ.* Toronto: Penguin Books.

Eysenck, H. J. (1994b). Synergistic interaction between psychosocial and physical factors in the causation of lung cancer. In C. Lewis, C. O'Sullivan, & J. Barraclough (Eds.), *The psychoimmunology of human cancer* (pp. 163–178). London: Oxford University Press.

Eysenck, H. J., & Eysenck, S. B. G. (1993). *Eysenck personality questionnaire* (Rev. ed.). London: Hodder & Stoughton Educational.

Fagot, B. I., & Hagan, R. (1991). Observations of parent reactions to sex-stereotyped behaviours: Age and sex effects. *Child Development, 62,* 617–628.

Fanselow, M. S., & Gale, G. D. (2003). The amygdala, fear, and memory. *Annals of the New York Academy of Sciences, 985,* 125–134.

Fantz, R. L. (1961). The origin of form perception. *Scientific American, 204,* 66–72.

Fantz, R. L. (1964). Visual experience in infants: Decreased attention to familiar patterns relative to novel ones. *Science, 146,* 668–670.

Faraone, S. V., Biederman, J., & Wozniak, J. (2012). Examining the comorbidity between attention deficit hyperactivity disorder and bipolar I disorder: A metaanalysis of family genetic studies. *The American Journal of Psychiatry, 169*(12), 1256–1266. doi:10.1176/appi.ajp.2012.12010087

Farthing, W. (1992). *The psychology of consciousness.* Upper Saddle River, NJ: Prentice-Hall.

Faucett, J., Gordon, N., & Levine, J. (1994). Differences in postoperative pain severity among four ethnic groups. *Journal of Pain Symptom Management, 9,* 383–389.

Fawzy, F. I., Fawzy, N. W., Hyun, C. S., Elashoff, R., Guthrie, D., Fahey, J. L., et al. (1993). Malignant melanoma effects of an early structured psychiatric intervention, coping, and affective state on recurrence and survival 6 years later. *Archives of General Psychiatry, 50*(9), 681–689.

Fazel-Rezai, R., & Peters, J. F. (2005). P300 wave feature extraction: Preliminary results. In *Proceedings of the 18th Annual Canadian Conference on Electrical and Computer Engineering (CCECE '05)* (pp. 390–393). Saskatoon, Saskatchewan, Canada.

Fazio, R. H., & Olson, M. A. (2003). Attitudes: Foundations, functions, and consequences. In M. A. Hogg & J. Cooper (Eds.), *The Handbook of Social Psychology* (pp. 139–160). London: Sage.

Fechner, G. T. (1860). *Elemente der Psykophysik.* Leipzig: Breitkopf und Härtel.

Fedoroff, I. C., & McFarlane, T. (1998). Cultural aspects of eating disorders. In S. S. Kazarian & D. R. Evans (Eds.), *Cultural clinical psychology: Theory, research and practice* (pp. 152–176). New York: Oxford University Press.

Feingold, A. (1992). Good-looking people are not what we think. *Psychological Bulletin, 111,* 304–341.

Feldman, D. H. (2003). Cognitive development in childhood. In I. B. Weiner, R. M. Lerner, M. A. Easterbrooks, & J. Mistry (Eds.), *Handbook of psychology: Developmental psychology: Vol. 6* (pp. 195–201). New York: Wiley.

Ferguson, C. J. (2010). Video games and youth violence: A prospective analysis in adolescents. *Journal of Youth and Adolescence.* doi:10.1007/s10964-010-9610-x

Fernald, A. (1984). The perceptual and affective salience of mothers' speech to infants. In L. Feagans, C. Garvey, & R. Golinkoff (Eds.), *The origins and growth of communication.* Norwood, NJ: Ablex.

Fernald, A. (1992). Human maternal vocalizations to infants as biologically relevant signals: An evolutionary perspective. In J. H. Barkow, L. Cosmides, & J. Tooby (Eds.), *The adapted mind: Evolutionary psychology and the generation of culture.* New York: Oxford University Press.

Feroah, T. R., Sleeper, T., Brozoski, D., Forder, J., Rice, T. B., & Forster, H. V. (2004, April 17–21). *Circadian slow wave sleep and movement behavior are under genetic control in inbred strains of rat.* Paper presented at the American Physiological Society Annual Conference, Washington, DC.

Festinger, L. (1954). A theory of social comparison processes. *Human Relations, 7,* 117–140.

Festinger, L. (1957). *A theory of cognitive dissonance.* Stanford, CA: Stanford University Press.

Festinger, L., & Carlsmith, J. (1959). $1/$20 experiment: Cognitive consequences of forced compliance. *Journal of Abnormal and Social Psychology, 58*(2), 203–210.

Fiatarone, M. A. (1996). Physical activity and functional independence in aging. *Research Quarterly for Exercise and Sport, 67,* 70–75.

Fincham, F. D., Harold, G. T., & Gano-Phillips, S. (2000). The longitudinal association between attributions and marital satisfaction: Direction of effects and role of efficacy expectations. *Journal of Family Psychology, 14,* 267–285.

Finger, S. (1994). *Origins of neuroscience: A history of explorations into brain function.* New York: Oxford University Press.

Fink, M. (1984). Meduna and the origins of convulsive therapy. *American Journal of Psychiatry, 141,* 1034–1041.

Finke, C., Esfahani, N. E., & Ploner, C. J. (2012). Preservation of musical memory in an amnesic professional cellist. *Current Biology, 22*(15), R59.

Finke, R. (1995). Creative realism. In S. Smith, T. Ward, & R. Finke (Eds.), *The creative cognition approach* (pp. 301–326). Cambridge, MA: Cambridge University Press.

Finkel, D., & McGue, M. (1997). Sex differences and nonadditivity in heritability of the Multidimensional Personality Questionnaire scales. *Journal of Personality and Social Psychology, 72,* 929–938.

Fischl, B., Liu, A., & Dale, A. M. (2001). Automated manifold surgery: Constructing geometrically accurate and topologically correct models of the human cerebral cortex. *IEEE Transactions on Medical Imaging, 20,* 70–80.

Fisher, M., Holland, C., Merzenich, M. M., & Vinogradov, S. (2009). Using neuroplasticity-based auditory training to improve verbal memory in schizophrenia. *The American Journal of Psychiatry, 166*(7), 805–811.

Fisher, R., Salanova, V., Witt, T., Worth, R., Henry, T., Gross, R., et al. (2010). Electrical stimulation of the anterior nucleus of thalamus for treatment of refractory epilepsy. *Epilepsia, 17,* 17.

Fiske, S. T. (1998). Stereotyping, prejudice, and discrimination. In D. T. Gilbert & S. T. Fiske (Eds.), *The handbook of social psychology* (4th ed., Vol. 2, pp. 357–411). New York: McGraw-Hill.

Fitzpatrick, M. (2004). *MMR and autism* (pp. 133–149). New York: Routledge.

Flaherty, J. A., & Adams, S. A. (1998). Therapist-patient race and sex matching: Predictors of treatment duration. *Psychiatric Times, 15*(1).

Flaskerud, J. H. (1991). Effects of an Asian client-therapist language, ethnicity and gender match on utilization and outcome of therapy. *Community Mental Health Journal, 27*, 31–42.

Flavell, J. H. (1999). Cognitive development: Children's knowledge about the mind. *Annual Review of Psychology, 50*, 21–45.

Flegal, K. M., Carroll, M. D. & Ogden, C. L. (2012). Prevalence of obesity and trends in the distribution of body mass index among US adults, 1999–2010. *Journal of the American Medical Association, 307*(5): 491–497.

Fleming, M. F., & Barry, K. L. (1992). Clinical overview of alcohol and drug disorders. In M. F. Fleming & K. L. Barry (Eds.), *Addictive disorders*. St. Louis: Mosby Year Book.

Flemons, W. W. (2002). Obstructive sleep apnea. *New England Journal of Medicine, 347*, 498–504.

Flynn, J. R. (2009). *What is intelligence? Beyond the Flynn effect*. New York: Cambridge University Press.

Folkard, S., Arendt, J., & Clark, M. (1993). Can melatonin improve shift workers' tolerance of the night shift? Some preliminary findings. *Chronobiology International: The Journal of Biological and Medical Rhythm Research, 10*(5), 315–320.

Folkman, S. (1997). Positive psychological states and coping with severe stress. *Social Science and Medicine, 45*, 1207–1221.

Folkman, S., & Lazarus, R. S. (1980). An analysis of coping in a middle-aged community sample. *Journal of Health and Social Behavior, 21*(3), 219–239.

Forbes, G., Zhang, X., Doroszewicz, K., & Haas, K. (2009). Relationships between individualism-collectivism, gender, and direct or indirect aggression: A study in China, Poland, and the U.S. *Aggressive Behavior, 35*(1), 24–30.

Fortuna, L. R., Alegria, M., & Gao, S. (2010). Retention in depression treatment among ethnic and racial minority groups in the United States. *Depression and Anxiety, 27*(5), 485–494. doi:10.1002/da.20685

Foulkes, D. (1982). *Children's dreams*. New York: Wiley.

Frank, E., Kupfer, D. J., Buysse, D. J., Swartz, H. A., Pilkonis, P. A., Houck, P. R., et al. (2007). Randomized trial of weekly, twice-monthly, and monthly interpersonal psychotherapy as maintenance treatment for women with recurrent depression. *American Journal of Psychiatry, 164*(5), 761–767.

Frankel, B. R., & Piercy, F. P. (1990). The relationship among selected supervisor, therapist, and client behaviors. *Journal of Marital and Family Therapy, 16*, 407–421.

Franklin, D. (1990). Hooked: Why isn't everyone an addict? *In Health, 4*(6), 38–52.

Fredrickson, B. L., Maynard, K. E., Helms, M. J., Haney, T. L., Siegler, I. C., & Barefoot, J. C. (2000). Hostility predicts magnitude and duration of blood pressure response to anger. *Journal of Behavioral Medicine, 23*, 229–243.

Freedman, J., & Fraser, S. (1966). Compliance without pressure: The foot-in-the-door technique. *Journal of Personality and Social Psychology, 4*, 195–202.

Freeman, A., Simon, K. M., Beutler, L. E., & Arkowitz, H. (Eds.). (1989). *Comprehensive handbook of cognitive therapy*. New York: Plenum Press.

Freeman, J. (2001). *Gifted children grown up*. London: David Fulton.

Freeman, W., & Watts, J. W. (1937). Prefrontal lobotomy in the treatment of mental disorders. *Southern Medical Journal, 30*, 23–31.

Frensch, P. A., & Runger, D. (2003). Implicit learning. *Current Directions in Psychological Science, 12*, 13–18.

Freud, A. (1946). *The ego and the mechanisms of defense* (American ed.). New York: I.U.P.

Freud, S. (1900). The interpretation of dreams. *S. E., 4–5*. (cf. J. Crick, Trans., 1999). London: Oxford University Press.

Freud, S. (1901). The psychopathology of everyday life. *S. E., 6*, 1–290.

Freud, S. (1904). *Psychopathology of everyday life*. New York: Macmillan; London: Fisher Unwin.

Freud, S. (1923). The ego and the id. *S. E., 19*, 12–66.

Freud, S. (1930). *Civilization and its discontents*. New York: Jonathon Cape and Co.

Freud, S. (1933). *New introductory lectures on psycho-analysis*. London: Hogarth Press.

Freud, S. (1940). Splitting of the ego in the process of defence. *International Journal of Psychoanalysis, 22*, 65. (1938, *S. E., 23*, 275–278).

Freud, S. (1977). *Inhibitions, symptoms and anxiety. Standard edition of the complete works of Sigmund Freud*. New York: W. W. Norton.

Freud, S., Strachey, J., & Riviere, J. (1990). *The ego and the id (The standard edition of the complete psychological works of Sigmund Freud)*. New York: W. W. Norton and Company.

Fridlund, A. J., Beck, H. P., Goldie, W. D., & Irons, G. (2012). Little Albert: A neurologically impaired child. *History of Psychology, 15*(4), 302–327.

Friederich, H.-C., Wu, M., Simon, J. J., & Herzog, W. (2013). Neurocircuit function in eating disorders. *International Journal of Eating Disorders, 46*(5), 425–432. doi:10.1002/eat.22099

Friedman, J. M. (2000). Obesity in the new millennium. *Nature, 404*, 632–634.

Friedman, J. M. (2003). A war on obesity, not the obese. *Science, 299*(5608), 856–858.

Friedman, J. M., & Halaas, J. L. (1998). Leptin and the regulation of body weight in mammals. *Nature, 395*, 763.

Friedman, M., & Kasanin, J. D. (1943). Hypertension in only one of identical twins. *Archives of Internal Medicine, 72*, 767–774.

Friedman, M., & Rosenman, R. H. (1959). Association of specific behavior pattern with blood and cardiovascular findings. *Journal of the American Medical Association, 169*, 1286–1296.

Frontera, W. R., Hughes, V. A., Lutz, K. J., & Evans, W. J. (1991). A cross-sectional study of muscle strength and mass in 45- to 78-year-old men and women. *Journal of Applied Physiology, 71*, 644–650.

Frydenberg, E., Lewis, R., Ardila, R., Cairns, E., & Kennedy, G. (2001). Adolescent concern with social issues: An exploratory comparison between Australian, Colombian and North Irish students. *Journal of Peace Psychology, 7*, 59–76.

Fulcher, J. S. (1942). "Voluntary" facial expression in blind and seeing children. *Archives of Psychology, 38*, 1–49.

Furumoto, L. (1979). Mary Whiton Calkins (1863–1930): Fourteenth president of the American psychological association. *Journal of the History of Behavioral Sciences, 15*, 346–356.

Furumoto, L. (1991). Portraits of pioneers in psychology. In G. A. Kimble, M. Wertheimer, & C. White (Eds.), *From "Paired associates" to a psychology of self: The intellectual odyssey of Mary Whiton Calkins* (pp. 57–72). Washington, DC: American Psychological Association.

Gable, R. S. (2004). Acute toxic effects of club drugs. *Journal of Psychoactive Drugs, 36*(1), 303–313.

Gado, M. (2004). A cry in the night: The Kitty Genovese murder. *Court TV's Crime Library: Criminal Minds and Methods*. Retrieved August 2, 2004, from www.crimelibrary.com/serial_killers/predators/kitty_genovese/1.html?sect=2

Galanter, M. (1983). Unification church ("Moonie") dropouts: Psychological readjustment after leaving a charismatic religious group. *American Journal of Psychiatry, 140*(8), 984–989.

Galanti, G. A. (1997). *Caring for patients from different cultures* (2nd ed.). Philadelphia: University of Pennsylvania Press.

Galea, S., Resnick, H., Kilpatrick, D., Bucuvalas, M., Gold, J., & Vlahov, D. (2002). Psychological sequelae of the September 11 terrorist attacks in New York City. *New England Journal of Medicine, 346*(13), 982–987.

Gallagher, R. P. (2009). *National Survey of Counseling Center Directors, 2009*. The American College Counseling Association (ACCA). Retrieved from http://www.counseling.org/docs/public-policy-resources-reports/2009-national-survey.pdf?sfvrsn=2

Gamwell, L., & Tomes, N. (1995). *Madness in America: Cultural and medical perspectives of mental illness before 1914*. Ithaca, NY: Cornell University Press.

Ganchrow, J. R., Steiner, J. E., & Munif, D. (1983). Neonatal facial expressions in response to different qualities and intensities of gustatory stimuli. *Infant Behavior Development, 6*, 473–478.

Ganis, G., Thompson, W. L., & Kosslyn, S. M. (2004). Brain areas underlying visual mental imagery and visual perception: An fMRI study. Brain research. *Cognitive Brain Research, 20*(2), 226–241.

Garb, H. N., Florio, C. M., & Grove, W. M. (1998). The validity of the Rorschach and the Minnesota Multiphasic Personality Inventory: Results from metaanalyses. *Psychological Science, 9*, 402–404.

Garcia, J., & Koelling, R. A. (1966). Relation of cue to consequence in avoidance learning. *Psychonomic Science, 4*, 123.

Garcia, J., Brett, L. P., & Rusiniak, K. W. (1989). Limits of Darwinian conditioning. In S. B. Klein & R. R. Mowrer (Eds.), *Contemporary learning theories: Instrumental conditioning theory and the impact of biological constraints on learning* (pp. 237–275). Hillsdale, NJ: Erlbaum.

Garcia-Campayo, J., Fayed, N., Serrano-Blanco, A., & Roca, M. (2009). Brain dysfunction behind functional symptoms: Neuroimaging and somatoform, conversive, and dissociative disorders. *Current Opinion in Psychiatry, 22*(2), 224–231.

Gardner, E. P., & Johnson, K. O. (2013). Sensory coding. In E. R. Kandel, J. H. Schwartz, T. M. Jessell, S. A. Siegelbaum, & A. J. Hudspeth (Eds.), *Principles of neural science* (5th ed., pp. 449–474). USA: McGraw-Hill.

Gardner, H. (1993a). *Creating minds: An anatomy of creativity seen through the lives of Freud, Einstein, Picasso, Stravinsky, Eliot, Graham, and Ghandi.* New York: Basic Books.

Gardner, H. (1993b). *Multiple intelligences: The theory in practice.* New York: Basic Books.

Gardner, H. (1998). Are there additional intelligences? The case for naturalist, spiritual, and existential intelligences. In J. Kane (Ed.), *Education, information, and transformation* (pp. 111–131). Upper Saddle River, NJ: Merrill-Prentice Hall.

Gardner, H. (1999a). *Intelligence reframed: Multiple intelligences for the 21st century.* New York: Basic Books.

Gardner, H. (1999b, February). Who owns intelligence? *Atlantic Monthly,* 67–76.

Gardner, H., Kornhaber, M. L., & Wake, W. K. (1996). *Intelligence: Multiple perspectives.* Orlando, FL: Harcourt Brace.

Gardner, R. J. M., & Sutherland, G. R. (1996). *Chromosome abnormalities and genetic counseling* (Oxford Monographics on Medical Genetics No. 29). New York: Oxford University Press.

Garland, E. J., & Smith, D. H. (1991). Simultaneous prepubertal onset of panic disorder, night terrors, and somnambulism. *Journal of American Academic Child and Adolescent Psychiatry, 30*(4), 553–555.

Garnier-Dykstra, L. M., Caldeira, K. M., Vincent, K. B., O'Grady, K. E., & Arria, A. M. (2012). Nonmedical use of prescription stimulants during college: Four-year trends in exposure opportunity, use, motives, and sources. *Journal of American College Health, 60*(3), 226–234.

Gazzaniga, M. S. (2006). *The ethical brain: The science of our moral dilemmas.* New York: HarperCollins.

Gazzaniga, M. S. (2009). *Human: The science behind what makes us unique.* New York: Harper Perennial.

Geddes, D. P. (Ed.). (1954). *An analysis of the Kinsey reports.* New York: New American Library.

Geen, R. G., & Thomas, S. L. (1986). The immediate effects of media violence on behavior. *Journal of Social Issues, 42*, 7–27.

Gelder, M. (1976). Flooding. In T. Thompson & W. Dockens (Eds.), *Applications of behavior modification* (pp. 250–298). New York: Academic Press.

Gelman, S. A., & Markman, E. M. (1986). Categories and induction in young children. *Cognition, 23*, 183–209.

Gershoff, E. T. (2002). Corporal punishment by parents and associated child behaviors and experiences: A meta-analytic and theoretical review. *Psychological Bulletin, 128*(4), 539–579. doi: 10.1037//0033-2909.128.4.539

Geschwind, D. H., & Iacoboni, M. (2007). Structural and functional asymmetries of the frontal lobes. In B. L. Miller & J. K. Cummings (Eds.), *The human frontal lobes* (2nd ed., pp. 68–91). New York: Guilford Press.

Ghaziri, J., Tucholka, A., Larue, V., Blanchette-Sylvestre, M., Reyburn, G., Gilbert, G., et al. (2013). Neurofeedback training induces changes in white and gray matter. *Clinical EEG and Neuroscience.* doi:10.1177/1550059413476031

Giancola, F. (2006). The generation gap: More myth than reality. *Human Resource Planning, 29*(4), 32–37.

Gibbons, J. L., Stiles, D. A., & Shkodriani, G. M. (1991). Adolescents' attitudes toward family and gender roles: An international comparison. *Sex Roles, 25*, 625–643.

Gibbons, R. D., Brown, C. H., Hur, K., Davis, J., & Mann, J. J. (2012). Suicidal thoughts and behavior with antidepressant treatment: Reanalysis of the randomized placebo-controlled studies of fluoxetine and venlafaxine. *Archives of General Psychiatry, 69*(6), 580–587.

Gilberg, C., & Coleman, M. (2000). *The biology of the autistic syndromes* (3rd ed.). London: MacKeith Press.

Gilbert, S. J. (1981). Another look at the Milgram obedience studies: The role of the graduated series of shocks. *Personality and Social Psychology Bulletin, 7*(4), 690–695.

Gill, S. T. (1991). Carrying the war into the never-never land of psi. *Skeptical Inquirer, 15*(1), 269–273.

Gillen-O'Neel, C., Huynh, V. W., & Fuligni, A. J. (2012). To study or to sleep? The academic costs of extra studying at the expense of sleep. *Child Development, 84*(1), 133–142.

Gillespie, M. A., Kim, B. H., Manheim, L. J., Yoo, T., Oswald, F. L., & Schmitt, N. (2002, June). The development and validation of biographical data and situational judgment tests in the prediction of college student success. Presented in A. M. Ryan (Chair), *Beyond g: Expanding thinking on predictors of college success.* Symposium conducted at the 14th Annual Convention of the American Psychological Society, New Orleans, LA.

Gillham, B., Tanner, G., Cheyne, B., Freeman, I., Rooney, M., & Lambie, A. (1998). Unemployment rates, single parent density, and indices of child poverty: Their relationship to different categories of child abuse and neglect. *Child Abuse and Neglect, 22*(2), 79–90.

Gilligan, C. (1982). *In a different voice: Psychological theory and women's development.* Cambridge, MA: Harvard University Press.

Gillund, G., & Shiffrin, R. M. (1984). A retrieval model for both recognition and recall. *Psychological Review, 91*, 1–67.

Ginzburg, K., Solomon, Z., Koifman, B., Keren, G., Roth, A., Kriwisky, M., et al. (2003). Trajectories of post-traumatic stress disorder following myocardial infarction: A prospective study. *Journal of Clinical Psychiatry, 64*(10), 1217–1223.

Gittelman-Klein, R. (1978). Validity in projective tests for psychodiagnosis in children. In R. L. Spitzer & D. F. Klein (Eds.), *Critical issues in psychiatric diagnosis* (pp. 141–166). New York: Raven Press.

Glenn, A. L., Raine, A., Mednick, S. A., & Venables, P. (2007). Early temperamental and psychophysiological precursors of adult psychopathic personality. *Journal of Abnormal Psychology, 116*(3), 508–518.

Glucksman, M. L. (2006). Psychoanalytic and psychodynamic education in the 21st century. *Journal of American Academy of Psychoanalysis, 34*, 215–222.

Glynn, S. M. (1990). Token economy approaches for psychiatric patients: Progress and pitfalls over 25 years. *Behavior Modification, 14*, 383–407.

Godden, D. R., & Baddeley, A. D. (1975). Context-dependent memory in two natural environments: On land and underwater. *British Journal of Psychology, 66*, 325–331.

Goel, V., & Grafman, J. (1995). Are the frontal lobes implicated in "planning" functions? Interpreting data from the Tower of Hanoi. *Neuropsychologia, 33*(5), 623–642.

Goin, M. K. (2005). Practical psychotherapy: A current perspective on the psychotherapies. *Psychiatric Services, 56*(3), 255–257.

Goldsmith, H. H., & Campos, J. (1982). Toward a theory of infant temperament. In R. Emde & R. Harmon (Eds.), *The development of attachment and affiliative systems: Psychobiological aspects* (pp. 161–193). New York: Plenum Press.

Goleman, D. (1995). *Emotional intelligence: Why it can matter more than IQ.* New York: Bantam Books.

Golkaramnay, V., Bauer, S., Haug, S., Wolf, M., & Kordy, H. (2007). The exploration of the effectiveness of group therapy through an Internet chat as aftercare: A controlled naturalistic study. *Pychotherapy and Psychosomatics, 76*, 219–225.

Goncalves, R., Pedrozo, A. L., Coutinho, E. S., Figueira, I., & Ventura, P. (2012). Efficacy of virtual reality exposure therapy in the treatment of

PTSD: A systematic review. *PLoS One, 7*(12), e48469. doi:10.1371/journal.pone.0048469

Gong-Guy, E., & Hammen, C. (1980). Causal perceptions of stressful events in depressed and nondepressed outpatients. *Journal of Abnormal Psychology, 89,* 662–669.

Gonsalves, B., Reber, P. J., Gitelman, D. R., Parrish, T. B., Mesulam, M. M., & Paller, K. A. (2004). Neural evidence that vivid imagining can lead to false remembering. *Psychological Science, 15,* 655–660.

Gonzaga, G. C., Turner, R. A., Keltner, D., Campos, B. C., & Altemus, M. (2006). Romantic love and sexual desire in close relationships. *Emotion 6,* 163–179.

Gonzales, P. M., Blanton, H., & Williams, K. J. (2002). The effects of stereotype threat and double-minority status on the test performance of Latino women. *Personality and Social Psychology Bulletin, 28*(5), 659–670.

Goodglass, H., Kaplan, E., & Barresi, B. (2001). *The assessment of aphasia and related disorders* (3rd ed.). Baltimore: Lippincott, Williams & Wilkins.

Goodman, E. S. (1980). Margaret Floy Washburn (1871–1939) first woman Ph.D. in psychology. *Psychology of Women Quarterly, 5,* 69–80.

Gotlib, I. H., Sivers, H., Canli, T., Kasch, K. L., & Gabrieli, J. D. E. (2001, November). Neural activation in depression in response to emotional stimuli. In I. H. Gotlib (Chair) (Ed.), *New directions in the neurobiology of affective disorders.* Symposium conducted at the annual meeting of the Society for Research in Psychopathology, Madison, WI.

Gottesman, I. I. (1991). *Schizophrenia genesis: The origins of madness.* New York: W. H. Freeman.

Gottesman, I. I., & Shields, J. (1976). A critical review of recent adoption, twin and family studies of schizophrenia: Behavioural genetics perspectives. *Schizophrenia Bulletin, 2,* 360–401.

Gottesman, I. I., & Shields, J. (1982). *Schizophrenia: The epigenetic puzzle.* New York: Cambridge University Press.

Gottesman, I. I., McGuffin, P., & Farmer, A. E. (1987). Clinical genetics as clues to the "Real" genetics of schizophrenia (A decade of modest gains while playing for time). *Schizophrenia Bulletin, 13,* 23–47.

Gottman, J. M., & Krokoff, L. J. (1989). Marital interaction and satisfaction: A longitudinal view. *Journal of Consulting and Clinical Psychology, 57,* 47–52.

Gough, H. G. (1995). *California Psychological Inventory* (3rd ed.). Palo Alto, CA: Consulting Psychologist-Press.

Gould, J. L., & Gould, C. G. (1994). *The animal mind.* New York: Scientific American Library.

Gould, S. J. (1996). *The mismeasure of man.* New York: W. W. Norton.

Goyal, M., Singh, S., Sibinga, E. M. S., Gould, N. F., Rowland-Seymour, A., Sharma, R., et al. (2014). Meditation programs for psychological stress and well-being: A systematic review and meta-analysis. *Journal of the American Medical Association: Internal Medicine.* doi:10.1001/jamainternmed.2013.13018

Graber, J. A., Brooks-Gunn, J., & Warren, M. P. (1995). The antecedents of menarcheal age: Heredity, family environment, and stressful life events. *Child Development, 66,* 346–359.

Graf, W. D., Nagel, S. K., Epstein, L. G., Miller, G., Nass, R., & Larriviere, D. (2013). Pediatric neuroenhancement: Ethical, legal, social, and neurodevelopmental implications. *Neurology, 80*(13), 1251–1260. doi:10.1212/WNL.0b013e318289703b

Grandjean, P., Weihe, P., White, R. F., Debes, F., Araki, S., Yokoyama, K., et al. (1997). Cognitive deficit in 7-year-old children with prenatal exposure to methylmercury. *Neurotoxicology and Teratology, 19*(6), 417–428.

Graven, S. N., & Browne, J. V. (2008). Sleep and brain development: The critical role of sleep in fetal and early neonatal brain development. *Newborn & Infant Nursing Review, 8,* 173–179.

Greeley, A. (1987). Mysticism goes mainstream. *American Health, 1,* 47–49.

Gregory, R. L. (1990). *Eye and brain, the psychology of seeing.* Princeton, NJ: Princeton University Press.

Gresham, L. G., & Shimp, T. A. (1985). Attitude toward the advertisement and brand attitudes: A classical conditioning prospective. *Journal of Advertising, 14*(1), 10–17, 49.

Grocer, S., & Kohout, J. (1997). *The 1995 APA survey of 1992 baccalaureate recipients.* Washington, DC: American Psychological Association.

Gross, C. G. (1999). A hole in the head. *The Neuroscientist, 5,* 263–269.

Grünbaum, A. (1984). *The foundations of psychoanalysis: A philosophical critique.* Berkeley: University of California Press.

Guilford, J. P. (1967). *The nature of human intelligence.* New York: McGraw-Hill.

Gummerman, K., Gray, C. R., & Wilson, J. M. (1972). An attempt to assess eidetic imagery objectively. *Bulletin of the Psychonomic Society, 28,* 115–118.

Gunderson, E. A., Gripshover, S. J., Romero, C., Dweck, C. S., Goldin-Meadow, S., & Levine, S. C. (2013). Parent praise to 1- to 3-year-olds predicts children's motivational frameworks 5 years later. *Child Development,* ePub ahead of print. doi:10.1111/cdev.12064

Guthrie, R. V. (2004). *Even the rat was white: A historical view of psychology.* Boston: Allyn & Bacon.

Haber, R. N. (1979). Twenty years of haunting eidetic imagery: Where's the ghost? *The Behavioral and Brain Sciences, 2,* 583–619.

Halbesleben, J. R. B., & Bowler, W. M. (2007). Emotional exhaustion and job performance: The mediating role of motivation. *Journal of Applied Psychology, 91,* 93–106.

Hall, A. P., & Henry, J. A. (2006). Acute toxic effects of 'Ecstasy' (MDMA) and related compounds: Overview of pathophysiology and clinical management. *British Journal of Anaesthesia, 96*(6), 678–685.

Hall, C. (1966). *Studies of dreams collected in the laboratory and at home.* Institute of Dream Research Monograph Series (No. 1). Santa Cruz, CA: Privately printed.

Hall, W., & Degenhardt, L. (2009). Adverse health effects of non-medical cannabis use. *Lancet, 374,* 1383–1391.

Hamilton, D. L., & Gifford, R. K. (1976). Illusory correlation in interpersonal perception: A cognitive basis of stereotypic judgments. *Journal of Experimental Social Psychology, 12,* 392–407.

Hampton, J. A. (1998). Similarity-based categorization and fuzziness of natural categories. *Cognition, 65,* 137–165.

Handel, S. (1989). *Listening: An introduction to the perception of auditory events.* Cambridge, MA: MIT Press.

Hargittai, E. (2007). Whose space? Differences among users and non-users of social network sites. *Journal of Computer-Mediated Communication, 13*(1), article 14. Retrieved from http://jcmc.indiana.edu/vol13/issue1/hargittai.html

Harlow, H. F. (1958). The nature of love. *American Psychologist, 13,* 573–685.

Harman, G. (1999). Moral philosophy meets social psychology: Virtue ethics and the fundamental attribution error. *Proceedings of the Aristotelian Society, 1998–99, 99,* 315–331.

Harris, B. (2011). Letting go of Little Albert: Disciplinary memory, history, and the uses of myth. *Journal of the History of the Behavioral Sciences, 47*(1), 1–17. doi:10.1002/jhbs.20470

Harris, J. L., & Qualls, C. D. (2000). The association of elaborative or maintenance rehearsal with age, reading comprehension, and verbal working memory performance. *Aphasiology, 14*(5–6), 515–526.

Harrison, P. J. (1999). The neuropathology of schizophrenia: A critical review of the data and their interpretation. *Brain, 122,* 593–624.

Harrison, T. L., Shipstead, Z., Hicks, K. L., Hambrick, D. Z., Redick, T. S., & Engle, R. W. (2013). Working memory training may increase working memory capacity but not fluid intelligence. *Psychological Science.* doi:10.1177/0956797613492984

Hart, P. (1998). Preventing group-think revisited: Evaluating and reforming groups in government. *Organizational Behavior and Human Decision Processes, 73*(2–3), 306–326.

Hartfield, E. (1987). Passionate and companionate love. In R. J. Sternberg & M. L. Barnes (Eds.), *The psychology of love* (pp. 191–217). New Haven, CT: Yale University Press.

Harvard Mental Health Letter (2010). Experts urge caution in using deep brain stimulation. *Harvard Mental Health Letter, 26*(8), 6–7.

Harvey, S., & Keashly, L. (2003). Predicting the risk for aggression in the workplace: Risk factors, self-esteem and time at work. *Social Behaviour and Personality: An International Journal, 31*(8), 807–814.

Hassan, S., Karpova, Y., Baiz, D., Yancey, D., Pullikuth, A., Flores, A., et al. (2013). Behavioral stress accelerates prostate cancer development in mice. *Journal of Clinical Investigation, 123*(2), 874–886. doi:10.1172/JCI63324

Hauck, S. J., & Bartke, A. (2001). Free radical defenses in the liver and kidney of human growth hormone transgenic mice. *Journal of Gerontology and Biological Science, 56,* 153–162.

Havighurst, R. J., Neugarten, B. L., & Tobin, S. N. S. (1968). Disengagement and patterns of aging. In B. L. Neugarten (Ed.), *Middle age and aging: A reader in social psychology* (pp. 161–172). Chicago: University of Chicago Press.

Hawks, S. R., Madanat, H. N., Merrill, R. M., Goudy, M. B., & Miyagawa, T. (2003). A cross-cultural analysis of "motivation for eating" as a potential factor in the emergence of global obesity: Japan and the United States. *Health Promotion International, 18*(2), 153–162.

Hay, P. (2013). A systematic review of evidence for psychological treatments in eating disorders: 2005–2012. *International Journal of Eating Disorders, 46*(5), 462–469. doi:10.1002/eat.22103

Hayflick, L. (1977). The cellular basis for biological aging. In C. E. Finch & L. Hayflick (Eds.), *Handbook of biology of aging* (p. 159). New York: Van Nostrand Reinhold.

Hayward, C., Killen, J. D., & Taylor, C. B. (1989). Panic attacks in young adolescents. *American Journal of Psychiatry, 146*(8), 1061–1062.

Hayward, C., Killen, J. D., Kraemer, H. C., & Taylor, C. B. (2000). Predictors of panic attacks in adolescents. *Journal of the American Academy of Child and Adolescent Psychiatry, 39*(2), 207–214.

Hazan, C., & Shaver, P. (1987). Romantic love conceptualized as an attachment process. *Journal of Personality and Social Psychology, 52,* 511–524.

Heavey, C. L., Layne, C., & Christensen, A. (1993). Gender and conflict structure in marital interaction: A replication and extension. *Journal of Consulting and Clinical Psychology, 61,* 16–27.

Hebb, D. O. (1955). Drives and the CNS (Conceptual Nervous System). *Psychological Review, 62,* 243–254.

Hegeman, R. (2007, July 4). *Police: Shoppers stepped over victim.* Associated Press. Retrieved from http://abcnews.go.com/US/wireStory?id=3342724

Heider, F. (1958). *The psychology of interpersonal relations.* New York: Wiley.

Heil, G., Maslow, A., & Stephens, D. (1998). *Maslow on management.* New York: Wiley.

Heilman, K. M., Watson, R., & Valenstein, E. (1993). Neglect and related disorders. In K. Heilman & E. Valenstein (Eds.), *Clinical neuropsychology.* New York: Oxford University Press.

Heimberg, R. G., & Becker, R. E. (2002). *Cognitive-behavioral group therapy for social phobia: Basic mechanisms and clinical strategies.* New York: Guilford Press.

Heimberg, R. G., & Magee, L. (2014). Social anxiety disorder. In D. H. Barlow (Ed.), *Clinical handbook of psychological disorders: A step-by-step treatment manual* (5th ed., pp. 114–154). New York: Guilford Press.

Heimer, L. (1995). *The human brain and spinal cord: Functional neuroanatomy and dissection guide.* New York: Springer-Verlag.

Heinicke, C. M., Goorsky, M., Moscov, S., Dudley, K., Gordon, J., Schneider, C., et al. (2000). Relationship-based intervention with at-risk mothers: Factors affecting variations in outcome. *Infant Mental Health Journal, 21,* 133–155.

Heinrich, B. (2000). Testing insight in ravens. In C. Heyes & L. Huber (Eds.), *The evolution of cognition.* Cambridge, MA: MIT Press.

Helfrich, C., Pierau, S. S., Freitag, C. M., Roeper, J., Ziemann, U., & Bender, S. (2012). Monitoring cortical excitability during repetitive transcranial magnetic stimulation in children with ADHD: A single-blind, sham-controlled TMS-EEG study. *PLoS One, 7*(11), e50073.

Helms, J. E. (1992). Why is there no study of cultural equivalence in standardized cognitive ability testing? *American Psychologist, 47*(9), 1083–1101.

Henningfield, J. E., Clayton, R., & Pollin, W. (1990). Involvement of tobacco in alcoholism and illicit drug use. *British Journal of Addition, 85,* 279–292.

Henningfield, J. E., Cohen, C., & Slade, J. D. (1991). Is nicotine more addictive than cocaine? *British Journal of Addiction, 86,* 565–569.

Herberman, R. B., & Ortaldo, J. R. (1981). Natural killer cells: Their role in defenses against disease. *Science, 214,* 24–30.

Herbst, J. H., Zonderman, A. B., McCrae, R. R., & Costa, P. T., Jr. (2000). Do the dimensions of the Temperament and Character Inventory map a simple genetic architecture? Evidence from molecular genetics and factor analysis. *American Journal of Psychiatry, 157,* 1285–1290.

Herman, L. M., Pack, A. A., & Morrell-Samuels, P. (1993). Representational and conceptual skills of dolphins. In H. L. Roitblatt, L. M. Herman, & P. E. Nachtigall (Eds.), *Language and communication: Comparative perspectives.* Hillsdale, NJ: Erlbaum.

Hernandez, D., & Fisher, E. M. (1996). Down syndrome genetics: Unravelling a multifactorial disorder. *Human Molecular Genetics, 5,* 1411–1416.

Herrnstein, R. J., & Murray, C. (1994). *The bell curve: The reshaping of American life by differences in intelligence.* New York: Free Press.

Hersh, S. M. (2004, May 10). Annals of national security: Torture at Abu Ghraib. *The New Yorker.* Retrieved from http://www.newyorker.com

Hershberger, S. L., Plomin, R., & Pedersen, N. L. (1995, October). Traits and metatraits: Their reliability, stability, and shared genetic influence. *Journal of Personality and Social Psychology, 69*(4), 673–685.

Herxheimer, A., & Petrie, K. J. (2001). Melatonin for preventing and treating jet lag. *Cochrane Database of Systematic Reviews, 1,* CD 001520.

Hetrick, S. E., McKenzie, J. E., Cox, G. R., Simmons, M. B., & Merry, S. N. (2012). Newer generation antidepressants for depressive disorders in children and adolescents. *Cochrane Database of Systematic Reviews (Online), 11,* CD004851. doi:10.1002/14651858.CD004851.pub3

Hewlin, P. F. (2009). Wearing the cloak: Antecedents and consequences of creating facades of conformity. *Journal of Applied Psychology, 94*(3), 727–741.

Hewstone, M., Rubin, M., & Willis, H. (2002). Intergroup bias. *Annual Review of Psychology, 53,* 575–604.

Heyes, C. M. (1998). Theory of mind in nonhuman primates. *Behavior and Brain Science, 21,* 101–148.

Hicklin, J., & Widiger, T. A. (2000). Convergent validity of alternative MMPI-2 personality disorder scales. *Journal of Personality Assessment, 75*(3), 502–518.

Higgins, E. T., & Scholer, A. A. (2010). When is personality revealed? A motivated cognition approach. In O. P. John, R. W. Robins, & L. A. Pervin (Eds.), *Handbook of personality: Theory and research* (pp. 182–207). New York: Guilford Press.

Hilgard, E. R. (1991). A neodissociation interpretation of hypnosis. In S. J. Lynn & J. W. Rhue (Eds.), *Theories of hypnosis* (pp. 83–104). New York: Guilford Press.

Hilgard, E. R., & Hilgard, J. R. (1994). *Hypnosis in the relief of pain* (Rev. ed.). New York: Brunner/Mazel.

Hill, D. (1990). Causes of smoking in children. In B. Durston & K. Jamrozik, *Smoking and health 1990—The global war. Proceedings of the 7th World Conference on Smoking and Health,* 1–5 April. Perth: Health Department of Western Australia, 205–209.

Hill, P. C., & Butter, E. M. (1995). The role of religion in promoting physical health. *Journal of Psychology and Christianity, 14*(2), 141–155.

Hillman, C. H., Pontifex, M. B., Raine, L. B., Castelli, D. M., Hall, E. E., & Kramer, A. F. (2009). The effect of acute treadmill walking on cognitive control and academic achievement in preadolescent children. *Neuroscience, 159*(3), 1044–1054.

Hilton, J. L., & von Hipple, W. (1996). Stereotypes. *Annual Review of Psychology, 47,* 237–271.

Hilts, P. J. (1998, August 2). Is nicotine addictive? It depends on whose criteria you use. *New York Times,* p. C3.

Hines, T. (2003). *Pseudoscience and the paranormal: A critical examination of the evidence.* Amherst, NY: Prometheus Books.

Hintze, J. M. (2002). Interventions for fears and anxiety problems. In M. R. Shinn, H. R. Walker, & G. Stoner (Eds.), *Interventions for academic and behavior problems II: Preventive and remedial approaches* (pp. 939–954). Bethesda, MD: National Association of School Psychologists.

Hnasko, T. S., Chuhma, N., Zhang, H., Goh, G. Y., Sulzer, D., Palmiter, R. D., et al. (2010). Vesicular glutamate transport promotes dopamine storage and glutamate corelease in vivo. *Neuron, 65,* 643–656.

Hobson, J. (1988). *The dreaming brain*. New York: Basic Books.

Hobson, J. A., & McCarley, R. (1977). The brain as a dream state generator: An activation-synthesis hypothesis of the dream process. *American Journal of Psychiatry, 134*, 1335–1348.

Hobson, J., Pace-Schott, E., & Stickgold, R. (2000). Dreaming and the brain: Towards a cognitive neuroscience of conscious states. *Behavioral and Brain Sciences, 23*(6), 793–1121.

Hochman, J. (1994). Buried memories challenge the law. *National Law Journal, 1*, 17–18.

Hodges, J. R. (1994). Retrograde amnesia. In A. Baddeley, B. A. Wilson, & F. Watts (Eds.), *Handbook of memory disorders* (pp. 81–107). New York: Wiley.

Hodgson, B. (2001). *In the arms of Morpheus: The tragic history of laudanum, morphine, and patent medicines*. New York: Firefly Books.

Hodson, D. S., & Skeen, P. (1994). Sexuality and aging: The hammerlock of myths. *The Journal of Applied Gerontology, 13*, 219–235.

Hoeft, F., Gabrieli, J. D. E., Whitfield-Gabrieli, S., Haas, B. W., Bammer, R., Menon, V., et al. (2012). Functional brain basis of hypnotizability. *Archives of General Psychiatry, 69*(10), 1064.

Hoffer, T. B., Hess, M., Welch, V., Jr., & Williams, K. (2007). *Doctorate Recipients from United States Universities: Summary Report 2006*. Chicago: National Opinion Research Center.

Hoffrage, U., Hertwig, R., & Gigerenzer, G. (2000). Hindsight bias: A by-product of knowledge updating? *Journal of Experimental Psychology: Learning, Memory, and Cognition, 26*, 566–581.

Hofstede, G. H. (1980). *Culture's consequences, international differences in work-related values*. Beverly Hills, CA: Sage.

Hofstede, G. J., Pedersen, P. B., & Hofstede, G. H. (2002). *Exploring culture: Exercises, stories, and synthetic cultures*. Yarmouth, ME: Intercultural Press.

Hogg, M. A., & Hains, S. C. (1998). Friendship and group identification: A new look at the role of cohesiveness in groupthink. *European Journal of Social Psychology, 28*(1), 323–341.

Holden, C., & Vogel, G. (2002). Plasticity: Time for a reappraisal? *Science, 296*, 2126–2129.

Hollon, S. D., & Beck, A. T. (1994). Cognitive and cognitive-behavioral therapies. In A. E. Bergin & S. L. Garfield (Eds.), *Handbook of psychotherapy and behavior change* (4th ed., p. 428). Chichester, UK: Wiley.

Hollon, S. D., These, M., & Markowitz, J. (2002). Treatment and prevention of depression. *Psychological Science in the Public Interest, 3*, 39–77.

Holmes, T. H., & Masuda, M. (1973). Psychosomatic syndrome: When mothers-in-law or other disasters visit, a person can develop a bad, bad cold. *Psychology Today, 5*(11), 71–72, 106.

Holmes, T. H., & Rahe, R. H. (1967). The Social Readjustment Rating Scale. *Journal of Psychosomatic Research II*, 213–218.

Hood, D. C. (1998). Lower-level visual processing and models of light adaptation. *Annual Review of Psychology, 49*, 503–535.

Hopfinger, J. B., Buonocore, M. H., & Mangun, G. R. (2000). The neural mechanisms of top-down attentional control. *Nature Neuroscience, 3*, 284–291.

Horney, K. (1939). *New ways in psychoanalysis*. New York: Norton.

Horney, K. (1973, 1967). *Feminine psychology*. New York: Norton.

Horowitz, D. L. (1985). *Ethnic groups in conflict*. Berkeley: University of California Press.

Hortaçsu, N. (1999). The first year of family and couple initiated marriages of a Turkish sample: A longitudinal investigation. *International Journal of Psychology, 34*(1), 29–41.

Hossain, P., Kawar, B., & El Nahas, M. (2007). Obesity and diabetes in the developing world—a growing challenge. *New England Journal of Medicine, 356*(9), 973.

Hovland, C. I. (1937). The generalization of conditioned responses. I. The sensory generalization of conditioned responses with varying frequencies of tone. *Journal of General Psychology, 17*, 1251–1248.

Hu, P., & Meng, Z. (1996, August). *An examination of infant-mother attachment in China*. Poster session presented at the meeting of the International Society for the Study of Behavioral Development, Quebec City, Quebec, Canada.

Huesmann, L. R., & Eron, L. (1986). *Television and the aggressive child: A cross-national comparison*. Hillsdale, NJ: Erlbaum.

Huesmann, L. R., & Miller, L. S. (1994). Long-term effects of repeated exposure to media violence in childhood. In L. R. Huesmann (Ed.), *Aggressive behavior: Current perspectives* (pp. 153–183). New York: Plenum Press.

Huesmann, L. R., Moise, J. F., & Podolski, C. L. (1997). The effects of media violence on the development of antisocial behavior. In D. M. Stoff, J. Breiling, & J. D. Maser (Eds.), *Handbook of antisocial behavior* (pp. 181–193). New York: Wiley.

Huesmann, L. R., Moise-Titus, J., Podolski, C. L., & Eron, L. D. (2003). Longitudinal relations between children's exposure to TV violence and their aggressive and violent behavior in young adulthood: 1977–1992. *Developmental Psychology, 39*(2), 201–221.

Huff, W., Lenartz, D., Schormann, M., Lee, S. H., Kuhn, J., Koulousakis, A., et al. (2010). Unilateral deep brain stimulation of the nucleus accumbens in patients with treatment-resistant obsessive-compulsive disorder: Outcomes after one year. *Clinical Neurology and Neurosurgery, 112*(2), 137–143.

Hugenberg, K., & Bodenhausen, G. V. (2003). Facing prejudice: Implicit prejudice and the perception of facial threat. *Psychological Science, 14*, 640–643.

Hughes, J. (1993). Behavior therapy. In T. R. Kratochwill & R. J. Morris (Eds.), *Handbook of psychotherapy with children and adolescents* (pp. 185–220). Boston: Allyn & Bacon.

Hull, C. L. (1943). *Principles of behavior*. New York: Appleton-Century.

Hull, J. G., Draghici, A. M., & Sargent, J. D. (2012). A longitudinal study of risk glorifying video games and reckless driving. *Psychology of Popular Media Culture, 1*(4), 244–253. doi:10.1037/a0029510

Hummer, R. A., Rogers, R. G., Nam, C. B., & Ellison, C. G. (1999). Religious involvement and U.S. adult mortality. *Demography, 36*(2), 273–285.

Humphries, L. L. (1987). Bulimia: Diagnosis and treatment. *Comprehensive Therapy, 13*, 12–15.

Hunt, M. (1993). *The story of psychology*. New York: Doubleday.

Hurlemann, R., Patin, A., Onur, O. A., Cohen, M. X., Baumgartner, T., Metzler, S., et al. (2010). Oxytocin enhances amygdala-dependent, socially reinforced learning and emotional empathy in humans. *Journal of Neuroscience, 301*, 4999–5007.

Hurley, D. (1989). The search for cocaine's methadone. *Psychology Today, 23*(7–8), 54.

Hurley, S., & Nudds, M. (Eds.). (2006). *Rational animals?* Oxford, UK: Oxford University Press.

Hurvich, L. M., & Jameson, D. (1957). An opponent-process theory of color vision. *Psychological Review, 64*, 384–404.

Hyde, J. S., & Kling, K. C. (2001). Women, motivation, and achievement. *Psychology of Women Quarterly, 25*, 264–378.

Hyde, J. S., & Plant, E. A. (1995). Magnitude of psychological gender differences. *American Psychologist, 50*, 159–161.

Hygge, S. A., & Öhman, A. (1976). The relation of vicarious to direct instigation and conditioning of electrodermal responses. *Scandinavian Journal of Psychology, 17*(1), 217–222.

Hyman, I. E., Gilstrap, L. L., Decker, K., & Wilkinson, C. (1998). Manipulating remember and know judgements of autobiographical memories. *Applied Cognitive Psychology, 12*, 371–386.

Hyman, I. E., Jr. (1993). Imagery, reconstructive memory, and discovery. In B. Roskos-Ewoldsen, M. J. Intons-Peterson, & R. E. Anderson (Eds.), *Imagery, creativity, and discovery: A cognitive perspective* (pp. 99–121). The Netherlands: Elsevier Science.

Hyman, I. E., Jr., & Loftus, E. F. (1998). Errors in autobiographical memories. *Clinical Psychology Review, 18*, 933–947.

Hyman, I. E., Jr., & Loftus, E. F. (2002). False childhood memories and eyewitness memory errors. In M. L. Eisen, J. A. Quas, & G. S. Goodman (Eds.), *Memory and suggestibility in the forensic interview* (pp. 63–84). Mahwah, NJ: Erlbaum.

Hyman, S. E., & Cohen, J. D. (2013). Disorders of mood and anxiety. In E. R. Kandel, J. H. Schwartz, T. M. Jessell, S. A. Siegelbaum, & A. J. Hudspeth (Eds.), *Principles of neural science* (5th ed., pp. 1402–1424). USA: McGraw-Hill.

Iacoboni, M., Woods, R. P., Brass, M., Bekkering, H., Mazziotta, J. C., & Rizzolatti, G. (1999). Cortical mechanisms of human imitation. *Science, 286*, 2526–2528.

Iber, C., Ancoli-Israel, S., Chesson, A. L., Jr., & Quan, S. F. (2007). *The AASM manual for the scoring of sleep and associated events: Rules, terminology and technical specifications.* Westchester, IL: American Academy of Sleep Medicine.

Imaizumi, Y. (1998). A comparative study of twinning and triplet rates in 17 countries, 1972–1996. *Acta Genetic Medicine and Gemellology, 47,* 101–114.

Insel, T. R., & Wang, P. S. (2010). Rethinking mental illness. *The Journal of the American Medical Association, 303*(19), 1970–1971.

Irwin, M., Mascovich A., Gillin, J. C., Willoughby, R., Pike, J., & Smith, T. L. (1994). Partial sleep deprivation reduces natural killer cell activity in humans. *Psychosomatic Medicine, 56,* 493–498.

Irwin, M., McClintick, J., Costlow, C., Fortner, M., White, J., & Gillin, J. C. (1996). Partial night sleep deprivation reduces natural killer and cellular immune responses in humans. *The Federation of American Societies for Experimental Biology Journal, 10,* 643–653.

Isabel, J. (2003). *Genetics: An introduction for dog breeders.* Loveland, CO: Alpine.

Isenberg, D. J. (1986). Group polarization: A critical review and meta-analysis. *Journal of Personality and Social Psychology, 50*(6), 1141–1151.

Iwamoto, E. T., & Martin, W. (1988). A critique of drug self-administration as a method for predicting abuse potential of drugs. *National Institute on Drug Abuse Research Monograph, 1046,* 81457–81465.

Izard, C. (1988). Emotion-cognition relationships and human development. In C. Izard, J. Kagan, & R. Zajonc (Eds.), *Emotions, cognition, and behavior.* New York: Cambridge University Press.

Jackson, L. A., & Wang, J.-L. (2013). Cultural differences in social networking site use: A comparative study of China and the United States. *Computers in Human Behavior, 29*(3), 910. doi:10.1016/j.chb.2012.11.024

Jackson, M. L., Gunzelmann, G., Whitney, P., Hinson, J. M., Belenky, G., Rabat, A., et al. (2013). Deconstructing and reconstructing cognitive performance in sleep deprivation. *Sleep Medicine Reviews, 17*(3), 215–225. doi:10.1016/j.smrv.2012.06.007

Jackson, R. (2001). *Plato: A beginner's guide.* London: Hoder & Stroughton.

Jackson, T., Iezzi, T., Gunderson, J., Fritch, A., & Nagasaka, T. (2002). Gender differences in pain perception: The mediating role of self-efficacy beliefs. *Sex Roles, 47,* 561–568.

Jaeggi, S. M., Buschkuehl, M., Jonides, J., & Perrig, W. J. (2008). Improving fluid intelligence with training on working memory. *Proceedings of the National Academy of Sciences, USA, 105*(19), 6829–6833.

James, W. (1884). What is an emotion? *Mind, 9,* 188–205.

James, W. (1890). *Principles of psychology.* New York: Henry Holt.

James, W. (1894). The physical basis of emotion. *Psychological Review, 1,* 516–529.

James, W. (2002, 1890). *The principles of psychology (Vols. 1 and 2).* Cambridge, MA: Harvard University Press.

Jameson, M., Diehl, R., & Danso, H. (2007). Stereotype threat impacts college athletes' academic performance. *Current Research in Social Psychology, 12*(5), 68–79.

Jang, K. L., Livesley, W. J., & Vernon, P. A. (1996). Heritability of the Big Five personality dimensions and their facets: A twin study. *Journal of Personality, 64,* 577–591.

Jang, K. L., McCrae, R. R., Angleitner, A., Riemann, R., & Livesley, W. J. (1998). Heritability of facet-level traits in a cross-cultural twin sample: Support for a hierarchical model of personality. *Journal of Personality and Social Psychology, 74,* 1556–1565.

Janis, I. (1972). *Victims of groupthink.* Boston: Houghton-Mifflin.

Janis, I. (1982). *Groupthink* (2nd ed.). Boston: Houghton-Mifflin.

Janos, P. M. (1987). A fifty-year follow-up of Terman's youngest college students and IQ-matched agemates. *Gifted Child Quarterly, 31,* 55–58.

January, D., & Kako, E. (2007). Re-evaluating evidence for linguistic relativity: Reply to Boroditsky (2001). *Cognition, 104*(2), 417–426.

Jehn, K., Northcraft, G., & Neale, M. (1999). Why differences make a difference: A field study of diversity, conflict, and performance in workgroups. *Administrative Science Quarterly, 44,* 741–763.

Jensen, A. R. (1969). How much can we boost IQ and scholastic achievement? *Harvard Educational Review, 39,* 1–123.

Jensen, M. P., Gertz, K. J., Kupper, A. E., Braden, A. L., Howe, J. D., Hakimian, S., et al. (2013). Steps toward developing an EEG biofeedback treatment for chronic pain. *Applied Psychophysiology and Biofeedback.* doi:10.1007/s10484-013-9214-9

Johnson, C. P., & Myers, S. M. (Council on Children with Disabilities). (2007). Identification and evaluation of children with autism spectrum disorders. *Pediatrics, 120*(5), 1183–1215.

Johnson, D., Johnson, R., & Smith, K. (1991). *Active learning: Cooperation in the college classroom.* Edna, MN: Interaction Book Company.

Johnson, G. (1995, June 6). Chimp talk debate: Is it really language? *New York Times.*

Johnson, J., Cohen, P., Pine, D. S., Klein, D. F., Kasen, S., & Brook, J. S. (2000). Association between cigarette smoking and anxiety disorders during adolescence and early adulthood. *Journal of the American Medical Association, 284*(18), 2348–2351.

Johnston, L. D., O'Malley, P. M., Bachman, J. G., & Schulenberg, J. E. (2007, September). *Monitoring the future national survey results on drug use, 1975–2006: Vol. 1. Secondary school students 2006.* Bethesda, MD: National Institute on Drug Abuse.

Jones, E. E., & Harris, V. A. (1967). The attribution of attitudes. *Journal of Experimental Social Psychology, 3,* 1–24.

Jones, E. J., Krupnick, J. L., & Kerig, P. K. (1987). Some gender effects in a brief psychotherapy. *Psychotherapy, 24,* 336–352.

Jones, G. W. (1997). Modernization and divorce: Contrasting trends in Islamic Southeast Asia and the West. *Population and Development Review, 23*(1), 95–113.

Jones, M. C. (1924). A laboratory study of fear: The case of Peter. *Pedagogical Seminary, 31,* 308–315.

Jones, M. K., & Menzies, R. G. (1995). The etiology of fear of spiders. *Anxiety, Stress and Coping, 8,* 227–234.

Judelsohn, R. G. (2007, November–December). Vaccine safety: Vaccines are one of public health's great accomplishments. *Skeptical Inquirer, 31*(6). Retrieved June 13, 2010, from http://www.csicop.org/si/show/vaccine_safety_vaccines_are_one_of_public_healthrsquos_great_accomplishment/

Juffer, F., & Rosenboom, L. G. (1997). Infant-mother attachment of internationally adopted children in the Netherlands. *International Journal of Behavioral Development, 20*(1), 93–107.

Julien, R. M., Advokat, C. D., & Comaty, J. E. (2011). *A primer of drug action: A comprehensive guide to the actions, uses, and side effects of psychoactive drugs* (12th ed.). New York: Worth Publishers.

Jung, C. (1933). *Modern man in search of a soul.* New York: Harcourt Brace.

Kabat-Zinn, J., Lipworth, L., & Burney, R. (1985). The clinical use of mindfulness meditation for the self-regulation of chronic pain. *Journal of Behavioral Medicine, 8,* 163–190.

Kabat-Zinn, J., Lipworth, L., Burney, R., & Sellers, W. (1986). Four year follow-up of a meditation-based program for the self regulation of chronic pain: Treatment outcomes and compliance. *Clinical Journal of Pain, 2,* 159–173.

Kable, J. A., Coles, C. D., Lynch, M. E., & Platzman, K. (2008). Physiological responses to social and cognitive challenges in 8-year olds with a history of prenatal cocaine exposure. *Developmental Psychobiology, 50*(3), 251–265.

Kagan, J. (1998). *Galen's prophecy: Temperament in human nature* (pp. 237–260, 270–274). New York: Basic Books.

Kagan, J. (2010). *The temperamental thread.* New York: Dana Press.

Kagan, J., Snidman, N., Kahn, V., & Towsley, S. (2007). The preservation of two infant temperaments into adolescence. *SRCD Monographs, 72*(2), 76–80.

Kahan, M., & Sutton, N. (1998). Overview: Methadone treatment for the opioid-dependent patient. In B. Brands & J. Brands (Eds.), *Methadone maintenance: A physician's guide to treatment* (pp. 1–15). Toronto, ON: Addiction Research Foundation.

Kahneman, D. (2011). *Thinking, fast and slow.* New York: Farrar, Straus and Giroux.

Kahneman, D., & Tversky, A. (1973). On the psychology of prediction. *Psychological Review, 80,* 237–251.

Kahneman, D., Slovic, P., & Tversky, A. (1982). *Judgment under uncertainty: Heuristics and biases*. New York: Cambridge University Press.

Kail, R., & Hall, L. K. (2001). Distinguishing short-term memory from working memory. *Memory and Cognition, 29*(1), 1–9.

Kakko, J., Svanborg, K. D., Kreek, M. J., & Heilig, M. (2003). 1-year retention and social function after buprenorphine-associated relapse prevention treatment for heroin dependence in Sweden: A randomised, placebo-controlled trial. *Lancet, 361*, 662–668.

Kales, A., Soldatos, C., Bixler, E., Ladda, R. L., Charney, D. S., Weber, G., et al. (1980). Hereditary factors in sleepwalking and night terrors. *British Journal of Psychiatry, 137*, 111–118.

Kandel, E. R., & Schwartz, J. H. (1982). Molecular biology of learning: Modulation of transmitter release. *Science, 218*, 433–443.

Kaplan, M. F., & Miller, C. E. (1987). Group decision making and normative versus informational influence: Effects of type of issue and assigned decision rule. *Journal of Personality and Social Psychology, 53*(2), 306–313.

Karau, S. J., & Williams, K. D. (1993). Social loafing: A meta-analytic review and theoretical integration. *Journal of Personality and Social Psychology, 65*, 681–706.

Karau, S. J., & Williams, K. D. (1997). The effects of group cohesiveness on social loafing and social compensation. *Group Dynamics: Theory, Research and Practice, 1*, 156–168.

Karney, B. R., & Bradbury, T. N. (2000). Attributions in marriage: State or trait? A growth curve analysis. *Journal of Personality and Social Psychology, 78*, 295–309.

Kastenbaum, R., & Costa, P. T., Jr. (1977). Psychological perspective on death. *Annual Review of Psychology, 28*, 225–249.

Kaufman, J., & Zigler, E. (1993). The intergenerational transmission of abuse is overstated. In R. J. Gelles & D. R. Loseke (Eds.), *Current controversies on family violence*. Newbury Park, CA: Sage.

Kaye, W. H., Fudge, J. L., & Paulus, M. (2009). New insights into symptoms and neurocircuit function of anorexia nervosa. *Nature Reviews Neuroscience, 10*(8), 573–584. doi:10.1038/nrn2682

Kaye, W. H., Wierenga, C. E., Bailer, U. F., Simmons, A. N., & Bischoff-Grethe, A. (2013). Nothing tastes as good as skinny feels: The neurobiology of anorexia nervosa. *Trends in Neurosciences, 36*(2), 110–120. doi:10.1016/j.tins.2013.01.003

Kazdin, A. E. (1980). Acceptability of time out from reinforcement procedures for disruptive behavior. *Behavior Therapy, 11*(3), 329–344.

Kazdin, A. E. (2008). Evidence-based treatment and practice: New opportunities to bridge clinical research and practice, enhance the knowledge base, and improve patient care. *American Psychologist, 63*(3), 146–159. doi:10.1037/0003-066x.63.3.146

Kearney, C. A., & Silverman, W. K. (1998). A critical review of pharmacotherapy for youth with anxiety disorders: Things are not as they seem. *Journal of Anxiety Disorders, 12*, 83–102.

Keel, P. K., & Forney, K. J. (2013). Psychosocial risk factors for eating disorders. *The International Journal of Eating Disorders, 46*(5), 433–439. doi:10.1002/eat.22094

Keillor, J., Barrett, A., Crucian, G., Kortenkamp, S., & Heilman, K. (2002). Emotional experience and perception in the absence of facial feedback. *Journal of the International Neuropsychological Society, 8*(1), 130–135.

Keirsey, D. (1998). *Please understand me ii: Temperament character intelligence*. Del Mar, CA: Prometheus Nemesis Book Company.

Keller, M. B., McCullough, J. P., Klein, D. N., Arnow, B., Dunner, D., Gelenberg, A., et al. (2000). A comparison of nefazodone, the cognitive behavioral-analysis system of psychotherapy, and their combination for the treatment of chronic depression. *New England Journal of Medicine, 342*(20), 1462–1470.

Kelly, I. (1980). The scientific case against astrology. *Mercury, 10*(13), 135.

Kelly, J. A., McAuliffe, T. L., Sikkema, K. J., Murphy, D. A., Somlai, A. M., Mulry, G., et al. (1997). Reduction in risk behavior among adults with severe mental illness who learned to advocate for HIV prevention. *Psychiatric Services, 48*(10), 1283–1288.

Kempf, L., & Weinberger, D. R. (2009). Molecular genetics and bioinformatics: An outline for neuropsychological genetics. In T. E. Goldberg & D. R. Weinberger (Eds.), *The genetics of cognitive neuroscience* (pp. 3–26). Cambridge, MA: MIT Press.

Kendler, K. S. (1985). Diagnostic approaches to schizotypal personality disorders: A historical perspective. *Schizophrenia Bulletin, 11*, 538–553.

Kendler, K. S., Czajkowski, N., Tambs, K., Torgersen, S., Aggen, S. H., Neale, M. C., et al. (2006). Dimensional representations of DSM-IV cluster A personality disorders in a population-based sample of Norwegian twins: A multivariate study. *Psychological Medicine, 36*(11), 1583–1591. doi:10.1017/s0033291706008609

Kenny, A. (1968). Mind and body. In *Descartes: A study of his philosophy* (p. 279). New York: Random House.

Kenny, A. (1994). Descartes to Kant. In A. Kenny (Ed.), *The Oxford history of Western philosophy* (pp. 107–192). Oxford, UK: Oxford University Press.

Keromoian, R., & Leiderman, P. H. (1986). Infant attachment to mother and child caretaker in an East African community. *International Journal of Behavioral Development, 9*, 455–469.

Kerwin, D. R., Zhang, Y., Kotchen, J. M., Espeland, M. A., Van Horn, L., McTigue, K. M., et al. (2010). The cross-sectional relationship between body mass index, waist-hip ratio, and cognitive performance in postmenopausal women enrolled in the women's health initiative. *Journal of the American Geriatric Society, 58*, 1427–1432. [Article first published online July 14, 2010]. doi:10.1111/j.1532-5415.2010.02969.x

Kessler, R. C., Petukhova, M., Sampson, N. A., Zaslavsky, A. M., & Wittchen, H. U. (2012). Twelve-month and lifetime prevalence and lifetime morbid risk of anxiety and mood disorders in the United States. *International Journal of Methods in Psychiatric Research, 21*(3), 169–184. doi:10.1002/mpr.1359

Kety, S. S., Wender, P. H., Jacobsen, B., Ingaham, L. J., Jansson, L., Faber, B., et al. (1994). Mental illness in the biological and adoptive relatives of schizophrenic adoptees. *Archives of General Psychiatry, 51*, 442–455.

Kiecolt-Glaser, J. K. (2009). Psychoneuroimmunology: Psychology's gateway to the biomedical future. *Perspectives on Psychological Science, 4*(4), 367.

Kiecolt-Glaser, J. K., Fisher, L. D., Ogrocki, P., Stout, J. C., Speicher, C. E., & Glaser, R. (1987). Marital quality, marital disruption, and immune function. *Psychosomatic Medicine, 49*, 13–34.

Kiecolt-Glaser, J. K., Glaser, R., Gravenstein, S., Malarkey, W. B., & Sheridan, J. (1996). Chronic stress alters the immune response to influenza virus vaccine in older adults. *Proceedings of the National Academy of Sciences, USA, 93*(7), 3043–3047.

Kiecolt-Glaser, J. K., Marucha, P. T., Malarkey, W. B., & Marcado, A. M. (1995). Slowing of wound healing by psychological stress. *Lancet, 346*, 1194–1196.

Kiecolt-Glaser, J. K., McGuire, L., Robles, T., & Glaser, R. (2002). Psychoneuroimmunology: Psychological influences on immune function and health. *Journal of Consulting and Clinical Psychology, 70*, 537–547.

Kihlstrom, J. F. (1985). Hypnosis. *Annual Review of Psychology, 36*, 385–418.

Kihlstrom, J. F. (1987). The cognitive unconscious. *Science, 237*, 1445–1452.

Kihlstrom, J. F. (1999). Conscious and unconscious cognition. In R. J. Sternberg (Ed.), *The nature of cognition* (pp. 173–203). Cambridge, MA: MIT Press.

Kihlstrom, J. F. (2001). Hypnosis and the psychological unconscious. In Howard S. Friedman (Ed.), *Assessment and therapy: Specialty articles from the encyclopedia of mental health* (pp. 215–226). San Diego, CA: Academic Press.

Kihlstrom, J. F. (2002). Memory, autobiography, history. *Proteus: A Journal of Ideas, 19*(2), 1–6.

Kihlstrom, J. F., Mulvaney, S., Tobias, B., & Tobis, I. (2000). The emotional unconscious. In E. Eich, J. Kihlstrom, G. Bower, J. Forgas, & P. Niedenthal (Eds.), *Cognition and emotion* (pp. 30–86). New York: Oxford University Press.

Kim, H., & Markus, H. R. (1999). Deviance or uniqueness, harmony or conformity? A cultural analysis. *Journal of Personality and Social Psychology, 77*, 785–800.

Kimura, D. (1999). *Sex and cognition*. Cambridge, MA: MIT Press.

Kimura, R., Mactavish, E., Yang, J., Westaway, D., & Jhamandas, J. H. (2012). Beta amyloid-induced depression of hippocampal long-term potentiation is mediated through the amylin receptor. *Journal of Neuroscience, 32*(48), 17401–17406. doi:10.1523/%u200BJNEUROSCI.3028-12.2012

King, M. W., Street, A. E., Gradus, J. L., Vogt, D. S., & Resick, P. A. (2013). Gender differences in posttraumatic stress symptoms among OEF/OIF veterans: An item response theory analysis. *Journal of Traumatic Stress, 26*(2), 175–183. doi:10.1002/jts.21802

Kinsey, A. C., Pomeroy, W. B., & Martin, C. E. (1948). *Sexual behavior in the human male.* Philadelphia: W. B. Saunders.

Kinsey, A. C., Pomeroy, W. B., Martin, C. E., & Gebhard, P. H. (1953). *Sexual behavior in the human female.* New York: W. B. Saunders.

Kirschvink, J. L., & L., G. J. (1981, March 13). Biogenic magnetite as a basis for magnetic field detection in animals. Retrieved October 29, 2014, from PubMed.gov website: http://www.ncbi.nlm.nih.gov/pubmed/7213948/biosystems

Kirmayer, L. J. (1991). The place of culture in psychiatric nosology: Taijin kyofusho and the DSM-III-TR. *Journal of Nervous and Mental Disease, 179,* 19–28.

Kirsch, I. (2000). The response set theory of hypnosis. *American Journal of Clinical Hypnosis, 42*(3–4), 274–292.

Kirsch, I., & Lynn, S. J. (1995). The altered state of hypnosis: Changes in the theoretical landscape. *American Psychologist, 50,* 846–858.

Kitamura, T., Saitoh, Y., Takashima, N., Murayama, A., Niibori, Y., Ageta, H., et al. (2009). Adult neurogenesis modulates the hippocampus-dependent period of associative fear memory. *Cell, 139*(4), 814–827.

Kitayama, S., & Markus, H. R. (1994). Introduction to cultural psychology and emotion research. In S. Kitayama & H. R. Markus (Eds.), *Emotion and culture: Empirical studies of mutual influence* (pp. 1–22). Washington, DC: American Psychological Association.

Kleinot, M. C., & Rogers, R. W. (1982). Identifying effective components of alcohol misuse prevention programs. *Journal of Studies on Alcohol, 43,* 802–811.

Klorman, R., Hilpert, P. L., Michael, R., LaGana, C., & Sveen, O. B. (1980). Effects of coping and mastery modeling on experienced and inexperienced pedodontic patients' disruptiveness. *Behavior Therapy, 11,* 156–168.

Kluft, R. P. (1984). Introduction to multiple personality disorder. *Psychiatric Annals, 14,* 19–24.

Klüver, H., & Bucy, P. C. (1939). Preliminary analysis of functions of the temporal lobes in monkeys. *Archives of Neurological Psychiatry, 42,* 979–1000.

Knight, A. (1996). *The life of the law: The people and cases that have shaped our society, from King Alfred to Rodney King.* New York: Crown Publishing Group.

Knight, J. A. (1998). Free radicals: Their history and current status in aging and disease. *Annals of Clinical and Laboratory Science, 28,* 331–346.

Kobasa, S. (1979). Stressful life events, personality, and health: An inquiry into hardiness. *Journal of Personality and Social Psychology, 37*(1), 1–11.

Koch, C., & Mormann, F. (2010). The neurobiology of consciousness. In G. Mashour (Ed.), *Consciousness, awareness, and anesthesia* (pp. 24–46). New York: Cambridge University Press.

Koenig, H. G., Hays, J. C., Larson, D. B., George, L. K., Cohen, H. J., McCullough, M. E., et al. (1999). Does religious attendance prolong survival? A six-year follow-up study of 3,968 older adults. *Journal of Gerontology, 54A,* M370–M377.

Koenig, H. G., McCullough, M. E., & Larson, D. B. (2001). *Handbook of religion and health.* Oxford, UK: Oxford University Press.

Koester, J., & Siegelbaum, S. A. (2013). Membrane potential and the passive electrical properties of the neuron. In E. R. Kandel, J. H. Schwartz, T. M. Jessell, S. A. Siegelbaum & A. J. Hudspeth (Eds.), *Principles of neural science* (5th ed., pp. 148–171). USA: McGraw Hill.

Koh, J. K. (1996). *A guide to common Singapore spiders* (BP Guide to Nature series). Singapore: Singapore Science Center.

Kohlberg, L. (1973). Continuities in childhood and adult moral development revisited. In P. Baltes & K. W. Schaie (Eds.), *Life-span development psychology: Personality and socialization.* San Diego, CA: Academic Press.

Köhler, W. (1925, 1992). *Gestalt psychology: An introduction to new concepts in modern psychology (reissue).* New York: Liveright.

Koob, G. F., & Le Moal, M. (2005). Plasticity of reward neurocircuitry and the 'dark side' of drug addiction. *Nature Neuroscience, 8*(11), 1442–1444.

Korn, S. (1984). Continuities and discontinuities in difficult/easy temperament: Infancy to young adulthood. *Merrill Palmer Quarterly, 30,* 189–199.

Kosfeld, M., Heinrichs, M., Zak, P. J., Fischbacher, U., & Fehr, E. (2005). Oxytocin increase trust in humans. *Nature, 435,* 673–676.

Kosslyn, S. M. (1983). Mental imagery. In Z. Rubin (Ed.), *The psychology of being human.* New York: Harper & Row.

Kosslyn, S. M., Alpert, N. M., Thompson, W. L., Maljkovic, V., Weise, S. B., Chabris, C. F., et al. (1993). Visual mental imagery activates topographically organized visual cortex: PET investigations. *Journal of Cognitive Neuroscience, 5,* 263–287.

Kosslyn, S. M., Ball, T. M., & Reiser, B. J. (1978). Visual images preserve metric spatial information: Evidence from studies of image scanning. *Journal of Experimental Psychology: Human Perception and Performance, 4,* 47–60.

Kosslyn, S. M., Ganis, G., & Thompson, W. L. (2001). Neural foundations of imagery. *Nature Reviews Neuroscience, 2,* 635–642.

Kosslyn, S. M., Pascual-Leone, A., Felician, O., Camposano, S., Keenan, J. P., Thompson, W. L., et al. (1999). The role of area 17 in visual imagery: Convergent evidence from PET and rTMS. *Science, 284,* 167–170.

Kotkin, M., Daviet, C., & Gurin, J. (1996). The *Consumer Reports* mental health survey. *American Psychologist, 51*(10), 1080–1082.

Kovacs, K., Lajtha, A., & Sershen, H. (2010). Effect of nicotine and cocaine on neurofilaments and receptors in whole brain tissue and synaptoneurosome preparations. *Brain Research Bulletin, 82*(1–2), 109–117.

Kozberg, M., Chen, B. R., De Leo, S. E., Bouchard, M. B., & Hillman, E. M. C. (2013). Resolving the transition from negative to positive blood oxygen level dependent responses in the developing brain. *Proceedings of the National Academy of Sciences of the United States of America (PNAS).* Published online ahead of print, February 20, 2013. doi:10.1073/pnas.1212785110

Kratofil, P. H., Baberg, H. T., & Dimsdale, J. E. (1996). Self-mutilation and severe self-injurious behavior associated with amphetamine psychosis. *General Hospital Psychiatry, 18,* 117–120.

Kriegstein, A., & Alvarez-Buylla, A. (2009). The glial nature of embryonic and adult neural stem cells. *Annual Review of Neuroscience, 32*(1), 149–184.

Kristensen, P., & Bjerkedal, T. (2007). Explaining the relation between birth order and intelligence. *Science, 316*(5832), 1717.

Kryger, M., Lavie, P., & Rosen, R. (1999). Recognition and diagnosis of insomnia. *Sleep, 22,* S421–S426.

Kübler-Ross, E. (1997). *The wheel of life: A memoir of living and dying.* New York: Touchstone.

Kuhn, H. W., & Nasar, S. (Eds.). (2001). *The essential John Nash.* Princeton, NJ: Princeton University Press.

Kuhn, J., Gründler, T. O. J., Lenartz, D., Sturm, V., Klosterkötter, J., & Huff, W. (2010). Deep brain stimulation for psychiatric disorders. *Deutsches Ärzteblatt International, 107*(7), 105–113.

Kumar, S., & Oakley-Browne, M. (2002). Panic disorder. *Clinical Evidence, 7,* 906–912.

Küntay, A., & Slobin, D. I. (2002). Putting interaction back into child language: Examples from Turkish. *Psychology of Language and Communication, 6,* 5–14.

Kuo, B. C. H. (2011). Culture's consequences on coping: Theories, evidences, and dimensionalities. *Journal of Cross-Cultural Psychology, 42,* 1084. doi: 10.1177/0022022110381126

Kupfer, D. J., & Reynolds, C. F., III. (1997). Management of insomnia. *New England Journal of Medicine, 336*(5), 341–346.

Kvavilashvili, L., Mirani, J., Schlagman, S., Foley, K., & Dornbrot, D. E. (2009). Consistency of flashbulb memories of September 11 over long delays: Implications for consolidation and wrong time slice hypotheses. *Journal of Memory and Language, 61*(4), 556–572.

LaBar, K. S., LeDoux, J. E., Spencer, D. D., & Phelps, E. A. (1995). Impaired fear conditioning following unilateral temporal lobectomy to humans. *Journal of Neuroscience, 15,* 6846–6855.

LaBerge, D. (1980). Unitization and automaticity in perception. In J. H. Flowers (Ed.), *Nebraska symposium on motivation* (pp. 53–71). Lincoln: University of Nebraska Press.

Labouvie-Vief, G. (1980). Beyond formal operations: Uses and limits of pure logic in lifespan development. *Human Development, 23,* 114–146.

Labouvie-Vief, G. (1992). A neo-Piagetian perspective on adult cognitive development. In R. Sternberg & C. Berg (Eds.), *Intellectual development* (pp. 197–228). Cambridge, UK: Cambridge University Press.

Lacayo, A. (1995). Neurologic and psychiatric complications of cocaine abuse. *Neuropsychiatry, Neuropsychology, and Behavioral Neurology, 8*(1), 53–60.

LaFromboise, T., Coleman, H. L. K., & Gerton, J. (1993). Psychological impact of biculturalism: Evidence and theory. *Psychological Bulletin, 114,* 395–412.

Lagopoulos, J., Xu, J., Rasmussen, I., Vik, A., Malhi, G. S., Eliassen, C. F., et al. (2009). Increased theta and alpha EEG activity during nondirective meditation. *The Journal of Alternative and Complementary Medicine, 15*(11), 1187.

Lal, S. (2002). Giving children security: Mamie Phipps Clark and the radicalization of child psychology. *American Psychologist, 57*(1), 20–28.

Lalancette, M.-F., & Standing, L. G. (1990). Asch fails again. *Social Behavior and Personality, 18*(1), 7–12.

Lambert, M. J., & Ogles, B. M. (2004). The efficacy and effectiveness of psychotherapy. In M. J. Lambert (Ed.), *Handbook of psychotherapy and behavior change* (5th ed., pp. 139–193). New York: Wiley.

Lambert, N., Fincham, F. D., Dewall, N. C., Pond, R., & Beach, S. R. (2013). Shifting toward cooperative tendencies and forgiveness: How partner-focused prayer transforms motivation. *Personal Relationships, 20*(1), 184. doi: 10.1111/j.1475-6811.2012.01411.x

Lance, C. J., LaPointe, J. A., & Fisicaro, S. (1994). Tests of three causal models of halo rater error. *Organizational Behavior and Human Decision Performance, 57,* 83–96.

Landrum, R. E. (2009). *Finding jobs with a psychology bachelor's degree.* Washington, DC: American Psychological Association.

Landrum, R. E., & Davis, S. F. (2007). *The psychology major: Career options and strategies for success* (3rd ed.). Upper Saddle River, NJ: Prentice Hall.

Lane, R. D., Kivley, L. S., DuBois, M. A. Shamasundara, P., & Schwartz, G. E. (1995). Levels of emotional awareness and the degree of right hemisphere dominance in the perception of facial emotion. *Neuropsychologia, 33,* 525–538.

Lang, J. W. B., & Lang, J. (2010). Priming competence diminishes the link between cognitive test anxiety and test performance. *Psychological Science, 21*(6), 811–819.

Lange, C. (1885). *The emotions.* Reprinted in C. G. Lange & W. James (Eds.), *The emotions.* New York: Harner.

Langer, E. J., & Rodin, J. (1976). The effects of enhanced personal responsibility for the aged: A field experiment in an institutional setting. *Journal of Personality and Social Psychology, 34,* 191–198.

Langone, M. C. (1996). Clinical update on cults. *Psychiatric Times, 13*(7), 1–3.

Lanphear, B. P., Dietrich, K., Auinger, P., & Cox, C. (2000). Cognitive deficits associated with blood lead concentrations <10 micrograms/dL in U.S. children and adolescents. *Public Health Reports, 115*(6), 521–529.

Lapierre, M. A., Vaala, S. E., & Linebarger, D. L. (2011). Influence of licensed spokescharacters and health cues on children's ratings of cereal taste. *Archives of Pediatric & Adolescent Medicine, 135*(3), 229–234. doi: 10.1001/archpediatrics. 2010.300

Lapsley, D. K., Milstead, M., Quintana, S. M., Flannery, D., & Buss, R. R. (1986). Adolescent egocentrism and formal operations: Tests of a theoretical assumption. *Developmental Psychology, 22,* 800–807.

Larsen, J. T., Berntson, G. G., Poehlmann, K. M., Ito, T. A., & Cacioppo, J. T. (2008). The psychophysiology of emotion. In M. Lewis, J. M. Haviland-Jones, & L. F. Barrett (Eds.), *Handbook of emotions* (3rd ed., pp. 180–195). New York: Guilford Press.

Larzelere, R. (1986). Moderate spanking: Model or deterrent of children's aggression in the family? *Journal of Family Violence, 1*(1), 27–36.

Lashley, K. S. (1938). The thalamus and emotion. *The Psychological Review, 45,* 21–61.

Lasnik, H. (1990). Metrics and morphophonemics in early English verse. In *University of Connecticut Working Papers in Linguistics: Vol. 3* (pp. 29–40). Storrs: University of Connecticut.

Latané, B., & Darley, J. M. (1969). Bystander "apathy." *American Scientist, 57*(2), 244–268.

Latané, B., Williams, K., & Harkins, S. (1979). Many hands make light the work: The causes and consequences of social loafing. *Journal of Personality & Social Psychology, 37*(6), 822–832.

Launer, L., Masaki, K., Petrovitch, H., Foley, D., & Havlik, R. (1995). The association between midlife blood pressure levels and late-life cognitive function. *Journal of the American Medical Association, 272*(23), 1846–1851.

Laungani, P. (1997). Death in a Hindu Family. In C. M. Parkes, P. Laungani, & B. Young (Eds.), *Death and bereavement across cultures* (pp. 52–72). London: Routledge.

Laviolette, S. R., Lauzon, N. M., Bishop, S. F., Sun, N., & Tan, H. (2008, August 6). Dopamine signaling through D1-like versus D2-like receptors in the nucleus accumbens core versus shell differentially modulates nicotine reward sensitivity. *Journal of Neuroscience, 28*(32), 8025–8033.

Laws, G., Davies, I., & Andrews, C. (1995). Linguistic structure and nonlinguistic cognition: English and Russian blues compared. *Language and Cognitive Processes, 10,* 59–94.

Lay, C., & Nguyen, T. T. I. (1998). The role of acculturation-related and acculturation non-specific daily hassles: Vietnamese-Canadian students and psychological distress. *Canadian Journal of Behavioural Science, 30*(3), 172–181.

Lazarus, R. S. (1991). *Emotion and adaptation.* New York: Oxford University Press.

Lazarus, R. S. (1993). From psychological stress to the emotions: A history of changing outlooks. *Annual Review of Psychology, 44,* 1–22.

Lazarus, R. S. (1999). *Stress and emotion: A new synthesis.* New York: Springer.

Lazarus, R. S., & Folkman, S. (1984). *Stress, appraisal and coping.* New York: Springer.

Leary, M. R., & Forsyth, D. R. (1987). Attributions of responsibility for collective endeavors. *Review of Personality and Social Psychology, 8,* 167–188.

Leask, J., Haber, R. N., & Haber, R. B. (1969). Eidetic imagery in children: II. Longitudinal and experimental results. *Psychonomic Monograph Supplements, 3,* 25–48.

Leccese, A. P., Pennings, E. J. M., & De Wolff, F. A. (2000). *Combined use of alcohol and psychotropic drugs. A review of the literature.* Leiden, The Netherlands: Academisch Ziekenhuis Leiden (AZL).

Leclerc, C. M., & Hess, T. M. (2007). Age differences in the bases for social judgments: Tests of a social expertise perspective. *Experimental Aging Research, 33*(1), 95–120.

LeDoux, J. (1994). Emotion, memory and the brain. *Scientific American, 270,* 32–39.

LeDoux, J. E. (1996). *The emotional brain: The mysterious underpinnings of emotional life.* New York: Simon & Schuster.

LeDoux, J. E., & Phelps, E. A. (2008). Emotional networks in the brain. In M. Lewis, J. M. Haviland-Jones, & L. F. Barrett (Eds.), *Handbook of emotions* (3rd ed., pp. 159–179). New York: Guilford Press.

Lee, F., Hallahan, M., & Herzog, T. (1996). Explaining real life events: How culture and domain shape attributions. *Personality and Social Psychology Bulletin, 22,* 732–741.

Lee, M., & Shlain, B. (1986). *Acid dreams: The complete social history of LSD: The CIA, the sixties, and beyond.* New York: Grove Press.

Lee, P. A. (1995). Physiology of puberty. In K. L. Becker (Ed.), *Principles and practice of endocrinology and metabolism* (pp. 822–830). Philadelphia: J. B. Lippincott.

Lehnert, B. (2007). Joint wave-particle properties of the individual photon. *Progress in Physics, 4*(10), 104–108.

Lehr, U., & Thomae, H. (1987). *Patterns of psychological aging. Results from the Bonne Aging Longitudinal Study (BOLSA).* Stuttgart, Germany: Enke.

LePort, A. K., Mattfeld, A. T., Dickinson-Anson, H., Fallon, J. H., Stark, C. E., Kruggel, F., et al. (2012). Behavioral and neuroanatomical investigation of Highly Superior Autobiographical Memory (HSAM). *Neurobiology of Learning and Memory, 98*(1), 78. doi:10.1016/j.nlm.2012.05.002

Leroy, C., & Symes, B. (2001). Teachers' perspectives on the family backgrounds of children at risk. *McGill Journal of Education, 36*(1), 45–60.

Levenson, R. W. (1992). Autonomic nervous system differences among emotions. *Psychological Sciences, 3,* 23–27.

Levy, B. R., Slade, M. D., Kunkel, S. R., & Kasl, S. V. (2002). Longevity increased by positive self-perceptions of aging. *Journal of Personality and Social Psychology, 83,* 261–269.

Lewis, D. K. (1996, June). A cross-cultural model for psychotherapy: Working with the African-American client. *Perspectives on Multiculturalism and Cultural Diversity,* VI(2).

Lewis, J. R. (1995). *Encyclopedia of afterlife beliefs and phenomenon.* Detroit, MI: Visible Ink Press.

Liechti, M. E., & Vollenweider, F. X. (2001). Which neuroreceptors mediate the subjective effects of MDMA in humans? A summary of mechanistic studies. *Human Psychopharmacology, 16,* 589–598.

Like, R., Steiner, P., & Rubel, A. (1996). Recommended core curriculum guidelines on culturally sensitive and competent care. *Family Medicine, 27,* 291–297.

Lilienfeld, S. O. (1999). Projective measures of personality and psychopathology: How well do they work? *Skeptical Inquirer, 23*(5), 32–39.

Lilienfeld, S. O., Wood, J. M., & Garb, H. N. (2000). The scientific status of projective techniques. *Psychological Science in the Public Interest, 1*(2), 27–66. doi:10.1111/1529-1006.002

Lim, Y. Y., Ellis, K. A., Pietrzak, R. H., Ames, D., Darby, D., Harrington, K., et al. (2012). Stronger effect of amyloid load than APOE genotype on cognitive decline in healthy older adults. *Neurology, 79*(16), 1645. doi:10.1212/WNL.0b013e31826e9ae6

Lin, C. S., Lyons, J. L., & Berkowitz, F. (2007). Somatotopic identification of language–SMA in language processing via fMRI. *Journal of Scientific and Practical Computing, 1*(2), 3–8.

Lin, P. J., & Schwanenflugel, P. J. (1995). Cultural familiarity and language factors in the structure of category knowledge. *Journal of Cross-Cultural Psychology, 26,* 153–168.

Lin, P. J., Schwanenflugel, P. J., & Wisenbaker, J. M. (1990). Category typicality, cultural familiarity, and the development of category knowledge. *Developmental Psychology, 26,* 805–813.

Lipsman, N., Woodside, D. B., Giacobbe, P., Hamani, C., Carter, J. C., Norwood, S. J., et al. (2013). Subcallosal cingulate deep brain stimulation for treatment-refractory anorexia nervosa: A phase 1 pilot trial. *Lancet, 381*(9875), 1361–1370. doi:10.1016/s0140-6736(12)62188-6

Lisanby, S. H., Maddox, J. H., Prudic, J., Devanand, D. P., & Sackeim, H. A. (2000). The effects of electroconvulsive therapy on memory of autobiographical and public events. *Archives of General Psychiatry, 57,* 581–590.

Livesley, J. W. (Ed.). (1995). *The DSM-IV personality disorders.* New York: Guilford Press.

Lizskowski, U., Carpenter, M., Striano, T., & Tomasello, M. (2006). 12- and 18-month-olds point to provide information for others. *Journal of Cognition and Development, 7,* 173–187.

Loehlin, J. C. (1992). *Genes and environment in personality development.* Newbury Park, CA: Sage.

Loehlin, J. C., McCrae, R. R., Costa, P. T., Jr., & John, O. P. (1998). Heritabilities of common and measure-specific components of the Big Five personality factors. *Journal of Research in Personality, 32,* 431–453.

Loehlin, J. C., Willerman, L., & Horn, J. M. (1985). Personality resemblances in adoptive families when the children are late-adolescent or adult. *Journal of Personality and Social Psychology, 48,* 376–392.

Loftus, E. (1975). Leading questions and the eyewitness report. *Cognitive Psychology, 7,* 560–572.

Loftus, E. F., Miller, D. G., & Burns, H. J. (1978). Semantic integration of verbal information into a visual memory. *Journal of Experimental Psychology: Human Learning, 4,* 19–31.

Loftus, J. (2001). America's liberalization in attitudes toward homosexuality, 1973 to 1998. *American Sociological Review, 66*(5), 762–782.

Loo, S. K., Hale, T. S., Macion, J., Hanada, G., McGough, J. J., McCracken, J. T., et al. (2009). Cortical activity patterns in ADHD during arousal, activation and sustained attention. *Neuropsychologia, 47*(10), 2114–2119.

Lord, T. R. (2001). 101 reasons for using cooperative learning in biology teaching. *The American Biology Teacher, 63*(1), 30–38.

Lovaas, O. I. (1987). Behavioral treatment and normal educational and intellectual functioning in young autistic children. *Journal of Consulting and Clinical Psychology, 55,* 3–9.

Lovaas, O. I., Berberich, J. P., Perloff, B. F., & Schaffer, B. (1966). Acquisition of imitative speech by schizophrenic children. *Science, 151,* 705–707.

Lu, S., & Ende, N. (1997). Potential for clinical use of viable pluripotent progenitor cells in blood bank stored human umbilical cord blood. *Life Sciences, 61,* 1113–1123.

Lubinski, D. (2000). Scientific and social significance of assessing individual differences: "Sinking shafts at a few critical points." *Annual Review of Psychology, 51,* 405–444.

Luborsky, L., Singer, B., & Luborsky, L. (1975). Comparative studies of psychotherapies: Is it true that "everyone has won and all must have prizes"? *Archives of General Psychiatry, 32,* 995–1008.

Luck, S. J., & Gold, J. M. (2008). The construct of attention in schizophrenia. *Biological Psychiatry, 64*(1), 34–39.

Lucy, J. A., & Shweder, R. A. (1979). Whorf and his critics: Linguistic and nonlinguistic influences on color memory. *American Anthropologist, 81,* 581–615.

Luria, A. R. (1965). Two kinds of motor perseveration in massive injury of the frontal lobes. *Brain, 88,* 1–10.

Luria, A. R. (1968). *The mind of a mnemonist* (pp. 24, 25). New York: Basic Books.

Lurito, J. T., Dzemidzic, M., Mathews, V. P., Lowe, M. J., Kareken, D. A., Phillips, M. D., & Wang, Y. (2000). Comparison of hemispheric lateralization using four language tasks. *Neuroimage, 11,* S358.

Lykken, D. T. (1995). *The antisocial personalities.* Hillsdale, NJ: Erlbaum.

Lykken, D. T., & Tellegen, A. (1996). Happiness is a stochastic phenomenon. *Psychological Science, 7,* 186–189.

Lynott, P. P., & Roberts, R. (1997). The developmental stake hypothesis and changing perceptions of intergenerational relations, 1971–1985. *The Gerontologist, 37,* 394–405.

Lytton, H., & Romney, D. M. (1991). Parents' sex-differentiated socialization of boys and girls: A meta-analysis. *Psychological Bulletin, 109,* 267–296.

MacCoun, R. J., & Kerr, N. L. (1988). Asymmetric influence in mock jury deliberation: Jurors' bias for leniency. *Journal of Personality and Social Psychology, 54,* 21–33.

MacDonald, A. P. (1970). Internal-external locus of control and the practice of birth control. *Psychological Reports, 27,* 206.

MacDonald, D., Kabani, N., Avis, D., & Evens, A. C. (2000). Automated 3D extraction of inner and outer surfaces of cerebral cortex from MRI. *Neuroimage, 12,* 340–356.

Maciejewski, P. K., Zhang, B., Block, S. D., & Prigerson, H. G. (2007). An empirical examination of the stage theory of grief. *The Journal of the American Medical Association, 297*(7), 716–723. doi:10.1001/jama.297.7.716

MacKenzie, S. B., Lutz, R. J., & Belch, G. E. (1986, May). The role of attitude toward the ad as a mediator of advertising effectiveness: A test of competing explanations. *Journal of Marketing Research, 23,* 130–143.

Macknik, S. L., & Martinez-Conde, S. (2009). Real magic: Future studies of magic should be grounded in neuroscience. *Nature Reviews: Neuroscience, 10*(3), 241–241.

Macknik, S. L., King, M., Randi, J., Robbins, A., Teller, Thompson, J., et al. (2008). Attention and awareness in stage magic: Turning tricks into research. *Nature Reviews: Neuroscience, 9*(11), 871–879.

Macquet, P., & Franck, G. (1996). Functional neuroanatomy of human rapid eye movement sleep and dreaming. *Nature, 383,* 163–166.

Macrae, C. N., & Bodenhausen, G. V. (2000). Social cognition: Thinking categorically about others. *Annual Review of Psychology, 51,* 93–120.

Madsen, K. M., Hviid, A., Vestergaard, M., Schendel, D., Wohlfahrt, J., Thorsen, P., et al. (2002). A population-based study of measles, mumps, rubella vaccine and autism. *New England Journal of Medicine, 347,* 1477–1482.

Mahoney, M. J. (2005). Constructivism and positive psychology. In C. R. Snyder & S. J. Lopez (Eds.), *Handbook of positive psychology* (pp. 745–750). New York: Oxford University Press.

Mahowald, M. W., & Schenck, C. H. (1996). NREM sleep parasomnias. *Neurologic Clinics, 14,* 675–696.

Maier, S. F., & Watkins, L. R. (1998). Cytokines for psychologists: Implications of bidirectional immune-to-brain communication for understanding behavior, mood, and cognition. *Psychological Review, 105,* 83–107.

Main, M., & Hesse, E. (1990). Parents' unresolved traumatic experiences are related to infant disorganized attachment status; is frightened and/or frightening parental behaviour the linking mechanism? In M. T. Greenberg, D. Cicchetti, & E. M. Cummings (Eds.), *Attachment in the preschool years: Theory, research and intervention* (pp. 161–182). Chicago: University of Chicago Press.

Main, M., & Solomon, J. (1990). Procedures for identifying infants as disorganized/disoriented during the Ainsworth Strange Situation. In M. T. Greenberg, D. Cicchetti, & E. M. Cummings (Eds.), *Attachment in the preschool years: Theory, research and intervention* (pp. 121–160). Chicago: University of Chicago Press.

Mandler, G. (1967). Organization and memory. In K. W. Spence & J. T. Spence (Eds.), *The psychology of learning and motivation,* (Vol. 1, pp. 327–372). New York: Academic Press.

Manning, R., Levine, M., & Collins, A. (2007). The kitty genovese murder and the social psychology of helping: The parable of the 38 witnesses. *American Psychologist, 62*(6), 555–562. doi: 10.1037/0003-066X.62.6.555

Manusov, V., & Patterson, M. L. (Eds.). (2006). *The Sage handbook of nonverbal communication* (p. 289). Thousand Oaks, CA: Sage.

March of Dimes Foundation, 2009. Organization of Teratology Information Specialists, 2011.

Margolin, S., & Kubic, L. S. (1944). An apparatus for the use of breath sounds as a hypnogogic stimulus. *American Journal of Psychiatry, 100,* 610.

Marik, P. E. (2000). Leptin, obesity, and obstructive sleep apnea. *Chest, 118,* 569–571.

Markovitz, J. H., Lewis, C. E., Sanders, P. W., Tucker, D., & Warnock, D. G. (1997). Relationship of diastolic blood pressure with cyclic GMP excretion among young adults (the CARDIA study): Influence of a family history of hypertension. *Journal of Hypertension, 15*(9), 955–962.

Marks, K. (2010, May 16). Round-the-world teenage sailor Jessica Watson gets hero's welcome in Australia. *The Christian Science Monitor.* Retrieved June 27, 2010, from http://www.csmonitor.com/World/Asia-Pacific/2010/0516/Round-the-world-teenage-sailor-Jessica-Watson-gets-hero-s-welcome-in-Australia

Markus, H. R., & Kitayama, S. (1991). Culture and the self: Implications for cognition, emotion, and motivation. *Psychological Review, 98*(2), 224–253.

Mars, A. E., Mauk, J. E., & Dowrick, P. (1998). Symptoms of pervasive developmental disorders as observed in prediagnostic home videos of infants and toddlers. *Journal of Pediatrics, 132,* 500–504.

Martin, C. L. (2000). Cognitive theories of gender development. In T. Eckes & H. M. Trautner (Eds.), *The developmental social psychology of gender* (pp. 91–121). Mahwah, NJ: Lawrence Erlbaum.

Martin, J. A., & Buckwalter, J. J. (2001). Telomere erosion and senescence in human articular cartilage chondrocytes. *Journal of Gerontology and Biological Science, 56*(4), 172–179.

Martínez-Frías, M. L., Bermejo, E., Mendioroz, J., Rodríguez-Pinilla, E., Blanco, M., Egüés, J., Félix, V., García, A., Huertas, H., Nieto, C., López, J. A., López, S., Paisán, L., Rosa, A., & Vázquez, M. S. (2009). Epidemiological and clinical analysis of a consecutive series of conjoined twins in Spain. *Journal of Pediatric Surgery, 44*(4), 811–820. doi: 10.1016/j.jpedsurg.2008.07.002

Martyn, A. C., De Jaeger, X., Magalhaes, A. C., Kesarwani, R., Goncalves, D. F., Raulic, S., et al. (2012). Elimination of the vesicular acetylcholine transporter in the forebrain causes hyperactivity and deficits in spatial memory and long-term potentiation. *Proceedings of the National Academy of Sciences, 109*(43), 17651–17656. doi:10.1073/pnas.1215381109

Maruta, T., Colligan, R. C., Malinchoc, M., & Offord, K. P. (2002, August). Optimism-pessimism assessed in the 1960s and self-reported health status 30 years later. *Mayo Clinic Proceedings, 77,* 748–753.

Maslow, A. (1943). A theory of human motivation. *Psychological Review, 50,* 370–396.

Maslow, A. (1954). *Motivation and personality.* New York: Harper & Row.

Maslow, A. (1971). *The farther reaches of human nature.* New York: Viking Press.

Maslow, A. (1987). *Motivation and personality* (3rd ed.). New York: Harper & Row.

Maslow, A., & Lowery, R. (Eds.). (1998). *Toward a psychology of being* (3rd ed.). New York: Wiley.

Massaro, D. W., & Cowan, N. (1993). Information processing models: Microscopes of the mind. *Annual Review of Psychology, 44,* 383–426.

Masson, J. M. (1984). *The assault on truth: Freud's suppression of the seduction theory.* New York: Farrar, Straus & Giroux.

Masters, J. C., Burish, T. G., Holton, S. D., & Rimm, D. C. (1987). *Behavior therapy: Techniques and empirical finding.* San Diego, CA: Harcourt Brace Jovanovich.

Masuda, T., & Kitayama, S. (2004). Perceiver-induced constraint and attitude attribution in Japan and the U.S.: A case for the cultural dependence of the correspondence bias. *Journal of Experimental Social Psychology, 40,* 409–416.

Matsumoto, D. (1993). Ethnic differences in affect intensity, emotion judgments, display rule attitudes, and self-reported emotional expression in an American sample. *Motivation and Emotion, 17*(2), 107–123.

Matsumoto, D. (1994). *People: Psychology from a cultural perspective* (pp. 144–147). Pacific Grove, CA: Brooks-Cole.

Matsumoto, D. (1999). *People: Psychology from a cultural perspective* (2nd ed.). Pacific Grove, CA: Brooks/Cole.

Matthew, N., & Dallery, J. (2007). Mercury rising: Exploring the vaccine-autism myth. *Skeptic, 13*(3). Retrieved May 3, 2010, from http://www.skeptic.com/eskeptic/07-06-20/#feature

Matthews, K. A., Gump, B. B., Harris, K. F., Haney, T. L., & Barefoot, J. C. (2004). Hostile behaviors predict cardiovascular mortality among men enrolled in the Multiple Risk Factor Intervention trial. *Circulation, 109,* 66–70.

Mavromatis, A. (1987). *Hypnagogia: The unique state of consciousness between wakefulness and sleep.* London: Routledge & Kegan Paul.

Mavromatis, A., & Richardson, J. T. E. (1984). Hypnagogic imagery. *International Review of Mental Imagery, 1,* 159–189.

Maxmen, J. S., Ward, N. G., & Kilgus, M. D. (2009). *Essential psychopathology and its treatment.* New York: W. W. Norton & Company.

Mayer, J. D., & Geher, G. (1996). Emotional intelligence and the identification of emotion. *Intelligence, 22,* 89–113.

Mayer, J. D., & Salovey, P. (1997). What is emotional intelligence? In P. Salovey & D. Sluyter (Eds.), *Emotional development and emotional intelligence: Educational implications* (pp. 3–31). New York: Basic Books.

Mayer, J. D., Roberts, R. D., & Barsade, S. G. (2008). Human abilities: Emotional intelligence. *Annual Review of Psychology, 59*(1), 507–536. doi:10.1146/annurev.psych.59.103006.093646

Mayer, J. D., Salovey, P., & Caruso, D. R. (2000). Models of emotional intelligence. In R. J. Sternberg (Ed.), *Handbook of human intelligence* (2nd ed., pp. 396–420). New York: Cambridge University Press.

Maziade, M., Bissonnette, L., Rouillard, E., Martinez, M., Turgeon, M., Charron, L., et al. (1997). 6P24-22 region and major psychoses in the Eastern Quebec population. *American Journal of Medical Genetics, 74,* 311–318.

McAdams, D. P., & Olson, B. D. (2010). Personality development: Continuity and change over the life course. *Annual Review of Psychology, 61,* 517–542. doi:10.1146/annurev.psych.093008.100507

McCann, S. J. H., & Stewin, L. L. (1988). Worry, anxiety, and preferred length of sleep. *Journal of Genetic Psychology, 149,* 413–418.

McCarty, C. A., Weisz, J. R., Wanitromanee, K., Eastman, K. L., Suwanlert, S., Chaiyasit, W., & Band, E. B. (1999). Culture, coping, and context: Primary and secondary control among Thai and American youth. *Journal of Child Psychology and Psychiatry, 40,* 809–818.

McCauley, C. (1998). Group dynamics in Janis's theory of groupthink: Backward and forward. *Organizational Behavior and Human Decision Processes, 73*(2–3), 142–162.

McClelland, D. C. (1961). *The achieving society.* Princeton, NJ: Van Nostrand.

McClelland, D. C. (1987). *Human motivation.* Cambridge, MA: Cambridge University Press.

McClelland, J. L., & Rumelhart, D. E. (1988). *Explorations in parallel distributed processing.* Cambridge, MA: MIT Press.

McCrae, R. R., & Costa, P. T., Jr. (1996). Toward a new generation of personality theories: Theoretical contexts for the five-factor model. In J. S. Wiggins (Ed.), *The five-factor model of personality: Theoretical perspectives* (pp. 51–87). New York: Guilford Press.

McCrae, R. R., & Terracciano, A. (2005). Universal features of personality traits from the observer's perspective: Data from 50 cultures. *Journal of Personality and Social Psychology, 88*(3), 547–561. doi:10.1037/0022-3514.88.3.547

McCrae, R. R., Martin, T. A., & Costa, P. T., Jr. (2005). Age trends and age norms for the NEO Personality Inventory-3 in adolescents and adults. *Assessment, 12*(4), 363–373. doi:10.1177/1073191105279724

McCrae, R. R., Terracciano, A., & 78 Members of the Personality Profiles of Cultures Project. (2005). Universal features of personality traits from the observer's perspective: Data from 50 cultures. *Journal of Personality and Social Psychology, 88*, 547–561.

McDermott, J. F. (2001). Emily Dickinson revisited: A study of periodicity in her work. *American Journal of Psychiatry, 158*(5), 686–690.

McDougall, W. (1908). *An introduction to social psychology.* London: Methuen & Co.

McEwen, B. S. (2000). The neurobiology of stress: From serendipity to clinical relevance. *Brain Research, 886*, 172–189.

McGaugh, J. L. (2004). The amygdala modulates the consolidation of memories of emotionally arousing experiences. *Annual Review Neuroscience, 27*, 1–28.

McGinn, L. K. (2000). Cognitive behavioral therapy of depression: Theory, treatment, and empirical status. *American Journal of Psychotherapy, 54*, 254–260.

McGinnis, J. M., & Foege, W. H. (1993). Actual causes of death in the United States. *Journal of the American Medical Association, 270*(18), 2207–2212.

McGrath, E., Keita, G. P., Strickland, B. R., & Russo, N. F. (1992). *Women and depression: Risk factors and treatment issues.* Washington, DC: American Psychological Association.

McGrath, R. E., & Carroll, E. J. (2012). The current status of 'projective' 'tests'. In H. Cooper, P. M. Camic, D. L. Long, A. T. Panter, D. Rindskopf, & K. J. Sher (Eds.), *APA handbook of research methods in psychology, Vol. 1: Foundations, planning, measures, and psychometrics* (pp. 329–348). Washington, DC: American Psychological Association.

McGregor, D. (1960). *The human side of enterprise.* New York: McGraw-Hill.

McLaughlin, S. K., & Margolskee, R. F. (1994). Vertebrate taste transduction. *American Scientist, 82*, 538–545.

McMahon, F. J., Akula, N., Schulze, T. G., Muglia, P., Tozzi, F., Detera-Wadleigh, S. D., et al. (2010). Meta-analysis of genome-wide association data identifies a risk locus for major mood disorders on 3p21.1. *Nature Genetics, 42*(2), 128–131. doi:10.1038/ng.523

McMonagle, T., & Sultana, A. (2002). Token economy for schizophrenia (Cochrane Review). In *The Cochrane Library, 2.* Oxford: Update Software.

McPherson, J. M., Smith-Lovin, L., & Cook, J. M. (2001). Birds of a feather: Homophily in social networks. *Annual Review of Sociology, 27*, 415–444.

Meador, B. D., & Rogers, C. R. (1984). Person-centered therapy. In R. J. Corsini (Ed.), *Current psychotherapies* (3rd ed., pp. 142–195). Itasca, IL: Peacock.

Mehrabian, A. (2000). Beyond IQ: Broad-based measurement of individual success potential or "emotional intelligence." *Genetic, Social, and General Psychology Monographs, 126*, 133–239.

Meikle, J., & Boseley, S. (2010, May 24). MMR row doctor Andrew Wakefield struck off register. *The Guardian* (London). Retrieved April 26, 2013, from http://www.guardian.co.uk/society/2010/may/24/mmr-doctor-andrew-wakefield-struck-off

Meineri, S., & Guéguen, N. (2008). An application of the foot-in-the-door strategy in the environmental field. *European Journal of Social Sciences, 7*, 71–74.

Mejía, O. L., & McCarthy, C. J. (2010). Acculturative stress, depression, and anxiety in migrant farmwork college students of Mexican heritage. *International Journal of Stress Management, 17*(1), 1–20.

Melzack, R., & Wall, P. D. (1996). *The challenge of pain.* London: Penguin Books.

Mennella, J. A., & Trabulsi, J. C. (2012). Complementary foods and flavor experiences: Setting the foundation. *Annals of nutrition & metabolism, 60*(Suppl. 2), 40–50. doi:10.1159/000335337

Menon, T., Morris, M., Chiu, C. Y., & Hong, Y. I. (1999). Culture and the construal of agency: Attribution to individual versus group dispositions. *Journal of Personality and Social Psychology, 76*, 701–727.

Mervis, C. B., & Rosch, E. (1981). Categorization of natural objects. *Annual Review of Psychology, 32*, 89–115.

Mesgarani, N., & Chang, E. F. (2012). Selective cortical representation of attended speaker in multi-talker speech perception. *Nature, 485*, 233–236. doi:10.1038/nature11020

Meyer, G. J., & Kurtz, J. E. (2006). Advancing personality assessment terminology: Time to retire 'objective' and 'projective' as personality test descriptors. *Journal of Personality Assessment, 87*(3), 223–225.

Meyrick, J. (2001). Forget the blood and gore: An alternative message strategy to help adolescents avoid cigarette smoking. *Health Education, 101*(3), 99–107.

Michaels, J. W., Blommel, J. M., Brocato, R. M., Linkous, R. A., & Rowe, J. S. (1982). Social facilitation and inhibition in a natural setting. *Replications in Social Psychology, 2*, 21–24.

Michalski, D., Mulvey, T., & Kohoout, J. (2010). *2008 American Psychological Association survey of psychology health service providers.* Retrieved April 5, 2010, from http://www.apa.org/workforce/publications/08-hsp/report.pdf

Mickelson, K. D., Kessler, R. C., & Shaver, P. R. (1997). Adult attachment in a nationally representative sample. *Journal of Personality and Social Psychology, 73*, 1092–1106.

Mikami, A. Y., Szwedo, D. E., Allen, J. P., Evans, M. A., & Hare, A. L. (2010). Adolescent peer relationships and behavior problems predict young adults' communication on social networking websites. *Developmental Psychology, 46*, 46–56.

Miles, D. R., & Carey, G. (1997). Genetic and environmental architecture of human aggression. *Journal of Personality and Social Psychology, 72*, 207–217.

Milgram, S. (1963). Behavioral study of obedience. *Journal of Abnormal and Social Psychology, 67*, 371–378. doi:10.1037/h0040525

Milgram, S. (1964b). Issues in the study of obedience: A reply to Baumrind. *American Psychologist, 19*, 848–852.

Milgram, S. (1974). *Obedience to authority: An experimental view.* New York: Harper & Row.

Miller, G. A. (1956). The magical number seven, plus or minus two: Some limits on our capacity for processing information. *Psychological Review, 63*, 81–97.

Miller, J. G. (1984). Culture and the development of everyday social explanation. *Journal of Personality and Social Psychology, 46*, 961–978.

Miller, L. H., & Smith, A. D. (1993). *The stress solution.* New York: Pocket Books.

Miller, M. E., & Bowers, K. S. (1993). Hypnotic analgesia: Dissociated experience or dissociated control? *Journal of Abnormal Psychology, 102*, 29–38.

Miller, M. N., & Pumariega, A. (1999). Culture and eating disorders. *Psychiatric Times, 16*(2), 1–4.

Miller, N. E., Sears, R. R., Mowrer, O. H., Doob, L. W., & Dollard, J. (1941). The frustration-aggression hypothesis. *Psychological Review, 48*, 337–342.

Miller, T. Q., Smith, T. W., Turner, C. W., Guijarro, M. L., & Hallet, A. J. (1996). A meta-analytic review of research on hostility and physical health. *Psychological Bulletin, 119*, 322–348.

Miller, T. Q., Turner, C. W., Tindale, R. S., Posavac, E. J., & Dugoni, B. L. (1991). Reasons for the trend toward null findings in research on type A behavior. *Psychological Bulletin, 110*, 469–485.

Mills, M. A., Edmondson, D., & Park, C. L. (2007). Trauma and stress response among Hurricane Katrina evacuees. *American Journal of Public Health, 97*(1), 116–123.

Milner, J. (1992, January). Risk for physical child abuse: Adult factors. *Violence Update*, 9–11.

Mintz, L. B., & Betz, N. E. (1988). Prevalence and correlates of eating disordered behaviors among undergraduate women. *Journal of Counseling Psychology, 35*, 463–471.

Mischel, W. (1966). A social learning view of sex differences in behaviour. In E. E. Maccoby (Ed.), *The development of sex differences* (pp. 56–81). Stanford, CA: Stanford University Press.

Mischel, W., & Shoda, Y. (1995). A cognitive-affective system theory of personality: Reconceptualizing situations, dispositions, dynamics, and invariances in personality structure. *Psychological Review, 102*, 246–268.

Mishell, D. R. (2001). Menopause. In M. A. Stenchever et al. (Eds.), *Comprehensive gynecology* (4th ed., pp. 1217–1258). St. Louis, MO: Mosby.

Missonnier, P., Hasler, R., Perroud, N., Herrmann, F. R., Millet, P., Richiardi, J., et al. (2013). EEG anomalies in adult ADHD subjects performing a working memory task. *Neuroscience.* doi:10.1016/j.neuroscience.2013.03.011

Mitchell, J. E., Pyle, R. L., & Eckert, E. D. (1981). Frequency and duration of binge-eating episodes in patients with bulimia. *American Journal of Psychiatry, 138,* 835–836.

Mitchell, J. E., Roerig, J., & Steffen, K. (2013). Biological therapies for eating disorders. *International Journal of Eating Disorders, 46*(5), 470–477. doi:10.1002/eat.22104

Mitchell, S. A., & Black, M. J. (1996). *Freud and beyond: A history of modern psychoanalytic thought* [Reprint ed.]. New York: HarperCollins.

Moffic, H. S. (2003). Seven ways to improve "cultural competence." *Current Psychiatry, 2*(5), 78.

Mogil, J. S. (1999). The genetic mediation of individual differences in sensitivity to pain and its inhibition. *Proceedings of the National Academy of Sciences, USA, 96*(14), 7744–7751.

Mokdad, A. H., Bowman, B. A., Ford, E. S., Dietz, W. H., Vinicor, F., Bales, V. S., et al. (2001). Prevalence of obesity, diabetes, and obesity related health risk factors. *Journal of the American Medical Association, 289,* 76–79.

Moldofsky, H. (1995). Sleep and the immune system. *International Journal of Immunopharmacology, 17*(8), 649–654.

Moll, H., & Tomasello, M. (2007). How 14- and 18-month-olds know what others have experienced. *Developmental Psychology, 43,* 309–317.

Möller, A., & Hell, D. (2002). Eugen Bleuler and forensic psychiatry. *International Journal of Law and Psychiatry, 25,* 351–360.

Money, J. (1994). *Sex errors of the body and related syndromes.* Baltimore: Paul H. Brookes.

Monson, C. M., Resick, P. A., & Rizvi, S. L. (2014). Posttraumatic stress disorder. In D. H. Barlow (Ed.), *Clinical handbook of psychological disorders: A step-by-step treatment manual* (5th ed., pp. 62–113). New York: Guilford Press.

Montgomery, C., & Fisk, J. E. (2008). Ecstasy-related deficits in the updating component of executive processes. *Human Psychopharmacology, 23*(6), 495–511.

Moody, R., & Perry, P. (1993). *Reunions: Visionary encounters with departed loved ones.* London: Little, Brown.

Moore, T. E. (1988). The case against subliminal manipulation. *Psychology and Marketing, 5,* 297–316.

Moore, T. H., Zammit, S., Lingford-Hughes, A., Barnes, T. R., Jones, P. B., Burke, M., et al. (2007). Cannabis use and risk of psychotic or affective mental health outcomes: A systematic review. *Lancet, 370,* 293–294, 319–328.

Moore-Ede, M. C., Sulzman, F. M., & Fuller, C. A. (1982). *The clocks that time us.* Cambridge, MA: Harvard University Press.

Moorhead, G., Neck, C. P., & West, M. S. (1998). The tendency toward defective decision making within self-managing teams: The relevance of groupthink for the 21st century. *Organizational Behavior and Human Decision Processes, 73*(2–3), 327–351.

Mora, G. (1985). History of psychiatry. In H. I. Kaplan & B. J. Sadock (Eds.), *Comprehensive textbook of psychiatry* (pp. 2034–2054). Baltimore: Williams & Wilkins.

Moreland, R. L., & Zajonc, R. B. (1982). Exposure effects in person perceptions: Familiarity, similarity, and attraction. *Journal of Experimental Social Psychology, 18*(5), 395–415.

Moreno-Manzano, V., Rodriguez-Jimenez, F. J., Acena-Bonilla, J. L., Fustero-Lardies, S., Erceg, S., Dopazo, J., et al. (2009). FM19G11, a new HIF modulator, affects stem cell differentiation status. *Journal of Biological Chemistry, 285*(2), 1333–1342.

Morgan, C. A., Rasmusson, A., Pietrzak, R. H., Coric, V., & Southwick, S. M. (2009). Relationships among plasma dehydroepiandrosterone and dehydroepiandrosterone sulfate, cortisol, symptoms of dissociation, and objective performance in humans exposed to underwater navigation stress. *Biological Psychiatry, 66*(4), 334–340.

Morgan, C. D., & Murray, H. A. (1935). A method for investigating fantasies: The Thematic Apperception Test. *Archives of Neurology and Psychiatry, 34,* 298–306.

Morishima, Y., Schunk, D., Bruhin, A., Ruff, C. C., & Fehr, E. (2012). Linking brain structure and activation in temporoparietal junction to explain the neurobiology of human altruism. *Neuron, 75*(1), 73–79. doi: 10.1016/j.neuron.2012.05.021

Morris, J. S., Friston, K. J., Buche, L. C., Frith, C. D., Young, A. W., Calder, A. J., et al. (1998). A neuromodulatory role for the human amygdala in processing emotional facial expressions. *Brain, 121,* 47–57.

Morris, M. W., & Peng, K. (1994). Culture and cause: American and Chinese attributions social and physical events. *Journal of Personality and Social Psychology, 67,* 949–971.

Morris, M., Nisbett, R. E., & Peng, K. (1995). Causal understanding across domains and cultures. In D. Sperber, D. Premack, & A. J. Premack (Eds.), *Causal cognition: A multidisciplinary debate* (pp. 577–612). Oxford, UK: Oxford University Press.

Morrow, C. E., Culbertson, J. L., Accornero, V. H., Xue, L., Anthony, J. C., & Bandstra, E. S. (2006). Learning disabilities and intellectual functioning in school-aged children with prenatal cocaine exposure. *Developmental Neuropsychology, 30*(3), 905–931.

Moscovici, S., & Zavalloni, M. (1969). The group as a polarizer of attitudes. *Journal of Personality and Social Psychology 12,* 125–135.

Mosher, W. D., Chandra, A., & Jones, J. (2005). *Sexual behavior and selected health measures: Men and women 15–44 years of age, United States, 2002* (Advance data from vital and health statistics; no 362). Hyattsville, MD: National Center for Health Statistics.

Motraghi, T. E., Seim, R. W., Meyer, E. C., & Morissette, S. B. (2013). Virtual reality exposure therapy for the treatment of posttraumatic stress disorder: A methodological review using consort guidelines. *Journal of Clinical Psychology.* doi:10.1002/jclp.22051

Mowat, F. (1988). *Woman in the mists: The story of Dian Fossey and the mountain gorillas of Africa.* New York: Warner Books.

Mroczek, D. K., Spiro, A., & Turiano, N. A. (2009). Do health behaviors explain the effect of neuroticism on mortality? Longitudinal findings from the VA Normative Aging Study. *Journal of Research in Personality, 43*(4), 653.

Muller-Oerlinghausen, B., Berghofer, A., & Bauer, M. (2002). Bipolar disorder. *Lancet, 359,* 241–247.

Murdock, B. B., Jr. (1962). The serial position effect in free recall. *Journal of Experimental Psychology, 64,* 482–488.

Murphy, L. R. (1995). Managing job stress: An employee assistance/human resource management partnership. *Personnel Review, 24*(1), 41–50.

Murray, S. L., Holmes, J. G., MacDonald, G., & Ellsworth, P. C. (1998). Through the looking glass darkly? When self-doubts turn into relationship insecurities. *Journal of Personality and Social Psychology, 75,* 1459–1480.

Muter, P. (1978). Recognition failure of recallable words in semantic memory. *Memory & Cognition, 6*(1), 9–12.

Myers, D. (1993). *The pursuit of happiness: Who is happy, and why?* New York: Avon.

Nadeau, K. G., Quinn, P., & Littman, E. (2001). *AD/HD self-rating scale for girls.* Springfield, MD: Advantage Books.

Najavits, L. M. (2007). Psychosocial treatments for posttraumatic stress disorder. In P. E. Nathan & J. M. Gorman (Eds.), *A guide to treatments that work* (3rd ed., pp. 513–530). New York: Oxford University Press.

Nasar, S. (1998). *A beautiful mind: A biography of John Forbes Nash, Jr., winner of the Nobel Prize in economics 1994.* New York: Simon & Schuster.

National Academy of Neuropsychology. (2001, May). *NAN definition of a clinical neuropsychologist* [Electronic version]. Retrieved April 13, 2010, from http://www.nanonline.org/NAN/Files/PAIC/PDFs/NANPositionDefNeuro.pdf

National Institute of Mental Health (NIMH). (2010). *The numbers count: Mental disorders in America.* Retrieved from http://www.nimh.nih.gov/health/publications/the-numbers-count-mental-disorders-in-america/index.shtml

National Institute of Mental Health. (2008). *Suicide in the U.S.: Statistics and Prevention* (NIH Publication No. 06-4594). Retrieved from http://www.nimh.nih.gov/health/publications/suicide-in-america/suicide-america-trifold_133257.pdf

National Institute on Alcoholism and Alcohol Abuse (NIAAA). (2007). *Data/statistical tables.* Retrieved July 25, 2007, from http://www.niaaa.nih.gov/Resources/DatabaseResources/QuickFacts/default.htm

National Institute on Drug Abuse (NIDA). (2002). Research report series—Prescription drugs: Abuse and addiction. National Institutes of Health (NIH). Retrieved July 19, 2008, from www.drugabuse.gov/ResearchReports/Prescription/prescription5.html

National Institute on Drug Abuse (NIDA). (2006, May). *NIDA Infofacts: MDMA (Ecstasy).* Retrieved May 5, 2010, from http://www.nida.nih.gov/Infofacts/ecstasy.html

National Safety Council. (2010). *National safety council estimates that at least 1.6 million crashes are caused each year by drivers using cell phones and texting.* Retrieved June 5, 2011, from http://www.nsc.org/Pages/NSCestimates16millioncrashescausedbydriversusingcellphonesandtexting.aspx

National Sleep Foundation (2009). Can't sleep? What to know about insomnia. Retrieved May 5, 2010, from http://sleepfoundation.org/sleep-disorders-problems/insomnia

Neale, M. C., Rushton, J. P., & Fulker, D. W. (1986). The heritability of items from the Eysenck Personality Questionnaire. *Personality and Individual Differences, 7,* 771–779.

Neimark, J. (1996). The diva of disclosure, memory researcher Elizabeth Loftus. *Psychology Today, 29*(1), 48–80.

Neimeyer, R. A., & Mitchell, K. A. (1998). Similarity and attraction: A longitudinal study. *Journal of Social and Personality Relationships, 5,* 131–148.

Neisser, U., & Harsch, N. (1992). Phantom flashbulbs: False recollections of hearing the news about challenger. In E. Winograd & U. Neisser (Eds.), *Affect and accuracy in recall: Studies of "flashbulb memories"* (pp. 9–31). New York: Cambridge University Press.

Nelson, C. A. (2011). Brain development and behavior. In A. M. Rudolph, C. Rudolph, L. First, G. Lister, & A. A. Gershon (Eds.), *Rudolph's pediatrics* (22nd ed.). New York: McGraw-Hill.

Nelson, D. B., Sammel, M. D., Freeman, E. W., Lin, H., Gracia, C. R., & Schmitz, K. H. (2008). Effect of physical activity on menopausal symptoms among urban women. *Medicine and Science in Sports & Exercise, 40*(1), 50–58.

Nestor, P. G., Kubicki, M., Niznikiewicz, M., Gurrera, R. J., McCarley, R. W., & Shenton, M. E. (2008). Neuropsychological disturbance in schizophrenia: A diffusion tensor imaging study. *Neuropsychology, 22*(2), 246–254.

Neto, F. (1995). Conformity and independence revisited. *Social Behavior and Personality, 23*(3), 217–222.

Neumarker, K. (1997). Mortality and sudden death in anorexia nervosa. *International Journal of Eating Disorders, 21,* 205–212.

Neville, H. J., & Bavelier, D. (2000). Specificity and plasticity in neurocognitive development in humans. In M. S. Gazzaniga (Ed.), *The new cognitive neurosciences* (2nd ed., pp. 83–99). Cambridge, MA: MIT Press.

Newcomb, M. D., & Harlow, L. L. (1986). Life events and substance use among adolescents: Mediating effects of perceived loss of control and meaninglessness in life. *Journal of Personality and Social Psychology, 51,* 564–577.

Nicholson, N., Cole, S., & Rocklin, T. (1985). Conformity in the Asch situation: A comparison between contemporary British and U.S. students. *British Journal of Social Psychology, 24,* 59–63.

Nickell, J. (1995). Crop circle mania wanes: An investigative update. *Skeptical Inquirer, 19*(3), 41–43.

Nickerson, R. S., & Adams, J. J. (1979). Long-term memory for a common object. *Cognitive Psychology, 11,* 287–307.

Niedermeyer, E. (2005). Historical aspects. In E. Niedermeyer & F. Lopes da Silva (Eds.), *Electroencephalography: Basic principles, clinical applications, and related fields* (5th ed., pp. 1–15). Philadelphia: Lippincott, Williams & Wilkins.

Nielsen, M., Suddendorf, T., & Slaughter, V. (2006). Mirror self-recognition beyond the face. *Child Development, 77,* 176–185.

Nieto, F., Young, T. B., Lind, B. K., Shahar, E., Samet, J. M., Redline, S., et al. (2000). Association of sleep-disordered breathing, sleep apnea, and hypertension in a large, community-based study. *Journal of the American Medical Association, 283*(14), 1829–1836.

Nigg, J. T. (2010). Attention-Deficit/Hyperactivity Disorder: Endophenotypes, structure, and etiological pathways. *Current Directions in Psychological Science, 19*(1), 24–29.

Nijenhuis, E. R. (2000). Somatoform dissociation: Major symptoms of dissociative disorders. *Journal of Trauma and Dissociation, 1*(4), 7–29.

Nikolajsen, L., & Jensen, T. S. (2001). Phantom limb pain. *British Journal of Anaesthesia, 87,* 107–116.

Nisbett, R. E., Aronson, J., Blair, C., Dickens, W., Flynn, J., Halpern, D. F., et al. (2012). Intelligence: New findings and theoretical developments. *American Psychologist, 67*(2), 130–159.

Nitsche, M. A., Boggio, P. S., Fregni, F., & Pascual-Leone, A. (2009). Treatment of depression with transcranial direct current stimulation (tDCS): A review. *Experimental Neurology, 219*(1), 14–19.

Nolen-Hoeksema, S. (1990). *Sex differences in depression.* Palo Alto, CA: Stanford University Press.

Nolen-Hoeksema, S. (2012). Emotion regulation and psychopathology: The role of gender. *Annual Review of Clinical Psychology, 8,* 161–187. doi:10.1146/annurevclinpsy-032511-143109

Norcross, J. C. (2005). A primer on psychotherapy integration. In J. C. Norcross & M. R. Goldfried (Eds.), *Handbook of psychotherapy integration* (2nd ed., pp. 3–23). New York: Oxford University Press.

Nordenskjold, A., von Knorring, L., & Engstrom, I. (2011). Predictors of time to relapse/recurrence after electroconvulsive therapy in patients with major depressive disorder: A population-based cohort study. *Depression Research and Treatment,* Article ID 470985. doi:10.1155/2011/470985

Norenzayan, A., Choi, I., & Nisbett, R. E. (1999). Eastern and Western perceptions of causality for social behavior: Lay theories about personalities and situations. In D. A. Prentice & D. T. Miller (Eds.), *Cultural divides* (pp. 239–272). New York: Russell Sage Foundation.

Norrbrink Budh, C., Lund, I., Hultling, C., Levi, R., Werhagen, L., Ertzgaard, P., et al. (2003). Gender-related differences in pain in spinal cord injured individuals. *Spinal Cord, 41,* 122–128.

Novella, S. (2007, November–December). The anti-vaccination movement. *Skeptical Inquirer.* Retrieved May 21, 2010, from http://www.csicop.org/si/show/anti-vaccination_movement/www.guardian.co.uk/science/2007/feb/24/badscience.uknews

Nyberg, L., & Tulving, E. (1996). Classifying human long-term memory: Evidence from converging dissociations. *European Journal of Cognitive Psychology, 8*(2), 163–183.

O'Connor, R. D. (1972). Relative efficacy of modeling, shaping, and the combined procedures for modification of social withdrawal. *Journal of Abnormal Psychology, 79,* 327–334.

Ocholla-Ayayo, A. B. C., Wekesa, J. M., & Ottieno, J. A. M. (1993). *Adolescent pregnancy and its implications among ethnic groups in Kenya* (Vol. 1, pp. 381–395). In International Population Conference, Montreal, Canada, International Union for the Scientific Study of Population.

Ochsner, K., & Kosslyn, S. M. (1994). Mental imagery. In V. S. Ramaschandran (Ed.), *Encyclopedia of human behavior.* New York: Academic Press.

Ohayon, M. M., Priest, R. G., Caulet, M., & Guilleminault, C. (1996). Hypnagogic and hypnopompic hallucinations: pathological phenomena? *British Journal of Psychiatry,169,* 459–467.

Öhman, A. (2008). Fear and anxiety. In M. Lewis, J. M. Haviland-Jones, & L. F. Barrett (Eds.), *Handbook of emotion* (3rd ed., pp. 709–729). New York: Guilford Press.

Olin, B. R. (Ed.). (1993). Central nervous system drugs, sedatives and hypnotics, barbiturates. In *Facts and comparisons drug information* (pp. 1398–1413). St. Louis, MO: Facts and Comparisons.

Oliver, J. E. (1993). Intergenerational transmission of child abuse: Rates, research, and clinical interpretations. *American Journal of Psychiatry, 150,* 1315–1324.

Ollendick, T. H., & King, N. J. (1998). Empirically supported treatments for children with phobic and anxiety disorders: Current status. *Journal of Clinical Child Psychology, 27*(2), 156–167.

Olsen, P. (1975). *Emotional flooding.* Baltimore: Penguin Books.

Olson, H. C., & Burgess, D. M. (1997). Early intervention for children prenatally exposed to alcohol and other drugs. In M. J. Guralnick (Ed.), *The effectiveness of early intervention* (pp. 109–146). Baltimore: Brookes.

Oman, C. M. (1990). Motion sickness: A synthesis and evaluation of the sensory conflict theory. *Canadian Journal of Physiological Pharmacology, 68,* 294–303.

Onken, L. S., Blaine, J. D., & Battjes, R. J. (1997). Behavioral therapy research: A conceptualization of a process. In S. W. Henggeler & A. B. Santos (Eds.), *Innovative approaches for difficult-to-treat populations* (pp. 477–485). Washington, DC: American Psychiatric Press.

Osshera, L., Flegala, K. E., & Lustiga, C. (2012). Everyday memory errors in older adults. *Aging, Neuropsychology, and Cognition, 20*(2), 220–242. doi:10.1080/13825585.2012.690365

Oster, J. R. (1987). The binge-purge syndrome: A common albeit unappreciated cause of acid-base and fluid-electrolyte disturbances. *Southern Medical Journal, 80,* 58–67.

Oswald, I. (1959). Sudden bodily jerks on falling asleep. *Brain, 82,* 92–103.

Overeem, S., Mignot, E., Gert van Dijk, J., & Lammers, G. J. (2001). Narcolepsy: Clinical features, new pathophysiological insights, and future perspectives. *Journal of Clinical Neurophysiology, 18*(2), 78–105.

Overmier, J. B., & Seligman, M. E. P. (1967). Effects of inescapable shock on subsequent escape and avoidance behavior. *Journal of Comparative Physiology and Psychology, 63,* 23–33.

Owen, A. M., Hampshire, A., Grahn, J. A., Stenton, R., Dajani, S., & Burns, A. S. (2010). Putting brain training to the test. *Nature, 465*(7299), 775–778.

Pajonk, F. G., Wobrock, T., Gruber, O., Scherk, H., Berner, D., Kaizl, I., et al. (2010). Hippocampal plasticity in response to exercise in schizophrenia. *Archives of General Psychiatry, 67*(2), 133–143.

Palva, J. M., Monto, S., Kulashekhar, S., & Palva, S. (2010). Neuronal synchrony reveals working memory networks and predicts individual memory capacity. *Proceedings of the National Academy of Sciences, USA, 107*(16), 7580–7585.

Pan, A. S. (2000). Body image, eating attitudes, and eating behaviors among Chinese, Chinese-American and non-Hispanic White women. *Dissertation Abstracts International, Section B: The Sciences and Engineering, 61*(1–B), 544.

Panksepp, J., Herman, B. H., Vilberg, T., Bishop, P., & Deeskinazi, F. G. (1980). Endogenous opioids and social behavior. *Neuroscience and Biobehavioral Reviews, 4,* 473–487.

Paparelli, A., Di Forti, M., Morrison, P. D., & Murray, R. M. (2011). Drug-induced psychosis: How to avoid star gazing in schizophrenia research by looking at more obvious sources of light. *Frontiers in Behavioral Neuroscience, 5,* 1. doi:10.3389/fnbeh.2011.00001

Pargament, K. I. (1997). *The psychology of religion and coping: Theory, research, and practice.* New York: Guilford Press.

Park, J., Turnbull, A. P., & Turnbull, H. R. (2002). Impacts of poverty on quality of life in families of children with disabilities. *Exceptional Children, 68,* 151–170.

Pavlov, I. P. (1906). The scientific investigation of the psychical faculties or processes in the higher animals. *Science, 24,* 613–619.

Pavlov, I. P. (1926). *Conditioned reflexes.* London: Oxford University Press.

Pavlov, I. P. (1927). *Conditioned reflexes: An investigation of the physiological activity of the cerebral cortex* (Translated and edited by G. V. Anrep). London: Oxford University Press.

Peng, K., Ames, D. R., & Knowles, E. D. (2000). Culture and human inference: Perspectives from three traditions. In D. Matsumoto (Ed.), *The handbook of culture and psychology* (pp. 245–264). New York: Oxford University Press.

Peplau, L. A., & Taylor, S. E. (1997). *Sociocultural perspectives in social psychology: Current readings.* Upper Saddle River, NJ: Prentice-Hall.

Pepperberg, I. M. (1998). Talking with Alex: Logic and speech in parrots. *Scientific American Presents: Exploring Intelligence, 9*(4), 60–65.

Pepperberg, I. M. (2007). Grey parrots do not always "parrot": The roles of imitation and phonological awareness in the creation of new labels from existing vocalizations. *Language Sciences, 29*(1), 1–13.

Pereira, M. A., Kartashov, A. I., Van Horn, L., Slattery, M., Jacobs, D. R., Jr., & Ludwig, D. S. (2003). Eating breakfast may reduce risk of obesity, diabetes, heart disease. Paper presented March 6 at the American Heart Association's 2003 Annual Conference on Cardiovascular Disease Epidemiology and Prevention in Miami, FL.

Perrin, S., & Spencer, C. P. (1980). The asch effect—a child of its time. *Bulletin of the British Psychological Society, 33,* 405–406.

Perrin, S., & Spencer, C. P. (1981). Independence or conformity in the Asch experiment as a reflection of cultural and situational factors. *British Journal of Social Psychology, 20*(3), 205–209.

Perrine, D. M. (1997). *The chemistry of mind-altering drugs.* Washington, DC: American Chemical Society.

Perry, W. G., Jr. (1970). *Forms of intellectual and ethical development in the college years: A scheme.* New York: Holt, Rinehart, and Winston.

Peters, W. A. (1971). *A class divided.* Garden City, NY: Doubleday.

Peterson, D. R. (1976). Need for the doctor of psychology degree in professional psychology. *American Psychologist, 31,* 792–798.

Peterson, D. R. (1982). Origins and development of the doctor of psychology concept. In G. R. Caddy, D. C. Rimm, N. Watson, & J. H. Johnson (Eds.), *Educating professional psychologists* (pp. 19–38). New Brunswick, NJ: Transaction Books.

Peterson, L. R., & Peterson, M. J. (1959). Short-term retention of individual items. *Journal of Experimental Psychology, 58,* 193–198.

Petitto, L. A., & Marentette, P. F. (1991). Babbling in the manual mode: Evidence for the ontogeny of language. *Science, 251,* 1493–1496.

Petitto, L. A., Holowka, S., Sergio, L. E., & Ostry, D. (2001). Language rhythms in baby hand movements. *Nature, 413,* 35.

Petri, H. (1996). *Motivation: Theory, research and application* (4th ed.). Belmont, CA: Wadsworth.

Petrides, G., Tobias, K. G., Kellner, C. H., & Rudorfer, M. V. (2011). Continuation and maintenance electroconvulsive therapy for mood disorders: A review of the literature. *Neuropsychobiology, 64*(3), 129–140. doi:10.1159/000328943

Petrova, P. K., Cialdini, R. B., & Sills, S., J. (2007). Compliance, consistency, and culture: Personal consistency and compliance across cultures. *Journal of Experimental Social Psychology, 43,* 104–111.

Pettigrew, J. D. (1999). *The Journal of Experimental Biology.* Retrieved October 29, 2014, from *The Journal of Experimental Biology* website: http://jeb.biologists.org/content/202/10/1447.full.pdf

Pettigrew, T. F., & Tropp, L. R. (2000). Does intergroup contact reduce prejudice? Recent meta-analytic findings. In S. Oskamp (Ed.), *Reducing prejudice and discrimination: Social psychological perspectives* (pp. 93–114). Mahwah, NJ: Erlbaum.

Petty, R. E. (1995). Attitude change. In A. Tesser (Ed.), *Advances in social psychology* (pp. 194–255). New York: McGraw-Hill.

Petty, R. E., & Cacioppo, J. (1986). *Communication and persuasion: Central and peripheral routes to attitude change.* New York: Springer-Verlag.

Petty, R. E., & Cacioppo, J. (1996). *Attitudes and persuasion: Classic and contemporary approaches* (reprint). Boulder, CO: Westview Press.

Petty, R. E., Wheeler, S. C., & Tormala, Z. L. (2003). Persuasion and attitude change. In T. Millon & M. J. Lerner (Eds.), *Handbook of psychology: Vol. 5: Personality and social psychology* (pp. 353–382). Hoboken, NJ: Wiley.

Pezdek, K., & Hodge, D. (1999). Planting false childhood memories in children: The role of event plausibility. *Child Development, 70,* 887–895.

Pezdek, K., Finger, K., & Hodge, D. (1997). Planting false childhood memories: The role of event plausibility. *Psychological Science, 8,* 437–441.

Phan, T., & Silove, D. (1999). An overview of indigenous descriptions of mental phenomena and the range of traditional healing practices amongst the Vietnamese. *Transcultural Psychiatry, 36,* 79–94.

Piaget, J. (1926). *The language and thought of the child.* New York: Harcourt Brace.

Piaget, J. (1952). *The origins of intelligence in children.* New York: Norton.

Piaget, J. (1962). *Play, dreams and imitation in childhood.* New York: Norton.

Piaget, J. (1983). Piaget's theory. In W. Kessen (Ed.), *Handbook of child psychology: Vol. 1: Theoretical models of human development* (pp. 103–128). New York: Wiley.

Pilkington, J. (1998). "Don't try and make out that I'm nice": The different strategies women and men use when gossiping. In J. Coates (Ed.), *Language and gender: A reader* (pp. 254–269). Oxford, UK: Blackwell.

Pinker, S. (1995). Language acquisition. In L. R. Gleitman & M. Liberman (Eds.), *An invitation to cognitive science* (2nd ed., pp. 135–182). Cambridge: MIT Press.

Pinker, S., & Bloom, P. (1990). Natural language and natural selection. *Behavioral and Brain Sciences, 13*(4), 707–784.

Pinsof, W. M., & Wynne, L. C. (1995). The efficacy of marital and family therapy: An empirical overview, conclusions, and recommendations. *Journal of Marital and Family Therapy, 21,* 585–613.

Pizarro, D. A., & Salovey, P. (2002). On being and becoming a good person: The role of emotional intelligence in moral development and behavior. In J. Aronson (Ed.), *Improving academic achievement: Impact of psychological factors on education* (pp. 247–266). San Diego, CA: Academic Press.

Plaut, D. C., & McClelland, J. L. (2010). Locating object knowledge in the brain: A critique of Bowers' (2009) attempt to revive the grandmother cell hypothesis. *Psychological Review, 117*, 284–288.

Plomin, R. (1994). The nature of nurture: The environment beyond the family. In R. Plomin (Ed.), *Genetics and experience: The interplay between nature and nurture* (pp. 82–107). Thousand Oaks, CA: Sage.

Plomin, R. N. L., Pederson, G. E., McClearn, J. R., Nesselroade, C. S., & Bergman, H. F. (1988). EAS temperaments during the last half year of the life span: Twins reared apart and twins raised together. *Psychology of Aging, 4*, 43–50.

Plomin, R., & DeFries, J. C. (1998, May). Genetics of cognitive abilities and disabilities. *Scientific American*, 62–69.

Plomin, R., & Spinath, F. M. (2004). Intelligence: Genetics, genes, and genomics. *Journal of Personality and Social Psychology, 86*(1), 112–129.

Plomin, R., Owen, M. J., & McGuffin, P. (1994). The genetic basis of complex human behaviors. *Science, 264*(5166), 1733–1739.

Plug, C., & Ross, H. E. (1994). The natural moon illusion: A multi-factor angular account. *Perception, 23*, 321–333.

Pogue-Geile, M. F., & Yokley, J. L. (2010). Current research on the genetic contributors to schizophrenia. *Current Directions in Psychological Science, 19*, 214–219. doi:10.1177/0963721410378490. Retrieved from http://cdp.sagepub.com/content/19/4/214.abstract

Polce-Lynch, M., Myers, B. J., Kilmartin, C. T., Forssmann-Falck, R., & Kliewer, W. (1998). Gender and age patterns in emotional expression, body image, and self-esteem: A qualitative analysis. *Sex Roles, 38*, 1025–1050.

Polgreen, L. (2010, July 31). India digs under top of the world to match rival. *New York Times*. Retrieved from http://www.nytimes.com/2010/08/01/world/asia/01pass.html

Pope, H. G., Poliakoff, M. B., Parker, M. P., Boynes, M., & Hudson, J. I. (2007). Is dissociative amnesia a culture-bound syndrome? Findings from a survey of historical literature. *Psychological Medicine, 37*(2), 225–233.

Pormerleau, C. S., & Pormerleau, O. F. (1994). Euphoriant effects of nicotine. *Tobacco Control, 3*, 374.

Posthuma, D., de Geus, E. J. C., & Deary, I. J. (2009). The genetics of intelligence. In T. E. Goldberg & D. R. Weinberger (Eds.), *The genetics of cognitive neuroscience*. Cambridge, MA: The MIT Press.

Postman, L. (1975). Tests of the generality of the principle of encoding specificity. *Memory and Cognition, 3*, 663–672.

Powell, R. A. (2010). Little Albert still missing. *American Psychologist, 65*(4), 299–300. doi:10.1037/a0019288

Powers, M. H. (1984). A computer-assisted problem-solving method for beginning chemistry students. *The Journal of Computers in Mathematics and Science Teaching, 4*(1), 13–19.

Pratkanis, A. R., & Greenwald, A. G. (1988). Recent perspectives on unconscious processing: Still no marketing applications. *Psychology and Marketing, 5*, 337–353.

Pratt, J. A. (1991). Psychotropic drug tolerance and dependence: Common underlying mechanisms? In E. Pratt (Ed.), *The biological bases of drug tolerance and dependence* (pp. 2–28). London: Academic Press/Harcourt Brace Jovanovich.

Preston, J. D., O'Neal, J. H., & Talaga, M. C. (2008). *Handbook of clinical psychopharmacology for therapists* (5th ed.). Oakland, CA: New Harbinger Publications.

Priester, J. M., & Petty, R. E. (1995). Source attributions and persuasion: Perceived honesty as a determinant of message scrutiny. *Personality and Social Psychology Bulletin, 21*, 637–654.

Prigerson, H. G., Bierhals, A. J., Kasi, S. V., Reynolds, C. F., Shear, M. K., Day, N., et al. (1997). Traumatic grief as a risk factor for mental and physical morbidity. *American Journal of Psychiatry, 154I*, 616–623.

Prochaska, J. O., & Norcross, J. C. (2003). *Systems of psychotherapy* (5th ed.). Belmont, CA: Wadsworth.

Prochaska, J. O., & Norcross, J. C. (2009). *Systems of psychotherapy: A transtheoretical analysis*. Belmont, CA: Brooks/Cole, Cengage Learning.

Puetz, T. W., Flowers, S. S., & O'Connor, P. J. (2008). A randomized controlled trial of the effect of aerobic exercise training on feelings of energy and fatigue in sedentary young adults with persistent fatigue. *Psychotherapy and Psychosomatics, 77*(3), 167–174.

Pumariega, A. J., & Gustavson, C. R. (1994). Eating attitudes in African-American women: The essence. *Eating Disorders: Journal of Treatment and Prevention, 2*, 5–16.

Putnam, S. P., & Stifter, C. A. (2002). Development of approach and inhibition in the first year: Parallel findings for motor behavior, temperament ratings and directional cardiac response. *Developmental Science, 5*, 441–451.

Quintero, J. E., Kuhlman, S. J., & McMahon, D. G. (2003). The biological clock nucleus: A multiphasic oscillator network regulated by light. *Journal of Neuroscience, 23*, 8070–8076.

Raaijmakers, J. G. W., & Shiffrin, R. M. (1992). Models for recall and recognition. *Annual Review of Psychology, 43*, 205–234.

Rabins, P., Appleby, B. S., Brandt, J., DeLong, M. R., Dunn, L. B., Gabriels, L., et al. (2009). Scientific and ethical issues related to deep brain stimulation for disorders of mood, behavior, and thought. *Archives of General Psychiatry, 66*(9), 931–937.

Rachman, S. (1990). The determinants and treatments of simple phobias. *Advances in Behavioral Research and Therapy, 12*(1), 1–30.

Rachman, S. J., & Hodgson, R. J. (1980). *Obsessions and compulsions*. Englewood Cliffs, NJ: Prentice Hall.

Raikkonen, K., Matthews, K. A., & Salomon, K. (2003). Hostility predicts metabolic syndrome risk factors in children and adolescents. *Health Psychology, 22*, 279–286.

Rainforth, M. V., Schneider, R. H., Nidich, S. I., Gaylord-King, C., Salerno, J. W., & Anderson, J. W. (2007). Stress reduction programs in patients with elevated blood pressure: A systematic review and meta-analysis. *Current Hypertension Reports, 9*, 520–528.

Ramachandran, V. S., & Blakeslee, S. (1998). *Phantoms in the brain*. New York: Quill William Morrow.

Ramon y Cajal, S. (1995). *Histology of the nervous system of man and vertebrates* (English translation by N. Swanson & L. M. Swanson). New York: Oxford University Press.

Rapoport, J. L., Addington, A. M., Frangou, S., & Psych, M. R. (2005). The neurodevelopmental model of schizophrenia: Update 2005. *Molecular Psychiatry, 10*(5), 434–449. doi:10.1038/sj.mp.4001642

Rapoport, J. L., Giedd, J. N., & Gogtay, N. (2012). Neurodevelopmental model of schizophrenia: Update 2012. *Molecular Psychiatry, 17*(12), 1228–1238. doi:10.1038/mp.2012.23

Ratey, J. J., & Hagerman, E. (2008). *Spark: The revolutionary new science of exercise and the brain*. New York: Little, Brown and Company.

Raynor, H. A., & Epstein, L. H. (2001). Dietary variety, energy regulation and obesity. *Psychological Bulletin, 127*(3), 325–341.

Reason, J. T., & Brand, J. J. (1975). *Motion sickness*. London: Academic Press.

Rechtschaffen, A., & Kales, A. (1968). *A manual of standardized terminology, techniques, and scoring system for sleep stages of human subjects*. Washington, DC: U.S. Department of Health, Education, and Welfare Public Health Service—NIH/NIND.

Reese, H. W. (2010). Regarding Little Albert. *American Psychologist, 65*(4), 300–301. doi:10.1037/a0019332

Reichborn-Kjennerud, T. (2008). Genetics of personality disorders. *Psychiatric Clinics of North America, 31*, 421.

Reichborn-Kjennerud, T., Czajkowski, N., Neale, M. C., Orstavik, R. E., Torgersen, S., Tambs, K., et al. (2007). Genetic and environmental influences on dimensional representations of DSM-IV cluster C personality disorders: A population-based multivariate twin study. *Psychological Medicine, 37*(5), 645–653. doi:10.1017/s0033291706009548

Reinders, A., Quak, J., Nijenhuis, E. R., Korf, J., Paans, A. M., Willemsen, A. T., & den Boer, J. A. (2001, June). *Identity state-dependent processing of neutral and traumatic scripts in dissociative identity disorder as assessed by PET*. Oral presentation at the 7th Annual Meeting of the Organisation for Human Brain Mapping, Brighton, UK.

Reiner, W. G. (1999). Assignment of sex in neonates with ambiguous genitalia. *Current Opinions in Pediatrics, 11*(4), 363–365.

Reiner, W. G. (2000, September 29). *The genesis of gender identity in the male: Prenatal androgen effects on gender identity and gender role*. Oral presentation at New York University Child Study Center, Grand Rounds Summary, New York.

Reisenzein, R. (1983). The Schachter theory of emotion: Two decades later. *Psychological Bulletin, 94,* 239–264.

Reisenzein, R. (1994). Pleasure-arousal theory and the intensity of emotions. *Journal of Personality and Social Psychology, 7*(6), 1313–1329.

Renchler, R. (1993). *Poverty and learning* (ERIC Digest No. 83). Eugene, OR: ERIC Clearinghouse on Educational Management. (ERIC Document Reproduction Service No. ED 357 433)

Renner, M. J., & Mackin, R. S. (1998). A life stress instrument for classroom use. *Teaching of Psychology, 25,* 47.

Rescorla, R. A. (1988). Pavlovian conditioning—it's not what you think. *American Psychologist, 43,* 151–160.

Rezvani, A. H., & Levin, E. D. (2001). Cognitive effects of nicotine. *Biological Psychiatry, 49,* 258–267.

Rice, W. R., Friberg, U., & Gavrilets, S. (2012). Homosexuality as a consequence of epigenetically canalized sexual development. *The Quarterly Review of Biology, 87*(4), 344–368.

Richards, C. F., & Lowe, R. A. (2003). Researching racial and ethnic disparities in emergency medicine. *Academic Emergency Medicine, 10*(11), 1169–1175.

Rideout, V. J., Foehr, U. G., & Roberts, D. F. (2010). *Generation M2: Media in the lives of 8- to 18-year-olds.* Menlo Park, CA: Henry J. Kaiser Family Foundation.

Ridley, M. (1999). *Genome: The autobiography of a species in 23 chapters.* London: Fourth Estate.

Ridley, M. (2002). Crop circle confession. *Scientific American.* Retrieved February 17, 2010, from http://www.scientificamerican.com/article/crop-circle-confession/

Rieber, R. W., & Robinson, D. K. (2001). *Wilhelm Wundt in history: The making of a scientific psychology.* New York: Kluwer Academic.

Rijsdijk, F. V., Gottesman, I. I., McGuffin, P., & Cardno, A. G. (2011). Heritability estimates for psychotic symptom dimensions in twins with psychotic disorders. *American Journal of Medical Genetics Part B, Neuropsychiatric Genetics, 156B*(1), 89–98. doi:10.1002/ajmg.b.31145

Ritchey, M., LaBar, K. S., & Cabeza, R. (2011). Level of processing modulates the neural correlates of emotional memory formation. *Journal of Cognitive Neuroscience, 4,* 757–775.

Ritts, V. (1999). *Infusing culture into psychopathology: A supplement for psychology instructors.* Retrieved June 19, 2004, from www.stlcc.cc.mo.us/mc/users/vritts/psypath.htm

Ro, E., & Clark, L. A. (2009). Psychosocial functioning in the context of diagnosis: Assessment and theoretical issues. *Psychological Assessment, 21*(3), 313–324.

Roberto, C. A., Baik, J., Harris, J. L., & Brownell, K. D. (2010). Influence of licensed characters on children's taste and snack preferences. *Pediatrics.* Retrieved from http://pediatrics.aappublications.org/content/early/2010/06/21/peds.2009-3433.abstract

Robinson, J. W., & Preston, J. D. (1976). Equal status contact and modification of racial prejudice: A reexamination of the contact hypothesis. *Social Forces, 54,* 911–924.

Robinson, P. (1993). *Freud and his critics.* Berkeley: University of California Press.

Rodin, J. (1981). Current status of the internal-external hypothesis for obesity. *American Psychologist, 36,* 361–372.

Rodin, J. (1985). Insulin levels, hunger, and food intake: An example of feedback loops in body weight regulation. *Health Psychology, 4,* 1–24.

Roediger, H. L. (1990). Implicit memory: Retention without remembering. *American Psychologist, 45,* 1043–1056.

Roediger, H. L., III, & Guynn, M. J. (1996). Retrieval processes. In E. L. Bjork & R. A. Bjork (Eds.), *Memory* (pp. 197–236). New York: Academic Press.

Roediger, H. L., III. (2000). Why retrieval is the key process to understanding human memory. In E. Tulving (Ed.), *Memory, consciousness and the brain: The Tallinn Conference* (pp. 52–75). Philadelphia: Psychology Press.

Roffman, R. A., Stephens, R. S., Simpson, E. E., & Whitaker, D. L. (1988). Treatment of marijuana dependence: Preliminary results. *Journal of Psychoactive Drugs, 20*(1), 129–137.

Roffwarg, H. P., Muzio, J. N., & Dement, W. C. (1966). Ontogenetic development of the human sleep-dream cycle. *Science, 152*(3722), 604–619.

Rogers, C. R. (1951). *Client-centered therapy.* Boston: Houghton Mifflin Co.

Rogers, C. R. (1961). *On becoming a person: A therapist's view of psychotherapy.* Boston: Houghton/Mifflin.

Rogers, R. W., & Mewborn, C. R. (1976). Fear appeals and attitude change: Effects of a threat's noxiousness, probability of occurrence, and the efficacy of the coping responses. *Journal of Personality and Social Psychology, 34,* 54–61.

Rogoff, B. (1994). Developing understanding of the idea of communities of learners. *Mind, Culture, and Activity, 1*(4), 209–229.

Rohde, P., Silva, S. G., Tonev, S. T., Kennard, B. D., Vitiello, B., Kratochvil, C. J., et al. (2008). Achievement and maintenance of sustained improvement during TADS continuation and maintenance therapy. *Archives of General Psychiatry, 65*(4), 447–455.

Roid, G. H. (2003). *Stanford-Binet intelligence scales* (5th ed.). Itasca, IL: Riverside.

Roper, G., Rachman, S., & Marks, I. (1975). Passive and participant modeling in exposure treatment of obsessive-compulsive neurotics. *Behaviour Research and Therapy, 13,* 271–279.

Ros, T., Theberge, J., Frewen, P. A., Kluetsch, R., Densmore, M., Calhoun, V. D., et al. (2013). Mind over chatter: Plastic up-regulation of the Fmri salience network directly after EEG neurofeedback. *Neuroimage, 65,* 324–335. doi:10.1016/j.neuroimage.2012.09.046

Rosch, E. (1973). On the internal structure of perceptual and semantic categories. In T. E. Moore (Ed.), *Cognitive development and the acquisition of language* (pp. 111–144). New York: Academic Press.

Rosch, E. (1977). Human categorization. In N. Warren (Ed.), *Advances in cross-cultural psychology* (Vol. 1, pp. 1–72). London: Academic Press.

Rosch, E., & Mervis, C. B. (1975). Family resemblances: Studies in the internal structures of categories. *Cognitive Psychology, 7,* 573–605.

Rosch-Heider, E. (1972). Universals in color naming and memory. *Journal of Experimental Psychology, 93,* 10–20.

Rosch-Heider, E., & Olivier, D. C. (1972). The structure of the color space in naming and memory for two languages. *Cognitive Psychology, 3,* 337–354.

Rose, S., Kamin, L. J., & Lewontin, R. C. (1984). *Not in our genes: Biology, ideology and human nature.* Harmondsworth, UK: Penguin.

Rosenbloom, T., Shahar, A., Perlman, A., Estreich, D., & Kirzner, E. (2007). Success on a practical driver's license test with and without the presence of another testee. *Accident Analysis & Prevention, 39*(6), 1296–1301.

Rosenhan, D. L. (1973), On being sane in insane places, *Science, 179,* 250–258.

Rosenman, R. H., Brand, R. I., Jenkins, C. D., Friedman, M., Straus, R., & Wurm, M. (1975). Coronary heart disease in the Western Collaborative Group Study, final follow-up experience of 2 years. *Journal of the American Medical Association, 233,* 812–817.

Rosenthal, A. M. (1964). *Thirty-eight witnesses: The Kitty Genovese case.* New York: McGraw-Hill.

Rosenthal, R., & Jacobson, L. (1968). *Pygmalion in the classroom.* New York: Holt, Rinehart & Winston.

Ross, H. E., & Ross, G. M. (1976). Did Ptolemy understand the moon illusion? *Perception, 5,* 377–385.

Rossini, P. M., Altamura, C., Ferreri, F., Melgari, J. M., Tecchio, F., Tombini, M., et al. (2007). Neuroimaging experimental studies on brain plasticity in recovery from stroke. *Eura Medicophys, 43*(2), 241–254.

Rothbaum, B. O., Hodges, L. F., Kooper, R., Opdyke, D., Williford, J. S., & North, M. (1995). Effectiveness of computer-generated (virtual reality) graded exposure in the treatment of acrophobia. *American Journal of Psychiatry, 152,* 626–628.

Rothbaum, R., Weisz, J., Pott, M., Miyake, K., & Morelli, G. (2000). Attachment and culture: Security in Japan and the U.S. *American Psychologist, 55,* 1093–1104.

Rotter, J. B. (1966). Generalized expectancies for internal versus external control of reinforcements. *Psychological Monographs, 80*(Whole no. 609).

Rotter, J. B. (1978). Generalized expectancies for problem solving and psychotherapy. *Cognitive Therapy and Research, 2,* 1–10.

Rotter, J. B. (1981). The psychological situation in social learning theory. In D. Magnusson (Ed.), *Toward a psychology of situations: An interactional perspective*. Hillsdale, NJ: Erlbaum.

Rotter, J. B. (1990). Internal versus external control of reinforcement: A case history of a variable. *American Psychologist, 45,* 489–493.

Rotton, J., & Frey, J. (1985). Air pollution, weather, and violent crime: Concomitant time-series analysis of archival data. *Journal of Personality and Social Psychology, 49,* 1207–1220.

Rotton, J., Frey, J., Barry, T., Milligan, M., & Fitzpatrick, M. (1979). The air pollution experience and physical aggression. *Journal of Applied Social Psychology, 9,* 397–412.

Rouru, J., Wesnes, K., Hänninen, J., Murphym M., Riordan, H., & Rinne, J. (2013, March 16–23). *Safety and efficacy of ORM-12741 on cognitive and behavioral symptoms in patients with Alzheimer's disease: A randomized, double-blind, placebo-controlled, parallel group, multicenter, proof-of-concept 12 week study.* Paper presented at American Academy of Neurology 65th Annual Meeting, San Diego, CA.

Rouse, B. A. (1998). *Substance and mental health statistics source book.* Rockville, MD: Department of Health and Human Services, Substance Abuse and Mental Health Services Administration (SAMHSA).

Rowan, J. (2001). *Ordinary ecstasy.* Hove, UK: Brunner-Routledge.

Roysircai-Sodowsky, G. R., & Maestas, M. V. (2000). Acculturation, ethnic identity, and acculturative stress: Evidence and measurement. In R. H. Dana (Ed.), *Handbook of cross-cultural and multicultural assessment* (pp. 131–172). Mahwah, NJ: Erlbaum.

Ruble, D., Alvarez, J., Bachman, M., Cameron, J., Fuligni, A., Garcia Coll, C., et al. (2004). The development of a sense of "we": The emergence and implications of children's collective identity. In M. Bennett & F. Sani (Eds.), *The development of the social self.* New York: Psychology Press.

Rudd, P., & Osterberg, L. G. (2002). Hypertension: Context, pathophysiology, and management. In E. J. Topol (Ed.), *Textbook of cardiovascular medicine* (pp. 91–122). Philadelphia: Lippincott, Williams & Wilkins.

Rudmin, F.W. (2010). Steps towards the renovation of acculturation research paradigms: What scientists' personal experiences of migration might tell science. *Culture and Psychology, 16*(3), 299–312, http://cap.sagepub.com/, accessed 9 October 2010.

Ruhe, H. G., Mason, N. S., & Schene, A. H. (2007). Mood is indirectly related to serotonin, norepinephrine and dopamine levels in humans: A meta-analysis of monoamine depletion studies. *Molecular Psychiatry, 12*(4), 331–359.

Ruiz, S., Birbaumer, N., & Sitaram, R. (2013). Abnormal neural connectivity in schizophrenia and fmri-brain-computer interface as a potential therapeutic approach. *Frontiers in Psychiatry, 4,* 17. doi:10.3389/fpsyt.2013.00017

Rumelhart, D. E., Hinton, G. E., & McClelland, J. L. (1986). A general framework for parallel distributed processing. In D. E. Rumelhart, J. L. McClelland, & the PDP Research Group (Eds.), *Parallel distributed processing: Explorations in the microstructure of cognition: Vol. 1. Foundations* (pp. 45–76). Cambridge, MA: MIT Press.

Ruscio, A. M., Borkovec, T. D., & Ruscio, J. (2001). A taxometric investigation of the latent structure of worry. *Journal of Abnormal Psychology, 110,* 413–422.

Russell, D. E. (1986). *The secret trauma: Incest in the lives of girls and women.* New York: Basic Books.

Rutherford, A. (2000). Mary Cover Jones (1896–1987). *The Feminist Psychologist, 27*(3), 25.

Ryan, R. M., & Deci, E. L. (2000). Intrinsic and extrinsic motivations: Classic definitions and new directions. *Contemporary Educational Psychology, 25,* 54–67.

Ryan, R. M., Chirkov, V. I., Little, T. D., Sheldon, K. M., Timoshina, E. L., & Deci, E. L. (1999). The American dream in Russia: Extrinsic aspirations and well-being in two cultures. *Personality and Social Psychology Bulletin, 25,* 1509–1524.

Sabatini, E., Della Penna, S., Franciotti, R., Ferretti, A., Zoccolotti, P., Rossini, P. M., et al. (2009). Brain structures activated by overt and covert emotional visual stimuli. *Brain Research Bulletin, 79*(5), 258–264.

Sackett, P. R., Borneman, M. J., & Connelly, B. S. (2008). High stakes testing in higher education and employment: Appraising the evidence for validity and fairness. *American Psychologist, 63*(4), 215–227. doi:10.1037/0003-066X.63.4.215

Sacks, D. P., Bushman, B. J., & Anderson, C. A. (2011). Do violent video games harm children? Comparing the scientific amicus curiae "experts" in *Brown v Entertainment Merchants Association. Northwestern University Law Review Colloquy, 106,* 1–12.

Sacks, O. (1990). *The man who mistook his wife for a hat and other clinical tales.* New York: HarperPerennial.

Sadker, M., & Sadker, D. (1994). *Failing at fairness: How America's schools cheat girls.* New York: Scribner.

Sadock, B. J., Kaplan, H. I., & Sadock, V. A. (2007). *Kaplan & Sadock's synopsis of psychiatry: Behavioral sciences/clinical psychiatry* (10th ed.). Philadelphia, PA: Lippincott Williams & Wilkins.

Sagan, C. (1977). *The dragons of Eden: Speculations on the evolution of human intelligence.* New York: Random House.

Saha, S., Chant, D., Welham, J., & McGrath, J. (2005). A systematic review of the prevalence of schizophrenia. *PLoS Medicine, 2*(5), e141.

Salamone, J. D., & Correa, M. (2012). The mysterious motivational functions of mesolimbic dopamine. *Neuron, 76*(3), 470–485.

Salend, S. J. (1987). Contingency management systems. *Academic Therapy, 22,* 245–253.

Salovey, P., & Mayer, J. D. (1990). Emotional intelligence. *Imagination, Cognition, and Personality, 9,* 185–211.

Salovey, P., Rothman, A. J., Detweiler, J. B., & Steward, W. (2000). Emotional states and physical health. *American Psychologist, 55,* 110–121.

Salthouse, T. A. (1984). The skill of typing. *Scientific American, 250*(2), 128–135.

Sanders, L. D., Weber-Fox, C. M., & Neville, H. J. (2008). Varying degrees of plasticity in different subsystems within language. In J. R. Pomerantz (Ed.), *Topics in integrative neuroscience: From cells to cognition* (pp. 125–153). New York: Cambridge University Press.

Sands, L. P., & Meredith, W. (1992). Intellectual functioning in late midlife. *Journal of Gerontological and Psychological Science, 47,* 81–84.

Sanes, J. R., & Jessell, T. M. (2013a). Experience and the refinement of synaptic connections. In E. R. Kandel, J. H. Schwartz, T. M. Jessell, S. A. Siegelbaum, & A. J. Hudspeth (Eds.), *Principles of neural science* (5th ed., pp. 1259–1283). USA: McGraw-Hill.

Sanes, J. R., & Jessell, T. M. (2013b). Repairing the damaged brain. In E. R. Kandel, J. H. Schwartz, T. M. Jessell, S. A. Siegelbaum, & A. J. Hudspeth (Eds.), *Principles of neural science* (5th ed., pp. 1284–1305). USA: McGraw-Hill.

Santhakumar, V., Wallner, M., & Otis, T. S. (2007). Ethanol acts directly on extrasynaptic subtypes of GABAA receptors to increase tonic inhibition. *Alcohol, 41*(3), 211–221.

Saper, C. B., Chou, T. C., & Scammell, T. E. (2001). The sleep switch: Hypothalamic control of sleep and wakefulness. *Trends in Neurosciences, 24,* 726–731.

Sapir, E. S. (1921). *Language: An introduction to the study of speech.* New York: Harcourt, Brace.

Sarbin, T. R., & Coe, W. C. (1972). *Hypnosis: A social psychological analysis of influence communication.* New York: Holt, Rinehart, & Winston.

Satterly, D. (1987). Piaget and education. In R. L. Gregory (Ed.), *The Oxford companion to the mind* (pp. 110–143). Oxford: Oxford University Press.

Sattler, J. M. (1977). The effects of therapist-client racial similarity. In A. S. Gurman & A. M. Razin (Eds.), *Effective psychotherapy: A handbook of research* (pp. 252–290). Elmsford, NY: Pergamon.

Savage, J., & Yancey, C. (2008). The effects of media violence exposure on criminal aggression: A meta-analysis. *Criminal Justice and Behavior, 35*(6), 772–791. doi:10.1177/0093854808316487

Savage-Rumbaugh, S., & Lewin, R. (1994). *Kanzi.* New York: Wiley.

Savage-Rumbaugh, S., Shanker, S., & Taylor, T. J. (1998). *Apes, language and the human mind.* Oxford, UK: Oxford University Press.

Scarpa, A., Raine, A., Venables, P. H., & Mednick, S. A. (1995). The stability of inhibited/uninhibited temperament from ages 3 to 11 years in Mauritian children. *Journal of Abnormal Child Psychology, 23,* 607–618.

Schachter, S., & Singer, J. E. (1962). Cognitive, social and physiological determinants of emotional states. *Psychological Review, 69,* 379–399.

Schafer, M., & Crichlow, S. (1996). Antecedents of groupthink: A quantitative study. *Journal of Conflict Resolution, 40*, 415–435.

Schaie, K. W., & Willis, S. L. (2010). *Handbook of the psychology of aging* (7th ed., pp. 27–29). Maryland Heights, Montana: Academic Press.

Schalock, R. L., Borthwick-Duffy, S. A., Buntinz, W. H. E., Coultier, D. L., & Craig, E. M. P. (2010). *Intellectual disability: Definition, classification, and systems of supports* (11th ed.). Washington, DC: American Association on Intellectual and Developmental Disabilities.

Scharnowski, F., Hutton, C., Josephs, O., Weiskopf, N., & Rees, G. (2012). Improving visual perception through neurofeedback. *The Journal of Neuroscience, 32*(49), 17830–17841. doi:10.1523/jneurosci.6334-11.2012

Schiller, P. H., & Carvey, C. E. (2005). The Hermann grid illusion revisited. *Perception, 34*(11), 1375–1397.

Schmitt, D. P. (2002). Personality, attachment and sexuality related to dating relationship outcomes: Contrasting three perspectives on personal attribute interaction. *British Journal of Social Psychology, 41*(4), 589–610.

Schmitt, D. P., Allik, J., McCrae, R. R., & Benet-Martinez, V. (2007). The geographic distribution of big five personality traits: Patterns and profiles of human self-description across 56 nations. *Journal of Cross-Cultural Psychology, 38*(2), 173–212. doi:10.1177/0022022106297299

Schmitt, K. C., & Reith, M. E. A. (2010). Regulation of the dopamine transporter. *Annals of the New York Academy of Sciences, 1187*, 316.

Schmitz, C., Wagner, J., & Menke, E. (2001). The interconnection of childhood poverty and homelessness: Negative impact/points of access. *Families in Society, 82*(1), 69–77.

Schnabel, J. (1994). *Round in circles* (pp. 267–277). London: Hamish Hamilton.

Schneider, et al. (2012). Stress reduction in the secondary prevention of cardiovascular disease: Randomized, controlled trial of transcendental meditation and health education in blacks. *Circulation: Cardiovascular Quality and Outcomes, 5*(6), 750–758. doi: 10.1161/circoutcomes.112.967406

Schneider, K. J., Bugental, J. F. T., & Fraser, J. F. (Eds.). (2001). *Handbook of humanistic psychology*. Thousand Oaks, CA: Sage.

Schneider, R. H., Staggers, F., Alexander, C. N., Sheppard, W., Rainforth, M., Kondwani, K., et al. (1995). A randomized controlled trial of stress reduction for hypertension in older African Americans. *Hypertension, 26*(5), 820–827.

Schneider, W., Dumais, S., & Shriffrin, R. (1984). *Automatic and control processing and attention*. London: Academic Press.

Schneidman, E. (1983). *Death of man*. New York: Jason Aronson.

Schneidman, E. (1994). *Death: Current perspectives*. New York: McGraw-Hill.

Schols, L., Haan, J., Riess, O., Amoiridis, G., & Przuntek, H. (1998). Sleep disturbance in spinocerebellar ataxias: Is the SCA3 mutation a cause of restless legs syndrome? *Neurology, 51*, 1603–1607.

Schroeder, S. R. (2000). Mental retardation and developmental disabilities influenced by environmental neurotoxic insults. *Environmental Health Perspectives, 108*(Suppl. 3), 395–399.

Schonhoff, T. A., & Ciordano, A. A. (2006). *Detection and estimation theory and applications*. Boston, MA: Prentice Hall.

Schroth, M. L., & McCormack, W. A. (2000). Sensation seeking and need for achievement among study-abroad students. *The Journal of Social Psychology, 140*, 533–535.

Schwanenflugel, P., & Rey, M. (1986). Interlingual semantic facilitation: Evidence from common representational system in the bilingual lexicon. *Journal of Memory and Language, 25*, 605–618.

Schwartz, C. E., Kunwar, P. S., Greve, D. N., Moran, L. R., Viner, J. C., Covino, J. M., et al. (2010). Structural differences in adult orbital and ventromedial prefrontal cortex predicted by infant temperament at 4 months of age. *Archives of General Psychiatry, 67*(1), 78–84. doi:10.1001/archgenpsychiatry.2009.171

Schwartz, J. H., & Javitch, J. A. (2013). Neurotransmitters. In E. R. Kandel, J. H. Schwartz, T. M. Jessell, S. A. Siegelbaum, & A. J. Hudspeth (Eds.), *Principles of neural science* (5th ed., pp. 289–306). USA: McGraw-Hill.

Schwartz, J. H., Barres, B. A., & Goldman, J. E. (2013). The cells of the nervous system. In E. R. Kandel, J. H. Schwartz, T. M. Jessell, S. A. Siegelbaum, & A. J. Hudspeth (Eds.), *Principles of neural science* (5th ed., pp. 71–99). USA: McGraw-Hill.

Schwartz, S. K. (2000). *Working your degree*. Retrieved March 6, 2010, from http://cnnfn.cnn.com/2000/12/08/career/q_degreepsychology/

Schweickert, R. (1993). A multinomial processing tree model for degradation and redintegration in immediate recall. *Memory and Cognition, 21*, 168–175.

Schwitzgebel, E. (1999). Representation and desire: A philosophical error with consequences for theory-of-mind research. *Philosophical Psychology, 12*, 157–180.

Security Director's Report. (2008). Experts identify four trends in workplace violence. *Institute of Management and Administration, Inc., 8*(6), 1–15.

Seedat, S., Scott, K. M., Angermeyer, M. C., Berglund, P., Bromet, E. J., Brugha, T. S., Kessler, R. C. (2009). Cross-national associations between gender and mental disorders in the world health organization world mental health surveys. *Archives of General Psychiatry, 66*(7), 785–795. doi: 10.1001/archgenpsychiatry.2009.36

Segall, M. H., Campbell, D. T., & Herskovits, M. J. (1966). *The influence of culture on perception*. Indianapolis, IN: Bobbs-Merrill.

Segerstrom, S. C., & Sephton, S. E. (2010). Optimistic expectancies and cell-mediated immunity: The role of positive affect. *Psychological Science, 21*(3), 448–455.

Segerstrom, S. C., Taylor, S. E., Kemeny, M. E., & Fahey, J. L. (1998). Optimism is associated with mood, coping, and immune change in response to stress. *Journal of Personality and Social Psychology, 74*(6), 1646–1655.

Seligman, M. (1975). *Helplessness: Depression, development and death*. New York: W. H. Freeman.

Seligman, M. (1989). *Helplessness*. New York: W. H. Freeman.

Seligman, M. (1995). The effectiveness of psychotherapy: The *Consumer Reports* study. *American Psychologist, 50*, 965–975.

Seligman, M. (1998). *Learned optimism: How to change your mind and your life* (2nd ed.). New York: Pocket Books.

Seligman, M. (2002). *Authentic happiness*. New York: Free Press.

Seligman, M. E. P. (2005). Positive psychology, positive prevention, and positive therapy. In C. R. Snyder & S. J. Lopez (Eds.), *Handbook of positive psychology* (pp. 3–9). New York: Oxford University Press.

Seligman, M. E. P., & Csikszentmihalyi, M. (2000). Positive psychology: An introduction. *American Psychologist, 55*(1), 5–14. doi:10.1037/0003-066x.55.1.5

Seligman, M., & Maier, S. F. (1967). Failure to escape traumatic shock. *Journal of Experimental Psychology, 74*, 1–9.

Selye, H. (1936). Syndrome produced by diverse nocuous agents. *Nature, 138*, 32.

Selye, H. (1956). *The stress of life*. New York: McGraw-Hill.

Selye, H. (1976). *The stress of life* (Rev. ed.). New York: McGraw-Hill.

Shadish, R., Cook, T. D., & Campbell, D. T. (2002). *Experimental and quasi-experimental designs for generalized causal inferences*. New York: Houghton Mifflin.

Shapiro, A. K., & Shapiro, E. (1997). *The powerful placebo*. Baltimore: Johns Hopkins University Press.

Shapiro, K. L., Jacobs, W. J., & LoLordo, V. M. (1980). Stimulus relevance in Pavlovian conditioning in pigeons. *Animal Learning and Behavior, 8*, 586–594.

Sharot, T., Delgado, M. R., & Phelps, E. A. (2004). How emotion enhances the feeling of remembering. *Nature Neuroscience, 7*(12), 1376–1380.

Shaver, K. (2007, June 17). Stay-at-home dads forge new identities, roles. *Washington Post*. Retrieved from http://www.washingtonpost.com/wp-dyn/content/article/2007/06/16/AR2007061601289.html

Shean, R. E., de Klerk, N. H., Armstrong, B. K., & Walker, N. R. (1994). Seven-year follow-up of a smoking-prevention program for children. *Australian Journal of Public Health, 18*, 205–208.

Sheldon, K. M. (2012). The self-determination theory perspective on positive mental health across cultures. *World Psychiatry, 11*(2), 101–102.

Sheldon, S. H. (2002). Sleep in infants and children. In T. L. Lee-Chiong, M. J. Sateia & M.A. Carskadon (Eds.), *Sleep medicine* (pp. 99–103). Philadelphia: Hanley & Belfus.

Shepard, R. N., & Metzler, J. (1971). Mental rotation of three-dimensional objects. *Science, 171*, 701–703.

Shepard, T. H. (2001). *Catalog of teratogenic agents* (10th ed.). Baltimore: Johns Hopkins University Press.

Sherif, M. (1936). *The psychology of social norms*. New York: Harper & Row.

Sherif, M., Harvey, O. J., White, B. J., Hood, W. R., & Sherif, C. W. (1961). *Intergroup conflict and cooperation: The Robber's Cave experiment*. Norman: University of Oklahoma Book Exchange.

Sherlin, L. H., Arns, M., Lubar, J., Heinrich, H., Kerson, C., Strehl, U., et al. (2011). Neurofeedback and basic learning theory: Implications for research and practice. *Journal of Neurotherapy: Investigations in Neuro-modulation, Neurofeedback and Applied Neuroscience, 15*(4), 292–304.

Shore, L. A. (1990). Skepticism in light of scientific literacy. *Skeptical Inquirer, 15*(1), 3–4.

Shorey, G. (2001). Bystander non-intervention and the Somalia incident. *Canadian Military Journal*, 19–27.

Shorter, E. (1997). *A history of psychiatry: From the era of the asylum to the age of Prozac*. New York: Wiley.

Showalter, E. (1997). *Hysteries: Hysterical epidemics and modern culture*. New York: Columbia University Press.

Shuglin, A. (1986). The background chemistry of MDMA. *Journal of Psycho-active Drugs, 18*(4), 291–304.

Siegel, R. K., & West, L. J. (Eds.). (1975). *Hallucinations: Behavior, experi-ence, and theory* (2nd ed.). New York: Wiley.

Siegel, S. (1969). Effects of CS habituation on eyelid conditioning. *Journal of Comparative and Physiological Psychology, 68*(2), 245–248.

Siegler, I. C., Costa, P. T., Brummett, B. H., Helms, M. J., Barefoot, J. C., Williams, R. B., et al. (2003). Patterns of change in hostility from col-lege to midlife in the UNC alumni heart study predict high-risk status. *Psychosomatic Medicine, 65*, 738–745.

Siegler, R. S. (1996). *Emerging minds: The process of change in children's thinking*. New York: Oxford University Press.

Simeon, D., Guralnik, O., Hazlett, E. A., Spiegel-Cohen, J., Hollander, E., & Buchsbaum, M. S. (2000). Feeling unreal: A PET study of depersonaliza-tion disorder. *American Journal of Psychiatry, 157*, 1782–1788.

Simon, D. A., & Bjork, R. A. (2001). Metacognition in motor learning. *Journal of Experimental Psychology: Learning, Memory, and Cognition, 27*(4), 907–912.

Singer, M. T., & Lalich, J. (1995). *Cults in our midst*. San Francisco: Jossey-Bass.

Singh-Manoux, A., Richards, M., & Marmot, M. (2003). Leisure activities and cognitive function in middle age: Evidence from the Whitehall II study. *Journal of Epidemiology and Community Health, 57*, 907–913.

Skinner, B. F. (1938). *The behavior of organisms: An experimental analysis*. New York: Appleton-Century-Crofts.

Skinner, B. F. (1956). A case history in scientific method. *American Psycholo-gist, 11*, 221–233.

Skinner, B. F. (1961). *Cumulative record: Definitive edition*. New York: Appelton-Century-Crofts.

Skinner, B. F. (1971). *Beyond freedom and dignity*. New York: Knopf.

Skinner, B. F. (1974). *About behaviorism*. New York: Knopf.

Skinner, B. F. (1989). The origins of cognitive thought. In *Recent issues in the analysis of behavior*. Princeton, NC: Merrill Publishing Company.

Skolnick, A. (1986). Early attachment and personal relationships across the life course. In P. B. Baltes, D. L. Featherman, & R. M. Lerner (Eds.), *Life-span development and behavior* (Vol. 7). Hillsdale, NJ: Erlbaum.

Slater, A. (2000). Visual perception in the young infant: Early organisation and rapid learning. In D. Muir & A. Slater (Eds.), *Infant development: The essential readings*. Oxford, UK: Blackwell.

Slater, M., Antley, A., Davison, A., Swapp, D., Guger, C., Barker, C., et al. (2006). A virtual reprise of the Stanley Milgram obedience experiments. *PLoS ONE, 1*(1), e39. doi:10.1371/journal.pone.0000039

Slipp, S. (1993). *The Freudian mystique: Freud, women and feminism*. New York: New York University Press.

Sloan, D. M., & Mizes, J. S. (1999). Foundations of behavior therapy in the contemporary healthcare context. *Clinical Psychology Review, 19*, 255–274.

Smith, D. (2001). Shock and disbelief. *Atlantic Monthly, 2*, 79–90.

Smolen, P., Baxter, D. A., Byrne, J. H., (2006). A model of the roles of essen-tial kinases in the induction and expression of late long-term potentia-tion. *Biophysical Journal, 90*, 2760–2775.

Snarey, J. R. (1985). Cross-cultural universality of social-moral development: A critical review of Kohlbergian research. *Psychological Bulletin, 97*(2), 202–232.

Snyder, C. R., & Lopez, S. J. (2005). The future of positive psychology. In C. R. Snyder & S. J. Lopez (Eds.), *Handbook of positive psychology* (pp. 751–767). New York: Oxford University Press.

Snyder, M., Tanke, E. D., & Berscheid, E. (1977). Social perception and in-terpersonal behavior: On the self-fulfilling nature of social stereotypes. *Journal of Personality and Social Psychology, 35*, 656–666.

Snyder, T. D., & Dillow, S. A. (2010). *Digest of education statistics 2009* (NCES Publication No. NCES 2010-013). Washington, DC: National Center for Education Statistics, Institute of Education Sciences, U.S. Department of Education.

Söderlund, J., Schröder, J., Nordin, C., Samuelsson, M., Walther-Jallow, L., Karlsson, H., et al. (2009). Activation of brain interleukin-1β in schizophrenia. *Molecular Psychiatry, 14*(12), 1069.

Sodowsky, G. R., Lai, E. W., & Plake, B. S. (1991). Moderating effects of socio-cultural variables on acculturation attitudes of Hispanics and Asian Americans. *Journal of Counseling & Development, 70*, 194–204.

Somerville, L. H., Jones, R. M., Ruberry, E. J., Dyke, J. P., Glover, G., & Casey, B. J. (2013). The medial prefrontal cortex and the emergence of self-conscious emotion in adolescence. *Psychological Science, 24*, 1554–1562.

Soomro, G. M. (2001). Obsessive-compulsive disorder. *Clinical Evidence, 6*, 754–762.

Sorkhabi, N. (2005). Applicability of Baumrind's parent typology to collective cultures: Analysis of cultural explanations of parent socialization effects. *International Journal of Behavioral Development, 29*(6), 552–563.

Spangler, W. D. (1992). Validity of questionnaire and TAT measures of need for achievement: Two meta-analyses. *Psychological Bulletin, 112*, 140–154.

Spangler, W. J., Cosgrove, G. R., Ballantine, H. T., Jr., Cassem, E. H., Rauch, S. L., Nierenberg, A., et al. (1996). Magnetic resonance image-guided stereo-tactic cingulotomy for intractable psychiatric disease. *Neurosurgery, 38*, 1071–1076.

Sparing, R., Mottaghy, F., Ganis, G., Thompson, W. L., Toepper, R., Kosslyn, S. M., et al. (2002). Visual cortex excitability increases during visual mental imagery—a TMS study in healthy human subjects. *Brain Research, 938*, 92–97.

Spearman, C. (1904). "General intelligence" objectively determined and mea-sured. *American Journal of Psychology, 15*, 201–293.

Speca, M., Carlson, L. E., Goodey, E., & Angen, E. (2000). A randomized wait-list controlled clinical trial: The effects of a mindfulness meditation-based stress reduction program on mood and symptoms of stress in can-cer outpatients. *Psychosomatic Medicine, 6*, 2613–2622.

Sperling, G. (1960). The information available in brief visual presentations. *Psychological Monographs, 74*(11), 1–29.

Sperry, R. W. (1968). Mental unity following surgical disconnection of the cerebral hemispheres. In *The Harvey lectures* (pp. 293–323). New York: Academic Press.

Spiegel, D., Bloom, J. R., & Gottheil, E. (1989). Effects of psychosocial treat-ment on survival of patients with metastatic breast cancer. *Lancet, 2*, 888–891.

Springer, S. P., & Deutsch, G. (1998). *Left brain, right brain: Perspectives from cognitive neuroscience* (5th ed.). New York: W. H. Freeman.

Squire, L. R., & Kandel, E. R. (2009). *Memory: From mind to molecules* (2nd ed.). Greenwoodvillage, CO: Roberts and Company Publishers.

Squire, L. R., & Slater, P. C. (1978). Anterograde and retrograde memory impairment in chronic amnesia. *Neuropsychologia, 16*, 313–322.

Squire, L. R., Knowlton, B., & Musen, G. (1993). The structure and organiza-tion of memory. *Annual Review of Psychology, 44*, 453–495.

Srivastava, S., John, O. P., Gosling, S. D, & Potter, J. (2003). Development of personality in early and middle adulthood: Set like plaster or per-sistent change? *Journal of Personality and Social Psychology, 84*(5), 1041–1053.

Stahl, S. M. (2013). *Stahl's essential psychopharmacology: Neuroscientific basis and practical applications* (4th ed.). New York, NY: Cambridge University Press.

Standing, L., Conezio, J., & Haber, R. N. (1970). Perception and memory for pictures: Single-trial learning of 2500 visual stimuli. *Psychonomic Science, 19,* 73–74.

Stanovich, K. E., & West, R. F. (2000). Individual differences in reasoning: Implications for the rationality debate? *Behavioral and Brain Sciences, 23*(5), 645–665; discussion 665–726.

Steele, C. M. (1992). Race and the schooling of Black Americans. *The Atlantic Monthly, 269*(4), 68–78.

Steele, C. M. (1997). A threat in the air: How stereotypes shape intellectual identity and performance. *American Psychologist, 52,* 613–629.

Steele, C. M. (1999, August). Thin ice: "stereotype threat" and Black college students. *The Atlantic Monthly, 284,* 44–54.

Steele, C. M., & Aronson, J. (1995). Stereotype threat and the intellectual test performance of African Americans. *Journal of Personality and Social Psychology, 69,* 797–811.

Steele, J., James, J. B., & Barnett, R. C. (2002). Learning in a man's world: Examining the perceptions of undergraduate women in male-dominated academic areas. *Psychology of Women Quarterly, 26,* 46–50.

Stein-Behrens, B., Mattson, M. P., Chang, I., Yeh, M., & Sapolsky, R. (1994). Stress exacerbates neuron loss and cytoskeletal pathology in the hippocampus. *Journal of Neuroscience, 14,* 5373–5380.

Steinberg, L., & Silverberg, S. B. (1987). Influences on marital satisfaction during the middle stages of the family life cycle. *Journal of Marriage and the Family, 49,* 751–760.

Stern, W. (1912). *The psychological methods of testing intelligence* (G. M. Whipple, Trans.) (Educational Psychology Monograph No. 13). Baltimore, MD: Warwick & York, Inc.

Sternberg, R. J. (1986). A triangular theory of love. *Psychological Review, 93,* 119–135.

Sternberg, R. J. (1988a). Triangulating love. In R. Sternberg & M. Barnes (Eds.), *The psychology of love* (pp. 119–138). New Haven, CT: Yale University Press.

Sternberg, R. J. (1988b). *The triarchic mind: A new theory of human intelligence.* New York: Viking-Penguin.

Sternberg, R. J. (1997a). Construct validation of a triangular love scale. *European Journal of Social Psychology, 27,* 313–335.

Sternberg, R. J. (1997a). Construct validation of a triangular love scale. *European Journal of Social Psychology, 27,* 313–335.

Sternberg, R. J. (1997b). The triarchic theory of intelligence. In P. Flannagan, J. L. Genshaft, & P. L. Harrison (Eds.), *Contemporary intellectual assessment: Theories, tests, and issues* (pp. 92–104). New York: Guilford Press.

Sternberg, R. J., & Grigorenko, E. L. (2006). Cultural intelligence and successful intelligence. *Group Organization Management, 31,* 27–39.

Sternberg, R. J., & Kaufman, J. C. (1998). Human abilities. *Annual Review of Psychology, 49,* 479–502.

Sternberger, R. R., Turner, S. M., Beidel, D. C., & Calhoun, K. S. (1995). Social phobia: An analysis of possible developmental factors. *Journal of Abnormal Psychology, 194,* 526–531.

Stevenson, M. B., Roach, M. A., Leavitt, L. A., Miller, J. F., & Chapman, R. S. (1988). Early receptive and productive language skills in preterm and full-term 8-month-old infants. *Journal of Psycholinguistic Research, 17*(2), 169–183.

Stiff, J. B., & Mongeau, P. A. (2002). *Persuasive communication* (2nd ed.). New York: Guilford Press.

Stipek, D. J., Gralinski, J. H., & Kopp, C. B. (1990). Self-concept development in the toddler years. *Developmental Psychology, 26*(6), 972–977.

Stowell, J. R., Kiecolt-Glaser, J. K., & Glaser, R. (2001). Perceived stress and cellular immunity: When coping counts. *Journal of Behavioral Medicine, 24*(4), 323–339.

Stratton, K., Gable, A., & McCormick, M. C. (Eds.). (2001a). *Immunization safety review: Thimerosal-containing vaccines and neurodevelopmental disorders.* Washington, DC: National Academies Press.

Strauss, A. S. (2004). The meaning of death in Northern Cheyenne culture. In A. C. G. M. Robben (Ed.), *Death, mourning, and burial: A cross-cultural reader* (pp. 71–76). Malden, MA: Blackwell.

Strawbridge, W. J., Cohen, R. D., Shema, S. J., & Kaplan, G. A. (1997). Frequent attendance at religious services and mortality over 28 years. *American Journal of Public Health, 87,* 957–961.

Strayer, D. L., & Drews, F. A. (2007). Cell-phone-induced driver distraction. *Current Directions in Psychological Science, 16,* 128–131.

Strayer, D. L., & Johnston, W. A. (2001). Driven to distraction: Dual-task studies of simulated driving and conversing on a cellular phone. *Psychological Science, 12,* 462–466.

Strayer, D. L., Drews, F. A., & Crouch, D. J. (2006). A comparison of the cell phone driver and the drunk driver. *Human Factors, 48,* 381–391.

Stromeyer, C. F., III, & Psotka, J. (1971). The detailed texture of eidetic images. *Nature, 237,* 109–112.

Strunk, D. R., Brotman, M. A., & DeRubeis, R. J. (2010). The process of change in cognitive therapy for depression: Predictors of early inter-session symptom gains. *Behaviour Research and Therapy, 48*(7), 599–606.

Sue, D. W., & Sue, D. (2008). *Counseling the culturally diverse.* Hoboken, NJ: John Wiley & Sons, Inc.

Sue, S. (1977). Community mental health services to minority groups: Some optimism, some pessimism. *American Psychologist, 32,* 616–624.

Sue, S. (1992). Ethnicity and mental health: Research and policy issues. *Journal of Social Issues, 48*(2), 187–205.

Sue, S., Zane, N., & Young, K. (1994). Research on psychotherapy in culturally diverse populations. In A. Bergin & S. Garfield (Eds.), *Handbook of psychotherapy and behavior change* (pp. 783–817). New York: Wiley.

Suleiman, J., & Watson, R.T. (2008). Social loafing in technology-supported teams. *Computer Supported Cooperative Work, 17,* 291–309.

Sullivan, P. F., Neale, M. C., & Kendler, K. S. (2000). Genetic epidemiology of major depression: Review and meta-analysis. *American Journal of Psychiatry, 157,* 1552–1562.

Sulzer, J., Sitaram, R., Blefari, M. L., Kollias, S., Birbaumer, N., Stephan, K. E., et al. (2013). Neurofeedback-mediated self-regulation of the dopaminergic midbrain. *Neuroimage, 75C,* 176–184. doi:10.1016/j.neuroimage.2013.02.041

Suryani, L., & Jensen, S. (1993). *Trance and possession in Bali: A window on western multiple personality, possession disorder, and suicide.* New York: Oxford University Press.

Sutherland, P. (1992). *Cognitive development today: Piaget and his critics.* London: Paul Chapman.

Swaab, D. F., Bao, A.-M., Garcia-Falgueras, A., Hofman, M. A., & Ishunina, T. A. (2012). Sex differences in the forebrain. In J. K. Mai & G. Paxinos (Eds.), *The human nervous system* (pp. 739–758). London, UK: Academic Press.

Swaab, D. F., Bao, A.-M., Garcia-Falgueras, A., Hofman, M. A., & Ishunina, T. A. (2012). Sex differences in the forebrain. In J. K. Mai & G. Paxinos (Eds.), *The human nervous system* (pp. 739–758). London, UK: Academic Press.

Swanbrow, D. (1998, March 25). Red fish, blue fish help clarify cultural aspects of emotion. *The University Record.* Retrieved from http://ur.umich.edu/9798/Mar25_98/fish.htm

Swann, J. (1998). Talk control: An illustration from the classroom of problems in analyzing male dominance of conversation. In J. Coates (Ed.), *Language and gender: A reader* (pp. 185–196). Oxford, UK: Blackwell.

Swayze, V. W., II. (1995). Frontal leukotomy and related psychosurgical procedures in the era before antipsychotics (1935–1954): A historical overview. *American Journal of Psychiatry, 152*(4), 505–515.

Swenson, D. D., & Marshall, B. (2005, May 14). Flash flood: Hurricane Katrina's inundation of New Orleans, August 29, 2005 (SWF). *Times-Picayune.*

Szell, M., & Thurner, S. (2013). How women organize social networks different from men. *Scientific Reports, 3,* 1214. doi:10.1038/srep01214

Taglialatela, J. P., Savage-Rumbaugh, E. S., & Baker, L. A. (2003). Vocal production by a language-competent bonobo (*Pan paniscus*). *International Journal of Comparative Psychology, 24,* 1–17.

Tajfel, H., & Turner, J. C. (1986). The social identity theory of intergroup behaviour. In S. Worchel & W. G. Austin (Eds.), *The psychology of intergroup relations* (Vol. 2, pp. 7–24). New York: Nelson Hall.

Talbott, G. D., & Crosby, L. R. (2001). Recovery contracts: Seven key elements. In R. H. Coombs (Ed.), *Addiction recovery tools* (pp. 127–144). Thousand Oaks, CA: Sage.

Tarrier, N., & Taylor, R. (2014). Schizophrenia and other psychotic disorders. In D. H. Barlow (Ed.), *Clinical handbook of psychological disorders: A step-by-step treatment manual* (5th ed., pp. 502–532). New York: Guilford Press.

Taylor, B., Miller, E., Farrington, C. P., Petropoulos, M. C., Favot-Mayaud, I., Li, J., et al. (1999). Autism and measles, mumps, and rubella vaccine: No epidemiological evidence for a causal association. *Lancet, 353,* 2026–2029.

Taylor, C., Manganello, J. A., Lee, S. J., & Rice, J. C. (2010). Mothers' spanking of 3-year-old children and subsequent risk of children's aggressive behavior. *Pediatrics, 125,* 1057–1065.

Teigen, K. (1994). Yerkes-Dodson: A law for all seasons. *Theory and Psychology, 4,* 525–547.

Temoshok, L., & Dreher, H. (1992). *The Type C connection: The behavioral links to cancer and your health.* New York: Random House.

Terman, L. M. (1916). *The measurement of intelligence.* Boston: Houghton Mifflin.

Terman, L. M. (1925). *Mental and physical traits of a thousand gifted children (I).* Stanford, CA: Stanford University Press.

Terman, L. M., & Oden, M. H. (1947). *The gifted child grows up: 25 years' follow-up of a superior group: Genetic studies of genius* (Vol. 4). Stanford, CA: Stanford University Press.

Tevis, M. (1994). George I. Sanchez. In L. Glenn Smith & Joan K. Smith (Eds.), *Lives in education: A narrative of people and ideas* (2nd ed., pp. 346–354). New York: St. Martin's Press.

Thase, M. E. (1999). When are psychotherapy and pharmacotherapy combinations the treatment of choice for major depressive disorders? *Psychiatric Quarterly, 70*(4), 333–346.

The University of Manchester. (2009). Virtual solution to driving phobias [Press release]. Retrieved from http://www.psych-sci.manchester.ac.uk/aboutus/press-releases/virtualdriving

Thomas, A., & Chess, S. (1977). *Temperament and development.* New York: Brunner/Mazel.

Thompson, W. W., Price, C., Goodson, B., Shay, D. K., Benson, P., Hinrichsen, V. L., et al. (2007). Early thimerosal exposure and neuropsychological outcomes at 7 to 10 years. *The New England Journal of Medicine, 357*(13), 1281–1292.

Thoresen, C. E., & Harris, H. S. (2002). Spirituality and health: What's the evidence and what's needed? *Annals of Behavioral Medicine, 24,* 3–13.

Thorndike, E. L. (1911). *Animal intelligence: Experimental studies.* New York: Macmillan.

Thorndike, E. L. (1920). A constant error on psychological rating. *Journal of Applied Psychology, 5,* 25–29.

Thornton, A., & Hui-Sheng, L. (1994). Continuity and change. In A. Thornton & Hui-Sheng (Eds.), *Social change and the family in Taiwan* (pp. 396–410). Chicago: University of Chicago Press.

Tienari, P., Wynne, L. C., Sorri, A., Lahti, I., Laksy, K., Moring, J., et al. (2004). Genotype-environment interaction in schizophrenia-spectrum disorder: Long-term follow-up study of Finnish adoptees. *The British Journal of Psychiatry, 184,* 216–222.

Tobach, E. (2001). Development of sex and gender. In J. Worell (Ed.), *Encyclopedia of women and gender* (pp. 315–332). San Diego, CA: Academic Press.

Toga, A. W., & Thompson, P. M. (2003). Mapping brain asymmetry. *Nature Reviews Neuroscience, 4,* 37–48.

Tolman, E. C., & Honzik, C. H. (1930). Introduction and removal of reward and maze learning in rats. *University of California Publications in Psychology, 4,* 257–275.

Tomasello, M., Carpenter, M., & Lizskowski, U. (2007). A new look at infant pointing. *Child Development, 78,* 705–722.

Torgersen, S., Czajkowski, N., Jacobson, K., Reichborn-Kjennerud, T., Roysamb, E., Neale, M. C., et al. (2008). Dimensional representations of DSMIV cluster B personality disorders in a population-based sample of Norwegian twins: A multivariate study. *Psychological Medicine, 38*(11), 1617–1625. doi:10.1017/s0033291708002924

Torrance, E. P. (1993). The Beyonders in a thirty-year longitudinal study of creative achievement. *Roeper Review, 15*(3), 131–135.

Trace, S. E., Baker, J. H., Penas-Lledo, E., & Bulik, C. M. (2013). The genetics of eating disorders. *Annual Review of Clinical Psychology, 9,* 589–620. doi:10.1146/annurev-clinpsy-050212-185546

Trappey, C. (1996). A meta-analysis of consumer choice and subliminal advertising. *Psychology and Marketing, 13,* 517–530.

Treisman, A. [M.]. (2006). How the deployment of attention determines what we see. *Visual Cognition, 14,* 411–443.

Treisman, A. M., & Gelade, G. (1980). A feature integration theory of attention. *Cognitive Psychology, 12,* 97–136.

Triandis, H. (1971). *Attitude and attitude change.* New York: Wiley.

Trocmé, N., MacLaurin, B., Fallon, B., Daciuk, J., Billingsley, D., Tourigny, M., et al. (2001). *Canadian incidence study of reported child abuse and neglect: Final report* (pp. 30–31). Ottawa, ON: Minister of Public Works and Government Services Canada.

Troncoso, X. G., Macknik, S. L., Otero-Millan, J., & Martinez-Conde, S. (2008). Microsaccades drive illusory motion in the enigma illusion. *Proceedings of the National Academy of Sciences, USA, 105*(41), 16033–16038.

Trujillo, K. A., & Chinn, A. B. (1996). *Drugs and the Brain: Antidepressants.* California State University. Retrieved July 20, 2004, from www.csusm.edu/DandB/AD.html#history

Trut, L. M. (1999). Early canid domestication: The Farm-Fox experiment. *Science, 283.*

Tsai, G. E., Condle, D., Wu, M.-T., & Chang, I.-W. (1999). Functional magnetic resonance imaging of personality switches in a woman with dissociative identity disorder. *Harvard Review of Psychiatry, 7,* 119–122.

Tsai, J. L., Simeonova, D. I., & Watanabe, J. T. (2004). Somatic and social: Chinese Americans talk about emotion. *Personality and Social Psychology Bulletin, 30*(9), 1226–1238.

Tsapogas, J. (2006). *Characteristics of Doctoral Scientists and Engineers in the United States: 2003,* NSF, 06-320. Arlington, VA: National Science Foundation, Division of Science Resources Statistics.

Tucker, E. W., & Potocky-Tripodi, M. (2006). Changing heterosexuals' attitudes toward homosexuals: A systematic review of the empirical literature. *Research on Social Work Practice, 16*(2), 176–190.

Tucker, M. A., Hirota, Y., Wamsley, E. J., Lau, H., Chaklader, A., & Fishbein, W. (2006). A daytime nap containing solely non-REM sleep enhances declarative but not procedural memory. *Neurobiology of Learning and Memory, 86*(2), 241–247.

Tukuitonga, C. F., & Bindman, A. B. (2002). Ethnic and gender differences in the use of coronary artery revascularisation procedures in New Zealand. *New Zealand Medical Journal, 115,* 179–182.

Tulving, E., & Thomson, D. M. (1973). Encoding specificity and retrieval processes in episodic memory. *Psychological Review, 80,* 352–373.

Turk, C. L., Heimberg, R. G., & Magee, L. (2008). Social anxiety disorder. In D. H. Barlow (Ed.), *Clinical handbook of psychological disorders* (pp. 123–163). New York: Guilford Press.

Underwood, M. K., Beron, K. J., & Rosen, L. H. (2009). Continuity and change in social and physical aggression from middle childhood through early adolescence. *Aggressive Behavior, 35*(5), 357–375.

Unger, R. (1979). Toward a redefinition of sex and gender. *American Psychologist, 34,* 1085–1094.

Vail, A. (1976). Factors influencing lower class, black patients' remaining in treatment. *Clinical Psychology, 29,* 12–14.

Valverde, R., Pozdnyakova, I., Kajander, T., Venkatraman, J., & Regan, L. (2007). Fragile X mental retardation syndrome: Structure of the KH1-KH2 domains of fragile X mental retardation protein. *Structure, 9,* 1090–1098.

Van de Castle, R. (1994). *Our dreaming mind.* New York: Ballantine Books.

van der Merwe, A., & Garuccio, A. (Eds.). (1994). *Waves and particles in light and matter.* New York: Plenum Press.

van der Stelt, O., van der Molen, M., Boudewijn Gunning, W., & Kok, A. (2010). Neuroelectrical signs of selective attention to color in boys with Attention-Deficit/Hyperactivity disorder. *Cognitive Brain Research, 12*(2), 245–264.

Van Dongen, H. P. A., Maislin, G., Mullington, J. M., & Dinges, D. F. (2003). The cumulative cost of additional wakefulness: Dose-response effects on neurobehavioral functions and sleep physiology from chronic sleep restriction and total sleep deprivation. *Sleep, 26,* 117–126.

Van Horn, J. D., Irimia,, A., Torgerson, C. M., Chambers, M. C., Kikinis, R., & Toga, A. W. (2012). Mapping connectivity damage in the case of phineas gage. *PLoS ONE, 7*(5), e37454. doi:10.1371/journal.pone.0037454

VandenBos, G. R., & Bulatao, E. Q. (Eds.). (1996). *Violence on the job: Identifying risks and developing solutions.* Washington DC: American Psychological Association.

Vartanian, L. R. (2000). Revisiting the imaginary audience and personal fable constructs of adolescent egocentrism: A conceptual review. *Adolescence, 35*(140), 639–661.

Vaughan, S. (2000). *Half empty, half full: The psychological roots of optimism.* New York: Harcourt.

Vernon, S. W., & Roberts, R. E. (1982). Use of RDC in a tri-ethnic community survey. *Archives of General Psychiatry, 39,* 47.

Villani, S. (2001). Impact of media on children and adolescents: A 10-year review of the research. *Journal of the American Academy on Child and Adolescent Psychiatry, 40*(4), 392–401.

Virkkunen, M., & Linnoila, M. (1996). Serotonin and glucose metabolism in impulsively violent alcoholic offenders. In D. M. Stoff & R. B. Cairns (Eds.), *Aggression and violence* (pp. 87–100). Mahwah, NJ: Erlbaum.

Visser, P. S., & Krosnick, J. A. (1998). Development of attitude strength over the life cycle: Surge and decline. *Journal of Personality and Social Psychology, 75*(6), 1389–1410.

Vokey, J. R., & Read, J. D. (1985). Subliminal messages: Between the devil and the media. *American Psychologist, 40,* 1231–1239.

Volkow, N. D., Wang, G.-J., Newcorn, J., Telang, F., Solanto, M. V., Fowler, J. S., et al. (2007). Depressed dopamine activity in caudate and preliminary evidence of limbic involvement in adults with Attention-Deficit/Hyperactivity Disorder. *Archives of General Psychiatry, 64*(8), 932–940.

von Helmholtz, H. (1852). On the theory of compound colours. *Philosophical Magazine, 4,* 519–535.

von Helmholtz, H. L. F. (1863, 1954). *Die Lehre von den Tonempfindungen als physiologische Grundlage fur die Theorie der Musik* [*On the sensations of tone as a physiological basis for the theory of music*] (Alexander J. Ellis, Trans.). New York: Dover.

Voss, M. W., Erickson, K. I., Prakash, R. S., Chaddock, L., Malkowski, E., Alves, H., et al. (2010). Functional connectivity: A source of variance in the association between cardiorespiratory fitness and cognition? *Neuropsychologia, 48*(5), 1394–1406.

Voyer, D., & Rodgers, M. (2002). Reliability of laterality effects in a dichotic listening task with nonverbal material. *Brain and Cognition, 48,* 602–606.

Voyer, D., Voyer, S., & Bryden, M. (1995). Magnitude of sex differences in spatial abilities: A meta-analysis and consideration of critical variables. *Psychological Bulletin, 117*(2), 250–270.

Vygotsky, L. S. (1962, 1934). *Thought and language.* Cambridge, MA: MIT Press.

Vygotsky, L. S. (1978). *Mind in society: The development of higher psychological processes.* Cambridge, MA: Harvard University Press.

Vygotsky, L. S. (1987). Thought and word. In R. W. Riebe & A. S. Carton (Eds.), *The collected works of L. S. Vygotsky: Vol. 1. Problems of general psychology* (pp. 243–288). New York: Plenum.

Wade, T. D., Gordon, S., Medland, S., Bulik, C. M., Heath, A. C., Montgomery, G. W., et al. (2013). Genetic variants associated with disordered eating. *The International Journal of Eating Disorders.* doi: 10.1002/eat.22133

Wahlsten, D. (1997). The malleability of intelligence is not constrained by heritability. In B. Devlin, S. E. Fienberg, & K. Roeder (Eds.), *Intelligence, genes, and success: Scientists respond to the bell curve* (pp. 71–87). New York: Springer.

Wakefield, A. J., Murch, S. H., Anthony, A., Linnell, J., Casson, D. M., Malik, M., et al. (1998). Ileal-lymphoid-nodular hyperplasia, non-specific colitis, and pervasive developmental disorder in children. *The Lancet, 351,* 9103.

Walker, L. J. (1991). Sex differences in moral reasoning. In W. M. Kurtines & J. L. Gewirtz (Eds.), *Handbook of moral behavior and development: Vol. 2. Research* (pp. 333–364). Hillsdale, NJ: Erlbaum.

Wampold, B. E. (1997). Methodological problems in identifying efficacious psychotherapies. *Psychotherapy Research, 7,* 21–43.

Wang, Z., David, P., Srivastava, J., Powers, S., Brady, C., D'Angelo, J., et al. (2012). Behavioral performance and visual attention in communication multitasking: A comparison between instant messaging and online voice chat. *Computers in Human Behavior, 28*(3), 968.

Ward, A. S., Li, D. H., Luedtke, R. R., & Emmett-Oglesby, M. W. (1996). Variations in cocaine self-administration by inbred rat strains under a progressive-ratio schedule. *Psychopharmacology, 127*(3), 204–212.

Ward, C., & Rana-Deuba, A. (1999). Acculturation and adaptation revisited. *Journal of Cross-Cultural Psychology, 30,* 422–442.

Ward, J., Mattic, K. R. P., & Hall, W. (1999). *Methadone maintenance treatment and other opioid replacement therapies.* Sydney, Australia: Harwood Academic.

Washburn, M. F. (1908). *The animal mind: A text-book of comparative psychology.* New York: Macmillan.

Wasserman, E. A., & Miller, R. R. (1997). What's elementary about associative learning? *Annual Review of Psychology, 48,* 573–607.

Waterman, A. S. (2013). The humanistic psychology–positive psychology divide: Contrasts in philosophical foundations. *American Psychologist, 68*(3), 124–133. doi:10.1037/a0032168

Watkins, C. E., Campbell, V. L., Nieberding, R., & Hallmark, R. (1995). Contemporary practice of psychological assessment by clinical psychologists. *Professional Psychology: Research and Practice, 26,* 54–60.

Watson, J. B. (1913). Psychology as the behaviorist views it. *Psychological Review, 20,* 158–177.

Watson, J. B. (1924). *Behaviorism.* New York: Norton.

Watson, J. B., & Rayner, R. (1920). Conditioned emotional responses. *Journal of Experimental Psychology, 3,* 1–14.

Watson, J. M., & Strayer, D. L. (2010). Supertaskers: Profiles in extraordinary multitasking ability. *Psychonomic Bulletin and Review, 17*(4), 479–485.

Watt, H. M. G. (2000). Measuring attitudinal change in mathematics and English over the 1st year of junior high school: A multi-dimensional analysis. *Journal of Experimental Education, 68,* 331–361.

Weaver, F. M., Follett, K., Stern, M., Hur, K., Harris, C., Marks, W. J., Jr., et al. (2009). Bilateral deep brain stimulation vs. best medical therapy for patients with advanced Parkinson disease: A randomized controlled trial. *Journal of the American Medical Association, 301*(1), 63–73.

Webb, W. B. (1992). *Sleep: The gentle tyrant* (2nd ed.). Bolton, MA: Ander.

Wechsler, D. (1975). *The collected papers of David Wechsler.* New York: Academic Press.

Wechsler, D. (2002). *WPPSI-III (Weschsler preschool and primary scale of intelligence—Third edition) administration and scoring manual.* San Antonio, TX: Pearson.

Wechsler, D. (2003). *WISC-IV (Weschsler Intelligence Scale for children—Fourth edition) administration and scoring manual.* San Antonio, TX: Pearson.

Wechsler, D. (2008). *WAIS-IV (Weschsler Adult Intelligence Scale—Fourth edition) administration and scoring manual.* San Antonio, TX: Pearson.

Wedding, D. (2004). Cross-cultural counseling and psychotherapy. In R. J. Corsini & D. Wedding (Eds.), *Current psychotherapies* (7th ed., p. 485). Itasca, IL: Peacock.

Weinberger, D. R. (1987). Implications of normal brain development for the pathogenesis of schizophrenia. *Archives of General Psychiatry, 44,* 660–668.

Weiner, B. (1985). An attributional theory of achievement motivation. *Psychological Review, 92,* 548–573.

Weiner, I. B. (1997). Current status of the Rorschach Inkblot Method. *Journal of Personality Assessment, 68,* 5–19.

Weiner, I. B. (2013). Applying Rorschach assessment. In G. P. Koocher, J. C. Norcross, & B. A. Greene (Eds.), *Psychologists' desk reference* (pp. 148–152). New York: Oxford University Press.

Weiner, R. D. (2000). Retrogade amnesia with electroconvulsive therapy: Characteristics and implications. *Archives of General Psychiatry, 57,* 591–592.

Weisman, A. (1972). *On dying and denying.* New York: Behavioral Publications.

Weissman, M. M., & Klerman, G. L. (1977). Sex differences and the epidemiology of depression. *Archives of General Psychiatry, 34,* 98–111.

Wells, J. E., Browne, M. O., Aguilar-Gaxiola, S., Al-Hamzawi, A., Alonso, J., Angermeyer, M. C., et al. (2013). Drop out from out-patient mental healthcare in the world health organization's world mental health survey initiative. *The British Journal of Psychiatry, 202*(1), 42–49. doi:10.1192/bjp.bp.112.113134

Wenneberg, S. R., Schneider, R. H., Walton, K. G., Maclean, C. R., Levitsky, D. K., Mandarino, J. V., Waziri, R., & Wallace, R. K. (1997). Anger expression correlates with platelet aggregation. *Behavioral Medicine, 22*(4), 174–177.

Wenneberg, S. R., Schneider, R. H., Walton, K. G., Maclean, C. R., Levitsky, D. K., Mandarino, J. V., et al. (1997). Anger expression correlates with platelet aggregation. *Behavioral Medicine, 22*(4), 174–177.

Werker, J. F., & Lalonde, C. E. (1988). Cross-language speech perceptions: Initial capabilities and developmental change. *Developmental Psychology, 24*, 672–683.

Wertheimer, M. (1982). *Productive thinking.* Chicago: University of Chicago Press.

Westen, D. (2005). Cognitive neuroscience and psychotherapy: Implications for psychotherapy's second century. In G. Gabbard, J. Beck, & J. Holmes (Eds.), *Oxford textbook of psychotherapy.* Oxford, UK: Oxford University Press.

Wetherell, J. L. (2002). Behavior therapy for anxious older adults. *Behavior Therapist, 25*, 16–17.

Wever, E. G. (1949). *Theory of hearing.* New York: John Wiley & Sons.

Wever, E. G., & Bray, C. W. (1930). The nature of acoustic response: The relation between sound frequency and frequency of impulses in the auditory nerve. *Journal of Experimental Psychology, 13*(5), 373–387.

Weyant, J. M. (1996). Application of compliance techniques to direct-mail requests for charitable donations. *Psychology and Marketing, 13*, 157–170.

White, G. L. (1980). Physical attractiveness and courtship progress. *Journal of Personality and Social Psychology, 39*, 660–668.

White, J. N., Hutchens, T., & Lubar, J. (2005). Quantitative EEG assessment during neuropsychological task performance in adults with attention deficit hyperactivity disorder. *Journal of Adult Development, 12*(2), 113–121.

Whorf, B. L. (1956). *Language, thought and reality.* New York: Wiley.

Wicker, A. W. (1971). An examination of the "other variables" explanation of attitude—behavior inconsistency. *Journal of Personality and Social Psychology, 19*, 18–30.

Wierenga, C. E., Stricker, N. H., McCauley, A., Simmons, A., Jak, A. J., Chang, Y. L., et al. (2010). Increased functional brain response during word retrieval in cognitively intact older adults at genetic risk for Alzheimer's disease. *Neuroimage, 15*, 15.

Williams, J. A., Pascual-Leone, A., & Fregni, F. (2010). Interhemispheric modulation induced by cortical stimulation and motor training. *Physical Therapy, 90*(3), 398–410.

Williams, M. E. (1995). *The American Geriatrics Society's complete guide to aging and mental health.* New York: Random House.

Williams, R. B. (1999). A 69-year-old man with anger and angina. *Journal of the American Medical Association, 282*, 763–770.

Williams, R. B. (2001). Hostility: Effects on health and the potential for successful behavioral approaches to prevention and treatment. In A. Baum, T. A. Revenson, & J. E. Singer (Eds.), *Handbook of health psychology.* Mahwah, NJ: Erlbaum.

Williams, R. B., Haney, T. L., Lee, K. L., Kong, Y. H., Blumenthal, J. A., & Whalen, R. E. (1980). Type A behavior, hostility, and coronary atherosclerosis. *Psychosomatic Medicine, 42*(6), 539–549.

Winningham, R. G., Hyman, I. E., Jr., & Dinnel, D. L. (2000). Flashbulb memories? The effects of when the initial memory report was obtained. *Memory, 8*, 209–216.

Winton, W. M. (1987). Do introductory textbooks present the Yerkes-Dodson law correctly? *American Psychologist, 42*(2), 202–203.

Wise, K., Alhabash, S., & Park, H. (2010). Emotional responses during social information seeking on Facebook. *Cyberpsychology, Behavior, and Social Networking, 13*(5), 555–562.

Wiseman, R. (2007). *Quirkology: How we discover the big truths in small things* (pp. 7–8, 28–29). New York: Basic Books.

Witelson, S. F. (1991). Neural sexual mosaicism: Sexual differentiation of the human temporo-parietal region for functional asymmetry. *Psychoneuroendocrinology, 16*, 131–153.

Wolberg, L. R. (1977). *The technique of psychotherapy.* New York: Grune & Stratton.

Wood, J. M., Nezworski, M. T., & Stejskal, W. J. (1996). The comprehensive system for the Rorschach: A critical examination. *Psychological Science, 7*(1), 3–10, 14–17.

Woodhouse, A. (2005). Phantom limb sensation. *Clinical and Experimental Pharmacology and Physiology, 32*(1–2), 132–134.

Wyman, P. A., Moynihan, J., Eberly, S., Cox, C., Cross, W., Jin, X., et al. (2007). Association of family stress with natural killer cell activity and the frequency of illnesses in children. *Archives of Pediatric and Adolescent Medicine, 161*, 228–234.

Wynne, C. (1999). Do animals think? The case against the animal mind. *Psychology Today, 32*(6), 50–53.

Yalom, I. (1995). *The theory and practice of group psychotherapy* (4th ed.). New York: Basic Books.

Yamaguchi, S., Isejima, H., Matsuo, T., Okura, R., Yagita, K., Kobayashi, M., et al. (2003). Synchronization of cellular clocks in the suprachiasmatic nucleus. *Science, 302*, 1408–1412.

Yerkes, R. M., & Dodson, J. D. (1908). The relation of strength of stimulus to rapidity of habit formation. *Journal of Comparative Neurology and Psychology, 18*, 459–482.

Yip, Y. L. (2002, Autumn). Pivot–Qi. *The Journal of Traditional Eastern Health and Fitness, 12*(3).

Yopyk, D., & Prentice, D. A. (2005). Am I an athlete or a student? Identify salience and stereotype threat in student-athletes. *Basic and Applied Social Psychology, 27*(4), 29–336.

Young, J. E., Rygh, J. L., Weinberger, A. D., & Beck, A. T. (2014). Cognitive therapy for depression. In D. H. Barlow (Ed.), *Clinical handbook of psychological disorders: A step-by-step treatment manual* (5th ed., pp. 275–331). New York: Guilford Press.

Young, S. N. (Ed.). (1996). Melatonin, sleep, aging, and the health protection branch. *Journal of Psychiatry Neuroscience, 21*(3), 161–164.

Yule, G. (1996). *Pragmatics.* Oxford, UK: Oxford University Press.

Zajonc, R. B. (1965). Social facilitation. *Science, 149*, 269–274.

Zajonc, R. B. (1968). Attitudinal effects of mere exposure. *Journal of Personality and Social Psychology Monographs, 9*(2), 1–27.

Zajonc, R. B. (1980). Feeling and thinking: Preferences need no inferences. *American Psychologist, 35*, 151–175.

Zajonc, R. B. (1984). On the primacy of affect. *American Psychologist, 39*, 117–123.

Zajonc, R. B. (1998). Emotions. In D. T. Gilbert & S. T. Fiske (Eds.), *Handbook of social psychology* (4th ed., Vol. 1, pp. 591–632). New York: McGraw-Hill.

Zajonc, R. B., Heingartner, A., & Herman, E. M. (1970). Social enhancement and impairment of performance in the cockroach. *Journal of Social Psychology, 13*(2), 83–92.

Zarate, C. A., Jr., Brutsche, N. E., Ibrahim, L., Franco-Chaves, J., DiazGranados, N., Cravchik, A., Zedler, B. (1995). Mary Whiton Calkins. In M. E. Waithe (Ed.), *A history of women philosophers: Vol. 4* (pp. 103–123). Netherlands: Kluwer Academic Publishers.

Zeidner, M., & Matthews, G. (2005). Evaluative anxiety. In A. Elliott & C. Dweck (Eds.), *Handbook of competence and motivation* (pp. 141–146). New York: Guilford Press.

Zeki, S. (2001). Localization and globalization in conscious vision. *Annual Review of Neuroscience, 24*, 57–86.

Zentall, T. R. (2000). Animal intelligence. In R. J. Sternberg (Ed.), *Handbook of intelligence.* Cambridge, MA: Cambridge University Press.

Zilles, K. (1990). Cortex. In G. Paxinos (Ed.), *The human nervous system* (pp. 757–802). San Diego, CA: Academic.

Zilles, K., & Amunts, K. (2012). Architecture of the cerebral cortex. In J. K. Mai & G. Paxinos (Eds.), *The human nervous system* (pp. 836–895). London, UK: Academic Press.

Zillmann, D., Baron, R., & Tamborini, R. (1981). Social costs of smoking: Effects of tobacco smoke on hostile behavior. *Psychology Journal of Applied Social, 11*, 548–561.

Zimbardo, P. G. (1970). The human choice: Individuation, reason, and order versus deindividuation, impulse, and chaos. In N. J. Arnold & D. Levine (Eds.), *Nebraska Symposium on Motivation, 1969.* Lincoln: University of Nebraska Press.

Zimbardo, P. G. (1971). The pathology of imprisonment. *Society, 9*(4–8), 4.

Zimbardo, P. G., & Hartley, C. F. (1985). Cults go to high school: A theoretical and empirical analysis of the initial stage in the recruitment process. *Cultic Studies Journal, 2,* 91–148.

Zimbardo, P., Maslach, C., & Haney, C. (2000). Reflections on the Stanford Prison Experiment: Genesis, transformations, consequences. In T. Blass (Ed.), *Obedience to authority: Current perspectives on the Milgram paradigm* (pp. 193–237). London: Lawrence Erlbaum.

Zlatin, D. M. (1995). Life themes: A method to understand terminal illness. *Omega: Journal of Death and Dying, 31*(3), 189–206. doi:10.2190/E4BA-ML04-E2BK-7YJE

Zorilla, E. P., Luborsky, L., McKay, J. R., Rosenthal, R., Houldin, A., Tax, A., et al. (2001). The relationship of depression and stressors to immunological assays: A meta-analytic review. *Brain, Behavior, and Immunity, 15,* 199–226.

Zuckerman, M. (1979). *Sensation seeking: Beyond the optimal level of arousal.* Hillsdale, NJ: Erlbaum.

Zuckerman, M. (1994). *Behavioral expression and biosocial bases of sensation seeking.* New York: Cambridge University Press.

Zuckerman, M. (2002). Zuckerman-Kuhlman Personality Questionnaire (ZKPQ): An alternative five-factorial model. In B. De Raad & M. Perugini (Eds.), *Big Five assessment* (pp. 377–396). Seattle, WA: Hogrefe & Huber.

Zuo, L., & Cramond, B. (2001). An examination of Terman's gifted children from the theory of identity. *Gifted Child Quarterly, 45*(4), 251–259.

Zvolensky, M. J., Schmidt, M. B., & Stewart, S. H. (2003). Panic disorder and smoking. *Clinical Psychology: Science and Practice, 10,* 29–51.

Credits

PHOTO CREDITS

Chapter 1

Page 2 StockImageGroup/Shutterstock; **Page 4** Anita Ponne/Shutterstock; **Page 5** Fancy/Alamy; **Page 6** Pearson Education; **Page 7** INTERFOTO/Alamy; **Page 7** Nancy R Cohen/Getty Images, Inc.; **Page 8** Pearson Education; **Page 8** The University of Akron/Archives of the History of American Psychology; **Page 9** Pearson Education; **Page 10** G. Paul Bishop; **Page 11** Courtesy, Dr. Arthur W. Toga, Laboratory of Neuro Imaging, UCLA School of Medicine; **Page 12** CREATISTA/Shutterstock; **Page 16** Anita Ponne/Shutterstock; **Page 17** Pearson Education; **Page 18** Adam Seward/Alamy; **Page 19** BSIP SA/Alamy; **Page 20** George Price/The New Yorker Collection/The Cartoon Bank; **Page 21** Pearson Education; **Page 22** Pearson Education; **Page 23** Bill Aron/PhotoEdit; **Page 23** Pearson Education; **Page 24** Pearson Education; **Page 25** John Henley/Corbis; **Page 25** Pearson Education; **Page 26** Pearson Education; **Page 26** Tom Chalkley/The New Yorker Collection/The Cartoon Bank; **Page 28** Anita Ponne/Shutterstock; **Page 39** Tom Chalkley/The New Yorker Collection/The Cartoon Bank.

Chapter 2

Page 40 Sebastian Kaulitzki/Fotolia; **Page 42** Sebastian Kaulitzki/Fotolia; **Page 43** Pearson Education; **Page 44** Secchi Lecaque/Photo Researchers, Inc./Science Source; **Page 45** Peter Arnold/Getty Images, Inc.; **Page 47** Image Source/Getty Images, Inc.; **Page 50** Pearson Education; **Page 50** Peter Hvizdak/The Image Works; **Page 51** Paul CC Collis/Alamy; **Page 55** Sebastian Kaulitzki/Fotolia; **Page 56** Noland White, Ph.D; **Page 56** Noland White, Ph.D; **Page 56** Richard T Nowitz/Photo Researchers, Inc./Science Source; **Page 57** Medical-on-Line/Alamy; **Page 57** Noland White, Ph.D; **Page 57** Philippe Psaila/Photo Researchers, Inc./Science Source; **Page 58** Pearson Education; **Page 59** moodboard/Corbis; **Page 61** Courtesy Walter L. Isaac, Phd.; **Page 64** Marcelo Santos/Getty Images, Inc.; **Page 68** Sebastian Kaulitzki/Fotolia; "**Page 69** Frank & Ernest reprinted by permission of Tom Thaves; **Page 71** CNRI/Science Photo Library/Science Source.

Chapter 3

Page 78 Agrus/Shutterstock; **Page 78** Venus Angel/Shutterstock; **Page 79** Nordling/Shutterstock; **Page 79** Valentyn Volkov/Shutterstock; **Page 80** Valentyn Volkov/Shutterstock; **Page 86** Noland White, Ph.D; **Page 88** Bryan Allen/Corbis; **Page 88** Fritz Goro/Getty Images, Inc.; **Page 90** Charles Barsotti/The New Yorker Collection/The Cartoon Bank; **Page 94** Giry Daniel/Corbis; **Page 95** Pearson Education; **Page 95** Science Source; **Page 96** Pearson Education; **Page 97** Pearson Education; **Page 97** Robin Sachs/PhotoEdit; **Page 99** Stephen Morton/Associated Press; **Page 100** Vince Streano/Corbis; **Page 102** Valentyn Volkov/Shutterstock; **Page 105** Mark Richards/PhotoEdit.; **Page 107** Creative Eye/Mira.com; **Page 107** Grant Faint/Getty Images, Inc.; **Page 107** sborisov/Fotolia; **Page 107** Shaen Adey/Dorling Kindersley Limited; **Page 109** Larry Landolfi/Photo Researchers, Inc./Science Source; **Page 110** Created by and courtesy of Dr. Akiyoshi Kitaoka, Ritsumeikan University.; **Page 110** Created by and courtesy of Jorge Otero-Millan, Martinez-Conde Laboratory, Barrow Neurological Institute; **Page 111** David H Wells/The Image Works; "**Page 111** Hill, "My Wife and My Mother-in- Law," Puck, p.11, 1915.; " **Page 112** Chris Connor/Newscom; **Page 119** Vince Streano/Corbis.

Chapter 4

Page 120 Eric Gevaert/Fotolia; **Page 120** Inara Prusakova/Shutterstock; **Page 122** Eric Gevaert/Fotolia; **Page 122** Pearson Education; **Page 123** Sunny S Unal/Corbis; **Page 124** AUGUST/Corbis; **Page 125** Stephen Frink/Corbis; **Page 125** SW Productions/Photodisc/Getty Images, Inc.; **Page 129** Charles Gullung/Corbis; **Page 129** Mark Seelen/Corbis; **Page 130** Envision/Corbis; **Page 130** Joe Dator/The New Yorker Collection/The Cartoon Bank; **Page 131** Bill Abbott/CartoonStock; **Page 132** Dana Fradon/The New Yorker Collection/The Cartoon Bank; **Page 133** Sven Hagolani/Corbis; **Page 135** Eric Gevaert/Fotolia; **Page 137** Bettmann/Corbis; **Page 140** Bettmann/Corbis; **Page 141** 68/Ocean/Corbis; **Page 141** Spencer Grant/PhotoEdit; **Page 142** Allstar Picture Library/Alamy; **Page 142** Stephen Fore/Fotolia; **Page 143** Lee Powers/Photo Researchers, Inc./Science Source; **Page 145** R. Wright/Corbis; **Page 151** Bettmann/Corbis; **Page 151** Bettmann/Corbis.

Chapter 5

Page 152 Ljupco Smokovsk/Fotolia; **Page 154** Production Perig/Fotolia; **Page 156** Pasieka/Photo Researchers, Inc./Science Source; **Page 156** Pearson Education; **Page 157** John Birdsall Photography/AGE Fotostock; **Page 157** Monkey Business Images/Shutterstock; **Page 159** Production Perig/Fotolia; **Page 161** BSIP SA/Alamy; **Page 161** Chad Ehlers/Alamy; **Page 161** Petit Format/Photo Researchers, Inc./Science Source; **Page 161** Petit Format/Photo Researchers, Inc./Science Source; **Page 163** Bloomimage/Corbis; **Page 163** Denise Hager, Catchlight Visual Services/Alamy; **Page 163** Elizabeth Crews/The Image Works; **Page 163** Laura Elliott/Pearson Education; **Page 163** UIG via Getty Images; **Page 164** Dave King/Dorling Kindersley Limited; **Page 164** Elizabeth Crews Photography/Elizabeth Crews Photography; **Page 164** Gelpi JM/Shutterstock; **Page 164** Geri Engberg Photography/Geri Engberg Photography; **Page 164** Jo Foord/Dorling Kindersley Limited; **Page 164** Jo Foord/Dorling Kindersley Limited; **Page 166** Pearson Education; **Page 167** David Tothill/Alamy; **Page 168** Dennis MacDonald/PhotoEdit; **Page 169** Mike Good/Dorling Kindersley Limited; **Page 169** Saturn Still/Science Photo Library/Science Source; **Page 170** Pearson Education; **Page 171** Radius Images/Corbis; **Page 172** University of Wisconsin/Harlow Primate Laboratory; **Page 176** Production Perig/Fotolia; **Page 179** Michael Gibson/Corbis; **Page 180** Pearson Education; **Page 180** Pearson Education; **Page 181** Mike Greenlar/The Image Works; **Page 182** Olivier Voisin/Photo Researchers, Inc./Science Source; **Page 190** Elizabeth Crews/The Image Works.

Chapter 6

Page 192 macgyverhh/Fotolia; **Page 192** Shutterstock; **Page 194** King Features Syndicate; **Page 194** Shutterstock; **Page 198** Benjamin Harris; **Page 199** StevenRussellSmithPhotos/Shutterstock; **Page 201** Shutterstock; **Page 202** Pearson Education; **Page 203** Pearson Education; **Page 205** Pearson Education; **Page 207** Bonnie Kamin/PhotoEdit; **Page 211** Shutterstock; **Page 212** SuperStock, Inc.; **Page 214** Albert Bandura; **Page 216** Shutterstock; **Page 217** Design Pics/Carson Ganci/Getty Images; **Page 219** Frans Lanting Studio/Alamy; **Page 226** Albert Bandura; **Page 226** Bonnie Kamin/PhotoEdit; **Page 227** Design Pics/Carson Ganci/Getty Images; **Page 227** Frans Lanting Studio/Alamy.

Chapter 7

Page 228 Odua Images/Shutterstock; **Page 230** Mrs. Opossum/Shutterstock; **Page 232** Pearson Education; **Page 236** Pearson Education; **Page 236** Pearson Education; **Page 236** The University of Akron/Archives of the History of American Psychology; **Page 238** Mrs. Opossum/Shutterstock; **Page 240** Pearson Education; **Page 242** Pearson Education; **Page 244** Bettmann/Corbis; **Page 244** Pearson Education; **Page 245** Allan Tannenbaum/Newscom; **Page 247** Bill Aron/PhotoEdit; **Page 248** Pearson Education; **Page 251** Pearson Education; **Page 252** Philip G. Zimbardo, Inc.; **Page 253** Pearson Education; **Page 261** Bettmann/Corbis.

Chapter 8

Page 262 igorborodin/Fotolia; **Page 263** maximino/Shutterstock; **Page 264** maximino/Shutterstock; **Page 265** Darrin Henry/Fotolia; **Page 265** Robert Kneschke/Shutterstock; **Page 266** PhotoAlto/James Hardy/Getty Images; **Page 271** Ian Cumming/Getty Images, Inc.; **Page 274** David R. Frazier/Alamy; **Page 275** Blue Jean Images/Alamy; **Page 275** Charles Barsotti/The New Yorker Collection/The Cartoon Bank; **Page 277** Mrs. Opossum/Shutterstock; **Page 277** maximino/Shutterstock; **Page 278** Donald Reilly/The New Yorker Collection/The Cartoon Bank; **Page 279** Pixtal/SuperStock; **Page 284** Ian Cumming/Getty Images, Inc.; **Page 285** Pixtal/SuperStock.

Chapter 9

Page 286 Pakhnyushcha/Shutterstock; **Page 286** sevenke/Shutterstock; **Page 287** Keith Bell/Shutterstock; **Page 287** Lightspring/Shutterstock; **Page 288** Lightspring/Shutterstock; **Page 289** Huw Evans/Associated Press; **Page 290** Bob Krist/Corbis; **Page 291** Dennis MacDonald/Alamy; **Page 292** Kathy Ferguson Johnson/PhotoEdit; **Page 292** Tim Pannell/Corbis; **Page 293** Alan Bailey/Shutterstock; **Page 293** Whisson/Jordan/Corbis RF; **Page 294** Dex Image/Corbis; **Page 296** Lightspring/Shutterstock; **Page 297** Frank Burek/Corbis; **Page 297** Pearson Education; **Page 298** Rainer Holz/Corbis; **Page 299** Don Shrubshell/Associated Press; **Page 299** Lee Lorenz/The New Yorker Collection/The Cartoon Bank; **Page 301** Bill Holden/AGE Fotostock; **Page 301** Pearson Education; **Page 302** zeljkodan/Shutterstock; **Page 303** Richard Lord/The Image Works; **Page 305** Lacy Atkins/Corbis.

Chapter 10

Page 312 alphaspirit/Fotolia; **Page 313** mtkang/Shutterstock; **Page 314** mtkang/Shutterstock; **Page 316** Eric Isselee/Shutterstock; **Page 318** Jennie Hart/Alamy; **Page 319** Brigette Sullivan/Alamy; **Page 321** SuperStock, Inc.; **Page 323** Hector Mata/Associated Press; **Page 325** mtkang/Shutterstock; **Page 326** Eastcott

Momatiuk/The Image Works; **Page 326** Mark Richards/PhotoEdit; **Page 328** Randy Olson/Aurora Photos; **Page 329** Stanford University Libraries; **Page 342** Eric Isselee/Shutterstock.

Chapter 11

Page 344 Pete Saloutos/Shutterstock; **Page 345** md3d/Fotolia; **Page 346** md3d/Fotolia; **Page 348** Greg Epperson/Shutterstock; **Page 348** Norbert Schaefer/Corbis; **Page 349** London Entertainment/Alamy; **Page 350** Pearson Education; **Page 351** Everett Collection; **Page 352** benng/Shutterstock; **Page 353** Ryan McVay/Thinkstock; **Page 353** Voisin/Phanie/Science Source; **Page 354** Trinette Reed/Corbis; **Page 356** David Roth/Getty Images, Inc.; **Page 359** md3d/Fotolia; **Page 360** Pearson Education; **Page 361** Barbara Penoyar/Getty Images, Inc.; **Page 361** Cheryl Casey/Shutterstock; **Page 361** Christopher J Briscoe/Photo Researchers, Inc./Science Source; **Page 361** Guido Alberto Rossi/AGE Fotostock America Inc.; **Page 361** Guido Alberto Rossi/AGE Fotostock America Inc.; **Page 361** Photo Researchers, Inc.; **Page 364** Jack Hollingsworth/Getty Images, Inc.; **Page 371** Pixland/Corbis; **Page 371** Pixland/Corbis.

Chapter 12

Page 372 Antonov Roman/Shutterstock; **Page 372** Atiketta Sangasaeng/Shutterstock; **Page 372** Bugtiger/Shutterstock; **Page 373** alice-photo/Shutterstock; **Page 377** Pearson Education; **Page 380** Pearson Education; **Page 381** Pearson Education; **Page 383** Andresr/Shutterstock; **Page 388** Pearson Education; **Page 395** alice-photo/Shutterstock; **Page 396** Pearson Education; **Page 397** Pearson Education; **Page 399** Bill Aron/PhotoEdit; **Page 399** Noland White/Noland White, Ph.D.

Chapter 13

Page 408 sabri deniz kizil/Shutterstock; **Page 408** tashka2000/Fotolia; **Page 409** Maksim Samasiuk/Fotolia; **Page 410** Maksim Samasiuk/Fotolia; **Page 412** Pearson Education; **Page 412** Pearson Education; **Page 415** Pearson Education; **Page 418** Maksim Samasiuk/Fotolia; **Page 418** Pearson Education; **Page 420** Pearson Education; **Page 421** Julie Dermansky/Corbis; **Page 422** Bernd Vogel/Corbis; **Page 425** Charles Platiau/Corbis; **Page 426** Pearson Education; **Page 427** Newscom/dpaphotos173512; **Page 428** Larry Brownstein/Newscom; **Page 436** Bernd Vogel/Corbis; **Page 437** Charles Platiau/Corbis.

Chapter 14

Page 437 Newscom/dpaphotos173512; **Page 438** jcfotografie/Fotolia; **Page 440** jcfotografie/Fotolia; **Page 441** Charles Ciccione/Photo Researchers, Inc./Science Source; **Page 442** Pearson Education; **Page 443** Lisa F. Young/Shutterstock; **Page 443** Pearson Education; **Page 444** Zigy Kaluzny/Getty Images, Inc.; **Page 445** Pearson Education; **Page 446** Bob Daemmrich/The Image Works; **Page 447** Pearson Education; **Page 448** Pearson Education; **Page 450** Pearson Education; **Page 453** Pearson Education; **Page 455** jcfotografie/Fotolia; **Page 458** P Berndt/Newscom; **Page 460** Bettmann/Corbis; **Page 460** Photo courtesy of Martijn Arns, http://www.brainclinics.com; **Page 464** Bebeto Matthews/Associated Press; **Page 464** Yonathan Weitzman/Corbis; **Page 470** Pearson Education; **Page 471** Bettmann/Corbis; **Page 471** Yonathan Weitzman/Corbis.

Chapter 15

Page 472 ifong/Shutterstock; **Page 473** BMCL/Shutterstock; **Page 473** MidoSemsem/Shutterstock; **Page 474** BMCL/Shutterstock; **Page 474** MidoSemsem/Shutterstock; **Page 474** Pearson Education; **Page 475** Robert Harbison Photography; **Page 477** Myrleen Pearson/PhotoEdit.; **Page 477** Pearson Education; **Page 478** Nathan Benn/Corbis; **Page 479** Gary Conner/PhotoEdit; **Page 482** Pearson Education; **Page 487** Ada Summer/Corbis; **Page 487** Adrian Weinbrech/Getty Images; **Page 487** Pearson Education; **Page 488** Victor Englebert/Science Source; **Page 490** Donald Reilly/The New Yorker Collection/The Cartoon Bank; **Page 492** Profimedia.CZ a.s./Alamy; **Page 493** Ronnie Kaufman/Corbis; **Page 499** Adrian Weinbrech/Getty Images.

Chapter 16

Page 500 wavebreakmedia/Shutterstock; **Page 504** Ted Foxx/Alamy RF; **Page 504** Ted Foxx/Alamy RF; **Page 508** Paul Conklin/PhotoEdit; **Page 508** Will & Deni McIntyre/Photo Reearchers; **Page 509** Erika Schultz/Newscom; **Page 510** Restyler/Shutterstock; **Page 511** AT&T Archives; **Page 512** Jim Michaud/Associated Press; **Page 514** Joel Page/Associated Press; **Page 518** Michael Heron/PhotoEdit; **Page 518** Michael Heron/PhotoEdit; **Page 519** Joel Page/Associated Press; **Page 519** Paul Conklin/PhotoEdit;

TEXT CREDITS

Chapter 1

Page 13 Figure 1.1a Tsapogas, J. Project Officer. 2006. Characteristics of Doctoral Scientists and Engineers in the United States: 2003, NSF, 06320. National Science Foundation.; **Page 13** Figure 1.1b Hoffer, T. B., Hess, M.,Welch, V., Jr., & Williams, K. (2007). Doctorate Recipients from United States Universities: Summary Report 2006. Chicago: National Opinion Research Center.

Chapter 2

Page 56 Figure 5.1 CT and MRI data courtesy of N. White.; **Page 57** Figure 5.2 EEG data courtesy of N. White.

Chapter 3

Page 86 Figure 7.4 Source: Based on information from St. Luke's Cataract & Laser Institute.; **Page 110** Figure 8.8 Created by and courtesy of Dr. Akiyoshi Kitaoka, Ritsumeikan University.; **Page 110** Figure 8.9 Created by and courtesy of Jorge Otero-Millan, Martinez-Conde Laboratory, Barrow Neurological Institute.

Chapter 4

Page 123 "Source: Koch, C., & Mormann, F. (2010). The neurobiology of consciousness. In G. Mashour (Ed.), Consciousness, awareness, and anesthesia (pp. 24–46). New York: Cambridge University Press. p. 1225".; **Page 125** Figure 9.1 from H. P. Roffwarg; J. N. Muzio; W. C. Dement, "Ontogenetic Development of the Human Sleep-Dream Cycle" Science, (1966), 152, pp. 604-619. Reprinted with permission from AAAS.; **Page 127** Figure 9.2 Dr. Leslie Sherlin. Used by permission.; **Page 128** Figure 9.3 Saundra Ciccarelli.

Chapter 5

Page 162 Table 12.1 Sources: March of Dimes Foundation (2009); Organization of Teratology Information Specialists (2011); Shepard, T. H. (2001).; **Page 172** Harlow, H. F. (1958). The nature of love. American Psychologist, 13, 573–685; **Page 173** Table 12.3 Source: Derived from Erikson, 1950.; **Page 178** Table 13.1 Source: Based on Kohlberg, L. (1969). Stage and sequence: the cognitive-developmental approach to socialization. In D. A. Goslin (Ed.), Handbook of socialization: Theory in research (pp. 347–480). Boston: Houghton-Mifflin.

Chapter 6

Page 197 Figure 14.2 CI Hovland, "The Generalization of Conditioned Responses: IV. The Effects of Varying Amount of Reinforcement Upon the Degree of Generalization of Conditioned Reponses," in Journal of Experimental Psychology (1937), 21, 261-267.; **Page 212** Figure 16.1 "Introduction and Removal of Reward and Maze Learning in Rats" by EC Tolman and CH Honziak, University of California Publication in Psychology (1930), 4, 257-275.

Chapter 7

Page 231 Figure 18.1 Source: Adapted from Asch, S. E. (1956). Studies of independence and conformity: A minority of one against a unanimous majority. Psychological Monographs, 70 (Whole no. 416).; **Page 233** Table 18.1 Janis 1972, 1988.; **Page 241** Figure 19.2 Source: Adapted from Festinger, L., & Carlsmith, J. (1959). $1/$20 experiment: Cognitive consequences of forced compliance. Journal of Abnormal and Social Psychology, 58(2), 203–210.

Chapter 9

Page 299 Loftus, E. (1975). Leading questions and the eyewitness report. Cognitive Psychology, 7, 560–572.

Chapter 10

Page 315 Figure 25.1 From "Visual Images Preserve Metric Spatial Information: Evidence from Studies of Image Scanning" by S. M. Kosslyn, T. M. Ball, and B. J. Reiser, Journal of Experimental Psychology: Human Perception and Performance (1978) 4, 47 60. Published by American Psychological Association.; **Page 331** Table 26.1 Source: Based on Stanford-Binet Intelligence Scales, Fifth Edition (SB5) (Roid, 2003) Roid, G. H. (2003). Stanford-Binet intelligence scales (5th ed.). Itasca, IL: Riverside.; **Page 332** Table 26.2 Source: Based on WECHSLER ADULT INTELLIGENCE SCALE Third Edition (WAIS III) by David Wechsler. Copyright © 1997 by NCS Pearson, Inc.

Chapter 11

Page 351 Figure 27.3 From MOTIVATION AND PERSONALITY 3rd edition by Abraham H. Maslow, edited by Robert D. Frager & James Fadiman. Copyright © 1987. Printed and electronically reproduced by permission of Pearson Education, Inc., Upper Saddle River, NJ 07458

Chapter 12

Page 387 Table 29.2 Source: Adapted from McCrae & Costa (1990). From PERSONALITY IN ADULTHOOD 2nd edition by Robert R. Mac- Crae and Paul T. Costa. Copyright © 1990 by Guilford Publications. Reprinted with permission of the Guilford Publications; **Page 434** Figure 11.5 Source: Data from Miller et al. (1991, 1996).

Chapter 13

Page 415 Table 31.1 Source: Adapted from National Institute of Mental Health (2013). Table uses terminology from both the DSM-IV and DSM-5 (American Psychiatric Association, 2000, 2013); **Page 429** Figure 32.1 Copyrighted by Pearson Education, Upper Saddle River, NJ.

Chapter 14

Page 444 Meador, B. D., & Rogers, C. R. (1984). Person- centered therapy. In R. J. Corsini (Ed.), Current psychotherapies (3rd ed., pp. 142–195). Itasca, IL: Peacock.; **Page 452** adapted from Wedding, D. (2004). Cross-cultural counseling and psychotherapy. In R. J. Corsini & D. Wedding (Eds.), Current psychotherapies (7th ed., p. 485). Itasca, IL: Peacock.

Chapter 15

Page 476 Table 35.1 Source: Adapted and abridged from Holmes & Rahe (1967). Holmes, T. H. & Rahe, R. H. (1967). The Social Readjustment Scale. Journal of Psychosomatic Research 11, 213 218. Copyright © 1967 by American Psychological Association.; **Page 482** Figure 35.2 Source: Cohen, S., Frank, E., Doyle, B. J., Skoner, D. P., Rabin, B. S., & Gwaltney, J. M. (1998). Types of stressors that increase susceptibility to the common cold. Health Psychology, 17, 214–223.

Name Index

Subject Index

Breland, Keller, 208
Breland, Marian, 208
Brightness, 85
Brightness constancy, 103
British Medical Council, 170
Broca, Paul, 63
Broca's aphasia, 220
Broca's area, 62–63, 219–220
Bulimia nervosa (bulimia), 426
Buprenorphine, 142
Bureau of Labor Statistics, 507
Burnout, 478
Bush, George W., 232
Bystander effect, 228, 254

C
Caffeine, 141
California police departments, 120
Calkins, Mary Whiton, 8
Camerino, Taria, 78
Cancer, 483
Cannabinoids, 143
Cannabis sativa, 143
Cannon, Walter, 361–362
Cannon-Bard theory of emotion, 361–362, 361f
Careers in psychology
  bachelor's degree, 505
  career options, 507–510
  degree requirements, 503–506
  master's degree, 504
  medical degree, 503
  other career field interaction, 507–510
  reasons to study, 501
  resources available, 507
Case study, defined, 19
Catastrophe, 475
Catatonia, 428
Catatonic schizophrenia, 428
Cattell, Raymond, 386
Cellular clock theory, 180
Centers for Disease Control and Prevention (CDC), 140, 141
Central nervous system (CNS), 47–48
Central-route processing, 240
Centration, 167
Cerebellum, 59, 59f, 60
Cerebral hemispheres, 61
Cerebrum, 64
Cerletti, Ugo, 458
Challenger, 232
Character, 374
Children
  psychopharmacology treatment, 460–461
China, 266–267
Chromosomes, 69–71, 157
Chronological age, 330
Chunking, 291
Circadian rhythms, 124
Class Divided, A (Peters), 246
Classical conditioning
  affecting emotions, 198–199
  clinical and experimental examples of, 198–199
  defined, 195, 196f
  in everyday life, 199
  principles of, 194–198
  psychotherapy, 445–446
Clinical psychology, 505
Cocaine, 140

Cochlea, 92
Cochlear implant, 93, 94f
Cocktail party effect, 290, 291f
Cognition, 314
Cognitive-behavioral therapy (CBT), 448
Cognitive development, 177
Cognitive differences, 278–279
Cognitive dissonance, 240–241, 241f
Cognitive health, 337
Cognitive learning theory, 211–213
Cognitive map, 212
Cognitive-mediational theory, 363
Cognitive neuroscience, 11
Cognitive perspective, 11
Cognitive psychology
  abnormal behavior, 413
  anxiety disorders, 421–422
  dissociative disorders, 423
Cognitive therapy, 447–449
Cognitive universalism, 218
Cohort effect, 155
Collective monologue, 218
Collective unconscious, 380
Collectivism, 267, 268
Collectivistic cultures, 269, 390
College Undergraduate Stress Scale (CUSS), 477
Color, perception of, 88–90
Color blindness, 89–90
Color-deficient vision, 89–90
Commitment, 250
Community psychology, 510
Companionate love, 251, 356
Comparative psychology, 506
Compliance, 234–235
Computed tomography (CT) scan, 56
Concepts, 315–317
Concrete operations stage, 167
Conditional positive regard, 385
Conditioned emotional response (CER), 198–199
Conditioned response (CR), 195–196
Conditioned stimulus (CS), 195–197
Conditioned taste aversion, 199
Conditioning, 9. See also Classical conditioning; Operant conditioning
Conduction hearing impairment, 93
Conductive hearing loss, 93
Confederate, 231
Confidentiality, 462
Confirmation bias, 323
Conformity, 230–232, 231f, 267
Confounding variable, 23
Congenital analgesia, 98
Congenital insensitivity to pain with anhidrosis (CIPA), 98
Conscience, 377
Conscientiousness, 386
Consciousness
  altered states of, 123
  definition of, 122–123
  drugs affecting, 144t
  hypnosis, 135–137
  meditation and, 137–138
  reasons to study, 121
  relaxation and, 137–138
  states of, 122–123
  waking, 123
Conservation, 167
Conservation experiment, 167f

Constructive processing, 301, 302
Contact comfort, 172–173
Context-dependent learning, 296
Continuous reinforcement, 204
Control group, 25–26
Convergence, 107–108
Convergent thinking, 320
Cooing, 168, 219
Coping strategies, 486–489
Cornea, 86
Coronary heart disease, stress, 482
Corpus callosum, 61, 64
Correlation, 20–22, 33
Correlation coefficient, 21, 33
Correlation method, 20–22
Cortex, 61, 61f
  association areas of, 62–63
  somatosensory, 63f
Costa, P. T., 387
Counseling psychology, 505
Counterconditioning, 10
Creativity, 320–321
  culture and, 270
Critical periods, 161
Cross-cultural psychology, 269–273
Cross-sectional design, 154
Cross-sequential design, 154
Crowe, Russell, 427
Csikszentmihalyi, Mihaly, 138
Cultural bias, 270–271, 335–336
Cultural explanations, 272–273
Cultural idioms of distress, 272–273
Cultural psychology, 11
Cultural relativity, 272, 413
Cultural syndromes, 272–273
Culture, cultural influences
  abnormal behavior and, 272–273, 413–414
  anxiety and, 273
  characteristics of, 264–265
  cognition and, 270–271
  conceptions of self, identity, 268
  conformity and, 267
  creativity and, 270
  cross-cultural psychology, 267–269
  defined, 264
  eating disorders and, 273, 353
  emotion, 271–272
  gender, 277–279
  immigration, acculturation, 267
  integration, 267
  personality and, 269–270, 390–391
  in psychology, 264–275
  psychotherapy, 452–453
  stress factors, 478–479, 488
  use and experience of drugs and, 145
  variations across time, place, 265–267
Culture-bound syndromes, 272, 413
Curve of forgetting, 302, 302f

D
Dark adaptation, 88
Darwin, Charles, 8, 71, 363
Data analysis, 28–34
Death, cross-cultural views on, 184–185

Death and dying, 183
Decay, 303
Deci, Edward, 351
Decibel, 91f
Decision making, 317–321, 322–323
Declarative memory, 293
Degrees in psychology, 503–506
Deindividuation, 252
Delta waves, 126
Delusional disorder, 424, 427
Delusions, 427
Dementia praecox, 427
Dendrites, 42, 48
Dennett, Daniel, 122
Dependent variable, 23
Depersonalization/derealization disorder, 423
Depolarization, 43
Depressants, 141
Depression, 213
  treating, 460–461, 467–468
Depth perception, 105–108
Descriptive statistics, 28–29
Desire, 214
Developmental psychology, 505
Deviation IQ scores, 333
Dexedrine, 140
Diabetes, 51
Diagnostic and Statistical Manual of Mental Disorders, Fifth Edition (DSM-5), 414–415
Diary of a Student Revolution, 300
Dichromatic vision, 89–90
Difficult babies, 170
Diffusion of responsibility, 254
Digit Span experiment, 291
Direct observation, 396
Discrimination, 245–246, 274–275
Disorganized-disoriented attachment, 171
Disorganized schizophrenia, 428
Displaced aggression, 492
Display rules, 271–272, 359
Dispositional cause, 242
Dissociation, 136
Dissociative amnesia, 422–423
Dissociative disorders, 422–423
Dissociative fugue, 422–423
Dissociative identity disorder, 423
Distress, 475
Distributed practice, 303
Divergent thinking, 320
Dizygotic twins, 160, 160f
DNA (deoxyribonucleic acid), 69
Doctorate, 503–504
Doctor of philosophy (Ph.D.), 503
Doctor of psychology (Psy.D.), 503
Domhoff, William, 133
Dominant genes, 69, 156
Double-blind experiment, 25
Downward social comparison, 489
Dreams, 133
  functions of, 131–133
  interpretation, 443
  as wish fulfillment, 131–132
Drive, 347
Drive-reduction theory, 347–348
Drugs
  affecting consciousness, 144t